Ethics for Everyday

Ethics for Everyday

David Benatar
University of Cape Town

Boston   Burr Ridge, IL   Dubuque, IA   Madison, WI   New York
San Francisco   St. Louis   Bangkok   Bogotá   Caracas   Kuala Lumpur
Lisbon   London   Madrid   Mexico City   Milan   Montreal   New Delhi
Santiago   Seoul   Singapore   Sydney   Taipei   Toronto

McGraw-Hill Higher Education

A Division of The *McGraw-Hill* Companies

ETHICS FOR EVERYDAY

Published by McGraw-Hill, a business unit of The McGraw-Hill Companies, Inc.,
1221 Avenue of the Americas, New York, NY 10020. Copyright © 2002 by The
McGraw-Hill Cjompanies, Inc. All rights reserved. No part of this publication
may be reproduced or distributed in any form or by any means, or stored in a
database or retrieval system, without the prior written consent of The McGraw-
Hill Companies, Inc., including, but not limited to, in any network or other
electonic storage or transmission, or broadcast for distance learning.

Some ancillaries, including electronic and print components, may not be
available to customers outside the United States.

This book is printed on acid-free paper.

1 2 3 4 5 6 7 8 9 0 QPF/QPF 0 9 8 7 6 5 4 3 2 1

ISBN 0-07-240889-8

Editorial Director: *Jane E. Karpacz*
Sponsoring editor: *Monica Eckman*
Editorial coordinator: *Hannah Glover/Shannon Morrow*
Marketing manager: *Daniel M. Loch*
Senior project manager: *Kay J. Brimeyer*
Production supervisor: *Kara Kudronowicz*
Coordinator of freelance design: *Michelle D. Whitaker*
Cover designer: *So Yon Kim*
Cover image: *© Jim Dandy/The Stock Illustration Source, Inc.*
Digital content specialist: *Candy M. Kuster*
Compositor: *GAC–Indianapolis*
Typeface: *10/12 Palatino*
Printer: *Quebecor World Fairfield, PA*

Library of Congress Cataloging-in-Publication Data

Ethics for everyday / [edited by] David Benatar.—1st ed.
 p.   cm.
Includes bibliographical references.
ISBN 0-07-240889-8 (alk. paper)
1. Ethical problems. 2. Applied ethics. I. Benatar, David.

BJ1031.E853   2002
170—dc21   2001030400
                                                       CIP

www.mhhe.com

To my grandmothers,

and in memory of my grandfathers.

Contents

Part 2
SEX

Chapter 5: Premarital Sex, Promiscuity, and Masturbation   154

Chapter 6: Adultery   198

Chapter 7: Homosexuality   241

Part 3
PARENTS AND CHILDREN

Chapter 8: Rearing Children   276

Chapter 9: Familial and Filial Duties   321

Part 6
BODY AND ENVIRONMENT

Part 7
VIRTUES AND VICES

Preface

Because there are dozens of applied ethics anthologies, the need for a new one should be defended. *Ethics for Everyday* is an anthology of papers on a notably neglected set of practical moral problems. These problems are those confronted by ordinary people in everyday life, not in their capacities as professionals, citizens, or lawmakers, but simply as people. More traditional applied ethics collections focus on problems in law, medicine, education, or business. Among the issues they include are capital punishment, civil disobedience, abortion, euthanasia, and affirmative action. By contrast, *Ethics for Everyday* is devoted to such issues as joke-telling, gossiping, adultery, the physical punishment of children, the keeping of pets, gambling, tipping, smoking, politeness, and gratitude. In many ways, these "everyday" issues are less exalted than the more traditional applied ethics fare. However, they are also much more relevant to the daily lives of most people. In that sense they are more urgent and of greater practical import to the vast majority of us.

In the introduction that follows this preface, I shall offer some comments about the structure and content of the book and offer an explanation of why ethical issues in everyday life have been relatively neglected. I shall then briefly outline some of the most influential normative ethical theories and the major criticisms of them. This will help those unfamiliar with these theories to understand references to them in many of the articles. Finally, for students new to philosophy, I shall say something about the practice of philosophy and the reading of philosophical articles.

Much of the general introduction, the summaries that introduce each of the readings, and the study questions that follow them are directed toward those who are relatively new to the study of philosophy. However, the anthology should also be of interest to many others, because the constituent articles are worthy of the attention of even seasoned philosophers.

A number of people have provided assistance in the production of this book:

For advice, encouragement, or suggestions, I should like to thank James Rachels and John Arthur, Tom Beauchamp, Laurence Goldstein, Samuel Gorovitz, Ned Hettinger, Hugh LaFollette, Michael Levine, Colin Lumb, Jacques Rousseau, and Alan Soble.

Reviewers for McGraw-Hill gave useful feedback and provided me with a better idea of how potential readers might react to various features of the anthology. For their comments, my thanks go to:

John Coker, *University of South Alabama*

John Langan, *Georgetown University*

Robert Hollinger, *Iowa State University*

Jessica Prata Miller, *University of Maine*

Bernard Rollin, *Colorado State University*

Clifford Anderson, *California State University, Sacramento*

Jeff Bell, *Southeastern Louisiana University*

Richard Spinello, *Boston College*

James Rachels, *University of Alabama*

Jose DaCruz, *Ozarks Technical Community College*

Barry Hallen, *Morehouse College*

Michelle Moody Adams, *Indiana University*

As is to be expected, the reactions of some reviewers often conflicted with those of others. However, even where I did not follow a reviewer's suggestions, I usually profited from considering them.

I should also like to thank those authors who either wrote or revised a paper especially for this volume: James Anderson and Ronald Sandler, David Carey, Peter Collins, Tibor Machan, Julia Meaton and David Morrice, and Gary Varner.

I could not have asked for more efficient and friendly editors and a project manager at McGraw-Hill than Monica Eckman, Hannah Glover, Shannon Morrow, and Kay Brimeyer. It has been a pleasure working with them, and I am very appreciative of all they have done.

Finally, I want to thank my parents and brothers for sharing my interest in this project and for the support and assistance each has provided. I am immensely grateful to them for this and for much more.

David Benatar
University of Cape Town

Introduction

Quotidian Ethics: Ethics for Everyday

The last few decades have witnessed the birth and burgeoning of philosophical attention to practical moral problems. The first such issues to which philosophers turned their attention were problems in medical practice or at the interface of morality and law or public policy. There are now countless articles and books on topics that include abortion, euthanasia, capital punishment, civil disobedience, and affirmative action.

By contrast, those problems that confront ordinary people in everyday life have been relatively ignored. That is to say, philosophers have said remarkably little about moral problems that people face daily, not in their capacities as professionals, citizens, or lawmakers, but simply as people. For example, very little has been written about the ethics of telling jokes or lies, gossiping, practicing adultery, gambling, smoking, corporal punishment of one's children, and copying copyrighted material.

It is useful to have a name by which to refer to philosophical inquiry into these sorts of issues, just as other areas of practical ethics are termed bioethics (or medical ethics), business ethics, legal ethics, and environmental ethics. I propose that we use the term "quotidian ethics" (from the Old French *cotidien* and the Latin *quotidianus*, meaning "every day"[1]). This book is devoted to problems of quotidian ethics, the moral problems of everyday life. It includes papers on many neglected topics in this area, as well as some on those problems—eating meat and the giving of aid, for example—that have received much more philosophical attention. Unlike these last two examples, it sometimes seems as though more has been written about a quotidian ethical issue than really is the case. This is because the focus on some practices often has not been on what I have called their quotidian features, but rather on what view the law or social policy should take of them. Thus, much has been written about homosexuality,

---

[1]See the *Shorter Oxford English Dictionary* (Oxford: Clarendon Press, 1973), 1734.

for example, but a large proportion of this literature (including, most recently, discussion of same-sex marriages) has focused on what the legal status of homosexuals and their relationships ought to be. Similarly, the use of recreational drugs has been the subject of philosophical discussion, but usually the focus has been on to what extent, if at all, such drug use should be legally regulated. In selecting papers for this anthology, I have considered only those, the primary focus of which is truly what I have called "quotidian."

The Structure and Content of This Book

Although there is a clear rationale behind the way the papers in this collection have been ordered and grouped, there are (overlapping but) different and equally good ways in which it could have been structured. Alternative groupings of essays would have made sense because there are many connections between the various papers. For instance, some of the issues raised in the chapter on Familial and Filial Duties—whether we have special duties arising from our relationships with particular people—have bearing on papers in the chapter on Giving Aid and on papers in the chapter on Pets. Similarly, there is overlap between the papers devoted to adultery and those that consider premarital sex and promiscuity. The paper about private car use is relevant to issues of the environment and consumption but also connects quite closely with the issues raised in the chapter on Substance and Sustenance. Similarly, the order of the chapters could have been different because no one chapter must, by every possible criterion, come first. The upshot of all this is that although a choice has had to be made in structuring this book, no reader or course instructor is bound to follow either the order or groupings I have chosen. Considerable flexibility is possible.

Most of the papers have been previously published, but a few are new. The aim has been to include papers representing different views on each topic, but this was not always possible. On some topics—tipping, for example—I am aware of only one published paper. Some quotidian problems are not included at all because I know of no papers that examine them. Hopefully the gaps will be filled as further philosophical work is stimulated in this interesting area.

This book includes a number of papers on sex. In defending the exclusion of such topics from his *Practical Ethics*, Peter Singer argued that even "in the era of AIDS, sex raises no unique moral issues at all. Decisions about sex may involve considerations of honesty, concern for others, prudence, and so on, but there is nothing special about sex in this respect, for the same could be said of decisions about driving a car."[2] He went on to say that there "are more important ethical issues to be considered."[3] I agree entirely that sex raises no *unique* moral issues and that morality has had an unduly exclusive association with sex in some people's minds. However, an activity does not need to raise unique moral issues in order to be worthy of moral discussion and evaluation. Nor does it need to be the most important moral issue imaginable to warrant

[2]Peter Singer, *Practical Ethics,* 2d ed. (Cambridge: Cambridge University Press, 1993), 2.
[3]Ibid.

attention. That is why I have included not only sex but also driving cars, telling jokes, smoking, drinking, and so many other activities, which all raise moral issues, whether or not they are either unique or supremely important moral issues. As it happens, though, at least some sexual activities, it seems to me, do raise very weighty moral issues, precisely because of HIV. Having sex with somebody can now be a way of killing that person, even if only negligently or unintentionally. That is not something to be treated lightly. Of course, this is not true of all sexual practices. Some sexual activities, of which masturbation is a notable example, cause no harm, either to others or oneself. For this reason, they may be thought by many people not to raise moral questions at all. I have no quarrel with that view. However, I also recognize that not everybody shares that view. There are some people for whom topics like masturbation are morally laden. This, I think, provides sufficient grounds for including such topics in this anthology. Even if it is the case that practices like masturbation are morally entirely unproblematic, there is a value in providing arguments for this conclusion, rather than simply asserting it.

The chapter entitled "Eating Meat and Wearing Leather" contains no papers that deal explicitly with the wearing of leather (and some that do not refer explicitly to eating meat either). However, all of these articles are relevant to both the eating of meat and the wearing of leather. By mentioning both these practices in the title of this chapter, I have sought to render more explicit the broader relevance of the papers in that chapter. It should be emphasized, however, that even this title does not exhaust the range of practices to which the articles are relevant. The use of those soaps, shampoos, glues, and so on, that contain animal flesh products raises related, even if not identical, moral concerns. The same is true of the eating of eggs that are produced by battery chickens—chickens that are intensively reared under conditions of great suffering. Clearly the title "Eating Meat and Wearing Leather" does not make explicit the constituent papers' relevance to all these topics. However, a title that did that surely would be either unwieldy or too vague.

There is an extensive literature about virtues and vices. Some people may wonder what motivated the selection of the particular topics I have included in the part of the book devoted to this topic. One important consideration was that much of the literature on virtues and vices is devoted to analyzing the nature of these character traits, often with a moral evaluation of the trait only tacked onto the end. Of course, understanding the nature of a trait is vital for assessing its worth, but it is the moral rather than conceptual issue that is the primary concern of this book. Accordingly I have attempted to select papers in this part that focus more on the normative issues than on the conceptual ones. It has not been possible to achieve the same degree of focus on normative issues across all the virtues that were included. The papers on modesty, for example, deal more with conceptual issues than do the papers in the rest of this part of the book. However, because the conceptual questions about modesty are unusually closely connected to the normative ones, I chose nonetheless to include this topic.

In the remainder of this introduction, I shall (*a*) offer an explanation of why quotidian ethics has been relatively neglected and say why this neglect is to be regretted; (*b*) briefly outline some major normative ethical theories and traditional criticisms of them, as this will help those unfamiliar with these theories to better understand references to them in the readings; (*c*) provide some insight, for readers new to philosophy, into how philosophy is practiced and what value the philosophical method has in tackling quotidian moral problems; and finally (*d*) offer some suggestions about how one might approach the reading of philosophical articles.

The Neglect of Quotidian Ethics

What accounts for the neglect of quotidian ethics?[4] The answer, I believe, is to be found in the recent history of philosophical ethics. A shift from very general to more particular concerns can be discerned in moral philosophy over the last century. In the early years of the twentieth century, philosophers, at least in the Anglo-American tradition of ethics, were almost exclusively concerned with what is called "metaethics." This branch of ethics does not seek to evaluate normative moral claims. Instead, it involves an analysis of the language of such claims. It is not itself an ethical inquiry but rather an inquiry about the nature of ethics. As metaethics lost some of its grip, there was a return to what is known as normative ethical theory. Normative ethical theories seek to explain, at a theoretical level, what makes some kinds of action morally right and others morally wrong. Until the birth—some would say rebirth—of the practical ethics tradition, normative ethical theory was discussed in abstraction from practical moral problems. Thus we can discern a shift from a concern with questions *about* ethics, to general theoretical questions *in* ethics, to particular practical

---

[4]In response to my noting, in a call for papers for a conference on quotidian ethics, that this area of moral inquiry had been relatively neglected, one philosopher responded with the claim that while mainstream philosophy had given it insufficient attention, feminist philosophy had not. This comment might be thought to draw on the feminist argument that mainstream philosophical ethics (which is contrasted with feminist ethics) reflects the experience of those who have done this work: men. Since men have traditionally occupied the *public* sphere, they have developed theories suited to and focused on problems that arise in that sphere. The experiences of women—traditionally restricted to the *private* sphere—have not been adequately represented in moral philosophy. (E.g., Samantha Brennan, "Recent Work in Feminist Ethics," *Ethics* 109 [1999]: 861.) Feminist ethics has indeed drawn attention to and cast light on important aspects of morality that had been ignored. The neglect of quotidian ethics, however, cannot adequately be understood by this feminist explanation. First, even though the public sphere has traditionally been the preserve of men, this does not mean that men have not also lived in the private realm. Accordingly, we need to ask how the predominance of men in the public realm explains philosophical neglect of personal morality. One answer could be that men have been so *distracted* by their public roles that they have ignored moral issues that confront them in their daily lives as ordinary people. However, if that were so, then one would expect that women, who were not so distracted, would have given more attention to quotidian moral problems. This brings us to a second problem with employing a feminist explanation of the neglect of quotidian ethics. Although feminists and female philosophers have given considerable attention to some quotidian moral problems, such as sexist speech, they have tended to focus on those issues of special relevance to the status of *women*. They, as far as I know, have said no more than other philosophers about topics like humor, lying, adultery, eating animals, keeping pets, violating copyright, tipping, giving aid, gambling, smoking, or taking drugs. This suggests that it is not only mainstream and male philosophers who have neglected quotidian ethics.

moral problems. In view of the historical trend, it is not surprising that even with the shift to practical moral problems, it was those problems whose focus was more general—social rather than personal—that received primary, even though not exclusive, attention. The professional and social problems are the "big" practical problems—the ones that concern what professions and societies should do and allow. The less grandiose questions that focus not on whole societies or constituent groups but on individual people took second place.

Why the Neglect Is Regrettable

It is regrettable that the social issues, in which the scope of a moral judgment ranges over many people, are seen as unequivocally more important. Of course, judgments that bind large groups of people are, in some respects, more important than ones that bind only individuals. However, there are other ways in which the personal questions are more important. This is well illustrated by the joke about the husband who described a division of labor between him and his wife: "I," he said, "take charge of all the *big* questions, like: Should our country wage war against another?; Should taxes be raised?; Who should be President? My wife takes charge of all the *small* questions, like: Where should we live?; What school should the children attend?; What food should we buy and eat?" The husband's attention to the "big" issues provides him with a false sense of his own role in deciding on them. His wife, by contrast, is concerned with decisions of a more limited scope, but her role is crucially important and what she decides is of the utmost importance to her and her family.

Those of one's decisions that affect the smaller number of people are usually the decisions that one is more capable of implementing. You may very well decide that capital punishment is or is not desirable, but unless you are your country's dictator, your ability to implement your decision will be limited (and often thwarted) by the complex social decision-making mechanisms. For this reason, deciding about questions of personal morality will often (although not always) have a greater effect than deciding about questions of social morality. They can also have a more immediate effect. If one decides today that eating meat is wrong or that tipping is inappropriate, one can effect the relevant changes in one's behavior forthwith. Of course, there will sometimes be psychological obstacles impeding the implementation of one's decisions. Thus one might decide that eating meat is wrong but be too weak-willed to give it up immediately. Or one might decide that tipping is inappropriate but feel intimidated by the undeserving taxi driver's resentful snarl into giving him a tip. However, these failures to act on one's judgments are themselves within one's control because, unlike the failure to implement one's judgments about issues in social morality, one *could* overcome them.

Normative Ethical Theory

The branch of philosophy devoted to the study of practical moral problems, including quotidian ones, is often called "applied ethics." Some people have taken issue with this appellation, suggesting instead the term "practical ethics."

They have argued that "applied ethics" suggests that work in this area amounts simply to the *application* of normative ethical theory to practical problems. This, they argue, is a misdescription because very rarely can one answer a practical moral problem simply by applying a moral theory. Practical moral problems are almost always more complicated than that, it is said. Whether or not this criticism of the term "applied ethics" is correct, it is clear that theoretical considerations do impact on practical moral issues. Arguments about such issues often cannot be understood without knowing something about normative ethical theory.

The Nature and Importance of Normative Ethical Theory

The aim of a normative ethical theory is to provide a *unifying explanation* of why particular acts are or would be right or wrong. To better understand this unifying explanatory function of theory, consider the case of scientific theory. When faced with an array of phenomena, the scientist, instead of suggesting that each and every phenomenon is explained in its own way, postulates a theory that would explain groups of these phenomena. For example, the observations that bricks, leaves, apples and cats fall to the ground when unsuspended in the atmosphere are given a common explanation: the theory of gravity. This theory makes sense of a variety of phenomena. We do not need to postulate different explanations for each of the objects we observe falling to the ground. Similarly, a moral theory seeks to provide a unifying explanation. It seeks to explain what makes individual right actions right or, in other words, what the rightness of any particular action is.

Many people suspect that ethical theory cannot be much use because morality is not an abstract cognitive activity. Consider the case of an extraordinarily clever philosopher who has attained great understanding about ethics and can mount marvelous arguments about what we should and should not do and yet behaves wickedly. Such a person is not moral, his cognitive skills notwithstanding. This observation is an important one. In addition to moral knowledge, one must be *motivated* to do what is right. However, just as moral knowledge is not sufficient, moral motivations are not sufficient. It is no use having the will to perform the moral action, if one does not know what the moral action is. Ethics classes in universities tend to be concerned with the cognitive aspects of morality—seeking to know what one ought to do. Moral motivations, which are best cultivated from early childhood even though their development can be a lifelong project, are largely beyond the scope of university ethics courses. Many would argue that it is appropriate that university ethics classes deal only with the cognitive aspects of morality.

Another suspicion some people have about ethical theory is that because religion tells us what we ought to do, ethical theorizing is superfluous. But such a judgment would be too hasty. First, the foundations of religious ethics are at least as controversial, and probably more so, than those of many ethical theories. That is to say, any religious account of what one ought to do would have to first establish the existence of God and that the source of the religious prescription—the Bible or the Koran, for example—was indeed the word of God. These are claims that are as or more difficult to defend than the philosophical ethical theories they are thought to render redundant. But the difficulties for a religious view of ethics extend further and apply even to those who do accept a religious worldview. For example, a diversity of moral views characterizes not only people of different religious traditions but even people of a single religious tradition. Even if one assumes that God exists and that the Bible is his word, it is still far from clear what God requires. The Bible has been subject to many varying interpretations. For instance, some people believe that the Bible prohibits blood transfusions, while others do not. It is also the case that most religions understand the moral requirements of God to have changed. Thus, the Bible permits a man to be married to more than one woman (at one time), to divorce a wife against her will, to marry a child and to have sex with her. The Bible also permits the buying, selling and keeping of slaves. Yet many religions and religious people today take these sorts of practices to be morally unacceptable. And there are practices that the Bible prohibits, such as having sex with or while a menstruating woman or consuming leaven on Passover, which people of many (but not all) religious groups take to be acceptable today. In short, then, it is hard to tell just by looking at the Bible or other such religious sources, what is religiously permitted and what is religiously prohibited. Finally, if God's judgments of what is right and wrong (whatever they may be) are presumed to be wise ones based on good reasons, rather than just arbitrary, then there must be some rationale that lies behind them. For those who have religious views, normative ethical theory can be seen as a way of attempting to uncover that rationale. Thus ethical theorizing is not incompatible with religious ethics and cannot be replaced by appeals to religious authority.

For over two millennia philosophers have thought and argued about competing ethical views. Many people find it frustrating that no answer has been agreed upon by everybody. Philosophers tend to be resigned to this. They realize that the philosophical enterprise is not simply about getting answers. It is also about attaining clarity and understanding, both of which can be achieved at least to some degree. In the process different thinkers settle on the particular answer they think is best, even if they fail to convince everybody else that their view is correct. Even then, however, there is something tentative about these answers for those who hold them. They must always remain open to philosophical challenges and thus there is the possibility that the answers will have to be rejected or refined in the light of these challenges.

As ethical theory is a vast area of inquiry in its own right, there is no way that this brief introduction can do justice to it. All I intend to do here is to outline some of the more influential theories and gesture at their commonly regarded strengths and weaknesses. This will provide some minimum background for understanding references to ethical theories in articles in this anthology.[5] I shall not probe the alleged strengths and weaknesses in order to evaluate them.

---

[5]Those wanting a more comprehensive introduction to normative theory should consult a text dedicated to that purpose, such as James Rachels's excellent book *The Elements of Moral Philosophy*.

Relativism

Relativism, or more specifically normative relativism, is the view that the moral value of an action is dependent on and relative to different societies or individuals. Thus, if a given society believes that an action is morally wrong, then it is actually morally wrong for that society. This view must be distinguished from another with which it is often confused: descriptive relativism. Descriptive relativism makes no normative claim. It merely notes that there are a variety of moral views, without passing judgment on them. Normative relativism does more than describe a difference in moral view. It also endorses each culture's (or individual's) views, claiming that they are actually, and not merely perceived to be, normatively binding for that culture (or individual). Although descriptive relativism and normative relativism are often confused with each other, it is important to realize that they are distinct and that the former does not entail the latter.

Normative relativism has had considerable appeal, not least because it seems to embody the value of *tolerance:* it suggests a policy of "each to his own." Critics of relativism suggest that despite this enlightened appearance, relativism is a sinister theory that justifies gross moral violations in the name of individual or group morality. For example, if a culture believes it is right to persecute some minority within its midst, such persecution would be deemed morally right by normative relativism. Other critics suggest that relativism, at least in its crudest forms, is an incoherent theory because it espouses a relativism of moral norms but implicit in it is a nonrelative moral judgment—that we should not interfere with other individuals or societies. If one thinks that a culture's moral beliefs dictate what is actually right and wrong for that culture, then how can one say that interfering with another culture is wrong for a culture that believes in interfering with other cultures?

Consequentialism

Consequentialism is the view that the right action is the one that has the best consequences. On this view we ought to do whatever we can to achieve the best outcome. Consequentialism is sometimes summarized as the view that "the end justifies the means." The "end" is the goal or set of consequences to which the "means" (or actions) are directed or which they produce. The most influential version of consequentialism is *utilitarianism.* This is the view that we ought to act in order to bring about the most utility. Utilitarians have been divided on what is meant by "utility." The hedonistic utilitarians understand it to be pleasure and the absence of pain. Others have adopted a broader view of utility, understanding it as the satisfaction of preferences. (Pleasure is one kind of preference one has, but one can also have preferences for things other than pleasure, even when satisfying those preferences causes one to have less pleasure.)

The attraction of consequentialism in general and utilitarianism in particular is that they suggest that it is better to have more rather than less of what is good. If utility is good and we can produce more rather than less of it, surely the right action is to produce more! The first problem utilitarianism faces is that we rarely know what all the consequences of an action will be. The future is notoriously unpredictable. Second, even if we were able to know all the consequences of our actions, it would be practically impossible to quantify the goodness of these consequences. How can we measure and compare the utility that different people would derive from two alternative possible actions? A further problem is that consequentialism is said to be an excessively demanding theory. It restricts the range of permissible actions (and omissions) to those that will produce the *most* good. At every juncture, unless one is producing the most good one could produce, one is doing wrong. By far the most worrying problem is that utilitarianism can require us to kill and torture individuals if that is what would produce more good. Accordingly, it is said that utilitarianism does not take individual rights seriously.

Deontology

Deontology maintains that the moral value of an action—whether it is right or wrong—is intrinsic to the action and not dependent on the consequences of the action. Some deontologists, notably Kantians (after the philosopher Immanuel Kant), believe that consequences are irrelevant—that one ought never to consider the consequences. Other deontologists are sensitive to the moral significance of the consequences of actions. They simply deny that these consequences have a monopoly in determining the moral value of that action. That is to say, they think that consequences are relevant, but not decisive in evaluating an action.

Deontology is attractive primarily for two reasons. First, it imposes restrictions on the way we may treat individuals. It says that there are some things that are so bad that they may never be done to an individual irrespective of the consequences of not doing them. Second, it holds us responsible only for what we do or do not do, and not (like consequentialism) for all consequences of our behavior even where these include the actions of others. Thus, if terrorists threaten to blow up an airplane filled with passengers unless I kill one innocent person, the deontologist says that were I to kill the one person, I would be responsible for that death. By contrast, if I refused to kill that person, then the terrorists, and not I, would not be responsible for the deaths of the people on the airplane.

Critics of deontology sometimes suggest that deontology is merely consequentialism in disguise. The argument is that although deontologists think that they can determine, independently of consequences, which actions are right, they surreptitiously appeal to consequences. To say, for example, that an intrinsically wrong action is one that one would not want all others to perform is merely to say, the argument goes, that performing those sorts of actions would have bad consequences. Other critics argue either that deontology is unable to explain adequately what makes some actions intrinsically right or that it is unacceptably rigid and lacks a mechanism for resolving conflict between moral principles.

Contractarianism

Contractarianism is the view that morality is the product of a social contract, either actual or hypothetical. On this view, the rules of morality are those which (on the actual-contract version) *are*, or (on the hypothetical-contract version) *would be* adopted by parties to the contract.

One appealing feature of contractarianism is that it can explain from where moral rules come and which rules there are. Critics of the actual-contract version deny that there is an actual contract that binds us. Critics of the hypothetical-contract version deny that a hypothetical contract is a kind of contract and thus deny that the rules of such a "contract" can be binding. Some opponents of contractarianism have suggested that it is unable to explain why we have duties to those, such as animals and severely handicapped people, who cannot be party to the social contract, either because they have nothing to offer in the contract or because they lack the capacity to enter into a contract.

Virtue Ethics

Virtue ethics has received considerable attention in the last few decades as some philosophers have begun to question the whole enterprise of modern moral philosophy.[6] These philosophers have suggested that instead of focusing on questions like "What actions are right?", as modern moral philosophy has tended to do, we should attempt to answer questions like "What sort of person is a good person?" In other words, they have suggested that morality is more fundamentally about *character*—that is, what kind of person one is—than about what one *does*. According to this view, theories like consequentialism and deontology answer the wrong kind of question: they tell us how to act rather than what sort of person to be. Critics of the virtue ethics school argue that although a focus on character is important, it cannot be a substitute for a focus on right action. Viewed as an alternative approach to morality it surely gets things the wrong way around. What makes a character good is its disposition to produce the right actions. It is not the case that an action is right simply because it is performed by somebody with a good character. How could a character trait be deemed a virtue without recourse to its impact on how people behave?

Faced with these theories, their strengths and weaknesses, some people want to pick and choose among them, depending on the particular problem at hand. When one theory provides the intuitively best solution to a particular problem, they want to employ that theory. And when another theory provides the intuitively best solution to another problem, they want to switch to that theory. Such people are "moral chameleons"—they change their theoretical colors depending on the problem. While color changes may be good for chameleons, they are not good for those theorizing about ethics. If a theory does not deliver the right answer in some situations, then we have to wonder whether it really is providing the correct explanation of the rightness of those actions with which it is congruent and which we think are right. This is not to say that some combination of theories is not possible. There are utilitarian accounts of virtue, for example, and contractarian accounts of deontology. In these cases, however, there has to be a coherent theoretical account that integrates the component parts.

[6]See, for example, G. E. M. Anscombe, "Modern Moral Philosophy," *Philosophy* 33 (1958): 1–19.

Practicing Philosophy

Philosophy is a difficult discipline. It is intellectually challenging, requiring one to master complex concepts and to think and argue in ways that meet demanding standards of rigor. Common sloppy ways of thinking and inclinations to oversimplification must be eschewed. But philosophy is difficult in another way too. One of its characteristic features is a commitment to questioning. This commitment is not an easy one.

Questioning

For the philosopher, there are no views that are immune to criticism. Of course, it would be impractical and silly to question everything all the time. Were one to do that, no argument could ever get off the ground. We do accept some views for the purposes of certain arguments, albeit tentatively. Thus if we are arguing about whether we have environmental duties, for example, we do not question the existence of the external world (the world beyond one's own mind) and suggest that pollution cannot be wrong because there is no environment it can damage. In environmental debates we assume that the external world exists. Nevertheless, no view—not even the view that the external world exists—is so sacrosanct that it may *never* be questioned. Philosophers do typically challenge (even though they do not always reject) beliefs that are ordinarily taken as obviously true. To many people, such questioning is, at best, childish or, worse, ludicrous. That dismissive attitude to philosophical questioning is too hasty, especially when it comes to moral issues. There are countless examples in human history of ideas that, although now recognized to be patently false, were once accepted as self-evidently true. For many of our human forebears, it was as clear as day that the world was flat, that some people were naturally suited to be slaves, that killing somebody for his religious beliefs was permissible or even desirable, or that women were too feeble-minded to have the vote and should have no place in the universities or professions. Philosophers have not been above holding such beliefs, even though other philosophers have disagreed with them. This shows that the practice of philosophy is no guarantee against falsehood. (Where two people hold contradictory beliefs, at least one party must be wrong.) Nevertheless, it remains true that only those who are prepared to question a view could ever come to reject it. It is because of this that the philosophical disposition to critical questioning is so important. It is extremely unlikely that *all* the beliefs that one holds are correct. To think otherwise is a kind of hubris. Although questioning one's views will not guarantee that one will come to hold only true beliefs, one stands a much greater chance of discovering erroneous beliefs if one is prepared to question the views held by oneself and by those around one.

This seems to be quite widely recognized in scientific circles. The scientific methodology is also a questioning one. What is odd, though, is how many people entertain scientific questions and demand evidence for scientific views, but are content to rely, without question, on whatever moral views happen to be current. One reason for this is the difficulty of questioning one's own moral (as well as political and religious) views. With some exceptions (notably those that impinge on religious, political, and moral ideas), scientific questioning does not challenge the values and beliefs that people hold dear. Philosophical inquiry in areas like ethics, political philosophy, and philosophy of religion requires us to subject to critical scrutiny those of our beliefs and values that are most important to us. This is an immensely difficult task, and most people fail miserably. Some are content never to question and simply to accept their views. Others are prepared to engage in superficial questioning, but only in order to search for arguments that will reinforce the position they already hold. Very few people are willing and able to give up views that cannot withstand scrutiny. Yet this is exactly what is required for good philosophy. It is not sufficient to have the cognitive skills necessary to understand and evaluate an issue. One must have the dispositional attribute of wanting to know the truth, even if it is uncomfortable. This is not to say that philosophy is only done well when it leads to the abandonment of one's beliefs. Sometimes one's views are correct, and when they are it would surely be wrong to reject them. Unfortunately, however, most people simply assume that most or all their opinions are right and do not sufficiently seriously consider the possibility that a view they hold deeply might be erroneous.

The topics covered in this book are ones that affect—often deeply affect— our daily lives. Accordingly, they are likely to be issues about which we have firm opinions. Sometimes this will be because we have thought about them, even if only glibly. On other occasions, although we may not have thought explicitly about them, the way we are accustomed to behave will cause us to have heavily vested interests in a view that endorses that behavior. For instance, gamblers may have a vested interest in defending gambling. Non-gamblers may be inclined to dismiss far too quickly the pleasures that gambling brings to gamblers and thereby rush to a negative judgment of gambling. Similarly, Microsoft executives may unreflectively condemn unauthorized copying of computer software, while impoverished students may rush to a defense of this practice. To earnestly engage quotidian and other ethical issues, one must subject one's own views to probing scrutiny as well as taking seriously the arguments of those philosophers with whom one disagrees. It sometimes helps to identify the interests one has in adopting one or other view. That is the first step in determining whether those interests are blinding one. Of course, sometimes one's interests will be happily congruent with the correct view, but we cannot simply assume that the comfortable answer is the right one. Very often it is not.

Answering Moral Questions

How can we tell whether a moral view should be accepted—whether or not it is right? Many people suggest that there really are no answers to moral questions. This is a view that, I suspect, is more often articulated than believed. Consider what the response would be of those who express this view, if one were to threaten to or actually inflict some harm on them (perhaps on account of their having expressed this view). More often than not, I imagine, they would be quick to denounce the injustice of one's (proposed) action. Moreover, most people think that those who disagree with their moral views have not simply a different view but a wrong one. None of this, it must be emphasized, shows that there is more to ethics than opinion. What it does show is that very few people actually believe this.

Ethics clearly is not characterized by the same degree of certainty as is mathematics. But this is not to say that ethics is merely a matter of opinion. There are scientific disciplines, such as medicine or archaeology, in which there is much less certainty than in mathematics, yet we do not conclude that in these areas any opinion is as good as any other. We think that the evidence and arguments can get us quite far, even if not as far as in mathematics, and we think that opinions in these areas can be better or worse. Even where the evidence is inconclusive, we do not infer that there is no answer—only that we do not know what it is. This should demonstrate that the relative uncertainty in ethics does not by itself show that there are no answers, or that any opinion is as good as any other. Indeed, it seems that reason can take us quite far in ethics. We can evaluate moral views, at least to a considerable extent. Whether we adopt or reject a moral view should depend on the strength of the arguments that can be advanced for or against it.

One standard to which we can appeal is that of *consistency*. A moral view that was inconsistent would be defective in the same sort of way that a contradiction is. If, for instance, a moral view endorses Jane's torturing John, but not John's torturing Jane, and no morally relevant differences between the two situations can be demonstrated, then the moral view is inconsistent and thus defective. Another way in which we can judge moral views is by examining *the truth of empirical claims* on which they rest. Some people have defended the infliction of injury on animals on the grounds that animals cannot feel pain. It has also been claimed that we are justified in treating some people less well because they are members of a less intelligent race. Such empirical claims can be assessed. The best scientific evidence available to us shows that they are false. Thus any view that rested on these grounds would be without adequate foundation.

It must be conceded that there can be both good and bad arguments for a view. Thus, demonstrating that one argument fails to support a given conclusion does not entail that the conclusion is false. It could be that one defense of lying, for example, is deeply flawed, but that another is extremely compelling. If, however, the advocates of a view fail to provide *any* reasonable defense of their view, then their view is without apparent foundation and is not worthy of adoption.

Reading Philosophy

Reading philosophy is not easy. Even when written in a clear, accessible style, the argument can be complicated and close attention may be required to fully understand it. One might be able to speed-read novels, but reading philosophy must be a more attentive process. Very often one will need to read the article a second or even third time.

It is sometimes helpful to *underline* words, phrases, or brief passages that mark the various stages of the argument or are otherwise important. One should be cautioned, however, against getting carried away and underlining (or highlighting) the bulk of the text. That undermines the point of the marking: to be able to return to only a few key elements of the paper in order to refresh one's memory about the argument.

Another helpful technique is to make *annotations* in the margins. Sometimes, while reading a paper, one thinks of an objection or a question. Writing it down in the margin is a way of preserving that thought and enabling one to return to it later. Marginal annotations may also serve to mark the various stages in the development of the argument.

Diligent students might also decide to write a *summary* of a philosophical article they read. Being able to do this is a good test of whether one has understood the paper. In this book, summaries of each paper are provided to help students understand the papers. This should not preclude students from writing summaries of their own, and perhaps then comparing them with the ones provided. In a summary, one should ask oneself what each author is saying. That is to say, one should ask oneself what view is being advocated and what arguments are being advanced in its defense.

It would be a mistake to think that the summaries that appear in this book may be read in lieu of the articles themselves. The summaries really are only an outline of the argument. They do not attempt to *evaluate* the papers, which students must do. To assess the argument, the articles themselves must be read. Some of the study questions provided at the end of each reading are aimed at facilitating such evaluation. Answering these questions will require reading the articles rather than only the summaries. In any event, reading only the summaries but pretending that one has read the full articles would be cheating, and that, surely, is not something one should do, least of all in an ethics class!

Suggestions for Further Reading

Becker, Lawrence C., and Charlotte B. Becker, eds. *Encyclopedia of Ethics*. New York: Garland, 1992.

Rachels, James. *The Elements of Moral Philosophy*, 3d ed. Boston: McGraw-Hill, 1999.

———. *Can Ethics Provide Answers?* Lanham, Md.: Rowman and Littlefield, 1997.

Singer, Peter. *A Companion to Ethics*. Oxford: Blackwell, 1993.

PART ONE

Communication

CHAPTER 1

Humor

Racist Acts and Racist Humor

Michael Philips

Michael Philips argues against what he calls the Agent-Centered Account of racist humor. On this account a joke cannot be racist unless it is told by a racist, and a racist is somebody who has racist beliefs or feelings. Thus, on this view, the jokes one tells cannot be racist if one has no racist beliefs or feelings. The author rejects this view in favor of what he calls an Act-Centered Theory, according to which the most basic sense in which the word 'racist' is used is in reference to actions. On this view, talk of racist people, beliefs, policies, and so on, must be understood in relation to racist acts. Thus, for example, racist beliefs are (roughly) those beliefs that are used to justify racist acts.

The Act-Centered Theory says that a person P performs a Basic Racist Act by doing (an action) A when "(a) P does A in order to harm Q because Q is a member of a certain ethnic group; or (b) (regardless of P's intentions or purposes) P's doing A can reasonably be expected to mistreat Q as a consequence of Q's being a member of a certain ethnic group." A strength of the Act-Centered Theory, says the author, is that it recognizes that what is essentially wrong with racism is what it does to the victim. It is acts rather than beliefs that are the immediate cause of that harm.

I

Racist jokes are often funny. And part of this has to do with their racism. Many Polish jokes, for example, may easily be converted into moron jokes but are not at all funny when delivered as such. Consider two answers to 'What has an I.Q. of 100?': (a) a nation of morons; or (b) Poland. Similarly, jokes portraying Jews as cheap, Italians as cowards, and Greeks as dishonest may be told as jokes about how skinflints, cowards, or dishonest people get on in the world. But they

Michael Philips, "Racist Acts and Racist Humor," *Canadian Journal of Philosophy*, vol. 14, no. 1, March 1984. Copyright 1984. Reprinted by permission of the University of Calgary Press.

are less funny as such (at least if one is not Jewish, Greek, or Italian). As this suggests, racist humor is 'put down' humor. We laugh, in part, because we find put-downs funny, sometimes even if they are about us. In many contexts, this tendency is relatively harmless; indeed, within reason, it may be therapeutic to join others in a good laugh at oneself. Why, then, all the commotion about racist humor?

'Racist' is a moral pejorative. To say that an act is racist is to say that it is prima facie wrong. Our problem, then, is to determine the range of cases that deserve this description. That is, we are trying to decide what forms of race-related behavior to discourage by means of this moral pejorative. In relation to humor, we face a nest of problems. Much racist humor, for example, attributes an unflattering characteristic to its target group. What if members of that group really have or tend statistically to have that characteristic? Surely we are allowed to notice this and to communicate this information to one another. Is truth a defense against the charge of racism? Also, what of the good-natured interplay between friends of different ethnic groups in which such jokes may play an important part? And what of exchanges of such jokes between members of ethnic groups about whom they are told? This paper will present an account of racist humor in relation to which we can answer these and related questions. What is said here about racist humor will also apply to sexist humor and to humor about national groups.

II

Not all humor that takes an ethnic group as its subject matter is racist. Some such humor is morally unobjectionable. Our first task, then, is to distinguish this sort of humor from racist humor. In other words, we need to determine why some humor about ethnic groups is morally unobjectionable while other humor is not.

Let me begin with a popular theory; or, in any case, a theory that is presupposed by a very common defense against the charge of having made a racist joke. This defense denies, in effect that joking remarks are racist so long as they are made by persons whose souls are pure. According to this view, a racist act presupposes a racist actor, and a racist actor is a person who acts from racist beliefs and/or racist feelings. I call this the Agent-Centered Account. Although a complete account of this view requires an account of the nature of racist beliefs and feelings, my purposes do not require this here. For now, suffice it to say that on this account one may innocently entertain one's fellow Rotarians with jokes like 'After shaking hands with a Greek, count your fingers,' so long as one harbors no racist beliefs or feelings about Greeks. If one's soul is pure, such jokes are all in good fun and ought to be accepted as such.

Before attacking this theory , I want to contrast it with my own account. The term 'racist' is used of books, attitudes, societies, epithets, actions, persons, feelings, policies, laws, etc., as well as of humor. Any account of 'racist' will explain some of these uses in relation to others. The Agent-Centered Theory explains racist humor in relation to racist persons, and racist persons in relation to racist beliefs and attitudes. And, to the extent that it can be generalized, moreover, it explains all other uses of 'racist' in this way as well. On my own view, 'racist' is used in its logically primary sense when it is attributed to actions. All other uses of 'racist,' I believe, must be understood directly or indirectly *in relation to* this one. Accordingly, racist beliefs are (roughly) beliefs about an ethnic group used to 'justify' racist acts, racist feelings are feelings about an ethnic group that typically give rise to such acts, and racist epithets are the stings and arrows by means of which certain such acts are carried out. Books and films are said to be racist, on the other hand, if they perpetuate and stimulate racist beliefs or feelings (which are in turn understood in relation to racist acts).

More precisely, on my view, 'racist' is used in its logically primary sense when it is used of what I shall call Basic Racist Acts. Roughly, P performs a Basic Racist Act by doing A when: (a) P does A in order to harm Q because Q is a member of a certain ethnic group; or (b) (regardless of P's intentions or purposes) P's doing A can reasonably be expected to mistreat Q as a consequence of Q's being a member of a certain ethnic group.[1] Note that, on this account, P's motives, beliefs, feelings, or intentions need not be taken into account in determining that P performed a racist act. If you refer to someone as 'a stinking little kike' in my company, I am harmed by your action because I am Jewish, whether you intended this result or not. If this harm counts as mistreatment, then, in my account, your remark is racist, And, I shall argue, this is so even if you have nothing at all against Jews, e.g., you are merely attempting to discredit a competitor in the eyes of an anti-Semite. I call my view the Act-Centered Theory.

Before arguing for the superiority of this view to the Agent-Centered view, two observations are in order. To begin with, condition (a), in effect, acknowledges an element of truth in the Agent-Centered Theory. For if P does A in order to harm Q simply because Q is Hispanic, P must have racist beliefs or feelings against Hispanics. And it follows from this that P's acting on such beliefs or feelings—i.e., P's acting as a racist by doing A—is a sufficient condition of A's being a racist act. Nonetheless, it is mistaken to focus on P's beliefs or feelings in our account of why P's act is wrong. Rather, we ought focus on what P's act means for its victims. For roughly, it is not the fact that racists act on mistaken beliefs or irrational feelings that make their actions wrong, i.e., it is not the state of mind of the actor that corrupts the act.[2] Rather, it is the meaning of the act for the victims

---

[1]I am using 'mistreatment' in (b) to include any morally objectionable injury to someone's interests. Note that 'harm' is not sufficient here. Affirmative Action, for example, may harm White males in virtue of their race, but is not 'reverse racism' unless it can be established that it mistreats them. I use 'harm' instead of 'mistreatment' in condition (a) to avoid counter-examples in which A acts within his rights by harming B, but would not harm B were B's race different (e.g. White landlord A evicts Black tenant B for delinquency, in paying the rent, but would not do so were B White). Although I would argue that this constitutes mistreatment, I do not want my criteria to depend on the arguable point that one may mistreat someone by choosing to exercise one's rights.

[2]Moreover, there are cases in which we cannot justifiably condemn the racist for his feelings and beliefs. For the feelings may be consequences of the beliefs and the beliefs may be those that any normal person in her position would adopt. Consider, for example, the adolescent who grows up in a

that makes us condemn both the act and the state of mind that prompted it. Indeed, if condition (b) is correct, P's being a racist—or even acting as a racist on some particular occasion—is not a necessary condition of P's act being a racist act. It is sufficient that his act can reasonably be expected to mistreat in the appropriate way. This is not, of course, to say that an act must succeed in mistreating someone in order to be racist. Were this the case, condition (a) would be unnecessary. But, in general, because we are entitled to assume a certain competence on the part of wrong-doers, it makes sense for us morally to condemn acts that would mistreat or victimize were their intention realized. Accordingly, we condemn lies that fail to deceive, assaults that fail to harm, and robberies that yield no stolen goods. We do not condemn these acts because they spring from some intention or state of mind that can be identified as morally corrupt independently of its likelihood of giving rise to some form of mistreatment. On the contrary, it is precisely in virtue of this likelihood that we condemn the intention.

In the second place, it is worth pointing out that the Act-Centered Theory and the Agent-Centered Theory each reflect a certain point of view. Roughly, the Agent-Centered Theory reflects the perspective of the morally troubled member of a persecuting group. Such persons are loathe to acknowledge their contributions to what they agree to be a morally indefensible system. The Agent-Centered Account permits them to escape unblemished so long as they are able to purge themselves of racist beliefs and feelings. Once purged, they may do what is 'necessary' to get on in a racist society without fear of moral censure. For example, they may prohibit their daughter to date a Black classmate on the grounds that this will jeopardize her future; or they may ask her not to invite her Black friends to her wedding on the grounds that this will be unsettling to old family friends. On the Agent-Centered Theory, if these are in fact their motives, they needn't think of their actions as racist, and they needn't think of

---

highly racist community. It may well be that everyone she respects in that community holds racist beliefs. And it may also be that the limited experience she has in relation to the victimized group tends to confirm these beliefs (suppose, e.g., she works in a liquor store that sells largely to poor Blacks). Now that the mass media has developed some degree of racial consciousness, of course, it is very likely that most such persons will also be exposed to countervailing views. But her authorities in the relevant community may have ways of discounting the media (e.g., by claiming that it is run by Communists and Jews). And if the adolescent in question does not read very well—indeed, if she lacks the proper research skills—she really hasn't the resources to determine whom to trust. In this case it is difficult to see how she could be blamed for holding the beliefs she holds. On the other hand, the greater her exposure to 'recalcitrant data' the more we have a right to expect her to reevaluate her beliefs. Racist societies typically discourage such reevaluations by formally or informally punishing those who undertake them; and, as a consequence of this, many people have a strong tendency to overlook data that conflicts with their racist beliefs when they encounter them (and a tendency to weigh confirming instances relatively more heavily than disconfirming instances). Given the consequences of these beliefs for action, however, these tendencies *are* morally objectionable. Where there is the opportunity for knowledge on such serious matters, ignorance is blameworthy. In any case, it is important to emphasize that whether or not we regard P's possession of such beliefs as blameworthy, we are entitled to condemn the actions that flow from them as racist, and therefore, as prima facie wrong. Again, our reason for this is that these actions victimize or are intended to victimize members of the relevant ethnic group.

themselves as complicit in a racist system. Indeed, this permits them to feel morally superior to those who discriminate out of feeling or conviction.

The Act-Centered conception, on the other hand, adopts the perspective of the victim, the accuser. The victim experiences racism as so many forms of mistreatment. If she is not invited to a friend's wedding because she is Black, she takes this to be a racist act. Since racist acts are wrong only prima facie, this does not necessarily mean that she condemns the act as wrong, or even that she considers her friend a racist (the relationship between racist acts and racist persons is more complex than this). Still, she is deprived of an invitation to which she is entitled as a friend because of her ethnicity. Accordingly, even if the act is justified, *she* is wronged.[3] And since this is so, the act is racist.

As this suggests, the term 'racism' marks a contested concept. Established English use places outside limits on what counts as an acceptable definition ('racist' can not be defined as ice cream) but there is plenty of room for disagreement within these parameters. Established English use does not and should not determine how we are to decide between the alternatives. When we choose between competing patterns of use we are deciding what forms of race-related behavior it is important for us as a society morally to disparage. In effect, then, a defense of an 'analysis' of this concept is a defense of a moral standard (or set of related standards). My defense of an act-centered account, then, is really a defense of the claim that that account yields the sorts of moral judgments we should be making in relation to race-related conduct. More specifically, I am arguing that this pattern of use better serves the purposes of combating racial injustice than its alternatives.[4]

III

To begin with, the Agent-Centered Theory has difficulty making sense of certain important uses of 'racist.' Consider racial epithets ('nigger,' 'kike,' 'wop,' etc.). On the Agent-Centered Theory, use of such epithets to insult or to assert undeserved power are racist *only if* the users have racist beliefs or feelings. But suppose that a white man calls a Black travelling-companion 'nigger' to remind him of his social status, e.g., as an insult or as a power move ('Look nigger, if push comes to shove, nobody's going to take your side here'). In determining whether this use is racist, do we need to consider what the White man believes

---

[3]To deny this is to fail to take wrongs seriously. Philosophers and bureaucrats sometimes do this. So long as an action is judged right, all things considered, there is a tendency on the part of some to deny that anyone is wronged by it. But this is mistaken. Suppose that we must jail an innocent person for two weeks to prevent a vendetta very likely to kill scores. Most of us, I think, would take this to be the right action. But isn't it also clear that the jailed party has been wronged? To deny this is to deny: (a) that we owe this person some recompense, and (b) that we have a reason to regret the jailing of this person that we would not have were he guilty of some offense. It seems to me, however, that not to accept (a) and (b) is to endorse ruthlessness.

[4]For an account of how moral standards are properly defended and criticized see chapters 4–6 of my book *Between Universalism and Skepticism*, Oxford University Press, 1994.

or feels about Blacks in general? Suppose that he harbors no beliefs or feelings to the effect that Blacks are inferior or deserve inferior treatment, and that he is 'putting his companion in his place' *merely* to have his own way. Still, he has used this epithet unfairly to threaten, insult, or assume unwarranted power over another person; and, obviously, his act has this consequence because of his companion's race. Accordingly, I believe, we would call such acts 'racist.' In any case, we should speak this way. For we want morally to condemn forms of victimization that are made possible by the victims' ethnic identity and this seems an unobjectionable way to do so.

The Agent-Centered Theory, moreover, prevents us from saying that certain paradigm cases of racist acts are racist. Consider the German soldier who volunteers to march Jewish victims to the gas ovens *out of simple patriotism,* or the Klansman who ties nooses at lynchings for *business reasons.* Each may (in principle) act with heart and mind uncorrupted by racist beliefs or feelings (though obviously this is unlikely). Does this mean that they have not acted in a racist manner? Suppose that all the German soldiers at Dachau acted out of patriotism and all the Klansmen at the lynching were there for business reasons. Would this mean that none of those who participated in such events were guilty of racist acts?

Note that I am not arguing that participants in such events are racists; only that they act in a racist manner. Indeed, there may be good reason to deny they are racist since we want to distinguish those who participate in victimization out of patriotism or self-interest from those participate in victimization out of race hate or authentic conviction. Still, it is the victimization, not the persons, we are primarily concerned to condemn and eliminate, and if we refuse to condemn acts of victimization as racist, it is unclear what moral category we could invoke to this end.

Racist societies encourage racist victimization by a system of rewards and punishments. Sometimes these are formal and explicit (e.g., apartheid laws), sometimes they are informal and subtle (e.g., subtle forms of social exclusion). In any case, this system creates a set of prudential reasons for *all* members of the victimizing race to participate in victimization, i.e., to be complicit in the mistreatment of the victimized group. By calling these forms of complicity 'racist,' we make them a matter of moral concern whatever their motivation, i.e., whether they are motivated by race hate or by prudence. It is important that we do this. Were we morally to condemn only those forms of victimization motivated by race hate or racist beliefs, we would leave equally important forms of victimization outside the realm of moral concern; or, at best, subject to moral evaluation only on utilitarian grounds. Suppose, for example, that Alice excludes a Black friend from her wedding list in order to not to upset one of Daddy's business associates. And suppose that this action produces just a little more happiness than unhappiness. If we do not describe this sort of complicity in the general pattern of victimization of Blacks as prima facie wrong, in itself, her action will be immune from moral criticism. Moreover, to the extent that we discount utilitarian considerations in our ethics such acts of complicity will be regarded simply as questions of prudence.

It could be replied that we could condemn the complicity in question without condemning it as racist. On this account, we would reserve 'racist' for those acts of victimization performed out of racist belief and feeling and coin some other term for the forms of complicity in question. This suggestion, however, seems weak. To begin with, the point of the category 'racist' is to eliminate a pervasive form of injustice. And to do this effectively, it is important that we focus attention on the actions that promote or are constituitive of it. It is clear, however, that most victimizing actions contribute equally to victimization whether motivated by self-interest or motivated by race hate. Thus, for the purposes of evaluating the action, there appears to be no good reason for introducing a distinction based on motive (assuming that the acts in question are intentional). Considerations of motive may be relevant to our moral assessment of the actor. But in this case, at least, they ought to be irrelevant to our moral consideration of the act.

In the second place, moreover, the suggestion that we introduce a second category of moral condemnation for self-interested victimization is impractical. Even were we capable of coining a term for this category that gained currency, it would take quite some time for this category to gain the familiarity and pejorative force the term 'racist' now enjoys. If our purpose is to combat victimization now, this strategy would cost us considerable time and effort.

IV

That the Agent-Centered Theory is false does not imply that the Act-Centered Theory is true. For it might be that racist acts can be defined in some other way. It would not be useful to explore all the possibilities here. Most are wildly implausible. One alternative, however, is likely to appeal intuitively to some philosophers, viz., the view that racist acts are acts which *presuppose* racist beliefs for their justification. On this view, to say that act A is racist is to say that A is justified if and only if certain racist beliefs are true. I shall call this the Belief-Centered Theory.

The problem with the Belief-Centered Theory emerges clearly when we consider what could be meant by a racist belief here. Note that a Belief-Centered theorist cannot characterize a racist belief as a belief that justifies racist acts, for then his account of each is circular in a way that renders both unilluminating. To define a racist act as an act justified by some racist belief and a racist belief as a belief that justifies racist acts is to say nothing that enables us better to understand either. There are, of course, two ways out of this circle. One is to define racist acts independently of racist beliefs (as I have done), and the other is to define racist beliefs independently of their role in justifying racist acts. But where could this second strategy lead?

One plausible way to characterize racist beliefs independently of their role in justifying racist acts is to describe them as beliefs to the effect that members of certain ethnic groups are inferior or subhuman. Here, of course, not just any form of inferiority will do. We are concerned, roughly, with those forms that are thought to justify restrictions or deprivations of rights or deserts. We can distinguish between two sorts of beliefs to the effect that groups are inferior in this way. They are: (a) beliefs which, if true, would justify such deprivations (e.g., Antebellum views to the effect that Blacks were much more like beasts of burden than human beings); and (b) beliefs which would not justify such deprivations whether they were true or false (e.g., beliefs that Jews are ambitious, pushy, and cheap).

The first thing to notice about all this, however, is that were we to accept the latter category as a category of racist beliefs, we must change the Belief-Centered Theory. A racist act can no longer be defined as an act that would be justified were some racist belief true, since beliefs of this type (b) do not in fact justify the acts they may be invoked to defend. On the other hand, it is clear that beliefs in this category are often used in defense of racist acts, and that they are important aspects of any racist ideology. Accordingly, we must include them in any reasonable account of racist beliefs. If we do so, however, we must amend the Belief-Centered Theory to read: 'A is a racist act if and only if it is *believed* that A is justified by some racist belief.' The obvious question to which this information gives rise is: 'Believed by whom?' And—if we are to avoid a return to the Agent-Centered Theory—the only remotely plausible answer to this is: 'Believed by members of the society in which A occurs.' Accordingly, the Belief-Centered definition of a racist act must further be amended to read: 'A is a racist act if and only if (some) members of society in which A occurs believe that A is justified by some racist belief that they take to be true.'

The need for such an amendment is also clear from the fact that on the unamended version, every wrong to another person turns out to be a racist act. Since everyone belongs to some ethnic group, every mistreatment of a person, P, could be justified were the appropriate racist belief about P's ethnic group true. The amended version avoids this consequence by restricting racist beliefs to those beliefs actually held in the relevant society.

The amended version, however, has two fatal difficulties. To begin, it remains a consequence of the amended version that every wrong against a member of an ethnic group that could be justified by a racist belief in his society is racist. But surely we want to allow that members of a persecuted group may be wronged in ways that have nothing to do with racism at all, despite the fact that such wrongs *could be* justified by some such racist belief. One might wrongfully harm a Black man, for example, because one is angry at *him*. So long as the attack is wholly personal, and so long as he is not attacked *as* a Black man (e.g., called a nigger), there may be no question of racism at all here. Note that if we further amend the Belief-Centered Theory to meet this objection by requiring that the racist belief belong to the perpetrator of the act, we have returned to the Agent-Centered Theory.

The second problem with the amended version is that if we loosen the connection between racist acts and racist beliefs from 'presupposes' to 'believed to be justified by,' it is impossible to identify racist beliefs by attending to their content. This is particularly clear in the case of beliefs in category (b). For these are beliefs that are *mistakenly* held to imply a certain conclusion and there is no way of deciding on the basis of the content of any belief what can *mistakenly* be inferred from it. Indeed, 'inferences' from the sorts of characteristics named in category (b) beliefs are notoriously inconsistent. For example, beliefs by Americans that Scots are cheap and drive hard bargains are never given as reasons for depriving Scots of rights or privileges. Indeed, these qualities are endearing in Scots, perhaps even virtues. With respect to Jews, however, it is another matter.

If the Belief-Centered theorist cannot identify racist beliefs on the basis of their content, how can he identify them? I can see no plausible answer. On the Act-Centered Account, however, the answer is clear. First, we identify Basic Racist Acts, and then we uncover the personal and/or social ideologies in relation to which these acts are believed to be justified. This move, of course, requires that we are capable of identifying Basic Racist Acts independently of racist beliefs and is not, therefore, open to the Belief-Centered theorist.

V

Before applying my account to the question of racist humor, I would like to anticipate one further objection, viz., that on my account too many actions which seem entirely unobjectionable turn out to be racist. The objector recognizes that on my account racist acts are wrong prima facie, and that there may be occasions on which one is morally justified in acting in a racist manner. His concern is that in other cases of prima facie wrongs it is *typically* wrong to act in the proscribed manner, but that this does not appear to be so in the case of racism. For once we begin to think about it, it is clear that there are myriad ways we may contribute to the victimization of members of victimized groups without doing anything wrong. Consider, for example, cases of distrust. You are walking down a dark street in a poor Black neighborhood at night. A large Black man approaches you from the opposite direction. You cross the street to avoid contact. You recognize that the odds are slim that this particular man will attack you (25 to 1?). But the consequences of being attacked are so great that you would be foolish to take the risk. By so acting, however, you exhibit distrust of a *particular* person. Moreover, chances are excellent that this person has been treated with fear and distrust by Whites throughout his adolescence and adulthood simply in virtue of his size and race. To be treated in such a way is to be victimized, and by crossing the street you are contributing to this victimization. Examples of this sort of distrust are commonplace. And, in many cases at least, this distrustful attitude—though unfair to the overwhelming majority who pose no threat—is nonetheless rational. For, though the odds against any particular attack may be much in one's favor—e.g., 25 to 1—if one is not distrustful in this way and one lives in an urban environment, it is likely that one will be attacked sooner or later. And again, the consequences of an attack are so severe that it is foolish to take the risk in any case. According to the objection, acts of this sort are not typically wrong. And if they are not typically wrong, the victimization they involve ought not be regarded as prima facie wrong either.

This objection is not a strong one. It is interesting, however, in that it brings into relief an important fact about moral relations in racist societies. The fact is that in any society in which racism is pervasive there will be a social chasm between the races that forces most members of every ethnic group to relate to members of other groups through racial stereotypes, at least most of the time. There is too little opportunity for most people to get to know members of other groups well enough to permit anything else. Moreover, as the present example suggests, there may be good reason to act on stereotypes, even where it is recognized that a stereotype applies to only a small number of persons within a group.[5] Now where the treatment dictated by the stereotype is negative, most persons in the victimized group (e.g., twenty-four or twenty-five) will be treated unfairly *as a matter of course* by most members of the victimizing group. The fact that this treatment *is* unfair, however, makes it prima facie wrong. The objector makes an obvious mistake in denying that victimization is prima facie wrong merely because it may typically be justified by overriding considerations. But he is correct in emphasizing the high price—perhaps even the impossibility—of avoiding complicity in this victimization. If we are members of a victimizing race, it is virtually certain that we will be complicit. It is the genius of a racist society to arrange that this is so. This does not mean that we are all racists. Nor does it mean that we are moral monsters. Again, there are times that even the best intentioned of us have no real choice. But in this case, what we have no choice about is whether to commit a racist act. This is the tragedy of living in a racist society for the morally sensitive members of the victimizing race.

VI

Belief- and Agent-Centered theories tend to direct our attention to the cognitive aspect of racist acts. In relation to humor, they incline us to focus on content. Accordingly, they direct our attention primarily to one form of humor—humor based on racist stereotypes and they incline us to consider such humor in a certain way, viz., in relation to the beliefs it may promote or express. Thus, if we adopt such an account, we are likely to consider the problem of characterizing racist humor as the problem of describing the sorts of beliefs such humor portrays or expresses. Accordingly, we shall probably begin by characterizing racist humor as humor which expresses false and unflattering beliefs about an ethnic group. And this beginning leads us inevitably to questions of truthfulness. For we must now decide how to characterize humor based on stereotypes which have some foundation in truth. For example, if it is statistically true that Blacks are significantly less literate than Whites, we will be inclined to ask whether it is racist to make jokes about problems created by Black illiteracy. It is likely,

---

[5]It is worth noting that given the social hiatus between victimizing and victimized groups in racist societies stereotypes need little confirmation to achieve widespread belief. Partly as a result of this social chasm confirming instances of a stereotype are far more accessible than disconfirming instances. Consider the Italian gangster stereotype, i.e., the view that most Italians are linked to organized crime. The confirming instances—Mafia personnel—are in the public eye. But it seems likely that those who take this stereotype seriously do not know many Italians personally, and have no way of knowing whether or not the Italians with whom they have contact (e.g., grocery store and restaurant owners) are connected with the Mafia.

moreover, that we see in this question a conflict between truth, on the one hand, and social justice, on the other. By freeing us from focusing narrowly on content, the Act-Centered Theory frees us from focusing on questions of truth. Moreover, in many cases, at least, it enables us to avoid formulating the question of the morality of certain jokes as questions that involve deciding in favor of truth, on the one hand, or of social justice, on the other.

Roughly speaking, then, the Act-Centered Theory holds that ethnic humor is racist: (a) when it is used with the intent to victimize a member of an ethnic group in virtue of her ethnicity; and (b) when it in fact promotes such victimization or can reasonably be expected to promote it (e.g., by contributing to an atmosphere in which it is more likely to occur).

To be more precise, let us use the expression 'a bit of humor' for a particular occurrence of humor, e.g., the telling of a joke, the mimicking of an accent, the appearance of a cartoon in a particular time and place. On my account, a bit of ethnic humor is racist if: (1) it is a Basic Racist Act, or (2) it can reasonably be expected to promote an atmosphere in which Basic Racist Acts are more likely to occur, or (3) it is intended to promote such an atmosphere. Of course, we also speak of jokes, books, films, etc. as racist 'in themselves,' i.e., apart from their particular occurrences. But if I am correct, this way of speaking is parasitic on the other. Roughly, we say that a joke 'itself' is racist because a typical act of telling it will be racist in at least one of the ways described; and analogous points hold for films, books, laws, etc. (though, of course, we may need to express these points somewhat differently). A consequence of this view is that a joke which embodies a discarded and forgotten racist stereotype—e.g., a scheming Phoenician—is not now racist. Indeed, where stereotypes have been forgotten, stereotyped characters in jokes (books and movies) will not be identified as such; their actions will be construed as the acts of individuals rather than as representative of ethnic groups. Upon discovering that these characters were stereotypes, we may decide to call the work in question 'racist.' But here we mean only that the work was racist *in its time.* This use of 'racist' does not have the same moral significance as our ordinary use. We do not mean to suggest by this, for example, that there is anything wrong with exhibiting or distributing this material now.

As suggested at the outset of this paper, at least much racist humor is 'put down' humor. Racial 'put downs,' of course, are at least often Basic Racist Acts. In any case, it is clear that they are when they are used to insult, humiliate, ridicule, or otherwise assault someone in consequence of his ethnic identity. Such bits of humor need not make use of ethnic stereotypes. It is sometimes enough merely to humiliate a member of a victimized group in some manner thought to be funny (e.g., in the American West, to cut the 'Chinaman's' pigtail). Such humor is often extremely cruel. Moreover, even where stereotypes are incorporated in ridicule or humiliation, use of these stereotypes is not racist merely because they promote racist beliefs. Indeed, their chief use may be to identify the form of insult or humiliation thought appropriate to the member of the victimized group. This form of humiliation, moreover, may be rather far removed from any racist belief that 'justifies' mistreatment. Thus, though Jews were not *mistreated* on the ground that they were believed (or said) to have large noses, some think it quite amusing to make jokes about 'Jewish noses.' Note that insults, ridicule, and humiliation do not, *in general*, require justification—or even a sham of justification—to do their work. All that is required is an attitude of derision on the part of the victimizer toward some characteristic that the victim is said to have (however insincere the attribution). Again, some stereotypes do not function so much to promote beliefs but to ridicule or humiliate in just this way. The main point of portraying Jews with enormous noses and Blacks with huge lips is not to perpetuate the belief that Jews or Blacks tend to look *that* way. Rather, it is to promote an *attitude* about looking that way, and *to take the position* that Jews and Blacks look that way *as a way of* insulting Jews and Blacks. What goes on here is similar to what goes on in the school yard when a group of children decide to humiliate another child by taunting him with accusations that are insulting merely in virtue of the attitudes expressed toward him. Again, almost any characteristic will do here and it doesn't really matter to anyone whether or not the victim *is* that way. In fact, it may be more effective if he is not. Then, in addition to insult, he suffers a further miscarriage of justice. The difference between school yard tauntings and the caricatures of Jews and Blacks in question is that the tone of school yard tauntings is often deadly earnest while the caricatures in question taunt through comic ridicule.

Moreover, jokes and cartoons which on some occasions create or reinforce racist stereotypes may be racist in contexts where they do not serve this end. For they may be used *simply* to insult, humiliate, or ridicule. The most obvious example is that of a stereotyping joke told with gleeful hostility to a member of a victimized group. If the victim and the victimizer are alone, there may be no question of spreading or perpetrating racist beliefs here.[6] What is racist about expressing such stereotypes is their use to insult or to humiliate. Where such jokes are told before 'mixed audiences,' they may be racist both because they insult and because they help to reinforce racist beliefs.

It is important to notice, moreover, that bits of humor that insult by the use of stereotypes may do so *however* close or far that stereotype is from a relevant statistical truth. As suggested, ridicule, insult, and humiliation are what they are whether or not the victims are as they are said to be; and, indeed, whether or not there is in fact something defficient about being as the victim is said to be. Note that children and insensitive adults may ridicule or humiliate retarded persons and spastics by imitating them *accurately*. In general, it may be insulting merely to point out some truth about a person that someone with respect for the feelings and well-being of others would pass over in silence.

Precisely what determines the conditions under which a person is humiliated, insulted, or ridiculed—as opposed to merely feeling that way—is a complex question that I cannot hope to answer here. It is clear, however, that context is extremely important. And here, two points are worthy of comment.

---

[6]Although such jokes may contribute to the sense of inferiority often suffered by members of victimized races. And when this occurs it could be said that they promote the belief that such people are inferior.

First, although it may occasionally be possible to exchange what would ordinarily be considered racial insults in an atmosphere of good will and comraderie, good will does not preclude the possibility of insults. One may insult or humiliate another with the purest of hearts and the best of intentions, so long as one is sufficiently stupid or insensitive (consider the high school principal who introduces a Japanese commencement speaker by 'assuling' the audience that he 'explesses the freerings of his frerrow immiglants').

Secondly, one may insult without saying or doing anything that is 'objectively insulting.' Sometimes it is enough simply to probe what ought to be recognized as a sensitive area. Typically, if we know that a friend is very touchy about, e.g., some characteristic, we avoid referring to it, even in jest. Indeed, unless there is some strong countervailing reason to refer to it, we insult him by so doing. And it does not matter whether or not we believe that our friend's sensitivity is rational, i.e., whether such remarks *ought to be* considered insulting or humiliating. If it is no great burden to respect his sensitivity, to fail to do so is insulting. And what holds for friends in this regard ought also to hold for acquaintances or even strangers. Typically, if we know that members of a victimized group are insulted by certain jokes made about them, we ought not to make such jokes in their presence (unless, e.g., we do this for therapeutic purpose). This standard, however, is too restrictive to govern communications before mass audiences, e.g., television. But even here we ought not require that sensitivities be perfectly rational in order to be respected. If a substantial number of the victimized group—say, a majority—is known to be offended by certain ways of portraying them, then it may be insulting to them to portray them in these ways simply because we ignore their sensitivities by so doing. If there is no overriding reason for portraying them in this way, we ought not to do so. Moreover, we ought to give special weight to the opinion of the victimized group that such portrayals *are* insulting in and of themselves. For it requires more empathy on the part of an outsider fully to appreciate the position of a victimized group than many of us have a right to claim. Consider, for example, the glee that the most educated among us take in telling Polish jokes.

But it is not only the immediate impact of racist humor on victimized groups that makes it racist. The impact on victimizers and potential victimizers is also important. Typically, discussion of this impact focuses on the cognitive side, i.e., on how racist humor spreads and reinforces racist beliefs. At least as important, I think, are the affective consequences. For, insofar as racist humor constitutes an assault on members of an ethnic group, it joins together those who participate—both performers and audience—in a community of feeling against that group. By appreciating such humor together, we take common joy in putting *them* down, e.g., in turning them into objects of scorn or contempt or into beings not to be taken seriously (wife jokes). Our mutual participation in this through shared laughter legitimizes this way of feeling about them. Those among us who fail to laugh—or who object to laughter—are immediately outsiders, perhaps even traitors. In general, the price of objecting is a small exile. By participating, however, one accepts membership in a racist association (albeit a temporary one). The seriousness of so doing, of course, is far less than, e.g., the seriousness of joining an official white supremacist organization. But notice that the difference in seriousness diminishes the greater one's participation in such informal communities of feeling.

It is important to note that this creation of a community of feeling is not contingent on the creation of a community of belief. Many people who entertain one another with Polish jokes do not thereby implicitly accept Polish slovenliness or stupidity as a fact. What they share is the pleasure of ridiculing Poles and they legitimize this pleasure by sharing it with one another. Typically, because they are innocent of racist beliefs and of hatred against Poles, they take this pleasure to be innocent (an Agent-Centered understanding). But one wonders how the Poles think of it. How do American philosophers of Polish descent feel knowing that their colleagues entertain themselves in this 'innocent' way? (Imagine a Black philosopher in a department of Whites who told Sambo and Rastus jokes.)

The reason most frequently given for describing a bit of humor as racist is that it expresses a racist belief. As we have seen, this view is inadequate where the belief expressed is identified with the belief of the speaker. Whether it is adequate where the belief in question is not that of the speaker, but rather a belief abroad in the land, depends a good deal on what we mean by 'express.' Where jokes work by stereotyping, the most natural way to understand this is to identify what belief a joke expresses with the stereotype on which the joke turns. The emphasis here is on content. But if we take 'express' in this way, the common view that bits of humor are racist in virtue of expressing racist beliefs is not quite accurate. For example, a comedian may tell a series of jokes which express such beliefs (embody such stereotypes) without committing a Basic Racist Act and without doing or intending to do anything that can reasonably be believed to contribute to an atmosphere in which such acts are more likely to occur. He might tell such jokes, for example, to make a point about racism in order to combat it. Understood as bits of humor—as performances—the jokes told by such a comedian are not racist.

A better way to make the point about stereotyping, I think, is to characterize bits of humor as racist if they can reasonably be expected *to promote* or to reinforce racist beliefs or if they are intended to do so. This way of putting things, moreover, frees us from an exclusive preoccupation with content and enables us more clearly to understand the importance of context.

Most racist jokes do not persuade *by argument* that a certain stereotype is true of a certain ethnic group. Rather, they promote such stereotypes by repeated assertion. At least part of what gives such assertions their power to establish and to reinforce belief is that they are invested with the authority of those who make them. Roughly, one promotes racist beliefs by means of racist humor when one lends one's authority to a joke that embodies some racist stereotype. One may do this simply by telling such a joke in the way jokes are ordinarily told (as one may lend one's authority to what one asserts merely by asserting it). However, if one's audience has antecedent reason to believe that one does not hold such beliefs, or if one provides it with such reasons, this relationship will not hold. In this case, one may tell a joke that embodies some such stereotype without committing a racist act. Whether one lends one's authority to a stereotype by telling a joke (or displaying a cartoon) depends in part on the context. Typically, for example, one does not lend one's authority to such stereotypes by telling such jokes where the context is scholarly, e.g., where the purpose is to examine the means by which racist beliefs are perpetuated (though it is *possible* to lend one's authority even here by telling such jokes with obvious glee and approval).

It is worth pointing out, moreover, that we cannot determine by an abstract or acontextual analysis of content whether a joke could reasonably be expected to promote a racist stereotype.

Consider the following Polish joke:

Q: How do you tell the groom at a Polish wedding?
A: He's the one in the clean bowling shirt.

To an audience familiar with the current American Polish stereotype, this joke will be understood to assert that Poles are deficient in the categories of style and hygiene. An audience unfamiliar with this stereotype—e.g., an audience that believes that Poles are reputed to be elegant and cultured—cannot be expected to understand these sentences in this way. Indeed, such an audience would be at a loss to see any joke here at all. Many jokes are like this. Still other jokes can reasonably be expected to be understood differently depending on who tells them, to whom they are told, in what spirit they are told, and under what circumstances. Consider:

WHITE FOREMAN: Washington, what the hell are you doing lying down on the job again? When I hired you, you said you never get tired.
BLACK WORKER: That's how I do it, sir.
WHITE FOREMAN: Don't talk in riddles, boy.
BLACK WORKER: I ain't. You see, the reason I never gets tired is as soon as I begins to get tired I jes lies down and takes myself a rest.

Depending on who tells this joke to whom and on how it is told, it may reasonably be expected to be understood as a joke about Blacks in general, a joke about Black laborers, or a joke about a particular Black man named Washington. Moreover, the joke may be understood to mean that Blacks are lazy, sly, or shiftless; or it may be understood to show how a clever Black worker can talk his way out of a tough spot; or, if Washington is an established character, it may be understood as another illustration of how Washington gets on in the world.[7] If we focus narrowly on content—if we focus on what is presupposed by 'the joke itself'—it is easy to miss the importance of context here.

VII

Defenders of the Belief-Centered Theory may object that some jokes are racist merely in virtue of 'embodying' racist beliefs and attitudes, whether or not the

---

[7]Of course, Washington could be an established character who, in effect, represented a Black 'type' or Blacks in general. Were this the case, the joke in question might be racist. Whether or not it is would depend, e.g., on what else is true of Washington as a character, and perhaps, on where the joke appears (e.g., whether in a predominantly Black or a predominantly White publication). Note that members of a victimized group are far less likely to mistake a survival strategy for a character trait than members of a victimizing group.

expressions of these beliefs and attitudes are Basic Racist Acts and whether or not they contribute or are intended to contribute to an atmosphere in which such acts occur. Suppose, for example, that a tribe of isolated Aborigines in the Australian outback happened onto a book of Polish jokes and began to entertain one another by generating new jokes in this genre. And suppose further that this group will never encounter Poles or encounter anyone who will be influenced by their attitudes toward Poles. Still, it might be maintained, such jokes are racist. And this seems a counter-example to my view.

It seems to me, however, that there is no real problem here. For our inclination to regard these jokes as racist is no stronger or no weaker than our inclination to regard the telling of them as a form of mistreatment. They may be regarded as such for a number of reasons. To begin with, it may be painful to some Poles to know that they are objects of ridicule and derision in the Australian outback, even though they are unlikely to suffer in any other way from this treatment. Further, even were the telling of these jokes to remain a secret, it could still be said that they constitute a form of mistreatment. Ridicule and derision are what they are whether the victim is aware of them or not. And to those who value their good name for its own sake, they do harm in either case. It is worth mentioning in this regard that some maintain that we may be harmed by those who ridicule or slander us after we are dead and buried. I am not arguing that these are good reasons for holding that Poles are wronged by such jokes. I am, rather, suggesting that we will regard the telling of these jokes in this context as morally objectionable to the degree that we accept them as good reasons.

There is, however, a derivative sense of 'racist' that has no moral force. This is the sense in which jokes that embody long-forgotten and dead stereotypes may be so described (e.g., jokes about scheming Phoenicians, assuming that these do not wrong Phoenicians by unfairly sullying their memory). To say that a joke is racist in this derivative sense is to say that typical acts of telling it were racist in the morally important sense at some time. It is not to say, however, that such acts are currently prima facie objectionable. If we are permitted to regard spacial isolation as analogous to temporal discontinuity, it may be that the Polish jokes in question are racist in this derivative sense. But again, to say this is not to say that it is prima facie wrong to tell them. And again, if we are inclined to say that they are racist in the morally important sense, I would suggest it is because we believe that unfairly to be made an object of ridicule or derision is to be mistreated, whether or not one knows that this has happened, and whether or not one suffers in some additional way in virtue of its so happening.

VIII

Let me conclude by summarizing my position and by applying it to the question of truth raised in the introductory section of this paper. To begin with, then, bits of humor may be racist in three ways: (1) They may insult (or be intended to insult), humiliate, or ridicule members of victimized groups in relation to their ethnic identity; (2) They may create (or be intended to create) a community of feelings against such a group; and (3) They may promote (or be intended to promote) beliefs that are used to 'justify' the mistreatment of such a group.

Whether a particular bit of humor is racist in one or more of these ways depends on a variety of contextual features. On this view, when we describe a joke or cartoon as racist 'in itself' we mean that a typical use of it will be racist in our culture. In making this judgment we presuppose a background of contextual features so familiar in our culture that they need not be specified. Given the history of racist cartoon caricatures of Blacks, a political cartoon that portrayed a prominent Black American with huge lips and bug eyes is a racist insult, despite the fact that he may have rather large lips and somewhat bulging eyes. Were it not for this history, however, such a caricature would be no more racist than any political cartoon that exaggerated the unusual anatomical features of its subject. And since it would not insult, it would not help to perpetuate a community of feeling against Blacks as well. Our judgment that any such cartoon is racist 'in itself' presupposes this history. As we have seen, moreover, a corresponding point holds in relation to the promotion of racist beliefs. Polish jokes cannot reasonably be expected to perpetuate or reinforce racist beliefs against Poles where the audience is familiar with a much different Polish stereotype (e.g., Poles as cultured and intelligent). In general, how an audience can reasonably be expected to understand such jokes will depend on what the audience already believes about the group in question. Compare:

QUESTION: What has an I.Q. of 100?
ANSWER 1: Poland
ANSWER 2: Israel

In general, to determine whether a bit of humor is racist in virtue of being insulting to a member of the relevant group may require a good deal of intelligence and sensitivity to feelings and to social dynamics. And the same may be said in relation to the creation of communities of feeling. For the formation of social alliances—and the use of humor to form them—may be very obvious or very subtle. Again, it may take a good deal of sensitivity to detect it.

Applying these findings to the questions raised in the introduction to this paper, it should be clear by now that truth is not a sufficient defense against the charge of racism. To begin with, racist victimization in a society may be supported by an ideology that consists—in part—of statistically true beliefs. For example, Blacks are statistically less literate than Whites. Such statistical truths, however, are abused in racist ideologies in two ways. First, they are used to support factual inferences that would not follow from them were all the evidence in (e.g., Blacks are genetically less capable of literacy than Whites); and secondly, they are used as premises in moral arguments for conclusions that do not follow from them (e.g., Blacks should have fewer rights than Whites). Most of us agree that it is racist to help to promote this ideology. Accordingly, we would judge ourselves amiss were we to mention the rate of Black literacy to someone who might come to be influenced by this ideology *and also* fail to give him an explanation of this fact. But this is just what we do when we tell such a person a joke in which Blacks are portrayed as illiterates. Even jokes that are grounded in statistically true stereotypes, then, may be racist in virtue of promoting racist ideology. Whether such jokes are racist for this reason, of course, is dependent on the audience to whom they are addressed. Where there is no question that the audience will be influenced in the direction of this racist ideology—e.g., where the audience consists of Black sociologists—the telling of such jokes need not be racist at all. Indeed, they could be used as a way of portraying just how bad things are (e.g., how Blacks have been deprived of educational opportunities).

As we saw, moreover, one can use the truth to insult, humiliate, or ridicule members of a victimized group, whether or not the truth ought to be considered shameful. Thus, Blacks are ridiculed for having big lips, Jews for having big noses, etc. It does not matter here whether or not this is true. Again, what is insulting here is the attitude of derision adopted toward the trait. Once members of a group are made to feel ashamed of being certain ways, it is insulting and humiliating to 'remind' them that they are—whether they are or not or whether the trait is shameworthy or not. Moreover, it is clear that a community of feeling against a group is created when members of another group adopt an attitude of derision toward some trait alleged in the first, whether or not this allegation is true. Accordingly, bits of humor may be racist in all three ways despite the fact that they are grounded in some truth.

Questions

1. Do you think that Michael Philips's Act-Centered Theory is correct? What reasons can you give to support your view?
2. Do you agree that we ought to avoid telling jokes which, although not what the author calls "objectively insulting," do offend people's (hyper-)sensitivities?
3. Can it be wrong to tell jokes which turn on stereotypes which are true of many or most members of the stereotyped group?

When Is It Wrong to Laugh?

Ronald de Sousa

Ronald de Sousa rejects three arguments for the view that there cannot be an Ethics of Laughter: (1) laughter is involuntary; (2) laughter is trivial; and (3) the funny is merely aesthetic. Instead of a consequentialist moral evaluation of laughter, the author recommends one based on laughter's origins. He calls the evil element in laughter Phthonos *("malicious envy") and suggests that laughter having this characteristic expresses an emotional attitude. He then argues that such attitudes cannot be hypothetically adopted and thus* phthonos *has what he calls an* anhypothetical *feature. This implies that one's finding a joke funny indicates that one actually shares the underlying emotional attitudes. If those attitudes are bad, says the author, then the laughter is wrong. Another way in which laughter can be wrong, he says, is when it involves an important kind of emotional self-deception. He rejects two additional moral criticisms of laughter: (1) that it is frivolous; and (2) that it distorts and oversimplifies the way the world is.*

I laughed in all Cathedrals, knowing they were mine.
—ELLEN ESTABROOK TAYLOR

The gift of laughter is often described as central to human nature. Rabelais, who had a stake in thinking well of laughter, said it defined the human essence: "Le rire est le propre de l'homme." Of the many differentiae suggested for our species, this has proved among the hardiest. "Featherless Biped" wouldn't do, as Diogenes proved by plucking a chicken, and our claim to be exclusive users of language and tools has been squeezed thin of late between apes and computers. The human cachinnophile will grant other species a sense of fun, a taste for play

Ronald de Sousa, "When is it Wrong to Laugh?" reprinted from *The Philosophy of Laughter and Humor* by John Morreall (ed.), by permission of the State University of New York Press © 1987, State University of New York. All rights reserved.

and even a capacity for mischief. But without repudiating the continuity of animal life, they will insist that if other animals turn out to laugh, this marks just one more way in which their intelligence and sociality is closer to ours than we thought. Before I proceed, a caveat about what I take my topic to include. Laughter is no mere class of sounds, not even if one of the defining conditions of the class is that they be produced by humans. Hysterical laughter is not laughter (though my account may implicitly suggest what the relation is between them), nor are the happy noises and cries of infants, or "laughing with pleasure." Laughter as I am concerned with it is a response of which the Formal Objects are the funny, the comical, the ridiculous.[1] I shall lump these together as *the Funny*. I shall be mostly interested in the Funny and our emotional response to it, rather than in laughing behavior. But the expression of an emotion may be of constitutive importance in defining the emotion itself, both as social reality and as subjective experience. So I shall not avoid speaking sometimes of actual laughter.

I shall not attempt to explain this fact, nor to provide a comprehensive account of laughter. Instead I shall ask how we can apply to it my contention that emotions can be rationally evaluated. Or rather, since we obviously do sometimes think it is irrational or even morally wrong to laugh, I shall ask whether we can rationalize the principles behind such assessments to construct an *Ethics of Laughter*.

This inquiry is intended as a prolegomenon to a more general discussion of the role of emotion in the moral life. In particular, it explores the idea that some principles of rationality constrain what emotions can coexist in relation to the same object. Most importantly, it will reveal an interesting characteristic that differentiates, I shall argue, emotional *attitudes* from mere beliefs. Finally, it will add a facet to our understanding of the ambivalence so prevalent in our emotional life. If indeed the Funny and our capacity to perceive it are central to human nature, that ambivalence is not surprising. For human nature has always been regarded, epecially in our tradition, as both angelic and demonic. Our vocabulary for the main emotions often comes in pairs of almost identical emotions, differing only in their sign. Love and Lust; Admiration and Envy; Indignation and Resentment. You know that one is good and one is bad, but you're neither quite sure which is which, nor even how to tell them apart. And that's how it is with laughter: "You're laughing at me!"—"No, I'm not laughing *at* you, I'm laughing *with* you." That there is a distinction seems clear; but how do we tell in practice when that retort is true?

Many a quotable word has been spoken by those who have focused exclusively on one side or the other of the ambivalence, praising or condemning laughter as such. The motto of Italian and French comedy, as one might expect, places laughter on the side of the angels: "Castigat Ridendo Mores," or loosely translated, the point of laughter is moral improvement. On the other hand, one Father of the Church claimed that while laughter was not itself a sin, it leads to

---

[1] I speak of a Formal Object as *what gives the point* of a representational state, as truth does of belief and good of wanting. I also define a special sense of *success* for propositional or representational states in which it means the attainment of the relevant formal object: a desire is then successful if its object is indeed good. This contrasts with satisfaction, which is merely the *truth* of the propositional object. For a fuller explanation, see my "The Good and the True," *Mind*, 83 (1974): 534–551.

sin. The poet Shelley seems to have agreed. He once wrote to a friend: "I am convinced that there can be no entire regeneration of mankind until laughter is put down."[2] Most of us are not so single-mindedly on one side or the other. We think of laughter as an occasionally risky pleasure, like sex, which is a good thing in itself, or at least when done in the right way and kept in its place. Like monarchs, we sometimes license fools to tell us truths which our friends will be too well brought up to speak. And apart from such licensed fools, the common sense Ethics of Laughter goes something like this: Laugh when it's funny, grow up and stop snickering at dirty jokes, don't laugh at cripples (unless you are one yourself), and *show respect.* To show respect means not to laugh, snicker, titter, chortle, giggle, or even chuckle when it's Too Sad, when it would be Unkind to, when it would Offend a Sacred Memory, and when it might be taken to Insult a Mother, a Country, or a Religion. But a few precepts don't add up to an Ethic. Can anything, indeed, properly be called the "Ethics of Laughter"?

THREE ARGUMENTS AGAINST
TAKING THE SUBJECT SERIOUSLY

I see three arguments that might be adduced against the very idea: that laughter is *involuntary*, that its consequences are *trivial*, and that its demands are at best *merely aesthetic.*

Laughter Is Involuntary

The first argument stems from the familiar doctrine of the emotions as passions, therefore passive. It urges that nothing that is not voluntary could be the subject of moral constraint. For, it is often repeated, ought implies can. But the sense in which morally significant actions must be in our power is not, as Aristotle pointed out, one that requires each one of our actions to be directly chosen among psychologically genuine alternatives. It is enough sometimes that we are responsible for being the kind of person who no longer has a choice in this situation. That's why a driver—who could less avoid the accident drunk than sober—is thereby not less but more culpable. To be sure, it is not unusual to hear that someone "ought to know better" than to find a certain sexist or racist joke funny. Besides, actual laughter (as opposed to the inclination to laugh) may generally be inhibited. And as Aristotle again sagaciously remarked with regard to a certain Adeimantus, who once burst out laughing but is not otherwise known, we don't blame someone for laughing if he's tried really hard not to.[3]

---

[2]For these and other opinions about laughter, see H.L. Mencken's *Dictionary of Quotations,* s.v. *laughter.* Milan Kundera adds this twist to the theme of ambivalence: the laughter of the angels is fanatical joy, that of the devils sceptical mockery. So there are two forms of laughter, perfectly antagonistic. (Milan Kundera, *The Book of Laughter and Forgetting,* tr. M.H. Heim, (Harmondsworth: Penguin Books, 1981). Which do *you* detest more?

[3]For Aristotle on the voluntary and responsibility for character, see *Nicomachean Ethics,* Books II and III.

Triviality

Still, it might be said that even if laughter betrays character, and even if we ought on occasion to contain it, this is merely a minor social duty, like the duty not to fart or burp. Failures of restraint can inconvenience others, perhaps embarrass or even offend them; but surely this is a matter of etiquette, not of Ethics. Rules of etiquette are typically relative to a particular group: "It's all right to use such language when you're at camp with your buddies; but it just won't do at your sister's wedding." The suggestion that there are categorical Laws of Etiquette is a familiar device of the comical—either ingenuous, as in the injunction to "Never Give a Lady a Restive Horse," or ingenious, like Oscar Wilde's rule that "the only way to make up for being occasionally a little overdressed is to be always immensely overeducated."[4]

This won't do, for two reasons, as a characterization of the difference between Ethics and social convention. For one thing, it is one of the anthropologist's tasks to find underlying universal structures beneath the surface of particular social conventions. And on the other hand, a case might be made that some genuinely moral rules are relative to conventional social structures. But surely it is a necessary condition of moral significance that an act and its consequence not be *trivial*. Can laughter pass this test?

The association of laughter with the frivolous means that we may be tempted to assume that it cannot be serious. Yet for many people laughter is a great revealer of character. It is natural to assume that in these cases information is coming to us through the object of laughter: we can react positively, as to revealed affinity, or negatively with shock and revulsion to the fact that someone finds a certain sort of joke or situation funny. In this way laughter is a powerful sorter. But it isn't always easy thus to pick out the object. To say what someone is laughing at, in the sense of exactly what target or scenario provokes laughter, is not always to specify *what's funny about it*—the motivating aspect. Moreover a sincere answer to that question is not always a true one. A partial guide to the nature of the true object is the character of the laughter itself, its actual sound, considered in isolation from its occasion. (Sometimes the sort of occasion it is can be easily inferred from the sound.) Imagine a man whose habitual sound of laughter is a *cackle*, or a *snicker*. Would you like your daughter to marry him? Even more interesting is a second-order thought experiment that can be carried out here. The example just given, to be imaginatively convincing, had to be gender specific. Our gender stereotypes dictate that it is not very feminine to *guffaw*, nor very manly to *giggle*. There are assumptions buried in these reactions to the sound of laughter which cut much deeper than etiquette:

> Self-loathing ladies titter; Hags and Harpies roar. Fembots titter at themselves when Daddy turns the switch. They totter when he pulls the string . . . Daddy's little Titterers try to intimidate women struggling for greatness. This is what

---

[4]Thomas E. Hill's Manuals of Etiquette, of which selections have been published in facsimile as *Never Give a Lady a Restive Horse* (Berkeley: Diablo Press, 1967). Wilde's advice is from *Phrases and Philosophies for the Use of the Young*.

they are made for and paid for. There is only one taboo for titterers: they must never laugh seriously at Father—only at his jokes.[5]

The Funny Is Merely Aesthetic

Those categories of expressiveness are coarse, as they have to be to be even roughly describable. But our ear is sensitive to much finer and less easily describable nuances of expressiveness. We can be attracted or repelled by the sound of a laugh even more surely than by that of a speaking voice, without quite knowing why. "Tell me what you laugh at and I will tell you who you are," but "Let me hear you laugh and I will know if I like you." When I find a personality disagreeable, it is a normal effect of moderate vanity to hope it is because there's something wrong with them, and not with me. Thus it is always satisfying to find the accident of personal distaste supplemented by a sound motive for moral disapproval. Is this possible here? Or are the preferences evoked by the expressiveness of laughter just aesthetic ones? This question is quite a different one from that concerning the triviality of laughter; for aesthetic questions can cut very deep, and still not be held to be moral. That we are dealing with merely aesthetic preferences is suggested by the variety of our reactions and by the difficulty of articulating them in terms of general principles. If this is so, the affinities or differences they reveal may not have moral significance.

ORIGINS AND CONSEQUENCES

To determine whether our attitudes to laughter can be governed by genuinely moral principles, let us first look at different types of moral consideration. Central to most moral systems is an interest in consequences, actual, probable, or merely possible. This contrasts with aesthetic interest, which characteristically focuses on some object in itself. Laughter, it may be conceded, does not have very significant consequences. The French philosopher Henri Bergson calls it a kind of "punishment," but stresses that it is only a social gesture: "society cannot here intervene with any material repression, since it is not hurt materially" by what laughter is intended to punish.[6] Leaving aside the curious optimism that prompts Bergson to assume that society will punish only symbolically what harms it only symbolically, what we should note here is that the material consequences of laughter are attributable only to the *meaning* of laughter: in this way laughter is essentially a sign, whose effect is based on convention. Yet— and this is the other side of the variety manifested by the sounds and object of laughter—laughter itself is natural to humans. It is universal, not just as a sound, but as a mode of communication. At least one important variety of this

---

[5]Mary Daly, *Gyn/Ecology: the Metaethics of Radical Feminism* (Boston: Beacon Press, 1978): p. 17.
[6]Henri Bergson, a philosopher otherwise best forgotten, wrote a fascinating little book on laughter: *Le Rire; Essai sur la Signification du Comique.* (Paris: Presses Universitaires de France, 1940). See pp. 15, 16.

mode, as we shall see, presupposes sociality in that it requires a recipient or butt: someone to whom the laughter is liable, perhaps indeed intended, to give offense.

Not any action that gives offense is thereby morally offensive. Its evaluation requires that we consider the reason that it is found offensive. Mixed marriages frequently give offense to racists, but that does not warrant moral regard. Explicitly sexual literature can be offensive to the "common decency" of "community standards." Such offenses are liable to draw upon themselves social and legal sanctions, but whether they warrant moral condemnation on the ground of offense alone is less clear. The power to create moral obligations should perhaps be ascribed to prevailing social conventions only insofar as they express or embody human values that depend on sociality itself. The existence of some particular social arrangement or public opinon would not be sufficient. Moreover what gives offense usually does so in virtue of its motivational origins. An observer acquainted with La Tourette's syndrome, for example, will not be offended by the verbal products (known as coprolalia, which is Greek for "shittalk") which spring directly from a neurological disorder and not from any even unconscious intent to utter offensive words. Similarly hebephrenic laughter is not, for our purposes, laughter at all. The sound of laughter is significant as laughter only if it's produced in the right way. Does it make sense then to speak of an "Ethics" of some class of acts that is discerned not primarily by their consequences, but by their origins?

A distinction is needed between two kinds of relevant origins. There is a classic sense, of course, in which all ethical assessments of particular acts are not of actual consequences but of "origin" in the sense of *motive*. For the Kantian, this judgment of the goodness of the Will is the only truly ethical evaluation. But this is not the sense in which I speak of evaluating laughter in terms of its origin. For although we can sometimes burst out laughing—or omit to restrain our laughter—on purpose, specifically with the intention of wounding someone, this is not the usual case, nor is it very problematical. More interesting is the criticism of laughter which arises from treating it as a *symptom*. There are cases in which we say: "If you can laugh at something like that, you must be insensitive, boorish cruel . . ." Such strictures are related to the Kantian criticism of motives, but they are not the same. For the Kantian looks at the origin of the act only in the sense of looking at the goal which it aims at. The "naturalness" of laughter makes it inappropriate for that kind of criticism. If we can answer the question "What did you intend to *achieve* by laughing?" then it was no genuine laughter at all.

The better parallel is with the assessment of cognitive rationality, or the "Ethics of Belief." Belief, like laughter, is not typically voluntary: On the contrary if it aims at some result—apart from the attainment of its Formal Object—its claim to be genuine belief is undermined. The evaluation of belief is in terms of the correctness of the *procedures* in which it originated. So to believe something in the face of the evidence because the consequences of believing it would be good is always a violation of the Ethics of Belief.

Such a violation might be required by overriding considerations; sometimes perhaps we should persuade ourselves of some comforting falsehood in order to preserve the moral strength to continue a worthwhile struggle. In some of those cases a "bootstrapping" principle may be operative, so that the belief seems almost to create its own justification,[7] and maybe it is even sometimes our duty to propagate a Noble Lie for the benefit of humankind. But these are cases where the intrinsic, universalizable Ethics of belief is overridden, not cases where it appeals to consequentialist criteria for the sake of its own Formal Object.

Much the same can be said of "Professional Ethics": medical, business, or legal. All of these, more obviously than the Ethics of Belief, may ultimately rest on consequentialist moral considerations, but they are rules about the best *procedures* in the transactions characteristic of each of these domains. And insofar as they admit of exceptions, they do not violate the principle of universalizability. For exceptions to principles of professional Ethics are due to features of circumstances, not to the vagaries of individual preference.

Might not the objection then be raised that all these "Ethics" are so called merely by courtesy, by convenience, or by analogy? A simple argument shows that this objection would be wrong. It is always an unequivocally ethical question whether in some particular case we should allow ethical considerations *simpliciter* to outweigh or override the principles of the special Ethics. If these "special Ethics" had no genuine ethical import, this would not be so. For suppose they merely had the status, say, of etiquette: then on most ethical principles they would automatically be of no weight at all if confronted with genuinely ethical objections. Although they might provide *indirect* reasons through people's reactions or hurt feelings, and so forth.

I conclude that there are genuine examples of Ethics where the considerations are ones of appropriateness in relation to origins, not of consequences either aimed at or achieved. That, in any case, is the sense in which I shall be speaking of the Ethics of Laughter. If the preceding considerations do not suffice to vindicate it, they may be taken merely to define it.

THE COMIC AND THE TRAGIC

When *Waiting for Godot* first made it to the suburbs of London, England, I went to a matinee performance at the Golders Green Hippodrome. During the intermission I struck up a conversation with an elderly woman in the next seat. She had laughed not at all, and she spoke mostly of how gloomy the play was. As she could no doubt see that I was only thirteen years old, she was anxious that

---

[7] By "bootstrapping" I mean our capacity to "make it so by thinking it so." For example: I take Vitamin C to ward off colds. What I have read about it has convinced me that, *pace* Linus Pauling, vitamin C is a placebo. But *I believe in placebos.* That belief seems entirely rational, because I have read in *Scientific American* that placebos are surprisingly effective in bringing about improvements.

I not be misled into thinking it a comedy. The theatre darkened again, and there came one of the play's moments of sheer clowning. The philosophical disquisitions of the two tramps are punctuated by the rapid tossing of a bowler hat, with machine-like precision and irrelevance. There is nothing funny in the telling of it: it was not a joke but pure slapstick, an excellently executed visual gag, which brought the house down. Under cover of the loud laughter, the lady bent down towards me and gravely hissed: *"But it isn't MEANT to be funny!"*

But on the contrary: these actors had worked very hard to be that funny.[8] The lady was right, I daresay, about the overall vision of the play; but what interested me, and still does, was the presupposition of her reproof: *If something is tragic then it can't be funny.*

Note that this doctrine, if true, would be of great interest for the present theory. For it would provide us with one of those elusive principles laying down the constraints on the coexistence of emotions, which as I pointed out a logic of the emotions ought to be able to provide. It is a doctrine that has in most ages passed either for common sense or at least for an indubitable principle of aesthetics. There have been some exceptions: in the *Symposium* Plato reports that Socrates, at the end of that long night of talking and drinking, "forced his companions to acknowledge that the genius of comedy was the same as that of tragedy." But he implies that they agreed mainly because "they were drowsy and didn't quite follow the argument." By and large, the Greeks separated Tragedy from Comedy. So did their classical French followers, who like most of the English eighteenth century thought Shakespeare exceeding vulgar for not knowing the difference. But even Shakespeare usually separated comic scenes from tragic ones. And although some authors view laughter as a substitute for tears, even they view them as incompatible, even though mutually substitutable: "Man alone," said Nietzsche "suffered so excruciatingly in the world that he was compelled to invent laughter." And Byron: "If I laugh at any mortal thing,—T'is that I may not weep."

But what could be the nature of such incompatibility? Let us begin by distinguishing two sources, or types, of incompatibility. Two emotions might be incompatible *in the subject* or *in relation to the object*. The first type applies characteristically to *moods*. If one cannot feel elated and depressed at the same time, this cannot be because of any incompatibility between the objects of these moods—for moods have no object. Depression and elation seem to be real contraries, not merely "opposites" in some vaguer sense. Thus if, in the traditional figure of the Tragic Clown, we are inclined to see someone that is both gloomy and merry, we can evade contradiction only by appealing to some sort of split level theory. Split levels, like Plato's Parts of the Soul, allow each level to be pure even while explaining the possibility of inner conflict. Plato's method is explicitly designed to split faculties two by two, and it has trouble generating more than two Parts of the Soul. There is also a problem about how, if it succeeds in that task, it avoids succeeding too well, and producing an

---

[8]Garrick is said to have remarked in warning to a young actor: "You can fool the town with Tragedy m'boy, but Comedy's a serious business."

indefinite proliferation of parts.[9] The application of the method, I argued, is fallacious, but the basic principle is just a version of Leibniz's law. It says that if some pair of properties are incompatible, then no *one* thing can have them both at the same time. And if one grants that there can be more than one "level," why not several?

If we adopt Plato's strategy, we implicitly construe the incompatibility on the model of the impossibility of being simultaneously and homogeneously red all over and green. But this can't be the correct account of the incompatibility between laughter and alternative reactions. For although we do occasionally get into a "laughing mood," under the influence of cannabis, for example, or following relief from great tension, laughter is not objectless, as moods are. To get a better idea of what is involved in inconsistency with regard to objects, let's return to the case of inconsistent objects of belief. It is not inconsistent to describe a subject as believing both that p and that not-p. But it does constitute an *ascription* of inconsistency. What's wrong with inconsistency? What's wrong with it is that it guarantees *at least one false belief.* This goes against the categorical imperative of the Ethics of Belief: *Believe (all and only?) what is true.* The criterion for that violation lies in the logical relations between the propositions believed—between the contents of the beliefs. In an emotional analogue to propositional content, the imperative of consistency would derive from the following principle of the Logic of Emotions:[10]

> If two emotional contents are incompatible, then that will guarantee that at least one of them is inappropriate.

Unfortunately examples are hard to pin down. For the objects of emotions have no criteria of identity even as dubiously clear as those of propositions. How then can we tell whether one's emotional contents are so structured as to guarantee that at least one is inappropriate? We must resort, it seems, to some unexplained notion of phenomenological incompatibility. Whether the comic and the tragic are phenomenologically incompatible seems a hopeless question: both are too complicated. Let us at least narrow the case down to the *funny* and the *bitter.* As practiced by a certain kind of comedian (Lenny Bruce, Richard Pryor) it seems as though the funniness is *in* the very bitterness itself. Some might find this unintelligible; but any disagreement here is likely to get bogged down in denials of each other's phenomenological reports. Let us then grant, at least, that some people sincerely report experiencing both responses at once. Should this report be disbelieved, or construed as self-deceptive?

We need some distinctions. Let us say that the Richard Pryor *schtick* is the *target.* The two *Formal Objects* are the Comic and the Tragic. The tricky question concerns *what's funny about* the target: I shall call it the *motivating aspect.* The

---

[9]Plato, *Republic,* Book IV, 436ff. Cf. Terry Penner, "Thought and Desire in Plato" (in G. Vlastos, ed., *Plato,* vol. II (New York: Anchor Books, 1971).

[10]See the excellent discussion by Patricia Greenspan, "A Case of Mixed Feelings; Ambivalence and the Logic of Emotions," in Amélie Oksenberg Rorty, ed. *Explaining Emotions* (Berkeley: University of California Press, 1980).

problem, then, is whether there are two distinct motivating aspects, and if so, what their relations are to the Comic and the Tragic as Formal Objects. The claim of incompatibility must be refined to distinguish the impossibility of joint *satisfaction* (incompatibility) from the impossibility of joint *success* (inconsistency). Recall that success was defined as the possession by a motivating aspect of the property that defines the Formal Object (e.g., the property *for* which I want something's being actually a *good*-making one.) Satisfaction is the actual possession by the target of the motivating property attributed to it by the intentional state (e.g., for a want: the proposition wanted actually being *true*). Now there are two possibilities:

(a) Suppose first that there are two motivating aspects, both present in the performance: the tone of Pryor's voice, perhaps, which is apprehended as Comic, and the content of his words, apprehended as Tragic. Then, since the Formal Objects (and the corresponding emotional responses) are being attributed to those different aspects, no argument could show them to be inconsistent. That would be like claiming that it is inconsistent to say of two different propositions that one is true and the other is false.

(b) But now take the second possibility: there is really only one motivating aspect. It is not only the same performance, but the very same *aspect* of it that arouses both emotions. Here true inconsistency is a possibility: perhaps the two Formal Objects are inconsistent *as criteria of success.*

The example of belief will help to make this clear. No single proposition could be both true and false, not because of some property that every proposition has which prevents it, but because that is part of the meaning of the opposition between truth and falsity. So might it be with Comic and Tragic: that they are by their very natures related as logical contraries.[11]

The trouble with this last supposition is that although it is coherent I cannot think of a way to establish its truth. This seems to be a place where nothing but phenomenology will give us any answer. And if indeed some people report having both types of response in regard to a single aspect, I find no argument to support the view that the two Formal Objects must be inconsistent.

But there remains to be explored a form of the charge of incompatibility, which proceeds with a quite different strategy.

---

[11]Though not, like true and false, as *contradictories*, since as we saw the number of Formal Objects of emotions is large, whereas for belief there is only one. This is one disanalogy which makes the emotional analogue of truth harder than truth. *Good* is already more complicated than True, in that it is subject to the "Monkey's Paw phenomenon": something good can turn out bad because of what it is conjoined with. (See "The Good and the True", art. cit., for details) Nothing true, by contrast, can turn out false because of what *it* is conjoined with. That complication certainly applies here as well. I have a hunch, not worked out as yet, that the multiplicity of Formal Objects may be responsible for yet a further complication to the latter, which might be traced to the possibility of *higher-order motivating aspects.* Even if it is the quality of Pryor's voice that is the relevant motivating aspect, yet perhaps there are two aspects of that quality, or two *aspects of some aspect* of that quality, which evoke the different responses. By this reasoning every situation of type (b), might ultimately be reconstrued as one of type (a).

FEELING AND THINKING: THE WALBERG VIEW

On this new version, the claim is not that Comic and Tragic are inconsistent emotions, but that the comic is incompatible with *emotion as such*. I shall refer to this as the *Walberg view*.[12] This is a radical view, not only because it is so sweeping, but for its claim that laughter itself does not stem from emotion at all, but contrasts with it.

Against the Walberg view I see two arguments. One is too simple. The other perhaps will seem too complicated. Such is the Philosophical Life.

The simple argument is that to compete with emotion, laughter needs to be *in the same game.* The Walberg view presupposes some sort of philosophical psychology, in which something like Faculties can enter into competition. Now obviously there might be models that do this which philosophers traditionally haven't thought of; but, the argument runs, all the models that have been thought of are basically variants of either the *Cartesian* or the *Platonic*. On the Cartesian, Intelligence (or Understanding) is viewed as a separate faculty from emotion (or Will). On the Platonic, they are more like the parts of the soul of the *Republic:* each one is in some sense dominated by a particular faculty and primarily identified with it, but every faculty is represented in each homunculus.

Consider first the Cartesian picture. It allows no competition between the faculties, for they perform quite different tasks. Their *organs* can of course compete for resources; but the *functions* themselves can no more conflict than the volume control of a radio can conflict with the tuning control.

But the Platonic picture fares no better. To be sure, it agrees well enough with the popular notion that some individuals are primarily analytical and others primarily empathic. But it gives us no particular reason to see this as an *incompatibility.* And that was just what we needed explaining.

[12]In honor of Hugh Walpole and Henri Bergson. Walpole's quip is often quoted: "This world," he said, "is a comedy to those who think, a tragedy to those who feel." In Bergson's view, "the comical demands . . . something like a momentary anesthesis of the heart. It speaks to pure intelligence . . . Laughter has no greater enemy than emotion." (Op. cit., ch 1, I). In naming it the Walberg view I wish to honor its authors without caring too much about how accurately the version of it which they inspired conforms to their own. For a recent defense of a similar view, see J. Morreall, "Humor and Emotion," *American Philosophical Quarterly,* 20/3 (1983): 297–305. Morreall argues, much like Bergson, that humor and emotion are *incompatible,* and indeed he suggests that it is precisely in this incompatibility that its evolutionary function resides. He writes:

> In [the] development of reason, emotions would have been not a boon but an encumbrance . . . Amusement by contrast, like artistic activities and science, would be helpful in the development of reason because it involves a breaking out of a practical and self-concerned frame of mind . . . The capacity of humor to block emotions would also have facilitated the development of rationality, for emotions would often get in the way of rational thinking . . . (302–3).

These points are unexceptionable in connection with wit or the laughter of incongruity, with which both Bergson and Morreall are chiefly concerned. But I now want to introduce a different species of Funny.

The diagnosis I suggest is this. The distinction so far sketched confounds two different contrasts. One is between *evaluative engagement* and neutrality or *detachment*. The other is between *identification* and *alienation*. We tend to associate detachment with alienation, and identification with empathy and therefore with evaluative engagement. But these are no more than associations: one can be evaluatively engaged with what is alien and one can be cold even while identifying with another person. I can regard *myself* coldly, for that matter, without ceasing to be or feel *myself*. This distinction is particularly important with regard to laughter; for laughter can be dispassionate, as when it is evoked by mere wit, or emotionally involving, whether we are laughing "with" someone, (involvement with identification) or "at" someone (involvement with alienation). The evaluative involvement characteristic of laughter has traditionally and, as I shall argue, at least some times correctly—been taken to involve some apprehension of evil. My hunch is that in an important class of cases there is an interaction between this element of evil and the dialectic of identification and alienation. This class of cases defines a kind of laughter that is particularly susceptible to moral condemnation, and which for reasons that I shall explain in the next section I call *phthonic laughter*. If this is right, then the Walberg view rests on a confusion between intellectualizing detachment and emotionally involved alienation.

PHTHONOS, WIT, AND ANHYPOTHETICAL HUMOR

To begin with, let us exorcise the evil element in laughter by giving it a name to distinguish it from wit and from mere amusement. I borrow from Plato the word *Phthonos*. The Greek word means something like "malicious envy"; it connotes both the involvement of something evil and the ambiguity between identification and alienation that characterizes jealousy. Plato applies it to the kind of laughter typically experienced at some ridiculous spectacle. Malicious ridicule, in Plato's book, is properly directed against our enemies; but it is a pleasure mixed with pain when directed at our friends. Of the many philosophers that have emphasized this element of evil,[13] Hobbes saw especially clearly that the phthonic element is distinguishable from wit: "That laughter consisteth in wit, or as they call it, in jest, experience confuteth, for man laughs at mischances and indecencies wherein lieth no wit nor jest at all."[14] But how is the distinction between phthonos and wit to be drawn? In reaching for a hypothesis, I need a joke of undiluted nastiness; one that is as devoid of wit as possible. A rape joke will do.

> Margaret Trudeau goes to visit the hockey team. When she emerges she complains that she has been gang-raped. Wishful thinking.

[13]For example, Cicero: "laughter has its spring in some kind of meanness or deformity"; Descartes: "The joy that comes from what is good is serious, while that which comes from evil is accompanied by laughter and mockery"; Spinoza: "A man hates what he laughs at."
[14]Thomas Hobbes, *Human Nature*, ch. 9, sec. 13.

I once had occasion to discuss this joke with a student editor who rather proudly claimed to be its author; an exaggeration, since all rape jokes are variants of the same basic joke. I pointed out to the "author" that the joke seems to imply certain beliefs. One is the belief that all women secretly want to be raped. But the "author" protested: I had entirely missed the point. What the joke was *really* about, he ingenuously explained, was the common knowledge that Margaret Trudeau was *promiscuous*.

In tendering this transparent reply, the young man was furthering my quest. That Margaret Trudeau is promiscuous is indeed a hypothetical assumption of the joke. And embedded in the very use of the word "promiscuous" in this context are something like the following propositions: that rape is just a variant form of sexual intercourse; that women's sexual desires are indiscriminate; and that there is something intrinsically objectionable or evil about a woman who wants or gets a lot of sex. These are sexist assumptions. But *merely to know this doesn't make the joke funny*. What's more, to laugh at the joke *marks you as sexist*. It is not a convincing defense to say: "I was merely going along with the assumptions required to get the point of the joke."

Why not? In every joke that is based on a story—as opposed to arising from some life situation—some assumptions, some background setting, need to be understood and accepted. "An Englishman," we begin, "a Scotsman, and an Irishman . . . ." So how are the sexist beliefs just mentioned unlike the ordinary presuppositions that every joke requires?

What seems to be needed is that the listener *actually share* these attitudes. This suggests an explanatory hypothesis:

> In contrast to the element of wit, the *phthonic* element in a joke requires *endorsement*. It does not allow of hypothetical laughter. The phthonic makes us laugh only insofar as the assumptions on which it is based are attitudes actually shared. Suspension of disbelief in the situation can and must be achieved for the purposes of the joke; suspension of attitudes cannot be.

We cannot come to find something funny by merely imagining that we share its phthonic assumptions. Nevertheless we intuitively know that sharing these assumptions is what would enable us to find it funny. This is a crucial point. For without the possibility of this sort of second order knowledge about the relation of attitudes to laughter there could be no *criticism* of other people's laughter. Indeed there probably could be no phthonic jokes at all. For in the standard case a phthonic joke requires a butt or victim, and the butt of the joke is someone who typically does not laugh but knows only too well what's funny to those who do.[15]

But perhaps someone remains unconvinced, because they do find the joke funny and disclaim the allegedly necessary attitudes. For such a man, no knockdown argument can be forthcoming, but a simple thought experiment might help. Just imagine either of two variants. In the first, some non sexual form of assault is substituted for rape. Apart from some tenuous connection with

[15]On the "victim or butt" cf. G. Legman, *Rationale of the Dirty Joke, First Series* (New York: Grove Press, 1968): p. 9.

masochism by which one might try to restore the original point, it will un-doubtedly cease to be funny to anyone. In the second variant, substitute some man who (a) is not assumed to be homosexual and (b) is not the object of any particularly hostile attitude. Again, the joke loses its point. And this cannot be remedied by my saying: "for the purposes of the joke, just ignore the sexist double standard, and pretend that you think that there is something evil or con-temptible about a man who fucks a lot."

My last sentence embodied a second thought-experiment, which both sup-ports my suggestion and imposes an amendment. If you snickered at my lan-guage, it's because you consider it *naughty*. That is an *attitude*. If you didn't, I'm unlikely to get a chuckle out of you by asking you, just for the present purposes, hypothetically to think my language naughty. Though there is apparently a possible exception here: but it is only apparent, and therefore "proves the rule." The supposition just made may raise a chuckle after all, but only because you agree with me, and therefore find it funny to suppose otherwise. So the chuckle would really only be raised by the meta-thought-experiment, and instead of a counterexample it would be merely an instance of the following principle:

> It can be funny to suppose that something that is not at all funny might be funny, but only if you actually think it isn't actually funny.[16]

(A number of Monty Python's jokes are based on this principle.) This confirms my hypothesis, as well as carrying the additional empirical implication that thinking something intrinsically funny (or unfunny) is itself an *attitude*, and not a mere belief. The modification to my thesis required by this last example is the following. My suggestion about the anhypothetical feature was originally con-fined to phthonic jokes, defined as those that in some way involved evil. But we now see that the moral is broader. Phthonic jokes are a species of jokes that rest not merely on beliefs, actual or hypothetical, but on *attitudes*. But not all atti-tudes involve evil, nor are such jokes all phthonic. How is an attitude different from a belief? The hypothesis I have defended yields the following definition: *attitudes are beliefs that one cannot hypothetically adopt.*[17]

This, I believe, reveals an interesting characteristic of the category of emo-tional attitudes: their anhypothetical nature.

---

[16]This principle was suggested to me in conversation by Birgit Worlidge.

[17]I am prompted to suggest a practical application. Most of us are not perturbed by the common charge that philosophy and humor are both useless, because we realize that only the intrinsically worthless can be purely useful. Nevertheless, we might be cheered by a concrete suggestion about how humor, at least, might be of use to philosophy. I am thinking of the task of selecting suitable ap-prentices to the profession. This is a tedious process, and the usual methods of selection are unsat-isfactory, because they concentrate more on such relatively irrelevant facts as talent, intelligence, knowledge, and so forth, when in fact the only important factor is that the candidate should display an appropriately philosophical *attitude*. The best aptitude test is an attitude test. If what I have ar-gued here is right, I can now justify an old dream: philosophical aptitude tests consisting entirely of jokes. The applicants' laughter would be carefully measured, classified, and graded, and since, as I have argued, attitudes cannot be adopted at will for the purposes of finding some joke funny, we need have no qualms of conscience about settling candidates' destiny entirely on the basis of their responses. The main practical obstacle to such a scheme is that the entire scale would have to be

THE SOCIAL FACTOR

The anhypothetical nature of attitudes is related to another feature of emotions—their *social* nature. One aspect of this factor, only implicit so far, is the social relativity of jokes. This forms the subject of one of Bergson's "fundamental observations on the Comical":

> A man was asked why he wasn't crying during a sermon which had everyone else in tears. "I'm not from the parish," he answered. What this man thought about tears is even more true of laughter. However frank it may seem, laughter always conceals a subconscious thought of community, one might almost say of complicity, with laughing companions real or imaginary." (Ibid., p. 5)

Since the community of laughers is allowed to be imaginary, it would be hard to refute Bergson's claim here. But when we actually laugh alone, what subsists of this imaginary community? At least the fact that certain attitudes are endorsed, and that if anyone else were also to endorse them they would presumably be laughing too. But also, more generally, there remains a set of social-biographical facts that constitute the paradigm scenarios definitive of the particular sort of Funny involved.

The notion of community is of independent importance, however; for in some circumstances the question of whether one belongs to a certain community, or shares in certain assumptions made in that community, admits of no ready answer. After long enough among the natives, the anthropologist might feel a sufficient sense of community to laugh at their jokes, even though in sober conscience she does not share their attitudes: she does not really believe, say, that chickens are dirty and pigeons are pure. A feeling of community can substitute for as well as engender a genuine adoption of attitudes, just as the adoption of certain attitudes can be both a criterion of membership and a sufficient ground for being adopted as a member. Here then we have a concrete example of the possibility of changes in emotional dispositions. The convertibility of emotional attitudes and community involvement ensures that in at least some cases new paradigm scenarios can continue to enlarge and refine our repertoire of emotions. But I need to say more about the significance of this notion of *community involvement*.

IDENTIFICATION AND ALIENATION: INSIDE AND OUTSIDE

We have seen that the notion of community is related both to the endorsement of common phthonic premises, and to the contrast of identification and

---

calibrated to a given person in a given mood; and the mood induced by the testing conditions would most likely leave all amusement below the threshold of differentiated observable response. But this is merely a technical difficulty—if indeed it is a difficulty at all. For should we really encourage those people to be philosophers who lose their sense of humor under stress?

alienation. It's time now to look more closely at the distinction between "inside" and "outside."

There are two characteristic manifestations of this distinction. First, there is our claim to have a right to laugh, by virtue of shared experience or community, at some things but not others. Second, there is the distinction we make between laughing *at* and laughing *with* someone. These are different distinctions, but they are related in the following way: I cannot really laugh with you, unless I have the right to laugh; and I only have a right to laugh at you if there is a clear possibility of identification with you. Cyrano de Bergerac makes fun of his own nose, but threatens with death anyone who does likewise:

> Je me les sers moi-même avec assez de verve
> Mais je ne permets pas qu'un autre me les serve.[18]

There is often a note of embarrassed reticence in the laughter of white people at the jokes of blacks about themselves. Yet the whites would, perhaps, readily laugh at the blacks, if the blacks weren't laughing at themselves. What causes the unease in the one case is the thought that *they* (who laugh) *have no right to laugh;* what lifts it in the other is the thought that they (the others) *won't find out.* The same dynamics can be observed even more commonly nowadays in the jokes of men about women. What is wrong with laughing at someone behind their back, when the same joke would be acceptable face to face? The answer is that if you were face to face, the alienation expressed by the joke itself would be offset by the reality of community signaled by the sharing of it.

An extreme example was related to me by someone who had been brought up among the miners of the Congo. Among these men to laugh at cripples was perfectly normal, and not condemned as especially rude or callous. Part of what the laughter expressed in those circumstances, in which the men were exposed to great danger, is that it could happen to anyone: it had happened to you and *it could have been me, but you are not me and it didn't.* The two movements, identification and alienation, are both clearly present here,[19] and I speculate that each is an essential element, linked with the evocation of some frightening evil, of true phthonic laughter.

I can now add one more layer of understanding to my previous analysis of what is wrong with laughing at a rape joke. It is not merely that it evinces its origins in sexist attitudes. It also involves the presence of a characteristic mix of phthonic fear, identification, and alienation. This combination makes it wrong to laugh, because it in effect involves an important variety of *emotional self-deception.* The identification is hidden by a false front of alienation, or the layer of alienation is hidden usually all too thinly by a second false front of identification or sympathy. For in the laughter of put-down or ridicule, the identification is part and parcel of the motivating conditions; but the *aim* of the joke is

---

[18]Edmond Rostand, *Cyrano de Bergerac,* I, 3.
[19]The element of identification is less obvious than the alienation: so in support I drag in the word of an expert: "The 'only' joke you know how to tell," says G. Legman, "is you." (Legman, op. cit., Second Series: p. 16).

alienation: it therefore constitutes a kind of denial of reality. (Just such a denial, perhaps, is what we foster when, in our well intentioned way, we try to repress laughter in children.)

A COGNITIVE PERSPECTIVE ON LAUGHTER

So far, I have argued that the Walberg view couldn't be giving us the right account of phthonic laughter (though it might be right for wit). For such laughter, far from abandoning emotion, presupposes a very definite emotional engagement. If laughter is wrong, it is because this engagement is wrong. I also speculated that certain forms of laughter may be wrong because they represent an act of harmful alienation founded on a distortion or denial of an underlying identification. These two conclusions converge in an unexpected way: the "unethical" in both cases involves a wrong *assessment of reality*. This brings confirmation of the parallels I have been urging between the appropriateness conditions of emotions and the truth of beliefs. The Ethics of Belief form not merely a remote parallel, I contend, but an actual *congeneric* of the Ethics of Laughter. Like belief, laughter is wrong when it is grounded in the deception of self or others. This is what is entailed by viewing the Funny as coming within the quasi-cognitive domain. It allows us to rephrase the title question of this chapter thus:

> When is laughter good or bad for the adequacy of our attitudes to the objective world?

That formulation of this chapter's central question suggests yet *a third* line of attack on the question of the incompatibility of the comic with other emotions. Given our limited capacity for attention, humor may distract us from more serious things. The charge of frivolity is often leveled against those who laugh too much, who have too much fun to attend to the serious business of life. But the problem here is one of authority: whom shall we trust to decree the criteria by which some things (the *serious* ones) are more important than others (the *frivolous* ones)? The champion of the Aesthetic says, with Oscar Wilde or Baudelaire, that "To be a useful man has always seemed to me a truly hideous thing."[20] Who is to say that laughing is not intrinsically more important than many of the serious activities with which it is deemed incompatible? (Certainly it's better for your health.)[21] But this should not count as relevant, since we have agreed that the cognitive model of the Ethics of Laughter is inhospitable to considerations of consequences.

---

[20]Quoted by Hannah Arendt in her Introduction to Walter Benjamin, *Illuminations* (New York: Schocken, 1978). One of Oscar Wilde's *Phrases and Philosophies for the Use of the Young* deplores the "many young men who start out with a beautiful profile and end up adopting a useful profession."
[21]Witness Norman Cousins's account of his successful therapeutic program of laughter, in *Anatomy of an Illness as Perceived by the Patient: Reflexions on Healing and Regeneration* (New York: Norton, 1979).

Here again, Bergson has another interesting idea, suggesting a *fourth* line of attack against the beleaguered Funny. He defines the difference between Comedy and Tragedy in terms of Tragedy's commitment to the particular, in contrast to Comedy's interest in general types. Indeed he claims that Comedy is "the only one of the arts that aims at the general." (Op. cit. p. 114.) But "the highest ambition of art is to reveal to us nature itself" (p. 119) which is incompatible with the aims of practical living, because "to live is to accept from objects only those impressions that are *useful,* so that we can respond in appropriate ways" (p. 115). In sum, then, Comedy is mid-way between the Utilitarian perception of everyday life, and the essential perception of the world in itself which only art can claim to give us. In these terms we might explain the cognitive defect of laughter not merely as diverting our attention from "more serious things," which in itself is meaningless, but in the necessary distortion and obfuscation of the world it purports to reveal, because of its reliance on generalities and stereotypes. The thesis has some plausibility even from the point of view of a consequentialist Ethics: for if others are screened from our attention by generalities, we are bound to treat them less adequately to who they really are. More generally, insofar as we have a duty to apprehend the world as clearly as possible, laughter must impede us in the execution of that duty.

Bergson is urging us here to pay attention to the *particularity* of those we encounter, as well as of the situations of life. And it would seem churlish to refuse. Nevertheless, interesting as it is, the proposal must be rejected. It rests on two unwarranted assumptions. One is that by eliminating stereotypes and simplifications, we can have direct access to a correct vision of reality and its singular contents. The second is that simplification acts by cutting out or concealing parts of reality. The assumption is that true reality—as opposed to utilitarian representations of reality—is captured by a direct intuition. If this is to involve art, it must make no use of categories and stereotypes.

But this view is not credible. To be sure, the significant patterns that we find in reality often owe their significance to the importance of practical concerns. But the idea of a reality devoid of salient significant patterns, but perceived through art nevertheless, is the mere shadow of a false contrast. Simplification can be effective in drawing our attention to a pattern, without for all that concealing or obscuring the background. It's just that now we see it *as* background, and we therefore see the whole as differently organized. Insofar as the general types of Comedy do this for us, therefore, they bring us closer to reality, not further away.

Moreover simplification can be a means to knowledge even when it does proceed by exclusion of some elements of reality. This is the normal procedure of science, which—consistently with the views I have cited—Bergson thought powerless to tell us anything about reality. Science standardly considers certain features in isolation, in order to understand them better. If Bergson is right about the Comic, then laughter is revelatory of the nature of reality just in the measure that science is. Those are credentials enough for me. To be sure, elements so isolated need to be reintegrated into their context for the resulting pattern to prove adequate to reality. And it is just so with laughter: a partial view may be required for certain patterns to become salient, but a partial view becomes a distortion when we rest content with it.

So laughter can never be wrong merely because it simplifies. It would only be wrong if one were to remain content to laugh at a single joke forever. (*Idyllic* laughter, too, even if there is no joke, is wrong in being repetitious. That is what is hateful about "angelic" laughter.) Luckily, human laughter seems naturally protected against that particular potential sin. As an avenue to knowledge, it has the great advantage that it is always seeking fresh perspectives. One can be frozen in pomposity, but only angels can be frozen in laughter.

Questions

1. Can we ever blame people for laughing at an inappropriate time or place if they tried hard not to?
2. Can one find a joke funny without actually sharing the stereotypes on which it turns?
3. Are there any ways, other than the ones Ronald de Sousa mentions, in which you think laughter can be wrong?

Prejudice in Jest: When Racial and Gender Humor Harms

David Benatar

This paper responds to two questions, one raised by Michael Philips and the other by Ronald de Sousa: (1) What makes a piece of humor racist or sexist? (2) Are jokes that embody negative racial and gender stereotypes necessarily racist and sexist? The author gives an account of humor ethics and defends this against rival views of racist and sexist humor. More specifically he argues that a harm-centered account is to be preferred to Michael Philips's Act-Centered theory. Then arguments are advanced for a negative answer to the second question. In doing so, Ronald de Sousa's arguments for a positive answer are rejected.

AN ACCOUNT OF HUMOR ETHICS

How can humor be immoral? Briefly, the answer is that it is immoral where it is intended to harm people or where there are good grounds for expecting it to harm people, and where the harm in question is wrongfully inflicted. Following Joel Feinberg, I understand harm in terms of negative effects on people's interests. However, my understanding of harm is, in two ways, broader than the one for which he opts in his work about the moral limits of the criminal law.[1] Firstly, because in the current context I have a more expansive interpretation of what interests are, my understanding of harm includes what he calls hurts, offenses and other disliked states which are insufficiently severe to warrant being termed harms for his purposes. Because I am concerned with the morality of humor rather than with the moral limits of legally restricting it, the inclusion of less severe though nonetheless disliked states is more appropriate. Secondly, for

---

[1] Joel Feinberg, *Harm to Others* (New York: Oxford University Press, 1984): pp. 34–36. See also, "Wrongful Life and the Counterfactual Element in Harming," in Joel Feinberg, *Freedom and Fulfilment* (Princeton: Princeton University Press, 1992): pp. 3–4.

Professor Feinberg, a harm is something that is wrongfully inflicted. That definition is the desired one in interpreting the liberal harm principle, but the broader non-moral definition, according to which the expression "wrongfully inflicted harm" is not tautologous, is better suited to my undertaking.

Interests range in importance, but typically those upon which immoral humor infringes are interests in not being demeaned, insulted, shocked or disgusted. In themselves these interests are weaker ones on the scale of interest strengths, but in certain cases their infringement can lead to harms of a greater order of magnitude. This is especially so against a background of sustained prejudice and discrimination against certain groups. Demeaning or insulting jokes about members of these groups may cause more profound harm than if similar jokes were told about groups who have not suffered past discrimination. However, even when the harm is only mild this still provides *prima facie* moral reason against the activity which causes it.

The appeal of this account is that the connection is preserved between the ethics of humor and an influential understanding of ethics generally. On this understanding, rightness and wrongness is to be explained in terms of benefits and harms to people (or other moral recipients). The problem, of course, is that harms and benefits usually have to be balanced against each other. This is why there is not a straightforward correlation between harm and wrong and between benefit and good. Nevertheless it remains true that, according to the view being discussed, right and wrong are understood *in terms* of benefit and harm.

The harm explanation of immoral humor, insofar as it relates to racist and sexist humor, is similar to a view for which Michael Philips argues and which he calls an Act-Centered account[2] of racism and racist humor. According to him the term "racist," when used in its logically primary sense, is applied to actions. Persons and beliefs are racist in a derivative sense. This is because racism must be understood in terms of what it *does to the victim*. Since acts, the argument implies, are what are done to people, it is acts that are the logically primary application of the term "racist." Any understanding of how persons or beliefs are racist must be derivative from this.

There is a subtle, but conceptually important, difference between the Act-Centered account and the account I have outlined. On my view X is wrong if, *ceteris paribus*, it harms. Now as a matter of fact, it is usually actions (broadly understood to include not only speech acts, facial expressions, and other manifest relations between people but also some omissions) that benefit or harm. However, logically what is of importance is not the act but the harm or benefit. It is this that makes for rightness and wrongness. If having beliefs or thoughts can harm and benefit others, then beliefs and thoughts are subject to moral evaluation in a non-derivative sense. We can certainly imagine a science fiction scenario in which mere mental states brought harm or benefit to others. Perhaps my hating somebody would sap his life even though I were careful to avoid any harmful actions. However, in pursuit of such imaginative examples we should not

---

[2]Michael Philips, "Racist Acts and Racist Humor," *Canadian Journal of Philosophy* 14, no. 1 (March 1984): 76ff.

overlook a significant but mild and non-physical harm which mere beliefs in fact do inflict. If I believe negative rumors about somebody, that person is harmed by my having the belief even if I fail to act on it (in the broad sense of acting outlined above). His reputation is damaged. Similarly imagine that one is loathed by everybody one knows. Even if those who loathe one never make their feelings known (verbally or via their actions) to either the object of their revulsion or to anybody else, the person who is held in contempt is harmed in an important way.[3] This is so because we have interests not only in being *treated* with regard, but also in *being well regarded*. Damaged reputations or being viewed (even if not treated) with contempt adversely affect these interests and so constitute harms. Racists who view blacks, for example, as inferior beings, damage certain interests of blacks—interests in being regarded as beings *worthy* of respect. Note here that a racist might treat with respect those whom he regards as contemptible, for reasons other than his actually having respect for them. Prudence is one reason. Social condemnation of racist talk and practice might be such that a racist does not give expression to his beliefs. Less sophisticated prudential considerations may sometimes also be operative, say where a white racist appears before a black judge or finds himself about to be operated upon by a black surgeon. The Act-Centered account does not take account of states of mind which harm.

There are a number of reasons why people may be unpersuaded by the argument that mere beliefs can harm in the way I have said. For one thing, they may doubt that we really have interests in being *regarded* independent of the effect this can have on how we are treated. That we have such interests is suggested by the preference most of us have for a world in which we were well regarded to a world in which, although we were treated *as if* we were well regarded, we were not so regarded. Now it might be objected that we prefer this because we prefer not to be deluded. Although I am inclined to think that this may provide a partial explanation for our preference for the one world over the other, our preference for being well regarded seems to run deeper than this. This seems to be demonstrated by the fact that our preferences can vary in intensity depending on what kind of regard is at stake. Consider the scenario in which one has recently patented a new soft drink flavor and the beverage is now commercially available. An acquaintance of one's hears of this and tries the drink. I suggest that one would prefer a world in which the acquaintance actually enjoys the drink to a world in which he merely acts as if he does. But it seems to me that one's preference here would not be as strong as it would be in a choice between a world in which one were regarded as a being worthy of respect and a world in which although one was treated as such, one was actually regarded as an unworthy and inferior being. The difference in intensity, I think, shows that the preference not to be misled cannot *fully* account for why we prefer the world in which we are well regarded to one in which people merely act as if we are. If the concern about delusion fully explained our preference, then I cannot see why our preferences in the two scenarios I described would differ in

---

[3]The fact that the object of contempt does not know about it is not in itself an indication that he is not harmed. See Joel Feinberg, *Harm to Others*, pp. 86–87.

intensity. We stand to be deluded in both cases. The only difference is what we are deluded about, but that should not matter if we have no interest (that runs deeper than our concern about delusion) in how people regard us.

Another reason why people may doubt that mere beliefs can harm is that the harms inflicted purely by beliefs are minuscule in comparison with harms mediated by or resulting from actions, especially actions like lynchings, beatings, and enslavings. However, it cannot be inferred from the fact that the harms caused by beliefs are relatively mild that they are not harms at all. It is a mistake, I believe, to fail to distinguish small harms from the complete absence of harm.

A related reason why some people may be reluctant to accept that states of mind can harm is that they think that the *mere* presence of a harm makes something wrong. The worry then is that merely thinking badly of somebody may be immoral, even if it has no *manifest* effect upon him. However, this is not an implication of my view. On the understanding of harm that I am employing, there is a difference between a harm and a wrong. Not all harms, understood as negative effects on interests, are wrongs. Sometimes a harm is justifiable, in which case it is not wrong. For example, sometimes the rumors we believe about people are true. On occasion people deserve our resentment or contempt. Even when the harm is not justified, however, there may be other reasons to preclude our terming it a wrong. For instance, harmful beliefs are often, to a greater or lesser extent, beyond our control. To the degree that they are, they cannot be wrongs, even if they are undesirable because they cause unjustified harms.

Among those beliefs that harm are racist (and sexist) beliefs. The contents of some such beliefs are negative stereotypes. Stereotyping involves viewing, judging, or regarding individuals not in their own right but in terms of a set of attributes they are presumed to have in virtue of their belonging to a group, where the group's essential features do not include the attributes in question. Although a stereotype is something that is "continued or constantly repeated without change"[4] it is, in our ordinary (figurative) usage, not something that is necessarily applied in an exceptionless way. That is to say, although stereotypes are applied repeatedly and unchangingly they are not necessarily applied in every instance. Most of those who entertain stereotypes admit exceptions, even if they continue to measure the exception against the stereotype rule. (It is this that explains why statements like "Some of my best friends are Jews" can be true without constituting a defense against a charge of prejudice.) It is only the most ideological of racists whose prejudicial beliefs are held to be exceptionless. But a stereotype is more than merely a working generalization. As a form of prejudice it has a much stronger grip on the bearer's mind and is less easily overcome in instances where it clearly does not apply. It is for this reason, in part, that stereotypes are troubling even when they contain an element of truth, that is, when they say something that is true of a significant proportion of the stereotyped group. The stereotyper is heavily (though not invariably) disposed to attribute the stereotyped charactersitics to individual members of the group

---

[4]*The Shorter Oxford English Dictionary*, 1973.

that lack those characteristics. And when the stereotyper does recognize that an individual does not match the stereotype there is often an ongoing sense of anomaly—a troubling awareness of the difference between the stereotype and the individual who is "meant" to fit it but is aberrant. Stereotypes may be positive—that is, characterize a group in some favorable way—but more often they are not. It is the negative stereotype that will concern me here.

Although racist beliefs harm, having such beliefs is not a sufficient condition for humor's being racist. In other words, I am not saying that a person's having racist beliefs is sufficient to make his jokes racist jokes. His racist beliefs might be unconnected with his jokes. Some of the jokes he tells may involve (negative) stereotypes other than those he endorses. When there is a connection between humor and racist beliefs—where the jokes express racist beliefs—then one condition for racist humor is met. The condition is a sufficient, but not a necessary, one. That is to say, the fact that a joke *expresses* racist beliefs is enough to make it racist. That is because such expressions are harmful and on racial grounds. When told to people who are members of the group targeted by the joke, the harm is typically a feeling of hurt or degradation. The joke acts as a form of insult. But when I say that a joke *expresses* racist beliefs I do not mean exclusively that it *communicates* such beliefs (to others). It can mean that, but jokes can be an expression of prejudice even when one is alone and, recalling a joke, one enjoys it inwardly.

That a joke expresses racist beliefs is sufficient to make it racist, but it is not necessary. Racial jokes can be harmful and racist even where they do not express racist beliefs. If renditions of jokes inculcate and spread racist views then they are harmful even if the person who tells them does not endorse the stereotypes embodied by them.

This explains in part why my view is not like another view which Michael Philips discusses—one he calls an Agent-Centered account of racist and sexist humor.[5] According to such an account the essential feature of a racist act is that it is performed by a racist, where a racist is understood as somebody who has racist beliefs. On this view, if it is true that a person has no racist beliefs then he cannot be described as a racist and it follows that his acts are not racist. In other words, according to this view racist beliefs are a necessary condition for racism. If there are no racist beliefs there is no racism. On my view, there can be racism in the absence of racist beliefs. That is to say, racist beliefs are not a necessary condition for racism. However, having and expressing such beliefs are sufficient conditions for racism.

ARE NEGATIVE RACIAL JOKES NECESSARILY RACIST?

I shall distinguish *racist* and *sexist* humor from *racial* and *gender* humor. Racist and sexist humor are those forms of humor which are intended to, or can reasonably be expected to, inflict harms on racial or gender grounds, where these

[5]Michael Philips, p. 76.

harms are wrongful. The terms "racist" and "sexist" denote moral defectiveness. The terms "racial" and "gender" humor denote no normative element. They refer to pieces of humor that turn on racial or gender stereotypes or images. The question I shall now tackle is whether negative racial and gender humor—humor embodying negative racial and gender stereotypes and images—is necessarily racist and sexist.

A popular view among those who have written on the ethics of humor is that one cannot appreciate a joke embodying gender or racial stereotypes unless one shares those stereotypes. We cannot find a joke funny merely by imagining, for the purposes of the joke, that we share its prejudicial assumptions. If we do not actually endorse them we cannot appreciate the joke. Because it is said that the prejudicial attitudes cannot be hypothetically adopted for the purpose of the joke, racist and sexist humor has been said to have this *anhypothetical* feature.[6] It is a consequence of this view that negative racial or gender jokes are necessarily racist or sexist. This is because they necessarily express racist or sexist views. I shall argue that this view is mistaken—that we can enjoy racial and gender humor without actually endorsing the stereotypes they embody.

Note that the question of whether the *mere* appreciation of negative racial or gender jokes morally taints that appreciation arises only if one accepts my harm explanation over Michael Philips's Act-Centered account of racist humor. On the Act-Centered account the appreciation of a joke *cannot* be morally tainted unless that appreciation is communicated to others or negatively affects how one treats others.

The anhypothetical feature is advanced partly as an intuitive datum.[7] One author, Ronald de Sousa, acknowledges that against those who are unconvinced no knock-down argument can be advanced, but he appeals to some thought experiments to support the view.[8] These center around the following joke:

> Margaret Trudeau goes to visit the hockey team. When she emerges she complains that she has been gang-raped. Wishful thinking.

Now my problem with following the subsequent thought experiments is that I simply do not find the joke funny. One possible reason is that when I first read the joke I did not know who Margaret Trudeau was. However, even now that I have been informed that she is commonly regarded as being promiscuous, I still do not find the joke funny. I see its point, but it is not a good joke. The same is true if I substitute "Margaret Trudeau" with the name of a woman whom I do know is commonly regarded as being promiscuous. Even though I take the Trudeau joke to be a bad one, I shall discuss it and Professor de Sousa's treatment of it. This is because I think it is important to respond to existing argument

---

[6]Ronald de Sousa's term. See his "When is it Wrong to Laugh?" in *The Philosophy of Laughter and Humor*, ed. John Morreall (Albany, N.Y.: State University of New York Press, 1987), p. 241.
[7]Ronald de Sousa says: We "intuitively know that sharing these assumptions is what would enable us to find it funny" in *The Philosophy of Laughter and Humor*, p. 240.
[8]Ibid.

about the anhypothetical element in racial and gender humor, and this has focused on the Trudeau joke.[9]

Professor de Sousa will say that, to my credit, I fail to appreciate the Trudeau joke because I do not endorse the assumptions underlying the word "promiscuous" implicit in the context of this joke. He says that these assumptions are something like the following:

a) "rape is just a variant form of sexual intercourse."
b) "women's sexual desires are indiscriminate."
c) "there is something intrinsically objectionable or evil about a woman who wants or gets a lot of sex."[10]

I disagree that, as they stand, these are indeed assumptions of the joke. It is not my aim here to provide a full account of how to determine what the assumptions of a joke are—that is to say, how to decide exactly what a joke is *about*. That would require an extensive discussion that would take me well beyond the topic of this paper—the ethics of humor. In brief, however, I think that something is an assumption of a joke if at least part of the funniness of the joke is dependent on it. (But because a joke can please in more than one way—that is, because it can be funny for more than one reason—it is not *necessarily* true that without a particular assumption the joke must be unfunny.) The Margaret Trudeau joke does not, as Professor de Sousa claims, make assumptions about all women. If it did, then any woman's name could be substituted, without cost, for Margaret Trudeau's. But, in fact, it is crucial to the joke that the woman mentioned be taken to be *promiscuous*. Perhaps some people who enjoy the joke make these assumptions about all women, but that is not what the joke requires. The joke turns only on the more restricted assumption. Furthermore, it is relevant that the men who are said to have raped the promiscuous woman are putative icons of masculinity, not wimpy or decrepit men. Thus, both a) and b) must be modified to reflect accurately the implicit assumptions:

a') For *promiscuous* women, rape is just a variant form of sexual intercourse.
b') *Promiscuous* women's sexual desires for macho men are indiscriminate.

Although these are assumptions of the joke, this does not make them true. They are false. Promiscuity does not entail absolute sexual indiscriminateness. Promiscuity is a matter of degree. One can be promiscuous without wanting to have sex with just anybody (or even any sexually attractive person) and at any time.

In support of his anhypothetical claim, Professor de Sousa asks us to imagine either of two variants on the joke. One is that some non-sexual form of assault is substituted for rape. Alternatively we can substitute some man who is

---

[9]Another writer who has followed Professor de Sousa's lead in citing the Trudeau joke and endorsing his claims about its anhypothetical nature is Merrie Bergman, "How Many Feminists Does it Take to Make a Joke? Sexist Humor and What's Wrong with It," *Hypatia* 1, no. 1 (Spring 1986). Claudia Mills, although she does not discuss the Trudeau joke, seems to endorse the views of Professors de Sousa and Bergman. See Claudia Mills, "Racist and Sexist Jokes: How Bad are They (Really)?" *Report from the Center for Philosophy and Public Policy* 7, no. 2/3 (Spring/Summer 1987).
[10]Ronald de Sousa, p. 239.

not assumed to be homosexual and is not the object of any particularly hostile attitude. In both cases we are told that the humor would be lost.

I think that we can explain why the humor might be lost by the first change. The joke is about promiscuity. Given that promiscuity is a sexual concept, changing the assault to a non-sexual form would lose the connection with promiscuity. The appropriate incongruity would vanish. If this is so, then Ronald de Sousa's explanation for why the humor is lost fails to establish the conclusion for which he argues. It is not, as he says, that we must endorse the assumption to find the joke funny. Rather, it is that the assumption (whether endorsed or not) makes the sexual element essential to the joke's funniness. To obviate this problem we could alter the promiscuous component as well. Then, if whatever humor the Trudeau joke has was not preserved, Professor de Sousa's argument would be vindicated. However, I am not convinced that the humor would be lost. I can imagine attempts at non-sexual humor that would have the same form as the Trudeau joke (although I doubt that they would be any funnier). Imagine, for example, McCarthy's claiming that America's problems were attributable to the stranglehold which the communists have over the country. A political satirist might well say that this was "wishful thinking"—both because it would be a simplistic diagnosis of the cause of complex social problems and because of McCarthy's personal interest in having communists (real or imagined) to expose.

What if we pursue Ronald de Sousa's second thought experiment and alter the sex of the butt of the joke? I think that whatever humor there is in the Trudeau joke could be preserved, or even enhanced. Imagine that James Bond was taken captive by a squad of exquisitely beautiful women and that when he escaped he complained to his superiors that he had been forced to engage in serial sexual intercourse with them. This may strike us as humorous given Bond's well-known promiscuity. There would be an incongruity between Bond's promiscuous reputation and his complaints about unwanted sexual activity. But, why should we think that Bond enjoyed this anymore than we think a promiscuous woman enjoys being raped?

Following Ronald de Sousa, we might say that the propositions that constitute the assumptions of this scene are:

a″) For *promiscuous men*, being forced to have sex is just a variant form of sexual intercourse;
b″) *Promiscuous men's* sexual desires for exquisitely beautiful women are indiscriminate; and
c′) There is something intrinsically objectionable or evil about a *man* who wants and gets a lot of sex.

Given that humor, like the Bond scene, that assumes a″), b″) and c′), can be at least as funny as humor, like the Trudeau joke, that assumes a′), b′) and c), it seems that Ronald de Sousa's claim, that the Trudeau joke and its assumptions are sexist, is false.

Suppose that Professor de Sousa concedes that his thought experiments fail to establish anhypothetical *sexist* premises. He might still insist that a′) and b′) and c), although not sexist, must be endorsed for the joke to be funny. He might say, in other words, that the choice of joke was a bad example because it turns out not to be a case of anhypothetical *sexist* beliefs. Nevertheless, he might add, my deliberations so far have failed to disprove the anhypothetical feature of some humor. If some humor is anhypothetical then if another joke has truly sexist premises (unlike the Trudeau joke), those premises would have to be endorsed for the joke to be appreciated. I shall now counter this possible objection by arguing against the anhypothetical nature of racist and sexist humor.

Professor de Sousa's argumentative strategy is to ask us to engage in various thought experiments about jokes and see whether we find the result funny. I want to employ this kind of argument to show that one can find a joke funny without sharing the underlying stereotype. The problem is that no single thought experiment will make the point as strongly as possible for everybody. The reason is that the best way to establish my point is for a person to consider a gender or ethnic joke that turns on a stereotype which the person knows he or she does not share. Although some people are well attuned to their psychological dynamics and can determine when they have and do not have prejudices, such acuity may be doubted by the subject himself or disputed by others. One can be most sure of the absence of a prejudice when one is a member of the sex, ethnic group, or race about which the prejudice is held. Of course, even here one can never be certain that one does not share the prejudice and that one is not suffering from self-hate. However, it would be a mistake to infer from this epistemic uncertainty that *whenever* one enjoys a joke embodying a stereotype that one shares the stereotype. That would be to *stipulate* that enjoyment of jokes embodying stereotypes constitutes an endorsement of the stereotype. The argument for the anhypothetical nature of racial and gender humor would then be both circular and unfalsifiable.

The project then for each person is to determine whether he or she enjoys a joke that turns on a negative stereotype about his or her own sex, ethnic group, or race.

Consider the following as an example:

QUESTION: Why do Jewish men like to watch pornographic movies backwards?
ANSWER: They like to see the prostitute giving the money back afterwards.

I know that I enjoy jokes such as this which incorporate negative Jewish stereotypes (such as Jewish miserliness) even though I am as confident as possible that I do not share the stereotypes. This suggests to me that one *can* hypothetically accept stereotypes for the purposes of a joke and find the joke funny.

A reasonable objection to this is that I could not hypothetically apply the stereotype to just any ethnic or racial group for the purposes of the joke (although I probably could apply it to some other groups). Imagine that the above joke had been about English men. The humor would be lost, even if I were told that, for the purposes of the joke, I should assume that the English are miserly. To understand why this is so we need to distinguish between i) merely stipulating a stereotype, ii) recognizing a stereotype, and iii) actually endorsing a stereotype. It is true that the incongruous elements of a joke, whether or not any of them are stereotypes, cannot merely be stipulated. A joke which is preceded by an explicit stipulation of assumptions is too contrived to please. This is especially so when we are aware of the group regarding which the stereotype is stipulated and the stereotype runs counter to prevailing stereotypes about that group. But endorsing a stereotype is not the only alternative to merely stipulating it. Recognition of the stereotype is sufficient for the joke to be enjoyed. This recognition is what facilitates a hypothetical acceptance of the stereotype.

There are two senses in which a stereotype can be recognized. The most obvious is where one is previously aware of the stereotype and thus some newly encountered instance of it is familiar to one. A less obvious sense is where, although one is not antecedently aware of the stereotype, on encountering a manifestation of it one perceives it as the stereotype that it is. It is for this reason that one can sometimes enjoy ethnic jokes even when one has never even heard of the ethnic group in question. Consider the following humor:

QUESTION: Why do Århusians have so many scars round their mouths on
   Mondays?
ANSWER: Because they practice eating with a knife and fork on Sundays.

I appreciated this humorous riddle even though, prior to reading it, I had never heard of the Århusians. This suggests that it may simply be the cleverness of an ethnic joke that we often find funny. Nevertheless, I think that the enjoyment is usually likely to be less than in those cases where one was previously aware of the stereotype.

The joke about Jewish men watching pornographic movies backwards is as funny as it is because I encounter the joke knowing that *there is* the stereotype that Jews are tightfisted. I suspect that were one not aware of this stereotype, one would not find the joke as funny. And, in the absence of *any* recognition of the stereotype, mere stipulation of the stereotype would not make the joke funny. If over the course of time one were to be told a number of jokes employing this stereotype, then the stereotype would become familiar to one and one would recognize it (in the obvious sense of "recognize" mentioned above). I suggest that this recognition would usually happen in a far shorter space of time than it would take to come to *endorse* the stereotype. My argument for this again appeals to personal introspections, in the way that Professor de Sousa's arguments do.

My grandmother, Suzette Benatar, told me a few Djoha jokes when I was a child. Djoha is the fool in the humor of the Jewish community in Turkey where she grew up. As I was unfamiliar with the character of Djoha, the jokes were not very funny at first, However, after hearing a few more Djoha jokes over time, I became familiar with the characterization of Djoha as fool and, recognizing this in further Djoha jokes, found them much funnier. I have subsequently attempted to establish whether there are ethnic overtones to Djoha jokes. As far as I can tell there are not—at least my grandmother is not aware of any—but imagine that my inquiries had revealed that there *were* such overtones. Obviously that would not show that I shared the ethnic stereotypes all along. This is born out by my experience of van der Merwe jokes which are the staple South African joke. Van der Merwe is the idiot of South African humor. I enjoyed these jokes for years before realizing that there were ethnic overtones. Van der Merwe is an Afrikaner surname and in some senses van der Merwe is the Afrikaner stereotype, but the jokes became no more enjoyable once I became aware of this.[11] One final example is that of the JAP (Jewish American Princess). The stereotype of the JAP as frigid was, until a few years ago, unknown to me. Moreover, it directly contradicts other stereotypes of Jewish women, namely that they are over-sexed. It was not long before I came to appreciate the jokes, again by recognizing the stereotype, not endorsing it. From the above reflections it can be concluded that we need not endorse gender and racial stereotypes in order to appreciate humor that turns on them. Racial and gender jokes do not necessarily express prejudice and thus are not necessarily morally defective. That my argument has been directed to establishing this reassuring but very limited conclusion should not obscure the unpleasant fact that racial and gender humor often do express, inculcate, or reinforce prejudice, or cause people to be insulted or demeaned.[12]

Postscript

Since this paper was first published, I have made further inquiries about Djoha jokes. These inquiries suggest that Djoha is indeed not an ethnic stereotype. He is the butt of jokes in many Arab countries. Interestingly, while Turkish Jews tell jokes about Djoha, the rest of the Turkish population tells exactly the same jokes about a character called Nasreddin Hoja who is indistinguishable from Djoha in everything but name.

Questions

1. Can one really be harmed by people's beliefs if these beliefs are never given any expression, either in word or deed? How does the author understand the concept of "harm"? Can you think of an alternative interpretation of this concept?
2. What is a stereotype?
3. Can you think of a racial, gender, or ethnic joke that you find funny but the assumptions of which you are sure you don't share? How can you be sure that you do not share the assumptions?

Suggestions for Further Reading on Humor

ARISTOTLE. "Wit." Book 4, chap. 8 in *Nicomachean Ethics*, translated by Terence Irwin, Indianapolis: Hackett, 1985: pp. 112–114.

---

[11]It is interesting to note that despite the racially oppressive nature of Apartheid (or perhaps because of it), van der Merwe was far more frequently the butt of jokes than were blacks, at least in English-speaking circles.

[12]I am grateful to Noël Carroll for encouraging and valuable comments on an earlier version of this paper. Marty Perlmutter, together with whom I have enjoyed many laughs, was a willing reader whose suggestions helped me to improve the paper. My thanks also go to anonymous reviewers for their helpful remarks, and to my colleague Laurence Goldstein for his interest and comments.

BERGMANN, MERRIE. "How Many Feminists Does It Take to Make a Joke? Sexist Humor and What's Wrong with It." *Hypatia* 1, no. 1 (spring 1986): pp. 63–82.

BOSKIN, JOSEPH. "The Complicity of Humor: The Life and Death of Sambo." In *The Philosophy of Laughter and Humor*, edited by John Morreall. Albany: State University of New York Press, 1987: pp. 250–263.

GAUT, BERYS. "Just Joking: The Ethics and Aesthetics of Humor." *Philosophy and Literature* 22 (1998): pp. 51–68.

GOLDSTEIN, LAURENCE. "Humor and Harm." *Sorites*, no. 3 (November 1995): pp. 27–42. http://www.ifs.csic.es/sorites/Issue_03/item4.htm

HARVEY, J. "Humor as Social Act: Ethical Issues." *Journal of Value Inquiry* 29, no. 1 (1995): pp. 19–30.

MORREALL, JOHN. *Taking Laughter Seriously.* Albany: State University of New York Press, 1983, chaps. 8 and 9.

ROBERTS, ROBERT C. "Humor and the Virtues." *Inquiry* 31, no. 2 (June 1988): pp. 127–149.

CHAPTER 2

Sexist Speech

JANICE MOULTON, The Myth of the Neutral 'Man'
CASEY MILLER & KATE SWIFT, Who Is Man?
MICHAEL LEVIN, Sexist Language

The Myth of the Neutral "Man"

Janice Moulton

Janice Moulton argues that irrespective of a speaker's intention in using words like "man" and "he," these words do not function as genuine gender-neutral terms. To this end, she notes that words like "man" and "he" do not function like ordinary un-marked terms. Unmarked terms are words like "tall," "long," "wide," "old," and "pure," that not only (1) refer to one of a pair of opposite qualities but also (2) describe the quality of which the two opposites are extremes. For example, "tall" can be used both (1) to mean the opposite of "short" and (2) to describe the quality of which "tall" (in the first sense) and "short" are extremes. Thus one can (1) say that a person is tall, the claim that he has the quality of being toward one end of the height spectrum, or one can (2) ask how tall a person is, which does not presuppose that the person is tall (in the first sense). Notice that marked terms, like "short,"
cannot be used properly in the second sense. Although one can ask how short a person is, phrasing the question that way suggests that the person is short(ish).

Janice Moulton argues that unlike words like "he" and "man," ordinary un-marked terms become disambiguated in certain restricted contexts where they are used neutrally. For example, although it is clear that the word "tall" is used in its neutral sense when the question "How tall is she?" is asked, it is very unclear whether the word "man" is intended to be used neutrally in the statement "Neanderthal man was a hunter." The author then proceeds to argue that words like "he" and "man" cannot be used to refer to a female human without it sounding strange, or ironic. For instance, there is something odd about saying "She is the best man for the job" or "Man has mammary glands."

Janice Moulton, "The Myth of the Natural Man," in *Sexist Language*, Mary Vetterling-Braggin (ed.) Littlefield, Adams and Co. Copyright 1981. Reprinted by permission of Rowman & Littlefield.

This paper owes a special thanks to G. M. Robinson and Cherin Elias for their comments and encouragement. Many other people at the Society for Women in Philosophy, the American Philosophical Association meetings, and the University of Maryland philosophy department gave me valuable comments. I would particularly like to thank Mary Vetterling-Braggin, Virginia Valian, Larry Stern, Christine Pierce, Susan Rae Peterson, Stan Munstat, Susan Moore, W. G. Lycan, Ron Laymon, Adele Laslie, Gale Justin, Carl Ginet, Alan Donagan, Richard Brandt, and H. D. Block.

I

Here are two riddles:

(1) A man is walking down the street one day when he suddenly recognizes an old friend whom he has not seen in years walking in his direction with a little girl. They greet each other warmly and the friend says, "I married since I last saw you, to someone you never met, and this is my daughter, Ellen." The man says to Ellen, "You look just like your mother." How did he know that?

(2) A boy and his father were driving when suddenly a large truck careened around a corner and hit their car head-on. The car was crushed, and when their bodies were removed from the wreck the father was already dead. The son, badly injured but still alive, was rushed to the hospital, where hasty preparations were made for immediate surgery. As the boy was brought in for the operation, the surgeon saw him and said, "I can't operate, that's my son." How is that possible?

If you have not heard these riddles before and they puzzle you, that's an important datum for this paper.

II

Recently it has been argued that the words "he," "man," etc. should not be used as gender-neutral terms because it is unfair to women; anyone who looks for the best *man* for the job or tells an applicant to send *his* credentials is less likely or less able to consider a female candidate fairly.

Two claims should be distinguished here. The first accepts that there is a gender-neutral meaning for terms like "he," "man," etc. Adherents of this view consider the gender-neutral uses of these terms an *effect* of, and an unpleasant reminder of, the lower status of women, and urge that the gender-neutral use be eliminated as a sign of good will and for symptomatic relief.

The second claim denies that terms such as "he" and "man" have gender-neutral uses. It argues that using these terms as if they were neutral terms *causes* unfairness. This is because not really being gender-neutral, the use of such terms leads one to apply the context to males, and makes it difficult to apply it to females.

The first claim is sometimes followed up with a shift to the second claim: once the first claim has been articulated, the second claim is thought to become true. Refusing to adopt this sign of good will indicates a lack of good will—that is, sexism. Continued use of "he" and "man" as neutral terms indicates that the attitude of the speaker is not gender-neutral. It will be recognized on some level of awareness that the speaker intends men to be preferred to women, and intends terms such as "he" or "man," although hitherto neutral, to apply primarily to men. Only people who have these intentions will continue to use these terms as if they were neutral. Such an argument defends and reinforces the first claim by appeal to the second claim.

The first claim, that there *are* neutral uses but they are symptoms of unfairness and should be eliminated, has greater initial plausibility than the second.

Using "he" and "man" as neutral terms may well be the result of the greater prominence of men in our culture. But once this use has been established, it appears that it can be both intended and understood neutrally. There is no initial reason to suppose that these terms are less likely to be applied to women than men, *if* used neutrally.

I am going to defend the second claim, but I would like to do so without appealing to any connection with the first claim. I believe that the second claim can be defended on its own, without appeal to sexist attitudes of the speakers. I shall try to show that however innocently and neutrally they are intended, the words "he," "man," etc. may not function as genuine gender-neutral terms; that their use is unavoidably somewhat gender-specific; and that male gender-specific descriptions make it difficult to recognize that descriptions in that context could apply to a female.

III

Let us first consider the criticism of the use of "he," "man," etc. as gender-neutral terms which, while allowing that the uses may be neutral, nevertheless requests relief from these symptoms of other injustices. This criticism reminds us that there are other neutral terms: One can look for the best *person* for the job, tell *applicants* to send their credentials to one, etc. It continues: If we change our language, we will increase awareness of past unfair treatment of women and save women from being constantly reminded of the male priority and domination that the neutral uses of "he" and "man" indicate. Although some of the suggested changes will be awkward at first, they will be signs of a spirit of sympathy and cooperation with the criticism and therefore with efforts of women to attain equal human status.

Once this request has been made, the continued use of "he" and "man" as gender-neutral terms does not *make* a person less likely to consider a woman for the job. Nevertheless it may be an indication that the person is not especially sympathetic to the problems of being automatically assigned a lower status, and therefore that the person may be less likely to consider a woman for the job. On this view, the gender-neutral use of "he," etc. is a consequence, or a symbol, not a cause, of existing unjust attitudes.

This request seems to be asking very little, just that a few words be changed, but is actually asking more than that. The change in language might also publicize a political position, or challenge friends and colleagues. In our language where a lower socioeconomic class is detectable by dialect variants such as the use of "gutter," "nylons," and "light bill," instead of "street" or "road," "stockings," and "electric bill," and a graduate education turns a "resume" into a "vita," a "convention" into "meetings," and "manuscripts" into "stuff" (as in "send me your stuff"), the change of few words is likely to announce a life style, broadcast a political position, or misdirect attention to the wrong issue.

If, after their relation to male status has been pointed out, "he" and "man" continue to be used in place of other neutral terms, it does not necessarily follow that the user lacks good will toward females. Small variations in language may have great social significance. It may not be a lack of good will, but a desire to concentrate on more significant issues or a shyness about taking political stands in casual conversations, that leaves the request unfulfilled.

IV

Perhaps you've recognized by now that the above riddles are intended to illustrate that assuming that a description (a surgeon, the friend of a man) applies to a male makes it difficult to recognize that the description could also apply to a female.

The second riddle is frequently presented as an illustration of our sexist presuppositions. We automatically assume that the surgeon has to be a man. But the first riddle has a similar effect without the presence of a professional description to receive the blame. I do not believe that the surgeon riddle does show sexism. What it shows is that once the assumption is made that a description is of a man, it is very, very hard to change that assumption. In the first riddle the assumption is probably made merely because an old friend of a man is somewhat more likely to be a man than a woman. (The assumption about gender need not have any empirical basis. There appears to be a tendency to assume that "my cousin," if spoken by a woman, refers to a female, and if spoken by a man, refers to a male.) Yet however weak the basis for the assumption, the perplexity caused by the riddles shows that it is still very hard to change one's assumptions about gender.

Note that these riddles do not show that the use of "he" or "man" in their alleged neutral sense makes it difficult to realize that a description in that context could be of a female. The only thing the riddles show is that if one assumes that a description applies to a male, it is hard to realize that the description could apply to a female. But genuine gender-neutral terms should not foster such an assumption. Therefore I still have to show that the alleged gender-neutral uses of these terms are, in fact, somewhat gender-specific.

V

It is not legitimate to assume that any use of "he" makes people think of a male instead of a female. Language has an influence on thought, but there are many other influences, too. Consider another example: "being doctored" has worse connotations than "being nursed." Things that have been doctored are in a worse condition than if left alone, whereas things that have been nursed are frequently in a better condition as a result. However, such linguistic usage does not prevent people from seeking doctors rather than nurses for serious illnesses. It seems very likely that these verb forms are derived from the functions of doctors and nurses. Yet there is no reason to suppose that use of these expressions causes discrimination against doctors in favor of nurses.

So even though the use of "he" as a gender-neutral pronoun is related to the position of males as compared with that of females in this culture,[1] and even though women are in a position inferior to men, it still has to be shown that gender-neutral uses of "he," "man," etc. affect people's thinking by preventing them from applying the context in question to women.[2]

The claim that there is no really neutral use might not need defense if there were no other terms that had both a neutral and non-neutral use. But such is not the case. Many adjectives that refer to one of a pair of opposite qualities can be used neutrally to indicate the dimension whose extremes are the opposites. One can ask "How tall is she?" of a short person, and "How wide is that?" of a narrow object. "Tall" and "wide" are used not only as opposites of "short" and "narrow," but as neutral terms to describe the quality or dimension of which the opposites are extremes. One *can* ask "How short is she?" or "How narrow is that?" but doing so expresses the expectation that the answer will lie on one end of the range of possible answers. In contrast, any tendency to suppose that anyone of whom it is asked how tall they are is in fact a tall person, is certainly very slight. Such uses of "short," "narrow," as well as "young," "impure," "bad," and "small" are called *marked* while similar uses of the opposite terms, "tall" and "long," "wide," "old," "pure," "good," and "big" are termed *unmarked*.[3]

In this respect, unmarked and marked adjectives behave very much like the he-she, man-woman, his-her pairs. The use of "he" or "man" may be either gendered or neutral. However, if one uses "she" or "woman," one conveys the expectation that a person who fits the description will be female, not male.[4] If one is going to argue that "he" and "man" cannot function as gender-neutral terms, it cannot be merely because such terms also have gender-specific meanings.

---

[1]Many people believe this claim, but Robin Lakoff in "Language and Woman's Place," *Language in Society* 2 (1973): 45–80, supports it with an impressive number of gender asymmetries in language whose best explanation appears to be the superior position of one gender in the culture. See also Mary Ritchie Key, *Male/Female Language* (Metuchen, N.J.: Scarecrow Press, 1975); and Casey Miller and Kate Swift, *Words and Women* (Garden City, N.Y.: Anchor Press/Doubleday, 1976).

[2]Even if the gender-neutral uses of "he," etc. prevent people from considering women in those contexts, there are some contexts where one does not want to be considered (for example, as a murder suspect). So one has also to show that the disadvantages of not being considered for jobs, awards, and consultation outweigh the advantages of not being considered for criminal activities, punishment, and obligations. Women who oppose the Equal Rights Amendment seem to disagree with other women, not on the actual unequal status of women, but rather on whether the advantages of this status outweigh the disadvantages.

[3]Although this terminology was originally applied to phonological distinctions (e.g., the third-person singular of regular verbs is marked with an "s"), it has been extended to the use I cite. See John Lyons, *Introduction to Theoretical Linguistics* (Cambridge: Cambridge University Press, 1971), p. 79.

[4]Porter C. Perrin and Karl W. Dykema, in *Writer's Guide and Index to English*, 3rd edition (Glenview, Ill.: Scott, Foresman, 1959), pp. 538–539, 551–552, say: "As we must often refer to nouns that name either or both male and female, the language has developed . . . ways of making up for the lack of an accurate pronoun: The usual way is to use *he* or *his* alone even when some of the persons are female . . . Sometimes when the typical invididuals or the majority of the group referred to would be women, *her* is used in the same way."

VI

It might be argued that, given that there are other neutral terms ("they," "one," "human," "person"), perpetuation of a neutral use of one of a pair of opposites gives that quality a priority or superiority over the opposite quality. There is some evidence that the unmarked term of a pair of opposites has higher positive associations. The use of a marked term often has a pejorative tone.[5] It is not an accident that "good" and "pure" are unmarked, "bad" and "impure" marked. If by perpetuating the neutral uses of "he" and "man" one encouraged the continuation of the unfair priority of males, then there would be a sense in which such uses were not really neutral.

Granted that people usually do have higher positive associations for the term with the neutral use than with its opposite.[6] And people have higher positive associations for "he" than "she." But it is far from clear that the positive association is a *result* of the neutral use; it may well be the other way around. The neutral uses of "tall," "wide," "high," "long," "big," etc. tell us that, in general, the larger size is better, or standard, or ideal. I suspect the reason for this is that children, during the time of first language learning, are expected to increase in size and are often praised for doing so and worried over when they do not. Thus at the outset they learn the term for the extreme that is their goal, and then come to use it to stand for the whole dimension.[7] (This would explain why "old" is unmarked even though youth is so much admired and valued. The post-adolescent youth that is valued is many years older than the language-learning child.) When one uses an adjective that can stand for one end of a dimension neutrally to name the dimension, one presents that end of the dimension as expected or standard. For example, "How cold is it?" vs. "How hot is it?"; "How hard is it?" vs. "How soft is it?". If one end of a dimension is a standard independently of a particular context, the term for that end would acquire a neutral use. If this explanation of the origin of unmarked adjectives is correct, the similarity to unmarked adjectives is no reason to suppose that the more positive evaluation of "he" is the *result* of its neutral use. It indicates, instead, that men's being more highly regarded than women promotes the neutral uses of male terms.

In any case, the higher positive associations of adjectives with neutral uses do not affect evaluations in particular cases. Although "wide" has a higher

---

[5]According to Lyons, *Theoretical Linguistics*, p. 467.

[6]Evidence for this is to be found in C. E. Osgood, Suci, and Tannenbaum, *The Measurement of Meaning* (Urbana: University of Illinois Press, 1957), especially pp. 36–62. Unmarked terms tend to be scored more positively by subjects on the semantic differential evaluative scale. But this is not always the case. It is worth remarking that "feminine" receives a higher positive evaluation than "masculine."

[7]Eve V. Clark in "What's in a Word? On the Child's Acquisition of Semantics in his First Language," in *Cognitive Development and the Acquisition of Language*, T. E. Moore, ed. (New York: Academic Press, 1973), pp. 65–110, points out that children learn to use the unmarked term of a pair before they learn the marked term.

positive association for people than "narrow," wider objects are not necessarily valued more than narrower objects. For example, pocket calculators are touted for their narrow dimensions (although in advertisements one is more likely to hear the term "slim" than "narrow"). And so there is no reason to suppose that using "he" and "man" as unmarked neutral terms affects evaluations of females in particular cases. If one is going to argue that such uses are not really neutral, one has to show something more about these terms—something other than that they have the properties of other unmarked terms.

VII

There are important differences between unmarked adjectives and words like "he" and "man." The neutral use of adjectives is quite unambiguous, restricted to contexts in which a quantity or amount of that dimension is the topic (i.e., three inches *high*, 99 & 44/100% *pure)*. The neutral uses of "he" and "man" have no restricted contexts to clarify them. Moreover, uses of these terms are frequently in need of clarification. We might be inclined to say that "man" in "The Neanderthal man was a hunter" was being used neutrally to mean "human." But this sentence could be used to describe just males. One might say, "The Neanderthal man was a hunter. The Neanderthal woman raised crops." In this context "man" is clearly intended to mean "male human." In an example from an introductory philosophy text, an apparently neutral use of "he" turns out to be intentionally gender-specific. This ambiguity is resolved only by the last word:

> Consider, firstly, two comparatively simple situations in which a cyberneticist might find himself. He has a servomechanism, or a computing machine, with no randomising element, and he also has a wife.[8]

Although "he" and "man" behave like unmarked adjectives in some respects, their double roles as both gender-specific and gender-neutral terms permit ambiguity in ways that the double roles of unmarked adjectives do not.

The ambiguity in the beginning of these examples allows an intended gender-specific "he" or "man" to be interpreted as a neutral term so that a context may be inadvertently applied to women. And ambiguity may also allow an intended neutral "he" to be interpreted as a gender-specific term so that the context is accidentally not applied to women. But if this is so, the culprit is ambiguity, which could be resolved without forsaking the neutral uses of male terms. Add that you are an equal-opportunity employer and there should be no gender-specific interpretation of "man" in "the best man for the job." One need not eliminate the neutral use of "he" and "man" in order to eliminate ambiguity. There will be other ways of resolving the ambiguity besides using other neutral terms that are not ambiguous.

[8]L. Jonathan Cohen, "Can There Be Artificial Minds?" in *Reason and Responsibility*, 2nd ed., Joel Feinberg, ed. (Encino, Calif.: Dickenson Publishing Co., 1971), p. 288.

VIII

Here's the problem: However the use of a term gets started, it would seem that if it was intended a certain way when used, and understood that way by others, then, on any available theory of meaning, that's what it means. If "man" or "he" are intended neutrally, as they often are, and if people know that, as they do, then it would seem that "man" and "he" do refer to the members of the human species, and that they are as neutral as "human" and "they."

In order to show that "man" and "he" and like terms are not really neutral, I propose to show that it is not enough that one *intend* a term to have a particular meaning for it to have that meaning; that intended neutral uses of "he," "man," etc. can fail to be neutral; and that such failures have implications for all other allegedly neutral uses.

Let's compare "he" and "man" with other terms whose gender neutrality is not in dispute, such as "one," "they," "human," and "person." One striking difference is the inability to use "he" and "man" to refer to a female human. It would be a rare person who could say without irony "She's the best *man* for the job" or say of a female, "He's the best." Yet the undisputed gender-neutral terms can indeed be used this way: "She's the best person;" "That one is the best" (of a female). If "he" and "man" are genuinely gender-neutral, then they ought to be applicable to any person regardless of gender.

One might argue that one does not say "he's the best" of a female for the same reason one does not merely say "I believe" when one knows. On Grice's account of the latter, it is not that believing *implies* not knowing, but that one does not usually convey less information than one can.[9] Therefore if one says one believes, people may assume one does not actually know. Similarly, one might argue, if it is clear in some context that the gender of a referent is known to the speaker, then the speaker is expected to specify that gender. It is not that uses of "he" and "man" *imply* that the referent is male, but simply that one does not convey less information than one can. If one uses "he" or "man," people may assume that either a male is being referred to or that the gender is not known.

This explanation, however, does not account for all the facts. It offers no explanation for why "She's the best man" is not permissible since gender *has* been specified. Moreover, it would predict that undisputed neutral terms could not be used if the gender were known. If the problem were only that speakers are expected to specify gender when known, the sentence "That's the best person" would be as inappropriate to say of either a male or a female as "That's the best man" is to say of a female.

On some theories of meaning, the meaning of a term is a function of its use. I have already pointed out that "he" and "man" do not have the same uses as undisputed gender-neutral terms. Recent theories of meaning have analyzed meaning as a function of the intentions of the speaker. Yet failures of gender-

---

[9]H. Paul Grice, "Logic and Conversation," in *Syntax and Semantics,* vol. 3, Peter Cole and Jerry L. Morgan, eds. (New York: Academic Press, 1975).

neutrality of "he" and "man" occur even though the speaker may intend a gender-neutral use. For example, Bertrand Russell in his classic paper "On Denoting" says:

> Suppose now we wish to interpret the proposition, "I met a man." If this is true, I met some definite man; but that is not what I affirm. What I affirm is, according to the theory I advocate:—"'I met x and x is human' is not always false."[10]

If Russell were correct, then parents familiar with his theory would have no cause for anxiety if their young female child, on arriving home several hours late from kindergarten, said, "I met a man." Russell did not notice that "man" is not used neutrally in his context. This example shows that one cannot account entirely for the meaning of a term by the intentions of the speaker on a particular occasion. The meaning of a term involves, among other things, its expected interpretation, the way it functions with other terms, and its use in linguistic enterprises such as reasoning. This is important for the next point.

"He" and "man" cannot be used in some contexts where undisputedly gender-neutral terms can. But what about other contexts? Suppose it can be shown that a familiar and paradigmatic example of a gender-neutral use of "man" or "men" is not really neutral at all? Then I think it can be argued that there is no real gender-neutral meaning of these terms. Consider the first line of the familiar syllogism:

All men are mortal.

Most people would agree that the occurrence of "men" is intended to be neutral; this is a statement about the whole human species. But if it is a neutral use, then this syllogism, that paradigm of valid syllogisms, is invalid, for the second line usually reads,

Socrates is a man.

The occurrence of "man" in this sentence is *not* a neutral use. If it were a neutral use, then replacing "Socrates" with the name of a female human being or a child would not affect the syllogism. Yet the usual interpretation of

Sophia is a man

makes it false, or insulting. It is not taken to mean that Sophia is a member of the human species.

Let me add two explanations here. (1) The meaning of a term is not determined by the interpretation of one person alone. How others will understand it must be considered as well. Although some people might argue that in this context the syllogism "Sophia is a man" can be read as "Sophia is a human being," they will recognize that many other people will not take it this way (this is due in part to our inability to use "man" to refer to a female in other contexts). Although *some* people might be able to *read* "man" neutrally in this context, it does not follow that this is what it means. Further examples where "man" and "his" fail to be gender-neutral will be given to convince those who can make a gender-neutral reading in one case.

---

[10]Bertrand Russell, "On Denoting," *Mind* 13 (1905): 479.

(2) It might be argued that I have changed the meaning of "man" in the syllogism by substituting "Sophia" for "Socrates." The original syllogism might have had a neutral occurrence of "man" which changed with the substitution. For example, if I substituted "The Outer Banks" for "savings and loan institutions" in "_____ are banks," I would change the meaning of "banks." However, if "man" *has* a gender-neutral use, it should retain that use regardless of the gender of the referent. There is no reason to claim that it has a gender-neutral meaning unless it has a use that can be applicable to females as well as males. Gender-neutral terms such as "human" and "person" are not affected by the substitution of a female name in their context.

Thus the inference from "All men are mortal" and "Socrates is a man" to "Socrates is mortal" is invalid if the occurrence of "men" is intended to be gender-neutral in the first premise. Instead of a paradigm of valid inference we would have an equivocation, because the meaning of the terms has changed. It would be just like the argument:

All banks are closed on Sunday.

The Outer Banks are banks.

Therefore, the Outer Banks are closed on Sunday.

That the occurrence of "men" in the first premise is believed to be gender-neutral, and that the syllogism is believed to be neither enthymematic nor invalid, is evidence either that we are confused about neutral uses or that we are confused about validity even in the simplest cases. There is further evidence that it is the former. Consider another example:

Man is a mammal.

This use of "man" is neutral if any use is. But if this is conjoined with the dictionary definition of "mammalia":

the highest class of Vertebrata comprising man and all other animals that nourish their young with milk, that have the skin usu. more or less covered with hair, that have mammary glands . . .[11]

it should be legitimate to conclude:

Man has mammary glands.

But this conclusion is less acceptable than:

Humans have mammary glands.

because "man" does not function in the same gender-neutral way as "human" in this context. A statement that members of the human species have mammary glands is not peculiar, but a statement that males have mammary glands is. Although both men and women have mammary glands, only the mature glands of women are ordinarily likely to be topics of conversation. If "man" could be used gender-neutrally, its occurrence in a context that applied to both male and female humans, particularly to female humans, would be given a gender-neutral interpretation. Instead, its occurrence in such a context is plainly gender-specific.

---

[11] *Webster's Third New International Dictionary.*

Alleged neutral uses of "he" are not as frequently found in syllogisms. But *if* it sounds strange to ask an applicant about the interests of his husband or wife, to instruct a child on the cleaning of his vagina or penis, or to compliment a guest on his gown or tuxedo, then something is less than neutral about "he" and "his" as well. Note that there is no ambiguity about these uses. The contexts make it clear that "man" and "his" are supposed to be understood to be gender-neutral, if possible. Other obvious failures of gender neutrality are:

Man has two sexes.

Some men are female.

There are many more contexts in which attempts to use terms such as "he" and "man" gender-neutrally produce false, funny, or insulting statements, even though the gender-neutrality was clearly intended.

The failure of "he," "man," etc. to be gender-neutral can be demonstrated in examples where a reference to a particular person, or a grammatical context in which these terms cannot be used neutrally occurs. But what about other cases? Surely I cannot *prove* that there is never a case in which "man" means human, you will say.

Similarly I could not prove that there was never a case in which "wash-bucket" meant "justice" or "Watch out!" (Imagine a feud in a laundry room.) But that's not the sense of meaning that's at issue here. As I've said earlier, the meaning of a term involves its expected interpretation, the way it functions with other terms and its use in reasoning and other discourse. And what we've seen with "he" and "man," etc. is that some uses which may appear gender-neutral at first turn out to be gender-specific because of what is said in some other place.

To give an idea of the variety of ways that gender-neutrality can fail, or can be shown to have failed, let me offer another example first pointed out by Ruth Lucier:

> All men and all women are philosophers; or, let us say, if they are not conscious of having philosophical problems, they have, at any rate, philosophical preju- dices. Most of these are theories which they unconsciously take for granted, or which they have absorbed from their intellectual environment or from tradi- tion.
>
> Since few of these theories are consciously held, they are prejudices in the sense that they are held without critical examination, even though they may be of great importance for the practical actions of people, and for their whole life.
>
> It is an apology for the existence of professional philosophy that men are needed who examine critically these widespread and influential theories.[12]

In these three paragraphs by Karl Popper, he begins by speaking of men and women, using the pronoun "they" and then in the third paragraph switches to "men." Were it not for his talk of men *and women*, we might be tempted to interpret his use of men as intended gender-neutrally. But because

[12]Karl R. Popper, "How I See Philosophy," in *The Owl of Minerva*, Charles J. Bontempo and S. Jack Odell, eds. (New York: McGraw Hill, 1975), p. 48.

there is a shift from men and women to men, whether deliberate or not, I believe that the reference to men is unquestionably gender-specific.

The difficulty is that there is no way of guaranteeing a gender-neutral use, because one cannot predict how that use will be connected with other discourse and behavior. One can imagine that an entire book might be written with attempted neutral uses of "he" and "man," while the title alone or some advertising copy shows that these uses are gender-specific (for example, the *SPLEEN OF THE DIABETIC MALE*, or *MEN OF THE FUTURE*—"essential reading for their wives and girlfriends"—I. M. Mailer).

One might want to claim that the gender-specific contexts do not make the other neutral uses gender-specific. Instead there has been a change in meaning—as if one had switched from a discussion of different color greens to salad greens, from sand banks to commercial banks.

However, a shift in meaning, like a pun, is usually noticeable and often a bit funny. This is not the case for the alleged shift with "he," "man," etc. If there is a shift it takes place smoothly, and usually goes unnoticed, particularly by the people who are most likely to claim that there has been one. The noticeable and funny examples occur only when a gender-neutral use is attempted (as in "Man has two sexes") and not when a gender-specific reference is made. Because the gender-specific references are *not* noticeable shifts in meaning, I think it is justified to conclude that they were not genuinely neutral uses in the first place.

One might argue that all uses of "he," "man," and like terms are simply gender-specific. But I think a weaker conclusion is easier to support: that attempts at gender-neutrality with these terms fail, not because they are simply gender-specific but because something else is going on. This conclusion is supported by empirical studies that show the use of "he" rather than "they" or "he or she," makes it more likely, but not inevitable, that people will think of males. I try to explain what else is going on in the next section.

IX

How can the failure of gender-neutrality be accounted for when people think they are using "he," "man," etc. in a gender-neutral sense? Rather than attribute the failure to peculiar properties of each context in an ad hoc fashion, I believe it is the result of a broader linguistic phenomenon: Parasitic Reference. Tissues are called Kleenex; petroleum jelly, Vaseline; bleach, Clorox; etc. to the economic benefit of the specific brands referred to and to the economic detriment of those brands that are ignored by this terminology. The alleged gender-neutral uses of "he," "man," etc. are just further examples of this common phenomenon. A gender-specific term, one that refers to a high-status subset of the whole class, is used *in place of* a neutral generic term. Many of us who deplore the efforts of drug companies to get us to use the brand name rather than the generic name of a product have failed to recognize that the use of "he," "man," etc. in place of "they," "one," "person," or "human" is a similar phenomenon with similar effects. Manufacturers realize that someone sent to buy "the cheapest Clorox" is less likely to return with the equal-strength half price store brand than someone sent to buy the cheapest bleach. And this is true even when the term "Clorox" is intended and understood to be synonymous with "bleach." The failure of "Clorox" to be brand-neutral and the failure of "he" and "man" to be gender-neutral appear to be instances of the same phenomenon.[13]

Regardless of the intentions of the speakers and hearers, and regardless of their beliefs about the meanings of the terms, if the terms refer parasitically, subjectivity can fail, inferences may not go through, and equivocations will be produced. This is true not merely for brand names but for other terms, such as "he" and "man," whose neutral performances have been advertised by lexicographers but which break down easily even under normal speaking conditions. The existence of Parasitic Reference requires that theories of reference and meaning recognize that the functioning of terms in one context may be affected by their uses in other contexts that are not explicitly present.

Questions

1. What are "marked" and "unmarked" adjectives, and in what way does Janice Moulton suggest that marked adjectives differ from words like "man" and "he"?
2. Can you think of any uses of words like "man" and "he" that are unambiguously neutral?
3. Can you think of any instances in which "man" or "he" is used to refer to a female human without its sounding strange or ironic?
4. What is meant by "Parasitic Reference"? Do you think that this is a good explanation of why people can (mistakenly?) think they are using "man" and "he" in a gender-neutral sense?

---

[13]Elizabeth Lane Beardsley, in "Referential Genderization," *Philosophical Forum* 5 (1973–74): 285–293, calls this phenomenon "linguistic imperialism."

Who Is Man?

Casey Miller and Kate Swift

Casey Miller and Kate Swift argue that although it may be grammatically correct to use the word "man" to refer to both female and male humans, this usage is constantly in conflict with its gender-specific meaning: human male. They cite studies which suggest that use of the word "man," even in the allegedly gender-neutral sense, disposes people to think more of males than of females. This, suggest the authors, shows that use of "man" encourages us to overlook women. The authors note that there was a time when the word "man" (and its earlier variants "mann" and "monn") had a genuinely gender-neutral meaning in English, as evidenced by some medieval usages of the word. They argue, however, that that time has passed and the meaning has narrowed.

"The Ascent of Man," Jacob Bronowski's acclaimed BBC television series on the evolution of human culture, opens with a program in which the significance of physical adaptation in early hominids is spun in lyric sequence to that watershed of human self-perception, the cave paintings of the Paleolithic period. The series as a whole is remarkable for its stunning and wide-ranging visuals. In this first program two particularly memorable sequences are used to illustrate musculoskeletal development in the only surviving hominid species: scenes of an adult male athlete running and pole-vaulting and poetically executed dissolve shots of a male baby crawling and raising himself to a standing position. The visualizations provide dramatic support for Dr. Bronowski's superb commentary on our beginnings as "man."

To follow the advice of a Bronowski aphorism—ask an impertinent question and you are on the way to a pertinent answer—why did the creators of the program not show either a female athlete or a female baby? If it occurred to them that including a female would provide a more complete and so more accurate image of the human race, why did they reject the idea? Did they feel, consciously or otherwise, that artistic harmony would somehow be compromised if the descriptions of "man" were matched with pictures of a person clearly not a man? They could scarcely have intended to convey the message that males alone participated in the evolution of humankind, yet through the use of imagery limited to males they effectively negated an inclusive, generic interpretation of their title subject.

In choosing the male to represent the norm, Bronowski and his colleagues were following a long-standing tradition in science. What is remarkable is that the habit persists today. In the 1950s, before the rise of black consciousness among whites in the United States, museum exhibits and textbooks on human evolution often showed a series of male figures or faces on an ascending scale with a Caucasian at the top, a black African one step below. The racist misinformation such graphs conveyed is exceeded in its arrogance only by the total exclusion of women from the human race.

The failure of the BBC epic either to conceive or to convey a generic interpretation of *man* in that opening program was confirmed by two additional circumstances. One was the treatment of a particularly important fossil skull as an anomaly: it was identified several times as "the skull of an adult female," although other skulls shown were not identified in terms of sex (the subject under discussion was man, of course). The second and stronger evidence emerged in an interview at the end of the hour-long program when, after a climax marked by homage to the cave painters, the host of the series chatted for a few minutes with a guest anthropologist about what women were doing during this early period in the ascent of man.

The use of *man* to include both women and men may be grammatically "correct," but it is constantly in conflict with the more common use of *man* as distinguished from *woman*. This ambiguity renders *man*, virtually unusable in what was once its generic sense—a sense all-too-accurately illustrated in Tennyson's line, "Woman is the lesser man." When Dr. Bronowski said that for years he had been fascinated by "the way in which man's ideas express what is essentially human in his nature,"[1] it is anybody's guess whether his vision included all the anonymous women of the past whose ideas and contributions to science and the arts are no less real for never having been identified.

The newspaper headline THREE-CENT PILL LAST HOPE OF MAN suggests that the story to follow may be an announcement by zero-population-growth researchers of a major contraceptive breakthrough, but actually the news item under that particular headline concerned the personal plight of a fifty-one-year-old Wichita, Kansas, man whose only chance for survival was an inexpensive drug called guanidine.[2] Examples of such ambiguity are endless, and the confusion they cause increases as women come to be seen less as the second sex and more as beings who are fully and essentially human.

[1]J. Bronowski, *The Ascent of Man*, Boston, Little, Brown and Company, 1973, p. 24.
[2]The *Middletown* (Conn.) *Press*, November 27, 1972.

Most dictionaries give two standard definitions of *man:* a human being, a male human being. A high school student, thinking about these two meanings, may well ask the obvious question, "How can the same word include women in one definition and exclude them in another?" At which point the teacher may dredge up the hoary platitude, "Man embraces woman"—which gets a laugh but leaves the question unanswered. And the student, perhaps distracted now by continuing snickers, may feel the question is too trivial (and somehow, if she is a girl, too demeaning) to pursue.

In 1972 two sociologists at Drake University, Joseph Schneider and Sally Hacker, decided to test the hypothesis that *man* is generally understood to embrace *woman.* Some three hundred college students were asked to select from magazines and newspapers a variety of pictures that would appropriately illustrate the different chapters of a sociology textbook being prepared for publication. Half the students were assigned chapter headings like "Social Man," "Industrial Man," and "Political Man." The other half were given different but corresponding headings like "Society," "Industrial Life," and "Political Behavior." Analysis of the pictures selected revealed that in the minds of students of both sexes use of the word *man* evoked, to a statistically significant degree, images of males only, filtering out recognition of women's participation in these major areas of life, whereas the corresponding headings without *man* evoked images of both males and females.[3] In some instances the differences reached magnitudes of 30 to 40 percent. The authors concluded, "This is rather convincing evidence that when you use the word man generically, people do tend to think male, and tend not to think female."[4]

The nature of the pictures chosen was interesting in another way, for they demonstrated that *man* calls up largely negative images of power and dominance. The originators of the research project describe the data gathered at their own university (the largest of three samples studied) as follows:

> When we said "Urban Man," as opposed to "Urban Life," students tended to give us pictures portraying sophisticated, upper middle class white males and their artifacts—stereos, cars, bachelor apartments, and so on. We also got pictures of disorganization, slums, demolition. The title "Urban Life" also stimulated pictures of ghettos, but in addition there existed a minor theme of hope—people in the park, building construction, and the like.
>
> When we said "Industrial Man" students gave us pictures of heavy, fairly clumsy machinery, and men doing heavy, dirty, or greasy work. We also got the industrial workers' boss—the capitalist, or corporate executive (e.g., of Mack Trucks, Inc., standing in front of a line of his products). When we said "Industrial Life," we more often received pictures of inside craft work, or of scientific-

[3]Joseph W. Schneider and Sally L. Hacker, "Sex Role Imagery and the Use of the Generic 'Man' in Introductory Texts: A Case in the Sociology of Sociology," paper presented at the section on Sociology of Sex Roles, American Sociological Association Annual Meetings, August 1972; New Orleans. The paper was published in *American Sociologist*, February 1973, pp. 12–18.

[4]Letter from Schneider and Hacker, summarizing the results of their study, sent to over one hundred publishers of sociology titles, April 19, 1972.

technical work—people operating precision optical instruments, oil refineries, etc.—and more pictures of machines without people.

"Economic Man" primarily yielded pictures of disorganization; people at the mercy of the economic system (cartoons of governmental corruption and waste, white collar crime, shots of unemployed workers, small businesses going bankrupt, store window signs indicating rising prices, etc.). A secondary theme was extravagant consumption of the very wealthy, or again, corporate executives, capitalists. The title "Economic Behavior" also stimulated pictures of disorganization and despair, but they tended toward abstract representation of the economic system in trouble, such as graphs, charts, and so on. But "Economic Behavior" appeared to elicit fewer pictures of capitalists than did the term "Economic Man."

"Political Man" was portrayed by pictures of Nixon or other politicians making speeches to mixed audiences. "Political Behavior" was represented by prominent political figures also, but contained a secondary theme of people, including women and minority males, in political protest situations.

"Social Man" was portrayed as a sophisticated white, party-going male (a third to half of the pictures included consumption of alcohol), usually with women around. "Society" involved scenes of disruption and protest, with a subtheme of cooperation among people—kids of various ethnic origins walking in the woods, for example. . . .

When normative white male behavior is portrayed, it is supposed to be cool, sophisticated, powerful, sometimes muscular, almost always exploitive—(getting more than their fair share). A sort of Norman Mailer ideal self is evoked by the use of the word "man." "Behavior" and "life," however, seem to evoke more comprehensively human imagery when people are portrayed. As the image of capitalist, playboy, and hard hat are called forth by the word "man," so it is the other side of the coin called forth by "behavior" or "life"—women, children, minorities, dissent and protest.[5]

These were the responses of young adults who knew, presumably, how dictionaries define *man*. What does the word mean to children, especially the very young? In dictionaries for beginning readers the "human being" definition of *man* is rarely included because it does not relate to anything in a very young child's experience.[6] To a toddler, a "man" may be someone who comes to repair the dishwasher, who puts gas in the car, or who appears on the television screen. In the Golden Picture Dictionary for Beginning Readers the full entry for the word is: "Man, men—A boy grows up to be a man. Father and Uncle George are both men."[7] A child may infer from this definition that mother and Aunt Jane are not men. Nobody, least of all a young child, learns the meaning of *man*

[5]Sally L. Hacker, Phyllis Blood, and Joseph Schneider, "Further Notes on Cultural and Structural Oppression of Women: Man's Language and His Publishing Houses." Photocopy, no date.

[6]Of eight dictionaries for young people consulted, only one, The Weekly Reader Beginning Dictionary, Grades 2 and 3 (William Morris, ed., New York, Grosset & Dunlap, 1974) defines *man* as "people in general" in addition to man as an adult male. The example provided was, "Man has invented many things to make life easy."

[7]The Golden Picture Dictionary for Beginning Readers, New York, Golden Press, 1972 edition, Western Publishing Company, Racine, Wis.

from a dictionary, but this limited definition does fit the child's experience. A word means what it means not because of what dictionaries say about it, but because most speakers of the language use it with a certain meaning in mind and expect others to use it with the same meaning. If Billy, at age three or four, were to see the "Avon lady" coming up the front walk and say to his mother, "Here comes a man," she would correct him. If at nursery school he were asked to draw a picture of a man and he drew a figure that appeared to be a woman, he might well be carted off to a psychiatrist.

In primary school, however, children begin to encounter *man* and *men* in contexts that include people like mother and Aunt Jane and the Avon lady. And despite a conflict with the meaning they already know, they are expected at this stage to acquire an understanding of the other, so-called generic meaning of *man*.

Little is known about how or to what extent this transition in understanding takes place, but Aileen Pace Nilsen touched on the subject in a 1973 study she conducted at the University of Iowa. Using a picture-selection technique with one hundred children ranging in grade level from nursery school through the seventh grade, Nilsen found that *man* in the sentences "Man must work in order to eat" and "Around the world man is happy" was interpreted by a majority of children of both sexes to mean male people and not to mean female people.[8] A correlative survey of beginning textbooks on prehistoric people, all having the word *man* (or *men*) in the title, suggests a possible reason for the children's response. Nilsen found that in these books illustrations of males outnumbered illustrations of females by eight to one.[9]

Prehistoric people were also the focus of a more extensive study involving some five hundred junior high school students in Michigan in 1974. Designed by Linda Harrison of Western Michigan University, the study was aimed at finding out how the students interpreted different terms used to refer to early human beings. Approximately equal numbers of boys and girls taking science courses were asked to complete a survey (which would not be graded) by drawing their impressions of early people as they were described in seven statements on human activities at the dawn of civilization—the use of tools, cultivation of plants, use of fire for cooking, pottery making, care of infants, and the like. The statements distributed to one group of students were all phrased in terms of "early man," "primitive men," "mankind," and "he." Students in a second group received the same statements rephrased to refer to "early people," "primitive humans," and "they." For a third group all the statements were worded in terms of "men and women" and "they." The students were also asked to label each character they depicted in the acts of cultivating plants, using tools, making pottery, and so forth, with a modern first name. The number of female and male characters drawn by the students in each group were then counted according to the names assigned. (Names that might have applied to either sex were not counted.)

[8]Alleen Pace Nilsen, "Grammatical Gender and Its Relationship to the Equal Treatment of Males and Females in Children's Books," Ph.D. diss., University of Iowa, 1973, pp. 106–7, 121–32.
[9]Ibid., p. 96.

In the group receiving the "man," "men," "mankind," and "he" statements, more students of both sexes drew male figures only than female figures only for every statement except one. The exception related to infant care, but even there 49 percent of the boys and 11 percent of the girls drew males only. Students of both sexes who illustrated the "people" and "humans" statements also tended to draw more males than females. Those who were given statements referring to "men and women" included the greatest number of female characters in their drawings, although here, too, more students of both sexes drew males only than females only.[10]

Harrison, who is a geologist, notes that the male dominance of the students' responses is probably a reflection not only of the language used on the survey but of the language in which human evolution is usually discussed. "The students' apparent impressions that females were not tool users or plant cultivators are not supported by fossil evidence and inferences about our early predecessors drawn from analogies with hunting and gathering cultures today," she wrote. "It seems likely that females contributed at least an equal share in the early development of agriculture, weaving, and pottery, and to the development of tools used in these endeavors—to the development of what is normally thought of as evidence of culture."[11]

Whatever may be known of the contributions females made to early human culture, an effective linguistic barrier prevents the assimilation of that knowledge in our present culture. Studies like those conducted by Harrison, Nilsen, and Schneider and Hacker clearly indicate that *man* in the sense of male so overshadows *man* in the sense of human being as to make the latter use inaccurate and misleading for purposes both of conceptualizing and communicating.

The "generic man" trap, in which "The Ascent of Man" was also caught, operates through every kind of medium whenever the human species is being talked about. Writing in a national magazine, the psychoanalyst Erich Fromm described man's "vital interests" as "life, food, access to females, etc."[12] One may be saddened but not surprised at the statement, "Man is the only primate that commits rape." Although, as commonly understood, it can apply to only half the human population, it is nevertheless semantically acceptable. But "man, being a mammal, breast-feeds his young" is taken as a joke.

Sometimes the ambiguity of *man* is dismissed on the grounds that two different words are involved and that they are homonyms, like a *row* of cabbages and a *row* on the lake. Two words cannot be homonyms, however, if one includes the other as does *man* in the first definition given by the most recent [1990] Webster's Collegiate Dictionary: "A human being, *especially* an adult male human." Since the definers do not explain whom their italicized "especially" omits, one is left to wonder. Women, children, and adolescent males,

[10]Linda Harrison, "Cro-Magnon Woman—In Eclipse," *The Science Teacher,* April 1975, pp. 8–11.
[11]Ibid., p. 11.
[12]Erich Fromm, "The Erich Fromm Theory of Aggression," *New York Times Magazine,* February 27, 1972.

perhaps? The unabridged Merriam-Webster Third New International Dictionary is more precise: man is "a member of the human race: a human being . . . now usually used of males except in general or indefinite applications. . . ."

The meaning of a homonym, like *row* or *bow* or *pool*, is usually clear from its context, but the overlapping definitions of *man* often make its meaning anything but clear. Can we be sure, without consulting the board of directors of the General Electric Company, what the slogan "Men helping Man" was supposed to convey? Since GE employs a large number of women, it should be a safe bet that both female and male employees were in the slogan writer's mind. Yet an ad for the company that ran during the same period as the slogan seems to tip the scales in the other direction: "As long as man is on earth, he's likely to cause problems. But the men at General Electric will keep trying to find answers."[13] Maybe the article *the* is the limiting factor, but it is hard to picture any of "the men at General Electric" as female men. Once again the conscious intention to describe man the human being has been subverted by the more persistent image of man the male.

If it were not for its ambiguity, *man* would be the shortest and simplest English word to distinguish humankind from all other animal species. The Latin scientific label *Homo sapiens* is long, foreign, and the *sapiens* part of questionable accuracy. But at least *homo*—like the Hebrew *'adham*—has the clear advantage of including both sexes. Its inclusiveness is demonstrated by the presence in Latin of the words *mas* and *vir*, both of which signify a male person only and distinguish him unequivocally from *femina* or *mulier*, Latin words for "woman." Nevertheless, *homo* is sometimes erroneously understood to mean "male person," and semantic confusion runs riot when it is mistakenly thought to occur in *homosexual*, thereby limiting that term to males. (The prefix *homo-*, as in *homosexual, homonym*, and *homogeneous*, comes from the Greek *homos* meaning "same," and its similarity to the Latin *homo* is coincidental.)

To get back to "humankind," the Greek word is *anthropos*, from which come words like *anthropology* and *philanthropy* as well as *misanthropy*, a blanket dislike of everybody regardless of sex. Like Latin and Hebrew, Greek has separate words for the sexes—*aner* for a male person (its stem form is *andr-*), *gune* (or *gyne*) for a female person. So in English *misandry* is the little-known partner of *misogyny*; but when the two Greek roots come together in androgyny, they form a word that is beginning to be used to describe the rare and happy human wholeness that counteracts the destructive linguistic polarization of the sexes.

Although they serve many uses in English, the words for humankind borrowed from classical Greek and Latin have not been called on to resolve the ambiguity of *man*. Native English grew out of a Teutonic branch of the Indo-European family of languages that also produced German, Danish, Norwegian, and Swedish. In the ancestor of all these tongues the word *man* meant a human being irrespective of sex or age. That sense survives in the modern derivatives *mensch* in German, *menneske* in Danish and Norwegian, and *människa* in Swedish, all of which can refer to a woman or a man, a girl or a boy.

---

[13]The ad appeared in *Time* magazine, October 4, 1971.

The language we speak has no counterpart for these words. However, when *man* was first used in English—as *mann* or sometimes *monn*—it too had the prevailing sense of a human being irrespective of sex and age. About the year 1000 the Anglo-Saxon scholar Aelfric wrote, "His mother was a Christian, named Elen, a very full-of-faith man, and extremely pious."[14] The Oxford English Dictionary cites numerous other examples, including a description written in 1325 of a husband and wife as "right rich men" and a statement from a sermon of 1597 that "the Lord had but one pair of men in Paradise."[15]

At one time English also had separate and unambiguous words to distinguish a person by sex: *wif* for a female, *wer* and *carl* for a male. *Mann*—a human being—dropped the second *n* in combined forms like *waepman* and *carlman*, both of which meant an adult male person, and *wifman*, an adult female person. *Wifman* eventually became *woman* (the plural, *women*, retains the original vowel sound in the pronunciation of the first syllable), while *wif* was narrowed in meaning to become *wife*. But *wer* and *waepman*, *carl* and *carlman* simply became obsolete; they were no longer needed once man was used to signify a male—especially. One cannot help but wonder what would have happened to the word that originally meant a human being if females rather than males had dominated the society in which English evolved through its first thousand years. Would *man* still mean a human being, but especially an adult female?

The question underlines the essential absurdity of using the same linguistic symbols for the human race in one breath and for only half of it in the next. Alma Graham, a lexicographer, draws these contrasts: "If a woman is swept off a ship into the water, the cry is 'Man overboard!' If she is killed by a hit-and-run driver, the charge is 'manslaughter.' If she is injured on the job, the coverage is 'workmen's compensation.' But if she arrives at a threshold marked 'Men Only,' she knows the admonition is not intended to bar animals or plants or inanimate objects. It is meant for her."[16]

Alleen Pace Nilsen notes that adults transfer to children their own lack of agreement about when the many compound words like *workman* and *salesman* apply to both sexes and when such compounds are to be used of males only. She offers some examples to illustrate the different levels of acceptability we sense in such words: "My mother's a salesman for Encyclopædia Britannica" and "Susy wants to be chairman of the dance" are acceptable to many people, but not to all, as is evident from the existence of the terms *saleswoman, chairwoman,* and *chairperson.* "Carol Burnett did a one-man show last night" and "Patsy is quite a horseman, isn't she?" are also acceptable, but they draw attention to the discrepancy between the masculine gender term and the subject's sex. "Miss Jones is our mailman" and "Stella Starbuck is KWWL's new weatherman" seem

---

[14]Quoted by Marjorie Anderson and Blanche Williams, *Old English Handbook,* Boston, Houghton Mifflin Company, 1935, p. 207.

[15]Both examples are given under the entry *man* in the Oxford English Dictionary. For convenience we have modernized the spelling.

[16]Alma Graham, "How to Make Trouble: The Making of a Nonsexist Dictionary," *Ms.,* December 1973, p. 16.

questionable, perhaps because of the newness in relation to women of the activities they describe. "My brother married a spaceman who works for NASA" and "That newsman is in her seventh month of pregnancy" are generally unacceptable.[17]

If adults cannot agree on when a compound of *man* may be a woman, these terms must be doubly confusing to young children, whose understanding of words is limited by their immediate experience. The meaning a child assigns to a word may be quite different from the meaning an adult assumes the child understands. One youngster, for example, when asked to illustrate the incident in the Garden of Eden story where God drives Adam and Eve from the garden, produced a picture of God at the wheel of a pickup truck, with Adam and Eve sitting in the back surrounded by an assortment of flowering plants for their new home. And there is the story of the children who were disappointed to discover that the "dog doctor" was not a dog at all, but an ordinary human being.

It is not really known at what point children begin to come to terms with the dual role the word *man* has acquired or with the generalized use of *he* to mean "either he or she." Certainly the experience is different for boys and girls—ego-enhancing for the former and ego-deflating for the latter. The four-year-old girl who hides her father's reading glasses and waits for a cue line from him to go find them is *not* expecting to hear, "If somebody will find my glasses, I'll give him a big hug." Yet the same child will sooner or later be taught that in such a sentence *him* can also mean *her*.

At a meeting of the Modern Language Association the story was told of twin girls who came home from school in tears one day because the teacher had explained the grammatical rule mandating the use of *he* when the referent is indefinite or unknown.[18] What emotions had reduced them to tears? Anger? Humiliation? A sense of injustice? It is unlikely that any woman can recapture her feelings when the arbitrariness of that rule first struck her consciousness: it happened a long time ago, no doubt, and it was only one among many assignments to secondary status.

In reporting on her work with children, Nilsen provides some insights on the different routes boys and girls travel in accepting the generic use of *he:*

> It is reasonable to conjecture that because of the egocentricity which psychologists describe as a normal developmental stage of all young children, a boy who is accustomed to hearing such words as *he, him,* and *his* used in relationship to himself will feel a closer affinity to these terms than will a young girl who has instead developed an emotional response to *she, her,* and *hers. . . .*
>
> A young boy who is accustomed to hearing himself and his possessions . . . referred to with masculine pronouns has excellent readiness for acquiring the standard formal rules guiding the treatment of gender in English. As he expands his world to include progressively larger circles of environment and acquaintances he simply expands the size of the body of things referred to with

[17]Nilsen, op. cit., pp. 86–87.
[18]Patricia C. Nichols, "The Uses of Gender in English," revision of a paper read before the Women's Forum of the Modern Language Association in December 1971 under the title "Gender in English: Syntactic and Semantic Functions"; photocopy, p. 11.

masculine pronouns. It's a very natural process for him to learn that every animate being not obviously female is treated as masculine. . . . The only unusual requirement is that at some stage in his development he learns to include females in the body of referents.[19]

For a boy, internalizing the generic interpretation of masculine pronouns is part of a continuum. He becomes aware that a symbol that applies to him is reflected throughout the animate world; a link is strengthened between his own sense of being and all other living things. For a young girl, no such continuum exists.

When she begins to expand her environment, unlike the boy, she does not simply enlarge her set of referents for the pronouns she is already accustomed to. Instead she has to do a reverse switch. . . .[20]

If a girl is not to experience a recurring violation of reality, she must look upon a familiar symbol for herself as something different and apart from the symbol used for animate beings in general. Older children are taught that we use *he* as a grammatical convention. In itself that is a slight to girls, but at least it is one they can come to grips with intellectually. Younger children have no way of knowing that the mouse or the turtle or the crocodile referred to as *he* is not necessarily a male. "Here he comes," says the TV personality of the woolly bear caterpillar as it marches across the screen.[21] "The groundhog won't see his shadow today," the weather forecaster begins. For several years a national brand of oatmeal was packaged in individual servings, each with an animal illustration and an "educational" note meant to appeal to children. For example: "White Tailed Deer. A native of North America, he was the main source of food for early American settlers." "Buffalo. This North American animal roamed the plains in large numbers. He furnished the Indians with food and warm clothing." "Leopard. A member of the cat family, he lives in Africa and Asia. He is a clever hunter."[22] Only ladybugs, cows, hens, and mother animals with their young are predictably called *she*.

The linguistic presumption of maleness is reinforced by the large number of male characters, whether they are human beings or humanized animals, in children's schoolbooks, storybooks, television programs, and comic strips. From Kukla and Ollie to the Cookie Monster, prestigious puppets and fantasized figures all speak with a male voice. And in Scotland, hunters of the Loch Ness monster tried to lure "him" with an artificial female monster.[23] In short, the male is the norm, and the assumption that all creatures are male unless they are known to be female is a natural one for children to make.

Some writers and speakers who recognize the generic masculine pronoun as a perpetuator of the male-is-norm viewpoint are making the effort required

---

[19]Nilsen, op. cit., pp. 16, 17.
[20]Ibid., p. 18.
[21]Gene Shalit, on the "Today Show," NBC Television, October 23, 1974.
[22]The Quaker Oats Company, Chicago, Ill., on packets containing maple and brown sugar oatmeal.
[23]"Plastic Monster Being Readied to Lure Nessie." *Manchester Guardian* news item reprinted in the *Middletown* (Conn.) *Press.* June 7, 1975.

to avoid it. Dr. Benjamin Spock, for example, acknowledged, "Like everyone else writing in the child-care field, I have always referred to the baby and child with the pronouns 'he' and 'him.' There is a grammatical excuse, since these pronouns can be used correctly to refer to a girl or woman . . . just as the word 'man' may cover women too in certain contexts. But I now agree with the liberators of women that this is not enough of an excuse. The fact remains that this use of the male pronoun is one of many examples of discrimination, each of which may seem of small consequence in itself but which, when added up, help to keep women at an enormous disadvantage—in employment, in the courts, in the universities, and in conventional social life."[24] A prominent child psychologist, Dr. Lee Salk, comments in the preface to a book written for parents, "An author interested in eliminating sexism from his or her work is immediately confronted with the masculine tradition of the English language. I personally reject the practice of using masculine pronouns to refer to human beings. Accordingly I have freely alternated my references, sometimes using the female gender and sometimes using the male gender."[25]

If pediatricians and child psychologists tend to be especially sensitive to the harm done by exclusionary language, some linguists are sensitive to what they see as a dangerous precedent when the conventional generic use is replaced by wording like Dr. Salk's "his or her work." James D. McCawley, professor of linguistics at the University of Chicago, once argued that the phrase "he or she" is actually more sexist than *he* alone, which, he said, "loses its supposed sexual bias if it is used consistently."[26] In other words, never, never, never qualify the generic pronoun and you will always be understood to include both sexes. "Why not give him or her a subscription to *XYZ* magazine?" asks a promotional letter. A sexist way to word the question, one imagines Professor McCawley advising the advertising agency: "*He or she* does as much to combat sexism as a sign saying 'Negroes admitted' would do to combat racism—it makes women a special category of beings that are left out of the picture unless extra words are added to bring them in explicitly."[27] McCawley's analogy would be relevant if the sign in question were posted by an organization calling itself "The White People." But nobody ever uses *white* to mean both white and black, the way *he* is sometimes used to mean both he and she. Alma Graham makes the problem clear by stating it as a mathematical proposition: "If you have a group half of whose members are A's and half of whose members are B's and if you call the group C, then A's and B's may be equal members of group C. But if you call the group A, there is no way that B's can be equal to A's within it. The A's will always be the rule and the B's will always be the exception—the subgroup, the subspecies, the outsiders."[28]

---

[24]Benjamin Spock, M.D., *Redbook*, November 1973, as quoted in *Today's Education*, September–October 1974, p. 110.
[25]Lee Salk, *Preparing for Parenthood*, New York. David McKay Company, 1974.
[26]James D. McCawley, Letter to the Editor, *New York Times Magazine*, November 10, 1974.
[27]Ibid.
[28]Alma Graham, Letter to the Editor, *The Columbia Forum*, Fall 1974.

Admittedly "he or she" is clumsy, and the reasonable argument that it should be alternated with "she or he" makes it still clumsier. Also, by the time any consideration of the pronoun problem gets to this stage, there is usually a large body of opinion to the effect that the whole issue is trivial. Observing that men more often take this view than women, the syndicated columnist Gena Corea has come up with a possible solution. All right, she suggests, "if women think it's important and men don't . . . let's use a pronoun that pleases women. Men don't care what it is as long as it's not clumsy so, from now on, let's use 'she' to refer to the standard human being. The word 'she' includes 'he' so that would be fair. Anyway, we've used 'he' for the past several thousand years and we'll use 'she' for the next few thousand; we're just taking turns."[29]

Men who work in fields where women have traditionally predominated—as nurses, secretaries, and primary school teachers, for example—know exactly how Corea's proposed generic pronoun would affect them: they've tried it and they don't like it. Until a few years ago most publications, writers, and speakers on the subject of primary and secondary education used *she* in referring to teachers. As the proportion of men in the profession increased, so did their annoyance with the generic use of feminine-gender pronouns. By the mid-1960s, according to the journal of the National Education Association, some of the angry young men in teaching were claiming that references to the teacher as "she" were responsible in part for their poor public image and, consequently, in part for their low salaries. One man, speaking on the floor of the National Education Association Representative Assembly, said, "The incorrect and improper use of the English language is a vestige of the nineteenth-century image of the teacher, and conflicts sharply with the vital image we attempt to set forth today. The interests of neither the women nor of the men in our profession are served by grammatical usage which conjures up an anachronistic image of the nineteenth-century schoolmarm."[30]

Here is the male-is-norm argument in a nutshell. Although the custom of referring to elementary and secondary school teachers as "she" arose because most of them were women, it becomes grammatically "incorrect and improper" as soon as men enter the field in more than token numbers. Because the use of *she* excludes men, it conflicts with the "vital image" teachers attempt to project today. Women teachers are still in the majority, but the speaker feels it is neither incorrect nor improper to exclude them linguistically. In fact, he argues, it is proper to do so because the image called up by the pronoun *she* is that of a schoolmarm. To be vital, it appears, a teacher's image must be male.

No "schoolmarm" was responsible for making *man* and *he* the subsuming terms they have become, though female schoolteachers—to their own disadvantage—dutifully taught the usages schoolmasters decreed to be correct. Theodore M. Bernstein and Peter Farb, respected arbiters of usage, also invoke

---

[29]Gena Corea, "Frankly Feminist," syndicated column dated June 28, 1974, reprinted in *Media Report to Women*, Vol. 3, No. 1, January 1, 1975.
[30]*Today's Education*, September–October 1974, p. 110.

"schoolmarms" when they want to blame someone for what they consider over-conservatism. Bernstein calls his scapegoat "Miss Thistlebottom" and Farb calls his "Miss Fiditch." But on the matter of generic singular pronouns, both men defend the rule that says *he* is the only choice.[31] Ethel Strainchamps, who eschews the role of arbiter, calls that "a recent Mr. Fuddydud 'rule'" and cites examples of contrary usage from the Oxford English Dictionary to prove her point.[32]

By and large, however, the "correctness" of using *man* and *he* generically is so firmly established that many people, especially those who deal professionally with English, have difficulty recognizing either the exclusionary power of these words or their failure to communicate reality. In fact the yearning to understand masculine terminology as including both sexes is sometimes so strong that it asserts itself in defiance of literary or historic evidence to the contrary. Of *course* Alexander Pope's admonition, "Know then thyself . . . the proper study of mankind is man," was intended to include women, we say. But the reader to whom these lines were addressed is made more specific by the author's later reference in the same work to "thy dog, thy bottle, and thy wife."

It was Pope's custom to write his philosophical poems in the form of epistles to particular individuals, and *An Essay on Man*, published in 1733, was written to his friend Henry St. John, Lord Bolingbroke. Today most readers probably infer that the particular is being made general, that the specific man, Bolingbroke, represents generic "man" in the poet's mind. Pope may have thought so too, but that doesn't solve the linguistic problem. In the unlikely event that he had addressed *An Essay on Man* to a woman instead of to a man, would he have made a categorical reference to her dog, her bottle, and her husband? The question is not as frivolous as it sounds, for the issue is essentially one of categories and what they are understood to include or omit. Women—and in this case wives—are understood to be a category included in generic man. When women are separated from man and grouped with other non-man items like dogs and bottles, the effect on generic man is scarcely noticeable: the subject of the "proper study" remains intact. But if men—and, by extension, husbands—were to be considered a discrete category and were separated from the whole, what would happen to generic man? Would "he" be allowed to consist entirely of women, as he is often allowed to consist entirely of men?

In the spring of 1776, when John Adams and his colleagues in Congress were preparing to dissolve the political bands that connected the thirteen colonies to Great Britain, Abigail Adams wrote to her husband: "In the new code of laws which I suppose it will be necessary for you to make, I desire you would remember the ladies and be more generous and favorable to them than your ancestors. Do not put such unlimited power in the hands of the husbands. Remember, all men would be tyrants if they could. If particular care and attention

---

[31]Theodore M. Bernstein, *The Careful Writer: A Modern Guide to English Usage*, New York, Atheneum, 1965, and *Watch Your Language*, Great Neck, N.Y., Channel Press, 1958; Peter Farb, *Word Play: What Happens When People Talk*, New York, Alfred A. Knopf, 1974.

[32]Ethel Strainchamps, review of Peter Farb, *Word Play*, in *The Village Voice, Voice Literary Supplement*, March 21, 1974. Examples are cited by the Oxford English Dictionary under entries for *they, their, them*, and *themselves*.

is not paid to the ladies, we are determined to foment a rebellion, and will not hold ourselves bound by any laws in which we have no voice or representation." Abigail Adams was plainly excluding women from her phrase "all men would be tyrants," for she went on to say, "That your sex are naturally tyrannical is a truth so thoroughly established as to admit of no dispute; but such of you as wish to be happy willingly give up the harsh title of master for the more tender and endearing one of friend."

To which John Adams replied: "As to your extraordinary code of laws, I cannot but laugh. We have been told that our struggle has loosened the bonds of government everywhere; that children and apprentices were disobedient; that schools and colleges were grown turbulent; that Indians slighted their guardians, and Negroes grew insolent to their masters. But your letter was the first intimation that another tribe, more numerous and powerful than all the rest, were grown discontented."[33]

When the Declaration of Independence was issued in Philadelphia a few months later, the self-evident truths that "all men are created equal" and that "governments are instituted among men, deriving their just powers from the consent of the governed," did not apply to women any more than they did to men who were slaves or to those original inhabitants of the country referred to in the document as "the merciless Indian savages."

Lessons in American history provide many more examples of how the part played by women has been distorted or omitted through the use of terminology presumed to be generic. Schoolchildren are taught, for instance, that the early colonists gained valuable experience in self-government. They learn that the Indians, though friendly at first, soon began to plunder the frontier settlements. They are told that pioneers pushed westward, often taking their wives, children, and household goods with them. A child may wonder whether women were involved in the process of self-government or were among the plunderers of frontier settlements, or the child may accept the implication that women were not themselves colonists or Indians or pioneers, but always part of the baggage.

"Man is the highest form of life on earth," the Britannica Junior Encyclopædia explains. "His superior intelligence, combined with certain physical characteristics, have enabled man to achieve things that are impossible for other animals."[34] The response of a male child to this information is likely to be "Wow!"—that of a female child, "Who? Do they mean me too?" Even if the female child understands that, yes, she too is part of man, she must still leap the hurdles of all those other terms that she knows from her experience refer to males only. When she is told that we are all brothers, that the brotherhood of man includes sisters, and that the faith of our fathers is also the faith of our mothers, does she really believe it? How does she internalize these concepts?

[33]The Abigail Adams letter of 31 March 1776, and John Adams's reply of 14 April 1776, are quoted from Miriam Schneir, ed., *Feminism: The Essential Historical Writings,* New York, Vintage Books, 1972, pp. 3–4.
[34]Volume 10, p. 48B, 1971 edition. The Britannica Junior Encyclopædia for Boys and Girls is compiled with the editorial advice of the Faculties of the University of Chicago and the University Laboratory Schools and published by Encyclopædia Britannica, Inc.

"We must understand that 'the brotherhood of man' does not exclude our beloved sisters," the eminent scholar Jacques Barzun wrote.[35] But how do we accomplish that feat? By an act of will? By writing it on the blackboard a hundred and fifty times?

The subtle power of linguistic exclusion does not stop in the schoolroom, and it is not limited to words like *man, men, brothers, sons, fathers,* or *forefathers.* It is constantly being extended to words for anyone who is not female by definition. Musing on the nature of politics, for example, a television commentator says, "People won't give up power. They'll give up anything else first—money, home, wife, children—but not power."[36] A sociologist, discussing the correlates of high status, reports that "Americans of higher status have more years of education, more children attending college, less divorce, lower mortality, better dental care, and less chance of having a fat wife."[37] Members of the women's movement in France were arrested for displaying the slogan "One Frenchman in Two Is a Woman"; it was taken by some outraged French males to mean that 50 percent of their number were homosexuals.[38]

If these items appear to be molehills, it must be remembered that the socializing process, that step-by-step path we follow in adapting to the needs of society, is made up of many small experiences that often go unnoticed. Given the male norm, it becomes natural to think of women as an auxiliary and subordinate class, and from there it is an easy jump to see them as a minority or a special-interest group. In 1971, Robert H. Bork, an authority on constitutional law, wrote: "Various kinds of claims are working their way through the judicial system, and the Supreme Court may ultimately have to face them—suits seeking judicial determination of abortion statutes, the death penalty, environmental issues, the rights of women, the Vietnam war."[39] If the Supreme Court is ever asked to make a judicial determination of "the rights of men," it will be a sign that the rights of women and the rights of men have finally become parallel and equal constituents of human rights.

Some authorities, including Professor Barzun, have insisted that *man* is still a universal term clearly understood to mean "person," but the mass of evidence is against that view. As early as 1752, when David Hume referred in his *Political Discourses* to "all men, male and female," the word had to be qualified if it was not to be misunderstood. Dr. Richard P. Goldwater, a psychotherapist, goes to the heart of the matter when he asks, "If we take on its merits [the] assertion that *man* in its deepest origin of meaning stands for both sexes of our race, then how did it come to mean *male*? Did we males appropriate *man* for ourselves at

---

[35]Jacques Barzun, "A Few Words on a Few Words," *The Columbia Forum,* Summer 1974, p. 19.

[36]Frank McGee, on the "Today Show," NBC Television, June 16, 1972.

[37]Theodore Caplow, *Elementary Sociology,* Englewood Cliffs, NJ., Prentice-Hall, 1971, p. 310, quoted by Schneider and Hacker, "Sex Role Imagery," fn. 9.

[38]Justine DeLacy, "How French Women Got That Way—And How to Handle Them," *New York Times,* January 13, 1974, "Travel and Resorts" section.

[39]Robert H. Bork, "We Suddenly Feel That Law Is Vulnerable," *Fortune* magazine, December 1971.

the expense of the self-esteem of our sisters? Did what we now call 'sexism' alter the flow of language through us?"[40]

Those who have grown up with a language that tells them they are at the same time men and not men are faced with ambivalence—not about their sex, but about their status as human beings. For the question "Who is man?" it seems, is a political one, and the very ambiguity of the word is what makes it a useful tool for those who have a stake in maintaining the status quo.

Questions

1. Do you have experiences that either confirm or disconfirm the claim that the use of "man" in contexts where it is intended to be gender-neutral disposes people to think more of men than of women?
2. If the word "man" once had a genuinely gender-neutral meaning, could that meaning return if we consciously used the word as it was used before? Would that be more or less preferable to substituting a word like "person" for "man"?
3. The authors claim that the use of "he or she" is a clumsy alternative to "he" when referring to people of both or indeterminate sex. Do you agree? What do you think of other alternatives, such as alternating between "he" and "she," always using "she," or using the plural "their" even when referring to a single person? Can you think of any other possible alternatives?

[40]Richard P. Goldwater, M.D., Letter to the Editor, *The Columbia Forum*, Fall 1974, p. 46.

Sexist Language

Michael Levin

Michael Levin argues against using substitutes for words like "man," "he" and "chairman." He suggests that there are four standard objections to the use of such words: (1) they reflect the inferior social status of women; (2) they perpetuate this status; (3) they falsely represent women as inferior to men; (4) they insult women by causing us to overlook them. He argues that these objections cannot be leveled simultaneously because they are inconsistent. For instance, if women do have an inferior social status to men, then words that reflect that do not misrepresent the way things are.

He then argues that it is unwise to attempt to change women's social position by attending to language because, he claims, past attempts to enforce linguistic reform have failed to change reality. Language, he suggests, can reflect inequalities, but it cannot cause them. He then argues that using terms like "man" and "he" is not insulting to women. He claims that an insulting word is one that is used with the intention of causing feelings of shame and inadequacy. Since "man" and "he" are not intended to have these effects, he concludes that they cannot be insulting.

> Words are wise men's counters, they do but reckon by them; but they are the money of fools.
>
> —Thomas Hobbes

Of all feminist initiatives, the attempt to alter language is the most apt to provoke derision. It is difficult to suppress a smile when "manholes" become "personholes." The Labor Department's replacement of "fisherman" and "newsboy" by "fisher" and "news carriers," the National Weather Service's scrupulous alternation of male with female names for hurricanes (which begin with male and female "A" names in alternate years), engage the sense of the absurd by their strenuous pursuit of the trivial.

Absurd or not, this campaign has been markedly successful, well beyond the embrace of linguistic guidelines by publishers and professional organizations. Executive officers have become chairpersons and chairs. Businessmen have become business professionals. Ships are no longer manned, but crewed by crewmembers. Hockey defensemen are "defenders" and "defensive players." "He/she's" populate public utterances and private memos. There are computer programs to insert "or she" after inadvertent "he's" (and to delete such words as *virile, manly,* and *manhood*). Schools encourage teachers to call their charges "children" instead of "boys and girls." "Man" as the inclusive name for the human biological species has become taboo, with parallel efforts under way to change other languages.

That natural language infuriates feminists is clear enough:

> Sexist language is no less noxious than racist language. As Kett and Underwood say in their recent book, "Avoiding *he* is equal to taking down the 'whites only' sign in a restaurant."[1]

What precisely is wrong with the inclusive use of "he" and related features of natural languages is less clear. These usages are said to be "biased," but language, which distributes nothing and takes nothing, cannot be directly assessed by the canons of justice. Speaking more analytically, there are four standard objections to current speech patterns: (1) They reflect the inferior state of women; (2) they perpetuate this inferior status; (3) they mendaciously represent women as inferior to or different front men; and (4) they insult women by making them "invisible." Many of these charges are made in *The Right Word*, a booklet prepared by the National Committee of the American Society for Public Administration. According to *The Right Word*, current language presents a "danger" to working women by its "perpetuation of myths and false generalizations . . . 'active' and 'passive' are descriptive of individual personality—not gender; sometimes men are quiet [and] women are insensitive." The pronoun "he" is objectionable because it results in "misleading and inaccurate communication" and "reinforces the perception of woman as an appendant to generic 'man,'" as well as "reinforcing inequity based on gender." Or, as Marie Shear puts it, "Male pronouns . . . imply that everyone who is anyone is male."[2] Similar theses are maintained in more scholarly works.[3]

These charges cannot all be leveled consistently. If women enjoy lower status than men and have been pushed by socialization from society's mainstream, it is not a lie to represent women in this light—assuming that it is *language* that can be properly said to represent anything, rather than *speakers* who

---

[1]Marie Shearer, "Solving the Great Pronoun Problem: Twelve Ways to Avoid the Sexist Singular," *Perspectives: The Civil Rights Quarterly* 13 (Spring 1981): 18.

[2]Ibid.

[3]See e.g. Robin Lakoff, *Language and Women's Place* (New York: Harper & Row, 1975); Mary Vetterling-Braggin, ed., *Sexist Language* (Totowa, N.J.: Littlefield, Adams, 1981).

represent things by use of the means language supplies. If some traits are for whatever reason more prevalent in one sex, it is not mythologizing to reserve the appropriate epithets for that sex. One cannot coherently complain that "he" refers basically to men, and that the masculine "he" refers to *both men and women*. In fact, before going further, we may dismiss the idea that masculine pronouns are misleading. Words are misleading when they mislead. If nobody is misled by a turn of phrase, it is not misleading, and there is no one over the age of three who has been fooled by "he" into thinking that women are un-persons. It is not possible to produce a woman who believed (until feminists cleared things up) that "He who hesitates is lost" did not apply to her. It is universally understood that "he" is used with the intention of referring to both men and women, and that this intention has settled into a convention. Nothing more is required for a purely designative expression like "he" to *mean* men and women both.

Possibly because the only difficulty created by ordinary language is that feminists do not like it, feminist linguistic reform has become a kind of ongoing referendum about feminism itself. In the absence of any clearer purpose, substituting "person" for "man" is a concession made to feminists just because feminists demand it. As a result, whatever thought is to be conveyed in the act of communication is consciously subordinated to equity, with the collateral effect of obscuring whatever is actually being said. When clergymen refer to "Our Father and Mother who art in Heaven," or "The God of Abraham and Sarah," as many now do, or when contemporary reworkings of the New Testament change the "Son of God" to "The Human One," they shift attention from religion to the struggle against sexism. Feminist linguistic reform is an attempt to make all thought whatsoever concern feminism to the exclusion of everything else.

Feminist linguistic reform is for this reason far from inconsequential. Linguistic change legislated to conform to a worldview makes people self-conscious about their own language, an uncomfortable state of mind that may properly be called oppressive. Language is the vehicle of thought, and in an important sense speakers must be unconscious of choosing their words if they are to express their thoughts. When we become entangled in decisions about how to talk, we lose contact with the reality our talk is supposed to be about. Like playing the piano, language is largely a system of acquired habits, and fluent speech accompanied by constant conscious decisions about which words to utter is as difficult as fluent pianism accompanied by constant conscious decisions about which keys to hit. The most uncomfortable moments in life—emotional scenes, first dates, delicate negotiations with the boss—are distinguished by precisely this need to anticipate what to say. There is no need to think about words when things go smoothly—the right words come unprompted. The distraction occasioned by the felt need not to offend the notional feminist watchperson hovering nearby makes everyone just that much more self-conscious about talking. As *The Right Word* admits, "the newly sensitized administrator is frequently tongue-tied." Feminists insist that this self-consciousness passes in a few weeks. The reader must judge the plausibility of this guarantee for himself.

LANGUAGE AND THOUGHT

At the end of this chapter we will look at attempts to enforce feminist linguistic reform by law. For now it suffices to remember that enforced ideological linguistic reform has been tried before, and failed. During the Reign of Terror that succeeded the French Revolution, all persons were addressed as "citizen" and "citizeness." Russians became "comrades" after the Bolshevik Revolution. In both cases these conventions swiftly became empty, for reality is not so obliging as to follow language. The ordinary worker may be officially entitled to address the First Secretary of the Party as "comrade," but that has not made them friends or equals in any substantial way. Russians must still privately distinguish genuine comrades from pro forma ones, thus undercutting the reform. The failure of "comrade" and "citizen" to induce political equality suggests that language does not and cannot shape thought in the manner or to the extent supposed by egalitarian reformers. Attempts to alter putatively biased thinking by altering the language which expresses this thinking reverse cause and effect. At the same time, these attempts have negative short-term effects of the sort mentioned in the previous section.

The beginning of wisdom on this complex subject is to reject the idea, advanced by a number of contemporary anthropologists and philosophers, that language shapes rather than reflects reality, and the related thesis, usually called the Whorf hypothesis, that a speaker's language is a significant factor in determining his conception of the world, particularly the social world.[4] In my view, the Whorf hypothesis completely reverses the direction of the causal arrows connecting language, thought, and reality.[5]

Speakers mark a distinction linguistically when the distinction becomes important, and name a phenomenon when the phenomenon becomes salient; things do not *become* important *because* the means to describe them have been enlarged. Imagine a community of cavemen who call all furry animals by the single word *furry* (or, to avoid anachronism, a word best translated into English as "furry".) Suppose that one kind of furry annual begins to attack members of the community. The community would almost certainly coin a special name for that special animal—"leopard," say. Cave children would thereafter be warned about leopards, and the next generation of adults would see leopards as particularly dangerous. It is surely implausible to attribute these changes in outlook to the addition of "leopard" to the communal vocabulary. The cavemen fear leopards because leopards attack them, not because "leopard" has fearsome connotations; quite the reverse—the coinage "leopard" acquired fearsome connotations because leopards themselves are menacing.

---

[4] See Benjamin Whorf, *Language, Thought, and Reality*, ed J.E. Carroll (Cambridge, Mass.: MIT press, 1956).
[5] See Michael Levin, *Metaphysics and the Mind-Body Problem* (London: Oxford University Press, 1979), pp. 152–56.

Feminist monitoring of language can be simulated in this situation by a shamanistic injunction to remove "leopard" from the cave vocabulary because using "leopard" is sinful. In that case, a viable cave community would simply *reinvent* a synonym for the old world *leopard*, or some handy descriptive device for capturing the difference between harmless and dangerous furry animals. The least likely outcome would be for speakers of the newly "leopard"-less language to cease fearing leopards. Speakers desirous of obeying the shaman would experience short-term difficulties in heeding the distinction between leopards and other things, to be sure, and aversion to the guilt attendant on verbalizing leopard-thoughts would generalize to aversion to leopard-thoughts themselves. No one would want to think about, much less talk about, leopards. Even though the use of "leopard" does not cause leopard-thoughts, thoughts are sufficiently associated with words for both to come to control a response originally keyed on just one. George Orwell was right to think that tinkering with language disrupts thought, but wrong to think that this was because language determines thought. The disruption is in fact the product of two vectors: positive reinforcement by reality for calling things as they are seen, and fear of pain conditioned by harassment for calling things as they are seen. The effect Orwell identified might be compared to the flickering of a flame caused by a blockage in the ventilation shaft.

The perception- and reality-dependence of language is illustrated by anthropological data commonly thought to illustrate the language-dependence of perception. Take the variety of Eskimo words for snow. In fact, Eskimos differ from speakers of English not in seeing as different what speakers of English see as similar, but in having short phrases for the different kinds of snow that speakers of English can distinguish only clumsily. The availability in Eskimo of distinct words for differently textured snow is a linguistic adaptation to the importance of weather in Eskimo life. English speakers can say whatever Eskimos can say and describe any kind of snow Eskimos can describe, albeit more long-windedly. There has been no pressure on speakers of English to compress the description "dry, powdery snow that cannot be packed into snowballs" because, in the environments in which the typical speaker of English finds himself, the texture of snow is unrelated to vital interests like the location of food. Or consider the Hopi, who use different words for the spilling and pouring of powders, but the same word for the spilling and pouring of liquids.[6] It is better to explain Hopi usage in terms of the Hopi sense of similarity—the Hopi find the spillage of different substances less similar than they do the spillage and pouring of the same substance—than to explain the Hopi sense of similarity in terms of Hopi usage. The latter explanation cannot address the question of where the Hopi usage itself came from, while numerous non-question-begging explanations can be suggested for the origin of particular similarity spacings. To have interesting empirical content, the Whorf hypothesis must predict that the

---

[6]See J.B. Carroll and J.B. Casagrande, "The Function of Language Classifications in Behavior," in *Communication and Culture*, ed. A.G. Smith (New York: Holt, Rinehart, & Winston, 1966), pp. 489–514.

Hopi *disregard* the difference between spilling and pouring liquids—that, for instance, Hopi mothers punish their children for naughtily pouring water from jugs *and* for accidentally spilling it, in contrast to English-speaking mothers who punish water mischief but not water accidents. So far as I know, this has not been observed to be a trait of Hopi behavior. In fact, so many observations are at variance with the Whorf hypothesis—primitive people with no word for "jet plane" notice and become quite worked up about the first jet plane that flies low over their heads—that its defenders usually reformulate it in terms of *inclinations* created by language to heed or ignore phenomena. It is not clear that hypotheses about inner mental models of the universe that lack behavioral manifestations are empirically significant.

I believe social scientists are led to suppose that speakers of differing languages see the world differently through identifying the expressibility of a thought in a language with the presence in that language of a single word for the thought. That this *is* an error is plain enough from the undoubted expressive equivalence of French with English despite the French use of pairs of syncategorematic potencies to express negation. Neither "ne" nor "pas" means quite what "not" means, yet "Je ne danse pas" means exactly what "I do not dance" means (to the extent that synonymy can survive the attacks of the philosopher Quine). Social scientists sometimes stumble over this point in their very attempt to describe incompatible linguistic frameworks. Carol Eastman writes: "American English does not have a kinship term which refers to one's daughter's husband's brother."[7] It does, of course—"one's daughter's husband's brother."

Still, might not concepts for which no single word exists be more *difficult* to utilize than those for which there is a single, familiar word? (So that it would be *harder* to be sexist in a gender-neutral language.) There is evidence that this is not so when the environment is sufficiently demanding. The Nigerian language Wolof contains no single word for "blue," a single word denoting both "red" and "orange," and a vague word most nearly equivalent to "yellow." Bruner, Greenfield, and Olver[8] found that children who speak Wolof classified toy trucks with respect to color and function just as French children do.

A language expresses a culture and its patterns of thinking—"A language is a form of life," in Ludwig Wittgenstein's Whorfian apothegm—in the sense that much may be inferred about the culture and environment of a group from its language, particularly its vocabulary. An observer can infer a great deal about the Eskimo's world from the large number of Eskimo words for "snow." In this sense, but in no stronger sense, language is continuous with culture. An observer, then, who knew nothing of the human race, could infer from its "sexist" languages that human beings perceive the sexes to be dimorphic. And, just as he would conclude that Eskimos would not have coined so many words for different kinds of snow unless there *were* different kinds of snow, he will conclude that human discourse probably reflects some truth about sex dimorphism.

[7]Carol Eastman, *Aspects of Language and Culture* (San Francisco: Chandler & Sharp, 1975), p. 88.
[8]*Studies in Cognitive Growth* (New York: Wiley, 1966), p. 385ff.

What really bothers feminists about language is that virtually every natural language records a fundamental recognition of sex differences. The feminist quarrel is not with language, but the reality behind language and the human recognition of this reality. When the demand is made that "men working" signs be replaced by "people working" signs (as the state of New York is spending ten million dollars over a ten-year period to accomplish), the aim is not fairness but the denial of sexual dimorphism. Feminists want language to be the way it would have been had the sexes been the same. Because the feminist argument reverses the causal arrow between the perception of sex differences and the origin of this perception, it is not altogether clear whether feminists expect a neutered language to change the reality behind it, or whether they simply regard the avoidance of acknowldgement of this reality as intrinsically desirable.[9] Either expectation is an attack on the messenger.

EXAMPLES

An example of the confusion of words with their referents is Robin Lakoff's observation that people look askance at men who have mastered the vocabulary of sewing. This observation, although correct, has nothing to do with language. People take mastery of any specialized vocabulary to indicate familiarity with its subject. Since in our culture most men are unfamiliar with seams, hems, and other details of sewing, a man who speaks competently about them is anomalous, and draws the suspicion normally directed at any anomaly, because he shows an anomalous familiarity with sewing itself. This is a fact about people's attitude toward men and sewing, not their attitude toward men and words about sewing. Assuming it desirable to change this attitude, this change cannot be induced by encouraging people to say "John fingered the damask" with a straight face (as Lakoff herself seems at times to realize.)

An extensive subgenre of feminist writing on language is directed against sexual slang.[10] Feminists correctly observe that sex described from the male point of view is always active (men "conquer" and "score," "screw" and "hump") while sex described from the female point of view is passive (women

---

[9]Robin Lakoff does acknowledge that "social change creates language change, not the reverse" (*Language and Women's Place*, p. 59), a conclusion very vexing to Virginia Valian: "While we are curing the disease, no overnight affair, we can use a little relief from the symptoms . . . not only is reduction of suffering a good in itself, it often gives the patient the strength to fight the disease more effectively. . . . The disease . . . is not social inequality but lack of power over one's life; all forms of oppression—be they economic, psychological, social, or linguistic—are merely symptoms of it" ("Linguistics and Feminism," in Vetterling-Braggin, p. 76). As the example mentioned at the beginning of the next section indicates, it is not clear that Lakoff herself is always consistent on the direction of the causal arrow.

[10]See e.g. Barbara Lawrence, "Four-Letter Words *Can* Hurt You," in *Philosophy and Sex*, ed. Robert Baker and Frederick Elliston (Buffalo, N.Y.: Prometheus, 1975); Stephanie Ross, "How Words Hurt: Attitudes, Metaphors, and Oppression," in *Sexist Language*, pp. 194–216; Robert Baker, "'Pricks' and 'Chicks': A Plea for Persons," in *Sexist Language*, pp. 161–82.

"put out" and are "satisfied"). The anger provoked by these idioms is probably beyond the reach of reason, but it is worthwhile pointing out that in sex men *do* aggress while women are receptive. A man must achieve erection and a woman must relax. The ability to sustain an erection no matter what is a point of pride for many men, whereas women do not regard the ability to relax sexually as a comparable achievement. It is hardly surprising that metaphors for sexual intercourse should reflect these facts, or that these metaphors should involve the insertion of prongs into orifices. Parental investment theory predicts that sex for men will be accompanied by feelings of mastery, and sex for women by feelings of surrender—psychological realities merely reflected in language.

The neologism *Ms.* also puts the linguistic cart before the horse of reality. "Ms." was explicitly introduced by feminists as a device to mask the marital status of women just as "Mr." does for men, it being felt that the "Miss./Mrs." distinction disadvantageously "defines" women in terms of their relations with men. More recently, there have been efforts to replace "Ms." by the even more sex-neutral convention of designating women by their last names alone in contexts in which men are so designated. Whether these notational changes can contribute to making marital status no more important for women than it is for men depends on the function of "Miss." and "Mrs." As the most adaptive strategy for K-selected males is the aggressive pursuit of many females, while the most adaptive strategy for females is monogamous surrender to the male who vanquishes his competitors, it must be the K-selected male who initiates courtships. So as not to waste calories pursuing already mated females, a male must be able to gauge the availability of females he encounters. The female, who does not initiate courtship needs no such gauge; a male's initiation of mating rituals—showing off his tailfeathers, requesting a date—is itself a signal of his interest. Every human society will evolve a device to signal the male about the availability of females. (Male philanderers send false signals by approaching females as if unattached; on the whole, married women are less inclined to stray because one mate is all a woman needs for maximum reproductive success. In any event, social signals evolve to fit the average.) The wish to collapse "Miss." and "Mrs." into Ms.'s who resemble Mr.'s is the wish that women be thought of as selecting sexual partners in the way and with the purposes characteristic of men. It is a wish for the terms of address and marital status that would have evolved had there been no differences in the sexual nature of men and women. (I suspect that the conventional prefixing of some title to female names reflects an unconscious desire to soften the harsh functionality of bare name reference, which *is* thought appropriate for men.)

The more deeply language is probed, the more traces it reveals of the beings that produce it. The cases of nouns in languages with masculine and feminine words are usually appropriate; "house" is usually feminine and "key" masculine. The neuter in classical Greek coincides with the masculine more often than with the feminine, and never with the feminine alone—perhaps reflecting some dim perception that men have a greater affinity with neutral things. The *absence* of cases from a language has no correspondence with a cultural history in which women experience unusual political equality with men or are accorded unusually extensive participation in male spheres. Turkish lacks cases, but Turkish women lack many rights enjoyed by women in countries with more "sexist" native tongues.

DOES LANGUAGE INSULT WOMEN?

That natural languages reflect sex differences makes natural languages anti-woman only on the assumption that typically male traits are better than typically female ones and that any reflection of sex differences is a reminder of female inferiority. In fact, language cannot be misogynistic (or be biased against anything else) for the simple reason that anything at all about men and women, indeed anything at all about anything, can be said in any natural language. Take the word *shrew,* whose presence in English is sometimes cited as an instance of linguistic bias against aggressive women. Now, English cannot force anybody to believe that there are strident women, for if it did it would be impossible to say in English that there are no shrewish women, which is easily done by uttering the sentence "There are no shrewish women." Nor does the admitted negative weight of "shrew" compel dislike of certain forms of female behavior, for English and other natural languages contain devices for neutralizing evaluative connotations. Anyone who does not mind the behavior normally called shrewish need only say "I don't mind the behavior normally called 'shrewish.'"

There remains the charge that "he," "mankind," and their cognates slight women by referring to them by words that are also used to refer to men alone, thereby implying that women are not important enough to deserve a name of their own. This charge is silly for the same reason it is silly to say that "he" does not refer to women. Just as reference is secured by a mutually recognized intention to refer—so that "he" refers to women as well as men because everyone realizes that it does—so an insult is a word or gesture used with the *intention* of causing affront through the recognition of that intention.[11] In the all-important point of their history, words like *he* and *man* are neutral names for the human race as a whole; whatever the reason that the collective name for males is also the collective name for males and females, nobody ever adopted this usage *with the intention* of causing feelings of shame and inadequacy, or with the intention of expressing contempt. The word *nigger,* by contrast, *is* intended to affront by expressing contempt. It has acquired this conventional force because its original usage was known to be accompanied by contempt, so that its continued use by a speaker, who would be presumed to know that feelings of contempt would be imputed to him, amounted to the intention of expressing contempt. The generic "he" has no similar history.

No matter what distress it may cause, a word or gesture is not insulting unless accompanied by or known to be conventionally associated with malice. If

---

[11]A large philosophical literature has developed a theory of linguistic meaning in terms of nested intentions; its primary contributors are H.P. Grice, P.F. Strawson, John Searle, Jonathan Bennett, David Lewis, J.L. Austin, and Stephen Schiffer.

my passing remark about your tie causes chagrin because of some event in your childhood unknown to me, I have not insulted you. Were ordinary pronouns insulting to women, every utterance ever voiced in English before 1970 was an insult. It would follow that Shakespeare unintentionally insulted women when he had Hamlet say "I'll make a ghost of him who lets me" without threatening Ophelia. The idea of an unintended insult makes no more sense than that of unintended discrimination.

The use of "he" has doubtless *become* provocative, but only because the feminist movement has made it so. By announcing that they will respond belligerently to "he," feminists have turned it into a fighting word. They have so raised linguistic consciousness that some decisions on pronouns have become unavoidable; if one is not profeminist in one's usage, one declares oneself defiantly antifeminist. It is of course the feminists' privilege to transform a previously inoffensive pronoun into a fighting word, as it is the privilege of the saloon brawler to announce that touching an intrinsically inoffensive chip on his shoulder will henceforth be construed as a challenge to fight. It is, however, quite absurd for feminists to decide to take offense at the English language and then complain that offensive remarks are constantly falling on their ears.

WHAT FEMINIST REFORM ACCOMPLISHES

Embedded sex differentiations do not desensitize language to social change. World War II produced "Rosie the Riveter," just as the popularity of Charles Dana Gibson's drawings produced the "Gibson girl" in a previous era. But such changes cannot be predicted, let alone dictated, for they arise from the same unconscious depths as speech itself and in response to the unpredictable contingencies in the extralinguistic world.

Because language reflects reality and not vice versa, universal adoption of feminist usages will do nothing to "upgrade" women. Indeed, there is an inconsistency between the claim that such coinages will beneficially raise consciousness and the demand that these coinages become the unconscious standard, for if "he or she" comes to be used as "he" now is (or was until very recently), namely as an indexical device, it will prompt no thoughts of sexual equality. The change will simply sprinkle a great many "she's" where none would otherwise have been found, a protocol as empty as calling everyone "comrade." If sprinkling "she's" is to have a point, the point must be kept in mind; if "he or she" becomes the *un*conscious norm, it will leave everything as it is. The same perceptions which once created "he" will continue to operate. Suppressing one or many of their linguistic manifestations will simply leave these perceptions in temporary tension with a language forbidden to express them—temporary, because they will find other expressions.

These points are unintentionally illuminated by an experiment taken by its designers to show that "he" suppresses thoughts of women.[12] It was found that

---

[12]Janice Moulton, George M. Robinson, and Cherin Elias, "Sex Bias in Language Use," *American Psychologist* (November 1978): pp. 1032–36.

people are more likely to think of a man first when "he" is used in sentences than when "he or she" is used. An alternative interpretation of this experiment comes to mind when its unsurprising result is redescribed as the greater readiness of people to think of a woman first when "he or she" is used than when "he" is used. It is surely more plausible to suppose that "he or she" prompts previously unentertained thoughts of women than that "he" quashes previously excogitated thoughts of women ready to enter consciousness. Consider the same experiment with "she" replaced by "a kangaroo." No doubt people are more likely to think of a human being first if "he" is used than if "he or a kangaroo" is, but does this mean that "he" inhibits thoughts of kangaroos, or that "he or a kangaroo" produces thoughts of kangaroos that would not otherwise have existed? The experiment as conducted relies on the current novelty value of "he or she." There is no reason to think the effect would continue should "he or she" simply *replace* "he" as the standard, unconscious conventional mode of reference used by English speakers from birth. People would continue to think first of whomever experience showed to lead the way in most activities, which would still be men.

It is extremely unlikely that "he or she," "he/she," "s/he" or similar neologisms will acquire purely indexical status, since they are syntactically complex. The mind seeing an "or," overt or disguised by a slash, wants to construct the meaning of the complex or-phrase from its components. The only practical replacement for "he" would have to be a completely new word bearing no syntactical relation to "he." The prospects for injecting such a word into a natural language by fiat are nil.

While its oppressiveness and clumsiness may sink feminist newspeak of its own weight, this tampering with language can, as noted, carry important negative consequences. Punishing words creates an aversion to the thoughts these words normally express, and while nothing can make people permanently disregard what they see, people can be made to *worry* about acknowledging what they see. This happened during the Victorian era, when an unwillingness to acknowledge sex openly drove people to clothe the "limbs" of tables and devise elaborate euphemisms for anything vaguely corporeal. Considerable damage was done in the way of hysteria and repression (although sex itself seems to have survived). Feminists seek to make taboo the acknowledgement of anything having to do with sex differences, and particularly with masculinity. For all their good words for forms of sexual behavior the Victorians would have abhorred, feminists are rather akin to Victorians.

LANGUAGE AND GOVERNMENT

Insofar as the feminist invasion of the mind is a private effort, there is nothing further to be said about it than to point out the errors on which it rests. It is up to each individual whether or not to lower his mental portcullis. The extent to which the government has taken the feminist side in this invasion is so far relatively minor. Still, neutering language is presented as a matter of rights, and the censoring of "discriminatory language" is increasingly equated with antidiscriminatory legislation.[13] Some feminists hold "sexist language" to violate Title VII and Title IX; during a television discussion in which I participated, it was asserted that control of the language of textbooks was a matter of "civil rights."[14]

The state has, somewhat tentatively, accepted the invitation to enter. In 1980, the secretary of health and human services prohibited the use of "sex biased" terms in departmental communications, and sent copies of *The Right Word* to all regional officers. A "right to be free of sexist language" is cited in Iowa's ban on language that "excludes women" in its public schools. This right is also cited in section 1604.11, the federal ban on "sexual harassment," which gives legal effect to the theory that language may serve as an oppressive force against women. As I noted in chapter 9, "sexual harassment" conjures up images of sexual blackmail, and there might be a case for treating sexual blackmail as a problem of some sort, if not perhaps a federal tort, if a precisely and narrowly defined case could be made for its prevalence. This condition is not met in section 1604.11, whose central provision runs as follows (emphasis added):

> Section (a)(3): *verbal* or physical conduct of a sexual nature constitute[s] sexual harassment when such conduct has the purpose *or effect* of unreasonably interfering with an individual's work performance or creating an intimidating, hostile or *offensive* work environment.
>
> Section (c): an employer is responsible for its acts and those of its agents and supervisory employees with respect to sexual harassment regardless of whether the specific acts complained of were authorized or even forbidden by the employer and *regardless of whether the employer knew or should have known* of their occurrence.
>
> Section (e): An employer may also be responsible for the acts of nonemployees.
>
> Section (f): An employer should take all steps necessary to prevent sexual harassment from occurring, such as affirmatively raising the subject, expressing strong disapproval, developing appropriate sanctions, informing employees of their right to raise and how to raise the issue of harassment under Title VII, and developing methods to sensitize all concerned.[15]

This language is aimed less at sexual blackmail than at any communication involving sex which, intentionally or unintentionally, bothers someone. It is consistent with (a)(3) that use of the epithet "bitch" is a tort; whether it actually is such will depend on the discretion of the federal judiciary. It is consistent with (a)(3) that all epithet need be directed at no particular individual to be harassing; if a woman is offended by an argument in the workplace using off-color language, she has standing and a prima facie case, as does a woman being pestered for a date. If a woman in a workplace dislikes a male coworker's sexual boasts, or the pin-ups in his locker, she may have a legally sound complaint;

---

[13]See Susan Salliday, Letter to the Editor, *Proceedings of the American Philosophical Association* 52 (August 1979): p. 869.

[14]*Straight Talk*, WOR-TV, New York, June 21, 1982.

[15]*Federal Register*, 45, 219, sec. 1604.11 (November 10, 1980), p. 74667. Sec. 1604.11 was issued by the EEOC as an implementing regulation of Title VII.

its "reasonableness" is a matter for judicial determination. Heated insistence on sex differences in an office argument will also be tortious if the federal courts see it as sufficient grounds for offense. (When section 1604 was issued for preliminary public comment before publication in the Federal Register, feminists argued strenuously for the deletion of the (a)(3) reasonableness test.)

The strict liability created by (c) for an employer for any sexual harassment by an employee or, per clause (e), any passerby, codifies *Miller,* in which the Bank of America was found responsible for a supervisor's firing a subordinate for denying him sexual favors. The application of a strict standard of liability is notable beyond its transformation of a tort that one would have thought inherently intentional. Strict liability, the threat to inflict punishment for events beyond the tort-feasor's control, is rare in the law. Some jurists regard it as a holdover from a time before the concept of individual responsibility had been developed. Jurists who do see a place for strict liability in Western law regard it as a means for promoting vigilance against serious mishaps. A restaurant owner is held strictly liable for his patrons' food poisoning even if he has taken reasonable precautions against it, on the theory that food poisoning constitutes such grave harm that restaurant owners must be made to take extraordinary precautions against it. In effect, section 1604 holds that remarks capable of giving sexual offense are as harmful as food poisoning.

Clause (f) outlines the measures an employer must take to maintain this heightened vigilance. In tandem with strict liability, the affirmative obligations of clause (f) strongly encourage employers to raise a commotion when there is no prior evidence of a need to. One thinks of the shock the required steps might bring to the average male and female office workers. They are probably not bothered by "sex harassment," and perhaps have never heard of it. They may enjoy the mild flirting that goes on, and, if unmarried, may hope to find a marriageable partner at work. Suddenly, on government orders transmitted by the local AA/EEO office, comes a flood of memoranda, posters, videotapes, lectures, warnings, instructions for bringing lawsuits and incitements to the anonymous grievances. An employer who takes section 1604 seriously may make periodic sweeps of the janitor's locker room, and to be on the safe side dismiss any employee who asks a co-worker for a date. Chase Manhattan Bank, fearful of 1604 litigation, now forbids all physical contact between employees and discourages "verbal pats on the back." The employer must still anticipate inadvertently offensive remarks by nonemployees who happen onto the premises. The owner of a diner might feel safest by putting signs around his parking lot warning "Don't whistle at our waitpersons."

This neo-Victorian obsession with sexual misbehavior is designed to mix everyone's awareness of sex with the thought of legal reprisal, to suppress speech with any sort of sexual content, and, ultimately, to chill normal relations between men and women. It is difficult to understand a "civil rights" policy which insists via quotas on "sexually integrating" the workplace, and then threatens reprisal when men and women placed in proximity, often in situations of stress, refuse to pretend they are neuters.

To place 1604 in perspective, the reader might recall the Supreme Court doctrine that no speech, however disrespectful, contemptuous, or advocatory of violent change, can be prohibited unless it is inciteful of and imminently likely to produce lawless action.[16] Under this doctrine the Supreme Court has protected topless dancing, American flags worn on the seat of the pants in public schools, and neo-Nazi marches through Jewish neighborhoods. Yet making a pass at work is no longer protected against state action.

Questions

1. To what extent does our language cause or reflect social reality? Can social change be brought about by linguistic change?
2. Is Michael Levin correct that for a word to be insulting it must be intended to be so? Does the fact that words like "man" and "he" cause offense make it wrong to use them?
3. Do you think that Michael Levin accurately represents the objections of people like Janice Moulton, Casey Miller, and Kate Swift? How might these authors respond to his arguments?

Suggestions for Further Reading on Sexist Speech

BAKER, ROBERT. "'Pricks' and 'Chicks': A Plea for Persons." In *Philosophy and Sex*. Rev. ed. Edited by Robert Baker and Frederick Elliston. Buffalo: Prometheus Books, 1984: pp. 249–267.

BODINE, ANN. "Androcentrism in Prescriptive Grammar: Singular 'They,' Sex-Indefinite 'He,' and 'He or She.'" In *The Feminist Critique of Language: A Reader*, edited by Deborah Cameron. London: Routledge, 1998: pp. 124–138.

KORSMEYER, CAROLYN. "The Hidden Joke: Generic Uses of Masculine Terminology." In *Feminism and Philosophy*, edited by Mary Vetterling-Braggin, Frederick A. Elliston, and Jane English. Littlefield, Adams, 1977: pp. 138–153.

LAKOFF, ROBIN. *Language and Woman's Place*. New York: Harper Colophon Books, 1975: pp. 43–50.

MILLER, CASEY and KATE SWIFT. *Words and Women: New Language in New Times*. New York: HarperCollins, 1991.

SATIRE, WILLIAM (alias Douglas R. Hofstadter). "A Person Paper on Purity in Language." In *Metamagical Themas*. New York: Basic Books, 1985: pp. 159–167.

SCHWARTZ, MARILYN, et al. *Guidelines for Bias-Free Writing*, Bloomington: Indiana University Press, 1995.

SPENDER, DALE. *Man Made Language*. 2nd ed. London: Routledge & Kegan Paul, 1985.

VALIAN, VIRGINIA. "Linguistics and Feminism." In *Feminism and Philosophy*, edited by Mary Vetterling-Braggin, Frederick A. Elliston, and Jane English, Totowa, N. J.: Littlefield, Adams, 1977.

VETTERLING-BRAGGIN, Mary, ed. *Sexist Language: A Modern Philosophical Analysis*. Totowa, N. J.: Littlefield, Adams, 1981.

WARREN, VIRGINIA. *Guidelines for Non-Sexist Use of Language*. American Philosophical Association Committee on the Status of Women in the Profession.

[16]See *Brandenburg v. Ohio*, 395 US 444 (1969).

CHAPTER 3

Gossip

The Logic of Gossip

Laurence Thomas

Laurence Thomas seeks to answer the question "What is gossip?" He notes that although all cases of gossip are instances of two or more people talking about someone who is not a party to the conversation, not all instances of such talk constitute gossip. By a clever use of examples designed to show up what kinds of talk we do and do not think are gossip, he arrives at a complex definition of gossip, labeled as (G) in his paper.

Gossip is best thought of as conversational embroidery. A small or large pattern can be embroidered on a piece of cloth. The extent to which the pattern on the cloth stands out depends on a number of things: its location, the character of the design, the color of the design, and so forth. A small pattern can be absolutely eye-catching or easily missed. On the other hand, a pattern that covers the entire cloth can be subtle or eye-catching, depending on color and design. Then, of course, there are the intricacies of the design. If gossip is like embroidery, then it is false to think of it as a sustained mode of conversation. By way of examples and analysis, I hope to offer an account of gossip that is true to this general way of framing the subject.

Though neither a bodily function nor a fulfillment of a basic human need, gossiping is an activity that just about everyone engages in to some extent, including many who disapprove of it. Gossiping is clearly a matter of two or more people talking about someone who is not a party to the conversation, though gossip does not occur every time two people talk about someone who is not a party to the conversation.

Consider:

(1) AUSTIN: Is Cohen going to the presidential address? I would like to talk to her about her recent paper on particle physics.

   LEE: I don't think so, since she will be accepting the Nobel Prize then.

Certainly we have no gossip here. The conversation is factual and without innuendo. But suppose the conversation continues:

(2) AUSTIN: I can't believe that they are awarding her the Nobel Prize in physics. Must be because she is a woman.
    LEE: To tell you the truth, I have been thinking the same thing myself.

This is surely gossip—perhaps even malicious gossip. The move from nongossip to gossip can happen ever so swiftly. Do we have gossip, however, if instead of (2), the conversation continues as follows:

(3) AUSTIN: Wonderful. They could not have picked a more deserving person!
    LEE: Absolutely. Everyone thinks that Cohen's work on the origins of the universe is just first-rate.

I doubt if many would call this gossip. But suppose the conversation began as follows:

(1′) SMITH: Hey Lee, guess who is getting the Nobel Prize in physics?—Cohen.
     LEE: Are you serious?
     SMITH: No kidding! I overheard the decision makers as they were leaving the room. They obviously did not think anyone was around. I wonder when they will go public with the announcement.

Professional gossip, as we have here, is not necessarily negative or malicious; for nothing about the context of (1′) reveals malice on the part of either Lee or Smith. On the contrary, we can imagine that both are good friends of Cohen and are absolutely delighted that she is being honored in this way. But if we have benign professional gossip in (1′), then what do we have in the following example:

(4) AUSTIN: Hey Paul, I just witnessed a most wonderful event: Just as a shark was being let into the pool at the museum, a three year old fell into the water. Without thinking, Cruz jumped into the water and saved the infant. The jaws of the shark missing them both by mere seconds.
    JONES: Incredible. If there are any saints in this profession, surely Cruz numbers among them. I don't know anyone who is as giving as he is.

This does not sound like gossip; indeed, the very idea that purely complimentary remarks about a third party amounts to gossip is counterintuitive. But how can it be that (1′) is gossip, but (4) is not? Any satisfactory account of gossip must explain this seeming difference between (1′) and (4).

Although conveying information can constitute gossiping, not every exchange of information does so, nor is it necessary to convey new information in order to be gossiping. Suppose long-time friends Baldwin and Gilbert are about to part for their separate offices when they see Johnson driving by in a new car with, apparently, a new lover. Baldwin and Gilbert meet later as is customary, and the conversation begins:

(5) BALDWIN: Well man, what do you think. With Johnson the pattern seems to be new car, new lover.
    GILBERT: I have never seen such rash behavior. Every lover is easily half Johnson's age.

There can be no doubt that we have gossip here, although the point of the conversation is not to convey new information about Johnson, since in fact both know much the same things about Johnson.

I imagine that for most of us (5) is what most readily comes to mind when we think of gossip. This is malicious gossip, though not as malicious as it can get. Now suppose a conversation similar to (5) takes place between a married couple:

(5*) HUSBAND: Johnson worries me. He has been going through cars and
    lovers like people go through handkerchiefs.
  WIFE: I know what you mean. I never would have suspected that
    inheriting $100 million would have affected him in this way. I wonder
    if we should speak to him, since we are perhaps his closest friends?

I believe that (5*) falls short of being gossip, although both (5) and (5*) are occasioned by Johnson's recent behavior.

Through examples of conversation, I have tried to indicate in an intuitive way when a conversation constitutes gossip and when it does not. The question now is whether any satisfactory account of when we do and do not judge a conversation to be gossip can be constructed. I propose the following:

(G) Gossip exists between A and B if and only if
    (i) A's motive in talking to B about (some aspect of) C's behavior is
        simply to comment on C's behavior; A neither intends to express
        admiration of C's behavior nor to elicit admiration from B regard-
        ing C's behavior, and there is no socially legitimate reason for
        commenting about C's behavior;
   (ii) A's purpose is to ventilate A's negative feelings about C, where
        the presumption on A's part is both that C's behavior does not,
        in and of itself, constitute morally admirable behavior and this is
        more or less evident to B.
  (iii) the information conveyed fails to be in keeping with the norms of
        social protocol when it comes to offering information concerning
        the well-being of another.

A gloss on (G)(ii) is in order. Usually a person gossips to another in the hopes that the other person will also gossip in return, either about the same individual or another individual. And that hope is realized often enough. It is certainly possible, however, that a person's gossiping will meet silence. (G)(i) captures the reality that gossip can be either benign or malicious. Plenty of conceptual space separates admiring and disparaging speech about someone else. Clearly, (iii) rules out as gossip "Did you hear, Jones just had a heart attack last night" or "Rubin gave birth this morning." The latter is not to be confused with "Rubin is pregnant," which is not covered by (iii). Only Rubin or her lover can make this announcement, unless the pregnancy is public knowledge or Rubin has indicated that she does not care who knows about her pregnancy.

According to (G), gossip does not exist when the point of a conversation is to find a way to cope with an individual's unacceptable behavior. If Johnson of (5) and (5*) above lives in an apartment building and has taken to having wild parties nightly the neighbors need not be gossiping if they gather to develop a strategy for dealing with him. It might be difficult to imagine that no one at the gathering would gossip about Johnson, but certainly it need not be that everyone does, including those who give evidence about Johnson's unruly behavior by offering a few sordid details. Some will be moved to embellish what they have to say; others will try as best they can to stick to the facts.

Now, (G) does not rule out the possibility that one can gossip about morally admirable behavior. A may call B to talk about C's saving a life, knowing full well that B will speak disparagingly of C's deed. After all, there are people who can find something negative to say about just about anything, including morally admirable behavior. The wording of (G), however, is meant to emphasize that A is not gossiping about C's morally admirable behavior if A draws B's attention to it simply as a way of expressing A's own admiration for C and eliciting B's. A's point is not at all to excite a negative reaction or to vent feelings, but to engage in a bit of mutual moral admiration. One way to show our admiration for the deeds of others is by speaking about them with the aim of expressing our own approval and eliciting approval from others.

Yet (G) allows for the unfortunate reality that people can gossip about what is in fact morally admirable behavior on the part of others. We have malicious gossip when A draws B's attention to C's behavior just to engage in demeaning it. But one need not do that; and in this regard so-called professional gossip comes readily to mind. Of course, professional gossip can be quite malicious, but it need not be so, and that it need not be malicious is no accident. Information about who is moving up the ladder of professional success, or just plain moving, can be conveyed without discussing personal aspects of a person's life. One can extrapolate without denigrating. Professional acquaintances are often interested in such information for its own sake, having no desire whatsoever to offer any assessment of the character of the individual involved.

This distinction between professional and nonprofessional gossip—personal gossip, let us call it—is rather illuminating. Both can avoid character assessment based on a person's behavior. Cases of admiration aside, however, it is generally very difficult to say much about a person's life that does not constitute a violation of the individual's privacy or that is not in some way malicious. It is difficult—but not impossible. We sometimes consider a person's behavior rather eccentric. We neither admire the behavior nor regard it as having any redeeming qualities. Nor, however, do we deem it inappropriate. For example, suppose Wong is compulsive about his teeth. He owns five or six toothbrushes, which he is constantly replacing, and he brushes his teeth four or five times a day. Or suppose Ahn is "crazy" about peanut-butter sandwiches, consuming at least five or six of them a day. To be sure, these things can be commented upon in a malicious way, but surely they need not be, and rarely would such comments about a person constitute a violation of privacy. Here we have paradigm examples of benign gossip.

By contrast what often is called professional gossip in no way comments on a person's private life. Moreover, the behavior in question generally counts as amoral, in the way that drinking a glass of water does; accordingly, the gossip does not involve an explicit or implicit moral assessment of the behavior. That "Briggs is accepting an offer at such-and-such" can be noted without any assessment of Briggs's character or any invitation to make such an assessment. Obviously there can be borderline cases, as when upon being informed that Briggs accepted the offer, the auditor remarks, "Briggs is moving again!"

Sometimes what is called gossip is not that at all; for example, conveying public information does not constitute gossip. Something can be made public without, at the same time, being generally known. Thus, when Susan Briggs posted on her door at 9 p.m. a note that she had accepted the offer from Chemistry for Everyone, she made that fact public, though not generally known. If a late-working colleague sees the note and calls across the country to tell a friend and professional acquaintance, the colleague is not gossiping about Briggs, any more than he would be if Briggs had taken out a very small back-page advertisement to the effect that she was accepting the offer and the colleague happened to have seen it and called the friend. The claim here, needless to say, is not that one cannot gossip about public information, but that the mere conveying of such information does not constitute gossip. Otherwise, a person would be gossiping if he merely conveyed the contents of a newspaper to someone who had not read it.

Consider a private marriage between two people who had a secret ceremony. Marriage is a public relationship in that a document of marriage must be filed with the state, and the fact that one is married is a matter of public record. Suppose, then, that the official recording the marriage for the state happens to be someone who knows the husband and wife. According to our analysis, for the official simply to inform yet another person of the couple's marriage does not constitute gossip. The official is at a party, and someone remarks, "What a wonderful wife so-and-so would make. She is so incredibly brilliant." To this, the official responds, "Well, I think you had better look elsewhere. She is legally spoken for." Given the distinction between information being public and its being publicly known, it follows that, strictly speaking, what often passes for professional gossip is not that at all, for quite often the content of so-called gossip is merely public information that is not yet widely known. Perhaps, then, one reason why professional gossip seems so benign is that it is not gossip at all.

I do not deny that people slip into gossip in the course of conveying information, though there are people able to convey appropriate information without engaging in editorial comment. They also refrain from remarking upon the editorial comments of others; in fact, some will make it clear that they are not interested in such comments. When Jones asks whether Cohen is accepting the Institute's offer, and Martin says that according to the Professional Physicists Bulletin she is, Martin is hardly gossiping. Perhaps Martin has quite an opinion on the matter but, characteristically, keeps it to himself.

Let us return to (5*) and the claim that this conversation, unlike its counterpart (5), falls short of being gossip. No doubt gossip often constitutes an exchange of useful information or offers speculation about a person's life. Not every exchange of useful information or bit of speculation about a person's life, however, constitutes gossip. Friends often have reason to discuss a person's behavior precisely in order to determine whether they should confront the person about it, and if so for what reasons and in what way. Consider a conversation that seems perhaps to be gossip, but which I maintain is not:

(6) BALDWIN: What's wrong? You have seemed so down lately.
   GILBERT: I still can't get over Jones's behavior. He is the very last person in the world I would have expected to make such a crass sexist remark.
   BALDWIN: Well, no one is perfect.
   GILBERT: We are not talking about perfection here, but a gross form of immoral behavior. There is just no excuse for him calling woman after woman at the reception "a cute whore." It is not just sexist, but indecent sexist behavior even among self-avowed male chauvinists. Have I been friends with such a dyed-in-the-wool sexist? What does that say about me?
   BALDWIN: Don't you think that you are being a little too hard on yourself? It is not as if you became friends with Jones knowing full well that he was given to uttering such remarks. Everyone at the party was taken by surprise.
   GILBERT: True. But you know that he did not apologize either then or later. I have sensed no shame on his part at all.

Clearly, we have the beginning of what could easily be a very long conversation that speculates about Jones's personality, motives, and behavior in all sorts of ways. Yet the conversation between Gilbert and Baldwin is not gossip.

There can be significant self-disclosure among friends and lovers. Indeed, this is a defining feature of deep friendships.[1] The point of the conversation is not to discuss Jones as such, but for Gilbert to achieve a measure of self-understanding and direction concerning his relationship with Jones. Baldwin is the vehicle through which this is being achieved. Baldwin and Gilbert are rather like the wife and husband scenario of (5*) above. In this regard, we suggest that deep friends are more like lovers or spouses than many are inclined to suppose.

Gossip is an extremely difficult notion to grasp, partly, I believe, because it is a mistake to think of any given conversation as either constituting gossip (in its entirety) or not. Gossip is not an all or nothing proposition. A conversation can be entirely free of gossip, except for a single remark limited to a single sentence. Or a conversation may be peppered with gossip. Or gossip may be the point of a conversation where little or no information alone is conveyed, as with (5) above. In just about any conversation, one can easily move from simply conveying information to a remark that constitutes gossip, or vice versa, for gossip lacks the conventional markers promises and introductions offer.

If my analysis is correct, gossip is tied conceptually to the motives behind the remarks being made. Given one motive, we have gossip; given another, we do not. Recall (5) and (6). Since we often do not know another person's motive, we can be quite mistaken about whether a person is engaging in gossip. What

---

[1]See the account of friendship in L. Thomas, *Living Morally: A Psychology of Moral Character* (Temple University Press, 1989), ch. 4.

may sound like gossip may not in fact be gossip at all. Some light falls, then, on the stereotype that women gossip far more than men. For what may seem to the ears of men to be gossip may not be that at all. The interests of men are not the only measure of things worthy of discussion.

Tying gossip to motives is important in another way. It is sometimes important to convey negative information about another to prevent a person from being harmed. Thus, a female graduate student might inform other females that if they work with a certain distinguished male professor they can expect to be propositioned by him. To be sure, the woman may simply be conveying this true information in order to damage the professor's reputation. But I take as obvious that conveying this information need not constitute gossip. Naturally, it is possible for a person to be mistaken or confused about why they are conveying such information. More than one motive may in fact be operating. I merely have to underline the reality that a negative comment about another person, if inspired by the right motives, does not constitute gossip.

Significantly, my analysis reveals that gossip need not in any way constitute an invasion of privacy. Gossip can be about what is widely known, although much gossip has to do with conveying private information about a third party—information which one has come by illegitimately, as a result of carelessness on the part of the possessor of the information, or by some structural inadequacy or foul-up of information control. The distinction between benign and malicious gossip helps us to understand why gossip that involves violations of privacy is often malicious. If nothing else, there can be little moral justification in conveying information about a person that she does not want revealed. And although I have claimed that gossip about private information is generally malicious; I did not mean to suggest that gossip about public information is not likely to be. Conversations about public information regarding the personal lives of public figures will in all likelihood be largely gossip unless it is a genuine expression of admiration. The fact that such gossip can be extremely malicious shows that the public status of information is no bar to malicious gossip about it.

I should like to emphasize, finally, that just about any conversation is likely to be a mixture of gossip and nongossip. Fortunately, though, not all gossip is malicious, and even better, we can talk about others with admiration in a way that does not constitute gossip at all. Recall the adage: "If you can't say anything good about a person, then don't say anything at all."

Questions

1. Does Laurence Thomas's definition (G) of gossip entail the judgment that all gossip is wrong?
2. Does his definition (G) account for why his example (1′) is gossip?
3. Consider the following example:

> JONES: I just heard that Smith was fired yesterday.
> BALDWIN: Wow, he sure has had a rough time lately.

Do you think that this is gossip? Is it gossip according to definition (G)?

Gossip

Sissela Bok

Sissela Bok shows how gossip has commonly been thought of in disparaging terms. Although she recognizes that gossip is often deserving of its bad reputation, she argues that it should not be defined as being bad. It can function in valuable ways, she says. She defines gossip as "informal personal communication about other people who are absent or treated as absent." She explains each element of this definition and distinguishes gossip from rumor. On her definition, she notes, gossip is not necessarily morally wrong. She then discerns and discusses three kinds of gossip she thinks are especially reprehensible: (1) gossip that breaches confidence; (2) gossip the speaker knows to be false; and (3) unduly invasive gossip. Finally, she considers the trivializing effect gossip can sometimes have.

DEFINITIONS

> Round the samovar and the hostess the conversation had been meanwhile vacillating . . . between three inevitable topics: the latest piece of public news, the theater, and scandal. It, too, came finally to rest on the last topic, that is, ill-natured gossip . . . and the conversation crackled merrily like a burning fagot-stick.

Tolstoy's group portrait from *Anna Karenina* brings to mind many a cluster of malicious gossips, delighting in every new morsel of ultimate information about others, the more scandalous the better.[1] So well do we recognize this temptation, and so often do we see it indulged, that it is easy to think of all gossip as petty, ill-willed, too often unfounded—as either trivial and thus demeaning to those whose lives it rakes over, or else as outright malicious. In either case, gossip seems inherently questionable from a moral point of view.

[1]Leo Tolstoy, *Anna Karenina*, trans. Constance Garnett (New York: Random House, Modern Library, 1950), p. 158.

Dictionary definitions reinforce the view of gossip as trivial. Thus the *American Heritage Dictionary* defines it as "trifling, often groundless rumor, usually of a personal, sensational, or intimate nature; idle talk."[2]

Thinkers who adopt a normative point of view often stress the more negative evaluation of gossip. Aristotle wrote of that tantalizing and yet strangely limited "great-souled man," who "claims much and deserves much," that he is no gossip [*anthropologos*],

> for he will not talk either about himself or about another, as he neither wants to receive compliments nor to hear other people run down . . .; and so he is not given to speaking evil himself, even of his enemies, except when he deliberately intends to give offense.[3]

Thomas Aquinas distinguished "talebearers" from "backbiters": both speak evil of their neighbors, but a talebearer differs from a backbiter "since he intends, not to speak ill as such, but to say anything that may stir one man against another," in order to sever friendship.[4]

Kierkegaard abhorred gossip. He spoke out against its superficiality and its false fellow-feeling. Gossip and chatter, he wrote, "obliterate the vital distinction between what is private and what is public" and thereby trivialize all that is inward and inherently inexpressible. He castigated his own age as one in which the expanding press offered snide and leveling gossip to a garrulous, news-hungry public.[5] Heidegger likewise, in pages echoing those of Kierkegaard, deplored idle talk as "something which anyone can rake up." He held that it perverts genuine efforts at understanding by making people think they already know everything.[6] And in their 1890 article on the right to privacy, Samuel Warren and Louis Brandeis spoke of gossip with similar distaste, assailing in particular its spread in the expanding yellow press: "Gossip is no longer the resource of the idle and vicious but has become a trade which is pursued with industry as well as effrontery."[7]

Cheap, superficial, intrusive, unfounded, even vicious: surely gossip can be all that. Yet to define it in these ways is to overlook the whole network of human exchanges of information, the need to inquire and to learn from the

---

[2]*The American Heritage Dictionary* (Boston: Houghton Mifflin & Co., 1969).

[3]Aristotle, *Nicomachean Ethics*, bk. 4, chap. 3, 31. Aristotle contrasted the "great-souled man" with the "small-souled man," on the one hand, who claims less than he deserves, and with the "vain man" on the other, who claims more than he deserves. I have used the traditional translation of Aristotle's *anthropos megalopsuchos*, as "great-souled man"; it must, needless to say, not be thought to refer to males only.

[4]Thomas Aquinas, *Summa Theologica* II-II. Ques. 73-74, trans. Fathers of the English Dominican Province (New York: Benziger Brothers, 1918), pp. 290–303.

[5]Soren Kierkegaard, *Two Ages* (1846), trans. Howard V. and Edna H. Hong (Princeton, N.J.: Princeton University Press, 1978). See esp. pp. 97–102.

[6]Martin Heidegger, *Being and Time* (New York: Harper & Row, 1962), p. 213. See p. 212 for Heidegger's view of the role of gossip and "scribbling" in "idle talk."

[7]Warren and Brandeis, "The Right to Privacy," pp. 193–220. For a discussion of this article and of the authors' distaste for gossip, see Dorothy J. Glancy, "The Invention of the Right to Privacy, *Arizona Law Review* 21 (1979): 1–39.

experience of others, and the importance of not taking everything at face value. The desire for such knowledge leads people to go beneath the surface of what is said and shown, and to try to unravel conflicting clues and seemingly false leads. In order to do so, information has to be shared with others, obtained from them, stored in memory for future use, tested and evaluated in discussion, and used at times to encourage, to entertain, or to warn.

Everyone has a special interest in personal information about others. If we knew about people only what they wished to reveal, we would be subjected to ceaseless manipulation; and we would be deprived of the pleasure and suspense that comes from trying to understand them. Gossip helps to absorb and to evaluate intimations about other lives, as do letters, novels, biography, and chronicles of all kinds. In order to live in both the inner and the shared worlds, the exchange of views about each—in spite of all the difficulties of perception and communication—is indispensable.[8]

Thanks to the illuminating studies of gossip by anthropologists and others—in villages around the world as in offices, working teams, schools, or conventions—we now have a livelier and clearer documentation of the role it actually plays.[9] These studies have disproved the traditional stereotype of women as more garrulous and prone to gossip than men, and have shown how such forms of communication spring up in every group, regardless of sex.[10] By tracing the intricate variations of gossip, these writings have led to a subtler understanding of how it channels, tests, and often reinforces judgments about human nature.

Before considering the moral problems that some forms of gossip clearly raise, we must therefore define it in a less dismissive way than those mentioned at the beginning of this chapter. We shall then be able to ask what makes it more or less problematic from a moral point of view, and weigh more carefully the dangers that Kierkegaard, Heidegger, and others have signaled.

I shall define gossip as informal personal communication about other people who are absent or treated as absent. It is informal, first of all, unlike communication in court proceedings or lectures or hospital records or biographies, in

[8]For the central role of gossip for information storage and retrieval in a society, see John M. Roberts, "The Self-Management of Cultures," in Ward H. Goodenough, *Explorations in Cultural Anthropology* (New York: McGraw-Hill Book Co., 1964), p. 441. And for an economic interpretation of information management through secrecy and gossip, see Richard A. Posner, "The Right to Privacy," *Georgia Law Review* 12 (Spring 1978): 398–422.

[9]See, among others, Max Gluckman, "Gossip and Scandal," *Current Anthropology* 4 (1963): 307–16; Don Handelman, "Gossip in Encounters: The Transmission of Information in a Bounded Social Setting," *Man*, n.s. 8 (1973): 210–27; Robert Paine, "What is Gossip About? An Alternative Hypothesis," *Man*, n.s. 2 (1967): 278–85; Ralph L. Rosnow and Gary A. Fine, *Rumor and Gossip: The Social Psychology of Hearsay* (New York: Elsevier, 1976); John Beard Haviland, *Gossip, Reputation, and Knowledge in Zinacantan* (Chicago: University of Chicago Press, 1977).

[10]We need not go back to Aesop, Plutarch, or the eighteenth-century moralists for vivid examples of such distinctions based on sex. Carl Fullerton Sulzberger permitted himself the following tortuous speculation, put forth as self-evident fact, in "Why It Is Hard to Keep Secrets," p. 42: "As we all know, most women habitually indulge in acquiring secrets only to give them away with celerity and obvious enjoyment. . . . When I once asked a patient why she was so eager to acquire and then spread secret rumors, her first association was, 'it is like adorning myself with borrowed feathers.'. . . the greater readiness of women to disseminate secrets entrusted to them is directly related to the working of the castration complex."

that it lacks formal rules setting forth who may speak and in what manner, and with what limitations from the point of view of accuracy and reliability. It is informal, too, in that it takes place more spontaneously and relies more on humor and guesswork, and in that it is casual with respect to who ends up receiving the information, in spite of the frequent promises not to repeat it that are ritualistically exacted along its path. (In each of these respects, gossip nevertheless has standards as well, though usually unspoken, as all who have tried to take part in gossip and been rebuffed have learned.) And the formal modes of discourse may themselves slip into more or less gossipy variations.

Secrecy is one of the factors that make gossip take the place of more formal communication about persons. Gossip increases whenever information is both scarce and desirable—whenever people want to find out more about others than they are able to. It is rampant, for instance, in speculations about the selection of prize-winners, or the marriage plans of celebrities, or the favors of a capricious boss. Gossip is more likely, too, when formal modes of discourse, though possible, have drawbacks for the participants. Thus hospital and school personnel gossip about their charges rather than entering the information on institutional records. And those who have the power to retaliate should they learn that their personal affairs are discussed are criticized in gossip rather than to their faces.

The seventeenth- and eighteenth-century New England Puritans illustrate in their writings the intensity with which human lives may be raked over, both in personal soul-searching and in talking about the lives of others. They labored with the strongest fears of not being among those who would turn out to be saved in the life to come; but they had no evidence for who was and who was not saved, and recognized no way to influence their fate, believing that it had been decided for them before birth. Might they nevertheless discern traces of such evidence in their own lives and in those of others? Might behavior and demeanor not hold some clues? Speculating about imperceptible yet all-important differences between persons took on an urgency rarely exceeded before or since. Hypocrisy naturally abounded. One of the foremost tasks of thinkers such as Thomas Shepard and Jonathan Edwards became the effort to separate the hypocrites from the sincere, and above all, to discern in self and others what they called the "inner hypocrisy" or self-deception that masked one's sins and doubts even from oneself.[11]

The second element in my definition of gossip is personal communication. The original source of what is said may be hidden or forgotten, but each time, gossip is communicated by one or more persons to others, most often in personal encounters, but also by telephone, by letter, or, in the last few centuries, in the mass media. This personal element, combined with the third—that the information is also *about* persons—makes gossip a prime vehicle for moral evaluation. Part of the universal attraction of gossip is the occasion it affords for comparing oneself with others, usually silently, while seeming to be speaking

---

[11]Michael McGiffert, ed., *God's Plot: The Paradoxes of Puritan Piety, Being the Autobiography and Journal of Thomas Shepard* (Amherst: University of Massachusetts Press, 1972); Jonathan Edwards, *Religious Affections* (Edinburgh, W. Laing & J. Matthews, 1789). See also Perry Miller, *The New England Mind: The Seventeenth Century* (New York: Macmillan Co., 1939).

strictly about someone else. Few activities tempt so much to moralizing, through stereotyped judgments and the head-shaking, seemingly all-knowing distancing of those speaking from those spoken about. The result is hypocrisy— judging the lives of others as one would hardly wish one's own judged. As one student of the anthropology of gossip has said:

> If I suggest that gossip and scandal are socially virtuous and valuable, this does not mean that I always approve of them. Indeed, in practice I find that when I am gossiping about my friends as well as my enemies I am deeply conscious of performing a social duty; but that when I hear they gossip viciously about me, I am rightfully filled with righteous indignation.[12]

Because gossip is primarily about persons, it is not identical with the larger category of rumor; there can be rumors of war or rumors of an imminent stock-market collapse, but hardly gossip.[13] And there can be stories, but not gossip, about the foibles and escapades of animals, so long as humans are not part of the plot, or the animals taken to represent individual persons or endowed with human characteristics.

Gossip, finally, is not only about persons but about persons absent, isolated, or excluded, rather than about the participants themselves. The subjects of gossip, while usually physically absent, can also be treated as if they were absent should they be part of the group engaging in gossip. While the conversation is directed past them and around them, they are then its targets, and are meant to overhear it. Least of all can people gossip about themselves, unless they manage to treat themselves as if they were absent, and as subjects of scandal or concern. Though it is hard to gossip about oneself, one can lay oneself open to gossip, or talk about one's doings that include others in such a way as to arouse gossip. Compare, from this point of view, the rumored divorce and the announced one, or the gossip about a young girl's pregnancy and her acknowledgment of it.

These four elements of gossip—that it is (1) informal (2) personal communication (3) about persons who (4) are absent or excluded—are clearly not morally problematic in their own right. Consider the many harmless or supportive uses of gossip: the talk about who might marry, have a baby, move to another town, be in need of work or too ill to ask for help, and the speculations about underlying reasons, possible new developments, and opportunities for advice or help. Some may find such talk uninteresting, even tedious, or too time-consuming, but they can hardly condemn it on moral grounds.

On the other hand, it is equally easy to conceive of occasions when the four elements do present moral problems. The informality and the speculative nature of what is said may be inappropriate, as it would be if gossip were the basis for firing people from their jobs. The communication about other persons may be of a degrading or invasive nature that renders it inappropriate, whether in gossip or in other discourse. And the talk about persons in their absence—

---

[12]Gluckman, "Gossip and Scandal," p. 315.
[13]See Gordon W. Allport and Leo Postman, *The Psychology of Rumor* (New York: Henry Holt & Co., 1947), and articles cited in note 9 above.

behind their backs—is sometimes of such a nature as to require that it either be spoken to their faces or not spoken at all. Pirandello's play *Right You Are! (If You Think So)* shows how irresistibly such gossip can build up among men and women in a small town, and the havoc it can wreak.[14]

For an example of gossip that is offensive on all such grounds, and as a contrast to the many forms of harmless gossip mentioned earlier, consider the alleged leak by an FBI official to a Hollywood columnist about the private life of the actress Jean Seberg. The leak indicated that she had engaged in extramarital relations with a member of the Black Panther Party, who was said to have fathered her unborn child.[15] It was meant to cast suspicion on her support of black nationalist causes. Reprinted by *Newsweek,* it was disseminated, as intended, throughout the world. Such uses of gossip have not been rare. They injure most directly the person whose reputation they are meant to call in question. But they debilitate as well those who take part in manufacturing and spreading the rumors and their superiors who are responsible for permitting such a scheme to go ahead; and thus they endanger still others who may be the targets of similar attacks. Such acts, with all their ramifications, overstep all bounds of discretion and of respect for persons. They are especially reprehensible and dangerous when undertaken in secrecy by a government agency in the name of the public's best interest.

In between these extremes of innocuousness and harm lie most forms of gossip: the savoring of salacious rumors, the passing on of unverified suspicions, the churning over seemingly self-inflicted burdens in the lives of acquaintances, and the consequent self-righteousness and frequent hypocrisy of those passing judgment in gossip. No testing ground for the exercise of discretion and indiscretion is more common than such everyday probing and trading of personal matters. Just as all of us play the roles of host and guest at different times, so all of us gossip and are gossiped about. Gossip brings into play intuitive responses to the tensions of insider and outsider, and forces us to choose between concealing and revealing, between inquisitiveness and restraint. Each of us develops some standards, however inarticulate, however often honored in the breach, for amounts and kinds of gossip we relish, tolerate, or reject. Can these standards be made more explicit? If so, how might we weigh them?

REPREHENSIBLE GOSSIP

> Why is gossip like a three-pronged tongue? Because it destroys three people: the person who says it, the person who listens to it, and the person about whom it is told. [The Babylonian Talmud]

---

[14]Luigi Pirandello, *Right You Are! (If You Think So)*, in Montrose J. Moses, ed., *Dramas of Modernism and their Forerunners* (Boston: Little, Brown & Co., 1931), pp. 239–75.

[15]"FBI Admits It Spread Lies About Actress Jean Seberg," *Los Angeles Times,* September 15, 1979, p. 1, and editorial, September 19.

Not all gossip, as I have defined it, is injurious or otherwise to be avoided. But when it is, it can harm all who take part in it, as the Babylonian Talmud warned.[16] Out of respect for oneself as much as for others, therefore, it matters to discern such cases. Three categories of gossip should be singled out as especially reprehensible: gossip in breach of confidence, gossip the speaker knows to be false, and unduly invasive gossip.

It is wrong, first of all, to reveal in gossip what one has promised to keep secret. This is why the gossip of doctors at staff meetings and cocktail parties about the intimate revelations of their patients is so inexcusable. True, pledges of confidentiality must at times be broken—to save the life of an adolescent who confides plans of suicide, for example. But such legitimate breaches could hardly be carried out through gossip, because of its lack of discrimination with respect to who ends up hearing it. Such information should, rather, be disclosed only to those who have a particular need to know, and with the utmost respect for the privacy of the individual concerned.

Must we then bar all gossip conveyed in spite of a pledge of silence? And would we then not exclude *most* gossip? After all, few pieces of information are more rapidly disseminated than those preceded by a "promise not to tell." At times such a promise is worthless, a more empty gesture, and both parties know it; one can hardly call the subsequent repeating of the "secret" a breach of confidence. Sometimes the person who asks for the promise before sharing his bits of gossip may believe it to be more binding than it turns out to be. But, as La Rochefoucauld asked, why should we imagine that others will keep the secret we have ourselves been unable to keep?[17] At still other times, a promise may have been sincere, but should never have been made to begin with. Many promises of secrecy are exacted with the aggressive intent of burdening someone, or of creating a gulf between that individual and others. The best policy is to be quite sparing in one's promises of secrecy about any information, but scrupulous, once having given such a promise, in respecting it.

Second, gossip is unjustifiable whenever those who convey it know that it is false and intend to deceive their listeners (unlike someone who makes it clear that he exaggerates or speaks in jest). Whether they spread false gossip just to tell a good story, or to influence reputations, perhaps even as a weapon—as when newly separated spouses sometimes overstate each other's misdeeds and weaknesses in speaking to friends—they are exceeding the bounds of what they owe to their listeners and to those whose doings they misrepresent. The same is true of the false gossip that can spring up in the competition for favor, as in office politics or in academic backbiting, and of collective strategies for deceit. Thus in the re-election campaign of President Nixon in 1972, some individuals had been assigned the task of spreading false rumors about his opponents. Conspiratorial groups and secret police have employed such methods through the ages. Whatever the reason, there can be no excuse for such dissemination of false gossip.

---

[16]The Babylonian Talmud, cited in Francine Klagsbrun, *Voices of Wisdom: Jewish Ideals and Ethics for Everday Living* (New York: Pantheon Books, 1980), p. 74.
[17]La Rochefoucauld, *Maximes et réflexions diverses* (1664; Paris: Gallimard, 1976), p. 143.

Might there not be exceptional circumstances that render false gossip excusable?* I argued, in *Lying,* that certain lies might be excusable, such as those that offer the only way to deflect someone bent on violence. But whatever lies one might tell such an assailant, false gossip about third parties would hardly provide the requisite help at such a time of crisis; and if by any chance the assailant could be stalled simply by talking about other persons, there would be no need to use falsehood in so doing.

Are there forms of false gossip that correspond to innocent white lies? Gossip to please someone on his deathbed, for instance, who has always enjoyed hearing about the seedy and salacious doings of his friends, by a wife who can think of nothing truthful that is sufficiently titillating? Should she then invent stories about neighbors or friends, thinking that no harm could come thereof, since her husband would not live to spread the stories further? Such a way out would be demeaning for both, even if it injured no one else: demeaning to the dying man in the unspoken judgment about what would most please him, and in the supposition that lying to him would therefore be acceptable; and demeaning to his wife, as she reflected back on her inability to muster alternative modes of silence and speech at such a time. No matter how well meant, falsehoods about the lives of others bear little resemblance to harmless white lies.

Much of the time, of course, those who convey false gossip do not know it to be false. It may rest on hearsay, or be unverified, or be pure speculation. Often the facts cannot easily *be* verified, or not without serious intrusion. Thus to spread rumors that a person is a secret alcoholic is made more serious because of the difficulty that listeners have in ascertaining the basis of the allegation. At times such gossip cannot be known to be true by the speakers, nor credibly denied by the subjects. This was one reason why the dissemination of the rumor about Jean Seberg's unborn baby was so insidious. She had no way before the baby's birth to demonstrate the falsity of the rumor.

In the third place, gossip may be reprehensible, even if one has given no pledge of silence and believes one's information correct, simply because it is unduly invasive. On this ground, too, planting the rumor about Jean Seberg's sexual life and the identity of the father of her unborn child was unjustifiable, regardless of whether the FBI thought the story accurate or not.

Is any gossip, then, unduly invasive whenever it concerns what is private, perhaps stigmatizing, often secret? If so, much of the gossip about the personal lives of neighbors, co-workers, and public figures would have to be judged inexcusable. But such a judgment seems unreasonable. It would dismiss many harmless or unavoidable exchanges about human foibles. To such strictures, the perspective of Mr. Bennett in Jane Austen's *Pride and Prejudice* should give

---

*One could imagine a club dedicated to false gossip, in which members vied with one another for who could tell the most outrageous stories about fellow human beings. So long as all knew the tales were false, and the stories went no farther, the practice would not be a deceptive one, and more allied to storytelling and fiction than to the intentional misleading about the lives of others that is what renders false gossip inexcusable. Such a club, however, would be likely to have but few members; for gossip loses its interest when it is *known* to be false.

pause: "For what do we live," he asked, "but to make sport for our neighbors and to laugh at them in turn?"[18]

How then might we sort out what is unduly invasive from all the gossip about private and secret lives? To begin with, there is reason to stop to consider whether gossip is thus invasive whenever those whose doings are being discussed claim to feel intruded upon. But these claims must obviously not be taken at face value: they are often claims to ownership of information about oneself. While such claims should give gossipers pause, they are not always legitimate. People cannot be said, for instance, to own aspects of their lives that are clearly evident to others and thus in fact public, such as a nasty temper or a manipulative manner, nor can they reasonably argue that others have no right to discuss them. Least of all can they suppress references to what may be an "open secret," known to all, and half-suspected even by themselves—a topic treated in innumerable comedies about marital infidelity. Similarly, more concealed aspects of their lives may be of legitimate interest to others—their mistreatment of their children, for example, or their past employment record. And the information that government leaders often try to withhold through claims to executive privilege is often such that the public has every right to acquire it. At such times, gossip may be an indispensable channel for public information.

Merely to *say* that gossip about oneself is unduly invasive, therefore, does not make it so. I would argue that additional factors must be present to render gossip unduly invasive: the information must be about matters legitimately considered private; and it must hurt the individuals talked about.* They may be aware of the spreading or of the harm; or else they may be injured by invasive gossip without ever knowing why—fail to keep their jobs, perhaps, because of rumors about their unspoken political dissent. But the speculations in bars or sewing circles concerning even the most intimate aspects of the married life of public figures is not intrusive so long as it does not reach them or affect their lives in any way. Such talk may diminish the speakers, but does not intrude on the persons spoken about.

While the three categories of reprehensible gossip—gossip in breach of confidence, gossip that is known to be false, and gossip that is clearly invasive—should be avoided, each one has somewhat uncertain boundaries and borderline regions. One cannot always be sure whether one owes someone silence, whether one is conveying false gossip, or whether what is said of an intimate nature about people will find its way back to them or otherwise hurt them. In weighing

---

[18]Jane Austen, *Pride and Prejudice* (New York: E. P. Dutton & Co., 1976), p. 384.

*For this reason, gossip should give pause whenever the speaker believes it may reach someone in a position to injure the person spoken of. If the listener is a judge, for instance, or an executive having the power to make decisions over someone's employment, the gossiper must weigh his words with care. Even when the listener is not in an official position, gossip directed to him is problematic if he is given to injurious responses: if he is malicious, slanderous, indiscreet, profiteering, or in any way likely to put the information to an inappropriate use. Gossip is problematic, too, if the listener is a poor intermediary: perhaps one who exaggerates gossip in conveying it further, or who is likely to misunderstand it and spread it in false garb, or is unable to discriminate in turn between listeners, so that he conveys the gossip to one who is incompetent or dangerous.

such questions, discretion is required; and, given the capacity of gossip to spread, it is best to resolve doubts in favor of silence.

Extra caution is needed under certain circumstances, when the temptation to indulge in any of the three forms may be heightened. At such times, the borderline cases carry an even stronger presumption against taking part in gossip. Discretion is then needed more than ever to prevent gossip from blending with one or more of the kinds earlier ruled out. The desire to have an effect, first of all, to impress people, perhaps to deal a blow, easily leads to greater pressure to breach secrecy or exaggerate in gossip or to speak intrusively about others. As soon as a speaker gains in any way from passing on gossip, these pressures arise. Prestige, power, affection, intimacy, even income (as for gossip columnists): such are the gains that gossipers envisage. It cannot be wrong to gain from gossip in its own right, since in one sense most gossip aims at a gain of some sort—if nothing else, in closeness to the listener, or in the status of someone who seems to be "in the know." But the prospect of such gain increases the likelihood that promises will be broken, unverified rumors passed on, privacy invaded. The misfortunes of another may then be used in such a way as to traffic in them. This is in part why the inside gossip of the former employee or the divorced spouse is more troubling when it is published for financial gain or as revenge.

A desire for gain of a different kind motivates those who take special pleasure in passing on discreditable gossip. Maimonides, like Aquinas and many others, distinguished the talebearer from the person who speaks to denigrate: the scandalmonger, or, as Maimonides expressed it, "the evil tongue."[19] He spoke, too, of "the dust of the evil tongue": the insinuations that sow suspicion without shedding light either on the implied offense or on the evidence concerning it. Before scandalmongers and insinuators are known as such, they can destroy trust among friends or in entire communities; in consequence they have been more distasteful to commentators than all others. And yet, all disparaging or discreditable personal information cannot be avoided. On the contrary, it must sometimes be conveyed, as when the deceitful or the aggressive or, indeed, the indiscreet are pointed out to put newcomers on their guard. Consider, as an illustration of such cautioning remarks, the following exchange in a Mexican village:

> Down the path someone spotted a young man named Xun, whose reputation as a drunkard made everyone anxious to be on his way.
>
> "If you meet him drunk on the path, he has no mercy. He won't listen to what you say, that Xun."
>
> "He doesn't understand what you say; you're right. If he's just a bit tight when you meet him on the path—puta, 'Let's go, let's go,' he'll say. You will be forced to drink."
>
> "But doesn't he get angry?"
>
> "No, no. He'll just say, 'Let's go have a little soft drink.'"
>
> "He's good-natured."
>
> "But he doesn't bother to ask if you're in a hurry to get someplace . . ."

---

[19]Maimonides, *Code*, "Laws Concerning Moral Dispositions and Ethical Conduct," chap. 7, secs. 1–4, quoted in Klagsbrun, *Voices of Wisdom*, p. 75.

"No, he's good-hearted . . ."

"If you find yourself in a hurry to get somewhere and you see him coming the best thing to do is hide . . ."

". . . or run away."

And with that, the various men went on about their business.[20]

TRIVIALIZING GOSSIP

Beyond such questions of avoiding reprehensible and harmful gossip lies a larger one: that of the tone gossip can lend to discourse about human lives. It is this tone that Kierkegaard and Heidegger aimed at, in arguing that gossip streamlines and demeans what is spoken. What is utterly private, and inward, Kierkegaard held, cannot be expressed; as a result, talking about it must necessarily distort and trivialize. Gossip therefore has a leveling effect, in conveying as shallow and ordinary what is unfathomable. It levels, moreover, by talking of all persons in the same terms, so that even the exceptionally gifted, the dissident, and the artist are brought down to the lowest common denominator. Finally, it erases and levels the differences between the different modes of talking, so that all is glossed over in the same superficial and informal chatter.

According to such a view, the informality with which we talk about the weather or the latest price rises can only trivialize what we say about human beings. And this informality of gossip can combine with the special liberties taken in the absence of those spoken about so as to permit the speaker to indulge in a familiarity disrespectful of their humanity and in turn of his own. It was this reflection that gossip casts on so many who convey it that made George Eliot compare it to smoke from dirty tobacco pipes: "it proves nothing but the bad taste of the smoker."[21]

Gossip can also trivialize and demean when it substitutes personal anecdote for a careful exploration of ideas. Someone incapable of taking up political or literary questions without dwelling endlessly on personalities can do justice neither to the ideas nor to the persons under debate.

Such gossip can be an intoxicating surrogate for genuine efforts to understand. It can be the vehicle for stereotypes—of class, for instance, or race or sex. It turns easily into a habit, and for some a necessity. They may then become unable to think of other human beings in other than trivial ways. If they cannot attribute scope and depth and complexity to others, moreover, it is unlikely that they will perceive these dimensions in themselves. All news may strike them as reducible to certain trite formulas about human behavior; all riddles seem transparent.

Many do not merely gossip but are known *as* gossips. They may serve an important group function; but such a role should cause concern to the individuals thus labeled. It is far more likely to tempt to breaches of confidence, to

---

[20]Haviland, *Gossip, Reputation, and Knowledge in Zinacantan*, p. 15.

[21]George Eliot, *Daniel Deronda*, Standard Edition, *The Works of George Eliot* (Edinburgh & London: William Blackwood & Sons, 1897), 1: 207.

falsehoods, to invasive gossiping—and thus to a general loss of discernment about reasons to avoid gossip and persons to shield from it. At the extreme of this spectrum is the pathological gossip, whose life revolves around prying into the personal affairs of others and talking about them.

Plutarch wrote of the garrulous that they deny themselves the greatest benefits of silence: hearing and being heard. In their haste to speak, they listen but poorly; others, in turn, pay little heed to their words.[22] And Heidegger expounded on the strange way in which gossip and all facile discourse, so seemingly open and free-ranging, turns out instead to inhibit understanding: "by its very nature, idle talk is a closing-off, since to go back to the ground of what is talked about is something which it *leaves undone.*"[23] Those whose casual talk stops at no boundaries, leaves no secret untouched, may thereby shut themselves off from the understanding they seem to seek. Gossip can be the means whereby they distance themselves from all those about whom they speak with such seeming familiarity, and they may achieve but spurious intimacy with those *with whom* they speak. In this way gossip can deny full meaning and depth to human beings, much like some forms of confession: gossip, through such trivializing and distancing; confession, through molding those who confess and overcoming their independence.

These warnings go to the heart of the meaning of discernment concerning human beings, including oneself, and of its links with the capacity to deal with openness and secrecy. Quite apart from the obvious problems with false or invasive gossip discussed earlier, all gossip can become trivializing in tone, or turn into garrulity.

Yet gossip need not deny meaning and debilitate thus. Those who warn against it often fail to consider its extraordinary variety. They ignore the attention it can bring to human complexity, and are unaware of its role in conveying information without which neither groups nor societies could function.[24] The view of all gossip as trivializing human lives is itself belittling if applied indiscriminately. When Kierkegaard and Heidegger speak out against idle talk, gossip, and chatter, and against "the public" and the "average understanding" taken in by such discourse, they erase differences and deny meaning in their own way.[25] One cannot read their strictures without sensing their need to stand aloof, to maintain distance, to hold common practices vulgar. In these passages, they stereotype social intercourse and deny it depth and diversity, just as much as gossip can deny those of individuals. When moral judgment takes such stereotyped form, it turns into moralizing: one more way in which moral language can be used to avoid a fuller understanding of human beings and of their efforts to make sense of their lives.

---

[22]Plutarch, "Concerning Talkativeness," *Moralia,* 6: 399.
[23]Heidegger, *Being and Time,* p. 213.
[24]See Elizabeth Drew, *The Literature of Gossip: Nine English Letter-Writers* (New York: W. W. Norton & Co., 1964), p. 26, for examples of gossipers who can "inspire the commonplace with an uncommon flavor, and transform trivialities by some original grace or sympathy or humor or affection."
[25]See, for example, Kierkegaard, *Two Ages,* p. 100, and Heidegger, *Being and Time,* p. 212.

Questions

1. Apply Sissela Bok's definition to the various examples Laurence Thomas provides. Can her definition satisfactorily account for which of those examples are gossip and which are not?
2. Do you agree with Sissela Bok's judgment about the false gossip the woman feeds to her dying husband?
3. Can you think of a way in which we might determine when gossip is unduly invasive?

In Praise of Gossip:
Indiscretion as a Saintly Virtue

Ronald de Sousa

Ronald de Sousa defends gossip. He says that because information empowers and gossip conveys information, gossip is a form of power—one that weaker groups might employ against those who hold more conventional power. He defines gossip as "conversation about other people's private lives." His main concern is to defend gossip against the objection that it constitutes a violation of privacy.

He argues that talking about people is not literally invasive. For this reason, he sees no basis for a right not to be the subject of talk. Sometimes, he says, shame or guilt explains why people do not want information about them spread. On other occasions people desire privacy for privacy's sake—not because they are ashamed or guilty about the information that might be conveyed. He dismisses such extreme desires for privacy as being childlike. He argues that such feelings provide no justification whatsoever for a moral prohibition on speaking about them. He argues that to keep "private" details secret diminishes our understanding of human nature. Gossip provides us with important information we would otherwise not have. Were it the case that all private information were made public we would, he says, "approach utopia." No longer could people be deceived, misunderstood, or betrayed.

Gossip has been the object of much malicious talk. But then, so have all forms of power—and gossip is power. It differs from ordinary power as information differs from brute force, but it is power nevertheless. Gossip is typically a subversive form of power: an attempt by the weak, and often, though far from exclusively, by women, to use the power of knowledge independently of those who wield more conventional power. As Patricia Meyer Spacks put it, "The ferocity of several centuries' attack on derogatory conversation about others

Ronald de Sousa: "In Praise of Gossip: Indiscretion as a Saintly Virtue," *Good Gossip*, Robert F. Goodman and Aaron Ben Ze'ev (eds.) Copyright 1994. Reprinted by permission of the University Press of Kansas; Lawrence, KA.

This paper grew out of remarks provoked by presentations by Louise Collins and Maryann Ayim at the Canadian Philosophical Association meetings in June 1990. It owes much to both those presentations.

probably reflects justifiable anxiety of the dominant about the aggressive impulses of the submissive."*

This aspect of gossip has motivated a minority of recent writers—including
some included in this volume—to come to the defense of gossip. Without conceding that gossip is exclusively a woman's occupation, for example, Maryann
Ayim[1] and Louise Collins[2] point out that gossip is a form of inquiry that remains available to women even when other avenues of inquiry are closed to
them by circumstance or convention. Similarly, it is a commonplace that the
novel, of all the arts, is the one in which women have been most successful at
competing directly with men. This is true of Western culture and even of oriental cultures, where the control and oppression of women have been perhaps
even more intense. You can write a novel in snatches, discreetly slipping the paper under the blotter when company comes, without the need for bulky, heavy
raw material, without sophisticated tools, and without fear of being given away
by the noise of the chisel or the smell of paint. Gossip is inherently democratic,
concerned with private life rather than public issues, and "idle" in the sense
that it is not instrumental or goal oriented. Yet it can serve to expand our understanding of life in ways that other modes of inquiry cannot.

What, then, are the standard objections to gossip? Gossip, it is said, is often
motivated by malice or envy; its enjoyment is often taken at the expense of others, whom it harms by exposing their vices and foibles to ridicule; and worst, it
often sacrifices the truth. These objections are, in fact, irrelevant. No doubt malice, envy, prevarication, and other vices often mar the character of those who
gossip. But such faults can no more be held against gossip in itself than they can
be held against love, marriage, or commerce, all of which notoriously provide
opportunities for the deployment of the very same vices. True, if gossip is defined as malicious and harmful talk about the private lives of others, for example, then to discuss its moral worth is superfluous. On the other hand, gossip
could be defined simply as conversation about other people's private lives,
which would leave open the substantive question of whether such conversations are necessarily, or usually, reprehensible for one reason or another. Clearly,
the methodologically superior approach is that which does not prejudge questions of value at the stage of initial definition of the subject matter.

Current discussions of pornography provide a case in point. They frequently get bogged down because some discussants want to define pornography in a morally neutral way, whereas others argue that if a representation can
be correctly described in a morally neutral way then that alone is sufficient to
establish that it is not pornography. Sometimes, pornography is defined as "depictions of sexual violence degrading to women." In that case, the debate about
the worth of pornography will be closed before it can be joined. On the other

---

*P. M. Spacks. 1985. *Gossip*. New York: Knopf: 30.

[1]Maryann Ayim, "Knowledge through the Grapevine: Gossip as Inquiry" in *Good Gossip*, Robert F.
Goodman & Aaron Ben Ze'ev (eds.) pp. 85–99.

[2]Louise Collins, "Gossip: A Feminist Defense" in *Good Gossip*, Robert F. Goodman & Aaron Ben
Ze'ev (eds.) pp. 106–116.

hand, if pornography is defined as "depictions of sexual activity intended primarily to occasion sexual arousal," we can discuss whether and when that is a bad thing. Perhaps pornography cannot be judged to be bad without appealing to evaluative terms such as "undue exploitation of" or "excessive emphasis on" sex. But in order to begin the discussion we need a morally neutral definition.[3] Similarly, if gossip is defined as malicious, we have gone too far, too fast, and we risk losing sight of that position in conceptual space occupied by uncensored, no-holds-barred—but private—talk about the private lives of others. We do better to endorse a morally neutral characterization of gossip, in order to decide when and whether activities of the type so defined should be condemned.

Of course, someone might claim that the neutrality of the definition in question is only apparent; that a Kantian analysis or its implications would show that it would in fact be incoherent to wish that gossip "become a universal law of nature."[4] Perhaps it is a psychological truth (though not a logical one) that talking about other people's private lives seems interesting only when it is driven by malicious motivation. But if everyone were driven by malicious motivation, it is hard to imagine a world in which this were not generally known. And if everyone knew that when others gossiped they were driven by malice, they would no more be inclined to take them seriously than people could be deceived by liars in a society where everyone lied. I shall give this Kantian form of argument a peculiar twist in a moment, urging that gossip is not only a virtue but, in a very specific sense, a saintly one. But such an argument will not work to attack gossip. For if the listener shares the malicious motivation of the speaker, the latter's gossip is hardly less likely to be credited: on the contrary, it then becomes a shared task of malice, and the argument might even be turned on its head to suggest that gossip is pointless unless it is conducted in a society of malicious participants. That would yield the rather conventional view that gossip is indeed universal because people are universally malicious in fact. This familiar view characterizes some of the more pessimistic satirists in classical literature.

I do not see any reason to grant the psychological speculation that grounds the argument just given. But even if it were sound, it still would not give us a reason to condemn gossip as such. At worst, the attribution of bad motives to those who gossip would condemn the practice as bad de facto because of its association with evil motivation. But suppose that gossip were not merely generally but always, even necessarily, driven by envy, malice, or any other combination of deplorable motives. Would this be sufficient to condemn it? In fact it would not, at least not from a reasonably Utilitarian point of view, for one could not infer from even the most constant association of gossip with bad motives that as a social institution gossiping was worse in its consequences than refraining from gossip. It might have benefits independent of its motivation.

---

[3]For examples of these terminological meanders, see D. Copp, and S. Wendell, eds. 1983. Pornography and censorship. In *New concepts in human sexuality*. Buffalo: Prometheus Books.

[4]Louise Collins has in fact made a similar suggestion. For the Kantian principle at stake, see I. Kant. *Fundamental principles of the metaphysics morals*. [Indianapolis: Bobbs-Merrill, 1949. First published 1785.]

Compare, for example, the relation of greed to capitalism. Someone might claim that the success of private enterprise rests entirely on the motivation of greed and thus deplore it. But that person might at the same time grant that the consequences of allowing greed free rein are, on the whole, preferable to the consequences of suppressing it altogether. Similarly, gossip could be a good thing on the whole, even if some of its individual consequences were indisputably deplorable and even if its motivation were invariably malicious.

Yet another defense of gossip might be posited: Gossip is morally defensible even though its actual consequences are not best on the whole. Because I wish to argue in this chapter for a defense of gossip as free speech extended to the private sphere, I must look at a different and more powerful set of objections to gossip that center on issues of privacy. The relevant sense of that somewhat multifarious word carries the suggestion that there exists a right to control information about oneself. Is there such a right?

In the most straightforward terms, what is at question here is simply the right not to be talked about. A friend once suggested that it is an infringement of my personal rights if you use me, without my permission, in your sexual fantasies, be they ever so private. If that were so, then surely, by analogy, would I not have the right not to be discussed or even thought about? In a newspaper article, the Canadian philosopher Tom Hurka recently endorsed this sentiment, claiming that for people to "analyze your deep motivations" is "invasive."* It's not easy to say anything objective about this. Obviously there is nothing literally invasive about merely talking or thinking about someone (that is how information differs from matter!). And I have no idea how the relevant metaphorical sense of "invasive" might be worked out to make sense of Hurka's point. So I don't see what the basis of such a right might be. Nevertheless, some people don't want to be talked about.

But why? Clearly such feelings are sometimes linked to shame or guilt. Indeed gossip not infrequently focuses on aspects of people's lives that are liable to evoke those emotions. But this is not always so: sometimes the feeling of not wanting to be observed is just that and does not depend on the object of observation's being engaged in anything disreputable. Some people, like J. D. Salinger, seem to desire secrecy for its own sake. Living behind high walls of stone and expensive lawyers, they actively repel any inquiry into any facts of their life. Some people do this even while cognizant of the importance to our knowledge of human nature that the whole truth be known about as many people as possible. Freud, for example, surely did more than anyone to break down the barrier between the public and the private, and yet he did his utmost to stop anyone from finding out the private truth about himself. By doing this he undermined the very exploration of human nature that he purported so fearlessly to lead.

This extreme desire for privacy resembles children's feelings that they don't want to be looked at or the "primitive" fear of being photographed. To this is added the characteristically adolescent desire to have "secrets." The difficulty of

*T. Hurka, 1990. "Principles." *Toronto Globe and Mail*, April 17.

rationalizing such feelings is that they run rather deep; an appropriate explanation for them belongs properly to depth psychology. Whatever their cause might be, they are no doubt at least partially to blame for the general bad press that gossip has received. But can such feelings justify that bad press? The answer to this question depends on the extent to which justification is linked to general approval. Suppose there is general disapproval of gossip and that people generally claim their disapproval is grounded in the "offensive" nature of gossip to their "feelings of privacy." In a strictly anthropological sense, that would constitute justification enough. But I am interested, perhaps quixotically, in further justification, a justification of the "feeling" itself. And from that perspective, it seems to me that the feelings in question can provide no justification at all.

Consider, first, attitudes to sexual practices. Some people argue that certain practices, while not in themselves wrong, ought nevertheless to be kept in the closet because they are offensive to the sensibilities of others. "I know there's nothing really wrong with homosexuality," we sometimes hear, "but I find it disgusting and I think you should give some weight to my feelings." Using a simplistic interpretation of Utilitarianism, I suppose any feelings of pleasure or unpleasure ought to be taken into consideration. But this supposition is unacceptable. In this case, for example, my own intuition is that the feelings of discomfort themselves are wrong and have no moral weight. Feelings only have moral weight if they reflect some real—that is, objective—value. In the absence of any real superiority of value to heterosexuality, the feelings of discomfort elicited by homosexuality have no moral weight at all.

The rhetorical force of my argument is weakened, I am well aware, by its presupposition of the existence of objective values. Since I don't have the space to defend this presupposition here,[5] let me turn to a second, less controversial analogy. I once met a man who explained to me that he and his wife had no prejudices at all against blacks, but that unfortunately his wife felt sick in close proximity with any African American. Did this strong feeling on her part not constitute a reason, though perhaps not an overriding one, in favor of segregation? No. Surely in this case the simplistic utilitarian view is seen to be without force. Her feelings are not merely overridden by other values; they constitute no reason *at all* for any action whatever, except therapeutic action to eliminate the feeling itself. Accordingly, sensibilities—feelings—can provide no convincing argument against gossip.

There is a second, slightly different, nuance of the putative "right to privacy" that might find an independent justification. The right to privacy in this sense is the right to keep secrets. In his newspaper column, Tom Hurka also articulates this objection. He writes that if we haven't broadcast information about ourselves, this is tantamount to signifying that we want it kept secret. But so what? "When [people] don't [license gossip about themselves,] we should

---

[5]In R. de Sousa, 1987. *The rationality of emotions*. Cambridge, Mass.: MIT Press. I have defended a notion of objective value, compatible with granting the relativity of value to human capacities and experiences, of which appropriate emotional response constitute the apprehension.

feel more than uneasy" about gossiping. He doesn't say why. Now to claim the right to keep things to ourselves is obviously more reasonable than to claim the right to censor other people's thoughts about you. Nevertheless, the former claim, too, rests on feelings that I have argued can have no moral claim on our respect.

Perhaps, then, there exists a right to keep certain things secret (if one can); but though we must recognize this right, we may deplore its exercise, for to keep some things secret is necessarily to manipulate information in ways that are bound to diminish our understanding of human nature. At the very least, such manipulation is likely to promote self-deception and hypocrisy. And because the things most likely to be kept secret concern areas, like personal relations and sex, about which people know too little and need to know as much as possible, it can significantly lower the capacity of ordinary people to thrive.

Let me put the argument as radically as I can. At question here is the freedom of speech, but applied to private speech about the private sphere: although the dissemination of private information may make some people uncomfortable, its importance must, as a matter of public policy, be deemed to outweigh that discomfort. (This argument has force even if my earlier claim that such feelings have no moral weight at all is rejected.) This is more or less recognized in countries like Canada and the United States that have laws guaranteeing "access to information" or "freedom of information." We might object that this argument applies only to the public sphere, for the private sphere is not important enough to justify a "need to know," and the damage done to private persons by public knowledge of their lives easily outweighs what little gain might still be claimed.

In fact, however, the opposite is true. In the absence of active censorship, public matters are by and large a matter of record. The private sphere is more elusive and quirky, and therefore more difficult to investigate. Indeed, gossip is especially valuable where a strict distinction is made between private and public life. In cultures that emphasize that distinction, the "private" sphere is often a euphemism for the freedom of men to abuse women and children. The concept of a private sphere, by definition, renders a whole domain of people's experience especially difficult to explore by any so-called objective or scientific means. And since that part of life, in terms of the actual quality of our lives, may well be the most important one, accurate knowledge about it is particularly crucial. This is the area that gossip alone can crack.

Here, then, is my radical twist on the Kantian theme:

To refrain from gossip is to be discreet and according to common prejudice, discretion is a virtue. Certainly discretion is often prudent as well as kind. But this makes it only an ordinary virtue. Indiscretion, by contrast, is a superior virtue, indeed a saintly one.

Unlike ordinary virtue, saintly virtue is not justified by its immediate consequences. On the Kantian schema, what justifies a practice is the consistency and desirability of a possible world in which it were universalized. The practice of saintly virtue, then, does not pretend to be crassly pragmatic. Heroes and saints are not supposed to be utilitarians. Their virtues challenge and enrich our understanding of moral possibilities. Thus it is that heroes and saints, however revered from afar, are detested close up, and generally end up drawn and quartered or burned at the stake. I suggest that the indiscretion of the gossip is, in a small way, a saintly virtue.

La Rochefoucauld taught us that hypocrisy is the tribute that vice pays to virtue. But what is discretion but hypocrisy in the third person? Discretion is the tribute paid in return to vice by virtue. Consider: if your friends had nothing worth keeping secret, there would be no use for discretion. (Remember that I have already set aside the claim based on the sole "feeling" of not wanting to be talked about.) What point would there be to discretion in Paradise? Without the thieves, the Good Samaritan would never have had his chance at memorable virtue. Similarly, the opportunity for discretion about our friends' unusual or not-so-unusual sexual preferences, say, arises only thanks to the society's prejudices.

Among the findings of the Kinsey reports on sexuality—a kind of glorified and systematic gossip—one of the most startling and revealing findings was that most people thought themselves abnormal: Most people, it seems, thought that most other people never did what they themselves mostly did.* This is precious information, which only a great deal of high-quality gossip might have anticipated. People can be harmed by the dissemination of such knowledge only because knowledge of that kind is generally withheld. Consider the harm that used to come from the revelation that someone was a homosexual: If every homosexual could have been "outed" at one fell swoop, the knowledge would most likely have been powerless to harm anyone. If all truths became public, we would approach utopia. We would no longer need to spend so much time on concealment. When petty crimes and mean thoughts can no more be hidden than nuclear warheads, then the deception industries, private and public, will wither away as the state was supposed to do. (Perhaps even the state would wither away, too.) Personal relationships would be far less likely to be poisoned by misunderstandings and disappointments. Love might still be painful, but betrayal would be far less common. No longer would ludicrous and harmful assumptions about human nature be fostered by chronic hypocrisy. Worldwide disarmament would soon follow, and enormous resources would be liberated to the benefit of humankind.

Well, perhaps I exaggerate. Universal knowledge of who was a Jew would not have helped the Jews under Hitler. (But perhaps in my utopia of universal knowledge, Hitler would never have gained power in the first place.) At any rate, it seems likely that a world in which all information were universally available would be preferable to a world where immense power resides in the control of secrets. If so, it is enough to make of indiscretion a saintly if not a pragmatic virtue, and enough to reject the reasons adduced to condemn gossip.

---

*A. C. Kinsey, W. B. Pomeroy, and C. E. Martin. 1948. *Sexual behavior in the human male*. Philadelphia: W. B. Saunders.

   A. C. Kinsey, W. B. Pomeroy, C. E. Martin, and P. H. Gebhard. 1953. *Sexual behavior in the human female*. Philadelphia: W. B. Saunders.

My analysis has a corroborating consequence: if it is at all correct, we can now better understand why in actual practice malice is so often associated with gossip. The reason lies in precisely the fact that makes gossip so necessary in the first place: our appalling ignorance of how people really work, about "what makes them tick." Given our ignorance, all but the more sophisticated among us live in constant fear that their own perverted natures will be exposed for all to see. Malicious gossip reassures them that others are no better than they are. The institutionalized gossip of *People* magazine and other such publications is particularly effective in that regard, because it allows us to believe that the rich and famous are no better than the rest of us. Of course, if information about the intimate lives of real men and women were not jealously hoarded, this would be public knowledge in the first place, and the thirst to expose others as no better than myself could not be slaked by such ordinary revelations.

Gossip is, I have suggested, an assault on the notion of a private sphere of life. Not exactly public, gossip most often occurs within a narrow social sphere.[6] And since the social circle in question is essentially restricted, the resulting judgments, as Spacks points out, are likely to remain conventional and conservative ones: "By generating shame in those who violate social standards, [gossip] helps to enforce agreed-upon values."[*] For anyone who is a strict social constructivist on matters of value, such a conclusion is acceptable; but for those who prize the subversive element in gossip, it is not radical enough. The progress of a culture depends on its mavericks, just as evolution in a species depends on its mutants; thus the extent to which social pressure in a small group enforces conformity should worry us. Here again anthropology offers a parallel damaging to my optimistic thesis. The social pressure to maintain the horrendous practices of ritual genital mutilation where these are traditionally part of the "culture" comes mainly from the women who are both perpetrators and victims. The critical, subversive pressure comes mainly if not entirely from outside the culture.[†] Even in "pluralistic cultures," like contemporary Canada, small subcultures have a remarkable capacity for retaining and enforcing within the group the most viciously narrow-minded views. My own instinct is always to resist the suggestion that where moral and psychological truths are in question "reality depends on the ultimate decision of the community."[7] Community is a Janus face: though one side wears the smile of social harmony, on the other lurks the scowl of fascism.

We should remember, however, that in the Peircean utopia just mentioned, the "community decision" endowed with criterial power is as Ayim phrases it

[6]Ayim, who compares the cooperative search for truth in gossip and the search for truth in science, observes that "the test for truth in investigative gossip [as in science] is inherently social." But she clearly acknowledges the problem of size.

[*]P. M. Spacks. 1985. *Gossip*. New York: Knopf: 141.

[†]J. P. Boddy. 1989. *Wombs and alien spirits: Women, men, and the Zar cult in northern Sudan.* Madison: University of Wisconsin Press.

[7]See C. S. Peirce. 1931–1958. *Collected papers,* vols. 1–8, C. Hartshorne, P. Weiss, and A. Burks, eds. Cambridge, Mass.: Harvard University Press. Quoted by Ayim.

"the ideal state of complete information." And since it is precisely the informational advantages of gossip that I have been insisting on, this Peircan point is one I can endorse in the spirit of what I have called "saintly virtue." In practice, the consensus of any subculture may be a narrow-minded and wrong-headed one, but the conditions under which a broader view might prevail surely include a universalized practice of radical and guiltless indiscretion, a world of transparent gossip such as I have envisaged in my perfectly indiscreet utopia.

Even in the real and imperfect world in which we live, falling far short of complete information, the cultural values articulated by gossip are not necessarily those of the dominant culture. On the contrary, they are at least as likely to be those of a subculture of the oppressed or at least of the less powerful. In this way, then, gossip could serve to articulate an alternative moral psychology as much as it might consolidate the dominant one. No doubt both functions are certainly served; in what proportion, though, is a matter for empirical investigation: I don't know how one could determine a priori which function is better served, the subversive or the conservative. It is up to each of us, as ethically responsible gossips, to find the right mix.

Questions

1. For what reason does Ronald de Sousa think that gossip may be acceptable even if it were always motivated by envy or malice?
2. For what reason does he think that feelings have no moral weight unless they reflect some objective value? Do you agree?
3. Do you think that some things, even if not disreputable in themselves, are best kept private? If yes, what and why? If not, why not?

Suggestions for Further Reading on Gossip

GOODMAN, ROBERT F., and AARON BEN-ZE'EV, eds. *Good Gossip.* Lawrence: University Press of Kansas, 1994.
HOLLAND, MARGARET G. "What's Wrong with Telling the Truth? An Analysis of Gossip." *American Philosophical Quarterly* 33, no. 2 (April 1996): pp. 197–209.

CHAPTER 4

Lying

IMMANUEL KANT, On a Supposed Right to Lie from Altruistic Motives

SISSELA BOK, Lying

THOMAS E. HILL JR., Autonomy and Benevolent Lies

On a Supposed Right to Lie from Altruistic Motives

Immanuel Kant

Immanuel Kant believes that it is **never** *morally permissible to lie. He rejects the view that we have a duty to tell the truth only to those who have a right to the truth. He considers an extreme case—that of somebody who cannot avoid answering a murderer's inquiry regarding the whereabouts of a potential victim. Even in such a situation, Immanuel Kant thought, one must tell the truth. To tell the truth, when one does not have the option of silence, is, he says, the duty of everyone, irrespective of its costs.*

Although, as an extreme deontologist, Immanuel Kant does not think that actions should be evaluated in terms of their consequences, he mentions that the consequences of lying to the murderer may turn out, contrary to expectations, to be worse than the consequences of telling the truth. It may happen that the potential victim is no longer where one thought he was and one's lie leads the murderer directly to where his intended victim is. When that happens, one would be responsible, says Immanuel Kant, for the victim's death. If, however, one had told the truth and that had led to the murderer's finding his victim, one would not be responsible, he says, for the murder. We have a duty to tell the truth, he thinks, because the acceptance of lying would cause all undertakings to lose their force and thereby wrong all humankind.

In the journal *France*[1] for 1797, Part VI, No. 1, page 123, in an article entitled "On Political Reactions"[2] by Benjamin Constant,[3] there appears the following passage:

---

[1] The journal *Frankreich im Jahre 1797. Aus den Briefen deutscher Manner in Paris,* published in Altona.
[2] *Des réactions politiques* had appeared in 1796 and was translated in this journal.
[3] Henri Benjamin Constant de Rebecque (1767–1830), the French writer, statesman, and orator.

Immanuel Kant, "On a Supposed Right to Lie from Altrustic Motives," in *Critique of Practical Reason and Other Writings in Moral Philosophy,* University of Chicago Press 1949.

The moral principle, "It is a duty to tell the truth," would make any society impossible if it were taken singly and unconditionally. We have proof of this in the very direct consequences which a German philosopher has drawn from this principle. This philosopher goes so far as to assert that it would be a crime to lie to a murderer who asked whether our friend who is pursued by him had taken refuge in our house.*

The French philosopher on page 124 refutes this principle in the following manner:

> It is a duty to tell the truth. The concept of duty is inseparable from the concept of right. A duty is that which in one being corresponds to the rights of another. Where there are no rights, there are no duties. To tell the truth is thus a duty; but it is a duty only in respect to one who has a right to the truth. But no one has a right to a truth which injures others.

The *proton pseudos* (false starting point) in this argument lies in the sentence: "To tell the truth is a duty, but it is a duty only toward one who has a right to the truth."

It must first be noted that the expression, "to have a right to truth" is without meaning. One must rather say, "Man has a right to his own truthfulness (*veracitas*)," i.e., to the subjective truth in his own person. For to have objectively a right to truth would mean that it is a question of one's will (as in questions of what belongs to individuals generally) whether a given sentence is to be true of false. This would certainly produce an extraordinary logic.

Now, the first question is: Does a man, in cases where he cannot avoid answering "Yes" or "No," have a right to be untruthful? The second question is: Is he not in fact bound to tell an untruth, when he is unjustly compelled to make a statement, in order to protect himself or another from a threatened misdeed?

Truthfulness in statements which cannot be avoided is the formal duty of an individual to everyone,** however great may be the disadvantage accruing to himself or to another. If, by telling an untruth, I do not wrong him who unjustly compels me to make a statement, nevertheless by this falsification, which must be called a lie (though not in a legal sense), I commit a wrong against duty

---

*"J. D. Michaelis[4] of Göttingen expressed this extraordinary opinion earlier than Kant. But the author of this essay has informed me that Kant is the philosopher spoken of in this passage."—K. F. Cramer.†[5]

†That this was really said by me somewhere I hereby admit, though I cannot now remember the place.[6]—I. Kant.

**I should not like to sharpen this principle to the point of saying, "Untruthfulness is a violation of duty to one's self." This principle belongs to ethics, but here we are concerned with a legal duty. [Ethics as a] theory of virtue sees in this transgression only worthlessness, which is the reproach the liar draws upon himself.

[4]Johann David Michaelis (1717–91), biblical scholar, professor in Göttingen.

[5]Karl Friedrich Cramer (1752–1807), the editor of *Frankreich . . .*, formerly professor of Greek and oriental languages and homiletics at Kiel, had been dismissed in 1794 because of his open sympathy for the Revolution.

[6]"Such a place is not to be found in Kant's previous works."—Heinrich Maier (editor of the Academy edition of this work).

generally in a most essential point. That is, so far as in me lies I cause that declarations should in general find no credence, and hence that all rights based on contracts should be void and lose their forcce, and this is a wrong done to mankind generally.

Thus the definition of a lie as merely an intentional untruthful declaration to another person does not require the additional condition that it must harm another, as jurists think proper in their definition (*mendacium est falsiloquium in praeiudicium alterius*). For a lie always harms another; if not some other particular man, still it harms mankind generally, for it vitiates the source of law itself.

This benevolent lie, however, can become punishable under civil law through an accident (*casus*), and that which escapes liability to punishment only by accident can also be condemned as wrong even by external laws. For instance, if by telling a lie you have prevented murder, you have made yourself legally responsible for all the consequences; but if you have held rigorously to the truth, public justice can lay no hand on you, whatever the unforeseen consequences may be. After you have honestly answered the murderer's question as to whether his intended victim is at home, it may be that he has slipped out so that he does not come in the way of the murderer, and thus that the murder may not be committed. But if you had lied and said he was not at home when he had really gone out without your knowing it, and if the murderer had then met him as he went away and murdered him, you might justly be accused as the cause of his death. For if you had told the truth as far as you knew it, perhaps the murderer might have been apprehended by the neighbors while he searched the house and thus the deed might have been prevented. Therefore, whoever tells a lie, however well intentioned he might be, must answer for the consequences, however unforseeable they were, and pay the penalty for them even in a civil tribunal. This is because truthfulness is a duty which must be regarded as the ground of all duties based on contract, and the laws of these duties would be rendered uncertain and useless if even the least exception to them were admitted.

To be truthful (honest) in all declarations, therefore, is a sacred and absolutely commanding decree of reason, limited by no expediency.

Mr. Constant makes a thoughtful and correct remark on decrying principles so strict that they are alleged to lose themselves in such impracticable ideas that they are to be rejected. He says, on page 23, "In every case where a principle which has been proved to be true appears to be inapplicable, the reason is that we do not know the middle principle which contains the means of its application." He adduces (p. 121) the doctrine of equality as the first link of the social chain, saying (p. 122):

> No man can be bound by any laws except those to the formulation of which he has contributed. In a very limited society this principle can be applied directly and needs no mediating principle in order to become a common principle. But in a society consisting of very many persons, another principle must be added to this one we have stated. This mediating principle is: the individuals can participate in the formulation of laws either in their own person or through their representatives. Whoever wished to apply the former principle to a large society without making use of the mediating principle would invariably bring

about the destruction of the society. But this circumstance, which would only show the ignorance or the incompetence of the legislator, proves nothing against the principle.

He concludes (p. 125) that "a principle acknowledged to be true must never be abandoned, however obviously danger seems to be involved in it." (And yet the good man himself abandoned the unconditional principle of truthfulness on account of the danger which it involved for society. He did so because he could find no mediating principle which could serve to prevent this danger; and, in fact, there is no principle to be interpolated here.)

If we wish to preserve the names of the persons as they have been cited here, the "French philosopher" confuses the action by which someone does harm (*nocet*) to another in telling the truth when he cannot avoid making a statement, with the action whereby he does the other a wrong (*laedit*). It was only an accident (*casus*) that the truth of the statement harmed the occupant of the house; it was not a free act (in a juristic sense). For to demand of another that he should lie to one's own advantage would be a claim opposed to all lawfulness. Each man has not only a right but even the strict duty to be truthful in statements he cannot avoid making, whether they harm himself or others. In so doing, he does not do harm to him who suffers as a consequence; accident causes this harm. For one is not at all free to choose in such a case, since truthfulness (if he must speak) is an unconditional duty.

The "German philosopher" will not take as one of his principles the proposition (p. 124): "To tell the truth is a duty, but only to him who has a right to the truth." He will not do so, first, because of the ambiguous formulation of this proposition, for truth is not a possession the right to which can be granted to one and denied to another. But he will not do so chiefly because the duty of truthfulness (which is the only thing in question here) makes no distinction between persons to whom one has this duty and to whom one can exempt himself from this duty; rather, it is an unconditional duty which holds in all circumstances. . . .

Questions

1. Why does Immanuel Kant think that a duty to tell the truth is not only owed to those who have a right to it?
2. Do you think that a person can be responsible for unforeseeable unfortunate consequences of altruistic lying but not be responsible for clearly foreseeable unfortunate consequences of truth-telling?

Lying

Sissela Bok

Sissela Bok first discusses the value of truthfulness in any society and explains the various ways in which lying can coerce people to act against their will. Next she considers the Kantian view that all lies are wrong. She notes that if force may be used to prevent a murder, then it seems odd to think that lying for the same purpose is wrong. She also argues against Immanuel Kant's view that one bears no responsibility for averting a murder one could easily have prevented by lying. She then turns to consider the consequentialist view on lying. Utilitarians, she notes, unlike Kantians, think that lies can vary in their degree of seriousness. She points, however, to the difficulties of determining and comparing the consequences of truthfulness and deception. She also points to the dangers of utilitarian rationalizations of deception. She argues, therefore, for a utilitarian presumption against lying. Finally, she discusses the question of "white lies," arguing that some are acceptable while others are not.

LYING AND CHOICE

Deceit and violence—these are the two forms of deliberate assault on human beings.[1] Both can coerce people into acting against their will. Most harm that can befall victims through violence can come to them also through deceit. But deceit

---

[1]See quotation . . . where Dante characterizes force and fraud as the two forms of malice aiming at injustice: "Of every malice that gains hatred in Heaven the end is injustice; and every such end, either by force or by fraud, afflicts another. But because fraud is an evil peculiar to man, it more displeases God, and therefore the fraudulent are the lower, and more pain assails them" (Dante, *The Divine Comedy: Inferno,* trans. Charles S. Singleton [Princeton, N.J.: Princeton University Press, 1940], canto II, p. III). See also Northrop Frye, *The Secular Scripture: A Study of the Structure of Romance* (Cambridge, Mass.: Harvard University Press, 1976), chap. 3.

Sissela Bok, *Lying: Moral Choice in Public and Private Life,* Harvester Press, Hassocks Sussex, 1978, pp 18–20, 38–42, 48–52, 57–61.

controls more subtly, for it works on belief as well as action. Even Othello, whom few would have dared to try to subdue by force, could be brought to destroy himself and Desdemona through falsehood.

The knowledge of this coercive element in deception, and of our vulnerability to it, underlies our sense of the *centrality* of truthfulness. Of course, deception—again like violence—can be used also in self-defense, even for sheer survival. Its use can also be quite trivial, as in white lies. Yet its potential for coercion and for destruction is such that society could scarcely function without some degree of truthfulness in speech and action.*

Imagine a society, no matter how ideal in other respects, where word and gesture could never be counted upon. Questions asked, answers given, information exchanged—all would be worthless. Were all statements randomly truthful or deceptive, action and choice would be undermined from the outset. There must be a minimal degree of trust in communication for language and action to be more than stabs in the dark. This is why some level of truthfulness has always been seen as essential to human society, no matter how deficient the observance of other moral principles. Even the devils themselves, as Samuel Johnson said, do not lie to one another, since the society of Hell could not subsist without truth any more than others.[2]

A society, then, whose members were unable to distinguish truthful messages from deceptive ones, would collapse. But even before such a general collapse, individual choice and survival would be imperiled. The search for food and shelter could depend on no expectations from others. A warning that a well was poisoned or a plea for help in an accident would come to be ignored unless independent confirmation could be found.

All our choices depend on our estimates of what is the case; these estimates must in turn often rely on information from others. Lies distort this information and therefore our situation as we perceive it, as well as our choices. A lie, in Hartmann's words, "injures the deceived person in his life; it leads him astray."[3]

To the extent that knowledge gives power, to that extent do lies affect the distribution of power; they add to that of the liar, and diminish that of the deceived, altering his choices at different levels.[4] A lie, first may misinform, so as to obscure some *objective,* something the deceived person wanted to do or obtain. It may make the objective seem unattainable or no longer desirable. It may even create a new one, as when Iago deceived Othello into wanting to kill Desdemona.

Lies may also eliminate or obscure relevant *alternatives,* as when a traveler is falsely told a bridge has collapsed. At times, lies foster the belief that there are

---

*But truthful statements, though they are not meant to deceive, can, of course, themselves be coercive and destructive; they can be used as weapons, to wound and do violence.

[2]Samuel Johnson, *The Adventurer* 50 (28 April 1753), in *Selected Essays from The Rambler, Adventurer, and Idler,* ed. W. J. Bate (New Haven and London: Yale University Press, 1968).

[3]Nicolai Hartmann, *Ethics,* 2: 282.

[4]The discussion that follows draws upon the framework provided by decision theory for thinking about choice and decision-making. This framework includes the *objectives* as they are seen by the decision maker, the *alternatives* available for reaching them, an estimate of *costs and benefits* associated with both, and a *choice rule* for weighing these.

more alternatives than is really the case; at other times, a lie may lead to the un-necessary loss of confidence in the best alternative. Similarly, the estimates of *costs and benefits* of any action can be endlessly varied through successful deception. The immense toll of life and human welfare from the United States' intervention in Vietnam came at least in part from the deception (mingled with self-deception) by those who channeled overly optimistic information to the decision-makers.

Finally, the degree of *uncertainty* in how we look at our choices can be ma-nipulated through deception. Deception can make a situation falsely uncertain as well as falsely certain. It can affect the objectives seen, the alternatives be-lieved possible, the estimates made of risks and benefits. Such a manipulation of the dimension of certainty is one of the main ways to gain power over the choices of those deceived. And just as deception can initiate actions a person would otherwise never have chosen, so it can prevent action by obscuring the necessity for choice. This is the essence of camouflage and of the cover-up—the creation of apparent normality to avert suspicion. . . .

Kant takes issue, first, with the idea that any generous motive, any threat to life, could excuse a lie. He argues that:

> Truthfulness in statements which cannot be avoided is the formal duty of an individual to everyone, however great may be the disadvantage accruing to himself or to another.[5]

This is the absolutist position, prohibiting all lies, even those told for the best of purposes or to avoid the most horrible of fates. For someone holding such a position, to be called a liar was a mortal insult—perhaps cause even for legal action or a duel; to be *proved* a liar could lead to self-exile out of shame.

Kant's view, if correct, would eliminate any effort to distinguish among lies, since he rejects them all. He takes the duty of truthfulness to be an "uncondi-tional duty which holds in all circumstances";[6] a lie, even if it does not wrong any particular individual, always harms mankind generally, "for it vitiates the source of law." It harms the liar himself, moreover, by destroying his human dignity and making him more worthless even than a mere thing.[7]

Kant also rejects the way around Augustine's prohibition that consists in defining certain falsehoods as not being lies. He defines a lie as "merely an in-tentional untruthful declaration to another person" and dismisses the idea that we owe the duty of speaking the truth only to those who have a right to the truth.[8] On the contrary, truthfulness is a duty which no circumstances can

---

[5]Kant, "On a Supposed Right to Lie."

[6]*Ibid.*

[7]Kant, *The Doctrine of Virtue*, p. 93.

[8]In "On a Supposed Right to Lie," Kant takes up this view as expressed by Benjamin Constant, in "Des réactions politiques," *France*, 1797, 6: 123. Kant claims that the expression "to have a right to truth" is without meaning.

In *The Doctrine of Virtue*, p. 92, Kant argues, "In the doctrine of Law an intentional untruth is called a lie only if it infringes on another's right. But it is clear of itself that in ethics, which derives no moral title to an action from its harmlessness [to others], every deliberate untruth in the expres-sion of one's thoughts deserves this harsh name."

abrogate. Whatever else may be said about Kant's position, it seems to have the virtue of clarity and simplicity. Others may argue about when to lie, but he makes a clean sweep.

CONFLICTS OF DUTY

But can we agree with Kant? His position has seemed too sweeping to nearly all his readers, even obsessive to some. For although veracity is undoubtedly an important duty, most assume that it leaves room for exceptions. It can clash with other duties, such as that of averting harm to innocent persons. Yet Kant holds[9] that "a conflict of duties and obligations is inconceivable," that if one does one's duty, one will turn out to have had no conflicting obligations. It is this refusal to consider conflicts of duty which drives Kant into such inflexible positions.

Most have held the contrary view—that there are times when truthfulness causes or fails to avert such great harm that a lie is clearly justifiable. One such time is where a life is threatened and where a lie might avert the danger. The traditional testing case advanced against the absolutist position is that discussed by Kant himself, where a would-be murderer inquires whether "our friend who is pursued by him had taken refuge in our house."[10] Should one lie in order to save one's friend? Or should one tell the truth?

This is a standard case, familiar from Biblical times, used by the Scholastics in many variations, and taken up by most commentators on deception. It assumes, of course, that mere silence or evasion will not satisfy the assailant. If this case does not weaken your resistance to all lies, it is hard to think of another that will.

In nineteenth-century England, the same case was taken up once more by Cardinal Newman. He was defending himself and Catholic scholars against charges of immorality and laxity regarding truthfulness. He argued that men of great rectitude, no matter what their faith, might resort to a lie in extreme circumstances. He quoted Samuel Johnson as stating:

> The General Rule is, that truth should never be violated; there must, however, be some exceptions. If, for instance, a murderer should ask you which way a man has gone.

Even so, Cardinal Newman added, Johnson might well have acted quite differently had he been put to the test:

> As to Johnson's case of a murderer asking which way a man has gone, I should have anticipated that, had such a difficulty happened to him, his first act would have been to knock the man down, and to call out for the police; and next, if he was worsted in the conflict, he would not have given the ruffian the

---

[9]Kant, "Introduction to the Metaphysic of Morals," *The Doctrine of Virtue*, p. 23.
[10]Kant, "On a Supposed Right to Lie."

information he asked at whatever risk to himself. I think he would have let himself be killed first.[11]

Cardinal Newman's supposition might well have astounded Johnson! Depending on the physical strength of the murderer, resistance by force might seem a very unplausible alternative to deception. Kant evidently does not even consider it; confronted with this test case, he takes his stand squarely with those objecting even to lies under such extreme circumstances.

Most others have argued that, in such cases, where innocent lives are at stake, lies are morally justified, if indeed they are lies in the first place. Kant believes that to lie is to annihilate one's human dignity; yet for these others, to reply honestly, and thereby betray one's friend, would in itself constitute a compromise of that dignity. In such an isolated case, they would argue, the costs of lying are small and those of telling the truth catastrophic.

Similarly, a captain of a ship transporting fugitives from Nazi Germany, if asked by a patrolling vessel whether there were any Jews on board would, for Kant's critics, have been justified in answering No. His duty to the fugitives, they claim, would then have conflicted with the duty to speak the truth and would have far outweighed it. In fact, in times of such crisis, those who share Kant's opposition to lying clearly put innocent persons at the mercy of wrongdoers.[12]

Furthermore, force has been thought justifiable in all such cases of wrongful threat to life. If to use force in self-defense or in defending those at risk of murder is right, why then should a lie in self-defense be ruled out? Surely if force is allowed, a lie should be equally, perhaps at times more, permissible. Both words and force, as I mentioned, can be used coercively, so as to alter behavior. And even though we need the strongest protection against such coercion, there are times when it must be allowed. Kant's single-minded upholding of truthfulness above all else nullifies the use of falsehoods in self-defense. Can the principle of veracity reasonably be made to carry such a burden?

This burden would clearly create guilt for many: guilt at having allowed the killing of a fellow human, rather than lie to a murderer. Kant attempts to assuage this guilt by arguing as follows: If one stays close to the truth, one cannot, strictly speaking, be responsible for the murderous acts another commits. The murderer will have to take the whole blame for his act. In speaking to him truthfully, one has done nothing blameworthy. If, on the other hand, one tells him a lie, Kant argues, one becomes responsible for all the bad consequences which might befall the victim and anyone else.[13] One may, for instance, point

---

[11]Cardinal Newman's *Apologia Pro Vita Sua*, pp. 274, 361. His book is a passionate defense of his life as a convert to Catholicism, wherein the subtleties of the long tradition of taking up cases of lying are upheld against Protestant critics. See also J. L. Altholz, "Truth and Equivocation: Liguri's Moral Theory and Newman's *Apologia*," *Church History* 44 (1975): 73–84.

[12]Compare James Martineau, *Types of Ethical Theory* (Oxford: Clarendon Press, 1875), 2:241: "Must the enemy, the murderer, the madman, be able to wreak his will upon his victim by our agency in putting him on the right track?"

[13]See the Introduction to "The Metaphysic of Morals" in *The Doctrine of Virtue*: "The good or bad effects of a due action . . . cannot be imputed to the subject" (p. 28).

the murderer in what one believes to be the wrong direction, only to discover with horror that that is exactly where the victim has gone to hide.

There is much truth in saying that one is responsible for what happens after one has done something wrong or questionable. But it is a very narrow view of responsibility which does not also take some blame for a disaster one could easily have averted, no matter how much others are also to blame. A world where it is improper even to tell a lie to a murderer pursuing an innocent victim is not a world that many would find safe to inhabit. . . .

THE ROLE OF CONSEQUENCES

Erasmus, well-acquainted with zealots, observed that a rigid condemnation of all falsehood is simply unworkable. All falsehoods are not lies, he wrote, and the idea put forth by many theologians, that not even one harmless lie should be told to save the bodies and souls of the whole human race, runs counter to common sense.[14]

Chief among those who have relied on a commonsense stance in ethics are the utilitarian philosophers and their precursors in antiquity. They did not accept the premise that God has ruled out all lies. They brought a great sense of freedom to those whom they could convince that what ought to be done was not necessarily what the soothsayer or the ruler or the priests required, but rather, quite simply, what brought about the greatest balance of good over evil. For utilitarians, an act is more or less justifiable according to the goodness or badness of its consequences. Their procedure for weighing moral choice is very similar to ways in which most of us do in fact approach many situations of moral conflict—close, therefore, to the workings of common sense.

Sidgwick, using such a method, assumed that certain lies, such as those told to invalids and children for their own good are necessary. His justification for this position is a consequentialist one—it compares the consequences of lying to those of not lying in particular cases:

> But if the lawfulness of benevolent deception in any case be admitted, I do not see how we can decide when and how far it is admissible, except by considerations of expediency; that is, by weighing the gain of any particular deception against the imperilment of mutual confidence involved in all violation of the truth.[15]

. . . [U]tilitarianism generates no controversies over how to *define* lying. It requires no special leeway for mental reservations in order to acknowledge some deception as justified; it need not define some falsehoods as not being true lies, nor yet some truthful statements as not being duties. Utilitarianism simply

---

[14]Erasmus, *Responsio ad Albertum Pium, Opera Omnia*, vol. 9 (Leiden, 1706; reprinted Hildesheim, 1962), cols. 1194–96.

[15]H. Sidgwick, "The Classification of Duties. Veracity," p. 316 (see Appendix). See also Hastings Rashdall, *The Theory of Good and Evil*, 2d ed. (New York and London: Oxford University Press, 1924), bk. I, pp. 192–93.

requires an evaluation of courses of action, be they deceptive or not. For those, on the other hand, who claim that all lies are absolutely wrong, the precise definition of a lie is obviously crucial.

Utilitarians also differ from Kant (though not . . . from Augustine) in stressing the differences in seriousness between one lie and another. They are therefore much closer to our actual moral deliberation in many cases where we are perplexed. In choosing whether or not to lie, we *do* weigh benefits against harm and happiness against unhappiness. We judge differently the lie to cover up an embezzlement and the lie to camouflage a minor accounting error. And we judge both of those to be different in turn from a sympathetic lie told to avoid hurting a child's feelings. In making such judgments, the difference has to do precisely with the degree to which the lie may cause or avoid harm, increase or decrease happiness.

But, as soon as more complex questions of truthfulness and deception are raised, the utilitarian view turns out to be unsatisfactory as well. First of all, the more complex the acts, the more difficult it becomes to produce convincing comparisons of their consequences. It is hard enough to make estimates of utility for one person, keeping in mind all the different alternatives and their consequences. But to make such estimates for several persons is often well-nigh impossible, except, once again, in the starkest cases. The result is that, even apart from lying, those conflicts which are most difficult to resolve, such as questions of suicide or capital punishment, cause as much disagreement among utilitarians as among everyone else.

A second reason to be wary of a simple-seeming utilitarian calculation is that it often appears to imply that lies, from their resultant harm and benefits, are in themselves neutral. It seems to say that a lie and a truthful statement which achieve the same utility are *equivalent.* Is there not, then, a contradiction between such a view and the principle of veracity? . . . For this principle holds, in effect, that before we even begin to weigh the good and bad aspects of a lie, the falsehood itself is negatively weighted; while such a negative weight may be overridden, it is there at the outset. To go back to Bentham's statement about falsehood,*. . . must it be taken to disagree with the premise that lies are to be negatively weighted from the outset? Not really. For in ordinary life, as Bentham would be the first to agree, falsehood cannot be taken "by itself"; most lies *do* have negative consequences for liars, dupes, all those affected, and for social trust.[16] And when liars evaluate these consequences, they are peculiarly likely

---

*"Falsehood, take it by itself, consider it as not being accompanied by any other material circumstances, nor therefore productive of any material effects, can never, upon the principle of utility, constitute any offense at all. Combined with other circumstances, there is scarce any sort of pernicious effect which it may not be instrumental in producing" (J. Bentham, *The Principles of Morals and Legislation*).

[16]Laurence Tribe, in "Policy Science: Analysis or Ideology?," *Philosophy and Public Affairs* 2 (1972): 66–110, criticizes the tendency in much modern philosophy including utilitarianism to focus on end results only rather than taking also into account "the *procedures* that shape individual and social activity." At root, I believe, the failure to discount for lying reveals such an attitude. See also R. Nozick, *Anarchy, State and Utopia* (New York: Basic Books, 1968), chap. 7.

to be biased; their calculations frequently go astray. Therefore, even strict utilitarians might be willing to grant the premise that in making moral choices, we should allow an initial presumption against lies.[17] There would be no need to see this presumption as something mysterious or abstract, nor to say that lies are somehow bad "in themselves." Utilitarians could view the negative weight instead as a correction, endorsed by experience, of the inaccurate and biased calculations of consequences made by any one liar.

The common assumption that lies can be evaluated on a risk-benefit scale determined by the liar can therefore be set aside on utilitarian grounds. The risks are different from those ignored in the moral vacuum conjured up by Bentham. And the chances for the liar to arrive at rationalizations in secret are unlimited. The long-range results of an acceptance of such facile calculations, made by those most biased to favor their own interests and to disregard risks to others, would be severe.[18]

This stumbling block, though not fundamental to the utilitarian tradition, is deeply entrenched in much actual utilitarian writing on deception. The subject of lying appears there, as it does so frequently in moral philosophy, merely as an illustration. A brief example is given, followed by a quick calculation of pros and cons, with no weight accorded to the lie at the outset of the calculation.[19] The result, most often, is an equally quick intuitive conclusion.

The well-known desert island examples of lying and promise-breaking exhibit this type of quick calculation. They ask what we should do in circumstances where a lie or a broken promise could accomplish a great deal of good, harm no one, and never be discovered.

> I have promised a dying man on a desert island, from which subsequently I alone am rescued, to give his hoard of gold to the South Australian Jockey Club. On my return I give it to the Royal Adelaide Hospital, which, we may suppose, badly needs it for a new X-ray machine. Could anybody deny that I had done rightly without being open to the charge of heartlessness? (Remember that the promise was known only to me, and so my action will not in this case weaken the general confidence in the social institution of promising.)[20]

Such textbook examples are designed to measure resistance to lying and promise-breaking in their own right, quite apart from any harm to the dying man or to society, which can never know about the act. They facilitate clear

---

[17]That part of the negative weight which stems from harm to the integrity of the liar, however, would be hard for Bentham to accept, so long as no *pain* is involved. Mill would not find this so difficult.

[18]D. H. Hodgson has shown, in *Consequences of Utilitarianism* (London: Oxford University Press, 1967), how a utilitarian approach to lying and truth-telling must cause trust in communication to deteriorate. (See reply by D. K. Lewis, "Utilitarianism and Truthfulness," *Australian Journal of Philosophy* 50 [1972]:17–19.)

[19]See, for example, Sidgwick, *Methods of Ethics*, p. 316, and Rashdall, *The Theory of Good and Evil*, p. 193.

[20]See J. J. C. Smart and Bernard Williams, *Utilitarianism, For and Against* (London: Cambridge University Press, 1973), p. 62.

thinking about whether or not we consider the breach of promise or the lie reprehensible. They also provide a vivid illustration of the profound disagreement which exists among us. For in most groups asked to consider the example, a substantial number will choose each of the two answers.

But those who see in this example a vacuum where no one can be harmed ignore the risks to the liar himself of personal discomfort and loss of integrity, of a greater likelihood, however slight, of having to lie again to shore up the first lie; and of a somewhat diminished resistance to lying for causes he may wish to further in the future. Whatever one may decide in the desert island case, then, one ought not to proceed on the assumption that the choice has no harmful consequences whatsoever.

Choices between lies and truthful statements, therefore, exhibit the difficulties often thought to beset utilitarianism as a method for coping with moral conflict. But the problems mentioned so far might in principle be counteracted within utilitarianism. They need not invalidate the general effort to weigh factors in a moral problem. The hard tasks of interpersonal utility estimates may even arise less often than is now thought, once the powerful reasons against most lies are taken into account. The presumption against lying before any consequences in a particular case are evaluated can be acknowledged and explored, and steps can be taken to diminish the bias with which liars judge their choices.

HARMLESS LYING

White lies are at the other end of the spectrum of deception from lies in a serious crisis. They are the most common and the most trivial forms that duplicity can take. The fact that they are so common provides their protective coloring. And their very triviality, when compared to more threatening lies, makes it seem unnecessary or even absurd to condemn them. Some consider *all* well-intentioned lies, however momentous, to be white; in this book, I shall adhere to the narrower usage: a white lie, in this sense, is a falsehood not meant to injure anyone, and of little moral import. I want to ask whether there *are* such lies; and if there are, whether their cumulative consequences are still without harm; and, finally, whether many lies are not defended as "white" which are in fact harmful in their own right.

Many small subterfuges may not even be intended to mislead. They are only "white lies" in the most marginal sense. Take, for example, the many social exchanges: "How nice to see you!" or "Cordially Yours." These and a thousand other polite expressions are so much taken for granted that if someone decided, in the name of total honesty, not to employ them, he might well give the impression of an indifference he did not possess. The justification for continuing to use such accepted formulations is that they deceive no one, except possibly those unfamiliar, with the language.

A social practice more clearly deceptive is that of giving a false excuse so as not to hurt the feelings of someone making an invitation or request: to say one "can't" do what in reality one may not *want* to do. Once again, the false excuse may prevent unwarranted inferences of greater hostility to the undertaking than one may well feel. Merely to say that one can't do something, moreover, is not deceptive in the sense that an elaborately concocted story can be.

Still other white lies are told in an effort to flatter, to throw a cheerful interpretation on depressing circumstances, or to show gratitude for unwanted gifts. In the eyes of many, such white lies do no harm, provide needed support and cheer, and help dispel gloom and boredom. They preserve the equilibrium and often the humaneness of social relationships, and are usually accepted as excusable so long as they do not become excessive. Many argue, moreover, that such deception is so helpful and at times so necessary that it must be tolerated as an exception to a general policy against lying. Thus Bacon observed:

> Doth any man doubt, that if there were taken out of men's minds vain opinions, flattering hopes, false valuations, imaginations as one would, and the like, but it would leave the minds of a number of men poor shrunken things, full of melancholy and indisposition, and unpleasing to themselves?[21]

Another kind of lie may actually be advocated as bringing a more substantial benefit, or avoiding a real harm, while seeming quite innocuous to those who tell the lies. Such are the placebos given for innumerable common ailments, and the pervasive use of inflated grades and recommendations for employment and promotion.

A large number of lies without such redeeming features are nevertheless often regarded as so trivial that they should be grouped with white lies. They are the lies told on the spur of the moment, for want of reflection, or to get out of a scrape, or even simply to pass the time. Such are the lies told to boast or exaggerate, or on the contrary to deprecate and understate;[22] the many lies told or repeated in gossip; Rousseau's lies told simply "in order to say something";* the embroidering on facts that seem too tedious in their own right; and the substitution of a quick lie for the lengthy explanations one might otherwise have to provide for something not worth spending time on.

Utilitarians often cite white lies as the *kind* of deception where their theory shows the benefits of common sense and clear thinking. A white lie, they hold, is trivial; it is either completely harmless, or so marginally harmful that the cost of detecting and evaluating the harm is much greater than the minute harm itself. In addition, the white lie can often actually be beneficial, thus further tipping the scales of utility. In a world with so many difficult problems, utilitarians might ask: Why take the time to weigh the minute pros and cons in telling someone that his tie is attractive when it is an abomination, or of saying to a guest

---

[21]See Appendix.

[22]Aristotle, in *Nicomachean Ethics* (pp. 239–45), contrasts these as "boasting" and "irony." He sees them as extremes between which the preferable mean of truthfulness is located.

*"Never have I lied in my own interest; but often I have lied through shame in order to draw myself from embarrassment in indifferent matters [. . .] when, having to sustain discussion, the slowness of my ideas and the dryness of my conversation forced me to have recourse to fictions in order to say something" (Jean-Jacques Rousseau, *Reveries of a Solitary*).

that a broken vase was worthless? Why bother even to define such insignificant distortions or make mountains out of molehills by seeking to justify them?

Triviality surely does set limits to when moral inquiry is reasonable. But when we look more closely at practices such as placebo-giving, it becomes clear that all lies defended as "white" cannot be so easily dismissed. In the first place, the harmlessness of lies is notoriously disputable. What the liar perceives as harmless or even beneficial may not be so in the eyes of the deceived. Second the failure to look at an entire practice rather than at their own isolated case often blinds liars to cumulative harm and expanding deceptive activities. Those who begin with white lies can come to resort to more frequent and more serious ones. Where some tell a few white lies, others may tell more. Because lines are so hard to draw, the indiscriminate use of such lies can lead to other deceptive practices. The aggregate harm from a large number of marginally harmful instances may, therefore, be highly undesirable in the end—for liars, those deceived, and honesty and trust more generally.

Just as the life-threatening cases showed the Kantian analysis to be too rigid, so the cases of white lies show the casual utilitarian calculation to be inadequate. Such a criticism of utilitarianism does not attack its foundations, because it does not disprove the importance of weighing consequences. It merely shows that utilitarians most often do not weigh enough factors in their quick assumption that white lies are harmless. They often fail to look at *practices* of deception and the ways in which these multiply and reinforce one another. They tend to focus, rather, on the individual case, from the point of view of the individual liar.

In the post-Watergate period, no one need regard a concern with the combined and long-term effects of deception as far-fetched. But even apart from political life, with its peculiar and engrossing temptations, lies tend to spread. Disagreeable facts come to be sugar-coated, and sad news softened or denied altogether. Many lie to children and to those who are ill about matters no longer peripheral but quite central, such as birth, adoption, divorce, and death. Deceptive propaganda and misleading advertising abound. All these lies are often dismissed on the same grounds of harmlessness and triviality used for white lies in general.

Questions

1. In which ways does Sissela Bok say that deceit can coerce people?
2. Is there a difference—that could be of relevance to Immanuel Kant—in the way that lies and physical force can coerce?
3. How would a utilitarian justify a presumption against lying?
4. Under which conditions, if any, do you think that "white lies" are morally permissible?

Autonomy and Benevolent Lies

Thomas E. Hill, Jr.

Thomas Hill examines the question of whether it is ever morally acceptable to tell benevolent lies that are told without any ulterior motives and are rather intended to and do benefit the person deceived without causing any harm. He provides three interesting examples of such benevolent lies. He notes that a number of common grounds for thinking lies to be wrong do not apply in the cases he considers. For instance, these lies involve no breach of promise not to lie and they are very unlikely to be discovered. The absence of these sorts of problems, says the author, enables us to focus on when and how lies can interfere with a person's autonomy. By manipulating the information available to the deceived, the liar closes off certain choices for the deceived. The author argues that although benevolent lies do not always interfere with autonomy, they sometimes do. Moreover, he argues, we should not be too hasty in assuming that a particular lie does not have such an effect. They do impede autonomy more often than we think.

Often it is easy to see what is wrong with lying.[1] Many lies are vicious: they are meant to hurt, and often do. Other lies are self-serving at the expense of others: they gain something for the liar but are detrimental to those who are deceived. Even well-intentioned lies are sometimes discovered, with consequent damage to valued relationships and to trust and credibility in general. Many lies are violations of professional obligations; others are breaches of promise to particular individuals. But there are also instances in which these explanations do not seem to apply and yet the lie is still not beyond moral question. We feel that

---

[1] I have had the benefit of helpful comments and criticisms from a number of students and colleagues, most notably Robert Adams, Gregory Kavka, Warren Quinn, a U.C.L.A. Law and Philosophy discussion group, and colloquium participants at the University of Utah and the University of California, Santa Barbara.

Thomas E. Hill, Jr., "Autonomy and Benevolent Lies," *Journal of Value Inquiry,* Vol 18, 1984. Copyright 1984. Reprinted by permission of Kluwer Academic Publishers.

there is at least something to be said against lying even then, but it is not obvious what this is. No promises or professional commitments are at stake; no harmful consequences are intended or expected; and yet the lie still seems at least *prima facie* objectionable. We naturally wonder, "why"? To rest the matter with the intuitive remark that truth-telling is always a *prima facie* obligation is hardly satisfying. To say that killing, maiming, and causing pain are *prima facie* wrong may arouse no further questions; but why, one wonders, should truth-telling be viewed this way, especially when a lie seems likely to result in more good than harm?

At least a partial answer, I suggest, is that lies often reflect inadequate respect for the autonomy of the person who is deceived. . . .

A former teacher related to me the following true story (which I have modified slightly). He had a student who showed in tutorial conversations signs of deep, suicidal depression. The student was later found dead, and the circumstances were such that others could easily have seen his death as accidental. The professor helped to gather up the boy's belongings to return to his mother, and no suicide note was found. But the mother, a devout Roman Catholic, was deeply worried about her son's soul, and she asked the professor point blank whether he had any reason to suspect suicide. The professor, an atheist, wanted to comfort her and so, by a quite deliberate lie, assured her that, as far as he knew, the boy had been in good spirits.

Another true story concerns a doctor who discovered that his mother, a very elderly but happy woman, had extremely advanced atheriosclerosis. Her doctor had apparently chosen to treat the problem as best he could without informing the woman how near death she was. The son had no objection to the medical treatment or her doctor's decision to withhold information. Though he thought his mother psychologically and physically capable of handling the truth, he believed that her last days would be happier if she did not know. The problem arose when she asked her son directly, "Do you think the doctor is telling me everything?" The son lied; but since the question concerned his opinion and he had learned of her condition in ways she did not suspect and without anyone else knowing that he knew, he felt confident that she would never discover his lie. He lied to make her more comfortable, and she was in fact happy until her death.

Consider, lastly, a dilemma which could occur even if it has not. Mary has made a painful break from her ex-lover, John, and though pulled towards him, is on the mend. Her roommate is pleased for her, as she knows that John and Mary were, and will remain, painfully incompatible. She is fearful, though, that John and Mary will get together again, causing both unnecessary misery before the inevitable final separation. Overhearing John talking with a friend, she learns that John is ready to "start over" if only he receives an encouraging sign; and she expects that Mary, ever the optimist, would give the sign. Later Mary asks the roommate, "Do you think he would want to try again if I asked him?" As an act of kindness, the roommate replies, "No, I am sure he knows it would never work."

These examples illustrate the special sort of benevolent lies I want to consider. The lies are benevolent because they are intended to benefit the person deceived, for no ulterior motives, and they actually succeed in giving comfort without causing pain. Despite the benevolent motives, there is no denying that deliberate lies were told. We are not dealing with examples of mere silence, evasion, ambiguous response, and the like. The lies, moreover, are not designed to protect incompetents from truths beyond their capacities to handle sanely and responsibly. In our sample cases a lie will protect someone from avoidable pain, but it is not needed to prevent serious physical or psychological damage, violent outbursts, gross misperception of reality, and so on.

Our examples also fall outside a range of special problem situations. Some lies, for example, are told in a context where the liar has rather little chance of being believed; but in our cases there is sufficient credibility to make the deception effective. Other lies concern matters which are, intuitively, "none of the business" of the questioner: for example, a lie told to a curious student who asked his teacher about his private sex life. But the questions in our examples are clearly not "out of bounds" in this way. What is asked for is information or opinion about what deeply concerns the questioner's own life. Also the lies in our stories cannot be deemed trivial. Unlike "little white lies," they are about matters of the utmost importance to the deceived: heaven or hell, life or death, reunion or separation from a loved one. Further, our examples concern lies between individuals, not lies from public officials or to institutions, and so certain questions of public responsibility are left aside. Finally, let us imagine that the deceived has not forfeited a right to know, for example, by his own repeated lying or by having a plain intent to misuse the truth.

Lies are often wrong at least in part because they are breaches of a promise to be truthful, but, to simplify matters, let us suppose that there were no such promises in our examples. It is easy to imagine that the professor, the dying woman's son, and the roommate never made an *explicit* promise to tell the truth as, for example, one is required to do before testifying in court. The more difficult matter is to remove the suspicion that they made a tacit or implicit promise to be truthful. Ross maintained that we make such an implicit promise every time we make an assertion, and so he viewed all lies as breaches of promise. But this position, surely, is implausible. Suppose, for example, two enemies distrust each other, have no desire to be honest with each other, and both know this. As seems to be common in international relations, they tell the truth to each other only when they expect that lying will not give them an advantage. In this situation when one asserts to the other, say, that he has documents damaging to the other's political ambitions, we cannot reasonably interpret this as a promise. Neither person believes that the speaker intends to put himself under obligation. Given their mutual understanding, the speaker cannot seriously intend to lead the other to believe that he is making it a matter of conscience to convey the truth. Furthermore if every assertion amounted to a promise to say what is true, we would not think, as in fact we do, that a lie preceded by an explicit promise to be truthful is usually worse than a lie not preceded by such a promise. There are, of course, implicit promises but it requires more than mere assertion to make one. Suppose, for example, Mary and her roommate had often discussed how they valued each other's honesty and frankness, and each had on other occasions insisted that the other tell the truth, however painful, and neither gave any hint of reservations about giving and counting on complete truthfulness between them. With this special background we might want to say that they had made implicit promises to tell each other the truth. However, to focus attention away from promises, let us suppose that in our examples there were no such special conditions to create implicit promises to be truthful.

Our examples are also meant to minimize the force of utilitarian considerations that so often tell against lying. Most importantly, the lies in our stories are extremely unlikely to be discovered. It is a moralist's fiction that lies can never remain hidden: perhaps a useful fiction, but untrue nonetheless. In each of our examples a person is asked about what he knows or believes, and if he is determined to stand by his response there is no practical way others can find out that he is lying. Even if the student's mother learns that her son committed suicide, she cannot know that the professor lied; the elderly woman can find out that she is seriously ill, but not that her son lied about his opinion; Mary may learn that John is still available, but she has no way of discovering that her roommate knew. There is, of course, always *some* chance, however remote, that those who lie will give themselves away; for example, they may talk in their sleep. If the discovery of the lie would be an utter disaster, then from a utilitarian point of view even this very small risk might not be warranted. But to simplify, let us suppose that in our cases discovery would not be disastrous. The persons deceived, let us say, have an unusually forgiving and trusting nature. If they realized the special circumstances and benevolent intent, they would forgive the lie; and, though disappointed, they would not become unreasonably suspicious and distrustful. Again, typical lies tend to multiply, one lie calling for another and each lie making successive ones easier; but we can imagine this not to be so in our example. Our professor, doctor/son, and roommate, let us suppose, are of firm character and would lie only in the special circumstances we have defined, and they do not need an entangled web of further deception to hide the first.

Lies of the sort pictured here are no doubt rare; but, by minimizing the usual considerations of utility and promises, they enable us to focus on other relevant considerations, which may be important in more typical cases as well. In particular, we can reflect on how lies can fail to respect persons' autonomy. . . .

Let us say that persons have autonomy, or live autonomously, in a final sense if the following is true: (1) they have the psychological capacities for rational decision making which are associated with autonomy; (2) they actually use these capacities when they face important choice situations; (3) they have the right of autonomy discussed previously, i.e. a right to make morally and legally permissible decisions about matters deeply affecting their own lives free from threats and manipulation by others; (4) other people actually respect this right as well as their other rights; (5) they are able and disposed to have distinctly human values; (6) others respect this capacity by not presuming that they value only good experiences for themselves and by not counting their comfort more important than their declared values; and, finally, (7) they have ample opportunities to make use of these conditions in living a life over which they have a high degree of control. . . .

. . . The ideal of developing the psychological capacities associated with autonomy may give some reason to hesitate to tell lies to protect people from painful realities, but not a reason that applies in all cases. Probably, as a rule, having to face unpleasant truths about matters deeply affecting one's life helps one to develop the capacity for mature, reflective decision making. If so, there would be a general presumption against benevolent lies, even if it would not always be persuasive as, for example, when we are dealing with the very elderly whose capacities have presumably already been developed as much as they will be.

If we believe in the *right* of autonomy, however, we have more reason to object to benevolent lies. This is most obvious in our example of the roommate lying to keep her friend from re-uniting with her ex-lover. The roommate manipulates her friend's decision (to call or not to call her "ex"-) by actively concealing pertinent information. If we accept the right of autonomy, this could only be justified if the reunion would have been so great a disaster that the right is over-ridden. In other cases the right of autonomy may be violated but in a less obvious way. The professor and the doctor/son, for example, did not lie in order to control the decisions of the people they deceived; they only wanted to spare them avoidable pain. Nevertheless, there were important, life-altering decisions which the deceived might have made if they had not been deprived of relevant information; and surely the professor and the doctor/son knew this. They knowingly prevented certain options presented by the real situation from ever being faced by the people they deceived: to pray or not, and, if so, how; to continue life as usual or to re-order one's priorities; to face death and tragedy stoically or to be open in a new way with friends.

Someone may object as follows: "Sometimes benevolent lies interfere with life-altering decisions, but not always; often benevolent lies merely keep people from suffering unnecessarily because of something which they can do nothing about. When, for example, a widow demands to know whether her husband suffered when he was killed in the war, there is little she can *do* if she is told truthfully that he died in horrible agony. And similarly, if the suicide's mother had been bedridden and terminally ill, the professor's lie would not have interfered with any important decisions."

The appropriate response, I think, is this: Benevolent lies do not necessarily or always violate the right of autonomy, but we should not be hasty in concluding that a particular lie does not concern any significant decisions. Good novelists and biographers know what philosophers too easily forget, namely, that the most important decisions in life are not always about external behavior, about what to *do* in the public world. How we face death, family tragedy, our own successes and failures, and the way others treat us, is partly a matter of decision, as Sartreans knew but exaggerated. Even *whether* to see a situation as success or failure, tragic or routine, is not simply a matter of perception of fact. We can also interfere with these life-altering decisions, or prevent a person from facing them, by keeping certain truths from him—even if he is immobile for the rest of his life.[2]

Consider next the principles associated with autonomy as a capacity for distinctly human values. Their implications for benevolent lies depend upon what we know about the preferences of the person to be deceived. Suppose, first, that we have no reason to doubt that the questioner wants an honest answer. His question is in effect an expression of a desire to know the truth. To give him less because we want to spare him pain would be to count his comfort more important than what he himself professes to value more and so would be contrary to our principles.

Sometimes, of course, people ask questions wanting to be reassured rather than to learn the truth. What should we do if we have indirect evidence that the questioner does not really want to know? Much depends, I think, on the nature and strength of the evidence. Suppose, for example, the evidence is rather evenly mixed: the person often shrinks from painful realities but, on the other hand, he asked in a serious tone, he never said in advance not to reveal the sort of fact in question, and the truth is not outside the range of answers he could anticipate. Often when we are in doubt whether a person really prefers what he professes, we can remove the uncertainty by asking further questions; but the peculiarity of the dilemma of the would-be benevolent liar is that he cannot resolve the uncertainty this way. To ask, "Would you *really* prefer the truth even though it will hurt?" is in effect to give away the answer. When faced with such mixed evidence and unresolvable uncertainty, one guided by our principles of autonomy would, I believe, again be disposed to tell the truth; for respecting a person's capacity for distinctly human values implies that, other things equal, it is worse to presume that someone prefers comfort to some other declared value than to presume the opposite.[3]

If there were definitive evidence that the questioner preferred not to learn the painful truth, then autonomy as a capacity for distinctly human values would not be relevant. This would be the case if, for example, the questioner had explicitly requested in advance not to be told the truth in specified circumstances, and then, later, those circumstances arose and ample evidence indicated that he had not changed his mind.

---

[2]Several have suggested to me that opposition to lying in these cases stems from the judgment that knowing the truth, or facing tragic realities, is intrinsically valuable regardless of the pain it causes; but I suspect that theories (such as G.E. Moore's) which make it a duty to promote an objective intrinsic value will repeatedly call for interference with autonomy. Robert Adams suggested that an ideal of autonomy might include *"living* one's own life", e.g. experiencing the tragic realities actually surrounding one, quite a aside from opportunities to make *decisions,* rational or otherwise; but I think that autonomy is so closely associated with the idea of "self-*governing*" that his ideal is probably better classified under some other conception.

[3]This may seem strange if one supposes (mistakenly) that we should give people what they want—truth or comfort, whichever they prefer. But the principle in question was in fact rooted in a different idea, namely, that persons are to be respected for their distinctly human (e.g. non-hedonistic) values. From this point of view, given uncertainty, it is worse to err in supposing that they prefer comfort to truth than to err in the opposite direction.

Such cases, however, are probably rare. Normally even if a person has previously asked not to be told the truth, his subsequent question raises legitimate doubts about his current preferences. Suppose the earlier request was not made in anticipation of a period of incompetence—like Ulysses' request to his crew before facing the Sirens ("Don't listen to what I say later"). Then the would-be liar is apparently faced with two conflicting requests: an earlier request for deception, and a later request for truth. Unless there are independent reasons for discounting the latter, or for not treating the later question as a request for truth, then one might argue that respect for autonomy gives precedence to the more recent request. Other things equal, we respect a person's autonomy more by allowing changes of mind, honoring what he *does* profess to value over what he *did* profess to value.

The many-sided *ideal* of autonomous living will usually give further reason for hesitating to tell benevolent lies. Even if benevolent lies do not violate a *right*, they still deprive people of a realistic picture of their situation. Insofar as having such a realistic picture is needed for genuine rational control over one's life, to that extent the benevolent liar fails to promote an ideal end.[4]

It may be objected that this argument supports the desirability of volunteering the truth just as much as it supports the desirability of not actively depriving someone of the truth; and yet, it might be said, it is counter-intuitive to suppose that we have as much reason to volunteer painful truths as to tell them when directly asked. The ideal does give reason to volunteer the truth, I think, but there are also reasons why lying in response to a direct question is worse than merely not volunteering the truth. There is a general presumption that one should not cause avoidable pain to others, but this presumption is at least partially set aside when the person requests the painful treatment for the sake of something he wants: e.g. painful medical tests. Thus, although there is a general presumption against expressing truths which cause pain, this presumption is at least partially set aside when a competent person asks for truth; but the presumption is not set aside when one simply volunteers the truth without being asked. Thus, though the ideal of autonomy gives some reason for volunteering painful information about someone's life, the case for volunteering is not as strong as the case for telling the truth when asked.

Another objection might be this: "Sometimes we need to lie in order to increase the chances that a person will make his own decisions (and so live autonomously). For example, when my son asked me where I wanted him to go to college, I lied, telling him that I did not care. Actually I wanted very much for him to go where I went; but I figured that he could make up his own mind better if I kept my preference to myself."

---

[4]It may be argued, rightly, that sometimes benevolent lies may promote the ideal of autonomous living in other respects. This might be so if, for example, coping with a painful truth, about which little could be done, would so preoccupy a person that other important aspects of life would be comparatively neglected. Sometimes, perhaps, too much information can also interfere with rational decision-making.

The objection points to a practical problem difficult to resolve in real cases, but it does not, I think, show that the ideal of autonomy unequivocally recommends lying even in the example just presented. *One* aspect of ideal, to be sure, was encouraging people to make their important decisions in a rational way free from inner psychological obstacles such as neurotic need for a father's approval. Thus, if the son in our example was so dominated by his father's opinions that he could not make a rational choice once his father expressed his desires, then one aspect of the ideal of autonomy would urge the father to hide his opinion. But let us suppose, as in our previous examples, the person deceived is rationally competent with respect to his choice problem and so is not a slave to his father's wishes. In this case another aspect of the ideal of autonomy would urge the father to express his wishes: he should make clear both that he prefers his son to go to his old college and also that he wants his son to decide on the basis of what he, the son, most wants. This puts the pertinent facts on the table, giving the son an opportunity he would have otherwise lacked, namely, to choose whether to give weight to his father's wishes or not and, if so, which wish to count more important. By lying, the father would have helped the son make a self-interested choice; but, as we have seen, one's autonomous choice is not always self-interested. To "make up one's own mind" is not necessarily to decide without regard for others' wishes but to decide maturely in the light of the facts about the situation.

So far we have considered ways in which principles and ideals of autonomy help to explain why we view even benevolent lies as to some degree objectionable; but we also have intuitive opinions about which sort of lies (or deceptions) are worse than others. Let us consider, then, whether considerations of autonomy help to explain these intuitions as well.

To consider several factors together, I suppose it is commonly accepted that deceptive responses to questions are worse, other things equal, when (a) the response is a direct lie rather than a merely evasive, misleading, or deceptively ambiguous response, (b) the person deceived trusts the deceiver and was encouraged to do so, and (c) the lie concerns the life of the deceived rather than matters only remotely touching him. The lies of the roommate and the doctor/son described earlier exemplify the first sort. An example of the second, less significant sort of deception might be this: A person asks me, simply from curiosity, "Do you know whether so-and-so is gay?", and, though I know, I answer, "How would I know?"

Now utilitarians will have familiar explanations why the first sort of lie is regarded as more serious than the second; but it is worth nothing that our principles and ideals of autonomy provide an alternative, or additional, explanation. In brief, one's opportunity to live in rational control of one's life is increased when there are people one can unmistakenly identify as prepared to give straight, honest answers to direct pointed questions. If one does not want to know, one can refrain from asking; if the first answer is evasive or ambiguous, suggesting a reluctance on the other's part to reveal the truth, then one can choose to put the question again more pointedly or to back off; and if one does insist ("I want a straight, honest answer!"), then, while allowing for honest errors, one can make important decisions with more confidence that one understands the real situation. To live in a world without people we can rely on in this way would be to live in a world in which we have less control over our lives. Utilitarians often stress the unpleasantness that results when lies which violate trust become discovered, and for this reason our examples were designed to minimize the risk of discovery. But now it emerges that ideals of autonomy not only oppose undiscoverable benevolent lies; they also oppose lies which risk discovery of a breach of trust, for discovery of such lies encourages us to be distrustful and suspicious and so less able to make use of even the honest answers trustworthy persons give us; and this limits our opportunities for rational control over our lives.

These conclusions, of course, are both hypothetical and intuitive: that is, the argument has been that if one accepts certain principles of autonomy, then one has reasons to refrain from benevolent lies. But imagine now an objection from a normative hedonist unwilling to rest the issue on intuitive principles. He argues that, intuitions aside, it is *irrational* to prefer truth to comfort, unless having the truth would maximize one's pleasure in the long run. Thus, he continues, when one aims to be benevolent towards another, it is *irrational* to give him the truth if a lie will contribute more to his total satisfaction.

The objection rests on the common, but mistaken, assumption that, at least when free from moral constraints, a fully rational person would always aim for his most favorable pleasure/pain ratio. But why so? As we have seen, people do in fact have (non-moral) concerns independent of any anticipated good experiences. Some, perhaps, make maximum pleasure their goal; and others do not. What determines whether one is rational is not, by itself, the content of one's aims, but how they are arrived at, how they fit into one's life plan, etc. More plausible than the hedonist's conception of rationality, I think, is that of John Rawls, who defines ideal rationality, roughly, as satisfying certain "counting principles" (means-end efficiency, inclusion, etc.) and then deciding in light of full information about one's desires, circumstances, etc. Given this conception and the falsity of *psychological* hedonism (i.e. that all seek only to maximize their pleasure), then the rational life will be different for different people. For some, maybe, it will be predominantly pursuit of pleasure; but, unless we suppose that all non-hedonistic desires would extinguish when exposed to more information, for many the rational life will include pursuit of other values, such as truth, independently of their pay-off in personal satisfaction.

The principles of autonomy which we have considered, though still ununified in a general theory, point toward a conception of morality quite different in spirit from familiar forms of utilitarianism, hedonistic and otherwise. The latter start with views about what is intrinsically valuable as an end, and then define morality, in one way or another, as what promotes this end. A theory of autonomy, following Kant, Rawls, and others, would first define principles for moral institutions and personal interactions, leaving each person, within these constraints, the freedom to choose and pursue whatever ends they will. Such a theory would not oppose benevolent lies on the ground that truth-telling will maximize some intrinsic value other than pleasure (e.g. self-awareness); rather, it would encourage truthfulness as, in general, a way of respecting people as free to choose their own ends.

Questions

1. Can you think of different situations in which considerations of autonomy would or would not render the telling of benevolent lies permissible?
2. Are all benevolent lies that do not interfere with autonomy morally acceptable?
3. What is the possible objection from the normative hedonist which Thomas Hill considers? What is the author's response to it?

Suggestions for Further Reading on Lying

BOK, SISSELA. *Lying*, Hassocks Sussex, England: Harvester Press, 1978.

CHISHOLM, RODERICK and THOMAS FEEHAN. "The Intent to Deceive." *Journal of Philosophy* 74, no. 3 (March 1977): pp. 143–159.

FRANKFURT, HARRY G. "On Bullshit." In *The Importance of What We Care About: Philosophical Essays*, Cambridge: Cambridge University Press, 1988: pp. 117–133.

KORSGAARD, CHRISTINE M. "The Right to Lie: Kant on Dealing with Evil." *Philosophy and Public Affairs* 15, no. 4 (Fall 1986): pp. 325–349.

KUPFER, JOSEPH. "The Moral Presumption against Lying." *Review of Metaphysics* 36 (September 1982): pp. 103–126.

MCMAHON, CHRISTOPHER. "Openness," *Canadian Journal of Philosophy* 20, no. 1 (March 1990): pp. 29–46.

RACHELS, JAMES. "Absolute Rules and the Duty Not to Lie." *The Elements of Moral Philosophy*. 3rd ed. Boston: McGraw-Hill, 1999: pp. 125–128.

PART TWO

Sex

CHAPTER 5

Premarital Sex, Promiscuity, and Masturbation

VINCENT C. PUNZO, Morality and Human Sexuality

FREDERICK ELLISTON, In Defense of Promiscuity

ALAN SOBLE, Masturbation

Morality and Human Sexuality

Vincent C. Punzo

Vincent Punzo argues against sex that takes place between people who have not made the deepest of commitments to one another. His argument, he states, will have no appeal to anybody who thinks that morality is only about avoiding harm. He says that it may be acceptable, however, to those who accept the notion of what he calls the "morality of aspiration," by which he means "the positive attempt to live up to what is best" in humans.

He argues that there is a morally significant difference between sex and other human activities. Sexual intercourse, he says, is "as intimate and as total a physical union of two selves as is possible of achievement." Given this, he argues, it would be odd to think that a man and a woman need give no more thought to whether they should have sex than they do to whether they should play tennis, for example. He sees the sexual union as involving not only the physical but also the non-physical dimensions of the partners. Moreover, he sees the self as being a historical as well as a physical being. He says that people are able to commit themselves

to sharing the future with each other. Within the context of such a commitment, which is what he thinks a marriage is, sex is a way of "asserting and confirming the fullness and totality of their mutual commitment." Those who engage in premarital sex and have made no such commitment "lack existential integrity," argues the author, because they allow a full physical union while consciously deciding not to unite other dimensions of themselves. Those who do this, he argues, treat their bodies and those of their partners as mere commodities, which can be exchanged in the way that things are exchanged at market.

The author notes that his argument is not against "preceremonial" sex—sex before a marriage ceremony. Rather his argument applies to cases where people have sex before having made the sort of commitment to one another that is characteristic of a marriage in its moral, rather than its technical legal, sense.

If one sees man's moral task as being simply that of not harming anyone, that is if one sees this task in purely negative

terms, he will certainly not accept the argument to be presented in the following
section. However, if one accepts the notion
of the morality of aspiration, if one accepts
the view that man's moral task involves
the positive attempt to live up to what is
best in man, to give reality to what he sees
to be the perfection of himself as a human
subject, the argument may be acceptable.

SEXUALITY AND THE HUMAN SUBJECT

[Prior discussion] has left us with the question as to whether sexual intercourse is a type of activity that is similar to choosing a dinner from a menu. This question is of utmost significance in that one's view of the morality of premarital intercourse seems to depend on the significance that one gives to the sexual encounter in human life. Those such as [John] Wilson and [Eustace] Chesser who see nothing immoral about the premarital character of sexual intercourse seem to see sexual intercourse as being no different from myriad of other purely aesthetic matters. This point is seen in Chesser's questioning of the reason for demanding permanence in the relationship of sexual partners when we do not see such permanence as being important to other human relationships.[1] It is also seen in his asking why we raise a moral issue about premarital coition when two people may engage in it, with the resulting social and psychological consequences being no different than if they had gone to a movie.[2]

Wilson most explicitly makes a case for the view that sexual intercourse does not differ significantly from other human activities. He holds that people think that there is a logical difference between the question "Will you engage in sexual intercourse with me?" and the question, "Will you play tennis with me?" only because they are influenced by the acquisitive character of contemporary society.[3] Granted that the two questions may be identical from the purely formal perspective of logic, the ethician must move beyond this perspective to a consideration of their content. Men and women find themselves involved in many different relationships: for example, as buyer-seller, employer-employee, teacher-student, lawyer-client, and partners or competitors in certain games such as tennis or bridge. Is there any morally significant difference between these relationships and sexual intercourse? We cannot examine all the possible relationships into which a man and woman can enter, but we will consider the employer-employee relationship in order to get some perspective on the distinctive character of the sexual relationship.

A man pays a woman to act as his secretary. What rights does he have over her in such a situation? The woman agrees to work a certain number of hours

---

[1]Eustace Chesser, *Unmarried Love* (New York: Pocket Books, 1965), p. 29.
[2]*Ibid.*, pp. 35–36, see also p. 66.
[3]John Wilson, *Logic and Sexual Morality* (Baltimore, Md.: Penguin Books, 1965). See footnote 1, p. 67.

during the day taking dictation, typing letters, filing reports, arranging appointments and flight schedules, and greeting clients and competitors. In short, we can say that the man has rights to certain of the woman's services or skills. The use of the word "services" may lead some to conclude that this relationship is not significantly different from the relationship between a prostitute and her client in that the prostitute also offers her "services."

It is true that we sometimes speak euphemistically of a prostitute offering her services to a man for a sum of money, but if we are serious about our quest for the difference between the sexual encounter and other types of human relationships, it is necessary to drop euphemisms and face the issue directly. The man and woman who engage in sexual intercourse are giving their bodies, the most intimate physical expression of themselves, over to the other. Unlike the man who plays tennis with a woman, the man who has sexual relations with her has literally entered her. A man and woman engaging in sexual intercourse have united themselves as intimately and as totally as is physically possible for two human beings. Their union is not simply a union of organs, but is as intimate and as total a physical union of two selves as is possible of achievement. Granted the character of this union, it seems strange to imply that there is no need for a man and a woman to give any more thought to the question of whether they should engage in sexual intercourse than to the question of whether they should play tennis.

In opposition to Wilson, I think that it is the acquisitive character of our society that has blinded us to the distinction between the two activities. Wilson's and Chesser's positions seem to imply that exactly the same moral considerations ought to apply to a situation in which a housewife is bartering with a butcher for a few pounds of pork chops and the situation in which two human beings are deciding whether sexual intercourse ought to be an ingredient of their relationship. So long as the butcher does not put his thumb on the scale in the weighing process, so long as he is truthful in stating that the meat is actually pork, so long as the woman pays the proper amount with the proper currency, the trade is perfectly moral. Reflecting on sexual intercourse from the same sort of economic perspective, one can say that so long as the sexual partners are truthful in reporting their freedom from contagious venereal diseases and so long as they are truthful in reporting that they are interested in the activity for the mere pleasure of it or to try out their sexual techniques, there is nothing immoral about such activity. That in the one case pork chops are being exchanged for money whereas in the other the decision concerns the most complete and intimate merging of one's self with another makes no difference to the moral evaluation of the respective cases.

It is not surprising that such a reductionistic outlook should pervade our thinking on sexual matters, since in our society sexuality is used to sell everything from shave cream to underarm deodorants, to soap, to mouthwash, to cigarettes, and to automobiles. Sexuality has come to play so large a role in our commercial lives that it is not surprising that our sexuality should itself come to be treated as a commodity governed by the same moral rules that govern any other economic transaction.

Once sexuality is taken out of this commercial framework, once the character of the sexual encounter is faced directly and squarely, we will come to see that Doctor Mary Calderone has brought out the type of questions that ought to be asked by those contemplating the introduction of sexual intercourse into their relationships: "How many times, and how casually, are you willing to invest a portion of your total self, and to be the custodian of a like investment from the other person, without the sureness of knowing that these investments are being made for keeps?"[4] These questions come out of the recognition that the sexual encounter is a definitive experience, one in which the physical intimacy and merging involves also a merging of the nonphysical dimensions of the partners. With these questions, man moves beyond the negative concern with avoiding his or another's physical and psychological harm to the question of what he is making of himself and what he is contributing to the existential formation of his partner as a human subject.

If we are to make a start toward responding to Calderone's questions we must cease talking about human selfhood in abstraction. The human self is an historical as well as a physical being. He is a being who is capable of making at least a portion of his past an object of his consciousness and thus is able to make this past play a conscious role in his present and in his looking toward the future. He is also a being who looks to the future, who faces tomorrow with plans, ideals, hopes, and fears. The very being of a human self involves his past and his movement toward the future. Moreover, the human self is not completely shut off in his own past and future. Men and women are capable of consciously and purposively uniting themselves in a common career and venture. They can commit themselves to sharing the future with another, sharing it in all its aspects—in its fortunes and misfortunes, in its times of happiness and times of tragedy. Within the lives of those who have so committed themselves to each other, sexual intercourse is a way of asserting and confirming the fullness and totality of their mutual commitment.

Unlike those who have made such a commitment and who come together in the sexual act in the fullness of their selfhood, those who engage in premarital sexual unions and who have made no such commitment act as though they can amputate their bodily existence and the most intimate physical expression of their selfhood from their existence as historical beings. Granting that there may be honesty on the verbal level in that two people engaging in premarital intercourse openly state that they are interested only in the pleasure of the activity, the fact remains that such unions are morally deficient because they lack existential integrity in that there is a total merging and union on a physical level, on the one hand, and a conscious decision not to unite any other dimension of themselves, on the other hand. Their sexual union thus involves a "depersonalization" of their bodily existence, an attempt to cut off the most intimate physical expression of their respective selves from their very selfhood. The mutual agreement of premarital sex partners is an agreement to merge with

---

[4]Mary Steichen Calderone, "The Case for Chastity," *Sex in America,* ed. by Henry Anatole Grunwald (New York: Bantam Books, 1964), p. 147.

the other not as a self, but as a body which one takes unto oneself, which one possesses in a most intimate and total fashion for one's own pleasure or designs, allowing the other to treat oneself in the same way. It may be true that no physical or psychological harm may result from such unions, but such partners have failed to existentially incorporate human sexuality, which is at the very least the most intimate physical expression of the human self, into the character of this selfhood.

In so far as premarital sexual unions separate the intimate and total physical union that is sexual intercourse from any commitment to the self in his historicity, human sexuality, and consequently the human body, have been fashioned into external things or objects to be handed over totally to someone else, whenever one feels that he can get possession of another's body, which he can use for his own purposes.[5] The human body has thus been treated no differently from the pork chops spoken of previously or from any other object or commodity, which human beings exchange and haggle over in their day-to-day transactions. One hesitates to use the word that might be used to capture the moral value that has been sacrificed in premarital unions because in our day the word has taken on a completely negative meaning at best, and, at worst, it has become a word used by "sophisticates" to mock or deride certain attitudes toward human sexuality. However, because the word "chastity" has been thus abused is no reason to leave it in the hands of those who have misrepresented the human value to which it gives expression.

The chaste person has often been described as one intent on denying his sexuality. The value of chastity as conceived in this section is in direct opposition to this description. It is the unchaste person who is separating himself from his sexuality, who is willing to exchange human bodies as one would exchange money for tickets to a baseball game—honestly and with no commitment of self to self. Against this alienation of one's sexuality from one's self, an alienation that makes one's sexuality an object, which is to be given to another in exchange for his objectified sexuality, chastity affirms the integrity of the self in his bodily and historical existence. The sexuality of man is seen as an integral part of his subjectivity. Hence, the chaste man rejects depersonalized sexual relations as a reduction of man in his most intimate physical being to the status of an object or pure instrument for another. He asserts that man is a subject and end in himself, not in some trans-temporal, nonphysical world, but in the historical-physical world in which he carries on his moral task and where he finds his fellow man. He will not freely make of himself in his bodily existence a thing to be handed over to another's possession, nor will he ask that another treat his own body in this way. The total physical intimacy of sexual intercourse will be an expression of total union with the other self on all levels of their beings. Seen from this perspective, chastity is one aspect of man's attempt to attain existential integrity, to accept his body as a dimension of his total personality.

---

[5] The psychoanalyst Rollo May makes an excellent point in calling attention to the tendency in contemporary society to exploit the human body as if it were only a machine. Rollo May, "The New Puritanism," *Sex in America*, pp. 161–164.

In concluding this section, it should be noted that I have tried to make a case against the morality of premarital sexual intercourse even in those cases in which the partners are completely honest with each other. There is reason to question whether the complete honesty, to which those who see nothing immoral in such unions refer, is as a matter of fact actually found very often among premarital sex partners. We may well have been dealing with textbook cases which present these unions in their best light. One may be pardoned for wondering whether sexual intercourse often occurs under the following conditions: "Hello, my name is Josiah. I am interested in having a sexual experience with you. I can assure you that I am good at it and that I have no communicable disease. If it sounds good to you and if you have taken the proper contraceptive precautions, we might have a go at it. Of course, I want to make it clear to you that I am interested only in the sexual experience and that I have no intention of making any long-range commitment to you." If those who defend the morality of premarital sexual unions so long as they are honestly entered into think that I have misrepresented what they mean by honesty, then they must specify what they mean by an honest premarital union. . . .

MARRIAGE AS A TOTAL HUMAN COMMITMENT

The preceding argument against the morality of premarital sexual unions was not based on the view that the moral character of marriage rests on a legal certificate or on a legal or religious ceremony. The argument was not directed against "preceremonial" intercourse, but against premarital intercourse. Morally speaking, a man and woman are married when they make the mutual and total commitment to share the problems and prospects of their historical existence in the world. . . .

. . . A total commitment to another means a commitment to him in his historical existence. Such a commitment is not simply a matter of words or of feelings, however strong. It involves a full existential sharing on the part of two beings of the burdens, opportunities, and challenges of their historical existence.

Granted the importance that the character of their commitment to each other plays in determining the moral quality of a couple's sexual encounter, it is clear that there may be nothing immoral in the behavior of couples who engage in sexual intercourse before participating in the marriage ceremony. For example, it is foolish to say that two people who are totally committed to each other and who have made all the arrangements to live this commitment are immoral if they engage in sexual intercourse the night before the marriage ceremony. Admittedly this position can be abused by those who have made a purely verbal commitment, a commitment which will be carried out in some vague and ill-defined future. At some time or other, they will unite their two lives totally by setting up house together and by actually undertaking the task of meeting the economic, social, legal, medical responsibilities that are involved in living this commitment. Apart from the reference to a vague and amorphous future time when they will share the full responsibility for each other, their commitment presently realizes itself in going to dances, sharing a box of popcorn at Saturday night movies, and sharing their bodies whenever they can do so without taking too great a risk of having the girl become pregnant.

Having acknowledged that the position advanced in this section can be abused by those who would use the word "commitment" to rationalize what is an interest only in the body of the other person, it must be pointed out that neither the ethician nor any other human being can tell two people whether they actually have made the commitment that is marriage or are mistaking a "warm glow" for such a commitment. There comes a time when this issue falls out of the area of moral philosophy and into the area of practical wisdom. . . .

The characterization of marriage as a total commitment between two human beings may lead some to conclude that the marriage ceremony is a wholly superfluous affair. It must be admitted that people may be morally married without having engaged in a marriage ceremony. However, to conclude from this point that the ceremony is totally meaningless is to lose sight of the social character of human beings. The couple contemplating marriage do not exist in a vacuum, although there may be times when they think they do. Their existences reach out beyond their union to include other human beings. By making their commitment a matter of public record, by solemnly expressing it before the law and in the presence of their respective families and friends and, if they are religious people, in the presence of God and one of his ministers, they sink the roots of their commitment more deeply and extensively in the world in which they live, thus taking steps to provide for the future growth of their commitment to each other. The public expression of this commitment makes it more fully and more explicitly a part of a couple's lives and of the world in which they live. . . .

Questions

1. Vincent Punzo thinks that the sexual union involves not only the physical but also the non-physical aspects of the partners. Does he offer any arguments for this claim? If somebody denied it, and thought that sex can be only physical, what effect would this have on the author's argument for the wrongfulness of premarital sex?

2. Although the author speaks about sex between a man and a woman, could his arguments about the nature of marital sex not apply equally well to two people of the same sex who have made a marital commitment to each other?

3. Is premarital oral-genital contact premarital *sex*? Is premarital touching of another's genitals or breasts premarital *sex*? Is premarital kissing premarital *sex*? What is sex?

In Defense of Promiscuity

Frederick A. Elliston

Frederick Elliston offers a qualified defense of promiscuity: he thinks that for some people, some of the time, promiscuity is a good thing. He first considers and points to shortcomings of some existing definitions before offering a definition of his own. On his view promiscuity is sex with a series of other adults, not directly related through marriage, with no commitments.

He then raises and rejects various arguments against promiscuity: (1) that promiscuous sex should be prohibited in order that children should be raised only in a loving and secure context; (2) that sex has two inseparable functions, to foster the physical, emotional and spiritual union of a man and woman, and to reproduce; (3) that promiscuity threatens monogamy; (4) that promiscuous people are untrustworthy and exploit others for their own sexual gratification; and (5) that promiscuous people lack self-discipline.

The author then argues that three models for understanding and directing sexual activities give a legitimate place to promiscuity: (1) the classical liberal model, under which promiscuity can be viewed as the freedom to explore nontraditional patterns of sexual behavior; (2) the model of sex as body language, under which promiscuity can be thought to enhance the repertoire of meanings sex can have; and (3) the existential model, under which authentic sexuality can be thought to require a sexual openness to others that commitments like monogamy restrict.

In concluding, the author suggests that an intentionally lifelong relationship is intrinsically more valuable than intentionally temporary relationships, but he denies that the latter have no value at all.

The Western tradition has been remarkably conservative in its reflections on sexual morality.[1] Whether this conservatism is due to the fact that practically every major philosopher before Hegel was a bachelor male dedicated to the pursuit of some form of reason is a moot point on which I shall not speculate. Whatever the explanation, most philosophers have tended to formulate and resolve sexual issues in favor of the status quo. Perhaps because sexual promiscuity (the only type I shall consider) has usually been a practice widely at variance with prevalent norms, it has scarcely arisen as an issue at all—much less been criticized or defended. Today, however, sexual norms have changed—at least for an increasingly significant number of society's members. This change challenges the philosophers to question the assumptions on which the conventions that regulate our sex lives are based, much as recent political changes have provided the motive for a radical critique of social practices and institutions.[2] My purpose here is to take up this challenge by offering a defense of promiscuity: first, I shall criticize current notions of promiscuity as inadequate and provide my own definition; second, I shall rebut some traditional arguments against promiscuity; and third, I shall defend it in terms of three sexual paradigms. I shall conclude with some reflections on the limits of my defense.

LINGUISTIC FORAYS

What is meant by "promiscuity"? It may be that the word has no descriptive content, but only emotive and/or hortatory force. On this view, to condemn a practice or person as promiscuous is simply to express feelings of disapproval, or to issue a prohibitive "Stop!" This position attempts to resolve the issue of meaning by limiting "promiscuity" to its emotional or prescriptive force.[3] Even this restriction, though, does not eliminate all of the problems. For not all people oppose promiscuity, and hence the intended overtones are not always negative. And this position leaves an important question unanswered: To what kinds of persons or actions does the term apply? Only when this question has been answered are we in a position to ask how we should feel about, act toward, or react to promiscuous people or behavior.

The *Oxford English Dictionary* defines "promiscuous" as: "without distinction, discrimination or order." *Webster's New Twentieth Century Dictionary* adds: "engaging in sexual intercourse indiscriminately or with many persons." The

---

[1] I am grateful to Professors Willard Enteman and Jan Ludwig for suggestions and criticisms that helped to rescue this paper from some of its more egregious errors and confusions.

[2] See, for example, Robert Paul Wolff's *In Defense of Anarchism* (New York: Harper & Row, 1970). Though I shall not pursue the parallels between political and sexual life, I believe anarchy represents a moment in Wolff's account of political obligation analogous to the promiscuous moment in sexual morality: each is marked by a radical freedom that serves as the transcendental ground for subsequent commitments and obligations.

[3] This thesis was advanced by A.J. Ayer in *Language, Truth and Logic* (New York: Dover, 1946), chap. 6, in order to account for the nonscientific (that is, nondescriptive) character of moral discourse. See C. L. Stevenson, *Ethics and Language* (New Haven: Yale University Press, 1944) and R. M. Hare, *The Language of Morals* (London: Oxford University Press, 1952) for subsequent refinements of this thesis.

root notion operative in these definitions is *indiscriminate*, sometimes signified quantitatively, according to *Webster's*.

But this definition is too broad and begs the question at hand. For the promiscuous person clearly does draw *some* distinctions: typically he or she does not derive sexual satisfaction from a lover's shoe or copulate with a dead body or a sibling. In such cases more precise terminology is applied—fetishism, necrophilia, or incest. Even a promiscuous person usually discriminates between things and persons, between living people and dead people, between people who are members of the family and those who are not. Since some distinctions are operative, the suggestion that a promiscuous person is *completely indiscriminate* is too strong.

Similar difficulties arise with *Webster's* numerical criterion: How many liaisons must a person engage in before he or she is promiscuous? Clearly more than one is required; anyone who has made love to only one person cannot (logically) be labeled "promiscuous." But is two enough? Perhaps a person who carries on two affairs would be called "promiscuous." But imagine someone who married at twenty and who remarried at forty, two years after his wife died. Clearly, under these conditions he is not promiscuous. If two is not enough, then increase the number to three and repeat the scenario: married at twenty, forty, and sixty, two years after each wife died. This twice-widowed "Romeo" satisfies *Webster's* numerical criterion, for he has engaged in sex with many (that is, three) people; and yet he is clearly not promiscuous. As more marriages are added it still remains uncertain at what point a person becomes promiscuous. And even if a clear line could be drawn, the question would immediately arise: Why draw it there, for what is the criterion for assessing the number of liaisons that suffice to justify the judgment "promiscuous"? This is a further legitimate question raised by *Webster's* definition but left unanswered.

Of course these examples deal with sequential liaisons, which may be more problematic than their simultaneous counterparts. But I think the basic problem remains: Is a person who carries on two serious loving affairs that endure for a lifetime promiscuous? I think not. Then again, if two are not enough, how many are required and on what grounds?

By these two counterattacks I am suggesting that it is *false* that a promiscuous person is indiscriminate and *facile* to assess promiscuity numerically. But what is it, then, that invites this judgment? More likely the condemnation arises not because such people do not discriminate *at all*, but because they fail to discriminate *according to the prevalent sexual code*. Promiscuous behavior challenges our sexual conventions, thereby giving this label its emotive force and prescriptive overtones.[4]

More precisely, promiscuity violates a very special principle that regulates our erotic life: "Sexual relations shall be exclusively heterosexual and . . . no

[4]What is true of promiscuity is also true of perversion: violations of the operative code tend to make our adrenalin flow. For one explanation of this emotional reaction to unnatural sexual acts see Michael Slote, "Inapplicable Concepts and Sexual Perversion," in *Philosophy and Sex*, 1st ed. (Amherst, N.Y.: Prometheus Books, 1975), pp. 261–67.

sexual activity shall take place outside monogamous unions which are, intentionally at least, life-long."[5] It is this "Western norm," as Ronald Atkinson terms it, that prescribes the *distinctions* to be drawn, the *discriminations* to be made, and the *order* to be upheld in our sex lives, to which the definition in the *Oxford English Dictionary* alludes.

But to say that promiscuity violates the Western norm is still too broad, for so does coprophilia. Though many people use the term in this vague sense, a more precise definition is needed.

Promiscuity is sometimes identified with "free love." This persuasive definition (or redefinition) may induce some to accept this sexual pattern because freedom, like motherhood, is a good everyone is supposed to espouse. But what exactly is the sexual freedom in question? If it means freedom from all sexual prohibitions (including, for example, those against perversions), then this rephrasing is again too broad. And if it means freedom from just the Western norm (which would allow perverted sex within marriage), then it is no improvement. Moreover "free love" is a misleading expression: like everything else, sex has its price—assessed in terms of time, effort, emotional tensions, and a tradeoff of other benefits and burdens.

Promiscuity may be identified with recreational sex—intercourse just for the fun of it. But this definition is disquieting because of what might be hidden under the adverb "just"; and the term "fun" would align the defenders of promiscuity with that "vulgar hedonism" that some may want to reject in favor of a broader conception of the good life. Though when it harms no one promiscuity may be defensible simply on the grounds that it provides pleasure, this justification should not be built into the definition. A more neutral definition is preferable in order to avoid this commitment at the outset and thereby leave open the question of its justification.

Neither the definitions of the *Oxford English Dictionary* nor *Webster's New Twentieth Century Dictionary,* nor any of the current philosophic or popular notions is satisfactory. In view of the failure of these linguistic forays to uncover a viable definition I shall offer my own. In so doing I cross a thin but significant boundary between linguistic analysis and linguistic revision. And conceding Wittgenstein's insight that language is a form of life, the dispute over the definition of promiscuity cannot be regarded as merely semantic.

With these caveats (or concessions), I shall offer the following definition, or redefinition: "promiscuity" means sex with a series of other adults, not directly related through marriage, with no commitments. Let me explain each component in turn.

First, promiscuity demands *copulation*—its *telos* is sexual intercourse. Someone who engages in the rituals of seduction without this goal is perhaps a flirt or a "tease"—but is not promiscuous. Of course not every seduction succeeds. But at least the intention to consummate the relation must be present on all occasions and realized on some. Whether the sex is "straight" or perverted is irrelevant, for these are two different phenomena. One can be perverted and not

---

[5]Ronald Atkinson, *Sexual Morality* (London: Hutchinson, 1965), p. 45.

promiscuous, or promiscuous and not perverted: a lifelong incestuous relation renders a person perverted but not promiscuous; and many promiscuous liaisons accord with the paradigm of natural sex—"the two-minute emissionary missionary male-superior ejaculation service."[6]

Second, *repetition* is essential—the pursuit of a new partner must recur. Promiscuity on only one occasion is logically impossible. If someone is remarkably casual about his or her one affair, he or she may be labeled "superficial" or "unfeeling," but cannot be called promiscuous. Different partners on several occasions must be sought. The *number* of affairs per se does not suffice to delineate promiscuity (the mistake of *Webster's* definition); plurality is a necessary but not a sufficient condition of promiscuity.

Third, both partners must be *adults*. If one partner is a child, then their behavior is pedophilia. If the child is a son or daughter, it is incest. In neither case is it promiscuity. Adulthood cannot be fixed chronologically; it signifies a degree of maturity some teenagers have and some elderly people lack. The other adult need not be of the opposite sex. Homosexuals and lesbians per se are not necessarily promiscuous. Some make significant personal sacrifices to maintain their relationship; though their behavior violates the Western norm, it is not promiscuous, because of the commitment their sacrifices signify.

Fourth, the couple cannot be directly related through *marriage*. It is logically impossible for husband and wife to engage in promiscuity with one another, though of course their sex play may sometimes bear a "family resemblance" to it. Similarly, sex between a brother and sister, even when they are adults, is a different phenomenon. It is possible to be promiscuous with distant cousins to whom one is not *directly* related through marriage; different societies draw the lines for incest in different ways.[7]

Finally and most decisively, promiscuity is *noncommittal* sex. It defies the traditional connection between sex and marriage—not just as a social institution, but as a symbol of a serious, loving, and intentionally lifelong relation. Promiscuity asserts a freedom from the obligation within or without marriage to "love, honor, and obey" and a freedom to engage in sex with any peer who agrees. These refusals to issue promissory notes for affection and support throughout an indefinite future and to issue a guarantee of sexual exclusivity are promiscuity's most significant departures from the traditional sexual norm.

[6]See Robert Solomon, "Sex and Perversion," *Philosophy and Sex*, 1st ed., p. 271.

[7]The boundaries of incest vary from society to society and, indeed, between groups within society. Freud sought to account for these differences in the incest taboo in terms of myth, Darwinism, and anthropology. See *Totem and Taboo* (New York: New Republic, 1931), pp. 249ff. Some have tried to show it is instinctive (see Robert H. Lowrie, *Primitive Society* [New York: Liveright, 1920]). Others explain the prohibition as a safeguard against biological degeneration due to inbreeding (see Lewis H. Morgan, *Ancient Society* [New York, 1877], pp. 69, 378, 424), or as a way of expanding and hence protecting the tribe (E. B. Tylor, "On a Method of Investigating the Development of Institutions; Applied to Laws of Marriage & Descent," *Journal of the Anthropological Institute* 18 [1888]: 245–69), or as a consequence of the prohibition against shedding the blood of one's own totemic group (Émile Durkheim, "La prohibition de l'incest et ses origins," *L'Annèe Sociologique* 1 [1898]: 1–70). For a more recent treatment see S. Kirson Weinberg, *Incest Behavior* (New York: Citadel, 1955).

Is such behavior defensible? I shall now turn to some familiar arguments against it.

REBUTTALS AND REJOINDERS

Several arguments can be offered in defense of the Western norm and hence in opposition to promiscuity. As I shall try to demonstrate in my rejoinders, none are sound.

1. *The Western Norm and Technology.* At one time a strong argument might have been made in defense of the Western norm by invoking the causal connection between sex and reproduction: unless the natural processes are interrupted, intercourse leads to procreation; for the sake of children, on whom society's future depends, promiscuity is rightly prohibited in order to confine sex to marriage, as that secure and loving context within which children can best be raised. As stated, this argument relies on two claims, the first factual and the second normative.

The first premise has been falsified by technology: the advances of medicine have made available reliable birth-control devices and reasonably safe techniques for sterilization and abortion, thereby making sex possible without the risk of conception or birth. Second, the absolute value of the nuclear family as the *only* context for child rearing is at least problematic: experiments in communal living and the increasing number of single parents provide some evidence that the needs of the child can be met either through a plurality of parent figures or through just one individual. Moreover, even granting the risk of pregnancy, despite precautions, and the value of the nuclear family, despite alternatives, the prohibitions against promiscuity would not follow. First, pregnancies can be terminated. With the exception of the Roman Catholic Church, many concede the legitimacy of abortion, at least during the first trimester. Second, even if this option is disregarded, it should be emphasized that promiscuity is *logically* compatible with *some* commitments to one's partner in the event of pregnancy and to the child in the event of its birth. Promiscuity does not preclude such contingent agreements; it rules out only emotional and sexual commitments as a precondition of sex—the promise to love the other exclusively and to share a life completely.

This rejoinder asserts that available technology should be used as a safeguard against undesirable consequences. But "can" does not always entail "ought": not everything science is capable of doing should be done. Some, notably Roman Catholics, have argued strongly against the use of such means.

2. *The Inseparability Premise and Promiscuity.* The Roman Catholic position is that the sex act[8] has two inseparable functions: to foster the physical, emotional, and spiritual union of man and woman, and to reproduce the species. If this

---

[8]To refer to this as the "conjugal act," as the Roman Catholic Church does, is to beg the question of sex outside marriage. This restriction has a long and venerable tradition within Roman Catholicism,

claim were true, then the use of birth-control devices or sterilization and abortion techniques would be prohibited. Promiscuity would then become more hazardous since without contraceptives the risk of pregnancy would be much greater; and it would become less frequent since only *coitus interruptus* and the rhythm method could be practiced to avoid conception. Of course abstinence and masturbation would be alternatives; but to practice them is to cease to be promiscuous.

The most recent defense of this inseparability premise is found in Pope Paul VI's *Humanae Vitae:* to violate the inseparability of the unitive and procreative aspect of sex is "to contradict the nature of both man and woman and of their most intimate relationship, and therefore it is to contradict also the plan of God and His will."[9]

Carl Cohen contends that this inseparability premise is false.[10] First, it has no basis in scripture or natural law, but rests only on a fallacious *argumentum ad verecundiam*. Second, the entailed prohibition against birth control would cause overpopulation and hunger. Third, the fear of pregnancy and the ensuing inhibitions thwart the conjugal love that the Church promulgates. Fourth, the assumption that all sexual processes must be completed is erroneous, for we recognize acts with erotic overtones that rightly remain unconsummated (for example, a father's love for his daughter). Fifth, the integrity of the spiritual and natural is frequently denied without transgressing a divine (or moral) command—for example, eating for pleasure rather than nourishment. And finally, if the Church sanctions drugs to promote physical health, it should permit drugs (for example, oral contraceptives) to promote sexual health.

Though Cohen's six points may not persuade all Catholics,[11] they do provide an impressive list of reasons for legitimizing birth control. Though admittedly his purpose is to defend their use within marriage, this limitation is not demanded by his logic. They serve to justify the use of the technology that severs the causal tie on which the earlier rebuttal of promiscuity depended.

3. *Promiscuity as a Threat to Monogamy.* Like adultery, promiscuity may be judged immoral on the grounds that it endangers one of our society's central and sacred institutions—monogamous marriage:[12] allowing people to achieve sexual gratification while escaping long-term commitments undermines this basic institution in a way that threatens the stability of our society; in self-defense, society rightly imposes social sanctions against the threatening promiscuous behavior.

---

beginning with St. Paul's warning that it is better to marry than to burn in hell. See the following: Augustine, *De Genesi ad Litteram,* Book IX, chap. 7, n. 12; Thomas Aquinas, *On the Truth of the Catholic Faith,* Book 3, parts 1 and 2; Pope Leo XIII, *Rerum Novarum* (1891); and Pope Pius XI, *Casti Connubii* (1930).

[9]Pope Paul VI, *Humanae Vitae,* "Faithfulness to God's Design," issued July 28, 1968, at Rome.

[10]Carl Cohen, "Sex, Birth Control, and Human Life," *Ethics* 79 (1969): 251–62.

[11]See, for example, E. D. Watt, "Professor Cohen's Encyclical," *Ethics* 80 (1970): 218–21.

[12]Richard Wasserstrom considers this point in his article "Is Adultery Immoral?" in *Today's Moral Problems,* ed. Richard Wasserstrom (New York: Macmillan Co., 1975).

This argument rests on two assumptions: first, that promiscuity has adverse effects on monogamy; and second, that monogamy is socially superior to the alternatives.

The first assumption is a questionable causal claim. For despite the recent weakening of sexual taboos, marriage continues to be a popular practice. Even conceding the high divorce rate does not weaken this claim, for many who are divorced remarry—thereby testifying to the value they accord this institution. Consequently, the so-called new morality is not clearly harming marriage. Indeed, two alternative hypotheses about the causal relation between promiscuity and monogamy are equally plausible: by providing for a broader range of sex partners from which to select a spouse promiscuity increases the probability of sexual compatibility within marriage, and hence the probability of a more "successful" marriage (at least according to this one criterion of success—the satisfaction of one need); and by eliminating the need to marry *merely* for sexual gratification (and hence to disregard those other factors that contribute to successful marriages, such as respect, considerateness, shared values, love, and compassion), promiscuity again increases the likelihood of a successful marriage. Perhaps the trouble with premarital unions, trial marriage, and open marriage is that they have not been tried, for the strong presumption that monogamy is the only way to institutionalize our sex life works against such experiments. Freeing sex of the monopoly of marriage could provide for new institutions that might satisfy more effectively the emotional and physical needs of society's members and offer greater scope for the exercise of personal freedom and initiative in creating new lifestyles. Though society once had the right to insist that its members have a "license to procreate," to use Michael Bayles's expression, with the development of new contraceptives it no longer has the right to insist on a license to copulate. Abolishing the demand for such a license by permitting promiscuity may ease the unnecessary and spurious pressures on monogamy, so as to promote rather than prevent healthy changes within this institution.

4. *Lying, Deceiving, and Exploiting.* According to the popular prototype, promiscuous people are unfaithful and unreliable: they break promises, say things that are not true, and use others for their own sexual gratification. If this prototype were true, promiscuity would indeed be wrong, because it would violate familiar moral rules: people are supposed to keep their promises, tell the truth, and not deceive or exploit others. But does promiscuity *necessarily* involve these forms of immorality?

At one time these subterfuges may have been necessary in order to obtain sex and yet avoid commitments. To circumvent the Western norm, which was justified when copulation entailed procreation, those who wanted *only* the "joys of sex" were forced to tease, tempt, and manipulate. Under these circumstances promiscuity is wrong—*not* because it is promiscuity, but because it violates well-established ethical principles. The moral fault lies not in noncommittal sex but in the lies, deceptions, and exploitation to which some *happen* to have recourse in order to have intercourse. Such immoral behavior is only contingently associated with promiscuity; logically, rather than empirically, it is not necessary. In some groups or societies openly promiscuous behavior is tolerated, if not encouraged. When the threat of pregnancy is minimized, sex for its own sake becomes possible, enjoyable, and desirable—thereby making many of the earlier reasons for lying, deceiving, and exploiting invalid. That promiscuity must involve immoral behavior then becomes an anachronism, an empirical claim that is no longer true. Promiscuity per se or prima facie is not wrong. At most, it is the immoral things promiscuous people sometimes happen to do that are wrong.

This defense is complicated by the fact that a double standard is operative within large segments of society: men are allowed to "sow their wild oats," whereas women are denigrated as "loose" or "fallen" for the same behavior. Though this sexual inequality may once have served to protect women who had more to lose through such "sins" (for it is women who become pregnant, and not men), now it discriminates against them. Because of this double standard, promiscuity is to the advantage of males and to the disadvantage of females. Consequently it becomes exploitive in a more subtle fashion: men receive sexual gratification; women receive social condemnation.

This argument invites the initial rejoinder that it is not promiscuity that is wrong, but the double standard. In this case it is not promiscuity that we should abandon, but the double standard that places promiscuous women at a disadvantage in comparison to promiscuous men. However, this response may be too facile, too theoretical in its disregard for the reality of the social inequality of the sexes. Yet, even conceding the inadequacy of this initial rejoinder, this argument against promiscuity on the grounds that it exploits women would not apply to all cases: women immune or indifferent to social reprobation and members of groups without a double standard could still be promiscuous and yet not necessarily exploit others or be exploited by them. Since promiscuity cannot be shown to be wrong in all cases, the charge that it necessarily violates generally accepted moral principles is false.

5. *Personal Emotional Security and Growth.* Peter Bertocci argues against premarital sex, and by implication against promiscuity, on the grounds, that it threatens "personal emotional security."[13] He contends that the demand for sex outside marriage exhibits a lack of self-discipline in people who cannot control their desires, and a failure to show respect and consideration for those on whom the demand is placed. Such undisciplined and inconsiderate behavior places needless strain on the relationship, threatening to destroy whatever values it embodies.

Is it true that a promiscuous person is completely lacking in self-discipline? The ritual of seduction frequently has its own carefully observed logic in the selection of a suitable consort, the finesse of the "first approach," and the rhythms of attracting and repulsing, until the ceremony reaches its *telos*.[14] What Bertocci

---

[13]See Peter Bertocci, *The Human Venture in Sex, Love and Marriage* (New York: Associated Press, 1949), chap. 2, and his *Sex, Love and the Person* (New York: Sheed & Ward, 1967).

[14]For an entertaining description of this ritual see Soren Kierkegaard. *Diary of a Seducer,* trans. K. Fick (Ithaca, N.Y.: The Dragon Press, 1935).

perceives as incoherent or irrational behavior is really a self-conscious refusal to be directed by the Western norm. But promiscuous people should not be faulted for failing to regulate their actions according to a principle they reject.

Does promiscuity entail inconsiderateness? The rejoinder here parallels the earlier refutation of the charge that promiscuity is necessarily exploitive. The fact that some promiscuous people are rude, brusque, or selfish does not establish this logical tie, any more than the fact that some doctors collect stamps establishes a logical tie between medicine and philately. Only if respect is defined in terms of the Western norm is promiscuity necessarily disrespectful. Though such a definition is possible, it would beg the question at hand, which must remain empirical. Acknowledging the other's freedom to engage or not engage in noncommittal sex demonstrates some degree of respect. And at each subsequent stage of the battle of the sexes, its dialectical impetus arises through the joint effort to preserve the other's freedom.[15] The reciprocity of initiatives whereby each person asserts his or her selfhood, presided over by moral rules that embody recognition for "man as an end in himself" (to use Kant's somewhat chauvinistic phrase), provides further testimony for respect.

Does promiscuity threaten what is valuable in the relation? Of course the answer depends in part on what is considered valuable; pleasure, freedom, and respect certainly *need not* be endangered. Bertocci believes that the emotional tensions and guilt feelings that arise from violating the taboos against nonmarital sex will corrode the relation. But this harm can alternatively be eliminated by abolishing the taboos instead, so that promiscuity would no longer count as an infraction and hence no longer generate the strain that it now does. Since the traditional supports for these taboos have collapsed through an advancing technology, abolishing the Western norm is the more rational solution.

It is not promiscuity that is bad, but the arguments that purport to rebut it. These rejoinders to those arguments, though, do not prove that promiscuity itself is morally good, for I have not considered all possible arguments against it. And even if I had, the conclusion would not follow logically: promiscuity could still be bad although no one has formulated a good argument to prove it.

Perhaps promiscuity is neither good nor bad in any moral sense, but purely a matter of individual taste. To categorize it as an aesthetic rather than ethical issue concedes its normative status, but removes it from the sphere of other-regarding virtues. But even granting this move, some critical issues would remain: Is promiscuity in good taste or bad taste, and how does one decide?

Alternatively, promiscuity might be dismissed as neither a moral nor an aesthetic issue but a prudential one—a question of what is to the advantage of the agent within the sphere of actions that affect only him or her. This approach too leaves critical issues unresolved: Is promiscuity to my advantage or disadvantage, and how do I decide? Moreover this reduction of the normative to the

---

[15]In *Being and Nothingness* (Part 3, chap. 3) Sartre transmutes the celebrated Hegelian dialectical battle for prestige between the master and slave of *The Phenomenology of Mind* (pp. 228–40) into the notorious battle of the sexes. The intervening link between Sartre and Hegel is Alexander Kojève; see his *Introduction to the Reading of Hegel*, trans. J. H. Nichols (New York: Basic Books, 1969), pp. 31–70.

prudential seems to disregard the fact that it takes two people (minimally) to be promiscuous—that is, others are involved.

Such attempts to categorize promiscuity presuppose a clarity and consensus on the nature of good taste and personal advantage that is altogether lacking in the literature. So I shall eschew these ways of demonstrating that promiscuity is positively a good thing in favor of a less traditional defense.

PARADIGMS AND ARCHETYPES

Development of a satisfactory sexual philosophy is hindered in part by lack of knowledge: Just what are the contingent ties between sexual intercourse, love, marriage, and the things or activities we find valuable? This difficulty is further compounded by linguistic confusions: the language at our disposal is notoriously vague and radically ambiguous. Moreover these two shortcomings are aggravated by a third: the absence of accepted paradigms for conceptualizing our sex life and of corresponding archetypes to give substance to our ideals. I shall now turn to three descriptive and normative models for understanding and directing sexual activities. In each case, I shall argue, promiscuity plays a legitimate role.

1. *A Classical Liberal Defense.* According to John Stuart Mill's principle of liberty, "the sole end for which mankind are warranted, individually or collectively, in interfering with the liberty of action of any of their number is self-protection. That the only purpose for which power can be rightfully exercised over any member of a civilized community, against his will, is to prevent harm to others. His own good, either physical or moral, is not a sufficient warrant."[16]

Promiscuity falls within this domain of individual liberty provided those who engage in it satisfy two conditions: they must observe some traditional moral rules, and they must exercise extreme care to avoid unwanted births. The conventional prohibitions against lying, deceit, and exploitation serve to prevent harm to others—most immediately to the person exploited or deceived and less immediately, but no less importantly, to others indirectly affected. The second proviso is designed to avoid illegitimacy, abortion, adoption, and forced marriage—not to mention the social stigma of an unwanted pregnancy, unmarried motherhood, or bastardy. Assuming then that promiscuity (as defined earlier) satisfies these two negative conditions, what can be said in its defense?

For at least some of the people some of the time sex is fun. Whatever else may be true of it, at the barest level sex remains an intensely pleasing physical activity. Like the satisfaction of an appetite (such as eating) or the release of tension (such as a good drive in golf), sex is physically enjoyable. Midst the mystification of sex it should not be forgotten that sex is and continues to be sensual; the erotic appeal of another engages all of our senses in a way equaled by few (if any) other physical activities. One paradigm that must be acknowledged by

---

[16]*The Essential Works of John Stuart Mill*, ed. Max Lerner (New York: Bantam, 1961), p. 263.

all is that sex is a type of bodily interaction that can be intensely pleasing. Granted the two earlier provisos, sex is good for this reason, if no other.

This defense does not entail that pleasure alone is good. The underlying hedonism is not "vulgar," to use Michael Bayles's term, for no attempt need be made to reduce sex merely to a sensation of pleasure.[17] A variety of things good in themselves can be acknowledged while still insisting that pleasure as "the joy of sex" is one of them. Insofar as promiscuity maximizes the pleasures that can be derived from sex, it is good; and insofar as the prohibition against promiscuity is a limitation on the pleasures to be derived from sex, it is unwarranted—in a word, "bad."

Despite his insistence that pleasure and pleasure alone is good in itself,[18] Mill himself gives evidence that he is not a vulgar hedonist. In defending his principle of liberty he suggests that happiness is not so much a sensation of pleasure as the full development of an individual's "higher faculties." Quoting Wilhelm von Humbolt with enthusiastic agreement, Mill asserts that the end of man is "the highest and most harmonious development of his powers to a complete and consistent whole."[19] This remark suggests a second defense of promiscuity within classical liberalism: the freedom to be promiscuous can contribute to the full growth of the human personality.

In many areas, such as clothing, vocation, and recreation, the need for experimentation and diversity is recognized and conceded. Mill defends his principle of liberty, not just in the intellectual arena by arguing for freedom of thought and discussion, but in the practical domain with his insistence on the individual's right to form and carry out his own "plan of life."[20] The lack of commitment that characterizes promiscuity is a freedom to explore patterns of sexual behavior at variance with the tradition. This exploration can engage one's "higher faculties" of reason, judgment, and good taste.[21] Promiscuity opens up to each person a broader range of sex partners and practices.

From the standpoint of classical liberalism, then, promiscuity may increase the pleasures of individuals, enhance the cultivation of their higher faculties (happiness in the eudaemonian sense) and enrich society with the ensuing institution.

2. *Sex as Body Language.* The sexual paradigm operative in the liberal defense of promiscuity has its limitations. For though sex is admittedly a form of bodily interaction that leads to pleasure, it is clearly more than that in some

---

[17]See Michael Bayles, "Marriage, Love, and Procreation," from Robert B. Baker, Kathleen J. Winninger & Frederick Elliston (eds.) *Philosophical Sex*, Third Edition, pp. 116–129 (Amherst, NY: Prometheus Books) 1998.

[18]Mill, *The Essential Works*, pp. 193ff.

[19]Ibid., p. 306.

[20]Ibid., p. 307. Mill's insistence on the freedom to create one's own mode of life and his emphasis on individuality and the cultivation of human faculties align him with the existential tradition of Sartre ("condemned to be free"; "fundamental project") and Heidegger (*Seinkönnen*—"potentiality for Being") more than Mill's interpreters have yet recognized. I quoted Wilhelm von Humbolt earlier because he (and Aristotle) may provide the historical link.

[21]Mill, *The Essential Works*, p. 323.

sense. In his papers "Sexual Paradigms" and "Sex and Perversion,"[22] Robert Solomon suggests what this "more" might be: As body language, sex has "meaning" that goes beyond its physical dimensions.

Just as words are more than marks and sounds, sex is more than thrusts and moans, caresses and sighs. Just as verbal language has a dimension of meaning beyond phonemes and morphemes,[23] so body language has a significance beyond the intertwining of two bodies. The sentences and words of verbal languages have their analogues in the gestures and particular movements of body language. As in all language, these latter are subject to rules that demarcate well-formed formulae. Body language has its own semantics and syntax.

This type of language can serve to express feelings, to state intentions, and to issue commands or invitations. An embrace can express genuine affection. A nod toward the bedroom door conjures up a familiar series of events. A sly glance may frequently initiate the rituals of seduction. Of course not all body language is sexual. Canadian Prime Minister Pierre Trudeau's infamous shrug communicates political indifference.[24] A policeman's hand signal issues a legal command. And holding open an elevator door is an invitation to enter something far more prosaic than what a coy smile offers. Meaning here as elsewhere depends on context. What imparts sexual significance to body language is the kind of possibility intimated—namely, intercourse, or some incomplete moment in the dialectical movement toward it.

Promiscuity has instrumental value in that it can facilitate the mastery of one kind of body language. To be in command of a language is to possess an extensive vocabulary, clear diction, and rhetorical devices for conveying meaning. These verbal skills are acquired through social interaction. Sexual body language is learned through sexual interaction.

Sexual experiences enable an individual to develop a repertoire of gestures for communicating desire and affection and of decisive movements that clearly state intentions of love or amusement. People can be moved not only by the things we *say* but by the things we *do*—with them, for them, or to them. Desire and satisfaction can be communicated not only through verbal exchanges such as "please" and "thank you," but through a lingering look and an appreciative caress. To a shattered ego a physical embrace may express far more reassurance than its verbal counterparts, and a kiss may convey desire more eloquently than pleas or poems. The subjectivity of another, their autonomy and individuality, is confirmed in the dialectics of sex: in the reversals of their roles as the initiator and the initiated, the aggressor and the pursued, the lover and the loved, each can experience his or her own incarnate freedom and acknowledge that of the other. Like verbal etiquette, the sexual rituals of flirtation and seduction are subject to rules that prohibit interruption while another is "speaking," that prescribe that each be allowed to participate fully in the conversation, and that

[22]R. C. Solomon, "Sexual Paradigms," *Journal of Philosophy* 71(1974): 336–45; and "Sex and Perversion."
[23]Max Black, *The Labyrinth of Language* (New York: Praeger, 1968). chap. 2, provides one explanation of this terminology.
[24]Those less familiar with the gallic (and galling) tendencies of Canadian politics should consult Walter Stewart, *Shrug: Trudeau in Power* (New York: Outerbridge, 1971).

exclude insults, attacks, and abuses. The observance of this etiquette is an acknowledgment of the selfhood of the other. The acquisition of it is one of the opportunities promiscuity provides.

Strict adherence to the Western norm places our sex lives in a straitjacket that curtails body language to "I love you," the *only* message to be delivered to just *one* person, with *fixed* diction and intonation—until the disillusioned pair have become bored by the repetition.

Sex and eating are frequently compared, since both are appetites whose satisfaction is socially regulated. Consider a society where the following etiquette is operative. Each man is allowed to dine with only one woman. Before their first meal begins, each receives a solemn injunction: "Thou shalt dine with none other, so long as you both shall live." Their partnership is exclusive; no one may be invited to the meal ("three is a crowd"). Only the utensils already provided and accepted by others may be used; bringing a new gadget to the meal is an innovation attempted by many, though (curiously) condemned by all. Throughout the remaining meals the menu is fixed on the grounds that meat and potatoes are the most nourishing foods. The ways in which these meals are prepared and consumed is subject to strict regulation: one is not supposed to touch the food with one's hands; everyone must keep an upright position (it is considered an insult for one to stand while the other lies). Interaction is drastically curtailed: one is not allowed to exchange dishes; one must feed only oneself (for a man to place his spoon in his partner's mouth is a mortal sin). These rules prescribe that each person gratify his own appetite, but in the company of a select other (to eat alone is forbidden, though many do).[25] During the meal a typical conversation consists of compliments—how good the meal is and how agreeable the company—regardless of their truthfulness.

If food and sex were only the satisfaction of appetites, these restrictions might be defensible—though the prohibitions against some changes would still be contentious. However, some innovations, at least for some people, not only could enhance the efficiency of such practices, but could add to their *meaning* as well. To "dine" with several different people can make eating not only more pleasant, but more enlightening too. To vary the "menu" is a safeguard against boredom that not only expands the topic of conversation, but also has nutritional value. To invite a guest similarly intensifies the conversation, which need not dissolve into monologues if considerateness is shown by all.[26] People should be allowed to get their fingers sticky (sex is wet) and to eat alone (masturbation makes neither your eyesight grow dim nor your hair fall out). Sometimes it may be more convenient to eat standing up or lying down: the exceptions of one society may elsewhere be the rule. More interaction can make the experience

[25]Lest the analogy seem far-fetched by this point, it is worth recalling that Kant was one respected moral philosopher who regarded sex as mutual masturbation, salvaged only by the sanctity of matrimony. See Immanuel Kant, *Lectures on Ethics,* trans. Louis Infield (London: Methuen, 1930), pp. 162–71.

[26]The conclusion that group sex is necessarily dissatisfying may be a faulty inference from the failures of its unskilled practitioners who have not yet mastered the complexities of multi-person corporeal conversations.

more significant; for example, switching dishes when the desires are different (to the dismay of many, they frequently only *look* different) provides variety that, after all, is still "the spice of life." If the food is not well-cooked and the company is no longer mutually attractive, admit these shortcomings; such honesty may lead to better meals. Only recently have the stereotypes that determined who issued the invitations, and who prepared the meal and did the serving, begun to dissolve. Exchanging traditional sex roles by allowing the woman to show greater initiative (if not aggression) can enhance mutual understanding and respect by dramatizing what it is to be in the other person's place.

Loosening the restrictions of the Western norm in these ways is tantamount to permitting, if not promulgating, promiscuity. The ensuing changes promise to make our sex lives not only physically more satisfying, but also more meaningful. This second defense of promiscuity has expanded the model of sexual behavior from mere bodily interaction for pleasure to a form of corporeal dialogue. With the third defense, to be offered next, these models are expanded further, to envelop man in the totality of his concrete existence.

3. *Authentic Sexuality: An Existential Defense of Promiscuity.* Heidegger's insistence that Being-with (*Mitsein*) is an essential structure of existence correctly stresses that the human personality is always situated within a social matrix.[27] My world includes others to whom I relate in various modes of solicitude. To this Heideggerian insight Merleau-Ponty adds that sexuality is an irreducible dimension of the being of the self as body subject: the erotic contours of the world reflect my incarnate being as sexual within that *gestalt* that is my existence taken as a whole.[28] Conjoining these two insights yields *eros* as a dimension of all modalities of social existence.

Among the three basic ways to be with others—against them, for them, or indifferently passing them by—Heidegger distinguishes two positive modes of "solicitude" (*Fürsorge*): to leap-in (*einspringen*) is to perform some task for another; to leap-ahead (*vorausspringen*) is to prepare another for their genuine or authentic (*eigentlich*) possibilities.[29] This authenticity stands in contrast to the inauthenticity of everyday life, which is lived under the domination of the "they-self" (*das Man*) and distinguished a lack of distinction in public, anonymous ways of thinking and acting.[30]

This everyday immersion in the commonplace, with its uncritical assimilation of the traditional, is disrupted by the call of conscience,[31] which summons

[27]See Martin Heidegger, *Being and Time,* trans. J. Macquarrie and E. Robinson (New York: Harper & Row, 1962), sec. 27.

[28]Maurice Merleau-Ponty, *The Phenomenology of Perception,* trans. Colin Smith (New York: Humanities Press, 1962), part 1, chap. 6.

[29]*Being and Time,* sec. 26. R. Weber, in "A Critique of Heidegger's Concept of 'Solicitude,'" *New Scholasticism* 42 (1965): 537–60, misinterprets mineness (*Jemeinigkeit*) and the non-relational character of death, thereby generating her spurious paradoxes. For a more faithful but less direct account see J. Macquarrie's excellent book *Existentialism* (Baltimore: Penguin, 1973), chap. 5, "Existence and Others."

[30]*Being and Time,* sec. 27. For an explication of inauthenticity see Ernest H. Freund, "Man's Fall in Martin Heidegger's Philosophy," *The Journal of Religion* 24 (1944): 180–87.

[31]*Being and Time,* secs. 54–57.

the self (*Dasein*) to the recognition and acceptance of its finitude, or what Heidegger somewhat misleadingly calls "guilt."[32] My choices (*Existenz*) are finite: in pursuing one path I must forego its alternatives. My power over the world into which I am thrown (*geworfen*) is finite: some aspects of my situation remain forever beyond my control. And finally, my genuine existence, even when attained, is bounded by inauthenticity: the accommodating and tranquilizing ruses of the mediocre (*durchschnittlich*), leveled-down public life constantly tempt me to abandon personal initiative and responsibility.[33] This finitude is also temporal: my death is the ever-present possibility of my no longer having a world in which to reside, an eventuality certain to overcome me, though the moment always remains indefinite.[34] Authenticity (*Eigentlichkeit*) arises as a resolve (*Entschluss*) to remain open (*Erschliessen*) to this finitude—to be responsive to the summons to guilt and to anticipate (*vorlaufen*) death.[35] In their everyday lives, and indeed throughout a philosophical tradition, people have closed themselves off (a kind of ontological untruth for Heidegger[36]) from guilt and death, hence from that reality that they are and from that totality of entities (*Ganzheit des Seienden*) to which they are inextricably bound.

Authentic sexuality—admittedly a rather un-Heideggerian conjunction—requires a similar openness to others. Commitments are chains that bind us to some and exclude us from others, blinders that narrow down the field of social praxis to a privileged one (monogamy) or few (friendship). To elicit the many facets of the human personality requires a dynamic network of social interaction. Full sexual growth similarly requires a receptivity to the many erotic dimensions of social existence. Promiscuity provides this openness through its freedom from emotional and sexual commitments.

In the Western tradition love has been mistakenly treated as exclusive because it is erroneously thought of as possessive (compare, to "have" a woman), or that in which I have invested my will, in Hegelian terms.[37] But another person (*Mitdaseiende*) is neither a tool (*Zuhandene*) to be appropriated to my ends, nor a mere object of cognition (*Vorhandene*) to be explored. Rather, others are

---

[32]Ibid., sec. 58. On Heidegger's existential notion of guilt see Michael Gelven, *Winter Friendship and Guilt* (New York: Harper & Row, 1972); D. V. Morano, *Existential Guilt: A Phenomenological Study* (Assen, The Netherlands: Van Gorcum, 1973); C. O. Schrag, *Existence and Freedom* (Evanston, Ill.: Northwestern University Press, 1961), chap. 6.

[33]*Being and Time*, secs. 25–27, 35–38.

[34]Ibid., division C, chap. 1.

[35]On Heidegger's existential notion of death see J. G. Gray, "Martin Heidegger: On Anticipating my own Death," *Personalist* 46 (1965): 439–58; R. Hinners, "Death as Possibility," *Continuum* 5 (1967): 470–82; and B. E. O'Mahoney, "Martin Heidegger's Existential of Death," *Philosophical Studies* (Ireland) 18 (1969): 58–75.

[36]Heidegger explicates his ontological notion of truth and relates this to the epistemological concepts in section 44 of *Being and Time* and in his essay "On the Essence of Truth," in *Being and Existence*, ed. W Brock (Chicago: Gateway, 1949). This central concept has attracted much discussion. Ernst Tugendhat's *Der Wahrheitsbegriff bei Husserl und Heidegger* (Berlin: W. de Gruyter, 1970) is perhaps the most noteworthy.

[37]G. W. F. Hegel, *The Philosophy of Right*, trans. T. M. Knox (London: Oxford University Press, 1942), pp. 40–56.

entities like me, with whom I share a world. Consequently love should be construed in Heideggerian terms as a leaping-ahead that affirms another's genuinely human possibilities, or in R. D. Laing's terms, as the confirmation of that which is true and good in another.[38]

The tradition has reversed the relation between sex and love—for reasons that once applied but, as previously pointed out, that are now anachronistic. The nakedness of sexual intercourse is not only physical, but psychological and emotional too: by laying bare not just our bodies, but our thoughts and feelings, two people can achieve a privileged moment from which they may *then* decide what kinds of commitments subsequently to make to one another. Promiscuity prepares for this moment through its "lack of commitment." To insist on an emotional involvement that closes off the future as a condition of this sexual self-revelation to others is, ironically, to frustrate the growth of the very love that such commitments are intended to cultivate. And to insist that this commitment as love can be made to only one other person is to succumb to the ontological fallacy of confusing people with things.

With its freedom from emotional and sexual restrictions promiscuity can play an important role in the achievement of authentic sexuality. This negative freedom-from is a positive freedom-for a genuinely human mode of social and sexual interaction.

CONCLUDING UNSCIENTIFIC POSTSCRIPT

My remarks might suggest that I believe promiscuity is *always* right. But this conclusion overstates my position. The claim I have sought to defend is more modest: for some of the people some of the time promiscuity is a good thing. Such behavior is curtailed by moral obligations to tell the truth, to be honest, and to respect others. It is also limited in time: for some, on occasion, promiscuity may not yet, or no longer, be good. To put my defense in perspective I shall conclude with a nod to Kierkegaard.

Kierkegaard's refutation of the Don Juan complex locates promiscuity as one stage on life's way.[39] Aping the Hegelian dialectic, of which he is both master and critic, he notes that the cause of its ultimate demise is boredom: despite the novelty achieved through the rotation method (varying the fields on which one's "seed" is sown), the full pursuit of the life of the senses ultimately succumbs to a cycle of sameness from which it can be rescued only by advancing to a higher mode of existence—the principled life of the ethical stage.[40]

Applied to the preceding sexual paradigms, Kierkegaard's insight suggests three corresponding resolutions of promiscuity. First, the good sex life

[38]R. D. Laing, *Self and Others* (Baltimore: Penguin, 1971), chap. 7.

[39]See Soren Kierkegaard, "The Rotation Method" (reprinted from *Either/Or*), in *A Kierkegaard Anthology*, ed. R. Bretall (New York: Modern Library, 1946), pp. 21–32.

[40]In his recourse to the rational to overcome the sensual (or the "aesthetic," as Kierkegaard somewhat misleadingly terms it), Kierkegaard's solution to the morality of sex resembles Kant's (see note 25).

cannot be achieved through physical gratification alone. The moral commitment represented by the Western norm is an attempt to achieve the advance Kierkegaard extols: wedded love regulated by reason seeks to overcome and yet to preserve (*aufheben*) the fleeting pleasures of the body. To deny this dialectical movement is to deny one's full humanity, to be arrested at a lower level of existence. Second, it may be noted that what the dialogue carried on through the body achieves in breadth it may lose in depth: having talked with many, we may discover that our most meaningful dialogue can be carried on with one. The commitment to this one person becomes, henceforth, a "natural" way to safeguard and foster this corporeal dialogue. The prohibitions against multiple dialogues were overthrown at the earlier stage so that this one person might be found and now they serve only as superfluous restrictions that need not be enforced to be observed. Finally, the openness of authentic sexuality may likewise achieve a moment at which a full commitment to a single other is its natural fruition; through its own catharsis the promiscuous life may discover a completion in Buber's I-Thou relation.[41] On such occasions promiscuity ceases to be of value in the sexual life of the individual. Indeed, from this point on not to abandon it would be as wrong as the prohibitions against it were at the earlier stage.

From this temporal perspective promiscuity has definite but limited value in the movement toward a sexual ideal. Michael Bayles is correct in his insistence that the intentionally lifelong relationship is intrinsically more valuable, but wrong in his (implicit) suggestion that intentionally temporary relations are of no value.[42] The principled life represented by the traditional commitment "to love, honor, and obey" signifies a higher mode of existence that partially transcends the vicissitudes of time. Whether this ideal is expressed in Platonic terms, as the longing for a love that is eternal,[43] or in Buber's terms, as a full awareness of the other in their unity, totality, and uniqueness, it must be wrung from man's historical existence. The value of promiscuity is located in the pursuit of just such ideals.

Questions

1. Is Frederick Elliston correct in thinking that paedophilic and incestuous sex cannot be promiscuous?
2. How does the author respond to each of the arguments against promiscuity?
3. Do you think that somebody could accept his arguments that promiscuity has some positive value, but argue that it has negative value which outweighs this?

---

[41]I have not tried to develop a notion of authentic sexuality on the model of Buber's I-Thou, though such an interpretation could be provided, because what I find lacking in Buber but present in Heidegger is a fuller recognition of the historicity of such ideals. For a Buberian interpretation of sexuality see M. Friedman, "Sex in Sartre and Buber," in *Sexuality and Identity,* ed. H. Ruitenbeek (New York: Bantam, 1970), pp. 84–99.

[42]Though Bayles does not quite say they are of no value whatsoever, he believes that they are not sufficiently valuable to warrant legal protection.

[43]See D. P. Verene, "Sexual Love and Moral Experience," in *Philosophy and Sex,* 1st ed. pp. 105–15; and his *Sexual Love and Western Morality* (New York: Harper & Row, 1972), pp. 10–47.

Masturbation

Alan Soble

Alan Soble first analyzes the concept of masturbation, examining different views about what it is and what it is not. He concludes that sexual acts, whether solitary or paired, are masturbatory to the extent that the person who performs them attempts to produce pleasure for the self rather than for another. He then shows how some influential philosophical accounts of sexuality suggest that masturbation is not sexual activity at all (Alan Goldman's view), is perverted (an implication of Thomas Nagel's account), or is "empty" (on Robert Solomon's account). Alan Soble responds to each of these. He then argues that male masturbation can be viewed, contrary to the views of some conservative feminists, as an act of "men's feminism." Finally, he defends masturbation against the attacks of the conservative thinkers John Finnis and Roger Scruton, before briefly expressing some doubt about masturbation.

This vice, which shame and timidity find so convenient, has a particular attraction for lively imaginations. It allows them to dispose, so to speak, of the whole female sex at their will, and to make any beauty who tempts them serve their pleasure without the need of first obtaining her consent.
—ROUSSEAU, *CONFESSIONS*, BOOK III

[I]f your right hand causes you to sin, cut it off and throw it away. It is better for you to lose one part of your body than for your whole body to go into hell.
—JESUS [ACCORDING TO MATTHEW 5: 30]

Alan Soble, "Masturbation" in Alan Soble (ed.) *The Philosophy of Sex,* Third Edition, copyright 1997, reprinted by permission of Rowman & Littlefield.

This essay began its life as "Sexual Desire and Sexual Objects," a paper presented at the Pacific Division meetings of the American Philosophical Association, San Francisco, March 1978. It was first published as "Masturbation" in *Pacific Philosophical Quarterly* 61 (1980): 233–44 and reprinted, greatly revised, as "Masturbation and Sexual Philosophy" in Alan Soble, ed., *Philosophy of Sex,* 2d ed. That version was again revised to become Chapter Two of my *Sexual Investigations* (New York University Press, 1996), of which the present version is an abbreviation and modification.

Reflecting on the special virtues, and not only the vices, of adultery, prostitution, homosexuality, bisexuality, group sex, sadomasochism, and sex with anonymous strangers is a valuable exercise. Indeed, when thinking philosophically about sexuality, it is mandatory to compare these practices with a privileged pattern of relationship in which two adult heterosexuals love each other, are committed and faithful to each other within a formal marriage, and look forward to procreation and family. Some people sincerely strive to attain this pattern; some live it effortlessly; the sexual lives of others are more complex, even chaotic. It does not matter whether the privileged pattern is actually a widespread form of behavior or a piece of ideology that attempts to influence behavior. Regardless, the contrast between the pattern and the practices mentioned above provides the material for the conceptual and ethical thinking that is the philosophy of sex.

Masturbation, too, violates the spirit and letter of the privileged pattern: it is unpaired, nonprocreative sex in which pleasure is relished for its own sake. Masturbation mocks the categories of our sexual discourse: it is sex with someone I care about, to whose satisfaction and welfare I am devoted; it is incestuous; if I'm married, it is sex with someone who is not my spouse and hence adulterous; it is homosexual; it is often pederastic; it is sex we occasionally fall into inadvertently ("if you shake it more than twice, you're playing with it"); and, with a Rousseauvian stretch, it is the promiscuous rape of every man, woman, or beast to whom I take a fancy. No wonder, then, that we advertise our marriages and brag about our affairs, but keep our masturbatory practices and fantasies to ourselves. The sexual revolution has made living together outside matrimony acceptable; it has encouraged toleration of homosexuality; it has even breathed life into the practices of the daughters and sons of the Marquis de Sade. But to call a man a "jerk off" is still derogatory. Masturbation is the black sheep of the family of sex, scorned, as we shall see, by both the Right and the Left.

THE CONCEPT

Conceptual questions about masturbation arise when we critically examine the paradigm case: a person in a private place manually rubs the penis or clitoris and produces an orgasm. The salient features of the paradigm case are conceptually unnecessary. (1) One can openly masturbate in the crowded waiting room of a bus terminal, with erect penis displayed for all to see or with fingers conspicuously rubbing the clitoris. (2) The hands do not have to be employed, as long as the target areas are pressed against a suitably shaped object of comfortable composition—the back of a horse, a bicycle seat, a rug. (3) Orgasm need not be attained, nor need it be the goal. Sexual pleasure is the point. (4) The penis or clitoris need not receive the most, or any, attention. There are other sensitive areas one can touch and press: the anus, nipples, thighs, lips. What remains in the paradigm case does seem indispensable: (5) the person who, by pressing the sensitive areas, causally produces the pleasurable sensations is the person who experiences them; the rubber is the rubbed. Masturbation, the "solitary vice" of "self-abuse," looks logically reflexive.

But *mutual* masturbation would be impossible if masturbation were logically solitary, and we have a paradigmatic case of mutual masturbation: two persons rubbing each other between the legs. Further, if it is conceptually possible for X and Y to masturbate each other, it must be possible for X to masturbate Y, while Y simply receives this attention, not doing anything to X. "To masturbate" is both transitive and intransitive; like respect and deception, it can take the self or other as object. Reflexivity, then, might be sufficient but it is not necessary for a sexual act to be masturbatory. But explaining why mutual masturbation *is* masturbation is not easy. Saying that these activities are masturbatory just because they involve the hands and genitals is awkward; we would end up claiming that all solitary sex acts are masturbatory, even those that do not involve the manual rubbing of the genitals, while paired acts are masturbatory exactly when they do involve the manual rubbing of the genitals. On this view, X's tweaking her own nipples is masturbatory, Y's doing it for X is not masturbatory, yet Y's tweaking X's clitoris is masturbatory.

One way to distinguish masturbatory from nonmasturbatory acts is to contrast sexual acts that do not involve any insertion and those that do. The idea is that without the insertion of something, no mixing together of two fleshes occurs, and so the participants remain isolated. Solitary acts of self-pleasuring would be masturbatory for the reason that no insertion occurs (but what about digital anal or vaginal masturbation?); the paradigm case of mutual masturbation also need not involve insertion (but it might, of fingers into vagina); and both male-female coitus and male-male anal coitus would not be masturbatory because they do involve insertion. This view entails that X's fellating Y is not a case of masturbation (which seems correct), it has the plausible implication that coitus between a human male and a female animal (a sheep), or a human female and a male animal (a dog), is not masturbatory (even though each activity involves only one *person* and is, in that sense, a solitary activity—unless mammals are persons), and it is consistent with the not incredible intuitions that frottage in a crowded subway car is masturbatory and that tribadism can be mutually masturbatory. But to distinguish between masturbatory and nonmasturbatory sexual activity by distinguishing between acts that do not and acts that do involve insertion is inadequate, as my examples have already hinted. Consider others. Cunnilingus might or might not involve insertion, in this case of the tongue or lips or nose; to say it is masturbatory when and only when it does not involve insertion implies that one continuous act of cunnilingus changes from masturbatory to not masturbatory and back again often in a few minutes. And what about a male who punctures a hole in a watermelon to make room for his penis, or a female who reaches for her g-spot with a zucchini inside her vagina? These acts are masturbatory yet involve insertion.

Some of these problem examples can be avoided by narrowing what counts as "insertion." Masturbation might be characterized more specifically as sexual activity not involving the insertion of a real penis into a hole of a living being. Then all lesbian sexuality is masturbatory, while many acts of male homosexuals would not be. Were we to decide that a male having intercourse with an animal is, after all, masturbating—that is, if there is no significant difference between this act and a man's rubbing his penis with a woman's panties—masturbation could be defined more specifically as sexual activity not involving the insertion of a real penis into a hole of a living human being. This refined view is literally phallocentric in characterizing sexual acts with reference to the male organ. As a result, the analysis implies a *conceptual* double standard: fellatio, oral sex done on a male, is not masturbatory, but cunnilingus, oral sex done on a female, always is. And an *evaluative* double standard looms when the usual disparagement of masturbation is added: fellatio is acceptable, real sex, cunnilingus is a fraud. This scholastic view (which is sexist but not heterosexist—its point does not depend on the sex/gender of the fellator) is similar to the claim (which is heterosexist but not necessarily sexist) that the paradigm case of natural sexual activity is male-female genital intercourse. What is conceptually emphasized in such a view—the most specific we can get—is the insertion of a real penis not into any hole of a living human being, but into a particular hole, the vagina. This suggests that masturbation be understood as any nonprocreative sexual activity, whether solitary or paired. If so, our sexual lives contain a lot more masturbation than we had thought.

There is usually a clear distinction between solitary and paired sexual activity. But suppose X is having sex with Y, and X's arousal is sustained by X's private fantasies. The act is solitary masturbation in the sense that the other person is absent from X's sexual consciousness. That which would arouse X during solitary masturbation is doing the same thing for X while X rubs his penis or clitoris on/with Y's body instead of X's hand. Even so, the difference between solitary and paired sex is not that between masturbatory and nonmasturbatory sex. But under certain descriptions of sexual activity, no difference exists between the paradigm case of mutual masturbation and two ordinary cases of nonmasturbatory sex: heterosexual genital intercourse and homosexual anal intercourse. Listen to helpful Alexander Portnoy offering his cheating father a redescription of adultery: "What after all does it consist of? You put your dick some place and moved it back and forth and stuff came out the front. So, Jake, what's the big deal?"[1] Adulterous coitus is redescribed, defined "downward," almost as if it were solitary masturbation. Portnoy's sarcasm suggests why there is no essential difference between mutual masturbation and genital or anal intercourse: *every* paired sexual act is masturbatory because the mutual rubbing of sensitive areas, the friction of skin against skin, that occurs during mutual masturbation is the same, physically, as the mutual rubbing of skin against skin that occurs during coitus. The only difference is that different parts of the body or patches of skin are involved in the rubbings; but no one patch or set of patches of skin has any ontological privilege over any other. Further, the difference between solitary and paired masturbation is only the number of people who accomplish these same rubbings.

---

[1]Philip Roth, *Portnoy's Complaint* (New York: Random House, 1969), 88.

A similar conclusion can be reached on Kantian grounds. For Kant, human sexual interaction by its nature involves a person's merely using another person for the sake of pleasure:

> [T]here is no way in which a human being can be made an Object of indulgence for another except through sexual impulse. . . . Sexual love . . . by itself . . . is nothing more than appetite. Taken by itself it is a degradation of human nature. . . . [A]s an Object of appetite for another a person becomes a thing.[2]

Kant is not asserting the physical indistinguishability of mutual masturbation and coitus. Instead, he is insisting that the intentions involved in both activities—to get pleasure for oneself through the vehicle of the other's body and compliance with one's wishes—are the same. But in portraying all sexual acts as objectifying and instrumental, Kant makes us wonder: is not celibacy required? He answers in the negative:

> The sole condition on which we are free to make use of our sexual desire depends upon the right to dispose over the person as a whole. . . . [I] obtain these rights over the whole person . . . [o]nly by giving that person the same rights over the whole of myself. This happens only in marriage. . . . In this way the two persons become a unity of will. . . . Thus sexuality leads to a union . . . and in that union alone its exercise is possible.[3]

Kant is not claiming that the marital pledge assures that even if the spouses are a means to each other's pleasure in the marriage bed, they are not treating each other only as means but also as ends, as persons to whom respect and consideration are due during sex, as well as before and after. Instead, Kant justifies marital sex by abolishing the possibility of instrumentality altogether; he literally unites two persons into one person by marriage.[4] This is to justify all marital sex by reducing or equating it to solitary masturbation, the sex of a single (even if larger or more complex) person.[5]

Kant's notion that the marital union of two people into one cleanses sexuality of its instrumentality apparently has two radical implications: that homosexual marriage would similarly cleanse same-sex sexuality[6] and that solitary masturbation is permissible. Kant resists both conclusions, asserting that masturbation and homosexuality are *crimina carnis contra naturam:*

> [O]nanism . . . is abuse of the sexual faculty without any object. . . . By it man sets aside his person and degrades himself below the level of animals. . . .

---

[2]Immanuel Kant, *Lectures on Ethics*, trans. Louis Infield (New York: Harper and Row, 1963), 162–71, at 163.

[3]*Lectures on Ethics*, 166–67.

[4]"If a fusion of one and the other truly exists, . . . the very possibility of using an *other* as a means no longer exists" (Robert Baker and Frederick Elliston, eds., *Philosophy and Sex* [Buffalo: Prometheus, 1975, 1984], 1st ed., 18; 2d ed., 26–27). Kantian fusion seems to make rape in marriage (a kind of use) logically impossible.

[5]"Masturbation" is thus the answer to Barbara Herman's question, "sex would then be what?" if Kant were right that (in her words) "we become parts of a new self that has two bodies" ("Could It Be Worth Thinking About Kant on Sex and Marriage?" in Louise M. Antony and Charlotte Witt, eds., *A Mind of One's Own* [Boulder: Westview, 1993], 49–67, at 61).

[6]Herman, "Could It Be Worth Thinking," 66 n. 22.

[I]ntercourse between *sexus homogenii* . . . too is contrary to the ends of humanity; for the end of humanity in respect of sexuality is to preserve the species.[7]

Kant concludes his denouncement of these aberrations nastily: "He," the masturbator or homosexual, "no longer deserves to be a person."

Kant has not provided a criterion for distinguishing paired masturbatory
sexual activity from paired nonmasturbatory sex—quite the opposite—but
Kant's thought suggests a criterion that concedes the *physical* similarity of mutual masturbation and coitus and focuses instead on a *mental* difference: sexual
activity between two persons, each of whom is concerned not only with her or
his own pleasure but also with the pleasure of the other person, is not masturbatory (regardless of what physical acts they engage in), while sexual activity in
which a person is concerned solely with her or his own pleasure is masturbatory. Conceiving of another person merely as a means might be a mark of the
immoral; here it is being regarded, in addition, as a mark of the masturbatory.
This view implies that inconsiderate husbands and rapists are largely the
authors of masturbatory acts. It also implies that mutual masturbation is *not*
masturbatory if the touchings are meant to produce pleasure not only for the
toucher but also for one's partner.

This Kantian criterion does not sufficiently distinguish between the definition and the evaluation of masturbation. What seems to be at the heart of masturbation is the effort to cause sexual pleasure for the self—full stop. It is not
part of the core idea that masturbation be solitary; the attempt to produce sexual pleasure for the self can causally involve other people, animals, the whole
universe. That masturbation is logically reflexive—*X* acts to produce sexual
pleasure for *X*—is neither equivalent to nor entails its being solitary. Given the
kind of physical creatures we are, attempting to please the self by acting on oneself is easier, even if not always successful. Our own bodies are handy. Hence
we misleadingly associate masturbation entirely with one form of it, the case in
which *X* touches and pleasures *X*. But the attempt to produce one's own pleasure can involve other people. Solitary and paired sexual acts are masturbatory,
then, to the extent that the actor attempts to produce pleasure for the self; paired
sex is not masturbatory when one person attempts to produce pleasure for another. This notion of masturbation is descriptive, not normative; it neither
praises nor condemns masturbation. That the attempt to produce, and the
search for, one's own sexual pleasure, either in solitary or paired acts, is selfish
or, instead, merely self-interested, or even benevolent (which is possible), is not
part of the core idea. Seeking to produce sexual pleasure for the self is that
which marks the masturbatory, not these other motivational factors that are
more directly relevant to a distinct moral evaluation of sexual acts.

FULFILLING DESIRE

Three contemporary philosophical accounts of sexuality, proffered by thinkers within the sexually liberal tradition, yield the conclusions that solitary

[7]*Lectures on Ethics,* 170.

masturbation is not a sexual activity at all (Alan Goldman), is perverted (Thomas Nagel), or is "empty" (Robert Solomon). These conclusions are surprising, given the sexual pedigree of these philosophers.[8] I propose to take a careful look at them.

Let's begin with Alan Goldman's definitions of "sexual desire" and sexual activity":[9]

> [S]exual desire is desire for contact with another person's body and for the pleasure which such contact produces; sexual activity is activity which tends to fulfill such desire of the agent. (40)

On Goldman's view, sexual desire is strictly the desire for the pleasure of physical contact itself, nothing else, and so does not include a component desire for, say, love, communication, or progeny. Goldman thus takes himself to be offering a liberating analysis of sexuality that does not tether sex normatively or conceptually to love, the emotions, or procreation. But while advocating the superiority of his notion of "plain sex," Goldman forgot that masturbation needed protection from the same (usually conservative) philosophy that obliged sex to occur within a loving marriage or to be procreative in order to be morally proper. On Goldman's analysis, solitary masturbation is not a sexual activity to begin with: it does not "tend to fulfill" sexual desire, viz., the desire for contact with another person's body. Solitary masturbation is unlike mutual masturbation, which does tend to fulfill the desire for contact, since it involves the desired contact and hence is fully sexual. Goldman seems not to be troubled that on his view solitary masturbation is not a sexual act. But it's funny that masturbation is, for Goldman, not sexual, for the conservative philosophy that he rejects would reply to his account like this: by *reducing* sexuality entirely to the meaningless desire for the pleasure of physical contact, what Goldman has analyzed is merely a form of masturbation.

The vague "tends to fulfill" in Goldman's analysis of sexual activity presents problems. Goldman intended, I think, a narrow causal reading of this phrase; actually touching another person's body is a sexual act just because by the operation of a simple mechanism the act fulfills the desire for that contact and its pleasure. The qualification "tends to" functions to allow bungled kisses to count as sexual acts, even though they did not do what they were intended to do; kisses tend to fulfill desire in the sense that they normally and effectively produce pleasure, prevented from doing so only by the odd interfering event (the braces get tangled; the hurrying lips land on the chin). It also functions to allow disappointing or bad sex, that which does not bring what anticipation promised, to count as sex. In this sense of "tends to fulfill," solitary masturbation is not sex. Suppose that X desires sex with Y, but Y declines the invitation, and so X masturbates thinking about Y. Goldman's view is not that X's masturbation satisfies X's desire for contact with Y only, or at least, a little and hence is

---

[8]A notable contrast is Russell Vannoy's treatment of masturbation, *Sex Without Love* (Buffalo: Prometheus, 1980), 111–17.

[9]"Plain Sex," *Philosophy and Public Affairs* 6 (1977): 267–87; reprinted in Alan Soble, ed., *Philosophy of Sex* (Totowa, NJ.: Rowman & Littlefield, 1980; Savage, Md., 1991), 1st ed., 119–38; 2d ed., 73–92.

a sexual act even if inefficient. This masturbation is not a sexual act at all, despite the sexual pleasure it yields for X, unlike the not pleasurable but still sexual bungled kiss. X's masturbation cannot "tend to fulfill" X's desire for contact with Y, since it excludes that contact.

Suppose we read "tends to fulfill" in a causally broader way. Then giving money to a prostitute—the act of taking bills out of a wallet and handing them to her—might be a sexual act (even if no sexual arousal accompanies it), because doing so allows the patron to fulfill his desire for contact with her body. Handing over $100 would be a *more efficient* sexual act than handing over a ten. Even on this broader reading, solitary masturbation would not be a sexual activity; despite the causal generosity, masturbation is still precluded from fulfilling sexual desire in Goldman's sense. (For similar reasons, someone masturbating while looking at erotic photographs is not engaged in a sexual act.) Indeed, masturbation will be a *contrasexual* act, on Goldman's view, if the more a person masturbates, the less time, energy, or interest he or she has for fulfilling the desire for contact with someone's body.

Goldman does acknowledge one sense in which masturbation is a sexual activity:

> Voyeurism or viewing a pornographic movie qualifies as a sexual activity, but only as an imaginative substitute for the real thing (otherwise a deviation from the norm as expressed in our definition). The same is true of masturbation as a sexual activity without a partner. (42)

Masturbation done for its own sake, for the specific pleasure it yields, is *not* sexual; masturbation is a sexual act only when done as a substitute for the not available "real thing." But on what grounds could Goldman claim that masturbation's being an "imaginative substitute" for a sexual act makes it a sexual act? In general, being a *substitute for* a certain kind of act does not make something an occurrence of that act-kind. To eat soy-burger as a beef substitute is not to eat hamburger, even if it tastes exactly like hamburger. Eating a hamburger as a substitute for the sex I want but cannot have does not make my going to Queen Burger a sexual event, not even if out of frustration I gorge myself on burgers as compensation.

On the other hand, given Goldman's analyses of sexual desire and activity, the claim that masturbation done for its own sake is not sexual makes some sense. If the masturbator desires the pleasure of physical contact, and masturbates trying (in vain) to get that pleasure, the act, by a stretch, is sexual, because it at least involves genuine sexual desire. By contrast, if the masturbator wants only to experience pleasurable clitoral or penile sensations, then the masturbator does not have sexual desire in Goldman's sense, and activity engaged in to fulfill this (on his view, nonsexual) desire is not sexual activity. But now we have a different problem: what are we to call the act of this masturbator? In what category does it belong, if not the sexual? Note that Goldman argues (41), along the same lines, that if a parent's desire to cuddle a baby is only the desire to show affection, and not the desire for the pleasure of physical contact itself, then the parent's act is not sexual. Goldman assumes that if the desire that causes or leads to the act is not sexual, neither is the act. But if so, a woman who performs fellatio on a man for the money she gets from doing so is not performing a sexual act. It does not fulfill the sexual desire "of the agent," for, like the baby-cuddling parent, she has no sexual desire to begin with. Thus the prostitute's contribution to fellatio must be called, instead, a "rent paying" or "food gathering" act, since it tends to fulfill her desires to have shelter and eat.

COMPLETENESS

Thomas Nagel's theory of sexuality was designed to distinguish, in human sexuality, between the natural and the unnatural (the perverted.)[10] Human sexuality differs from animal sexuality in the role played by a spiral phenomenon that depends on self-consciousness. Suppose (1) X looks at Y or hears Y's voice or smells Y's hair—that is, X "senses" Y—and as a result is sexually aroused. Also suppose (2) Y senses X, too, and as a result becomes aroused. X and Y are at the earliest stage of sexual interaction: the animal level of awareness, response, and arousal. But if (3) X becomes aroused further by noticing (or "sensing") that Y is aroused by looking at X, and (4) Y becomes further aroused by noticing that X is aroused by sensing Y, then X and Y have reached the first level of natural human sexuality. Higher iterations of the pattern are also psychologically characteristic of human sexuality: (5) X is aroused even further by noticing (4). On Nagel's view of human sexuality, when X senses Y at the purely animal stage of sexual interaction, X is in X's own consciousness a subject and only a subject; while Y is for X at this stage only an object of sexual attention. But when X advances to the first distinctively human level of sexuality, and notices that Y is aroused by sensing X, X becomes in X's own consciousness also an object, and so at this level X experiences X-self as both subject and object. If Y, too, is progressing up the spiral, Y's self-consciousness is also composed of feeling Y-self as subject and object. For Nagel, the awareness of oneself as *both subject and object* in a sexual interaction marks it as "complete," that is, psychologically natural.

Nagel's theory, because it is about natural sex and not the essence of the sexual, does not entail that masturbation is not sexual. However, the judgment that solitary masturbation is perverted *seems* to follow from Nagel's account. Solitary masturbation, unlike mutual masturbation, does not exhibit the completeness of natural sexuality; it lacks the combination of an awareness of the embodiment of another person and an awareness of being sensed as embodied, in turn, by that person. This is apparently, why Nagel claims that "narcissistic practices"—which for him seem to include solitary masturbation—are "stuck at some primitive version of the first stage" (17) of the spiral of arousal; they are sexually perverted because they are "truncated or incomplete versions of the complete configuration" (16). There is a world of difference between narcissism

---

[10]"Sexual Perversion," *Journal of Philosophy* 66 (1969): 5–17; reprinted in Soble, *Philosophy of Sex,* 1st ed., 76–88; 2d ed., 39–51.

in some technical sense and masturbation, so even if looking upon one's own body in a mirror with delight is a sexual perversion, a theorist of sex should not feel compelled for that reason to judge perverted the prosaic practice of solitary masturbation. Nagel claims that shoe fetishism is perverted (9); "intercourse with . . . inanimate objects" is incomplete (17). But just because shoe fetishism might be a perversion that involves masturbation, a theory of sex need not entail that shoeless masturbation is perverted.

A case can be made, however, that the nature of effective sexual fantasy allows masturbation to be complete enough to be natural. Consider someone who masturbates while looking at erotic photographs. This sexual act avoids incompleteness insofar as the person is aroused not only by sensing the model's body (the animal level) but by recognizing the model's intention to arouse or by sensing her real or feigned arousal (the human level), as much as these things are captured by the camera or read into the photograph by the masturbator. Completeness seems not to require that X's arousal and pleasure as a result of X's awareness of Y's arousal occur at the same time as Y's arousal. Nor does it require that X and Y be in the same place: X and Y can arouse and cause each other pleasure by talking over the telephone. Further, if X masturbates while fantasizing, *sans* photograph, about another person, X might be aroused by the intentions expressed or arousal experienced by the imagined partner. (Nagel does allow [14] that X might become aroused in response to a "purely imaginary" Y.) A masturbator having a powerful imagination can conjure up these details and experience heightened pleasure as a result. If the masturbator is aroused not only by sensing, in imagination, the other's body, but also aroused by noticing (having created the appropriate fantasy) that the other is aroused by sensing X's body, then X can be conscious of X-self as both subject and object, which is the mark of complete sexuality.

COMMUNICATION

Robert Solomon, like Nagel, wants to distinguish between animal and human sexuality.[11] On Solomon's view, human sexuality is differentiated by its being "primarily a means of communicating with other people" (*SAP*, 279). Sensual pleasure is important in sex, but it is not the main point of sexual interaction or its defining characteristic ("Sexual Paradigms," 26; *SAP*, 277–79). Sexuality is, instead, "first of all language" (*SAP*, 281). As "a means of communication, it is . . . *essentially* an activity performed with other people" (*SAP*, 279). Could such a view of sexuality be kind to solitary masturbation? Apparently not:

> If sexuality is essentially a language, it follows that masturbation, while not a perversion, is a deviation. . . . Masturbation is not "self-abuse" . . . but it is, in an important sense, self-denial. It represents an inability or a refusal to say

[11] "Sexual Paradigms," *Journal of Philosophy* 71 (1974): 336–45; reprinted in Soble, *Philosophy of Sex*, 1st ed., 89–98; 2d ed., 53–62; and "Sex and Perversion," Baker and Elliston, *Philosophy and Sex*, 1st ed., 268–87 (references to this essay are preceded by *SAP*).

what one wants to say. . . . Masturbation is . . . essential as an ultimate retreat, but empty and without content. Masturbation is the sexual equivalent of a Cartesian soliloquy. (*SAP,* 283)

If sexuality is communicative, solitary masturbation can *be* sexual; conversing with oneself is not impossible, even if not the paradigm case. The distinctive flaw of masturbation, for Solomon, is that communicative intent, success, or content is missing. Hence solitary masturbation is "empty," a conclusion that seems to follow naturally from the idea that sexuality is "essentially" a way persons communicate *with each other.*

But denouncing masturbation as a "refusal to say what one wants to say" slights the fact that one might not have, at any given time, something to say (without being dull); or that there might be nothing worthy of being said, and so silence is appropriate. Solomon's communication model of sexuality seems to force people to talk to each other, to have empty sex, even when there is nothing to be said. Further, even if the masturbator is merely babbling to himself, he still enjoys this harmless pastime as much as does the infant who, for the pure joy of it, makes noises having no communicative intent or meaning. Thus to call masturbation "self-denial" is wrongheaded, but at least a change from the popular criticism of masturbation as a *failure* of self-denial, a giving-in to temptation, an immersing of the self in the hedonistic excesses of self-gratification.

The simple point is that there is no warrant to conclude, within a model that likens sexuality to linguistic behavior, that solitary masturbation is inferior.[12] Solomon meant the analogy between masturbation and a "Cartesian soliloquy" to reveal the shallowness of solitary sexuality. But Descartes's philosophical soliloquies are hardly uninteresting, and I suspect many would be proud to masturbate as well as the *Meditations* does philosophy. Diaries are not often masterpieces of literature, but that does not make them "empty." Some of the most fruitful discussions one can have are with oneself, not as a substitute for dialogue with another person, or as compensation for lacking it, but to explore one's mind, to get one's thoughts straight. This is the stuff of intellectual integrity, not preparation for public utterances.

Solomon acknowledges that not only "children, lunatics, and hermits" talk to themselves; "poets and philosophers" do so as well (*SAP,* 283). This misleading concession plays upon the silly notion that philosophers and poets are a type of lunatic. Where are the bus drivers and cooks? Solomon's abuse of masturbation trades unfairly on the fact that talking to oneself has always received bad publicity—unfair because we all do it, lips moving and heads bouncing, without damning ourselves. Solomon admits, in light of the fact that philosophers speak to themselves—a counterexample to his argument that "sexuality is a language . . . and primarily communicative" and hence masturbation *must* be deviant—that "masturbation might, *in different contexts,* count as wholly different extensions of language" (*SAP,* 283; italics added). But this qualification

---

[12]See Goldman, "Plain Sex," 45–48; Hugh Wilder, "The Language of Sex and the Sex of Language," in Alan Soble, ed., *Sex, Love, and Friendship* (Amsterdam: Editions Rodopi, 1997), 23–31.

implies that Solomon's negative judgment of masturbation is unjustified. Sometimes we want to converse with another person; sometimes we want to have that conversation sexually. In other contexts—in other moods, with other people, in different settings—we want only the pleasure of touching the other's body or of being touched and no serious messages are communicated. To turn around one of Solomon's points: sometimes pleasure is the goal of sexual activity, and even though communication might occur it is not the desired or intended result but only an unremarkable or merely curious side effect. In still other contexts, we will not want to talk with anyone at all, but spend time alone. We might want to avoid intercourse, of both types, with human beings, those hordes from whose noisy prattle we try to escape by running off to Montana— not an "ultimate retreat" but a blessed haven. For Solomon to call masturbation "empty" in the face of such obvious facts about the importance of context to human sexuality in its many forms is to confess that he did not understand his own qualification.

MEN'S LIBERATION

One of the conspicuous curiosities of the late 20th century is that telling the liberal from the conservative is no longer easy. Consider the views of John Stoltenberg, a student of the feminists Catharine MacKinnon and Andrea Dworkin. Stoltenberg rightly complains about the "cultural imperative" according to which men in our society must "fuck" in order to *be* men, and he rightly calls "baloney" the idea that "if two people don't have intercourse, they have not had real sex."[13] Stoltenberg also observes that "sometimes men have coital sex . . . not because they particularly feel like it but because they feel they *should* feel like it." This is a reasonable philosophy of men's liberation and men's feminism. But from these observations Stoltenberg fails to draw the almost obvious masturbatory conclusion. Indeed, it is jolting to behold Stoltenberg, in an argument reminiscent of religious objections to contraception (it makes women sexual objects), laying a guilt trip on men who masturbate with pornography:

> Pay your money and imagine. Pay your money and get real turned on. Pay your money and jerk off. That kind of sex helps . . . support an industry committed to making people with penises believe that people without are sluts who just want to be ravished and reviled—an industry dedicated to maintaining a sex-class system in which men believe themselves sex machines and men believe women are mindless fuck tubes. (35–36)

Given Kant's dismal view of human sexual interaction as essentially instrumental, and Stoltenberg's criticism of the social imperative that men must fuck women to be men, surely *something* can be said on behalf of solitary masturbation. The men's movement attack on oppressive cultural definitions of masculinity and feminist worries about the integrity of sexual activity between

[13]*Refusing to Be a Man* (Portland, Ore.: Breitenbush Books, 1989), 39.

unequally empowered men and women suggest that men's masturbation is at least a partial solution to a handful of problems. A man pleasing himself by masturbating is not taking advantage of economically and socially less powerful women; he is not refurbishing the infrastructure of his fragile ego at the expense of womankind. He is, instead, flouting cultural standards of masculinity that instruct him that he must perform sexually with women in order to be a man. Yet it is fantasizing and the heightened sexual pleasure that the imagination makes possible (44)—the things I mentioned in arguing that masturbation is complete, in Nagel's sense—that Stoltenberg points to as constituents of wrongful sexual objectification. He does not merely condemn masturbating with pornography (35–36, 42–43, 49–50). Fantasy *per se* is a fault: Stoltenberg condemns men's masturbating with memories of and passing thoughts about women, even when these fantasies are not violent (41–44). According to Stoltenberg, a man's conjuring up a mental image of a woman, her body, or its various parts, is to view her as an object, as a thing.

The mental objectification involved in sexual fantasy is, for Stoltenberg, both a cause and a result of our social system of "male supremacy" (51, 53–54). Further, mental sexual objectification contributes to violence against women (54–55). Stoltenberg's reason for thinking this is flimsy. He supposes that when a man fantasizes sexually about women, he reduces them from persons to objects. Further, when a man thinks of women as things, he has given himself *carte blanche* in his behavior toward them, including violence: regarding an object "you can do anything to it you want" (55). Of course the last claim is false; there are innumerable lifeless objects to which I would never lay a hand, either because other people value them, and I value these people, or because I dearly value the objects. Therefore, reducing a woman to a thing—or, to describe it more faithfully to men's experiences than Stoltenberg: emphasizing for a while the beauty of only one aspect of a person's existence—does not mean, either logically or psychologically, that she can or will be tossed around the way a young girl slings her Barbie.

Stoltenberg vastly underestimates the nuances of men's fantasies about women; his phenomenological account of what occurs in the minds of fantasizing men—the purported reduction of persons to things—is crude. Her smile, the way she moves down the stairs, the bounce of her tush, the sexy thoughts in her own mind, her lusty yearning for me—these are mere parts of her. But fantasizing or imagining them while masturbating, or driving my car, or having coffee, need not amount to, indeed is *the opposite of,* my reducing her to plastic. These are fantasies about people, not things. My fantasy of her (having a) fantasy of me (or of my [having a] fantasy of her) is structurally too sophisticated to be called objectification. The fantasizer makes himself in his consciousness both subject and object and imagines his partner as both subject and object. Recognizing the imagined person ontologically as a person is hardly a superfluous component of men's—or women's—fantasies. That Stoltenberg overlooks the complex structure of men's fantasies about women is not surprising; the primitive idea that men vulgarly reduce women to objects in their fantasies is precisely what would occur to someone who has already objectified men, who has reduced men from full persons having intricate psychologies to robots with penises.

CONJUGAL UNION

The conservative philosopher and legal scholar John Finnis claims, plausibly, that there are morally worthless sexual acts in which "one's body is treated as instrumental for the securing of the experiential satisfaction of the conscious self."[14] Out of context, this seems to be condemning rape, the use of one person by another for mere "experiential satisfaction." But rape is the farthest thing from Finnis's mind; he is talking not about coerced sex, but that which is fully voluntary. When is sex instrumental, and hence worthless, even though consensual? Finnis immediately mentions, creating the impression that these are his primary targets, that "in masturbating, as in being . . . sodomized, the body is just a tool of satisfaction. As a result of one's body being used, a person undergoes "disintegration": in masturbation and homosexual anal intercourse "one's choosing self [becomes] the quasi-slave of the experiencing self which is demanding gratification." We should ask—since Finnis sounds remarkably like the Kant who claims that sex by its nature is instrumental and objectifying—how acts other than sodomy and masturbation avoid this problem. Finnis's answer is that they do not; the worthlessness and disintegration attaching to sodomy attach to "all extramarital sexual gratification." The physical character of the act is not the decisive factor; the division between the wholesome and the worthless, for Finnis, is between "conjugal activity" and everything else.

The question, then, is: what is special about the conjugal bed that allows marital sex to avoid promoting disintegration? Finnis replies that worthlessness and disintegration attach to masturbation and sodomy in virtue of the fact that in these activities "one's conduct is not the actualizing and experiencing of a real common good." Marriage, on the other hand,

> with its double blessing—recreation and friendship—is a real common good . . . that can be both actualized and experienced in the orgasmic union of the reproductive organs of a man and a woman united in commitment to that good.

Maybe being married *is* conducive to the worthiness of sexual activity. Even so, what is wrong with sex between two single consenting adults who care about and enjoy pleasing each other in bed? Does not this mutual pleasuring avoid shamefulness and worthlessness? No: the friends might only be seeking pleasure for its own sake, as occurs in sodomy and masturbation. And although Finnis thinks that "pleasure is indeed a good," he qualifies that concession with "*when it is the experienced aspect of one's participation in some intelligible good*" (italics added). For Finnis's argument to work, he must claim that pleasure is a good *only when* it is an aspect of the pursuit or achievement of some other good. This is not quite what he says. Perhaps he does not say it because he fears his readers will reject such an extreme reservation about pleasure, or because he realizes it is false: the pleasure of tasting food is good in itself, regardless of whether the eating is part of the goods of securing nutrition or sharing table.

---

[14]John Finnis and Martha Nussbaum, "Is Homosexual Conduct Wrong? A Philosophical Exchange," *The New Republic* (15 November 1993), 12–13.

What if the friends say that they do have a common good, their friendship, the same way a married couple has the common good that is their marriage? If "their friendship is not marital . . . activation of their reproductive organs cannot be, in reality, an . . . actualization of their friendship's common good." The claim is obscure. Finnis tries to explain, and in doing so reveals the crux of his sexual philosophy:

> the common good of friends who are not and cannot be married (man and man, man and boy, woman and woman) has nothing to do with their having children by each other, and their reproductive organs cannot make them a biological (and therefore a personal) unit.

Finnis began with the Kantian intuition that sexual activity involves treating the body instrumentally, and he concludes with the Kantian intuition that sex in marriage avoids disintegrity since the couple is a (biological) "unit," or insofar as "the orgasmic union of the reproductive organs of husband and wife really unites them biologically." In order for persons to be part of a genuine union, their sexual activity must be both marital and procreative. The psychic falling apart each person would undergo in nonmarital sex is prevented in marital sex by their joining into one; this bolstering of the self against a metaphysical hurricane is gained by the tempestuous orgasm, of all things. At the heart of Finnis's philosophy is a scientific absurdity, and further conversation with him becomes difficult. But the argument, even if it shows the worthlessness of sterile homosexuality and solitary masturbation, has no relevance for heterosexual friends, for those who are not, but could be, married. After all, if marriage has the "double blessing" of procreation and friendship, heterosexual friendship can have the same double blessing. Does Finnis want to claim that if these friends are committed to each other for a lifetime and plan to, or do, have children by each other, they are *married* and hence their sexual interactions are fine? That claim might be true, but Finnis does not and would not assert it. Others in his school make it clear that marriage requires more than an informal agreement between people to spend their lives together indefinitely; no genuine commitment (or love, or union) exists without a formal compact, since a promise too easily fled is no promise at all.

TRANSCENDENTAL ILLUSIONS

For Finnis, the self is so fragile metaphysically that sex for the sheer pleasure of it threatens to burst it apart. For Roger Scruton, another conservative who condemns masturbation, the ephemeral self is in continual danger of being exposed as a fraud: "In my [sexual] desire [for you] I am gripped by the illusion of a transcendental unity behind the opacity of [your] flesh."[15] We are not transcendental selves but material beings; "excretion is the final 'no' to all our transcendental illusions" (151). We are redeemed only through "a metaphysical illusion residing in the heart of sexual desire" (95). Our passions make it *appear* that we

---

[15]*Sexual Desire: A Moral Philosophy of the Erotic* (New York: Free Press, 1986), 130.

are ontologically more than we really are. Sexuality must be treated with kid gloves, then, lest we lose the socially useful and spiritually uplifting reassurance that we humans are the pride of the universe.

The requirement that sex be approached somberly translates, for Scruton, not only into the ordinary claim that sex must be educated to be the partner of heterosexual love, but also into a number of silly judgments. While discussing the "obscenity" of masturbation, Scruton offers this example:

> Consider the woman who plays with her clitoris during the act of coition. Such a person affronts her lover with the obscene display of her body, and, in perceiving her thus, the lover perceives his own irrelevance. She becomes disgusting to him, and his desire may be extinguished. The woman's desire is satisfied at the expense of her lover's, and no real union can be achieved between them. (319)

Feminism has contested the tradition, revived by Scruton, in which the clitoris, the organ of women's masturbation and pleasure and a symbol of their autonomy, is suspicious.[16] Even if in rubbing herself during coitus, a woman asserts independence from her partner, must that be bad? One reply to Scruton, then, is that without masturbation, *her* desire might be extinguished and *his* desire satisfied at the expense of hers, and still there is no union. We could, instead, recommend to the man who "perceives his own irrelevance" that he become more involved in his partner's pleasure by helping her massage her clitoral or some other region or doing the rubbing for her; even when they are linked together coitally, he will find the arms long and the body flexible. But Scruton's claim is false (in this country) that most men would perceive a woman's masturbation during coitus as "disgusting." Her doing so can even help the couple attain the very union Scruton hopes for as the way to perpetrate our metaphysical illusion, by letting them experience and recognize the mutual pleasure, perhaps the mutual orgasm, that results.

Why does Scruton judge the woman's masturbation an "obscene display"? One part of his thinking is this. When masturbation is done in public (say, a bus station), it is obscene; it "cannot be witnessed without a sense of obscenity." Scruton then draws the astounding conclusion that *all* masturbation is obscene, even when done privately, on the grounds that "that which cannot be witnessed without obscene perception is itself obscene" (319). Scruton seems not to notice that his argument proves too much; it implies that heterosexual coitus engaged in by a loving, married couple in private is also obscene, if we assume—as I think he would—that this act "cannot be witnessed," in public, "without obscene perception." The fault lies in the major premise of Scruton's syllogism. Whether an act is obscene might turn exactly on whether it is done publicly or privately. Scruton has failed to acknowledge a difference between exposing oneself to anonymous spectators and opening oneself to the gaze of a lover.

All masturbation is obscene, for Scruton, also because it "involves a concentration on the body and its curious pleasures" (319). Obscenity is an "obsession . . . with the organs themselves and with the pleasures of sensation" (154),

---

[16]See Shere Hite, *The Hite Report: A Nationwide Study on Female Sexuality* (New York: Dell, 1976).

and even if the acts that focus on the body and its pleasures are paired, they are "masturbatory" (recall how the conservative criticized Goldman's "plain sex"). "In obscenity, attention is taken away from embodiment towards the body" (32), and there is "a 'depersonalized' perception of human sexuality, in which the body and its sexual function are uppermost in our thoughts" (138). A woman's masturbation during coitus is obscene since it leads the pair to focus too sharply on the physical; she is a depersonalized body instead of a person-in-a-body. Thus, for Scruton, this obscene masturbation cannot sustain, indeed threaten, the couple's metaphysical illusion. But if a woman's masturbation during coitus is greeted with delight by a partner, rather than with disgust, and increases the pleasure they realize and recognize in the act together, then, contrary to Scruton, either not all masturbation is obscene (the parties have not been reduced altogether to flesh) or obscenity, all things considered, is not a total sexual, normative, or metaphysical disaster.

GUILT

A common platitude says, "there is not one shred of evidence that masturbation is harmful. . . . The only harm that can result from masturbation is if the individual is plagued with feelings of guilt."[17] Thus, in reply to the oft-heard advice that we should not masturbate because doing so will make us feel anxious, depressed, or guilty, it is just as often mentioned that only because philosophy, medicine, theology, and popular opinion treat the act in a disparaging way do we run the risk of experiencing anxiety or guilt in the first place. That is to some extent true, but to repeat this rejoinder might no longer be convincing. Maybe we have gone too far in reaction against views critical of masturbation and it is time for a swing back to traditional intuitions, if not thermoelectrocautery. There are other reasons for the moral criticism of fantasy and masturbation, some of which have emerged from feminist thought, especially among those who have continued to press the question of pornography: if pornography is morally objectionable, seriously degrading to women, making heterosexual men feel guilty for masturbating with such horrible stuff might be legitimate. Maybe Rousseau was right, after all, to imply that sexual fantasy, a mental depiction, is little different from rape.

Questions

1. Do you agree with Alan Soble that "mutual masturbation" is a logically possible category?
2. Are those paired sexual acts in which each person aims at producing pleasure for the self as well as for the other person, masturbatory or nonmasturbatory on Alan Soble's account?

---

[17]James Haynes, "Masturbation," in V. Bullough and B. Bullough, eds., *Human Sexuality: An Encyclopedia* (New York: Garland, 1994), 381–85, at 384.

3. Why does Thomas Nagel think that masturbation is perverted? Why are John Finnis and Roger Scruton opposed to masturbation? Do you agree with any of their arguments?

4. Do Vincent Punzo's arguments in "Morality and Human Sexuality" have any bearing on masturbation? If so, what? If not, why not?

Suggestions for Further Reading on Premarital Sex, Promiscuity, and Masturbation

AQUINAS, THOMAS. "Moderation in Sex." In *Summa Theologiae: A Concise Translation,* edited by Timothy McDermott, Westminster, Md.: Christian Classics, 1989: pp. 429–432.

AQUINAS, THOMAS. "The Purpose of Sex." In *Philosophy and Sex.* 3d ed. Edited by Robert B. Baker, Kathleen J. Wininger, and Frederick A. Elliston. Amherst, N.Y.: Prometheus Books, 1998: pp. 91–95.

FORTUNATA, JACQUELINE. "Masturbation and Women's Sexuality" In *The Philosophy of Sex.* Edited by Alan Soble, Totowa, NJ: Rowman and Littlefield, 1980: pp. 389–408.

GOLDMAN, ALAN H. "Plain Sex." *Philosophy and Public Affairs* 6, no. 3 (1977): pp. 267–287.

KANT, IMMANUEL. "Duties towards the Body in Respect of Sexual Impulse." In *Lectures in Ethics,* translated by Louis Infield, New York: Harper & Row, 1963: pp. 162–168.

KIELKOPF, CHARLES. "Masturbation: A Kantian Condemnation." *Philosophia* 25, nos. 1–4 (April 1997): pp. 223–246.

MAPPES, THOMAS A. "Sexual Morality and the Concept of Using Another Person." In Thomas A. Mappes and Jane S. Zembaty, *Social Ethics: Morality and Social Policy.* 4th ed. New York: McGraw-Hill, 1992: pp. 203–216.

POPE PAUL VI. "Humanae Vitae." In *Philosophy and Sex.* 3d ed. Edited by Robert B. Baker, Kathleen J. Wininger, and Frederick A. Elliston, Amherst, N.Y.: Prometheus Books, 1998: pp. 96–105.

PRIMORATZ, IGOR. *Ethics and Sex.* London: Routledge, 1999.

CHAPTER 6

Adultery

Is Adultery Immoral?

Richard A. Wasserstrom

One argument for the immorality of adultery, notes Richard Wasserstrom, is that adultery involves the breaking of a promise—a promise of sexual exclusivity. Since this promise is a particularly important one (for a variety of reasons he mentions), breaking it is seriously wrong. Another argument for the wrongfulness of adultery focuses on the frequent connection between adultery and deception. When this connection exists and insofar as deception is wrong, adultery is wrong.

The most obvious form of deception is where the unfaithful spouse hides the infidelity. However, the author suggests that there might be another form of deception. This arises in cultures where there is a connection between sexual intimacy and feelings of love and affection. Different levels of sexual intimacy are indicators of different levels of love and affection. Given such a framework, if the adulterous spouse

does not have the feelings for the extramarital partner (or for the nonparticipating spouse) that are commensurate with the act(s) of sexual intercourse with that person, then the adulterous spouse deceives the sexual partner.

The author then asks what might be said against adultery if one rejected either the idea that sex should be connected to love or the idea that sexual love had to be exclusive. What, in other words, would be wrong with an "open marriage"? This leads the author to a discussion of two issues: (1) whether the parties to an "open marriage" can properly be characterized as being married to each other; and (2) whether the requirement for sexual exclusivity is instrumentally valuable in preserving marriages and the nuclear family (assuming, of course, that these are worth preserving).

Many discussions of the enforcement of morality by the law take as illustrative of the problem under consideration the regulation of various types of sexual behavior by the criminal law. It was, for example, the Wolfenden

Richard Wasserstrom, "Is Adultery Immoral?" in R. Wasserstrom (ed.) *Today's Moral Problems*, Second Edition, Macmillan, NY, 1979, pp. 288–300.

Report's recommendations concerning homosexuality and prostitution that led Lord Devlin to compose his now famous lecture, "The Enforcement of Morals." And that lecture in turn provoked important philosophical responses from H. L. A. Hart, Ronald Dworkin, and others.

Much, if not all, of the recent philosophical literature on the enforcement of morals appears to take for granted the immorality of the sexual behavior in question. The focus of discussion, at least, is whether such things as homosexuality, prostitution, and adultery ought to be made illegal even if they are immoral, and not whether they are immoral.

I propose in this paper to think about the latter, more neglected topic, that of sexual morality, and to do so in the following fashion. I shall consider just one kind of behavior that is often taken to be a case of sexual immorality—adultery. I am interested in pursuing at least two questions. First, I want to explore the question of in what respects adulterous behavior falls within the domain of morality at all: For this surely is one of the puzzles one encounters when considering the topic of sexual morality. It is often hard to see on what grounds much of the behavior is deemed to be either moral or immoral, for example, private homosexual behavior between consenting adults. I have purposely selected adultery because it seems a more plausible candidate for moral assessment than many other kinds of sexual behavior.

The second question I want to examine is that of what is to be said about adultery, without being especially concerned to stay within the area of morality. I shall endeavor, in other words, to identify and to assess a number of the major arguments that might be advanced against adultery. I believe that they are the chief arguments that would be given in support of the view that adultery is immoral, but I think they are worth considering even if some of them turn out to be nonmoral arguments and considerations.

A number of the issues involved seem to me to be complicated and difficult. In a number of places I have at best indicated where further philosophical exploration is required without having successfully conducted the exploration myself. The paper may very well be more useful as an illustration of how one might begin to think about the subject of sexual morality than as an elucidation of important truths about the topic.

Before I turn to the arguments themselves there are two preliminary points that require some clarification. Throughout the paper I shall refer to the immorality of such things as breaking a promise, deceiving someone, etc. In a very rough way, I mean by this that there is something morally wrong that is done in doing the action in question. I mean that the action is, in a strong sense, of *"prima facie"* *prima facie* wrong or unjustified. I do not mean that it may never be right or justifiable to do the action; just that the fact that it is an action of this description always does count against the rightness of the action. I leave entirely open the question of what it is that makes actions of this kind immoral in this sense of "immoral."

The second preliminary point concerns what is meant or implied by the concept of adultery. I mean by "adultery" any case of extramarital sex, and I want to explore the arguments for and against extramarital sex, undertaken in a variety of morally relevant situations. Someone might claim that the concept of adultery is conceptually connected with the concept of immorality, and that to characterize behavior as adulterous is already to characterize it as immoral or unjustified in the sense described above. There may be something to this. Hence the importance of making it clear that I want to talk about extramarital sexual relations. If they are always immoral, this is something that must be shown by argument. If the concept of adultery does in some sense entail or imply immorality, I want to ask whether that connection is a rationally based one. If not all cases of extramarital sex are immoral (again, in the sense described above), then the concept of adultery should either be weakened accordingly or restricted to those classes of extramarital sex for which the predication of immorality is warranted.

One argument for the immorality of adultery might go something like this: what makes adultery immoral is that it involves the breaking of a promise, and what makes adultery seriously wrong is that it involves the breaking of an important promise. For, so the argument might continue, one of the things the two parties promise each other when they get married is that they will abstain from sexual relationships with third persons. Because of this promise both spouses quite reasonably entertain the expectation that the other will behave in conformity with it. Hence, when one of the parties has sexual intercourse with a third person he or she breaks that promise about sexual relationships which was made when the marriage was entered into, and defeats the reasonable expectations of exclusivity entertained by the spouse.

In many cases the immorality involved in breaching the promise relating to extramarital sex may be a good deal more serious than that involved in the breach of other promises. This is so because adherence to this promise may be of much greater importance to the parties than is adherence to many of the other promises given or received by them in their lifetime. The breaking of this promise may be much more hurtful and painful than is typically the case.

Why is this so? To begin with, it may have been difficult for the nonadulterous spouse to have kept the promise. Hence that spouse may feel the unfairness of having restrained himself or herself in the absence of reciprocal restraint having been exercised by the adulterous spouse. In addition, the spouse may perceive the breaking of the promise as an indication of a kind of indifference on the part of the adulterous spouse. If you really cared about me and my feelings—the spouse might say—you would not have done this to me. And third, and related to the above, the spouse may see the act of sexual intercourse with another as a sign of affection for the other person and as an additional rejection of the nonadulterous spouse as the one who is loved by the adulterous spouse. It is not just that the adulterous spouse does not take the feelings of the spouse sufficiently into account, the adulterous spouse also indicates through the act of adultery affection for someone other than the spouse. I will return to these points later. For the present, it is sufficient to note that a set of arguments can be developed in support of the proposition that certain kinds of adultery are wrong just because they involve the breach of a serious promise which, among other things, leads to the intentional infliction of substantial pain by one spouse upon the other.

Another argument for the immorality of adultery focuses not on the existence of a promise of sexual exclusivity but on the connection between adultery and deception. According to this argument, adultery involves deception. And because deception is wrong, so is adultery.

Although it is certainly not obviously so, I shall simply assume in this paper that deception is always immoral. Thus the crucial issue for my purposes is the asserted connection between extramarital sex and deception. Is it plausible to maintain, as this argument does, that adultery does involve deception and is on that basis to be condemned?

The most obvious person on whom deceptions might be practiced is the nonparticipating spouse; and the most obvious thing about which the nonparticipating spouse can be deceived is the existence of the adulterous act. One clear case of deception is that of lying. Instead of saying that the afternoon was spent in bed with A, the adulterous spouse asserts that it was spent in the library with B, or on the golf course with C.

There can also be deception even when no lies are told. Suppose, for instance, that a person has sexual intercourse with someone other than his or her spouse and just does not tell the spouse about it. Is that deception? It may not be a case of lying if, for example, the spouse is never asked by the other about the situation. Still, we might say, it is surely deceptive because of the promises that were exchanged at marriage. As we saw earlier, these promises provide a foundation for the reasonable belief that neither spouse will engage in sexual relationships with any other persons. Hence the failure to bring the fact of extramarital sex to the attention of the other spouse deceives that spouse about the present state of the marital relationship.

Adultery, in other words, can involve both active and passive deception. An adulterous spouse may just keep silent or, as is often the fact, the spouse may engage in an increasingly complex way of life devoted to the concealment of the facts from the nonparticipating spouse. Lies, half-truths, clandestine meetings, and the like may become a central feature of the adulterous spouse's existence. These are things that can and do happen, and when they do they make the case against adultery an easy one. Still, neither active nor passive deception is inevitably a feature of an extramarital relationship.

It is possible, though, that a more subtle but pervasive kind of deceptiveness is a feature of adultery. It comes about because of the connection in our culture between sexual intimacy and certain feelings of love and affection. The point can be made indirectly at first by seeing that one way in which we can, in our culture, mark off our close friends from our mere acquaintances is through the kinds of intimacies that we are prepared to share with them. I may, for instance, be willing to reveal my very private thoughts and emotions to my closest friends or to my wife, but to no one else. My sharing of these intimate facts about myself is from one perspective a way of making a gift to those who mean the most to me. Revealing these things and sharing them with those who mean the most to me is one means by which I create, maintain, and confirm those interpersonal relationships that are of most importance to me.

Now in our culture, it might be claimed, sexual intimacy is one of the chief currencies through which gifts of this sort are exchanged. One way to tell someone—particularly someone of the opposite sex—that you have feelings of affection and love for them is by allowing to them or sharing with them sexual behaviors that one doesn't share with the rest of the world. This way of measuring affection was certainly very much a part of the culture in which I matured. It worked something like this. If you were a girl, you showed how much you liked someone by the degree of sexual intimacy you would allow. If you liked a boy only a little, you never did more than kiss—and even the kiss was not very passionate. If you liked the boy a lot and if your feeling was reciprocated, necking, and possibly petting, was permissible. If the attachment was still stronger and you thought it might even become a permanent relationship, the sexual activity was correspondingly more intense and more intimate, although whether it would ever lead to sexual intercourse depended on whether the parties (and particularly the girl) accepted fully the prohibition on nonmarital sex. The situation for the boy was related, but not exactly the same. The assumption was that males did not naturally link sex with affection in the way in which females did. However, since women did, males had to take this into account. That is to say, because a woman would permit sexual intimacies only if she had feelings of affection for the male and only if those feelings were reciprocated, the male had to have and express those feelings, too, before sexual intimacies of any sort would occur.

The result was that the importance of a correlation between sexual intimacy and feelings of love and affection was taught by the culture and assimilated by those growing up in the culture. The scale of possible positive feelings toward persons of the other sex ran from casual liking at the one end to the love that was deemed essential to and characteristic of marriage at the other. The scale of possible sexual behavior ran from brief, passionless kissing or hand-holding at the one end to sexual intercourse at the other. And the correlation between the two scales was quite precise. As a result, any act of sexual intimacy carried substantial meaning with it, and no act of sexual intimacy was simply a pleasurable set of bodily sensations. Many such acts were, of course, more pleasurable to the participants because they were a way of saying what the participants feelings were. And sometimes they were less pleasurable for the same reason. The point is, however, that in any event sexual activity was much more than mere bodily enjoyment. It was not like eating a good meal, listening to good music, lying in the sun, or getting a pleasant back rub. It was behavior that meant a great deal concerning one's feelings for persons of the opposite sex in whom one was most interested and with whom one was most involved. It was among the most authoritative ways in which one could communicate to another the nature and degree of one's affection.

If this sketch is even roughly right, then several things become somewhat clearer. To begin with, a possible rationale for many of the rules of conventional sexual morality can be developed. If, for example, sexual intercourse is associated with the kind of affection and commitment to another that is regarded as characteristic of the marriage relationship, then it is natural that sexual intercourse should be thought properly to take place between persons who are married to each other. And if it is thought that this kind of affection and commitment is only to be found within the marriage relationship, then it is not surprising that sexual intercourse should only be thought to be proper within marriage.

Related to what has just been said is the idea that sexual intercourse ought to be restricted to those who are married to each other as a means by which to confirm the very special feelings that the spouses have for each other. Because the culture teaches that sexual intercourse means that the strongest of all feelings for each other are shared by the lovers, it is natural that persons who are married to each other should be able to say this to each other in this way. Revealing and confirming verbally that these feelings are present is one thing that helps to sustain the relationship; engaging in sexual intercourse is another.

In addition, this account would help to provide a framework within which to make sense of the notion that some sex is better than other sex. As I indicated earlier, the fact that sexual intimacy can be meaningful in the sense described tends to make it also the case that sexual intercourse can sometimes be more enjoyable than at other times. On this view, sexual intercourse will typically be more enjoyable where the strong feelings of affection are present than it will be where it is merely "mechanical." This is so in part because people enjoy being loved, especially by those whom they love. Just as we like to hear words of affection, so we like to receive affectionate behavior. And the meaning enhances the independently pleasurable behavior.

More to the point, moreover, an additional rationale for the prohibition on extramarital sex can now be developed. For given this way of viewing the sexual world, extramarital sex will almost always involve deception of a deeper sort. If the adulterous spouse does not in fact have the appropriate feelings of affection for the extramarital partner, then the adulterous spouse is deceiving that person about the presence of such feelings. If, on the other hand, the adulterous spouse does have the corresponding feelings for the extramarital partner but not toward the nonparticipating spouse the adulterous spouse is very probably deceiving the nonparticipating spouse about the presence of such feelings toward that spouse. Indeed, it might be argued, whenever there is no longer love between the two persons who are married to each other, there is deception just because being married implies both to the participants and to the world that such a bond exists. Deception is inevitable, the argument might conclude, because the feelings of affection that ought to accompany any act of sexual intercourse can only be held toward one other person at any given time in one's life. And if this is so, then the adulterous spouse always deceives either the partner in adultery or the nonparticipating spouse about the existence of such feelings. Thus extramarital sex involves deception of this sort and is for this reason immoral even if no deception vis-á-vis the occurrence of the act of adultery takes place.

What might be said in response to the foregoing arguments? The first thing that might be said is that the account of the connection between sexual intimacy and feelings of affection is inaccurate. Not inaccurate in the sense that no one thinks of things that way, but in the sense that there is substantially more divergence of opinion than that account suggests. For example, the view I have delineated may describe reasonably accurately the concepts of the sexual world in which I grew up, but it does not capture the sexual *weltanschauung* of today's youth at all. Thus, whether or not adultery implies deception in respect to feelings depends very much on the persons who are involved and the way they look at the "meaning" of sexual intimacy.

Second, the argument leaves to be answered the question of whether it is desirable for sexual intimacy to carry the sorts of messages described above. For those persons for whom sex does have these implications, there are special feelings and sensibilities that must be taken into account. But it is another question entirely whether any valuable end—moral or otherwise—is served investing sexual behavior with such significance. That is something that must be shown and not just assumed. It might, for instance, be the case that substantially more good than harm would come from a kind of demystification of sexual behavior: one that would encourage the enjoyment of sex more for its own sake and one that would reject the centrality both of the association of sex with love and of love with only one other person.

I regard these as two of the more difficult, unresolved issues that our culture faces today in respect to thinking sensibly about the attitudes toward sex and love that we should try to develop in ourselves and in our children. Much of the contemporary literature that advocates sexual liberation of one sort or another embraces one or the other of two different views about the relationship between sex and love.

One view holds that sex should be separated from love and affection. To be sure sex is probably better when the partners genuinely like and enjoy each other. But sex is basically an intensive, exciting sensuous activity that can be enjoyed in a variety of suitable settings with a variety of suitable partners. The situation in respect to sexual pleasure is no different from that of the person who knows and appreciates fine food and who can have a very satisfying meal in any number of good restaurants with any number of congenial companions. One question that must be settled here is whether sex can be so demystified; another, more important question is whether it would be desirable to do so. What would we gain and what might we lose if we all lived in a world in which an act of sexual intercourse was no more or less significant or enjoyable than having a delicious meal in a nice setting with a good friend? The answer to this question lies beyond the scope of this paper.

The second view seeks to drive the wedge in a different place. It is not the link between sex and love that needs to be broken; rather, on this view, it is the connection between love and exclusivity that ought to be severed. For a number of the reasons already given, it is desirable, so this argument goes, that sexual intimacy continue to be reserved to and shared with only those for whom one has very great affection. The mistake lies in thinking that any "normal" adult will only have those feelings toward one other adult during his or her lifetime—or even at any time in his or her life. It is the concept of adult love, not ideas about sex, that, on this view, needs demystification. What are thought to be both unrealistic and unfortunate are the notions of exclusivity and possessiveness that attach to the dominant conception of love between adults in our and other cultures. Parents of four, five, six, or even ten children can certainly claim and sometimes claim correctly that they love all of their children, that they love them all equally, and that it is simply untrue to their feelings to insist that the numbers involved diminish either the quantity or the quality of their love. If this is an idea that is readily understandable in the case of parents and children, there is no necessary reason why it is an impossible or undesirable ideal in the case of adults. To be sure, there is probably a limit to the number of ultimate, "primary" relationships that any person can maintain at any given time without the quality of the relationship being affected. But one adult ought surely be able to love two, three, or even six other adults at any one time without that love being different in kind or degree from that of the traditional, monogomous, lifetime marriage. And as between the individuals in these relationships, whether within a marriage or without, sexual intimacy is fitting and good.

The issues raised by a position such as this one are also surely worth exploring in detail and with care. Is there something to be called "sexual love" which is different from parental love or the nonsexual love of close friends? Is there something about love in general that links it naturally and appropriately with feelings of exclusivity and possession? Or is there something about sexual love, whatever that may be, that makes these feelings especially fitting here? Once again the issues are conceptual, empirical, and normative all at once: What is love? How could it be different? Would it be a good thing or a bad thing if it were different?

Suppose, though, that having delineated these problems we were now to pass them by. Suppose, moreover, we were to be persuaded of the possibility and the desirability of weakening substantially either the links between sex and love or the links between sexual love and exclusivity. Would it not then be the case that adultery could be free from all of the morally objectionable features described so far? To be more specific, let us imagine that a husband and wife have what is today sometimes characterized as an "open marriage." Suppose, that is, that they have agreed in advance that extramarital sex is—under certain circumstances—acceptable behavior for each to engage in. Suppose, that as a result there is no impulse to deceive each other about the occurrence or nature of any such relationships, and that no deception in fact occurs. Suppose, too, that there is no deception in respect to the feelings involved between the adulterous spouse and the extramarital partner. And suppose, finally, that one or the other or both of the spouses then has sexual intercourse in circumstances consistent with these understandings. Under this description, so the agreement might conclude, adultery is simply not immoral. At a minimum, adultery cannot very plausibly be condemned either on the ground that it involves deception or on the ground that it requires the breaking of a promise.

At least two responses are worth considering. One calls attention to the connection between marriage and adultery; the other looks to more instrumental arguments for the immorality of adultery. Both issues deserve further exploration.

One way to deal with the case of the "open marriage" is to question whether the two persons involved are still properly to be described as being married to each other. Part of the meaning of what it is for two persons to be married to each other, so this argument would go, is to have committed oneself to have sexual relationships only with one's spouse. Of course, it would be added, we know that that commitment is not always honored. We know that persons who are married to each other often do commit adultery. But there is a difference between being willing to make a commitment to marital fidelity even though one may fail to honor that commitment, and not making the commitment at all. Whatever the relationship may be between the two individuals in the case described above, the absence of any commitment to sexual exclusivity requires the conclusion that their relationship is not a marital one. For a commitment to sexual exclusivity is a necessary although not a sufficient condition for the existence of a marriage.

Although there may be something to this suggestion, as it is stated it is too strong to be acceptable. To begin with, I think it is very doubtful that there are many, if any, *necessary* conditions for marriage; but even if there are, a commitment to sexual exclusivity is not such a condition.

To see that this is so, consider what might be taken to be some of the essential characteristics of a marriage. We might be tempted to propose that the concept of marriage requires the following: a formal ceremony of some sort in which mutual obligations are undertaken between two persons of the opposite sex; the capacity on the part of the persons involved to have sexual intercourse with each other; the willingness to have sexual intercourse only with each other; and feelings of love and affection between the two persons. The problem is that we can imagine relationships that are clearly marital and yet lack one or more of these features. For example, in our own society, it is possible for two persons to be married without going through a formal ceremony, as in the common-law marriages recognized in some jurisdictions. It is also possible for two persons to get married even though one or both lacks the capacity to engage in sexual intercourse. Thus, two very elderly persons who have neither the desire nor the ability to have intercourse can, nonetheless, get married, as can persons whose sexual organs have been injured so that intercourse is not possible. And we certainly know of marriages in which love was not present at the time of the marriage, as, for instance, in marriages of state and marriages of convenience.

Counterexamples not satisfying the condition relating to the abstention from extramarital sex are even more easily produced. We certainly know of societies and cultures in which polygamy and polyandry are practiced, and we have no difficulty in recognizing these relationships as cases of marriages. It might be objected, though, that these are not counterexamples because they are plural marriages rather than marriages in which sex is permitted with someone other than with one of the persons to whom one is married. But we also know of societies in which it is permissible for married persons to have sexual relationships with persons to whom they were not married, for example, temple prostitutes, concubines, and homosexual lovers. And even if we knew of no such societies, the conceptual claim would still, I submit, not be well taken. For suppose all of the other indicia of marriage were present: suppose the two persons were of the opposite sex, suppose they had the capacity and desire to have intercourse with each other, suppose they participated in a formal ceremony in which they understood themselves voluntarily to be entering into a relationship with each other in which substantial mutual commitments were assumed. If all these conditions were satisfied, we would not be in any doubt about whether or not the two persons were married even though they had not taken on a commitment of sexual exclusivity and even though they had expressly agreed that extramarital sexual intercourse was a permissible behavior for each to engage in.

A commitment to sexual exclusivity is neither a necessary nor a sufficient condition for the existence of marriage. It does, nonetheless, have this much to do with the nature of marriage: like the other indicia enumerated above, its presence tends to establish the existence of a marriage. Thus, in the absence of a formal ceremony of any sort, an explicit commitment to sexual exclusivity would count in favor of regarding the two persons as married. The conceptual role of the commitment to sexual exclusivity can, perhaps, be brought out through the following example. Suppose we found a tribe which had a practice in which all the other indicia of marriage were present but in which the two parties were *prohibited* ever from having sexual intercourse with each other. Moreover, suppose that sexual intercourse with others was clearly permitted. In such a case we would, I think, reject the idea that the two were married to each other and we would describe their relationship in other terms, for example, as some kind of formalized, special friendship relation—a kind of heterosexual "blood-brother" bond.

Compare that case with the following. Suppose again that the tribe had a practice in which all of the other indicia of marriage were present, but instead of a prohibition on sexual intercourse between the persons in the relationship there was no rule at all. Sexual intercourse was permissible with the person with whom one had this ceremonial relationship, but it was no more or less permissible than with a number of other persons to whom one was not so related (for instance, all consenting adults of the opposite sex). Although we might be in doubt as to whether we ought to describe the persons as married to each other, we would probably conclude that they were married and that they simply were members of a tribe whose views about sex were quite different from our own.

What all of this shows is that a *prohibition* on sexual intercourse between the two persons involved in a relationship is conceptually incompatible with the claim that the two of them are married. The *permissibility* of intramarital sex is a necessary part of the idea of marriage. But no such incompatibility follows simply from the added permissibility of extramarital sex.

These arguments do not, of course, exhaust the arguments for the prohibition on extramarital sexual relations. The remaining argument that I wish to consider—as I indicated earlier—is a more instrumental one. It seeks to justify the prohibition by virtue of the role that it plays in the development and maintenance of nuclear families. The argument, or set of arguments, might, I believe, go something like this.

Consider first a farfetched nonsexual example. Suppose a society were organized so that after some suitable age—say 18, 19, or 20—persons were forbidden to eat anything but bread and water with anyone but their spouse. Persons might still choose in such a society not to get married. Good food just might not be very important to them because they have underdeveloped taste buds. Or good food might be bad for them because there is something wrong with their digestive system. Or good food might be important to them, but they might decide that the enjoyment of good food would get in the way of the attainment of other things that were more important. But most persons would, I think, be led to favor marriage in part because they preferred a richer, more varied, diet to one of bread and water. And they might remain married because the family was the only legitimate setting within which good food was obtainable. If it is important to have society organized so that persons will both get married and stay married, such an arrangement would be well suited to the preservation of the family, and the prohibitions relating to food consumption could be understood as fulfilling that function.

It is obvious that one of the more powerful human desires is the desire for sexual gratification. The desire is a natural one, like hunger and thirst, in the sense that it need not be learned in order to be present within us and operative upon us. But there is in addition much that we do learn about what the act of sexual intercourse is like. Once we experience sexual intercourse ourselves—and in particular once we experience orgasm—we discover that it is among the most intensive, short-term pleasures of the body.

Because this is so, it is easy to see how the prohibition upon extramarital sex helps to hold marriage together. At least during that period of life when the enjoyment of sexual intercourse is one of the desirable bodily pleasures, persons will wish to enjoy those pleasures. If one consequence of being married is that one is prohibited from having sexual intercourse with anyone but one's spouse, then the spouses in a marriage are in a position to provide an important source of pleasure for each other that is unavailable to them elsewhere in the society.

The point emerges still more clearly if this rule of sexual morality is seen as of a piece with the other rules of sexual morality. When this prohibition is coupled, for example, with the prohibition on nonmarital sexual intercourse, we are presented with the inducement both to get married and to stay married. For if sexual intercourse is only legitimate within marriage, then persons seeking that gratification which is a feature of sexual intercourse are furnished explicit social directions for its attainment; namely marriage.

Nor, to continue the argument, is it necessary to focus exclusively, on the bodily enjoyment that is involved. Orgasm may be a significant part of what there is to sexual intercourse, but it is not the whole of it. We need only recall the earlier discussion of the meaning that sexual intimacy has in our own culture to begin to see some of the more intricate ways in which sexual exclusivity may be connected with the establishment and maintenance of marriage as the primary heterosexual, love relationship. Adultery is wrong, in other words, because a prohibition on extramarital sex is a way to help maintain the institutions of marriage and the nuclear family.

Now I am frankly not sure what we are to say about an argument such as this one. What I am convinced of is that, like the arguments discussed earlier, this one also reveals something of the difficulty and complexity of the issues that are involved. So, what I want now to do—in the brief and final portion of this paper—is to try to delineate with reasonable precision what I take several of the fundamental, unresolved issues to be.

The first is whether this last argument is an argument for the *immorality* of extramarital sexual intercourse. What does seem clear is that there are differences between this argument and the ones considered earlier. The earlier arguments condemned adulterous behavior because it was behavior that involved breaking of a promise, taking unfair advantage, or deceiving another. To the degree to which the prohibition on extramarital sex can be supported by arguments which invoke considerations such as these, there is little question but that violations of the prohibition are properly regarded as immoral. And such a claim could be defended on one or both of two distinct grounds. The first is that things like promise-breaking and deception are just wrong. The second is that adultery involving promise-breaking or deception is wrong because it involves the straightforward infliction of harm on another human being—typically the nonadulterous spouse—who has a strong claim not to have that harm so inflicted.

The argument that connects the prohibition on extramarital sex with the maintenance and preservation of the institution of marriage is an argument for the instrumental value of the prohibition. To some degree this counts, I think, against regarding all violations of the prohibition as obvious cases of immorality. This is so partly because hypothetical imperatives are less clearly within the domain of morality than are categorical ones, and even more because instrumental prohibitions are within the domain of morality only if the end they serve or the way they serve it is itself within the domain of morality.

What this should help us see, I think, is the fact that the argument that connects the prohibition on adultery with the preservation of marriage is at best seriously incomplete. Before we ought to be convinced by it, we ought to have reasons for believing that marriage is a morally desirable and just social institution. And this is not quite as easy or obvious a task as it may seem to be. For the concept of marriage is, as we have seen, both a loosely structured and a complicated one. There may be all sorts of intimate, interpersonal relationships which will resemble but not be identical with the typical marriage relationship presupposed by the traditional sexual morality. There may be a number of distinguishable sexual and loving arrangements which can all legitimately claim to be called *marriages.* The prohibitions of the traditional sexual morality may be effective ways to maintain some marriages and ineffective ways to promote and preserve others. The prohibitions of the traditional sexual morality may make good psychological sense if certain psychological theories are true, and they may be purveyors of immense psychological mischief if other psychological theories are true. The prohibitions of the traditional sexual morality may seem obviously correct if sexual intimacy carries the meaning that the dominant culture has often ascribed to it, and they may seem equally bizarre when sex is viewed through the perspective of the counterculture. Irrespective of whether instrumental arguments of this sort are properly deemed moral arguments, they ought not to fully convince anyone until questions like these are answered.

Questions

1. Ought sexual intimacy to have the meaning Richard Wasserstrom describes, or should sex be treated just like any other pleasure, such as eating?
2. Is a marriage without an undertaking of sexual exclusivity really a marriage?
3. Must sexual love be exclusive or can it, like parental love, be felt equally toward more than one person?

Adultery and Fidelity

Mike W. Martin

Mike Martin thinks that a rule-oriented approach to morality is inadequate to the task of answering the questions about adultery which Richard Wasserstrom raises. He prefers, instead, an expanded conception of morality that encompasses ideals and virtues—most especially the moral ideals of love (including honesty, trust, and fairness) and the virtues that enable one to pursue those ideals. The ideals, he says, are morally optional, but for those who do embrace them, strong obligations to avoid adultery arise. The author's discussion of the ethics of adultery is divided into two parts: making commitments and keeping them.

He takes marriage to be a commitment to love, which he understands not as a commitment to have continuous feelings of strong affection, but rather as a commitment to create and sustain a relationship that is conducive to such feelings.

He thinks that sexual exclusivity expresses and protects love, partly because so many people take adultery to be so threatening to love and marriage, and partly because sex is, for many people, so important an expression of love. The value of sexual exclusivity is thus instrumental rather than intrinsic. It facilitates the attainment of certain ideals of love for couples who have embraced them.

Turning to the keeping of commitments, the author indicates his agreement with Richard Wasserstrom that the prohibition against adultery (even in traditional relationships) is prima facie. He then discusses four complicating factors: instances where (1) the partners change their commitments, (2) love is lost, (3) one spouse falls in love with an additional person, and (4) extramarital affairs facilitate an often much-needed self-affirmation by the adulterous spouse.

Adultery has recently entered prominently into evaluations of public figures. Bill Clinton's 1992 presidential campaign was nearly derailed by allegations about a twelve-year extramarital affair. Shortly thereafter England's royal family engaged in extensive damage control as public revelations surfaced

Mike W. Martin, "Adultery and Fidelity" *Journal of Social Philosophy*, Vol. 25, No. 3, Winter 1994.

about the love trysts of Prince Charles and Lady Diana. Earlier, in 1987, Gary Hart's "womanizing" forced his withdrawal as the leading democratic presidential candidate. About the same time, charges of adultery contributed to the downfall of the leading television evangelist Jim Bakker.[1]

It is not clear what most upsets (or intrigues) the public in such cases. Is it the adultery *per se*, the deception used to conceal it (from spouses or the public), the hypocrisy in professing contrary religious beliefs, or the poor judgment in failing to keep it discrete (including the bravado of Gary Hart in baiting the press to uncover his affairs)? Nor is it clear how the adultery itself is pertinent to public service, even if we think the adultery is immoral. Character is not a seamless web, and integrity can be present in one context (public service) and absent in another setting (sexual conduct).[2] Many notable leaders had extramarital affairs, including Franklin D. Roosevelt, Dwight Eisenhower, John F. Kennedy, and Martin Luther King, and public scrutiny of marital intimacy might discourage worthy candidates from seeking public office.

It is clear, however, that adultery is morally complex. Philosophers have devoted little attention to it,[3] largely leaving it as a topic for theology, social science, and literature. Certainly novelists have had much to say: "To judge by literature, adultery would seem to be one of the most remarkable of occupations in both Europe and America. Few are the novels that fail to allude to it."[4] In any case, whether as moral judges assessing the character of adulterers or as moral agents confronted with making our own decisions about adultery, we often find ourselves immersed in confusions and ambiguities that are both personally and philosophically troublesome.

I will seek a middle ground between conventional absolute prohibitions and trendy permissiveness. A humanistic perspective should embrace a pluralistic moral outlook that affirms a variety of forms of sexual relationships, including many traditional marriages. It can justify a strong presumption against adultery for individuals who embrace traditional marital ideals.

The ethics of adultery divides into two parts: making commitments and keeping them. The ethics of making commitments centers primarily on commitments to love, where love is a value-guided relationship, and secondarily on the promise of sexual exclusivity (the promise to have sex only with one's spouse) which some couples make in order to support the commitment to love. The ethics of keeping commitments has to do with balancing initial marital commitments against other moral considerations.

[1]Charles E. Shepard, *Forgiven: The Rise and Fall of Jim Bakker and the PTL Ministry* (New York: Atlantic Monthly Press, 1989).

[2]*Cf.* Owen Flanagan, *Varieties of Moral Personality* (Cambridge: Harvard University Press, 1991).

[3]R. J. Connelly, "Philosophy and Adultery," in Philip E. Lampe (ed.) *Adultery in the United States* (Buffalo: Prometheus Books, 1987), pp. 131–164.

[4]Denis de Rougemont, *Love in the Western World*, rev. ed., trans. Montgomery Belgion (New York: Harper and Row, 1974), p. 16. Two illuminating literary critics are Tony Tanner, *Adultery in the Novel: Contract and Transgression* (Baltimore: The Johns Hopkins University Press, 1979) and Donald J. Greiner, *Adultery in the American Novel: Updike, James, and Hawthorne* (Columbia, SC: University of South Carolina Press, 1985).

MAKING COMMITMENTS

What is adultery? Inspired by the *New Testament*, some people employ a wide definition that applies to any significant sexual interest in someone besides one's spouse: "You have heard that it was said, 'Do not commit adultery.' But I tell you that anyone who looks at a woman lustfully has already committed adultery with her in his heart."[5] Other people define adultery narrowly to match their particular scruples: for them extramarital genital intercourse may count as adultery, but not oral sex; or falling in love with someone besides one's spouse may count as adultery but not "merely" having sex.[6] Whatever definition we adopt there will always be borderline cases, if only those created by "brinkmanship"—going as far as possible without having intercourse (e.g., lying naked together in bed).[7]

In this paper, "adultery" refers to married persons having sexual intercourse (of any kind) with someone other than their spouses.[8] I am aware that the word "adultery" is not purely descriptive and evokes a range of emotive connotations. Nevertheless, I use the word without implying that adultery is immoral; that is a topic left open for investigation in specific cases. Like "deception," the word "adultery" raises moral questions about possible misconduct but it does not answer them. By contrast, I will use a wider sense of "marriage" that refers to all monogamous (two-spouse) relationships formally established by legal or religious ceremonies *and* closely analogous moral relationships such as committed relationships between homosexual or heterosexual couples who are not legally married.

A moral understanding of adultery turns on an understanding of morality. If we conceive morality as a set of rules, we will object to adultery insofar as it violates those rules. "Do not commit adultery" is not an irreducible moral principle, but many instances of adultery violate other familiar rules. As Richard Wasserstrom insightfully explained, much adultery violates one or more of these rules: Do not break promises (*viz.*, the wedding vows to abjure outside sex, vows which give one's partner "reasonable expectations" of sexual fidelity); do not

---

[5]*Matthew* 5: 27–28. *New International Version.* In targeting males, this scripture presupposes that husbands are the primary adulterers. That presupposition is not surprising given a long history of indulging profligate husbands while severely punishing wayward wives, based in part on the view that wives are their husbands' property, duty-bound to maintain male lines of progeny, and in part on the view that women are chaste creatures who can be held to a higher standard than males. Today, husbands continue to lead in adultery statistics—well over half of them have extramarital affairs—although women are catching up. Annette Lawson cautiously estimates that somewhere between 25–50% of women have at least one extramarital lover during any given marriage, and 50–65% of husbands engage in adultery by the age of forty. *Adultery: An Analysis of Love and Betrayal* (New York: Basic Books, 1988), p. 75. A humanistic approach regards male and female adultery as on a par and also proceeds without invoking religious beliefs that condemn all adultery as sinful.
[6]Morton Hunt, *The Affair* (New York: The World Publishing Company, 1969), p. 9.
[7]This is not an imaginary case. See *ibid.*, p. 80.
[8]Michael J. Wreen plausibly widens the term "adultery" to apply to nonmarried persons who have sex with married persons, but since my focus is spouses, I will not widen the definition. "What's Really Wrong with Adultery?" *Journal of Applied Philosophy*, 3 (1986), pp. 45–49.

deceive (whether by lying, withholding information, or pretending about the affair); do not be unfair (by enjoying outside sex forbidden to one's spouse); and do not cause undeserved harm (to one's spouse who suspects or learns of the affair).[9] Wasserstrom points out that all these rules are *prima facie*: In some situations they are overridden by other moral considerations, thereby justifying some instances of adultery.

Moreover, adultery is not even *prima facie* wrong when spouses have an "open marriage" in which they give each other permission to have extramarital affairs. In this connection Wasserstrom raises questions about the reasonableness of traditional marital promises of sexual exclusivity. Wouldn't it be wiser to break the conventional ties between sex and love, so that the pleasures of adultery can be enjoyed along with those of marriage? Alternatively, should we maintain the connection between sex and love but break the exclusive tie between sexual love and one's spouse, thus tolerating multiple simultaneous loves for one's spouse and for additional partners? No doubt the linking of love, sex, and exclusivity has an *instrumental* role in promoting marriages, but so would the patently unreasonable practice of allowing people to eat decent meals (beyond bread and water) only with their spouses.

In my view, a rule-oriented approach to morality lacks the resources needed to answer the important questions Wasserstrom raises. We need an expanded conception of morality as encompassing ideals and virtues, in particular the moral ideals of love which provide the point of marital commitments and the virtues manifested in pursuing those ideals. The ethics of adultery centers on the moral ideals of and commitments to love—which include ideals of constancy (or faithfulness), honesty, trust, and fairness—that make possible special ways of caring for persons. The ideals are morally optional in that no one is obligated to embrace them. Nevertheless, strong obligations to avoid adultery arise for those couples who embrace the ideals as a basis for making traditional marital commitments. The primary commitment is to love each other, while the commitment of sexual exclusivity is secondary and supportive. This can be seen by focusing on three ideas that Wasserstrom devotes little attention to: love, commitments to love, and trust.

1. What is *love?* Let us set aside the purely descriptive (value-neutral) senses in which "love" refers to (a) a strong positive attraction or emotion[10] or (b) a complex attitude involving many emotions—not only strong affection, but also

---

[9] Richard Wasserstrom, "Is Adultery Immoral?" *Philosophical Forum*, 5 (1974), 513–528. Wasserstrom's preoccupation with rules explains why the most interesting part of his essay—the discussion of the connections between sex, love, and sexually-exclusive loving relationships—is approached so indirectly, in terms of "deeper deceptions" that violate the rule against deception, rather than directly in terms of violating moral ideals embedded in love.

[10] Wasserstrom sometimes uses "love" this way, as on p. 518. But on p. 522 he hints at the value-laden meaning of "love": "the issues are conceptual, empirical, and normative all at once: What is love? How could it be different? Would it be a good thing or a bad thing if it were different?" These questions, which are posed but not pursued, adumbrate my approach.

excitement, joy, pride, hope, fear, jealousy, anger, and so on.[11] Let us focus instead on the normative (value-laden) sense in which we speak of "true love" or "the real thing." Cogent disputes arise concerning the values defining true love, though ultimately individuals have a wide area of personal discretion in the ideals they pursue in relationships of erotic love.

In its value-laden senses, "love" refers to special ways of valuing persons.[12] As an attitude, love is valuing the beloved, cherishing her or him as unique. Erotic love includes sexual valuing, but the valuing is focused on the person as a unity, not just a body. As a relationship, love is defined by reciprocal attitudes of mutual valuing. The precise nature of this valuing turns on the ideals one accepts, and hence those ideals are part of the very meaning of "love."

2. According to the traditional ideal (or set of ideals) of interest here, marriage is based on a *commitment to love:* "to have and to hold from this day forward, for better for worse, for richer for poorer, in sickness and in health, to love and to cherish, till death us do part." This is not a commitment to have continuous feelings of strong affection—feelings which are beyond our immediate voluntary control. Instead, it is a commitment to create and sustain a relationship conducive to those feelings, as well as conducive to the happiness and fulfillment of both partners. Spouses assume responsibility for maintaining conditions for mutual caring which in turn foster recurring emotions of deep affection, delight, shared enthusiasm, and joy. The commitment to love is not a promise uttered once during a wedding ceremony; it is an ongoing willingness to assume responsibility for a value-guided relationship.

The commitment to love implies a web of values and virtues. It is a commitment to create a lifelong relationship of deep caring that promises happiness through shared activities (including sexual ones) and through joining interests in mutually supportive ways involving shared decision-making, honesty, trust, emotional intimacy, reciprocity, and (at least in modern versions) fair and equal opportunities for self-expression and personal growth. This traditional ideal shapes how spouses value each other, both symbolically and substantively. Commitments to love throughout a lifetime show that partners value each other as having paramount importance and also value them as a unity, as persons-living-throughout-a-lifetime. Time-limited commitments, such as to remain together only while in college, express at most a limited affirmation of the importance of the other person in one's life.

Valuing each other is manifested in a willingness to make accommodations and sacrifices to support the marriage. For most couples, some of those sacrifices are sexual. The promise of sexual exclusivity is a distinct wedding vow

---

[11]*Cf.* Annette Baier, "Unsafe Loves," in *The Philosophy of (Erotic) Love,* ed. Robert C. Solomon and Kathleen M. Higgins (Lawrence, KS: University Press of Kansas, 1991), pp. 444 and 449, n. 29.

[12]Irving Singer, *The Nature of Love,* 2nd ed. (Chicago: University of Chicago Press, 1984), 1, pp. 3 ff. In the third volume of this work, Singer sets forth a subjectivist view of the worth of persons. (Chicago: University of Chicago Press, 1987), III, p. 403. I share the more objectivist view of the unique worth of persons defended by Jeffrey Blustein in *Care and Commitment* (New York: Oxford University Press, 1991), pp. 203–216.

whose supportive status is symbolized by being mentioned in a subordinate clause, "and, forsaking all others, keep thee only unto her/him." Hopefully, couples who make the vow of sexual exclusivity are not under romantic illusions that their present sexual preoccupation with each other will magically abolish sexual interests in other people and temptations to have extramarital affairs. They commit themselves to sexual exclusivity as an expression of their love and with the aim of protecting that love.

How does sexual exclusivity express and protect love? In two ways. First, many spouses place adultery at the top of list of actions which threaten their marriage. They are concerned, often with full justification, that adultery might lead to another love that would damage or destroy their relationship. They fear that the affection, time, attention, and energy (not to mention money) given to an extramarital partner would lessen the resources they devote to sustaining their marriage. They also fear the potential for jealousy to disrupt the relationship.[13] As long as it does not become excessive, jealousy is a healthy reaction of anger, fear, and hurt in response to a perceived loss of an important good.[14] Indeed, if a spouse feels no jealousy whatsoever, the question is raised (though not answered) about the depth of love.

Second, sexual exclusivity is one way to establish the symbolism that "making love" is a singular affirmation of the partner. The love expressed is not just strong affection, but a deep valuing of each other in the ways defined by the ideals embedded in the marriage. Sex is especially well-suited (far more than eating) to express that love because of its extraordinary physical and emotional intimacy, tenderness, and pleasure. The symbolic meaning involved is not sentimental fluff; it makes possible forms of expression that enter into the substance of love.

In our culture sex has no uniform meaning, but couples are free to give it personal meanings. Janet Z. Giele notes two extremes: "On the one hand, the body may be viewed as the most important thing the person has to give, and sexual intercourse therefore becomes the symbol of the deepest and most far-reaching commitment, which is to be strictly limited to one pair-bond. On the other hand, participants may define sexual activity as merely a physical expression that, since it does not importantly envelop the whole personality nor commit the pair beyond the pleasures of the moment, may be regulated more permissively."[15] Between the two extremes lie many variations in the personal symbolism that couples give to sex, and here we are exploring only those variations found in traditional marital vows.

3. *Trust* is present at the time when couples undertake commitments to love, and in turn those commitments provide a framework for sustaining trust. Trust implies but is not reducible to Wasserstrom's "reasonable expectations" about a

---

[13]Roger Scruton, *Sexual Desire* (New York: Free Press, 1986), p. 339.

[14]For an illuminating historical study of changing attitudes see Peter N. Stearns, *Jealousy* (New York: New York University Press, 1989).

[15]Janet Z. Giele, as quoted by Philip E. Lampe, "The Many Dimensions of Adultery," in *Adultery in the United States*, p. 56.

partner's conduct. Expectations are epistemic attitudes, whereas trust is a moral attitude of relying on others to act responsibly, with good will, and (in marriage) with love and support.[16] We have a reasonable expectation that the earth will continue to orbit the sun throughout our lifetime, but no moral relationship of trust is involved. As a way of giving support to others, underwriting their endeavors, and showing the importance of their lives to us, trust and trustworthiness is a key ingredient in caring.

To be sure, trust is not always good. It is valuable when it contributes to valuable relationships, in particular to worthwhile marriages.[17] Marital trust is confidence in and dependence upon a spouse's morally responsible love. As such, it provides a basis for ongoing intimacy and mutual support. It helps spouses undergo the vulnerabilities and risks (emotional, financial, physical) inherent in intimate relationships.

The trust of marital partners is broad-scoped. Spouses trust each other to actively support the marriage and to avoid doing things that might pull them away from it. They trust each other to maintain the conditions for preserving intimacy and mutual happiness. Violating marital trust does more than upset expectations and cause pain. It violates trust, honesty, fairness, caring, and the other moral ideals defining the relationship. It betrays one's spouse. And it betrays one's integrity as someone committed to these ideals.

To sum up, I have avoided Wasserstrom's narrow preoccupation with the promise of sexual exclusivity. Commitments of sexual exclusivity find their rationale in wider commitments to love each other *if* a couple decides that exclusivity will support their commitments to love *and* where love is understood as a special way to value persons within lasting relationships based on mutual caring, honesty, and trust. Accordingly, marital faithfulness (or constancy) in loving is the primary virtue; sexual fidelity is a supporting virtue. And sexual fidelity must be understood in terms of the particular commitments and understandings that couples establish.

I have also avoided saying that sexual exclusivity is intrinsically valuable or a feature of all genuine love, unlike Bonnie Steinbock: "[sexual] exclusivity seems to be an intrinsic part of 'true love.' Imagine Romeo pouring out his heart to both Juliet *and* Rosaline! In our ideal of romantic love, one chooses to forgo pleasure with other partners in order to have a unique relationship with one's beloved."[18] In my view, the intrinsic good lies in fulfilling love relationships, rather than sexual exclusivity *per se*, thereby recognizing that some couples sustain genuine love without sexual exclusivity. For some couples sexual exclusivity does contribute to the goods found in traditional relationships, but other

---

[16]*Cf.* H.J.N. Horsburgh, "The Ethics of Trust," *The Philosophical Quarterly*, 10 (1960), 343–354; Annette Baier, "Trust and Antitrust," *Ethics*, 96 (1986), 231–260; Lawrence Thomas, "Trust, Affirmation, and Moral Character: A Critique of Kantian Morality," in *Identity, Character, and Morality: Essays in Moral Psychology* (Cambridge, MA: MIT Press, 1990), pp. 235–257; and Mike W. Martin, "Honesty in Love," *The Journal of Value Inquiry* (1993).

[17]Michael Slote, *Goods and Virtues* (Oxford: Clarendon Press, 1983), pp. 49, 65.

[18]Bonnie Steinbock, "Adultery," in Alan Soble (ed.), *The Philosophy of Sex* (Savage, Maryland: Rowman & Littlefield, 1991), p. 191.

couples achieve comparable goods through nontraditional relationships, for example open marriages that tolerate outside sex without love.[19] We can recognize the value of traditional relationships while also recognizing the value of alternative relationships, as chosen autonomously by couples.[20]

KEEPING COMMITMENTS

A complete ethics of keeping commitments of exclusivity would focus on the virtues of responsibility, faithfulness, and self-control. Here, however, I wish to defend Wasserstrom's view that even in traditional relationships the prohibition against adultery is *prima facie*. However strong the presumption against adultery in traditional relationships, it does not yield an exceptionless, all-things-considered judgment about wrongdoing and blameworthiness in specific cases. I will discuss four of many complicating factors.[21] What if partners wish to change their commitments? What happens when love comes to an end? What if one spouse falls in love with an additional partner? And what about the sometimes extraordinary self-affirmation extramarital affairs may bring?

(i) *Changing Commitments.* Some spouses who begin with traditional commitments later revise them. Buoyed by the exuberance of romance, most couples feel confident they will not engage in adultery (much less be among the fifty percent of couples who divorce). Later they may decide to renegotiate the guidelines for their marriage in light of changing attitudes and circumstances, though still within the framework of their commitments to love each other.[22] One study suggests that 90% of couples believe sexual exclusivity to be essential when they marry, but only 60% maintain this belief after several years of marriage (with the changes occurring primarily among those who had at least one affair).[23]

---

[19]See Russell Vannoy, *Sex Without Love* (Buffalo, NY: Prometheus, 1980).

[20]I am assuming that the consent involved in agreements between couples is fully voluntary and that a dominant partner does not exert pressures that make consent "intellectual" rather than emotionally wholehearted. Cf. J.F.M. Hunter, *Sex and Love* (Toronto: Macmillan, 1980), p. 42. To be sure, autonomy is not the sole value governing the making of marital commitments. There are reasons which need to be weighed in deciding what kind of commitments to make. Are partners being realistic in choosing between an exclusive relationship (with its element of sexual restriction) or an open relationship (with its risks of jealousy and new loves) as the best way to promote their happiness and love each other? And would permitting extramarital affairs negatively affect third parties (perhaps children)?

[21]These are not the only factors—a book would be needed to discuss all relevant factors. For example, what about the effects on third parties, not just children and other family, but the extramarital lover? Ellen Glasgow describes the joys of her affair with a married man as "miraculous" *The Woman Within* (New York: Hill and Wang, 1980), p. 156. Again, there are factors about how affairs are conducted, including the risk of contracting AIDS and giving it to one's spouse.

[22]The mutual renegotiation of relationships is a central aspect of marital equality, as argued by Robert C. Solomon, *About Love* (New York: Simon and Schuster, 1980), pp. 283–300.

[23]Lawson, *Adultery*, pp. 72–73.

Vita Sackville-West and Harold Nicolson provide an illuminating if unusual example. They married with the usual sexual attraction to each other and for several years were sexually compatible. As that changed, they gave each other permission to pursue extramarital affairs, primarily homosexual ones. Yet their original commitment to love each other remained intact. Indeed, for forty-nine years, until Vita died in 1962, their happy marriage was a model of mutual caring, deep affection, and trust: "What mattered most was that each should trust the other absolutely. 'Trust,' in most marriages, means [sexual] fidelity. In theirs it meant that they would always tell each other of their infidelities, give warning of approaching emotional crises, and, whatever happened, return to their common centre in the end."[24] Throughout much of their marriage they lived apart on weekdays, thereby accommodating both their work and their outside sexual liaisons. On weekends they would reunite as devoted companions, "berthed like sister ships."[25]

Just as we respect the mutual autonomy of couples in forming their initial understanding about their relationship, we should also respect their autonomy in renegotiating that understanding. The account I have offered allows us to distinguish between the primary commitment to love and the secondary commitment of sexual exclusivity. The secondary commitment is made in order to support the primary one, and if a couple agrees that it no longer is needed they are free to revoke it. Renegotiations can also proceed in the reverse directions: Spouses who initially agree on an open marriage may find that allowing extramarital affairs creates unbearable strains on their relationship, leading them to make commitments of exclusivity.

Changing commitments raise two major difficulties. First, couples are sometimes less than explicit about the sexual rules for their relationship. One or both partners may sense that their understandings have changed over the years but fail to engage in discussions that establish explicit new understandings. As a result, one spouse may believe that something is acceptable to the other spouse when in fact it is not. For example, Philip Blumstein and Pepper Schwartz interviewed a couple who, "when it came to a shared understanding about extramarital sex, . . . seemed not to be in the same marriage."[26] The man reported to them, "Sure we have an understanding. It's: 'You do what you want. Never go back to the same one [extramarital partner],'" presumably since that would threaten the relationship. By contrast, the wife reports: "We've never spoken about cheating, but neither of us believe in it. I don't think I'd ever forgive him [if he cheated on me]." Lack of shared understanding generates moral vagueness and ambiguity concerning adultery, whereas periodic forthright communication helps establish clear moral boundaries.[27]

---

[24]Nigel Nicolson, *Portrait of a Marriage* (New York: Atheneum, 1973), p. 188.

[25]*Ibid*, p. 231.

[26]Philip Blumstein and Pepper Schwartz, *American Couples* (New York: William Morrow, 1983), pp. 286–287.

[27]*Cf*. J.E. and Mary Ann Barnhart, "Marital Faithfulness and Unfaithfulness," *Journal of Social Philosophy* 4 (April 1973): 10–15.

Second, what happens when only one partner wants to renegotiate an original understanding? The mere desire to renegotiate does not constitute a betrayal, but nor does it by itself justify adultery if one's spouse refuses to rescind the initial vow of sexual exclusivity. In such cases the original presumption against adultery continues but with an increased risk that the partner wishing to change it may feel adultery is more excusable. Such conflicts may or may not be resolved in a spirit of caring and compromise that enables good relationships to continue. Lacking such resolution, the moral status of adultery may become less clear-cut.

(ii) *Lost Love.* Couples who make traditional commitments sometimes fall out of love, singly or together, or for other reasons find themselves unwilling to continue in a marriage. Sometimes the cause is adultery, and sometimes adultery is a symptom of irresponsibility and poor judgment that erodes the relationship in additional ways.[28] But other times there is little or no fault involved. Lasting love is a creation of responsible conduct *and* luck.[29] No amount of conscientiousness can replace the good fortune of emotional compatibility and conducive circumstances.

In saying that traditional commitments to love are intended to be lifelong, we need not view them as unconditional.[30] Typically they are based on tacit conditions. One condition is embedded in the wedding ceremony in which *mutual* vows are exchanged, namely, that one's spouse will take the marital vows seriously. Others are presupposed as background conditions, for example, that the spouse will not turn into a murderer, rapist, spouse-beater, child-abuser, or psychopathic monster. Usually there are more specific tacit assumptions that evolve before the marriage, for example, that the spouses will support each other's careers. Above all, there is the background hope that with sincere effort the relationship will contribute to the overall happiness of both partners. All these conditions remain largely tacit, as a matter of faith. When that faith proves ill-founded or just unlucky, the ethics of adultery becomes complicated.

As relationships deteriorate, adultery may serve as a transition to new and perhaps better relationships. In an ideal world, marriages would be ended cleanly before new relationships begin. But then, in an ideal world people would be sufficiently prescient not to make traditional commitments that are unlikely to succeed. Contemplating adultery is an occasion for much self-deception, but at least sometimes there may be good reasons for pursuing alternative relationships before officially ending a bad marriage.[31]

---

[28]E.g., Herbert S. Strean, *The Extramarital Affair* (New York: Free Press, 1980); and Frank Pittman, *Private Lies: Infidelity and the Betrayal of Intimacy* (New York: W.W. Norton, 1989).

[29]Cf. Martha C. Nussbaum, *The Fragility of Goodness* (New York: Cambridge University Press, 1980), pp. 259–362.

[30]Contrary to Susan Mendus, "Marital Faithfulness," *Philosophy*, 59 (1984), p. 246. For criticisms of Mendus, see Alan Soble *The Structure of Love* (New Haven, CN: Yale University Press, 1990), p. 166; and Mike W. Martin, "Love's Constancy," *Philosophy* 68 (1993): 63–77.

[31]An interesting example of deciding *against* adultery is the subject of Lotte Hamburger and Joseph Hamburger, *Contemplating Adultery* (New York: Fawcett Columbine, 1991).

(iii) *New Loves.* Some persons claim to (erotically) love both their spouse and an additional lover. They may be mistaken, as they later confess to themselves, but is it impossible to love two (or more) people simultaneously? "Impossible" in what sense?

Perhaps for some people it is a psychological impossibility, but, again, other individuals report a capacity to love more than one person at a time. For many persons it is a practical impossibility, given the demands of time, attention, and affection required in genuine loving. But that would seem to allow that re-sourceful individuals can finesse (psychologically, logistically, financially, and so forth) multiple simultaneous relationships. I believe that the impossibility is moral and conceptual—*if* one embraces traditional ideals that define marital love as a singular affirmation of one's spouse and *if* a couple establishes sex as a symbolic and substantive way to convey that exclusive love.[32] Obviously peo-ple can experience additional romantic attractions after they make traditional vows, but it is morally impossible for them to actively engage in loving rela-tionships with additional partners without violating the love defined by their initial commitments.

Richard Taylor disagrees in *Having Love Affairs*, a book-length defense of adultery. No doubt this book is helpful for couples planning open marriages, but Taylor concentrates on situations where traditional vows have been made and then searches for ways to minimize the harm to spouses that results from extramarital love affairs.[33] In that regard his book is morally subversive in that it systematically presents only one side of the story. Here are five examples of this one-sidedness.

First, with considerable panache Taylor develops a long list of rules for *non*adulterous partners who should be tolerant of their partner's affairs. (a) "Do not spy or pry," since that is self-degrading and shows a lack of trust in one's spouse. (But is a commitment-breaking spouse trustworthy?) (b) "Do not con-front or entrap," because that would humiliate the spouse. (But what about being humiliated oneself?) (c) "Stay out of it," since good marriages survive adultery. (No empirical support is offered for that generalization!) (d) "Stop being jealous," since jealousy disrupts marriages. (But what about the case for not provoking jealousy in the first place?)

Taylor also offers rules for the spouse having the affair: Maintain fidelity with one's lover, be honest with one's lover, be discreet rather than boasting about the affair, and do not betray or abandon the lover. In discussing these rules Taylor is oblivious to the infidelity, betrayal of trust, and failure to value one's spouse in the way called for by traditional commitments and the shared understanding between spouses.

Second, Taylor defines infidelity as "a betrayal of the promise to love" and faithfulness as "a state of one's heart and mind," rather than "mere outward

---

[32]Robert Nozick develops a slightly different argument based on the intimate mutual identification involved in forming a couple or a "we." See *The Examined Life* (New York: Simon and Schuster, 1989), pp. 82, 84.

[33]Richard Taylor, *Having Love Affairs* (Buffalo, NY: Prometheus, 1982), pp. 67–68.

conformity to rules." Infidelity can be shown in ways unrelated to adultery, such as in neglecting the spouse's sexual needs, selfishly using shared financial resources, and failing to be caring and supportive.[34] It is true that infidelity takes other forms, but what about the infidelity in violating marital vows and understandings? Moreover, the only place we are reminded that "inner states" of faithfulness are manifested in outward conduct is when Taylor condemns infidelity toward an extramarital lover, not one's spouse.

Third, love affairs are natural and avoiding them is unhealthy. "A man, by nature, desires many sexual partners"; "The suppression of the polygamous impulse in a man is . . . bought at a great price" of frustrated and rueful longing for outside love affairs.[35] Granted, most people (male and female) have desires for multiple sexual partners. Yet many people also have monogamous impulses, as shown in their decisions to enter into traditional marriages. The resulting conflicts make sexual exclusivity notoriously difficult, but they need not result in frustration; often they contribute greatly to overall sexual satisfaction within secure and trusting relationships.

Fourth, "No one can tell another person what is and is not permissible with respect to whom he or she will love. . . . However inadvisable it may be to seek love outside the conventional restraints, the *right* to do so is about as clear as any right can be."[36] Taylor is equivocating of "right," which can mean that (1) others are obligated to leave one alone or (2) that one's conduct is all right. Having a right not to be interfered with by society as one engages in adultery does not imply that one's conduct is "all right" or morally permissible. Indeed, couples who make traditional commitments waive some rights in relation to each other; in particular they waive the right to engage in adultery which violates their marital agreements.

Fifth, and most important, Taylor praises love affairs as inherently good and even the highest good: "the joys of illicit and passionate love, which include but go far beyond the mere joys of sex, are incomparably good."[37] On the same page he says, "This does not mean that love affairs are better than marriage, for they seldom are. Love between married persons can, in the long run, be so vastly more fulfilling" than affairs. I find it difficult to reconcile these claims: Those marriages which are vastly more fulfilling would thereby seem to provide the incomparable goods, not extramarital affairs which violate the commitments defining the marriage. Of course many people find joy in extramarital sex, and for some the joy may be the greatest they find in life. But Taylor provides no basis for saying that happy traditional marriages never produce comparable joys. Nor does he ever explain how extramarital joys are morally permissible for individuals who make traditional marriage vows.

---

[34]*Ibid.*, pp. 59–60.

[35]*Ibid.*, pp. 70, 72–73. The possible frustrations of monogamy are discussed by Edmund Leites in his illuminating book, *The Puritan Conscience and Modern Sexuality* (New Haven: Yale University Press, 1986).

[36]*Ibid.*, p. 48. For these and other ambiguities of "rights" see Ronald Dworkin, *Taking Rights Seriously* (Cambridge: Harvard University Press, 1977), pp. 188–189.

[37]*Ibid.*, p. 12.

Bonnie Steinbock affirms an opposite view. She suggests that to fall in love with someone other than one's spouse is already a betrayal: "Sexual infidelity has significance as a sign of a deeper betrayal—falling in love with someone else. It may be objected that we cannot control the way we feel, only the way we behave; that we should not be blamed for falling in love, but only for acting on the feeling. While we may not have direct control over our feelings, however, we are responsible for getting ourselves into situations in which certain feelings naturally arise."[38] I agree that spouses who make traditional vows are responsible for avoiding situations that they know (or should know) foster extramarital love.[39] Nevertheless, deeply committed people occasionally do fall in love with third parties without being blameworthy for getting into situations that spark that love. Experiencing a strong romantic attraction is not by itself an infidelity, and questions of betrayal may arise only when a person moves in the direction of acting on the love in ways that violate commitments to one's spouse.

Having said all this, I know of no argument that absolutely condemns all love-inspired adultery as immoral, all things considered and in all respects, even within traditional relationships. Nonetheless, as I have been concerned to emphasize, there is a serious betrayal of one's spouse. But to say that ends the matter would make the commitment to love one's spouse a moral absolute, with no exceptions whatsoever. Tragic dilemmas overthrow such absolutes, and we need to set aside both sweeping condemnations and wholesale defenses of love-inspired adultery.

To mention just one type of case, when marriages are profoundly unfulfilling, and when constricting circumstances prevent other ways of meeting important needs, there is a serious question whether love-inspired adultery is sometimes justifiable or at least excusable—witness *The Scarlet Letter, Anna Karenina, Madame Bovary, Lady Chatterley's Lover,* and *The Awakening.* Moreover, our deep ambivalence about some cases of love-inspired adultery reflect how there is some good and some bad involved in conduct that we cannot fully justify nor fully condemn.

(iv) *Sex and Self-Esteem.* Extramarital affairs are often grounded in attractions less grand than love. Affection, friendship, or simple respect may be mixed with a desire for exciting sex and the enhanced self-esteem from being found sexually desirable. The sense of risk may add to the pleasure that one is so desirable that a lover will take added risks. Are sex and self-esteem enough to justify violating marital vows? It would seem not. The obligations created through marital commitments are moral requirements, whereas sex and self-esteem pertain to one's self-interest. Doesn't morality trump self-interest?

But things are not so simple. Morality includes rights and responsibilities to ourselves to pursue our happiness and self-fulfillment. Some marriages are sexually frustrating or damaging in other ways to self-respect. Even when marriages

[38]Bonnie Steinbock, "Adultery," in Alan Soble (ed.), *The Philosophy of Sex,* p. 192.
[39]For an interesting example, see Janice Rosenberg "Fidelity," in Laurie Abraham *et al., Reinventing Love* (New York: Plume, 1993), pp. 101–106.

are basically fulfilling, more than a few individuals report their extramarital affairs were liberating and transforming, whether or not grounded in love. For example, many women make the following report about their extramarital affair: "It's given me a whole new way of looking at myself . . . I felt attractive again. I hadn't felt that way in years, really. It made me very, very confident."[40]

In addition, the sense of personal enhancement may have secondary benefits. Occasionally it strengthens marriages, especially after the extramarital affair ends, and some artists report an increase in creative activity. These considerations do not automatically outweigh the dishonesty and betrayal that may be involved in adultery, and full honesty may never be restored when spouses decide against confessing an affair to their partners.[41] But nor are considerations of enhanced self-esteem and its secondary benefits irrelevant.

I have mentioned some possible justifications or excuses for specific instances of adultery after traditional commitments are made. I conclude with a caveat. Specific instances are one thing; general attitudes about adultery are another. Individuals who make traditional commitments and who are fortunate enough to establish fulfilling relationships based on those commitments ought to maintain a general attitude that for them to engage in adultery would be immoral (as well as stupid). The "ought" is stringent, as stringent as the commitment to sexual exclusivity. Rationalizing envisioned adultery with anecdotes about the joys of extramarital sex or statistics about the sometimes beneficial effects of adultery is a form of moral duplicity. It is also inconsistent with the virtues of both sexual fidelity and faithfulness in sustaining commitments to love.

Questions

1. Does Mike Martin's expanded conception of morality enable one to understand the ethics of adultery any better than Richard Wasserstrom's account does? Can it say any more about the evaluation of "open marriages"—marriages in which the partners specifically avoid making a commitment of sexual exclusivity?
2. May a commitment to be sexually exclusive ever be overturned?
3. To what extent, if any, can a person who has made a commitment to love a spouse be blamed for ceasing to have strong affections for that person?

---

[40]Lynn Atwater, *The Extramarital Connection* (New York: Irvington Publishers, 1982), p. 143. The same theme is developed in Dalma Heyn, *The Erotic Silence of the American Wife* (New York: Signet, 1993).

[41]Dalma Heyn (*ibid.*) urges that not confessing adultery to one's spouse is especially justified for women whose adultery is likely to provoke physical abuse or a divorce that would leave them and their children impoverished. Others argue that even when the adultery is immoral that confession wreaks more harm than the benefits of restoring full honesty in the relationship. (E.g., Laura Green, "Never Confess," in *Reinventing Love*, pp. 192–197.) The case for promoting honesty by confessing to one's spouse an infidelity is made by Frank Pittman in *Private Lies*.

Virtue Ethics and Adultery

Raja Halwani

Raja Halwani begins by outlining some recent concerns about Kantian (or deontological) and consequentialist ethics before explaining what a virtue ethics approach is. He then addresses what he takes to be the shortcomings of Kantian approaches to the question of adultery. He suggests that to evaluate adultery, as Kantianism does, in terms of rules (such as those concerning the keeping of promises) is to oversimplify a matter that involves highly complex emotions, beliefs, and histories. Moreover, he claims that a promise of sexual exclusivity is not a promise in relation to a specific act, but rather a promise to be a certain kind of person—a sexually faithful one. Since being this kind of person is very hard and something over which one does not have complete control, a promise of sexual exclusivity should not be seen as an ordinary kind of promise but rather as a promise to attempt to be sexually exclusive. As a result, he says, applying ordinary judgments about the keeping and breaking of promises to adultery will be misleading and unrealistic.

The author thinks that a virtue ethics approach to adultery is much richer. He takes fidelity to be an ideal in a marriage because infidelity tends to undermine the emotional commitment on which marriage is based. Given the ideal of fidelity, a virtuous person would strive to uphold it. This is done by fostering love, trust, and affection—emotions that tend to be undermined by adulterous behavior. This virtue account of adultery also helps, says the author, to deal with nonideal cases. Thus, for example, in a marriage no longer characterized by emotional commitments, adultery will be less bad (even though it will still involve the breaking of a promise of sexual exclusivity).

The paper concludes with some arguments about why consequentialism provides a less satisfactory account of adultery than virtue ethics does. Regarding act utilitarianism, the author refers to the notorious problem that it sometimes requires the performance of unjust acts. He argues, too, that on such a theory, actions that appear bad at the time they are performed can

*turn out to be good because of the unfore-
seen beneficial consequences that result
from their performance. Rule utilitarian-* *ism, he says, suffers from the same sorts of
problems as Kantianism in focusing on
rules rather than on character.*

When philosophers have turned their attention to the topic of adultery, even though this has been rare,[1] they did so primarily under the terms of Kantian ethics. Thus we find Michael Wreen giving a Kantian argument against adultery, and we find Richard Wasserstrom arguing that under a Kantian model adultery is still permissible.[2] I would like to take a look at adultery from the standpoint of an ethics of virtue, the reason being that such an ethics allows better for the complexities surrounding the topic.

In the first section, I list and briefly explain some of the most important misgivings that the friends of virtue ethics have with Kantian theory (and consequentialism). I also briefly explain the salient features of an ethics of virtue, some of its salient problems, and some possible replies to these problems. In the second section, I point out some of the deficiencies that result from assessing the morality of adultery from a Kantian standpoint. In the third and final section, I discuss what an ethics of virtue has to say on adultery.

1. AN OUTLINE OF VIRTUE ETHICS

Recently, there has been some dissatisfaction with modern moral philosophy, that is, Kantian ethics, consequentialism, and their offshoots, such as social contract ethics and rights theory. Elizabeth Anscombe, Philippa Foot, Alasdair MacIntyre, and Bernard Williams[3] are among the first philosophers to inveigh against modern moral philosophy, and their views have prompted the

[1]The following is an inexhaustive list of some of the recent literature. David Carr, "Chastity and Adultery," *American Philosophical Quarterly,* vol. 23, no. 4, Oct. 1986, Raja Halwani, "The Morality of Adultery," *Dialogue,* vol. 38, issue 2/3, April 1996; Mike W. Martin, "Adultery and Fidelity," *Journal of Social Philosophy,* vol. 25, no. 3, Winter 1994; Bonnie Steinbock, "Adultery," in *Philosophy of Sex,* ed. by Alan Soble (Savage, Md.: Rowman and Littlefield, 1991); Richard Taylor, *Having Love Affairs* (Buffalo: Prometheus Books, 1982); Richard Wasserstrom, "Is Adultery Immoral?", in *Philosophy and Sex,* ed. by Robert Baker and Frederick Elliston (Buffalo: Prometheus Books, 1984); and Michael Wreen, "What's Really Wrong with Adultery," in *Philosophy of Sex,* ed. by Soble. Carr's discussion is Christian in its approach and focuses on the logic of the concept of the virtue of chastity; Halwani, Wasserstrom, and Wreen approach the topic from a Kantian perspective; Martin, Steinbock and Taylor have views highly amenable to virtue ethics.
[2]Wasserstrom does not explicitly say that he is operating from within a Kantian framework. I will discuss these positions in some detail in section 2 below.
[3]Here's a sample. Elizabeth Anscombe, "Modern Moral Philosophy," *Philosophy,* 33: 1–19, 1958; Philippa Foot, *Virtues and Vices* (Berkeley: University of California Press, 1978); Alasdair MacIntyre,

search for an alternative ethical theory. The most important candidate is virtue ethics, an ethics that has its roots in Aristotle's views on the nature of the ethical life.

A number of components of modern moral philosophy have come under attack. Very briefly, the notion of duty has been attacked on the grounds that (i) such a notion presupposes the idea of a set of laws laid down by a certain authority, but that with respect to moral duties and obligations, it is difficult to find the principles and laws that would adequately justify such duties, and (ii) that the notion of moral obligation has its roots in a religious conception which is no longer viable. Moreover, the idea of moral duty is in tension with moral luck. The former seems to imply that morality is immune to luck, since it requires that agents carry out their moral duties, and this can be done only if it is within our ability to do so. But it also seems that luck is a pervasive phenomenon, and so duty and luck are in conflict. A third problem is concerned with principles: modern moral philosophy, in its emphasis on principles has failed to supply us with ones that can guide our actions, and one reason for this is the generality and abstractness of such principles. Such principles assume agents which are without context and history. In addition, we rarely conduct our ethical life by invoking such principles.[4]

Most philosophers who have attacked modern moral philosophy have gathered around an ethics of virtue, an ethics which is still in its infancy insofar as its theoretical articulation is concerned. The core idea in an ethics of virtue is that the basic judgments in ethics are not judgments about acts but about character. According to Gregory Trianosky, "a pure ethics of virtue makes two claims. First it claims that at least some judgments about virtue can be validated independently of any appeal to judgments about the rightness of actions. Second . . . it is this antecedent goodness of traits which ultimately makes any right act right."[5] Under deontological and utilitarian conceptions, the notion of right behavior or acts is logically prior to that of virtues. An ethics of virtue flips such a conception around: it is right behavior which is justified in terms of the virtues.

The question now of course is from what do the virtues themselves derive their justification. The answer usually given is that the virtues derive their justification from the notion of well-being or human flourishing. The virtues can then be thought of as being either *necessary* for well-being or as *constitutive* of it. However, and according to Statman, the linkage between the virtues and well-being is not essential to an ethics of virtue. What is essential is the claim that judgments about character are prior to judgments about the rightness or

---

After Virtue (Notre Dame: University of Notre Dame Press, 1984); Michael Slote, *From Morality to Virtue* (New York: Oxford University Press, 1992); Michael Stocker, "The Schizophrenia of Modern Ethical Theories," *Journal of Philosophy*, 73: 453–466, 1976; Bernard Williams, *Ethics and the Limits of Philosophy* (Cambridge: Harvard University Press, 1985).
[4]Daniel Statman, ed., *Virtue Ethics*, unpublished, p. 6.
[5]Gregory Trianosky, "What is Virtue Ethics All About?", *American Philosophical Quarterly*, vol. 27, no. 4, October 1990, p. 336.

wrongness of behavior.[6] Such a claim can be a moderate one—that although most judgments are judgments of character, still, some actions can be evaluated independently of character—or it can be an extreme one. Under an extreme formulation, we can hold either a reductionist view or a replacement one. The former states that deontic concepts such as rightness and duty are useful, but that they are nevertheless derived from concepts of character. The latter, which is the most extreme formulation, states that deontic notions should be entirely discarded by an ethics of virtue and be replaced by other concepts, such as those of courage, benevolence, and generosity—the "thick concepts" of Bernard Williams.[7]

A good person is someone who is good because of the virtues he or she possesses. So not only are acts justified in terms of the virtues, but also whether a person is good or not will depend on the virtues, or lack thereof, that she has. This raises the question of what kind of an account of the virtues can be given. Typically, the understanding of the virtues has been dispositional: to have a certain virtue is to be disposed to act in certain ways given certain conditions. Such an understanding has been attacked by Mary Ella Savarino on the grounds that virtues do not turn out to be fundamental: "the focus is not on the virtue itself (courage), but on the person's behavior."[8] Savarino herself favors an account of virtues which takes them to be first actualities in the Aristotelian sense. In any case, the issue is still open: an adequate account of the virtues is needed.

It is obvious that virtue ethics has a number of advantages. For example, it makes room for the idea that it is not the case that for any moral problem there is only one right answer. Two virtuous people may act differently from one another when faced with the same situation, and yet both their actions can be right. A mother in poor health who has to work in the fields, who has five children, and who has an abortion upon her sixth pregnancy is not to be described as self-indulgent. Another mother in a similar situation might decide to go ahead with the pregnancy, and she is surely heroic. Both the actions are right despite the fact that the mothers acted differently. Second, virtue ethics is not in tension with the phenomenon of moral luck. As Statman put it, "According to Virtue Ethics, judgments of character, such as, 'Barbara is a friendly woman', 'Tom is unbearably arrogant', are not touched by the discovery that these traits are the result of genes, education, and circumstances, over which the agent had very limited control."[9]

Another important advantage of an ethics of virtue is its rejection of the distinction between the moral and the nonmoral. For if virtue ethics is concerned with the evaluation of character, then other nonmoral traits would be

[6]Statman, p. 8.

[7]Ibid., p. 9. Michael Slote, *From Morality to Virtue*, advocates the moderate view. Anscombe advocates the replacement view. Williams seems to hold the reductionist view. See also Philipp Montague, "Virtue Ethics: A Qualified Success Story," *American Philosophical Quarterly*, vol. 29, no. 1, January 1992.

[8]Mary Ella Savarino, "Toward an Ontology of Virtue Ethics", *Journal of Philosophical Research*, vol. 18, 1993, p. 245.

[9]Statman, p. 17.

important, especially if the notion of well-being is taken to be primary. What enters into the well-being or flourishing of a person is not only what has been traditionally dubbed as "moral," but also a host of other "nonmoral" considerations, such as love, marriage, and sexual relations.

But it is also obvious that an ethics of virtue still has some difficulties to overcome. Two difficulties are especially pernicious. The first concerns the justification of the virtues: from what do the virtues derive their justification? One answer has been that they get their justification from the idea of well-being or human flourishing. The problem would then consist of giving an account of flourishing which itself does not rely on the notion of the virtues in order to avoid circularity. Sarah Conly[10] has argued that such an account is not forthcoming because it faces a dilemma: either we define flourishing in terms of one important feature, or we define it broadly, such that it would contain a number of human goods, and such that people can flourish in a variety of ways. A narrow understanding of flourishing would yield the implausible result that one feature (the defining feature) can capture all that goes into the notions of the good life and the good character. If, however, flourishing is defined broadly, then the problem would be the possibility of someone flourishing without the virtues. Conly gives the example of Lorenzo the Magnificent, who was rich, powerful, and a patron of the arts. Plausibly, he flourished and was happy. Yet he was notoriously unjust: he assassinated his enemies, he was "ruthless and pitiless," and he never cared for the rights of others (p. 92).

The second important difficulty that faces an ethics of virtue is that of its inability to provide us with principles and rules to help us guide our actions. What is ironic about this problem, of course, is that it is the same one that the friends of virtue ethics have accused modern moral philosophy of. This difficulty is connected to the one above, for one possibility of providing guidance would be to follow in the footsteps of what a flourishing person would do in the situation of a moral dilemma. But imagining what such a virtuous person would do would at best yield vague results.

Such difficulties do not constitute knock-down arguments against virtue ethics. There are replies for them. For example, Slote argues that it is true that the virtues cannot be strictly justified, that is, cannot be derived from first principles, but that they can be justified in the sense that they cohere with our moral intuitions. Of course, one can still attempt to give an account of human flourishing, an account that would evade Conly's dilemma. With respect to rules and principles, Kantian and consequentialist ethics are in no better position, and perhaps it is a mistake to look for principles to begin with: moral problems require the exercise of judgment, sensitivity, and imagination, at least in order to be able to decide on the course of action to be taken. A virtuous person is not necessarily someone who possesses an excellent set of principles and meta-principles. We have to remember also that in everyday life we often make correct moral judgments, and we do not typically make them by appealing to utilitarian or Kantian

---

[10]Sarah Conly, "Flourishing and the Failure of the Ethics of Virtue," *Midwest Studies in Philosophy,* vol. 13. Page references are to this journal.

principles. So it is not the case that without such theories we are bereft of rules. An ethics of virtue can rely on the rules of thumb used in everyday life, it can rely on a broad enough conception of what a good person is, and it can rely on specific virtues if the question is that of guidance.

It is not my purpose here to give a theoretical defense of what virtue ethics is. Such a task is extremely difficult and, I suspect, pointless. I myself prefer a moderate version of virtue ethics, a version which does not attempt to eliminate or reduce all judgments about acts to judgments about character. After all, certain acts are so horrific that they are bad no matter what kind of person commits them. In such a moderate version, the primacy of character is what is central to ethical thinking and evaluation, and hard and fast moral principles are avoided. What is retained is a paradigmatic set of virtues, virtues that are universal (such as courage, honesty, fairness, and love), and that one and the same person can possess. Moreover, deliberation about how to act and evaluation of acts are intimately connected to the history of the person who deliberates and commits these acts.

It is important to mention that an ethics of virtue is not in tension with feminist ethics, generally speaking.[11] To begin with, they both agree in many of their criticisms of modern moral philosophy. Moreover, their positive claims are in harmony. For example, an ethics of care, such as that advocated by Carol Gilligan, emphasizes that what is important about some of our acts from an ethical point of view is that one does them because one cares, and not because it is one's duty to do them. This claim, of course, would be embraced by an ethics of virtue.

2. TWO EXISTENT PHILOSOPHICAL VIEWS ON ADULTERY

In "What's Really Wrong with Adultery," Michael Wreen[12] advances an argument, based on Kantian considerations, to show that adultery is morally wrong. His argument is as follows: adultery is wrong because it involves a contradiction (the Kantian consideration), on the part of the married adulterer, in two policies: the policy of sexual exclusivity and the policy of engaging in sexual behavior with someone not included in the former policy. The contradiction arises because these two policies cannot be universalized consistently (p. 181). The conclusion is that adultery is wrong. However, it is prima facie wrong, and such wrongness can be overridden in some circumstances, in a case, for instance, in which committing adultery is the only way to save a marriage (p. 185).

Wreen's argument is not sound, because one of its premises is false. Adultery is typically not a matter of policy; one does not engage in adultery as a mat-

---

[11]Some important work in feminist ethics is the following: Annette Baier, "What Do Women Want in a Moral Theory?", *Nous*, 19: 53–63, 1985, and "Extending the Limits of Moral Theory," *Journal of Philosophy*, 83 (10): 538–45, 1986; Carol Gilligan, *In a Different Voice* (Cambridge: Harvard University Press, 1982); Nel Noddings, *Caring: A Feminine Approach to Ethics and Moral Education* (Berkeley and Los Angeles: University of California Press, 1984).

[12]In *The Philosophy of Sex*, ed. by Soble. All page references in my paper are to this anthology.

ter of policy. Sometimes "things just happen," and often, when engaging in an extramarital affair,[13] one pursues the affair simply because of the lack of sufficient willpower not to. It is *possible* to pursue adultery as a policy, but it is not typical. And surely Wreen does not want to have a premise of his argument resting on the untypical.

I am not really concerned with finding faults in specific arguments. What is crucial, I think, is the general framework from which Wreen approaches the topic. According to Wreen, the morality of adultery stems from a contradiction, "social and personal" though it may be, and sexual exclusivity and extramarital engagements are given the status of policies. There is something very unrealistic about treating such matters in these ways, and I have hinted at this by claiming that adultery is rarely a matter of policy. The attempt at sexual exclusivity and the committing of adultery involve highly complex emotions, beliefs, and histories that resist such simplification and tidiness. A woman who has an affair because her husband has consistently neglected her—and not just sexually— cannot be condemned in a sweeping fashion such as Wreen's. And often one cannot just leave a marriage if one's spouse is being neglectful; sometimes there are things at stake. To categorically condemn adultery in the way that Wreen does displays insensitivity to these phenomena. We simply cannot go by strict rules here. Moreover, hedging these considerations by introducing the 'prima facie' rider will not do it. For if it turns out that in most cases of adultery there is always the need to take into account the details of the situation, details that would make the application of such rules difficult, then the usefulness of the rider is called into question. As the proponents of an ethics of virtue have emphasized, going by strict rules is both simplistic and unfaithful to the way we ethically think and behave.

Richard Wasserstrom in "Is Adultery Immoral?"[14] replies to two arguments that are typically given against adultery. The first is that adultery is wrong because it is an instance of promise-breaking, and any instance of promise-breaking is wrong. The second argument is that adultery is wrong because it is a form of deception, and deception is wrong. Wasserstrom's response to both arguments is embodied in the possibility, and the actuality, of open marriages. If this is so, then neither of the above two arguments would go through, for in cases of open marriages, there is neither promise-breaking—no promises of sexual exclusivity have been made to begin with—nor deception (p. 101).

Insofar as these two arguments go, Wasserstrom is correct. They are invalid because not every case of marriage need involve promise-making, and not every case of adultery in a marriage need involve deception. Again, however, the framework within which Wasserstrom operates is impoverished. Let me start by saying a couple of things about the institution of promise-making in marriage.

---

[13]Unless explicitly noted, I use "marriage" and "marital" in a broad sense, covering also heterosexual and homosexual couples, who are married for all practical purposes, although not formally so. Of course, I also use the terms for those who are formally and legally married.

[14]In *Today's Moral Problems* (New York: Macmillan, 1975). Also reprinted in *Philosophy and Sex*, ed. Baker and Elliston. Page references in my paper are to the latter anthology.

To begin with, the promise of being faithful to one's spouse ranges over two kinds of things: acts and emotions. One promises not to have sexual relations outside marriage, and one promises not to love (romantically) anyone else other than one's spouse. Such promises are interesting. Under one usual understanding of what it is to make a promise, when I make a promise to someone, the promise is in relation to a *specific act*; I promise to meet her at a certain time and place, I promise to return the money to him, and so forth. The operative idea here is that to make a promise is to make a commitment to do something (or not to) that is within one's power to do. I simply cannot promise to do something that I believe I am not able to perform. In this, promise-making is similar to deliberation: one cannot deliberate about what is not within one's power to do. When it comes, however, to promises regarding habits and character traits, things look a bit different. "I promise to be honest" is a void one if uttered by a pathological liar, and is a rash one if uttered by someone who has been lying most of his life. Promises that range over character traits are problematic in the sense that what is promised cannot be easily assumed to be within the agent's immediate control. Such promises are perhaps better understood to be elliptical: "I promise to be honest" is short for "I promise to try to be honest."

With these points in mind, the promise of sexual fidelity does not range over one specific individual, that is, I do not promise my spouse not to have sex just with John. Rather, I promise my spouse not to have sex with anyone other than my spouse. In this regard, such a promise ranges over an open-ended list of potential, typically unknown, sexual partners. This sets the promise of sexual fidelity apart from other instances of promise-making, in which the promise ranges over some specific act. This, in and of itself, is not strange, for we often make promises such as, "I promise not to do this anymore," or "I promise to be more attentive," or "I promise to be more honest." These promises range over habits and character traits. But the fact that the promise of sexual exclusivity is a promise about what kind of person one is going to be—a sexually faithful one— and not about a specific act should caution us from thinking that a violation of such a promise is a simple act of promise-breaking in the same way as not meeting my friend after I had promised her that I would. For often being a certain kind of person is a hard thing to do. The promise of sexual exclusivity is best understood as the promise to try to be sexually faithful. If not, our judgments of those who fail in their promises might very well be unnecessarily harsh.

In regard to the promise of romantic exclusion, there is something very strange about promising someone to have, or to maintain, a certain emotion or emotions. The reason is that emotions are often not the kind of thing that is within our immediate control. If one is the kind of person who does not react with indignation in the appropriate circumstances, then "I promise to feel indignation next time" has a false ring to it, because to feel indignation is not a matter of sheer willpower. The having of certain emotions requires toil, practice, placing oneself in certain situations, and so on. When it comes to love, things look similar. Love is not the kind of thing that can be acquired at the drop of a hat, and whether one feels love or not is not a matter of direct control. Many factors come into shaping and having the emotion of love, and these factors are sometimes beyond the agent's control. How can I promise to love someone for all eternity when I know that I can have a change of heart, and when I know that my change of heart is often not up to me?

I am not arguing that we should never promise to love or to be sexually faithful. What I am arguing, however, is that looking at the ethics of adultery and love from the perspective of promise-making is misleading and unrealistic to the kind of beings that we are. To recapitulate, promises to sexual exclusivity do not involve specific acts, but character traits and virtues: to promise to be sexually faithful is to promise to be a certain kind of person. Furthermore, being a certain kind of person is not a simple matter of willpower or of refraining from doing specific acts. It is a matter of education, training, desires, luck, *and* will power. Hence, to commit adultery is to deviate, at least temporarily, from being that kind of person. Moreover, if our focus is on characters and virtues, then surely, whether adultery is wrong or not cannot be approached from the perspective of acts, that is, whether adultery is wrong or not is not a matter of whether it is an instance of a wrong kind of act (promise-breaking) or not.

3. ADULTERY AND VIRTUE ETHICS

In *Having Love Affairs*,[15] Richard Taylor gives us an interesting case of a married couple, the upshot of which is that whereas it is the wife who commits adultery, she is not the one to be described as unfaithful. The husband has been married to the same woman for a long time, and he has never been sexually unfaithful to her. He believes that sexual fidelity is of utmost importance, and he frowns upon any act of adultery committed by others. However, it is not in his nature, so to speak, to be sexually active. As a matter of fact, "[h]is intimacy with his own wife is perfunctory, infrequent, dutiful, and quite devoid of joy for himself or his spouse" (pp. 59–60). Moreover, it appears to others that the couple are of moderate financial means but hard-working. However, the husband, in complete secrecy from his wife and others, has a number of savings accounts which collectively contain a huge sum of money accumulated over the years. The wife, on the other hand, gets sick with cancer and undergoes a mastectomy, "[w]hereupon whatever small affection her husband ever had for her evaporates completely" (p. 60). The husband neglects her to the point of being "dimly aware" of her presence. In addition, the wife has always been an ardent writer of good poetry, and she meets a man who appreciates her talents. The man is oblivious to her physical scars, and loves her for who she is. Although Taylor does not explicitly say it, it seems that the wife has an affair with this man. The question that Taylor poses is, "Who has been faithless to whom?" (p. 60). The answer, of course, is, "The husband."[16]

---

[15]Buffalo: Prometheus Books, 1982. Page references in my paper are to this book.

[16]It is debatable whether such a case can be dealt with from a Kantian standpoint by relying on the prima facie rider: adultery is permissible because the wife had a duty that overrides her promise of sexual fidelity to her husband. From Wreen's perspective, my guess is that he would not allow it. The case he gives is of a couple who experience sexual dysfunction, such that the only way to save

I have gone into the details of this story because it gives us a good starting point as to how an ethics of virtue would deal with the issue of adultery. The picture we get from Taylor's story is that of a man (the husband) who lies, deceives, and is not to be commended for his sexual fidelity. He is the kind of person who is calculative, cold, selfish, and emotionally distant. Moreover, the fact that he did not commit adultery has nothing to do with his amazing ability to withstand sexual temptations, and has everything to do with the facts that he has never been tempted and that he is of a sexually passive nature. The wife, out of sheer bad luck, gets sick with cancer, suffers from its effects, and suffers from her husband's increased neglect. That she has an affair with another man is not only understandable, but even recommended, given her need for affirmation and love.

Under a Kantian picture, we are at a loss as to how to deal with Taylor's case. Did the wife violate her promise of sexual fidelity? Yes. Was her violation permissible in this case, that is, did she have a duty that can override her duty to keep her promise to her husband? If yes, what duty would that be? The duty to be happy? That would surely be a very strange duty, for under a Kantian scheme we do not have a duty to promote our own happiness. Does the fact that the husband violated his duty to love his wife justify her violation of the promise to sexual fidelity? Surely not, for if her violation is wrong, then, as the saying goes, two wrongs do not make a right, and if her violation is permissible, surely it is not because her husband violated his own promise. Perhaps a good way to think of this would be the following: had the husband done what he did, without having made any promises, he would still be a despicable person. The wife might very well have broken her promise of sexual fidelity and so violated a right that her husband has against her. But as Rosalind Hursthouse suggests in her paper on abortion and virtue ethics, "in exercising a moral right I can do something cruel, or callous, or selfish, light-minded, self-righteous, stupid, inconsiderate, disloyal, dishonest,—that is, act viciously."[17] Similarly but oppositely, in violating a right one might sometimes do what is morally correct. Violation of promises is not what is at stake here.

Does virtue ethics have any general picture to give us about adultery? Yes, and the answer can be approached from two perspectives: the nature of love and the nature of the virtuous person.

The wrongness of adultery stems from the fact that adultery occurs in the context of marriage or a love relationship, the basis of which is an emotional commitment. Although it is perhaps meaningful to speak of adultery when it occurs in the context of a purely sexual relationship between two people, the act of the adulterer does not appear to be so horrific in such a case. What seems to be horrible about adultery is that it indicates a more fundamental betrayal, namely, that of love. As Bonnie Steinbock puts it, "[s]exual infidelity has significance as a sign of a deeper betrayal—falling in love with someone else."[18] Logically

---

their marriage is for one of them (the relevant party) to commit adultery. Crucial to this case is the goal (duty?) to save the marriage, a goal which is not operative in the case given by Taylor.

[17]"Virtue Theory and Abortion," *Philosophy and Public Affairs*, vol. 20, no. 3, 1991, p. 235.

[18]"Adultery," in *Philosophy of Sex*, p. 192. Page references in my paper are to this anthology.

speaking, of course, there is no necessary connection between sex and love, as gay male orgy rooms aptly demonstrate. Indeed, one can argue that given that it is possible for love and sex to be disconnected, the permissibility of adultery follows. An argument that tries to show the immorality of adultery by arguing that since sex is connected with love, then sexual betrayal is tantamount to emotional betrayal, and hence adultery is wrong, is an invalid one, because there is no necessary connection between love and sex. This kind of reasoning[19] is correct but naive. It is true that sex is a pleasurable activity in and of itself, but sex is also typically an intimate activity. It requires a substantial amount of trust, it involves a good amount of self-exposure, and it is accompanied by the exchange of affection. We do not typically have sex in ways that are depicted in pornography movies, in which the partners have sex purely for sex's sake. Moreover, sex is connected to love precisely because it is a pleasurable activity: "People naturally have feelings of affection for those who make them happy, and sex is a very good way of making someone extraordinarily happy" (Steinbock, p. 190).

The fact that sex is intimately connected with love indicates the wrongness of adultery in two important ways. On the part of the adulterous spouse, the spouse, upon committing adultery, puts himself in a position in which emotional betrayal might be involved, and in which there is the possibility of increased affection between himself and the person he is having sex with. On the part of the nonadulterous spouse, the amount of pain and hurt upon the discovery is bad in itself, and it could lead to the destruction of the marriage. It could destroy the trust and affection that have been built over the years, and it could leave either party, if not both, emotionally and mentally damaged. I then endorse Steinbock's conclusion that sexual fidelity is an ideal in a marriage or in a romantic commitment.

If fidelity is an ideal in marriage, then a virtuous person would strive to stick to this ideal in a relationship. Moreover, a virtuous spouse would strive to maintain and foster the love, trust, and affection that exist between him and his spouse. These are healthy emotions and are an important part, surely, of any conception of a virtuous and flourishing person. To this end, adultery is to be avoided. This is a difficult endeavor, for it seems that we are not by nature sexually monogamous: we find people other than our spouses to be also sexually desirable, and we sometimes fantasize about them. Moreover, it is a fact that with time, the novelty of sex with one person wears out, and the temptation to seek sexual encounters with new partners increases. These facts warn us that sometimes failure to conform to the ideal is understandable. Be this as it may, it is crucial to strive for the ideal of fidelity. If the person is in love with someone, and if the person wants to be with that person for an indefinite period of time, then it is essential to strive for fidelity, given that adultery can damage the relationship and the persons involved. But to maintain the ideal of fidelity requires one to be a certain kind of person, a sexually faithful person, not because being sexually faithful guarantees the flourishing of the relationship and the people involved, but because in most cases it is pre-required by such flourishing.

---

[19]This reasoning is used by Wasserstrom.

A virtuous person is one who is to a large extent wise, courageous, fair, honest, moderate, caring, compassionate, benevolent, loving. Some of these virtues go a long way in helping to maintain the ideal of fidelity: the wisdom not to put oneself in tempting situations and in situations in which one cannot easily resist temptation (e.g., drunkenness), the wisdom to know when one is ready for a commitment, the wisdom to know whether one is the kind of person who is capable of being in a committed relationship, the courage to resist temptation, the compassion, care, and love for one's spouse that would form one's basis for refusing to commit adultery, and the honesty to one's spouse in the case of committing adultery. Other virtues do not seem to have room with respect to adultery. Adultery does not, for example, admit of moderation.[20]

But perhaps the important question is what virtue ethics tells us about the failure to conform to the ideal.[21] If in a drunken moment a spouse goes ahead and commits adultery, this would be a sorry and sad situation, but it would not be a tragedy, for the chances of emotional betrayal here are minimal, and to throw away a marriage, especially if it is good, because of what one spouse did in a moment of drunkenness is uncalled for. The fact that one might commit adultery in a drunken moment does not indicate that the marriage was going sour (the question, "Why else would one commit adultery?" often embodies this mistaken reasoning). As I mentioned, it does not seem to be in our nature to be sexually monogamous, and being drunk can often unleash our inhibited desires. But this is no good reason to throw away a good marriage.

If a woman is abused by her spouse, treated as an object, neglected, or all of these, she cannot be described as self-indulgent if she has an affair with another person. Her self-worth and happiness are at stake, and an affair can go a long way in healing her scars. To argue that the wife should first get a divorce before she has an affair with another man is simplistic. Often there are important factors at play that block such a way out. The wife might have no independent economic means by which she can sustain herself. There might be children involved, and sometimes the wife reasons that it is not in their best interests if a divorce occurs. Also, the wife might wish to stay in the marriage in the hope that it will get better, even if she does not envision a clear way of how this would happen.

In communities, such as those of Renaissance Florence and some Middle Eastern countries, in which marriage is often not based on love, the risk that there is a mismatch between the two married people is high, and often in such communities dissolving the marriage is not an easy matter, given that much rests on the continuation of the marriage, such as family honor, money, and political alliances. If one of, or both, the spouses commits adultery, this would be understandable, and perhaps even encouraged. Being stuck with a person that

---

[20]Except in some special cases. A couple in an open relationship might want to be moderate in their extramarital sexual activities perhaps to avoid the higher risk of contracting diseases, especially the potentially fatal HIV. A person who is allowed by his or her spouse (for some reason or another) to engage in extramarital sex might still want to be moderate in what they do during their sexual escapades and in the frequency of such escapades.

[21]In what follows, I owe much to Steinbock's "Adultery" and Hursthouse's "Virtue Theory and Abortion."

one does not want to be with is not a trivial matter, and having an extramarital affair can make the situation a bit more bearable.

Furthermore, sometimes the decision to commit adultery is the right one, although it might still be a case of moral failing. A husband who thinks that his wife is not treating him well, who feels that his marital life falls short of what it should be, who is as a result miserable, but who fails to be honest about his thoughts and feelings because he is too cowardly to talk to his wife, or because he lacks the perception to realize that his wife is simply unaware of the results of her actions, might very well make the right decision in having an affair with someone who satisfies his psychological and emotional needs. But the husband has also failed by allowing the situation to reach the point where he feels the need for an affair. He lacked the requisite courage and honesty to deal with these problems with his wife.

A person who knows from experience that his sexual drive is very strong, and who feels unable to be sexually monogamous simply because he loves sex too much, and yet who desires to be in a relationship with some specific individual, should be quite honest about what the sexual expectations of such a relationship would be. A sexually open relationship might be the most desirable form. Many gay couples, for example, have such relationships. Yet the form of extramarital sex that they allow themselves to have is highly impersonal so as to avoid the possibility of emotional intimacy with the new sexual partner. Hence, they resort to cruising in parks, they resort to dark rooms in gay bars and discos, and these are places in which there is minimal or no verbal and emotional communication.

One last issue I would like to discuss briefly is the question of why utilitarianism cannot account, as successfully as virtue ethics, for the wrongness of adultery. After all, a utilitarian might advise married couples not to commit adultery because the consequences might be bad: loss of love between the spouses, possible anguish for the children, and so forth.[22]

As far as act utilitarianism goes, I find it unsuccessful to deal with this issue for two major reasons. The first is that act utilitarianism has certain undesirable consequences, and hence is in itself a bad theory *in general*. Act utilitarianism could justify acts of murder, of punishing the innocent, and of trampling on the rights of others if such acts proved to have a net effect of good consequences (typically, happiness) over bad ones. The second reason is that act utilitarianism, insofar as it is a utilitarian theory—which it is—is not concerned only with the effects that adultery has on the family in question. Insofar as it is a utilitarian theory, it is concerned with the effects it has on everyone. Hence, and at least in principle, act utilitarianism could justify an act of adultery by appealing to the overall consequences. For example, suppose that John is married to Judith, that they have no children because Judith cannot have them, and that they both refuse to adopt. Suppose further that on one dark night John finally succumbs to lust and has an affair with his secretary Jezebel. They fall in love with each other, and they get married after John and Judith get a divorce. John and Jezebel

---

[22]This suggestion was given by a reader from *The Journal of Social Philosophy*.

proceed to have three children, one who grows up to be a physicist and who ends up solving the problems of quantum mechanics, one who grows up to be a doctor and who finds a decisive cure for AIDS, and the third who grows up to be a famed economist who solves the problem of the incompatibility of price inflation and high employment. It would seem, then, that act utilitarianism could justify wrong acts of adultery.

Rule utilitarianism, which states that certain kinds of acts are wrong because they violate certain rules, and which justifies these rules by appealing to the principle of utility, suffers from its own defects. In general, when certain rules conflict, a rule utilitarian, being a utilitarian, must resort to solving the problem by appealing to the consequences of each act. Hence, in cases when there is a conflict of rules, rule utilitarianism becomes act utilitarianism. Furthermore, when it comes to adultery, rule utilitarianism is not as well equipped as virtue ethics is to handle this problem. Rule utilitarianism becomes similar to Kantian ethics in telling us that adultery is wrong because it violates a certain rule (adultery is wrong; do not commit adultery). By not appealing to character traits, the history of the agents involved, and the circumstances at hand (because these are not part and parcel of this doctrine), rule utilitarianism is as ineffective as Kantian ethics. We have seen, however, that virtue ethics is equipped to give us good explanations and justifications for certain cases of adultery precisely because it is a theory which takes certain factors into account, factors that have hitherto been left out by deontological and consequentialist theories of ethics.[23]

There is no one single answer to the question, "Would a virtuous person refrain from committing adultery?" Part of what it is to be a virtuous person is to be sensitive to the details of the situation and to be sensitive to the fact that one is a member of a certain kind of community or culture. Virtue ethics does not lapse into a vicious form of relativism or particularism. It tells us that a virtuous spouse should strive to maintain the ideal of fidelity, difficult though this may be. But virtue ethics does not give us one formula for treating the issue, and this, I believe, is a positive aspect of virtue ethics. As Aristotle remarked, we should not demand exactness from a subject that is not exact.

Questions

1. Is the promise of sexual exclusivity best understood as a promise to be a certain sort of person? Does the fact that keeping such a promise may be very difficult give us real reason for thinking that it is not a typical sort of promise? Are not many promises hard to keep?

---

[23]The reader from the journal also mentioned character utilitarianism, and why such a view cannot explain the wrongness of adultery as well as virtue ethics. I have never been entirely clear on what character utilitarianism exactly amounts to. As far as I understand it, it is the view that we should strive to have good characters. Stated in this way, it would seem to be a species of virtue ethics, and so, on my view, benign. But I still need to find a more articulate and coherent formulation of the view.

2. Raja Halwani cites Richard Taylor's example of a married couple in which the wife commits adultery but is not unfaithful. Can you think of a way in which a deontologist could explain why the wife's adultery is not wrong?
3. What do Mike Martin's and Raja Halwani's arguments have in common? How do they differ?

Suggestions for Further Reading on Adultery

GOLDSTEIN, LAURENCE. "Love and Fidelity." Chap. 15 in *The Philosopher's Habitat*. Routledge, London, 1990.

MENDUS, SUSAN. "Marital Faithfulness." In *Philosophy and Sex*, Third Edition. Edited by Robert B. Baker, Kathleen J. Wininger, and Frederick A. Elliston. Amherst NY: Prometheus Books, 1998: pp. 130–138.

PRIMORATZ, IGOR. "Marriage, Adultery, Jealousy." In *Ethics and Sex*. London: Routledge, 1999: pp. 69–87.

STEINBOCK, BONNIE. "Adultery." *Report from the Center for Philosophy and Public Affairs* 5, no. 4 (fall 1985).

TAYLOR, RICHARD. "The Ethics of Having Love Affairs." In *Philosophy and Sex*. New rev. ed. Edited by Robert Baker and Frederick Elliston. Buffalo: Prometheus Books, 1984: pp. 71–78.

WREEN, MICHAEL J. "What's Really Wrong with Adultery." *The International Journal of Applied Philosophy* 3, no. 2 (Fall 1986): pp. 45–49.

CHAPTER 7

Homosexuality

MICHAEL LEVIN, Why Homosexuality is Abnormal

BURTON M. LEISER, Homosexuality, Morals, and the Law of Nature

Why Homosexuality
Is Abnormal

Michael Levin

Michael Levin's thesis is that homosex-uality is abnormal and undesirable—not that it is immoral. Nevertheless, he thinks that his view has moral implications. Ho-mosexuality is abnormal, he says, because it involves a misuse of the genitals. Ac-cording to his account, the purpose—or proper use—of a bodily part is that activ-ity which explains why it came to be se-lected in the evolutionary process. Thus just as the purpose of teeth is chewing, so the purpose of the genitals is procreation.

Because nature makes the proper use of one's bodily parts rewarding, the exclusive misuse of one's bodily parts, including one's genitals, is likely to cause unhappi-ness and is thus undesirable. Homosexu-als, he argues, tend to be less happy than heterosexuals, and this, he says, is ex-plained by their misuse of their genitals rather than by negative societal views of homosexuals. In conclusion, the author discusses the moral and social policy im-plications of his argument.

1. INTRODUCTION

This paper defends the view that homosexuality is abnormal and hence unde-sirable—not because it is immoral or sinful, or because it weakens society or hampers evolutionary development, but for a purely mechanical reason. It is a misuse of bodily parts. Clear empirical sense attaches to the idea of *the use* of such bodily parts as genitals, the idea that they are *for* something, and conse-quently to the idea of their misuse. I argue on grounds involving natural selec-tion that misuse of bodily parts can with high probability be connected to unhappiness. I regard these matters as prolegomena to such policy issues as the rights of homosexuals, the rights of those desiring not to associate with homo-sexuals, and legislation concerning homosexuality, issues which I shall not discuss systematically here. However, I do in the last section draw a seemingly evident corollary from my view that homosexuality is abnormal and likely to lead to unhappiness.

I have confined myself to male homosexuality for brevity's sake, but I believe that much of what I say applies *mutatis mutandis* to lesbianism. . . .

2. ON "FUNCTION" AND ITS COGNATES

To bring into relief the point of the idea that homosexuality involves a misuse of bodily parts, I will begin with an uncontroversial case of misuse, a case in which the clarity of our intuitions is not obscured by the conviction that they are untrustworthy. Mr. Jones pulls all his teeth and strings them around his neck because he thinks his teeth look nice as a necklace. He takes pureéd liquids supplemented by intravenous solutions for nourishment. It is surely natural to say that Jones is misusing his teeth, that he is not using them for what they are for, that indeed the way he is using them is incompatible with what they are for. Pedants might argue that Jones's teeth are no longer part of him and hence that he is not misusing any bodily parts. To them I offer Mr. Smith, who likes to play "Old MacDonald" on his teeth. So devoted is he to this amusement, in fact, that he never uses his teeth for chewing—like Jones, he takes nourishment intravenously. Now, not only do we find it perfectly plain that Smith and Jones are misusing their teeth, we predict a dim future for them on purely physiological grounds; we expect the muscles of Jones's jaw that are used for—that *are* for—chewing to lose their tone, and we expect this to affect Jones's gums. Those parts of Jones's digestive tract that are for processing solids will also suffer from disuse. The net result will be deteriorating health and perhaps a shortened life. Nor is this all. Human beings enjoy chewing. Not only has natural selection selected in muscles for chewing and favored creatures with such muscles, it has selected in a tendency to find the use of those muscles reinforcing. Creatures who do not enjoy using such parts of their bodies as deteriorate with disuse, will tend to be selected out. Jones, product of natural selection that he is, descended from creatures who at least tended to enjoy the use of such parts. Competitors who didn't simply had fewer descendants. So we expect Jones sooner or later to experience vague yearnings to chew something, just as we find people who take no exercise to experience a general listlessness. Even waiving for now my apparent reification of the evolutionary process, let me emphasize how little anyone is tempted to say "each to his own" about Jones or to regard Jones's disposition of his teeth as simply a deviation from a statistical norm. This sort of case is my paradigm when discussing homosexuality. . . . An organ is for a given activity if the organ's performing that activity helps its host or organisms suitably related to its host, *and* if this contribution is how the organ got and stays where it is. . . . This definition . . . distinguishes what something is for from what it may be *used* for on some occasion. Teeth are for chewing—we have teeth because their use in chewing favored the survival of organisms with teeth—whereas Jones is using his teeth for ornamentation. . . .

3. *APPLICATIONS TO HOMOSEXUALITY*

The application of this general picture to homosexuality should be obvious. There can be no reasonable doubt that one of the functions of the penis is to introduce semen into the vagina. It does this, and it has been selected in because it does this. (Sexual intercourse itself can probably be explained by the evolutionary value of bisexual reproduction. For $n > 2$, n-sexual reproduction would increase genetic variety at the cost of hardly ever occurring: (see e.g., [3].) The advantages accruing to relatively motile gametes seems to account for the emergence of bisexual reproduction itself.) Nature has consequently made this use of the penis rewarding. It is clear enough that any proto-human males who found unrewarding the insertion of penis into vagina have left no descendants. In particular, proto-human males who enjoyed inserting their penises into each other's anuses have left no descendants. This is why homosexuality is abnormal, and why its abnormality counts prudentially against it. Homosexuality is likely to cause unhappiness because it leaves unfulfilled an innate and innately rewarding desire. And should the reader's environmentalism threaten to get the upper hand, let me remind him again of an unproblematic case. Lack of exercise is bad and even abnormal not only because it is unhealthy but also because one feels poorly without regular exercise. Nature made exercise rewarding because, until recently, we had to exercise to survive. Creatures who found running after game unrewarding were eliminated. Laziness leaves unreaped the rewards nature has planted in exercise, even if the lazy man cannot tell this introspectively. If this is a correct description of the place of exercise in human life, it is by the same token a correct description of the place of heterosexuality.

It hardly needs saying, but perhaps I should say it anyway, that this argument concerns tendencies and probabilities. Generalizations about human affairs being notoriously "true by and large and for the most part" only, saying that homosexuals are bound to be less happy than heterosexuals must be understood as short for "Not coincidentally, a larger proportion of homosexuals will be unhappy than a corresponding selection of the heterosexual population." There are, after all, genuinely jolly fat men. To say that laziness leads to adverse affective consequences means that, because of our evolutionary history, the odds are relatively good that a man who takes no exercise will suffer adverse affective consequences. Obviously, some people will get away with misusing their bodily parts. Thus, when evaluating the empirical evidence that bears on this account, it will be pointless to cite cases of well-adjusted homosexuals. I do not say they are non-existent; my claim is that, of biological necessity, they are rare.

My argument might seem to show at most that heterosexual behavior is (self-) reinforcing, not that homosexuality is self-extinguishing—that homosexuals go without the built-in rewards of heterosexuality, but not that homosexuality has a built-in punishment. This distinction, however, is merely verbal. They are two different ways of saying that homosexuals will find their lives less rewarding than will heterosexuals. Even if some line demarcated happiness from unhappiness absolutely, it would be irrelevant if homosexuals were all happily above the line. It is the comparison with the heterosexual life that is at issue. A lazy man might count as happy by some mythic absolute standard, but he is likely to be less happy than someone otherwise like him who exercises.

Another objection to my argument, or conjectural evolutionary scenario, is that heterosexuality might have been selected in not because it favors survival, but as a by-product of some other inclusively fit structure or behavior. A related suggestion is that what really has been selected in is some blend of dominant heterosexual and recessive homosexual genes. As for the former, it seems extraordinarily unlikely, given how long life has reproduced itself by sexual intercourse, that the apparently self-reinforcing character of heterosexuality is a by-product of some other fitness-enhancing trait. If heterosexual intercourse is not *directly* connected to propagation, what is? Biologists have no trouble determining when bird plumage is there to attract mates, and hence favors survival. It would be astounding if the same could not be said for heterosexual intercourse.

The sophisticate might complain that I am not giving "by-product" hypotheses their due. And indeed at this point sociobiological hypotheses come thick and fast. I will be discussing some others later in this paper, and making some overall observations about sociobiology and homosexuality. Here it is appropriate to examine one hypothesis of the "by-product" school, that of Hutchinson (see [11]). Fact: there can be recessive genes for a trait that inhibits the reproduction of and even kills organisms which exhibit it, but which, when co-occurring with the dominant trait-suppressing allele, give rise to an organism or phenotype more inclusively fit than a comparable organism with two of the dominant alleles. In such cases, the "bad" allele will be passed along in fit heterozygous organisms and its associated trait will occasionally surface. For example, sickle-cell anemia persists because the heterozygote Cc (Non-sickle-cell C, sickle-cell c) confers resistance to malaria. Perhaps a recessive gene predisposing to homosexuality persists in this way. Organisms of genotype Hh—a dominant allele H for heterosexuality, a recessive allele h for homosexuality—might be most fit, and then of course organisms with hh genotype will surface with some regularity.

Without even considering the empirical likelihood of this elegant hypothesis, it is clearly consistent with my chief claim. For as it stands it represents sickle-cell anemia and the perpetuation of the c allele as *unfortunate by-products* of a process that selects in resistance to malaria; and, presumably, the same would go for homosexuality. For what does it mean to say that sickle-cell anemia is a by-product? Precisely this: had immunity to malaria not been associated with the Cc genotype, the "gene" for malarial immunity would have been selected in anyway; however, had the Cc genotype and hence sickle-cell anemia not been associated with malarial immunity or some other inclusive-fitness-enhancing trait, the c allele would have disappeared. Recurring to our definition of "function," the cause of the persistence of the c allele and the Cc genotype, what that genotype is for, is fending off malaria. Sickle-cell anemia is a maladaptive by-product of the Cc genotype since, had it not been associated with what is in fact the function of the Cc genotype, sickle-cell anemia would have caused the disappearance of the Cc genotype. Nothing, not even the c allele, has sickle-cell anemia as its function. The key question, of course, is whether a maladaptive by-product, so understood, is reinforcing. On the present model, it is not. For suppose sickle-cell anemia could be contracted voluntarily, and there was a gene which (a) made contracting or becoming vulnerable to it reinforcing, but (b) was not connected with malarial immunity. A strain with the tastes this gene confers would soon be selected out. Therefore, surviving humans who get sickle-cell anemia do not find it in any way reinforcing. So the "heterozygote fitness" hypothesis (and the kin-selection hypothesis: see below) predict, consistently with my view, that homosexuality is associated with unhappiness; and, conversely, wide-spread homosexual unhappiness would confirm that homosexuality is a maladaptive by-product.

An important methodological corollary of this discussion is that a trait or tendency may be "in the genes" but still be abnormal. It is normal only if it is in the genes because it itself enhances fitness, not because it is associated with something else that enhances fitness on independent grounds. Sickle-cell anemia is a malfunction of its victims' blood, which was selected in to oxygenate the muscles. A comparable story for homosexuality would involve a gene that instructed its organism to make just a little testosterone. This might have survival value by raising phenotypic verbal sensitivity, and perhaps low testosterone is the only way nature has figured out to secure this inclusively fit trait. Suppose, too, that a disposition to homosexuality was a causal consequence, a by-product, of low testosterone—but not so disadvantageous a by-product that the gene was selected out. Homosexuality would then be a necessary condition for advantageous verbal ability, but it would not follow that homosexuality was selected in because it conduced to verbal ability, or for any other reason. It would not follow that homosexuality is the least reinforcing. Unhappy homosexuals might be the price nature pays for verbal ability, homosexuality being no more a cause of verbal ability than sickle-cell anemia is a cause of malarial resistance.

Talk of what is "in the genes" inevitably provokes the observation that we should not blame homosexuals for their homosexuality if it is "in their genes." True enough. Indeed, since nobody decides what he is going to find sexually arousing, the moral appraisal of sexual object "choice" is entirely absurd. However, so saying is quite consistent with regarding homosexuality as a misfortune, and taking steps—this being within the realm of the will—to minimize its incidence, especially among children. Calling homosexuality involuntary does not place it outside the scope of evaluation. Victims of sickle-cell anemia are not blameworthy, but it is absurd to pretend that there is nothing wrong with them. Homosexual activists are partial to genetic explanations and hostile to Freudian environmentalism in part because they see a genetic cause as exempting homosexuals from blame. But surely people are equally blameless for indelible traits acquired in early childhood. And anyway, a blameless condition may still be worth trying to prevent. (Defenders of homosexuality fear Freud at another level, because his account removes homosexuality from the biological realm altogether and deprives it of whatever legitimacy adheres to what is "in the genes.")

My sociobiological scenario also finds no place for the fashionable remark that homosexuality has become fitness-enhancing in our supposedly over-populated world. Homosexuality is said to increase our species' chances by easing the population pressure. This observation, however correct, is irrelevant. Even if homosexuality has lately come to favor species survival, this is no part of how homosexuality is created. Salvation of the human species would be at best a fortuitous by-product of behavior having other causes. It is not easy, moreover, to see how this feature of homosexuality could get it selected in. If homosexuality enhances inclusive fitness precisely because homosexuals don't reproduce, the tendency to homosexuality cannot get selected for by a filtering process when it is passed to the next generation—it doesn't get passed to the next generation at all. The same applies, of course, to any tendency to find homosexuality rewarding.

The whole matter of the survival advantage of homosexuality is in any case beside the point. Our organs have the functions and rewards they do because of the way the world was, and what favored survival, many millions of years ago. *Then*, homosexuality decreased fitness and heterosexuality increased it; an innate tendency to homosexuality would have gotten selected out if anything did. We today have the tendencies transmitted to us by those other ancestors, whether or not the race is going to pay a price for this. That 50 years ago certain self-reinforcing behavior began to threaten the race's future is quite consistent with the behavior remaining self-reinforcing. Similarly, widespread obesity and the patent enjoyment many people experience in gorging themselves just show that our appetites were shaped in conditions of food scarcity under which gorging oneself when one had the chance was good policy. Anyway, the instability created by abundance is, presumably, temporary. If the current abundance continues for 5000 generations, natural gluttons will almost certainly disappear through early heart disease and unattractiveness to the opposite sex. The ways in which the populous human herd will be trimmed is best left to speculation.

I should also note that nothing I have said shows bisexuality or sheer polymorphous sexuality to be unnatural or self-punishing. One might cite the Greeks to show that only exclusive homosexuality conflicts with our evolved reinforcement mechanism. But in point of fact bisexuality seems to be a quite rare phenomenon—and animals, who receive no cultural conditioning, seem instinctively heterosexual in the vast majority of cases. Clinicians evidently agree that it is possible for a person to be homosexual at one period of his life and heterosexual at another, but not at the same time. Some statistics in [5] confirm this. 18% of the male homosexuals interviewed had been married; while 90% reported having intercourse with their wives during the first year of marriage, 72% reported having homosexual fantasies during intercourse, and 33% reported this "often" ([5], tables 17.1–17.7). So only 4.5% of the sample had "reciprocal" heterosexual intercourse. This coheres well with table 22.4 in [5], which indicates that roughly 95% of male homosexuals in the Bell-Weinberg sample were "exclusively homosexual." But one mustn't move too quickly or dogmatically here. On the face of it, telling its host body "Put your penis in any reasonably small, moist opening" is a sufficiently adaptive gene strategy to ensconce a gene that follows it in the gene pool. A body controlled by such a gene would reproduce itself and hence the gene often enough. The flaw in the plan is that a competitor gene might evolve to tell its body: "Put your penis only in vaginas, i.e., moist openings with a certain feel and which are accompanied by such visual clues as breasts and wide hips." The second gene would reproduce itself even more often and—waiving by-products—would eventually displace the first. But our bisexual gene isn't finished. It might evolve the following strategy: "Body, insert your penis in vaginas most of the time, but insert your penis in male anuses frequently enough to keep other males, who are competing with you for females, occupied." A body with such a gene could keep a harem pregnant. A male who put other males out of commission for n hours by stimulating them to orgasm might himself seem vulnerable to exhausting himself, but he can avoid this by refraining from orgasm during homosexual acts. The fly in *this* ointment is the counterstrategy that purely heterosexual genes could evolve: "Avoid erect penises heading for your anus." If even one such gene appeared in a population of bisexuals it would reproduce itself a little more readily, since it would never waste time spiking the guns of its competitors.

By now we are lost in speculation. There is no way to disprove the existence of a hardy bisexual gene, or to prove that heterosexual countermeasures always evolved. It is *possible,* but not likely and not suggested by anything currently known, that a bisexual gene has achieved stable existence in the human gene pool. It is also quite unlikely, on equivalent analytical grounds and the virtual nonexistence of polymorphous animal sexuality in the wild, that males are primed only for an undifferentiated enjoyment of sex that is shaped by culture into heterosexuality.

Utilitarians must take the present evolutionary scenario seriously. The utilitarian attitude toward homosexuality usually runs something like this: even if homosexuality is in some sense unnatural, as a matter of brute fact homosexuals take pleasure in sexual contact with members of the same sex. As long as they don't hurt anyone else, homosexuality is as great a good as heterosexuality. But the matter cannot end here. Not even a utilitarian doctor would have words of praise for a degenerative disease that happened to foster a certain kind of pleasure (as sore muscles uniquely conduce to the pleasure of stretching them). A utilitarian doctor would presumably try just as zealously to cure diseases that feel good as less pleasant degenerative diseases. A pleasure causally connected with great distress cannot be treated as just another pleasure to be toted up on the felicific scoreboard. Utilitarians have to reckon with the inevitable consequences of pain-causing pleasure.

Similar remarks apply to the question of whether homosexuality is a "disease." A widely-quoted pronouncement of the American Psychiatric Association runs:

> Surely the time has come for psychiatry to give up the archaic practice of classifying the millions of men and women who accept or prefer homosexual object choices as being, by virtue of that fact alone, mentally ill. The fact that their alternative life-style happens to be out of favor with current cultural conventions must not be a basis in itself for a diagnosis.

Apart from some question-begging turns of phrase, this is right. One's taste for mutual anal intercourse is nothing "in itself" for one's psychiatrist to worry about, any more than a life of indolence is anything "in itself" for one's doctor to worry about. In fact, in itself there is nothing wrong with a broken arm or an occluded artery. The fact that my right ulna is now in two pieces is just a fact of nature, not a "basis for diagnosis." But this condition is a matter for medical science anyway, because it will lead to pain. Permitted to persist, my fracture will provoke increasingly punishing states. So if homosexuality is a reliable sign of present or future misery, it is beside the point that homosexuality is not "by virtue of that fact alone" a mental illness. High rates of drug addiction, divorce and illegitimacy are in themselves no basis for diagnosing social pathology. They support this diagnosis because of what else they signify about a society which exhibits them. Part of the problem here is the presence of germs in paradigm diseases, and the lack of a germ for homosexuality (or psychosis). I myself am fairly sure that a suitably general and germ-free definition of "disease" can be extruded from the general notion of "function" exhibited in Section 2, but however that may be, whether homosexuality is a disease is a largely verbal issue. If homosexuality is a self-punishing maladaptation, it hardly matters what it is called.

4. EVIDENCE AND FURTHER CLARIFICATION

I have argued that homosexuality is "abnormal" in both a descriptive and a normative sense because—for evolutionary reasons—homosexuals are bound to be unhappy. In Kantian terms, I have explained how it is possible for homosexuality to be unnatural even if it violates no cosmic purpose or such purposes as we retrospectively impose on nature. What is the evidence for my view? For one thing, by emphasizing homosexual unhappiness, my view explains a ubiquitous fact in a simple way. The fact is the universally acknowledged unhappiness of homosexuals. Even the staunchest defenders of homosexuality admit that, as of now, homosexuals are not happy. (Writers even in the very recent past, like Lord Devlin, could not really believe that anyone could publicly advocate homosexuality as intrinsically good: see [6], 87.) A conspicuous exception to this is [5], which has been widely taken to show that homosexuals can be just as happy as heterosexuals. A look at their statistics tells a different story—an important matter I have dealt with in some detail in the Appendix.

The usual environmentalist explanation for homosexuals' unhappiness is the misunderstanding, contempt and abuse that society heaps on them. But this not only leaves unexplained why society has this attitude, it sins against parsimony by explaining a nearly universal phenomenon in terms of variable circumstances that have, by coincidence, the same upshot.[1] Parsimony urges that we seek the explanation of homosexual unhappiness in the nature of homosexuality itself, as my explanation does. Having to "stay in the closet" may be a

---

[1] A number of authors trace the present culture's taboo against "homophilia" (Wilson's term) to the Old Testament proscription against nonreproductive practices, and summarily dismiss it as "simplistic" and "archaic" nonsense (see [27], 142–43; also the Appendix). While I have no sympathy for theological teleology, it should be recalled that the ban on homosexuality in Leviticus is one of just three rules set down as absolutely binding. Another one prohibits the shedding of innocent blood. This prohibition against using convenient victims for ulterior purposes is the basis for Western law and morality, and I trust Wilson does not find it simplistic or archaic.

great strain, but it does not account for all the miseries that writers on homosexuality say is the homosexual's lot.

Incorporating unhappiness into the present evolutionary picture also smooths a bothersome ad-hocness in some otherwise appealing analyses of abnormality. Many writers define abnormality as compulsiveness. On this conception, homosexuality is abnormal because it is an autonomy-obstructing compulsion.[2] Such an analysis is obviously open to the question, What if an autonomous homosexual comes along? To that, writers like van den Haag point out that homosexuality is, in fact, highly correlated with compulsiveness. The trouble here is that the definition in question sheds no light on why abnormal, compulsive, traits are such. The present account not only provides a criterion for abnormality, it encapsulates an explanation of *why* behavior abnormal by its lights is indeed compulsive and bound to lead to unhappiness.

One crucial test of my account is its prediction that homosexuals will continue to be unhappy even if people altogether abandon their "prejudice" against homosexuality. This prediction, that homosexuality being unnatural homosexuals will still find their behavior self-punishing, coheres with available evidence. It is consistent with the failure of other oppressed groups, such as American Negroes and European Jews, to become warped in the direction of "cruising," sado-masochism and other practices common in homosexual life (see [16]). It is consistent as well with the admission by even so sympathetic an observer of homosexuality as Rechy ([19]) that the immediate cause of homosexual unhappiness is a taste for promiscuity, anonymous encounters, and humiliation. It is hard to see how such tastes are related to the dim view society takes of them. Such a relation would be plausible only if homosexuals courted multiple anonymous encounters *faute de mieux*, longing all the while to settle down to some sort of domesticity. But, again, Europeans abhorred Jews for centuries, but this did not create in Jews a special weakness for anonymous, promiscuous sex. Whatever drives a man away from women, to be fellated by as many different men as possible, seems independent of what society thinks of such behavior. It is this behavior that occasions misery, and we may expect the misery of homosexuals to continue.

In a 1974 study, Weinberg and Williams ([25]) found no difference in the distress experienced by homosexuals in Denmark and the Netherlands, and in the U.S., where they found public tolerance of homosexuality to be lower. This would confirm rather strikingly that homosexual unhappiness is endogenous,

---

[2]Summarizing a wide body of work on this subject, Sagarin writes: "Sick is, of course, a stigmatizing categorization when applied to mental and emotional disorders, but this does not mean that it is scientifically invalid. The misuse of a concept for political purposes is not an argument against its validity. Is homosexuality a sickness, or a behavioral symptom of a sickness? There seems to be a great deal of evidence in favor of the latter formulation. . . . [T]he evidence is strong that homosexuality arises in most instances from faulty childhood development, is often accompanied by poor sex-role identification, and is overwhelmingly concomitant with compulsivity, inability to relate to others, poor self-image, low feeling of self-worth, and a great deal of what Bergler called 'injustice collecting'" ([20], 10).

unless one says that Weinberg's and Williams's indices for public tolerance and distress—chiefly homosexuals' self-reports of "unhappiness" and "lack of faith in others"—are unreliable. Such complaints, however, push the social causation theory toward untestability. Weinberg and Williams themselves cleave to the hypothesis that homosexual unhappiness is entirely a reaction to society's attitudes, and suggest that a condition of homosexual happiness is positive endorsement by the surrounding society.[3] It is hard to imagine a more flagrantly *ad hoc* hypothesis. Neither a Catholic living among Protestants nor a copywriter working on the great American novel in his off hours asks more of society than tolerance in order to be happy in his pursuits.

It is interesting to reflect on a natural experiment that has gotten under way in the decade since the Weinberg-Williams study. A remarkable change in public opinion, if not private sentiment, has occurred in America. For whatever reason—the prodding of homosexual activists, the desire not to seem like a fuddy-duddy—various organs of opinion are now hard at work providing a "positive image" for homosexuals. Judges allow homosexuals to adopt their lovers. The Unitarian Church now performs homosexual marriages. Hollywood produces highly sanitized movies like *Making Love* and *Personal Best* about homosexuality. Macmillan strongly urges its authors to show little boys using cosmetics. Homosexuals no longer fear revealing themselves, as is shown by the prevalence of the "clone look." Certain products run advertising obviously directed at the homosexual market. On the societal reaction theory, there ought to be an enormous rise in homosexual happiness. I know of no systematic study to determine if this is so, but anecdotal evidence suggests it may not be. The homosexual press has been just as strident in denouncing pro-homosexual movies as in denouncing Doris Day movies. Especially virulent venereal diseases have very recently appeared in homosexual communities, evidently spread in epidemic proportions by unabating homosexual promiscuity. One selling point for a presumably serious "gay rights" rally in Washington D.C. was an "all-night disco train" from New York to Washington. What is perhaps most salient is that, even if the changed public mood results in decreased homosexual unhappiness, the question remains of why homosexuals in the recent past, who suffered greatly for being homosexuals, persisted in being homosexuals.

But does not my position also predict—contrary to fact—that any sexual activity not aimed at procreation or at least sexual intercourse leads to unhappiness? First, I am not sure this conclusion is contrary to the facts properly understood. It is universally recognized that, for humans and the higher animals, sex is more than the insertion of the penis into the vagina. Foreplay is

---

[3]This is the impression they leave, although it is hard to find them asserting it. Thus their reviewer: "the authors . . . start the book with asserting as their creed and point of departure the 'societal reaction theory', [and] try to minimize the issue by a modification, namely that tolerance is probably not enough, that is to say, it is not the same as full acceptance" ([4], 339–40; most of this review appears in [21]). Perhaps Weinberg and Williams are so inexplicit because, starting from wholly environmentalist premises, they regard the insufficiency of tolerance as the conclusion to be drawn from their data rather than as just one hypothesis to explain them.

necessary to prepare the female and, to a lesser extent, the male. Ethologists have studied the elaborate mating rituals of even relatively simple animals. Sexual intercourse must therefore be understood to include the kisses and caresses that necessarily precede copulation, behaviors that nature has made rewarding. What my view does predict is that exclusive preoccupation with behaviors normally preparatory for intercourse is highly correlated with unhappiness. And, so far as I know, psychologists do agree that such preoccupation or "fixation" with, e.g., cunnilingus, is associated with personality traits independently recognized as disorders. In this sense, sexual intercourse really is virtually necessary for well-being. Only if one is antecedently convinced that "nothing is more natural than anything else" will one confound foreplay as a prelude to intercourse with "foreplay" that leads nowhere at all. One might speculate on the evolutionary advantages of foreplay, at least for humans: by increasing the intensity and complexity of the pleasures of intercourse, it binds the partners more firmly and makes them more fit for child-rearing. In fact, such analyses of sexual perversion as Nagel's ([18]), which correctly focus on the interruption of mutuality as central to perversion, go wrong by ignoring the evolutionary role and built-in rewards of mutuality. They fail to explain why the interruption of mutuality is disturbing.

It should also be clear that my argument permits gradations in abnormality. Behavior is the more abnormal, and the less likely to be rewarding, the more its emission tends to extinguish a genetic cohort that practices it. The less likely a behavior is to get selected out, the less abnormal it is. Those of our ancestors who found certain aspects of foreplay reinforcing might have managed to reproduce themselves sufficiently to implant this strain in us. There might be an equilibrium between intercourse and such not directly reproductive behavior. It is not required that any behavior not directly linked to heterosexual intercourse lead to maximum dissatisfaction. But the existence of these gradations provides no entering wedge for homosexuality. As no behavior is more likely to get selected out than rewarding homosexuality—except perhaps an innate tendency to suicide at the onset of puberty—it is extremely unlikely that homosexuality can now be unconditionally reinforcing in humans to any extent.

Nor does my position predict, again contrary to fact, that celibate priests will be unhappy. My view is compatible with the existence of happy celibates who deny themselves as part of a higher calling which yields compensating satisfactions. Indeed, the very fact that one needs to explain how the priesthood can compensate for the lack of family means that people do regard heterosexual mating as the natural or "inertial" state of human relations. The comparison between priests and homosexuals is in any case inapt. Priests do not simply give up sexual activity without ill-effect; they give it up for a reason. Homosexuals have hardly given up the use of their sexual organs, for a higher calling or anything else. Homosexuals continue to use them, but, unlike priests, they use them for what they are not for.

I have encountered the thought that by my lights female heterosexuality must be abnormal, since according to feminism women have been unhappy down the ages. The datum is questionable, to say the least. Feminists have offered no documentation whatever for this extravagant claim; their evidence is usually the unhappiness of the feminist in question and her circle of friends.

Such attempts to prove female discontent in past centuries as [9] are transparently anachronistic projections of contemporary feminist discontent onto inappropriate historical objects. An objection from a similar source runs that my argument, suitably extended, implies the naturalness and hence rewardingness of traditional monogamous marriage. Once again, instead of seeing this as a *reductio*, I am inclined to take the supposed absurdity as a truth that nicely fits my theory. It is not a theoretical contention but an observable fact that women enjoy motherhood, that failure to bear and care for children breeds unhappiness in women, and that the role of "primary caretaker" is much more important for women than men. However, there is no need to be dogmatic. This conception of the family is in extreme disrepute in contemporary America. Many women work and many marriages last less than a decade. Here we have another natural experiment about what people find reinforcing. My view predicts that women will on the whole become unhappier if current trends continue. Let us see.[4]

Not directly bearing on the issue of happiness, but still empirically pertinent, is animal homosexuality. I mentioned earlier that the overwhelmingly heterosexual tendencies of animals in all but such artificial and genetically irrelevant environs as zoos cast doubt on sheer polymorphous sexuality as a sufficiently adaptive strategy. By the same token, it renders implausible the claim in [15] that human beings are born with only a general sex drive, and that the objects of the sex drive are *entirely* learned. If this were so, who teaches male tigers to mate with female tigers? Who teaches male primates to mate with female primates? In any case, the only evidence Masters and Johnson cite is the entirely unsurprising physiological similarity between heterosexual and homosexual response. Plainly, the inability of the penile nerve endings to tell what is rubbing them has nothing to do with the innateness of the sexual object. The inability of a robin to tell twigs from clever plastic look-alikes is consistent with an innate nest-building instinct.

The work of Beach ([2]) is occasionally cited (e.g., in [27]) to document the existence of animal homosexuality and to support the contention that homosexuality has some adaptive purpose, but Beach in fact notes certain important

---

[4]Feminists are understandably hostile to sociobiology, which offers a plausible theoretical underpinning for the observable differences between the sexes. Such being the temper of the times, sociobiologists themselves get awfully cold feet when facing off against feminists. Barash hems and haws when considering if sociobiology is "sexist," a word which conveys no clear sense to him or anyone else—but which has evidently acquired powers of intimidation (see my [13]). After documenting the innateness of numerous psychophysiological gender differences, Wilson recommends a system of quotas and indoctrination for eliminating all consequences of sexual differentiation as preferable to a society of free individuals in which sexual differences would naturally manifest themselves. One would like to see a Wilsonian army take on a traditional one, like the Soviet Union's. Michael Ruse, a philosophical commentator, has even written a book with the astounding title *Is Science Sexist?*, as if the truth about men and women might be ideologically suspect. Sociobiologists tend to be braver taking on socialism, which demands an indifference to the claims of one's family that no gene which hoped to reproduce itself could permit. A sound point, but one would have thought socialism's absurdity required less arcane demonstration. Anyway, Wilson seems not to recognize that his egalitarian utopia would require far more interference with natural impulses than the most authoritarian socialism.

disanalogies between mammalian homosexual behavior in the wild and human homosexuality. Citing a principle of "stimulus-response complementarity," he remarks that a male chimpanzee will mount another male if the latter emits such characteristically female behavior as display of nether parts. Male homosexual humans, on the other hand, are attracted to maleness. More significantly, the male chimpanzee's mounting is unaccompanied by erection, throusting or, presumably, intromission. Beach suggests that this display-mounting sequence may be multipurpose in nature, signalling submission and dominance when it occurs between males. In the same vein, Barash ([1], 60) cites male-male rape in *Xylocanis maculipennis,* but here the rapist's sperm is deposited in the rape victim's storage organs. This is a smart evolutionary move reminiscent of the gun-spiking strategy mentioned in an earlier section, but it is not comparable in its effects to homosexuality in humans. . . .

5. *ON POLICY ISSUES*

Homosexuality is intrinsically bad only in a prudential sense. It makes for unhappiness. However, this does not exempt homosexuality from the larger categories of ethics—rights, duties, liabilities. Deontic categories apply to acts which increase or decrease happiness or expose the helpless to the risk of unhappiness.

If homosexuality is unnatural, legislation which raises the odds that a given child will become homosexual raises the odds that he will be unhappy. The only gap in the syllogism is whether legislation which legitimates, endorses or protects homosexuality does increase the chances that a child will become homosexual. If so, such legislation is *prima facie* objectionable. The question is not whether homosexual elementary school teachers will molest their charges. Pro-homosexual legislation might increase the incidence of homosexuality in subtler ways. If it does, and if the protection of children is a fundamental obligation of society, legislation which legitimates homosexuality is a dereliction of duty. I am reluctant to deploy the language of "children's rights," which usually serves as one more excuse to interfere with the prerogatives of parents. But we do have obligations to our children, and one of them is to protect them from harm. If, as some have suggested, children have a right to protection from a religious education, they surely have a right to protection from homosexuality. So protecting them limits somebody else's freedom, but we are often willing to protect quite obscure children's rights at the expense of the freedom of others. There is a movement to ban TV commercials for sugar-coated cereals, to protect children from the relatively trivial harm of tooth decay. Such a ban would restrict the freedom of advertisers, and restrict it even though the last clear chance of avoiding the harm, and thus the responsibility, lies with the parents who control the TV set. I cannot see how one can consistently support such legislation and also urge homosexual rights, which risk much graver damage to children in exchange for increased freedom for homosexuals. (If homosexual behavior is largely compulsive, it is falsifying the issue to present it as balancing risks to children against the freedom of homosexuals.) The right of a homosexual to work for the Fire Department is not a negligible good. Neither is fostering a legal atmosphere in which as many people as possible grow up heterosexual.

It is commonly asserted that legislation granting homosexuals the privilege or right to be firemen endorses not homosexuality, but an expanded conception of human liberation. It is conjectural how sincerely this can be said in a legal order that forbids employers to hire whom they please and demands hours of paperwork for an interstate shipment of hamburger. But in any case legislation "legalizing homosexuality" cannot be neutral because passing it would have an inexpungeable speech-act dimension. Society cannot grant unaccustomed rights and privileges to homosexuals while remaining neutral about the value of homosexuality. Working from the assumption that society rests on the family and its consequences, the Judaeo-Christian tradition has deemed homosexuality a sin and withheld many privileges from homosexuals. Whether or not such denial was right, for our society to grant these privileges to homosexuals *now* would amount to declaring that it has rethought the matter and decided that homosexuality is not as bad as it had previously supposed. And unless such rethinking is a direct response to new empirical findings about homosexuality, it can only be a revaluing. Someone who suddenly accepts a policy he has previously opposed is open to the same interpretation: he has come to think better of the policy. And if he embraces the policy while knowing that this interpretation will be put on his behavior, and if he knows that others know that he knows they will so interpret it, he is acquiescing in this interpretation. He can be held to have intended, meant, this interpretation.[5] A society that grants privileges to homosexuals while recognizing that, in the light of generally known history, this act can be interpreted as a positive re-evaluation of homosexuality, is signalling that it now thinks homosexuality is all right. Many commentators in the popular press have observed that homosexuals, unlike members of racial minorities, can always "stay in the closet" when applying for jobs. What homosexual rights activists really want, therefore, is not access to jobs but legitimation of their homosexuality. Since this is known, giving them what they want will be seen as conceding their claim to legitimacy. And since legislators know their actions will support this interpretation, and know that their constituencies know they know this, the Gricean effect or symbolic meaning of passing anti-discrimination ordinances is to declare homosexuality legitimate (see [26]).

Legislation permitting frisbees in the park does not imply approval of frisbees for the simple reason that frisbees are new; there is no tradition of banning them from parks. The legislature's action in permitting frisbees is not interpretable, known to be interpretable, and so on, as the reversal of long-standing disapproval. It is because these Gricean conditions are met in the case of abortion that legislation—or rather judicial fiat—permitting abortions and mandating their public funding are widely interpreted as tacit approval. Up to now, society has deemed homosexuality so harmful that restricting it outweighs putative homosexual rights. If society reverses itself, it will in effect be deciding that homosexuality is not as bad as it once thought.

---

[5]For this general conception of the meaning of a speech-act, see [10], [14], and [23]. For a cognate application to political philosophy, see [24].

Appendix

The best case for inevitable homosexual unhappiness comes from [5], a study which received much attention when it appeared. As their subtitle suggests, Bell and Weinberg claim to have shown that there is no such thing as homosexuality *per se;* there are different types of homosexuals, some of whom can be as well-adjusted, on the average, as heterosexuals. Bell and Weinberg admit that demonstrating this was the aim of their study: "We are pleased at the extent to which the aims of our investigation of homosexual men and women have been realized. The tables . . . clearly show that homosexuals are a remarkably diverse group" (217). They always refer to commonly held beliefs about homosexuals as "myths" (15) and "stereotypes" (73), and blame society's "homoerotophobia" (188) on the preoccupation of Jews with survival and the Christian Church with sin (149, 195). Working on the principle that a position is seriously weakened if the evidence marshalled by its friends disconfirms it, let us look at the Bell-Weinberg data.

Bell and Weinberg studied 686 San Francisco Bay area male homosexuals (and 293 lesbians, whom I ignore as in the body of the paper). One might question their methods: apart from the nonrandomness of their sample (22), the authors are oddly credulous about their informants' reports. They determined the level of their informants' health, and that of the informants in their heterosexual control group, by simply asking them how their health was (484). Not surprisingly, 87% of the white homosexuals and 91% of the black homosexuals reported that they were in good to excellent health, about the same as for the heterosexuals. But this accords ill with their table 19.2, which shows that 58% of all homosexuals spend 3 or more nights a week out. Common sense agrees with Satchel Paige that the social whirl isn't restful, but in any case the authors use none of the standard objective measures of health—visits to the doctor, use of medication, drugs, average amount of sleep, and the like. This, incidental though it is, warrants scepticism about self-report methodology in a matter like homosexuality.

Of the 206 pages of tables, 3 entries are particularly noteworthy as measures of homosexual unhappiness. The first (337, 339) is that 27% of all homosexuals experience either some or a great deal of regret about being homosexual. Taken with the 24% who experience "very little" regret, this prompts one to ask if only 49% of a random sample of heterosexuals would report no regrets about their heterosexuality. Would 27% of heterosexuals agree or agree strongly that their condition is an emotional disorder? (cf. 339; the control group disappears at this juncture). More strikingly, homosexuals are more than 6 times as likely as heterosexuals to attempt suicide—a criterion of unhappiness independent of the subject's report. The authors try to explain this statistic with an aside to the effect that the suicide rate in San Francisco is very high (211–12), a testimony to their faith in the explanatory power of nonprojectible predicates. (Perhaps not all philosophers would find this explanation defective. When I asked a well-known social philosopher critical of capital punishment why the murder rate had gone up in states where capital punishment had been abandoned, he said "the crime rate is going up everywhere.") In any case, the heterosexual sample was drawn from the same population, and homosexuals constitute a significant portion of San Francisco's population, so the San Francisco suicide rate is high, in part, because so many homosexuals commit suicide.

Perhaps the most striking trait revealed—or stereotype confirmed—is the extreme impersonality and frequency of homosexual contacts. Roughly speaking, 75% of the respondents reported having had more than 100 sexual partners, and 43% reported having had 500 or more (308). These numbers are not easy to believe. Even taken *cum grano,* they should be compared to the reader's own experience of sex as he tries to imagine what it would be like to move so promiscuously among anonymous encounters—79% of the respondents reported that more than half their partners were strangers. Surely having these many partners is a criterion for maladjustment and compulsivity, a chronic inability to find anyone satisfactory. A harder datum than these numbers is the report that 56% of the respondents usually spend several hours or less with a partner (305); in fact, the authors distinguish "several hours" from "all night." Only 2% usually spend as much as a weekend with a partner successfully "cruised." (I interpret this statistic to make it consistent with the amount of "close-coupledness" reported: see below.) Incidentally, the authors say that "the largest numbers of our respondents spent all night with their partners" (77), but this is misleading. 41% of the respondents usually spent all night, and this is the modal number; but, as noted, *most* homosexuals spend considerably less than a whole night with a partner.

What Bell and Weinberg want to emphasize, however, is that their sample tended to cluster around five "types" of homosexuals, one of which—the "close-coupled"—seem on the whole to be as well-adjusted as heterosexuals. The finding was duplicated for lesbians. Close-coupled homosexuals are those involved in a sort of marriage, living monogamously with a partner of the same sex, not cruising, not experiencing any extraordinary amount of "tension" or regret about homosexuality, and displaying much "joy and exuberance in their particular life-style" (231). This, the authors contend, shows that homosexuality "is not necessarily related to pathology" (ibid.).

The existence of close-coupled homosexuals by no means implies that homosexuality is not pathological. As I have noted, there are almost no significant exceptionless generalizations in human affairs. My evolutionary hypothesis implies only that homosexuals are more likely to be unhappy than their heterosexual counterparts. The pertinent questions are, how many "close-coupled" homosexuals are there, and how many homosexuals exhibit "stereotypic" personality disorders? In point of fact, [5] assigns only 67 homosexuals to the "close-coupled" category, less than 10% of the sample. By contrast, 12% fell into the "dysfunctional" category, tormented souls who regret their homosexuality, cruise frequently, and have many sexual partners. An additional 16% were "Asexuals," homosexuals who tend to live alone without lovers or friends, and whose suicide rate is the highest among homosexuals. On the evidence presented, sociopathic homosexuals outnumber well-adjusted ones 2.8 to 1. If one adds to these at least some of the "functionals"—"men and women [who] seem to organize their lives around their sexual experience" (223)—deeply troubled homosexuals outnumber happy ones by at least 3 to 1.

The authors mislead the reader when they say that close-coupled homosexuals are on the average as happy and well-adjusted as heterosexuals. For this is to compare the best-adjusted homosexual subtype with the homogeneous heterosexual control group, and that is special pleading. It would be more appropriate to compare close-coupled homosexuals to happily married men, something Bell and Weinberg admit in passing but for which they offer no statistics. Since a random sample of heterosexuals will include a number of lonely, twisted individuals, the adjustment level of happily "coupled" heterosexuals must be considerably higher than that of the best-adjusted homosexuals. So viewed, monogamous homosexual coupling looks like a vain attempt at marriage—and homosexual cruising looks perhaps like a realization, of sorts, of adolescent male fantasy. "Dysfunctionals and Asexuals have a difficult time of it, but there are certainly equivalent groups among heterosexuals" (231). Certainly. But do such groups make up 28% of all heterosexuals and 41% of all classifiable heterosexuals, as the Dysfunctionals and Asexuals jointly comprise 41% of all classifiable homosexuals in the Bell-Weinberg sample (346, table 13.5)? Moreover, the authors go only so far as to say that close-coupled men "did less cruising" than the homosexual average (132; also see table 13.7, p. 349), leaving the impression that even close-coupled men do sometimes cruise. No quantitative comparisons are offered between such cruising and extra-marital straying for heterosexual males. Table 22.4 shows that 1% of the coupleds cruise at least once a week, but there are no statistics on how many have cruised in, say, the preceding year. Incomplete though it is, this figure should be contrasted with the heterosexual case. It seems unlikely that 1% of the married male readership of this paper had anonymous sexual encounters last week.

Bell and Weinberg's peroration is a textbook example of circular reasoning:

> It would appear that homosexual adults who have come to terms with their homosexuality, who do not regret their sexual orientation, and who can function effectively sexually and socially, are no more distressed psychologically than are heterosexual men and women (216).

Obviously, anyone who can "function effectively sexually and socially" will not be especially "distressed psychologically." But even going by the Bell-Weinberg sample drawn from volunteers from the "good scene" (27) of the Bay area, the chances that a homosexual will fall into this category are rather low.

Note

Arthur Caplan, R. M. Hare, Michael Slote, Ed Erwin, Steven Goldberg, Ed Sagarin, Charles Winnick, Robert Gary, Thomas Nagel, David Benfield, Michael Green and my wife Margarita all commented helpfully on earlier drafts of this paper, one of which was read to the New York chapter of the Society for Philosophy and Public Policy. My definition of naturalness agrees to some extent with Gary's in [13], and I have benefited from seeing an unpublished paper by Michael Ruse.

References

1. Barash, D. *The Whispering Within*. New York: Harper & Row, 1979.
2. Beach, F. "Cross-Species Comparisons and the Human Heritage." *Archives of Sexual Behavior* 5 (1976): 469–85.
3. Beadle, G. and M. *The Language of Life*. New York: Anchor, 1967.
4. Beigl, H. Review of [34]. *Journal of Sex Research* 10: 339–40.
5. Bell, A. and M. Weinberg. *Homosexualities*. New York: Simon and Schuster, 1978.
6. Devlin, P. *The Enforcement of Morals*. Oxford: Oxford University Press, 1965.
7. Dworkin, G. Review of [36]. *Philosophical Review* 88: 660–63.
8. Gary, R. "Sex and Sexual Perversion." *Journal of Philosophy* 74 (1978): 189–99.
9. Greer, G. *The Obstacle Race*. New York: Farrar, Strauss & Giroux, 1979.
10. Grice, H. "Utterer's Meaning, Sentence-Meaning, and Word-Meaning." *Foundations of Language* 4 (1968): 1–18.
11. Hutchinson, G. "A Speculative Consideration of Certain Possible Forms of Sexual Selection in Man." *American Naturalist* 93 (1959): 81–91.
12. Karlen, A. *Sexuality and Homosexuality: A New View*. New York: Norton, 1967.
13. Levin, M. "'Sexism' is Meaningless." *St. John's Review* XXXIII (1981): 35–40.
14. Lewis, D. *Convention*. Cambridge, MA: Harvard University Press, 1970.
15. Masters, W. and V. Johnson. *Homosexuality in Perspective*. Boston, MA: Little, Brown and Company, 1979.
16. McCracken, S. "Replies to Correspondents." *Commentary*, April 1979.
17. Nagel, E. "Teleology Revisited." *Journal of Philosophy* 74 (1977): 261–301.
18. Nagel, T. "Sexual Perversion." *Journal of Philosophy* 66 (1969): 5–17.
19. Rechy, J. *The Sexual Outlaw*. New York: Grove Press, 1977.
20. Sagarin, E. "The Good Guys, the Bad Guys, and the Gay Guys." *Contemporary Sociology* (1973): 3–13.
21. Sagarin, E. and R. Kelley. "The Labelling of Deviance," in W. Grove, ed., *The Labelling of Deviance*. New York: Wiley & Sons, 1975.
22. Sayre, K. *Cybernetics and the Philosophy of Mind*. Atlantic Highlands, NJ: Humanities Press, 1976.
23. Schiffer, S. *Meaning*. Oxford: Oxford University Press, 1972.
24. Singer, P. *Democracy and Disobedience*. Oxford: Oxford University Press, 1968.
25. Weinberg, M. and C. Williams. *Male Homosexuals: Their Problems and Adaptations*. Oxford: Oxford University Press, 1974.
26. Will, G. "How Far Out of the Closet?" *Newsweek*, 30 May 1977, p. 92.
27. Wilson, E. *On Human Nature*. Cambridge, MA: Harvard University Press, 1978.

Questions

1. What does Michael Levin say are the implications of his analysis for bisexuality?
2. Is the case of Jones and his teeth a good analogy for homosexuality?
3. The author says that homosexuals tend to be less happy as a result of misusing parts of their bodies. In what ways, if any, are they less well off than heterosexuals as a result of how each group uses its genitals?
4. Is the author's distinction between homosexuals and celibate priests regarding the question of happiness a satisfactory one?

Homosexuality, Morals, and the Law of Nature

Burton M. Leiser

Burton Leiser first considers some utilitarian and other arguments that can be raised against some kinds of homosexual behavior, such as conduct that is likely to spread the HIV virus or acts of pedophilia. He points out, however, that some heterosexual activity can be as susceptible to such objections and much homosexual behavior—safe sex between consenting adults—is immune to such criticisms. He then considers the common objection that homosexual behavior is wrong because it is unnatural. He responds to a number of variants of this objection:

(1) The first of these is that homosexuality violates the laws of nature. In responding to this objection, he distinguishes between ordinary laws and laws of nature. In contrast to ordinary laws, laws of nature are discovered rather than enacted, and are descriptive rather than prescriptive. Moreover, laws of nature, unlike social laws, simply cannot be violated.

(2) The author then considers the related view that what is artificial or synthetic is unnatural and therefore immoral. The error of that view is that clearly the wearing of glasses, the filling of teeth, and the taking of painkillers, though artificial, are not wrong. In any event, he notes, homosexuality is not artificial in the sense that it is not synthetic.

(3) A third variant of the argument from unnaturalness is that what is statistically abnormal (i.e., uncommon) is unnatural and thus wrong. But if this were so, then genius would be immoral because it is certainly uncommon.

(4) The fourth version of the argument is that it is unnatural and therefore wrong to use an organ contrary to its principal purpose or function. In response to this, the author notes that an organ can have more than one purpose. Thus the genitals may be used for procreation, but they can also be used for the production of

Burton Leiser, "Homosexuality, Morals, and the Law of Nature," in *Ethics in Practice*, Hugh LaFollette (ed), Blackwells, Oxford, 1997, pp 242–253 pleasure. If only procreative sex were permissible, then it would be wrong for older and infertile married couples to engage in sex, yet almost nobody thinks that that is so.

(5) A final version of the argument from unnaturalness says that "unnatural" just means wrong. However, notes the author, that argument simply begs the question of whether homosexuality is unnatural (in the relevant sense). Having concluded that there are no good arguments supporting the view that homosexuality is wrong, he concludes his paper with a discussion of the rights and responsibilities of homosexuals.

Philosophers and others have insisted for centuries that homosexuality is immoral. The Bible proclaims that it is an abomination (e.g., Leviticus 18:22), but in ancient Greece and in some other societies, homosexuality was accepted as a normal form of sexual activity. In our own time, some nations have repealed laws discriminating against homosexuals and others have given legal recognition to homosexual relationships.

Arguments in support of the thesis that homosexual behavior is immoral and ought to be outlawed run the gamut from utilitarian arguments—that homosexuality causes harm to innocent persons or to society as a whole—to those based on the theory that homosexual relations are contrary to the laws of nature. In addition to these attempts to justify an anti-gay stance on philosophical grounds, substantial numbers of people have powerful emotional reactions to the very thought of homosexual relations, while others, relying upon Scripture or religious tradition as the source of their moral judgments, need no philosophical justifications for their feelings.

This article will critically examine the principal arguments that have been advanced in favor of the proposition that homosexuality is wrong. It will then consider some of the responsibilities that gays and lesbians have in relation to others who may be associated with them, as well as the responsibilities that others have toward gays and lesbians; and finally, some of the moral issues that have arisen as a result of recent attitudes and developments in this area.

I. UTILITARIAN ARGUMENTS AGAINST HOMOSEXUALITY

The Greeks and Romans of ages past believed that earthquakes and volcanic eruptions were often brought about by homosexual behavior. Readers of the biblical book of Genesis might infer from the story of the destruction of Sodom and Gomorra that entire cities could be engulfed in fire and their inhabitants annihilated by homosexual activities. If homosexual relations were likely to cause fire and brimstone to descend upon a city's inhabitants, convulsing the earth and inducing it to open up and swallow innocent human beings alive, that would certainly be an excellent reason for condemning such behavior and enacting the most rigid legal prohibitions against it. But no one with a scintilla of scientific training could reasonably believe that there is any such causal connection between homosexuality and volcanic eruptions or earthquakes.

Nevertheless, there is ample reason to believe that unprotected anal intercourse (a form of sexual behavior that is often engaged in by homosexual males) contributes to the spread of the HIV virus that causes the Auto-Immune Deficiency Syndrome (AIDS), an incurable, invariably fatal disease that has caused the deaths of countless victims since it was first discovered less than two decades ago. Anyone—whatever his or her sexual orientation—who engages in such sexual behavior knowing that there is a significant risk of spreading the disease, and fails to take appropriate measures to protect against infection, is rightly held to be morally, if not legally, culpable for recklessly endangering the lives of others. It may be argued, with some legitimacy, that homosexual sex has not only contributed immensely to human suffering and misery, but has also robbed the world of the services of some extraordinarily talented, creative persons whose contributions might have enhanced the quality of life for vast numbers of other people.

It has also been argued that homosexual relations are a threat to the integrity of vital social institutions and are inconsistent with the moral perceptions of ordinary people. In an influential essay he prepared for the British House of Lords long before the AIDS epidemic, Sir Patrick Devlin, one of England's most respected legal experts, responded to a committee that had been charged with recommending legislation on homosexual relations. The committee (known as the Wolfenden Committee) had concluded that consensual sodomy (that is, anal or oral intercourse to which the parties consent—assuming that they are of age and are mentally competent to make such decisions for themselves) should be legalized. Lord Devlin concluded that the committee's conclusion was erroneous, and that the British Parliament should adhere to the traditions of the past, under which homosexual behavior was legally forbidden and violators were subject to severe penalties. The law is not designed solely for the protection of the individual, he said, but for the protection of society. So-called victimless crimes, or crimes to which the "victim" has consented, are criminal nevertheless, for *society as a whole* is the victim in every such case. A murderer who acts with the consent of his victim, or even at the victim's request, is still a murderer, because the purpose of the law is the preservation of "one of the great moral principles upon which society is based, . . . the sanctity of human life." Thus, acts committed in private and with consent, such as dueling, suicide, and incest, may nevertheless be criminal.

The institution of marriage, Devlin argued, is one of the moral foundations of society. Consequently, adultery is not merely a private matter. It is a concern of the public as well, for it strikes at the very heart of the institution of marriage. The same is true of homosexuality, he said, for no society can exist without a shared sense of morals and ethics—common bonds of thought that constitute the glue that holds a society together. A common morality, he argued, is part of the price we pay to live in a civil society, for a society can be as readily destroyed from within, by the destruction of its moral standards, a loosening of its moral bonds, as it can from without. Therefore, he concluded, the suppression of vice is very much the law's business, and it is perfectly reasonable to prohibit homosexual relations.

But what criterion ought to be employed in determining what ought to be the moral standards upon which such legislation should rest? The test of a society's morals, Devlin said, is the standard of the ordinary man in the street. Immorality, he said, is what "every right-minded person is presumed to consider immoral." When ordinary people feel a deep sense of reprobation and disgust, and there is evidence that the practice in question is injurious to society, then, according to Devlin, we have reached the outer limits of toleration, the point at which the practice may be outlawed.

Devlin does not consider the possibility that a society's moral standards, as measured by "the ordinary man" test, might change or that they might differ from place to place, as they clearly do in various regions of the United States. In a very real sense, that "community of ideas" that is fundamental to Devlin's thesis simply does not exist in the vast, multicultural society that stretches across an entire continent and encompasses communities as diverse as Boise, Idaho, Anita, Iowa, New York City, and San Francisco. Nor, for that matter, is it likely to exist in any part of the industrialized world where the government does not impose severe restrictions on movement or the free exchange of ideas. The ordinary person on the streets of the Bronx is likely to have rather different attitudes from his or her counterpart in Charleston, South Carolina, and those differences are likely to be reflected in the persons elected to the state legislature, to Congress, and to the courts.

The community of interests that Devlin supposes must exist in a given society may not be very evident in the diverse societies with which we are familiar, at least in the areas of ethics and social mores. So far as the United States is concerned, the Supreme Court held as recently as 1986 that the prosecution of homosexuals for private, consensual acts is not inconsistent with the Constitution. Although some states have considered allowing homosexuals to enter into marriage or some relationship comparable to it, most have refused to remove statutes forbidding homosexual relations. Some states have explicitly refused to recognize the right of homosexuals to be treated as entitled to the rights that have been extended to women and members of racial and ethnic minorities who have been perceived as having been discriminated against in the past. Colorado voters adopted an amendment to the State Constitution in 1992 that specifically provided that neither the state nor any state agency or subdivision could adopt any statute, regulation, or policy under which homosexuals, lesbians, or bisexuals would have the status of or be permitted to claim to be a protected minority. The Colorado Supreme Court subsequently held that the amendment violated the United States Constitution. The United States Supreme Court has upheld this decision on the grounds that it violates the equal protection of rights of homosexuals. The vote of the people of Colorado suggests, however, that a substantial number of persons in the United States believe that homosexuals are unworthy of the protections that have been accorded, for example, to racial, religious, and ethnic minorities and to women.

II. OTHER REASONS FOR CONDEMNING HOMOSEXUAL BEHAVIOR

Philosophers, theologians, and social critics have come up with a number of other reasons for condemning homosexuality. None of them, however, seems to hold up under critical analysis. Most, in fact, would apply equally to heterosexuals, if the logic were consistently carried to its ultimate conclusion.

It has been argued, for example, that homosexuals tend to molest children, and that once a young person has been seduced by a gay or lesbian individual, he or she is likely to be initiated irreversibly into that way of life. But the offense being denounced is not homosexuality as such, but pedophilia—having sexual relations with minors. Persons guilty of pedophilia should be strongly denounced and their behavior should remain punishable under criminal statutes. The law has always presumed that minors are not capable of giving meaningful consent to sexual relations with adults, since they are not mature enough or well enough informed to understand the full implications of what they are doing. Criminal sanctions have been imposed upon adults who take advantage of their greater age and authority to seduce youngsters who are under the age of consent, regardless of the alleged willingness of the youngster to participate in such sexual conduct. Thus, an adult who has sexual relations with a 14-year-old may be tried and convicted of statutory rape despite the youngster's express willingness to enter into a sexual liaison with him. There should be no distinction, however, between homosexual and heterosexual relations of this type. Indeed, heterosexuals are guilty of far more acts of pedophilia than homosexuals.

The critics claim that homosexuals are afflicted by such serious psychological problems as feelings of guilt, insecurity, and constant fear of disgrace and ruin, and that homosexuality itself is a psychological problem. There is some truth to this, but as homosexuals "come out of the closet," becoming more open about their sexual preferences, it is becoming less so. One who has openly exposed his or her sexual preferences need no longer fear exposure. One who proudly claims to be a homosexual has conquered much, if not all, of the guilt that he or she might once have felt. The fear of disgrace and ruin is predicated entirely upon the judgment that the critics make: that homosexuals are bad people and that their sexual orientation renders them unfit for a bank loan, for the jobs they hold, or for the homes in which they live. However, if society—or, more specifically, banks, employers, and landlords—abandons its negative judgment on homosexuals and bases individual judgments upon the record of an individual's performance, gays and lesbians would have no more reason to fear exposure or feel insecure than "straight" individuals.

As for homosexual orientation being a psychological "problem," a condition is a problem only when the individual who has it feels that it is one, or when it objectively interferes with the achievement of that individual's goals in life. If homosexuals do not see their sexual preferences as problematic, but (as many evidently do) as liberating, then they are simply *not* problems, psychological or otherwise. And if those preferences do not interfere with the achievement of a homosexual's goals, except to the extent that society, its institutions, and the individuals who run them stand in the way because of an emotional need to condemn people who are different, then the "problem" is not a psychological one, but a social, political, and legal one that must be addressed as those problems are customarily addressed: through the political process.

The charge that homosexuals are unreliable and are poor security risks is true only if society perceives homosexuality to be evil or imposes criminal or social sanctions on those who are homosexual. A person cannot be blackmailed if the threat is exposure of a trait or practice that is deemed by all concerned to be socially acceptable. The fear that a teacher or scoutmaster might sexually abuse his or her charges is no more and no less rational in the case of a homosexual than it is in the case of a "straight" person. Pedophilia, not homosexuality, is the issue.

Homosexuals who engage in tasteless public displays of affection, cross-dressing, and solicitation or street walking for purposes of prostitution may appropriately be censured, reproached, or, where the offense is particularly egregious, punished. But the same is true of heterosexuals who engage in similarly crude and unseemly behavior in public.

III. HOMOSEXUAL BEHAVIOR AND THE LAW OF NATURE

By far the most interesting of the reasons offered by philosophers, theologians, and legal thinkers for declaring that homosexuality is wrong is the claim that it is contrary to the laws of nature. Homosexuals, it is said, violate natural law when they misuse their genital organs in ways that frustrate nature's intention that they be employed exclusively for purposes of reproduction. The critics claim that this violation of nature's laws and of God's design deserves the most severe reprobation. Indeed, many of the statutes that criminalize homosexual relations refer to them as the "infamous crime against nature."

Whether they believe that homosexual behavior should be punishable by law or not, many people seem to feel that anal intercourse, for example, is "unnatural." It takes a bit of a jump to infer that because something is *unnatural* or *contrary to the laws of nature*, it is wicked or wrong. A careful analysis of these concepts will reveal that the inference is completely unwarranted.

Descriptive Laws of Nature

To begin, consider the concept of *law*. In the ordinary sense of the word, laws have the following characteristics:

- They are social conventions, differing from one society to another, and sometimes between various groups within a society.

- They are *prescriptive*. That is, they prescribe or command that people engage in certain forms of behavior, that they either do or refrain from doing certain things. (For example, the law in the United States commands that every resident file an income tax return on the fifteenth of April, that no one assault anyone else, and that no government agency interfere with the free exercise of religion.)
- It is possible to violate them. (A person may fail to file an income tax return; he may assault his neighbor in defiance of the law; and a municipality may pass an ordinance that interferes with religious freedom.)
- Violators may be subject to penalties or other sanctions.
- Penalties or sanctions are imposed and carried out formally by government or institutional officials, or informally by members of the community.
- The laws of a state are not discovered by its citizens. Rather, the citizens are expected to *know* them so that they can obey them. People learn of the state's laws by being informed about them after they have been promulgated.
- The laws of a state may be abolished or modified by suitable governmental enactments.

Now consider what scientists call the laws of nature—i.e., such laws as the law of gravity, Boyle's Law, or Newton's laws of motion.

- They are not mere conventions, and are not variable from one society to another or from one place to another, but are universal.
- They are *descriptive*. That is, they merely *describe* what actually happens and do not command or order anything or anyone. (See the discussion that follows.)
- It is impossible to violate them. A person may not violate the law of gravity, for example. Anyone who attempts to "defy" that law by leaping from the observation deck of the Empire State Building will be treated, within a few seconds, to a dramatic proof of this fact. Astronauts who fly to the moon and balloonists who float above the trees and soar to great heights do not violate the law of gravity or any other natural law, but act in full accordance with them.
- Since it is impossible to violate a law of nature, there are no penalties for doing so. There are *consequences*, however, some of which are perfectly predictable. The hard landing that a person who leaps from a tall building makes on the concrete below is not a punishment, but a predictable consequence of his action. The force of his impact and the speed with which he will strike the concrete are easily calculable by any high school student of physics who is given the height of the building and the weight—or more properly, the mass—of the jumper.
- The laws of nature cannot be abolished by any government. Nor can any government enact a natural law. The laws of nature are *discovered*. They are not created by men.

A simple example of a natural law is Boyle's Law, discovered over three hundred years ago by Robert Boyle. The law states simply that if a given quantity of a gas is kept under constant temperature, its volume will be inversely proportional to the pressure exerted upon it. Thus, an air bubble rising from deep in the ocean to the surface will expand as it rises because the pressure exerted upon it is constantly decreasing as it moves closer to the surface. A helium-filled balloon, lifting from the surface of the earth, will expand as it climbs to ever greater altitudes, because the pressure diminishes as it ascends toward the stratosphere. Eventually, the balloon will burst because the expansion of the gases within it will be greater than the thin skin of the balloon is able to withstand. When the balloon bursts, it is not being punished for "violating" Boyle's Law. It is simply undergoing the inevitable consequences of "obedience" (if we can call it that) to Boyle's Law. Scuba divers must bear in mind a vitally important practical application of Boyle s Law: A diver who has descended to any significant depth at all (even six feet) must not hold her breath as she returns to the surface, for her lungs will act like the balloon just described. As she rises closer to the surface of the water, the pressure diminishes very rapidly, and the volume of the air in her lungs will increase correspondingly, causing severe injury or death. To prevent this from happening, she must exhale, or continue to breathe normally during the ascent in order to relieve the pressure within her lungs. A diver who fails to follow this procedure and suffers serious lung damage has not been *punished* for failing to obey Boyle's Law. The air in her lungs has acted completely in accordance with Boyle's Law, and she has simply suffered the inevitable tragic consequences.

Note that at the beginning of the last paragraph, I wrote that Robert Boyle "discovered" the law that was named after him. He did not create it, but through scientific methods of observation and experimentation, he formulated the general rule as to how gases behave under certain conditions.

None of this is remotely like the sort of thing that critics of homosexuality have in mind when they say that it is wrong because it violates the laws of nature. It is simply not possible to violate a law of nature: A gas cannot help but expand when the pressure on it is relieved, and when support is pulled out from under a stone or a person, neither of them can avoid moving toward the center of the earth (what we call "falling"). Since the descriptive laws of nature cannot be violated, it is sheer nonsense to say that homosexual behavior is wrong because it violates such laws.

All is not lost, however, since there are several other senses in which one might interpret the meaning of the claim that "homosexual behavior is wrong because it violates the laws of nature."

What Is Artificial Is Unnatural

When we speak of something as being unnatural or not natural, we sometimes mean that it is artificial or synthetic, that it is the product of human artifice.

In recent years, for example, chains of stores have grown up promoting what they call "natural" foods, and cosmetics that they claim are made of "natural ingredients." The implication is that there is something unnatural, or contrary to nature, in the foods and cosmetics that are sold in other stores or under different labels. The difference, presumably, is to be found in the fact that "natural" foods are grown and treated with substances that are found in nature rather than with substances that are manufactured or compounded artificially. Manure would be a natural fertilizer under this definition, since it is collected directly from the source—a farmer's herd of cattle, for example—while powders that the farmer purchases from a chemical manufacturer for the same purpose would be regarded as unnatural because they are synthetic. Similarly, a farmer who fights the insects that attack his crops with praying mantises or ladybugs might call his crops "natural," while one who applies commercial insecticides might not, inasmuch as the compounds he applies are artificial or synthetic, having been created out of a variety of ingredients ranging from petroleum to gases extracted from the air.

There may be some benefits, ecologically and otherwise, to the "organic" or "natural" approach to the production of products such as foods and cosmetics. However, it is a considerable leap from that to the conclusion that non-organic or artificial substances are harmful or—to go to the ultimate extreme—evil. On the contrary, many artificial, synthetic substances and products are vital to life as we know it. The only alternatives might be quite unappealing, if we thought about them.

If I were to walk into my classroom one day in a completely natural state, without any of the artificial garments that I ordinarily wear, I am confident not only that my students and colleagues would be quite shocked and offended, but that my job would be in jeopardy. Consider what you are wearing as you read these words: your clothes undoubtedly consist in large part of synthetic materials, such as nylon, orlon, and rayon, created in the very chemical plants that manufacture the farmer's fertilizers and insecticides, in more or less the same manner and out of the same raw materials. The metals that went into making the rivets, zippers, and buckles you wear were mined, smelted, and formed using techniques that must all be deemed to be artificial. It is obvious that the clothes we wear are not found in nature, but must all be manufactured. If you wear corrective lenses, as I do, you are probably as grateful as I am for the optician's art and for the brilliance of the scientists and engineers who have created the substances out of which our plastic lenses and frames are formed. The artificial fillings in our teeth are certainly superior to the only "natural" way of dealing with toothache—having the offending teeth pulled out. The synthetic substances we take to cure our headaches—whether aspirin or Tylenol—are certainly to be preferred over doing nothing at all for them, or employing unproved, possibly ineffective, and potentially harmful "natural" remedies. And the very book you are reading is an artificial object whose existence was made possible only because of the technological expertise of many people who formulated the artificial inks, papers, and glues that went into its production, and the printing presses and other machines that printed and folded and bound it.

In short, industry and its products are not evil, even though they are "unnatural" in this sense of the word. Nor is interference with nature evil or wrong. On the contrary, we are free of many diseases, and can be cured of many others, only because we have interfered with nature in many ways. Only our ability to turn nature's laws to our own advantage has enabled us to escape the diseases, the insects, the ravages of floods and cold and heat that would otherwise make our lives miserable.

Homosexual behavior simply cannot be considered unnatural in this sense. There is nothing *artificial* about it. On the contrary, to those who engage in it, it is the most natural thing in the world. Even if it *were* unnatural in this sense, it is difficult to see how that would justify calling it wrong.

The Uncommon or Abnormal Is Unnatural

It may be suggested that homosexuality should be condemned because it is "unnatural" in the sense of being uncommon or "abnormal" (i.e., not usual). But this proves no more to the point than the previous suggestions. Many of our most esteemed scientists, artists, musicians, and scholars do things that are quite out of the ordinary, but we don't scorn them for that. Of all the thousands of students who have attended my classes during the years I have been teaching, only one, so far as I can recall, played the harp, and one other played the oboe. Both of them engaged in uncommon or unusual behavior, but the fact that they did so simply set them apart as having unusual interests and uncommon talent. The geniuses like Thomas Alva Edison, Albert Einstein, and Jonas Salk, who gave the world the phonograph and the electric light bulb, the theory of relativity, and a vaccine that has saved millions of people from the ravages of polio, deserve praise rather than condemnation for their extraordinary (i.e., abnormal or uncommon) contributions. If homosexuality is wrong, it cannot be because it is "unnatural" in this sense of the word.

The Use of an Organ or Instrument in a Way That Is Contrary to Its Principal Purpose or Function Is Unnatural

Screwdrivers are admirably suited for their intended function: driving screws; hammers for pounding nails; the eyes for seeing; the teeth for chewing. Abuse of any of these instruments or organs can lead to trouble. One who uses a screwdriver to pound a nail may get hurt, and one who uses his teeth to pry the cap from a beer bottle is likely to end up with less than a full set of teeth. By the same token, it has been suggested that it is inconsistent with the proper function or purpose of one's sex organs to use them for anything but reproduction, that any such use (or abuse) is unnatural, and that it is therefore wrong and worthy of condemnation.

In the absence of technology capable of cloning people from cells scraped from inside their cheeks, it appears that the only way for people to reproduce is via the more or less traditional methods associated with the genital organs. Even though it is now possible to fertilize an ovum in a test tube without either the mother or the father having sexual intercourse, the resulting embryo will die unless it is transplanted into the uterus of a woman who is willing to carry it and nurture it until it has reached a stage of development at which it can exist more or less on its own. The sperm cells and the ova must in any event be collected from men and women who are willing to donate them. Therefore, although medical technology has developed so far that human reproduction can take place without actual sexual intercourse, the human sexual apparatus is still essential for its successful achievement.

Because the sex organs are obviously and uniquely designed for the purpose of procreation, it is argued, any use of them for any other purpose is abusive, abnormal, unnatural, and therefore wrong. Masturbation, homosexual relations, and heterosexual intercourse that deliberately frustrates the design of the sex organs are therefore deemed to be perversions that are or ought to be prohibited in any right-thinking society.

But the matter is not so straightforward. Both tools and body organs *can* be used for a multitude of tasks which we ordinarily consider to be perfectly acceptable. Although a screw driver's original purpose might have been to drive screws, it is not considered a misuse of such a tool, much less a perversion, to use it to pop the cap from a soda bottle or as a wedge or a lever, or for any number of other useful purposes. Teeth seem to be well designed for chewing, to be sure; but they can also be quite attractive, and add considerably to the beauty of a smile or the ferocity of a threatening glare. A person's ears are uniquely adapted for hearing. If a comedian wiggles his ears in order to draw a laugh from his audience, only an utterly humorless crank would accuse him of being perverse and wicked for using his ears to entertain his neighbors when they were designed for hearing.

The sex organs seem to be well suited, not only for reproduction, but also for the production of intense pleasure in oneself and in others. Their being so well suited for that purpose would seem to be utterly inconsistent with calling anyone who uses them merely to produce pleasure, either in himself or in another, while ignoring or frustrating procreation, perverse or wicked simply on the ground that he or she has committed an "unnatural" act. Since sex organs fulfill the function of producing pleasure so admirably, employing them for that purpose scarcely seems to be perverse or wicked on that account alone.

Moreover, it is quite obvious that human sex organs are used to express, in the deepest and most intimate way, the love of one person for another. Even those who most ardently oppose "unfruitful" intercourse concede this point, in practice if not in words, when they permit older married people who are beyond the age of reproduction to have sexual intercourse with one another. Similarly, when a woman is pregnant and thus incapable of becoming pregnant, she and her husband are nevertheless permitted to engage in sexual relations with one another without the slightest thought that what they are doing is perverse or "unnatural" because it is sure to be unfruitful. Under these circumstances, no one thinks that it is perverse or unnatural to engage in sexual relations that one knows will not lead to pregnancy. Sex organs, like other things that we are capable of manipulating, can be put to many uses. In themselves, those uses do not seem to be wicked, perverse, or unnatural, though some may be more common than others, at least in some societies or among some groups within a given society.

The fact that people *are* condemned for using their sex organs for their own pleasure or profit, or for that of others, reveals a great deal about the prejudices and irrational taboos of our society. The assumption that any organ has one and only one "proper" function is indefensible. The identification of such a "proper" or "natural" use when there are others is arbitrary and without foundation in scientific fact. To say that any use of an organ that is contrary to its principal purpose or function is unnatural and therefore evil or depraved proves nothing, for it merely begs the question.

That Which Is Natural Is Good, and Whatever Is Unnatural Is Bad

We asked at the beginning what definition of "unnatural" might reasonably lead to the conclusion that homosexual behavior, being unnatural, was therefore evil or wrong. Perhaps this is the key to the solution of our problem. Other senses of the word "unnatural" do not work: some "unnatural" things, such as artificial or synthetic things, are quite good and highly desirable; others, such as the uncommon or "abnormal," may also be good and praiseworthy. In other senses of the word, the unnatural simply cannot exist: the descriptive laws of nature admit of no exceptions. Therefore, nothing can be unnatural if that word is understood to refer to what is contrary to or inconsistent with the laws of nature.

But perhaps there is a sense of the word "unnatural" which simply *means* that which is wrong, perverse, depraved, or wicked. Then if homosexuality is unnatural, it would logically follow that it is wrong, perverse, depraved, or wicked!

But this is not very helpful, for it explains nothing at all. This is what it amounts to:

> Whatever is unnatural is, by definition, wicked, wrong, perverse, and depraved.
> Now, why is homosexuality wicked, wrong, perverse, and depraved?
> Because it is unnatural.

Now let's substitute the *definition* of "unnatural" for the *word* "unnatural" in this sentence: **Homosexuality is wicked, wrong, perverse, and depraved because it is *unnatural*.**

And we come up with the result: **Homosexuality is wicked, wrong, perverse, and depraved because it is *wicked, wrong, perverse, and depraved*.**

What is the end result? A tautology—a sentence that is true by definition, but is completely worthless since it communicates no information about anything whatever. In other words, if "unnatural" means wicked, wrong, perverse, and depraved, then it provides no support whatever for the argument that homosexuality is wicked, wrong, perverse, and depraved *because* it is unnatural. The argument is question-begging, and should be completely unconvincing to anyone who is at all familiar with elementary logic.

IV. IS HOMOSEXUALITY IMMORAL?

Upon careful analysis, we have seen that those arguments that are advanced most often with the intention of supporting the thesis that homosexuality is wrong simply do not hold up. We have not established that *no* valid argument exists to support that thesis. But a diligent search of the literature fails to discover one.

For some people, the fact that the Bible expresses very strong disapproval of homosexuality is sufficient to establish the fact that it is wicked. For them, no further argument is needed. Others are so disgusted by what they consider to be gross practices, more or less on the same level as bestiality or the consumption of rats or insects, that no intellectual arguments are likely to overcome their powerful emotional reactions. But such reasons are not philosophical, and are not likely to persuade anyone who chooses to base her moral judgments on reason rather than on ancient authority or pure emotionalism.

Despite the weight of tradition, the burden is on those who advocate the ostracism of homosexuals to demonstrate that there are cogent reasons for so punishing human beings whose only crime, if it is one, is to engage in the only form of love-making that they feel capable of. Nor is there any intellectually acceptable justification for the imposition of civil or criminal sanctions against gays and lesbians, or depriving them of the benefits of legal privileges that are available to people whose sexual inclinations are more in accordance with the views of most other people—such privileges as the right to inherit, to enjoy tax relief that is open to married couples, and perhaps to adopt children. (I say "perhaps" because further considerations may be relevant to that policy issue.) Some adult gays and lesbians have adopted their lovers, with their lovers' consent, in order to establish a kind of family relationship that would be recognized by the law. That they have had to resort to this rather strange use of adoption laws is an unfortunate consequence of the law's refusal to recognize long-term, stable relationships between them. Legislatures have generally refused to change the law to make it more favorable to homosexual relationships because many legislators and their constituents view homosexuality as immoral and are unwilling to confer legal recognition upon it.

V. HOMOSEXUALS: RIGHTS AND RESPONSIBILITIES

The moral issues surrounding homosexuality are not exhausted, however, by this discussion. Even if our communities recognize the rights of gays and lesbians to pursue their way of life without legal interference, there remain exceedingly delicate questions of the relations of gays and lesbians with their families and associates, and the moral dimensions of some of those relationships. Since none of the philosophical arguments against homosexuality holds up under critical analysis, it would seem to be reasonable to conclude that there remains no cogent justification for discriminating against homosexuals, either legally or in social relations. At the same time, however, it is reasonable to expect homosexuals to behave responsibly toward others, including those who—for whatever reason—find their way of life unacceptable.

Gays and lesbians who have demonstrated in St. Patrick's Cathedral in New York City, for example, disrupting services by raucous chanting designed to draw attention to their displeasure with the Church's policies toward people with their orientation, seem to have overstepped the bounds of decency and propriety. The gay and lesbian organization "Act Up" has mounted numerous rowdy demonstrations and marches, protesting what its participants see as injustices perpetrated against homosexuals. Far from winning sympathy for their cause, such incidents are likely to drive potential supporters away. But there is a larger question of the moral propriety of their behavior.

The American legal tradition exempts religious institutions from governmental control. The public policy behind this tradition derives from the theory that private associations should be free to determine their own policies, so long as they do not seriously jeopardize the fundamental rights of others. That principle implies that religious institutions, and other private associations, should be free to change their ancient strictures against homosexuality if their leaders choose to do so; but that they ought also to be free to *refuse* to abandon those practices and restrictions, as they see fit. Neither the First Amendment nor liberal views on free speech sanction the disruption of religious services, however worthy the cause. Nor do they authorize gays and lesbians to appoint themselves as censors to delete Biblical passages that unequivocally condemn homosexuality, however hurtful those passages might be.

Consider a man who pays surreptitious visits to a married woman, sends her flowers, writes amorous notes to her, and frequently calls her on the phone when her husband is out. These attentions threaten the integrity and stability of her marriage and the happiness of her husband and children, even if the relationship never develops into an overtly sexual one. Substitute a woman for the man (i.e., the third party) in this example, so that the outsider, a woman, is paying loving attention to the wife, and the morality of the situation undergoes no change at all. If the affection that develops between them becomes so deep and passionate that it alienates the married party from her spouse, then it is wrong—whether the new relationship is heterosexual or not. And if the new relationship becomes a sexual one, then it appears to be adulterous, whatever the sexual orientation of the parties. Although we gave up prosecuting adulterers and adulteresses long ago, and no longer permit people to sue for the damage done to them and their families through what the law used to call criminal conversation—adulterous cohabitation—or alienation of a spouse's affections, moral reprobation would seem to be appropriate in such cases, considering the hurt and the damage that they cause. What is true of heterosexuals seems no less true of homosexuals.

Many gays and lesbians, having been hurt by others, may have become callous toward persons who do not share their views on sexuality. Intent on pursuing their own inclinations—perhaps with justification—they may fail to realize how much hurt they cause to others in the process. No doubt it can be extremely painful for the traditional parents of a person to accept the strange (to them) way of life that their son or daughter has adopted. The natural desire of the gay son or daughter to be accepted by his or her parents should, one would think, be accompanied by an understanding of the difficulty the parents must have in accepting what must seem to them to be an outrageous, immoral way of life.

On the other hand, it is difficult to think of anything more cruel and heartless than the utter abandonment of a dying AIDS victim by his or her family because of self-righteousness, religious zealotry, or disapproval of homosexuality. Too many victims of that awful disease have withered, suffered, and died with no one to comfort them but their lovers, who are often weakened by the same affliction. Those who should be closest to them—their fathers and mothers, brothers and sisters—may be so preoccupied with nursing their own anger, their hurts, and their grievances that they have lost the capacity to be understanding or compassionate toward those to whom they have the closest possible biological connections. In some ways, this is one of the most grievous moral afflictions of our time. If there were a law of nature, one might wish that it would teach us, if not incline us, to care for our sons and daughters, despite our disagreements with them over matters that touch us deeply, particularly when they are suffering. Some have, indeed, responded to that call in heroic measure. But all too many have not.

Like every real human problem, the issues surrounding homosexual relations are complex and fraught with deep emotions. Philosophers may be able to shed some light on the arguments, but in the final analysis, only compassion and good will on all sides will lead to the kind of understanding and acceptance that may ultimately lead to a resolution of the most painful of them.

Questions

1. Why can laws of nature not be *violated*?
2. Burton Leiser responds to the argument that homosexuality involves the misuse of one's sexual organs. Could Michael Levin offer any rebuttal of this response?
3. Do you think Burton Leiser has neglected to consider any important objections to homosexuality?

Suggestions for Further Reading on Homosexuality

ATKINSON, RONALD. "The Morality of Homosexual Behavior." In *Today's Moral Problems*. Second Edition. Edited by Richard A. Wasserstrom, New York: Macmillan, 1979: pp. 311–315.

BAIRD, ROBERT M., and KATHERINE BAIRD, eds. *Homosexuality: Debating the Issues*. Amherst, N.Y.: Prometheus Books, 1995.

FINNIS, JOHN, and MARTHA NUSSBAUM, "Is Homosexual Conduct Wrong? A Philosophical Exchange." In *Homosexuality: Debating the Issues*, edited by Robert M. Baird and Katherine Baird. Amherst, N.Y.: Prometheus Books, 1995: pp. 44–48.

LEVIN, MICHAEL. "Homosexuality, Abnormality and Civil Rights." *Public Affairs Quarterly* 10, no. 1 (January 1996): pp. 31–48.

PRIMORATZ, IGOR. "Homosexuality." In *Ethics and Sex*. London: Routledge, 1999: pp. 110–132.

RUSE, MICHAEL. "The Morality of Homosexuality." In *Philosophy and Sex*. New rev. ed. Edited by Robert Baker and Frederick Elliston. Amherst, N.Y.: Prometheus Books, 1984: pp. 370–390.

PART THREE

Parents and Children

CHAPTER 8

Rearing Children

The Child in the Moral Order

Francis Schrag

Francis Schrag describes a society, the Namuh, in which one group, the Tluda, treat another group, the Dlihc in paternalistic ways that we would condemn, even though we typically treat children in exactly these ways. He asks whether the distinction between adults and children can support the moral weight it is thought to bear—namely, that paternalism toward children, but not toward (normal) adults, is acceptable.

He suggests that the one form of paternalism could be acceptable without the other if there were some relevant capacity that children lack and adults have. He considers some possible capacities: (1) the development of locomotion; (2) the development of linguistic competence; (3) sexual maturity; and (4) rational choice. None of these, he thinks, can justify our current practices. (1) and (2) are devel-oped to a basic level of competence by age six and (3) occurs by the early teens rather than around eighteen or twenty-one when we currently think paternalism ceases to be acceptable. (4) may appear to be a more promising criterion, but some probing, suggests the author, reveals that it too is inadequate. On a vague definition of "rationality," this capacity is developed so gradually and continuously that there is not even a rough age at which it can be said to arise. Understood in a more precise way as the capacity for "formal operations," it is present by age twelve.

Having failed to find any suitable criterion, Francis Schrag offers a modified utilitarian defense of paternalism toward children. He notes, however, that he is not committed to the current age of majority. There are good reasons, he says, for lowering it to fourteen or fifteen.

In the early 1700s the Flemish explorer Sicnarf Garhcs discovered a society, the Namuh, which he described in his two-volume compendium of primitive societies. As this society bears on my present topic, I begin with a summary of its salient features:

Francis Schrag, "The Child in the Moral Order," *Philosophy* 52 (1977): 167–177.

(1) It consists of two classes of people, the Tluda and the Dlihc, whom I shall hereafter refer to as the T's and the D's. Relative to the D's, the T's are (on the average) strong, intelligent and knowledgeable about the world. The D's are (with some exceptions) weak, ignorant and dim-witted.

(2) The society is divided into several communities and each community in turn into households. The T's offer protection and the necessities of life to the D's of their own household. The D's in return do the bidding of the T's and are required to adopt the beliefs and religion of the household. They are free to pursue their own enjoyments only within the boundaries arbitrarily determined by those T's who protect them. These boundaries vary from household to household and often from day to day within the same household.

(3) The T's retain the right to punish D's for transgressions of the rules, and punishment is often meted out on the basis of the flimsiest and most circumstantial evidence. Occasionally D's are allowed the opportunity to explain and defend themselves against an accusation but there is not even a semblance of due process.

Garhcs was able, through an interpreter, to question several of the T's about the reasons for their seemingly barbaric handling of the D's. Apparently it was thought that the sometimes harsh and unpredictable regime under which they live is a necessary part of an evolutionary process. At the conclusion of this process, Garhcs was told, the D's are 'ogtel' or 'emancipated' by the T's. 'Since they are unable to choose what is best for themselves, we make their choices for them. The necessity for occasional infliction of pain and deprivation is a manifestation of our love and concern for the growth of the soul', Garhcs' informant tells him. Garhcs apparently gives some credence to this response for he emphasizes the affection which T's and D's often seem to display towards each other, yet he remains hesitant about crediting this story about the emancipation of the D's. 'In my two month sojourn with the Namuh I only witnessed one such emancipation, and in this case the D was, I think, a freak of some sort, for his appearance was closer to that of a T than to that of a D.' So much for Garhcs.

How would we judge this society from within our own moral framework? There is little doubt, I think, that any such hierarchically ordered society would be universally condemned by almost every writer on ethics since Kant (and no doubt many before). Such a society denies to an entire class the fundamental right of freedom to pursue one's own life (limited only by the equal rights of others), a right claimed by writers as diverse as Locke, Kant, Bentham, Mill, or in our own day, H. L. A. Hart, John Rawls and Robert Nozick, to name only a few. The fact that the T's claim to restrict the D's in the latter's own 'true' interests would only partially mitigate this judgment. Even supposing that they are indeed 'emancipated' after a period of several years or decades this would hardly cause us to alter our judgment. Does one of us have a right forcibly to bend another to his will for a week or even a day even in the name of the latter's future happiness or freedom? Such a question is surely rhetorical.

Let us try, however, as an exercise whose purpose will become clear presently, to justify the Namuh society from within our own ethical traditions. It is possible to defend Namuh society from two different points of view. (1) A utilitarian defence would focus on the amount of happiness realized in Namuh society compared to a more egalitarian alternative. To be convincing, such a defence would have to show not only that total happiness was greater among the Namuh but that the subordinate class, the D's prospered. (2) A rigorous paternalistic defence would hold the right to freedom inviolable while at the same time ascribing less than human status to the D's inferior class. As Isaiah Berlin once pointed out, 'conceptions of freedom directly derive from views of what constitutes a self, a person, a man. Enough manipulation with the definition of man, and freedom can be made to mean whatever the manipulator wishes.'[1]

I said that the Namuh society bears on our own topic of the child in the moral order. In what way? As will no doubt be obvious, Namuh society *is* our own human society, the two classes being adults and children. The point of introducing the topic in such a deceitful way is to jar the reader's sensibilities in order to free them from their customary perspective. This perspective, shared by virtually every philosopher in our tradition, has two salient defects: it presents a distorted view of the *human* moral order; and it appears to solve certain difficult problems by concealing them without being aware that it is so doing.

I

In what way is the customary view a distortion? Seen from its perspective, human freedom is an inviolable right. From this it follows naturally that in a just society paternalism (the coercion of people in their own interest) is virtually absent; that the human right to freedom extends to any person at any time, and that what has been called the negative conception of liberty will be cherished, the positive conception rejected.[2] But from a broader perspective that encompasses the entire *life-span*, it is clear that no actual society nor any philosopher's ideal cherishes negative liberty to the exclusion of the positive conception, accords human children the right to freedom, or fails to endorse a paternalism which embraces every person for at least a quarter of his or her life. I do not think this point needs documentation. The fiercest opponents of paternalism, such as Mill, Berlin and Robert Nozick, do not hesitate to accept it for children. So Berlin's own tradition manipulates the definition of man in just the way he decries embracing the doctrine of equal liberty for adults while reserving paternalism for children. Or, to put the matter more judiciously, perhaps, an enormous philosophical weight is made to rest on the adult/child distinction, yet the basis of the distinction is left unexamined.[3]

The important question which I see at stake here may be put like this: the ancient philosophers (or at least most of the prominent ones) took it for granted that there were marked differences in the capacities of men, differences which

[1]Isaiah Berlin, 'Two Concepts of Liberty', *Four Essays on Liberty* (Oxford University Press, 1969), 134.
[2]Contemporary exemplars of this perspective, in addition to Berlin and Rawls, would include Richard Wasserstrom in 'Rights, Human Rights, and Discrimination', *Human Rights*, A. I. Melden (ed.) (Belmont, CA: Wadsworth Publishing Company, 1970), 96–110; and Robert Nozick, *Anarchy, State and Utopia* (New York: Basic Books, Inc., 1974).
[3]The one philosopher I have located who perceives this point plainly is J. Fitzjames Stephen, *Liberty, Equality, Fraternity* (Cambridge: Cambridge University Press, 1967), 141–142.

were not capable of being obliterated and which therefore would be and should be reflected in the social order. A hierarchical paternalistic society was neither unnatural nor unjust from the point of view of Plato or Aristotle. Following Locke and Kant the modern philosophers, to generalize somewhat crudely, reject this doctrine totally. They assume that no differences among adults in the morally relevant attributes approach the difference between adults and children. They further assume—at least I have never seen evidence to the contrary—that childhood ends at about the traditional age of majority, that is at the age of twenty-one. These two assumptions could be combined and formulated precisely like this: if we classify human beings according to the characteristics relevant to paternalism, then the *only* defensible system of classification (1) is based on degree of maturation as measured by chronological age and (2) divides the human population into two groups by drawing a line in the neighbourhood of twenty-one years of age.[4] I see no reason why this should be *assumed*, and I am not at all sure that it is true.

Unless the defender of the conventional view can illuminate the nature of the adult/child distinction, it is not clear how he can defend his radically divergent attitude towards human children and adults. Let us canvass some of the possible criteria which could be said to constitute the morally relevant differences between the two stages. These differences need not manifest themselves in a single, sudden metamorphosis such as is found occasionally in the animal kingdom. Still, we seek a qualitative difference rather than a very gradual development of powers which are always present to some degree, of if a gradual development, at least one that does not stretch out over the entire life span. Otherwise the line we conventionally draw at about the age of twenty-one could as well be drawn at ten or at forty, revealing a degree of arbitrariness which should make the defender of the conventional view uncomfortable.

Three relatively dramatic formations come to mind, the development of locomotion and of linguistic competence in early childhood and the achievement of sexual maturity at puberty. In the case of the first two, the attributes could well be related to the human creature's ability to survive in the world as an independent being. There is, of course, a sense in which we develop our linguistic and locomotor abilities well into adolescence and beyond, but both personal observation and rigorous research confirm that most children have developed a basic competence in these areas by the age of six.[5] If either or both of these are the differentiating factors, we could in no way justify the protracted period of paternalistic rule over children typical in Western society. No theorist, to my knowledge, has taken this view. The development of the capacity to reproduce with its attendant transformations in physique and psyche occurs closer to the conventional child/adult boundary, and indeed serves, I would guess, as the chief visible basis for discriminating between the two 'stages'. But I do not see

---

[4]I have discussed the justification for using chronological age as a criterion in 'The Child's Status in the Democratic State', *Political Theory*, November 1975.
[5]See Paul Mussen, *The Psychological Development of the Child*, Chap. III (Englewood Cliffs, N.J.: Prentice-Hall, 1973).

any clear way in which these developments relate to the justification of paternalism. It is much easier to coerce a person of reduced size and strength, which might explain why parents usually abandon paternalistic regime after their children reach physical muturity. But how does relative physical strength bear on the question of whether or not adults *ought* to continue paternalistic domination well beyond the beginning of adulthood or perhaps abandon it much earlier?

The ability to make rational decisions is usually given as a necessary condition for independence. The conception of rationality is often rather vague, however, as can be seen from a remark by G. J. Warnock. To be a rational being, says Warnock, one must be able to 'achieve some understanding of the situations in which one may be placed, to envisage alternative courses of action in those situations, to grasp and weigh considerations for or against those alternatives, and to act accordingly'.[6] This conception of rationality seems to be germane to the question of paternalism. If one is like a child, unable or inadequately able to understand and think, . . . or unable or not fully able to choose and to act in accordance with one's thoughts',[7] one is hardly able to act in one's own best interests and consequently needs paternalistic protection. The problem with such a vague notion of rationality, from our point of view, is that its development is so gradual and continuous an affair that it seems hard to draw a line at any point in the sequence from infancy to old age in order to separate humanity into those who require paternalistic protection and those who do not. I am *not* merely referring to the arbitrariness of taking a particular point rather than a neighbouring one, e.g., twenty-one rather than eighteen or twenty-three. I am talking about the absence of any compelling rationale to draw the line in the neighbourhood of twenty-one rather than eleven or thirty-one. The problem is not, to make this quite clear, like that of identifying the point at which night becomes day. For here, although we do not have a sudden, dramatic change, we can identify a neighbourhood. We can say, e.g., that from the point of view of the presence or absence of daylight there is a qualitative difference between 4 and 7 a.m. not matched by the difference between 7 a.m. and any other time until evening. Moreover, this vague notion of rationality allows for the possibility that some older adults stand in relation to the average twenty-one-year-old as the latter does to the average twelve-year-old. We adults are likely to recoil at the suggestion that others might be better placed than we, ourselves, to make decisions regarding our own welfare. But why do we not recoil from the idea that *we* are so placed with regard to our own children's welfare? Might not my psychoanalyst, for example, have a better understanding of my situation and its possibilities and limitations than I do myself?

One might seek to remedy the inadequacy of a very vague conception of rationality by seeking a more precise, technical conception, if possible one which is also known to be related to human development. The work of the Swiss psychologist Jean Piaget provides us with a promising candidate. Piaget

---

[6]G. J. Warnock, *The Object of Morality* (Oxford: Oxford University Press, 1973), 144.
[7]Ibid.

has identified several stages in human cognitive development, the highest of which, the stage of 'formal operations', begins 'at about age twelve and is consolidated during adolescence'.[8] This stage can be characterized in general terms. '... the adolescent's system of mental operations has reached a high degree of equilibrium. This means among other things, that the adolescent's thought is flexible and effective. He can deal efficiently with problems of reasoning ... can imagine the many possibilities inherent in a situation. Unlike the concrete-operational child, whose thought is tied to the concrete, the adolescent can transcend the immediate here and now.'[9] This general conception seems also to have a clear bearing on the person's ability to minister to his own needs and to seek his own good in his own way. Its chief virtue lies, however, in its being translatable into a set of precisely defined operations whose presence or absence is capable of being verified empirically. There are, for example, sixteen 'binary operations' e.g. 'negation', 'conjunction', 'conjunctive negation'.[10] The ability of a person to use theses operations is determined by observing him as he attempts to solve scientific problems such as identifying factors affecting a pendulum's frequency of oscillation.

But what this more rigorous approach to defining rationality gains in precision it loses in relevance. The ability to perform the sorts of logical operations described by Piaget seems to be neither necessary nor sufficient to be a basis for adopting paternalistic rule. We all know people able to perform such operations who are quite impotent to act on their conclusions. We also know some children, precocious intellectually, whose experience of people in the real world is so limited as to make them very unlikely to survive should they have to look after themselves. On the other hand, someone lacking these sophisticated logical abilities might be sufficiently canny and determined to succeed admirably in the world. Stories abound of very young children, such as those orphaned by war, who already been partially confirmed turns out to be true, namely that many *adults* do not reach the stage of formal operations.[11] What do we do then? Consider the attainment of the previous stage, the stage of concrete operations, sufficient? On what grounds? Piaget believes that this stage is normally reached between seven and eleven.[12] Ought we, therefore, to lower the age of majority by ten years? The lack of any clear answer here reveals the arbitrariness of relating paternalistic policies to Piaget's stages of cognitive development.[13]

The problem with using the notion of rationality as a criterion for distinguishing children from adults is this: the most relevant conception is too vague to draw a clear distinction between adults and children. But the more precisely the notion is formulated the less clear is its relevance to the question

---

[8]Herbert Ginzberg and Sylvia Opper, *Piaget's Theory of Intellectual Development: An Introduction* (Englewood Cliffs, N.J.: Prentice-Hall, 1969), 181
[9]Ibid.
[10]Ibid., 195.
[11]See Beth Stephens *et al.*, *The Development of Reasoning, Moral Judgment, and Moral Conduct in Retardates and Normals, Interim Progress Report* (Philadelphia, Pa., Temple University, January, 1972), 42.
[12]Ginzberg and Opper, op. cit., 133.
[13]Lawrence Kohlberg's scheme of stages of moral development, which might be thought to be a plausible candidate, does not really bear on the question of paternalistic rule.

of paternalism. Not much argument is required to see that if the notion of rationality suffers from this defect, a notion like 'maturity' would fare even worse.

Kant suggests one other candidate which we might consider, the ability to be self-sufficient: in society 'The Children of the House . . . attain *majority* and become Master of Themselves *(Majorennes, sui juris)*, even without a Contract of Release from their previous state of Dependence, by their actually attaining to the capability of self-maintenance.'[14] This is a plausible candidate because such ability is usually achieved at about the time we conventionally distinguish the end of childhood, and because it seems as if those unable to sustain themselves are in need of the protection and sustenance of others. But a moment's reflection will reveal that this candidate is not suitable either. 'Self-sufficiency' may mean something as vague as 'maturity' in which case it does not allow us to draw the sort of sharp line we want to. Or it might be defined more narrowly as ability to sustain oneself financially. But then it is both too strong and too weak a condition. A very young child might be capable of earning enough money to support himself, by modelling for instance, but this does not imply that he is incapable of assuming control of his own life. On the other hand there are numerous individuals incapable of supporting themselves, the crippled, the sick, the elderly, the unemployed, whose disability seems connected with their being able to live their own life only in the sense that they are not able to carry out their plans. They may require assistance from others, but there is no reason to suppose that they require to be *coerced* in their own best interests. It might be argued that any person who was unable to be self-sufficient, in this sense, *forfeited* the right to seek his own good in his own way. Regardless of whether this doctrine is palatable or not, it is clear that it could not be used to justify paternalism for children without at the same time embracing a sizeable portion of the adult population.

Unless I have overlooked something here, I am prepared to assert the following: the conventional view which endorsed paternalism for children while rejecting it for adults cannot be maintained on the basis of some allegedly clear distinction between children and adults, for no such distinction has any basis which survives scrutiny. In particular no criterion can be found such that: (1) it dramatically distinguishes older from younger human beings, (2) it has a clear bearing on a human being's ability to live free of paternalistic domination, and (3) it occurs in the neighbourhood of the conventional boundary between the two stages.

II

Holders of strongly anti-paternalistic views are therefore faced with a dilemma. Either they must abandon their claim that 'to be able to choose is a good that is independent of the wisdom of what is chosen', to cite Gerald Dworkin's paraphrase of Mill;[15] or they must be prepared to reject paternalism for children, at least for all those able to choose, that is, able to speak and give reasons for their

[14]Immanuel Kant, *The Philosophy of Law,* trans, W. Hastie (Edinburgh: T. & T. Clark, 1887), 118.
[15]Gerald Dworkin, 'Paternalism', *Morality and the Law,* R.A. Wassertrom (ed.) (Belmont, CA: Wadsworth Publishing Company, 1971), 117.

actions. As Dworkin has it, '. . . better ten men ruin themselves than one man be unjustly deprived of liberty'.[16] Yet this second course seems too drastic, I daresay. It invites the 'ruin' not of just ten but of millions rather than deprive them of liberty. As J. F. Stephen observed, 'If children were regarded by law as the equal of adults, the result would be something infinitely worse than barbarism. It would involve a degree of cruelty to the young which can hardly be realized even in imagination.'[17]

Faced with such a prospect, let us formulate a defence of the current arrangements by invoking the modified utilitarian rationale discussed earlier with respect to the Namuh, a rationale which would go like this: the purpose of social arrangements is the maximization of human happiness. Any person with some experience and understanding of the world is likely to have the keenest interest in and be the best judge of what will make him happy. As Mill said, 'Mankind are greater gainers by suffering each other to live as seems good to themselves, than by compelling each to live as seems good to the rest.'[18] For those of limited understanding and experience, however, this generalization does not hold, as even Mill does not hesitate to acknowledge. In the case of children, the chances of their achieving happiness if left to pursue their own good in their own way are slim. They must submit for a time to the paternalistic rule of others. (Note that this resolution is a severely constrained utilitarianism, for we do not allow some to thrive at the expense of others. Rather we say that even the children, whose desires are often frustrated, are better off than they would otherwise be.)

What is attractive about this solution is that it does not presuppose any dramatic difference in capabilities between children and adults. It acknowledges that the development of an understanding of the sources of personal satisfaction and the ability to act on that understanding is a gradual process; that the identification of a precise point at which the risks of unwise personal choices are outweighed by the risks of unwise choices by parents or guardians is impossible and therefore necessarily arbitrary to some extent. This helps us to accept the fact that the establishment of such a point can safely be left to convention. The stress on understanding and experience, moreover, rather than on the acquisition of particular powers or faculties, makes it reasonable for emancipation to follow puberty, so that a young person's initial encounters with the wider world and with members of the opposite sex, encounters likely to engender powerful, unfamiliar emotions, can be initially guided to some extent by those familiar with such emotions.

There is something troubling about this view of the moral order, which construes freedom as merely a means to securing happiness. What is troubling is the possibility, left open on this view, that this relationship of means to end need not always be so, that most men might be generally misled about the sources of their own happiness. The growing complexity of civilization, the increasing interdependence of spheres of activity, allows us to envisage a future world in which most adults are like our own children. We say that our children will come

---

[16]Ibid., p. 126.
[17]Stephen, op. cit., p. 193.
[18]J. S. Mill, *On Liberty*, R. B. McCallum (ed.) (Oxford: Basil Blackwell, 1947), 11.

to agree that we were acting in their interests when we refuse to allow them to risk their future happiness by remaining unschooled, to take an example. We say that they could not possibly appreciate the consequences twenty years hence of entering the world uneducated. But can we not imagine farsighted individuals able to recognize that much that we do now is not merely injurious to others and to future generations but shortsighted in just the same way—that in twenty years we ourselves will profoundly regret the choices we have made, choices, for example, in the areas of diet or resource conservation or family planning. If maximizing the chances for happiness in the future is the test, such farsighted individuals would be justified in restraining us in our own interest. This possibility seems remote, but still remains a possibility.

Dworkin suggests that Mill himself was sensitive to this, which is why he spoke at times as if he attributed value to freedom 'independent of the wisdom of what is chosen'. Dworkin's own principle, namely that paternalism be justified only to preserve a wider range of freedom for the individual, is not much more satisfactory than the principle of securing future happiness.[19] In the absence of a precise notion of a 'range of freedom', especially those which pose a risk to life or health in the name of expanding future options. Why not prevent people from eating certain foods now in the name of making possible a broader range of choices when they pass sixty?

If we cannot place an absolute value on freedom without risking our very survival, or at least that of our children, and if we dare not consider freedom as a mere means either to future happiness or to future freedom without risking our own freedom or that of our descendants, is there some alternative view which would protect both values while allowing us to preserve the conventional child/adult distinction? Suppose we posited a threshold of experience, beyond which freedom had an absolute value, whereas before this threshold was reached freedom of choice was but one among several goods. Now we have to question the basis for saying that prior to reaching this threshold, freedom did *not* hold absolute sway. Here presumably the costs outweigh the benefits, the risks are too high. Now what could these risks be but the risks of making disastrous choices, that is choices threatening future happiness or even survival? But once we have allowed for this possibility, what *guarantee* can we provide that now or in the future this threshold will be reached for all or most human beings? If the freedom of some may justifiably be limited by others under certain circumstances may not our freedom be justifiably limited in analogous circumstances? So the spectre of extensive paternalism beyond childhood would continue to haunt us.

III

I have presented two ways of looking at the child's status in the moral order. If we adopt one view, we can retain a rigorous anti-paternalism for adults by positing a sharp distinction between them and children. This by and large is the

---

[19]Dworkin, op. cit., pp. 118–126.

view of our philosophic tradition, at least since Mill. As we have seen, however, the facts about human development do not entitle us to erect such a clear boundary, at least not in the neighbourhood where most of us would like to, i.e. somewhere beyond the onset of puberty. The second view is far more consonant with the ways in which human beings actually develop. It does not require us to endow the relatively dramatic, visible changes occurring at adolescence with an unwarranted moral significance. Yet this closer fit to the 'data' is purchased at a price, the opening of the door to the possibility of an extension of paternalism beyond childhood, a possibility which could provide a basis for the kind of hierarchical society we abhor. It might be said that this opening amounts to no more than a crack for several reasons. First of all there is no reason to believe that most adults are not the best judges of their own interests. Second, there is no reason to believe that if some adults were not, others could be found to assume the role of benevolent 'parent' over them. If the past is any guide, such paternalistic relations would be almost certain to degenerate to the vilest exploitation, in which 'children' lost both their freedom and their happiness. For here the natural sympathy between parents and their children, which often acts as a bar to such exploitation, would no longer be present.

Yet even in our present society, which creates a sharp distinction between children and adults, there are areas where adults are treated as children, too ignorant to be trusted to look after their own interests. For example, no adult is permitted to purchase powerful drugs without a physician's authorization. If one imagines a world of increasing complexity, a world of vastly enlarged technical knowledge of antecedent and consequent in such areas as health, interpersonal relations and vocational satisfaction, and a world in which the adult/child distinction is no longer taken as absolute, the crack in the door does not seem so trifling.

These speculations highlight the question of what criteria to apply in deciding between the two views. If the views are taken as theories to be assessed against the data they organize, then the second view is clearly more adequate. There is more at stake here than the scientific adequacy of a theory, however. Each 'theory' takes a different view of the process of human development, the one positing two distinct segments where the other perceives a continuum. One view reinforces the existing cultural patterns while the other undermines them. Such cultural patterns are not neutral with respect to their impact on people's lives. As the anthropologist Clifford Geertz has suggested, these patterns should rather be viewed as programmes:

Culture patterns—religious, philosophical, aesthetic, scientific, ideological—are 'programs'; they provide a template or blueprint for the organization of social and psychological processes, much as genetic systems provide a template for the organization of organic processes.[20]

The choice between the two views is therefore a moral choice, in that it is one capable of having an impact on how human beings perceive and hence act

---

[20]Clifford Geertz, 'Ideology as a Cultural System', *Ideology and Discontent*, David Apter (ed.) (New York: The Free Press of Glencoe, 1964), 62.

towards each other. In view of the risks, slight though they be, of undermining a powerful bar to the encroachment of paternalism into our lives, I would opt for the first view. It makes a gamble also, one must admit, a gamble that in seeking their own good in their own way, most adults will fare better than most children would. Relative to the gamble of obtaining a benevolent paternalism, however, the former would seem to be a 'sure thing'.

In opting for the first view, I do not mean to endorse the particular age of majority recognized in our own society. A good case could be made for lowering the age to fourteen or fifteen. All I am arguing for here is maintaining the idea of a firm boundary between the two stages. Perhaps some will consider this a decision to support a kind of 'noble lie', but if so it is not one in which a few deceive the masses for their own good, but rather one in which we *all* believe for *our own* good.

Questions

1. Do you think that there are differences between the way adults treat children and the way that we are told the Tluda treat the Dlihc?
2. Do you think that there are capacities that are developed in the wake of sexual maturation that could be relevant to the issue of paternalism toward children?
3. Do you think that Francis Schrag's modified utilitarian defense of paternalism toward children is satisfactory?

The Case against Equal Rights for Children

Laura Purdy

In these selections from Laura Purdy's book In Their Best Interest?: The Case against Equal Rights for Children, *it is argued that a more robust understanding of "rationality" than child liberationists employ must be used to determine when paternalism is and is not justified. Laura Purdy argues that children lack the necessary experience and background information that are essential for being able to see and choose between the various options open to them. She argues that children also lack the necessary character traits to be able to carry out plans and decisions they might make.*

The author then surveys the psychological literature on permissive child-rearing. She refers to Diana Baumrind's distinction between two kinds of permissive parenting: in the democratic variety, *parents involve children in decision making, provide them with reasons for the rules, and accept children's views when these are reasonable; in laissez-faire parenting, the parents do not evaluate the children's behavior but rather accept and affirm the child's impulses, desires, and actions. Psychological research suggests that laissez-faire parenting is associated with impulsiveness, irresponsibility, disorganization, aggression, and general immaturity. Democratic parenting in a warm family environment is associated with the opposite traits. What this suggests is that in order to mature morally, children should not be given the freedom that adults enjoy. Instead they should be guided by adults who show warmth and who reason with them rather than imposing rules in a blind authoritarian way.*

RATIONALITY AS THE CRITERION FOR EQUAL RIGHTS

Talk about rationality tends to figure largely in discussions of equal rights for children. This is hardly surprising, given the importance attributed to rationality in the history of Western thought.[1] What *is* surprising is the ambivalence demonstrated by proponents of equal rights about its proper role here. In particular, although they tend to base their argument on the claim that rationality is the morally relevant difference upon which access to adult rights should be based, they often seem unsure of its nature or value.

We know well enough that there is a great deal of disagreement about the precise definition of rationality.[2] In an attempt to undermine appeal to anything but the most minimal notion of rationality, for example, the liberationist Bob Franklin points out the many possibilities here. Some have thought that rationality is entailed by a given IQ level, or by the ability to infer consequences of choices. Others emphasize thoughts and actions based on empirical knowledge and logic. Given these differences, he asks, how do we justify the choice of any given definition as a basis for granting rights?[3]

This question should not be the end of the line. Despite much argument on the part of philosophers and other, it seems to me that most of us have a rough working definition of what we mean by the concept. At its core is the notion that we need good reasons for believing and acting. Furthermore, rational action involves some awareness of alternative courses of action together with a judgment about which are better and which worse. Definitions of rationality can be more or less demanding with respect to thoroughness, of course, as well as with respect to the moral quality of ends. But the necessity for ongoing debate about such matters needn't preclude adopting some such approach as the one described here. What matters is not the elaboration of some Platonic form of rationality but deciding what it should take to qualify for adult rights.

Liberationists favor weak definitions of reason. In fact, Howard Cohen, because he denies the necessity for any distinction between the rights of children and those of adults, cannot, strictly speaking, require of children any reasoning ability at all.[4] He believes that their desire to make choices would not, in general, outstrip their developing competence at using them well. What at first appears to be an argument for equal rights based on justice turns out to depend in a fundamental way upon a utilitarian judgment, the judgment that the possible harm would not outweigh the benefits provided by those rights.

John Harris, more typically—and somewhat more plausibly—suggests that a sufficient criterion for equal rights would be having "a life to lead." Having

---

[1]See, e.g., Nicholas Rescher, *Rationality* (Oxford: Clarendon, 1988): "The ancients saw a man as the 'rational animal,' set apart from other creatures by capacities for speech and deliberation. Under the precedent of Greek philosophy, Western thinkers have generally deemed the use of thought for the guidance of our proceedings to be at once the glory and the duty of *Homo sapiens*" (p.1). The role of reason in morality has been especially emphasized from Plato on down.

[2]See, e.g., Max Black, "Ambiguities of Rationality," in *Naturalism and Rationality*, ed. Newton Garver and Peter H. Hare (Buffalo, N.Y.: Prometheus, 1986). For a particularly useful discussion of various aspects of the concept, see Mario Bunge, "Seven Desiderata for Rationality," in *Rationality: The Critical View*, ed. Joseph Agassi and Ian Charles Jarvie (The Hague: Martinus Nijhoff, 1987). For other recent work on rationality see Rescher, *Rationality*; and Martin Tamny and K. D. Irani, eds., *Rationality in Thought and Action* Greenwich, Conn.: Greenwood, 1986).

[3]Bob Franklin, *The Rights of Children* (Oxford: Basil, Blackwell, 1986), p. 28.

[4]Cohen, *Equal Rights for Children*, p. viii.

such life means "to have decisions and plans to make and things to do, it is to be aware of doing it all, to understand roughly what doing it all involves and to value the whole enterprise." This position sounds quite demanding until he fleshes it out somewhat more by saying that it would be important to be able to "see the connection between action (and inaction) and consequence, and [to have] some rudimentary understanding of the nature of consequences." A requirement of this sort turns out, in his view, to entail only awareness of elementary survival facts, such as that "fire burns, knives and broken glass cut, roads are dangerous, not everything can be safely eaten and that these things hold for others too."[5] So the position to be evaluated seems to be that once children are capable of avoiding the obvious physical dangers, they should be left free to plan their lives, just as adults are. It is important to keep in mind here just what this position implies in reality. It implies, among other things, that a six-year-old's announcement that she's not going to school today (or ever) should be respected. Isn't that at wildly implausible stand?

What could be said in its favor? Insofar as it is more demanding than Cohen's minimalist approach, it is likely to lead to less harm. Yet it is still weak enough to constitute an attractive escape from the very real difficulties inherent in making certain kinds of distinctions, difficulties that have in the past helped to rationalize serious injustice. The human track record with respect to such judgments is shameful: sex, color, and some other clearly irrelevant characteristics have all too often been used to deny people basic rights. Given this history, the appeal of erring on the side of generosity is understandable. It is reinforced by the general problem of defining boundaries: any given location may appear arbitrary and therefore vulnerable to slippery-slope arguments. This consideration is especially alluring in the case at hand, as children's gradual development over time makes extremely difficult the exact distinctions liberationists hold to be essential when basic rights are at issue. So there seem to be compelling reasons for adhering to the least demanding standard: only thus can the unjust inconsistent treatment of children and adults be avoided.

Nevertheless, the costs of retreating to such a weak criterion of rationality are so great that they undermine the case for liberation. In general, refusing to make distinctions can cause us to treat unlike cases alike, ignoring differing needs, capacities, and desires. Consider the consequences for women if society grants equal rights to fetuses: most abortions would unjustifiably be prohibited. In general, then, despite the advantages of adopting more inclusive standards, we cannot be blind to the possibly overridingly bad consequences of doing so. The details of the particular question at hand ought to determine which path is chosen. Unlike the liberationists, I believe not only that there is a great deal to lose by opting for a low standard here but that we are able to justify and apply a more demanding one. In short, in some situations, such as this one, we must resist the charms of generosity and return to the hard labor of making distinctions trusting democratic discussion to protect against oppression.

[5]Harris, "Political Status of Children,"p. 48.

At issue here is the question of minimum qualitative standards in decision making. Let us reflect for a moment on some of the differences between more or less competent decisions. A more competent decision about ends reflects some understanding of the variety of possible ends, as well as their probable consequences. Even if we doubt the possibility or wisdom of evaluating ends in terms of prudence or morality, a case can be made for emphasizing the importance of being aware of a wide range of possibilities before one chooses. Such awareness is, after all, one of the central values of the kind of liberal moral theory most likely to undergird the argument for equal rights. Decisions about means require the same kind of awareness of alternative routes between one's starting position and a given end.

Such knowledge about the world as these inferences require is accumulated only gradually (as Hume reminds us), so that young children are less likely to be well equipped with it than people with more experience.[6] And general background knowledge is critical to intelligent behavior, as even those parents blessed with unusually bright children can observe. A course of action that looks perfectly reasonable given an inaccurate set of premises becomes comically inept given more accurate ones. The plans of even quite mature adolescents provide their parents with many a good laugh; were they to be carried out, however, this amusement would in some cases turn to horror. What if your fourteen-year-old daughter decided to celebrate Halloween by going trick-or-treating as a nudist?

Even college-age students can be deficient in background knowledge to a worrisome degree, though they generally are noticeably better provisioned than younger teens.[7] Howard Kahane emphasizes how important it is for them (and by extension for younger children) to learn that reasoning validly from premises to conclusions is not enough.[8] What you already believe determines how well you can evaluate new information: "Even the most brilliant person cannot successfully evaluate everyday rhetoric without bringing to bear sufficient relevant background information, and that is why the need to have accurate background beliefs should be emphasized at least as much as the rules of validity so dear to logicians."[9] According to Jean Piaget, the intellectual tools for reasoning logically are acquired around the age of puberty. If he is right; then if background knowledge were not so important, it might be quite appropriate to recognize equal rights for children at the age of twelve or thirteen. But background knowledge is crucial, and in anything like the present circumstances it is hard to picture children acquiring enough of it to manage their lives well much before their late teens. When we imagine the various possible degrees of competence in

[6]David Hume, *An Enquiry Concerning Human Understanding* (Oxford: Clarendon, 1748), sec. IV, pt. I.

[7]I argue in chap. 2 that such a difference in degree *is* morally relevant here.

[8]In response to the liberationist "Aha!" in response to this point, it seems worth noting that this state of affairs could plausibly be attributed to American adolescents' general immaturity and inadequate education as compared to, say, the average European.

[9]Howard Kahane, *Logic and Contemporary Rhetoric: The Use of Reason in Everyday Life,* instructor's manual (Belmont, Calif.: Wadsworth, 1988), p. vi.

choosing means and ends, we see a vast range of levels of accuracy in conceptions of the whole interlocking network of cause and effect created by sequences of decision making over the course of time. The differences in function these levels represent may be a matter of degree, but the degrees are of such magnitude that for all practical purposes they constitute differences in kind.

Surely these points should also help lay to rest worries about the gray area where individual judgment plays such a large role in defining rational behavior. There will undoubtedly always be room for disagreement about whether some choices are wise, but it doesn't follow that there are no guidelines for evaluating decision making. Such considerations should help to show why the weak criteria for rights espoused by liberationists won't do; there are others, as well. Harris seems to equate his notion of children's "having a life to lead" with having the capacity for planning systematic utility-enhancing projects.[10] The two seem to me to be quite different, however; the requirements for the latter would surely require far more of a child than the mere ability to avoid obvious physical threats.[11] It would, in fact, entail knowing a great deal more about the workings of the world than the average five- or even ten-year-old.

Why would fixing on the capacity for planning systematic utility- enhancing projects as the relevant criterion for equal rights change the picture so much? Background knowledge is only the beginning. The decision to bake up a pan of brownies after school, for instance, constitutes a utility-enhancing project: one knows how to make brownies and one knows that one likes them.

It is undeniable that children routinely plan and successfully carry out projects of this sort. But does a series of such projects constitute a truly *systematic* approach to *utility enhancement*? The answer is clearly negative, on two counts. First, even if utility is defined only with an eye to our own pleasure, it must involve more than short-term gratification; enlightened self-interest, in fact. This point quickly leads to the second, that doing what is in our interest rather than what is immediately gratifying requires us to put our various goals into a broader context. So if a child bakes brownies every day and eats half the pan, she is not engaged in systematic utility enhancement.

In other words, a more sophisticated view of utility enhancement immediately suggests something like having a rational life plan, a criterion for equal rights proposed by Ann Palmeri. Now although Palmeri herself leaves us quite in the dark about what she means, the phrase hints at something rather more demanding than the criteria proposed by other liberationists, something more thought out and thorough, including perhaps some moral component.[12]

This notion presumably is borrowed from John Rawls, who says that we are "to suppose . . . that each individual has a rational plan of life drawn up subject to the conditions that confront him. This plan is designed to permit the

---

[10]Harris, "Political Status of Children," p. 41.

[11]One might well question Harris's minimal criterion here, even on its own grounds. Contemporary life is full of subtle threats that it would be well beyond most children to discern or deal with; why discount them just because they are not so immediate as the kind of threat he mentions?

[12]Palmeri, "Childhood's End," p. 112.

harmonious satisfaction of his interests. It schedules activities so that various desires can be fulfilled without interference. It is arrived at by rejecting other plans that are either less likely to succeed or do not provide for such an inclusive attainment of aims." Rawls then goes on to argue, as will I, that although people's plans may have different ends, any such plan will require certain goods he describes as "primary goods." He is concerned mainly, however, with what he calls "natural goods," such as intelligence and health, and "social goods" that are supplied by society, such as wealth and opportunity.[13] I concentrate instead on individual characteristics that, although based on natural factors, develop as a result of personal and social effort.

What such primary goods might be implied by this notion of a rational life plan? It would surely have to assume considerable competence at instrumental reasoning; it must also assume a capacity for evaluating ends and not just in terms of immediate pleasure. Evaluating ends requires both routine checks for coherence with respect to ends and the capacity to judge some ends to be more important than others. Thus the prerequisites for being able to plan systematic utility-enhancing projects and having a rational life plan look very much alike. Any difference between them might most plausibly be seen as a matter of degree, with a rational life plan requiring a better-organized and more comprehensive approach.

Before going any further here, it is important to notice that liberationists stress *capacities* much more than *actions*: they talk about the capacity for instrumental reasoning or the capacity for planning systematic utility-enhancing projects. Conspicuously lacking in emphasis is the carrying out of plans. Why is that? Tests of rational behavior rather than rational plans, they assert, would fail to differentiate adequately between children and adults: members of both classes would fail to pass any action-based test. Cohen suggests that we excuse adults who do not behave sensibly, without being tempted to withdraw their rights, by attributing their failures to circumstances beyond their control or to a conscious choice not to do so, whereas children are held to lack the ability to behave sensibly even when they want to.[14] He provides no real evidence for his assertion, but is relieved of the need to do so by his view that even if children did lack the ability to behave sensibly and adults had that ability, that difference would not be morally relevant. Cohen, as we shall see later, attempts to justify this unpromising claim by positing child agents who supply children with the necessary abilities.

Even if child agents could help children plan intelligently, however, they would be unable to make them behave intelligently. There is simply more to this question than Cohen is prepared to recognize. The capacity to make plans is one thing; acting on them is another. The first involves mainly cognitive capacities; the second, mainly character traits. Cognitive capacities help us figure out what

---

[13]Rawls, *Theory of Justice*, p. 61. Rawls's "natural goods" seem to me also to depend significantly on personal effort and social support.
[14]Cohen, *Equal Rights for Children*, p. 47.

to do, character traits are necessary to help us to do it.[15] Since planning, by itself, is not a particularly valuable endeavor, it is hard to see why it should be regarded as triggering rights unless it is accompanied by appropriate action. Children's capacity for planning, if we assume for the sake of argument that it is on a par with that of adults, wouldn't therefore be a very persuasive reason for recognizing equal rights for them. What is required in addition is the character traits that enable children to *carry out* their plans. Even if some adults have such weak characters that they are relatively lacking in the ability to act on their plans, that is not ... sufficient reason to ask less of children. So the ability to carry out systematic utility-enhancing projects or having a life plan requires both the cognitive capacity to judge what is in one's own interest and the character traits necessary to act on it.

PSYCHOLOGICAL RESEARCH

A large body of research has examined the effects of various kinds of treatment on children. Particularly revealing is the literature on permissiveness. "Permissiveness" has a broad array of meanings, including granting permission, tolerance, and allowing discretion. These are very broad categories—too broad, as researchers have found, to deal with the array of behavior that is of interest to us. Contemporary childrearing literature therefore distinguishes among types of permissiveness.[16] The most useful distinctions are provided by Diana Baumrind, who differentiates between "democratic" and "laissez-faire" styles. "Democratic" permissiveness consists of actively involving children in decision making and providing them with reasons for rules.[17] Differing opinions are

---

[15]This is a somewhat inaccurate description of the situation but it will do as a rough approximation for now. Once we add a moral dimension to this picture, which so far includes only prudence, the dichotomy will break down still further.

[16]The distinction represents progress in understanding the mixed results of early studies on permissiveness. For example, a classic study of development examined two dimensions of parental treatment of children: democracy and control. Children of democratic parents were planful, and fearless, good leaders, but aggressive and sometimes cruel in getting what they wanted from others. The writers nonetheless concluded that a democratic approach (which included a voice in family affairs and many choices about one's own activities) was the best, despite their opinion that this strategy might lead to resistance to the demands of adult society. They preferred the products of this method to those of both highly controlling parents (obedient, suggestible, fearful children lacking in tenacity) and undemocratic, controlling ones (obedient, suggestible, lacking in curiosity and creativity). Neither of the latter approaches led to quarrelsome, aggressive, cruel children. See A. L. Bladwin, J. Kalhorn, and E. H. Breese, *Psychological Monographs* 58, no.3. (1945): 493–94. Eleanor Maccoby suggests several problems with this study, and implies that some of the results can be explained by the failure to distinguish different elements of permissiveness: *Social Development: Psychological Growth and the Parent-Child Relationship* (San Diego: Harcourt Brace Jovanovich, 1980), pp. 368–71.

[17]Denise Kandel and Gerald S. Lesser, "Parent-Adolescent Relationships and Adolescent Independence in the U.S. and Denmark," in *Influences on Human Development*, ed. Urie Bronfenbrenner (Hinsdale, Ill.: Dryden, 1972), p. 637.

aired and evaluated. Children's views are treated with respect, and prevail when they are judged sound. The "laissez-faire" style provides a sharp contrast. Baumrind describes the laissez-faire parent as one who

> attempts to behave in a nonevaluative, acceptant and affirmative manner toward the child's impulses, desires and actions. She consults with him about policy decisions and gives explanations for family rules. She makes few demands for household responsibility and orderly behavior. She presents herself to the child as a resource for him to use as he wishes, not as an ideal for him to emulate, nor as an active agent responsible for shaping or altering his ongoing or future behavior. She allows the child to regulate his own activities as much as possible, avoids the exercise of control, and does not insist that he obey externally defined standards. She attempts to use reason and manipulation, but not overt power, to accomplish her ends.[18]

In other words, a laissez-faire permissive parent attempts to get children to do what she wants by manipulation or reason; when they fail, she lets them have their own way. In this respect, laissez-faire permissiveness mimics the situation in a liberated household where children make their own decisions without overt coercion from parents or teachers.

These two types of permissiveness have in common the practices of consulting about important decisions and explaining rules. In other respects, however, they differ radically. The democratic style, unlike the laissez-faire model, is not inconsistent with high demands, parental control of the child's impulses, and modeling by the parent. Laissez-faire permissiveness, on the contrary, attempts to persuade but lets the child have its own way when persuasion fails. It is therefore studies of laissez-faire permissiveness, with its implicit growth model of human development, that are likely to generate the kind of knowledge we seek.

An early article by David Levy suggests that psychopathy, a psychiatric condition characterized by subnormal ability to control impulses, can be caused by extreme permissiveness. People with this problem always put their own desires before those of others.[19] In his 1964 review of the literature, Wesley Becker reports that studies generally support what he calls the common-sense idea that more uninhibited behavior is the result of permissiveness. He describes a 1931

---

[18]Diana Baumrind, "Some Thoughts about Childrearing," in Bronfenbrenner, *Influences on Human Development*, p. 402. The comparison with both Rousseau and the psychoanalytic pedagogical ideal should be obvious.

[19]David M. Levy, "The Deprived and the Indulged Forms of Psychopathic Behavior," *American Journal of Orthopsychiatry* 21 (1951): 250–54, cited in Daniel G. Freedman, "The Origins of Social Behavior," in Bronfenbrenner, *Influences on Human Development*. Freedman describes his own interesting experiments on dogs, based on Levy's ideas. Although different breeds behaved in distinct ways, in general he discovered support for the hypothesis that permissiveness leads to weaker impulse control than firm discipline (p. 53). By the age of nine weeks, dogs subjected to alternate forms of discipline were very different: "The subsequent history of these two [permissively raised] pups was not a happy one. Although people were initially taken with them because of their uninhibited friskiness, they were passed from home to home as each owner found something else to complain about. They seemed to have become untrainable" (p. 54).

study that found that "children of submissive (permissive) parents were more disobedient, irresponsible, disorderly in the classroom, lacking in sustained attention, lacking in regular workhabits, and more forward and expressive.[20]

The picture is complicated by another powerful factor: whether the family environment is warm or hostile overall. Even in warm households, permissiveness leads to the kind of undesirable traits described here; permissiveness combined with hostility appears to be especially harmful. Becker points out that this combination "maximizes aggressive, poorly-controlled behavior." Many studies show a significant relation between permissiveness (especially in hostile households) and delinquency. In "normal" boys, aggression is likewise associated with permissiveness, or with inconsistently permissive and controlling behavior.[21] N. Kent and D. R. Davis found that children of parents who use "unconcerned" discipline also had lower IQ and reading scores than those of demanding parents.[22]

Eleanor Maccoby underscores these kinds of findings. Comparing permissive and nonpermissive families, she finds that the highest rates of aggressive behavior occur among children whose permissive parents sometimes respond punitively to transgressions.[23] In her discussion of impulsive adolescents, histories of permissive treatment are frequent. These youngsters

> were less able to wait for things they wanted and demanded immediate gratification and gave little attention to consequences. Their expression of emotions was often explosive and unregulated. They had poor ability to maintain attention and commitment to tasks they undertook. Their behavior had a superficial, unorganized, flitting quality, and they changed their minds and their enthusiasms frequently.

Their backgrounds were often troubled by parents in conflict, especially with respect to childrearing ideas. These parents "did not take the time or trouble to transmit age-appropriate skills to the children," rarely expected chores or other responsible behavior, and did not demand high achievement from them.[24]

Maccoby gives a comprehensive account of Baumrind's work, which is of central importance for us. In her first study, Baumrind found that parents of children who rated low on self-reliance and self-control were moderately nurturant, but "conspicuously low in exercising control."[25] Her more recent work

---

[20]Wesley C. Becker, "Consequences of Different Kinds of Parental Discipline," in *Review of Child Development Research*, ed. Martin L. Hoffman and Lois Wladis Hoffman (New York: Russell Sage Foundation, 1964), p. 191. He also notes problems with the studies given the wide range of definitions of permissiveness.

[21]Ibid., p. 193.

[22]N. Kent and D. R. Davis, "Discipline in the Home and Intellectual Development," in Bronfenbrenner, *Influences on Human Development*, p. 438.

[23]See Maccoby, *Social Development*, p. 135. These studies do not examine the children of overly abusive families.

[24]Ibid., p. 197. These studies presumably control for "normal" hyperactivity.

[25]Diana Baumrind, "Child Care Practices Anteceding Three Patterns of Preschool Behavior," *Genetic Psychology Monographs* 75 (1967): 43–88, quoted in Maccoby, *Social Development*, p. 375.

generally supports these early findings. It describes three distinct models of parenting, authoritarian, authoritative, and permissive.[26] Among the findings were that children of permissive parents "conspicuously lacked social responsibility" and were unusually dependent. Permissive parenting caused boys (but not girls) to be angry and defiant.[27] A follow-up study of preschoolers found that at age eight or nine "the children who are self-confident and oriented toward achievement . . . do not usually have highly permissive parents. And at this age the children continue to show the positive effects (if one values agency, that is!) of their parents' authoritative behavior when the children were preschoolers. Furthermore, agency was enhanced if the parents continued to demand mature behavior and enforce rules firmly as the child entered school.[28] One particularly telling finding is that low demands for such mundane habits as politeness and help around the house is associated with high aggression, undercontrol of impulse, and immaturity.[29]

Maccoby points out that recent studies provide inconsistent results with respect to high levels of parental control. Her discussion suggests, however, that a major part of the problem is that widely varying definitions of control have been used, and it is plausible to believe that different kinds of control have different results. After all, when the same word is used to denote high but

[26]Authoritarian parents "attempt to shape, control, and evaluate the behavior and attitudes of their children in accordance with an absolute set of standards; value obedience, respect for authority, work, tradition, and preservation of order; discourage verbal give and take." Authoritative parents, on the other hand, were likely to: attempt to direct the child in a rational, issue-oriented manner; encourage verbal give and take, explain the reasons behind demands and discipline but also use power when necessary; expect the child to conform to adult requirements but also to be independent and self-directing; recognize the rights of both adults and children; set standards and enforce them firmly. These parents did not regard themselves as infallible but also did not base decisions primarily on the child's desires. [Baumrind, "Some Thoughts about Childrearing," cited in Maccoby, *Social Development*, p. 376]

[27]Diana Baumrind, "Current Patterns of Parental Authority," *Developmental Psychology Monographs*, 4, no. 1, pt. 2 (1971), cited in Maccoby, *Social Development*, p. 378.

[28]Diana Baumrind, "Socialization Determinants of Personal Agency, "paper presented at the biennial meetings of the Society for Research in Child Development, New Orleans, 1977; cited in Maccoby, *Social Development*, p. 378. Maccoby describes "agency" as "the tendency to take initiative, assume control of situations, and make efforts to deal with the daily problems that arose." She sees two dimensions to the quality: (1) "social agency" involves active participation and leadership in group activity; (2) "cognitive agency" involves a clear sense of identity, striving to decide on and strive for standards, rising to meet intellectual challenges (and liking the process), and originality (p. 377). There is every reason to evaluate these qualities positively.

[29]Maccoby, *Social Development*, p. 383. Maccoby points out the importance here of age-appropriate demands, however. In a permissive environment, it is sometimes difficult to know what such demands might be. It is clearly important to make sure that the child has the requisite skills, and skills, Maccoby emphasizes, are achieved by training. Children can be trained to avoid quarreling, tolerate frustration, and be helpful, as well as to acquire such mundane skills as tying shoelaces. She attributes these good consequences of high demands (especially a feeling of competence) to the learning required for meeting them: "The children of demanding parents acquire a wide range of skills on which they can subsequently draw for their own enterprises outside the parents' home. In other words, high parental demands that are appropriate to the child's age and are accompanied by training can provide a steppingstone to self-reliance" (ibid.).

reasonable demands in a warm household and authoritarian parenting, there are bound to be differences in the outcomes.[30]

In general, the picture emerging here associates impulsiveness, irresponsibility, disorganization, aggression, and general immaturity with laissez-faire permissiveness. Conversely, democratic permissiveness that is characterized by some kinds of high control, coupled with rational explanation and warmth, is related to the opposite traits.[31] These studies are remarkably consistent, given the difficulties inherent in such work; there appears to be no solid evidence refuting them.

[30]The children of authoritarian parents, who demand high control by fiat rather than reasoning, lack empathy, have low self-esteem, only weakly internalize moral standards, lack spontaneity, affection, curiosity, and creativity, and do not establish good relationships with peers. This kind of parenting is also associated with aggressive children who are more likely to become juvenile delinquents. The traits that predominate appear to be related to the warmth of the household.

[31]Thus Maccoby reports that the results of Baumrind's first study showed that "children who were happy, self-reliant, and able to meet challenging situations directly . . . had parents who exercised a good deal of control over their children and demanded responsible, independent behavior from them but who also explained, listened, and provided emotional support" (*Social Development,* pp. 374–75). Her second study showed that children of authoritative parents "had independent and socially responsible children" (p. 377). The third showed that desirable kinds of agency (active, independent, original behavior) were "enhanced if the parents continued to demand mature behavior and enforce rules firmly as the child entered school" (p. 378). Consistent enforcement of demands and rules helps children to control aggression and coercion; high demands lead to low aggression and altruistic, competent behavior (pp. 381–83).

One of the most interesting research projects involved studying the family backgrounds of older student protesters. Jeanne H. Block, Norma Haan, and M. Brewster Smith, "Socialization Correlates of Student Activism," in Bronfenbrenner, *Influences on Human Development,* noted substantial differences in the upbringing of "activists" and "dissenters." "Activists" engage in more constructive social action and more protest action than the mean of the whole sample. They attempt to remedy suffering and injustice. They also believe that society does not live up to its ideals and protest to change the situation. "Dissenters" score above the mean on protest activities but below it on constructive social action. In short, they concentrate on negative demonstrations of their beliefs (p. 645).

Activists' parents are in some respects permissive: "They encourage the individuation and self-expression of the child, are more accepting of sexuality, and reject harsh punitive disciplinary methods." However, they demand independence, responsibility, and maturity from their children. They control aggression. These practices contrast with those of parents of dissenters: "dissenters' parents were described as making relatively minimal demands upon the child for independent mature behavior, being laissez-faire with respect to limits and discipline, being tolerant of self-assertiveness, and de-emphasizing self-control" (p. 655).

Thus the parents of the more admirable protesters exhibited exactly the characteristics found in other studies. It is interesting to note that this kind of research was undertaken at a time when many people were condemning protesters as "spoiled brats." They were indeed unpopular in many circles, partly because they were regarded as troublemakers by those content with the gap between rhetoric and practice in domestic and foreign policy. Seeing such discrepancies and trying to do something about them is surely something we want to foster in children; otherwise we will never have a more just society. But some individuals used violent and unjustifiable means to try to achieve their ends, and some were in the movement because it was exciting and fashionable. Much less favorable evaluation of them is appropriate. In particular, the distinction made by Block and her colleagues between constructive activists and mere dissenters is worth considering. We need people who work toward their goals in ways that go beyond mere protest.

They are, of course, subject to the usual caveats about research on humans.[32] Nonetheless, such findings are highly suggestive. It would obviously be foolish to believe that they are the last word on the topic of childrearing styles, but it would be even more foolish to ignore them: what empirical evidence we have points firmly against laissez-faire permissiveness if we value certain traits. Therefore, the burden of proof is upon those who argue for this kind of permissiveness to show either that the evidence is fatally flawed or that the traits are undesirable.

The recent psychological studies on laissez-faire permissiveness are of interest because they examine households where children are left quite free to make their own decisions, where parents are reluctant to override children's wishes except perhaps when they risk serious harm to themselves or others. This is the kind of home environment recommended by proponents of equal rights for children.

Questions

1. Why do weak criteria of rationality tend to support the views of child liberationists?
2. Do you think that the criterion of possessing "general background knowledge" is sufficient to distinguish adults from children? Could it be argued that since background knowledge is constantly being acquired, thirty-year-olds do not have as much as sixty-year-olds and for this reason paternalism toward thirty-year-olds can be justified in the same way? If not, why not?

---

[32]Maccoby suggests the following: First, most of the studies deal only with early and middle childhood. Second, although the relationships are statistically significant, they are not especially strong: children are also affected by nonparental elements of their environment. Third, descriptions of patterns of behavior must necessarily simplify the many complex interactions in families. Fourth, different children may react differently to given practices; gender certainly appears to alter outcomes. Fifth, inferences about causality are not always certain. Influence may flow in both directions. Just as warm or hostile parents may elicit loving or aggressive reactions from children, compliant or defiant children elicit warm and democratic or hostile and authoritarian reactions from parents: *Social Development*, pp. 406-7.

Corporal Punishment

David Benatar

This paper seeks to counter the extreme but commonly held view that corporal punishment of children in homes and schools is always morally wrong. The author argues that while physical punishment is inflicted far too often and, in many cases, unacceptably severely, the arguments against these excesses fail to support the extreme view that corporal punishment is never justified.

A number of arguments in favor of the extreme view are considered and rejected. These arguments claim that corporal punishment: (a) leads to abuse, (b) is degrading, (c) is psychologically damaging, (d) stems from and causes sexual deviance, (e) teaches the wrong lesson, (f) arises from and causes poor relationships between teachers or parents and children, and (g) does not deter.

Then the case for the permissibility (rather than the requirement) of limited corporal punishment is considered. It is suggested that (a) because corporal punishment punishes only the guilty, it may sometimes be preferable to alternative punishments; (b) corporal punishment has a significant role to play on the scale of punishments; (c) because being beaten is not a good in itself, it may sometimes be preferable to alternative punishments; and (d) condemning or prohibiting all corporal punishment without adequate evidence for its always being wrong is an unjustified interference with parents' liberty interests.

Finally, a number of conditions for the just infliction of physical punishment are discussed. It is suggested that corporal punishment (a) should be infrequent and not cause injury; (b) should not be inflicted in a discriminatory fashion (for example, by subjecting only boys and not also girls to this form of punishment); (c) should only be inflicted after due process; (d) should be inflicted with due attention to considerations about timing, which vary depending on the age of the child being punished; and (e) should be subject to constraints that safeguard against excess. The author concludes by arguing that finding the idea of corporal punishment unpleasant is compatible with thinking that it is sometimes permissible.

David Benatar, "Corporal Punishment," *Social Theory and Practice*, Vol. 24, No. 2, Summer 1998, pp. 237–260.

1. INTRODUCTION

Opponents of the corporal punishment of children are rightly critical of its extensive use and the severity with which it is all too often inflicted. They have been at pains to show that corporal punishment is not used merely as a last resort, but is inflicted regularly and for the smallest of infractions.[1] They have also recorded the extreme harshness of many instances of corporal punishment.[2]

I have no hesitation in joining the opposition to such practices, which are correctly labeled as child abuse. Where I believe that opponents of corporal punishment are wrong is in saying that physical punishment should *never* be inflicted. The popular as well as the educational and psychological debates about corporal punishment are characterized largely by polarization. Those who are opposed want to rule it out entirely. Those who are in favor tend to have a cavalier defense of the practice that is insensitive to many reasonable concerns about the dangers and abuses of this form of punishment.

It is surprising that the moral question of corporal punishment has escaped the attention of philosophers to the extent that it has. In this paper I want to consider the various standard arguments that are advanced against corporal punishment and show why they fail to establish the conclusion in defense of which they are usually advanced—that such punishment should be entirely abandoned. However, in doing so I shall show that some of the arguments have *some* force—sufficient to impose significant moral limitations on the use of corporal punishment—thereby explaining at least in part, why the abuses are beyond the moral pale.

After examining and rejecting the arguments that corporal punishment should be entirely eliminated, I shall briefly consider some positive arguments for corporal punishment before outlining what I take to be some requirements for its just infliction. However, before turning to any of this, some preliminary remarks will help to focus the subject matter I shall be discussing.

---

[1]For an horrific list of offenses for which school children in South Africa have been physically punished, see T.L. Holdstock, "Violence in Schools: Discipline," in Brian McKendrick and Wilma Hoffmann (eds.), *People and Violence in South Africa* (Cape Town: Oxford University Press, 1990), pp. 348, 349. There is extensive record of the kinds of offenses for which children in American schools have been subject to physical punishment. See, for example, Adah Maurer, "It Does Happen Here," in Irwin Hyman and James Wise (eds.), *Corporal Punishment in American Education* (Philadelphia: Temple University Press, 1979).

[2]The most well-known case that was brought before the United States courts is that of *Ingraham v. Wright*. Briefly, the facts of the case are that on 6 October 1970 a group of pupils at Drew Junior High School in Florida were slow in leaving the stage of the school auditorium when a teacher asked them to do so. The principal, Willie Wright, Jr. took the pupils to his office to be paddled. One pupil, 14-year-old James Ingraham, refused to accept the punishment. An assistant principal and an assistant to the principal held Ingraham prone across a table while Wright hit the child over twenty times with a paddle. The beating caused a hematoma, from which fluid later oozed. A doctor had to prescribe painkillers, laxatives, sleeping pills and ice packs. The child had to rest at home for over ten days and could not sit comfortably for three weeks. There are numerous other instances of corporal punishment in American schools that are less well known but no less serious.

a. What Is Corporal Punishment?

Corporal punishment is, quite literally, the infliction of punishment on the body. Even once it is differentiated from "capital punishment," "corporal punishment" remains a very broad term. It can be used to refer to a wide spectrum of punishments ranging from forced labor to mutilating torture. My focus in this paper will be on a form of corporal punishment that seems to me to be the pivotal area of controversy—the infliction of physical pain without injury.[3] I am not suggesting that this is the most problematic form of corporal punishment, but I shall focus on it because it seems to be the mildest level of corporal punishment at which the disagreement enters. Furthermore, the infliction of pain without injury appears to be the variety of corporal punishment that is at stake in the debate, even though opponents of corporal punishment make frequent reference to those instances of corporal punishment that result in injury.

Corporal punishment goes by a variety of names including, but not limited to, "beating," "hitting," "spanking," "paddling," "swatting," and "caning." Some of these terms are generic, others are specific to the severity of the punishment or the instrument used to inflict it. I shall use some of these terms interchangeably as general terms for corporal punishment.

b. Corporal Punishment in Homes and Schools

There are a number of settings in which corporal punishment has been used, but my focus will be on homes and schools. These places share a number of important features that together set them aside from other possible settings for corporal punishment. In both homes and schools *children* are punished by adults—either parents or teachers. Similarly, in both contexts punishment is often inflicted without formal trials and often for nonstatutory offenses—offenses that are not proscribed by some home or school statute, but that are rather deemed (at least in the more justifiable cases of punishment) to be moral wrongdoings.

There are some significant differences between the home and school settings. Parents are more likely to have their children's interests close to heart and to love and care for them. Parents are also more likely to know their children better than teachers know their pupils. Teachers, after all, have relatively little contact with their pupils and the little they do have is usually in large classes. While some people are opposed to corporal punishment anywhere, even by parents in the home, others oppose only its practice outside the home. They might suggest that the differences between the home and the school are morally

---

[3]I mean here physical injury. To include psychological injury would be to rule out many objections to corporal punishment—those that suggest that all physical punishment results in psychological injury. I want to reject this view, but by argument rather than stipulation. I am happy to stipulate the absence of physical injury because the claim that all corporal punishment results in such injury is more demonstrably false.

relevant and show why corporal punishment would be acceptable in the home but not in the school.

I do not think that the differences support this conclusion. Institutional punishment can never replicate the close connections of the family situation. That has some disadvantages and some advantages. One of the advantages is that the judgment of behavior and decision about punishment will not be blinded by love. (How many parents would sentence their homicidal offspring to lengthy prison terms?—"He's a good boy really!")

Moreover, not all institutional settings are equally impersonal. Schools are much more personal than state courts. Teachers know their pupils better and are likely to care more for them than judges do for the accuseds that stand before them. Punishment in schools can thus be seen as serving a useful educational purpose. It facilitates the move from the jurisdiction of the family to the jurisdiction of the state, teaching the child that punishment is not always inflicted by close people who love one and know one. This is not to say that teachers, like judges, should not inquire into relevant aspects of a wrongdoer's background before inflicting a severe punishment.

2. RESPONDING TO ARGUMENTS AGAINST CORPORAL PUNISHMENT

Those who oppose corporal punishment do not normally do so on the basis of a single argument. Usually they muster a battery of reasons to support their view. They do not root their arguments in particular theories of punishment—theories that justify the institution of punishment—and say why corporal punishment fails to meet the theoretical requirements. In many cases, this may be because they lack a theory of punishment. However, it should be said in their favor that having a theory of punishment is little help, by itself, in determining whether corporal punishment is ever morally acceptable. This is because the traditional theories of punishment in themselves do not commit one to accepting or rejecting corporal punishment. A number of issues mediate the application of the theories to the question of corporal punishment. For example, for consequentialist theories of punishment, the relevant considerations include the effectiveness of corporal punishment, either as a deterrent or reform, and the extent of any adverse side effects. For retributivists, punishment is justified if it is deserved. Retributivists are not concerned about the consequences of punishment, but they do consider the means of punishment. Thus, an important question for them is whether corporal punishment is an unacceptably cruel or degrading form of punishment. Retributivism per se says nothing about what constitutes an unacceptable form of punishment, just as utilitarianism itself cannot tell what kinds of punishment are effective or harmful. Thus we cannot turn to the theories themselves for answers to these questions. I shall not probe the theoretical foundations or venture any view about which theory of punishment is correct. This is because I take the theoretical background to be largely beyond the scope of this paper. There is a vast literature on whether punishment can be justified and I cannot hope to contribute to that here. Instead, I restrict my attention to the question of *corporal* punishment.

The arguments raised by those who believe that corporal punishment should never be inflicted are that corporal punishment 1) leads to abuse; 2) is degrading; 3) is psychologically damaging; 4) stems from and causes sexual deviance; 5) teaches the wrong lesson; 6) arises from and causes poor relationships between teachers (or parents) and children; and 7) does not deter. I shall now consider each of these arguments in turn.[4]

a. Corporal Punishment Leads to Abuse

Opponents of corporal punishment make regular reference to the frequency and severity of physical punishments that are inflicted upon children. They suggest that corporal punishment "escalates into battering,"[5] or at least increases the risk that those who punish will "cross the line to physical abuse."[6]

Clearly there are instances of abuse and of abusive physical punishment. But that is insufficient to demonstrate even a correlation between corporal punishment and abuse, and a fortiori a causal relationship. Research into possible links between corporal punishment and abuse has proved inconclusive so far. Some studies have suggested that abusive parents use corporal punishment more than nonabusive parents, but other studies have shown this not to be the case.[7] The findings of one study,[8] conducted a year after corporal punishment by parents was abolished in Sweden, suggested that Swedish parents were as prone to serious abuse of their children as were parents in the United States, where corporal punishment was (and is) widespread. These findings are far from decisive, but they caution us against hasty conclusions about the abusive effects of corporal punishment.

The fact that there are some parents and teachers who inflict physical punishment in an abusive way does not entail the conclusion that corporal punishment should never be inflicted by anybody. If it did have this entailment, then, for example, the consumption of *any* alcohol by anybody prior to driving would have to be condemned on the grounds that some people cannot control how

---

[4]There is a further argument—that corporal punishment violates constitutional provisions against cruel punishment. I shall not attend to this argument here, but I do so in "The Child, the Rod and the Law" in *Acta Juridica*, 1996, pp. 197–214; repr. in Raylene Keightley (ed.), *Children's Rights* (Kenwyn: Juta and Co., 1996).

[5]Adah Maurer, "The Case Against Corporal Punishment in Schools," in John Cryan (ed.), *Corporal Punishment in the Schools: Its Use Is Abuse* (Toledo: University of Toldedo, 1981), p. 22.

[6]Murray A. Straus, *Beating the Devil Out of Them: Corporal Punishment in American Families* (New York: Lexington Books, 1994), p. 81. He does concede, however, that not all studies have supported the idea that abusive parents use corporal punishment more than nonabusive parents, p. 84.

[7]For references to both kinds of study, see Straus, *Beating the Devil Out of Them*, pp. 83–84.

[8]Richard J. Gelles and Ake W. Edfeldt, "Violence Towards Children in the United States and Sweden," *Child Abuse and Neglect* 10 (1986): 501–10.

much alcohol they consume before driving. Just as we prohibit the excessive but not the moderate use of alcohol prior to driving, so should we condemn the abusive but not the nonabusive use of corporal punishment.

b. Corporal Punishment Is Degrading

One argument that is intended as an attack on both mild and severe cases of corporal punishment makes the claim that physically punishing people degrades them. I understand degradation to involve a lowering of somebody's standing, where the relevant sense of standing has to do with how others regard one, and how one regards oneself. It is the interplay between the way we understand how others view us and the way that we view ourselves that produces feelings such as shame. Thus one way in which one might be degraded is by being shamed.

In order to respond satisfactorily to the objection that corporal punishment is degrading, clarification is required about whether the term "degrade" is taken to have a normative content, or, in other words, whether it is taken to embody a judgment of wrongfulness. If it is not, then it will not be sufficient to show that corporal punishment is degrading. It will have to be shown that it is *unacceptably* so before it can be judged to be wrong on those grounds. If, by contrast, "degrade" *is* taken to embody a judgment of wrongfulness then a demonstration that corporal punishment is degrading will suffice to show that it is wrong. But then the argumentative work will have to be done in showing that corporal punishment is degrading because it will have to be shown that it amounts to an *unacceptable* lowering of somebody's standing.

Either way, the vexing question is whether corporal punishment involves an unacceptable lowering of somebody's standing. Here it is noteworthy that there are other forms of punishment that lower people's standing even more than corporal punishment, and yet are not subject to similar condemnation. Consider, for example, various indignities attendant upon imprisonment, including severe invasions of privacy (such as strip-searches and ablution facilities that require relieving oneself in full view of others) as well as imposed subservience to prison wardens, guards, and even to more powerful fellow inmates. My intuitions suggest that this lowering of people's standing surpasses that implicit in corporal punishment per se, even though it is obviously the case that corporal punishment could be meted out in a manner in which it were aggravated. If corporal punishment is wrong because it involves violating the intimate zone of a person's body, then surely the extreme invasions of prison inmates' privacy, which seem worse, would also be wrong. It is true that corporal punishment involves the application of direct and intense power to the body, but I do not see how that constitutes a more severe lowering of somebody's standing than employing indirect and mild power in the course of a strip-search, for example. It is true too that the prison invasions of privacy to which I have referred would be inflicted on adults whereas corporal punishment would be imposed on children, but again I fail to see how that difference makes physical punishment of children worse. In the case of young children especially, it seems that the element of shame would be less than that of adults given that the capacities for shame increase between the time one is a toddler and the time one becomes an adult. Therefore, if we think that current practices in prison life are not wrong on grounds of degradation, then we cannot consistently say that all corporal punishment is wrong on these grounds.

c. *Corporal Punishment Is Psychologically Damaging*

It is claimed that corporal punishment has numerous adverse psychological effects, including depression, inhibition, rigidity, lowered self-esteem and heightened anxiety.[9]

Although there is evidence that excessive corporal punishment can significantly increase the chances of such psychological harm, most of the psychological data are woefully inadequate to the task of demonstrating that mild and infrequent corporal punishment has such consequences. One opponent of corporal punishment who has provided data on even mild and infrequent physical chastisement is Murray Straus.[10] His research, which is much more sophisticated than most earlier investigations into corporal punishment, does lend support to the view that even infrequent noninjurious corporal punishment can increase one's chances of being depressed. However, for two reasons this research is inadequate to the task of demonstrating that mild corporal punishment is wrong. First, the studies are not conclusive. The main methodological problem is that the studies are not experiments but post facto investigations based on self-reports.[11] Murray Straus recognizes this[12] but nevertheless thinks that the studies are compelling. The second point is that even if Professor Straus's findings are valid, the nature of the data is insufficiently marked to justify a moral condemnation of mild and infrequent corporal punishment. For instance, the increase of depression, according to his study, is not substantial for rare physical punishment. The increments on his Mean Symptoms Index of depression are only slight for one or two instances of corporal punishment during one's teen years. The increments are somewhat more substantial for three to nineteen incidents of corporal punishment but, surprisingly, for twenty to twenty-nine incidents the Mean Symptoms Index falls again nearly to the level of two episodes of corporal punishment.[13] The chances of having suicidal thoughts, according to this study, decreases marginally with one incident

---

[9]E.g., Holdstock. "Violence in Schools: Discipline," pp. 356, 357; Richard Dubanoski, Michel Inaba, and Kent Gerkewicz, "Corporal Punishment in Schools: Myths, Problems and Alternatives," *Child Abuse and Neglect* 7 (1983): 271–78, p. 274: Straus, *Beating the Devil Out of Them*, chap. 5.

[10]Straus, *Beating the Devil Out of Them*.

[11]E.g., John Rosemond, "Should the Use of Corporal Punishment By Parents Be Considered Child Abuse?—No," in Mary Ann Mason and Eileen Gambrill (eds.), *Debating Children's Lives: Current Controversies on Children and Adolescents* (Thousand Oaks, Cal.: Sage Publications, 1994), p. 215.

[12]Straus, *Beating the Devil Out of Them*, p. 167.

[13]Ibid., p. 70. The (adjusted) increase for one episode of corporal punishment is only two points on the index. For two episodes of corporal punishment, there is a decrease of nearly one point on the index. The index then rises five points for nineteen instances of corporal punishment.

of corporal punishment during adolescence, then rises slightly for three to five episodes of corporal punishment. For ten to nineteen instances of physical punishment the likelihood of having suicidal thoughts is approximately the same as it is for those who are not beaten at all during adolescence. The probability increases markedly for more than twenty-nine episodes of corporal punishment during one's teens,[14] as one would expect when many beatings are administered. Professor Straus does not provide data about how physical punishment during (preteen) childhood affects the likelihood of depression, which would have been interesting given that one might expect corporal punishment to be psychologically more damaging to adolescents than to younger children.

Given that even the data suggesting that very rare instances of mild corporal punishment do have some negative effects also suggest that the effects are not substantial, there is a strong likelihood that they could be overridden by other considerations in a consequentialist calculation. In other words, showing some negative effects is not sufficient to make a consequentialist case against all corporal punishment. Other considerations, including possible advantages of corporal punishment, would have to be taken into account. Moreover, because the available evidence shows no serious harm from mild and infrequent corporal punishment, there seem to be poor grounds for suggesting that for retributivists the punishment should be regarded as unacceptably severe.

d. *Corporal Punishment Stems from and Causes Sexual Deviance*

Those who want to outlaw corporal punishment often argue that there are disturbing sexual undercurrents in the practice.[15] This objection is, in part, a special instance of the argument about adverse psychological effects. In part it is a separate, but related objection. The argument is that corporal punishment stems from some sexual perversity (on the part of the person inflicting the punishment) and can in turn cause sexual deviance (in the person punished). In some versions of this argument, it is claimed that sadomasochistic relationships can develop between the beater and the beaten. In other versions, only one party—usually but not always the beater—may experience sexual excitement through the beating. The beaten person may become sexually repressed. It is no accident, the argument goes, that the buttocks are often chosen as the site on the body to which the punishment is administered.

Those who advance the objection that corporal punishment fosters masochism are rarely clear about the nature of the masochistic inclinations that they say are produced. Yet, it is crucial to be clear about this. Studies show that most people have been sexually aroused, either in fantasy or in practice, by at

---

[14]Ibid., p. 73. I have described the data that were adjusted to control for other variables.
[15]See, for example, Adah Maurer, "Corporal Punishment," *American Psychologist* (August 1974), p. 621; Holdstock, "Violence in Schools: Discipline," pp. 358–59; Straus, *Beating the Devil Out of Them*, chap. 8.

least some mild masochistic activity, such as restraint or play fights.[16] Thus, some masochistic tendencies seem to be statistically normal. That does not preclude their being undesirable, but it is hard to see how, in an era of increased tolerance of diversity in sexual orientation and practice, we can *consistently* label mild masochism as perverse. If such inclinations increase opportunities for sexual pleasure without concomitant harms, then there is at least a prima facie case for the view that such inclinations are not to be regretted. And if one objects to those masochistic inclinations that seek gratification in more serious pain, injury, and bondage, there is no evidence of which I am aware that mild and infrequent corporal punishment fosters such inclinations. The available evidence linking corporal punishment and masochism makes the connection only with milder forms of masochistic fantasy and practice.

It is, of course, a concern that some parents or teachers might derive sexual gratification from beating children, but is it a reason to eliminate or ban the practice? Someone might suggest that it is, if the anticipated sexual pleasure led to beatings that were inappropriate—either because children were beaten when they should not have been, or if the punishment were administered in an improper manner. However, if this is the concern, surely the fitting response would be to place limitations on the use of the punishment and, at least in schools, to monitor and enforce compliance. Here we are not without examples to follow. For example, given the intimacy of a medical examination, the doctor-patient relationship is one that is prone to sexual undercurrents. Needless to say, it is a disturbing thought that doctors may be sexually aroused while examining patients, but we cannot (easily) monitor that. Our response then, is to lay down guidelines to curb any abuses that might ensue. I am aware that medical examinations are necessary in a way in which corporal punishment is not, but corporal punishment might nonetheless fulfill an important function.

e. *Corporal Punishment Teaches the Wrong Lesson*

It is often said that punishing a wrongdoer by inflicting pain conveys the message that violence is an appropriate way to settle differences or to respond to problems.[17] One teaches the child that if one dislikes what somebody does, it is acceptable to inflict pain on that person.

This implicit message is believed to reach the level of a contradiction in those cases where the child is hit for having committed some act of violence—like assaulting another child. Where this happens, it is claimed, the child is given the violent message that violence is wrong. The child is told that he was wrong to commit an act of violence and yet the parent or the teacher conveys this message through violence.

---

[16]Straus, *Beating the Devil Out of Them*, pp. 126–29.
[17]E.g., Irwin Hyman, Anthony Bongiovanni, Robert Friedman, and Eileen McDowell, "Paddling, Punishing and Force: Where Do We Go From Here?" *Children Today* 6 (Sept.–Oct. 1997): 17–23; p. 20; Adah Maurer, "The Case Against Corporal Punishment in Schools," p. 19.

Not only are such messages thought to be wrong in themselves, but it is claimed that they are then acted upon by the child who is hit.[18] In the short term, those who are physically punished are alleged to commit violence against other children, against teachers and against school property.[19] As far as long term effects are concerned, it is alleged that significant numbers of people who commit crimes were physically punished as children. It is these arguments that lie behind the adage "violence breeds violence." Three defenses of (limited) corporal punishment can be advanced against this objection.

First, there is a *reductio ad absurdum*. The argument about the message implicit in violence seems to prove too much. If we suggest that hitting a wrongdoer imparts the message that violence is a fitting means to resolve conflict, then surely we should be committed to saying that detaining a child or imprisoning a convict conveys the message that restricting liberty is an appropriate manner to deal with people who displease one. We would also be required to concede that fining people conveys the message that forcing others to give up some of their property is an acceptable way to respond to those who act in a way that one does not like. If beatings send a message, why don't detentions, imprisonments, fines, and a multitude of other punishments convey equally undesirable messages? The argument proves too much because it proves that *all* punishment conveys inappropriate messages and so is wrong. It is a *reductio* because this conclusion is absurd. Those who want to replace punishment with therapy would not be immune to the *reductio* either. Providing therapy would convey the message that people with whom one disagrees are to be viewed as sick and deserving of treatment.

This leads to the second argument. The objection takes too crude a view of human psychology and the message that punishment can impart. There is all the difference in the world between legitimate authorities—the judiciary, parents, or teachers—using punitive powers responsibly to punish wrongdoing, and children or private citizens going around beating each other, locking each other up, and extracting financial tributes (such as lunch money). There is a vast moral difference here and there is no reason why children should not learn about it. Punishing children when they do wrong seems to be one important way of doing this. To suggest that children and others cannot extract *this* message, but only the cruder version that the objection suggests, is to underestimate the expressive function of punishment and people's ability to comprehend it.

There is a possible response to my arguments. Perhaps it is true that, conceptually, the message that punishment conveys is more sophisticated. Nevertheless, those who are beaten do commit violence against others. It might not be that they got this *message* from the punishment, but that being subject to the willful infliction of pain causes rage and this gets vented through acts of violence on others. This brings me to my third response. There is insufficient evidence that the properly restricted use of corporal punishment causes increased violence. Although Murray Straus's study suggests that there is a correlation

---

[18]Maurer, "The Case Against Corporal Punishment in Schools," p. 20.
[19]Dubanoski et al., "Corporal Punishment in Schools," p. 274.

between rare corporal punishment and increased violence, the study has some significant defects, as I noted earlier, and the significance of his findings has been questioned in the light of other studies.[20] Nevertheless, Professor Straus's findings cannot be ignored and they suggest that further research, this time of an experimental sort, should be conducted. Note again, however, that even if it were shown that there is some increase in violence, something more is required in order to make amoral case against the corporal punishment that causes it. On a consequentialist view, for example, one would have to show that this negative effect is not overridden by any benefits there might be to corporal punishment.

f. Corporal Punishment, Pupils, Teachers, and Authority

Next there is a cluster of arguments about the relationship between corporal punishment and teacher-pupil relations.[21] These arguments make reference to what physical punishment says about such relations, what it does to them, and the impact that this has on education.

First, it is claimed that for a teacher to employ corporal punishment indicates that the teacher has failed to discourage pupil wrongdoing in other ways—by moral authority, by a system of rewards, or by milder punishments.

I am sympathetic to the claim that far too many teachers fail to foster an atmosphere of mutual respect between their pupils and themselves. They lack the ability or the inclination verbally to communicate expectations to children— first gently and then more strenuously. They do not first employ milder forms of punishment but rather resort to the cane in the first instance. Some might not believe in rewarding good behavior, only in punishing bad. However, from the claim that corporal punishment *often* indicates teacher failure, we cannot infer that it *necessarily* demonstrates such failure or even that as a matter of fact it *always* does. It is true that when the teacher resorts to corporal punishment this indicates that his prior efforts to discourage the wrongdoing failed. However, there is a big difference between this, a failure in the pupil, and a failure in the teacher. In either case it is true, in some sense, that the teacher failed to discourage the child from doing wrong—failed to prevent failure in the child. However, it is not a failure for which the teacher necessarily is *responsible*. I am well aware that the responsibility for children's wrongdoing is all too often placed exclusively at the door of children themselves, without due attention to the influences to which they are subjected. However, there is a danger that in rejecting this incorrect evaluation, teachers (and parents) will be blamed for *all* shortcomings in children.

This argument can be strengthened further. If we say that corporal punishment indicates the failure of prior efforts, then we must concede that the

---

[20]Robert Larzelere, "Should the Use of Corporal Punishment By Parents Be Considered Child Abuse?—No," in Mason and Garnbrill (eds.), *Debating Children's Lives*, pp. 204–9.
[21]E.g., Holdstock, "Violence in Schools: Discipline," pp. 353–54, 360–61; Hyman et al., "Paddling, Punishing and Force," p. 20.

immediately prior effort—say, detaining the child—equally indicate the failure of the still earlier efforts—admonition—that indicate the failure of yet earlier efforts—moral example. Once we see this, it becomes clearer why, although it is the case that earlier efforts may have failed, it is not sufficient to say that the failure is in the teacher. To reject this would lead to the conclusion that the teacher is responsible for the child's not following the teacher's moral example. We can now also see why the argument that corporal punishment indicates failure is as much an argument against any of the prior attempts (except the first) to prevent wrongdoing.

Just as school corporal punishment is seen by its opponents as originating in failed pedagogical relationships, so it is believed to compromise them further. Thus it is perceived as exacerbating the very problems from which it arises. The pupils, it is said, begin to fear their teachers and view them as enemies rather than concerned custodians charged with furthering their well-being and development, both mental and otherwise. Education does not thrive in an atmosphere in which children live in fear of those who teach them.[22] This opens the way for another objection in this cluster of arguments—that physically punishing children leads to an unquestioning acceptance of authority. If children fear their teachers, they are unlikely to ask questions or challenge views that their teachers present to them. The idea here is that children can be beaten into submission to authority.

Again, I have some sympathy for these arguments—if they are seen to be making the weaker claim that sometimes (even often) teacher-pupil relations are damaged by corporal punishment. I agree too that children can and have been beaten into unquestioning acceptance of authority. Where teachers regularly resort to using the cane and then use it with excessive force, I can well imagine their relationships with their pupils being compromised. Teachers who regularly and severely hit pupils are feared, not respected (though characteristically such teachers are unable to distinguish between the two). In such circumstances it would not surprise me at all if the inquiring, critical capacities of children were dampened or extinguished. However, I disagree that these are inevitable consequences of corporal punishment per se. I cannot see any reason for thinking that infrequent and mild corporal punishment would be likely to have any of these effects.

Furthermore, we should note that it is not only corporal punishment that can impact negatively on the educational relationship. Children who are frequently detained, banished from the classroom, or even rebuked (especially when this is done scathingly and publicly) can suffer feelings of alienation from their teachers. One does not have to resort to sticks to force children into submission. The tongue can do just as well. My argument here is not to justify one evil by the existence of another. The point is that just as in these cases we attack the excesses not the practices themselves, so should we attack only the abusive use of corporal punishment.

[22]E.g., Holdstock, "Violence in Schools: Discipline," p. 353; Dubanoski et al., "Corporal Punishment in Schools," p. 273.

It makes a big difference not only how frequently and severely corporal punishment is inflicted, but also the kinds of behavior for which it is administered. Where children are beaten for expressing unpopular ideas or for asking too many questions, the argument that it will lead to subservience to authority is greatly strengthened. Similarly, if children are paddled for not displaying servile deference to teachers, the relationship between them and their teachers is sure to suffer. However, if children are punished for genuine wrongdoing—lying, cheating, stealing, bullying—then the message is that *this* behavior is unacceptable. Teachers can foster critical inquiry and support the right to express even unpopular opinions, while at the same time punishing genuine wrongdoing. Children are able to distinguish between these.

g. *Corporal Punishment Does Not Deter*

Some opponents of corporal punishment have suggested that it is not an *effective* form of punishment because it does not deter those punished from further wrongdoing. If the argument were sound, it would be significant for those whose justification of punishment is consequentialist. However, the argument would have no force against a retributivist theory, according to which a punishment can be deserved whether or not it is effective.

Some of the arguments for why corporal punishment does not deter draw on research that suggests that for punishment to be effective it must meet certain conditions—conditions that would be impossible (and perhaps also undesirable) to fulfill. Thus, it is argued that effective punishment must follow wrongdoing instantaneously.[23] It is also claimed that for punishment to be effective it would have to follow every (or, at least, nearly every) act of wrongdoing,[24] and therefore would have to be inflicted even more regularly than it already is. It has been suggested too that punishment that is inflicted by surprise is more effective than punishment that is expected. Insofar as the research methodology is sound and actually supports these conclusions—conditions that I do not think are met—the conclusions would apply equally to other forms of punishment. In other words, the argument is not specifically against corporal punishment, but against punishment generally. This implication is all too often not made explicit.

Deterrence is not an all-or-nothing matter. A punishment might have some deterrent effect without being extremely effective. Once this is recognized, the mere continued existence of wrongdoing does not demonstrate the failure of punishment as a deterrent, as many have thought. To know how effective punishment is one must know what the incidence of the wrongdoing would be if prior punishments for it had not been inflicted. To establish this, much more

---

[23]One study cited by opponents of corporal punishment is that of Richard Walters and Lillian Dernkow, "Timing of Punishment as a Determinant of Response Inhibition," *Child Development* 34 (1963): 207–14. The study is not specifically about corporal punishment. The punishment used was a loud unpleasant sound from a buzzer.

[24]Hyman et al., "Paddling, Punishing and Force," p. 19.

research needs to be done. However, there is already some evidence of the deterrent effect of corporal punishment, at least with very young children.[25] Such findings cannot be considered decisive, but neither can they be ignored.

Finally, while we might expect increased frequency to improve the deterrent effect, there is good reason to think that the reverse might be true. The expressive function as well as the aura surrounding a particular form of punishment might well be enhanced by inflicting it less often. If one uses physical punishment infrequently, it can speak louder than if one inflicts it at every turn. The special status accorded it by its rare use might well provide psychological reason to avoid it out of proportion to its actual severity.

h. Do the Arguments Gain Strength in Numbers?

Up to now I have considered in turn each of the objections to corporal punishment. I have argued that each by itself fails. Do they gain any strength in numbers?

We need to distinguish between two ways an objection may fail: 1) because it rests on premises for which there is insufficient or no evidence; or 2) because the premises, although substantiated by sufficient evidence, do not lead to the desired conclusion. Objections that fail for the first reason cannot be strengthened by association with others. They fail whether they stand alone or in company. For example, if there is no evidence that corporal punishment causes severe masochism, then the evidence is not increased because there is some distinct argument that says something quite different about corporal punishment. However, it is another matter where an objection is flawed because although there is evidence for its premises, the premises are insufficiently strong to support the objection. If, as I have argued is not the case, the evidence were compelling that mild and infrequent corporal punishment slightly elevated the chances of violent physical abuse, then, *ex hypothesi*, the premise that such corporal punishment has this effect would be substantiated. However, this premise by itself would be insufficient to demonstrate the wrongfulness of corporal punishment. A mere increase in the chance of abuse is inadequate by itself, but it might be one consideration that, when added to others, contributes to a satisfactory case against corporal punishment.

I have argued that the objections to mild and infrequent corporal punishment fail because there is insufficient evidence for their premises. Accordingly, they are not stronger when considered together. I have indicated that some recent studies suggest that further research might yield satisfactory evidence. Other studies, including a review of 35 peer-reviewed empirical investigations about the outcomes of corporal punishment by parents cast doubt on this.[26] But

---

[25]Robert E. Larzelere, William N. Schneider, David B. Larson, and Pabicia L. Pike, "The Effects of Discipline Responses in Delaying Toddler Misbehavior Recurrences," *Child and Family Behavior Therapy* 18 (1996): 35–57.

[26]Robert E. Larzelere, "A Review of the Outcomes of Parental Use of Nonabusive or Customary Physical Punishment," *Pediatrics* 98, Supplement (1996): 824–28.

if further research does assuage these doubts and bolster the premises of the objections to corporal punishment, then a further question will arise: Are the harms that the research demonstrates sufficiently strong, when considered together, to render the practice morally wrong? But until we have the data this question cannot be answered.

3. CONSIDERING THE CASE FOR CORPORAL PUNISHMENT

Having rejected the arguments that support the total abandonment of corporal punishment, I shall now raise some positive arguments for preserving the option of limited corporal punishment.

a. Corporal Punishment Punishes Only the Guilty

It has been argued that one advantage that corporal punishment has over other forms of punishment is that it punishes only the guilty.[27] Detaining students often places a burden on parents who fetch children from school. They are then required to fetch the detained child at a later time, which may be inconvenient. If the parent has more than one child at the school, then detention of one of the children can result in two separate trips to the school. These consequences seem unjust to some because not only the guilty suffer.

I think that this argument has some force. In other words, there might well be certain instances in which this morally relevant consideration will tip the balance in favor of inflicting corporal punishment, rather than opting for some other form of punishment. However, there will often be other competing considerations. These include the concerns about the dangers of frequent use of canings. Thus, if excessive use of corporal punishment would lead to unacceptable psychological damage, then inflicting an alternative form of punishment might be justified even if it imposes some burden on family members.

Members of a family do not stand in isolation from one another. They are affected by what each of the others does and by what happens to each. When one member of a family performs a meritorious deed or has some good fortune, others in the family benefit. Similarly, if someone in the family does wrong or suffers some harm, this negatively affects the others. To a certain extent these "spill-overs" are an expected and legitimate part of family life.

Here we see an important distinction arising, one which is conflated by the argument that corporal punishment punishes only the guilty. It ignores the distinction by using the term "punish" in a weak sense. It claims that by detaining a wrongdoer, we also punish his family. But, of course, we do not *punish* the family. The detention may well cause the hardship, but that is quite different from punishing it. Punishment is not simply the suffering of hardship. First, it

---

[27]Graeme Newman, *Just and Painful: A Case for Corporal Punishment of Criminals* (New York: Macmillan, 1983), p. 43.

must be *imposed*. It is at least a matter of controversy whether the hardship is imposed on the family, or whether it is merely an unfortunate consequence. Second, the hardship the family suffers carries none of the condemnation that punishment conveys.[28] Some, but not all, of the force of the argument at hand is derived from glossing over these differences.

b. *Corporal Punishment in the Scale of Punishments*

A more compelling argument in favor of the limited use of corporal punishment is that it plays a significant role on the scale of punishments. In the context of a school, it fills an important position between punishments like detention on the one hand, and expulsion on the other. There is some value in having a scale of punishments of discernibly increasing severity. It is true that some scale could be introduced without corporal punishment. One might, for example, replace corporal punishment with detention of longer duration. However, having different forms of punishment that vary in severity can enhance the expressive function of punishment by making the varying degrees of condemnation more explicit.

c. *Being Beaten Is Not a Good in Itself*

Corporal punishment has another advantage. Many teachers are concerned that assigning extra work or requiring community service ought not to be used as punishments. This is because work and community service are seen by teachers as being good in themselves. While a child might not want to perform these activities, and so requiring them would be to inflict a hardship, one would be reinforcing the child's resistance to these practices. Not only would the child continue to dislike working or helping in the community, but he would come to associate these activities with punishment. This is why some teachers, when punishing children, prefer to require activities like detention or writing lines that are not good in themselves and are unpleasant. In this regard, corporal punishment is like these latter activities. It differs from these others in the intensity of its unpleasantness. This consideration reinforces the argument that corporal punishment occupies an important place in the scale of punishments. It becomes a significant substitute for something like community service.

d. *Child-Rearing and Parents' Liberty Interests*

We have seen that there is room for reasonable people to disagree about the value of corporal punishment in rearing and educating a child. Contrary to the views of those who oppose all physical punishment, it is not implausible to think that such punishment, if inflicted under the appropriate conditions, might do some good. If corporal punishment does indeed have some benefit, then this would be lost if the practice were abandoned. From the perspective of public

---

[28]However, as in other forms of punishment, there may be a moral stigma for the family.

policy, prohibiting corporal punishment would constitute a serious interference with the liberty interests of those parents who judge the possibility of corporal punishment to benefit their children. Such liberty interests would be overridable if there were compelling evidence of the harmfulness of corporal punishment, but the inconclusive data we currently have provide no such grounds.

4. SOME REQUIREMENTS FOR THE JUST INFLICTION OF CORPORAL PUNISHMENT

Corporal punishment can be unjust in a multitude of ways. Here I shall discuss a partial list of conditions for just corporal punishment.

a. Infrequent pain without injury

Given the overwhelming evidence about the evils of frequent and severe beatings, they should be judged to be wrong. If children are to be hit it should be only infrequently and then so as to cause pain without injury.

If one accepts the pain without injury view (or something close to it), there are a number of conditions that will be important. One of these is the site on the body where the punishment will be administered. We would have to rule out those parts of the body where injury is likely to result. Attention would also have to be given to the implement used. Implements that are more prone to cause injury would be ruled out. Finally, the number and intensity of the blows would have to be calculated to avoid any chance of injury. The difficulties of measuring force are often cited. One would have to err on the side of caution. The courts are often called upon to pass judgment on questions of "reasonableness," even "reasonable force." There is no reason why, with more appropriate legislation to provide guidelines, similar judgments could not be made in cases in which excessive corporal punishment is charged.

b. Non-discrimination

It is well known that often minority groups and especially males receive a disproportionate share of corporal punishment.[29] In some countries, corporal punishment of females is outlawed, while it is legal and widely practiced on males.

If corporal punishment is to be just, it must be inflicted without consideration for differences in race and sex. If girls are not caned for the same offenses for which boys are caned, then the boys are the victims of discriminatory treatment. Discrimination against women and girls in many areas has justifiably been an object of concern. However, there has been scant attention to those social practices that discriminate against men and boys. It seems clear to me that the discriminatory use of corporal punishment on the basis of race and sex is

---

[29]E.g., Steven Shaw and Jeffrey Braden, "Race and Gender Bias in the Administration of Corporal Punishment," *School Psychology Review* 19 (1990): 378–83.

immoral. I should like to think that little if any argument is required to convince people in our society of this. However, I cannot discount the possibility that some will think that gender differences are relevant. Some might suggest, for example, that girls ought to be treated more gently than boys because girls have a more delicate constitution. I do not see how this kind of view can be reconciled with the widespread views in western society that it is wrong to treat people differently on the basis of gender (or racial or religious) stereotypes. While some girls may be more delicate and sensitive than some boys, some boys are more delicate and sensitive than some girls. To treat people differently on the basis of gender rather than on an individual basis is to engage in unfair discrimination. I realize that not all societies share this view. It would be beyond the scope of this paper to examine which view is correct, though my sympathies are clear. Societies that do accept the liberal principles of nondiscrimination must consistently apply these principles.

Treating males and females equally with regard to corporal punishment would have the added benefit of countering the cult of machismo that sometimes surrounds physical punishment. If females are known to be subject to the same punishments, there will be nothing specifically "manly" about a caning. This may even increase the deterrent effect of the punishment because boys would feel less need to prove themselves by inviting it, and girls would know that they were not immune. Equally punishing boys and girls undermines rather than perpetuates gender stereotypes.

c. Due Process

Due process is important for any theory of punishment. On a retributivist theory, for any punishment to be just it must be inflicted only on guilty parties and then only in proportion to the wrongdoing. Due process is required to determine innocence or guilt and its extent. Utilitarians are also concerned about punishing only the guilty and in proportion to wrongdoing, even if their concern about these conditions is merely instrumental and so theoretically overridable.

Due process is no less important for punishments inflicted on children in families and schools—primarily for reasons of justice but additionally for the purposes of teaching moral lessons about retributive justice. It would be a mistake, however, to think that we are required to institute fully fledged trials before independent judges, with defense attorneys and prosecutors, before punishment is justified in homes and schools. That would be impractical and invasive of the privacy of families. It seems sufficient for a parent or teacher to inquire into a matter in order to establish the facts and to allow a child to defend himself against the accusation of wrongdoing.

d. Timing

There is some debate about the appropriate timing for punishment of children in general. Some think that it should follow as soon after he wrongdoing as possible in order to make explicit the connection between the offense and the punishment. In the case of very young children I am inclined to agree. They, like the animals on whom "punishment" studies are done, are unable to draw the connection between a wrong done at one time and a punishment inflicted much later. However, I believe that children at school already have the capacity to understand that a punishment inflicted now can be for a wrong committed at some significantly earlier time.

There are two additional reasons to favor (somewhat) delayed punishment. First, it allows time for due process. It would be completely inappropriate to rush into punishment without the necessary inquiries. However, the second reason provides important grounds for delaying corporal punishment. This is the idea that it would be wrong to beat a child in anger. Some think that this is precisely the only time when one should hit a child—to eliminate the aura of a *cold-blooded* assault,[30] or to show the child that the beating was a natural reaction to the wrongdoing. Quite to the contrary, I think that we need to avoid spur-of-the-moment beatings of passion. They are and appear to be more of a loss of temper and control than a punishment. Similarly, the punishment must *not* be and look like a reflex reaction to wrongdoing. Not only would beatings in anger remove the possibility of due process, but they would also teach the wrong lessons about what just punishment ought to be—cool and methodical, not passionate. Children are likely to be punished more often and more severely if it is done in anger. The parent or teacher should allow some time to elapse before inflicting corporal punishment. With tempers cooled and the perspective of some temporal distance from the event, the punishing adult is in a better situation to conduct a fair inquiry and determine an appropriate punishment. The child also has the opportunity to reflect on the wrongdoing prior to the punishment. Children, like adults, are often more susceptible to repentant feelings during the period between doing wrong and being punished than in the time following punishment.

e. Safeguards

It might be asked what safeguards could be introduced in order to prevent unjust corporal punishment. In schools there are numerous possibilities. First there could be restrictions on 1) the offenses for which the child may be physically punished; 2) the implement used to inflict the punishment; 3) the number of blows; 4) the places on the body to which such punishment may be administered. These and other requirements could be monitored in a variety of ways. For example, it could be required that all punishments and reasons for punishments be approved by the principal, or that a teacher other than the punisher be present during punishment, or that parents be notified of all physical punishments. School psychologists or inspectors could interview children from time to time about punitive practices. Punishment within families is less easily monitored, at least if we are to respect people's privacy. But because it is even more

---

[30]George Bernard Shaw, cited with approval by Gertrude J. Rubin Williams, "Corporal Punishment: Socially Sanctioned Assault and Battery," in Cryan (ed.), *Corporal Punishment in the Schools*, p. 37.

difficult to monitor parental compliance with an unqualified ban on corporal punishment than it is to monitor parental compliance with a ban on only severe physical punishment, this monitoring problem provides no support for the elimination of all corporal punishment in homes. Rather what is called for is a sensitization of those (such as doctors and teachers as well as children themselves) who are well placed to detect abusive punishment. That is the very mechanism we use to detect other forms of abuse of children.

5. CONCLUSION

I have argued that corporal punishment is not always immoral. With appropriate restrictions and safeguards, it is sometimes permissible. There is a danger that the position I have advanced will be misunderstood. This danger lies partly in the polarization of views about corporal punishment, such that those who hold the polar views are not sensitive to an intermediate position. However, it is also partly attributable to the form this paper has taken. I have suggested a battery of arguments against the opponent of corporal punishment. Some positive arguments for this form of punishment were also raised. This may create the impression that mine is a vigorous defense of beating children for wrongdoing. In fact, nothing could be further from the truth.

In the first instance, my arguments, although lengthy, have been directed against a radical yet commonly held view—that corporal punishment should never be inflicted. I have sought to show that this position is untenable, even though the arguments for it do show that frequent and severe physical punishment is morally wrong.

Second, although I think that corporal punishment is sometimes justified, I nevertheless feel uncomfortable about the idea of people being punished physically. I have a distinct distaste for the practice, and in the years that I taught school children I never resorted to corporal punishment. It may seem, then, as though my moral intuitions do not match my theoretical commitments. However, I think that an unease about corporal punishment is perfectly compatible with my theoretical position. There are many unpleasant practices that, although sometimes justified, should never be gleefully embraced. For example, it is sometimes justified to take another person's life, as in the case of self-defense, yet even in these circumstances we would judge the killer to be morally defective if he enjoyed or even failed to detest his killing of the aggressor. A killing is to be regretted even when it is justified.

Finally, many of the arguments about corporal punishment rest, at least in part, on empirical questions. Indeed, as I have said, these are difficult matters to settle. My view is that the empirical data, insofar as I have understood them, are insufficient to defend the extreme view that physical punishment should never be administered. Nevertheless we should remain open to the fruits of further research and be prepared to adapt our views accordingly.[31]

---

[31] I wish to thank the anonymous reviewers whose comments have helped me improve this paper.

Questions

1. Do you think that the strength of any of the arguments against corporal punishment varies depending on the age of the child?
2. Can you think of any arguments for or against corporal punishment that are not mentioned in this article?
3. Is a parent's inability to avoid gender discrimination in the infliction of corporal punishment adequate grounds for avoiding such punishment entirely?
4. Is a desire to "err on the safe side" good grounds for *never* inflicting physical punishment?

Suggestions for Further Reading on Rearing Children

ARCHARD, DAVID. *Children: Rights and Childhood.* Routledge: London, 1993.

BENATAR, DAVID. "The Child, the Rod and the Law," *Acta Juridica* (1996): pp. 197–214. (Reprinted in Keightley, Raylene, ed. *Children's Rights.* Kenwyn: Juta, 1996.)

HOULGATE, LAURENCE D. "Children, Paternalism and Rights to Liberty." In *Having Children*, edited by Onora O'Neill and William Ruddick, New York: Oxford University Press, 1979: pp. 266–274.

PURDY, LAURA. *In Their Best Interest?: The Case against Equal Rights for Children*, Ithaca, N.Y.: Cornell University Press, 1992.

REED, T.M., AND PATRICIA JOHNSTONE. "Children's Liberation." *Philosophy* 55 (1980).

SCARRE, GEOFFREY. "Children and Paternalism." *Philosophy* 55 (1980): pp. 117–124.

STRAUS, MURRAY A. *Beating the Devil out of Them: Corporal Punishment in American Families.* New York: Lexington, 1994.

CHAPTER 9

Familial and Filial Duties

Morality, Parents, and Children

James Rachels

Taking an ancient debate in Chinese philosophy as his starting point, James Rachels asks whether parents have obligations to their own children that they do not have to other children. Most people are inclined to think that they do, but, notes the author, this conflicts with the understanding of morality as requiring impartiality. If that understanding of morality is correct, as he suggests it is, either we need to find some relevant impartial way of justifying special treatment of one's own children or we must reject the idea that parents owe their own children anything more than they owe other children. The author argues that because what one is owed should not depend on the luck of having been born to particular parents, there is a strong reason why one should not favor one's own children. Why, for instance, should one's own children, but not starving orphans, be owed food because of the luck of having been born to parents who are able to provide for their needs.

The author considers and shows the limitations of three arguments that might be advanced in defense of special duties to one's own children: (1) that parenthood (together with its special duties) constitutes a vital social role; (2) that parents' proximity to their own children makes it sensible for them to have special responsibility for those children; and (3) that because loving relationships (like parenting) that involve special concern are very important personal goods, such partiality is morally justified. However, he shows that in a utopia where strict impartiality were practiced, some of the values underlying these arguments would be preserved and special obligations would have some place.

Finally, the author turns to the question of what duties parents have, not in utopia but in our own society. He rejects three answers to this question before defending a fourth one.

James Rachels, "Morality, Parents, and Children, in George Graham and Hugh LaFollette *Person to Person* (Philadelphia: Temple University Press, 1989), 46–62.

THE PROBLEM

At about the same time Socrates was being put to death for corrupting the youth of Athens, the great Chinese sage Mo Tzu was also antagonizing his community. Unlike the Confucianists, who were the social conservatives of the day, Mo and his followers were sharply critical of traditional institutions and practices. One of Mo's controversial teachings was that human relationships should be governed by an "all-embracing love" that makes no distinctions between friends, family, and humanity at large. "Partiality," he said, "is to be replaced by universality" (Fung, 1960, 92). To his followers, these were the words of a moral visionary. To the Confucianists, however, they were the words of a man out of touch with moral reality. In particular, Mo's doctrine was said to subvert the family, for it recommended that one have as much regard for strangers as for one's own kin. Meng Tzu summed up the complaint when he wrote that "Mo Tzu, by preaching universal love, has repudiated the family" (Rubin, 1976, 36). Mo did not deny it. Instead, he argued that universal love is a higher ideal than family loyalty, and that obligations within families can be properly understood only as particular instances of obligations to all mankind.

This ancient dispute has not disappeared. Do parents have special obligations to their own children? Or, to put the question a bit differently: Do they have obligations to their own children that they do not have to other children, or to children in general? Our instincts are with the Confucianists. Surely, we think, parents do have a special obligation to care for their own. Parents must love and protect their children; they must feed and clothe them; they must see to their medical needs, their education, and a hundred other things. Who could deny it? At the same time, we do not believe that we have such duties toward strangers. Perhaps we do have a general duty of beneficence toward them, but that duty is not nearly so extensive or specific as the duties we have toward our own young sons and daughters. If faced with a choice between feeding our own children and sending food to orphans in a foreign country, we would prefer our own, without hesitation.

Yet the Mohist objection is still with us. The idea that morality requires us to be impartial, clearly articulated by Mo Tzu, is a recurring theme of Western moral philosophy. Perhaps the most famous expression of this idea was Bentham's formula, "Each to count for one and none for more than one." Mill's formulation was less memorable but no less emphatic: He urged that, when weighing the interests of different people, we should be "'as strictly impartial as a disinterested and benevolent spectator" (Mill, 1957, 22). Utilitarianism of the kind espoused by Bentham and Mill has, of course, often been criticized for conflicting with common-sense morality, and so to will probably come as no great surprise that utilitarian notions clash with the common-sense idea of special parental obligations. However, the idea that morality requires impartiality is by no means exclusively a utilitarian doctrine. It is common ground to a considerable range of theories and thinkers.[1]

---

[1]"The good of any one individual is of no more importance, from the point of view (if I may say so) of the Universe, than the good of any other," says Sidgwick (1907, 382). "We [must] give equal

The problem, in its most general form, is this. As moral agents, we cannot play favorites—at least, not according to the conception of morality as impartiality. But as parents, we do play favorites. Parental love is partial through and through. And we think there is nothing wrong with this; in fact, we normally think there is something wrong with the parent who is *not* deeply partial where his own children are concerned. Therefore, it would seem, one or the other of these conceptions has to be modified or abandoned.

Of course, exactly the same is true of our relations with friends, spouses, and lovers. All these relationships, and others like them, seem to include, as part of their very nature, special obligations. Friends, spouses, and lovers are not just members of the great crowd of humanity. They are all special, at least to the one who loves them. The problem is that the conception of morality as impartiality seems to conflict with *any* kind of loving personal relationship. Mo Tzu not-withstanding, it seems to conflict with love itself.[2] In this essay I discuss only the question of parental obligations to children, but it should be kept in mind that the deeper issue has to do with personal relationships in general.

POSSIBLE SOLUTIONS

There are three obvious approaches to solving our problem: First, we might reject the idea of morality as impartiality; second, we might reject the idea of special parental obligations; or third, we might try to find some way of understanding the two notions that would make them consistent. The first approach has recently attracted some support among philosophers, who think that although the conception of morality as impartiality seems plausible when

---

weight in our moral deliberations to the like interests of all those affected by our actions," says Singer (1971, 197). "Moral rules must be for the good of everyone alike," says Baier (1958, 200). "A rational and impartial sympathetic spectator is a person who takes up a general perspective: he assumes a position where his own interests are not at stake and he possesses all the requisite information and powers of reasoning. So situated he is equally responsive and sympathetic to the desires and satisfactions of everyone affected by the social system. . . . Responding to the interests of each person in the same way, an impartial spectator gives free reign to his capacity for sympathetic identification by viewing each person's situation as it affects that person," says Rawls (1971, 186). In an interesting discussion, R. M. Hare argues that virtually all the major moral theories incorporate a requirement of impartiality and adds that his own "universal prescriptivism" is no exception.

[2]The point is a familiar one that pops up in all sorts of philosophical contexts. For example: In his recent book *On the Plurality of Worlds* David Lewis discusses an ethical objection to his thesis that all possible worlds are equally real, a thesis he calls modal realism. The objection is that, if modal realism is true, then our actions will have no effect whatever on the total amount of good or evil that exists. If we prevented an evil from occurring in *this* world, it would still exist in some *other* world. As Lewis puts it, "The sum total of good throughout the plurality of worlds is non-contingently fixed and depends not at all on what we do." Thus we might as well forget about trying to maximize the good. Lewis comments, "But if modal realism subverts only a 'truly universalistic ethics,' I cannot see that as a damaging objection. What collapses is a philosopher's invention, no less remote from common sense than modal realism itself. An ethics of our own world is quite universalistic enough. Indeed, I dare say that it is already far too universalistic; it is a betrayal of our particular affections" (1986, 128).

stated abstractly, it is refuted by such counter-examples as parental obligation. Their thought is that we should reject this conception and look for a new theory of morality, one that would acknowledge from the outset that personal relationships can be the source of special obligations.

Rejecting the idea of impartiality has a certain appeal, for it is always exciting to learn that some popular philosophical view is no good and that there is interesting work to be done in formulating an alternative. However, we should not be too quick here. It is no accident that the conception of morality as impartiality has been so widely accepted. It seems to express something deeply important that we should be reluctant to give up. It is useful, for example, in explaining why egoism, racism, and sexism are morally odious, and if we abandon this conception we lose our most natural and persuasive means of combating those doctrines. (The idea of morality as impartiality is closely connected to modern thoughts about human equality. That humans are in some sense equals would never have occurred to the Confucianists, which perhaps explains why they saw nothing plausible in Mo's teaching.) Therefore, it seems desirable to retain the notion of moral impartiality in some form. The question is, can we find some way of keeping both ideas—morality as impartiality, and special parental obligations? Can we understand them in a way that makes them compatible with one another?

As it turns out, this is not a difficult task. It is fairly easy to interpret impartiality in such a way that it no longer conflicts with special parental obligations. We can say, for example, that impartiality requires us to treat people in the same way *only when there are no relevant differences between them*. This qualification is obviously needed, quite apart from any considerations about parents and children. For example, it is not a failure of impartiality to imprison a convicted criminal, while innocent citizens go free, because there is a relevant difference between them (one has committed a crime; the others have not) to which we can appeal to justify the difference in treatment. Similar examples come easily to mind. But once we have admitted the need for this qualification, we can make use of it to resolve our problem about parental obligations: We can say that there is a relevant difference between one's own children and other children that justifies treating one's own children better. The difference will have something to do with the fact that they are one's own.

We might call this the compromise view. It is appealing because it allows us to retain the plausible idea of morality as impartiality, without having to give up the equally plausible idea that we have special obligations to our own children. Having found this solution to our problem, we might be tempted to stop here. That, however, would be premature. There is a further issue that needs to be addressed, and when we do, the compromise view will begin to look less attractive.

We are not free to call just any differences between individuals relevant. Suppose a racist claimed that there is a relevant difference between blacks and whites that justifies treating whites better—the difference being that they are members of different races. We would think this mere bluster and demand to know why *that* difference should count for anything. Similarly, it is only hand-waving to say that there is a relevant difference between one's own children and others that justifies treating one's own better—the difference being that they are one's own. We need to ask why *that* difference matters.

WHY SHOULD IT MATTER THAT A CHILD IS ONE'S OWN?

Why should it matter, from a moral point of view, that a child is one's own? Our natural tendency is to assume that it *does* matter and to take it as a mere philosophical puzzle to figure out why. Why should anyone want to resist this tendency? The feeling that our own children have a superior natural claim on our attention is among the deepest moral instincts we have. Can it possibly be doubted? I believe there is powerful reason for doubting that this feeling is morally legitimate—the fact that a child is one's own may *not* matter, or at least it may not matter nearly as much as we usually assume. That reason has to do with luck.

The point about luck can be brought out like this. Suppose a parent believes that, when faced with a choice between feeding his own children and feeding starving orphans, he should give preference to his own. This is natural enough. But the orphans need the food just as much, and they are no less deserving. It is only their bad luck that they were not born to affluent parents; and why should luck count, from a moral point of view? Why should we think that a moral view is correct, if it implies that some children should be fed, while others starve, for no better reason than that some were unlucky in the circumstances of their birth? This seems to me to be an extremely important matter—important enough, perhaps, that we should take seriously the possibility that a child's being one's own does not have the moral importance that we usually assume it has.

With this in mind, let us look at some of the arguments that support the Compromise View. The idea that one's own children have a superior claim to one's care might be defended in various ways. Let us consider the three arguments that seem most important.

1. *The Argument from Social Roles.* The first line of reasoning begins with some observations about social roles. It is not possible for an isolated individual to have anything resembling a normal human life. For that, a social setting is required. The social setting provides roles for us to fill—thus in the context of society we are able to be citizens, friends, husbands and wives, hospital patients, construction workers, scientists, teachers, customers, sports fans, and all the rest. None of us (with rare heroic exceptions) creates the roles we play; they have evolved over many centuries of human life, and we encounter them as simply the raw materials out of which we must fashion our individual lives.

These roles define, in large measure, our relations with other people. They specify how we should behave toward others. Teachers must wisely guide their students; friends must be loyal; husbands should be faithful; and so on. To the extent that you fail in these respects, you will be an inferior teacher, a bad friend, a poor husband. You can avoid these obligations by declining to enter into these roles: Not everyone will be a teacher, not everyone will marry, and some unfortunate people will not even have friends. But you can hardly avoid *all* social roles, and you cannot fill a social role without at the same time acknowledging the special responsibilities that go with it.

Now, parenthood is a social role, and like other such roles it includes special duties as part of its very nature. You can choose not to have children, or, having had a child, you may give it up for adoption. But if you *are* a parent, you are stuck with the responsibilities that go with the role. A parent who doesn't see to his children's needs is a bad parent, just as a disloyal friend is a bad friend, and an unfaithful husband is a poor husband. And that is why (according to this argument) we have obligations to our own children that we do not have to other children.

The argument from social roles is plausible; but how far should we be persuaded by it? The argument has at least four apparent weaknesses.

(i) We need to distinguish two claims: first, that our obligations to our own children *have a different basis* from our obligations to other children; and second, that our obligations to our own children *are stronger than* (take precedence over) our obligations to other children. If successful, the argument from social roles would show only that our obligations to our own children are based on different consideration than our obligations to other children. We have a social relationship with our own children that is the basis of our obligation to them, while our obligations to other children are based on a general duty of beneficence. The argument would not show that the former obligations are *stronger*. Thus a critic of the idea of special parental obligations could continue the dispute at another level. It could be argued that, even if one's duties to one's own children have a different basis, they nevertheless are *no stronger than* one's duties to other children.

(ii) The second point is related to the first. The argument from social roles trades on the notion of what it means to be a bad father or a bad mother. Now, suppose we admit that a man who ignores the needs of his own children is a bad father. It may also be observed that a man who ignores the cries of orphans, when he could help, is a bad *man*—a man lacking a proper regard for the needs of others. While it undesirable to be a bad father (or mother), it is also undesirable to be a bad man (or woman). So, once again, the argument from social roles does nothing to show that our obligations to other children are weaker.

(iii) Third, there is the point about luck that I have already mentioned. The system of social roles acknowledged in our society makes special provision for children lucky enough to live in homes with parents. This system favors even more those lucky enough to have affluent parents who can provide more for them than less affluent parents are able to provide. Even granting this, we can still ask: Is it a morally decent system? The system itself can be subject to criticism.

We do not have to look far to find an obvious objection to the system. The system does well enough in providing for some children; but it does miserably where others are concerned. There is no social role comparable to the parent-child relationship that targets the interests of orphans, or the interests of children whose parents are unable or unwilling to provide for them. Thus in this system luck plays an unacceptably important part.

(iv) Finally, students of social history might find the argument from social roles rather naïve. The argument draws much of its strength from the fact that contemporary American and European ideals favor families bound together by love. Anyone who is likely to read these words will have been influenced by that ideal—consider how the reader will have passed over the second paragraph of this essay, with its easy talk of parents loving and protecting their children, without a pause. Yet the cozy nuclear family, nourished by affectionate relationships, is a relatively recent development. The norm throughout most of Western history has been very different.

In his acclaimed book *The Family, Sex and Marriage in England 1500–1800*, Lawrence Stone points out that as recently as the seventeenth century affectionate relations between husbands and wives were so rare as to be virtually nonexistent, and certainly were not expected within normal marriages. Among the upper classes, husbands and wives occupied separate stations within large households and rarely saw one another in private. Children were sent away immediately after birth to be looked after by wet-nurses for 12 to 18 months; then, returning home, they would be raised largely by nurses, governesses, and tutors. Finally they would be sent away to boarding school when they were between 7 and 13, with 10 the commonest age (Stone, 1979, 83–84). The children of the poor were of course worse off: They would leave home at an equally early age, often to go and work in the houses of the rich. Stone writes,

> About all that can be said with confidence on the matter of emotional relations within the sixteenth- and early seventeenth-century family at all social levels is that there was a general psychological atmosphere of distance, manipulation, and deference. . . . Family relationships were characterized by interchangeability, so that substitution of another wife or another child was easy. . . . It was a structure held together not by affective bonds but by mutual economic interests (Stone, 1979, 88).

And what of parental duties? Of course there has always been a recognition of *some* special parental duties, but in earlier times these were much more restricted and were not associated with bonds of affection. Until some time in the eighteenth century, it seems, the emphasis in European morals was almost entirely on the duties owed by children to parents, rather than the other way around. Children were commonly said to owe their parents absolute obedience, in gratitude for having been given life. The French historian Jean Flandrin notes that "In Brittany the son remained subject to the authority of his father until the age of sixty, but marriage contracted with the father's consent emancipated him" (Flandrin, 1979, 130). Pity the man whose father lived to a ripe old age and refused consent for marriage—his only emancipation would be to flee. Both Stone and Flandrin make it clear that, while parental *rights* is an old idea, the idea of extensive parental *obligations* is a notion of much more recent vintage. (The debate between Mo Tzu and the Confucianists was also conducted in such terms—for them, the primary issue was whether children had special duties to their fathers, not the other way around.)

These observations about social history should be approached with care. Of course they do not refute the idea of special parental obligations. However, they do go some way toward undermining our easy confidence that present-day social arrangements only institutionalize our natural duties. That is the only moral to be drawn from them, but it is an important one. In this area, as in so many others, what seems natural just depends on the conventions of one's society.

2. *The Argument from Proximity.* The second argument goes like this. It is reasonable to accept a social arrangement in which parents are assigned special responsibility for their own children because parents are *better situated* to look after their own. Granted, all children need help and protection. But other children are remote, and their needs are less clear, while a parent's own children live in the same house, and the parent is (or ought to be) intimately familiar with their needs. Other things being equal, it makes sense to think that A has a greater responsibility for helping B than for helping C, if A is better situated to help B. This is true in the case of helping one's own children versus helping other children; therefore, one's obligation in the first instance is greater.

This argument is plausible if we concentrate on certain kinds of aid. Children wake up sick in the middle of the night; someone must attend to them, and that someone is usually Mother or Father. The parents are in a position to do so, and (most of the time) no one else is. The complaint that you nursed your own children, but you didn't help the other children who woke up sick elsewhere in the world is obviously misguided. The same goes for countless other ways that parents assist their children, by making them take their medicine, by stopping them from playing in the roadway, by bundling them up against the cold, and so on. These are all matters of what we might call *day-to-day care*.

Day-to-day care involves a kind of personal attention that a parent *could not* provide for many others, because it is physically impossible. The importance of physical proximity is that it makes these kinds of caring behaviors possible; the impossibility of doing the same for other children is just the impossibility of being in two places at once. So if there is partiality here, it is a partiality that we need not worry about because it cannot be avoided. There is little doubt, then, that parents are normally in a better position to provide day-to-day care for their own children than for others.

This type of argument is less plausible, however, when we consider more general, fundamental needs, such as food. Is a parent in a better position to feed his own children than to provide for others? At one time this might have been the case. Before the advent of modern communications and transportation, and before the creation of efficient relief agencies, people might have been able to say that while they could feed their own, they were unable to do much about the plight of children elsewhere. But that is no longer true. Today, with relief agencies ready to take our assistance all over the world, needing only sufficient resources to do so, it is almost as easy to provide food for a child in Africa as to provide for one's own. The same goes for providing basic medical care:

International relief agencies carry medical assistance around the world on the same basis.

Therefore, the argument from proximity is, at best, only partially successful. Some forms of assistance (such as getting up in the middle of the night to attend to sick children) do require proximity but others (such as providing food) do not. The argument might show that, where day-to-day care is concerned, parents have special duties. But the same cannot be said for the provision of fundamental needs.

3. *The Argument from Personal Goods.* The third argument hinges on the idea that loving relationships are personal goods of great importance: To love other people and be loved in return are part of what is involved in having a rich and satisfying human life. A loving relationship with one's children is, for many parents, a source of such happiness that they would sacrifice almost anything else to preserve it. But as we have already observed, love necessarily involves having a special concern for the well-being of the loved one, and so it is not impartial. An ethic that required absolute impartiality would therefore require forgoing a great personal good.

The intuitive idea behind this argument may seem plain enough. Nevertheless, it is difficult to formulate the argument with any precision. Why, exactly, is a loving relationship with another person such a great good? Part of the answer may be that pacts of mutual assistance enable all of us to fare better. If *A* and *B* have this sort of relationship, then *A* can count on *B's* assistance when it is needed, and vice versa. They are both better off. Of course, deals of this kind could be made between people who are not joined by bonds of affection, but affection makes the arrangement more dependable: People who love one another are more apt to remain faithful when the going is hard. But there is more. Bonds of affection are more than just instrumentally good. To be loved is to have one's own value affirmed; thus it is a source of self-esteem. This is important for all of us, but especially for children, who are more helpless and vulnerable than adults. Moreover, there is, at a deep level, a connection between love and the meaning of life (although I cannot go into this very deeply here). We question whether our lives have meaning when we find nothing worth valuing, when it seems to us that "all is vanity." Loving relationships provide individuals with things to value, and so give their lives this kind of meaning. That is why parents who love their children, and who strive to see that they do well, can find in this meaning for their lives.

These are important points, but they do not prove as much as they are sometimes taken to prove. In the first place, there is a lot about parental love that *is* consistent with a large measure of impartiality. Loving someone is not only a matter of preferring their interests. Love involves, among other things, intimacy and the sharing of experiences. A parent shows his love by listening to the child's jokes, by talking, by being a considerate companion, by praising, and even by scolding when that is needed. It may be objected that these kinds of behavior also show partiality, since the parent does not do these things for all children. But these are only further instances of the day-to-day care that requires proximity; again, if this is partiality, it is partiality that cannot be avoided.

And there is another difference between these kinds of support and such things as providing food and medical care. The companionship, the listening, the talking, and the praising and scolding are what make personal relationships *personal*. That is why the psychic benefits that accompany such relationships are more closely associated with these matters than with such relatively impersonal things as being fed.

Moreover, it is not necessary, in order to have a loving relationship with one's children and to derive from it the benefits that the argument from personal goods envisions, to regard their interests as *always* having priority, especially when the interests in question are not comparable. One could have a loving relationship that involves all the intimacies of day-to-day care and the provision of life's necessities, while acknowledging at the same time that when it comes to choosing between luxuries for them and food for orphans, the orphans' needs should prevail. At the very least, there is nothing in the argument from personal goods that rules out such an approach.

THE MORAL POINT OF UTOPIAN THINKING

There is another approach to our problem, favored by the Mohists, that we have not yet considered: Clinging to the ideal of impartiality, we could simply reject the idea of special parental duties. This goes against our intuitions, and it is opposed by the (partially successful) arguments we have just examined. Nevertheless, we may ask whether there is anything to be said in favor of this approach.

In fact, there is a lot that might be said in its favor. Suppose we forget, for a moment, the imperfections of actual human life, and try to imagine what it would be like if everyone behaved in a morally blameless manner. What would relations between adults and children be like in such a utopia? Here is one plausible picture of such a world. In it, children with living parents able to provide for them would be raised by their parents, who would give them all the love and care they need. Parents who through no fault of their own were unable to provide for their children would be given whatever assistance they need. Orphans would be taken in by families who would raise and love them as their own. The burdens involved in such adoptions would be shared by all.

It is fair to say that, in such a world, the ideal of impartiality is realized. In this world people do not act as if any child is more deserving than any other: One way or another, equal provision is made for the needs of all. Moreover, luck plays no part in how children will fare: The orphans' needs are satisfied too. When it is said by the Mohists that "love is universal," or by their counterparts, the utilitarians, that we should "promote impartially the interests of everyone alike," this might be the point: In the morally best world, we would not recognize many of the distinctions that we do recognize in the real world we inhabit.

But the idea of special obligations has crept back in. In the utopian world I have sketched, some special obligations are acknowledged, because particular adults (most often parents) are assigned special responsibility for looking after particular children. However, two points need to be emphasized: First, the *reason* for this arrangement is consistent with the principle of impartiality (and inconsistent with the thought that one's own children somehow have a natural superior claim on one's attention); the reason is that this is the best way to see that the needs of all children are satisfied. Second, the recognition of some special obligations might be *welcomed*, even in utopia; it need not be merely something that is grudgingly admitted. The arguments we have already considered suggest that there are special benefits to be derived from a social system in which particular adults are assigned responsibility for particular children—the benefits that go with loving personal relationships. This gives us reason to think that such an assignment would be part of the best social system—a system that would at the same time make adequate provision for all.

Of course we do not live in a utopia, and it might be objected that in the real world we inhabit, it would be ether silly or disastrous to start telling parents to stop favoring their own children—silly because no one would listen, or disastrous because if some did, their children would suffer greatly. (There might be, in current terms, a coordination problem: It might not be wise for some to adopt the best strategy unless all do.) So what is the point of thinking about utopia? I suggest this: A picture of utopia gives us an idea, not only of what we should strive for, but of what is in one sense objectively right and wrong. Conditions may exist in our own world that make it wrong, in some circumstances, to act as though we lived in utopia. But that is only because in our world human behavior is flawed. It may nevertheless be true that, in a deep sense, the utopian behavior is morally best.

Let me try to make this clearer by giving a different sort of example. It has been argued by many philosophers that there is nothing immoral in mercy-killing, when it is requested by a dying person as a humane alternative to a slow, painful death. Others have objected that if mercy-killing were permitted it would lead to further killings that we would not want—we might begin by killing people at their own request to put them out of misery, it is said, but then we would begin to pressure sick people into making such requests, and that would lead to killing old people who have not requested it (for their own good, of course), and then we would go on to killing the feeble-minded, and so on. I do not believe these things would happen.[3] But suppose they would. What would follow? It would not follow that mercy-killing is immoral in the original case. The objection would show, paradoxically, that there are good reasons why we should not perform actions that *are* moral and humane. Those reasons would have to do with the imperfections of human beings—the claim is that people are so flawed that they would slide down the slippery slope from the (moral) practice of euthanasia to the additional (immoral) practices described.

This suggests that moral philosophy might be idealistic in a way that applied ethics is not. Moral philosophy describes the ideals that motivate perfect

---

[3]For a complete discussion see Rachels (1986, chap. 10).

conduct, the conduct of people in utopia.[4] In utopia, as Thomas More observed in his book of that name, euthanasia would be accepted (More, 1965, 102), and the slippery-slope argument would be irrelevant because people in utopia do not abuse humane practices. Applied ethics, however, takes into account the messy details of the real world, including the prejudices, faults, and vices of real human beings, and recommends how we should behave considering all *that* as well as the ideals of perfect conduct.

What does this mean for the question of special parental obligations? It means that there is a point to the philosophical insistence that all children are equal, even if in the real world it would be unwise to urge particular parents to stop providing preferential care for their own. The practical question is, therefore, how nearly we can expect to approach the ideal system in the real world and what specific recommendations should be made, in light of this, to particular parents.

PRACTICAL IMPLICATIONS

How should parents, living not in utopia but in our society, who are concerned to do what is morally best, conceive of the relation between their obligations to their own children and their obligations to other children? Here are four contrasting views; each is implausible, but for different reasons.

1. *Extreme Bias.* On this view, parents have obligations to provide for their own children, but they have *no obligations at all* to other children. Anything done for other children is at best supererogatory—good and praiseworthy if one chooses to do it, but in no way morally mandatory. On this view, parents may provide not only necessities but also luxuries for their own children, while other children starve, and yet be immune from moral criticism.

Extreme bias is not plausible, because it makes no provision whatever for a duty of general beneficence. It is hard to believe that we do not have *some* obligation to be concerned with the plight of the starving, whoever they are, even if that obligation is less extensive than our obligations to our own kin.[5] Thus it will not be surprising if this view turns out to be unacceptable.

2. *Complete Equality.* The opposite view seems to be implied by the idea of morality as impartiality—the view that all children are equal and that there is

---

[4]On this point I am following Richard Brandt, although he does not put it in just this way. Brandt writes: "What I mean by 'is objectively wrong' or 'is morally unjustified' is 'would be prohibited by the set of moral rules which a rational person would prefer to have current or subscribed to in the consciences of persons in the society in which he expected to live a whole life, as compared with any other set of moral rules or none at all'" (1975, 367). Clearly, this is a set of rules appropriate for a utopia, where it is assumed that people will actually live according to the rules. In the real world we can make no such assumption, and sometimes this will mean we should do things that, according to this definition, would be objectively wrong.

[5]For arguments concerning the extensiveness of our obligations toward others, see Singer (1972) and Rachels (1979).

no difference at all between one's moral obligations toward one's own children and one's moral obligations toward other children. This view denies that there are any good moral grounds for preferring to feed one's own child rather than an orphan in a foreign country. In our society anyone who accepted and acted on such a view would seem to his neighbors to be morally deranged, for doing so would seem to involve a rejection of one's children—a refusal to treat them with the love that is appropriate to the parent-child relationship.

3. *The Most Common View.* What, in fact, do people in our society seem to believe? Most people seem to believe that one has an obligation to provide the necessities of life for other children only after one has already provided a great range of luxuries for one's own. On this view, it is permissible to provide one's own children with virtually everything they need in order to have a good start in life—not only food and clothing, but, if possible, a good education, opportunities for travel, opportunities for enjoyable leisure, and so forth. In the United States children of affluent families often have TV sets, stereos, and now computers, all laid out in their own rooms. They drive their own cars to high school. Few people seem to think there is anything wrong with this—parents who are unable to provide their children with such luxuries nevertheless aspire to do so.

The most common view imposes *some* duty regarding other children, but not much. In practical terms, it imposes a duty only on the very rich, who have resources left over even after they have provided ample luxuries for their own children. The rest of us, who have nothing left after doing as much as we can for our own, are off the hook. It takes only a little reflection to see that this view is also implausible. How can it be right to spend money on luxuries for some children, even one's own—buying them the latest trendy toys, for example while others do not have enough to eat? Perhaps, when confronted with this, many people might come to doubt whether it is correct. But certainly most affluent people act as if it were correct.

Is there a better alternative? Is there a view that escapes the difficulties of extreme bias, complete equality, and the most common view, and is consistent with the various other points that have been made in our discussion? I suggest the following.

4. *Partial Bias.* We might say that, while we do have a substantial obligation to be concerned about the welfare of all children, our own nevertheless come first. This vague thought needs to be sharpened. One way of making it more precise is this. When considering similar needs, you may permissibly prefer to provide for the needs of your own children. For example, if you were faced with a choice between feeding your own children or contributing the money to provide food for other children, you could rightly choose to feed your own. But if the choice were between some relatively trivial thing for your own and necessities for other children, preference should be given to helping the others. Thus if the choice were between providing trendy toys for your own already well-fed children or feeding the starving, you should feed the starving.

This view will turn out to be more or less demanding, depending on what one counts as a "relatively trivial thing." We might agree that buying trendy toys for some children, even for one's own, while other children starve is indefensible.

But what about buying them nice clothes? Or a college education? Am I justified in sending my children to an expensive college? Clearly, the line between the trivial and the important can be drawn at different places. (One will be pushed toward a more demanding interpretation as one takes more seriously the point about the moral irrelevance of luck.) Nevertheless, the intuitive idea is plain enough. On this view, you may provide the necessities for your own children first, but you are not justified in providing them luxuries while other children lack necessities. Even in a fairly weak form, this view would still require much greater concern for others than the view that is most common in our society.

From the point of view of the various arguments we have considered, partial bias clearly stands out as the superior view. It is closer to the utopian ideal than either extreme bias or the most common view; it is morally superior in that it makes greater provision for children who have no loving parents; it is consistent with the arguments we have considered concerning the benefits to be derived from loving relationships; and it is perhaps as much as we could expect from people in the real world. It is not, in fact, very far from the utopian ideal. If we begin with Complete Equality, and then modify it in the ways suggested in our discussion of utopia, we end up with something very much like partial bias.

What would the adoption of partial bias mean for actual families? It would mean that parents could continue to provide loving day-to-day care for their own children, with all that this involves, while giving them preferential treatment in the provision of life's necessities. But it would also mean preferring to provide the necessities for needier children, rather than luxuries for their own. Children in such families would be worse off, in an obvious sense, than the children of affluent parents who continued to live according to the dictates of extreme bias or the most common view. However, we might hope that they would not regard themselves as deprived, for they might learn the moral value of giving up their luxuries so that the other children do not starve. They might even come to see their parents as morally admirable people. That hope is itself utopian enough.

Questions

1. Do you agree with James Rachels that the moral irrelevance of luck imposes on those who would defend special obligations to one's own children the argumentative burden that he says it does?
2. What are the shortcomings, according to the author, of the "argument from proximity" and the "argument from personal goods"?
3. What conclusion does the author reach about how we, who do not live in utopia, should conceive of the relationship between our obligations to our own children and to other people's children?

References

BAIER, KURT. 1958. *The Moral Point of View.* Ithaca: Cornell University Press.
BRANDT, RICHARD B. 1975. "The Morality and Rationality of Suicide." In James Rachels, ed. *Moral Problems.* New York: Harper & Row.

FLANDRIN, JEAN. 1979. *Families in Former Times*. Richard Southern, trans. Cambridge: Cambridge University Press.

FUNG YU-LAN. 1960. *A Short History of Chinese Philosophy*. New York: Macmillan.

HARE, R. M. 1972. "Rules of War and Moral Reasoning." *Philosophy and Public Affairs*, 1, 166–81.

LEWIS, DAVID. 1986. *On the Plurality of Worlds*. Oxford: Blackwell.

MILL, JOHN STUART. 1957. *Utilitarianism*. Indianapolis: Bobbs-Merrill. This work, first published in 1861, is today available in many editions.

MORE, THOMAS. 1965. *Utopia*. Harmondsworth: Penguin. This work, first published in Latin in 1516, is today available in many editions. The Penguin translation is by Paul Turner.

RACHELS, JAMES. 1979. "Killing and Starving to Death." *Philosophy*, 54, 159–71.

———1986. *The End of Life: Euthanasia and Morality*. Oxford: Oxford University Press.

RAWLS, JOHN. 1971. *A Theory of Justice*. Cambridge: Harvard University Press.

RUBIN, VITALY A. 1976. *Individual and State in Ancient China*. New York: Columbia University Press.

SIDGWICK, HENRY. 1907. *The Methods of Ethics*, 7th. ed. London: Macmillan.

SINGER, PETER. 1972. "Famine, Affluence, and Morality." *Philosophy and Public Affairs*, 1, 229–43.

———1978. "Is Racial Discrimination Arbitrary?" *Philosophia*, 8, 185–203.

STONE, LAWRENCE. 1979. *The Family, Sex and Marriage in England 1500–1800*. New York: Harper & Row.

What Do Grown Children Owe Their Parents?

Jane English

Jane English thinks that although children have duties to their parents, they do not owe them anything. This, she says, is because the sacrifices that parents voluntary make for their children do not create debts that need to be repaid. Instead they tend to create love or friendship, and the duties of grown children to the parents are those of friends. Regarding such duties, she says, talk of "owing" is not apt. She argues that favors create debts that can be owed, but that friendship is not characterized by debts. Friends help one another whenever the help is needed. Moreover, they do so purely because of love, rather than to repay or create a debt. Another difference between the debts created by favors and the duties of friendship is that the latter last only so long as the friendship.

The author argues that although the sacrifices that parents make for their children have an important causal role in creating ongoing friendship, those sacrifices are not the justification for filial duties. The duties children have to help their parents (so long as they are friends) are determined not by how much parents sacrificed for them but by the needs of parents.

What do grown children owe their parents? I will contend that the answer is "nothing." Although I agree that there are many things that children *ought* to do for their parents, I will argue that it is inappropriate and misleading to describe them as things "owed." I will maintain that parents' voluntary sacrifices, rather than creating "debts" to be "repaid," tend to create love or "friendship." The duties of grown children are those of friends and result from love between them and their parents, rather than being things owed in repayment for the parents' earlier sacrifices. Thus, I will oppose those philosophers who use the word "owe" whenever a duty or obligation exists. Although the "debt" metaphor is appropriate in some moral circumstances, my argument is that a love relationship is not such a case.

Misunderstandings about the proper relationship between parents and their grown children have resulted from reliance on the "owing" terminology. For instance, we hear parents complain, "You owe it to us to write home (keep up your piano playing, not adopt a hippie lifestyle), because of all we sacrificed for you (paying for piano lessons, sending you to college)." The child is sometimes even heard to reply, "I didn't ask to be born (to be given piano lessons, to be sent to college)." This inappropriate idiom of ordinary language tends to obscure, or even to undermine, the love that is the correct ground of filial obligation.

1. FAVORS CREATE DEBTS

There are some cases, other than literal debts, in which talk of "owing,"though metaphorical, is apt. New to the neighborhood, Max barely knows his neighbor, Nina, but he asks her if she will take in his mail while he is gone for a month's vacation. She agrees. If, subsequently, Nina asks Max to do the same for her, it seems that Max has a moral obligation to agree (greater than the one he would have had if Nina had not done the same for him), unless for some reason it would be a burden far out of proportion to the one Nina bore for him. I will call this a *favor*: when A, at B's request, bears some burden for B, then B incurs an obligation to reciprocate. Here the metaphor of Max's "owing" Nina is appropriate. It is not literally a debt, of course, nor can Nina pass this IOU on to heirs, demand payment in the form of Max's taking out her garbage, or sue Max. Nonetheless, since Max ought to perform one act of similar nature and amount of sacrifice in return, the term is suggestive. Once he reciprocates, the debt is "discharged"—that is, their obligations revert to the condition they were in before Max's initial request.

Contrast a situation in which Max simply goes on vacation and, to his surprise, finds upon his return that his neighbor has mowed his grass twice weekly in his absence. This is a voluntary sacrifice rather than a favor, and Max has no duty to reciprocate. It would be nice for him to volunteer to do so, but this would be supererogatory on his part. Rather than a favor, Nina's action is a friendly gesture. As a result, she might expect Max to chat over the back fence, help her catch her straying dog, or something similar—she might expect the development of a friendship. But Max would be chatting (or whatever) out of friendship, rather than in repayment for mown grass. If he did not return her gesture, she might feel rebuffed or miffed, but not unjustly treated or indignant, since Max has not failed to perform a duty. Talk of "owing" would be out of place in this case.

It is sometimes difficult to distinguish between favors and non-favors, because friends tend to do favors for each other, and those who exchange favors tend to become friends. But one test is to ask how Max is motivated. Is it "to be nice to Nina" or "because she did *x* for me"? Favors are frequently performed by total strangers without any friendship developing. Nevertheless, a temporary obligation is created, even if the chance for repayment never arises. For instance, suppose that Oscar and Matilda, total strangers, are waiting in a long checkout line at the supermarket. Oscar, having forgotten the oregano, asks Matilda to watch his cart for a second. She does. If Matilda now asks Oscar to return the favor while she picks up some tomato sauce, he is obliged to agree. Even if she had not watched his cart, it would be inconsiderate of him to refuse, claiming he was too busy reading the magazines. He may have a duty to help others, but he would not "owe" it to her. But if she has done the same for him, he incurs an additional obligation to help, and talk of "owing" is apt. It suggests an agreement to perform equal, reciprocal, canceling sacrifices.

2. THE DUTIES OF FRIENDSHIP

The terms "owe" and "repay" are helpful in the case of favors, because the sameness of the amount of sacrifice on the two sides is important; the monetary metaphor suggests equal quantities of sacrifice. But friendship ought to be characterized by *mutuality* rather than reciprocity: friends offer what they can give and accept what they need, without regard for the total amounts of benefits exchanged. And friends are motivated by love rather than by the prospect of repayment. Hence, talk of "owing" is singularly out of place in friendship.

For example, suppose Alfred takes Beatrice out for an expensive dinner and a movie. Beatrice incurs no obligation to "repay" him with a goodnight kiss or a return engagement. If Alfred complains that she "owes" him something, he is if operating under the assumption that she should repay a favor, but on the contrary his was a generous gesture done in the hopes of developing a friendship. We hope that he would not want her repayment in the form of sex or attention if this was done to discharge a debt rather than from friendship. Since, if Alfred is prone to reasoning in this way, Beatrice may well decline the invitation or request to pay for her own dinner, his attitude of expecting a "return" on his "investment" could hinder the development of a friendship. Beatrice should return the gesture only if she is motivated by friendship.

Another common misuse of the "owing" idiom occurs when the Smiths have dined at the Joneses' four times, but the Joneses at the Smiths' only once. People often say, "We owe them three dinners." This line of thinking may be appropriate between business acquaintances, but not between friends. After all, the Joneses invited the Smiths not in order to feed them or to be fed in turn, but because of the friendly contact presumably enjoyed by all on such occasions. If the Smiths do not feel friendship toward the Joneses, they can decline future invitations and not invite the Joneses; they owe them nothing. Of course, between friends of equal resources and needs, roughly equal sacrifices (though not necessarily roughly equal dinners) will typically occur. If the sacrifices are highly out of proportion to the resources, the relationship is closer to servility than to friendship.[1]

---

[1] Cf. Thomas E. Hill, Jr., "Servility and Self-Respect," *Monist* 57 (1973). Thus, during childhood, most of the sacrifices will come from the parents, since they have most of the resources and the child has most of the needs. When children are grown, the situation is usually reversed.

Another difference between favors and friendship is that after a friendship ends, the duties of friendship end. The party that has sacrificed less owes the other nothing. For instance, suppose Elmer donated a pint of blood that his wife Doris needed during an operation. Years after their divorce, Elmer is in an accident and needs one pint of blood. His new wife, Cora, is also of the same blood type. It seems that Doris not only does not "owe" Elmer blood, but that she should actually refrain from coming forward if Cora has volunteered to donate. To insist on donating not only interferes with the newlyweds' friendship, but it belittles Doris and Elmer's former relationship by suggesting that Elmer gave blood in hopes of favors returned instead of simply out of love for Doris. It is one of the heart-rending features of divorce that it attends to quantity in a relationship previously characterized by mutuality. If Cora could not donate, Doris's obligation is the same as that for any former spouse in need of blood; it is not increased by the fact that Elmer similarly aided her. It *is* affected by the degree to which they are still friends, which in turn may (or may not) have been influenced by Elmer's donation.

In short, unlike the debts created by favors, the duties of friendship do not require equal quantities of sacrifice. Performing equal sacrifices does not cancel the duties of friendship, as it does the debts of favors. Unrequested sacrifices do not themselves create debts, but friends have duties regardless of whether they requested or initiated the friendship. Those who perform favors may be motivated by mutual gain, whereas friends should be motivated by affection. These characteristics of the friendship relation are distorted by talk of "owing."

3. PARENTS AND CHILDREN

The relationship between children and their parents should be one of friendship characterized by mutuality rather than one of reciprocal favors. The quantity of parental sacrifice is not relevant in determining what duties the grown child has. The medical assistance grown children ought to offer their ill mothers in old age depends upon the mothers' need, not upon whether they endured a difficult pregnancy, for example. Nor do one's duties to one's parents cease once an equal quantity of sacrifice has been performed, as the phrase "discharging a debt" may lead us to think.

Rather, what children ought to do for their parents (and parents for children) depends upon (1) their respective needs, abilities, and resources and (2) the extent to which there is an ongoing friendship between them. Thus, regardless of the quantity of childhood sacrifices, an able, wealthy child has an obligation to help his needy parents more than does a needy child. To illustrate, suppose sisters Cecile and Dana are equally loved by their parents, even though Cecile was an easy child to care for, seldom ill, Dana was often sick and caused some trouble as a juvenile delinquent. As adults, Dana is a struggling artist living far away, while Cecile is a wealthy lawyer living nearby. When the parents need visits and financial aid, Cecile has an obligation to bear a higher proportion of these burdens than her sister. This results from her abilities, rather than from the quantities of sacrifice made by the parents earlier.

Sacrifices have an important causal role in creating an ongoing friendship, which may lead us to assume incorrectly that it is the sacrifices that are the source of the obligation. That the source is the friendship instead can be seen by examining cases in which the sacrifices occurred but the friendship, for some reason, did not develop or persist. For example, if a woman gives up her newborn child for adoption, and if no feelings of love ever develop on either side, it seems that the grown child does not have an obligation to "repay" her for her sacrifices in pregnancy, For that matter, if the adopted child has an un-impaired love relationship with the adoptive parents, he or she has the same obligations to help them as a natural child would have.

The filial obligations of grown children are a result of friendship, rather than owed for services rendered. Suppose that Vance married Lola despite his parents' strong wish that he marry within their religion, and that as a result, the parents refuse to speak to him again. As the years pass, the parents are unaware of Vance's problems, his accomplishments, the birth of his children. The love that once existed between them, let us suppose, has been completely destroyed by this event and thirty years of desuetude. At this point, it seems Vance is under no obligation to pay his parents' medical bills in their old age, beyond his general duty to help those in need. An additional, filial obligation would only arise from whatever love he may still feel for them. It would be irrelevant for his parents to argue, "But look how much we sacrificed for you when you were young," for that sacrifice was not a favor but occurred as part of a friendship which existed at that time but is now, we have supposed, defunct. A more appropriate message would be, "We still love you, and we would like to renew our friendship."

I hope this helps to set the question of what children ought to do for their parents in a new light. The parental argument, "You ought to do x because we did y for you," should be replaced by, "We love you and you will be happier if you do x," or "We believe you love us, and anyone who loved us would do x." If the parents' sacrifice had been a favor, the child's reply, "I never asked you to do y for me," would have been relevant; to the revised parental remarks, this reply is clearly irrelevant. The child can either do x or dispute one of the parents' claims by showing that a love relationship does not exist, or that love for some-one does not motivate doing x or that he or she will not be happier doing x.

Seen in this light, parental requests for children to write home, visit, and of-fer them a reasonable amount of emotional and financial support in life's crises are well founded, so long as a friendship still exists. Love for others does call for caring about and caring for them. Some other parental requests, such as for more sweeping changes in the child's lifestyle or life goals, can be seen to be in-supportable, once we shift the justification from debts owed to love. The termi-nology of favors suggests the reasoning, "Since we paid for your college education, you owe it to us to make a career of engineering, rather than becom-ing a rock musician." This tends to alienate affection even further, since the tu-ition payments are depicted as investments for a return rather than done from love, as though the child's life goals could be "bought." Basing the argument on love leads to different reasoning patterns. The suppressed premise, "If A loves B, then A follows B's wishes as to A's lifelong career" is simply false. Love does not even dictate that the child adopt the parents' values as to the desirability of alternative life goals. So the parents' strongest available argument here is, "We love you, we are deeply concerned about your happiness, and in the long run you will be happier as an engineer." This makes it clear that an empirical claim is really the subject of the debate.

The function of these examples is to draw out our considered judgments as to the proper relation between parents and their grown children, and to show how poorly they fit the model of favors. What is relevant is the ongoing friendship that exists between parents and children. Although that relationship developed partly as a result of parental sacrifices for the child, the duties that grown children have to their parents result from the friendship rather than from the sacrifices. The idiom of owing favors to one's parents can actually be destructive if it undermines the role of mutuality and leads us to think in terms of quantitative reciprocal favors.

Questions

1. Do you agree with Jane English that one can have a duty to somebody without owing that person anything? Can one speak of a duty that is not owed?
2. What does the author mean by a "favor"? Why does she think that the sacrifices parents make for their children are not favors?
3. Given that bonds of friendship can be stronger or weaker, what implication would this have, on the author's account, for the duties grown children have to their parents?
4. What would James Rachels say about filial duties?

Filial Morality

Christina Hoff Sommers

Whereas James Rachels thinks that the re-
quirement of impartiality in morality
must be preserved, Christina Hoff Som-
mers argues that it should be abandoned.
She describes three cases that she takes to
be examples of filial impiety, and then
briefly outlines the history of views about
filial morality.

The author describes the requirement
of impartiality as the equal-pull (EP)
thesis and contrasts this with a view she
defends—the differential-pull (DP) thesis. *According to DP, what Robert Nozick*
calls the "ethical pull" of a moral patient
will depend in part on "how that moral
patient is related to the moral agent on
whom the pull is exerted." In other words,
one can have special duties to some people
as a result of how one is related to them.

How special duties are shaped by the par-
ticular circumstances and conventions is a
complex matter, the author says.

She argues that DP better accounts
for our pretheoretical moral judgments
than do either EP or the view of those she
calls the "sentimentalists." The sentimen-
talists (among whom she includes Jane
English) are those who, to use Carol Gilli-
gan's terminology, want an "ethic of care"
instead of an "ethic of rights" and who ob-
ject to talk of "owing" in reference to filial
morality. Finally, the author argues that
DP is not a form of ethical relativism be-
cause, unlike relativism, it can pass moral
judgment on whole societies. She says,
however, that DP does capture "ethical
relativism's large grain of truth."

> We not only find it hard to say exactly how much a son owes his parents, but
> we are even reluctant to investigate this.
>
> —HENRY SIDGWICK[1]

Christina Hoff Summers, "Filial Morality," *Journal of Philosophy*, vol. LXXXIII, no. 8 (August 1986):
439–456. © 1986 by The Journal of Philosophy, Inc.

This paper has benefited from lengthy discussion with Fred Sommers and from critical comments by A. I. Melden, Diana Meyers, Marcia Baron, David Wong, Michael Lockwood, Jonathan
Adler, and Patrick Derr.
[1]*The Methods of Ethics* (New York: Dover, 1966), p. 243.

What rights do parents have to the special attentions of their adult children? Before this century there was no question that a filial relationship defined a natural obligation; philosophers might argue about the nature of filial obligation, but not about its reality. Today, not a few moralists dismiss it as an illusion, or give it secondary derivative status. A. John Simmons[2] expresses "doubts . . . concerning the existence of 'filial' debts," and Michael Slote[3] seeks to show that the idea of filial obedience is an illusion whose source is the false idea that one owes obedience to a divine being. Jeffrey Blustein[4] argues that parents who have done no more than their duty may be owed nothing, and Jane English[5] denies outright that there are any filial obligations not grounded in mutual friendship.

The current tendency to deny or reconstrue filial obligation is related to the more general difficulty that contemporary philosophers have when dealing with the special duties. An account of the special obligations to one's kin, friends, community or country puts considerable strain on moral theories such as Kantianism and utilitarianism, theories that seem better designed for telling us what we should be doing for everyone impartially than for explaining something like filial obligation. The moral philosopher of a utilitarian or Kantian persuasion who is concerned to show that it is permissible to give some biased vent to family feeling *may* go on to become concerned with the more serious question of accounting for what appears to be a special obligation to care for and respect one's parents—but only as an afterthought. On the whole, the question of special agent-related duties has not seemed pressing. In what follows I shall be arguing for a strong notion of filial obligation, and more generally I shall be making a case for the special moral relations. I first present some anecdotal materials that illustrate the thesis that a filial duty to respect one's parents is not an illusion.

I. THE CONCRETE DILEMMAS

I shall be concerned with the filial duties of adult children and more particularly with the duty to honor and respect. I have chosen almost randomly three situations each illustrating what seems to be censurable failure on the part of adult children to respect their parents or nurturers. It would not be hard to add to these cases and real life is continually adding to them.

1. An elderly man was interviewed on National Public Radio for a program on old age. This is what he said about his daughter.

> I live in a rooming house. I lost my wife about two years ago and I miss her very much . . . My little pleasure was to go to my daughter's house in Anaheim and have a Friday night meal. . . . She would make a meal that I would enjoy. . . . So my son-in-law got angry at me one time for a little nothing and ordered me out of the house. That was about eight months ago. . . . I was back

[2]*Moral Principles and Political Obligations* (Princeton, N.J.: University Press, 1979), p. 162.
[3]"Obedience and Illusion," in Onora O'Neill and William Ruddick, eds., *Having Children* (New York: Oxford, 1979), pp. 319–325.
[4]*Parents and Children: The Ethics of the Family* (New York: Oxford, 1982).
[5]"What Do Grown Children Owe Their Parents?", in O'Neill and Ruddick, *op. cit.*, pp. 351–356.

once during the day when he was working. That was about two and a half or three months ago. I stayed for about two hours and left before he came home from work. But I did not enjoy the visit very much. That was the last time I was there to see my daughter.

2. An eighty-two year old woman (call her Miss Tate) spent thirty years working as a live-in housekeeper and baby-sitter for a judge's family in Massachusetts. The judge and his wife left her a small pension which inflation rendered inadequate. After her employers died, she lost contact with the children whom she had virtually brought up. One day Miss Tate arranged for a friend of hers to write to the children (by then middle-aged) telling them that she was sick and would like to see them. They never got around to visiting her or helping her in any way. She died last year without having heard from them.

3. The anthropologist Barbara Meyerhoff did a study of an elderly community in Venice, California.[6] She tells about the disappointment of a group of elders whose children failed to show up at their graduation from an adult education program:

> The graduates, 26 in all, were arranged in rows flanking the head table. They wore their finest clothing bearing blue and white satin ribbons that crossed the breast from shoulder to waist. Most were solemn and flushed with excitement. . . . No one talked openly about the conspicuous absence of the elders' children (87, 104).

I believe it may be granted that the father who had dined once a week with his daughter has a legitimate complaint. And although Miss Tate was duly salaried throughout her long service with the judge's family, it seems clear that the children of that family owe her some special attention and regard for having brought them up. The graduation ceremony is yet another example of wrongful disregard and neglect. Some recent criticisms of traditional conceptions of filial duty (e.g., by Jane English and John Simmons) make much of examples involving unworthy parents. One may agree that exceptional parents can forfeit their moral claims on their children. (What, given his behavior, remains of Fyodor Karamozov's right to filial regard?) But I am here concerned with what is owed to the average parent who is neglected or whose wishes are disregarded when they could at some reasonable cost be respected. I assume that such filial disregard is wrong. Although the assumption is dogmatic, it can be defended—though not by any quick maneuver. Filial morality is but one topic in the morality of special relations. The attempt to understand filial morality will lead us to a synoptic look at the moral community as a whole and to an examination of the nature of the rights and obligations that bind its members.

II. SHIFTING CONCEPTIONS

Jeffrey Blustein's *Parents and Children (op. cit.)* contains an excellent historical survey of the moral issues in the child-parent relationship. For Aristotle the

---

[6]*Number Our Days* (New York: Simon & Schuster, 1978).

obligation to serve and obey one's parents is like an obligation to repay a debt. Aquinas too explains the commandment to honor one's parents as "making a return for benefits received."[7] Both Aristotle and Aquinas count life itself as the first and most important gift that the child is given.

With Locke[8] the topic of filial morality changes: the discussion shifts from a concern with the authority and power of the parent to concern with the less formal, less enforceable, right to respect. Hume[9] was emphatic on the subject of filial ingratitude, saying, "Of all the crimes that human creatures are capable, the most horrid and unnatural is ingratitude, especially when it is committed against parents." By Sidgwick's time the special duties are beginning to be seen as problematic: "The question is on what principles . . . we are to determine the nature and extent of the special claims of affection and kind services which arise out of . . . particular relations of human beings" (242). Nevertheless, Sidgwick is still traditional in maintaining that "all are agreed that there are such duties, the non-performance of which is ground for censure," and he is himself concerned to show how "our common notion of Justice [is] applicable to these no less than to other duties" (243).

If we look at the writings of a contemporary utilitarian such as Peter Singer,[10] we find no talk of justice or duty or rights, and *a fortiori*, no talk of special duties or parental rights. Consider how Singer, applying a version of R. M. Hare's utilitarianism, approaches a case involving filial respect. He imagines himself about to dine with three friends when his father calls saying he is ill and asking him to visit. What shall he do?

> To decide impartially I must sum up the preferences for and against going to dinner with my friends, and those for and against visiting my father. Whatever action satisfies more preferences, adjusted according to the strength of the preferences, that is the action I ought to take (101).

Note that the idea of a special obligation does not enter here. Nor is any weight given to the history of the filial relationship which typically includes some two decades of parental care and nurture. According to Singer, "adding and subtracting preferences in this manner" is the only rational way of reaching ethical judgment.

Utilitarian theory is not very accommodating to the special relations. And it would appear that Bernard Williams is right in finding the same true of Kantianism. According to Williams,[11] Kant's "moral point of view is specially characterized by its impartiality and its indifference to any particular relations to particular persons." In my opinion, giving no special consideration to one's kin commits what might be called the *Jellyby fallacy*. Mrs. Jellyby, a character in Charles Dickens' *Bleak House*,[12] devotes all of her considerable energies to the

---

[7]*Summa Theologiae*, vol. 34, R. J. Batten, trans. (New York: Blackfriars, 1975), 2a2ae.

[8]John Locke, *Two Treatises of Government*, P. Laslett, ed. (New York: New American Library, 1965), Treatise 1, sec. 100.

[9]David Hume, *A Treatise on Human Nature*, Bk. III, p. 1, sec. 1.

[10]*The Expanding Circle: Ethics and Sociobiology* (New York: Farrar, Straus & Giroux, 1981).

[11]"Persons, Character and Morality," in Moral Luck (New York: Cambridge, 1982), p. 2.

[12]New York: New American Library, 1964.

foreign poor to the complete neglect of her family. She is described as a "pretty diminutive woman with handsome eyes, though they had a curious habit of seeming to look a long way off. As if they could see nothing nearer than Africa" (52). Dickens clearly intends her as someone whose moral priorities are ludicrously disordered. Yet by some modern lights Mrs. Jellyby could be viewed as a paragon of impartial rectitude. In the next two sections I will try to show what is wrong with an impartialist point of view and suggest a way to repair it.

III. THE MORAL DOMAIN

By a *moral domain* I mean a domain consisting of what G. J. Warnock[13] calls "moral patients." Equivalently, it consists of beings that have what Robert Nozick[14] calls "ethical pull." A being has *ethical pull* if it is ethically "considerable"; minimally, it is a being that should not be ill treated by a moral agent and whose ill treatment directly wrongs it. The extent of the moral domain is one area of contention (Mill includes animals; Kant does not). The nature of the moral domain is another. But here we find more uniformity. Utilitarians and deontologists are in agreement in conceiving of the moral domain as constituted by beings whose ethical pull is equal on all moral agents. To simplify matters, let us consider a domain consisting only of moral patients that are also moral agents. (For Kant, this is no special stipulation.) Then it is as if we have a gravitational field in which the force of gravitation is not affected by distance and all pairs of objects have the same attraction to one another. Or, if this sort of gravitational field is odd, consider a mutual admiration society no member of which is, intrinsically, more attractive than any other member. In this group, the pull of all is the same. Suppose that Buridan's ass was not standing in the exact middle of the bridge but was closer to one of the bags of feed at either end. We should still say that he was equally attracted to both bags, but also that he naturally would choose the closer one. So too does the utilitarian or Kantian say that the ethical pull of a needy East African and that of a needy relative are the same, but we can more easily act to help the relative. This theory of equal pull but unequal response saves the appearances for impartiality while acknowledging that, in practice, charity often begins and sometimes ends at home.

This is how the principle of impartiality appears in the moral theories of Kant and Mill. Of course their conceptions of ethical pull differ. For the Kantian any being in the kingdom of ends is an embodiment of moral law whose force is uniform and unconditional. For the utilitarian, any being's desires are morally considerable, exerting equal attraction on all moral agents. Thus Kant and Mill, in their different ways, have a common view of the moral domain as a domain of moral patients exerting uniform pull on all moral agents. I shall refer to this as the *equal-pull (EP) thesis*. It is worth commenting on the underlying assumptions that led Kant and Mill to adopt this view of the moral domain.

[13]*The Object of Morality* (London: Methuen, 1971), p. 152.
[14]*Philosophical Explanations* (Cambridge, Mass.: Harvard, 1981), p. 451.

It is a commonplace that Kant was concerned to free moral agency from its psychological or "anthropological" determinations. In doing so he offered us a conception of moral agents as rational beings which abstracts considerably from human and animal nature. It is less of a commonplace that utilitarian theory, in its modern development, tends also to be antithetical to important empirical aspects of human nature. For the Kantian, the empirical demon to be combatted and exorcized lies within the individual. For the utilitarian it is located within society and its customs, including practices that are the sociobiological inheritance of the species. According to an act utilitarian like Singer, reason frees ethical thought from the earlier moralities of kin and reciprocal altruism and opens it to the wider morality of disinterestedness and universal concern: "The principle of impartial consideration of interests . . . alone remains a rational basis for ethics" *(op. cit.,* 109). The equal-pull thesis is thus seen to be entailed by a principle of impartiality, common to Kantian and utilitarian ethics, which is seen as liberating us from the biased dictates of our psychological, biological, and socially conventional natures.[15]

IV. DIFFERENTIAL PULL

The doctrine of equal ethical pull is a modern development in the history of ethics. It is certainly not attributable to Aristotle or Aquinas, nor, arguably, to Locke. Kant's authority gave it common currency and made it, so to speak, foundational. It is, therefore, important to state that EP is a dogma. Why should it be assumed that ethical pull is constant regardless of circumstance, familiarity, kinship and other special relations? The accepted answer is that EP makes sense of impartiality. The proponent of the special duties must accept this as a challenge: alternative suggestions for moral ontology must show how impartiality can be consistent with differential ethical forces.

I will refer to the rival thesis as the *thesis of differential pull (DP).* According to the DP thesis, the ethical pull of a moral patient will always partly depend on how the moral patient is related to the moral agent on whom the pull is exerted. Moreover, the "how" of relatedness will be determined in part by the social practices and institutions in which the agent and patient play their roles. This does not mean that every moral agent will be differently affected, since it may be that different moral agents stand in the same relation to different moral patients. But where the relations differ in certain relevant ways, there the pull will

---

[15]See Alasdair MacIntyre, *After Virtue* (Notre Dame, Ind.: University Press, 1981). When one contrasts this modern approach to morality with classical approaches that give full play to the social and biological natures of moral agents in determining the range of moral behavior, one may come to see the history of ethics in terms of a MacIntyrean Fall; MacIntyre speaks of the "crucial moral opposition between liberal individualism in some version or other and the Aristotelian tradition in some version or other" (241). For MacIntyre, the Enlightenment is a new Dark Age both because of its abstract conception of the autonomous individual and because of the neglect of parochial contexts in determining the special obligations that were once naturally understood in terms of social roles.

differ. The relevant factors that determine ethical pull are in a broad sense circumstantial, including the particular social arrangements that determine what is expected from the moral agent. How particular circumstances and conventions shape the special duties is a complex question to which we cannot here do justice. We shall, however, approach it from a foundational standpoint which rejects EP and recognizes the crucial role of conventional practice, relationships, and roles in determining the nature and force of moral obligation. The gravitational metaphor may again be suggestive. In DP morality the community of agents and patients is analogous to a gravitational field where distance counts and forces vary in accordance with local conditions.

V. FILIAL DUTY

Filial duty, unlike the duty to keep a promise, is not self-imposed. But keeping the particular promise one has made is also a special duty, and the interplay of impartiality and specific obligation is more clearly seen in the case of a promise. We do well, therefore, to look at the way special circumstances shape obligations by examining more carefully the case of promise making.

A. I. Melden[16] has gone into the morality of promise keeping rather thoroughly, and I believe that some features of his analysis apply to the more general description of the way particular circumstances determine the degree of ethical pull on a moral agent. Following Locke, Melden assumes the natural right of noninterference with one's liberty to pursue one's interests (including one's interest in the well-being of others) where such pursuit does not interfere with a like liberty for others. Let an interest be called *invasive* if it is an interest in interfering with the pursuit of someone else's interests. Then the right that every moral patient possesses is the right not to be interfered with in the pursuit of his or her noninvasive interests. (In what follows 'interest' will mean noninvasive interest.)

According to Melden, a promiser "gives the promisee the action as his own." The promise-breaking failure to perform is then "tantamount to interfering with or subverting endeavours he [the promisee] has a right to pursue" (47). The promisee is "as entitled to [the action] as he is, as a responsible agent, to conduct his own affairs." What is special about this analysis is the formal grounding of the special positive duty of promise keeping in the minimalist negative obligation of noninterference. The negative, general, and indiscriminate obligation not to interfere is determined by the practice of promise making as a positive, specific, and discriminate obligation to act. Note how context here shapes and directs the initial obligation of noninterference and enhances its force. Given the conventions of the practice of promise making, the moral patient has novel and legitimate expectations of performances caused by the explicit assurances given by the promiser, who, in effect, has made over these

[16]*Rights and Persons* (Los Angeles: California UP, 1977).

performances to the promisee. And given these legitimate expectations, the agent's nonperformance of the promised act is invasive and tantamount to active interference with the patient's rights to its performance.

It is in the spirit of this approach to make the attempt to analyze other special obligations in the same manner. We assume a DP framework and a minimal universal deontological principle (the duty to refrain from interfering in the lives of others). This negative duty is refracted by the parochial situation as a special duty which may be positive in character, calling on the moral agent to act or refrain from acting in specific ways toward specific moral patients. This view of the special obligations needs to be justified. But for the present I merely seek to state it more fully.

The presumption of a special positive obligation arises for amoral agent when two conditions obtain: (1) In a given social arrangement (or practice) there is a specific interaction or transaction between moral agent and patient, such as promising and being promised, nurturing and being nurtured, befriending and being befriended. (2) The interaction in that context gives rise to certain conventional expectations (e.g., that a promise will be kept, that a marital partner will be faithful, that a child will respect the parent). In promising, the content of the obligation is verbally explicit. But this feature is not essential to the formation of other specific duties. In the filial situation, the basic relationship is that of nurtured to nurturer, a type of relationship which is very concrete, intimate, and long-lasting and which is considered to be more morally determining than any other in shaping a variety of rights and obligations.

Here is one of Alasdair MacIntyre's descriptions of the denizens of the moral domain:

> I am brother, cousin, and grandson, member of this household, that village, this tribe. These are not characteristics that belong to human beings accidentally, to be stripped away in order to discover "the real me". They are part of my substance, defining partially at least and sometimes wholly my obligations and my duties (32).

MacIntyre's description takes Aristotle's dictum that man is a social animal in a sociological direction. A social animal has a specific social role whose prerogatives and obligations characterize a particular kind of person. Being a father or mother is socially as well as biologically descriptive: it not only defines what one is; it also defines who one is and what one owes.

Because it does violence to a social role, a filial breach is more serious than a breach of promise. In the promise the performance is legitimately expected, being, as it were, explicitly made over to the promisee as "his." In the filial situation the expected behavior is implicit, and the failure to perform affects the parent in a direct and personal way. To lose one's entitlements diminishes one as a person. Literature abounds with examples of such diminishment; King Lear is perhaps the paradigm. When Lear first becomes aware of Goneril's defection, he asks his companion: "Who am I?" to which the reply is "A shadow." Causing humiliation is a prime reason why filial neglect is tantamount to active interference. One's sense of dignity varies with temperament. But dignity itself—in the context of an institution like the family—is objective, being inseparable from one's status and role in that context.

The filial duties of adult children include such things as being grateful, loyal, attentive, respectful and deferential to parents (more so than to strangers). Many adult children, of course, are respectful and attentive to their parents out of love, not duty. But, as Melden says: "The fact that, normally, there is love and affection that unites the members of the family . . . in no way undercuts the fact that there is a characteristic distribution of rights and obligations within the family circle" (67).

The mutual understanding created by a promise is simplicity itself when compared with the range of expected behavior that filial respect comprises. What is expected in the case of a promise is clearly specified by the moral agent, but with respect to most other special duties there is little that is verbally explicit. Filial obligation is thus essentially underdetermined, although there are clear cases of what counts as disrespect—as we have seen in our three cases. The complexity and nonspecificity of expected behavior which is written into the domestic arrangements do not affect what the promissory and the filial situation have in common: both may be viewed as particular contexts in which the moral agent must refrain from behavior that interferes with the normal prerogatives of the moral patient.[17]

By taking promising as a starting point in a discussion of special duties, one runs the risk of giving the impression that DP is generally to be understood as a form of social-contract theory. But a more balanced perspective considers the acts required by any of the special duties as naturally and implicitly "made over" within the practices and institutions that define the moral agent in his particular role as a "social animal." Within this perspective promising and other forms of contracting are themselves special cases and not paradigmatic. Indeed, the binding force of the obligation to fulfill an explicit contract is itself to be explained by the general account to be given of special duties in a DP theory.

VI. GRATEFUL DUTY

One group of contemporary moral philosophers, whom I shall tendentiously dub *sentimentalists*, has been vocal in pointing out the shortcomings of the mainstream theories in accounting for the morality of the special relations. But they would find my formal and traditional approach equally inadequate. The sentimentalists oppose deontological approaches to the morality of the parent-child

---

[17]Our account of the special moral relations is concentrating on the way the universal duty to refrain from invasive interference is refracted through circumstance into a variety of positive and discriminate duties. But a particular arrangement may produce the opposite effect: it may qualify the universal obligation to refrain from invasive interference by allowing the moral agent liberties normally forbidden. A fair amount of invasive behavior is the norm in certain private and voluntary arrangements where there is an understanding that exceptional demands may be made. My particular concern with the positive (filial) obligations has led me to confine discussion to the way context obligates moral agents to perform and not with how or to what extent it may license them.

relationship, arguing that *duties* of gratitude are paradoxical, that the "owing idiom" distorts the moral ideal of the parent-child relationship which should be characterized by love and mutual respect. For them, each family relationship is unique, its moral character determined by the idiosyncratic ties of its members. Carol Gilligan[18] has recently distinguished between an "ethic of care" and an "ethic of rights." The philosophers I have in mind are objecting to the aridity of the "rights perspective" and are urging moral philosophers to attend to the morality of special relations from a "care perspective." The distinction is suggestive, but the two perspectives are not necessarily exclusive. One may recognize one's duty in what one does spontaneously and generously. And just as a Kantian caricature holds one in greater esteem when one does what is right against one's inclination, so the idea of care, responsibility and personal commitment, without formal obligation, is an equally dangerous caricature.

Approaches that oppose care and friendship to rights and obligations can be shown to be sadly inadequate when applied to real-life cases. The following situation described in this letter to Ann Landers is not atypical:

> Dear Ann Landers:
> We have five children, all overachievers who have studied hard and done well. Two are medical doctors and one is a banker. . . . We are broke from paying off debts for their wedding and their education. . . . We rarely hear from our children. . . . Last week my husband asked our eldest son for some financial help. He was told 'File bankruptcy and move into a small apartment.' Ann, personal feelings are no longer a factor: it is a matter of survival. Is there any law that says our children must help out?[19]

There are laws in some states that would require that these children provide some minimal support for their indigent parents. But not a few contemporary philosophers could be aptly cited by those who would advocate their repeal. A. John Simmons, Jeffrey Blustein, and Michael Slote, for example, doubt that filial duty is to be understood in terms of special moral debts *owed* to parents. Simmons offers "reasons to believe that [the] particular duty meeting conduct [of parents to children] does not generate an obligation of gratitude on the child" (*op. cit.*, 182). And Blustein opposes what he and Jane English call the "owing idiom" for services parents were obligated to perform. "If parents have any right to repayment from their children, it can only be for that which was either above and beyond the call of parental duty, or not required by parental duty at all"[20] (The "overachievers" could not agree more.) Slote finds it "difficult to believe that one has a *duty* to show gratitude for benefits one has not requested" (320). Jane English characterizes filial duty in terms of the duties one good friend owes another. "[A]fter a friendship ends, the duties of friendship end" (354, 356).

Taking a sentimentalist view of gratitude, these philosophers are concerned to remove the taint of onerous duty from what should be a spontaneous and

---

[18]*In a Different Voice* (Cambridge, Mass.: Harvard, 1983).

[19]*The Boston Globe,* Thursday, March 21, 1985.

[20]Blustein, p. 182. According to Blustein, parents who are financially able are *obligated* to provide educational opportunities for children who are able to benefit from them.

free desire to be considerate of one's parents. One may agree with the sentimentalists that there is something morally unsatisfactory in being considerate of one's parents *merely* out of duty. The mistake lies in thinking that duty and inclination are necessarily at odds. Moreover, the *having* of certain feelings and attitudes may be necessary for carrying out one's duty. Persons who lack feeling for their parents may be morally culpable for that very lack. The sentimentalist objection that this amounts to a paradoxical duty to *feel* (grateful, loyal, etc.) ignores the extent to which people are responsible for their characters; to have failed to develop in oneself the capacity to be considerate of others is to have failed morally, if only because many duties simply cannot be carried out by a cold and unfeeling moral agent.[21] Kant himself speaks of "the universal duty which devolves upon man of so ordering his life as to be fit for the performance of all moral duties."[22] And MacIntyre, who is no Kantian, makes the same point when he says, "moral education is an 'education sentimentale'" (151).

Sentimentalism is not harmlessly false. Its moral perspective on family relationships as spontaneous, voluntary, and duty-free is simply unrealistic. Anthropological observations provide a sounder perspective on filial obligation. Thus Corinne Nydegger[23] warns of the dangers of weakening the formal constraints that ensure that obligations are met: "No society, including our own, relies solely on affection, good will and enlightened self-interest." She notes that the aged in particular "have a vested interest in the social control of obligations" (30).

It should be noted that the sentimentalist is arguing for amorality that is sensitive to special relations and personal commitment; this is in its own way a critique of EP morality. But sentimentalism ignores the extent to which the "care perspective" is itself dependent on a formal sense of what is fitting and morally proper. The ideal relationship cannot be "duty-free," if only because sentimental ties may come unraveled, often leaving one of the parties at a material disadvantage. Sentimentalism then places in a precarious position those who are not (or no longer) the fortunate beneficiaries of sincere personal commitments. If the EP moralist tends to be implausibly abstract and therefore inattentive to the morality of the special relations, the sentimentalist tends to err on the side of excessive narrowness by neglecting the impersonal "institutional" expectations and norms that qualify all special relations.

VII. DP MORALITY: SOME QUALIFICATIONS

It might be thought that the difference between EP and DP tends to disappear when either theory is applied to concrete cases, since one must in any case look

---

[21]See Marcia Baron, "The Alleged Moral Repugnance of Acting from Duty," this JOURNAL, LXXXI, 4 (April 1984): 197–220, especially pp. 204/5. She speaks of "the importance of the attitudes and dispositions one has when one performs certain acts, especially those which are intended to express affection or concern" and suggests that these attitudes constitute "certain parameters within which satisfactory ways of acting from duty must be located."

[22]Immanuel Kant, "Proper Self-respect," from *Lectures on Ethics,* Louis Enfield, trans. (New York: Harper & Row, 1963).

[23]"Family Ties of the Aged in Cross-cultural Perspective," *The Gerontologist,* XXIII, 1 (1983): 30.

at the circumstances to determine the practical response. But this is to underestimate how what one *initially* takes to be the responsibility of moral agents to patients affects the procedure one uses in making practical decisions in particular circumstances. Recall again how Peter Singer's EP procedure pits the preferences of the three friends against the preferences of the father, and contrast this with a differential-pull approach that assumes discriminate and focused obligations to the father. Similarly, the adult children of the graduating elders and the children raised by Miss Tate gave no special weight to filial obligation in planning their day's activities.

There are, then, significant practical differences between a DP and an EP approach to concrete cases. The EP moralist is a respecter of the person whom he sees as an autonomous individual but no respector of the person as a social animal within its parochial preserve. Moreover, a DP theory that grounds duty in the minimal principle of noninterference is sensitive to the distinction between strict duty and benevolence. Behaving as one is dutybound to behave is not the whole of moral life. But duty (in the narrow sense) and benevolence are not commensurate. If I am right, the Anaheim woman is culpably disrespectful. But it would be absurd if (in the manner of Mrs. Jellyby) she were to try to compensate for excluding her father by inviting several indigent gentlemen to dine in his stead.

I am arguing for a DP approach to the morality of the special relations. Williams, Nozick, MacIntyre, and others criticize: utilitarianism and Kantianism for implausible consequences in this area. I believe that their objections to much of contemporary ethics are symptomatic of a growing discontent with the EP character of the current theories. It may be possible to revise the theories to avoid some of the implausible consequences. Rule utilitarianism seems to be a move in this direction. But, as they stand, their EP character leaves them open to criticism. EP is a dogma. But so is DP. My contention is that DP moral theories more plausibly account for our preanalytic moral judgments concerning what is right and wrong in a wide variety of real cases. Having said this, I will acknowledge that the proper antidote to the malaise Williams and others are pointing to will not be effectively available until DP moral theories are given a theoretical foundation as well worked out as those of the mainstream theories. Alasdair MacIntyre is a contemporary DP moralist who has perhaps gone furthest in this direction. Nozick and Williams are at least cognizant that a "particularistic" approach is needed.[24]

The DP moral theory is in any case better able to account for the discriminate duties that correspond to specific social roles and expectations. But of course not all duties are discriminate: there are requirements that devolve on

---

[24]Unfortunately, Nozick's particularism is "sentimentalist": "[Some] views will countenance particularism on one level by deriving it from 'universalistic' principles that hold at some deeper level. This misconstrues the moral weight of particularistic ties it seems to me; it is a worthwhile task, one I cannot undertake explicitly here, to investigate the nature of a more consistently particularistic theory—particularistic all the way down the line" [*Philosophical Explanations* (New York: Cambridge, 1981), 456/7]. The particularistic ties Nozick has in mind are not objectively institutional but subjectively interpersonal ("valuing the particularity of the other").

everyone. This not only includes the negative requirement to refrain from harming one's fellowman, but also, in certain circumstances, to help him when one is singularly situated to do so. I am, for example, expected to help a lost child find its parent or to feed a starving stranger at my doorstep. Failure to do so violates an understanding that characterizes the loosest social ties binding us as fellow human beings. The "solitariness" that Hobbes speaks of is a myth; we are never in a totally unrelated "state of nature." The DP moralist recognizes degrees of relatedness and graded expectations. The most general types of positive behavior expected of anyone as a moral agent obey some minimal principle of Good Samaritanism applicable to "the stranger in thy midst."

Perhaps the most serious difficulty facing the DP approach is that it appears to leave the door wide open to ethical relativism. We turn now to this problem.

VIII. DP AND ETHICAL RELATIVISM

A theory is nonrelativistic if it has the resources to pass moral judgments on whole societies. My version of DP moral theory avoids ethical relativism by adopting a deontological principle (noninterference) which may be deployed in assessing and criticizing the moral legitimacy of the traditional arrangements within which purportedly moral interactions take place. We distinguish between unjust and merely imperfect arrangements. Arrangements that are essentially invasive are unjust and do not confer moral legitimacy on what is expected of those who are party to them. To correct the abuses of an unjust institution like slavery or a practice like suttee is to destroy the institution or practice. By contrast, an institution like marriage or the family will often contain some unjust features, but these are usually corrigible, and the institution itself is legitimate and morally determining in a straightforward sense.

In any case the DP moralist is in a position to hold that not all social arrangements impose moral imperatives. It is not clear to me that DP can avoid relativism without *some* deontological minimal ground. But conceivably a principle other than noninterference might better serve as universal ground of the special duties. What is essential to any deontologically grounded DP morality is the recognition that the universal deontological principle is differentiated and specified by local arrangements that determine what is legitimately expected of the moral agent.

It may now be clear in what sense I believe DP theories to be plausible. A moral theory is plausible to the extent that it accounts for our pretheoretical moral judgments. Such intuitive judgments are admittedly idiosyncratic and prejudicial, being conditioned by our upbringing and the traditions we live by. The EP moralist nobly courts implausibility by jettisoning prejudice and confronting moral decisions anew. By contrast, the DP moralist jettisons only those prejudices which are exposed as rooted in and conditioned by an unjust social arrangement. But for those institutions which are not unjust, our common-sense judgments of "what is expected" (from parents, from citizens, from adult children) are generally held to be reliable guides to the moral facts of life.

The version of DP that I favor accepts the Enlightenment doctrine of natural rights in the minimal form of a universal right to noninterference and the correlative duty of moral agents to respect that right. MacIntyre's version of DP is hostile to Enlightenment "modernism," abjuring all talk of universal rights or deontic principles of a universal character. It is in this sense more classical. An adequate version of DP must nevertheless avoid the kind of ethical relativism that affords the moral philosopher no way to reject some social arrangements as immoral. MacIntyre appears to suggest that this can be achieved by accepting certain teleological constraints on good societies. Pending more detail, I am not convinced that a teleological approach can by itself do the critical job that needs to be done if we are to avoid an unacceptable ethical relativism. But other non-deontic approaches are possible. David Wong[25] has argued for a Confucian condition of adequacy that grades societies as better or worse depending on how well they foster human flourishing. My own deontic approach is not opposed to teleological or Confucianist ways of judging the acceptability of social arrangements. If a given arrangement is degenerate, then that is in itself a good reason to discount its norms as morally binding. But conceivably even a flourishing society could be unjust; nevertheless its civic norms should count as morally vacuous and illegitimate. It seems to me, therefore, that MacIntyre's version of DP morality probably goes too far in its rejection of all liberal deontic principles.

I have argued that DP best explains what we intuitively accept as our moral obligations to parents and other persons who stand to us in special relations. And though my version of DP allows for criticizing unjust social arrangements, it may still seem unacceptably relativistic. For does it not allow that what is right for a daughter or son in one society is wrong for them in another? And does this not run afoul of the condition that what is right and wrong must be so universally? It should, I think, be acknowledged that the conservatism that is a feature of the doctrine of differential pull is somewhat hospitable to ethical relativism. Put another way: differential pull makes sense of ethical relativism's large grain of truth, but it does so without losing claim to its ability to evaluate morally the norms of different societies and institutions. Institutions that allow or encourage interference with noninvasive interests are unjust, and we have noted that the adherent of differential pull is in as good a position to apply a universal principle in evaluating an institution as anyone of an EP persuasion. But application of DP will rule out some institutions while allowing *diverse* others to count as legitimate and just. Only a just institution can assign and shape a moral obligation for those who play their roles within it. However, there are many varieties of just institutions, and so, in particular, are there many ways in which filial obligations are determined within different social and cultural contexts. What counts as filial respect in one context may not count as filial respect in another context. It is a virtue of our account that it not only tolerates but shows the way to justify different moral norms.

---

[25]*Moral Relativity* (Berkeley: California UP, 1984).

IX. COMMON SENSE

The sociologist Edward Shils[26] warns about the consequences of the modern hostility to tradition in ways reminiscent of ecologists warning us about tampering with delicate natural systems that have taken millenia to evolve. The EP character of much of modern philosophy encourages a hasty style of playing fast and loose with practices and institutions that define the traditional ties binding the members of a family or community. And a duty-free sentimentalism is no kinder to traditional mores.

The appeal to common sense is often a way of paying proper attention to the way that particular circumstance and social practice enter into the shaping of obligations. This, to my mind, is Sidgwick's peculiar and saving grace. But many a moral philosopher lacks Sidgwick's firm appreciation of the role of accepted practice or common sense. I shall illustrate this by way of a final example.

Richard Wasserstrom in "Is Adultery Immoral?"[27] raises the question of whether the (alleged) obligation not to commit adultery might be explained by reasons that would apply to any two persons generally. It is, for example, wrong for any person to deceive another. And he discusses the destructive effects adultery has on the love that the marital partners bear to one another. What is missing from Wasserstrom's account is any hint that the obligations of marriage are shaped by the institution as it exists and that being "faithful" is a legitimate institutional expectation informing the way that the partners may treat each other. Wasserstrom does say that "we ought to have reasons for believing that marriage is a morally desirable and just social institution" (300). But what follows if it is? Wasserstrom does not say. What we want here is an account of how and why a married person who commits adultery may be wronging the partner. How, in particular, might an act of adultery be construed as unwarranted interference? The shift from the examination of an obligation that has its locus and form within a given institution to evaluating the institution itself is legitimate; but it is all too often a way of avoiding the more concrete and immediate investigation which is the bread and butter of normative ethics.

EP is ethics without ethos. So too is sentimentalism. Both have a disintegrative effect on tradition. Where EP and sentimentalism sit in judgment on ethos, DP respects it and seeks to rationalize it. The EP moralist is reformist in spirit, tending to look upon traditional arrangements as obstacles to social justice. John Rawls,[28] for example, is led to wonder whether the family is ethically justifiable:

> It seems that even when fair opportunity (as it has been defined) is satisfied, the family will lead to unequal chances between individuals. Is the family to be

[26]Edward Shils, *Tradition* (Chicago: University of Chicago Press, 1981).
[27]In Wasserstrom, ed., *Today's Moral Problems*, pp. 288–300. Michael Tooley's arguments for the moral legitimacy of infanticide provide another example of the consequences of uninhibited EP zeal. See his book *Abortion and Infanticide* (New York: Oxford, 1984), and my critical review "Tooley's Immodest Proposal," *Hastings Center Report*, xv, 5 (June 1985): 39–42.
[28]*A Theory of Justice* (Cambridge, Mass.: Harvard, 1971).

abolished then? Taken by itself and given a certain primacy, the idea of equal opportunity inclines in this direction. But within the context of the theory of justice as a whole, there is less urgency to take this course (511).

Not urgent perhaps, but not unreasonable either. A defender of filial morality cannot with equanimity entertain the idea of abolishing the family. Here Sidgwick is the welcome antidote. For him the suggestion that ethical principles might require the elimination of something so central to "established morality" betrays a misconception of the job of ethics, instead, Sidgwick demands of philosophers that they "repudiate altogether that temper of rebellion . . . into which the reflective mind is always apt to fall when it is first convinced that the established rules are not intrinsically reasonable" (475).[29]

Reporting on how he arrived at his way of doing moral philosophy, Sidgwick tells of his rereading of Aristotle:

> [A] light seemed to dawn upon me as to the meaning and drift of [Aristotle's] procedure. . . . What he gave us there was the Common Sense Morality of Greece, reduced to consistency by careful comparison: given not as something external to him but as what "we"—he and others—think, ascertained by reflection . . . Might I not imitate this: do the same for our morality here and now, in the same manner of impartial reflection on current opinion? (xx)

Questions

1. What is the "theory of equal pull but unequal response" that Christina Hoff Sommers describes?
2. What two conditions does the author say must be met for a presumption of a special obligation to arise?
3. Do you think that DP can avoid the charge of being a form of ethical relativism? How and why does the author think it differs from ethical relativism?

Suggestions for Further Reading on Familial and Filial Duties:

BLUSTEIN, JEFFREY. *Parents and Children: The Ethics of the Family.* Oxford: Oxford University Press, 1982.

COLLINGRIDGE, MICHAEL and SEAMUS MILLER. "Filial Responsibility and the Care of the Aged." *Journal of Applied Philosophy* 14, no 2 (1997): pp. 119–128.

DIXON, NICHOLAS. "The Friendship Model of Filial Obligations." *Journal of Applied Philosophy* 12, no. 1 (1995): pp. 77–87.

SLOTE, MICHAEL. "Obedience and Illusions." In *Having Children*, edited by Onora O'Neill and William Ruddick, New York: Oxford University Press, 1982: pp. 319–325.

[29]C. D. Broad especially cautions utilitarian readers of Sidgwick to take this side of him seriously. "When all the relevant facts are taken into consideration it will scarcely ever be right for the utilitarian to break the rules of morality commonly accepted in his society" [*Five Types of Ethical Theory* (New York: Humanities, 1951), p. 157].

PART FOUR

Animals

CHAPTER 10

Eating Meat and Wearing Leather

All Animals Are Equal

Peter Singer

Peter Singer argues that just as the equality of men and women and people of different races is not undermined by the differences between them, so the differences between humans and non-human animals do not negate equality of the species. This is because equality is a moral idea—a prescription of how we should treat beings—and not a descriptive claim. He hastens to clarify that the principle of equality, whether applied to different sexes, different races, or different species, does not require identical treatment, *but only* equal consideration.

Treating beings differently is justified where there is some relevant *factual difference between them. That humans do and dogs do not have the capacities necessary to vote makes it acceptable to grant humans but deny dogs the vote. However, the unequal intellectual or rational capacities of animals and humans, like the intellectual inequalities between individual humans, is not relevant to determining whether a being is worthy of equal consideration. The relevant capacity for equal consideration, says the author, is the capacity of suffering and enjoyment. This*

capacity, he says, is a prerequisite for having interests at all.

Those for whom the interests of their own species are more important than the same interests of other species are guilty of "speciesism," a term that, like "racism" and "sexism," refers to a form of wrongful discrimination. Most humans, the author claims, are speciesists because they accept the sacrifice of the most important interests of non-human animals in order to serve even the most trivial interests of humans (as happens when animals are subjected to extremely painful treatments and living conditions in order to provide meat or eggs for humans).

The author argues that we have no good reasons for thinking that animals (at least those, such as mammals and birds, which are most like us) do not feel pain. Given that they feel pain, the principle of equality requires that we treat their pain in the same way as we treat the same levels of pain in humans. That is to say, if it is wrong to inflict a particular level of pain on a human without good reason, then it must be equally wrong to inflict the same level of pain on an animal

Peter Singer, "All Animals Are Equal," in *Animal Liberation* (New York: Avon Books, 1990).

without the same degree of justification. He concludes with some comments about the value of human and animal life, arguing that often a human life will be worth more than an animal life but that sometimes an animal life will be worth more than a human life.

"Animal Liberation" may sound more like a parody of other liberation movements than a serious objective. The idea of "The Rights of Animals" actually was once used to parody the case for women's rights. When Mary Wollstonecraft, a forerunner of today's feminists, published her *Vindication of the Rights of Woman* in 1792, her views were widely regarded as absurd, and before long an anonymous publication appeared entitled *A Vindication of the Rights of Brutes.* The author of this satirical work (now known to have been Thomas Taylor, a distinguished Cambridge philosopher) tried to refute Mary Wollstonecraft's arguments by showing that they could be carried one stage further. If the argument for equality was sound when applied to women, why should it not be applied to dogs, cats, and horses? The reasoning seemed to hold for these "brutes" too; yet to hold that brutes had rights was manifestly absurd. Therefore the reasoning by which this conclusion had been reached must be unsound, and if unsound when applied to brutes, it must also be unsound when applied to women, since the very same arguments had been used in each case.

In order to explain the basis of the case for the equality of animals, it will be helpful to start with an examination of the case for the equality of women. Let us assume that we wish to defend the case for women's rights against the attack by Thomas Taylor. How should we reply?

One way in which we might reply is by saying that the case for equality between men and women cannot validly be extended to non-human animals. Women have a right to vote, for instance, because they are just as capable of making rational decisions about the future as men are; dogs, on the other hand, are incapable of understanding the significance of voting, so they cannot have the right to vote. There are many other obvious ways in which men and women resemble each other closely, while humans and animals differ greatly. So, it might be said, men and women are similar beings and should have similar rights, while humans and non-humans are different and should not have equal rights.

The reasoning behind this reply to Taylor's analogy is correct up to a point, but it does not go far enough. There are obviously important differences between humans and other animals, and these differences must give rise to some differences in the rights that each have. Recognizing this evident fact, however, is no barrier to the case for extending the basic principle of equality to non-human animals. The differences that exist between men and women are equally undeniable, and the supporters of Women's Liberation are aware that these differences may give rise to different rights. Many feminists hold that women have the right to an abortion on request. It does not follow that since these same feminists are campaigning for equality between men and women they must support the right of men to have abortions too. Since a man cannot have an abortion, it is meaningless to talk of his right to have one. Since dogs can't vote, it is meaningless to talk of their right to vote. There is no reason why either Women's Liberation or Animal Liberation should get involved in such nonsense. The extension of the basic principle of equality from one group to another does not imply that we must treat both groups in exactly the same way, or grant exactly the same rights to both groups. Whether we should do so will depend on the nature of the members of the two groups. The basic principle of equality does not require equal or identical *treatment*; it requires equal consideration. Equal consideration for different beings may lead to different treatment and different rights.

So there is a different way of replying to Taylor's attempt to parody the case for women's rights, a way that does not deny the obvious differences between human beings and non-humans but goes more deeply into the question of equality and concludes by finding nothing absurd in the idea that the basic principle of equality applies to so-called brutes. At this point such a conclusion may appear odd; but if we examine more deeply the basis on which our opposition to discrimination on grounds of race or sex ultimately rests, we will see that we would be on shaky ground if we were to demand equality for blacks, women, and other groups of oppressed humans while denying equal consideration to non-humans. To make this clear we need to see, first, exactly why racism and sexism are wrong. When we say that all human beings, whatever their race, creed, or sex, are equal, what is it that we are asserting? Those who wish to defend hierarchical, inegalitarian societies have often pointed out that by whatever test we choose it simply is not true that all humans are equal. Like it or not we must face the fact that humans come in different shapes and sizes; they come with different moral capacities, different intellectual abilities, different amounts of benevolent feeling and sensitivity to the needs of others, different abilities to communicate effectively, and different capacities to experience pleasure and pain. In short, if the demand for equality were based on the actual equality of all human beings, we would have to stop demanding equality.

Still, one might cling to the view that the demand for equality among human beings is based on the actual equality of the different races and sexes. Although, it may be said, humans differ as individuals, there are no differences between the races and sexes as such. From the mere fact that a person is black or a woman we cannot infer anything about that person's intellectual or moral capacities. This, it may be said, is why racism and sexism are wrong. The white racist claims that whites are superior to blacks, but this is false; although there are some differences among individuals, some blacks are superior to some whites in all of the capacities and abilities that could conceivably be relevant. The opponent of sexism would say the same: a person's sex is no guide to his or her abilities, and this is why it is unjustifiable to discriminate on the basis of sex.

The existence of individual variations that cut across the lines of race or sex, however, provides us with no defense at all against a more sophisticated opponent of equality, one who proposes that, say, the interests of all those with IQ scores below 100 be given less consideration than the interests of those with ratings over 100. Perhaps those scoring below the mark would, in this society, be made the slaves of those scoring higher. Would a hierarchical society of this sort really be so much better than one based on race or sex? I think not. But if we tie the moral principle of equality to the factual equality of the different races or sexes, taken as a whole, our opposition to racism and sexism does not provide us with any basis for objecting to this kind of inegalitarianism.

There is a second important reason why we ought not to base our opposition to racism and sexism on any kind of factual equality, even the limited kind that asserts that variations in capacities and abilities are spread evenly among the different races and between the sexes: we can have no absolute guarantee that these capacities and abilities really are distributed evenly, without regard to race or sex, among human beings. So far as actual abilities are concerned there do seem to be certain measurable differences both among races and between sexes. These differences do not, of course, appear in every case, but only when averages are taken. More important still, we do not yet know how many of these differences are really due to the different genetic endowments of the different races and sexes, and how many are due to poor schools, poor housing, and other factors that are the result of past and continuing discrimination. Perhaps all of the important differences will eventually prove to be environmental rather than genetic. Anyone opposed to racism and sexism will certainly hope that this will be so, for it will make the task of ending discrimination a lot easier; nevertheless, it would be dangerous to rest the case against racism and sexism on the belief that all significant differences are environmental in origin. The opponent of, say, racism who takes this line will be unable to avoid conceding that if differences in ability did after all prove to have some genetic connection with race, racism would in some way be defensible.

Fortunately there is no need to pin the case for equality to one particular outcome of a scientific investigation. The appropriate response to those who claim to have found evidence of genetically based differences in ability among the races or between the sexes is not to stick to the belief that the genetic explanation must be wrong, whatever evidence to the contrary may turn up; instead we should make it quite clear that the claim to equality does not depend on intelligence, moral capacity, physical strength, or similar matters of fact. Equality is a moral idea, not an assertion of fact. There is no logically compelling reason for assuming that a factual difference in ability between two people justifies any difference in the amount of consideration we give to their needs and interests. *The principle of the equality of human beings is not a description of an alleged actual equality among humans: it is a prescription of how we should treat human beings.*

Jeremy Bentham, the founder of the reforming utilitarian school of moral philosophy, incorporated the essential basis of moral equality into his system of ethics by means of the formula: "Each to count for one and none for more than one." In other words, the interests of every being affected by an action are to be taken into account and given the same weight as the like interests of any other being. A later utilitarian, Henry Sidgwick, put the point in this way: "The good of any one individual is of no more importance, from the point of view (if I may say so) of the Universe, than the good of any other." More recently the leading figures in contemporary moral philosophy have shown a great deal of agreement in specifying as a fundamental presupposition of their moral theories some similar requirement that works to give everyone's interests equal consideration—although these writers generally cannot agree on how this requirement is best formulated.[1]

It is an implication of this principle of equality that our concern for others and our readiness to consider their interests ought not to depend on what they are like or what abilities they may possess. Precisely what our concern or consideration requires us to do may vary according to the characteristics of those affected by what we do: concern for the well-being of children growing up in America would require that we teach them to read; concern for the well-being of pigs may require no more than that we leave them with other pigs in a place where there is adequate food and room to run freely. But the basic element—the taking into account of the interests of the being, whatever those interests may be—must, according to the principle of equality, be extended to all beings, black or white, masculine or feminine, human or non-human.

Thomas Jefferson, who was responsible for writing the principle of the equality of men into the American Declaration of Independence, saw this point. It led him to oppose slavery even though he was unable to free himself fully from his slaveholding background. He wrote in a letter to the author of a book that emphasized the notable intellectual achievements of Negroes in order to refute the then common view that they had limited intellectual capacities:

> Be assured that no person living wishes more sincerely than I do, to see a complete refutation of the doubts I myself have entertained and expressed on the grade of understanding allotted to them by nature, and to find that they are on a par with ourselves . . . but whatever be their degree of talent it is no measure of their rights. Because Sir Isaac Newton was superior to others in understanding, he was not therefore lord of the property or persons of others.[2]

Similarly, when in the 1850s the call for women's rights was raised in the United States, a remarkable black feminist named Sojourner Truth made the same point in more robust terms at a feminist convention:

> They talk about this thing in the head; what do they call it? ["Intellect," whispered someone nearby.] That's it. What's that got to do with women's rights or Negroes' rights? If my cup won't hold but a pint and yours holds a quart, wouldn't you be mean not to let me have my little half-measure full?[3]

---

[1]For Bentham's moral philosophy, see his *Introduction to the Principles of Morals and Legislation*, and for Sidgwick's see *The Methods of Ethics*, 1907 (the passage is quoted from the seventh edition; reprint, London: Macmillan, 1963), p. 382. As examples of leading contemporary moral philosophers who incorporate a requirement of equal consideration of interests, see R. M. Hare, *Freedom and Reason* (New York: Oxford University Press, 1963), and John Rawls, *A Theory of Justice* (Cambridge: Harvard University Press, Belknap Press, 1972). For a brief account of the essential agreement on this issue between these and other positions, see R. M. Hare, "Rules of War and Moral Reasoning," *Philosophy and Public Affairs* 1 (2) (1972).

[2]Letter to Henry Gregoire, February 25, 1809.

[3]Reminiscences by Francis D. Gage, from Susan B. Anthony, *The History of Woman Suffrage*, vol. 1; the passage is to be found in the extract in Leslie Tanner, ed., *Voices From Women's Liberation* (New York: Signet, 1970).

It is on this basis that the case against racism and the case against sexism must both ultimately rest; and it is in accordance with this principle that the attitude that we may call "speciesism," by analogy with racism, must also be condemned. Speciesism—the word is not an attractive one, but I can think of no better term—is a prejudice or attitude of bias in favor of the interests of members of one's own species and against those of members of other species. It should be obvious that the fundamental objections to racism and sexism made by Thomas Jefferson and Sojourner Truth apply equally to speciesism. If possessing a higher degree of intelligence does not entitle one human to use another for his or her own ends, how can it entitle humans to exploit non-humans for the same purpose?[4]

Many philosopher and other writers have proposed the principle of equal consideration of interests, in some form or other, as a basic moral principle; but not many of them have recognized that this principle applies to members of other species as well as to our own. Jeremy Bentham was one of the few who did realize this. In a forward-looking passage written at a time when black slaves had been freed by the French but in the British dominions were still being treated in the way we now treat animals, Bentham wrote:

> The day *may* come when the rest of the animal creation may acquire those rights which never could have been withholden from them but by the hand of tyranny. The French have already discovered that the blackness of the skin is no reason why a human being should be abandoned without redress to the caprice of a tormentor. It may one day come to be recognized that the number of the legs, the villosity of the skin, or the termination of the *os sacrum* are reasons equally insufficient for abandoning a sensitive being to the same fate. What else is it that should trace the insuperable line? Is it the faculty of reason, or perhaps the faculty of discourse? But a full-grown horse or dog is beyond comparison a more rational, as well as a more conversable animal, than an infant of a day or a week or even a month, old. But suppose they were otherwise, what would it avail? The question is not, Can they *reason*? nor Can they *talk*? but, Can they *suffer*?[5]

In this passage Bentham points to the capacity for suffering as the vital characteristic that gives a being the right to equal consideration. The capacity for suffering—or more strictly, for suffering and/or enjoyment or happiness—is not just another characteristic like the capacity for language or higher mathematics. Bentham is not saying that those who try to mark "the insuperable line" that determines whether the interests of a being should be considered happen to have chosen the wrong characteristic. By saying that we must consider the interests of all beings with the capacity for suffering or enjoyment Bentham does not arbitrarily exclude from consideration any interests at all—as those who draw the line with reference to the possession of reason or language do. The capacity for suffering and enjoyment is *a prerequisite for having interests at all*, a con-

---

[4]I owe the term "speciesism" to Richard Ryder. It has become accepted in general use since the first edition of this book, and now appears in *The Oxford English Dictionary*, second edition (Oxford: Clarendon Press, 1989).

[5]*Introduction to the Principles of Morals and Legislation*, chapter 17.

dition that must be satisfied before we can speak of interests in a meaningful way. It would be nonsense to say that it was not in the interests of a stone to be kicked along the road by a schoolboy. A stone does not have interests because it cannot suffer. Nothing that we can do to it could possibly make any difference to its welfare. The capacity for suffering and enjoyment is, however, not only necessary, but also sufficient for us to say that a being has interests—at an ab-solute minimum, an interest in not suffering. A mouse, for example, does have an interest in not being kicked along the road, because it will suffer if it is.

Although Bentham speaks of "rights" in the passage I have quoted, the ar-gument is really about equality rather than about rights. Indeed, in a different passage, Bentham famously described "natural rights" as "nonsense" and "nat-ural and imprescriptable rights" as "nonsense upon stilts." He talked of moral rights as a shorthand way of referring to protections that people and animals morally ought to have; but the real weight of the moral argument does not rest on the assertion of the existence of the right, for this in turn has to be justified on the basis of the possibilities for suffering and happiness. In this way we can ar-gue for equality for animals without getting embroiled in philosophical contro-versies about the ultimate nature of rights.

In misguided attempts to refute the arguments of this book, some philoso-phers have gone to much trouble developing arguments to show that animals do not have rights.[6] They have claimed that to have rights a being must be au-tonomous, or must be a member of a community, or must have the ability to re-spect the rights of others, or must possess a sense of justice. These claims are irrelevant to the case for Animal Liberation. The language of rights is a conve-nient political shorthand. It is even more valuable in the era of thirty-second TV news clips than it was in Bentham's day; but in the argument for a radical change in our attitude to animals, it is in no way necessary.

If a being suffers there can be no moral justification for refusing to take that suffering into consideration. No matter what the nature of the being, the princi-ple of equality requires that its suffering be counted equally with the like suf-fering—insofar as rough comparisons can be made—of any other being. If a being is not capable of suffering, or of experiencing enjoyment or happiness, there is nothing to be taken into account. So the limit of sentience (using the term as a convenient if not strictly accurate shorthand for the capacity to suffer and/or experience enjoyment) is the only defensible boundary of concern for the interests of others. To mark this boundary by some other characteristic like intelligence or rationality would be to mark it in an arbitrary manner. Why not choose some other characteristic, like skin color?

Racists violate the principle of equality by giving greater weight to the in-terests of members of their own race when there is a clash between their inter-ests and the interests of those of another race. Sexists violate the principle of equality by favoring the interests of their own sex. Similarly, speciesists allow

[6]See M. Levin, "Animal Rights Evaluated," *Humanist* 37: 14–15 (July/August 1977); M. A. Fox, "An-imal Liberation: A Critique," *Ethics* 88: 134–138 (1978); C. Perry and G. E. Jones, "On Animal Rights," *International Journal of Applied Philosophy* 1: 39–57 (1982).

the interests of their own species to override the greater interests of members of other species. The pattern is identical in each case.

Most human beings are speciesists. . . .[O]rdinary human beings—not a few exceptionally cruel or heartless humans, but the overwhelming majority of humans—take an active part in, acquiesce in, and allow their taxes to pay for practices that require the sacrifice of the most important interests of members of other species in order to promote the most trivial interests of our own species.

There is, however, one general defense of [these] practices . . . that needs to be disposed of before we discuss the practices themselves. It is a defense which, if true, would allow us to do anything at all to non-humans for the slightest reason, or for no reason at all, without incurring any justifiable reproach. This defense claims that we are never guilty of neglecting the interests of other animals for one breathtakingly simple reason: they have no interests. Non-human animals have no interests, according to this view, because they are not capable of suffering. By this is not meant merely that they are not capable of suffering in all the ways that human being are—for instance, that a calf is not capable of suffering from the knowledge that it will be killed in six months time. That modest claim is, no doubt, true; but it does not clear humans of the charge of speciesism, since it allows that animals may suffer in other ways—for instance, by being given electric shocks, or being kept in small, cramped cages. The defense I am about to discuss is the much more sweeping, although correspondingly less plausible, claim that animals are incapable of suffering in any way at all; that they are, in fact, unconscious automata, possessing neither thoughts nor feelings nor a mental life of any kind.

Although, . . . the view that animals are automata was proposed by the seventeenth-century French philosopher Renè Descartes, to most people, then and now, it is obvious that if, for example, we stick a sharp knife into the stomach of an unanesthetized dog, the dog will feel pain. That this is so is assumed by the laws in most civilized countries that prohibit wanton cruelty to animals. Readers whose common sense tells them that animals do suffer may prefer to skip the remainder of this section, moving straight on to page 372 since the pages in between do nothing but refute a position that they do not hold. Implausible as it is, though, for the sake of completeness this skeptical position must be discussed.

Do animals other than humans feel pain? How do we know? Well, how do we know if anyone, human or non-human, feels pain? We know that we ourselves can feel pain. We know this from the direct experience of pain that we have when, for instance, somebody presses a lighted cigarette against the back of our hand. But how do we know that anyone else feels pain? We cannot directly experience anyone else's pain, whether that "anyone" is our best friend or a stray dog. Pain is a state of consciousness, a "mental event," and as such it can never be observed. Behavior like writhing, screaming, or drawing one's hand away from the lighted cigarette is not pain itself; nor are the recordings a neurologist might make of activity within the brain observations of pain itself. Pain is something that we feel, and we can only infer that others are feeling it from various external indications.

In theory, we *could* always be mistaken when we assume that other human beings feel pain. It is conceivable that one of our close friends is really a cleverly constructed robot, controlled by a brilliant scientist so as to give all the signs of feeling pain, but really no more sensitive than any other machine. We can never know, with absolute certainty, that this is not the case. But while this might present a puzzle for philosophers, none of us has the slightest real doubt that our close friends feel pain just as we do. This is an inference, but a perfectly reasonable one, based on observations of their behavior in situations in which we would feel pain, and on the fact that we have every reason to assume that our friends are beings like us, with nervous systems like ours that can be assumed to function as ours do and to produce similar feelings in similar circumstances.

If it is justifiable to assume that other human beings feel pain as we do, is there any reason why a similar inference should be unjustifiable in the case of other animals?

Nearly all the external signs that lead us to infer pain in other humans can be seen in other species, especially the species most closely related to us—the species of mammals and birds. The behavioral signs include writhing, facial contortions, moaning, yelping or other forms of calling, attempts to avoid the source of pain, appearance of fear at the prospect of its repetition, and so on. In addition, we know that these animals have nervous systems very like ours, which respond physiologically as ours do when the animal is in circumstances in which we would feel pain: an initial rise of blood pressure, dilated pupils, perspiration, an increased pulse rate, and, if the stimulus continues, a fall in blood pressure. Although human beings have a more developed cerebral cortex than other animals, this part of the brain is concerned with thinking functions rather than with basic impulses, emotions, and feelings. These impulses, emotions, and feelings are located in the diencephalon, which is well developed in many other species of animals, especially mammals and birds.[7]

We also know that the nervous systems of other animals were not artificially constructed—as a robot might be artificially constructed—to mimic the pain behavior of humans. The nervous systems of animals evolved as our own did, and in fact the evolutionary history of human beings and other animals, especially mammals, did not diverge until the central features of our nervous systems were already in existence. A capacity to feel pain obviously enhances a species' prospects of survival, since it causes members of the species to avoid sources of injury. It is surely unreasonable to suppose that nervous systems that are virtually identical physiologically, have a common origin and a common evolutionary function, and result in similar forms of behavior in similar circumstances should actually operate in an entirely different manner on the level of subjective feelings.

It has long been accepted as sound policy in science to search for the simplest possible explanation of whatever it is we are trying to explain. Occasionally it has been claimed that it is for this reason "unscientific" to explain the

---

[7]Lord Brain, "Presidential Address," in C. A. Keele and R. Smith, eds., *The Assessment of Pain in Men and Animals* (London: Universities Federation for Animal Welfare, 1962).

behavior of animals by theories that refer to the animal's conscious feelings, de-sires, and so on—the idea being that if the behavior in question can be ex-plained without invoking consciousness or feelings, that will be the simpler theory. Yet we can now see that such explanations, when assessed with respect to the actual behavior of both human and non-human animals, are actually far more complex than rival explanations. For we know from our own experience that explanations of our own behavior that did not refer to consciousness and the feeling of pain would be incomplete; and it is simpler to assume that the similar behavior of animals with similar nervous systems is to be explained in the same way than to try to invent some other explanation for the behavior of non-human animals as well as an explanation for the divergence between hu-mans and non-humans in this respect.

The overwhelming majority of scientists who have addressed themselves to this question agree. Lord Brain, one of the most eminent neurologists of our time, has said:

> I personally can see no reason for conceding mind to my fellow men and deny-ing it to animals. . . . I at least cannot doubt that the interests and activities of an-imals are correlated with awareness and feeling in the same way as my own, and which may be, for aught I know, just as vivid.[8]

The author of a book on pain writes:

> Every particle of factual evidence supports the contention that the higher mam-malian vertebrates experience pain sensations at least as acute as our own. To say that they feel less because they are lower animals is an absurdity; it can eas-ily be shown that many of their senses are far more acute than ours—visual acuity in certain birds, hearing in most wild animals, and touch in others; these animals depend more than we do today on the sharpest possible awareness of a hostile environment. Apart from the complexity of the cerebral cortex (which does not directly perceive pain) their nervous systems are almost identical to ours and their reactions to pain remarkably similar, though lacking (so far as we know) the philosophical and moral overtones. The emotional element is all too evident, mainly in the form of fear and anger.[9]

In Britain, three separate expert government committees on matters relating to animals have accepted the conclusion that animals feel pain. After noting the obvious behavioral evidence for this view, the members of the Committee on Cruelty to Wild Animals, set up in 1951, said:

> . . . we believe that the physiological, and more particularly the anatomical, ev-idence fully justifies and reinforces the commonsense belief that animals feel pain.

And after discussing the evolutionary value of pain the committee's report con-cluded that pain is "of clear-cut biological usefulness" and this is "a third type of evidence that animals feel pain." The committee members then went on to consider forms of suffering other than mere physical pain and added that they

---

[8]Lord Brain, "Presidential Address," p. 11.
[9]Richard Serjeant, *The Spectrum of Pain* (London: Hart Davis, 1969), p. 72.

were "satisfied that animals do suffer from acute fear and terror." Subsequent reports by British government committees on experiments on animals and on the welfare of animals under intensive farming methods agreed with this view, concluding that animals are capable of suffering both from straightforward physical injuries and from fear, anxiety, stress, and so on.[10] Finally, within the last decade, the publication of scientific studies with titles such as *Animal Thought, Animal Thinking,* and *Animal Suffering: The Science of Animal Welfare* have made it plain that conscious awareness in non-human animals is now generally accepted as a serious subject for ɪvestigation.[11]

That might well be thought enough to settle the matter; but one more objection needs to be considered. Human beings in pain, after all, have one behavioral sign that non-human animals do not have: a developed language. Other animals may communicate with each other, but not, it seems, in the complicated way we do. Some philosophers, including Descartes, have thought it important that while humans can tell each other about their experience of pain in great detail, other animals cannot. (Interestingly, this once neat dividing line between humans and other species has now been threatened by the discovery that chimpanzees can be taught a language.[12]) But as Bentham pointed out long ago, the ability to use language is not relevant to the question of how a being ought to be treated—unless that ability can be linked to the capacity to suffer, so that the absence of a language casts doubt on the existence of this capacity.

This link may be attempted in two ways. First, there is a hazy line of philosophical thought, deriving perhaps from some doctrines associated with the influential philosopher Ludwig Wittgenstein, which maintains that we cannot meaningfully attribute states of consciousness to beings without language. This position seems to me very implausible. Language may be necessary for abstract thought, at some level anyway; but states like pain are more primitive, and have nothing to do with language.

The second and more easily understood way of linking language and the existence of pain is to say that the best evidence we can have that other creatures are in pain is that they tell us that they are. This is a distinct line of argument, for it is denying not that non-language-users conceivably *could* suffer, but only that we could ever have sufficient reason to *believe* that they are suffering. Still, this line of argument fails too. As Jane Goodall has pointed out in her study of chimpanzees, *In the Shadow of Man,* when it comes to the expression of feelings and emotions language is less important than nonlinguistic modes of

---

[10]See the reports of the Committee on Cruelty to Wild Animals (Command Paper 8266, 1951), paragraphs 36–42; the Departmental Committee on Experiments on Animals (Command Paper 2641, 1965), paragraphs 179–182; and the Technical Committee to Enquire into the Welfare of Animals Kept under Intensive Livestock Husbandry Systems (Command Paper 2836, 1965), paragraphs 26–28 (London: Her Majesty's Stationery Office).

[11]See Stephen Walker, *Animal Thoughts* (London: Routledge and Kegan Paul, 1983); Donald Griffin, *Animal Thinking* (Cambridge: Harvard University Press, 1984); and Marian Stamp Dawkins, *Animal Suffering: The Science of Animal Welfare* (London: Chapman and Hall, 1980).

[12]See Eugene Linden, *Apes, Men and Language* (New York: Penguin, 1976); for popular accounts of some more recent work, see Erik Eckholm, "Pygmy Chimp Readily Learns Language Skill," *The New York Times,* June 24, 1985; and "The Wisdom of Animals," *Newsweek,* May 23, 1988.

communication such as a cheering pat on the back, an exuberant embrace, a clasp of the hands, and so on. The basic signals we use to convey pain, fear, anger, love, joy, surprise, sexual arousal, and many other emotional states are not specific to our own species.[13] The statement "I am in pain" may be one piece of evidence for the conclusion that the speaker is in pain, but it is not the only possible evidence, and since people sometimes tell lies, not even the best possible evidence.

Even if there were stronger grounds for refusing to attribute pain to those who do not have a language, the consequences of this refusal might lead us to reject the conclusion. Human infants and young children are unable to use language. Are we to deny that a year-old child can suffer? If not, language cannot be crucial. Of course, most parents understand the responses of their children better than they understand the responses of other animals; but this is just a fact about the relatively greater knowledge that we have of our own species and the greater contact we have with infants as compared to animals. Those who have studied the behavior of other animals and those who have animals as companions soon learn to understand their responses as well as we understand those of an infant, and sometimes better.

So to conclude: there are no good reasons, scientific or philosophical, for denying that animals feel pain. If we do not doubt that other humans feel pain we should not doubt that other animals do so too.

Animals can feel pain. As we saw earlier, there can be no moral justification for regarding the pain (or pleasure) that animals feel as less important than the same amount of pain (or pleasure) felt by humans. But what practical consequences follow from this conclusion? To prevent misunderstanding I shall spell out what I mean a little more fully.

If I give a horse a hard slap across its rump with my open hand, the horse may start, but it presumably feels little pain. Its skin is thick enough to protect it against a mere slap. If I slap a baby in the same way, however, the baby will cry and presumably feel pain, for its skin is more sensitive. So it is worse to slap a baby than a horse, if both slaps are administered with equal force. But there must be some kind of blow—I don't know exactly what it would be, but perhaps a blow with a heavy stick—that would cause the horse as much pain as we cause a baby by slapping it with our hand. That is what I mean by "the same amount of pain," and if we consider it wrong to inflict that much pain on a baby for no good reason then we must, unless we are speciesists, consider it equally wrong to inflict the same amount of pain on a horse for no good reason.

Other differences between humans and animals cause other complications. Normal adult human beings have mental capacities that will, in certain circumstances, lead them to suffer more than animals would in the same circumstances. If, for instance, we decided to perform extremely painful or lethal

---

[13]*In the Shadow of Man* (Boston: Houghton Mifflin, 1971), p. 225. Michael Peters makes a similar point in "Nature and Culture," in Stanley and Roslind Godlovitch and John Harris, eds., *Animals, Men and Morals* (New York: Taplinger, 1972). For examples of some of the inconsistencies in denials that creatures without language can feel pain, see Bernard Rollin, *The Unheeded Cry: Animal Consciousness, Animal Pain, and Science* (Oxford: Oxford University Press, 1989).

scientific experiments on normal adult humans, kidnapped at random from public parks for this purpose, adults who enjoy strolling in parks would become fearful that they would be kidnapped. The resultant terror would be a form of suffering additional to the pain of the experiment. The same experiments performed on non-human animals would cause less suffering since the animals would not have the anticipatory dread of being kidnapped and experimented upon. This does not mean, of course, that it would be *right* to perform the experiment on animals, but only that there is a reason, which is *not* speciesist, for preferring to use animals rather than normal adult human beings, if the experiment is to be done at all. It should be noted, however, that this same argument gives us a reason for preferring to use human infants—orphans perhaps—or severely retarded human beings for experiments, rather than adults, since infants and retarded humans would also have no idea of what was going to happen to them. So far as this argument is concerned non-human animals and infants and retarded humans are in the same category; and if we use this argument to justify experiments on non-human animals we have to ask ourselves whether we are also prepared to allow experiments on human infants and retarded adults; and if we make a distinction between animals and these humans, on what basis can we do it, other than a bare-faced—and morally indefensible— preference for members of our own species?

There are many matters in which the superior mental powers of normal adult humans make a difference: anticipation, more detailed memory, greater knowledge of what is happening, and so on. Yet these differences do not all point to greater suffering on the part of the normal human being. Sometimes animals may suffer more because of their more limited understanding. If, for instance, we are taking prisoners in wartime we can explain to them that although they must submit to capture, search, and confinement, they will not otherwise be harmed and will be set free at the conclusion of hostilities. If we capture wild animals, however, we cannot explain that we are not threatening their lives. A wild animal cannot distinguish an attempt to overpower and confine from an attempt to kill; the one causes as much terror as the other.

It may be objected that comparisons of the sufferings of different species are impossible to make and that for this reason when the interests of animals and humans clash the principle of equality gives no guidance. It is probably true that comparisons of suffering between members of different species cannot be made precisely, but precision is not essential. Even if we were to prevent the infliction of suffering on animals only when it is quite certain that the interests of humans will not be affected to anything like the extent that animals are affected, we would be forced to make radical changes in our treatment of animals that would involve our diet, the farming methods we use, experimental procedures in many fields of science, our approach to wildlife and to hunting, trapping and the wearing of furs, and areas of entertainment like circuses, rodeos, and zoos. As a result, a vast amount of suffering would be avoided.

So far I have said a lot about inflicting suffering on animals, but nothing about killing them. This omission has been deliberate. The application of the principle of equality to the infliction of suffering is, in theory at least, fairly straightforward. Pain and suffering are in themselves bad and should be prevented or minimized, irrespective of the race, sex, or species of the being that suffers. How bad a pain is depends on how intense it is and how long it lasts, but pains of the same intensity and duration are equally bad, whether felt by humans or animals.

The wrongness of killing a being is more complicated. I have kept, and shall continue to keep, the question of killing in the background because in the present state of human tyranny over other species the more simple, straightforward principle of equal consideration of pain or pleasure is a sufficient basis for identifying and protesting against all the major abuses of animals that human beings practice. Nevertheless, it is necessary to say something about killing.

Just as most human beings are speciesists in their readiness to cause pain to animals when they would not cause a similar pain to humans for the same reason, so most human beings are speciesists in their readiness to kill other animals when they would not kill human beings. We need to proceed more cautiously here, however, because people hold widely differing views about when it is legitimate to kill humans, as the continuing debates over abortion and euthanasia attest. Nor have moral philosophers been able to agree on exactly what it is that makes it wrong to kill human beings, and under what circumstances killing a human being may be justifiable.

Let us consider first the view that it is always wrong to take an innocent human life. We may call this the "sanctity of life" view. People who take this view oppose abortion and euthanasia. They do not usually, however, oppose the killing of non-human animals—so perhaps it would be more accurate to describe this view as the "sanctity of *human* life" view. The belief that human life, and only human life, is sacrosanct is a form of speciesism. To see this, consider the following example.

Assume that, as sometimes happens, an infant has been born with massive and irreparable brain damage. The damage is so severe that the infant can never be any more than a "human vegetable," unable to talk, recognize other people, act independently of others, or develop a sense of self-awareness. The parents of the infant, realizing that they cannot hope for any improvement in their child's condition and being in any case unwilling to spend, or ask the state to spend, the thousands of dollars that would be needed annually for proper care of the infant, ask the doctor to kill the infant painlessly.

Should the doctor do what the parents ask? Legally, the doctor should not, and in this respect the law reflects the sanctity of life view. The life of every human being is sacred. Yet people who would say this about the infant do not object to the killing of non-human animals. How can they justify their different judgments? Adult chimpanzees, dogs, pigs, and members of many other species far surpass the brain-damaged infant in their ability to relate to others, act independently, be self-aware, and any other capacity that could reasonably be said to give value to life. With the most intensive care possible, some severely retarded infants can never achieve the intelligence level of a dog. Nor can we appeal to the concern of the infant's parents, since they themselves, in this imaginary example (and in some actual cases) do not want the infant kept alive. The only thing that distinguishes the infant from the animal, in the eyes of those who claim it has a "right to life," is that it is, biologically, a member of the species Homo sapiens, whereas chimpanzees, dogs, and pigs are not. But to use *this* difference as the basis for granting a right to life to the infant and not to the other animals is, of course, pure speciesism.[14] It is exactly the kind of arbitrary difference that the most crude and overt kind of racist uses in attempting to justify racial discrimination.

This does not mean that to avoid speciesism we must hold that it is as wrong to kill a dog as it is to kill a human being in full possession of his or her faculties. The only position that is irredeemably speciesist is the one that tries to make the boundary of the right to life run exactly parallel to the boundary of our own species. Those who hold the sanctity of life view do this, because while distinguishing sharply between human beings and other animals they allow no distinctions to be made within our own species, objecting to the killing of the severely retarded and the hopelessly senile as strongly as they object to the killing of normal adults.

To avoid speciesism we must allow that beings who are similar in all relevant respects have a similar right to life—and mere membership in our own biological species cannot be a morally relevant criterion for this right. Within these limits we could still hold, for instance, that it is worse to kill a normal adult human, with a capacity for self-awareness and the ability to plan for the future and have meaningful relations with others, than it is to kill a mouse, which presumably does not share all of these characteristics; or we might appeal to the close family and other personal ties that humans have but mice do not have to the same degree; or we might think that it is the consequences for other humans, who will be put in fear for their own lives, that makes the crucial difference; or we might think it is some combination of these factors, or other factors altogether.

Whatever criteria we choose, however, we will have to admit that they do not follow precisely the boundary of our own species. We may legitimately hold that there are some features of certain beings that make their lives more valuable than those of other beings; but there will surely be some non-human animals whose lives, by any standards, are more valuable than the lives of some humans. A chimpanzee, dog, or pig, for instance, will have a higher degree of self-awareness and a greater capacity for meaningful relations with others than a severely retarded infant or someone in a state of advanced senility. So if we

---

[14]I am here putting aside religious views, for example the doctrine that all and only human beings have immortal souls, or are made in the image of God. Historically these have been very important, and no doubt are partly responsible for the idea that human life has a special sanctity. . . . Logically, however, these religious views are unsatisfactory, since they do not offer a reasoned explanation of why it should be that all humans and no non-humans have immortal souls. This belief too, therefore, comes under suspicion as a form of speciesism. In any case, defenders of the "sanctity of life" view are generally reluctant to base their position on purely religious doctrines, since these doctrines are no longer as widely accepted as they once were.

base the right to life on these characteristics we must grant these animals a right to life as good as, or better than, such retarded or senile humans.

This argument cuts both ways. It could be taken as showing that chimpanzees, dogs, and pigs, along with some other species, have a right to life and we commit a grave moral offense whenever we kill them, even when they are old and suffering and our intention is to put them out of their misery. Alternatively one could take the argument as showing that the severely retarded and hopelessly senile have no right to life and may be killed for quite trivial reasons, as we now kill animals.

Since the main concern of this book is with ethical questions having to do with animals and not with the morality of euthanasia I shall not attempt to settle this issue finally.[15] I think it is reasonably clear, though, that while both of the positions just described avoid speciesism, neither is satisfactory. What we need is some middle position that would avoid speciesism but would not make the lives of the retarded and senile as cheap as the lives of pigs and dogs now are, or make the lives of pigs and dogs so sacrosanct that we think it wrong to put them out of hopeless misery. What we must do is bring non-human animals within our sphere of moral concern and cease to treat their lives as expendable for whatever trivial purposes we may have. At the same time, once we realize that the fact that a being is a member of our own species is not in itself enough to make it always wrong to kill that being, we may come to reconsider our policy of preserving human lives at all costs, even when there is no prospect of a meaningful life or of existence without terrible pain.

I conclude, then, that a rejection of speciesism does not imply that all lives are of equal worth. While self-awareness, the capacity to think ahead and have hopes and aspirations for the future, the capacity for meaningful relations with others and so on are not relevant to the question of inflicting pain—since pain is pain, whatever other capacities, beyond the capacity to feel pain, the being may have—these capacities are relevant to the question of taking life. It is not arbitrary to hold that the life of a self-aware being, capable of abstract thought, of planning for the future, of complex acts of communication, and so on, is more valuable than the life of a being without these capacities. To see the difference between the issues of inflicting pain and taking life, consider how we would choose within our own species. If we had to choose to save the life of a normal human being or an intellectually disabled human being, we would probably choose to save the life of a normal human being; but if we had to choose between preventing pain in the normal human being or the intellectually disabled one—imagine that both have received painful but superficial injuries, and we only have enough painkiller for one of them—it is not nearly so clear how we ought to choose. The same is true when we consider other species. The evil of pain is, in itself, unaffected by the other characteristics of the being who feels the pain; the value of life is affected by these other characteristics. To give just

---

[15]For a general discussion of these questions, see my *Practical Ethics* (Cambridge: Cambridge University Press, 1979), and for a more detailed discussion of the treatment of handicapped infants, see Helga Kuhse and Peter Singer, *Should the Baby Live?* (Oxford: Oxford University Press, 1985).

one reason for this difference, to take the life of a being who has been hoping, planning, and working for some future goal is to deprive that being of the fulfillment of all those efforts; to take the life of a being with a mental capacity below the level needed to grasp that one is a being with a future—much less make plans for the future—cannot involve this particular kind of loss.[16]

Normally this will mean that if we have to choose between the life of a human being and the life of another animal we should choose to save the life of the human; but there may be special cases in which the reverse holds true, because the human being in question does not have the capacities of a normal human being. So this view is not speciesist, although it may appear to be at first glance. The preference, in normal cases, for saving a human life over the life of an animal when a choice *has* to be made is a preference based on the characteristics that normal humans have, and not on the mere fact they are members of our own species. This is why when we consider members of our own species who lack the characteristics of normal humans we can no longer say that their lives are always to be preferred to those of other animals. . . . In general, though, the question of when it is wrong to kill (painlessly) an animal is one to which we need give no precise answer. As long as we remember that we should give the same respect to the lives of animals as we give to the lives of those humans at a similar mental level, we shall not go far wrong.[17]

In any case, the conclusions that are argued for [here] . . . flow from the principle of minimizing suffering alone. The idea that it is also wrong to kill animals painlessly gives some of these conclusions additional support that is welcome but strictly unnecessary. Interestingly enough, this is true even of the conclusion that we ought to become vegetarians, a conclusion that in the popular mind is generally based on some kind of absolute prohibition on killing. . . .

Questions

1. What is the difference between "identical treatment" and "equal consideration"? Which of these is required by a principle of equality?
2. What is speciesism?
3. Do you agree with Jeremy Bentham and Peter Singer that sentience is the criterion for having interests?
4. When does Peter Singer think that the life of an animal is worth more than the life of a human?

[16]For a development of this theme, see my essay, "Life's Uncertain Voyage," in P. Pettit, R. Sylvan and J. Norman, eds., *Metaphysics and Morality* (Oxford: Blackwell, 1987), pp. 154–172.

[17]The preceding discussion, which has been changed only slightly since the first edition, has often been overlooked by critics of the Animal Liberation movement. It is a common tactic to seek to ridicule the Animal Liberation position by maintaining that, as an animal experimenter put it recently, "Some of these people believe that every insect, every mouse, has as much right to life as a human." (Dr. Irving Weissman, as quoted in Katherine Bishop, "From Shop to Lab to Farm, Animal Rights Battle is Felt," *The New York Times,* January 14, 1989.) It would be interesting to see Dr. Weissman name some prominent Animal Liberationists who hold this view. Certainly (assuming only that he was referring to the right to life of a human being with mental capacities very different from those of the insect and the mouse) the position described is not mine. I doubt that it is held by many—if any—in the Animal Liberation movement.

The Case for Animal Rights

Tom Regan

Tom Regan thinks that although the suffering that is inflicted on animals in the production of meat compounds the wrong that is done to the animals, this is not the fundamental wrong. The fundamental wrong is that in rearing and killing animals for food, we violate their rights by treating them merely as resources for our use.

He begins his argument by surveying a variety of views that, he says, have a defective understanding of the moral status of animals (and others). First, he rejects the view that although we may have duties concerning animals (indirect duties), we have no duties to animals (direct duties). Animals, unlike windshields, feel pain. Moreover, their pain matters to them. Thus, whereas one's duty not to smash a windshield is owed to its owner and not to it, duties not to inflict pain on animals are owed to the animals themselves. The author then considers contractarian arguments for the view that we have only indirect duties

to animals. On this view, animals are not party to the social contract that imposes moral rules on us and thus we cannot owe them anything directly, even though they feel pain and care about their pain. He argues that this sort of view fails to recognize not only the moral status of animals but also the moral status of those humans, such as infants and mentally defective people, who are unable to enter into the contract.

The author then turns to considering two views that do recognize direct duties to animals but that, in his opinion, are defective for other reasons. The first of these is what he calls the "cruelty-kindness" view. According to this view, we have a direct duty to be kind to animals and a direct duty not to be cruel to them. This view fails, he says, because one can be kind while doing wrong and do wrong without being cruel. The second view that allows direct duties to animals is utilitarianism (of which Peter Singer is a proponent). Although the

Tom Regan, "The Case for Animal Rights," in *In Defense of Animals,* edited by Peter Singer (New York: HarperCollins Publishers, 1985), 15–26.

author endorses the egalitarianism of this theory—that it counts everyone's interests equally—he says that utilitarianism's shortcoming is that it accords value only to interests and not to the beings whose interests they are. In place of these other

theories, he suggests what he calls the rights view. On this view all "experiencing subjects of a life," which includes not only humans but also animals, have inherent value.

I regard myself as an advocate of animal rights—as a part of the animal rights movement. That movement, as I conceive it, is committed to a number of goals, including:

- the total abolition of the use of animals in science;
- the total dissolution of commercial animal agriculture;
- the total elimination of commercial and sport hunting and trapping.

There are, I know, people who profess to believe in animal rights but do not avow these goals. Factory farming, they say, is wrong—it violates animals' rights—but traditional animal agriculture is all right. Toxicity tests of cosmetics on animals violates their rights, but important medical research—cancer research, for example—does not. The clubbing of baby seals is abhorrent, but not the harvesting of adult seals. I used to think I understood this reasoning. Not any more. You don't change unjust institutions by tidying them up.

What's wrong—fundamentally wrong—with the way animals are treated isn't the details that vary from case to case. It's the whole system. The forlornness of the veal calf is pathetic, heart wrenching; the pulsing pain of the chimp with electrodes planted deep in her brain is repulsive; the slow, tortuous death of the raccoon caught in the leg-hold trap is agonizing. But what is wrong isn't the pain, isn't the suffering, isn't the deprivation. These compound what's wrong. Sometimes—often—they make it much, much worse. But they are not the fundamental wrong.

The fundamental wrong is the system that allows us to view animals as *our resources,* here for *us*—to be eaten, or surgically manipulated, or exploited for sport or money. Once we accept this view of animals—as our resources—the rest is as predictable as it is regrettable. Why worry about their loneliness, their pain, their death? Since animals exist for us, to benefit us in one way or another, what harms them really doesn't matter—or matters only if it starts to bother us, makes us feel a trifle uneasy when we eat our veal escalope, for example. So, yes, let us get veal calves out of solitary confinement, give them more space, a little straw, a few companions. But let us keep our veal escalope.

But a little straw, more space and a few companions won't eliminate—won't even touch—the basic wrong that attaches to our viewing and treating these animals as our resources. A veal calf killed to be eaten after living in close confinement is viewed and treated in this way: but so, too, is another who is raised (as they say) 'more humanely'. To right the wrong of our treatment of farm animals requires more than making rearing methods 'more humane'; it requires the total dissolution of commercial animal agriculture.

How we do this, whether we do it or, as in the case of animals in science, whether and how we abolish their use—these are to a large extent political questions. People must change their beliefs before they change their habits. Enough people, especially those elected to public office, must believe in change—must want it—before we will have laws that protect the rights of animals. This process of change is very complicated, very demanding, very exhausting, calling for the efforts of many hands in education, publicity, political organization and activity, down to the licking of envelopes and stamps. As a trained and practising philosopher, the sort of contribution I can make is limited but, I like to think, important. The currency of philosophy is ideas—their meaning and rational foundation—not the nuts and bolts of the legislative process, say, or the mechanics of community organization. That's what I have been exploring over the past ten years or so in my essays and talks and, most recently, in my book, *The Case for Animal Rights*. I believe the major conclusions I reach in the book are true because they are supported by the weight of the best arguments. I believe the idea of animal rights has reason, not just emotion, on its side.

In the space I have at my disposal here I can only sketch, in the barest outline, some of the main features of the book. It's main themes—and we should not be surprised by this—involve asking and answering deep, foundational moral questions about what morality is, how it should be understood and what is the best moral theory, all considered. I hope I can convey something of the shape I think this theory takes. The attempt to do this will be (to use a word a friendly critic once used to describe my work) cerebral, perhaps too cerebral. But this is misleading. My feelings about how animals are sometimes treated run just as deep and just as strong as those of my more volatile compatriots. Philosophers do—to use the jargon of the day—have a right side to their brains. If it's the left side we contribute (or mainly should), that's because what talents we have reside there.

How to proceed? We begin by asking how the moral status of animals has been understood by thinkers who deny that animals have rights. Then we test the mettle of their ideas by seeing how well they stand up under the heat of fair criticism. If we start our thinking in this way, we soon find that some people believe that we have no duties directly to animals, that we owe nothing to them, that we can do nothing that wrongs them. Rather, we can do wrong acts that involve animals, and so we have duties regarding them, though none to them. Such views may be called indirect duty views. By way of illustration: suppose your neighbour kicks your dog. Then your neighbour has done something wrong. But not to your dog. The wrong that has been done is a wrong to you. After all, it is wrong to upset people, and your neighbour's kicking your dog upsets you. So you are the one who is wronged, not your dog. Or again: by kicking your dog your neighbour damages your property. And since it is wrong to damage another person's property, your neighbour has done something wrong—to you, of course, not to your dog. Your neighbour no more wrongs your dog than your car would be wronged if the windshield were smashed.

Your neighbour's duties involving your dog are indirect duties to you. More generally, all of our duties regarding animals are indirect duties to one another—to humanity.

How could someone try to justify such a view? Someone might say that your dog doesn't feel anything and so isn't hurt by your neighbour's kick, doesn't care about the pain since none is felt, is as unaware of anything as is your windshield. Someone might say this, but no rational person will, since, among other considerations, such a view will commit anyone who holds it to the position that no human being feels pain either—that human beings also don't care about what happens to them. A second possibility is that though both humans and your dog are hurt when kicked, it is only human pain that matters. But, again, no rational person can believe this. Pain is pain wherever it occurs. If your neighbour's causing you pain is wrong because of the pain that is caused, we cannot rationally ignore or dismiss the moral relevance of the pain that your dog feels.

Philosophers who hold indirect duty views—and many still do—have come to understand that they must avoid the two defects just noted: that is, both the view that animals don't feel anything as well as the idea that only human pain can be morally relevant. Among such thinkers the sort of view now favoured is one or other form of what is called *contractarianism*.

Here, very crudely, is the root idea: morality consists of a set of rules that individuals voluntarily agree to abide by, as we do when we sign a contract (hence the name contractarianism). Those who understand and accept the terms of the contract are covered directly; they have rights created and recognized by, and protected in, the contract. And these contractors can also have protection spelled out for others who, though they lack the ability to understand morality and so cannot sign the contract themselves, are loved or cherished by those who can. Thus young children, for example, are unable to sign contracts and lack rights. But they are protected by the contract none the less because of the sentimental interests of others, most notably their parents. So we have, then, duties involving these children, duties regarding them, but no duties to them. Our duties in their case are indirect duties to other human beings, usually their parents.

As for animals, since they cannot understand contracts, they obviously cannot sign; and since they cannot sign, they have no rights. Like children, however, some animals are the objects of the sentimental interests of others. You, for example, love your dog or cat. So those animals that enough people care about (companion animals, whales, baby seals, the American bald eagle), though they lack rights themselves, will be protected because of the sentimental interests of people. I have, then, according to contractarianism, no duty directly to your dog or any other animals, not even the duty not to cause them pain or suffering; my duty not to hurt them is a duty I have to those people who care about what happens to them. As for other animals, where no or little sentimental interest is present—in the case of farm animals, for example, or laboratory rats—what duties we have grow weaker and weaker, perhaps to vanishing point. The pain and death they endure, though real, are not wrong if no one cares about them.

When it comes to the moral status of animals' contractarianism could be a hard view to refute if it were an adequate theoretical approach to the moral status of human beings. It is not adequate in this latter respect, however, which makes the question of its adequacy in the former case, regarding animals, utterly moot. For consider: morality, according to the (crude) contractarian position before us, consists of rules that people agree to abide by. What people? Well, enough to make a difference—enough, that is, *collectively* to have the power to enforce the rules that are drawn up in the contract. That is very well and good for the signatories but not so good for anyone who is not asked to sign. And there is nothing in contractarianism of the sort we are discussing that guarantees or requires that everyone will have a chance to participate equally in framing the rules of morality. The result is that this approach to ethics could sanction the most blatant forms of social, economic, moral and political injustice, ranging from a repressive caste system to systematic racial or sexual discrimination. Might, according to this theory, does make right. Let those who are the victims of injustice suffer as they will. It matters not so long as no one else— no contractor, or too few of them—cares about it. Such a theory takes one's moral breath away . . . as if, for example, there would be nothing wrong with apartheid in South Africa if few white South Africans were upset by it. A theory with so little to recommend it at the level of the ethics of our treatment of our fellow humans cannot have anything more to recommend it when it comes to the ethics of how we treat our fellow animals.

The version of contractarianism just examined is, as I have noted, a crude variety, and in fairness to those of a contractarian persuasion it must be noted that much more refined, subtle and ingenious varieties are possible. For example, John Rawls, in his *A Theory of Justice*, sets forth a version of contractarianism that forces contractors to ignore the accidental features of being a human being—for example, whether one is white or black, male or female, a genius or of modest intellect. Only by ignoring such features, Rawls believes, can we ensure that the principles of justice that contractors would agree upon are not based on bias or prejudice. Despite the improvement a view such as Rawls's represents over the cruder forms of contractarianism, it remains deficient: it systematically denies that we have direct duties to those human beings who do not have a sense of justice—young children, for instance, and many mentally retarded humans. And yet it seems reasonably certain that, were we to torture a young child or a retarded elder, we would be doing something that wronged him or her, not something that would be wrong if (and only if) other humans with a sense of justice were upset. And since this is true in the case of these humans, we cannot rationally deny the same in the case of animals.

Indirect duty views, then, including the best among them, fail to command our rational assent. Whatever ethical theory we should accept rationally, therefore, it must at least recognize that we have some duties directly to animals, just as we have some duties directly to each other. The next two theories I'll sketch attempt to meet this requirement.

The first I call the cruelty-kindness view. Simply stated, this says that we have a direct duty to be kind to animals and a direct duty not to be cruel to them. Despite the familiar, reassuring ring of these ideas, I do not believe that this view offers an adequate theory. To make this clearer, consider kindness. A kind person acts from a certain kind of motive—compassion or concern, for example. And that is a virtue. But there is no guarantee that a kind act is a right act. If I am a generous racist, for example, I will be inclined to act kindly towards members of my own race, favouring their interests above those of others. My kindness would be real and, so far as it goes, good. But I trust it is too obvious to require argument that my kind acts may not be above moral reproach—may, in fact, be positively wrong because rooted in injustice. So kindness, notwithstanding its status as a virtue to be encouraged, simply will not carry the weight of a theory of right action.

Cruelty fares no better. People or their acts are cruel if they display either a lack of sympathy for or, worse, the presence of enjoyment in another's suffering. Cruelty in all its guises is a bad thing, a tragic human failing. But just as a person's being motivated by kindness does not guarantee that he or she does what is right, so the absence of cruelty does not ensure that he or she avoids doing what is wrong. Many people who perform abortions, for example, are not cruel, sadistic people. But that fact alone does not settle the terribly difficult question of the morality of abortion. The case is no different when we examine the ethics of our treatment of animals. So, yes, let us be for kindness and against cruelty. But let us not suppose that being for the one and against the other answers questions about moral right and wrong.

Some people think that the theory we are looking for is utilitarianism. A utilitarian accepts two moral principles. The first is that of equality: everyone's interests count, and similar interests must be counted as having similar weight or importance. White or black, American or Iranian, human or animal—everyone's pain or frustration matter, and matter just as much as the equivalent pain or frustration of anyone else. The second principle a utilitarian accepts is that of utility: do the act that will bring about the best balance between satisfaction and frustration for everyone affected by the outcome.

As a utilitarian, then, here is how I am to approach the task of deciding what I morally ought to do: I must ask who will be affected if I choose to do one thing rather than another, how much each individual will be affected, and where the best results are most likely to lie—which option, in other words, is most likely to bring about the best results, the best balance between satisfaction and frustration. That option, whatever it may be, is the one I ought to choose. That is where my moral duty lies.

The great appeal of utilitarianism rests with its uncompromising *egalitarianism:* everyone's interests count and count as much as the like interests of everyone else. The kind of odious discrimination that some forms of contractarianism can justify—discrimination based on race or sex, for example—seems disallowed in principle by utilitarianism, as is speciesism, systematic discrimination based on species membership.

The equality we find in utilitarianism, however, is not the sort an advocate of animal or human rights should have in mind. Utilitarianism has no room for the equal moral rights of different individuals because it has no room for their equal inherent value or worth. What has value for the utilitarian is the satisfaction of an individual's interests, not the individual whose interests they are. A universe in which you satisfy your desire for water, food and warmth is, other things being equal, better than a universe in which these desires are frustrated. And the same is true in the case of an animal with similar desires. But neither you nor the animal have any value in your own right. Only your feelings do.

Here is an analogy to help make the philosophical point clearer: a cup contains different liquids, sometimes sweet, sometimes bitter, sometimes a mix of the two. What has value are the liquids: the sweeter the better, the bitterer the worse. The cup, the container, has no value. It is what goes into it, not what they go into, that has value. For the utilitarian you and I are like the cup; we have no value as individuals and thus no equal value. What has value is what goes into us, what we serve as receptacles for; our feelings of satisfaction have positive value, our feelings of frustration negative value.

Serious problems arise for utilitarianism when we remind ourselves that it enjoins us to bring about the best consequences. What does this mean? It doesn't mean the best consequences for me alone, or for my family or friends, or any other person taken individually. No, what we must do is, roughly, as follows: we must add up (somehow!) the separate satisfactions and frustrations of everyone likely to be affected by our choice, the satisfactions in one column, the frustrations in the other. We must total each column for each of the options before us. That is what it means to say the theory is aggregative. And then we must choose that option which is most likely to bring about the best balance of totalled satisfactions over totalled frustrations. Whatever act would lead to this outcome is the one we ought morally to perform—it is where our moral duty lies. And that act quite clearly might not be the same one that would bring about the best results for me personally, or for my family or friends, or for a lab animal. The best aggregated consequences for everyone concerned are not necessarily the best for each individual.

That utilitarianism is an aggregative theory—different individuals' satisfactions or frustrations are added, or summed, or totalled—is the key objective to this theory. My Aunt Bea is old, inactive, a cranky, sour person, though not physically ill. She prefers to go on living. She is also rather rich. I could make a fortune if I could get my hands on her money, money she intends to give me in any event, after she dies, but which she refuses to give me now. In order to avoid a huge tax bite, I plan to donate a handsome sum of my profits to a local children's hospital. Many, many children will benefit from my generosity, and much joy will be brought to their parents, relatives, and friends. If I don't get the money rather soon, all these ambitions will come to naught. The once-in-a-lifetime opportunity to make a real killing will be gone. Why, then, not kill my Aunt Bea? Oh, of course I *might* get caught. But I'm no fool and, besides, her doctor can be counted on to cooperate (he has an eye for the same investment and I happen to know a good deal about his shady past). The deed can be done . . . professionally, shall we say. There is *very* little chance of getting caught. And as for my conscience being guilt-ridden, I am a resourceful sort of fellow and will take more than sufficient comfort—as I lie on the beach at Acapulco—in contemplating the joy and health I have brought to so many others.

Suppose Aunt Bea is killed and the rest of the story comes out as told. Would I have done anything wrong? Anything immoral? One would have thought that I had. Not according to utilitarianism. Since what I have done has brought about the best balance between totalled satisfaction and frustration for all those affected by the outcome, my action is not wrong. Indeed, in killing Aunt Bea the physician and I did what duty required.

This same kind of argument can be repeated in all sorts of cases, illustrating, time after time, how the utilitarian's position leads to results that impartial people find morally callous. It *is* wrong to kill my Aunt Bea in the name of bringing about the best results for others. A good end does not justify an evil means. Any adequate moral theory will have to explain why this is so. Utilitarianism fails in this respect and so cannot be the theory we seek.

What to do? Where to begin anew? The place to begin, I think, is with the utilitarian's view of the value of the individual—or, rather, lack of value. In its place, suppose we consider that you and I, for example, do have value as individuals—what we'll call *inherent value.* To say we have such value is to say that we are something more than, something different from, mere receptacles. Moreover, to ensure that we do not pave the way for such injustices as slavery or sexual discrimination, we must believe that all who have inherent value have it equally, regardless of their sex, race, religion, birthplace and so on. Similarly to be discarded as irrelevant are one's talents or skills, intelligence and wealth, personality or pathology, whether one is loved and admired, or despised and loathed. The genius and the retarded child, the prince and the pauper, the brain surgeon and the fruit vendor, Mother Teresa and the most unscrupulous used-car salesman—all have inherent value, all possess it equally, and all have an equal right to be treated with respect, to be treated in ways that do not reduce them to the status of things, as if they existed as resources for others. My value as an individual is independent of my usefulness to you. Yours is not dependent on your usefulness to me. For either of us to treat the other in ways that fail to show respect for the other's independent value is to act immorally, to violate the individual's rights.

Some of the rational virtues of this view—what I call the rights view—should be evident. Unlike (crude) contractarianism, for example, the rights view *in principle* denies the moral tolerability of any and all forms of racial, sexual or social discrimination; and unlike utilitarianism, this view *in principle* denies that we can justify good results by using evil means that violate an individual's rights—denies, for example, that it could be moral to kill my Aunt Bea to harvest beneficial consequences for others. That would be to sanction the disrespectful treatment of the individual in the name of the social good, something the rights view will not—categorically will not—ever allow.

The rights view, I believe, is rationally the most satisfactory moral theory. It surpasses all other theories in the degree to which it illuminates and explains the foundation of our duties to one another—the domain of human morality. On this score it has the best reasons, the best arguments, on its side. Of course, if it were possible to show that only human beings are included within its scope, then a person like myself, who believes in animals rights, would be obliged to look elsewhere.

But attempts to limit its scope to humans only can be shown to be rationally defective. Animals, it is true, lack many of the abilities humans possess. They can't read, do higher mathematics, build a bookcase or make *baba ghanoush*. Neither can many human beings, however, and yet we don't (and shouldn't) say that they (these humans) therefore have less inherent value, less of a right to be treated with respect, than do others. It is the *similarities* between those human beings who most clearly, most non-controversially have such value (the people reading this, for example), not our differences, that matter most. And the really crucial, the basic similarity is simply this: we are each of us the experiencing subject of a life, a conscious creature having an individual welfare that has importance to us whatever our usefulness to others. We want and prefer things, believe and feel things, recall and expect things. And all these dimensions of our life, including our pleasure and pain, our enjoyment and suffering, our satisfaction and frustration, our continued existence or our untimely death—all make a difference to the quality of our life as lived, as experienced, by us as individuals. As the same is true of those animals that concern us (the ones that are eaten and trapped, for example), they too must be viewed as the experiencing subjects of a life, with inherent value of their own.

Some there are who resist the idea that animals have inherent value. 'Only humans have such value,' they profess. How might this narrow view be defended? Shall we say that only humans have the requisite intelligence, or autonomy, or reason? But there are many, many humans who fail to meet these standards and yet are reasonably viewed as having value above and beyond their usefulness to others. Shall we claim that only human beings belong to the right species, the species *Homo sapiens?* But this is blatant speciesism. Will it be said, then, that all—and only—humans have immortal souls? Then our opponents have their work cut out for them. I am myself not ill-disposed to the proposition that there are immortal souls. Personally, I profoundly hope I have one. But I would not want to rest my position on a controversial ethical issue on the even more controversial question about who or what has an immortal soul. That is to dig one's hole deeper, not to climb out. Rationally, it is better to resolve moral issues without making more controversial assumptions than are needed. The question of who has inherent value is such a question, one that is resolved more rationally without the introduction of the idea of immortal souls than by its use.

Well, perhaps some will say that animals have some inherent value, only less than we have. Once again, however, attempts to defend this view can be shown to lack rational justification. What could be the basis of our having more inherent value than animals? Their lack of reason, or autonomy, or intellect? Only if we are willing to make the same judgement in the case of humans who are similarly deficient. But it is not true that such humans—the retarded child, for example, or the mentally deranged—have less inherent value than you or I. Neither, then, can we rationally sustain the view that animals like them in being the experiencing subjects of a life have less inherent value. *All* who have inherent value have it *equally*, whether they be human animals or not.

Inherent value, then, belongs equally to those who are the experiencing subjects of a life. Whether it belongs to others—to rocks and rivers, trees and glaciers, for example—we do not know and may never know. But neither do we need to know, if we are to make the case for animal rights. We do not need to know, for example, how many people are eligible to vote in the next presidential election before we can know whether I am. Similarly, we do not need to know how many individuals have inherent value before we can know that some do. When it comes to the case for animals rights, then, what we need to know is whether the animals that, in our culture, are routinely eaten, hunted, and used in our laboratories, for example, are like us in being subjects of a life. And we do know this. We do know that many—literally, billions and billions— of these animals are the subjects of a life in the sense explained and so have inherent value if we do. And since, in order to arrive at the best theory of our duties to one another, we must recognize our equal inherent value as individuals, reason—not sentiment, not emotion—reason compels us to recognize the equal inherent value of these animals and, with this, their equal right to be treated with respect.

That, *very* roughly, is the shape and feel of the case for animal rights. Most of the details of the supporting argument are missing. They are to be found in the book to which I alluded earlier. Here, the details go begging, and I must, in closing, limit myself to four final points.

The first is how the theory that underlies the case for animal rights shows that the animal rights movement is a part of, not antagonistic to, the human rights movement. The theory that rationally grounds the rights of animals also grounds the rights of humans. Thus those involved in the animal rights movement are partners in the struggle to secure respect for human rights—the rights of women, for example, or minorities, or workers. The animal rights movement is cut from the same moral cloth as these.

Second, having set out the broad outlines of the rights view, I can now say why its implications for farming and science, among other fields, are both clear and uncompromising. In the case of the use of animals in science, the rights view is categorically abolitionist. Lab animals are not our tasters; we are not their kings. Because these animals are treated routinely, systematically as if their value were reducible to their usefulness to others, they are routinely, systematically treated with a lack of respect, and thus are their rights routinely, systematically violated. This is just as true when they are used in trivial, duplicative, unnecessary or unwise research as it is when they are used in studies that hold out real promise of human benefits. We can't justify harming or killing a human being (my Aunt Bea, for example) just for these sorts of reason. Neither can we do so even in the case of so lowly a creature as a laboratory rat. It is not just refinement or reduction that is called for, not just larger, cleaner cages, not just more generous use of anaesthetic or the elimination of multiple surgery, not just tidying up the system. It is complete replacement. The best we can do when it comes to using animals in science is—not to use them. That is where our duty lies, according to the rights view.

As for commercial animal agriculture, the rights view takes a similar abolitionist position. The fundamental moral wrong here is not that animals are kept in stressful close confinement or in isolation, or that their pain and suffering, their needs and preferences are ignored or discounted. All these *are* wrong, of course, but they are not the fundamental wrong. They are symptoms and effects of the deeper, systematic wrong that allows these animals to be viewed and treated as lacking independent value, as resources for us—as, indeed, a renewable resource. Giving farm animals more space, more natural environments, more companions does not right the fundamental wrong, any more than giving lab animals more anaesthesia or bigger, cleaner cages would right the fundamental wrong in their case. Nothing less than the total dissolution of commercial animal agriculture will do this, just as, for similar reasons I won't develop at length here, morality requires nothing less than the total elimination of hunting and trapping for commercial and sporting ends. The rights view's implications, then, as I have said, are clear and uncompromising.

My last two points are about philosophy, my profession. It is, most obviously, no substitute for political action. The words I have written here and in other places by themselves don't change a thing. It is what we do with the thoughts that the words express—our acts, our deeds—that changes things. All that philosophy can do, and all I have attempted, is to offer a vision of what our deeds should aim at. And the why. But not the how.

Finally, I am reminded of my thoughtful critic, the one I mentioned earlier, who chastised me for being too cerebral. Well, cerebral I have been: indirect duty views, utilitarianism, contractarianism—hardly the stuff deep passions are made of. I am also reminded, however, of the image another friend once set before me—the image of the ballerina as expressive of disciplined passion. Long hours of sweat and toil, of loneliness and practice, of doubt and fatigue: those are the discipline of her craft. But the passion is there too, the fierce drive to excel, to speak through her body, to do it right, to pierce our minds. That is the image of philosophy I would leave with you, not 'too cerebral' but *disciplined passion*. Of the discipline enough has been seen. As for the passion: there are times, and these not infrequent, when tears come to my eyes when I see, or read, or hear of the wretched plight of animals in the hands of humans. Their pain, their suffering, their loneliness, their innocence, their death. Anger. Rage. Pity. Sorrow. Disgust. The whole creation groans under the weight of the evil we humans visit upon these mute, powerless creatures. It *is* our hearts, not just our heads, that call for an end to it all, that demand of us that we overcome, for them, the habits and forces behind their systematic oppression. All great movements, it is written, go through three stages: ridicule, discussion, adoption. It is the realization of this third stage, adoption, that requires both our passion and our discipline, our hearts and our heads. The fate of animals is in our hands. God grant we are equal to the task.

Questions

1. What is the difference between indirect duties and direct duties? Do you think we have direct duties to animals and babies?
2. Can you think of a way in which a contractarian could incorporate the notion of direct duties to animals?
3. What is inherent value?
4. What do you think that Tom Regan means by "experiencing subjects of a life"? Is this an acceptable criterion for having inherent value?

Rights, Interests, Desires, and Beliefs

R. G. Frey

Raymond Frey examines the question of whether animals are the sort of beings to which rights can be ascribed. He argues that they are not. He notes that a number of philosophers have accepted the claim that all and only beings that (can) have interests (can) have moral rights. Some of these philosophers then conclude that because animals, like humans, (can) have interests, animals (can) have moral rights.

The author disputes the claim that animals can have interests in the relevant sense. To demonstrate this he distinguishes between two senses of "interest": (1) interest as well-being and (2) interest as want. The word is used in its first sense when we say, "Good health is in John's interests." And it is used in its second sense when we say, "John has an interest in good health."

Raymond Frey agrees that animals have interests in the first sense. That is to say, animals have a good or well-being that can be harmed or benefited. This, however, is of little use because not only animals but also inanimate objects like tractors have interests in this sense since there are things that can be good or bad for tractors. Yet tractors clearly do not have rights and thus this first sense of "interest" must be insufficient for possessing rights.

Now tractors do not have interests in the second sense: they cannot want to be well functioning, for example. The second sense of "interest" thus seems to be the sense relevant to the possessing of rights. But do animals have interests in the second sense? The author argues that they do not. This, he says, is because to have such interests, one must have desires and to have desires one must have beliefs. Because animals do not have language they cannot have beliefs. His argument can be laid out as follows:

a. To desire X, one must believe that one does not currently have X.

b. To believe that one does not currently have X is to believe that "'I have X' is false."

R. G. Frey, "Rights, Interests, Desires, and Beliefs," *American Philosophical Quarterly*, vol. 16, no. 3 (July 1979). Copyright 1979. Reprinted by permission.

c. One cannot have such a belief unless one knows how language connects with the world.

d. One cannot know how language connects with the world if one does not have language.

e. Animals do not have language.

f. Therefore, animals cannot have desires.

g. If one does not have desires, then one cannot have interests (in the second sense).

h. Therefore, animals do not have interests (in the second sense).

i. If one does not have interests (in the second sense), then one cannot have rights.

j. Therefore, animals cannot have rights.

I

The question of whether non-human animals possess moral rights is once again being widely argued. Doubtless the rise of ethology is partly responsible for this: as we learn more about the behavior of animals, it seems inevitable that we shall be led to focus upon the similarities between them and us, with the result that the extension of moral rights from human beings to non-human animals can appear, as the result of these similarities, to have a firm basis in nature. (Of course, this way of putting the matter assumes that human beings have moral rights, and on another occasion I should perhaps wish to challenge this assumption.) But the major impetus to renewed interest in the subject of animal rights almost certainly stems from a heightened and more critical awareness, among philosophers and non-philosophers alike, of the arguments for and against eating animals and using them in scientific research. For if animals *do* have moral rights, such as a right to live and to live free from unnecessary suffering, and if our present practices systematically tread upon these rights, then the case for eating and experimenting upon animals, especially when other alternatives are for the most part readily available, is going to have to be a powerful one indeed.

It is important, however, not to misconstrue the question: the question is not about *which* rights animals may or may not be thought to possess or about *whether* their alleged rights in a particular regard are on a par with the alleged rights of humans in this same regard, but rather about the more fundamental issue of whether animals—or, in any event, the "higher" animals—are a kind of being which can be the logical subject of rights. It is this issue, and a particular position with respect to it, that I want critically to address here.

II

The position I have in mind is the widely influential one which links the possession of rights to the possession of interests. In his *System of Ethics*, Leonard Nelson is among the first, if not the first, to propound the view that all and only beings which have interests can have rights,[1] a view which has attracted an increasingly wide following ever since. For example, in his paper "Rights," H. J. McCloskey embraces this view but goes on to deny that animals have interests;[2] whereas Joel Feinberg, in his seminal paper "The Rights of Animals and Unborn Generations," likewise embraces the view but goes on to affirm that animals do have interests.[3] Nelson himself is emphatic that animals as well as human beings are, as he puts it, "carriers of interests,"[4] and he concludes, accordingly, that animals possess rights, rights which both deserve and warrant our respect. For Nelson, then, it is because animals have interests that they can be the logical subject of rights, and his claim that animals *do have* interests forms the minor premiss, therefore, in an argument for the moral rights of animals:

> All and only beings which (can) have interests (can) have moral rights; Animals as well as humans (can) have interests; Therefore, animals (can) have moral rights.

Both McCloskey and Feinberg accept the major premiss of this argument, which I shall dub the interest thesis, but disagree over the truth of the minor premiss; and it is apparent that the minor premiss is indeed the key to the whole matter. For given the truth of the major premiss, given, that is, that the possession of interests *is* a criterion for the possession of rights, it is nevertheless only the truth of the minor premiss that would result in the inclusion of creatures other than human beings within the class of right-holders. This premiss is doubtful, however, and the case against it a powerful one, or so I want to suggest.

This case is not that developed by McCloskey, whose position is not free of a rather obvious difficulty. He makes the issue of whether animals have interests turn upon their failure and/or inability to grasp and so behave in accordance with the prescriptive overtone which he takes talk of "*X* is in *A*'s interests" to have, when it is not obvious that expressions like "*X* is in *A*'s interests" do have a prescriptive overtone and certainly not obvious that a prescriptive overtone is part of the meaning of such expressions. I have elsewhere tried to show how a McCloskey-like position on interests might be sustained;[5] but I do not think his way of tackling the claim that animals have interests a particularly fruitful one, and I neither adopt nor rely upon it in what follows.

III

To say that "Good health is in John's interests" is not at all the same thing as to say that "John has an interest in good health." The former is intimately bound

---

[1] Leonard Nelson, *System of Ethics*, tr. by Norbert Guterman (New Haven, 1956), Part I, Section 2, Chapter 7, pp. 136–144.
[2] H. J. McCloskey, "Rights," *Philosophical Quarterly*, vol. 15 (1965), pp. 115–127.
[3] Joel Feinberg, "The Rights of Animals and Unborn Generations," in W. T. Blackstone, (ed.), *Philosophy and Environmental Crisis* (Athens, Georgia, 1974), pp. 43–68.
[4] Nelson, *op. cit.*, p. 138.
[5] See my paper "Interests and Animal Rights," *Philosophical Quarterly*, vol. 27 (1977), pp. 254–259.

up with having a good or well-being to which good health is conducive, so that we could just as easily have said "Good health is conducive to John's good or well-being," whereas the latter—"John has an interest in good health"—is intimately bound up with wanting, with John's wanting good health. That these two notions of "interest" are logically distinct is readily apparent: good health may well be in John's interests, in the sense of being conducive to his good or well-being, even if John does not want good health, indeed, even if he wants to continue taking hard drugs, with the result that his health is irreparably damaged; and John may have an interest in taking drugs, in the sense of wanting to take them, even if it is apparent to him that it is not conducive to his good or well-being to continue to do so. In other words, something can be *in* John's interests without John's *having* an interest in it, and John can *have* an interest in something without its being *in* his interests.

If this is right, and there are these two logically distinct senses of "interest," we can go on to ask whether animals can have interests in either of these senses; and if they do, then perhaps the minor premise of Nelson's argument for the moral rights of animals can be sustained.

IV

Do animals, therefore, have interests in the first sense, in the sense of having a good or well-being which can be harmed or benefited? The answer, I think, is that they certainly do have interests in this sense; after all, it is plainly not good for a dog to be fed certain types of food or to be deprived of a certain amount of exercise. This answer, however, is of little use to the Nelsonian cause; for it yields the counterintuitive result that manmade/manufactured objects and even things have interests, and, therefore, on the interest thesis, have or at least are candidates for having moral rights. For example, just as it is not good for a dog to be deprived of a certain amount of exercise, so it is not good for prehistoric cave drawings to be exposed to excessive amounts of carbon dioxide or for Rembrandt paintings to be exposed to excessive amounts of sunlight.

If, nevertheless, one is inclined to doubt that the notion of "not being good for" in the above examples shows that the objective or thing in question, "has a good," consider the case of tractors: anything, including tractors, can have a good, a well-being, I submit, if it is the sort of thing that can be good of its kind; and there are obviously good and bad tractors. A tractor which cannot perform certain tasks is not a good tractor, is not good of its kind; it falls short of those standards tractors must meet in order to be good ones. Thus, to say that it is in a tractor's interests to be well-oiled means only that it is conducive to the tractor's being a good one, good of its kind, if it is well-oiled. Just as John is good of his kind (i.e., human being) only if he is in health, so tractors are good of their kind only if they are well-oiled. Of course, farmers *have an interest* in their tractors being well-oiled; but this does not show that being well-oiled is not in a tractor's interest, in the sense of contributing to its being good of its kind. It *may* show that what makes good tractors good depends upon the purposes for which *we* make them; but the fact that we make them for certain purposes in no way shows that, once they are made, they cannot have a good of their own. Their good is being good of their kind, and being well-oiled is conducive to their being good of their kind and so, in this sense, in their interests. If this is right, if tractors do have interests, then on the interest thesis they have or can have moral rights, and this is a counter-intuitive result.

It is tempting to object, I suppose, that tractors cannot be harmed and benefited and, therefore, cannot have interests. My earlier examples, however, suffice to meet this objection. Prehistoric cave drawings are (not benefited but) positively harmed by excessive amounts of carbon dioxide, and Rembrandt paintings are likewise certainly harmed through exposure to excessive amounts of sunlight. It must be emphasized that it is these objects themselves that are harmed, and that their owners are harmed only in so far as and to the extent that the objects themselves undergo harm. Accordingly, on the present objection, interests are present, and the interest thesis once again gives the result that objects or things have or can have moral rights. To accommodate those, should there be any, who just might feel that objects or things can have moral rights, when these objects or things are, e.g., significant works of art, the examples can be suitably altered, so that what is harmed is, e.g., a quite ordinary rug. But if drawings, paintings and rugs can be harmed, why not tractors? Surely a tractor is harmed by prolonged exposure to rain? And surely the harm the tractor's owner suffers comes through and is a function of the harm to the tractor itself?

In short, it cannot be in this first sense of "interest" that the case for animals and for the truth of Nelson's minor premiss is to be made: for though animals do have interests in this sense, so, too, do tractors, with awkward results.

V

Do animals, therefore, have interests in the second sense, in the sense of having wants which can be satisfied or left unsatisfied? In this sense, of course, it appears that tractors do not have interests: for though being well-oiled may be conducive to tractors being good of their kind, tractors do not *have an interest* in being well-oiled, since they cannot *want* to be well-oiled, cannot, in fact, have any wants whatever. But farmers can have wants, and they certainly have an interest in their tractors being well-oiled.

What, then, about animals? Can they have wants? By "wants," I understand a term that encompasses both needs and desires, and it is these that I shall consider.

If to ask whether animals can have wants is to ask whether they can have needs, then certainly animals have wants. A dog can need water. But *this* cannot be the sense of "want" on which having interests will depend, since it does not exclude things from the class of want-holders. Just as dogs need water in order to function normally, so tractors need oil in order to function normally; and just as dogs will die unless their need for water is satisfied, so trees and grass and a wide variety of plants and shrubs will die unless their need for water is satisfied. Though we should not give the fact undue weight, someone who in ordinary discourse says "The tractor wants oiling" certainly means the tractor needs oiling, if it is not to fall away from those standards which make tractors good of their kind. Dogs, too, need water, if they are not to fall away from the standards which make them good of their kind. It is perhaps worth emphasizing, moreover, as the cases of the tractor, trees, grass, etc., show, that needs to not require the presence either of consciousness or of knowledge of the lack which makes up the need. If, in sum, we are to agree that tractors, trees, grass, etc., do not have wants, and, therefore, interests, it cannot be the case that wants are to be construed as needs.

This, then, leaves desires, and the question of whether animals can have wants as desires. I may as well say at once that I do not think animals can have desires. My reasons for thinking this turn largely upon my doubts that animals can have beliefs, and my doubts in this regard turn partially,[6] though in large part, upon the view that having beliefs is not compatible with the absence of language and linguistic ability. I realize that the claim that animals cannot have desires is a controversial one; but I think the case to be made in support of it, complex though it is, is persuasive. This case, I should stress, consists in an analysis of desire and belief and of what it is to have and to entertain beliefs, and *not* in the adoption of anything like Chomsky's account of language as something radically unlike and completely discontinuous with animal behavior.

VI

Suppose I am a collector of rare books and desire to own a Gutenberg Bible: my desire to own this volume is *to be traced* to my belief that I do not now own such a work and that my rare book collection is deficient in this regard. By "to be traced" here, what I mean is this: if someone were to ask *how* my belief that my book collection lacks a Gutenberg Bible is connected with my desire to own such a Bible, what better or more direct reply could be given that that, without this belief, I would not have this desire? For if I believed that my rare book collection *did* contain a Gutenberg Bible and so was complete in this sense, then I would not desire a Gutenberg Bible in order to make up what I now believe to be a notable deficiency in my collection. Of course, I might desire to own more than one such Bible, but this contingency is not what is at issue here.

Now, what is it that I believe? I believe that my collection lacks a Gutenberg Bible: that is, I believe that the sentence "My collection lacks a Gutenberg Bible" is true. In constructions of the form "I believe that . . . " what follows upon the "that" is a declarative sentence: and *what* I believe is that that sentence is true. The same is the case with constructions of the form "He believes that . . .": what follows upon the "that" is a declarative sentence, and what the "he" in question

---

[6]I express doubts of a different kind elsewhere: see note 6.

believes is that that sentence is true. The difficulty in the case of animals should be apparent: if someone were to say, e.g., "The cat believes that the door is locked," then the person is holding, as I see it, that the cat holds the declarative sentence "The door is locked" to be true; and I can see no reason whatever for crediting the cat or any other creature which lacks language, including human infants, with entertaining declarative sentences and holding certain declarative sentences to be true.

Importantly, nothing whatever in this account is affected by changing the example, in order to rid it of sophisticated concepts like "door" and "locked," which in any event may be thought beyond cats, and to put in their place more rudimentary concepts. For the essence of this account is not about the relative sophistication of this or that concept but rather about the relationship between believing something and entertaining and regarding as true certain declarative sentences. If what is believed is that a certain declarative sentence is true, then no creature which lacks language can have beliefs; and without beliefs, a creature cannot have desires. And this is the case with animals, or so I suggest; and if I am right, not even in the sense, then, of wants as desires do animals have interests, which, to recall, is the minor premiss in the Nelsonian argument for the moral rights of animals.

But is what is believed that a certain declarative sentence is true? I think there are three arguments of sorts, that shore up the claim that this *is* what is believed.

First, I do not see how a creature could have the concept of belief without being able to distinguish between true and false beliefs. When I believe that my collection of rare books lacks a Gutenberg Bible, I believe that it is true that my collection lacks a Gutenberg Bible; put another way, I believe that it is false that my collection contains a Gutenberg Bible. I can distinguish, and do distinguish, between the sentences "My collection lacks a Gutenberg Bible" and "My collection contains a Gutenberg Bible," and it is only the former I hold to be true. According to my view, what I believe in this case is that this sentence is true; and sentences are the sorts of things we regard as or hold to be true. As for the cat, and leaving aside now all questions about the relative sophistication of concepts, I do not see how it could have the belief that the door is locked unless it could distinguish this true belief from the false belief that the door is unlocked. But what is true or false are not states of affairs which correspond to or reflect or pertain to these beliefs: states of affairs are not true or false but either are or are not the case, either do or do not obtain. If, then, one is going to credit cats with beliefs, and cats must be able to distinguish true from false beliefs, and states of affairs are not true or false, then what exactly is it that cats are being credited with distinguishing as true or false? Reflection on this question, I think, forces one to credit cats with language, in order for there to be something that can be true or false in belief; and it is precisely because they lack language that we cannot make this move.

Second, if in order to have the concept of belief a creature must be possessed of the difference between true and false belief, then in order for a creature to be able to distinguish true from false beliefs that creature must—simply must, as I see it—have some awareness of, to put the matter in the most general terms, how language connects with, links up with the world; and I see no reason to credit cats with such an awareness. My belief that my collection lacks a Gutenberg Bible is true if and only if my collection lacks a Gutenberg Bible; that is, the *truth* of this belief cannot be entertained by me without it being the case that I am aware that the truth of the sentence "My collection lacks a Gutenberg Bible" is *at the very least* partially a function of how the world is. However difficult to capture, it is this relationship between language and the world a grasp of which is necessary if a creature is to grasp the difference between true and false belief, a distinction which it must grasp, if it is to possess the concept of belief at all.

Third, I do not see how a creature could have an awareness or grasp of how language connects with, links up with the world, to leave the matter at its most general, unless that creature was itself possessed of language; and cats are not possessed of language. If it were to be suggested, for example, that the sounds that cats make do amount to a language, I should deny it. This matter is far too large and complex to be tackled here; but the general line of argument I should use to support my denial can be sketched in a very few words. Can cats lie? If they cannot, then they cannot assert anything: and if they lack assertion, I do not see how they could possess a language. And I should be strict: I do not suggest that, lacking assertion, cats possess a language in some attenuated or secondary sense: rather, I suggest that, lacking assertion, they do not possess a language *at all*.

VII

It may be suggested, of course, that there might possibly be a class of desires— let us call them simple desires—which do not involve the intervention of belief, in order to have them, and which do not require that we credit animals with language. Such simple desires, for example, might be for some object or other, and we as language-users might try to capture these simple desires in the case of a dog by describing its behavior in such terms as "The dog simply desires the bone." (This position may have to be complicated, as the result of questions about whether the dog possesses the concept "bone" or even more general concepts such as "material object," "thing" and "thing in my visual field"; but these questions I shall leave aside here.) If all the dog's desires are simple desires, and this is the point, then my arguments to show that dogs lack beliefs may well be beside the point.

A subsidiary argument is required, therefore, in order to cover this possibility. Suppose, then, the dog simply desires the bone: is the dog aware that it has this simple desire or not? If it is alleged to have this desire but to be unaware that it has it, to want but to be unaware that it wants, then a problem arises. In the case of human beings, unconscious desire can be made sense of, but only because we first make sense of conscious desire; but where no desires are conscious ones, where the creature in question is alleged to have only unconscious desires, what cash value can the use of the term "desire" have in such a case? This question must be appreciated against the backdrop of what appears to ensue as a result of the present claim. On the strength of the dog's behavior, it is claimed that the dog simply desires the bone; the desire we claim for it is one which, if we concede that it has it, it is unaware that it has; and no distinction between conscious and unconscious desire is to be drawn in the dog's case. Consider, then, a rubber plant which shuns the dark and through a series of movements, seeks the light; by parity of reasoning with the dog's case, we can endow the plant with an unconscious desire for the light, and claim as we do so that it, too, is a type of creature for whom no distinction between conscious and unconscious desire is possible. In other words, without an awareness-condition of some sort, it would seem that the world can be populated with an enormous number of unconscious desires in this way, and it no longer remains clear what, if anything, the cash value of the term "desire" is in such cases. If, however, the dog is alleged to have a simple desire for the bone and to be aware that is has this desire, then the dog is aware that it simply desires the bone; it is, in other words, self-conscious. Now my objection to regarding the dog as self-conscious is not merely founded upon the view that self-consciousness presupposes the possession of language, which is too large a subject to go into here; it is also founded upon the fact that there is nothing the dog can do which can express the difference between desiring the bone and being aware of desiring the bone. Yet, the dog would have to be capable of expressing this difference in its behavior, if one is going to hold, *on the basis of that behavior,* that the dog is aware that it has a simple desire for the bone, aware that it simply desires the bone.

Even, then, if we concede for the sake of argument that there are simple desires, desires which do not involve the intervention of belief in order to have them, the suggestion that we can credit animals with these desires, without also having to credit them with language, is at best problematic.

VIII

I want, finally, to comment upon a contention that is not exactly an objection to my earlier remarks so much as a thesis which might be thought to serve as a possible rallying point for opponents.

In *Belief, Truth and Knowledge,* D. M. Armstrong proposes a way of interpreting "that"-clauses used of animals, such as the attribution of beliefs to animals in sentences of the form "The dog believes that . . ." remains intelligible but does not commit us to characterizing the exact content of animal beliefs.[7] Briefly, Armstrong suggests that "that"-clauses used of animals be treated as referentially transparent (as opposed to opaque) constructions, so that, "in saying that the dog believes that his master is at the door we are, or should be, attributing to the dog a belief whose exact content we do not know but which can be obtained by substituting *salva veritate* in the proposition 'that his master is at the door,'"[8] There are problems here, as Armstrong says, with the use of human

---

[7]D. M. Armstrong, *Belief, Truth and Knowledge* (Cambridge, 1973), pp. 24–37.
[8]*Ibid*, p. 26.

concepts to describe the actual content of animal beliefs, and further problems, which Armstrong does not go into, about the actual categories of things which animals recognize; and these two clusters of problems together, I suspect, prove highly damaging to Armstrong's analysis. But at least his way of proceeding, he claims, "shows that we need not give up our natural inclination to attribute beliefs to animals just because the descriptions we give of the beliefs almost certainly do not fit the beliefs' actual content."[9]

My problem with Armstrong's position is this: on the strength of the dog's behavior, we say "The dog believes that his master is at the door": but our attributing this belief to the dog is not the same thing as showing that it actually has this belief. What we require, if we are to move from our saying "The dog believes that p" to holding that the dog actually has the belief *that p,* is some account of the connection, not between behavior and our attribution of belief, but between behavior and belief. Now if, as Armstrong, one allows belief to have any propositional content whatever, even propositional content that is to be regarded and treated as referentially transparent; and if, as Armstrong, one is prepared to concede that dogs do not possess language; then it must be the case, if one is going to claim that dogs actually do have beliefs, but that they have some grasp (a term which the reader is to interpret as liberally as he desires) of this propositional content and that non-linguistic behavior alone can suffice to show that they have such a grasp. I have two difficulties here. First, I do not understand how non-linguistic behavior can *show* that a dog possesses the belief *that p* unless it is the case that that non-linguistic behavior is connected with the belief *that p* in such a way that same piece of non-linguistic behavior is not compatible with the belief *that q* or *that r* or *that s.* For if the dog's non-linguistic behavior is compatible both with the belief *that p* and with these other beliefs, then I do not understand how it can be concluded on the basis of that behavior that it has the belief *that p* or that it has a grasp of the propositional content of the belief *that p.* For example, yesterday, my dog wagged its tail when its master was at the door, but it also wagged its tail when its lunch was about to be prepared and when the sun was being eclipsed by the moon. On all three occasions, it barked and jumped about. So far as I could see, its non-linguistic behavior was the same on the last two occasions as it was on the first, and I am not clear how on the basis of that behavior it can possible be concluded that the dog *had* the belief that his master was at the door or that the dog *had* a grasp of the propositional content of the belief that its master was at the door. Second, I do not understand how a piece of non-linguistic behavior could be connected with the belief *that p* in such a way that we could conclude on the basis of the presence of that piece of behavior

---

[9]*Ibid,* p. 27. In this section, because I am addressing Armstrong and others who analyze belief propositionally or at least allow it to have propositional content, I shall allow myself to speak of the belief *that p,* where *that p* is a proposition. I remind the reader, however, that my own account of belief in Section VII is in terms of sentences. What I say here is consistent with what I say there, since in each instance where belief is analyzed propositionally here, I should resort to Quine's method for eliminating propositions in belief contexts in favor of sentences.

that the dog actually had the belief *that p* or had actually grasped the propositional content of the belief *that p* unless it were the case that there were some intrinsic connection between that piece of non-linguistic behavior and the proposition *that p* itself. The dog allegedly believes *that p*: according to Armstrong, *that p* is, even if in a referentially transparent fashion, what is believed, and *that p* is a proposition. In order to show that the dog grasps the proposition *that p*, its behavior must suffice; but if its behavior is in fact to show that it grasps just this particular proposition, just this proposition *that p*, then surely there must be some intrinsic connection between that behavior *and that proposition?* But there is no intrinsic connection between the dog's wagging its tail and its barking and jumping about and the proposition "Its master is at the door," since that behavior is compatible with the widely different propositions "Lunch is about to be served" and "The sun in being eclipsed by the moon." We can describe the dog's behavior in propositional terms, describe it as believing *that p* or as having grasp of the propositional content of the belief *that p*; but the fact that the dog wags its tail, barks and jumps about does not show that the dog has grasped the proposition *that p* and *could not* show this, I think, unless wagging its tail, barking and jumping about were intrinsically connected with just that proposition, which they are not, any more than they are so connected with any other proposition.

Put succinctly, then, my complaint against Armstrong is that, even if his analysis of the use of "that"-clauses in respect of animals is correct, it still has not been shown *either* that the dog has a grasp of the proposition *that p* or the propositional content of the belief *that p* or that non-linguistic behavior alone can suffice to establish such a grasp. But it is precisely these things which must be shown, if we are to pass from merely attributing beliefs to animals on the strength of their behavior to concluding on the strength of their behavior that they actually have some beliefs.[10]

IX

I conclude, then, that the Nelsonian position on the moral rights of animals is not a sound one: the truth of the minor premiss in his argument—that animals have interests—is doubtful at best, and animals must have interests if, in accordance with the interest thesis, they are to be a logical subject of such rights. For animals either have interests in a sense which allows objects and things to have interests, and so, on the interest thesis, to have or to be candidates for having moral rights or they do not have interests at all, and so, on the interest thesis, do

---

[10]One may, of course, try to get round my argument by analyzing belief non-propositionally (e.g., by trying to develop a reductionism of belief to behavior in the case of animals), but this is not Armstrong's tack in his discussion of animals. Nor, as will be apparent from my arguments in this paper, is it one that I think capable of showing that animals actually have the concept of belief, since a reductionism would appear to leave no room for a distinction between true and false belief, a grasp of which is necessary, in my view, if a creature is to have the concept of belief at all.

not have and are not candidates for having moral rights. I have reached this conclusion, moreover, without querying the correctness of the interest thesis itself, without querying, that is, whether the possession of interests *really is* a criterion for the possession of moral rights.[11]

Questions

1. Can you think of a third sense of "interest" that would apply to humans and animals but not to tractors? Do Peter Singer and Raymond Frey agree on what interests are?
2. Is it true that animals lack: (*a*) beliefs, (*b*) desires, and (*c*) language? If so, could it be right that because of this, animal pain is morally inconsiderable?

---

[11]An earlier version of this paper was read to a discussion group in Oxford and to a conference on the philosophy of Leonard Nelson in the University of Gottingen. I am indebted to the participants in each for helpful comments and suggestions.

A Defense of Meat Eating

Jan Narveson

Jan Narveson argues from a contractarian perspective for the moral permissibility of meat eating. He rejects Rawlsian contractarianism, according to which the terms of the contract are decided by beings who lack specific information about themselves. John Rawls imposes this condition of ignorance because he thinks that it makes the contract fairer, but Jan Narveson rejects it, perhaps because it entails a contract that is not actually agreed to by real people. (Unlike John Rawls himself, Jan Narveson thinks that Rawlsian contractarianism can quite easily be extended to support direct duties to animals.)

In place of Rawlsian contractarianism, Jan Narveson offers a contractarian theory in which the parties to the contract know who they are and what they want. The purpose of such a contract, he says, is to voluntarily limit one's own actions in order to reap the long-term benefits of the reciprocal forbearance of others. The advantage of this view of morality, he says, is that it explains both why we have morality and who is party to it. On this view, the point of morality is to secure one's long-term self-interest and those who are party to it are those who both (a) stand to gain (in the long run) from adhering to the contract and (b) are capable of entering into and keeping an agreement. On this view, animals lack moral standing because (a) humans generally have nothing to gain from entering into agreements with them and (b) animals are not able to enter into and adhere to contracts.

Jan Narveson then considers the problem of "marginal cases"—those humans, such as infants and the severely mentally defective, who do not pose any threat to the rest of us and who are incapable of entering into and keeping agreements. The author provides three reasons why such beings (unlike animals) should nonetheless be granted moral standing.

Jan Narveson, "A Defense of Meat Eating," published as "Animal Rights Revisited," in H. Miller and W. Williams (eds.), *Ethics and Animals* (Clifton, N.J.: Humana Press, 1983), 56–59.

The tendency in the past few years has been to take John Rawls' well-known theory of justice as the model of contractualist moral theory. I must therefore begin by explaining why that is a mistake.

On the contract view of morality, morality is a sort of agreement among rational, independent, self-interested persons, persons who have something to gain from entering into such an agreement. It is of the very essence, on such a theory, that the parties to the agreement know who they are and what they want—what they in particular want, and not just what a certain general class of beings of which they are members generally tend to want. Now, Rawls' theory has his parties constrained by agreements that they would have made if they *did not* know who they were. But if we can have that constraint, why should we not go just a little further and specify that one is not only not to know *which* person he or she is, but also whether he or she will be a person *at all*: reason on the assumption that you might turn out to be an owl, say, or a vermin, or a cow. We may imagine that *that* possibility would make quite a difference . . . (Some proponents of vegetarianism, I believe, are tempted by it, and do extend the veil of ignorance that far.)

The "agreement" of which morality consists is a voluntary undertaking to limit one's behavior in various respects. In a sense, it consists in a renunciation of action on unconstrained self-interest. It is, however, self-interested overall. The idea is to come out ahead in the long run, by refraining, contingently on others' likewise refraining, from certain actions, the general indulgence in which would be worse for all and therefore for oneself. There are well-known solutions for them. I only claim that this is an important and plausible conception of morality, worth investigating in the present context.

A major feature of this view of morality is that it explains why we have it and who is a party to it. We have it for reasons of long-run, self-interest, and parties to it include all and only those who have *both* of the following characteristics: (1) they stand to gain by subscribing to it, at least in the long run, compared with not doing so, and (2) they are *capable* of entering into (and keeping) an agreement. Those not capable of it obviously cannot be parties to it, and among those capable of it, there is no reason for them to enter into it if there is nothing to gain for them from it, no matter how much the others might benefit.

Given these requirements, it will be clear why animals do not have rights. For there are evident shortcomings on both scores. On the one hand, humans have nothing generally to gain by voluntarily refraining from (for instance) killing animals or "treating them as mere means." And on the other, animals cannot generally make agreements with us anyway, even if we wanted to have them do so. Both points are worth expanding on briefly.

(1) In saying that humans have "nothing generally to gain" from adopting principles restraints against behavior harmful to animals, I am in one respect certainly overstating the case, for it is possible that animal food, for instance, is bad for us, or that something else about animals, which requires such restraint from us, would be for our long-term benefit. Those are issues I mostly leave on one side here, except to note that some people may think that we gain on the score of purity of soul by treating animals better. But if the purity in question is

moral purity, then that would be question-begging on the contractarian conception of morality. In any case, those people are, of course, welcome to treat animals as nicely as they like. The question is whether others may be prevented from treating animals badly, e.g., by eating them, and the "purity of soul" factor cannot be appealed to in that context.

A main motive for morality on the contract view is, of course, diffidence. Humans have excellent reason to be fearful about each other. Our fellows, all and sundry, are quite capable of doing damage to us, and not only capable but often quite interested in doing so; and their rational (or at least, calculative) capacities only make things worse. There is compelling need for mutual restraint. Now, animals can, many of them, be harmful to us. But the danger is rather specialized and limited in most cases, and in those cases we can deal with it by such methods as caging the animals in question, or by shooting them, and so on. There is no general need for moral methods, and there is also the question whether they are available. In any case, we have much to gain from eating them, and if one of the main planks in a moral platform is refraining from killing merely for self-interest, then it is quite clear that such a plank, in the case of animals, would not be worth it from the point of view of most of us. Taking our chances in the state of nature would be preferable.

(2) What about the capability of entering into and keeping such agreements? Animals have been pretty badly maligned on this matter in the past, I gather. Really beastly behavior is a phenomenon pretty nearly unique to the human species. But still, when animals refrain from killing other animals or people just for the fun of it, there is no good reason to think that they do so out of moral principle. Rather, it is just that it is not really their idea of fun!

There remains a genuine question about the eligibility of animals for morality on the score of their abilities. A very few individuals among some animals species have been enabled, after years of highly specialized work, to communicate in fairly simple ways with people. That does not augur well for animals' entering quite generally into something as apparently sophisticated as an agreement. But of course agreements can be tacit and unwritten, even unspoken. Should we postulate, at some such inexplicit level, an "agreement" among humans, it is largely tacit there. People do not enter into agreements to refrain from killing each other, except in fairly specialized cases; the rule against killing that we (virtually) all acknowledge is one we adopt out of common sense and antecedent inculcation by our mentors. Still, it is reasonable to say that when one person does kill another one, he or she is (among other things) taking *unfair advantage* of the restraint that one's fellow have exercised with regard toward one over many years. But can any such thing be reasonably said of animals? I would think not.

On the whole, therefore, it seems clear that contractarianism leaves animals out of it, so far as rights are concerned. They are, by and large, to be dealt with in terms of our self-interest, unconstrained by the terms of hypothetical agreements with them. Just exactly what our interest in them is may, of course, be matter for debate; but that those are the terms on which we may deal with them is, on this view of morality, overwhelmingly indicated.

There is an evident problem about the treatment of what I have called "marginal cases" on this view, of course: infants, the feeble-minded, and the incapacitated are in varying degrees in the position of the animals in relation to us, are they not? True: but the situation is very different in several ways. For one thing, we generally have very little to gain from treating such people badly, and we often have much to gain from treating them well. For another, marginal humans are invariably members of families, or members of other groupings, which makes them the object of love and interest on the part of other members of those groups. Even if there were an interest in treating a particular marginal person badly, there would be others who have an interest in their being treated well and who are themselves clearly members of the moral community on contractarian premises. Finally, it does have to be pointed out that there is genuine question about the morality of, for instance, euthanasia, and that infanticide has been approved of in various human communities at various times. On the whole, it seems to me not an insurmountable objection to the contractarian account that we grant marginal humans fairly strong rights.

It remains that we may think that suffering is a bad thing, no matter whose. But although we think so, we do not think it is so bad as to require us to become vegetarians. Here by "we," of course, I mean most of us. And what most of us think is that, although suffering is too bad and it is unfortunate for animals that they are turned into hamburgers at a tender age, we nevertheless are justified on the whole in eating them. If contractarianism is correct, then these attitudes are not inconsistent. And perhaps it is.

Questions

1. How does Jan Narveson think that Rawlsian contractarianism can be extended to include animals?
2. What would Tom Regan say about Jan Narveson's defense of meat eating? What would Peter Singer say about it?
3. Is Jan Narveson's response to the problem of "marginal cases" satisfactory? That is to say, can he consistently grant moral standing to human infants and severely mentally defective humans while withholding it from animals?

A New Argument for Vegetarianism

Jordan Curnutt

Jordan Curnutt presents an argument for vegetarianism that seeks to avoid traditional approaches—those that appeal to utilitarianism, to rights-based theories, or to pain and suffering. These traditional approaches, suggests the author, have led to a stalemate, and a new argument is needed. He sketches and then explains a seven-step argument that he thinks will serve the necessary purpose. This argument does not appeal to utility, rights, or pain and suffering. Instead it rests on the idea that causing harm is prima facie wrong.

Philosophical discussion of vegetarianism has been steadily decreasing over the last ten years or so. This follows a prolific period in the 1970s and 1980s when a veritable flood of books and journal articles appeared, devoted wholly or in part to various defenses and rejections of vegetarianism. What has happened? Have the relevant problems been solved? Have philosophers simply lost interest in the topic? I don't think so. My hypothesis is that the major theoretical approaches to the issue which have been most rigorously pursued have produced a stalemate: appeal to some form of utilitarian theory, or to rights-based theories, or to pain and suffering, have not proved fruitful for resolving the problems.

I would like to present an alternative to these traditional approaches. This alternative avoids the difficulties which result in the stalemate, successfully eludes subsequent objections, and justifies a moral requirement to refrain from eating animals. I will first briefly explain why the old arguments have not been helpful. The remainder of the paper is devoted to the explanation and defense of a new argument for vegetarianism, one which does not depend on

Jordan Curnutt, "A New Argument for Vegetarianism," *Journal of Social Philosophy*, vol. 28, no. 3 (winter 1997). Copyright 1997. Reprinted by permission of *Journal of Social Philosophy*.

calculations of utility, any particular conception of rights, or the imposition of pain and suffering.[1]

OLD ARGUMENTS FOR VEGETARIANISM

Peter Singer has been the leading utilitarian defender of vegetarianism for more than twenty years.[2] He has often cited the vast amounts of pain and suffering experienced by domesticated animals "down on the factory farm" as they await and inevitably succumb to their fate as food for human consumption.[3] A utilitarian of any species is required to produce that state of affairs in which aggregations of certain positive and negative mental states exceed (or at least equal) such aggregations of any alternative state of affairs. Singer has argued that factory farming woefully fails to meet this standard. Vegetarianism is morally obligatory simply because it maximizes utility, precisely what utilitarians say we are supposed to do. Animal-eating promotes disutility, precisely what we are supposed to avoid.

But several philosophers have urged that utilitarianism is a perilous ally for the vegetarian. One major problem is that the end of animal-eating produces disutilities which must be accounted for in the utilitarian ledger. When that is done, animal-eating may not emerge as morally wrong after all. For example, R. G. Frey has claimed that the demise of the meat industry and its satellites which would attend a wholesale conversion to vegetarianism would be catastrophic to human welfare, and so could not be given a utilitarian justification.[4] Frey lists fourteen different ways in which rampant vegetarianism would deleteriously affect human affairs, mainly in the form of economic losses for those employed in the industry. In the face of this, his utilitarian calculation yields the result that we are permitted to eat animals at will, but we must strive to reduce the amount of suffering they experience.[5]

Not only does vegetarianism produce disutilities, but animal-eating can actually maximize utility: utilitarianism may *require* animal-eating. Roger Crisp

---

[1]There is another defense of vegetarianism based on the value of ecosystems, for example Peter Wenz's "An Ecological Argument for Vegetarianism," *Ethics and Animals* 5 (1984): 2–9. This approach is rare even though the ecologically destructive effects of raising cattle and sheep have been frequently noted in the scientific literature and are not uncommon in philosophical discussions of the environment. Such ecological arguments (as Wenz acknowledges, p. 2) depend on accepting that an ecosystem itself has a moral status. Here I assume the view is mistaken, so we need not consider the argument. The best cases for the moral value of ecosystems can be found in J. Baird Callicott, *In Defense of the Land Ethic*, State University of New York Press, 1989, and Holmes Rolston, *Environmental Ethics*, Temple University Press, 1989. However, both Callicott and Rolston reject vegetarianism.

[2]In many works, but most notably *Animal Liberation*, Avon, 1st ed., 1975, 2nd ed., 1990; and *Practical Ethics*, Cambridge, 1st ed., 1979, 2nd ed., 1993.

[3]For example, *Animal Liberation*, chap. 3. See also *Animal Factories*, Harmony Books, rev. ed., 1990, coauthored with Jim Mason.

[4]*Rights, Killing, and Suffering*, Basil Blackwell, 1983.

[5]Frey: 197–202.

contends that this theory leads to what he calls the "Compromise Require-ment view."[6] According to Crisp, "nonintensively-reared animals lead worth-while lives: and humans derive gustatory pleasure, satisfaction, or some other positive mental state from eating them. Vegetarianism would put an end to these two sources of utility. Thus, given the requirement to maximize util-ity, raising and eating animals in these circumstances becomes a utilitarian obligation.[7]

These philosophers, among others, have pinpointed why the utilitarian case for vegetarianism is a shaky one. Like any other utilitarian calculation, the issue here is an empirical and hence contingent one: vegetarianism is at the mercy of such capricious factors as the number of humans who eat meat relative to the number of animals eaten, and the negative and positive mental states attendant on a wide variety of animal husbandry situations and human living conditions. A similar contingency concerning methods of livestock-rearing also obtains for any argument premised on the pain and suffering caused to the animals eaten, whether or not these experiences are deployed in a utilitarian schema.[8] More-over, this theory requires summing and comparing the positive and negative mental states of *billions* of individuals of several different species.[9] That prospect alone certainly makes it appear as though the problem is an intractable one. The lesson to be learned is that a successful argument for vegetarianism must be in-dependent of any current or possible method of livestock-rearing and must ap-peal to factors which are fairly clear and manageable.

The leading contender to utilitarian theory in this area has been the rights-based perspective of Tom Regan. His dedication to defending animals in gen-eral and vegetarianism in particular nearly matches Singer's in duration and production.[10] In brief, Regan's position is that mammals of at least one year old are "subjects-of-a-life": they are conscious beings with a wide variety of mental states, such as preferences, beliefs, sensations, a sense of self and of the future. These features identify animals as rightsholders and possessors of "inherent" value. One implication of this view is that killing animals for food, whether or not this is done painlessly and independently of the quality of the animals' life, is a violation of their right to respectful treatment, since it uses them as a means to our own ends. Hence, vegetarianism is morally required.

---

[6]"Utilitarianism and Vegetarianism," *International Journal of Applied Philosophy* 4 (1988): 41–49.
[7]Crisp: 44. However, utility is not maximized by eating the products of factory farming. Crisp ar-gues against Frey, that utilitarian considerations do not permit us to eat "intensively-reared" ani-mals. But Frey asserts that "millions upon millions" of animals are not intensively-reared anyway (pp. 33-34).
[8]See, for example, Stephen Clark's *The Moral Status of Animals,* Clarendon, 1977.
[9]About 120 million cows, pigs, and sheep and about 5.5 billion birds (mostly chickens) are killed an-nually in this country alone (Jim Mason and Peter Singer, *Animal Factories:* 96). Global figures are unknown. There are about 10 million vegetarians in the U.S., which leaves more than 230 million animal-eaters.
[10]Principally in a series of papers beginning with "The Moral Basis of Vegetarianism," *Canadian Jour-nal of Philosophy* 5 (1975): 181–214, and culminating in *The Case for Animal Rights,* University of Cal-ifornia Press, 1983.

Regan is one of many philosophers who advocate the view that nonpersons in general or animals in particular (or both) qualify as moral rightsholders.[11] These philosophers tend to identify rightsholders according to their possession of certain affective capacities, such as interests or desires, and a number of them argue that animals do have these capacities. On the other hand, many other philosophers prefer cognitive criteria, confining rightsholders to beings with certain more advanced mental capacities—rationality and autonomy are the favorites—and explicitly or by implication disqualifying animals from this category.[12]

The Case for Animal Rights represents the *opus classicus* of the deontological approach to animal issues. Through more than four hundred pages of dense and tightly argued text, Regan has canvassed the philosophical problems of human-animal relationships more thoroughly than anyone has ever done. Even so, his view has been subjected to some quite damaging criticisms, ranging from concern over the mysterious and controversial nature of "inherent value" to charges of inconsistency and implausibility when the rights of humans and those of animals come into conflict.[13] This fact, along with the formidable argu-/ments marshaled by those who champion cognitive requirements for rights-holding, suggest that basing a case for vegetarianism upon the foundation of moral rights is an onerous task. The major problem is that the topic is exceedingly complex. A study of rights must address such daunting question as: What are rights? Are they real independently existing entities (natural rights) or human inventions (political, legal) or both? What is needed to qualify as a rights-holder? Exactly what rights are held by whom and why? How are conflicts among rights settled?

Thus, we have a very complicated theoretical endeavor marked by profound differences, yielding an area of philosophical debate which is highly

[11]For example: Joel Feinberg, "The Rights of Animals and Unborn Generations" *Philosophy & Environmental Crisis,* William T. Blackstone, ed., University of Georgia, 1974: 43–68, and "Human Duties and Animal Rights," *On the Fifth Day,* R. Morris and M. Fox, eds., Acropolis Books, 1978: 45–69; James Rachels, "Do Animals Have A Right to Liberty?" *Animal Rights and Human Obligations,* T. Regan and P. Singer, eds., Prentice Hall, 1976: 205–223; Stephen R. L. Clark, "The Rights of Wild Things," *Inquiry* 22 (1979): 171–78; Robert Elliot, "Moral Autonomy, Self-Determination and Animal Rights," *The Monist* 70 (1987): 83–97; Bernard Rollin, *Animal Rights and Human Morality,* Prometheus Books, rev. ed., 1990.

[12]For example: H. J. McCloskey, "Rights," *Philosophical Quarterly* 15 (1965): 113–27; "Moral Rights and Animals," *Inquiry* 22 (1979): 23–54; John Passmore, *Man's Responsibility for Nature,* Scribner's, 1974; Jan Narveson, "Animal Rights Revisited," *Ethics and Animals,* H. Miller and W. Williams, eds., Humana Press, 1983; Richard A. Watson, "Self-Consciousness and the Rights of Nonhuman Animals," *Environmental Ethics* 1 (1979): 99–129; Philip Montague, "Two Concepts of Rights," *Philosophy and Public Affairs* 9 (1980): 372–84; L. W. Sumner, *The Moral Foundations of Rights,* Oxford, 1987; Tibor Machan, "Do Animals Have Rights?" *Public Affairs Quarterly* 5 (1991): 163–73.

[13]For example: Paul Taylor, "Inherent Value and Moral Rights," and Jan Narveson, "On a Case for Animals Rights," both in *The Monist* 70 (1987): 15–49; David Ost, "The Case Against Animal Rights," *The Southern Journal of Philosophy* 24 (1986): 365–73; Mary Anne Warren, "Difficulties with the Strong Animal Rights Position," *Between the Species* 2 (1987): 163–73; and J. Baird Callicott, "Review of Tom Regan, *The Case For Animal Rights:* repr. in *In Defense of the Land Ethic,* State University of New York Press, 1989: 39–47.

unsettled. This tells us that a new argument for vegetarianism should traverse a relatively uncontroversial theoretical region which is stable and fixed.

A NEW ARGUMENT FOR VEGETARIANISM (NEW)

NEW makes no appeal to utility, rights, or pain and suffering:

[1] Causing harm is prima facie morally wrong.
[2] Killing animals causes them harm.
[3] Therefore, killing animals is prima facie morally wrong.
[4] Extensive animal-eating requires the killing of animals.
[5] Therefore, animal-eating is prima facie morally wrong.
[6] The wrongness of animal-eating is not overridden.
[7] Therefore, animal-eating is ultima facie morally wrong.

Premise [1] is an assumption: harming is wrong, not because it violates some right or because it fails to maximize utility, but simply because it is wrong. As "prima facie," however, the wrongness may be overridden in certain cases. I discuss premise [6] in the last section of the paper, and there I argue that the wrongness of the harm which eating animals causes them is not overridden, that it is "all things considered" or ultima facie wrong.

The term "extensive" in premise [4] indicates that the target of NEW is the industrialized practice of killing billions of animals as food for hundreds of millions of people, what has been referred to as "factory farming." NEW allows small-scale subsistence hunting, and eating animals who died due to accidents, natural causes, or other sources which do not involve the deliberate actions of moral agents.

The term "animal" used here and throughout this paper refers to any vertebrate species. For reasons I will make clear, NEW is more tentative with regard to invertebrate species. NEW is concerned with the harm caused by the killing and eating of animals, so it does not prohibit uses of animals which do not directly result in their deaths, in particular, those characteristic of the egg and dairy industries. Thus, the argument claims that "ovolacto vegetarianism" is morally required.

I now proceed to defend the remainder of NEW: how killing animals causes them harm (premise [2]); why the prima facie wrongness of killing animals (conclusion [3]) means that eating animals is also prima facie wrong (conclusion [5]); and why the wrongness is not overridden (premise [6]).

KILLING AND HARM

The claim that killing animals causes them harm might seem too obvious to warrant much discussion. However, its importance here is to distance NEW more clearly from other defenses of vegetarianism. As we will see, killing is harmful—and therefore morally wrong—whether or not any rights are

violated, and whether or not any pain or suffering occurs or some other conception of utility fails to be maximized.

Joel Feinberg's analysis of harm is especially useful here. To harm a being is
to do something which adversely affects that individual's *interests*. According to
Feinberg, harming amounts to "the thwarting, setting back, or defeating of an
interest."[14] Interests are not univocal. Some interests are more important than
others depending on their function in maintaining the basic well-being or welfare of the individual concerned. The most critical and essential interests that
anyone can have are what Feinberg calls "welfare interests":

> In this category are the interests in the continuance for a foreseeable interval of
> one's life, the interests in one's own physical health and vigor, the integrity and
> normal functioning of one's body, the absence of absorbing pain and suffer-
> ing . . . , emotional stability, the absence of groundless anxieties and resent-
> ments, the capacity to engage normally in social intercourse . . . , a tolerable so-
> cial and physical environment, and a certain amount of freedom from
> interference and coercion.[15]

Welfare interests are "the very most important interests . . . cry[ing] out for protection" not only because they are definitive of basic well-being, but also because their realization is necessary before one can satisfy virtually any other
interest or do much of anything with one's life. We cannot achieve our (ulterior)
interests in a career or personal relationships or material goods if we are unhealthy, in chronic pain, emotionally unstable, living in an intolerable social and
physical environment, and are constantly interfered with and coerced by others.
Feinberg concludes that when welfare interests are defeated, a very serious
harm indeed has been done to the possessor of those interests.[16]

What does it take to have an interest? Feinberg points out that there is a
close connection between interests and desires: if A does in fact have an interest
in x, we would typically not deny that A wants x.[17] However, we do speak of x
being in A's interest, whether A wants x or not; this seems to be especially so
when we are considering the welfare interests described above. We believe that
normally an individual's life, physical and mental health, and personal freedom
are in his or her interest even if these things are not wanted by that individual.
This suggests to Feinberg that interests of this kind obtain independently of and
are not derived from desires.[18]

We have here all that is needed to defend the claim that killing an animal
causes it harm and is therefore (by the moral principle assumed in premise [1])
morally wrong. Moreover, killing is perhaps the most serious sort of harm that

---

[14]*Harm to Others*, Oxford University Press, 1984: 33.
[15]Feinberg: 37. Welfare interests are contrasted with "ulterior interests," which presuppose but also
require as a necessary condition that certain welfare interests are satisfied. Feinberg lists raising a
family, building a dream house, advancing a social cause, and others as examples of ulterior interests.
[16]Ibid.
[17]Ibid.: 38.
[18]Ibid.: 42.

can be inflicted upon an animal by a moral agent; this is so not only because of the defeat of an animal's welfare interests—in life, health, and bodily integrity—but also because these are likely the only kind of interests animals have. One understanding of such interests appeals to the desire the animal has to live in a healthy, normal state of well-being. On Feinberg's analysis, another understanding of these interests makes no appeal to any such desire. This implies that killing defeats welfare interests independently of whether or not animals have a desire for life and well-being. They have an interest in this which is defeated when agents cause their deaths.

Some might object here that this is much too fast. Although it is true that x can be in A's interest even when A does not desire x, still x cannot be in A's interest if A has no desires whatever. Otherwise, we would be allowing that plants have interests, and that, some might think, is clearly absurd. Therefore, in order for this analysis of harm to be applicable to animals, it must be shown that they have some desires, preferably desires for that which agents are defeating.

DESIRE

Let us agree that the morally relevant sense of interest we want here is one constituted by certain desires. So why would anyone think that animals do not have desires? We attribute desires to animals routinely on much the same basis that we attribute desires to other people: as an explanation of their behavior. To say that some animal A wants x, uttered because A is doing something, is an extremely common locution for those who are in contact with animals everyday and seems to cause no problem for those who rarely ever encounter an animal. This creates a strong presumption in favor of animal desire. Since nobody denies that humans have desires, what do we have which animals do not have?

An answer that has been given, and perhaps the only answer available, is that animals do not have language. R. G. Frey holds this view that it is linguistic ability which makes desires possible. He maintains that for A to desire x, A must believe that something about x obtains.[19] However, "in expressions of the form '[A] believe that . . . ' what follows the 'that' is a sentence, and what [A] believes is that the sentence is true."[20] Since animals do not have a language, they cannot believe that any sentence is true. It follows that animals have neither beliefs nor desires.[21]

This argument has serious defects. Consider first: Frey does not give us any reason to accept the implication that belief is a necessary condition for desire. This is not obvious: the relationship between belief and desire is a complex one

---

[19]*Interests and Rights,* Clarendon, 1980: 72. Actually, Frey holds that desiring x requires that "I believe that I am deficient in respect of" x. This is too strong. I have amended the belief statement to a weaker claim, leaving it open what exactly A believes about x.

[20]Frey: 87.

[21]Ibid. Frey considers and rejects the notion that primates can possess a genuine language (pp. 93-99). I will not contest this point.

which has not been thoroughly investigated by philosophers.[22] Some have held that the relation is one of correlativity,[23] while others argue against it.[24] And what can be called "primitive" desires do not seem to be attended by any particular beliefs: if I desire food or drink or sex or sleep, just what is it that I believe? That I am hungry, thirsty, aroused, or tired? But are these distinguishable from the desires themselves? I might believe that satisfying the desire will bring pleasure or satiation. But I might not. It is by no means clear that there must be some belief lurking about in order to genuinely have a desire.

Consider next Frey's claim that when A believes something, what A believes is that a certain sentence is true. So, for example, Harry's belief that the Chicago Cubs will win the pennant is his believing that the sentence 'The Cubs will win the pennant' is true. But in that case, his belief that this sentence is true must itself be the belief that some other sentence is true, namely, the sentence "The sentence 'The Cubs will win the pennant' is true" is true. But then if Harry believes *that* sentence is true, he has to believe another sentence about this sentence about a sentence is true, and so on. What Frey needs is some way to stop this regress.

Assume there is some nonarbitrary and convincing way to stop the regress; the belief under consideration is Harry's believing that the sentence 'The Cubs will win the pennant' is true. But this is not what Harry believes. What he believes is *the Cubs will win the pennant*, that is, he believes that a group of men playing baseball will win more games than any team in their division over the course of the entire season, and then beat the winner of the other division four times in a playoff series. Harry's belief is about certain states of affairs in the world involving complex sets of persons, objects, and events, extended over a significant amount of time. His belief is clearly not about the truth value of a sentence.

So Frey has not shown that belief is a necessary condition for desire, and his argument that animals do not have desires fails. The next move would be to attack the specific desire in question. I have argued that killing an animal is morally wrong because of the harm the killing does; this harm is constituted by the defeat of welfare interests, and this interest is primarily a desire to live. One could then deny that animals have *this* desire. Ruth Cigman takes this approach when she denies that animals have "categorical desires," these being required to genuinely suffer death as a harm or "misfortune":

> to discover whether [death] is a misfortune for an animal, we must ask whether, or in what sense, animals don't want to die. . . . [A categorical desire] . . . answers the question whether one wants to remain alive . . . I reject the suggestion that a categorical desire is attributable to animals [because] . . . animals

---

[22]In his "Introduction" to *The Ways of Desire*, Precedent Publishing, 1986, editor Joel Marks comments (p. 13) that although the relationship between desire and belief "has long been sensed...it has seldom been the subject of scrutiny in its own right."
[23]For example, Robert Stalnaker, *Inquiry*, MIT Press, 1984: 15.
[24]For example, Dennis Stampe, "Defining Desire," *The Ways of Desire*: 149–73. Stampe's definition makes no mention of beliefs or a linguistic requirement.

would have to possess essentially the same conceptions of life and death as persons do [and] . . . understand death as a condition which closes a possible future forever. . . .[25]

Cigman is denying that animals have this desire because it requires understanding certain *concepts:* life, death, the future, the value of life, and others.

The difficulties with Frey's argument suggest that concepts, or language generally, are not required in order to have desires (or beliefs), but these "categorical" kind are presumably supposed to be very special and hard to obtain. Let us assume that there really are these sorts of desires and they are as Cigman has described them. The question is: Why does a being need "categorical desires" in order to have a desire to live?

Cigman does not say. She simply notes that Bernard Williams says the desire to remain alive is a categorical desire and then proceeds to detail what such a desire involves in a way which excludes animals. She has given us no argument for the view that the observations we make of animal activities are not enough to attribute a desire to live to them: fleeing from predators and enemies, seeking cover from severe weather, tending to injuries (such as they can), struggling to extricate themselves from potentially fatal situations, and exhibiting palpable fear in the face of threats to their lives are just the sorts of behaviors which exhibit this desire. Cigman might respond here that such actions only show that animals are "blindly clinging on to life"[26] rather than manifesting a genuine desire to live; it is instinct or some automatic response, not intentional action. But these activities are not blind clutchings, they are purposive and deliberate with a particular point to them, namely, to maintain that life. We would make precisely the same attributions to humans who acted in this way, without pausing to consider whether or not they had the concepts. Cigman asserts are requisite. And if we were to learn that these humans did not have these concepts, we would not and should not withdraw our judgment and chalk it all up to instinct.

CONSCIOUS AND NONCONSCIOUS DESIRES

Peter Carruthers concedes that animals do have desires, but he claims that [1] the desires of animals are not conscious ones, and [2] nonconscious mental states are unworthy of moral consideration.[27] It follows from these two claims that it is not morally wrong to defeat an animal's welfare interest arising from its desire to live. Now in order to complete this portion of the defense of NEW,

---

[25]"Death, Misfortune, and Species Inequality," *Philosophy and Public Affairs* 10 (1980): 57–58. The concept of a "categorical desire" is adopted from Bernard Williams. I am taking "misfortune" and "harm" as synonymous, though Cigman herself never equates the two.

[26]Cigman: 57.

[27]*The Animals Issue,* Cambridge University Press, 1992. He agrees that at least all mammals have desires (chaps. 3 and 6); animals also have sensations, including pain, but these too are nonconscious (pp. 187–89). Since NEW does not depend on the imposition of pain, I will not discuss this aspect of Carruthers' view.

only one or the other of these two claims needs to be rejected. But it would significantly strengthen NEW if we can find good grounds to reject both of them. I think we can do so.

Carruthers' contention that animal desire is nonconscious begins with his "proposal" that "a conscious, as opposed to a nonconscious, mental state is one that is available to conscious thought—where a conscious act of thinking is itself an event that is available to be thought about similarly in turn." Carruthers does not define conscious desire, but his definition of conscious belief can be readily adapted: a "conscious [desire] (*qua* dormant state) is one that is apt to emerge in a conscious thinking with the same content. . . . What makes my [desire that the Cubs win the pennant] a conscious one is that I am disposed in suitable circumstances to think to myself ['I want the Cubs to win the pennant']."[28] All this leads predictably to Carruthers' assertion that animals do not "think things to themselves," apparently because they do not have a natural language by which they express their thoughts.[29] Such an articulate thought as "I want to live" never crosses an animal's mind. Therefore, all of their mental states are nonconscious.

Are there such things as nonconscious mental states? There are some good reasons to think that there are not. For the last thirty minutes or so, I have had a desire for the piece of pizza in my lunch bag. I claim this desire has all along been a conscious one; I have certainly been quite vividly aware of it. But at no time during the last thirty minutes did I ever think to myself, "I want that piece of pizza." Carruthers would respond that what makes the desire a conscious one is not the necessity of actually stating it to myself, it is sufficient that I merely be "disposed" to state it to myself in "suitable circumstances": if someone had come along and asked me, I would have said "I want that piece of pizza."

This is a strange idea: from a description of some *counter*factual state of affairs, it follows that some other *actual* state of affairs presently obtains. Jack has a disposition to change lanes abruptly, ignore stop signs, and exceed the speed limit; this disposition often manifests itself in reckless driving. The disposition clearly does not mean that Jack is now driving recklessly. He isn't; he's sitting there listening to "Crash Test Dummies." Likewise, Jill is disposed to be friendly, sympathetic, and conversational; this disposition often manifests itself in Jill discussing personal problems with other people. The disposition clearly does not mean that Jill is now having such a discussion. She isn't; she's sitting there reading "Dear Abby." So why would a disposition to think some sentence to myself in some circumstance which *does not now* obtain mean that I am *now* having a conscious mental state? Carruthers does not say.

Another reason to reject this theory concerns its consequences for humans who do not have any natural language. Prelinguistic children and individuals who are nonlinguistic because of mental dysfunction do not think things to themselves, which means that they do not have conscious mental states, a result

---

[28]Carruthers: 180–81.
[29]Ibid.: 184.

which parents and caretakers will find quite surprising. Also surprising is that Carruthers never mentions this obvious implication of his view.[30] Indeed, he thinks that tying conscious mental states so closely with language mastery is an advantage.[31] But this is a distinct liability. First, it is incompatible with my memories, and memories others have related to me, of experiences which occurred *before* we acquired language mastery. To take just one example, I have a clear recollection of waking in the middle of the night and feeling very sick; I wandered through the house looking for my parents, but they had gone next door for a moment. I remember many details of the experience itself, especially a strong desire for my parents to be there. My mother has told me that I was not yet two years old at the time. I was not then capable of thinking any sentences to myself. So according to Carruthers, I had no conscious experiences. But how could I have a memory from a time when I was not conscious? Probably most of us have some such memories from infancy, before language acquisition, but on Carruthers' view we were not then conscious.

The second and most troublesome aspect of this language requirement leads us to Carruthers' second claim: nonconscious mental states are unworthy of moral consideration. This would have to include not only animals, but these pre- and nonlinguistic humans, leaving them without moral standing. Very few philosophers or ordinary moral agents would find such a view acceptable; a theory with this implication is highly unlikely to be correct. But even if this result were not so thoroughly counterintuitive, it turns out that the claim is either poorly supported or not really supported at all.

Why are nonconscious mental states not morally considerable? Carruthers' answer in this chapter is sympathy.[32] Although it is not clearly developed, the idea seems to be that moral standing arises from a sympathetic identification with the object of concern; since a nonconscious experience does not feel like anything, there is nothing to identify with: the animal doesn't care, so why should we? Carruthers surprises again here. He had earlier advocated contractualism as the most defensible ethical theory,[33] and, as is well known, animals are typically denied moral standing by this theory because rational, self-interested agents would not have any reason to accord them this status. In the initial situation, the contractors are concerned to formulate principles for the guidance of social interaction by assigning various rights and duties to moral persons, and animals cannot engage in such interaction or fulfill such assignments. Carruthers follows suit.[34] But sympathy plays no role whatever in contractualism: the contractors are apathetic toward others, not sympathetic. Has Carruthers suddenly switched from a constructivist metaethical theory in which fellow-feeling does not exist, to an antirealist metaethic where some projected positive attitude is precisely what is necessary to invest individuals with

---

[30]The problem is mentioned in his "Brute Experience," *Journal of Philosophy* 86 (1989): 269, but only in regard to the pain experiences of babies. NEW is not concerned with pain.
[31]Carruthers: 183.
[32]Ibid.: 189–91.
[33]Chap 2.
[34]Carruthers, 98–105.

moral value? This is unclear. The appeal to sympathy seems to come out of nowhere, but if Carruthers has made this switch, he now owes us a defense of moral antirealism. He must do more than simply presuppose that theory—if that is what he is doing—before his position is to be at all convincing. But aside from the issue of metaethical foundations, why think whether or not someone feels sympathy for another is even relevant to the question of moral appraisal, let along decisive? Carruthers does not say.

At this juncture, Carruthers could abandon the appeal to sympathy altogether and fall back to his earlier espoused contractualism. At least he does have some defense of this theory. Unfortunately, that defense is feeble,[35] but I do not want to dwell on what might be wrong with his contractualism generally. Instead, I want to focus on the specific point Carruthers needs to establish in the context of this discussion: since both groups are nonconscious, he needs some contractualist strategy which retains moral standing for children and the mentally dysfunctional, but disallows this standing for animals:

> The strategy depends on the fact that there are no sharp boundaries between a baby and an adult, between a not-very-intelligent adult and a severe mental defective, or between a normal old person and someone who is severely senile. The argument is then that the attempt to accord moral [standing] only to rational agents (normal adults) would be inherently dangerous and open to abuse. . . . The suggestion is that if we try to deny moral [standing] to some human beings, on the grounds that they are not rational agents, we shall be launched on a slipper slope which may lead to all kinds of barbarisms against those who *are* rational agents.[36]

This argument rests on two factual claims: [1] there is no clear distinction between humans with developed linguistic and rational capacities and humans without those capacities, and [2] according moral standing only to rational, language-users would lead to "barbarisms" directed against them. But both claims are false. In the terms which Carruthers takes to be relevant here—language proficiency and rationality—there is a vast and readily apparent gulf between a normal adult and a child of, say, less than one year old. The adult's command of language and problem solving abilities far eclipses those of a child who has no language whatever and is unable to recognize that a round peg fits a circular hole, skills which are also beyond the abilities of the severely mentally dysfunctional. Of course there will be borderline cases, but, inexplicably, Carruthers seems to think that every case is a borderline case. I do not see how this sharp divide could be reasonably denied, and I have yet to encounter anyone besides Carruthers who does deny it. In any event, he offers no reasons to reject the divide; he simply asserts, without argument, that there isn't one.

The claim that according moral standing only to rational humans would cause widespread moral abuse is also merely asserted and not defended. Excellent evidence for such a claim would cite cultures why deny children and the

---

[35] For a series of forceful criticisms, see Peter Wenz, "Contracts, Animals, and Ecosystems," *Social Theory and Practice* 19 (1993): 317–25.
[36] Carruthers: 114.

mentally dysfunctional moral standing while perpetrating all manner of atrocities against those who are recognized to have moral standing. Unfortunately, Carruthers offers no such citations. This is not surprising since it is highly unlikely there are any such cultures. My own research on moral relativism has led me to peruse a fair amount of anthropological literature, and I have never there encountered a culture which did not accord some sort of moral standing to its children. So this empirical claim cannot be verified empirically. But even if there were such cultures, establishing that the lack of moral standing for some was the cause of abuse for those with standing would be enormously difficult to do. How would that be shown? Carruthers gives no clue. And independent of any real world consideration, why would such a slippery slope occur in the first place? Once again, Carruthers does not say.

Our final verdict on his case against the nature and moral status of animal desire must be that it is either inadequately defended or not defended at all.

RECAPITULATION AND ELABORATION

At this point in the defense of NEW, we have firmly established the following:

[1] Causing harm is prima facie morally wrong.
[2] Killing animals causes them harm.
[3] Therefore, killing animals is prima facie morally wrong.

We have seen why killing animals harms them, and we have successfully countered challenges to the analysis of animal harms. We understand why this is one of the worst harms an animal can undergo, which indicates that this is a very serious (though prima facie) wrong when perpetrated by a moral agent. We can also now see the advantages of NEW over the old arguments for vegetarianism. NEW is not contingent upon any current or possible methods of raising animals for humans to eat: no matter how it is done, supplying food for millions of animal-eaters means the defeat of animal welfare interests. NEW does not employ any theoretical contructs which are unsettled and divisive: the analysis of harm in terms of interests and desires which are exhibited by certain behaviors is widely accepted and intuitively appealing. NEW does not introduce any indeterminacy or unwieldy ratiocination into the discussion: the desires and interests of animals, and the wrongness of defeating them, are plainly evident for all those who would simply look and see.

We can also now understand two further aspects of the vegetarianism required by NEW. Killing any creature with certain desires defeats its welfare interests, and is therefore harmful, but not all living things have such desires and interests. The judgment that some being has the requisite mental states must be formed on the basis of behavior and physiological evidence. Since invertebrates and plants either do not exhibit the appropriate behavior or they do not possess the appropriate physiological equipment (or both), consuming them is permitted. Although I do not hold that "interest-less" forms of life have no moral status whatever, I cannot here develop the notion of degrees of moral value or consider what else besides interests would qualify an entity for a moral status. It will have to suffice to say that beings with certain mental states are of greater moral worth than those without them, from the moral point of view it is better (*ceteris paribus*) to kill and eat a plant than an animal. Moreover, much vegetable matter can be eaten without killing anything: most vegetarian fare consists of the fruits and flowers of plants which are not killed or are harvested at the end of annual life cycles.

THE MORAL WRONGNESS OF EATING ANIMALS

The next step is to link the wrongness of *killing* animals with the wrongness of *eating* them:

[3] Therefore, killing animals is prima facie morally wrong.
[4] Animal-eating requires the killing of animals.
[5] Therefore, animal-eating is prima facie morally wrong.

Many might regard this step as especially problematic. All that has been shown so far is that moral agents who kill animals are engaged in actions which are prima facie wrong; how can it follow from this that different actions, done by different agents, are also prima facie wrong? After all, very few of those who consume animal flesh have personally killed the animals they eat. Those who actually do the killing—slaughterhouse workers—act impermissibly, while those who merely eat the body parts of dead animals supplied by those workers do not. How could the wrongness of one set of agents and actions *transfer* to an entirely different set?

One response would point out that purchasing and consuming the products of "factory farming" contributes to a morally abhorrent practice and thus perpetuates future wrongdoing. So although it is the killing which constitutes what is wrong with the practice of animal-eating, and conceding that very few animal-eaters actually kill what they eat, this contribution to and perpetuation of the killing should prompt us to act *as if* eating the animals is itself wrong.[37]

Hud Hudson has shown that this response does not work. It rests on the empirical claim that an individual's refraining from eating animals will make some difference to "factory farming" as an ongoing activity. But as a matter of economic fact, my refraining from eating animals will not affect the meat industry in the least. The loss of my financial contribution will not spare a single animal from harm, nor produce the slightest setback to the business; I will be preventing no future wrongdoing whatever by becoming a vegetarian.[38]

---

[37]See Tom Regan in "The Moral Basis of Vegetarianism" (repr. in *All That Dwell Therein*, University of California Press, 1982: 24). He says that the consumer of animal flesh is "causally implicated" in the continuance of a morally impermissible activity. As far as I know, he has not taken up this issue in any of the subsequent work on vegetarianism.

[38]"Collective Responsibility and Moral Vegetarianism," *Journal of Social Philosophy* 24 (1993): 94.

Hudson's solution to the problem is to widen our perspective from the individual vegetarian to groups of individuals, attributing "collective responsibility" for the harm caused to the animals eaten. This might look like a promising approach since it is precisely the fecklessness of individual action to prevent future wrongdoing which undermined the initial response to this objection. Hudson writes:

> [I]f enough nonvegetarian consumers of factory farmed products can be identified as the members of some loosely structured group which could prevent harms . . . by devising a decision-making procedure through which they would collectively cease purchasing and consuming such products, then the failure to prevent those harms through the collective inaction of that group is something for which the members are morally responsible. . . . [C]ertain individuals, by virtue of their membership in a loosely structured group, are at least partially morally responsible for not collectively preventing certain harms . . . , even though none of the individuals could have prevented the harm by acting independently.[39]

Unfortunately, this response will not work either.[40] Say I am a member of "some loosely structured group which could prevent harms . . . by devising a decision-making procedure through which they would collectively cease purchasing and consuming" animal flesh. On Hudson's view, this means that I am "at least partially morally responsible" for the wrongs perpetrated by the meat industry. Yet this is so despite the fact that these are harms I can do nothing about. It is a strange theory which burdens one with a responsibility that is virtually impossible to fulfill. But the situation is even worse than this. Say I decide to become a vegetarian, so I stop purchasing and eating animal flesh. On Hudson's view I am even so still partially responsible for the harm, because it is still necessary for collective action to occur if the wrongdoing is to be stopped or at least severely curtailed, and this will not happen as a result of my individual action. Hudson, however, claims that this is not the case, that acting individually in this manner will "eliminate [my] share of the responsibility resulting from the wrongful, collective inaction" of my group.[41] But why? According to Hudson's theory, the reason why I have some degree of responsibility in the first place has *nothing* to do with any actions I take or fail to take; it is precisely the ineffectual nature of my abstinence from animal flesh which gave rise to the objection and it is my membership in a group which could prevent wrongdoing through a coordinate effort which leads to the ascription of responsibility. My refusal to eat animals changes none of this.

What has gone awry here is the concession that we must find some way to think of animal-eating *as if* it were wrong, because in actuality it is not itself wrong; the killing is the wrong, not the eating of what has been killed by others. This led to the construction of the rather bizarre theory of responsibility

---

[39]Hudson: 97.
[40]Hudson himself recognizes the problem but then brushes it aside on pp. 98–99.
[41]Hudson: 99.

outlined above. We must not make this concession. Animal-eating is itself wrong, but this is not due to any "transference" of wrongness from the act of killing to the act of purchasing and eating animal flesh. The purchasing and consuming are two parts of the same wrong.

To see this, consider this modification of the objection which concerns us now:

> This is a lovely lamp. You say its base is made from the bones and its shade from the skin of Jews killed in concentration camps? Well, so what? I didn't kill them. Of course what the Nazis did was wrong, a very great moral evil. But my not buying the lamp is obviously not going to bring any of them back. Nor will it prevent any future harm: this sort of thing doesn't even occur any more, so there is no future wrongdoing to prevent even if my refusal to buy were effective in this way, which of course it wouldn't be. So what's wrong with buying and using the lamp?

What makes eating animals wrong has nothing to do with collective responsibility or any impact an individual might or might not have on the meat industry. We do not need to find some way to understand this activity which will allow it to be construed "as if" it were wrong (but really isn't). Animal-eating is wrong for much the same reason that purchasing and using the products of a concentration camp or those of slave labor generally is wrong; it is wrong for the same reason that buying stolen property or accepting any of the ill-gotten gains of another is wrong: a person who eats animals, or buys and uses lamps from Auschwitz or cotton clothing from the antebellum South, or a hot stereo from a hoodlum is profiting from, benefiting from a morally nefarious practice. Doing so, and especially doing so when morally innocuous alternatives are readily available, not only indicates support for and the endorsement of moral evil, it is also to participate in that evil. It is an act of complicity, partaking in condemnable exploitation, reaping personal advantages at a significant cost to others. This is so whether or not an individual's abstinence from the practice has any effect whatsoever on its perpetuation. It strikes me as quite uncontroversial to say that one who concurs and cooperates with wrongdoing, who garners benefits through the defeat of the basic welfare interests of others, is himself doing something which is seriously morally wrong.

OVERRIDING THE MORAL WRONGNESS
OF EATING ANIMALS

The final step in the defense of NEW is to support premise [6]: the prima facie wrongness of animal-eating is not defeated by additional factors which serve as overriding reasons; from this it will follow that animal-eating is ultima facie morally wrong (the conclusion [7]). There are at least four grounds for overriding this wrong: [1] traditional-cultural; [2] esthetic; [3] convenience; [4] nutrition. Do any of these supply an overriding reason which would morally justify the very serious harm that killing animals for food causes them?

[1] People eat animals because they have been raised on that diet, as have their parents and grandparents and on back through the generations. Animal-eating is a social practice which is deeply embedded into modern culture. Slavery, the oppression of women, and institutionalized racism also once had this status; however, few if any suppose that this status is what makes practices morally right or wrong. Slavery, for example, is wrong because it requires the persistent exploitation, coercion, and degradation of innocent people, not because it happens to be extinct in our society. The fact that a practice has the weight of tradition on its side and a prominent place in a given culture does not in itself carry any moral weight.[42]

[2] Animal flesh is regarded by most people as esthetically pleasing. Animal body parts are prepared for consumption in hundreds of different ways, employing many cooking techniques, spices, and accompaniments. Yet the esthetic attractions of other practices are regarded as irrelevant to their moral appraisal. Heliogabalus had masses of people gathered in fields, only to be mercilessly slaughtered solely for the pleasing effect he found in the sign of red blood on green grass.[43] Or consider "snuff films" whose "plot" is centered around the filming of an actual murder of a person apparently chosen at random. Who would not condemn such cinema in the strongest possible terms, even if it were directed by Orson Welles or Martin Scorcese and starred Dustin Hoffman or Meryl Streep? Yet one has only to enter the nearest slaughterhouse with a video camera on any given day of the week to produce a movie every bit as horrific as the most polished "snuff film."

[3] The convenience of animal-eating is largely a function of the other two factors. The pervasiveness of the desire to eat animals and its prominence within a variety of social functions naturally provokes free market economies to supply meat relatively cheaply and easily. Again, this seems to say nothing about whether or not animal-eating is morally permissible. It is often quite inconvenient and very difficult to keep a promise or discharge a parental duty or make a sacrifice for a stranger—or a friend; it is often quite convenient and very easy to conceal the trust or pocket merchandise without paying or take advantage of powerless persons. Few of us believe that convenience and ease have much of anything to do with whether these actions are morally right or wrong. Why should it be any different when it comes to killing animals for food?

It might be said that the difference is that human interests in convenience, in tradition, and esthetic pleasure override animal interests in life and well-being. This is because the defeat of an *animal* welfare interest, though morally wrong, is not a serious moral wrong. But what is it about humans which gives these nonbasic interests a moral priority over the most basic and important interests an animal can have? And what is it about animals which prevents a severe harm to them from being a serious moral problem? Certainly the nonbasic

---

[42]A point forcefully made by means of a macabre device in the classic short story by Shirley Jackson, "The Lottery."

[43]As reported by R. M. Hare in *Freedom and Reason,* Clarendon Press, 1963: 161.

interests of some humans do not have a moral priority over the welfare interests of other humans, and there is no question that the gravity of a wrong increases with the severity of harm caused to humans. So in order to sustain the objection, some feature, unique to our species, must be identified which accounts for the disparity between human and animal harms and wrongs. Two such distinguishing features, already encountered, immediately present themselves as possibilities: rationality and language. However, appeal to one or both of these capacities raises two immediate problems. First, neither feature is uniquely absent in animal species. No one would seriously contend that a taste for human baby flesh morally overrides anything, nor would anyone claim that the defeat of a child's welfare interest was not a serious moral wrong. Second, why does the proposed feature make such an enormous moral difference? The suggestion is that rationality or language justifies a gap in treatment so vast that it means utmost respect and consideration for humans but allows killing animals out of habit and pleasure. This seems very implausible. The lack of the requisite capacities might reasonably justify *some* difference in treatment, but not a difference which requires a dignified life for those who are favored and permits an ignominious death for those who are not.

[4] Nutrition. Most recent debate about vegetarianism has focused on the question of the adequacy of a meatless diet for human nutrition. This could provide the best reason for overriding the wrongness of killing animals. Let us assume as a fundamental principle that no moral agent can be required to destroy his or her own health and basic welfare for the sake of others; therefore, a diet having this consequence is not morally justified. Does vegetarianism seriously endanger an individual's health and well-being?

Kathryn Paxton George has argued that a vegetarian diet would make large numbers of humans worse off than they would otherwise be if they ate animals. She lists seven groups of people for whom such abstinence possess a significant risk to personal health.[44] Evelyn Pluhar has disputed many of George's findings, especially those regarding the benefits of iron and the threat of osteoporosis. Supported by numerous nutrition studies, she argues that vitamin and mineral supplementation, as well as the utilization of appropriate plant sources, will alleviate any deficiencies; furthermore, Pluhar contends that the correlation between consuming animal products and meeting certain health requirements is a dubious one.[45] George responded that Pluhar had either misinterpreted or willfully ignored certain facts of the studies she had herself cited.[46] The exchange continues; a journal has devoted an entire issue to their disagreement.[47]

Fortunately, we need not enter this particular debate; George's target is what she calls "strict vegetarianism," the vegan diet totally devoid of any

---

[44]"So Animal a Human…, or the Moral Relevance of Being An Omnivore," *Journal of Agricultural Ethics* 3 (1990): 172–86. Her list (pp. 175–78) includes children, pregnant and lactating women, the elderly, the poor, and the "undereducated."

[45]"Who Can be Morally Obligated to be a Vegetarian?" *Journal of Agricultural and Environmental Ethics* 5 (1992): 189–215.

[46]"The Use and Abuse of Scientific Studies," *Journal of Agricultural and Environmental Ethics* 5 (1992): 217–33.

[47]*Journal of Agricultural and Environmental Ethics* 7 (1994).

animal product. Both George and Pluhar admit that eggs and dairy products, which are allowed by NEW, would fulfill all or most of the required protein, vitamin, and mineral intake. I am not aware of any humans who, as a matter of basic welfare, must consume animal flesh in addition to eggs and dairy products, but if there are any such people, NEW would allow them to eat animals: we are under no moral requirement to significantly harm ourselves so that others, human or non-human, may benefit.

On the other hand, Jack Weir has maintained that

> worldwide ovolactovegetarianism would produce problems of unimaginable scope. . . . The animals would probably suffer horribly . . . ecological stress, increased agricultural monism, and immense pain for many of the animals [would result]. . . . Feeding the unproductive [animals] would consume valuable resources in a poorly diversified agricultural system overburdened by producing enough milk and eggs for the huge population of ovolactovegetarians.[48]

Weir's concerns are misguided. He assumes that this universal conversion would occasion drastic and ecologically destructive changes in the current scale of egg and dairy production. But this is very unlikely. The U.S. alone already produces far more eggs and dairy products than are actually consumed by Americans or sold overseas.[49] In that case, pervasive ovolacto-vegetarianism either encourages the status quo or is consistent with Weir's own advocacy of a return to the small family farm; this is his alternative to factory farming and one which would (presumably) yield a comparable production.[50] I assume the set of "unproductive" animals would be dominated by males; since they are still needed to bring more of the productive animals (females) into existence, and since there are already far fewer of them than there are females, they would hardly be the useless drain on resources that he apparently takes them to be. Nor is there any reason to think that these animals would necessarily lead miserable, painful lives, and Weir does not provide such a reason.

I conclude that none of [1]–[4] serve as a sufficiently compelling reason to override the wrongness of harming the animals eaten. If there are any individuals who must eat animal flesh (rather than just eggs and dairy products) in order to avoid a pronounced deterioration of their health, they are not prohibited from doing so by NEW. This possible case notwithstanding, the eating of animal flesh is ultima facie morally wrong.

The success of NEW indicates the direction in which future philosophical discussion of vegetarianism ought to proceed. That path avoids the intractable, contingent, and highly controversial nature of rights-based theories and utilitarianism, focusing instead on the more manageable and less contentious areas

---

[48]"Unnecessary Pain, Nutrition, and Vegetarianism," *Between the Species* 7 (1991): 18, 19.

[49]In 1991, U.S. farmers produced about 154 billion pounds of milk and dairy products, but only 135.6 billion pounds were consumed. In the same year, hens laid almost 5800 million dozen eggs; 4900 million dozen were consumed and 862 million dozen were either exported or used for hatching. This still leaves a surplus of about 456 million eggs. See *Statistical Abstract of the United States: 1993*, U.S. Bureau of the Census, Washington DC, 1993: 142, 675–76.

[50]Weir: 22.

of the wrongness of harming as a basic moral principle, the analysis of harm as a defeat of interests, and the understanding of interests in terms of certain desires. Much work remains to be done: the philosophy of mind which accounts plausibly for attributions of the appropriate mental states to animals needs to be specified; a fuller analysis of moral status (especially regarding the status of plant life) and the respective natures of basic and nonbasic interests will go a long way toward explaining the conditions under which various moral judgments are overridden; that project will lead to a certain ontological understanding of moral value and the general metaethical underpinnings of the normative ethic employed here. For now, the failure of arguments intended to deny animals the requisite interests and desires, and the failure of those intended to undermine NEW by appeal to overriding reasons and the wrong done by the consumer of animal flesh, means that vegetarianism emerges as a moral requirement as compelling as many of those that are more readily acknowledged and more assiduously practiced.

Questions

1. Would a vegetarian diet, if *gradually* adopted by all humans, have the negative economic effects that R. G. Frey is cited as suggesting would occur?
2. How does Jordan Curnutt respond to R. G. Frey's argument that animals do not have desires?
3. Does the author succeed in showing that if *killing* animals is prima facie wrong, then *eating* animals is prima facie wrong?
4. Which four reasons does the author say are sometimes thought to override the prima facie wrongfulness of animal-eating? Do you agree with the author that they fail to justify the harm inflicted on animals?

Suggestions for Further Reading on Eating Meat and Wearing Leather

ALWARD, PETER."The Naïve Argument against Moral Vegetarianism." *Environmental Values* 9 (2000): pp. 81–89.

BENATAR, DAVID."Why the Naïve Argument against Moral Vegetarianism Really Is Naïve. *Environmental Values* 10 (2001): pp. 103–12.

DEGRAZIA, DAVID. *Taking Animals Seriously: Mental Life and Moral Status*, Cambridge: Cambridge University Press, 1996.

DIAMOND, CORA."Eating Meat and Eating People." *Philosophy* 53 (1978): pp. 465–479.

FEINBERG, JOEL."The Rights of Animals and Unborn Generations." In *Rights, Justice and the Bounds of Liberty: Essays in Social Philosophy*, Princeton, N.J.: Princeton University Press, 1980: pp. 159–183.

FREY, R. G. *Interests and Rights: The Case against Animals*. Oxford: Oxford University Press, 1980.

———. *Rights, Killing and Suffering*, Oxford: Blackwell, 1983.

LEAHY, MICHAEL P. T. *Against Liberation: Putting Animals in Perspective*, London: Routledge, 1991.

MILLER, HARLAN B., AND WILLIAM H. WILLIAMS, eds. *Ethics and Animals*, Clifton, N.J.: Humana Press, 1983.

NOZICK, ROBERT."Constraints and Animals," In *Anarchy, State and Utopia*, Oxford: Blackwell, 1974: pp. 35–42.

REGAN, TOM. *The Case for Animal Rights*, Berkeley: University of California Press, 1983.

REGAN, TOM, AND PETER SINGER, eds. *Animal Rights and Human Obligations*, 2nd ed. Englewood Cliffs, N.J.: Prentice Hall, 1989.

ROWLANDS, MARK."Contractarianism and Animal Rights." *Journal of Applied Philosophy* 14, no. 3 (1997): pp. 235–247.

SINGER, PETER. *Animal Liberation* (2nd ed.) , New York: New York Review of Books, 1990.

———, *In Defense of Animals*, New York: Harper & Row, 1985.

CHAPTER 11

Pets

KEITH BURGESS-JACKSON, Doing Right by our Animal Companions

GARY VARNER, Pets, Companion Animals, and Domesticated Partners

Doing Right by Our Companion Animals[*]

Keith Burgess-Jackson

Keith Burgess-Jackson notes that almost without exception, the philosophical literature about our duties to animals ignores pets or companion animals. The assumption, he says, is that "whatever obligations humans have to any animals are had to all animals." He argues against this assumption and in favor of the view that humans "have special responsibilities to the animals they voluntarily bring into their lives—precisely because they bring them into their lives." For example, just as people who adopt a child acquire parental responsibilities to that child, so people who adopt animals acquire responsibilities to those animals.

One explanation for the philosophical neglect of the pets issue, says the author, is that the leading philosophical exponents of animal welfare have been impartialists. That is to say, they have thought that there are no special duties owed to those with whom one has special relationships—that people's duties to their own children are no different from their duties to other children. Unlike these theorists, however, most people accept partialism, the view that there can be special duties based on relational rather than intrinsic properties. The author shows why partialism is a reasonable view and why it does not exclude the possibility of duties based on intrinsic rather than relational properties. He argues that those who accept the partialist view regarding duties to humans should extend it to duties owed to animals.

In the final section of the paper, the author argues that our primary responsibility to companion animals is to provide for their needs. Taking dogs as an example, he discusses what their needs are.

[*]Nobody (aside from two anonymous reviewers late in the process) helped me with this essay, so I have nobody to thank, blame, flatter, or humiliate. It is dedicated to Sophie and Ginger, my beloved (and loving) canine companions—and to all non-human animals similarly situated. E-mail address: kbj@uta.edu: homepage: www.uta.edu/philosophy/faculty/burgess-jackson

Keith Burgess-Jackson, "Doing Right by Our Animal Companions," *The Journal of Ethics* 2 (1998): 159–185.

Apart from the universal rights they possess in common with all intelligent beings, domestic animals have a special claim on man's courtesy and sense of fairness, inasmuch as they are not his fellow-creatures only, but his fellow-workers, his dependents, and in many cases the familiar associates and trusted inmates of his home.[1]

The duties of a parent involve giving special weight to the interests and needs of his own children, precisely because they are his. And the same goes for our obligations to those others with whom we have a close and special relationship.[2]

Many of us live our lives in the company of animals[3]—dogs, cats, birds, fish and assorted reptiles and rodents. We share our homes with them. Depending on the species, we sleep with them, recreate with them, travel with them, care for them, play with them, teach them, learn from them, and in general consider their companionship a part of the good life. We are attuned to their material, psychic, and social needs. We worry when they are lost, ill or injured; we take satisfaction in their growth and development; we exult when they prevail in a competition, learn a trick, or give birth; and we grieve, sometimes protractedly, when they die. For better or for worse, animals are caught up in the many comedies and tragedies of our lives—and we in theirs.[4]

The more thoughtful among us do not simply delight in the *fact* of companionship; we reflect on it. We wonder, sporadically or systematically, whether we are being responsive to the many and diverse needs of our animal companions.[5]

---

[1]Henry S. Salt, *Animals' Rights Considered in Relation to Social Progress*, with a Preface by Peter Singer (Clark's Summit, PA: Society for Animal Rights, 1980), pp. 43–44. Salt's book was originally published in 1892.

[2]John Cottingham, "Ethics and Impartiality," *Philosophical Studies* 43 (1983), p. 97.

[3]Throughout the essay I use "animals" as an abbreviation for "animals other than human." This is not unproblematic. See Tom Regan, "The Moral Basis of Vegetarianism," *Canadian Journal of Philosophy* 5 (1975), p. 184, n. 7 ("The fact that this is an ordinary use of the word ["animal" for "animal other than human"], despite the fact that humans *are* animals, suggests that this is a fact that we are likely (and perhaps eager) to forget. It may also help to account for our willingness to treat (mere) animals in certain ways that we would not countenance in the case of humans" [italics in original]). For an insightful essay on nomenclature, see Kenneth Shapiro, "Language: Referring to Animals Other Than Humans," *ISAZ [International Society for Anthrozoology]—The Newsletter* (November 1997), pp. 20–23.

[4]The number of human-animal companionships is staggering. As of 1980, there were nearly half a *billion* (475.4 million) companion animals in the United States alone. This figure includes forth-eight million dogs (in thirty-two million households), 27.2 million cats, 25.2 million birds, 250 million fish, and 125 million other animals (including raccoons, hamsters, gerbils, rabbits, reptiles, rodents, and guinea pigs). See Alan M. Beck, "Animals in the City," in Aaron Honori Katcher and Alan M. Beck (eds.), *New Perspectives on Our Lives with Companion Animals* (Philadelphia: University of Pennsylvania Press, 1983), p. 238.

[5]I prefer "animal companion" or "companion animal" to "pet" on grounds that the first and second of these terms, but not the third, imply (or at least do not preclude) equality and mutuality. Nothing substantive—that is, nothing in my argument—hinges on this terminological choice. For a different approach to the matter, see Carol J. Adams, "Bringing Peace Home: A feminist Philosophical Perspective on the Abuse of Women, Children, and Pet Animals," *Hypatia* 9 (1994), p. 64.

We do not regard them as having merely instrumental value to us but as having a worth, dignity, integrity, and well-being of their own—a well-being that we, through action or omission, in knowledge or ignorance, can thwart or promote. We know, as surely as we know anything, that matters can go well or poorly for our animal companions, and we wish them to go well.

This wonder, if allowed to grow (and certainly if cultivated), gives rise to a number of philosophical questions concerning the nature, basis, and extent of our obligations to animal companions. Just what do we owe them, and why? When one turns to the philosophical literature for edification and guidance, however, one finds . . . next to nothing. The great manifestoes of our age, *Animal Liberation*[6] and *The Case for Animal Rights*,[7] say little or nothing about companion animals. The issue of our responsibility to them is not even broached. The assumption seems to be that whatever obligations humans have to *any* animals are had to *all* animals, wild or domestic, stray or companion, chosen or unchosen. Animals are viewed as an undifferentiated mass.[8]

That assumption, plausible as it may seem to some, is woefully mistaken, and my aim is to show why. I argue that human beings have special responsibilities to the animals they voluntarily bring into their lives—precisely *because* they bring them into their lives.[9] Before supporting this claim I want to clarify it, defend it against certain misconceptions, and diagnose its philosophical neglect, for the neglect is instructive. Since my conclusion is abstract, it will be useful to make the discussion concrete. In doing so, I focus on the case of dogs, which, among animal species, I know best.[10] Needs vary by species, of course,

---

[6]Peter Singer, *Animal Liberation* (New York: Avon Books, 1975; 2nd ed., 1990). All citations are to the second edition of this work.

[7]Tom Regan, *The Case for Animal Rights* (Berkeley and Los Angeles: University of California Press, 1983).

[8]One happy exception to this generalization is Bernard E. Rollin, *Animal Rights & Human Morality* (Buffalo: Prometheus Books, 1981; rev. ed., 1992). (All citations are to the revised edition of this work.) Rollin's book is divided into four chapters: the first on moral theory; the second on rights; the third on research; and the fourth, amounting to twenty-eight pages, on "Morality and Pet Animals." (Note that Rollin, like Adams, uses "pet" rather than "animal companion.") Rollin is a pioneer of what has come to be known as "veterinary ethics." He has also published an important work on animal pain. See Bernard E. Rollin, *The Unheeded Cry: Animal Consciousness, Animal Pain and Science*, with a Foreword by Jane Goodall (Oxford: Oxford University Press, 1989; paperback ed., 1990).

[9]This is not a claim of or about legal responsibility. It is a moral claim. For the sake of simplicity (and with only a few exceptions) I omit the word "moral throughout the essay. Nonetheless, the law illuminates the concept of special responsibility. Innkeepers are deemed by law to have special responsibilities toward their guests, lifeguards toward their charges, common carriers toward their passengers, and so on. These responsibilities go beyond the general duty (which everyone has) of reasonable care under the circumstances. See James A. Henderson, Jr., and Richard N. Pearson, *The Torts Process* (Boston: Little, Brown and Company, 1975), pp. 281, 369–396. Note that in each of these cases, the role is voluntarily assumed. Nobody is *required* to be an innkeeper, lifeguard, or common carrier. By the same token, nobody is *required* to assume the role of companion to an animal.

[10]"The domestic dog is one of the most popular companion animals with an estimated population of 90 million in Western Europe and the USA. One in every four households in Western Europe owns a dog, and the figure rises to two in every five households in the USA." Chris Thorne, "Feeding Behavior of Domestic Dogs and the Role of Experience," in James Serpell (ed.), *The Domestic*

and even by breed and individual within species.[11] I will ignore these complexities and describe what a typical dog needs in the way of basic care. What I saw about dogs applies, *mutatis mutandis*, to other species.

There is one other issue that needs to be raised and set aside.[12] The question of what one owes to a particular animal that one voluntarily brings into one's life is separate from the question of whether one should bring that animal into one's life. Is it permissible, morally, to make a companion of a wild animal such as a boa constrictor, deer, or tiger? These are not domesticated species. Unlike dogs and cats they have no history of living with and among human beings. *Given* that one makes a companion of a wild animal, one has responsibilities to it; but *it does not follow that doing so is or was permissible*. In fact, I believe it is almost always wrong to remove an animal from the wild (i.e., from its natural habitat), whether for companionship or for some other purpose. Only if one has harmed the animal and is confining it temporarily prior to releasing it into the wild may one deprive it of its liberty.[13] In what follows, I bracket the primary question of whether one should bring an animal into one's life and focus on the secondary question of what responsibilities one has toward an animal *given that* one has brought it into one's life.

I

My thesis, as indicated, is that the act of bringing an animal into one's life—the act of forming a bond or relationship with a particular sentient being—generates a responsibility to care for its needs.[14] I am not arguing for the different

---

Dog: Its Evolution, Behaviour, and Interactions with People (Cambridge: Cambridge University Press, 1995), p. 104. The focus on dogs is appropriate for another, more troubling reason."[H]umane society statistics reveal that dogs are by far the most common animal victims of human negligence and abuse." James Serpell, "From Paragon to Pariah: Some Reflections on Human Attitudes to Dogs," in James Serpell (ed.), *The Domestic Dog: Its Evolution, Behaviour, and Interactions with People* (Cambridge: Cambridge University Press, 1995), p. 252.

[11]On species-specificity, see Paul W. Taylor, *Respect for Nature: A Theory of Environmental Ethics* (Princeton: Princeton University Press, 1986), p. 68. With respect to diversity among dogs, it should be noted that there are 400 breeds in the world today, many of which are the product of selective breeding. See Juliet Clutton-Brock, Origins of the Dog: Domestication and Early History," in James Serpell (ed.), *The Domestic Dog: Its Evolution, Behaviour, and Interactions with People* (Cambridge: Cambridge University Press, 1995), p. 16.

[12]I am indebted to an anonymous reviewer for raising this issue.

[13]Here I agree with Paul Taylor, who argues for a "principle of restitutive justice" with respect to harmed organisms, species-populations, and biotic communities. See Taylor, *Respect for Nature*, pp. 186–192, 194–195, 196–197. This principle (he also calls it a rule) arises where "an agent has broken a valid moral rule an by doing so has upset the balance of justice between himself or herself and a moral subject." Ibid, p. 186. Taylor's four rules of duty are nonmaleficience, noninterference, fidelity, and restitutive justice. See ibid., chap. 4.

[14]Stated differently, I am arguing for an acquired duty toward (certain) animals. For a discussion of the distinction between acquired and unacquired duties, see, e.g., Regan, *The Case for Animal Rights*, pp. 273–276. Regan, quoting John Rawls, says that unacquired duties (what Rawls calls "natural" duties) "apply to us without regard to our voluntary acts" and "irrespective of . . . institutional

claim that because humans *collectively* have domesticated certain species of animals (dogs, for example),[15] they (humans) are responsible for the well-being of
those species. This argument is suggested by a passage from the zoologist
Michael W. Fox:

> Some may demean domesticated animals as being degenerate or inferior forms
> of their wild ancestors or counterparts. Others may see them as merely utilitar-
> ian "tools," manmade to serve humanity, in order to satisfy and gratify our
> many and diverse needs. Yet do we fully understand our enormous obligation
> and debt to them, which is ethically far greater perhaps than our debt to wild
> forms? While the latter may be in our trust and we their stewards, the former
> are *our own creations*. Being so, what kind of creator are we, and are we to be-
> come? Our debt to them is unmeasurable, for we have learned and are still
> learning from them to become more fully human: responsible and compassion-
> ate. We can learn through them in countless ways about nature and about our
> own nature as well.[16]

This collective-responsibility argument (as I term it) is compatible with my
argument, for one might claim that an individual human is responsible both *qua*
individual (to dogs he or she takes in) and *qua* human (to dogs generally). But
this argument creates additional challenges, such as spelling out the nature,
ground, distribution, and limits of collective responsibility. These challenges
may or may not be met. My claim, in contrast, is that *individual* humans, by acting in certain ways, incur responsibilities to *individual* animals.

Nor am I arguing that when a person takes an animal in, he or she is contracting with it, tacitly or otherwise. My argument is not, in other words, contractarian.[17] If any legal doctrine applies here, it is promissory estoppel. This is

---

relationships." Acquired duties, in contrast, arise "because of our voluntary acts or our place in institutional arrangements." Ibid, p. 273 (the first two quotations are from John Rawls, *A theory of Justice* [Cambridge: Harvard University Press, 1971], pp. 114–115). I do not argue (in this essay, at any
rate) for the existence of institutional duties toward animals.

   On an unrelated note, I have been criticized by an anonymous reviewer for using the pronouns
"it" and "its" (possessive case) to refer to nonhuman animals. The criticism is that this objectifies animals, which (allegedly) undermines the thesis of the essay. I am not convinced by the criticism; but
even if the use does objectify, it is interesting to observe that humans are also routinely objectified
in this way—usually when the context is abstract, as it is here. Jane Flax, for example, writes that
"The initial euphoria present in the discovery of the child's owns powers and skills diminishes as *it*
discovers the limitations as well as the possibilities of *its* developing skills. The child painfully
learns that not only is *it* not omnipotent, but that the mother, too, is not all powerful." Jane Flax,
"Political Philosophy and the Patriarchal Unconscious: A Psychoanalytic Perspective on Epistemology and Metaphysics," in *Discovering Reality: Feminist Perspectives on Epistemology, Metaphysics,
Methodology, and Philosophy of Science*, ed. Sandra Harding and Merrill B. Hintikka (Dordrecht, Holland: D. Reidel Publishing Company, 1983), p. 252 (emphasis added). Bernard Rollin, who can
hardly be accused of insensitivity to animals, also uses "it" to refer to particular animals where their
sex is irrelevant. See Rollin, *Animal Rights & Human Morality*, p. 216.

[16]Michael W. Fox, *The Dog: Its Domestication and Behavior* (New York and London: Garland STPM
Press, 1978), p. 262 (emphasis added).

[17]For a sketch of such an argument, see Bernard E. Rollin, "Morality and the Human-Animal Bond,"
in Aaron Honori Katcher and Alan M. Beck (eds.), *New Perspectives on Our Lives with Companion Animals* (Philadelphia: University of Pennsylvania Press, 1983), p. 504 ("[P]et animals, at least, *do* stand
in precisely this relationship to man, behaviorally [sic], biologically, and evolutionarily. There is a

the doctrine that one is bound by one's unilateral (unreciprocated) promises that one has reason to believe will generate, and do in fact generate, detrimental reliance (through expectation).[18] But I do not rest my conclusion on either expectations or reliance. I believe this fits our attitudes toward parental responsibility as well. As Annette Baier puts it, "Parental and filial responsibility does not rest on deals, actual or virtual, between parent and child."[19] The responsibility of a parent *qua* parent or of a sibling *qua* sibling has some other basis.

It might be objected that the very idea of a special responsibility or special obligation is misconceived. The objection is not that there *is* no special responsibility to companion animals, but that in the nature of things there *cannot* be, since judgments of responsibility and obligation, being moral judgments, must be universalizable, and those involving special responsibilities and special obligations are not universalizable.[20]

The objection is confused. The judgment that one is responsible to beings who are related to one in a particular way is, contrary to the assertion, universalizable. Take the judgment that Jennifer is responsible for the welfare of Ginger, the dog she brought home from the pound. The universalized form of this judgment is that *anyone* (that is, anyone in Jennifer's situation) who brings a dog home from the pound is responsible for the animal's welfare (or, more generally, that anyone who takes in a dog, from whatever source, is responsible).[21] I am

---

strong social contract between man and dog" [italics in original]). See also Rollin, *Animal Rights & Human Morality*, pp. 216–220. For doubts about the usefulness of a contractual mode, see Carole Pateman, "The Sexual Contract and the Animals," *Journal of Social Philosophy* 27 (1996), pp. 70–72 (arguing that since animals cannot refuse to enter into contracts, and since the possibility of refusal is "the basic criterion for the existence of a genuine practice of contract" [ibid., p. 72], animals cannot be contractors).

[18]See, e.g., *Black's Law Dictionary*, 5th ed. (St. Paul, MN: West Publishing Company, 1979), p. 1093 (s.v."Promissory estoppel") and John D. Calamari and Joseph M. Perillo, *The Law of Contracts*, 2nd ed. (St. Paul, MN: West Publishing Company, 1977), pp. 202–203. To estop is to stop, so estoppel is the act of stopping (i.e., preventing) someone from doing something. *Promissory* estoppel is the *doctrine* that one ought, legally, to be stopped or prevented from breaking one's promise. For a gesture in this direction with respect to human obligations to animals, see Roslind Godlovitch, "Animals and Morals," *Philosophy* 46 (1971), p. 25 ("The function of the practice of promising is to incur 'special' obligations . . .").

[19]Annette C. Baier, *Moral Prejudices: Essays on Ethics* (Cambridge: Harvard University Press, 1995), p. 110.

[20]An anonymous reviewer has suggested that this is "something of a straw man objection" since "Common moral practice, and more moral theory, certainly recognizes special obligations, e.g., to our loved ones, one's own community, etc." I agree that common moral practice recognizes special obligations, but I deny that the main moral theories do so. Consequentialists, for example, have a notoriously difficult time accommodating special obligations. See the discussion and references in Part III. It may be—and here I speculate—that this is why the main moral theories fail to resonate with ordinary people. I say this as someone who has taught practical and theoretical ethics for many years and who assumes that beginning students are "ordinary people." For a discussion of where, in my view, moral theory goes bad, see Keith Burgess-Jackson, "The Problem with Contemporary Moral Theory," *Hypatia* 8 (1993), pp. 160–166 (arguing that moral theory is unacceptably foundational).

[21]Here I concur with Philip Pettit, who writes: "Considering the repeatable features of his situation, each parent must acknowledge, not just his duty to look after his child, but the duty on all parents

not saying that the universalizability of the judgment *validates* it; I am saying that it insulates it from the criticism that it is nonuniversalizable, hence not a moral judgment. In other words, it passes the universalizability test. The problem with the objection is that it confuses generality and universality. There can be universalizable judgments about special (i.e., nongeneral) relationships.[22]

Note also that by arguing for the existence of special responsibilities to the animals one takes in, I am not ruling out the possibility or existence of general responsibilities, by which I mean responsibilities to "stranger" animals. The two types of responsibility can co-exist, as most of us think they do in the case of humans. Most of us believe that we have responsibilities to human strangers, although there may well be disagreement concerning the nature and extent of that responsibility (i.e., what it entails). For example, some of us believe that we have affirmative responsibilities to strangers (to sustain their lives), while others maintain that our only responsibility is negative: not to harm them.[23] But everyone allows that there is an obligation (overridable perhaps) not to harm strangers.[24] This is the shared core of belief.

The same is true of animals. One can have a general (overridable) obligation not to harm animals at the same time that one has an affirmative responsibility to promote the interests of particular animals. Indeed, I can have both types of obligation with respect to the same animals. *Qua* dog, *qua* sentient being, or *qua*

---

to take like care of their progeny." Philip Pettit, "Social Holism and Moral Theory: A Defence of Bradley's Thesis," *Proceedings of the Aristotelian Society*, n.s., 86 (1985/86), p. 183. See also Andrew Oldenquist, "Loyalties," *The Journal of Philosophy* 79 (1983), p. 174.

[22]See R. M. Hare, *Moral Thinking: Its Levels, Method, and Point* (Oxford: Clarendon Press, 1981), p. 41 ("[G]enerality is the opposite of specificity, whereas universality is compatible with specificity, and means merely the logical property of being governed by a universal quantifier and not containing individual constants."). I do not address the more fundamental question whether, in order for a judgment to *count* as a moral judgment, it must be universalizable. I assume so. For a discussion of this point, see ibid., p. 55; see also Cottingham, "Ethics and Impartiality," *passim*.

[23]Rawls addresses this point when he distinguishes two types of natural duty (the contrast being to nonnatural or acquired duty). Positive natural duties are duties "to do something good for another," while negative natural duties "requires us not to do something that is bad." Rawls, *A Theory of Justice*, p. 114. Rawls finds it "plausible to hold that, when the distinction is clear, negative duties have more weight than positive one." Ibid. He does not, however, argue the point.

The two distinctions (natural/acquired and positive/negative) cut across one another, generating the following four types: (1) positive natural duties; (2) negative natural duties; (3) positive acquired duties; and (4) negative acquired duties. An example of a positive natural duty would be providing aid to a stranger (this is Rawls's example). An example of a negative natural duty would be refraining from harming a stranger (also one of Rawls's examples). An example of a positive acquired duty would be educating one's child or keeping a promise. An example of a negative acquired duty would be not harming one's child. My argument, cast in Rawlsian terminology, is that we have duties of type 3 *and* 4 with respect to companion animals. The voluntary act of taking an animal in generates both positive and negative duties toward it. This does *not* entail that we *lack* duties of type 1 or 2.

[24]Perhaps "everyone" is extreme. An ethical egoist, for example, might deny that there are natural duties (positive *or* negative) in Rawls's sense. If one's governing principle is the maximization of self-interest, as it is to a rational egoist, then in a particular case one may be *required* to harm others, whether stranger or nonstranger.

living organism, Sophie (my canine companion) has a right that I not harm her; *qua* animal that I have taken in, she has a right that I attend to her needs.[25] Those who reject affirmative obligations, whether to humans or to animals, typically do so not on grounds that such obligations are incoherent or incompatible with negative obligations, but for substantive reasons.[26] They believe, for example, that affirmative obligations unduly restrain liberty, or that they blur the line between the obligatory (justice) and the supererogatory (charity), or that they generate irresolvable coordination problems.

II

Having clarified my thesis, let me state its grounds. My argument is *ad hominem* in nature.[27] It is addressed to anyone who believes that responsibility can be voluntarily undertaken or assumed—that is, to anyone who believes that certain actions, in virtue of being the actions they are, with the consequences they have, generate responsibilities or obligations to others.[28] The basic idea, which I

---

[25]I use the language of rights loosely. It is not my aim to defend any kind of rights for animals in this essay. But by the same token, I do not deny their existence or possibility. In this regard I part ways with Paul Taylor, with whom I am otherwise in agreement. See Taylor, *Respect for Nature,* Chap. 5 (arguing that moral rights, strictly and properly conceived, are such that it is impossible for animals—or plants—to be bearers of moral rights, but conceding that there is an extended sense of "moral right" in which animals—as well as plants—may be said to have moral rights). My argument is about human responsibility and duty, which may or may not correlate with animals rights. Stated differently, I do not embrace the correlativity thesis, which maintains that every right entails a duty and every duty a right. For a formal statement and discussion of the correlativity thesis, see Keith Burgess-Jackson, "Duties, Rights, and Charity," *Journal of Social Philosophy* 18 (1987), pp. 3–12.
[26]I say "typically" because there are exceptions. It has been argued, for example, that there are logical limits on the sorts of rights that might exist. See Hillel Steiner, "The Structure of a Set of Compossible Rights," *The Journal of Philosophy* 74 (1977), pp. 767–775. I thank an anonymous reviewer for bringing this essay to my attention.
[27]By "*ad hominem*" I mean addressed to particular people with particular beliefs, values, ideals, principles, and commitments. This is the Lockean sense of the term. See John Locke, *An Essay Concerning Human Understanding,* ed. with a foreword by Peter H. Nidditch (Oxford: Clarendon Press, 1975: 1st ed., 1689), Bk. IV, Chap. XVII, Sec. 21, p. 686 ("A third way [to persuade] is, to press a Man with Consequences drawn from his own Principles, or Concessions. This is already known under the Name of *Argumentum ad Hominem*" [italics in original]). Joel Feinberg describes this method, which he employs throughout his tetralogy, as follows: "The appeal in [ad hominem] arguments is made directly 'to the person' of one's interlocutor, to the convictions he or she is plausibly assumed to possess already. If the argument is successful, it shows to the person addressed that the judgment it supports coheres more smoothly than its rivals with the network of convictions he already possesses, so that if he rejects it, then he will have to abandon other judgments that he would be loath to relinquish." Joel Feinberg, *The Moral Limits of the Criminal Law,* vol. 1: *Harm to Others* (New York: Oxford University Press, 1984), p. 18. This sort of *ad hominem* argument should not be confused with the fallacious sort. There is a difference, however one marks it, between (1) dismissing a person's argument on the basis if irrelevant personal characteristics (attack *on* the person) and (2) drawing out the consequences of someone's beliefs, values, ideals, principles, or commitments (appeal *to* the person). Only the first of these is fallacious.
[28]I agree with Christina Hoff Sommers that "The contemporary philosopher is, on the whole, actively unsympathetic to the idea that we have *any* duties defined by relationships that we have not

believe is widely shared, is that one is responsible for what one does, and what one does is at least partly specified by its foreseeable consequences. One is responsible, that is to say, for conditions one brings about through voluntary action. If I shoot my rifle into a crowd of people, I am responsible (answerable) for any resultant harm, even if strictly speaking the harm is unintended. What we say in such a case is that I *should have known* of the grave risk of harm I created. My action was reckless. A responsible agent is one whose actions are one's own, who can and must respond to others for what one does.

Animals, no less than humans, have needs, not all of which, in this human-made world, can be fulfilled naturally or on their own.[29] Among other things, animals need protection from human beings and from human activities (e.g., the spraying of pesticides and herbicides), projects (building construction, warfare, sporting events), and objects (nails, culverts, toxic chemicals, automobiles.[30] Human beings who take custody of animals—who make companions of them—close off opportunities for those animals to fulfill their needs in any other way (as by being taken in by another human). This closing off of opportunities makes the animals vulnerable and dependent,[31] which, I maintain, generates a responsibility in its producer. The vulnerability is a direct consequence of what one does.

The situation is analogous to having or adopting a child, a fact that I exploit for argumentative purposes.[32] Why are parents responsible for, and to, their

---

voluntarily entered into." Christina Hoff Sommers, "Philosophers Against the Family," in George Graham and Hugh LaFollette (eds.), *Person to Person* (Philadelphia: Temple University Press, 1989), p. 82 (italics in original). The prevailing idea seems to be that all duties are self-imposed. I do not share this belief, but that is neither here nor there as far as my argument in this essay is concerned. My argument is addressed to those who *have* this belief. I try to show them that their principles commit them to acknowledging duties to companion animals.

[29] According to Beck, "Most companion animals . . . are domesticated or captive-born species that thrive better in captivity than when free of human care." Beck, "Animals in the City," p. 240. Note that this is a comparative judgment. Beck is not saying that *all* companion animals thrive. If he were, and if he were correct, there would be no need to write this essay. He is making a claim about species, not specimens.

[30] "[T]here is evidence that loose [unconstrained] dogs account for more than 6 percent of all automobile accidents . . ." Ibid., p. 24. This is not to blame the animals who cause such accidents but to suggest the degree of danger to which they are exposed. Beck advocates leash laws as a way to minimize this loss. See ibid.

[31] See, e.g., Harlan B. Miller, "Introduction: 'Platonists' and 'Aristotelians'," in Harlan B. Miller and William H. Williams (eds.), *Ethics and Animals* (Clifton, NJ: Humana Press, 1983), p. 10.

[32] I am not the first to notice or draw the analogy. See Leslie Pickering Francis and Richard Norman, "Some Animals Are More Equal Than Others," *Philosophy* 53 (1978), p. 523 ("[H]uman beings can be something like the voluntary parents of animals—their pets. However, . . . the human role in such cases will normally be 'parental' only in the sense of being a protective and nurturing one; the distinctive developmental features which we have stressed in the human parent-child relation will be present to a very small degree, if at all, in the relations between human beings and their pets. Even so, such relations may be treated as bearing some moral resemblance to the parent-child relationship; a pet owner would not be blamed for rescuing his/her pet rather than someone else's"). Francis and Norman are not here concerned to deny the possibility of special responsibilities to animals. What they claim is that not all animals are so related to humans. Rollin has also made the adoption comparison. See Rollin, *Animal Rights & Human Morality*, p. 230 ("[A]cquiring an animal is morally more like adopting a child than it is like buying a wheelbarrow").

children? Because the voluntary actions of the parents brought the child—a helpless, dependent, vulnerable being—into existence.[33] Of course, while I am responsible *for* everything I bring into existence, I am not responsible *to* everything I bring into existence. If I bake a cake, I do not thereby incur responsibility to the cake (for its welfare). But that is because the cake *has* no welfare; it makes no sense to say, of a cake, that things are going well or poorly for it. The cake is not sentient; it has no interests; nothing matters to it. But dogs and other animals are sentient; they have interests.[34] Things can go well or poorly for them in the same sense and in many of the same ways in which things can go well or poorly for you, me, or a human infant. Baier alludes to this parallel between animals and human infants when she says that

> we need a morality to guide us in our dealings with those who either cannot or should not achieve equality of power (animals, the ill, the dying, children while still young) with those with whom they have unavoidable and often intimate relationships.[35]

It is the *fact* of vulnerability, therefore, conjoined with causal responsibility for that condition, that generates moral responsibility.[36] It is not, I hasten to add, that parents contract with their children to respond to their children's needs, for infants and children are incapable of contracting. Nor is it that the parent is related to the child genetically, for we would (and do) say the same about the responsibility of those who adopt children as about those who conceive and bear their own. Simply put: If you believe that a parent is responsible for his or her children, then, by parity of reasoning, you should believe that humans are responsible for the animals they bring into their lives.[37] If you do *not* believe that a parent is responsible for his or her children, then my argument will not persuade you.

---

[33]See, e.g., Jeffrey Blustein, "Procreation and Parental Responsibility," *Journal of Social Philosophy* 28 (1997), pp. 79–86.

[34]See Rollin, "Morality and the Human-Animal Bond, pp. 500–501; Taylor, *Respect for Nature*, p. 17. There may be nonsentient animals—insects and mollusks, for example—but these are not likely to be human companions.

[35]Baier, *Moral Prejudices*, p. 116.

[36]Here I deviate from my announced practice of using the unadorned "responsibility," but only to distinguish it from causal responsibility, which, in and of itself, has no normative or evaluative significance. For a discussion of the psychic dependency of dogs on their human companions, see Fox, *The Dog*, pp. 250–257. See generally Rollin, *Animal Rights & Human Morality*, p. 217 ("The dog in its current form is essentially dependent upon humans for its physical existence, behavioral needs, and for fulfillment of its social nature").

[37]James Rachels examines three arguments in favor of what he calls "the Compromise View," which is the "idea that one's own children have a superior claim [vis-á-vis other children] to one's care." James Rachels, "Morality, Parents, and Children," in George Graham and Hugh LaFollette (eds.), *Person to Person* (Philadelphia: Temple University Press, 1989), p. 50. The first argument asserts that parenthood is a role and that certain responsibilities and obligations (as well as rights) inhere in roles. Since one occupies the parental role only in relation to one's own children, one has responsibilities and obligations only to them. The second argument maintains that parents have special responsibility to their own children (as opposed to the children of others) because they (the parents) are "better situated to look after their own." Ibid, p. 53 (italics omitted). The third argument

III

Why have philosophers neglected the line of argument I have just advanced?[38] Why does the literature of animal rights/welfare/liberation, which is now extensive, say so little about human responsibility to companion animals (as opposed to animals *per se*)? I believe there are several explanations for the lacuna.[39] The first is a fear (by those who have written on the moral status of animals) of negative practical repercussions. We know that there is a lively debate among moral philosophers and moralists concerning the extent of one's responsibility to other humans. So-called impartialists maintain that our responsibility to

---

maintains that love is a personal good of great importance and that, without special relationships, it would be unrealizable. As Rachels puts it, "An ethic that required absolute impartiality would therefore require forgoing a great personal good." Ibid, p. 54.

None of these arguments captures what I take to be the basis of our responsibility to companion animals. I have not argued for the existence of a social role involving companion animals, much less tried to give content to such a role. Thus, I do not use the term "special responsibility" in the way Philip Pettit (for example) uses "special duty." Pettit defines "special duties" as "those that belong to the occupants of certain social roles." Pettit, "Social Holism and Moral Theory," p. 173. Some—but not all—special responsibilities derive from roles (elsewhere in his essay Pettit uses the term "special duties" more broadly. See ibid., p. 180. I am arguing for special duties in that broader sense).

Nor is it my contention that we have special responsibilities to companion animals because we are best situated (spatiotemporally or otherwise) to provide for their needs. This may be true in many or most cases, but it is not the basis of my argument. Finally, I do not rest my case for responsibility on emotions such as love, however good and valuable they may be. While there is undoubtedly genuine affection (perhaps amounting to love) between many humans and their companion animals, this is not the basis of the responsibility humans have toward them. Rather, the responsibility flows from the act of acquisition and the fact of vulnerability. Oddly, Rachels does not consider this possibility. When he compares his own children to other children, he finds no relevant differences. One morally relevant difference is that he, Rachels, has brought some of these children (but not others) into existence. See Oldenquist, "Loyalties," p. 186.

[38]A computerized search of *The Philosopher's Index* for the years 1940 through March 1998 (inclusive) turned up only ten references to the conjunction of "companion" and "animal (or variants thereof), ten references to "pet(s)," and sixty-five references to "dog(s)." Many of the references to dogs concern their cognitive and linguistic abilities rather than questions of moral status. Only a handful of the eighty-five items address the subject of this essay, and will, accordingly, be discussed herein. One of the best-known anthologies in the field, published in 1983, contains twenty-six essays arrayed in eight sections. Seventeen of the contributors are listed as philosophers. Not *one* of the essays, or even a section of an essay, is devoted to companion animals, let alone to human responsibilities to companion animals. See Harlan B. Miller and William H. Williams (eds.), *Ethics and Animals* (Clifton, NJ: Humana Press, 1983). The second edition of another widely used anthology contains thirty-nine essays arrayed in nine sections. At least twenty-three of the contributors, by my count, are philosophers. Again, not one section of one essay is devoted to companion animals. See Tom Regan and Peter Singer (eds.), *Animal Rights and Human Obligations,* 2nd ed. (Englewood Cliffs, NJ: Prentice Hall, 1989; 1st ed., 1976).

[39]I am pleased to report that since the completion of this essay I discovered a brief but serious discussion, by a philosopher, of the morality of keeping companion animals. David DeGrazia argues for a principle (one of fifteen he sets out) to the following effect: "Provide for the basic physical and psychological needs of your pet, and ensure that she has a comparably good life to what she would likely have if she were not a pet." David DeGrazia, *Taking Animals Seriously: Mental Life and Moral Status* (Cambridge: Cambridge University Press, 1996), p. 280. One hopes, that other, more detailed studies follow.

others is vast and unlimited; that if we have affirmative obligations to anyone, we have affirmative obligations to everyone, even strangers. These individuals argue that it is misguided, if not irrational, to think that one can have special responsibilities to particular humans or groups of humans. This is thought to be an arbitrary and indefensible preference.[40] Partialists, on the other hand, deny this claim, insisting that it is neither misguided nor irrational to believe that one has special responsibilities. Partialists believe that one can and does have special responsibilities to friends, relatives, colleagues, compatriots, and so forth, and that this is not arbitrary.[41]

The impartialist fear seems to be that, by acknowledging the existence of *special* responsibilities, we dilute the more general responsibilities of (and to) humanity. The temptation would be to ignore or devalue those to whom one does not stand in a special relation. We ask only how our family, friends, neighbors, and compatriots are doing (perhaps how members of our race, sex, or religion are doing) rather than how people in general are doing. We exhibit tribalism. Strategically, impartialists believe, it is better to treat everyone the same, whether lover, friend, acquaintance, or stranger. Humans are humans. They have the same needs, interests, capacities, desires, and character. Humans are morally, if not materially, indistinguishable.[42] In economic terms, they are fungible.

It so happens that those who have been most active in defense of animals—Peter Singer and Tom Regan—are impartialists.[43] I believe they have the fears just described and that they project those fears onto human attitudes toward animals. The fear is that, if we acknowledge special responsibilities of the sort I advocate in this essay, so-called stranger animals, animals whom no human has taken in, or to whom no human is affectively related (perhaps because they lack "cuddliness"), will be ignored and devalued—will fall outside the moral community. We humans will divide the animal kingdom into two mutually exclusive and exhaustive categories, conferring moral status on members of one category but not on members of the other. The fear, in short, is that we will treat

---

[40]The term "impartialist" is Cottingham's. See Cottingham, "Ethics and Impartiality," *passum*. Impartialists are so called because they embrace the impartiality thesis, which "implies that when we are making moral decisions (e.g., about how to allocate goods and resources), we ought not to give any special weight to our own desires and interests; instead of giving preferential treatment to ourselves, or to members of our own particular social group, we should try to adopt a neutral standpoint, detaching ourselves as far as possible from our own special desires and involvements." Ibid, p. 83. Cottingham's essay is a sustained argument *against* the impartiality thesis.

[41]For another and more recent critique of impartialism (and therefore a partial defense of partialism), see Stephen R. L. Clark, "Enlarging the Community: Companion Animals," in Brenda Almond (ed.), *Introducing Applied Ethics* (Oxford and Cambridge, MA: Blackwell Publishers, 1995), pp. 318–330. Despite his title, Clark says very little about companion animals.

[42]This, I believe, is the thrust of Thomas Jefferson's immortal phrase "all men are created equal" (from the Declaration of Independence). See Brian L. Blakeley and Jacquelin Collins, *Documents in English History: Early Times to the Present* (New York: John Wiley & Sons, 1975), p. 271. Jefferson is saying that in spite of obvious material differences, humans are morally alike.

[43]Singer, not surprisingly, is one of Cottingham's targets. See Cottingham, "Ethics and Impartiality," pp. 83–84.

noncompanion animals—rats, pigs, cows, wolves, chimpanzees—as badly as, perhaps worse than, we treat human strangers.[44]

Another (by no means incompatible) explanation of the philosophical neglect of companion animals has to do with a metaphysical assumption rather than a strategic imperative. It is thought that responsibility to a being must— *logically* must—rest on some intrinsic property of the being rather than on, say, a relation between it and a responsible agent.[45] Despite their substantive differences, which are many and profound, Singer and Regan share this assumption.[46] Singer argues that the morally salient fact about animals (or certain animals) is their sentience, which he defines as "the capacity to suffer and/or

---

[44]This fear pervades *Animal Liberation,* where Singer insists that rats (for example) are "as capable of suffering as dogs are." Singer, *Animal Liberation,* p. 30. He then speculates about why dogs and rats are viewed differently: "People tend to care about dogs because they generally have more experience with dogs as companions." Ibid.; see also ibid., pp. 214, 218–219. Singer is worried that we will limit our moral attention to familiar, friendly, or cuddly animals, of which dogs are an exemplar. What Singer ignores is the possibility that the greater care and concern for dogs than for rats is a function of greater *responsibility* for the former, which in turn stems from having taken them in. In other words, the difference is moral, not psychological. One wonders whether people care more about feral or stray dogs than about rats. I suspect not.

[45]The same mindlessness, if I may call it that, attends the abortion debate. Until recently, when radical (as opposed to liberal) feminists began to address the subject, it was assumed that the moral status of a fetus must be a function of its intrinsic properties rather than of its relation to the woman in whom it develops (or to other humans). The only question was *which* properties were relevant to this status. For a pioneering discussion of this issue, see Lynn M. Morgan, "Fetal Relationality in Feminist Philosophy: An Anthropological Critique," *Hypatia* 11 (1996), pp. 47–70.

[46]I am by no means the first to point this out. Twenty years ago Cora Diamond criticized a line of argument that she called, revealingly, "the Singer-Regan approach." Cora Diamond, "Eating Meat and Eating People," *Philosophy* 53 (1978), p. 467. Diamond writes: "It is a mark of the shallowness of these discussions of vegetarianism that the only tool used in them to explain what differences in treatment are justified is the appeal to the *capacities* of the beings in question." Ibid., p. 468 (emphasis added); see also ibid., p. 479. This *sounds* like a critique of what I am calling "intrinsicalism." Diamond does not, however, emphasize relationships, as I do. Instead, she stresses the fact that other animals are "fellow creatures." Ibid., p. 474. But even wild (i.e., nondomesticated) animals such as songbirds (her example is a titmouse) turn out to be fellow creatures, so she is not concerned, after all, with those particular animals with whom we form relationships.

For a more recent and slightly different critique of Singer and Regan, see Richard Sorabji, *Animal Minds and Human Morals: The Origins of the Western Debate* (Ithaca, NY: Cornell University Press, 1993), p. 213. ("I can now state my chief doubt about the two principal modern theories [those of Singer and Regan], and that is that they take only one main consideration into account: preference satisfaction (supplemented by pleasure and pain equations) or inherent value. But there are so many other considerations"). If I understand him correctly, Sorabji's complaint is that Singer and Regan are *monists.* This is brought out by the title of the chapter in which he discusses their work: "The one-dimensionality of ethical theories."

In an important essay, Mary Anne Warren has urged rejection of "two common assumptions about the theoretical foundations of moral rights," namely, "the intrinsic-properties assumption" and "the single-criterion assumption." Mary Anne Warren, "The Moral Significance of Birth," *Hypatia* 4 (1989), p. 47. The former "is the view that the only facts that can justify the ascription of basic moral rights or moral standing to individuals are facts about *the intrinsic properties of those individuals.*" Ibid. (citations omitted; italics are original). The latter "is the view that there is some single property, the presence or absence of which divides the world into those things which have moral rights or moral standing, and those things which do not." Ibid. I agree with Warren not only that these assumptions are widespread, but that they should be rejected.

experience enjoyment." [47] Regan claims that the morally salient fact about (certain) animals is that they are "subjects of a life," which he defines as a being who has

> beliefs and desires; perception, memory, and a sense of the future, including their own future; an emotional life together with feelings of pleasure and pain; preference- and welfare-interests; the ability to initiate action in pursuit of their desires and goals; a psychophysical identity over time; and an individual welfare in the sense that their experiential life fares well or ill for them, logically independently of their utility for others and logically independently of their being the object of anyone else's interests.[48]

Both sentience (Singer) and subjecthood (to abbreviate Regan's phrase) are intrinsic properties; neither is dependent on how the being in question is related to others. A particular animal either has or lacks the property, and this is unaffected by its relations to others. If an animal has the property, then, according to these theorists, it has moral status.[49]

It will come as no surprise to the reader that philosophers disagree about what the relevant intrinsic properties are—as well as which extant beings have them.[50] My point is simply that there is a reigning assumption to the effect that moral status *is* supervenient on some such property. Robert Nozick summarizes the situation as follows:

> The traditional proposals for the important individuating characteristic connected with moral constraints [moral status] are the following: sentient and self-conscious; rational (capable of using abstract concepts, not tied to responses to immediate stimuli); possessing free will; being a moral agent capable of guiding its behavior by moral principles and capable of engaging in mutual limitation of conduct; having a soul.[51]

---

[47]Singer, *Animal Liberation*, pp. 8–9. In an early critique of Singer's arguments for vegetarianism, Francis and Norman point out that he is, in my terms, an intrinsicalist: "What is notable is that the properties he [Singer] considers as likely candidates [for distinguishing between humans and other animals] are all *non-relational:* possessing reason, being able to feel pain, having interests. We suggest that what are important are the *relations* in which human beings stand to one another and that with few exceptions they do not stand in the same relations to animals." Francis and Norman, "Some Animals Are More Equal Than Others," p. 518 (italics in original). The exceptions, of course, are crucial, for my argument is that we have special responsibilities to those animals we voluntarily bring into our lives and homes.

[48]Regan, *The Case for Animal Rights*, p. 243.

[49]Two points. First, according to Regan, being a subject of a life is not a matter of degree."One either *is* a subject of a life, in the sense explained, or one *is not*. All those who are, are so equally. The subject-of-a-life criterion thus demarcates a categorical status shared by all moral agents and those moral patients with whom we are concerned." Ibid., p. 245 (italics in original). Second, being a subject of a life is (for Regan) sufficient but not necessary for having moral status (what he calls "inherent value"). Ibid., pp. 245–246. But see Deborah Slicer, "Your Daughter or Your Dog? A Feminist Assessment of the Animal Research Issue," *Hypatia* 6 (1991), p. 110, who maintains that for Regan, "the possession of preference interests [is] a necessary condition" for "being owed moral consideration." Singer, in contrast, makes sentience both necessary and sufficient for having interests. See Singer, *Animal Liberation*, p. 8. Presumably, for Singer, all and only beings with interests have moral status.

[50]See, e.g., Francis and Norman, "Some Animals Are More Equal Than Others," pp. 513–518, who take issue with Singer and Regan both individually and collectively.

[51]Robert Nozick, *Anarchy, State, and Utopia* (New York: Basic Books, 1974), p. 48.

Much philosophical ink has been spilled in arguing for or against a particular property as being the morally salient one. As soon as we relax the metaphysical assumption about intrinsic properties, however, we see the importance of the many and varied relations in which humans stand to animals. The fact that I stand in such-and-such a relation to animal, *A,* may itself give rise to an obligation on my part—an obligation that effectively elevates *A*'s moral status. (To be the beneficiary of an obligation, I assume, is to have moral status—to count morally, to take up moral space.)[52]

Let us apply this thinking to the case of companion animals. Two dogs alike in all intrinsic properties can stand in different relations to me, with the result that I can have a responsibility to one of them that I do not have to the other. There is nothing logically suspect about this.[53] Nor is it particularly odd from a moral point of view, for, as we saw, most of us believe that one is responsible to/for one's own child but not to/for someone else's child *even though the children are alike in all relevant respects*—that is, even though they have the same intrinsic properties. The relation itself is thought to have moral significance. Indeed, it is an essential part of the explanation of why one has the obligations one has.[54]

[52]Regan devotes several paragraphs of his book to analyzing the case of the lifeboat, which goes as follows. Four humans and one dog (of the same size and weight) are in a lifeboat that can hold only four individuals. Someone—a human or a dog—must be thrown overboard if any of them are to survive. Who should it be? Regan says it should be the dog (although not *because* it is a dog). See Regan, *The Case for Animal Rights,* p. 324. At no point in his discussion does Regan consider the relation of the dog to any of its lifeboat companions, or, more specifically, whether any of the humans has undertaken responsibility for the dog's welfare. One wonders whether Regan would ignore this relational aspect if the dog were a mildly retarded *human being* who happened to be the child of one of the others in the lifeboat. Would the fact that the parent is responsible to/for the child make a difference to his assessment? *If so,* they why should it *not* make a difference to his assessment of the dog case? I am not saying that the relational aspect is dispositive; I am saying that it is relevant.

[53]Cottingham puts it nicely: "The maxim that a person should give preference to those who stand in some specific relationship with him is, from the logical point of view, a perfectly coherent one. There is nothing 'magical' about relational properties, nor is there anything necessarily irrational about maxims which refer to them." Cottingham, "Ethics and Impartiality," p. 89.

[54]Impartialists find this puzzling. Rachels, for instance, says that, "Like everyone else, I have a deep feeling, that I cannot shake, that my responsibilities to my own children are special. If I have to choose between feeding my own children, and giving the food to starving orphans, I am going to feed my own." James Rachels, "Moral Philosophy as a Subversive Activity," in Earl R. Winkler and Jerrold R. Coombs (eds.), *Applied Ethics: A Reader* (Oxford and Cambridge, MA: Blackwell Publishers, 1993), p. 114. But Rachels has qualms."[M]y children were merely lucky to have the same needs and are equally deserving, were unlucky to have gotten stuck with their situation. Why should the just distribution of life's goods, right down to food itself, be determined in this way?" Ibid., p. 115.

Rachels's puzzlement is puzzling. It appears to stem from his unarticulated assumption that only intrinsic properties of individuals are relevant to other people's responsibility to/for them. Notice how he emphasizes "the same needs" of the children, as well as the fact that they are "equally deserving." These are intrinsic properties. What he fails to notice is that there is a morally relevant difference between the children, namely, their relations to *him*. Rachels assumed responsibility for his children when he brought them into existence (or into his life). He performed no such act with respect to the orphans, however needy and however deserving they may be. This relational asymmetry is sufficient to explain his "deep feeling . . . that [his] responsibilities to [his] own children are special."

Consider the following chart:

		Beneficiary of Obligation	
		Human	Animal
Basis of obligation	Intrinsic properties of beneficiary	1	2
	Relational properties of beneficiary	3	4

Category 1 represents obligations to humans based on their intrinsic properties. Category 2 represents obligations to animals based on their intrinsic properties. Category 3 represents obligations to humans based on their relation to the person obligated. Category 4 represents obligations to animals based on their relation to the person obligated.

In his well-known and much-discussed essay "Famine, Affluence, and Morality,"[55] Singer argues that we have obligations of Type 1—that Category 1 is not empty. Human beings who are unknown to us (i.e., to whom we stand in no special relationship) but who are suffering and dying from lack of food, fuel, shelter, and medical care, are relevantly similar to human beings who are known/related to us and are in the same condition. Their interests are the same. So if we have obligations to the latter, as most of us believe, then we have obligations to the former. Rational consistency pushes us from Category 3 to Category 1. That is, if Category 3 has members, so does Category 1.

In *Animal Liberation*, Singer argues for obligations of Type 2. Animals, he says, are no less sentient than humans, which means that both animals and humans have an interest in not suffering. This intrinsic property of animals—their sentience, their capacity to suffer as well as experience pleasure and happiness—must be taken into account in our deliberations. To do otherwise would be to violate the principle of equal consideration of interests.[56] Singer's aim here, unlike before, is to push us from Category 1 to Category 2. Animals matter morally (he says) because of the kind of beings they are, not because they are related to humans (or to particular humans) in certain ways.

What *I* am arguing in *this* essay is that there are obligations of Type 4, obligations that do not rest on (although they may well presuppose the existence of) intrinsic properties of animals. I am trying to push the reader from Category 3 to Category 4. Singer, interestingly, does not address this argument, perhaps for

---

[55]Peter Singer, "Famine, Affluence, and Morality," *Philosophy & Public Affairs* 1 (1972), pp. 229–243.
[56]See Singer, *Animal Liberation*, p. 2. Singer takes pains, and rightly so, to distinguish equal treatment and equal consideration."The basic principle of equality does not require equal or identical *treatment*; it requires equal consideration. Equal consideration for different beings may lead to different treatment and different rights." Ibid. (italics in original).
[57]I said that one explanation of the philosophical neglect of companion animals is a fear that if special responsibilities to animals are acknowledged, a person may be more likely to reject general

one or more of the reasons adumbrated.[57] Notice, incidentally, that there is no incompatibility in arguing for obligations of all four types. In fact, I believe there *are* obligations of all four types. We are responsible to both humans and animals because of the sorts of beings they are; but we are also responsible to humans and animals in virtue of the relations in which we stand to them. Unfortunately, most philosophical work to date has focused on obligations of Types 1, 2, and 3. My essay is designed to fill this lacuna in the literature by arguing for obligations of Type 4.[58]

---

responsibilities to humans, which Singer (for one) believes to be unacceptable. We can see this strategic move graphically. The fear is that by acknowledging obligations of Type 4, we increase the likelihood of not (or no longer) acknowledging obligations of type 1. In other words, we come to see all obligations—even obligations to humans—as being based on relational properties. Singer, it would appear, consciously risks losing 4 in order not to lose 1.

I should mention in passing a third explanation of the philosophical neglect of companion animals. It may reflect an assumption that animals are "other"—that the lives of animals and humans are distinct and independent. This may in turn reflect as assumption that animals, but not humans, are part of nature. On one side (so the thinking goes) there are humans and the culture they produce; on the other side there are animals and nature. It is tempting, when laboring under this assumption, to view the moral status of animals as but one aspect of the larger question of the moral status of the natural world (or of human responsibilities thereto). This would explain why philosophical anthologies tend to lump the subjects together. See., e.g., James P. Sterba, ed., *Morality in Practice,* 5th ed. (Belmont, CA: Wadsworth Publishing Company, 1997), the eleventh chapter of which is entitled "Animal Liberation and Environmental Justice."

This is an egregious category mistake. The lives of many animals—especially dogs and cats—are interwoven with the lives of human beings. Dogs and cats are not misplaced, pitiable wild creatures, longing for some imagined freedom; they are urban and suburban denizens like their human companions. See., e.g., Rollin, *Animals Rights & Human Morality,* p. 227. This point is ignored by certain writers, such as Lori Gruen, who says that "When humans bring animals into their homes, the animals are forced to conform to the rituals and practices of the human's [sic] that live there. Cats and dogs are often denied full expression of their natural urges when their "owners' keep them indoors or put bells around cats' necks to prevent them from hunting or forbid dogs from scavenging for food." Lori Gruen, "On the Oppression of Women and Animals," *Environmental Ethics* 18 (1996), p. 443. I do not know whether Gruen believes that every human-animal relationship is of this sort. It seems clear to me that some, perhaps many, are not, and that only those that are *of this sort* are objectionable.

If dogs and cats are to be viewed as unauthentic or infantile versions of their wild cousins, then, for the sake of consistency, human beings should be viewed as unauthentic or infantile versions of the primates from which *they* descended and to whom *they* are presently related. Dogs, cats, and other companion animals are viable and contributing members of *human* culture. If we are to make sense of this fact, as Rosemary Rodd notes, we must refuse to see animals as just "part of the environment." See Rosemary Rodd, *Biology, Ethics, and Animals* (Oxford: Clarendon Press, 1990), p. 105.

[58]Unlike Singer and others, I do not fear the backsliding effect described in a previous note. I do not fear that by arguing for obligations of Type 4, I risk undermining people's belief that there are obligations of Type 1. In part this is because people tend to compartmentalize their beliefs about humans and animals. I see potential for a Pareto-superior move (for an explication and discussion of this and related concepts, such as Pareto-optimality, see Jules L. Coleman, *Markets, Morals and the Law* [Cambridge: Cambridge University Press, 1988], Chaps. 3 and 4). We can secure obligations of Type 4 for animals without risking the loss of obligations to anyone else, human or animal. In saying this, I rely on the fact that most people acknowledge obligations of Type 3. My argument, recall, is analogical. Why should relationships with particular humans give rise to obligations when relationships with particular animals do *not* give rise to obligations?

IV

If what I have argued is correct, then the proposition that we are responsible to (and for) the animals we take in is not only coherent but plausible. It makes sense and there is reason to accept it. The next set of questions concerns the nature, scope, and content of that responsibility, so let us turn to those matters. There are, in general, two types of responsibility, and both apply here. The first is what I call "meta-responsibility," which is responsibility in the undertaking and discharge of responsibilities. The objects of meta-responsibility are themselves responsibilities. The second is what I call "primary responsibility." Our primary responsibility to companion animals is to provide for their needs (about which more in a moment). Thus, there are responsibilities both before and after one takes in an animal (just as there are in the case of children). These responsibilities are mutually reinforcing and derive from the same source—namely, our voluntarily acts.

What do dogs need? In what ways are they vulnerable to harm? Dogs need many of the same things humans need, such as ample, nutritious food;[59] clean, fresh water and air; shelter from the elements (excessive heat and cold, precipitation, wind, noise, and so forth); medical care for injuries, bruises, abrasions, and disease;[60] and vigorous, regular exercise.[61] They need protection against parasites and pests (including, but not limited to, fleas, ticks, and worms);[62] immunization against the many diseases to which canines are subject (rabies, distemper, leukemia); treatment of allergies; plenty of sleep and rest (in the form of naps, for example); and regular bathing, trimming, and grooming. These may be considered the material, physical, or biological needs of dogs.

---

[59]See National Research Council, *Nutrient Requirements of Dogs,* rev. ed. (Washington, DC: National Academy Press, 1985).

[60]Some medical care is made necessary by human ignorance or neglect. See Rollin, *Animal Rights & Human Morality,* p. 226 ("Our lack of understanding of the animals' nutritional and biological needs results in myriad medical problems that arise out of bad diet, overfeeding, and lack of exercise"). Ignorance is particularly problematic."To put it bluntly, the average person is either ignorant or misinformed about dog and cat behavior, training, biology, nutrition, in short, about the animal's nature." Ibid., p. 223.

[61]Dogs, like humans, suffer from obesity, which is causally linked to other health problems (such as diabetes and heart, kidney, and liver disease). It has been estimated that "one-third of the British population of pet dogs is obese." Roger A. Mugford, "Canine Behavioural Therapy," in James Serpell (ed.), *The Domestic Dog: Its Evolution, Behaviour, and Interactions with People* (Cambridge: Cambridge University Press, 1995), p. 150; see also Robert Hubrecht, "The Welfare of Dogs in Human Care," in James Serpell (ed.), *The Domestic Dog: Its Evolution, Behaviour, and Interactions with People* (Cambridge: Cambridge University Press, 1995), p. 180. Veterinarian Ron Epps of Bedford, Texas, says that "About 60 percent of dogs are overweight." Stacy Ann Thomas, "Free Weight Checks Stick to the Ribs," *The Dallas Morning News* 148 (8 June 1997), p. 40A. It may be—and here I speculate—that obesity is more of a problem for dogs in affluent nations than for dogs in nonaffluent nations.

[62]Dogs suffer from many types of worms, the most common of which are ringworms, roundworms, hookworms, tapeworms, whipworms, and heartworms. All are internal parasites, which, if allowed to grow, can cause severe illness and even death to the host.

In addition, dogs, like humans, have a variety of psychic and social needs (although these tend to be ignored).[63] Dogs need the sort of stimulation that humans refer to as attention, entertainment, or recreation.[64] Dogs need to be rubbed, scratched, petted, and hugged (forms of tactile stimulation);[65] they need to be engaged in various forms of play (structured or unstructured) with their human companions; they need to develop and use their senses; and most importantly, they need to interact with other dogs.[66] Dogs are social beings. They are no less social than humans are, and while it is *possible* for a human or a dog to survive without interaction (think of a human being in solitary confinement), no human would count it an adequate existence, let alone a fulfilled one. It is a sad fact about our world that many dogs are kept penned or chained in back yards with no chance of seeing, much less sniffing, touching, or playing with, other canines.[67]

---

[63]For a discussion of various animal needs, see Regan, *The Case for Animal Rights*, pp. 88–94. Under "psychological and social needs," Regan lists "companionship, security and liberty." Ibid., p. 90. According to Michael W. Fox, dogs are similar to human infants in their emotional needs: "The dog has basically the same limbic or emotional structures capable of generating specific feelings or affects reflected in overt emotional reactions and also in changes in sympathetic and parasympathetic activity which are linked with psychosomatic and emotional disorders." Fox, *The Dog*, p. 258. This structural parallel between humans and dogs explains why dogs suffer from some of the same behavioral disorders as humans. These disorders range from "psychogenic epilepsy to asthma-like conditions, compulsive eating, sympathy lameness, hypermotility of the intestines with hemorrhagic gastroenteritis, possibly ulcerative colitis, not to mention sibling rivalry, extreme jealousy, aggression, depression, and refusal to eat food (anorexia nervosa)." Ibid., p. 259. Dogs also suffer from stress, which, as in the case of humans, can produce gastric ulcers, heart conditions, impairment of the immune system, and reproductive and growth problems. See Hubrecht, "The Welfare of Dogs in Human Care," p. 184.

[64]"All too often, a veterinarian is asked to kill a dog, sometimes a puppy, but more often an older dog, that is tearing up the house or urinating on the bed. The owners have tried beating, yelling, caging; nothing has worked. They are shocked to learn that the dog, as a social animal, is lonely. Often the older dog has been played with every day for years by children who have now gone to college. Often the dog has been accustomed to extraordinary attention from his mistress, a divorcee, who suddenly has a new boyfriend and has forgotten the dog's needs. Often the dog has been a child substitute for a young couple who now have a new baby, and the dog is being ignored and is jealous." Rollin, *Animal Rights & Human Morality*, p. 224.

[65]See Fox, *The Dog*, pp. 183–184; see also James Serpell, *In the Company of Animals: A Study of Human-Animal Relationships*, rev. and updated ed. (Cambridge: Cambridge University Press, 1996), p. 131. For my review of Serpell's book, see *Ethics and the Environment* 3 (1998), pp. 105–110. Hubrecht writes that "human social contact is important for dog welfare, possibly even more important than canine contact." Hubrecht, "The Welfare of Dogs in Human Care," p. 192.

[66]According to one longtime observer, the thing dogs most want is . . . to be around other dogs. See Elizabeth Marshall Thomas, *The Hidden Life of Dogs* (New York: Pocket Books, 1993), pp. 111, 134.

[67]This state of affairs is both intrinsically and instrumentally bad—bad because of what it is and bad because of what it does (causes). Among other things, "Long periods of daily social isolation or abandonment by the owner may . . . provide adult separation problems and excessive barking," James Serpell and J. A. Jagoe, "Early Experience and the Development of Behaviour," in James Serpell (ed.), *The Domestic Dog: Its Evolution, Behaviour, and Interactions with People* (Cambridge: Cambridge University Press, 1995), p. 98.

Not every human need is a dog need, obviously. We must not be mindless or anthropomorphic about it. Annette Baier has compiled a list of goods that human parents are responsible for providing to their children:

> The goods which a trustworthy parent takes care of for as long as the child is unable to take care of them alone, or continues to welcome the parent's help in caring for them, are such things as nutrition, shelter, clothing, health, education, privacy, and loving attachment to others.[68]

Of these items, clothing, education, and privacy (at least as normally understood) are inapplicable to dogs. There are, however, analogues. Dogs do not need clothing, but they need protection from the elements, which (among other things) is what clothing is designed to provide. They do not need education, but they need guidance and instruction in dealing with human and other risks (they need to be acculturated). Dogs do not need privacy, at least in the informational sense, but they need space of their own in which to relax, nap, eat, recreate, and care for their young. They need to be given room to breathe and choices to make. They need to be free of unwanted intrusion and domination.

The other "goods" on Baier's list—nutrition, shelter, health, and loving attachment to others—transfer quite readily from human children to dogs, so I will say little about them. Just as a responsible parent attends to the varied needs of his or her child, with the aim of making that child's life flourish, a responsible human attends to the needs of his or her canine companion(s).[69]

One further comment. The needs of children are not to be confused with either their wants or their inclinations. One can need something without wanting or being inclined toward it—and conversely (put differently, not everything a child is interested in is in its interest)[70]. This is where parental wisdom, vision, and authority come into play: to protect and promote the child's interests. Paternalism is objectionable only when the person being paternalized is an autonomous adult (who, as such, is presumed to know his or her interests and be able to protect and pursue them). No adult appreciates being treated like a child. When the state rather than an individual does the paternalizing, it is particularly demeaning.

---

[68]Baier, *Moral Prejudices,* p. 108.

[69]Throughout the essay I have been concerned with what I call the *needs* of companion animals. I have argued that human companions are responsible for fulfilling those needs. Most of us, however, make a distinction between needs (necessities) and mere wants (luxuries). I have not argued—indeed I deny—that one has an obligation to go beyond a companion animal's needs. Rachels argues (convincingly, in my opinion) that one "may provide the necessities for [one's] own children first, but [one is] not justified in providing them luxuries while other children lack necessities." Rachels, "Morality, Parents, and Children," p. 60. The same is true, *mutatis mutandis,* with respect to one's companion animals. Our responsibility to them is to provide fully for their *needs,* which are, as I have shown, many and varied. Once we reach that point we must turn our attention to other animals (or to humans). For examples of the lengths to which some humans go to "pamper" their animals companions, see Serpell, *In the Company of Animals,* pp. 28–30, 54–55. Rollin says that he is "morally certain that much of this money is spent to assuage the guilt consciences of animal owners [sic] who deny the animals something far more precious: time, love, and personal interaction." Rollin, *Animal Rights & Human Morality,* p. 219.

[70]For a discussion of this difference, see Regan, *The Case for Animal Rights,* pp. 87–88.

But children are children. As such, they lack the capacities constitute of autonomy. A parent would be irresponsible *not* to paternalize his or her child. A child may wish to stay up past midnight, carry or shoot a gun, drive a motor vehicle, or eat nothing but junk food day after day. A wise parent knows that these activities are not in the child's interest, so restriction is necessary (and, unless excessive, justified). The same is true of one's companion animals.[71] Dogs may in some sense want to run free through a neighborhood (or more widely), to eat chicken bones without supervision, or to ride in the bed of a pickup truck, but these activities are not in their interest. A responsible human companion restrains a dog's impulses—limits its liberty, frustrates its will—in order to protect it from known or foreseeable dangers. Exactly which rules and restrictions are appropriate for guarding against various dangers must be determined on a case-by-case basis.[72] My point is a theoretical one.[73]

How exactly does one incur or undertake responsibility for a companion animal? Is there more than one way to "take a dog in?" The most common way in which one incurs responsibility is by purchasing a dog from another individual (or accepting the dog as a gift). It makes no difference to one's responsibility whether the dog is old or young at the time of acquisition, although the dog's needs (therefore the content of one's responsibility) may well depend on the animal's age (as well as its other characteristics). Another way is by adopting a stray, either through a formal adoption procedure (such as going to a local pound or Humane Society office) or by taking the animal off the street. A third

---

[71]Regan has a valuable discussion of paternalism toward animals in ibid., Sec. 3.6. I agree with Regan as against certain of his critics that the concept of paternalism applies (literally) to animals. I find it odd, however, that Regan's *example* of parentalism toward animals is that of frightening a hungry raccoon away from a leghold trap. See ibid., pp. 104, 108. There would seem to be many and better examples drawn from our lives with companion animals. Perhaps Regan intended to show that paternalism is justified *even* in cases where one has no special relation to the beneficiary. If so, then *a fortiori* paternalism is justified in cases where one stands in a special relation (for example, to one's children or friends). For a brief discussion of paternalism toward animals, see Beth A. Dixon, "The Feminist Connection Between Women and Animals," *Environmental Ethics* 18 (1996), p. 188.

[72]Let me cite one example—to my mind a clear case—of irresponsibility. Elizabeth Marshall Thomas allowed dogs in her care to run free in an urban area (Cambridge, Massachusetts). She admits that the traffic in this area was dangerous and marvels at how one particular dog, Misha, avoided injury during his many nocturnal excursions. Thomas estimates that Misha had "a home range of approximately 130 square miles," a range that subsequently "expanded considerably." Thomas, *The Hidden Life of Dogs*, p. 2.

[73]I am *not* saying that all paternalism of companion animals is justified. Like Regan and Taylor, I believe that there can be unjustified infringements of animal liberty or autonomy. See Regan, *The Case for Animal Rights*, pp. 91–92; Taylor, *Respect for Nature*, pp. 173–179. The autonomy of animals may be of a different or lesser sort than that of humans, however, Regan calls it "preference autonomy," which he defines as the ability "to initiate action to satisfy [one's] desires and preferences." Regan, *The Case for Animal Rights*, p. 92.

As in the case of humans, there is a danger of overpaternalism. Dogs, like children, can suffer in various ways from being indulged and protected ("smothered"). The main way they suffer is by becoming excessively dependent on their "mother" or "father," which can result in behavioral problems such as depression, aggression, and separation anxiety. See Fox, *The Dog*, pp. 259–261. A wise person (parent) finds the right mix of paternalism and autonomy for his or her animal companion (child).

way is by allowing one's dog to procreate. The puppies so generated have been "taken in" just as if they had been purchased or adopted.

Procreation raises an interesting set of problems that I cannot deal with in this essay. But let me say this: If one is to avoid responsibility for the offspring of one's canine companions, one must ensure that the companions do not reproduce. One way (although not the only way) to do this is to have the dogs spayed or neutered.[74] I do not believe, nor do I argue here, that there is a general obligation to spay or neuter one's dogs (or other companion animals). One's responsibility, rather, is to ensure that *if* one's dog reproduces, the needs of the resultant puppies are fulfilled. This is but an application of the aforementioned meta-responsibility. Canine reproduction by its nature produces additional dogs for which—and to which—one is responsible. One has a meta-responsibility not to allow this state of affairs to obtain if one cannot (or in all likelihood will not) be able to assume primary responsibility for the offspring.[75]

Unfortunately, circumstances arise in which one can no longer care for one's companion animals, or cannot provide them with certain types of essential care. A person who has become physically impaired may be unable to exercise his or her canine companions. In this case the person must arrange for someone else to do so. Suppose I learn that I am allergic to dogs (or to a particular dog) to the point where my own health is endangered by continuing to live with my canine companion. I have an obligation in such a case to find another home for the animal, and not just someone who will take the dog in. My responsibility is to find someone who will fulfill the dog's primary needs *just as I would, if I could.* The meta-responsibility is to see that the primary responsibility is adequately discharged.

What is to be done when a person dies, leaving one or more animal companions? If there is another human in the household, there may be no problem, provided he or she can and will discharge the relevant responsibilities.[76] But what if the human companion lived alone? Each of us must reflect on this possibility and take steps to see that our animal companions receive adequate care in the event of our demise. We must see to it that the fulfillment of their needs is not contingent on our continued existence or good health. This, I hasten to

---

[74]One incidental benefit of spaying and neutering (sterilization) is that "Sterilized animals . . . tend to live longer and less restricted lives than intact animals." Hubrecht, "The Welfare of Dogs in Human Care," p. 182. While this does not by itself justify the procedure—any more than it would in the case of humans—it is a relevant consideration.

[75]Another example of meta-responsibility is the taking in of more animals than can be properly cared for. James Serpell reports that "So-called 'animal collectors'—people with a compulsion to adopt stray animals in such numbers that they eventually overwhelm the person's ability to provide them with adequate care—are an increasingly common problem in Europe and North America." Serpell, *In the Company of Animals*, p. 32.

[76]This raises the question of joint responsibility for companion animals. If a family of two or more individuals adopts a dog, is each member responsible for and to it? Perhaps the moral analogue of the legal doctrine of joint and several responsibility applies here, meaning that each individual is severally (i.e., individually) responsible for the animal and that the set of people is jointly responsible. I cannot pursue this matter here.

point out, is not a radical idea. Human parents are expected to make arrangements for the care of dependent children when they (the parents) die; why should humans be any less responsible for the posthumous care of their animal companions?[77] Doing right by them requires no less.

Questions

1. What are special responsibilities? Why does Keith Burgess-Jackson say that special responsibilities are universalizable? What is the difference, with respect to duties, between generality and universality?
2. The author distinguishes between duties that are based on "intrinsic properties" and those that are based on "relational properties." What is the difference between these two kinds of properties?
3. What are the three ways in which the author says one can incur responsibility for a companion animal?
4. In what way is the author's argument about what we owe companion animals at odds with the arguments James Rachels advances in "Morality, Parents, and Children" and consistent with Christina Hoff Sommers's arguments in her "Filial Morality"? (Both of the latter papers can be found in the chapter on "Familial and Filial Duties" in this book.)

---

[77]Children are provided for by means of trusts, inheritance (wills and intestacy), and insurance proceeds. There is no reason, legally or morally, why these instruments cannot be used for the benefit of companion animals. If the laws do not currently allow it, then reform is necessary. I hope that this essay goes some way toward effecting such reform.

Pets, Companion Animals, and Domesticated Partners

Gary Varner

Gary Varner's paper addresses both conceptual and normative questions about pets. Answering the conceptual question—"What are pets?"—is essential, he says, for grappling with the normative questions—such as "What do we owe pets?" Drawing with only minor modification on Deborah Barnbaum's treatment of the conceptual issues, he suggests (with some reservation and qualification) that for something to be one's pet it must meet four conditions: (a) One must have affection for it. (b) It must live in an area that is significantly under one's control and must either be prevented from leaving that area or voluntarily choose to remain there. (c) It must lead a dramatically different kind of life from one's own, and not be simply smaller and furrier than oneself. (d) It must be dependent on one and have an interest in its continued existence.

The author then distinguishes pets from companion animals and domesticated partners.

Turning to the normative questions, the author first argues that for at least some kinds of animals the practice of petkeeping is morally justified. This is because it genuinely benefits the pets and the humans that keep them. The author then considers the content of one's obligations to one's pets. He concludes that those who keep pets should: (a) provide for pets' psychological and physical needs; (b) ensure that the pets have a life that compares favorably with the life they would likely have had had they not been pets; (c) all things being equal, keep pets that are also domesticated partners or companion animals; and (d) cultivate a domestic partnership with their companion animals, insofar as this is practicable.

Gary Varner wrote "Pets, Companion Animals, and Domesticated Partners" for this volume.

INTRODUCTION

Pets are ubiquitous in human society. Most domesticated species are agricultural, and we tend to think of the first domestication, of the dog between 12,000 and 14,000 years ago, as a practical part of the transition from paleolithic hunter-gathering to neolithic agriculture. However, in his excellent overview of pet ownership, ethologist James Serpell notes that in one early burial site, dated to about 12,000 years ago in what is now northern Israel, an elderly human was buried with a five month old domesticated dog."The most striking thing about these remains," he says, "was the fact that whoever presided over the original burial had carefully arranged the dead person's left hand so that it rested, in a timeless and eloquent gesture of attachment, on the puppy's shoulder" (Serpell 1996, p. 58). By three to four thousand years ago, the Egyptians were worshiping cats in ways that would make the most eccentric contemporary pet owner look ordinary by comparison. And, as Serpell notes, almost all "tribal peoples" studied in modern times have kept pets of various kinds. He concludes that "The existence of pet-keeping among so called 'primitive' peoples poses a problem for those who choose to believe that such behaviour is the product of Western wealth, decadence and bourgeois sentimentality" (p. 53).

Although philosophers have written much about the moral status of non-human animals (henceforth animals) since the 1970s, they have had little to say about pets specifically, despite the fact that over half of all households in the developed nations today include pets.[1] Of the three best-known books on animal welfare and animal rights, only Bernard Rollin's *Animal Rights and Human Morality* (1992 [1981]) contains more than a passing reference to pets. In *The Case for Animal Rights,* Tom Regan mentions pets only in the course of discussing the concept of euthanasia (1983, p. 114), and the index to the book does not even mention pets or companion animals. And in the preface to *Animal Liberation,* Peter Singer (1990 [1975]) went out of his way to emphasize that he was not "inordinately fond of dogs, cats, or horses in the way that many people are: (p. ii), later mentioning pets only when giving the address of an organization to contact concerning vegetarian diets for them (p. 257) and in relation to the U.S. Animal Welfare Act (pp. 72, 76), which was originally motivated by concern about pets being stolen and sold as research animals.

A computerized search of *The Philosopher's Index* for 1940 through July 2000 returned only 13 titles or abstracts of English language works including the words "pet" or "pets."[2] Ten of these contained no discussion of pet animals:

---

[1]Serpell cites European Pet Food Federation statistics for 1994 indicating that over half of European Union households included pets. In August of 2000, I gathered the following statistics from internet sources. According to The American Veterinary Medical Association's Pet Ownership & Demographics Sourcebook, http://www.avma.org/pubinfo/pidemosb.htm, 58.9% of U.S. households own pets. And "Pet Net" of Australia, http://www.petnet.com.au/statistics.html, brags that the nation leads the world with 64% of all households owning pets and 53% of those without pets wishing they had one or more.

[2]A search in all languages returned only one additional hit, an article on the general question of interspecific justice, published in Dutch and Flemish: Wouter Achterberg, "Interspecifieke Rechtvaardigheid," *Algemeen Nederlands Tijdschrift voor Wijsbegeerte,* 74 (1982), pp. 77–98.

three referred to medical "PET scans," one to "polynomial-time equivalence types," two to "pet peeves" or "pet theories," and four merely used pet animals in examples not directly concerned with the ethics of keeping them. Two (Adams 1994 and Pateman 1996) concerned parallels between mistreatment of women and of animals. Only one, Deborah Barnbaum's short piece, "Why Tamagatchis Are Not Pets" (1998), was a philosophical analysis of what it means for something to be a pet. A search for "companion animals" returned only three hits,[3] one of which consisted of unsystematic reflections by a non-philosopher (Fullberg 1988 is the text of an address given by the ASPCA President to the New York State Humane Association Conference on Pet Overpopulation, September 12, 1987) and one of which (Clark 1995) was primarily historical. Only Keith Burgess-Jackson's recent essay, "Doing Right by Our Animal Companions" (1998), directly addressed philosophical questions about the content and basis of moral responsibilities to pets.

Aside from Barnbaum's analysis of what it means for something to be a pet, and Burgess-Jackson's and Rollin's discussions of the content and basis of our obligations to pets, I know of only one other systematic treatment of such conceptual and normative questions by an academic philosopher. David DeGrazia formulates a two part principle describing the obligations of pet owners in *Taking Animals Seriously: Mental Life and Moral Status* (1996, pp. 274–275). In this essay, I take up the conceptual and normative questions in turn, focusing in each case on what has been said by these four philosophers. The conceptual issues which I spend a great deal of time on first are not "merely semantic." What pets are is essential to a complete understanding of who owes them what, and when assessing the morality of pet ownership it is important to keep in mind the different kinds of pets there are.

CONCEPTUAL QUESTIONS: WHAT ARE PETS?

To date, only Barnbaum has discussed such conceptual questions in the philosophical literature. In "Why Tamagatchis Are Not Pets," she defends the following set of conditions which she argues are individually necessary and jointly sufficient for something being a pet (I have reordered them for purposes of exposition here).

> 1. *The affection criterion:* "While a pet may not necessarily feel affection towards the one who has it as a pet, the one who has a pet feels affection towards it" (p. 41).

It is hard to imagine a spider feeling affection for its owner, but the pet keeper's feeling affection for his or her charge seems central to our notion of having a pet. The *Oxford English Dictionary* offers the following definition of the noun in modern English: "Any animal that is domesticated or tamed and kept as a favorite, or treated with indulgence and fondness." While the etymology of the noun is uncertain, the verb "to pet—a gesture of affection—was formed from it, and the noun was originally applied to "cade lambs," lambs abandoned by their mothers and reared by hand. The centrality of affection to our notion of a pet explains why it seems wrong to call an animal one keeps only for work or profit, like a draft horse or a milk cow, a pet. Similarly, a dog who has been abandoned to a tether in the back yard and for whom no one any longer feels affection hardly seems to be a pet anymore.

Implicit in the OED's characterization of pets are two of Barnbaum's other conditions:

> 2. *The domicile criterion:* "The domicile criterion implies that many pets live 'unnatural lives', for they must live in our world. If they continue to live in their natural habitats, they fail to be pets" (p. 42).

Pets are "kept"—they don't "run wild" (except temporarily)—they typically are kept around the home, and even cade lambs on a farm are "made part of the household" by being hand-raised. But, as Barnbaum correctly observes, a child is not one's pet, because pets are profoundly different from us.

> 3. *The discontinuity criterion:* "Pets lead dramatically different lives than we do. The differences are not merely differences in quantity—they are differences in kind. I could not have a pet that was capable of doing all the same kinds of things that I do—read philosophy, go to the movies, order food in restaurants—but was merely smaller than me, or furrier than me, or had a shorter lifespan" (p. 41).

To call a member of our own species "a pet" is considered profoundly insulting. But Barnbaum is correct to call this "the discontinuity criterion," rather than, say, "the different species criterion," because if there were now another species on earth with capacities sufficiently similar to those of humans, it would be similarly insulting to talk of us keeping them as pets. Recent evolutionary history suggests how a real-world example could actually have arisen. In paleolithic times, Cro-Magnons (the immediate progenitors of modern humans) and Neanderthals (a subspecies of *Homo sapiens* which was either driven extinct or absorbed by Cro-Magnons) coexisted in Europe (Richards 1987, pp. 31, 284–91). But to call Neanderthals kept in captivity by Cro-Magnons (or vice-versa) "pets" would be to understate what was being done to these prisoners or slaves. Barnbaum also correctly observes that this criterion does not rule out humans being made the pets of a profoundly different species (p. 43).[4]

---

[4]A related question, which Barnbaum does not broach, is whether it makes sense to call profoundly retarded human beings pets, because they do meet all three criteria discussed so far as well as the fourth criterion, discussed below. One tack would be to claim that the domicile condition implies that pets' natural habitat is in non-human nature. But that is dead wrong about fully domesticated species like the dog and numerous agricultural animals. My own intuition is that just as being a member of a *different* species is not what makes an individual pass the discontinuity criterion, neither is being a member of the *same* species what makes an individual fail it. But since nothing of substance regarding non-human pets hangs on this question, I leave it unanswered here.

However, not just any profoundly different thing that one is fond of and keeps in the house can literally be said to be a pet. Several years ago "pet rocks" and "Tamagotchis" were marked as "pets" in the United States. Barnbaum herself owns a Tamagotchi for which she proclaims affection:

> The Tamagotchi has a liquid-crystal display, which shows a small creature. My Tamagotchi has several functions, all controllable via three buttons. I can push buttons that allow the small creature [to] appear to eat sandwiches and candy, play games, and give it medicine if it appears to be sick. The Tamagotchi beeps at me if it wants attention. If I fail to attend to the Tamagotchi in the proper fashion, the display will tell me that I have killed the small creature. I admit that I have gotten attached to my Tamagotchi, and if the display tells me that I have killed it, I will feel sad, feel that I have failed it somehow. (p. 41)

As a non-living thing, Barnbaum notes, a Tamagotchi has no interests which its owner affects. It fails what she proposes as a fourth and final criterion for pethood:

> 4. *The dependency criterion:* "The dependency criterion requires that there is something external to me which depends on me, and which has an interest in its continued existence."

However fond one is of a Tamagotchi, or a computer or a car, and however inclined one is to feel sad if one fails to meet its needs, these things are not really pets, and the explanation seems to be, as Barnbaum's characterization of the dependency criterion suggests, that their needs do not define interests. Barnbaum does not analyze the notions of "need" and "interest," but an interest, I take it, is any *morally significant* need or desire. More precisely, one has an interest in the fulfillment of one's needs and desires if and only if their fulfillment creates intrinsic value. Fulfilling the needs of a car is a good thing, but only because cars are of value to humans—fulfilling the needs of artefacts creates only instrumental value. To have interests, a thing must have a good of its own which makes the world a better place when life goes well for it (Varner 1998, pp. 6, 25).

Barnbaum assumes that all living things have interests in this sense. Elsewhere I have defended this claim at length (1998, chapter three), but I disagree with Barnbaum about one implication she draws from it. At one point she writes, "By my mind, plants and fish are equally dull pets. A Venus Flytrap is a slightly more interesting pet than a Ficus Tree, but not by much (but that is merely a personal bias)" (p. 42). By Barnbaum's criteria, houseplants are pets, because they are profoundly different than us, we are fond of them, we keep them in the house, and they have interests, the fulfillment of which depends on us tending to their needs. But to me it sounds like a category mistake to call a Ficus tree, or even a Venus Flytrap, a pet. Why? I think it is because plants cannot *move*, in the sense of voluntarily deciding to go, nor does it make sense to speak of holding them captive. This is why I would modify Barnbaum's domicile criterion in the following way:

> 2'. *The modified domicile criterion:* If something is your pet, it must live in an area that is significantly under your control or influence, and it must either be prevented from leaving that area or voluntarily choose to remain there.

A horse in a barn farm from its owner's house meets this condition, as do housecats who return after being let outside, and fish in a livingroom tank. The cats stay voluntarily. The horse might or might not choose to stay, but it is every bit as much prevented from leaving as the fish. Still, it is not literally a category mistake to call a plant a pet. For if an extraordinary species of plant were found which did occasionally pull up its roots and go, it would not seem to me like a misuse of the term to talk about such plants being kept as pets. Indeed, among what have not been classified as animals since the taxonomic revisions of the 1980s, members of both the Monera and Protista Kingdoms are capable of motion, and while they would make very unusual pets, both bacteria (in the Monera Kingdom) and paramecia (in the Protista Kingdom) could satisfy the modified domicile condition. And among what remain classified as animals, some fail the modified domicile criterion, for instance barnacles and sponges. So it seems to me that while an animal as simple as a starfish can be a pet, the barnacles and sponges it shares a tank with cannot.

For the purposes of this paper, I adopt Barnbaum's four criteria with the above modification to the domicile criterion. It is notoriously difficult to define words in a natural language in terms of necessary and sufficient conditions, and the above criteria might seem to imply the wrong thing in some cases. For instance, are fish who have been breeding for generations in a backyard pond pets? I am inclined to say that they are, but others think this stretches the notion of a pet too far. Are the anoles, spiders and cockroaches inhabiting my house pets? I think that stretches the notion too far, but these animals have been breeding for generations right inside the house, and if the house were sealed well, they would be prevented from leaving. So the above conditions may not be, strictly speaking, individually necessary and jointly sufficient. We could try to handle such cases in various ways, e.g., by specifying in the modified domicile criterion that someone must intend to prevent them from leaving. That would take care of my cockroach problem (at least conceptually), but many contemporary philosophers doubt that specifying necessary and sufficient conditions is the right way to go about defining terms in natural languages. Nevertheless, the four criteria discussed above characterize a "family resemblance" among paradigm examples of pets (domestic[5] dogs and cats, caged birds and fish, and horses or agricultural animals who are treated like pets), and although they imply that a broad range of other things can be pets—including lizards, spiders, lobsters, starfish, insects, and even slugs—it seems to me that calling these animals pets does not do violence to our pre-theoretic conception of a pet.

Still, these criteria raise a number of interesting conceptual questions, two of which it is important to discuss here, because they are directly relevant to the question of what we owe pets. One question is: Are there non-conscious pets? I believe the answer to this is "yes." I cannot go into my reasons here, but I

---

[5]Although authors (e.g. Waring 1983) commonly use "domestic" and "domesticated" interchangeably, strictly speaking, a "domestic animal" would be an animal kept in the house, which may or may not be domesticated. Thus many working animals, and farm animals, even if they are treated as pets, are not "domestic" animals, and some domestic animals, e.g., tamed wild ones, are not "domesticated."

believe that slugs, insects, starfish, lobsters, and spiders all lack consciousness of any kind. Obviously they perceive things in their environments and react to them, but I believe that they do so non-consciously. In particular, I believe that all invertebrates, with the exception of cephalopods (octopus, squid, and cuttlefish) probably do not feel pain, and among vertebrates, I believe that while mammals and birds have conscious desires, fish may well not (Varner 1998, chapter two). I know that many readers will disagree; some will draw lines regarding consciousness of pain and desire elsewhere in the animal kingdom. But for the sake of discussion in the next section, I will assume the truth of the foregoing claims about fish and invertebrates, and most will agree that at least *some* animals kept as pets (if only insects or starfish) lack consciousness. The significance is that on such a view morally appropriate treatment of a pet mammal or bird may involve much more than morally appropriate treatment of an invertebrate, or even a fish. Most obviously, there cannot be a duty not to cause pain to a non-sentient organism, and there cannot be a duty to fulfill the desires of an organism that has none.

Another question is whether working animals, like draft horses and service dogs, but also those who perform in zoos or theme parks, are pets. I say yes, at least to the extent that their owners, handlers or trainers feel genuine affection for them. For they clearly meet the discontinuity, dependency and modified domicile criteria, so to the extent that their owners, keepers or trainers feel genuine affection for them, they are indeed pets, albeit "working" ones (as are their non-working conspecifics to the extent that they are the objects of similar affection).

The answers I have given to these two questions motivate the introduction of two additional terms, in part because the associated concepts help to chart further the conceptual space that pets occupy, but also because, in the next section, I want to make some claims about the relative value of keeping pets of various kinds.

The first additional term is suggested by the point made just above about working animals. Working animals sometimes have a special kind of partnership with their trainers and handlers. The clearest example of this is the working dog, and to understand why, we must remember that dogs are the paradigm case of a fully domesticated animal, they are highly social, and they readily accept the dominance of humans in a hierarchical command structure. To say that the dog is fully domesticated is to say that it is natural for dogs to live among humans, and although individual wolves and coyotes can sometimes be tamed and coexist fruitfully with humans, dogs need humans in a way their wild cousins do not. As Rollin puts it,

> [M]an is responsible for the shape the dog has taken—physically, psychologically, and behaviorally. The dog is our creation. And just as God is alleged in the Catholic tradition to be not only the initial creator of the universe, but also its sustaining cause at each moment of time, so too are humans to the dog. If dogs were suddenly turned loose into a world devoid of people, they would be decimated. Aside from the obvious case of chihuahuas, bulldogs, and others who could simply not withstand the elements or who are too small, slow, or clumsy to be successful predators, the vast majority of dogs of any sort would not do

well. We know from cases of dogs who have gone feral that they still live primarily on the periphery of human society, existing on handouts, garbage, and vulnerable livestock such as poultry and lambs. Without vaccination, overwhelming numbers would succumb to disease. The dog in short has been developed to be dependent on us . . . (Rollin 1992, p. 220)

And owned dogs who escape and run in packs illustrate how much they need humans as surrogates of alpha canids:

All evidence indicates that it is packs of owned dogs rather than feral animals that are most dangerous to people and, most tragically, to children, who are most often severely maimed and even killed in unprovoked dog attacks. . . . These packs of owned dogs are often responsible for savage attacks on livestock in which the dogs pathologically, and unlike any wild canids, kill for no reason. . . . A pack of pet dogs can be very much like a mob or ordinary citizens—totally benign when taken singly, but literally possessed by mindless destructiveness when formed into a group. In domesticating the dog, man has assumed the rule of pack leader; to allow the formation of random packs is an abrogation of biological as well as moral responsibility. (Rollin 1992, pp. 226–27)

Indeed, one of the most common sources of "misbehavior" among pet dogs is their owners' failure to understand this. To avoid certain behavior problems, owners must understand that dogs expect to live in and act in accordance with a dominance hierarchy. When family members adopt what appears to the dog as a submissive attitude, problems ranging from unruly behavior to mauling are liable to arise (Serpell 1996, pp. 127–28; Rollin 1992 [1981], p. 226 and 1999, pp. 159–61).

Because they are fully domesticated and readily adopt a subordinate attitude in a command structure, working with humans can be very good for dogs. Regarding hunting and herding, specifically, Serpell writes:

The dog, after all, is descended from a wild predator, and it therefore shows a natural inclination to chase or hunt other animals. Dogs do not need to be forced to do these things, although they do require discipline and training to perform the tasks well. In other words, the aims and objectives of the hunter or the shepherd and his dog are roughly compatible. The animal seems to enjoy the work, so the person has little reason to feel guilty about using it. (Serpell 1996, p. 175)

And more generally, dogs who are highly trained and appropriately supervised compare to untrained and undisciplined "lap dogs" the way industrious humans compare to "couch potatoes." In an essay with an ultimately epistemological focus which is well beyond the scope of this paper, Vicki Hearne describes animals as working "at liberty" when they voluntarily cooperate with their handlers or trainers based on a mutual understanding of rules and goals.

The term "at liberty" here does not mean "free." Indeed, an animal at liberty, whose condition frees her to make the fullest use of some or all of her powers— in, say, search and rescue or in a "clever disobedience act"—may seem to be the most restrained of animals, just as the person whose submission to discipline may, paradoxically, free him to otherwise unattainable achievements. (Hearne 1995, p. 25)

She characterizes this as "a constraint in the way understanding of music is a constraint on the violinist who is not at war with herself" (p. 27). There is evidence of such profound understanding of constraints during cooperative pursuit of a goal in so-called "clever disobedience acts," as an example of which she describes how one of her dogs "created" the "strategic down" of police and military dogs:

> One day I was teaching a lesson and had my Airedale, Texas, with me for backup. The handler was having trouble with her dog, a Mastiff, so I had to take over. The Mastiff went for me. Texas left his "down" and put himself between me and the Mastiff. Once things were under control again, he, without prompting from me, returned to his "down" position at the edge of the training area. Here the simple "down" exercise became a lively and thoughtful posture police dog handlers sometimes call the "strategic down." It was the dog's grasping and acting on his own understanding that here expanded meaning. Before the incident, "Down" for this young dog has simple meant, "Lie down and hold still until you hear from me again." In the course of the incident with the Mastiff, Texas both created and learned a strategic down. A police officer, or a soldier, or a robber might leave her dog on a down with a view of one entrance while she went to cover the other; with a little experience, dogs come to understand the strategy in question. Once they grasp the point of the arrangement, they are controlled by their own understanding of the strategy, just as their handlers are. (Hearne, pp. 28–29)

And for animals to do such creative work "at liberty," the work must itself be interesting and gratifying, as Hearne says it is for search dogs: "For a dog with the capacity for it, search work is thrilling, transcending . . ." (Hearne 1995, p. 31).

Dogs working "at liberty," and in ways that emphasize and exercise the animal's mental and/or physical faculties in a healthy and satisfying way (for the dog), are the paradigm case of what I call *domesticated partners*. The partnership they have with their humans includes the affection and care owners typically give to pets, but the working dog exercises its faculties in a setting and command structure that are both natural to and healthy for it.

Aside from the dog, a range of animals seem more or less suited to becoming domesticated partners. Because they are widely used in a variety of ways—agriculture (as draft animals, cutting horses, etc.), for transportation, and in entertainment—horses are, along with dogs, the most visible working animals, and like dogs they are well suited to becoming fully fledged domesticated partners. Horses were domesticated in various places between 1500 and 6000 years ago (cf. Clabby 1976, p. 52, Waring 1983, p. 10, and Budiansky 1997, p. 40). By modern times the wild horse (*Equis przewalskii*, the progenitor of the domesticated horse) was left only in Mongolia (Clabby 1976, photo caption opposite p. 52), and now only in zoos (Waring 1983, p. 2). Although people sometimes think of horses as solitary animals, they are intensely social, living in herds of from three or four to twenty or so in the wild (Waring 1983, p. 142). Indeed, so-called "stable vices" (behaviors such as gnawing on wood, excessive water consumption, stereotypes, and "cribbing" the upper incisors against fence posts [Budiansky 1997, pp. 102–03]) may result from solitary life being imposed on such a highly social animal (Clabby 1976, p. 78).[6] Horses develop a variety of relationships with other horses. Mares and their foals groom and play (Waring 1983, p. 61), but all horses normally develop long-lasting peer relationships in the herd. Peer group "friends" engage in mutual grooming and generally spend time close together (Waring 1983, pp. 155–56).

> Horses removed from a herd will also readily form attachments to surrogates, including their human owners or even a barn cat. It is this instinct that humans draw upon in establishing their relationship with domesticated horses. An extreme, but extremely effective, method used by some trainers to deal with recalcitrant or aggressive horses that refuse to accept human control is to deprive them of any social companionship for as much as 23 hours a day; social contact (even with a nonequine) becomes so valuable to a socially deprived horse that it very quickly comes to accept and bond with its trainer. Our horses' affection for us, their owners, is unquestionably real, grounded in a basic instinct to form friendship bonds; it is slightly bruising to our egos, though, to realize that they bond with us only for lack of better company. (Budiansky 1997, pp. 84–85)

Horses also understand and act in accordance with dominance hierarchies. Mares are herded by stallions in the wild, and in captivity mares sometimes take over this function (Waring 1983, p. 146). Training horses is easy if started while they are young, and the direction a rider gives the horse is at least loosely analogous to mares being herded and to horses' general tendency to "follow the leader" in dangerous situations (Clabby 1976, pp. 78, 84). Thus although feral horses fare better than feral dogs and, unlike dogs, horses typically require restraint to prevent them from straying at least temporarily (especially in the company of other horses), horses are well suited to becoming domesticated partners. While I doubt that draft horses much enjoy their work, I find it entirely plausible that other sorts of working horses, for instance dressage horses and thoroughbreds, do, at least sometimes or under the best circumstances. Budiansky observes that both thoroughbreds and dressage horses appear to be playing when they work: "Training and learning may explain why a horse can be made to perform these tasks, but seem inadequate to explain the undeniable enthusiasm that many horses show for these pursuits" (Budiansky 1997, pp. 99–101).

Some tamed wild animals probably also enjoy, and genuinely benefit from, working with humans. For instance, Sea World San Antonio features performing orcas, dolphins, and sea lions, but they also have both sea lions and dolphins who do not "perform" aside from begging for fish from visitors during designated feeding hours. After comparing the lot of the two during a visit, I feel confident that the performing animals are far better off. First, because the training process provides far more mental stimulation than does begging from tourists. To learn a complex performance routine, an animal must solve a long series of problems over the course of months of training. The begging animals,

[6]Another factor probably is that confinement prevents horses from spending most of their time foraging and walking. Wild horses spend half or more of their time grazing and nearly 10% of it walking or running (Budiansky 1997, p. 105 and Waring 1983, p. 222).

by contrast, gets only one puzzle to solve. And especially given the kinds of shows dolphins and orcas are typically trained to put on—involving lots of fast swimming and jumping high out of the water—these performing animals get enormously more physical exercise than their begging cousins. Also, to the extent that captive animals enjoy contact with their trainers, the trained animals enjoy some additional contact which the beggars miss out on. However, such animals may never become fully fledged domesticated partners, for two reasons. First, they may leave if allowed unrestrained access to the ocean. As Serpell notes, dogs and cats are uniquely suited to be pets in part because they are almost unique among captive animals in their willingness to remain with their human keepers when not fenced in, caged, or tethered (Serpell 1996, p. 126). Second, even if these tamed wild animals enjoy their work and are better off for doing it, they may die younger than their wild conspecifics (although reliable statistics are still not available—Reeves and Mead 1999, pp. 426–27), in contrast to horses, who live much longer in domestication than in the wild, where their life expectancy is as low as five or six years (Waring 1983, p. 144).

A related point is that the goals of humans and their domesticated partners may be similar or different. Hunting dogs probably share their handlers' goal of subduing prey, and rescue dogs seem to genuinely understand that they are helping to save people. Maybe to the extent that dressage and racing horses are playing, they have at least a roughly similar goal while working as the humans who train and ride them. But just as clearly, the goals of human trainers and their animals often diverge. A trainer of circus lions may not think of what he is doing as "play" at all, and presumably the lions have nothing about mass entertainment in mind. So the goals of the animals and their humans may diverge, but insofar as the animal is still the object of genuine affection and the work in question exercises the animal's mental and/or physical faculties in a healthy way, I still call the pets in question domesticated partners.

I continue to refer generally to "pets," rather than using the politically correct "companion animals," because the latter term suggests a level of interaction which, although much less sophisticated than the partnerships described above, is unattainable with many pets. I have known a number of people who kept fish as pets, some who keep snakes, and one who keeps tarantulas. Some of these people talk to their pets and claim that the animals respond to them in various ways. But surely it is a stretch to call a fish or a spider a "companion." Healthy companionship is a two-way street, and I doubt that either spiders or fish would stay with their owners for the sake of human companionship the way dogs, cats, and horses commonly do. Although I cannot say exactly what criteria must be met for an individual animal's relationship with human beings to qualify, by a *companion animal* I mean, roughly, a pet who receives the affection and care owners typically give to pets, but who also has significant social interaction and would voluntarily choose to stay with the owner, in part for the sake of this companionship (rather than, say, just to get food and shelter).

As dogs working "at liberty" are the paradigm case of what I call domesticated partners, cats are the paradigm example of pets who are well suited to be companion animals, but who rarely become domesticated partners. Although cats are not as robustly social as dogs and horses, the popular image of cats as aloof exaggerates the extent to which they are asocial. When food and shelter are plentiful, cats both domestic and feral form friendly, cooperative communities (including females "babysitting" each others' kittens and bringing food to nursing mothers), they maintain complicated dominance and territorial arrangements, and, as anyone who has had several cats "get along" with each other in a household knows, these relationships are not always a Hobbesian war of all against all—cat "friends" groom each other regularly and often play good naturedly with each other, although with males this depends to some extent on their being castrated (Wright and Walters 1980, pp.126–29). Feral cats probably fare better than feral dogs, in part because selective breeding has not (yet) been used to change the physical form of the cat or its behavioral repertoire as much as it has been used to change the dog's, so cats do not *need* humans in the same way dogs do (Fox 1974, p. 81). Nevertheless, cats can be companions for humans in ways no fish can, and cats can live very healthy, satisfying lives in a kind of partnership with humans.

Cats have large eyes and small chins, giving their faces the cherubal look of neonatal humans, which naturally evokes human expressions of care and affection. Cats appear to reciprocate, in part because their pupils are large and dilated pupils are a sign of affection between human beings (Serpell 1996, p. 138), but they also behave in ways humans do when attentive to each other. Cats, like dogs, greet their owners, welcoming them home with "chirps," meows and leg-rubbing. They appear to enjoy being in the company of humans, and they sometimes favor certain humans. They purr, cuddle and nuzzle, and they appear to enjoy physical contact with humans, such as being petted and sleeping together. Cats clearly give the impression that they feel affection for their keepers. But is cats' affection for us genuine? Some of these apparent expressions of affection may be misinterpreted by humans, because some of these behaviors are said to be neotenies (a neoteny is a "retention of infantile or juvenile behavior patterns into adulthood"—Serpell 1996, p. 82). Kittens purr and knead around their mothers' teats at nursing time, and this is thought to signal the mother to "let down" her milk. So although most owners probably think that their cats are expressing a general affection, the cats could be seen as treating their keepers as surrogate mothers at an age when any normal cat should be independent of its mother. It could even be said that cats' habit of sticking their tails straight up upon greeting humans is a neoteny, because kittens greet their mothers this way. And I have frequently read popular accounts of cat behavior making the similarly deflationary claim that their repetitive rubbing of their humans' legs, and of their whisker pads against legs, faces, etc., are "merely" marking behaviors, since cats scent mark using various glands by behaving analogously in the wild.[7]

---

[7]Wright and Walters 1980 offer a less deflationary explanation of the leg rubbing: they say it is a modification of the way cats gather odors from each other for future recognition (p. 129). Similarly, they note that "Adult cats raise their tails as a greeting gesture towards friendly humans and other cats" (p. 127) and that "Within any cat group, individual members greet each other affectionately with nose kisses, body-rubbing and sniffing at anal regions" (p. 126).

Nevertheless, my own view, based on the lack of scientific evidence to the contrary, coupled with my own fairly extensive experience with cats, is that their affection for their humans is genuine. The fact that cats' apparently affectionate behavior has biological functions unrelated to affection entails neither that the behavior is not affectionate nor that it is misplaced. Remember that cats (and all other domesticated animals) lack the expressive potential afforded by the syntactic structure of language. So if cats do seek to express affection for their human keepers, they must use whatever vocabulary of expressive sounds and gestures they have at their disposal, and this vocabulary is limited to a range of signals that evolved to manage relations among cats prior to domestication. Consequently, in evaluating deflationary claims like those in the preceding paragraph, it is significant to note which such signals cats do in fact use with their humans. First, note that we do not hear of tom cats marking their humans with urine, the way they mark territory in the wild (and household objects when confined). Cats "marking" of humans with scent glands on their faces and necks, that would be reserved for marking landmarks in the wild, should hardly be dismissed as unaffectionate behaviors, given that cats in domestic settings are dealing with animals with whom they entered into communal living very recently in evolutionary terms. Similarly, that they adapted other parts of their limited expressive vocabulary to a new use, including behaviors previously reserved for kitten-mother interactions, should hardly surprise us, given the domestic cat's heavy dependence on us and their species' relatively recent domestication.

So I believe that cats really feel affection for their human keepers, but I also know that cats are more difficult to train than dogs and many other animals. Cats do not readily accept command hierarchies the way dogs and horses do, they are most effectively trained with rewards rather than punishments, and, when punishment is used, it is best arranged so that it looks unrelated to the human administering it (Wright and Walters 1980, p. 153), which makes it hardly count as "punishment" at all. Cats *can* be trained, though. Although I have never heard of rescue cats or drug sniffing cats, skilled trainers do turn them into movie "actors," and an owner with enough patience and a good understanding of how to train them can teach cats to respond to simple commands like "no," "come," "get down," "collar on," etc.; not to do certain things, like jump up on the kitchen counters or try to go out the front door of the house; and even where to sleep on the bed, e.g. next to the non-allergic partner in a human couple (all of these are things I have taught my own cats). Cats who have access to a safe outdoor environment or a sufficiently interesting indoor environment can be endlessly stimulated mentally and physically, so while cats are less likely to become fully fledged domesticated partners, they are eminently suited to be companion animals.

The discussion in this section reveals that the notion of a pet is surprisingly complex. So far I have made the following distinctions:

A *pet* is any entity which meets the affection, discontinuity, dependence and modified domicile criteria.

A *companion animal* is a pet who receives the affection and care owners typically give to pets, but who also has significant social interaction with its owner and would voluntarily choose to stay with the owner, in part for the sake of the companionship.

A *domesticated partner* is a companion animal who works with humans in ways that emphasize and exercise the pet's mental and/or physical faculties in a healthy way.

Here I add just one more:

A *mere pet* is a pet which[8] is neither a companion animal nor a domesticated partner.

Some animals, like spiders and fish, are congenitally incapable of being more than "mere pets" for humans. Spiders and fish, I am assuming, have no conscious desires, and so if they stay with their human keepers, it is not out of any conscious desire for human companionship. Other animals are quite capable of being companion animals, or even domesticated partners, but fail to be only because their relationship with their human keepers is insufficiently friendly and caring. For instance, the dog abandoned to a tether in the back yard, for whom no one feels affection, may very well crave human companionship, but the affection is not reciprocated. And a human could love a dog who, through previous mistreatment perhaps, is incapable of reciprocal affection.

NORMATIVE QUESTIONS: WHAT DO WE OWE PETS AND WHICH KINDS ARE PREFERABLE?

In approaching normative questions about pet keeping, it is important to keep the above distinctions in mind. For I think that some of the above kinds of relationships we can have with pets are morally preferable to others, and of the philosophers who have directly addressed the normative questions of what principle(s) ought to govern our treatment of pets and why, none has had much to say about animals other than dogs, or about dogs as anything other than companion animals. In this section, I will summarize Rollin's, Burgess-Jackson's and DeGrazia's discussions of the content and basis of owners' obligations to pets, noting how what they say might apply to a wider range of animals, and then clarify and defend my claim that some kinds of relationships we can have with pets are preferable to others.

First, however, something should be said about the general question of whether keeping pets is justifiable at all. In light of the foregoing discussion, the answer would seem to be yes, for at least *some* kind of pets. This is not the place to stake out a stance among traditional ethical theories such as utilitarianism versus rights views. Although not a rights theorist myself, elsewhere I have

---

[8]I say "a pet *who*" when speaking of a pet whom I believe to have a robust conscious life. I say "a pet *which*" when speaking of a pet which I believe lacks such a robust conscious life.

argued that various uses of animals, including some medical research, can be justified even on a strong animals rights view (Varner 1994), and I have myself adopted a roughly utilitarian stance on evaluating various claims about animals and the rest of non-human nature (Varner 1998). But on any plausible ethical theory, the keeping of pets who meet the conditions for being companion animals and domesticated partners is almost surely going to be permissible. At a bare minimum, dogs to a significant degree *need* to live among humans in order to live well. Where the animals enjoy genuine companionship with humans, and especially when they work with humans in ways that exercise their native physical or mental faculties, it is hard to see how pet ownership could be condemned, especially when the benefits to humans are significant, as they often are.

Humans obviously benefit from domesticated partners insofar as "service dogs" help the visually and hearing impaired, and the physically disabled function day to day; they help locate victims amid rubble, sniff out drugs and so on; and horses perform all manner of tasks. But recently, scientific studies have begun to confirm diverse benefits of interactions with companion animals. The term "pet therapy" was coined in 1964 when psychiatrist Boris Levinson noticed that severely withdrawn children readily struck up relationships with his dog (Serpell 1996, p. 89). In the 1970's, careful statistical studies first showed that heart attack survival rates were positively affected by pet ownership (Serpell 1996, pp. 97ff.). Since then "animal facilitated therapies" (AFTs) or "pet facilitated therapies" (PFTs) have been developed for a broad range of clients, including the elderly, victims of Alzheimer's disease, cerebral palsy and seizures, psychiatric patients, patients recovering from surgery, prison inmates, and developmentally challenged youths (Beck 2000); and the benefits of these therapies have been scientifically confirmed (see generally Fine 2000).

Outside of the clinical milieu, pet animals may be of significant value to human families, although scientists have so far devoted relatively little time to studying the benefits of companion animals in domestic settings, and, to my knowledge, none to the benefits of working with domesticated partners. Sandra Triebenbacker, a professor of child development and family relations, writes:

> Given the obvious visibility of companion animals in families, it seems odd that considerable research has focused on the psychological, social, and physical benefits of dyadic human-animal interactions, but limited attention has focused on the roles and functions of companion animals within the family unit. . . . Albert and Bulcroft surmise that perhaps pets have been overlooked in family studies because some social scientists have difficulty considering these companion animals as members of the family system. (Triebenbacker, p. 358)

But, she argues, the family is legitimately regarded as an evolving system, within which companion animals commonly play diverse roles during various stages of family development: from newly weds' "dress rehearsal" for parenthood, through education of various kinds for children, to "surrogate children" for the childless or elderly. I would add one related speculation: whatever benefits humans get from living with companion animals, living and *working* with domesticated partners probably is, for those who do it, far more satisfying in certain ways than merely keeping an animal companion around the house.

The burgeoning literature on animal assisted therapies, coupled with this call for research on the role of pets in human families, clearly indicates that pets are of significant value to human beings, and both companion animals and domesticated partners—at least as defined in the foregoing section—themselves get a lot out of the bargain. Obviously there will be disputes about which species of animals are suited to becoming companion animals or domesticated partners, but these questions are more empirical than philosophical. Are working elephants in India really domesticated partners? What about camels among Bedouins, and sled dogs among Inuits? I do not know enough to say, but at a minimum, we cannot say, *a priori*, that they never are. Similarly, the question of whether some wild animals kept as pets are true companion animals is not analytic. Maybe tamed wolves often count as companion animals while the average captured opossum does not. In any event, there are complex empirical questions here. In terms of the above definitions, the answers hinge on to what extent the animals value the human companionship enough to stay, and, in the case of domesticated partners, whether their work with humans exercises the animals' mental or physical faculties in a healthy way.

It seems then, on the face of it, that the keeping of companion animals and domesticated partners can be justified to the extent that both keeper and pet genuinely benefit from the relationship. As Evelyn Pluhar puts it: "Companion animals can benefit at least as much as the human animals who are lucky enough to offer them homes (often, the non-human is the one who does the choosing)" (1995, p. 271). And as Budiansky points out, domesticated animals in general are said to have "chosen" us as much as we chose them, because domestication has been attempted unsuccessfully with other species such as antelope and hyenas (1997, p. 10). The scare quotes are necessary around "chosen," because the choice was made at the level of an evolving species, not any conscious individual. Still, the metaphor is apt because it conveys how the *telos* of a species changes to accommodate cohabitation with humans during the process of domestication.

I turn now to the content and basis of owners' obligations to their pets. Rollin (1992 [1981]), Burgess-Jackson (1998), and DeGrazia (1996) are in broad agreement about both. Regarding the basis of owners' obligations to their pets, the three agree that, roughly speaking, we acquire special obligations as a result of taking animals in as pets, obligations which we have to no other animals (neither wild animals nor other peoples' pets). The three differ, however, on some related details. Rollin chooses to describe the special obligations as grounded in an almost literal "social contract" in which dogs, for instance, "gave up their free, wild, pack nature to live in human society in return for care, leadership, and food, which people 'agreed' to provide in return for the dog's role as sentinel, guardian, hunting companion, and friend" (pp. 216–17). Burgess-Jackson intentionally eschews this language of contract (p. 164), and, noting that some ethicists are loathe to recognize duties grounded in relational properties, spends much of the article developing an argument to this conclusion (pp. 167–71). For his part, DeGrazia grounds part of owners' duties to pets in the general "principle of nonmaleficence" (pp. 259, 274). These differences of detail on the basis of obligations to pets need not concern us here; Burgess-Jackson speculates that part of the reason philosophers writing on animal rights issues have tended to ignore pets is a worry that pointing up special obligations to pets would de-emphasize obligations to " 'stranger' animals" (p. 166), but the general idea that we acquire special duties to the animals we keep as pets comports with common sense.

As to the content of these duties, the three are again in broad agreement, but here the differences of detail are interesting in various ways. Burgess-Jackson characterizes the duty of pet owners as simply to "provide for their needs" (p. 179), which he illustrates using dogs as his only example."Not every human need is a dog need" (p. 181), he emphasizes, distinguishing between basic biological needs for nutrition, shelter, exercise, and medical care (179–180), and things like privacy and full-blown education, which are genuine social needs for humans, but have no strict analog among dogs. Nevertheless, he acknowledges that

> Dogs need the sort of stimulation that humans refer to as attention, entertainment, or recreation. Dogs need to be rubbed, scratched, petted, and hugged (forms of tactile stimulation); they need to be engaged in various forms of play (structured or unstructured) with their human companions; they need to develop and use their senses; and most importantly, they need to interact with other dogs. Dogs are social beings. They are no less social than humans are, and while it is *possible* for a human or a dog to survive without interaction (think of a human being in solitary confinement), no human would count it an adequate existence, let alone a fulfilled one. It is a sad fact about our world that many dogs are kept penned or chained in back yards with no chance of seeing, much less sniffing, touching, or playing with, other canines. (pp. 180–81)

Here I think Burgess-Jackson overstates dogs' need for contact with conspecifics. To the extent that humans really substitute for alpha animals in dogs' social environment, dogs may be able to lead perfectly healthy lives (at least as adults) without regular contact with other dogs. To some extent he may be conflating isolation per se with isolation from conspecifics, because in a footnote to the above passage Burgess-Jackson quotes an essay in which James Serpell and coauthor J. A. Jagoe say that "Long periods of daily social isolation or abandonment *by the owner* may . . . provoke adult separation problems and excessive barking" (p. 181, note #67—emphasis added).

Doubtless contact with conspecifics is good for dogs, as I believe it is for cats, and it may be a more important need for some other animals. My cats initiate play with each other more frequently than with the humans they are familiar with, and although my cats spend time nearby and sleep with us at night, they spend a great deal more time in close contact with each other. Not all cats learn to get along in these ways, but they commonly do, and for this reason it is generally good to have two or three cats rather than just one. And if the remarks about horses quoted in the preceding section are correct, they may have a more deep-seated need than dogs for contact with conspecifics. Commenting on horses' formation of peer relationships with members of other species, Budiansky states that they do this only when isolated from other horses or trained by humans, concluding that "they bond with us only for lack of better company" (Budiansky 1997, p. 85).

DeGrazia's treatment of pets runs less than two pages (1996, pp. 274–75). Like Burgess-Jackson, he acknowledges a general duty to "Provide for the basic physical and psychological needs of your pet," but he adds that by acquiring a pet, one takes on an additional duty to "ensure that she has a comparably good life to what she would likely have if she were not a pet." He argues that the general "principle of nonmaleficense" implies this additional duty, because "animals should not be made worse off for becoming a pet, since making them worse off would be an unnecessary harm." As DeGrazia recognizes, this "comparable-life requirement" could have strikingly different implications for different animals: "A hopelessly domesticated poodle might simply starve if she were not a pet—in which case, a pretty crummy domesticated life could meet this standard," but "A flourishing monkey . . . might lose a lot by being captured and domesticated." However, he notes, the other obligation, to take care of pets' physical and psychological needs, "picks up the ethical slack" in the case of misshapen animals like the poodle.

Rollin's chapter on pets in *Animal Rights and Human Morality* (1992 [1981], pp. 213–240) is largely anecdotal, and does not articulate any specific principles describing the duties of pet owners. However, his chapter builds directly on his discussion, earlier on the book, of the (roughly Aristotelian) notion of a *"telos,"* and how this can be used to articulate contemporary common sense views about how we ought to treat animals—what he came to call in later works "the new social ethic"[9] for our treatment of animals (1995a, pp. 139–168; 1995b, pp. 4–22; and 1999, pp. 35–44). So before discussing Rollin's anecdotes, we should recall his general account of the new social ethic for animals.

Rollin argues that until this century, the ways humans lived and worked with animals basically forced us to respect animals' biological needs and natural desires. Most use of animals was agricultural until recently, and the extensive methods of animal husbandry which predominated made it impossible to systematically neglect animals' needs without also sacrificing profits. In the second half of the 20th century, however, two things changed. First, agriculture moved towards more intensive and confinement-based systems, in poultry, egg, and swine production, but also to some extent in other areas where specialized feeds, hormones, and genetic engineering were used to significantly increase yields. Second, the use of animals in scientific research, including but not limited to biomedical research, blossomed and was increasingly subject to public scrutiny. As a result of these changes, the old social ethic regarding animals, which Rollin characterizes as simply forbidding *cruelty* ("that is, deliberate, sadistic, useless, unnecessary infliction of pain, suffering, and neglect on animals"—1995b, p. 5) became outmoded and has been replaced. The new social ethic

---

[9]By a "social ethic" Rollin means, "The portions of ethical rules that we believe to be universally binding on all members of society, and socially objective" (1999, p. 9).

is not opposed to animal use; it is opposed to animal use that goes against the animal's natures and tries to force square pegs into round holes, leading to friction and suffering. If animals are to be used for food and labor, they should, as they traditionally did, live lives that respect their natures. If animals are to be used to probe nature and cure disease for human benefit, they should not suffer in the process. Thus this new ethic is conservative, not radical, harking back to the animal use that necessitated and thus entailed respect for the animals' nature. (1995b, p. 18)

In his earlier book, Rollin made extensive use of the notion of a *telos* in articulating the new social ethic. The basic idea is that each living thing has "a nature, a function, a set of activities intrinsic to it, evolutionarily determined and genetically imprinted" (1992 [1981], p. 75). The new social ethic condemns agricultural practices which violate this *telos,* and scientific research which does so without good reason. Similarly, according to this new social ethic, keeping a pet is impermissible if the way it is treated seriously violates the *telos* of the animal in question.

Rollin's chapter on pets is basically a catalogue of practices that violate the *telos* of pet animals and of suggestions for associated reforms, with the vast majority of his examples involving dogs. The practices Rollin sees as inconsistent with the emerging new social ethic for animals fall into four categories. First, there is what he characterizes as "the mass extermination of pet animals" (p. 223). He notes that estimates of the number of pet animals killed yearly range from 6 to 14 million (p. 220), and he claims that they commonly are killed for trivial reasons:

People bring animals in to be killed because they are moving and do not want the trouble of traveling with a pet. People kill animals because they are moving to a place where it will be difficult to keep an animal or where animals are not allowed. People kill animals because they are going on vacation and do not want to pay for boarding and, anyway, can always get another one. People kill animals because their son or daughter is going away to college and can't take care of it. People kill animals because they are getting divorced or separated and cannot agree on who will keep the animal. People kill animals, rather than attempt to place them in other homes, because "the animal could not bear to live without me." People kill animals because they cannot housebreak them, or train them not to jump on the furniture, or not to chew on it, or not to bark. People kill animals because they have moved or redecorated and the animals no longer match the color scheme. People kill animals because the animals are not mean enough or too mean. People kill animals because they bark at strangers, or don't bark at strangers. People kill animals because they feel themselves getting old and are afraid of dying before the animal. People kill animals because the semester is over and Mom and Dad would not appreciate a new dog. People kill animals because they only wanted their children to witness the "miracle of birth" and have no use for the puppies or kittens. People kill animals because they have heard that when Doberman pinschers get old, their brain gets too big for their skills, and they go crazy. People kill animals because they have heard that when Great Danes get old, they get mean. People kill animals because they are no longer puppies and kittens and are no longer cute, or are too big. (1992 [1981], pp. 220–21)

Every time Rollin mentions specific animals above, they are either dogs or cats, but what he says clearly applies to many other kinds of pets, including the proverbial flushing of unwanted, but still very much alive, fish.

Presumably Rollin would regard true cases of euthanasia as *telos*-respecting, but none of the above cases can fairly be characterized as such. The one time Regan mentions pets in *The Case for Animal Rights* is during his discussion of euthanasia, where he proposes the following necessary conditions for a killing to qualify:

1. The individual must be killed by the least painful means available.
2. The one who kills must believe that the death of the one who is killed is in the interests of the latter.
3. The one who kills must be motivated to end the life of the one who is killed out of concern for the latter's interests, good, or welfare. (1983, p. 110)

Regan characterizes animal euthanasia as "paternalistic" because animals lack long-term preferences about their futures and we must substitute our own judgments about what is in their best interests. When the judgment that it would be in the animal's best interests to die is reasonable, killing it painlessly counts as paternalistic euthanasia. However, when the judgment is not reasonable, "we have (at most) well-intentioned killing, not euthanasia" (p. 115). The only example in Rollin's litany which could even qualify as "well-intentioned killing" would be the Doberman pinschers example, but in that case the owner's decision is based on the kind of "outrageously false information" about animals which Rollin notes is woefully widespread (1992 [1981], p. 223). And, Regan argues, even if shelters were full only of strays, killing animals because they are overcrowded and there is no place to send them would not constitute euthanasia, for:

> The question at issue is not which policy is *morally* preferable—the one where healthy animals are, or the one where they are not, routinely killed, if they have not been adopted in a given length of time. The question at issue is *conceptual.* It is *whether* animals are *euthanized* when shelters rely on the practice of killing animals if they have not been adopted after a given length of time. The answer must be, no. (p. 115—italics in original)

It may be unfeasible for us to do what is best for them, but killing unadopted pound animals is not in those individual's best interests.

The second general way Rollin describes owners commonly violating their pets' *telos* involves restricting their natural behavioral repertoire, as when small, high-strung dogs like poodles are kept in small apartments or where they cannot be constantly active (situations more suited to much larger, but lethargic dogs like Great Danes—p. 224), or when people fail to understand how to train and discipline dogs (p. 226). Here again, Rollin's examples involve dogs, but equally or more striking examples are afforded by other pets, for instance confining birds to small cages.

Third, animals are routinely mutilated in various ways for their owners' convenience or vanity. Rollin mentions debarking of dogs, declawing of cats, and docking of dogs' tails to meet American Kennel Club standards (p. 225), but here again striking examples are afforded by other kinds of pets, e.g., clipping birds' wings. A few pages later, Rollin mentions castration and spaying[10] in a similar tone, reminding us that "animals probably enjoy sexual congress as much as we do, and it is for this reason that I support vasectomies for male pet animals, rather than castration, and the development of effective contraceptives" (p. 227). Although Rollin does not mention it, an analogous option is available for females: tying off their fallopian tubes v. removing their ovaries ("spaying" them). I am skeptical, however, that neutering is as serious a violation of animals' *telos* as Rollin suggests by effectively comparing it with the declawing of cats and debarking of dogs. I do not doubt that intact animals enjoy sexual congress. However, humans probably tend to exaggerate what the loss of sexual activity means to animals like dogs and cats, first and foremost, because animals like dogs and cats are not sexually active all the time the way we are. Usually female cats and dogs only show an interest in sex when in heat, and males usually only become sexually aroused around females who are in heat. But there are also various health benefits of neutering. Regarding cats, specifically, intact females are seven times more likely than spayed females to develop mammary cancer (Shojai 1998, p. 360), and toms wander and fight much more than castrated males. Apart from war wounds, I believe that access to the outdoors, especially more "natural" areas, is particularly psychologically stimulating to cats, so an intact male's being prone to wander farther from home is a distinct liability, if there are roads and other hazards in the area. All in all, then, it seems to me that what cats lose through neutering may be less than they gain, and this could well be the case for other animals, for similar reasons. So although neutering is a clear example of the violation of animals' *telos*, it may well be a violation that is justified, all things considered. By contrast, declawing cats deprives them of parts of their anatomy (not only their claws, but part or all of their terminal toe bones—Wright and Walters 1980, p. 157) which they use daily in diverse ways, and the problems which lead to declawing (scratching where humans would prefer they not, aggression, etc.) can themselves be handled in a variety of other, less invasive ways. Similar things could be said about debarking dogs.

Finally, Rollin notes that many purebred lines perpetuate harmful genetic defects, including breathing difficulties and heart problems in bulldogs, hip problems in German shepherds, spinal disease in Dachshunds and Manx cats, deafness and bladder stones in Dalmations, cross-eyes in Siamese cats, and plain stupidity in Irish setters (p. 162). Here again Rollin's examples involve dogs and less so cats. This makes sense insofar as there are far more standardized breeds of dogs than of cats, but other animals kept as pets may also suffer from selective breeding. For instance, the stud book for thoroughbreds was "closed" in 1791, meaning that only horses descended from horses then in the book count as thoroughbreds. As a result, two thoroughbreds picked at random will on average have more genes in common that half-siblings, and the costs of 200+ years of inbreeding are apparent in several ways. First, despite premium

---

[10]It is only squeamishness that makes us refer to "neutering" males rather than castrating them."Spay" is indeed easier to pronounce that "ovariectomy," but "castrate" rolls right off the tongue, so we should only say "neuter" when referring to both castration and spaying.

prices being paid for outstanding studs, the winning times for thoroughbreds have not improved for over a hundred years. Second, "More than 80 percent of yearlings show some signs of congenital cartilage deterioration at the joints, and more than 95 percent have upper respiratory problems that can affect breathing" (Budiansky 1997, p. 248).[11]

In my discussions of Burgess-Jackson, DeGrazia, and Rollin, I have emphasized how restricted their examples are: they focus almost exclusively on dogs. I have indicated in passing how some of what they say might apply to cats, horses, and a few other animals, but it is also significant that none of the three distinguishes, as I did in the preceding section, among companion animals, domesticated partners, and mere pets. First, because there are good reasons to think that domesticated partners are preferable in a way to companion animals, and that companion animals are similarly preferable to mere pets. And second, pets capable of being companion animals who are treated like mere pets lead worse lives than those who become fully fledged companion animals or domesticated partners.

As I have defined the terms, what distinguishes a companion animal from a mere pet is that the former gets social interaction with its owner significant enough to make it want to stay for that reason. And as defined above, a domesticated partner is "a companion animal who works with humans in ways that emphasize and exercise the pet's mental and/or physical faculties in a healthy way." Thus a domesticated partner gets all the benefits of being a companion animal, and then some, and a companion animal gets all the benefits of being a mere pet, and then some. So, other things being equal, keeping a companion animal is better than keeping a mere pet, and keeping a domesticated partner is preferable to keeping a companion animal who fails to be a domesticated partner.[12]

Burgess-Jackson and DeGrazia both hold that pet owners should:

1. Provide for pets' psychological and physical needs.

And, DeGrazia adds:

2. Ensure that they have a comparably good life to what they would likely have if they were not pets.

For the above reasons, I believe we should add that:

3. Other things being equal, it is better to keep a domesticated partner or a companion animal than a mere pet, and
4. Pet owners should cultivate a domestic partnership with their companion animals to the extent practicable.

---

[11]The information on horses in this paragraph is all drawn from Budiansky 1997, pp. 242–43 and 248. Budiansky notes that inbreeding is also a problem is Przewalski's horse, which is the only truly wild horse and exists today only in zoos, but he describes the problem for *Equis Przewalski* in terms of lost diversity (the entire population is descended from 13 individuals) without mentioning any specific health problems (Budiansky 1997, pp. 265–66).

[12]In Varner 1998, chapter four, I defend a variant of Ralph Barton Perry's (1926) "principle of inclusiveness" which underwrites such judgements.

Of course, "other things" are almost never "equal," and what is "practicable" varies.

Some people who don't have the time required to turn a dog into any kind of domesticated partner could still get a lot out of a companion animal relationship, and I used cats as my paradigm example of pets who are eminently suited to being companion animals but rarely become domesticated partners, in part because they are more difficult to train than dogs. But do I think that therefore cat owners err in their selection of pets, or that dog owners who fail to develop domesticated partnerships with their dogs are morally remiss? No. Responsible people balance many commitments in their lives, almost never giving all they could to any one of them, and just as it is not necessarily unreasonable to devote extra time to work at the expense of family (or vice versa) it is not necessarily unreasonable to keep cats as companion animals because dogs are more trouble to keep, or to have a dog without spending a great deal of time training it. However, it is regrettable if a dog or cat ends up spending less time or less quality time with its keepers because they haven't bothered to train it in basic ways, since with proper basic training both the pet and its humans would get more out of the relationship. I am loathe to say that such keepers *violate an obligation* to their pets, but they are open to reasonable criticism: it is reasonable to expect owners of dogs and cats to learn enough about their pets to avoid or correct common behavior problems which can detract from their relationships with their pets.

Similarly, some people lack the time or facilities to maintain fully fledged companion animals. I noted that on the criteria adopted in the preceding section, lizards, fish, lobsters, starfish, insects, and slugs can all be pets, but that none of these are capable of being fully fledged companion animals (let alone domesticated partners). I do not think it wrong for people to keep such animals as pets, so long as in doing so they live up to the minimal criteria articulated by Burgess-Jackson and DeGrazia. Animals incapable of becoming fully fledged companions range from vertebrates with highly sophisticated central nervous systems (e.g. lizards and fish), to invertebrates with very simple ones (e.g. spiders and slugs). Their psychological needs will vary accordingly. I assume that lizards are capable of simple desires, but fish may not be. Nevertheless, both can feel pain and have a basic psychological need to avoid it. However, I assume that the neurologically simplest animals under discussion, e.g. spiders and slugs, are not conscious in any way, shape, or form, and thus have no psychological needs whatsoever.[13] Especially when animals lack psychological needs, I think it is easy to justify keeping them as pets. So long as such animals' physical needs are met at least as well as in their native habitats, I see nothing wrong with keeping them (other things being equal—e.g. they are not members of endangered species), even if the benefits humans get from doing so are no more significant than the benefits of having a waterfall or fireplace in the house. Studies show that some of the health benefits of keeping pets can be had from such distractions, or even from working with plants (Serpell 1996, p. 102; Nebbe

[13]Again, these things are simply assumed in this essay, but my reasons are given in Varner 1998, chapter two.

2000, pp. 388–91). But if the needs of animals incapable of being more than mere pets are met, as well or better than in their native habitats, then I see nothing wrong with keeping them.

It must be emphasized, however, that owners are probably as or more likely to be ignorant of such animals' basic needs as they are to be ignorant of the natural history of and training strategies for cats and dogs. Relatedly, it would be interesting to compare the life expectancies of fish, lizards, spiders, etc. when kept as pets by knowledgeable owners, when kept by the average (presumably much less knowledgeable) owner, and in their native habitats. This might tell us something about how difficult it really is to meet their physical needs in captivity.

CONCLUSION

Much has been omitted from this already lengthy essay. I have not discussed what legal arrangements might be appropriate in light of the moral considerations advanced here, and I have left out other, more philosophical questions of some import. I have not discussed the connotations and possible effects of thinking of pets as "owned" rather than "kept" or "cared for." In talking about the consciousness of fish and lizards I have not distinguished between "pain" and "suffering" (compare DeGrazia 1996, pp. 116ff). I have not discussed environmental reasons against keeping certain kinds of pets, e.g. outdoor cats, especially in Australia, or animals collected from the wild in environmentally harmful ways. And just as people sometimes stay in abusive relationships, in part out of real—but pathological—affection for their abusers, we can imagine some pets' status as companion animals or domesticated partners resting on pathological affection for their keepers. Obviously I do not mean to condone the keeping of such pets.

Certainly there are many other philosophical issues I have not even touched on here. Nevertheless, as detailed in the introduction, philosophers writing on the moral status of animals have so far generally neglected conceptual and normative questions about pets, despite the evident importance of pets in many (indeed most) humans' daily lives. I therefore hope that the present discussion, as tentative and incomplete as it is, will encourage more attention to what I think is an important practical issue with legitimate philosophical dimensions.[14]

Questions

1. Would the four conditions for something's being a pet be met by human infants or profoundly retarded humans? Why?
2. Do you agree with Gary Varner that a nonconscious thing can be a pet? Why?
3. What are the differences between pets, companion animals, and domesticated partners, as Gary Varner describes these?

---

[14]Colin Allen, Deborah Barnbaum, Heather Gert, and Jason Mallory read drafts of this paper and gave me valuable feedback. Mallory also tells me that he once kept a slug as a pet.

4. Do you think that the following practices are morally acceptable? If so, why? If not, why not? (*a*) Docking dogs' tails. (*b*) Declawing cats. (*c*) Preserving "thoroughbred" lines. (*d*) Spaying or neutering pets. What do the normative principles Gary Varner outlines imply about these practices?

Sources Cited

ADAMS, CAROL. 1994."Bringing Peace Home: A Feminist Philosophical Perspective on the Abuse of Women, Children, and Pet Animals." *Hypatia* vol. 9, no. 2 (Spring 1994), pp. 63–84.

BARNBAUM, DEBORAH. 1998."Why Tamagatchis Are Not Pets." *Thinking: The Journal of Philosophy for Children,* vol. 13, no. 4 (1998), pp. 41–43.

BECK, ALAN M. 2000."The Use of Animals to Benefit Humans: Animal-Assisted Therapy." In Aubrey Fine, ed. *Animal-Assisted Therapy: Theoretical Foundations and Guidelines for Practice*, pp. 21–40. San Diego: Academic Press.

BUDIANSKY, STEPHEN. 1997. *The Nature of Horses: Exploring Equine Evolution, Intelligence, and Behavior.* New York: The Free Press.

BURGESS-JACKSON, KEITH. 1998."Doing Right by Our Animal Companions." *The Journal of Ethics* 2, pp. 159–185.

CLABBY, JOHN. 1976. *The Natural History of the Horse.* London: Weidenfeld and Nicolson.

CLARK, STEPHEN R. L. 1995."Enlarging the Community: Companion Animals." In Brenda Almond, ed., *Introducing Applied Ethics*, pp. 318–330. Oxford: Blackwell Publishers.

DEGRAZIA, DAVID. 1996. *Taking Animals Seriously: Mental Life and Moral Status.* New York: Cambridge University Press.

FINE, AUBREY, ed. 2000. *Animal-Assisted Therapy: Theoretical Foundations and Guidelines for Practice.* San Diego: Academic Press.

FOX, MICHAEL W. 1974. *Understanding Your Cat.* New York: Coward, McCann & Geoghegan.

FULLBERG, JOHN F. 1988."Reflections on Companion Animals." *Between the Species* 4, pp. 135–138.

HEARNE, VICKI. 1995."A Taxonomy of Knowing: Animals Captive, Free-Ranging, and at Liberty." In Arien Mack, ed., *Humans and Other Animals.* Columbus: Ohio State University Press.

NEBBE, LINDAL "Nature Therapy." In Aubrey Fine, ed. *Animal-Assisted Therapy: Theoretical Foundations and Guidelines for Practice*, pp. 385-414. San Diego: Academic Press.

PATEMAN, CAROLE. 1996."The Sexual Contract and the Animals." *Journal of Social Philosophy* vol. 27, no. 1 (Spring 1996), pp. 65–80.

PERRY, RALPH BARTON. 1926. *General Theory of Value.* New York: Longman's, Green, and Co.

PLUHAR, EVELYN. 1995. *Beyond Prejudice: The Moral Significance of Human and Nonhuman Animals.* Durham: Duke University Press.

REEVES, RANDALL R. AND JAMES G. MEAD. 1999."Marine Mammals in Captivity." In *Conservation and Management of Marine Mammals*, pp. 412–36. Washington: Smithsonian Institution Press.

REGAN, TOM. 1983. *The Case for Animal Rights.* Berkeley: University of California Press.

RICHARDS, GRAHAM. 1987. *Human Evolution: An Introduction for the Behavioural Sciences.* New York: Routledge & Kegan Paul.

ROLLIN, BERNARD. 1992 (1981). *Animal Rights and Human Morality,* revised edition. Buffalo, New York: Prometheus Press.

————. 1995a. *The Frankenstein Syndrome: Ethical and Social Issues in the Genetic Engineering of Animals.* New York: Cambridge University Press.

————. 1995b. *Farm Animal Welfare: Social, Bioethical, and Research Issues.* Ames: Iowa State University Press.

————. 1999. *An Introduction to Veterinary Medical Ethics: Theory and Cases.* Ames: Iowa State University Press.

SERPELL, JAMES. 1996. *In the Company of Animals.* Cambridge: Cambridge University Press.

SHOJAI, AMY D. 1998. *The Purina Encyclopedia of Cat Care.* New York: Ballantine Books.

SINGER, PETER. 1990 [1975]. *Animal Liberation.* New York: Avon Books.

TRIEBENBACKER, SANDRA LOOKABAUGH. 2000."The Companion Animal within the Family System: The Manner in Which Animals Enhance Live within the Home." In Aubrey Fine, ed. *Animal-Assisted Therapy: Theoretical Foundations and Guidelines for Practice,* pp. 357–374. San Diego: Academic Press.

VARNER, GARY E. 1994."The Prospects for Consensus and Convergence in the Animal Rights Debate." *Hasting's Center Report* January/February, pp. 23–27.

————. 1998. *In Nature's Interests? Interests, Animal Rights, and Environmental Ethics.* New York: Oxford University Press.

WARING, GEORGE H. 1983. *Horse Behavior: The Behavioral Traits and Adaptations of Domestic and Wild Horses, Including Ponies.* Park Ridge, New Jersey: Noyes Publications.

WRIGHT, MICHAEL AND SALLY WALTERS, eds. 1980. *The Book of the Cat.* New York: Summit Books.

Suggestions for Further Reading on Pets

BARNBAUM, DEBORAH."Why Tamagatchis Are Not Pets," *Thinking: The Journal of Philosophy for Children* 13, no. 4, (1998): pp. 41–43.

DEGRAZIA, DAVID. *Taking Animals Seriously: Mental Life and Moral Status.* New York: Cambridge University Press, 1996: pp. 274–275.

ROLLIN, BERNARD."Morality and Pet Animals." In *Animal Rights & Human Morality*, rev, ed. Buffalo: Prometheus, 1992: pp. 216–221, 223–227.

PART FIVE

Money Matters

CHAPTER 12

Copyright Violation

HELEN NISSENBAUM, Should I Copy My Neighbor's Software?

DAVID CAREY, Should Millie Copy?

Should I Copy My Neighbor's Software?[1]

Helen Nissenbaum

Helen Nissenbaum rejects two extreme views about copying copyrighted material: (1) that it is never morally permissible and (2) that it is always morally permissible. She defends the view that it is sometimes morally acceptable to copy.

She first considers and rejects two consequentialist arguments for the extreme no-copy view. Copying of software in some circumstances, she says, will not lead to a decline in software production or a rise in software prices. She argues that some copying may even increase utility in various ways.

Next she turns to deontological, or rights-based, arguments against copying. She is prepared to concede that programmers own and therefore have property rights in the software they create, but she denies that this entails the extreme no-copy view. The nature and extent of property rights, she says, have to be determined in part by the justified claims of others. She thinks that private end users' claims are such that copying does not violate the property rights of programmers.

Finally, she considers and responds to some objections to her argument.

INTRODUCTION

Consider the following situation: Millie Smith is pleased with the way the home bookkeeping application, Quicken, organizes her financial records, even printing checks. Knowing how useful this would be to a good friend of hers, Max Jones, who lives precariously from one paycheck to the next, and yet

[1]An earlier version of this paper was presented at the Fifth Annual Computers and Philosophy Conference, Stanford University, August 8–11, 1990. Several members of the audience, with their sharp criticisms and suggestions, helped clarify my thinking a great deal. I'd also like to thank members of Partha Dasgupta's Applied Ethics Seminar at Stanford (1989) for useful and creative comments.

Helen Nissenbaum, "Should I Copy My Neighbor's Software?" in *Computers, Ethics, and Social Values,* edited by Deborah G. Johnson and Helen Nissenbaum (Upper Saddle River, N.J.: Prentice Hall, 1995), 201–213.

knowing that the program's price tag puts it outside of Max's financial reach, Millie is tempted to help Max out by offering him a copy of hers. She has read the lease agreement on the outside package which prohibits making copies of the diskette for any purpose other than archival backup, so she suspects she might be breaking the law. However, Millie is not as concerned about breaking the law (nor about the second-order question of the morality of law breaking) as she is about violating moral principles. If she is to copy Quicken for Max would her doing so be justifiable "not so much in a court of law as in the court of conscience"?[2] For private consumers of commercial software Millie's situation is all too familiar.

Although the majority of these private end-users admit to frequently making and sharing unauthorized copies, they experience a nagging and unresolved sense of wrong-doing. Posing as the "conscience" of these wayward software copiers, a vocal group, whom I refer to as supporters of a "strong no-copy view," urges users like Millie Smith to refrain from unauthorized copying[3] saying that it is always wrong. Jon Barwise, for example, in promoting a strong no-copy position, concludes in a series of scenarios whose protagonists must decide whether or not to copy an $800 piece of software, that even in the case of a professor providing a copy of his diskette to a student who needs it to finish a dissertation, "we should answer all of the (above) questions no."[4] Green and Gilbert, in an article directed specifically to users in educational institutions, recommend that "campuses should view and treat illegal copying as a form of plagiarism or theft" and that they should pursue ways of reducing "illegal and unethical copying."[5]

In the following discussion I challenge the no-copy position, arguing that it emphasizes the moral claims and interests of software producers while failing to consider other morally relevant claims—most notably, those of the private end-user. Accordingly, Millie would not be violating moral principles if she were to share a copy with Max. I show that there are morally compelling factors that motivate many acts of software copying, not simply brazen self-interest, irrationality, or weakness of the will. Although I argue that in *some* cases copying is not a violation, I do not support the position on the other end of the ideological spectrum, which completely rejects the constraints of software copy protection. Rather, we need to judge distinct types of situations according to their individual merits. In some situations there will be an overriding case in favor of copying, in others not. In still others, agents confront a genuine dilemma, trying to respond to equally convincing sets of opposing claims.

To reach this conclusion I focused on the arguments, both consequentialist and rights based, that have been proffered in support of the strong no-copy

[2]David Lyons, "The New Indian Claims and Original Rights to Land" in *Reading Nozick: Essays on Anarchy, State and Utopia*, (Ed) Jeffrey Paul, Rowman and Littlefield, Totowa, New Jersey. 1981.
[3]I will not be dealing with unlikely cases in which copy in software might save a life or avert a war. I assume that even those committed to a no-copy position would find rationale to permit those acts.
[4]Jon Barwise, "Computers and Mathematics: Editorial Notes." in *Notices of the A.M.S.*
[5]K. Green and S.W. Gilbert, "Software Piracy: Its Cost and Consequences" in *Change*, pp. 47–49. January/February 1987.

position. Upon analysis I find that, as a universal position, a strong no-copy position is not defensible.

Two Caveats

First, a word on how I set about recreating the justifications for a strong no-copy position. I've drawn from pieces written for computing trade publications, other non-philosophical journals, electronic-mail communications, as well as conversations. Although the arguments given in a favor of a moral prohibition on copying are generally not presented here in a framework of traditional ethical theory, I find this framework useful in organizing and evaluating them. For example, I classify the arguments that predict undesirable consequences of unauthorized copying under the general heading "consequentialist arguments." In a second working category, I classify arguments that claim unauthorized copying to be violations of moral rights and respect for persons. Although this group is more a grab bag, the label "deontological/rights-based" captures its hybrid spirit. My first caveat, however, is that while the philosophical categories are enlightening, suggestive of potential strengths and weaknesses of the arguments, they should be viewed as rough guides only. Moreover, because few of the commentators offer explicit or complete treatments, I've taken liberties in filling in steps. While I fleshed out the arguments and filled in gaps, I tried to stay strictly within the parameters set by their originators.

Second, in order to simplify the discussion I assume throughout this discussion that programs are written and owned by a single programmer. In the real world of commercial software, teams of software developers rather than single programmers create software products. And for many products, the title usually goes to the software corporation, rather than directly to its employees, the program's authors. In other instances, it goes to intermediate agents such as marketing firms, or vendors. The assumption of a single programmer, should not affect the substantive moral thesis.

Consequentialist Arguments

According to the arguments in this category, it is morally wrong to make unauthorized copies because doing so would have negative consequences. Although copying might appear to offer a short-term gain for the copier, the longer term and broader ramifications will be a loss for both consumers and producers alike. Barwise, for example, charges, ". . . software copying is a very serious problem. It is discouraging the creation of courseware and other software, and is causing artificially high prices for what software that does appear."[6]

Barwise's remarks suggest that we can expect at least two types of negative consequences. The first is a probable decline in software production. Because copying reduces the volume of software sales it deprives programmers of income. With an erosion of potential revenues, fewer individuals will be attracted

---

[6]Jon Barwise, "Computers and Mathematics: Editorial Notes." in *Notices of the A.M.S.*, 1989.

into software production. A smaller population of programmers and other software personnel will result in a reduction of available software. Furthermore, a slowing in software development would have a dampening effect on general welfare. The second negative impact of copying is a projected rise in software prices. Wishing to recoup anticipated losses caused by unauthorized copying, programmers will charge high prices for their software. Giving as an example Wolfram's *Mathematica*, which in 1989 was priced at $795, Barwise blames copying for the artificially high prices of software applications. How good are these arguments?

Embodied in the consequentialist line of arguments are a number of empirical assumptions and predictions which, I contend, are open to challenge. For consequentialist arguments to provide a moral as well as a prudential rationale, they must demonstrate links between copying and reduced income, between reduced income and decline in the software industry, and decline in production and an overall decline in society's welfare. If copying hurts the software industry but has no effect on general welfare a prohibition is not morally justifiable on consequentialist grounds. If copying is not directly related to income, nor income to a decline in the industry, then too, the argument breaks down. On close scrutiny these links don't stick. Furthermore, even if some damage could be attributed to unauthorized copying, I conclude that it's insufficient to warrant the all-out prohibition of the strong no-copy position.

Consider the claim that unauthorized copying leads to loss of sales. Although on the face of it, the argument is compelling, the implied link between copying and reduced sales is not always direct. Imagine a situation in which you are deciding whether to buy software application A or copy it from a friend. Although the consequentialists would have us think of all instances of copying as situations in which an agent must decide between the exclusive alternatives, buy A, or copy A, in many real-life situations this is not so. Computer users copy software that they would not buy for a number of reasons: because they could not afford it; are not yet sure that they want the product; or quite simply, have placed higher priority on other needs. For them, the choice is: copy A, or not have A.

Moreover, copying can actually lead to an increase in overall spending on computer software, at least for some individuals. Software sharing opens opportunities for trial and experimentation to otherwise timid users who thereby grow more comfortable with computers and software. As a result they become more active and diversified consumers of software than they would have been without those opportunities. We also find that users who are impressed by a particular piece of copied software, in order to own the manual and enjoy some of the additional benefits of "registered users," will go on to buy the application. In other words, much unauthorized copying would not result in loss of sales and some, in fact, would lead to increases.

The prediction that reduced income will discourage further creation of software belies a complicated story about motivation, action, and reward. Whereas wholesale fluctuations and extreme reductions probably would discourage would-be programmers, the effects of smaller fluctuations are not clear. Richard

Stallman[7] ably makes the point that directly tying software production to monetary reward paints an overly simplistic picture of the rewards that motivate programmers. Well-known for his active support of an open environment for information technology, Stallman suggests that besides the satisfaction of contributing to a social good, the fascination with programming itself will keep many of the most talented programmers working. He also raises the question of how much is enough. Although we would not expect many good programmers to have a monk-like devotion to programming and can agree that people work better when rewarded, it's not clear that any increment in reward will make them work proportionately better. (Furthermore, as suggested earlier, we still do not have a realistic idea of the extent to which cases like Millie Smith's actually affects potential earnings.)

Turning the tables on the usual consequentialist chain of reasoning, Stallman counters that prohibitions on copying, and other restrictions on the free distribution of computer code, has the opposite effect on computer technology. It is slowing progress rather than encouraging it. He and others suggest that the free exchange of ideas and code characteristic of the early days of systems and software development was responsible for the remarkable pace of progress, whereas limiting free exchange would dampen innovation and progress; moreover, laws restricting access to software would favor large, powerful and generally more conservative software producers. With a greater capacity to exert legal clout, they could control the production, development, and distribution of software, gradually squeezing out of the commercial arena the independent-minded, creative software-engineer, or "hacker". Even if we see a proliferation of commercially available software, we may also see a slowing of the cutting edge. If Stallman's predictions are sound, they offer moral justification for promoting free copying of software, and not the reverse.

So far, I have questioned the empirical basis for the claims that link copying with loss of revenue; claims that link loss of revenue with a decrease in software production; and, more generally, claims that link copying with a loss to the software industry as a whole. What about effects on general welfare? At this level of generality it is probably impossible to draw a meaningful connection between software and welfare. To the extent that software is a social good, it is surely through high-quality, well-directed software and not sheer quantity.[8] To discourage a potential copier, an extreme no-copy position must show the clear social benefits of abstaining without which there is little to offset the immediate loss. This question deserves more thorough exploration than I'm able to give it here because the connection between software production and overall utility or welfare, is complex. It does suggest, however, that the effects on general welfare of a particular act of copying would vary according not only to the context of

---

[7]R. Stallman, "The GNU Manifesto" in *GNU Emacs Manual.* Copyright 1987 Richard Stallman.
[8]Joseph Weizenbaum in Chapter 1 of *Computer Power and Human Reason,* San Francisco, Freeman, 1976, makes suggestive comments arguing that consumerism needn't necessarily lead to greater choices among genuinely distinct products. A conservative market might remain unimaginatively "safe," coming up with only trivially diverse products.

copying, but also to the type of software being copied. It would also need to be measured against the projected utility to the potential copier.

Let us now consider the alleged connection between copying and cost and the claim that producers are forced to charge high prices in anticipation of losses through copying. An obvious rejoinder to software producers, like Wolfram, is that if software applications were more reasonably priced, consumers would be less tempted to copy. If products were appropriately priced, the marginal utility of buying over copying would increase. This pattern holds true in the case of recorded music which could provide a model for computer software.[9] Because the cost of a tape, for example, fits many budgets, it is more convenient to buy the tape than search for someone who might have it. Though both the claim and rejoinder appear to hold genuine insights, they leave us in an uncomfortable standoff. Looking at high prices, pointing at consumers, critics say: "It's your fault for copying." Whereas consumers point back claiming: "It's your fault for charging such high prices." The average user apparently cannot afford to buy software at the current rates, and the programmer cannot afford to drop his or her price. Though we may agree that this is not a desirable equilibrium, it's not easy to see who should take the first step out of this circle of accusations. Resolving the standoff requires asking difficult questions about burden. Upon whom do we place the burden of maintaining a healthy software industry—consumer or producer? This question brings me to my concluding comments.

I agree with defenders of a consequentialist line that a prolific software industry with a high-quality output, which provides genuine choices to a wide variety of consumers, is a goal worth striving for. I disagree, however, that prohibiting copying is the only, or best, way of ensuring this. First, I have tried to show that the empirical grounds upon which they support their claims are open to dispute. Moreover, if a consequentialist approach is to be at all useful in guiding decisions about unauthorized copying, then it must distinguish among different types of copying—for their consequences surely differ. For example, cases like Millie's sharing a copy with Max would have a vastly different effect than cases in which a user places a copy on the software on a public network. Consequentialist moral injunctions should recognize these differences.

Finally, the no-copy position unreasonably focuses on private end-users, placing on their shoulders the onus of maintaining the health of the software market. But consumer copying is but one variable, among many, that affect the software industry. Holding fixed the other variables might serve some interests, but it gives disproportionate weight to the effects of copying. Decisions by commercial hardware manufacturers and even government agencies can significantly impact software. For example, if a hardware manufacturer perceives that a particular software product is critical to the sale of its machines it may, quite rationally, decide to support the software.[10] In addition, software companies have the capability to influence the actions of potential users by offering not

---

[9]Although some claim that the loss in sound-quality is a major reason for recorded music being less frequently copied, this doesn't tell the story for all (the average) listeners.

[10]Both Stallman, *ibid.* and Barwise, *ibid.* (and probably others) have made similar points.

only a good product as code on a diskette, but by also including attractive services such as consulting, good documentation, and software updates. In this way they make it worthwhile for the user to buy software, rather than copy it. The many flourishing software companies stand as evidence that good products and marketing works, despite alleged copying. Because other players—namely, government, hardware producers, software companies—have the power to significantly affect the software industry, we should not ignore their responsibilities when we assess the burden of maintaining the strength of software production. It is wrong for the private consumer to be unfairly burdened with responsibility.

Deontological/Rights-Based Arguments

In urging individual consumers not to make unauthorized copies some supporters refer to the "rights of programmers" and "respect for their labor". Regardless of its effects on the general welfare, or on the software industry, copying software without permission is immoral because it constitutes a violation of a moral right, a neglect of moral obligations. Depriving a programmer of earnings is wrong not only because of its undesirable ramifications, but because it is unjust and unfair. And even if programmers' earnings are not appreciably affected by copying, we have an obligation to respect their desire that we not make unauthorized copies. The obligation is absolute, not broken merely at the discretion of the private end-user.[11] Millie ought not make a copy of Quicken for Max because doing so would be unfair, it would violate the programmers' rights. But what are the rights to which these commentators refer; and does all copying, in fact, violate them?

Rights-based justifications of no-copy require a satisfactory resolution to both questions. They not only must identify the rights of programmers relevant to the questions of unauthorized copying, but must demonstrate that copying always violates these rights. Supporters usually cite property rights as relevant to the question of copying. A justification of the position should, accordingly, ask whether programmers do in fact qualify as owners of their programs so that they would have the appropriate rights of private property over them. But justification does not stop here. For even if we resolve that programmers do own their programs, it doesn't follow necessarily that all copying will violate their property rights. Or to put it another way, it is not obvious that property rights over programs include the right to restrict copying to the extent desired. A justification of the no-copy position needs a second step, to follow the finding that programmers own their programs. And that is, to show that copying violates these property rights. Many commentators fail to recognize the need for the second step, simply concluding that owning implies an unlimited right to restrict copying.

---

[11]Though strictly speaking, a rule-based approach could ultimately be grounded in utilitarian terms, the ones I consider here merge the rights-based and deontological styles of moral reasoning. They cite programmers' rights, inferring from them absolute obligations on the parts of software users.

In the discussion that follows I will spell out the two steps in a rights-based position beginning with the question of private ownership, and then moving to the question of whether owning a program implies the right to place absolute limits on reproduction. I will conclude that the second step is the weak one. As before, in recreating the arguments I've worked from informal written pieces, electronic mail messages, and verbal communications. In some cases this has meant filling in missing steps; steps that I judge necessary to making the best possible case for a rights-based justification. Finally, though recognizing that some might object to the very fabric of rights-based justifications of moral injunctions, I offer my criticisms from within this framework, and will not challenge the very idea of a rights-based approach.

Programming and Private Property

First, let's examine the following claim: Because a programmer writes, or creates, software he or she owns it. For some, this claim is so obvious as to not even need justification. To them, a program is an extension of the person's self and so, obviously, belongs to that person. For others, labor theories of property such as John Locke's, which claims that when individuals invest labor in a previously unowned item they earn property rights over it, offer a more traditional moral grounding for private ownership over programs. Locke writes, "Thus Labour, in the beginning, gave a right of property, wherever any one was pleased to employ it upon what was common."[12] Because programmers invest labor in creating a program, they are entitled to the "fruits of their labor." Although Locke's theory addresses the somewhat different issue of private acquisition of physical property, such as parcels of land and harvests, and focuses on the taking of initial title over a previously unowned item (or one held in common), his theory adapts well to intellectual labor. In fact, the case of intellectual property is somewhat easier for a labor theory in that it avoids a common pitfall identified by Locke's critics who, in the context of physical items, worry about the morally "correct" mix of labor with the physical entity.[13] I will concede then, that a programmer, in producing a program, accrues property rights over it, accepting as justification for this claim—if it is even needed—basic ideas of a labor theory of property.

Some have questioned the justice of extensive property rights over programs claiming that software creation is an essentially cumulative activity. Most programs, draw heavily on work that has preceded them so that giving rights to the programmer who happened to write the line of code in question rests on the unwarranted assumption that we can tell accurately where one programmer's labor really begins and the other's ends. For example, most commercial software on today's market is the product of a long line of cumulative work

---

[12]John Locke, Section 45 in *Second Treatise of Government*, originally published 1690, Hackett Publishing Company, Indianapolis, 1980.

[13]Nozick discusses this problem quite extensively in *Anarchy, State, and Utopia*, Basic Books, Inc. 1974.

most notably Lotus 1-2-3.[14] However, this objection does not challenge, rather it implicitly adopts, a form of the labor theory because it suggests that *all* those who contributed their effort toward creating a software product deserve proprietary rights over it, and not just those who happen to cross some arbitrary finishing line first. Just because they have made a bigger marketing effort, happen to be more worldly, belong to a large organization, or have good legal representation, does not vest in them a stronger moral claim. Although the question of just rewards for joint labor is an important one in light of the history of the development of computer software, for the remainder of my discussion, I will assume that we can talk meaningfully about *the* programmer who contributed most significantly to a program's creation. It is about this programmer that the discussion about property rights that follows applies.

As stated earlier, showing that programmers own their programs is not sufficient for a no-copy position. Its supporters must still demonstrate that owning a piece of software implies a moral right to restrict copying to the extent desired (and thus the duty in others to refrain from copying). How might I demonstrate this "second step," required of a rights-based justification of strong no-copy? In the next section I will examine whether a universal prohibition on copying software necessarily follows from general property rights over it.

Owning Software and Prohibiting Copying

In general, ownership implies a set of rights, rights defining the relationship between an owner and piece of property. Typically the rights of an owner over private property fall into a number of set categories including: one that covers conditions on initial acquisition over a previously unowned object;[15] another that refers to the extent of use and enjoyment an owner may exercise over that property; a third that determines the extent to which an owner may restrict access to her property (or alienate others from her property), and a fourth that endows upon an owner the power to determine the terms of transfer of title. Thus abstractly conceived, the concept of private ownership yields a fairly well-defined set of rights. When instantiating these rights in actual cases of owning a specific given item, the specific rights an owner has over that item, can vary considerably according to a host of factors. First, at the most general level, certain social, economic, political, and cultural factors greatly affect our ideas about private property rights, their nature and extent, and what sorts of objects can be owned privately in the first place. To simplify matters, for purposes of this discussion, I will assume a common background of roughly Western, free-market, principles. A second variable that also significantly determines the specific rights an owner can have over an item[16] is its metaphysical character, or

---

[14]For an interesting history of software inter-dependence see Bill Machrone's, "The Look-and-Feel Issue: The Evolution of Innovation" in *Computers, Ethics, & Society,* M.D. Ermann, M. B. Williams, C. Gutierrez, Oxford University Press, New York, 1990.

[15]This was Locke's central preoccupation.

[16]Metaphysical character can co-vary with cultural-social factors to make for an even more complex picture. Consider the potentially diverse views of descendents of European traditions and those of Native American traditions on property rights over land, sea, and air.

type. For example, the specific rights a child has over his peanut butter sandwich might include the rights to consume it, to chop it into twenty pieces and to decide whether to share it or not with a friend. But such rights make no sense in the case of landowners and plots of land, pet owners and their pets, car owners and their vehicles, and so forth. When we determine the appropriate set of rights instantiating the general rights of use and enjoyment, restricting access, terms of sale, on items of varying metaphysical character, we come up with distinct sets of specific rights. Whereas intellectual property stretches classical ideas of locking away or fencing ("restricting access"), consuming ("use and enjoyment"), and bartering ("transfer of title") deciding what it means to own software poses an even harder puzzle.

Computer software has raised a host of challenges to property theory, testing the traditional concepts and rationales in novel ways. Because even relatively simple programs have numerous components and moreover have various aspects, the first problem is to define, or identify, the "thing" that is *the* program, the thing that is the proper subject of private ownership. A program can be identified by its source code and object code, a formal specification defining what the program does, its underlying algorithm, and its user interface, or "look and feel." Each of the various components—or aspects—has a distinct metaphysical character and consequently suggests a distinct set of property rights. For example, because a program's source code is considered similar to a written work, it is considered by most to be covered by copyright laws. By contrast some judge a program's algorithm to be a process (and not a mathematical formula) and thus claim that it is patentable. Legal debates address the issue of whether one can abstract a program's so-called look and feel and claim to own that, in addition to, and independently of, the code, algorithm, and so on. And if so, they argue over whether legal protection ought to be through copyright, patent, or something else. There are many instructive works dedicated to the question of the optimal form of legal protection of all these aspects of software in a growing literature which is written from legal, philosophical, and technical perspective.[17]

Fortunately, we need not wait for a resolution to the entire range of puzzles that software ownership raises in order to gain a better understanding of Millie's dilemma. We acknowledge, in her case, that she explicitly duplicated object code, and thus we bypass many of the complexities. However, it is important to note the existing backdrop of uncertainty over how to categorize the metaphysics of software, and thus, how to fit it into our network of ideas on property rights. We are drawing conclusions about software ownership on the basis of imperfect analogies to other forms of private property. This leaves open the possibility of significant differences.

[17]See, for example: M. Gemignani, "The Regulation of Software," *Abacus,* vol. 5, no. 1, Fall 1987, pp. 57–59; D.G. Johnson, "Should Computer Programs Be Owned?", *Metaphilosophy,* vol. 16, no. 4, October 1985, pp. 276–288, P. Samuelson, "Why the Look and Feel of Software User Interfaces Should Not Be Protected by Copyright Law." *Communications of the ACM,* vol. 32, no. 5, May 1989, pp. 563–572.

We are ready now to return to this section's central question of how one might derive a prohibition on copying from ownership. On the basis of earlier observations about private property we can conclude that a programmer, or owner, has rights over the program including rights to restrict access and rights of use and enjoyment. Presumably, the programmer's right to generate earnings from his program would instantiate the latter. The programmer could choose to give others limited access to her program by selling diskettes, upon which she has copied the program, at a price she determines. But because the programmer still owns the program itself, she may impose restrictions on its use—in particular she retains the right to prevent buyers of the diskettes from making copies of the program that she has not explicitly authorized. Thus, we drive the programmer's specific right to restrict unauthorized copying from the general right property owners have to restrict access by others to their property. To distinguish transactions of this type from other types of sales, commercial software vendors adopt the jargon "software license" rather than "software sale." Thus, the argument from rights would dictate that Millie not copy because doing so would violate a programmers' valid claim to both use and enjoy his or her property (by depriving them earnings) and restrict access by others to it (by making unauthorized copies).

But this picture leaves out an important component of property theory. Like other rights, property rights restrict the freedoms of others by imposing certain obligations on them. For example a promisee's rights imply an obligation on the part of the promiser to keep the promise; a landowner's rights implies an obligation on would-be trespassers not to cross his or her land. As I stated earlier, the precise nature of property restrictions will vary according to the metaphysical character of the property. But there is yet another factor that shapes the extent and nature of property—and in fact all—rights. Even theorists of a libertarian bent, who support extensive rights over private property, recognize that these rights are not absolute. For example, Locke argued that morality allowed the appropriation of previously owned property only "where there is enough, and as good, left in common for others."[18] And Nozick, also recognizing limitations on property rights, illustrates one source of these restrictions with his colorful example: "My property rights in my knife allow me to leave it where I will, but not in your chest."[19] In other words, although owning a knife implies extensive rights of use and enjoyment, these rights are constrained by justified claims, or rights, of others—in this case, their right not to be harmed. While I wish to avoid either endorsing or criticizing the more far-reaching agendas of these two authors, I want to draw attention to an important insight they offer about private property rights: that property rights are subject to the limitations of countervailing claims of others.

Actual practice demonstrates that, as a rule rather than an exception, when we determine the nature and extent of property rights, we acknowledge the justified claims of others. For example, in determining the rights of the owner of a

---

[18]Locke, *ibid,* Chapter 5 Section 27.
[19]*Anarchy, State, and Utopia* by Robert Nozick p. 171.

lethal weapon we're influenced not only by its general metaphysical features (when we determine the types of actions that constitute use and enjoyment), but are concerned about the well-being of others. And so we restrict the way people may carry lethal weapons—either concealed or unconcealed depending on the accepted wisdom of the city or state in which they happen to live. We regulate construction projects of urban property owners for far less concrete counter-claims than freedom from bodily harm, but in the interest of values like aes-thetic integrity of a neighborhood, effects on the quality of life of immediate neighbors, and so forth. We restrict the rights of landowners over water tra-versing their land, preventing them, for example, from damming a flowing river. We also constrain the behavior of motor vehicle drivers. In all these cases where we perceive a threat to justified claims of other individuals, or of a social order, we limit the extent of owners' rights over their property. It makes sense to carry this principle over to the case of software asking not only about the claims of programmers, but the claims of end-users.

Does Millie Smith have a reasonable counter-claim that might limit the ex-tent to which Quicken's owners can constrain her actions. She would like to du-plicate her Quicken software for Max, an act of generosity, helping satisfy a friend's need. Despite the programmer's preferring that Millie not share a copy, Millie is motivated by other values. She views making a copy as a generous act which would help a friend in need. Copying software is a routine part of com-puter use. Millie's proposed action is limited; she has no intention of making multiple copies and going into competition with the programmer, she wouldn't dream of plagiarizing the software or passing it off as a product of her own cre-ation. The entire transaction takes places within the private domain of friends and family. She would view offering a copy to Max as a simple act of kindness, neither heroic nor extraordinary. Interfering with the normal flow of behavior, especially as pursued in the private realm, would constitute unreasonable re-striction of an agent's liberty. Thus, Millie's countervailing claim is the freedom to pursue the virtue of generosity within the private circle of friends and family.

The conclusion of this line of reasoning is *not* that, from a perspective of rights, *all* unauthorized duplication of software is morally permissible. I am sug-gesting merely that we decide the question whether to share or not to share in a case by case fashion. Although in some cases a programmer's desire that the user not copy software is a defensible instantiation of the right to restrict access to pri-vate property, in others the restriction will not be defensible because it conflicts with the valid claims of another agent. And even in the cases where making a copy would not be immoral it would not follow that the programmer has some-how lost all the property rights over his or her program. Commentators like Green and Gilbert are right to draw attention to programmers' claims over their software, and to encourage respect for intellectual labor; but they overlook the possibility of relevant, conflicting, counterclaims. When, at the beginning of the paper, I referred to the copier's dilemma, it was the dilemma created by conflict-ing obligations: on the one hand an obligation to respect a programmer's prop-erty rights, which in some cases includes the right to restrict copying; and on the other an obligation to help others, tempered by the belief that one ought not have one's behavior unduly restricted within the private domain.

Consider some objections. One objection is that no matter what Millie might think about helping Max, you just cannot get away from the fact that she's violating the programmer's property rights. And this is the reason that her copying—and all unauthorized copying—is immoral.

This objection fails to recognize that counterclaims can substantively affect what counts as a moral (property) right, in any given situation. Consider the rights of a landlord with respect to a leased apartment. When that apartment is vacant, the owner may come and go as he wishes; he may renovate it, choose to rent it, or to let it stand empty. However, once the apartment is leased, the landlord's rights of entry are limited by a tenant's competing right to privacy. Even if it would suit a landlord to stipulate in his lease the right to make surprise checks, this wish would be overridden by the justified claims of his tenants not to be disturbed, not to have their privacy violated. We would not say that the landlord's property rights are violated by the tenant; we would say that the landlord no longer has the right of free entry into his leased property. Consider another example. Let's say someone buys a word-processing package. On the outside of the customary sealed envelope containing the diskette, the buyer finds not only the usual terms of a lease agreement, but one further condition. The programmers stipulate that consumers are free to use the word processor any way they want, except to produce a document that promotes abortion. They reason that the abortion stipulation is merely an additional instantiation of their rights as owners to restrict access by others to their property. However, I think that the buyer could quite reasonably object that despite the programmer's intellectual property rights over the word processor, these rights do not include the right to control its use to the extent that it overrides valid, competing, claims to freedom of expression. Similarly, Millie, judging that in the private domain she should be largely unrestricted, could argue that the moral arm of the programmer does not extend into the private domain. We conclude, therefore, that in copying for Max she does not violate a moral right.

In a second objection, a critic could charge that if we judge Millie Smith's copying to be morally permissible, this would open the door to a total disregard for the rights of programmers. There would be no stopping agents from making multiple, unauthorized, copies and selling them in competition with the original programmer.

This objection doesn't hold because Millie's case, being significantly different from those other cases, would not lead us down a slippery slope. A potential copier must show a justifiable claim that conflicts with the programmer's. In the objector's example, and even in the case of a do-gooder who decides to place a piece of privately owned software on a public domain network,[20] copying takes place in a public domain lacking Millie's personal and private motivations. They lack the compelling counterclaim. Specifically for the public, commercial arena, we would expect to generate a network of laws and regulations to cover the many cases which moral principles alone could not decide.

---

[20]I confess to being stymied by cases such as that of a school teacher in a poor ghetto school deciding to make unauthorized copies of a software application that he believes would help his students, who would not ordinarily be able to afford it.

Another objection asserts that Millie would be acting immorally in making a copy for Max because copying is stealing. But this objection begs the question because it *assumes* that copying is stealing. In this section we've been examining whether or not copying always violates property rights and therefore constitutes wrongful seizure of another's possession. In other words, whether copying is stealing. This objection assumes that we've satisfactorily established that copying is theft, and thus assumes the issue we're trying to establish.

Conclusion

There is a prevailing presumption—in my opinion a disturbing one—that were we to follow the dictates of moral conscience, we would cease completely to make unauthorized copies of software. Yet when we examine the arguments given in support of that presumption we find that they fall short of their universal scope. The soundness of a rights-based rationale depends on successfully showing that owning software entails a right to restrict copying. I have argued that this step is not obvious, and that at least in some well-defined cases the entailment fails—notably, cases in which there are strong counterclaims. In practice this means that we should give equal consideration to the rights of end-users as well as to those of programmers. To simply insist that property rights override end-user freedoms is to beg the issue at hand.

Consequentialist rationales are also equivocal in that they rest on a number of sweeping empirical assumptions—many of which exaggerate the effects of copying, some of which are open to doubt. Moreover, it places squarely on the shoulders of private end-users the onus of maintaining a flourishing industry when in fact there are other agents well placed to share the burden. Many software manufacturers who have been vocal in their complaints, despite current levels of copying, appear to be enjoying overwhelming successes. Perhaps because they offer incentives like good consulting services, free upgrades, and reasonable prices they raise the marginal utility of buying over copying.

Finding that there are insufficiently strong moral grounds for universally prohibiting copying, I conclude not that all unauthorized copying is morally acceptable, but that that some copying is acceptable. There is sufficient variability in the types of situations in which software users copy to suggest that we ought to evaluate them case-by-case. In cases like Millie's and Max's, the argument against copying is not a compelling one.

Finally, some critics insist that the best approach to solving this issue is a hard-line economic one. Clearly, a rights-based approach, which unearths the usual set of conflicting rights is not helpful and leads us to a deadlock. Let the free market decide. We ought to allow software producers to place any conditions whatever on the sale of their software, and in particular, any limits on duplication. Consumers will soon make their preferences known. Defenders of no-copy say that current commercial software conditions are more or less in that position today, except that users are not keeping up their end of the bargain when they make copies of software. But even from this hard-line economic standpoint, a no-copy line is disturbing because it lets the robustness of a market depend on a mode of behavior to which most do not conform, and many find distasteful, that is, restricting the inclination to private acts of beneficence and generosity. Unless we alter human nature, experience suggests that this would be a shaky equilibrium.

On a final idealistic note, I echo strains of Richard Stallman in observing that if we can eradicate copying only when individuals ignore a natural tendency to respond to the needs of those close to them, we may not be maximizing expected utility after all.

Questions

1. In what ways does Helen Nissenbaum think that some copying can increase utility?
2. What does the author mean by the "metaphysics of software"? How, if at all, is this relevant to the moral questions of copying software?
3. How can one determine when the claims of private end-users justify the copying of software and other copyrighted material? Does the author give us a way of making this determination?

Should Millie Copy?[1]

David Carey

David Carey responds to Helen Nissenbaum's argument that Millie may make a copy of her expensive home bookkeeping program for her friend Max who cannot afford to buy one for himself. Whereas Helen Nissenbaum's paper examines the question from the perspective of two different theories—consequentialism and deontology— David Carey prefers to argue against the backdrop of a Thomistic view (named after St. Thomas Aquinas), which, he says, is a more comprehensive and integrated approach. He lists three conditions that must all be met in order for an action to be acceptable according to this view.

David Carey then argues that whether ownership of an original work unilaterally limits the copying of others is determined in the context of a legal system. Some legal systems, he says, do indeed forbid any copying by others (without permission of the owner). He agrees that there are some exceptions to the prohibition against copying—such as where copying would be necessary to save a life or avert a war—but says that these are not the sorts of circumstances in which Millie finds herself. Finally, the author says a contract, freely entered by the owner and user of intellectual property, may place restrictions over and above those determined by the rights of each party. Were Millie to make a copy for Max, she would be violating the license contract between her and the owner of the software.

In "Should I Copy My Neighbor's Software?" Helen Nissenbaum presents this case: Millie considers giving a copy of an expensive home-bookkeeping program to a friend Max, although she "suspects" that doing so would violate her license to use the program and so might be illegal. Her greater concern, though, is "about violating moral principles." She is motivated by concern for her friend

[1]I am grateful to David Benatar for his helpful comments on an earlier draft of this paper.

David Carey, "Should Millie Copy?," is printed by permission of the author.

Max, "who lives precariously from one paycheck to the next" (201) and so cannot now afford to buy (or "lease") a legal copy for himself.

In analyzing this case, Nissenbaum seeks to establish a universal negative ("Millie would not be violating moral principles if she were to share a copy with Max" (201)—that is, there is no moral principle that would be violated by her doing so). To establish this thesis, she considers two types of moral theory separately: consequentialism and deontology. She admits that these categories "should be viewed as rough guides only" to the sorts of arguments that she has encountered in "computer trade publications, other non-philosophical journals, electronic-mail communications, as well as conversations."[2] A more integrated analysis, however, would not consider consequences, duties, and rights as three independent and rival criteria, such that an action may pass consequentialist muster but fail to satisfy the deontologist. Rather, all relevant criteria can form a single complex-but-integrated standard. Perhaps the most venerable moral theory of this sort is the one developed by Aquinas, building on the insights of Aristotle. Because of its integration and comprehensiveness, we adopt it here.[3]

According to this theory, for an action to be morally justified, three conditions must be jointly met: (1) the chosen action must not be inherently disordered in itself (that is, essentially incompatible with one's ultimate end),[4] (2) the purpose or intention in choosing it must accord with one's ultimate end, and (3) the relevant circumstances (including the immediate consequences) must accord with the action's goodness as determined by the first two criteria. Thus, the morality of an action depends on *what* is done, *why* it is done, and *how* (when, where, to whom, etc.) it is done. For ease of reference, let us call these three criteria the criterion of object, the criterion of intention, and the criterion of circumstance, respectively. If a particular action meets *all* of these criteria, it is morally good; if it fails *any* one of them, it is morally bad.[5]

In the case at hand, there are (at least) three issues:

A. Does ownership of an original work unilaterally limit copying by others?
B. If so, is such a limitation exceptionless?
C. Can copying be further limited by contract?

---

[2]*Ibid.*, p. 202. To show the "hybrid spirit" of the second category, she actually calls it "deontological/rights-based," but for the sake of simplicity and elegance I've reduced her label to "deontology" or "deontological."

[3]St. Thomas Aquinas, *Summa Theologiae*, Ia-IIae, q. 18.

[4]An action is "essentially incompatible" with a goal just in case there is no way to perform that action and simultaneously advance toward that goal. So, for instance, theft (unjust taking of, or withholding, the property of another) is essentially incompatible with a happy life, that is a life expressing virtue, since theft violates the virtue of justice, which is the habitual intention to give all their due.

[5]According to this Thomistic theory, every particular human action is either morally good or morally bad; none is ever morally indifferent. *Kinds* of actions, however, can be good, bad, or indifferent: Helping a neighbor is a good kind of action, theft is always bad, using a computer is generally indifferent. A good kind of action can be bad in particular circumstances—e.g., helping a neighbor by theft. An action bad in kind, however, can never be made good. A particular instance of an indifferent *kind* of action, though, is either good or bad. As I argue, Millie's use of a computer to make an unauthorized copy for Max is a bad instance under the circumstances.

A. UNILATERAL LIMITATION

The rights associated with ownership are fully determined only in the context of a given legal system. Any natural rights of ownership (whether due to labor or some other cause) must be made particular by a given body of law. Thus there is no extra-legal or pre-legal answer to the first question, "Does ownership of an original work unilaterally limit copying by others?" In those legal systems in which intellectual property is defined and protected by copyright, patent, contract, or trademark, original ownership may well include the right to forbid any and all copying by others or to license such copying under terms agreeable to the owner. A common justification for this right, at least in legal systems derived from English common law, is the consequentialist theory that such a right benefits society in the long run by offering an incentive to entrepreneurs to risk time, talent, and capital in developing goods and services that eventually become freely available in the common domain. Accordingly, some sort of consequentialist principle (e.g., the principle of utility[6]) is a relevant moral principle for the case at hand.

On this point, Nissenbaum quotes Barwise's argument that software copying "is a very serious problem. It is discouraging the creation of courseware and other software, and is causing artificially high prices for what software does appear."[7] Nissenbaum objects both that "links" between illegal copying and "reduced income" have not been sufficiently demonstrated and also that such copying can actually lead to *increased* income for software vendors by stimulating demand for their products. Furthermore, she argues, creative people are not motivated simply by financial rewards (203). As for social benefit ("general welfare"), she says, "At this level of generality it is probably impossible to draw a meaningful connection between software and welfare" (204). Note that Nissenbaum is not challenging consequentialism *in principle* here but only the application of consequentialist reasoning to the case at hand. She seems to settle for "an uncomfortable standoff" (204) as to whether empirical research will corroborate Barwise's position or hers.

In the light of the robust requirements of the Thomistic theory that we have adopted, an analysis that considers merely the consequences is obviously inadequate. If copying in a particular case does more harm than good, knowledge of this preponderance of harm would be a sufficient reason to avoid the act of copying, since it would violate the criterion of circumstance. Conversely, though, the mere absence of such knowledge is never sufficient for justifying an action. An action could still fail to satisfy the other two criteria (of object and intention). Clearly, Nissenbaum's empirical "standoff" is insufficient justification for her claim that Millie's copying violates *no* moral principle (201).

---

[6]A typical formulation of the principle of utility is this: "Among available courses of action, choose the action which on balance does the most good for the most people."

[7]Nissenbaum gives the following citation: Jon Barwise, "Computers and Mathematics: Editorial Notes" in *Notices of the A.M.S.*, 1989.

Nissenbaum is aware of this, for she goes on to consider a second kind of moral principle, namely, deontological or "rights based" (201). She points out that a rights-based prohibition against copying requires two steps: (1) that a programmer does in fact have a right to prohibit copying of her program and (2) that unauthorized copying *always* violates this right. For the sake of argument, she grants the first step and addresses the second, which she considers "the weak one" (206). In the next section, we consider reasons for agreeing that the right to prohibit copying is not exceptionless or absolute. Even in showing that no deontological argument succeeds in justifying the prohibition against all unauthorized copying, however, she still would not have exhausted all the relevant principles. Respecting *rights* and fulfilling *duties*, although they are necessary conditions, are not by themselves sufficient conditions for moral goodness, any more than the avoidance of harmful consequences is sufficient.

Similarly, good intentions (such as "beneficence and generosity" (211) are never sufficient by themselves to justify an action that violates either of the other two criteria (of object and circumstance). In doing evil, no one is ever justified merely by intending that good may come of it. Certainly, Millie is to be commended for the neighborly intention to help her friend, but there are just and fair ways of fulfilling this intention (for example, doing Max's bookkeeping for him or buying for him a legal copy of the bookkeeping software).

Thus, both on consequentialist and on deontological grounds, a programmer (or other software owner) may well be justified in unilaterally prohibiting copying by others, even without a formal contract or other kinds of particular consent by other parties.[8] Others are morally required to respect such a prohibition.

We turn now to the second issue: Does unauthorized copying *always* violate this right? In other words, is the prohibition exceptionless?

B. EXCEPTIONLESS PROHIBITION AGAINST COPYING

In general, property rights over things (non-persons) are subordinate to the common good of the human community. For instance, the right to deploy capital is subordinate to the rights of workers. This is because goods that are merely auxiliary or instrumental goods (non-persons, material resources, capital, etc.) are subordinate to goods which are ends in themselves (persons and communities of persons). Conversely, more fundamental rights (e.g., the human right to life) trump less fundamental rights (e.g., external property rights). So, for example, ownership of basic necessities such as food, clothing, and shelter is

---

[8]As we noted above, many legal systems rely on a general and implied social contract concerning intellectual property: the inventor or discoverer is granted temporary monopoly rights over her work in return for relinquishing those rights to the public domain when the patent or copyright has expired. In the context of such a system, a programmer may be said to exercise such rights "unilaterally" with respect to other individuals. That is, the general social contract need not be formally ratified for each particular case.

subordinate to the human right to life. Thus a wealthy restaurant owner is unjustified in withholding food from an innocent, starving child. To take food for the child from the owner, in the extreme case that there is no other way of feeding the child, is not theft, even if the food is taken against the owner's will, since the owner's property right is subordinate to the child's right to life. Clearly, then, there will be cases in which an owner's prohibition against copying must be subordinated and restricted to "save a life or avert a war" (in Nissenbaum's words in n.3).

In this context, we should agree with Nissenbaum's thesis "that in *some* cases copying is not a violation" (or is a justifiable violation) of an owner's rights, but we should disagree with the wide scope that she gives to such exceptions, vastly expanded to include the case of Millie and Max. This case is hardly as exceptional as saving a life or averting a war. Rather, we should regard the usual and customary commercial prohibitions against copying as *prima facie* morally binding. That is, a violation of their terms is immoral under foreseeable circumstances, but may be justifiable in the truly rare cases of catastrophe or emergency (of the magnitude of the starving child).

C. CONTRACTUAL RESTRICTIONS

Finally, in addition to conduct that is already constrained by the rights of all parties, an owner of intellectual property and a user of that property may freely, by contract, further specify permitted and forbidden actions.[9] If implied, general social contracts are *prima facie* morally binding, all the more so are particular contracts mutually and explicitly undertaken by owners and users. A software license agreement, explicitly endorsed by the user's breaking of the shrinkwrap, is such a contract.

Hence, in Nissenbaum's example, Millie is not justified in giving Max a copy of the software. Doing so violates the criterion of object because it is essentially incompatible with the license contract and is not justified by an unforeseen emergency or catastrophe. The goodness of Millie's intention (generosity) is insufficient by itself (by the criterion of intention) to justify what amounts to theft.

So far, we have discussed reasons for respecting an owner's prohibition against copying, but nothing precludes generosity on the part of the owner, as well. If sound moral reasoning often upholds the rights of owners, it also challenges owners to exercise their rights of ownership in a manner that most

---

[9]Nissenbaum raises the issue of side-constraints on contracts: "Even if it would suit a landlord to stipulate in his lease the right to make surprise checks, this wish would be overridden by the justified claims of his tenants not to be disturbed, not to have their privacy violated" (210). What makes the tenants' claim "justified"? Is the alleged right to privacy a *natural* right, obtaining universally, no matter the culture or legal system? Or is it a *civil* right granted in some legal systems but not in others? However, we resolve this issue, the larger point remains that contracts are not made in moral and legal vacuums. No matter how freely both parties agree to the terms of a contract, they are not completely unfettered in making those terms.

contributes to the common good. Indeed, the very justification for private property developed in the Aristotelian-Thomistic tradition includes the larger consideration that all goods are ultimately destined for the common good of humans and their societies. Private ownership is justified, when it is justified, by the greater likelihood that clearly defined responsibility, peace, and order resulting from private ownership are more conducive to the common good than shared or common ownership would be.[10] The social contract justifying intellectual property (the bargain between society and inventors, authors, entrepreneurs, etc.) adds a more specific justification to this general justification of private ownership. Accordingly, the owner of the software in question may well be inclined to offer Max a steeply discounted copy, not merely as a marketing ploy but as an act of generosity. But this is a decision for the owner rather, than the user, to make.

Hence, in Millie's case, she would do well to help Max, but not by giving him a pirate copy of commercial software.

Questions

1. Why does David Carey think that there is not an extra-legal answer to the question of whether ownership of an original work limits copying by others?
2. Why does the author say that good intentions cannot justify copying?
3. The author agrees with Helen Nissenbaum that there are *some* exceptions to the prohibition against copying. Saving a life or averting a war are among these exceptional circumstances. Although Millie does not find herself in such circumstances, do you think that Helen Nissenbaum could argue that Millie's circumstances are also relevantly exceptional?

Suggestions for Further Reading on Copyright Violation

BRINGSJORD, SELMER."In Defense of Copying." *Public Affairs Quarterly* 3, no. 1 (January 1989): pp. 1–9.

JOHNSON, DEBORAH G."The Ownership of Computer Programs." In *Computer Ethics*, Englewood Cliffs, N.J.: Prentice Hall, 1985: pp. 87–103.

---

[10]St. Thomas Aquinas, *Summa Theologiae*, IIa-IIae, q. 66, a. 2, following Aristotle's *Politics*, 1263a35ff.

CHAPTER 13

Giving Aid

Rich and Poor

Peter Singer

Peter Singer argues that most people in rich countries have robust duties to assist the world's poor. A sizable proportion of the world's human population live in conditions of "absolute poverty," which means that they lack sufficient resources to meet the most basic biological needs for food, clothing, and shelter. While millions of such people die every year from malnutrition and poverty-induced disease, most people in the developed countries have resources not only for the basics but also for innumerable luxuries. Such people live in "absolute affluence."

By not giving more than we do to the world's poor, says the author, the affluent are allowing vast numbers of people in absolute poverty to die. He discusses the question of whether this failure to help is the moral equivalent of murder. His conclusions here lead him to adopt a different, non-comparative approach to the question of absolute poverty. He argues for an obligation to assist those in this condition.

The starting point for this argument is an analogy of the small child drowning in the university pond. Everyone thinks that we have a duty to save this child, even if it means getting one's clothes wet. A plausible principle supporting this duty, says the author, is that "if it is in our power to prevent something very bad from happening, without thereby sacrificing anything of comparable moral significance, we ought to do it." *This principle, he claims, should be supported by both consequentialists and nonconsequentialists. As this principle applies to the relief of absolute poverty by those of us who can afford luxuries, the author concludes that we have duties to assist the poor. The author then considers and rejects a number of objections to his argument.*

Peter Singer, "Rich and Poor," in *Practical Ethics,* 2d ed. Reprinted by permission of Cambridge University Press.

SOME FACTS ABOUT POVERTY

. . . Consider these facts: by the most cautious estimates, 400 million people lack the calories, protein, vitamins and minerals needed to sustain their bodies and minds in a healthy state. Millions are constantly hungry; others suffer from deficiency diseases and from infections they would be able to resist on a better diet. Children are the worst affected. According to one study, 14 million children under five die every year from the combined effects of malnutrition and infection. In some districts half the children born can be expected to die before their fifth birthday.

Nor is lack of food the only hardship of the poor. To give a broader picture, Robert McNamara, when president of the World Bank, suggested the term 'absolute poverty'. The poverty we are familiar with in industrialised nations is relative poverty—meaning that some citizens are poor, relative to the wealth enjoyed by their neighbours. People living in relative poverty in Australia might be quite comfortably off by comparison with pensioners in Britain, and British pensioners are not poor in comparison with the poverty that exists in Mali or Ethiopia. Absolute poverty, on the other hand, is poverty by any standard. In McNamara's words:

> Poverty at the absolute level . . . is life at the very margin of existence. The absolute poor are severely deprived human beings struggling to survive in a set of squalid and degraded circumstances almost beyond the power of our sophisticated imaginations and privileged circumstances to conceive.

> Compared to those fortunate enough to live in developed countries, individuals in the poorest nations have:

> An infant mortality rate eight times higher
> A life expectancy one-third lower
> An adult literacy rate 60 per cent less
> A nutritional level, for one out of every two in the population, below acceptable standards;
> And for millions of infants, less protein than is sufficient to permit optimum development of the brain.

McNamara has summed up absolute poverty as 'a condition of life so characterised by malnutrition, illiteracy, disease, squalid surroundings, high infant mortality and low life expectancy as to be beneath any reasonable definition of human decency'.

Absolute poverty is, as McNamara has said, responsible for the loss of countless lives, especially among infants and young children. When absolute poverty does not cause death, it still causes misery of a kind not often seen in the affluent nations. Malnutrition in young children stunts both physical and mental development. According to the United Nations Development Programme, 180 million children under the age of five suffer from serious malnutrition. Millions of people on poor diets suffer from deficiency diseases, like goitre, or blindness caused by a lack of vitamin A. The food value of what the poor eat is further reduced by parasites such as hookworm and ringworm, which are endemic in conditions of poor sanitation and health education.

Death and disease apart, absolute poverty remains a miserable condition of life, with inadequate food, shelter, clothing, sanitation, health services and education. The Worldwatch Institute estimates that as many as 1.2 billion people—or 23 per cent of the world's population—live in absolute poverty. For the purposes of this estimate, absolute poverty is defined as "the lack of sufficient income in cash or kind to meet the most basic biological needs for food, clothing, and shelter." Absolute poverty is probably the principal cause of human misery today.

SOME FACTS ABOUT WEALTH

This is the background situation, the situation that prevails on our planet all the time. It does not make headlines. People died from malnutrition and related diseases yesterday, and more will die tomorrow. The occasional droughts, cyclones, earthquakes, and floods that take the lives of tens of thousands in one place and at one time are more newsworthy. They add greatly to the total amount of human suffering; but it is wrong to assume that when there are no major calamities reported, all is well.

The problem is not that the world cannot produce enough to feed and shelter its people. People in the poor countries consume, on average, 180 kilos of grain a year, while North Americans average around 900 kilos. The difference is caused by the fact that in the rich countries we feed most of our grain to animals, converting it into meat, milk, and eggs. Because this is a highly inefficient process, people in rich countries are responsible for the consumption of far more food than those in poor countries who eat few animal products. If we stopped feeding animals on grains and soybeans, the amount of food saved would—if distributed to those who need it—be more than enough to end hunger throughout the world.

These facts about animal food do not mean that we can easily solve the world food problem by cutting down on animal products, but they show that the problem is essentially one of distribution rather than production. The world does produce enough food. Moreover, the poorer nations themselves could produce far more if they made more use of improved agricultural techniques.

So why are people hungry? Poor people cannot afford to buy grain grown by farmers in the richer nations. Poor farmers cannot afford to buy improved seeds, or fertilisers, or the machinery needed for drilling wells and pumping water. Only by transferring some of the wealth of the rich nations to the poor can the situation be changed.

That this wealth exists is clear. Against the picture of absolute poverty that McNamara has painted, one might pose a picture of 'absolute affluence'. Those who are absolutely affluent are not necessarily affluent by comparison with their neighbours, but they are affluent by any reasonable definition of human needs. This means that they have more income than they need to provide themselves adequately with all the basic necessities of life. After buying (either directly or through their taxes) food, shelter, clothing, basic health services, and education, the absolutely affluent are still able to spend money on luxuries. The absolutely affluent choose their food for the pleasures of the palate, not to stop hunger; they buy new clothes to look good, not to keep warm; they move house to be in a better neighbourhood or have a playroom for the children, not to keep out the rain; and after all this there is still money to spend on stereo systems, video-cameras, and overseas holidays.

At this stage I am making no ethical judgments about absolute affluence, merely pointing out that it exists. Its defining characteristic is a significant amount of income above the level necessary to provide for the basic human needs of one-self and one's dependents. By this standard, the majority of citizens of Western Europe, North America, Japan, Australia, New Zealand, and the oil-rich Middle Eastern states are all absolutely affluent. To quote McNamara once more:

> "The average citizen of a developed country enjoys wealth beyond the wildest dreams of the one billion people in countries with per capita incomes under $200." These, therefore, are the countries—and individuals—who have wealth that they could, without threatening their own basic welfare, transfer to the ab-solutely poor.

At present, very little is being transferred. Only Sweden, the Netherlands, Norway, and some of the oil-exporting Arab states have reached the modest tar-get, set by the United Nations, of 0.7 per cent of gross national product (GNP). Britain gives 0.31 per cent of its GNP in official development assistance and a small additional amount in unofficial aid from voluntary organisations. The to-tal comes to about £2 per month per person, and compares with 5.5 per cent of GNP spent on alcohol, and 3 per cent on tobacco. Other, even wealthier nations, give little more: Germany gives 0.41 per cent and Japan 0.32 per cent. The United States gives a mere 0.15 per cent of its GNP.

THE MORAL EQUIVALENT OF MURDER?

If these are the facts, we cannot avoid concluding that by not giving more than we do, people in rich countries are allowing those in poor countries to suffer from absolute poverty, with consequent malnutrition, ill health, and death. This is not a conclusion that applies only to governments. It applies to each ab-solutely affluent individual, for each of us has the opportunity to do something about the situation; for instance, to give our time or money to voluntary organ-isations like Oxfam, Care, War on Want, Freedom from Hunger, Community Aid Abroad, and so on. If, then, allowing someone to die is not intrinsically dif-ferent from killing someone, it would seem that we are all murderers.

Is this verdict too harsh? Many will reject it as self-evidently absurd. They would sooner take it as showing that allowing to die cannot be equivalent to killing than as showing that living in an affluent style without contributing to an overseas aid agency is ethically equivalent to going over to Ethiopia and shooting a few peasants. And no doubt, put as bluntly as that, the verdict is too harsh.

There are several significant differences between spending money on luxuries instead of using it to save lives, and deliberately shooting people.

First, the motivation will normally be different. Those who deliberately shoot others go out of their way to kill; they presumably want their victims dead, from malice, sadism, or some equally unpleasant motive. A person who buys a new stereo system presumably wants to enhance her enjoyment of music—not in itself a terrible thing. At worst, spending money on luxuries instead of giving it away indicates selfishness and indifference to the sufferings of others, characteristics that may be undesirable but are not comparable with actual malice or similar motives.

Second, it is not difficult for most of us to act in accordance with a rule against killing people: it is, on the other hand, very difficult to obey a rule that commands us to save all the lives we can. To live a comfortable, or even luxurious life it is not necessary to kill anyone; but it is necessary to allow some to die whom we might have saved, for the money that we need to live comfortably could have been given away. Thus the duty to avoid killing is much easier to discharge completely than the duty to save. Saving every life we could would mean cutting our standard of living down to the bare essentials needed to keep us alive.[1] To discharge this duty completely would require a degree of moral heroism utterly different from that required by mere avoidance of killing.

A third difference is the greater certainty of the outcome of shooting when compared with not giving aid. If I point a loaded gun at someone at close range and pull the trigger, it is virtually certain that the person will be killed; whereas the money that I could give might be spent on a project that turns out to be unsuccessful and helps no one.

Fourth, when people are shot there are identifiable individuals who have been harmed. We can point to them and to their grieving families. When I buy my stereo system, I cannot know who my money would have saved if I had given it away. In a time of famine I may see dead bodies and grieving families on television reports, and I might not doubt that my money would have saved some of them; even then it is impossible to point to a body and say that had I not bought the stereo, that person would have survived.

Fifth, it might be said that the plight of the hungry is not my doing, and so I cannot be held responsible for it. The starving would have been starving if I had never existed. If I kill, however, I am responsible for my victims' deaths, for those people would not have died if I had not killed them.

These differences need not shake our previous conclusion that there is no intrinsic difference between killing and allowing to die. They are extrinsic

---

[1]Strictly, we would need to cut down to the minimum level compatible with earning the income which, after providing for our needs, left us most to give away. Thus if my present position earns me, say, $40,000 a year, but requires me to spend $5,000 a year on dressing respectably and maintaining a car, I cannot save more people by giving away the car and clothes if that will mean taking a job that, although it does not involve me in these expenses, earns me only $20,000.

differences, that is, differences normally but not necessarily, associated with the distinction between killing and allowing to die. We can imagine cases in which someone allows another to die for malicious or sadistic reasons; we can imagine a world in which there are so few people needing assistance, and they are so easy to assist, that our duty not to allow people to die is as easily discharged as our duty not to kill; we can imagine situations in which the outcome of not helping is as sure as shooting; we can imagine cases in which we can identify the person we allow to die. We can even imagine a case of allowing to die in which, if I had not existed, the person would not have died—for instance, a case in which if I had not been in a position to help (though I don't help) someone else would have been in my position and would have helped.

Our previous discussion of euthanasia illustrates the extrinsic nature of these differences, for they do not provide a basis for distinguishing active from passive euthanasia. If a doctor decides, in consultation with the parents, not to operate on—thus to allow to die—a Down's syndrome infant with an intestinal blockage, her motivation will be similar to that of a doctor who gives a lethal injection rather than allow the infant to die. No extraordinary sacrifice or moral heroism will be required in either case. Not operating will just as certainly end in death as administering the injection. Allowing to die does have an identifiable victim. Finally, it may well be that the doctor is personally responsible for the death of the infant she decides not to operate upon, since she may know that if she had not taken this case, other doctors in the hospital would have operated.

Nevertheless, euthanasia is a special case, and very different from allowing people to starve to death. (The major difference being that when euthanasia is justifiable, death is a good thing.) The extrinsic differences that *normally* mark off killing and allowing to die do explain why we *normally* regard killing as much worse than allowing to die.

To explain our conventional ethical attitudes is not to justify them. Do the five differences not only explain, but also justify, our attitudes? Let us consider them one by one:

1. Take the lack of an identifiable victim first. Suppose that I am a travelling salesperson, selling tinned food, and I learn that a batch of tins contains a contaminant, the known effect of which, when consumed, is to double the risk that the consumer will die from stomach cancer. Suppose I continue to sell the tins. My decision may have no identifiable victims. Some of those who eat the food will die from cancer. The proportion of consumers dying in this way will be twice that of the community at large, but who among the consumers died because they ate what I sold, and who would have contracted the disease anyway? It is impossible to tell; but surely this impossibility makes my decision no less reprehensible than it would have been had the contaminant had more readily detectable, though equally fatal, effects.

2. The lack of certainty that by giving money I could save a life does reduce the wrongness of not giving, by comparison with deliberate killing; but it is insufficient to show that not giving is acceptable conduct. The motorist who speeds through pedestrian crossings, heedless of anyone who might be on

them, is not a murderer. She may never actually hit a pedestrian; yet what she does is very wrong indeed.

3. The notion of responsibility for acts rather than omissions is more puzzling. On the one hand, we feel ourselves to be under a greater obligation to help those whose misfortunes we have caused. (It is for this reason that advocates of overseas aid often argue that Western nations have created the poverty of third world nations, through forms of economic exploitation that go back to the colonial system.) On the other hand, any consequentialist would insist that we are responsible for all the consequences of our actions, and if a consequence of my spending money on a luxury item is that someone dies, I am responsible for that death. It is true that the person would have died even if I had never existed, but what is the relevance of that? The fact is that I do exist, and the consequentialist will say that our responsibilities derive from the world as it is, not as it might have been.

One way of making sense of the non-consequentialist view of responsibility is by basing it on a theory of rights of the kind proposed by John Locke or, more recently, Robert Nozick. If everyone has a right to life, and this right is a right *against* others who might threaten my life, but not a right to assistance from others when my life is in danger, then we can understand the feeling that we are responsible for acting to kill but not for omitting to save. The former violates the rights of others, the latter does not.

Should we accept such a theory of rights? If we build up our theory of rights by imagining, as Locke and Nozick do, individuals living independently from each other in a 'state of nature', it may seem natural to adopt a conception of rights in which as long as each leaves the other alone, no rights are violated. I might, on this view, quite properly have maintained my independent existence if I had wished to do so. So if I do not make you any worse off than you would have been if I had had nothing at all to do with you, how can I have violated your rights? But why start from such an unhistorical, abstract and ultimately inexplicable idea as an independent individual? Our ancestors were—like other primates—social beings long before they were human beings, and could not have developed the abilities and capacities of human beings if they had not been social beings first. In any case, we are not, now, isolated individuals. So why should we assume that rights must be restricted to rights against interference? We might, instead, adopt the view that taking rights to life seriously is incompatible with standing by and watching people die when one could easily save them.

4. What of the difference in motivation? That a person does not positively wish for the death of another lessens the severity of the blame she deserves; but not by as much as our present attitudes to giving aid suggest. The behaviour of the speeding motorist is again comparable, for such motorists usually have no desire at all to kill anyone. They merely enjoy speeding and are indifferent to the consequences. Despite their lack of malice, those who kill with cars deserve not only blame but also severe punishment.

5. Finally, the fact that to avoid killing people is normally not difficult, whereas to save all one possibly could save is heroic, must make an important difference to our attitude to failure to do what the respective principles demand.

Not to kill is a minimum standard of acceptable conduct we can require of everyone; to save all one possibly could is not something that can realistically be required, especially not in societies accustomed to giving as little as ours do. Given the generally accepted standards, people who give, say, $1,000 a year to an overseas aid organisation are more aptly praised for above average generosity than blamed for giving less than they might. The appropriateness of praise and blame is, however, a separate issue from the rightness or wrongness of actions. The former evaluates the agent; the latter evaluates the action. Perhaps many people who give $1,000 really ought to give at least $5,000, but to blame them for not giving more could be counterproductive. It might make them feel that what is required is too demanding, and if one is going to be blamed anyway, one might as well not give anything at all.

(That an ethic that put saving all one possibly can on the same footing as not killing would be an ethic for saints or heroes should not lead us to assume that the alternative must be an ethic that makes it obligatory not to kill, but puts us under no obligation to save anyone. There are positions in between these extremes, as we shall soon see.)

Here is a summary of the five differences that normally exist between killing and allowing to die, in the context of absolute poverty and overseas aid. The lack of an identifiable victim is of no moral significance, though it may play an important role in explaining our attitudes. The idea that we are directly responsible for those we kill, but not for those we do not help, depends on a questionable notion of responsibility and may need to be based on a controversial theory of rights. Differences in certainty and motivation are ethically significant, and show that not aiding the poor is not to be condemned as murdering them; it could, however, be on a par with killing someone as a result of reckless driving, which is serious enough. Finally the difficulty of completely discharging the duty of saving all one possibly can makes it inappropriate to blame those who fall short of this target as we blame those who kill; but this does not show that the act itself is less serious. Nor does it indicate anything about those who, far from saving all they possibly can, make no effort to save anyone.

These conclusions suggest a new approach. Instead of attempting to deal with the contrast between affluence and poverty by comparing not saving with deliberate killing, let us consider afresh whether we have an obligation to assist those whose lives are in danger, and if so, how this obligation applies to the present world situation.

THE OBLIGATION TO ASSIST

The Argument for an Obligation to Assist

The path from the library at my university to the humanities lecture theatre passes a shallow ornamental pond. Suppose that on my way to give a lecture I notice that a small child has fallen in and is in danger of drowning. Would anyone deny that I ought to wade in and pull the child out? This will mean getting my clothes muddy and either cancelling my lecture or delaying it until I can find something dry to change into; but compared with the avoidable death of a child this is insignificant.

A plausible principle that would support the judgment that I ought to pull the child out is this: if it is in our power to prevent anything very bad from happening, without thereby sacrificing anything of comparable moral significance, we ought to do it. This principle seems uncontroversial. It will obviously win the assent of consequentialists; but non-consequentialists should accept it too, because the injunction to prevent what is bad applies only when nothing comparably significant is at stake. Thus the principle cannot lead to the kinds of actions of which non-consequentialists strongly disapprove—serious violations of individual rights, injustice, broken promises, and so on. If non-consequentialists regard any of these as comparable in moral significance to the bad thing that is to be prevented, they will automatically regard the principle as not applying in those cases in which the bad thing can only be prevented by violating rights, doing injustice, breaking promises, or whatever else is at stake. Most non-consequentialists hold that we ought to prevent what is bad and promote what is good. Their dispute with consequentialists lies in their insistence that this is not the sole ultimate ethical principle: that it is an ethical principle is not denied by any plausible ethical theory.

Nevertheless the uncontroversial appearance of the principle that we ought to prevent what is bad when we can do so without sacrificing anything of comparable moral significance is deceptive. If it were taken seriously and acted upon, our lives and our world would be fundamentally changed. For the principle applies, not just to rare situations in which one can save a child from a pond, but to the everyday situation in which we can assist those living in absolute poverty. In saying this I assume that absolute poverty, with its hunger and malnutrition, lack of shelter, illiteracy, disease, high infant mortality, and low life expectancy, is a bad thing. And I assume that it is within the power of the affluent to reduce absolute poverty, without sacrificing anything of comparable moral significance. If these two assumptions and the principle we have been discussing are correct, we have an obligation to help those in absolute poverty that is no less strong than our obligation to rescue a drowning child from a pond. Not to help would be wrong, whether or not it is intrinsically equivalent to killing. Helping is not, as conventionally thought, a charitable act that it is praiseworthy to do, but not wrong to omit; it is something that everyone ought to do.

This is the argument for an obligation to assist. Set out more formally, it would look like this.

First premise: If we can prevent something bad without sacrificing anything of comparable significance, we ought to do it.

Second premise: Absolute poverty is bad.

Third premise: There is some absolute poverty we can prevent without sacrificing anything of comparable moral significance.

Conclusion: We ought to prevent some absolute poverty.

The first premise is the substantive moral premise on which the argument rests, and I have tried to show that it can be accepted by people who hold a variety of ethical positions.

The second premise is unlikely to be challenged. Absolute poverty is, as McNamara put it, 'beneath any reasonable definition of human decency' and it would be hard to find a plausible ethical view that did not regard it as a bad thing.

The third premise is more controversial, even though it is cautiously framed. It claims only that some absolute poverty can be prevented without the sacrifice of anything of comparable moral significance. It thus avoids the objection that any aid I can give is just 'drops in the ocean' for the point is not whether my personal contribution will make any noticeable impression on world poverty as a whole (of course it won't) but whether it will prevent some poverty. This is all the argument needs to sustain its conclusion, since the second premise says that any absolute poverty is bad, and not merely the total amount of absolute poverty. If without sacrificing anything of comparable moral significance we can provide just one family with the means to raise itself out of absolute poverty, the third premise is vindicated.

I have left the notion of moral significance unexamined in order to show that the argument does not depend on any specific values or ethical principles. I think the third premise is true for most people living in industrialised nations, on any defensible view of what is morally significant. Our affluence means that we have income we can dispose of without giving up the basic necessities of life, and we can use this income to reduce absolute poverty. Just how much we will think ourselves obliged to give up will depend on what we consider to be of comparable moral significance to the poverty we could prevent: stylish clothes, expensive dinners, a sophisticated stereo system, overseas holidays, a (second?) car, a larger house, private schools for our children, and so on. For a utilitarian, none of these is likely to be of comparable significance to the reduction of absolute poverty; and those who are not utilitarians surely must, if they subscribe to the principle of universalisability, accept that at least some of these things are of far less moral significance than the absolute poverty that could be prevented by the money they cost. So the third premise seems to be true on any plausible ethical view—although the precise amount of absolute poverty that can be prevented before anything of moral significance is sacrificed will vary according to the ethical view one accepts.

Objections to the Argument

Taking Care of Our Own

Anyone who has worked to increase overseas aid will have come across the argument that we should look after those near us, our families, and then the poor in our own country, before we think about poverty in distant places.

No doubt we do instinctively prefer to help those who are close to us. Few could stand by and watch a child drown; many can ignore a famine in Africa. But the question is not what we usually do, but what we ought to do, and it is difficult to see any sound moral justification for the view that distance, or community membership, makes a crucial difference to our obligations.

Consider, for instance, racial affinities. Should people of European origin help poor Europeans before helping poor Africans? Most of us would reject such a suggestion out of hand: . . . people's need for food has nothing to do with their race, and if Africans need food more than Europeans, it would be a violation of the principle of equal consideration to give preference to Europeans.

The same point applies to citizenship or nationhood. Every affluent nation has some relatively poor citizens, but absolute poverty is limited largely to the poor nations. Those living on the streets of Calcutta, or in the drought-prone Sahel region of Africa, are experiencing poverty unknown in the West. Under these circumstances it would be wrong to decide that only those fortunate enough to be citizens of our own community will share our abundance.

We feel obligations of kinship more strongly than those of citizenship. Which parents could give away their last bowl of rice if their own children were starving? To do so would seem unnatural, contrary to our nature as biologically evolved beings—although whether it would be wrong is another question altogether. In any case, we are not faced with that situation, but with one in which our own children are well-fed, well-clothed, well-educated, and would now like new bikes, a stereo set, or their own car. In these circumstances any special obligations we might have to our children have been fulfilled, and the needs of strangers make a stronger claim upon us.

The element of truth in the view that we should first take care of our own, lies in the advantage of a recognised system of responsibilities. When families and local communities look after their own poorer members, ties of affection and personal relationships achieve ends that would otherwise require a large, impersonal bureaucracy. Hence it would be absurd to propose that from now on we all regard ourselves as equally responsible for the welfare of everyone in the world; but the argument for an obligation to assist does not propose that. It applies only when some are in absolute poverty, and others can help without sacrificing anything of comparable moral significance. To allow one's own kin to sink into absolute poverty would be to sacrifice something of comparable significance; and before that point had been reached, the breakdown of the system of family and community responsibility would be a factor to weigh the balance in favour of a small degree of preference for family and community. This small degree of preference is, however, decisively outweighed by existing discrepancies in wealth and property.

Property Rights

Do people have a right to private property, a right that contradicts the view that they are under an obligation to give some of their wealth away to those in absolute poverty? According to some theories of rights (for instance, Robert Nozick's), provided one has acquired one's property without the use of unjust means like force and fraud, one may be entitled to enormous wealth while others starve. This individualistic conception of rights is in contrast to other views, like the early Christian doctrine to be found in the works of Thomas Aquinas, which holds that since property exists for the satisfaction of human needs, 'whatever a man has in superabundance is owed, of natural right, to the poor for their sustenance'. A socialist would also, of course, see wealth as belonging to the community rather than the individual, while utilitarians, whether socialist or not, would be prepared to override property rights to prevent great evils.

Does the argument for an obligation to assist others therefore presuppose one of these other theories of property rights, and not an individualistic theory like Nozick's? Not necessarily. A theory of property rights can insist on our *right* to retain wealth without pronouncing on whether the rich *ought* to give to the poor. Nozick, for example, rejects the use of compulsory means like taxation to redistribute income, but suggests that we can achieve the ends we deem morally desirable by voluntary means. So Nozick would reject the claim that rich people have an 'obligation' to give to the poor, in so far as this implies that the poor have a right to our aid, but might accept that giving is something we ought to do and failing to give, though within one's rights, is wrong—for there is more to an ethical life than respecting the rights of others.

The argument for an obligation to assist can survive, with only minor modifications, even if we accept an individualistic theory of property rights. In any case, however, I do not think we should accept such a theory. It leaves too much to chance to be an acceptable ethical view. For instance, those whose forefathers happened to inhabit some sandy wastes around the Persian Gulf are now fabulously wealthy, because oil lay under those sands; while those whose forefathers settled on better land south of the Sahara live in absolute poverty, because of drought and bad harvests. Can this distribution be acceptable from an impartial point of view? If we imagine ourselves about to begin life as a citizen of either Bahrein or Chad—but we do not know which—would we accept the principle that citizens of Bahrein are under no obligation to assist people living in Chad?

Population and the Ethics of Triage

Perhaps the most serious objection to the argument that we have an obligation to assist is that since the major cause of absolute poverty is overpopulation, helping those now in poverty will only ensure that yet more people are born to live in poverty in the future.

In its most extreme form, this objection is taken to show that we should adopt a policy of 'triage'. The term comes from medical policies adopted in wartime. With too few doctors to cope with all the casualties, the wounded were divided into three categories: those who would probably survive without medical assistance, those who might survive if they received assistance, but otherwise probably would not, and those who even with medical assistance probably would not survive. Only those in the middle category were given medical assistance. The idea, of course, was to use limited medical resources as effectively as possible. For those in the first category, medical treatment was not strictly necessary; for those in the third category, it was likely to be useless. It has been suggested that we should apply the same policies to countries, according to their prospects of becoming self-sustaining. We would not aid countries that even without our help will soon be able to feed their populations. We would not aid countries that, even with our help, will not be able to limit their population to a level they can feed. We would aid those countries where our help might make the difference between success and failure in bringing food and population into balance.

Advocates of this theory are understandably reluctant to give a complete list of the countries they would place into the 'hopeless' category; Bangladesh has been cited as an example, and so have some of the countries of the Sahel region of Africa. Adopting the policy of triage would, then, mean cutting off assistance to these countries and allowing famine, disease, and natural disasters to reduce the population of those countries to the level at which they can provide adequately for all.

In support of this view Garrett Hardin has offered a metaphor: we in the rich nations are like the occupants of a crowded lifeboat adrift in a sea full of drowning people. If we try to save the drowning by bringing them aboard, our boat will be overloaded and we shall all drown. Since it is better that some survive than none, we should leave the others to drown. In the world today, according to Hardin, 'lifeboat ethics' apply. The rich should leave the poor to starve, for otherwise the poor will drag the rich down with them.

Against this view, some writers have argued that overpopulation is a myth. The world produces ample food to feed its population, and could, according to some estimates, feed ten times as many. People are hungry not because there are too many but because of inequitable land distribution, the manipulation of third world economics by the developed nations, wastage of food in the West, and so on.

Putting aside the controversial issue of the extent to which food production might one day be increased, it is true, as we have already seen, that the world now produces enough to feed its inhabitants—the amount lost by being fed to animals itself being enough to meet existing grain shortages. Nevertheless population growth cannot be ignored. Bangladesh could, with land reform and using better techniques, feed its present population of 115 million; but by the year 2000, according to United Nations Population Division estimates, its population will be 150 million. The enormous effort that will have to go into feeding an extra 35 million people, all added to the population within a decade, means that Bangladesh must develop at full speed to stay where it is. Other low-income countries are in similar situations. By the end of the century, Ethiopia's population is expected to rise from 49 to 66 million; Somalia's from 7 to 9 million, India's from 853 to 1041 million, Zaire's from 35 to 49 million.[2]

---

[2]Ominously, in the twelve years that have passed between editions of this book, the signs are that the situation is becoming even worse than was then predicted. In 1979 Bangladesh had a population of 80 million and it was predicted that by 2000 its population would reach 146 million; Ethiopia's was only 29 million, and was predicted to reach 54 million; and India's was 620 million and predicted to reach 958 million.

What will happen if the world population continues to grow? It cannot do so indefinitely. It will be checked by a decline in birth rates or a rise in death rates. Those who advocate triage are proposing that we allow the population growth of some countries to be checked by a rise in death rates—that is, by increased malnutrition, and related diseases; by widespread famines; by increased infant mortality; and by epidemics of infectious diseases.

The consequences of triage on this scale are so horrible that we are inclined to reject it without further argument. How could we sit by our television sets, watching millions starve while we do nothing? Would not that be the end of all notions of human equality and respect for human life? . . . Don't people have a right to our assistance, irrespective of the consequences?

Anyone whose initial reaction to triage was not one of repugnance would be an unpleasant sort of person. Yet initial reactions based on strong feelings are not always reliable guides. Advocates of triage are rightly concerned with the long-term consequences of our actions. They say that helping the poor and starving now merely ensures more poor and starving in the future. When our capacity to help is finally unable to cope—as one day it must be—the suffering will be greater than it would be if we stopped helping now. If this is correct, there is nothing we can do to prevent absolute starvation and poverty, in the long run, and so we have no obligation to assist. Nor does it seem reasonable to hold that under these circumstances people have a right to our assistance. If we do accept such a right, irrespective of the consequences, we are saying that, in Hardin's metaphor, we should continue to haul the drowning into our lifeboat until the boat sinks and we all drown.

If triage is to be rejected it must be tackled on its own grounds within the framework of consequentialist ethics. Here it is vulnerable. Any consequentialist ethics must take probability of outcome into account. A course of action that will certainly produce some benefit is to be preferred to an alternative course that may lead to a slightly larger benefit, but is equally likely to result in no benefit at all. Only if the greater magnitude of the uncertain benefit outweighs its uncertainty should we choose it. Better one certain unit of benefit than a 10 per cent chance of five units; but better a 50 per cent chance of three units than a single certain unit. The same principle applies when we are trying to avoid evils.

The policy of triage involves a certain, very great evil: population control by famine and disease. Tens of millions would die slowly. Hundreds of millions would continue to live in absolute poverty, at the very margin of existence. Against this prospect, advocates of the policy place a possible evil that is greater still: the same process of famine and disease, taking place in, say, fifty years' time, when the world's population may be three times its present level, and the number who will die from famine, or struggle on in absolute poverty, will be that much greater. The question is: how probable is this forecast that continued assistance now will lead to greater disasters in the future?

Forecasts of population growth are notoriously fallible, and theories about the factors that affect it remain speculative. One theory, at least as plausible as any other, is that countries pass through a 'demographic transition' as their standard of living rises. When people are very poor and have no access to modern medicine their fertility is high, but population is kept in check by high death rates. The introduction of sanitation, modern medical techniques, and other improvements reduces the death rate, but initially has little effect on the birth rate. Then population grows rapidly. Some poor countries, especially, in sub-Saharan Africa, are now in this phase. If standards of living continue to rise, however, couples begin to realise that to have the same number of children surviving to maturity as in the past, they do not need to give birth to as many children as their parents did. The need for children to provide economic support in old age diminishes. Improved education and the emancipation and employment of women also reduce the birth-rate, and so population growth begins to level off. Most rich nations have reached this stage, and their populations are growing only very slowly, if at all.

If this theory is right, there is an alternative to the disasters accepted as inevitable by supporters of triage. We can assist poor countries to raise the living standards of the poorest members of their population. We can encourage the governments of these countries to enact land reform measures, improve education, and liberate women from a purely child-bearing role. We can also help other countries to make contraception and sterilisation widely available. There is a fair chance that these measures will hasten the onset of the demographic transition and bring population growth down to a manageable level. According to United Nations estimates, in 1965 the average woman in the third world gave birth to six children, and only 8 per cent were using some form of contraception; by 1991 the average number of children had dropped to just below four, and more than half the women in the third world were taking contraceptive measures. Notable successes in encouraging the use of contraception had occurred in Thailand, Indonesia, Mexico, Colombia, Brazil, and Bangladesh. This achievement reflected a relatively low expenditure in developing countries—considering the size and significance of the problem—of $3 billion annually, with only 20 per cent of this sum coming from developed nations. So expenditure in this area seems likely to be highly cost-effective. Success cannot be guaranteed; but the evidence suggests that we can reduce population growth by improving economic security and education, and making contraceptives more widely available. This prospect makes triage ethically unacceptable. We cannot allow millions to die from starvation and disease when there is a reasonable probability that population can be brought under control without such horrors.

Population growth is therefore not a reason against giving overseas aid, although it should make us think about the kind of aid to give. Instead of food handouts, it may be better to give aid that leads to a slowing of population growth. This may mean agricultural assistance for the rural poor, or assistance with education, or the provision of contraceptive services. Whatever kind of aid proves most effective in specific circumstances, the obligation to assist is not reduced.

One awkward question remains. What should we do about a poor and already overpopulated country that, for religious or nationalistic reasons, restricts the use of contraceptives and refuses to slow its population growth? Should we nevertheless offer development assistance? Or should we make our offer conditional on effective steps being taken to reduce the birthrate? To the latter course, some would object that putting conditions on aid is an attempt to impose our own ideas on independent sovereign nations. So it is—but is this imposition unjustifiable? If the argument for an obligation to assist is sound, we have an obligation to reduce absolute poverty; but we have no obligation to make sacrifices that, to the best of our knowledge, have no prospect of reducing poverty in the long run. Hence we have no obligation to assist countries whose governments have policies that will make our aid ineffective. This could be very harsh on poor citizens of these countries—for they may have no say in the government's policies—but we will help more people in the long run by using our resources where they are most effective. (The same principles may apply, incidentally, to countries that refuse to take other steps that could make assistance effective—like refusing to reform systems of land holding that impose intolerable burdens on poor tenant farmers.)

Leaving It to the Government

We often hear that overseas aid should be a government responsibility, not left to privately run charities. Giving privately, it is said, allows the government to escape its responsibilities.

Since increasing government aid is the surest way of making a significant increase to the total amount of aid given, I would agree that the governments of affluent nations should give much more genuine, no-strings-attached, aid than they give now. Less than one-sixth of one per cent of GNP is a scandalously small amount for a nation as wealthy as the United States to give. Even the official UN target of 0.7 per cent seems much less than affluent nations can and should give—though it is a target few have reached. But is this a reason against each of us giving what we can privately, through voluntary agencies? To believe that it is seems to assume that the more people there are who give through voluntary agencies, the less likely it is that the government will do its part. Is this plausible? The opposite view—that if no one gives voluntarily the government will assume that its citizens are not in favour of overseas aid, and will cut its programme accordingly—is more reasonable. In any case, unless there is a definite probability that by refusing to give we would be helping to bring about an increase in government assistance, refusing to give privately is wrong for the same reason that triage is wrong: it is a refusal to prevent a definite evil for the sake of a very uncertain gain. The onus of showing how a refusal to give privately will make the government give more is on those who refuse to give.

This is not to say that giving privately is enough. Certainly we should campaign for entirely new standards for both public and private overseas aid. We should also work for fairer trading arrangements between rich and poor countries, and less domination of the economics of poor countries by multinational corporations more concerned about producing profits for shareholders back home than food for the local poor. Perhaps it is more important to be politically active in the interests of the poor than to give to them oneself—but why not do both? Unfortunately, many use the view that overseas aid is the government's responsibility as a reason against giving, but not as a reason for being politically active.

Too high a standard? The final objection to the argument for an obligation to assist is that it sets a standard so high that none but a saint could attain it. This objection comes in at least three versions. The first maintains that, human nature being what it is, we cannot achieve so high a standard, and since it is absurd to say that we ought to do what we cannot do, we must reject the claim that we ought to give so much. The second version asserts that even if we could achieve so high a standard, to do so would be undesirable. The third version of the objection is that to set so high a standard is undesirable because it will be perceived as too difficult to reach, and will discourage many from even attempting to do so.

Those who put forward the first version of the objection are often influenced by the fact that we have evolved from a natural process in which those with a high degree of concern for their own interests, or the interests of their offspring and kin, can be expected to leave more descendants in future generations, and eventually to completely replace any who are entirely altruistic. Thus the biologist Garrett Hardin has argued, in support of his 'lifeboat ethics', that altruism can only exist 'on a small scale, over the short term, and within small, ultimate groups'; while Richard Dawkins has written, in his provocative book *The Selfish Gene:* 'Much as we might wish to believe otherwise, universal love and the welfare of the species as a whole are concepts which simply do not make evolutionary sense.' I have already noted, in discussing the objection that we should first take care of our own, the very strong tendency for partiality in human beings. We naturally have a stronger desire to further our own interests, and those of our close kin, than we have to further the interests of strangers. What this means is that we would be foolish to expect widespread conformity to a standard that demands impartial concern, and for that reason it would scarcely be appropriate or feasible to condemn all those who fail to reach such a standard. Yet to act impartially, though it might be very difficult, is not impossible. The commonly quoted assertion that 'ought' implies 'can' is a reason for rejecting such moral judgments as 'You ought to have saved all the people from the sinking ship', when in fact if you had taken one more person into the lifeboat, it would have sunk and you would not have saved any. In that situation, it is absurd to say that you ought to have done what you could not possibly do. When we have money to spend on luxuries and others are starving, however, it is clear that we can all give much more than we do give, and we can therefore all come closer to the impartial standard proposed in this chapter. Nor is there, as we approach closer to this standard, any barrier beyond which we cannot go. For that reason there is no basis for saying that the impartial standard is mistaken because 'ought' implies 'can' and we cannot be impartial.

The second version of the objection has been put by several philosophers during the past decade, among them Susan Wolf in a forceful article entitled 'Moral Saints'. Wolf argues that if we all took the kind of moral stance defended in this chapter, we would have to do without a great deal that makes life interesting: opera, gourmet cooking, elegant clothes, and professional sport, for a start. The kind of life we come to see as ethically required of us would be a single-minded pursuit of the overall good, lacking that broad diversity of interests and activities that, on a less demanding view, can be part of our idea of a good life for a human being. To this, however, one can respond that while the rich and varied life that Wolf upholds as an ideal may be the most desirable form of life for a human being in a world of plenty, it is wrong to assume that it remains a good life in a world in which buying luxuries for oneself means accepting the continued avoidable suffering of others. A doctor faced with hundreds of injured victims of a train crash can scarcely think it defensible to treat fifty of them and then go to the opera, on the grounds that going to the opera is of a well-rounded human life. The life-or-death needs of others must take priority. Perhaps we are like the doctor in that we live in a time when we all have an opportunity to help to mitigate a disaster.

Associated with this second version of the objection is the claim that an impartial ethic of the kind advocated here makes it impossible to have serious personal relationships based on love and friendship; these relationships are, of their nature, partial. We put the interests of our loved ones, our family, and our friends ahead of those of strangers; if we did not do so, would these relationships survive? I have already indicated, in the response I gave when considering the objection that we should first take care of our own, that there is a place, within an impartially grounded moral framework, for recognising some degree of partiality for kin, and the same can be said for other close personal relationships. Clearly, for most people, personal relationships are among the necessities of a flourishing life, and to give them up would be to sacrifice something of great moral significance. Hence no such sacrifice is required by the principle for which I am here arguing.

The third version of the objection asks: might it not be counterproductive to demand that people give up so much? Might not people say: 'As I can't do what is morally required anyway, I won't bother to give at all.' If, however, we were to set a more realistic standard, people might make a genuine effort to reach it. Thus setting a lower standard might actually result in more aid being given.

It is important to get the status of this third version of the objection clear. Its accuracy as a prediction of human behaviour is quite compatible with the argument that we are obliged to give to the point at which by giving more we sacrifice something of comparable moral significance. What would follow from the objection is that public advocacy of this standard of giving is undesirable. It would mean that in order to do the maximum to reduce absolute poverty, we should advocate a standard lower than the amount we think people really ought to give. Of course we ourselves—those of us who accept the original argument, with its higher standard—would know that we ought to do more than we publicly propose people ought to do, and we might actually give more than we urge others to give. There is no inconsistency here, since in both our private and our public behaviour we are trying to do what will most reduce absolute poverty.

For a consequentialist, this apparent conflict between public and private morality is always a possibility, and not in itself an indication that the underlying principle is wrong. The consequences of a principle are one thing, the consequences of publicly advocating it another. A variant of this idea is already acknowledged by the distinction between the intuitive and critical levels of morality, of which I have made use in previous chapters. If we think of principles that are suitable for the intuitive level of morality as those that should be generally advocated, these are the principles that, when advocated, will give rise to the best consequences. Where overseas aid is concerned, those will be the principles that lead to largest amount being given by the affluent to the poor.

Is it true that the standard set by our argument is so high as to be counterproductive? There is not much evidence to go by, but discussions of the argument, with students and others have led me to think it might be. Yet, the conventionally accepted standard—a few coins in a collection tin when one is waved under your nose—is obviously far too low. What level should we advocate? Any figure will be arbitrary, but there may be something to be said for a round percentage of one's income like, say, 10 per cent—more than a token donation, yet not so high as to be beyond all but saints. (This figure has the additional advantage of being reminiscent of the ancient tithe, or tenth, that was traditionally given to the church, whose responsibilities included care of the poor in one's local community. Perhaps the idea can be revived and applied to the global community.) Some families, of course, will find 10 per cent a considerable strain on their finances. Others may be able to give more without difficulty. No figure should be advocated as a rigid minimum or maximum; but it seems safe to advocate that those earning average or above average incomes in affluent societies, unless they have an unusually large number of dependents or other special needs, ought to give a tenth of their income to reducing absolute poverty. By any reasonable ethical standards this is the minimum we ought to do, and we do wrong if we do less.

Questions

1. Peter Singer argues that there are no intrinsic differences between murder and allowing people to die. What moral significance, if any, do extrinsic differences have?
2. Do you think that the case of the child in the pond is a good analogy for the problem of absolute poverty?
3. Can you think of a less demanding principle than that suggested by Peter Singer, but one that would still explain why we ought to save the drowning child.
4. Do you think that nonconsequentialists would accept the principle that "if it is in our power to prevent something very bad from happening, without thereby sacrificing anything of comparable moral significance, we ought to do it"?

Famine Relief and the Ideal Moral Code[1]

John Arthur

John Arthur responds to what he calls Peter Singer's "greater moral evil principle" that "if it is in our power to prevent something bad from happening, without thereby sacrificing anything of comparable moral importance, we ought . . . to do it." John Arthur says that Peter Singer's argument for this principle is not simply that it explains our feelings about the drowning child. Part of the rule's appeal is that it gives an important place to the idea that like amounts of suffering or happiness are of equal moral significance, irrespective of who is experiencing them. This sense of moral equality is an important part of our moral code.

However, says the author, there are other features of our moral code that Peter Singer ignores, namely, two forms of entitlement: rights and deserts. For example, the loss to me should I give up one of my kidneys would very likely be less than the benefit to somebody who will die without my kidney. Yet our moral code does not require me to give up one of my kidneys. This is because I have, and others do not have, a right to my kidneys. Or consider desert. All things being equal, those who work hard are taken to deserve more than those who are lazy. Our moral code, says John Arthur, gives weight to both the "greater moral evil principle" and the entitlements of rights and desert.

He argues that reforming the code by excluding rights and just deserts would be unreasonable. The moral code that it is rational for us to support, he says, is one that must be practical, and for it to be practical it must take account of human psychology. It cannot, for instance, even if it requires some altruism, expect people to be less unselfish than they are. He provides an alternative principle, which can be formulated as: "If it is in our power to prevent death of an innocent without sacrificing anything of 'substantial significance' then we ought morally to do it."

INTRODUCTION

Wħat do those of us who are relatively affluent owe, from a moral standpoint, to those who are hungry, sick, and may die without assistance? Peter Singer offers a provocative and interesting answer in which he defends what he terms an "uncontroversial" moral principle, that we ought to prevent evil whenever we can do so without sacrificing something of comparable moral significance. In doing so, he argues there is a duty to provide aid whenever others are in greater need and will suffer without our help.[2] Other philosophers, relying on the principle that all human life is of equal value, have reached similar conclusions.[3] My first concern, then, is to assess such arguments on their own terms, asking whether these argument do, in fact, establish a duty to give aid. I will argue, in response, that our moral "intuitions" include not only the commitments they emphasize, but also entitlements, which suggests that people who deserve or have rights to their earnings may be allowed to keep them.

But the fact that our social moral code includes entitlements is not a complete answer, for it is possible that contemporary moral attitudes are mistaken and our accepted code is defective. So in the final sections I ask whether a moral reformer might reasonably claim that an "ideal" moral code would reject entitlements, arguing that in fact it would not.

A DUTY TO PREVENT EVIL?

What do we intuitively believe, based on our accepted moral views, about helping people in desperate need? Some have argued that the ideal of treating people equally requires that we do much more to aid others than is usually supposed. Richard Watson, for example, emphasizes what he calls the "principle of equity." Since "all human life is of equal value," and difference in treatment should be "based on freely chosen actions and not accidents of birth or environment," he thinks that we have "equal rights to the necessities of life."[4] To distribute food unequally assumes that some lives are worth more than others, an assumption which, he says, we do not accept. Watson believes, in fact, that we put such importance on the "equity principle" that it should not be violated even if unequal distribution is the only way for anybody to survive. (Leaving aside for the moment whether or not he is correct about our code, it seems to me that if it really did require us to commit mass suicide rather than allow inequality in wealth, then we would want to abandon it for a more suitable set of moral rules. But more on that later.)

---

[2]Peter Singer, "Famine, Affluence, and Morality," *Philosophy and Public Affairs* Vol. 1, No. 3 (1972), pp. 229–243 and *Practical Ethics*, (New York: Cambridge University Press, 1979).
[3]For example Richard Watson, "Reason and Morality in a World of Limited Food" in William Aiken and Hugh LaFollette, eds., *World Hunger and Moral Obligation* (Englewood Cliffs, NJ: Prentice-Hall, 1977).
[4]*Ibid.*, pp. 117–118.

Begin with the premise: Is Watson correct that all life is of equal value? Did Adolph Hitler and Martin Luther King, for example, lead equally valuable lives? Clearly one did far more good, the other far more harm; and who would deny that while King fought for people's rights, Hitler violated them on a massive scale? Nor are moral virtues like courage, kindness, and trustworthiness equally distributed among people. So there are many important senses in which people are not, in fact, morally equal: some lives are more valuable to others, and some people are just, generous and courageous while others are unjust, cheap, and cowardly.

Yet all the same the ideal of equality is often thought to be a cornerstone of morality and justice. But what does it mean to say all people are "equal"? It seems to me that we might have in mind one of two things. First is an idea that Thomas Jefferson expressed in the *Declaration of Independence*."All men are created equal" meant, for him, that no man is the moral inferior of another, that, in other words, there are certain rights which all men share equally, including life and liberty. We are entitled in many areas to pursue our own lives without interference from others, just as no person is the natural slave of another. But, as Jefferson also knew, equality in that sense does not require equal distribution of the necessities of life, only that we not interfere with one another, allowing instead every person the liberty to pursue his own affairs, so long as he does not violate the rights of others.

Some people, however, have something different in mind when they speak of human equality. To develop this second idea, we will turn to Singer's argument. . . . Singer argues that two general moral principles are widely accepted, and then that those principles imply an obligation to eliminate starvation.

The first of the two principles he thinks we accept is simply that "suffering and death from lack of food, shelter and medical care are bad." Some may be inclined to think that the mere existence of such an evil in itself places an obligation on others, but that is, of course, the problem which Singer addresses. I take it that he is not begging the question in this obvious way and will *argue* from the existence of evil to the obligation of others to eliminate it. But how, exactly, does he establish this? The second principle, he thinks, shows the connection, but it is here that I wish to raise some questions. This second principle, which I will call the *"greater moral evil principle,"* states that:

> If it is in our power to prevent something bad from happening, without thereby sacrificing anything of comparable moral importance, we ought, morally, to do it.[5]

In other words, people are entitled to keep their earnings only if there is no way for them to prevent a greater evil by giving them away. Providing others with food, clothing, and housing would generally be of more importance than

---

[5]Singer also offers a "weak" version of this principle that, it seems to me, is *too* weak. It requires giving aid only if the gift is of *no* moral significance to the giver. But since even minor embarrassment or small amounts of unhappiness are not completely without moral importance, this weak principle would imply no obligation to aid, even to the drowning child.

buying luxuries, so the greater moral evil principle now requires substantial re-distribution of wealth.

Certainly few of us live by that principle, although as Singer emphasizes, that hardly shows we are *justified* in behaving that way. We often fail to live up to our own standards. Why does Singer think our shared morality requires that we follow the greater moral evil principle? What argument does he give for it?

He begins with an analogy. Suppose you came across a child drowning in a shallow pond. Certainly we feel it would be wrong not to help. Even if saving a child meant we must dirty our clothes, we would emphasize that those clothes are not of comparable significance to the child's life. The greater moral evil principle thus seems a natural way of capturing why we think it would wrong not to help.

But the argument for the greater moral evil principle is not limited to Singer's claim that it explains our feelings about the drowning child or that it appears "uncontroversial." Moral equality also enters the picture, in the following way.[6] Besides the Jeffersonian idea that we share certain rights equally, most of us are also attracted to another conception of equality, namely that like amounts of suffering (or happiness) are of equal significance, no matter who is experiencing them. I cannot reasonably say that, while my pain is no more se-vere than yours, I am somehow special and it's more important, objectively speaking, that mine be alleviated. Impartiality requires us to admit the oppo-site—that no one has a unique status warranting such special consideration.

But if we fail to give to famine relief and instead purchase a new car when the old one will do, or buy fancy clothes for a friend when his or her old ones are perfectly good, are we not assuming that the relatively minor enjoyment we or our friends may get is as important as another person's life? And that, it seems, is a form of prejudice; we are acting as if people were not equal in the sense that their interests deserve equal consideration. We are giving special con-sideration to ourselves or to our group, rather like a racist does. Equal consid-eration of interests thus leads naturally to the greater moral evil principle.

ENTITLEMENTS

Equal consideration seems to require that we should prevent harm to others if in doing so we do not sacrifice anything of comparable moral importance. But there is also another side to the coin, which Singer ignores. This idea can be ex-pressed rather awkwardly by the notion of entitlements, by which I have in mind the thought that having either a right or justly deserving something can also be important as we think about our obligations to others. A few examples will show what I mean.

One way we could help others is by giving away body parts. While your life may be shortened by the loss of a kidney or less enjoyable if lived with only

---

[6]See for example Singer's, "Postscript" to "Famine, Affluence and Morality" in Aiken and LaFol-lette, *Ibid.*, p. 36.

one eye, those costs are probably not comparable to the loss experienced by a person who will die without any kidney or who is totally blind. Or perhaps, using Judith Thomson's analogy, somebody needs to remain hooked up to you for an extended period of time while awaiting a transplant.[7] It seems clear, however, that our code does not *require* such heroism; you are entitled to your second eye and kidney and to control who uses your body, and that entitlement blocks the inference from the fact you could prevent harm to the conclusion you ought to let others have or use your body.

We express these ideas in terms of rights; it's your body, you have a right to it, and that weighs against whatever duty you have to help. To give up your right to your kidney for a stranger is more than is required, it's heroic. Unless, of course, you have freely agreed to let the person use your body, which brings us to the next point.

There are two types of rights, negative and positive. Negative rights are rights against interference by others. The right to life, for example, is a right not to be killed by others; the right against assault is a right that others not physically harm us. The right to one's body, the right to property, the right to privacy, and the right to exercise religious freedom are also negative, requiring only that people leave others alone and not interfere. Positive rights, however, are rights to receive some benefit. By contracting to pay wages, employers acquire the duty to employees who work for them to be paid, so if the employer backs out of the deal, the employees' positive right to receive a paycheck is violated.

Negative rights also differ from positive in that the former are natural or human, in the sense that they depend on what you are, not what you've done. All persons, we assume, have the right to life. If lower animals lack negative moral rights to life or liberty it is because there is a relevant difference between them and us. But the positive rights you may have are not natural in that sense; they arise because others have promised, agreed, or contracted to do something, just as you may have an obligation to let them use your property or even body if you agreed. The right not to be killed does not depend on anything you or anybody else has done; but the right to be paid a wage makes sense only on the basis of prior agreements.

None of that is to say that rights, whether negative or positive, are beyond controversy. Rights come in a variety of shapes and sizes, and people often disagree about both their shape and size. And while some rights are part of our generally shared moral code and widely accepted, others are controversial and hotly disputed.

Normally, then, a duty to help a stranger in need is not based on a *right* the person has, but instead on the general duty all people have to aid those in need (as Singer's drowning child illustrates). A genuine right to be aided requires something more, such as a contract or promise to accept responsibility for the child. Consider, for example a baby sitter who agrees to watch out for someone else's children but instead allows a child to drown. We would think that under these circumstances the parent whose child drowns would in fact be doubly

---

[7]Judith Jarvis Thomson, "A Defense of Abortion," *Philosophy and Public Affairs* Vol. 1, No. 1 (1971).

wronged. First, like everybody else the person who agreed to watch the child should not have cruelly or thoughtlessly let it drown. But it's also the case that here, unlike Singer's example, we can also say there are rights at stake; promises were made imposing special obligations on the baby sitter. Other bystanders also act wrongly by cruelly ignoring the child, but the baby sitter violates rights as well.

Moral rights are therefore one—but only one—factor to be weighed; we also have other obligations that should be considered. I am therefore not suggesting that rights are all we need to take into account. That view, like the greater moral evil principle, is an oversimplification. In reality, our moral code expects us to help people in need *as well as* to respect negative and positive rights. But it also seems clear that, besides being asked by our moral code to respect the rights of others, we are entitled, at least sometimes, to invoke our own rights as justification for what we do. It is not as if we promised to help, or are in any way responsible for the person's situation. Our social moral code teaches that although passing by a drowning child whom we can easily save is wrong we need not ignore our own rights and give away our savings to help distant strangers based solely on the greater moral evil principle.

A second form of entitlement involves just deserts: the idea that sometimes people deserve to keep what they have acquired. To see its role in our moral code, imagine an industrious farmer who manages through hard work to produce a surplus of food for the winter while a lazy neighbor spends the summer relaxing. Must our industrious farmer give the surplus away because that neighbor, who refused to work, will suffer? Under certain circumstances we might say because of the greater moral evil principle the farmer should help, but not necessarily. What this shows is that once again we have more than one factor to weigh. Besides the evil that could be prevented, we (and the hard working farmer too) should also consider the fact that one person earned it, through hard work. And while it might be the case that just desert is outweighed by the greater need of a neighbor, being outweighed is in any case not the same as weighing nothing!

Sometimes just desert can be negative in the sense of unwanted, as we well as something regarded as a good. The fact that the Nazi war criminals did what they did means they deserve punishment: We have a good reason to send them to jail, based on just desert. Other considerations, for example the fact that nobody will be deterred or that the criminal is old and harmless, may weigh against punishment and we may even decide not to pursue the case for that reason. But again that does not mean deserving to be punished is irrelevant, just that we've decided for other reasons to ignore desert in this case. But again I repeat: a principle's being outweighed is not the same as its having no importance.

Our social moral code thus honors both the greater moral evil principle and entitlements. The former emphasizes equality, claiming that from an objective point of view all comparable suffering, whoever its victim, is equally significant. It encourages us to take an impartial look at all the various effects of our actions, and is therefore forward looking. When we consider entitlements, however, our attention is directed to the past. Whether we have rights to money, property, or even our body depends on how we came to possess them. If money was stolen, for example, then the thief has no right to it. Or perhaps a person has promised to trade something, which would again (under normal circumstances) mean loss of entitlement. Like rights, just desert is also backward-looking, emphasizing past effort or past transgressions that now warrant responses such as reward, gratitude, or punishment.

I am suggesting, then, that expressing both equality and entitlements, our social moral code pulls in different directions. How then are we to determine when one principle is more important? Unless we are moral relativists, the mere fact that equality and entitlements are both part of our moral code does not in itself justify a person who relies on them, any more than the fact that our moral code once condemned racial mixing while condoning sexual discrimination and slavery should convince us that those principles are justified. We all assume (I trust) that the more enlightened moral code—the one we now subscribe to—is better in part just because it condemns discrimination and slavery. Because we know the rules defining acceptable behavior are continually changing, and sometimes changing for the better, we must allow for the replacement of inferior principles with more reasonable guidelines.

Viewed in that light, the issue posed by Singer's argument is really whether we should reform our current social moral code and reject entitlements, at least insofar as they conflict with the greater moral evil principle. What could justify our practice of evaluating actions by looking backward to rights and just desert instead of just to their consequences? To pursue these questions, we need to look more closely at how we might justify the moral rules and principles comprising a society's moral code; we will then be able to ask whether, though entitlements are part of our current code, we would improve our code—bring it closer to an ideal code—if they were not included.

THE CONCEPT OF A SOCIAL MORAL CODE

So I suggest that we first say something more about the nature and purpose of social moral codes in general; then we will turn to entitlements. We can begin with the obvious: A moral code is a system of principles, rules and other standards serving to guide people's conduct.[8] As such, it has characteristics in common with other systems of rules and standards such as the rules of organizations. Social clubs, sports leagues, corporations, bureaucracies, professional associations, even *The* Organization all have standards governing the behavior of members.

---

[8]Ronald Dworkin argues that there are important differences between principles and rules: while rules apply in an "all or nothing" fashion, and have specific exceptions, principles are not either/or, but instead have "weight" that must be considered in light of competing principles. Both of these can also be distinguished from moral ideals, which guide people toward the best, most valuable life. For purposes of this essay, however, these distinctions are not important; I do assume, however, that standards can compete, as Dworkin's analogy with the "weight" of principles suggests.

Such rules function in various ways, imposing different sanctions depending on the nature of the organization. Violation of a university's code of conduct leads to one sort of punishment, while different types of sanctions would typically be imposed by a social club or the American Bar Association.

Some standards of conduct are not limited to members of a specific organization but instead apply more broadly, and it is to those that we now turn. Law, for example, is a social practice rather than an organization. So are etiquette and customs. All these codes apply broadly, not just to members of an organization who have chosen to join. It will be most helpful in our thinking about the nature of a moral code to compare it with these other social practices, along a variety of dimensions.

As we noted with organizations, here too the form sanctions take vary among the different types of codes.[9] While in our legal system transgressions are punished by fines, jail, or even execution, informal sanctions of praise, criticism, and ostracism encourage conformity to the standards of morality and etiquette. Besides the type of sanctions, a second difference among these codes is that while violation of moral principles is always a serious affair, this need not be so for legal rules or the norms of etiquette and custom. Many of us think it unimportant whether a fork is on the left side of a plate or whether an outmoded and widely ignored Sunday closing law is violated. But violation of a moral principle is not ignored or thought trivial; indeed, the fact that a moral principle has lost its importance is often indicated by its "demotion" to mere custom.

A third contrast, besides differences in sanctions and importance, is that unlike morality, custom, and etiquette, legal systems include, besides criminal and civil rules, other "constitutional" rules governing how those laws are to be created, modified and eliminated.[10] Under the U.S. Constitution, for instance, if Congress acts to change the tax laws, then as of the date stated in the statute the rules are changed.[11] Moral rules, etiquette and customs also change, of course, but they do so without benefit of any agreed procedure identifying who or how the changes occur or when they take effect.

So far, then, we've noted that different codes and standards of behavior can vary widely, along a number of dimensions. Some apply narrowly, only to members of a specific organization, while others extend broadly. And while all codes include rules or other standards to guide conduct, the sanctions that are imposed by different codes differ widely, as do the ways rules change and the importance assigned to violations of the different codes.

The final point I want to make about rules generally, before looking specifically at morality, is that all standards serve a purpose, though what that is will

---

[9]This discussion follows H.L.A. Hart, *The Concept of Law*, 2nd edition (Oxford: Oxford University Press, 1995).

[10]But Ronald Dworkin has argued that legal interpretation is partly moral and normative, making this claim more difficult to make in that context. See, for example, *Law's Empire* (Cambridge: Harvard University Press, 1986), Chapters 2 and 7.

[11]Assuming, of course, the courts do not hold the law unconstitutional.

again vary with the organization or practice in question. Rules governing games, for example, are often changed, either informally among players or by a governing organization like the National Football League. This is done in order to more effectively achieve the goals, though the goals often vary and are sometimes open to dispute. Sometimes, for example, rules may be changed to improve safety (car design in auto racing, for example) or even to make the sport more exciting but less safe. Other times rules might be changed to accommodate younger players, such as abolishing the walk in kid's baseball. Similar points can be made about organizations, as for instance when a corporation changes its standards governing how many hours people work, or a university the deadline for dropping a class.

Like the rules of games and organizations like universities and corporations, legal and moral rules and principles also change in ways that serve their purposes either better or worse. But here enters one final, important point—because there can be deep disagreement about the purposes of such practices, there will also be disagreement about the rules themselves, including when there should be exceptions, what they exactly require, and the circumstances under which they can be ignored. Such a dispute about rules governing a social group such as a fraternity or sorority, for example, can rest on deeper, sometimes hidden disagreements about the purposes of the organization, just as differences between fundamentalists and liberals over religious rules and principles can also uncover disagreements about the purposes of religious practices.

Turning to morality, first consider a traditional rule such as the one prohibiting homosexual behavior. Assuming people could agree that the rule serves no useful purpose, but instead only increases the burden of guilt, shame, and social rejection borne by a significant portion of society, then it seems people would have good reason to alter their rules about sexual conduct and no longer condemn homosexuality. But people who see morality serving another purpose, for instance encouraging behavior that is compatible with God's will or with "natural" law, might oppose such a change. Or suppose, less controversially, that rules against killing and lying help us to accomplish what we want from a moral code. In that case, we have good reason to include those rules in our "ideal" moral code.

My suggestion, then, is that there is a connection between what we ought to do and how well a code serves its purposes. If a rule serves well the goals of a moral code, then we have reason to obey it. But if, on the other hand, a rule is useless, or if it frustrates the purposes of morality, we have reason neither to support it, teach it, nor to follow it. (Assuming, as I said, we agree what the purpose of a social moral code is.)

This suggests, then, the following conception of a right action: Any action is right if and only if it conforms with an ideal moral code for the society in which we are living. We will say more about this shortly, but most basically we must consider what, exactly, an *ideal* moral code is. In order to answer that, we must first ask ourselves the purpose that we hope to accomplish by creating, teaching and enforcing a moral code for society.

THE IDEAL SOCIAL MORAL CODE

One possibility, already suggested, is that morality's purpose depends on God—that morality serves to encourage people to act in accord with God's will. But I want to suggest, and very briefly defend, another view, namely that the ideal moral code is the one that, when recognized and taught by members of society, would have the best consequences. By best consequences, I mean that it would most effectively promote the collective well-being of those living under it.[12] (It's worth noting right off, however, that a religious person need not reject this out of hand but instead might reason that the general well-being is also what God would wish for creation.)

In pursuing this idea, it is helpful to return to the comparison between legal and moral standards. Clearly, both morality and law serve to *discourage* some of the same types of behavior—killing, robbing, and beating—while they both also *encourage* other acts such as repaying debts, keeping important agreements, and providing for one's children. The reason for rules discouraging acts like killing and beating seems clear enough, for imagine the disastrous consequences for human life absent such moral and legal rules. This idea is further substantiated when we think about how children are taught it is wrong to hit a baby brother or sister. Parents typically explain such rules in terms of their purpose, emphasizing that it hurts and can harm others when we hit them. At root, then, it seems at least plausible to suppose that these rules of morality and law function to keep people from causing unjustified harm to each other. A world in which people were allowed to kill and assault each other, without fear of legal or moral sanctions, would be far more miserable than a world in which such behavior is discouraged. Concern for general welfare explains how we learn moral standards as children and why we support them as adults.

In addition to justifying rules preventing harmful behavior, the other rules I mentioned, that encourage different types of behavior, can also be justified by their social consequences. Our own well-being as well as that of our friends, family, and indeed society as a whole depends on people generally keeping promises and fulfilling agreements. Without laws and moral rules to encourage such behavior, the institutions of promising and contracting would likely be unsustainable, and with their passing would be lost all the useful consequences flowing from our ability to bind ourselves and others by promising and contracting.

Moral rules thus promote our own welfare by discouraging acts of violence and creating and maintaining social conventions like promising and paying debts, and second, they perform the same service for our family, friends, and indeed all of us. A life wholly *without* legal and moral codes would be in danger of deteriorating into what Thomas Hobbes long ago feared: a state of nature in which life is solitary, poor, nasty, brutish and short.

---

[12]I leave aside here just how we can best understand "well-being" except to note that it should include whatever states of affairs have intrinsic value, however that is understood.

Many may find these thoughts fairly uncontroversial, thinking it obvious that moral codes are justified by their good consequences. But what more might be said to those who remain skeptical? One suggestion, from David Hume, emphasizes the importance of sentiment and feeling in human actions. It is, said Hume, only on the basis of feelings and sentiment that people can be moved to act at all, so that the key to understanding morality is that human nature is marked not only by self-interest but also by a sentimental attachment to the well-being of others. We take pleasure, Hume thinks, in the thought that others are happy as well as in our own happiness. This can be seen, he reasoned, from the fact that we

> frequently bestow praise on virtuous actions, performed in very distant ages and remote countries; where the utmost subtlety of imagination would not discover any appearance of self-interest, or find any connection with our present happiness and security with events so widely separated from us.[13]

Hume might have added that besides common sense there is also evidence that sympathy and concern for others' well-being are a natural part of our biological heritage. Some biologists, for example, think that many animals, particularly higher ones, take an interest in the welfare of other members of their species because such altruistic attitudes enable the species to survive better.[14] Others emphasize the inevitability of acquiring such sentiments through learning, arguing that feelings of benevolence originate naturally, via classical conditioning. We first develop negative associations with our own pain behavior (we associate screaming and writhing with our own pain) and this negative attitude is then generalized to the pain behavior of anybody.[15]

But whatever the reason behind sympathy, Hume concludes from this that we must renounce any moral theory

> which accounts for every moral sentiment by the principle of self-love. We must adopt a more public affection, and allow, that the interests of society are not, even on their own account, indifferent to us.[16]

Moral approval and condemnation, Hume is claiming, rest finally on sentiments rather than reason; but such sentiments extend beyond our own happiness to encompass the whole of humanity. Given such universal, sympathetic feelings for the well-being of others, he concludes, it is natural to understand a social moral code in terms of its utility or consequences on everybody's well-being.

But suppose that not everybody shares these sympathetic attitudes towards others. It might seem that such a person would therefore have reason to reject the idea that the ideal moral code is the one with the best over-all consequences. Instead, such an egoist might say, the truly best code would be the one maximizing *his own* welfare, even if others are not benefited at all. Caring for nobody else, he might regard as "ideal" a code giving him absolute power over the lives

[13]David Hume, *An Enquiry Concerning the Principles of Morals*, Sect. V, Part I, 175.
[14]Stephen Jay Gould, "So Cleverly Kind an Animal" in *Ever Since Darwin* (New York: W. W. Norton Co., 1977).
[15]Richard B. Brandt, *A Theory of the Good and the Right* (New York: Oxford University Press, 1979).
[16]Hume, *Ibid.*, Sect. V, Part II, 178.

and property of others, for example. How then should such a person be responded to by somebody who, like me, thinks the ideal code is the one that would have the best consequences for everybody and not just one individual?

One possibility, of course, is to acknowledge that such a person has a mistaken view of morality precisely because the ideal code would not only benefit one person, but to admit that such a person cannot be reasoned with let alone refuted. But while that may seem right, it would of course leave the egoist unpersuaded and without any reason to behave in accord with the ideal moral code. Yet why should we care if we cannot convince such a person that the ideal code would be one that has the best consequences for everybody? Some people may remain unmoved by moral considerations, but maybe that should not concern those of us who are.

But that said, it's instructive that we still do, in fact, have available a response to our imaginary egoist—based on the social nature of a social moral code. Suppose we were to ask the rational egoist concerned only to promote his own well-being to consider whether it really would be rational for him to *publicly* support the moral code benefiting only himself. How, we might ask, would he expect others to react to the idea that society recognize and teach a code that serves only his interest? The answer seems clear: any egoist who spent time supporting such a code, defending it in public and trying to have it adopted by others, would not in fact be acting rationally. For that reason, even the egoist who cares only about his own well-being would be driven toward a conception of the ideal moral code (understood, for him, in the egoistic way as the one it is in his self-interest to recognize and encourage others to adopt) that is not just acceptable from the perspective of a single person, but that could be supported by others as well. But that means, in turn, that even our egoist's conception of the ideal moral code begins to look more like the one that other people with more normal, sympathetic feelings would find ideal, namely the one that would have the best consequences for everybody. A social moral code must be one that could function in the world, which means it must be able to win general public support.

This line of thought, emphasizing the practical side of the ideal moral code, brings us finally to the issue with which we began: Would an ideal moral code (which I will now assume is the one that would have the best consequences generally, not just for one person) include principles respecting rights and just deserts, or would it, as Singer suggested, reject them completely in favor of the greater moral evil principle? The answer, I will argue, rests on the fact that an ideal moral code must not only be one that can hope to win public support, but must be practical and workable in other important ways as well. The ideal code is one that works for people as they are, or at least can be encouraged to become.

ARE RIGHTS PART OF THE IDEAL CODE?

What we want to know is whether rights (and also just desert) would be included in the ideal code, understood as the one that, in the real world, would have the best consequences. Initially, it may seem they would not, since it appears the best consequences could be realized by substituting the greater moral evil principle for entitlements, requiring people to prevent something bad whenever the cost to them is less significant than the benefit to another. That is because, unlike entitlements, the greater moral evil principle more clearly and directly expresses the consequentialism I have been defending.

But would such a single moral principle, recognized by society as their ideal, really have the best consequences? I want to suggest that the ideal code would not in fact ignore rights, for two reasons. Each is based on the fact that the ideal moral code must rest on realistic, accurate assumptions about human beings and our life in this world.

The first takes us back to the discussion of self-love and altruism. Although I did suggest, following Hume, that we ought not ignore people's altruistic side, it is also important that a social moral code not assume people are *more* altruistic than they are. Rules that would only work only for angels are not the ideal ones for a society of human beings. While we do care about others' well-being, especially those we love, we also care very deeply about ourselves. It will therefore be quite difficult to get people to accept a code requiring that they give away their savings or extra organs to a stranger simply because doing so would avoid even more evil as the greater moral evil rule would require if not balanced by entitlements. Many people simply wouldn't do as that rule would require; they care too deeply about their own lives and welfare, as well as the welfare of loved ones.

Indeed, were the moral code to attempt to require such saintliness despite these problems, three results would likely follow. First, because many would not live up to the rules, despite having been taught they should, feelings of guilt would increase. Second, such a code would encourage conflict between those who meet what they think of as their moral obligations and those who do not. Such a situation is in contrast, of course, to one in which people who give generously and selflessly are thought of as heroes who have gone beyond what is morally required. In that event, unlike instances when people don't live up to society's demands of them, the normal response is to praise them for exceeding the moral minimum. And, finally, a realistic code that doesn't demand more than people can be expected to do might actually result in more giving than one that ignores rights in favor of the greater moral evil rule. Think about trying to influence how children spend their money. Perhaps they will buy less candy if rules allow them to do so occasionally, but they are praised for spending on other things, than if its purchase is prohibited. We cannot assume that making what is now a charitable act into a requirement will always encourage such behavior. So, impractical rules would not only create guilt and social conflict, neither of which are compatible with the ideal code, but they often tend to encourage the opposite of the desired result. By giving people the right to keep their property yet praising those who do not exercise the right but help others instead, we have struck a good balance.

My second point is that an ideal moral code must not assume people are more objective, informed and unbiased than they are. People often tend, we know, to rationalize when their interests are at stake—a fact that has many implications for the sorts of principles we would included in an ideal, welfare maximizing code. For example, we might at first be tempted to discourage slavish conformity to counterproductive rules, teaching people to break promises whenever doing so would have the best consequences. But again practicality enters: an ideal code would not be blind to people's tendency to give special weight to their own welfare, or to their inability always to be objective in tracing the effects of different actions even when they want to be. So while an ideal code would not teach that promises must never be broken no matter what the consequences, we also would not want to encourage breaking promises whenever people convince themselves it would produce less evil to break their word.

Similar considerations apply to property. Imagine a situation where a person contemplates preventing an evil to herself or himself by taking something from a large store where it wouldn't be missed. Such theft could easily be rationalized by the greater moral evil principle on grounds that if stealing prevents something bad from happening (to the person deciding to steal) without sacrificing anything of comparable moral significance (the store won't miss the goods). So although a particular act of theft may sometimes be welfare maximizing, it does not follow that a *principle* like Singer's is part of an ideal code. To recognize and teach that theft is right whenever the robber is preventing greater evil, even to himself, would work only if people were far more objective, less liable to self-deception, and more knowledgeable about the long-term consequences than they are. So here again, including rights that block such conclusions in our moral code serves a useful role, discouraging the tendency to rationalize our behavior by underestimating the harm we may cause to others or exaggerating the benefits that may accrue to ourselves.

IS JUST DESERT PART OF THE IDEAL MORAL CODE?

Similar practical considerations argue for including desert as well as rights in the ideal moral code. The case of the farmers, recall, was meant to illustrate that our current social moral code encourages the attitude that people who work hard deserve to be rewarded, just as people who behave badly deserve to be punished. Most of us feel that while it be nice of the hard worker to help out a lazy neighbor, the worker also has reason—based on past effort—to refuse. But as I have stressed, it's still an open question whether an ideal code would allow such "selfishness."

But as we did with rights, here again we must be careful that our conception of an ideal code is realistic and practical, and does not assume people are more altruistic, informed or objective than they are. To see why this is relevant to the principle of just desert, we should first notice that for many people, at least, working and earning a living is not their favorite activity. People would often prefer to spend time doing something else, but know they must work if they and their family hope to have a decent life. Indeed, if humans generally are to live well then goods and services must be produced and made available for wide use, which means (I want to argue) incentives to work are an important factor in motivating people.

One such incentive, of course, is income. A moral code can encourage hard work by allowing people to keep a large part of what they earn, both through respecting rights and the principle of just desert."I worked hard for it, so I can keep it" is a familiar thought that expresses this attitude.

But suppose we eliminated the notion of deserving what we work for from our code, and asked people to follow the greater moral evil rule instead. What might happen? There are three possibilities. One is that they continue to produce as before, only this time motivated by the desire—derived from their social moral code—to prevent whatever evil they can, as long as the cost to them of doing so is not greater evil. But again that seems to me quite unrealistic: though people are not egoists, neither are they that saintly and altruistic.

Given that, one of two other outcomes could be expected. One is that people would stop working as hard, feeling that it is no longer worth the effort to help strangers rather than themselves or their family since they are morally required to give away all but what they can use without imposing a greater evil on anybody else. Suppose, to make it vivid, that the tax system enforces the greater moral evil rule, taking away all income that could be used to prevent a greater evil befalling somebody else. The result would be less work done, less total production of useful commodities, and therefore a general reduction in people's well-being. The other possibility is that people would simply fail to live up to the standards of society's moral code (having replaced desert with the greater moral evil rule), leading to widespread feelings of guilt and resentment by those (few?) who do behave as the code commands. In either case, I am suggesting, replacing the principle of just desert with the greater moral evil principle would actually worsen the situation. Like rights, the principle of just desert is also part of an ideal code.

CONCLUSION

The first sections of this paper attempted to show that our moral code is a bit schizophrenic. It seems to pull us in opposite directions, sometimes toward helping people who are in need based and other times toward the view that rights and desert justify keeping things we have even if greater evil could be avoided were we to give away our extra eye or our savings account. This apparent inconsistency led us to a further question: Is the emphasis on rights and desert really defensible, or should we try to resolve the tension in our own code by rejecting entitlements in favor of the greater moral evil rule? In the last sections I have considered this question, focusing on the idea that we should understand the ideal moral code as the one that if acknowledged and taught would have the over-all best consequences. Having suggested why it might seem sensible to conceive the ideal code this way, as the one that would produce the best consequences, I concluded by showing that an ideal code would not reject entitlements in favor of the greater moral evil rule. Concern that our moral code encourage effort and not fail because it unrealistically assumes people are more altruistic, informed, or objective than they are means that our rules giving people rights to their possessions and encouraging distribution according to desert are part of an ideal moral code. The ideal moral code would therefore not teach people to try to seek the best consequences in each individual case, insisting they give entitlements no weight whatsoever. But neither have I argued, nor do I believe, that an ideal moral code would allow people to overlook those in desperate need by making entitlements absolute, any more than it would ignore entitlements in favor of the greater moral evil rule discussed earlier.

But where would it draw the line? It's hard to know, of course, but the following seems to me to be a sensible stab at an answer. Concerns of the sort I have outlined argue strongly against expecting too much of people's selflessness or ability to make objective and informed decisions. A more modest proposal would require people to help strangers when there is no substantial cost to themselves, that is, when what they are sacrificing would not mean *significant* reduction in their own or their families' level of happiness. Since most people's savings accounts and nearly everybody's second kidney are not insignificant, entitlements would in those cases outweigh another's need. But if what is at stake is truly trivial, as dirtying one's clothes would normally be, then an ideal moral code would not allow rights to override the greater evil that can be prevented.

Another point is that, again mindful of the need to be realistic in what it expects of people, an ideal code might also distinguish between cases in which the evil is directly present to a person (as in the drowning child) and cases involving distant people. The reason, of course, is again practical: people will be more likely to help people with whom they have direct contact and can see immediately the evil they will prevent than they are to help distant strangers. So while such a distinction may seem morally arbitrary, viewed from the perspective of an ideal moral code it seems to make good sense.

Despite our code's unclear and sometimes schizophrenic posture, it seems to me that these conclusions are not that different from our current moral attitudes; an ideal moral code thus might not be a great deal different from our own. We tend to fault selfish people who give little or nothing to charity, and expect those with more to give more. Yet we do not ask people to make large sacrifices of their own or their family's well-being in order to aid distant strangers. What Singer's arguments do remind us of, however, is that entitlements are not absolute and we all have some duty to help. But the greater moral evil rule expresses only part of the story, and is not needed to make that point.[17]

---

[17]One final qualification is worth emphasizing. The subject of this essay has been the ideal moral code that we should adopt for our *private*, non-political relations, not the character of a just constitution and tax structure. It is therefore possible to argue that while the ideal moral code correctly captures the personal duties we owe to everybody, including foreigners and strangers, a just political order requires more extensive help to fellow citizens with whom we share the basic institutions of society. Many reasons could be given for making such a distinction, including the fact that it may be more practical to expect people to provide welfare when undertaken collectively, by government, than to do so on their own in the form of private charity enforced only by morality's informal sanctions. People may also be more inclined to look to the needs of people near home, who share a common national identity and history. Nor, finally, should we conclude that political justice must be

Questions

1. Why does John Arthur think that distant strangers have no right to our assistance?
2. John Arthur thinks that any moral code that required as much of us as Peter Singer suggests is required of us would be impractical. To what extent can current levels of altruism be taken as an indication of the levels of altruism of which members of our species are capable?
3. What does John Arthur's revised principle say about the drowning child case? On this principle, how extensive are our duties to the world's absolute poor?

---

understood in the same, utilitarian way that I have been defending here. While understanding private morality in terms of an ideal moral code that has the best over-all consequences, we might nevertheless conceive of political relationships and social justice in terms of the social contract, asking which constitutional arrangements could win universal consent. [The major proponent of this view of course is John Rawls's, *A Theory of Justice* (Cambridge: Harvard University Press, 1971).] It is therefore possible that justice is both philosophically distinct and also more demanding than is the ideal social moral code. Tax provisions securing a minimum income and fair equality of opportunity, for example, may be owed to other citizens on grounds of social justice (though many of the points I made earlier would apply in both contexts, including especially the need to provide incentives.) That Rawlsian approach to political justice seems to me quite consistent with the idea that we need not, as private citizens, give away our savings merely because we can prevent evil to another human being who would benefit more from them.

Famine and Charity

John M. Whelan Jr.

John Whelan argues both that (1) no purchase one makes, no matter how frivolous, can be faulted morally for being a failure to give charity and that (2) giving to famine relief charities is not morally optional in the way that giving to the local symphony is. Although the combination of these two views may seem contradictory, there is a difference, he says, between what one is morally required to do and what one morally ought to do even though one is not required to do it.

He considers an analogy—inspired by, and similar to, Peter Singer's drowning child—of a starving child next to the Coke machine. One has the choice of either buying oneself a Coke or giving her one's Coke money so that she can buy food for herself. In such a case, the author says that one ought to give one's Coke money to the child (even though one is not required to do so in that the child has no right to the money). He denies, however, that one ought to ask, before one makes any purchase, whether there is some starving person somewhere who could benefit more from the money that one is about to spend. He advances two reasons for this. (a) First, contributing to famine relief charities does not prevent anyone who would have starved from starving. This is, in part, because famine relief agencies do not increase the amount of food they provide as a result of receiving one's $25 contribution. (b) Second, if one views one's contribution not as the saving of a single additional life but as a fractional share of the whole famine relief enterprise, then one needs to compare that benefit (some exceedingly small fraction of the overall benefit, say, one-thirteenth-millionth) with the benefit one could have secured for oneself with that money. The author's claim is not that the benefit to the needy is less than the benefit to oneself. Instead, his claim is that the benefits simply cannot be compared and thus spending the money on oneself cannot be unfavorably compared to contributing it to charity.

He anticipates the objection that if everybody reasoned in this way then nobody would give to charity and that would be very bad. He replies that this objection would be a good one only if he were arguing against the view that people ought to give to charity. Although we are not required in any given instance to give to

John Whelan Jr., "Famine and Charity," *Southern Journal of Philosophy*, vol. 29, no. 1 (1991): 149–166.

charity, failure to ever give would consti-
tute complete neglect of the suffering of

the others and that is something that is
susceptible to negative moral evaluation.

Glancing through my favorite magazine I read: 'Five things you can do for 72 cents or less . . . 1. Enjoy a cup of coffee. 2. Pick up a newspaper. 3. Buy a few stamps. 4. Have a soft drink. Or 5. Make a lasting difference in the life of a child and family overseas through Foster Parents Plan'. I opt for the soft drink. Is my purchase of it and consequent failure to help the family a failure to do something that I am morally required to do, as for example a failure to save a child from drowning would be? Or is it a failure to do something that I morally ought to do even though I am not morally required to do it, as for example a failure to hold the door for someone carrying a heavy package would be? Or is it just a failure to be as generous as I possibly could be, and therefore, merely a matter of doing less than the ideal? Or is there some other possibility?

The view I will try to defend is that, on the one hand, no purchase of mine, no matter how frivolous, can be faulted morally for being a failure to give to charity; and on the other, that giving to charities like the Foster Parents Plan is not morally optional in the way that, for example, giving to the local symphony is.

My view is closely related, obviously, to the traditional view about charity. And both views face two problems. The first is suggested by the customary phrase 'duty of charity': it seems contradictory to say that anyone has a duty to do what she does not have to do. And my conclusions seem to be similarly paradoxical: how can it be true, as my view seems to suggest, that giving to charity is both optional and also something that ought to be done? Second, many philosophers and others believe that my first claim is false; they believe that many of our purchases can be faulted morally for being failures to give, for example, to famine relief.[1] In support of this they note that the world has changed radically since the traditional view was formulated; disparities in wealth are much greater; and it is possible to prevent terrible suffering in other parts of the world by giving to charity. As a result, they believe that many of our more frivolous purchases *can* be faulted morally for being failures to give to charity.

---

[1]Among philosophers, Peter Singer is notable for producing a careful argument for this conclusion. But roughly the same argument has regularly been made from one or another pulpit for a long time. Versions of Singer's argument appear in the following places: 'Famine, Affluence, and Morality', *Philosophy and Public Affairs*, v1, (1972); 'Reconsidering the Famine Relief Argument', *Food Policy: The Responsibility of the U.S. in the Life and Death Choices,* Peter Brown and Henry Shue (eds.), (New York: The Free Press, 1977); *Practical Ethics* (New York: Cambridge, 1979) pp. 158–181. In this last he explicitly mentions stylish clothes, color televisions, second cars, private schools, and expensive meals as examples of purchases that probably ought to be foregone in favor of charitable giving.

In the remainder of this essay I will try to show, first, that the line of reasoning I just sketched is fallacious, so that whatever else can be said about our more frivolous purchases, they are not morally defective for being failures to give to charity; and, second, that we ought to give to charity, even though we do not have, in any serious sense, a duty or obligation to.[2]

I

The questions with which I began this essay distinguished what I am morally required to do from what I morally ought to do even though I am not required to do it. And in my opinion discussions of charity are hampered by not attending to this distinction. In particular it is commonly assumed that if I am not morally required on some occasion to give to charity, then it must be the case that giving to charity on that occasion is strictly optional: a nice thing to do, but not something that ought to be done.[3] It is important to be clear that this assumption is false, so I want to say a bit about the distinction.

Let me begin with two definitions: Jones is morally required to do x on some occasion if and only if there is a *moral requirement* on Jones to do x on that occasion and there is not a more important reason for Jones to refrain from doing x. Jones ought to but is not required to do x on some occasion if and only if there is a *moral reason* for Jones to do x on that occasion, the moral reason does not amount to a moral requirement, and there is not a more important reason for Jones to refrain from doing x.

Some Examples of Moral Requirements. Moral requirements can be specified against assault, theft, lying, cheating, breaking promises, failing to do your duty, and so on. Examples could easily be multiplied, but each would be an example of an obligation voluntarily taken on, as in the case of a promise, or of a duty associated with some particular social role and (for the most part) voluntarily assumed, as when someone becomes a parent or policeman or professor, or of what are traditionally (and in my view misleadingly) called 'natural duties', like the requirements against assault, theft, cheating, lying, and so forth.

---

[2]Let me emphasize here that my essay has a quite specific focus: are any of our purchases morally defective for being failures to give to charities which try to help people who are starving? This focus is quite different from, for example, Onora O'Neill's in *Faces of Hunger* (London: Allen and Unwin, 1986). In that essay she argues for "far reaching political activity which transforms the basic principles of economic and social structures." (*op. cit.* p. 145.) Perhaps such a transformation is needed, but meanwhile each of us must confront the question of whether he or she has an obligation to do something about poverty and starvation by contributing to charity.

[3]To cite just a few examples, in a book devoted to this topic, William Aiken and Hugh La Follette (eds.) *World Hunger and Moral Obligation* (Englewood Cliffs, New Jersey: Prentice Hall, 1977) the following authors explicitly assume that if there is no duty or requirement to give to charity, then giving is, strictly speaking, optional: Aiken and La Follette, 'Introduction', pp. 2–3; John Arthur, 'Rights and the Duty to Bring Aid', p. 48; Jan Narveson, 'Morality and Starvation', p. 52; William Aiken, 'The Right to be Saved from Starvation', p. 86.

Some Examples of Moral Reasons That Do Not Amount to Requirements (Hereafter I Will Refer to These Simply as Moral Reasons). Jones can easily open the door for someone who is carrying a large package; so there is a moral reason for her to do so, but not a requirement. Smith can give candy to all of the Halloween 'trick-or-treaters'; consequently there is a moral reason for him to do so, but he does not violate a requirement even if he refrains out of prejudice from giving candy to the one black child. Brown coerces (but does not force) her teenage son into dressing and grooming as *she* chooses. There is a moral reason for her not to do this, but it does not amount to a requirement. White tells Smith a true, but embarrassing story he has heard, let us say at twelfth hand, about Jones. There is a moral reason for him not to gratuitously hurt Jones's reputation like this, but it is not a requirement. Blue goes out of his way to do a favor for Green; there is a moral reason for Green to express his gratitude to Blue, but he is not required to.

Two Comments. In saying there is no moral requirement against doing (or failing to do) any of these things, I do not mean to imply that doing any of them is morally acceptable. On the contrary, if there is a moral reason against doing something, then it ought not to be done unless there is a more important reason in favor of doing it. And I do not mean to imply either that moral requirements ought always to prevail over moral reasons in our deliberations about what to do.

So what do I mean to imply? Giving a full answer to this question, every point clarified and defended, would take me too far from my main topic; however, the most important part of that answer would be this: if there is a moral requirement on Jones to do x and there is not a more important reason for Jones to refrain from doing x, then someone may *demand* that Jones do x; whereas if Jones merely ought to do x, then, although Jones is liable for moral criticism for failing to do x, no one may demand that she do it. Further, if Jones is required to do x and she fails to do it, then someone may demand that Jones offer an apology, explanation, compensation, or rectification (whichever is appropriate); but if Jones fails to do what she merely ought to do, then no one may make such a demand.

This condition fits my reaction to cases: for example on the occasions when Jones is required to keep her promise, Smith may demand that Jones keep it, and if Jones breaks it, and Smith does not know why, then Smith may demand an explanation, and depending on what the explanation is perhaps also an apology. And if Smith suffered a serious loss as a result, then possibly he can demand compensation as well. However, if Jones fails to do what she ought but is not required to do, then perhaps explanations or apologies will be *expected*, but they may not be demanded. For example if Blue does a big favor for Green, then, as we say, Green 'owes Blue a debt of gratitude', but this "debt" is precisely unlike a debt incurred as a result of a contract in that payment cannot be demanded. Reactions diverge with respect to Smith and the Halloween candy: some share my reaction that Smith has not violated a requirement; others disagree. But to the best of my knowledge reactions do not diverge about this: *if* Smith violates a requirement by refusing to give the black child some candy, then others may demand that he rectify the situation.

The expression 'may demand' of course means is permitted morally to demand, and on my view the permission to demand compliance with it is essentially involved in the justification of any moral requirement; so the permission is justified in whatever way the requirement is justified. By contrast no one is permitted morally to demand that I do what there is merely a moral reason that I do: persuasion and criticism are the only "weapons" we may use to get people to do what they ought but are not required to do.

I am aware that what I have just written raises all sorts of questions, but for present purposes I hope this much can be conceded: 'Jones morally must do x' is stronger than 'Jones morally ought to do x'; and therefore there may be circumstances in which it is true that Jones morally ought to do something even though it is not true that she must do it, and similarly that it may be true that she ought to do something even though it is not true that she is required or has a duty or obligation to do it.

If I am right about this, then we should expect to find circumstances in which Jones, for example, is required to prevent harm, and also circumstances in which she ought to prevent it even though she is not required to. I believe this expectation is met. For example, most people believe that there is a moral requirement to save someone from drowning when it would be easy to do so, and most believe that there is a moral reason to hold the door for someone whose arms are filled with heavy packages. Roughly speaking, what distinguishes the first sort of case from the second is this: there is a requirement on Jones to prevent harm to Smith when there is sufficient reason to believe that the harm she can prevent is serious and undeserved, when there is also sufficient reason to believe that she can prevent this harm at little or no cost to herself, and also that preventing the harm will benefit Smith; and when, in addition, there is *not* sufficient reason to believe that Smith or anyone else will prevent the harm if she does not prevent it. By contrast the conditions under which there is a moral reason for Jones to prevent harm to Smith are much looser. The harm need not be serious, the cost to Jones need not be small in absolute terms only small in relation to the seriousness of the harm that Jones can prevent, and it does not matter whether others will help if Jones does not. What matters is whether Jones's failure to help favors her own relatively unimportant interest at the expense of an interest of Smith's which is much more important; whether, in other words, Jones favors her own interest in an objectionably selfish way. Very roughly and in sum: Jones *must* prevent harm to Smith when the harm she can prevent is serious, and it will not get prevented unless Jones prevents it; whereas Jones ought but is not required to prevent harm to Smith when it would be objectionably selfish not to.

II

Now I can take up two of the main questions of this essay: Does it follow from the fact that there are occasions when I am required to prevent harm that there are occasions when I am required to give to charity? And does it follow from the fact that there are occasions when I ought but am not required to prevent harm that there are occasions when I ought but am not required to give to charity? In my view the answer to both questions is 'No'. And I will try to show that this answer is correct by showing that there are no occasions when anyone *ought* to give, since if there are no occasions when the loose conditions described above are met, then there can be none when the more strict conditions for a requirement are met, and so none when anyone has a duty to forego some purchase and give the money she thereby saves to charity; and, if it is assumed that rights and requirements are connected, then this will also show that no one has a right against anyone that she forego some purchase and give the money to charity.

However, I must admit that a strong argument can be made for the opposite conclusion. Informal reasoning for that conclusion might go something like this. Suppose after reading the advertisement for the Foster Parents Plan, I head off for the Coke machine with fifty cents in my pocket, and when I get there, a child is standing next to it who manifestly needs money for food much more than I need the Coke. Not that she will die if she does not eat soon, and not that she may not be able to get food somewhere else, but she is very hungry now, and I can easily buy her something to eat at no sacrifice to myself. In circumstances like these it seems obvious that I ought to give her my Coke money, though of course I am not required to, have no duty to, and the child has no right against me that I do so. And it can also seem obvious that it is only my callousness and lack of imagination which prevents me from seeing that the actual situation when I buy a Coke is often in all morally relevant ways exactly like this hypothetical situation. After all, it is often true that my need for the Coke is small, and a starving child's need for food is always great. If this is correct, then what follows is that *I ought to use the need of a starving child as a kind of yardstick whenever I buy anything.* Before each purchase I ought to ask myself: is this purchase objectionably selfish given that I could send the money to a charity which will help people who are starving? And if the answer is 'Yes' and I make the purchase anyway, then in making it I will have done something just as wrong as turning my back on the hungry child at the Coke machine. I will not have violated a requirement or failed at any duty that I have, but I will have done something I ought not to have done.

These informal reflections lead to the following argument: 1. No one ought to do anything which constitutes an objectionably selfish failure to prevent harm. 2. A purchase constitutes such a failure if the money spent on it could be used to prevent harm, and preventing that harm is much more important than the benefit produced by the purchase. 3. Many of our purchases are for relatively unimportant things, the money spent on them could be sent to charities which prevent hunger and disease, and preventing those harms is much more important than making those purchases. Therefore, 4. many of our purchases ought not to be made.

This argument seems to me to be both radical in its implications and difficult to fault. Radical in its implications because not many of us think that each and every one of our purchases ought to be justified by comparing its importance to us with the importance of food to a starving child, nor do we think that it is wrong to make purchases which cannot be justified in that way. Difficult to fault because, as I will show in the next section, none of the objections typically made to roughly similar arguments undermine this one.

But before I get to that let me make two comments by way of clarification. First, a defender of this argument need not claim that many are now to *blame* for the objectionably selfish way they spend their money. Not many realize they are being objectionably selfish when they buy a Coke, and perhaps they are not to blame for failing to realize it. However, this does not invalidate the conclusion that they are spending their money in a way that they ought not to spend it.

Second, as should be obvious, the argument above is indebted to Peter Singer's well-known article 'Famine, Affluence, and Morality'.[4] That article elicited a powerful response when it was first published in 1972. Why? Certainly not because Singer argued that we ought to give money to charities designed to help people who are starving: that conclusion has been a commonplace in our moral tradition for a long time. Rather it was because Singer's article suggested this different conclusion: no purchase is morally justified unless the money spent on it brings about a benefit which is at least as important, impartially considered, as the harm that could be prevented if that money were used to prevent people from starving. Singer derived that conclusion from this premise: 'if we can prevent something bad from happening without sacrificing something of comparable moral significance, then we ought to do it'. Many philosophers would now reject that premise because they believe that we need not act based on the result of this sort of impartial comparison: doing so, in their view, demands too much of us.[5] These philosophers believe that it is acceptable morally to give our own projects and desires weight out of proportion to the weight they have when considered from an impartial point of view.[6] However, my argument shows that this objection can be avoided. Someone is objectionably selfish only if she favors herself *too much*. And a defender of my argument can admit (even insist) that there are irresolvable differences about when that point is reached. These differences arise on account of differences in the relative importance people assign to preventing various sorts of harm as opposed to making particular purchases, and also to differences about how great people think the gap between the two needs to be before it is objectionably selfish to make the purchase. For this, and other reasons, judgments about which purchases are objectionably selfish may differ somewhat. Be that as it may, all but the most heartless egoist must admit that there comes a point where favoring her own relatively unimportant interest over someone else's much more important

---

[4]*Loc. cit.*

[5]Bernard Williams' name is most often associated with this claim, but many philosophers echo it. See for example, Bernard Williams, 'A Critique of Utilitarianism', J. J. C. Smart and Williams, *Utilitarianism: For and Against* (New York: Cambridge, 1973); 'Persons, Character, and Morality', and 'Utilitarianism and Moral Self-Indulgence', both reprinted in his *Moral Luck* (New York: Cambridge, 1981). For a dissenting view, see Shelly Kagan's intricate and comprehensive discussion of these issues in his *The Limits of Morality* (Oxford: Clarendon Press, 1989).

[6]This way of putting the point derives from Samuel Scheffler *The Rejection of Consequentialism* (New York: Oxford, 1982).

interest is objectionably selfish, and consequently ought not to be done. My argument would therefore seem to demonstrate not merely the commonplace that we ought on occasion to give something to charity, but also the unsettling conclusions that some and possibly many of our purchases can be faulted morally for being failures to give to charity, and also that each and every one of them ought to be justified in the light of a starving child's need for food.

III

It would be wrong not to buy food for the child by the side of the Coke machine, why would it not therefore be wrong for someone to purchase a Coke when she could easily do without it, and could then send the money to charity which would prevent children from starving? And more generally, why does it not follow that we ought to measure each of our purchases against the need of a starving child for food?

Some think the reason is distance: one child is far away, the other is close at hand.—'Out of sight out of mind' is undoubtedly a psychological truth, and for that reason perhaps we ought not to blame those who do not give, but it is not a moral truth, so it is hard to see that it has anything to do with whether we ought to give.

'If the child is close at hand, we can be *certain* that our money will do her some good; if we send it to a charity in another part of the world, who knows? Perhaps the food will rot on the dock; perhaps it will be used for political purposes; perhaps the charity will be run by unscrupulous men for their own profit'. Perhaps. But there are reputable charities, and with respect to them, these risks are slight.

'The sick and starving are to blame for their poverty; so we should not help them'. This is dubious (though many people believe it) but suppose it were true. . . . Suppose a child was drowning because she ignored a warning sign, would it then be morally acceptable to allow her to drown?

'Giving to famine relief will only lead to more children, and therefore to more of a problem in the long run'. This is probably not true as a matter of fact, but suppose it were. . . . What follows is that we ought to give to charities which provide more than food, not that we ought not give to charity.

'Others with much more money can give more easily than I can'. True, but not enough money will be given; I can sometimes give without sacrificing anything important, my money will do some good, so it would seem that I ought to give it.

Many philosophers identify morality with what they are required to do, obligated to do, with what it is their responsibility or duty to do, with what others have a right against them that they do. So they make objections like this: 'Maybe it would be *nice* if I gave to charity, but it is not something that I *have* to do; therefore it is not something that I am wrong for not doing'. But this simply does not follow. True, it is not the case that I *have* to give, but it does not follow that it is not the case that I *ought* to give. And certainly it is wrong to fail to do what I ought to do. Put another way: to be objectionably selfish is not merely to fail to be nice.

'My money is just a drop in the bucket; I cannot help everyone'. Suppose there are more hungry children by the Coke machine than I have money to help, does it follow that I should not help any of them? What would seem to follow is that, on that occasion, I ought to help as many as I can up to the point where it would not be objectionably selfish to fail to help more.

And if this is what I ought to do on that occasion, then this is what I ought to do on every occasion; I ought to monitor each of my purchases with the thought of a starving child: before each purchase I should ask myself, would it be objectionably selfish to buy *this* given that the money spent on it could prevent a child from starving? And what follows from the argument in Section II is that no purchase which it would be objectionably selfish to make in the face of the need of a starving child ought to be made, and the money saved thereby ought to be sent to a charity designed to help people who are poor and suffering.

IV

Arguments of the kind I described in Section II are basically arguments from analogy which lead to the conclusion that many of our purchases are currently unrecognized instances of a familiar pattern: I do not hold the door for someone whose arms are filled with packages when I easily could; I do not give the starving child by the side of the Coke machine money for food when I have no important use for it; my wife and I do not eat at the cheaper restaurant for $45, but eat instead at the extravagant one for $70 when the difference in our enjoyment is not great, and the $25 saved could buy food and make a significant difference in the lives of starving children. The conclusion seems inescapable that this last purchase, and potentially many others, is objectionably selfish.

I will criticize this sort of argument in two stages: first, I will show that it is impossible, by contributing to any actual charity, to prevent people from starving in the way that those who argue as I described above typically suppose; second, I will show that the actual benefit paid for by giving money to a charity cannot unfavorably be compared with the benefit paid for by any frivolous purchase.

In moods when I am troubled by the argument above, I dimly imagine something like this: my $25 is sent to some charity and starving people get to eat $25 worth of food; my money is not sent and these people continue to starve: I imagine that my money can make this significant difference in the life of these starving people, and I wonder how, in the face of their need, I can use it to bring about small pleasures.

But these thoughts are a delusion; my money cannot make that difference. No charitable organization will alter the amount of money budgeted for food because my $25 does or does not arrive. Furthermore, it is senseless to think that my money could be, so to speak, "tracked" and we could thereby determine what effect its arriving on some particular day has or lacks. Finally, charities need to pay for all sorts of things—salaries, vacations, paper, advertising, equipment, and so forth—so my $25 cannot be said to make the difference between no food or $25 worth of food for people who are starving. If I do not send my money to some charity, then that charity will have that much less money to pay for all of the things that it needs to buy; it's ability to help people who are starving will be slightly less because I will have failed to pay for a fractional share of all the kinds of things the charity buys.

These considerations are enough to prove the following: I cannot send $25 to a charity and bring it about that starving people will get to eat $25 worth of food that they would not have gotten to eat otherwise; therefore, if it is objectionably selfish to eat at the more expensive restaurant, it is not because by doing so I fail to make this significant difference in the lives of the people who are starving. If there is a comparison which calls my purchase of the expensive meal into question, it is not this one.

But perhaps that purchase is objectionably selfish for another reason; perhaps it is selfish because it is a failure to pay for a fractional share of everything that a reputable charity needs to buy in order to help people who are starving. In order to get a feel for what this benefit might amount to, consider CARE. In 1989 CARE USA employed approximately 7500 people in 36 developing countries. These people helped provide emergency relief assistance: flood in Bangladesh, earthquake in Armenia, hurricane in the Caribbean, drought and civil war in the Sudan, Ethiopia, Somalia, and Mozambique; CARE claims to have distributed approximately 230,000 tons of food; estimates vary about the number of people who got the food, but the number is certainly in the millions. In addition CARE employees helped vaccinate 600,000 children, helped build water systems, distributed food supplements, helped plant 29 million trees, taught farmers about safer, more efficient growing techniques, helped thousands of people start and sustain small businesses, and many other things. The cost for doing all of this was $325 million. This means that each failure to contribute $25 to CARE in 1989 was a failure to increase by about one thirteen millionth the net benefit produced by CARE in that year. However, each failure to contribute $25 to charities which help people who are starving was not just a failure to contribute to CARE: it was a failure to contribute to each of the charities which do more or less what CARE does; so it was a failure to increase a much larger benefit by a much smaller fraction. Nonetheless, for my purposes it will be enough to focus on this question: is one thirteen millionth of the just described benefit significantly larger or smaller than the benefit produced by spending $25 for a more extravagant meal?

In my view the answer to that question is completely obvious: it has no answer. And if I am right about this, then it follows that no purchase of mine is objectionably selfish because it is a failure to give to a charity like CARE because there is no way to make the comparison which needs to be made if any purchase is to be called into question for being a failure to give to CARE. Note: my conclusion is *not* that the benefit brought about by my contribution is small in relation to the benefit brought about by my purchase of the meal; my conclusion is that there is no way to make this comparison.

Suppose someone disagreed with me about this, suppose she thinks it is obvious that one thirteen millionth of the benefit produced by CARE is vastly more important than the benefit produced by the more expensive meal. Or suppose she thinks the benefit brought about by a contribution to CARE is less important, could she defend her assertion? And in general, how do we defend claims of this kind?

Consider: someone disagrees that the benefit brought about by holding the door for someone whose arms are filled with heavy packages is more important than the exertion she would have to make to bring it about, what could I say to her? For one thing I could ask her to consider what she would want if roles were reversed. But suppose she is a self-reliant egoist . . . then I could ask instead which of these two things would be worse if it happened: you have to struggle through some door with your arms filled with heavy packages or you have to make the exertion necessary to open that same door (not the emotional exertion necessary to open it *for* someone, just the exertion necessary to open it)? The answer, I take it, is obvious. And again: which would be worse, that you have to forego the enjoyment of a Coke or that you have to continue starving? Again obvious. And now compare: which is worse, that you have to give up the pleasure of a more expensive meal or that each of the people who benefit from CARE in a year have to give up one thirteen millionth of the benefit?

With respect to this last question, it seems obvious to me that we have absolutely no idea what the answer is, and no idea how to find out. And this feeling of mine can be supported like this: our normal use of predicates like 'objectionably selfish' presupposes that we can confidently sort comparisons of individual well-being into one of three categories: that x happens to A is worse than that y happens to B, or that x happens to A is better than that y happens to B, or that reasons can be given for either answer, and so we must agree that the answer is uncertain. For example, I can remember as a child arguing about whether it would be worse for someone to lose his sight or his hearing. The argument was interesting because we could think of reasons to argue both sides: it was possible to try to extend our experience; to imagine and compare. But nothing like this is even *possible* when what we are trying to compare is some individual benefit with the result of the following pseudo-calculation: add the roughly estimated number of benefits of a roughly "estimated" magnitude that CARE, for example, brings about in a year, then subtract the roughly estimated number of losses of the roughly "estimated" magnitude that CARE also produces in a year, divide the result by 325 million, and then multiply by the cost of the frivolous individual benefit.

To call something objectionably selfish, to say that it belongs in the same category as the refusal to give a starving child money that was to buy a Coke, is to make a serious charge of immorality. If the charge is to be defensibly made, then it must be anchored in comparative judgments of well-being that almost all of us can immediately appreciate. That is why people are troubled by the (delusory) thought that the money spent on their more frivolous purchases could make a significant difference in the lives of people who are starving. And that is also why the charge cannot defensibly be made when it depends on a comparison between some individual benefit and the fractional part of a net benefit paid for by a contribution to, for example, CARE.

At this point someone might make the following objection: "True, each person's failure to give may only make a slight difference; so no one of those failures is objectionably selfish. But if everyone reasoned as you do, then no one would give to charity, and that would make a large difference to the well-being of lots of people."[7] This would be a good objection if I were arguing that it is not the case that people ought to give to charity because failing to give only makes a slight difference. But that is not what I have been arguing. My conclusion so far is only that a particular argument is defective; an argument which has the quite radical conclusion that many of my purchases are objectionably selfish for not being contributions to charity, and also that each of my purchases ought to be justified in the light of a starving child's need for food. It is one thing to show that this argument is defective, and that these conclusions are unsupported, and quite another to show that it is not the case that we ought on occasion to give to charity.

In my view philosophers equate attempting to refute this argument with attempting to argue that it is not the case that we ought to give to charity because they assume that people will give to charity only under the delusion that their contributions will make a significant difference in the lives of some of those who are starving—certainly advertisements of the kind that I mentioned at the beginning of this essay aim to keep that delusion alive. Nevertheless, the fact that people give to, for example, cancer research, shows that they will give to charities even if they are well aware that their contribution will have no individually important effect.

Furthermore, I made two criticisms of the argument of Section II and neither of them had anything to do with claiming that contributions to charity only make a slight difference: I claimed first that my, for example, $25 contribution cannot make the difference in the lives of people who are starving that the purchase of $25 worth of food could make; and I claimed second that there is no way to compare the effect that my contribution in fact does have with the benefit I would have to forego in order to make it.

---

[7]My consideration of this objection is prompted by reflection on "Five Mistakes in Moral Mathematics", Chapter 3 of Derek Parfit's *Reasons and Persons* (Oxford: Oxford University Press, 1987). Parfit tries to show there that I may have a reason to contribute to some project *because of the effect that contribution has* even in circumstances where that effect is imperceptible. I agree.

He considers a case where I have to choose whether to add the water in my one pint water bottle to 999 other pints which have already been poured into a water cart which is about to go into the desert to help 1000 thirsty men. This case would be analogous to the actual situation when we have to decide whether to give to charity if it were changed in at least the following ways: people are always thirsty and always in the desert, the water cart is always leaving, there are lots of uses, though many of them are frivolous, to which the water might be put by those who have to decide whether to donate, one pint donated does not mean one pint received, there are costs associated with getting the water to the thirsty men which those sending the water have to pay, and finally those sending the water have to decide *not* whether they would have a reason in these circumstances to donate their water (I believe they would), and *not* whether in these circumstances they ought sometimes to donate their water (I believe they sometimes should), but whether not sending some particular pint and using it for something else is objectionably selfish on some particular occasion.

To summarize: the argument I sketched in Section II is unsound; as a result it does not follow that I ought to think about what to give to charity by comparing the importance of each of my purchases with the importance of the harm I could prevent by foregoing it. And it also does not follow that what I ought to give in a month (day? year?) is what is left over after all of my not objectionably selfish purchases have been made. However, it does not follow from either of these conclusions that it is not the case that I sometimes ought to give to charities which aim to help people who are starving.

V

Before going on to the final part of this, let me try to put what I have argued so far into a larger perspective. In the background of the debate over consequentialism, understood as the doctrine that agents ought to perform the act with the best consequences impartially considered, has been the thought that if consequentialism is true, then many of our purchases can be faulted morally for being failures to give to charity; and if consequentialism is not true, then our current attitudes toward charitable giving are justified.[8]

I have tried to challenge both of these assumptions. In Section II I showed that a strong argument can be made for the conclusion that many of our purchases can be faulted morally for being failures to give to charity without assuming that consequentialism is true: a much weaker premise calls many of our purchases into question. And in Section IV I showed why that argument failed. An implication of what I had to say in that section is that it does not follow that I ought to give to famine relief even if consequentialism is true: the idea that it does follow assumes that giving and failing to give to charity have effects on the well-being of individuals which these acts cannot have.

VI

I said at the beginning of this essay that we ought to give to some charities, and now let me add, to charities which effectively attempt to prevent various sorts of serious harm. Giving to charities like these is not merely nice; it is something that we ought to do. In view of the foregoing, I need to clarify this last clause. Obviously I do not mean that any particular purchase can be faulted morally for being a failure to give to charity. And if moral evaluation were ultimately only a matter of evaluating acts and failures to act, then my view would be paradoxical because I would be saying about some act both that I ought to perform it, and that performing it is optional. Further, if acts and failures to act were the only objects of moral evaluation, then the dissatisfaction many morally sensitive people feel at the amount of their charitable giving would have to be attributed to confusion: no reasonable person ought to feel dissatisfied about failing to do what is, after all, optional, strictly speaking.

---

[8]This thought is explicit on the first page of *The Limits of Morality.*

But despite what many moral theorists assume, acts and failures to act are not the only objects of moral evaluation. And despite what others assume, acts, failures to act, and dispositions to act are not the only objects either. When people feel dissatisfied at the inadequacy of their response to famine relief, for example, they are not dissatisfied with themselves for failing to give on some particular occasion when they ought to have given—as someone would doubtless feel dissatisfied with herself for not saving someone from drowning when she easily could have. Nor are they dissatisfied with themselves for lacking some disposition to act. Rather they are dissatisfied with a set of their expenditures when that set is viewed in the light of the world's need; and so perhaps they say to themselves, "I ought to give more."

Those who believe moral evaluation has only to do with acts and failures to act must believe that our expenditures either succeed or fail to pass moral muster one by one. And I tried to show in Section IV that from that point of view none of our expenditures, not even the most frivolous, can be faulted morally for being a failure to give to charity. Nonetheless, I also believe that if I do not work enough charitable giving into my budget, then an entire set of my expenditures is morally defective in an important way; and therefore, giving to some charities is something that I sometimes ought to do.

In sum, the paradox I have mentioned is resolved like this: each of my charitable contributions is, strictly speaking, optional; however, giving to a charity at least once within an indeterminate period of time is not optional. Put another way: I am not blamable morally for failing to give to charity on any occasion, but if a large enough set of my purchases lacks a contribution to charity, then I *am* blamable morally for that.

This last conclusion needs defense from at least three points of view. First, it might be claimed that the effect of my earlier arguments is to undermine the only reason anyone could have to give to charity. I have already responded to this objection. People do not need to believe that they personally are preventing harm to anyone in order to be motivated to give to charity: many of us find that the desire to marginally improve the ability of institutions to prevent hunger and starvation is a completely adequate motive. People do not need the illusion that their contributions are individually important when they give to cancer research, and they do not need it when they contribute to CARE or Oxfam.

Second, it might be claimed that my conclusion is much too weak: it is not merely that we ought to give to certain kinds of charity from time to time, but that we ought to give a determinate amount, or that we ought to forego particular purchases and give to charity instead. I tried to defeat the only plausible argument for these conclusions that I know of in Section IV. I will not repeat those arguments here.

Third, it could be argued that my conclusion is too strong; it is not the case that we *ought* ever give to charity: giving to charity is a nice thing to do when we do it, but there is nothing bad even about never giving.

I have already conceded that there is no obligation to give, and also that failing to give on a particular occasion is not objectionably selfish. But it does not follow from either of these conclusions that there is nothing bad about not giving ever. Further, if anything is bad about not giving ever, it would appear to be this: such a failure would constitute, among people who have money to spend on inessentials, complete neglect of the suffering of other people. Therefore, the following argument would appear to justify the conclusion that many of us ought on occasion to give to charities which help people who are poor: 1. Completely neglecting the suffering of other people when you can do something about it at small cost to yourself is a bad thing. 2. Not giving at all to institutions which reduce the suffering of other people constitutes complete neglect of that suffering. 3. Therefore, those who have money to spend on inessentials ought to give some of that money to charities which reduce suffering.

Obviously this argument will not convince everyone. If someone does not accept 1., I have no general arguments guaranteed to convince her that she should. Two things can be said in favor of 2. One is that most of us hold people liable for blame if they do not sometimes give to charity, and I do not believe that conclusion can be supported without accepting something like 2. The other is that holding someone liable for blame because some set of her acts lacks a particular element is not confined to the case of charity. Parents have no duty to play with their children, and each time they do, they are doing something optional; but that parents sometimes play with their children is not optional. Friends have no duty to do favors for one another, and each time one friend does a favor for one another, what she has done is optional; but that friends sometimes do favors for one another is not optional.

What do we owe the poor? If the question means what are we obligated to give to private charities which benefit the poor, then the answer is nothing: no one and no government may demand that we contribute to charity. But if it means what ought we to do about hunger and poverty in addition to paying taxes, then the answer is that most of us ought to give to charities which are trying to eliminate it.[9]

Questions

1. Is the distinction between what one is required to do and what one ought to do an acceptable one?
2. Do you agree with John Whelan that the benefit of $25 to me and the fractional benefit it would bring to a vast number of recipients of famine relief *cannot be compared*?
3. Do John Whelan's arguments have any bearing on situations in which one lives in very close proximity to people who are "absolutely poor" in the sense described by Peter Singer?

[9]Many people helped me with this essay, but let me single out A. P. D. Maritninch for assistance with an early draft; Richard Brook, Owen Herring, and Oliver Larmi similarly for a more recent draft; and J. L. A. Garcia similarly for a still more recent draft.

The Life-Saving Analogy

Garrett Cullity

Garrett Cullity considers two objections to the life-saving analogical argument of people like Peter Singer (1) that even if aid agencies do benefit the poor, the effect of one's contributions to these agencies is not the saving of life; (2) that a situation, like Peter Singer's drowning child, where there is a single threatened life, is not a fitting analogy for famine relief situations, in which very many lives are at stake, and thus no inferences can be drawn from the one sort of case to the other.

There are two justifications for the first objection: (a) most aid agencies, instead of providing life-saving aid, work to prevent the need for such aid; (b) the food purchased with one's contribution to those aid agencies which do save lives is not used to save an extra life, but is rather spread over a fixed group of hungry people to whom one's contribution makes an imperceptible difference. In response to the arguments for (1), the author offers an argument from transitivity: Since aid agencies that earmark additional contributions to feed additional people are worse—morally and in terms of efficiency—than those that do not earmark (and rather share all available resources among the needy pool), and since spending all one's money on oneself is worse than giving to an aid agency that earmarks funds, it follows (transitively) that it is worse to spend all one's money on oneself than to contribute to an aid agency that does not earmark funds (even though the difference one makes to individual beneficiaries is imperceptible).

Turning to objection (2), the author notes that this affects not whether failing to help is wrong, but rather how much help one is required to give. Peter Singer thinks that we should give until we reach the level of marginal utility. To reach this conclusion, notes Garrett Cullity, Peter Singer must think that the Life-Saving Analogy can be iterated—applied repeatedly for each starving person. But is this

Garrett Cullity, "The Life Saving Analogy," in William Aiken and Hugh LaFollette, *World Hunger and Morality*, 2d ed. (Upper Saddle River, N.J.: Prentice Hall, 1996), 51–69.

right? Why not aggregate (by considering one's total *life-saving contributions) rather than iterate? Aggregation is supported by a true analogy of famine relief—not a single drowning child but a sea teeming with drowning people. In such a case it is far from intuitively obvious that we do wrong if we fail to spend every waking moment saving lives of the drowning.*

This is a serious blow to Peter Singer's analogical argument. There is, however, a serious challenge to the aggregative conclusion, which the author considers. In the end, he is unsure how to decide between the iterative and aggregative approaches. Either way, he concludes, our duties to give aid are much extensive than they are usually thought to be.

"It is morally wrong for affluent people not to help the chronically poor." Many people read this remark in a way that allows them to agree with it, while believing that they're not personally doing anything wrong—perhaps even that no individual is. They read it as maintaining that we are collectively acting wrongly. But on a second reading, it issues a direct personal challenge: It is wrong for affluent *individuals* not to help the world's poor, in failing to contribute their own time and money to voluntary international aid agencies. In this essay, I discuss the most prominent argument for this personal challenge.

To argue that individual noncontribution to aid agencies[1] is wrong, you need to identify a morally significant relation in which each affluent individual stands to destitute people. Your argument can take one of two forms. Let's call it a *derivative* argument if it seeks to derive this relation (one between affluent *individuals* and the destitute) from a morally significant relation in which affluent people *collectively* stand to the destitute. *Nonderivative* arguments, by contrast, seek to establish the existence of a morally significant relation between affluent individuals and the destitute more directly, without mediating the relation through group membership in this way.

One method available to both derivative and nonderivative arguments is to argue by analogy. This method begins by identifying a relation that is clearly morally significant, then argues that, since the relation of the affluent to the destitute is relevantly similar, we should attribute the same moral significance to it. Various analogies are used by different writers in this way: according to the most forceful of them, noncontribution to aid agencies is like failing to take some simple measure to save a life threatened right in front of you.[2] This is the "Life-Saving Analogy."

Arguments that invoke the Life-Saving Analogy to support the wrongness of individual noncontribution I shall call Life-Saving Arguments. These differ, depending on the moral relation which the analogy is being used to establish. Some of them maintain that I *violate the threatened person's right* to be saved. I *infringe a duty* to save him, or both.[3] The best-known Life-Saving Argument,

---

[1] I use "aid agencies" throughout to refer to voluntary, nongovernment, international aid agencies. "Noncontribution" will always refer to affluent individuals' failure to contribute time and money to aid agencies of this kind.

[2] For other arguments by analogy, see Nagel (1977: 58) and Brown (1977: 71), where the analogy concerns property-ownership, and Gorovitz (1977: 132–133, 141), where it concerns bigotry.

though—Peter Singer's—attributes moral significance to a simpler relation.[4] If you could easily save a stranger's life—you could save a drowning child, say, by wading into a pond—then failing to do so would be seriously wrong. And according to Singer, this shows that the following relation is morally significant: *being able to avert a very great harm to a person* (in this case, the loss of his life) *at small personal cost.* Any plausible normative ethical theory, he maintains, must agree. But every affluent individual stands in this relation towards those destitute people whose lives are threatened by illness or hunger: each of us can help them, at small personal cost, through the agency of aid organizations.[5] Undoubtedly, there are differences between the two cases: we could sum them up by saying that in his example, you could save a life *directly,* whereas with the distant poor you can do so only indirectly. But unless those differences are *morally relevant,* noncontribution to aid agencies remains as seriously wrong as failing to save a life directly.

Now the most fundamental kind objection to Life-Saving Arguments attacks the method of arguing by analogy itself. This method begins with one kind of situation where it seems "intuitively" (i.e., pretheoretically) obvious that inaction is morally wrong, and then maintains that unless a moral disanalogy can be found, inaction must be regarded as equally wrong in a second kind of situation. But what prevents us from arguing in the reverse direction? It seems intuitively obvious to most people that noncontribution to aid agencies is not seriously morally wrong: why not argue that unless there are morally relevant differences, refusing to save a life directly is not seriously wrong? Alternatively, why not argue that since it seems intuitively obvious to most people that inaction is seriously wrong in one case but not the other, there must be a moral disanalogy? The essence of the objection is this: if you appeal to one set of widespread moral intuitions in order to challenge another, what entitles you to be more confident about the first than the second?

This first, methodological challenge is a serious one, but I have argued elsewhere that it can be met.[6] A different kind of objection accepts the method of argument by analogy itself, but attacks the Life-Saving Analogy in particular. One familiar objection of this kind maintains that aid agencies confer no net benefit on the poor, and perhaps even impose a net cost: contributing to aid agencies, far from being like saving a life, is more like exacerbating the threat.[7] But I shall concentrate here on two less familiar objections. The first questions whether,

---

[3]See e.g., O'Neill (1975).

[4]Singer (1972). For a similar argument for an even stronger conclusion, see Rachels (1979).

[5]At the time of writing, the last year for which Oxfam was able to supply me with an estimate of the cost of sustaining the lives of its beneficiaries was 1991. In that year, it claimed that £23 would feed one person for 6 months in Ethiopia, Mozambique, Sudan, Angola, Malawi and Liberia—that is, about a dollar-and-a-half per week.

[6]See Cullity (1994).

[7]See e.g., Hardin (1974) and (1983), Lucas and Ogletree (1976) (especially the contributions by Fletcher, Englehardt and Hardin), Paddock and Paddock (1967), Ehrlich (1971), and Meadows et al. (1972).

even if aid agencies do confer a net benefit on the very poor, the effect of my contributions of time and money to those agencies will be the saving of life. And the second questions whether one can begin (as Singer does) with a situation involving a single threat to life, and draw his conclusions concerning a situation involving an enormous number of potential beneficiaries of our help.

Why concentrate on these two objections? One reason is that they challenge more than just Life-Saving Arguments. We shall find that the first objection threatens *any* argument for the wrongness of individual noncontribution, derivative or nonderivative, and whether arguing by analogy or not; and that the issue raised by the second affects all nonderivative arguments too. The other reason is that both objections are good ones: in its simple form, the Life-Saving Argument must be rejected.

I: SAVING LIFE

Singer's argument by analogy, as I read it, maintains that an affluent person's contributions to aid agencies will avert threats to people's lives.[8] However, this claim is false. The reason for this is not that the net effect of the activity of aid agencies fails to benefit the very poor. (I think a clear case can be mounted for opposing such a view.)[9] Rather, there are two better reasons.

Disaster Prevention and Disaster Relief

The first is simply that most nongovernment agencies are now primarily concerned with preventing future harm to poor people and improving their lives, rather than conducting emergency relief operations. To prevent the perpetuation of food scarcity, aid agencies have been concerned since the 1960s not simply to provide hungry people with food, but to implement programmes aiming to reduce communities' vulnerability to further crop failures, and to foster improvements in basic medicine and education. Many nongovernment agencies do seek to supplement governmental emergency relief operations, but this is becoming a progressively smaller part of their activities. Most of what they do, therefore, amounts not to providing life-saving aid, but rather preventing the need for it. It is not so much saving a drowning person as funding a swimming education program.

Clearly, however, this first objection does not apply to the disaster relief activities to which some aid agencies do devote themselves entirely, and many others in part. Here, a second objection applies.

---

[8]Another reading is possible. Singer's conclusion is clearly that *individual* noncontribution is wrong, but he might be read as offering a derivative argument for it—as inferring it from our *collective* ability to avert very great harm to the destitute at a relatively insignificant cost. However, the difficulties for the inference from collective to individual wrongness will be discussed later.

[9]The extensive literature supporting this case includes Sen (1981), Drèze and Sen (1989) and (1990), Meier (1984), Singer et al. (1987), and Maskrey (1989).

Spreading the Effect of My Donation

Suppose that, in response to a distant food crisis, I donate enough money to an aid agency to sustain one person for its likely duration. What will the effect of my donation be? Hopefully, it will enable the agency to buy more food.[10] But the extra food bought with my money will not be used (nor would it be proper for it to be used) to feed one extra person. It will be sent to a food distribution camp, and shared among the hungry people there. Had I refrained from making my donation, no one would have failed to receive food: the available food would have been spread a little more thinly across everyone. And only very slightly more thinly. If there are a thousand people in the camp, their each receiving a thousandth of a food ration more or less each day will not make much difference. Indeed, the effect of this increment of food on a person's hunger and health is likely to be imperceptible. (Even for those people whose bodies have a fairly definite threshold with regard to malnutrition—so that at a certain level of food intake, reducing it only slightly will put them suddenly in a precarious state—it is unlikely to be my noncontribution which makes this difference, rather than, for instance, the method of food allocation at the camp.)

This is not to deny that contributors to aid agencies collectively make a significant difference to the destitute. But I do not make such a difference. Any hungry person should be quite indifferent to whether I donate or not. Indeed, notwithstanding my far greater wealth, I probably lose more by making such donations than anyone gains from them. Let us call this the imperceptibility objection.[11]

The challenge to the Life-Saving Argument is plain. Its analogy, it seems, should be revised as follows: I'm invited to contribute to a fund for employing lifeguards to patrol a certain stretch of water, but am told that my donation won't make the difference between anyone's living and dying. Surely my refusal seems intuitively less wrong than failing to rescue a person drowning right next to me.

Generalizing the Imperceptibility Objection

The imperceptibility objection, therefore, threatens the Life-Saving Argument. But next, notice that it challenges all other arguments for the same conclusion.

---

[10]I say "hopefully" because a donation of $20 to $30 is actually rather unlikely to do this. World food trade is conducted in tons, and at 1993 prices of $123, $137, and $250 for a ton of wheat, cassava or rice, the likelihood that *my* donation will make the difference between an aid agency's buying an extra ton and not doing so is small. (FAO 1994: 76, 85, 74.) However, this point by itself does not undermine the Life-Saving Analogy: if I know that spending a small amount of money has a 10 percent chance of saving several lives, it still seems wrong to refuse.

[11]For versions of this objection, see Whelan (1991: 158–161), and Goodin (1985: 162–163). However, neither concludes that contributing nothing to aid agencies is morally acceptable, and it is unclear why not. Why should noncontribution be wrong if it makes no difference to anyone whether or not I contribute?

At the outset, I divided arguments for the wrongness of individual noncontribution to aid agencies into two categories. Derivative arguments derive the claim that there is a morally significant relation between affluent individuals and the destitute from the claim that the affluent collectively stand in a morally significant relation to the destitute; nonderivative arguments do not.

So far, we have been considering one kind of nonderivative argument: an argument by analogy for attributing moral significance to the relation of being *able to avert a very great harm at relatively small cost to yourself*. The imperceptibility objection has shown that the affluent do not stand in this relation even to the starving. Therefore, whether they argue by analogy or not, nonderivative arguments seeking to establish *this* relation fall. But the difficulties can be extended to the other relations which nonderivative arguments seek to establish—a right not to be hungry, for instance, or a duty of beneficence borne by the fortunate towards the needy. If my contributions to an aid agency will not themselves substantially help anyone, how can my not making them violate such a right, or abrogate such a duty?

It is tempting to think that derivative arguments escape these problems. After all, the imperceptibility objection does not impugn our ability *collectively* to avert great harm to the destitute at relatively small cost. The difficulty, though, is to spell out the derivation of *individual* moral wrongness from this or any other collective relation to the destitute. The most natural route for such a derivation would be this: given a group which collectively acts wrongly in failing to achieve a certain result, any member of the group who fails to contribute to achieving that result is individually acting wrongly. But the imperceptibility objection has blocked this route: my donating money to an aid agency will not, in any straightforward sense, contribute to feeding the hungry. If I donate it they will be no less hungry than if I don't.

It might seem that what is needed here is a universalization argument: what makes my individual noncontribution wrong is that if everyone acted in the same way, the destitute would be left unassisted. However, for a start, this pattern of argument seems to run into clear counterexamples. Suppose we ought collectively to build a fence to protect a vulnerable fellow villager and each of us owns ten fenceposts. If few others are doing anything, surely I'm not morally bound to erect my ten posts anyway? And more seriously, consider *why* this is a counterexample. What is ridiculous about my unilaterally erecting the posts is that this personally troublesome action makes no contribution to the end of protecting the villager. But as we have seen, there is a clear sense in which my donating money to an aid agency makes no contribution to the end of helping the destitute—it makes no difference to them whether or not I do it—although it makes a difference to me.

The imperceptibility objection, then, challenges *all* arguments for the wrongness of individual noncontribution. However, there is a reply to it.[12]

---

[12]For a different response to the imperceptibility objection, see Glover (1975) and Parfit (1984: 75–86). They try to show that it has consequences that even its proponents will find counterintuitive.

The Argument from Transitivity

Consider a famine relief scheme which operates as follows: each donation is used to buy a particular parcel of food, which is allocated to a particular needy individual. No such scheme exists,[13] but if it did, it would clearly circumvent the imperceptibility objection—my contribution would make a perceptible difference to the scheme's beneficiaries. A Life-Saving Argument for the wrongness of failing to contribute to *this* sort of scheme remains unchallenged. The failure to contribute *would* be a failure to avert threats to life.

But there is a good reason why such schemes do not exist. It would be perverse to adopt the earmarking policy in preference to the actual one, of using donations collectively to fund a food supply shared among the occupants of a food distribution camp. The earmarking policy would be perverse (quite apart from considerations of unfairness) because of its inefficiency—which is to say that more people would suffer more greatly under this policy than under the actual one. If so, it is clear what I morally ought to do if I could decide whether aid agencies were to conform to the earmarking model or the existing one. People would be left perceptibly worse off by the earmarking policy; therefore there is a clear reason for anyone concerned about other people's welfare to choose the nonearmarking policy, and none favoring the alternative. Again, the imperceptibility objection is no objection to this.

But I don't have any such power; so how does this help to address the imperceptibility objection? To see the counterargument, we need to think about the transitivity of judgments of moral wrongness. Consider, first, inferences of the following form:

1. Given only alternatives A and B, it would be uniquely wrong to choose A.
2. Given only alternatives B and C, it would be uniquely wrong to choose B.
3. Therefore given only alternatives A and C, it would be uniquely wrong to choose A.

When I say that doing something would be "uniquely wrong" given a certain set of alternatives, what I mean is that it is the only thing that would be wrong given those alternatives. (That is, if there can be cases where all your alternatives are wrong, this is not one of them.) With this clarification, this form of inference is easily supported. If, given only two alternatives, choosing one would be uniquely wrong, then it would be worse to choose it; and "worse than" is a paradigm of a transitive relation. If A is worse than B, and B is worse than C, then A must be worse than C.

But now consider a second kind of inference:

1. Given only alternatives A and B, it would be uniquely wrong to choose A.
2. If one had to choose between being given only alternatives A and B, and being given only alternatives A and C, it would be uniquely wrong to choose to be given only alternatives A and B.

---

[13]Child-sponsorship schemes for the relief of poverty do, although most of these target aid at an entire community rather than a single child or family.

3. Therefore given only alternatives A and C, it would be uniquely wrong to choose A.

Let's apply the same line of thought here. According to premise (2), choosing to be put in a first situation (where one must choose between A and B) would be worse than choosing to be put in a second (where one must choose between A and C). And premise (1) tells us, as before, that choosing A would be worse than choosing B. Suppose for a moment that choosing A were not worse than choosing C. If so, (2) would tell us that choosing the first situation, where the best one could do is to choose B, would be *worse* than choosing the second, where one could not do better than to choose A. But this implies, given premise (1), that choosing to be able to choose the better of two alternatives would be worse than choosing to be able to choose the worse of the two. And this is false. Therefore the supposition must be false: A must be worse than C. So the conclusion, (3), must be true if the premises are true.

The second form of inference, then, is also valid. And if so, an argument of this form refutes the imperceptibility objection. For A, read "spending all my money on myself"; for B, "contributing some money to an aid agency of the earmarking kind"; and for C, "contributing some money to an aid agency of the existing, nonearmarking kind." We saw earlier that it would be uniquely wrong to keep one's money to oneself, rather than contributing to an earmarking agency, if these were one's only alternatives. But we also saw that it would be uniquely wrong to choose to have earmarking rather than nonearmarking ones, were one given that choice. If so, it must be wrong to keep one's money to oneself instead of contributing to a nonearmarking agency.

This deals with the second, imperceptibility objection to the claim that my contributions to aid agencies save lives. But notice that the same strategy of argument also succeeds against the first—the objection that those aid agencies are primarily working to prevent threats to life instead. For again, given a choice between preventing such threats from arising and averting them once they have arisen, it would be uniquely wrong not to choose the former. However, if averting present poverty-related threats to life were the only option, failing to do so would be uniquely wrong, thanks to the life-saving analogy. The transitivity of moral wrongness again implies that where the preventive option is also available, refusing to take either can hardly be less wrong.

So far, I have considered two reasons for believing that an affluent individual's contributions to aid agencies are unlikely to avert a threat to anyone's life. Many voluntary aid agencies are more concerned with preventing future threats than addressing present ones, and the effects of my contributions will be spread over many people rather than concentrated on a few. In reply, I have not denied any of this. Noncontribution to aid agencies is not a failure to save life. However, I have shown that noncontribution remains morally *analogous* to the failure to save life: a Life-Saving Argument remains intact. If we consider any contribution large enough to have saved someone's life through an earmarking agency (and it seems that we're talking of something like $30 here),[14] then even

---

[14]See note 5.

if it will not actually save anyone's life, the argument from transitivity shows that failing to make it is as wrong as failing to save life. Any alternative non-derivative or derivative argument can handle the imperceptibility objection in the same way.

II: SAVING LIVES

I have examined a first challenge to the Life-Saving Analogy between non-contribution to aid agencies and the direct and unextenuated failure to save a life. The effect of my contributions of time and money to those agencies will almost certainly not be the saving of life. However, this point has been met, leaving a Life-Saving Argument intact. Now for a second disanalogy. It affects, not *whether* the Life-Saving Analogy supports a conclusion concerning the wrongness of individual noncontribution, but rather the strength of that conclusion.

So far, we have simply been discussing the conclusion that noncontribution to aid agencies is as wrong as letting someone die in front of you. This, I think, is a striking conclusion. However, it is compatible with holding that no one who has made one donation to an aid agency acts wrongly in stopping there. A Life-Saving Argument which claimed only this would perhaps be criticizing relatively few affluent people.

Singer goes much further. His full conclusion is that "we ought to give until we reach the level of marginal utility—that is, the level at which, by giving more, I would cause as much suffering to myself or my dependents as I would relieve by my gift. This would mean, of course, that one would reduce oneself to very near the material circumstances of a Bengali refugee."[15] How does he arrive at this extremely demanding claim?

Iteration

Singer's thought is evidently this: the Life-Saving Analogy can be iterated. Suppose that, confronted by two drowning children, I can only be bothered to save one. No doubt, more can be said morally for me than someone who saved neither, but my failure to save the second child remains morally wrong, and for the same reason as before: the cost of helping is trifling compared to what's at stake for him. The Life-Saving Analogy then instructs us to say the same about someone who refuses to make a second contribution to an aid agency. And the same goes for every successive contribution. Not making it will be wrong provided only that, *considered in isolation* (that is, apart from any contributions I have already made), not making it remains comparable to the direct and unextenuated failure to save a life.

[15]Singer (1972: 241).

It is sometimes maintained that the most that can be morally demanded[16] of any of us towards helping the destitute is that one do one's share."Why must I sacrifice nearly all of my own interests and projects to relieve this suffering when my being required to sacrifice this much is only the result of the indifference of nearly everyone else, and of their failure to help at all[?] This imposes an unfairly large sacrifice and burden on me. What morality requires is a fair distribution, to all those capable of sharing it, of the burden of helping those in need."[17] However, the counterargument is clear.[18] To the example of the two drowning children, add a second bystander. If the other bystander walks off and leaves me to deal with both of them, then no doubt this is contemptible. However, this surely does not allow me to save the first child and abandon the second, in accordance with my share of the required help. The underlying point is simply that, when an accusation of immoral callousness is made against someone who won't avert threats to other people's lives, protestations concerning one's share of the cost are irrelevant. Given the Life-Saving Analogy, the corresponding claim concerning world poverty—that morality demands only doing one's share towards alleviating it, even when one knows that others are not doing theirs—is no more credible.

Now there is one way in which, even on the iterative reading of the Life-Saving Argument, whether further contributions to aid agencies are morally demanded of me will depend on my previous contributions. The greater my contributions to aid agencies, the poorer I'll become, and as I become poorer, donating the same amount of money will become a progressively greater sacrifice. Eventually, that sacrifice might become too severe to demand it of me even to save a life directly. How severe is that? The common view seems to be that if saving someone's life would mean endangering my own, suffering a serious and permanent physical injury, or something comparable, and *this* deters me, then my inaction would not be wrong—rather, saving the life would have been heroic. If this is right, then once the sacrifice in making a further $30 donation has become this severe, my subsequent noncontribution will no longer be wrong. On the iterative reading, then, I will be morally required to keep giving money until either I reach this point, or there are no more destitute people to help. And the latter condition is unlikely to be met soon.[19]

---

[16]What I mean in saying that an action is morally demanded is simply that it would be morally wrong not to perform it.

[17]Brock (1991: 912), who calls this the "Why me?" objection. See Kagan (1991: 924–925) for a reply.

[18]This observation is not new. See Feinberg (1970: 244); Bennett (1981: 84); Fishkin (1982: Ch. 10); Barry (1982: 222); Goodin (1985: 134–144).

[19]The World Bank estimated in 1990 that over a billion people had an annual income of less than $370, and that 630 million had less than $275 (in 1985 "purchasing parity power" U.S. dollars). The $275 to $370 range spans its estimated poverty lines—the incomes required to sustain a minimum standard of nutrition and other basic necessities, as well as the estimated cost of "participating in the everyday life of society"—for a number of countries among those with the lowest average incomes: Bangladesh, Egypt, India, Indonesia, Kenya, Morocco, and Tanzania. See The World Bank (1990: 26–27).

Thus, on this iterative interpretation of the Life-Saving Argument, its full conclusion is the following:

The Iterative Conclusion

Ceasing to contribute to aid agencies will only be permissible when I have become so poor that making any further $30 contribution (one large enough to be comparable to averting a threat to someone's life) would itself be such a great sacrifice that it would not be wrong to let someone die in front of me at that cost.

The conventional view of how great that sacrifice must be has just been described. To be sure, this view has been attacked as unjustifiably lenient—Singer evidently thinks so, in concluding that we ought to reduce ourselves to the level below which we would cause more suffering to ourselves than we would relieve in our beneficiaries.[20] But notice that, even on the conventional view of the magnitude of a heroic sacrifice, the Iterative Conclusion generates severe demands. For even on the conventional view, it demands that I reduce myself to the level below which giving up another $30 would be the same as submitting myself to a serious and permanent physical injury. And surely I can only claim to have reached this point by becoming very poor indeed.

Aggregation

We wanted to know when the Life-Saving Argument will allow us to *stop* contributing to aid agencies. The Iterative Conclusion seems a persuasive answer. Its persuasiveness comes from its simplicity: if noncontribution is morally comparable to not saving a life directly, and if the grounds for the wrongness of not saving a life are iterative, then the grounds for the wrongness of noncontribution must also be iterative.

But isn't there a way of answering our question which is simpler still? According to the Life-Saving Argument, noncontribution is morally comparable to not saving lives directly; we want to know when we may permissibly stop contributing; so why not simply ask: when may we permissibly stop saving lives directly? And putting the matter this way reveals that the Life-Saving Analogy with which we have been working can be improved. A potential contributor to aid agencies is more closely analogous to someone confronted by a great many drowning people than to someone confronted by one. So why not simply examine our intuitions concerning the more closely analogous case? Suppose, then, that what I come across is not a pond containing one or two drowning children, but the nightmarish scene of a lake, or even a sea, teeming with them. And suppose (to complete the analogy) that many other people could help to save them, but relatively few are doing so. But now, it is surely far from intuitively obvious that it would be wrong of me not to spend practically every waking moment saving lives. This is what the iterative approach would require: I may only stop when the five minutes necessary to save one further individual

[20]See Singer (1972: 241). For a detailed challenge to the conventional view concerning heroic sacrifices, see Kagan (1989).

would itself be a severe sacrifice. But if there is any intuitive response to such a case, it is surely not this. No doubt, saving no one would be wrong, but would it be obviously wrong, say, to spend my mornings pulling people out of the water and my afternoons pursuing my own life?

It might seem that if intuition says this, intuition must be confused. If we think that the case against abandoning the second of two drowning children is the same as the case against abandoning the first, how can we resist the demanding conclusion concerning the case where many lives are threatened? If the moral considerations relating to a second victim simply iterate those relating to the first, they must be iterated for every subsequent victim as well.

However, there need be no confusion. For we needn't explain the wrongness of abandoning the second of two drowning children in terms of iteration. The iterative approach uses the following method to derive a conclusion concerning what an agent is morally required to do when presented with more than one person in extreme need: begin with what you would have been required to do for a single needy person, then iterate this for every other. But there is an alternative approach to such situations: begin instead by assessing the magnitude of the overall collective need of the people who could be helped, then ask directly what overall sacrifice can be morally demanded of you in response to that collective need. This aggregative approach, to be sure, does not as such preclude conclusions as strong as or even stronger than those generated by the iterative approach. But versions of it do yield weaker conclusions: and we saw some intuitive support for one of them in considering the imagined case of a sea of drowning children. According to such aggregative approaches, I may permissibly stop saving lives on the ground that I have given up as much as is demanded of me on their collective behalf, even though the sacrifice involved in saving one more life remains small. And on such an approach, the judgments about the two drowning children and the sea of drowning children can be reconciled. The complaint against someone who saves only one of two drowning children will not concern the trifling cost of saving the second child, but the trifling cost of saving *both* lives. This removes the obstacle to agreeing that the failure to save the second child is wrong, while rejecting the extreme demands generated by the iterative approach. The two intuitions are not contradictory after all.

The aggregative approach draws a different conclusion from the Life-Saving Argument. We can state it thus:

The Aggregative Conclusion

Ceasing to contribute to aid agencies will only be permissible when I have become so poor that any further contribution would make my *total* sacrifice greater than can be demanded of me to save other people's lives.

This formulation leaves it open just how the magnitude of the sacrifice which can be demanded of me relates to the number of lives to be saved. According to the very weakest version of the aggregative approach, this magnitude is constant, irrespective of the number of lives in question: I'm not required to sacrifice more for a hundred people than I am for one. However, only the weakest version claims this. There is a range of aggregative approaches which are progressively more demanding than this weakest version, but whose conclusions remain weaker than the Iterative Conclusion.

Generalizing the Issue between the Two

This gives us the Life-Saving Analogy's second challenge. A potential contributor to an aid agency is more like someone confronted by many drowning people than someone confronted by one, and this appears to support a weaker, Aggregative Conclusion rather than the stronger, Iterative Conclusion sought by Singer. In discussing the first challenge—that my contributions to aid agencies will not save life—I showed that it threatened not only the Life-Saving Argument, but all other arguments for the wrongness of individual noncontribution as well. Does the issue between the Aggregative and Iterative Conclusions also generalize to those other arguments, affecting this time not their validity as such, but the strength of their conclusions?

Yes: but this time, not all of them. Nonderivative arguments do all seem to confront this issue. Recall that they assert a morally significant relation between an affluent individual such as myself and the destitute which makes my noncontribution to aid agencies wrong, and which is not derived from a morally significant relation between the affluent collectively and the destitute. Now either the asserted relation holds between me and destitute individuals, or it holds between me and the destitute taken collectively. If the former, then it is hard to see how the moral relation—whether it concerns rights, duties, or potential benefaction—can fail to be the same in respect of *each* destitute person. But then I stand to each of them in my relation whose moral significance suffices to make a noncontribution to aid agencies wrong; if so, the route to an extremely demanding conclusion by iteration lies open. If the latter, then it is hard to see how my making a contribution which is morally comparable to saving only one life can fulfill any duty I owe to the destitute collectively, satisfy their collective right to be helped, or meet the demand incurred through any other moral relation I bear to them collectively; again, the case for iteration seems clear.

With derivative arguments, however, the situation is different. They derive the wrongness of my noncontribution from my membership of an affluent group which bears a collective responsibility to help the destitute. It is easy to see how the derivative individual demand could simply be to do my share towards the group's discharging that responsibility.

(However, we have seen the implausibility of requiring me only to do my share if a second bystander leaves me to deal with two drowning children—which is to say that it's implausible to derive the moral demand on me in this case from a collective responsibility. If the Life-Saving Analogy can be upheld, as I claim, then the attempt to derive the wrongness of noncontribution from collective responsibility is equally implausible.)

Adjudicating between the Two

I have suggested that intuition favors the Aggregative over the Iterative Conclusion. When considering someone confronted directly by many threatened lives, we do not readily draw the severely demanding analogue of the Iterative Conclusion. But how strong a source of support for the Aggregative Conclusion is this intuitive judgment?

It is certainly a serious blow to any argument for the Iterative Conclusion which uses Singer's methodology. As we noted at the outset, he begins with a case where the moral status of inaction seems intuitively obvious, then argues that unless a morally relevant disanalogy can be established, we should accord the same moral status to noncontribution to aid agencies. This methodology would seem committed to following our intuitive judgments about the more closely analogous case, and drawing the weaker conclusion. Of course, nothing privileges these intuitive judgments—especially when they concern such a quickly described and far-fetched situation. However, as I have already suggested, the Life-Saving Analogy itself cannot support such an attack. One may try arguing that since not saving a first person at small cost is wrong, and there is no good reason against saying the same for any subsequent threatened person, the weaker conclusion must be mistaken; but this begs the question. According to the aggregative approach, the point about a lone threatened person is not that *that person* can be saved at small cost, but that the entire number of threatened people can be.

Thus, the Aggregative Conclusion is not refuted by the Life-Saving Argument itself. There is, however, a strong and simple challenge to it, of the following form. Why should my failure to save the hundred-and-first, or the thousand-and-first person be any more excusable than my failure to save the first, if the cost remains trifling compared to what is at stake for that person? My having already saved a thousand lives does nothing to alter the fact that I could save *this* person at an insignificant cost. Intuition is telling me, in effect, to lump all the threatened people together, and assess my sacrifice in relation to this collective entity; but this ignores the very real plight of the individuals conglomerated in this way.

This is hardly the end of the story. It is easy to think of replies offered by various normative ethical theories. An indirect consequentialist may appeal to the beneficial consequences of setting ourselves achievable moral standards.[21] Theories of a contractualist kind may support a resuscitation of the requirement that each of us does one's moral share.[22] And some virtue theorists will want to argue as follows: my having already saved a thousand lives may not alter the fact that the person in front of me could be saved at an insignificant cost, but it does help to show that I am not a callous person, and therefore (since the moral assessment of actions derives from that of agents) that my leaving the thousand-and-first person is not wrong. What is difficult, though, is to see how to resolve the issue between the Aggregative and Iterative Conclusions without examining the plausibility of such general normative theories.[23] So I'll have to leave it unresolved here.

---

[21]See Hooker (1991).

[22]See Murphy (1993: 290–292), who seeks to distinguish affluent people's relation to the destitute from that of two bystanders to two drowning people.

[23]Difficult, but not impossible, it seems to me. Defending a nontheoretical resolution of the issue between the aggregative and iterative conclusions requires much more space than I have here, though.

Conclusion

I have concentrated on one kind of argument for the wrongness of affluent individuals' not contributing money to voluntary international aid agencies: one which draws an analogy between failing to contribute money to aid agencies and failing to make some small effort to save a life threatened right in front of you. However, in examining two different attacks on this analogy, I have shown that both raise challenges of wider significance. The first attack established that the effect of my contributions to aid agencies will almost certainly not be the saving of anyone's life. This threatened to undermine *all* arguments for the wrongness of individual noncontribution. However, my reply, appealing to relations of transitivity between our moral judgements, left a Life-Saving Argument intact.

The second attack opposed the attempt to use an analogy concerning a threat to a single life to support an extremely demanding conclusion concerning threats to many lives. This challenge concerned not the validity of the argument as such, but the strength of its conclusion; again, we found the issues here to be of wider significance, applying to all nonderivative arguments.

Whether the second attack succeeds is unclear. Even if it does, though, the Life-Saving Analogy still supports the aggregative conclusion. At its very weakest, this claims that you are morally required to keep contributing your time and money to aid agencies, until you have become so poor that any further contribution would make your total sacrifice so great that it would not be wrong to let someone die in front of you at that cost. This is still a much stronger standard than most of us are prepared to live up to.

Questions

1. What is the difference between what Garrett Cullity calls "derivative" and "nonderivative" arguments for a morally significant relation in which each rich person stands to very poor people? On this definition, is Peter Singer's analogical argument of the drowning child a derivative or nonderivative argument? Which of the objections to the analogical argument does Garrett Cullity think can be extended to all arguments for the morally significant relation he discusses?
2. Do you think that there is some way of adjudicating between the iterative and aggregative approaches?

Sources Cited

BARRY, BRIAN, 1982."Humanity and Justice in Global Perspective," Nomos 24: 219–252.

BENNETT, JONATHAN, 1981."Morality and Consequences," S.M. McMurrin, ed. *The Tanner Lectures on Human Values 2*. Cambridge: Cambridge University Press, pp. 45–116.

BROCK, DAN W., 1991."Defending Moral Options," *Philosophy and Phenomenological Research* 51: 909–913.

BROWN, PETER G., 1977."Food as National Property," Brown, Peter, and Shue Henry, eds. *Food Policy: The Responsibility of the United States in the Life and Death Choices*. New York: The Free Press, pp. 65–78.

CULLITY, GARRETT, 1994."International Aid and the Scope of Kindness," *Ethics* 105: 99–127.

DRÈZE, JEAN, AND SEN, AMARTYA, 1989. *Hunger and Public Action*. Oxford: Clarendon Press.

DRÈZE, JEAN, AND SEN, AMARTYA, eds. 1990. *The Political Economy of Hunger,* vol. 2: *Famine Prevention.* Oxford: Clarendon Press.

EHRLICH, PAUL, 1971. *The Population Bomb.* New York: Ballantine Books.

FEINBERG, JOEL, 1970. *Doing and Deserving.* Princeton, NJ: Princeton University Press.

FISHKIN, JAMES S., 1982. *The Limits of Obligation.* New Haven, CT: Yale University Press.

FOOD AND AGRICULTURAL ORGANIZATION (FAO) 1994. *Commodity Review and Outlook 1993–94.* Rome: FAO.

GLOVER, JONATHAN, 1975."It Makes No Difference Whether or Not I Do It," *Proceedings of the Aristotelian Society.* (Suppl.) 49:171–90.

GOODIN, ROBERT E., 1985. *Protecting the Vulnerable: A Reanalysis of Our Social Responsibilities.* Chicago: University of Chicago Press.

GOROVITZ, SAMUEL, 1977."Bigotry, Loyalty, and Malnutrition," Brown, Peter, and Shue, Henry, eds. *Food Policy: The Responsibility of the United States in the Life and Death Choices.* New York: The Free Press, pp. 129–142.

HARDIN, GARRETT, 1974."Lifeboat Ethics: The Case Against Helping the Poor," *Psychology Today,* reprinted in James Rachels, ed. *Moral Problems,* 3rd ed. New York: Harper and Row, 1979, pp. 279–291.

HARDIN, GARRETT, 1983."Living on a Lifeboat," in Jan Narveson, ed. *Moral Issues,* Toronto: Oxford University Press, pp. 166–178.

HOOKER, BRAD, 1991."Rule-Consequentialism and Demandingness: A Reply to Carson," *Mind* 100: 270–276.

KAGAN, S., 1989. *The Limits of Morality.* Oxford: Clarendon Press.

KAGAN, S., 1991."Replies to My Critics," *Philosophy and Phenomenological Research* 51: 919–928.

LUCAS, GEORGE R., JR., AND OGLETREE, THOMAS W., eds. 1976. *Lifeboat Ethics: The Moral Dilemmas of World Hunger.* New York: Harper & Row.

MASKREY, ANDREW, 1989. *Disaster Mitigation: A Community-Based Approach.* Oxford: Oxfam Publications.

MEADOWS, DONELLA H., MEADOWS, DENNIS L., RANDERS, JORGEN, AND BEHRENS, WILLIAM W., III, 1972. *The Limits of Growth: A Report for the Club of Rome's Project on the Predicament of Mankind.* London: Pan Books.

MEIER, GERALD M., 1984. *Emerging from Poverty.* New York: Oxford University Press.

MURPHY, LIAM B., 1993."The Demands of Beneficence," *Philosophy and Public Affairs* 22: 267–292.

NAGEL, THOMAS, 1977."Poverty and Food: Why Charity Is Not Enough," Brown, Peter, and Shue, Henry, eds. *Food Policy: The Responsibility of the United States in the Life and Death Choices.* New York: The Free Press, pp. 54–62.

O'NEILL, ONORA, 1975."Lifeboat Earth," *Philosophy and Public Affairs* 4: 273–292.

PADDOCK, PAUL, AND PADDOCK, WILLIAM, 1967. *Famine—1975!* Boston: Little, Brown & Co.

PARFIT, DEREK, 1984. *Reasons and Persons.* Oxford: Clarendon Press.

RACHELS, JAMES, 1979."Killing and Starving to Death," *Philosophy* 54: 159–171.

SEN, AMARTYA, 1981. *Poverty and Famines: An Essay on Entitlement and Deprivation.* Oxford: Clarendon Press.

SINGER, H., WOOD, J., AND JENNINGS, T., 1987. *Food Aid: The Challenge and the Opportunity.* Oxford: Clarendon Press.

SINGER, PETER, 1972."Famine, Affluence and Morality," *Philosophy and Public Affairs* 1: 229–243.

WHELAN, JOHN M. JR., 1991."Famine and Charity," *The Southern Journal of Philosophy* 29: 149–166.

THE WORLD BANK, 1990. *World Development Report 1900: Poverty.* New York: Oxford University Press.

Suggestions for Further Reading on Giving Aid

AIKEN, WILLIAM, AND HUGH LAFOLLETTE, eds. *World Hunger and Moral Obligation.* Englewood Cliffs, N.J.: Prentice Hall, 1977 (2d ed., 1996).

CONWAY, DAVID."Is Failing to Save Lives as Bad as Killing?" *Journal of Applied Philosophy* 5, no. 1 (1988): pp. 109–112.

FILICE, CARLO."On the Obligation to Keep Informed about Distant Atrocities." In *Applied Ethics: A Multicultural Approach,* 2d ed., edited by Larry May, Shari Collins-Chobanian, and Kai Wong, Upper Saddle River, N.J.: Prentice Hall, 1998: pp. 236–247.

HARDIN, GARRETT."Lifeboat Ethics: The Case against Helping the Poor." In *World Hunger and Moral Obligation,* edited by William Aiken and Hugh LaFollette, Englewood Cliffs, N.J.: Prentice Hall, 1977: pp. 12–21.

NARVESON, JAN."Feeding the Hungry." In *The Right Thing to Do,* 2d ed., edited by James Rachels, Boston: McGraw-Hill, 1999: pp. 177–189.

O'NEILL, ONORA."The Moral Perplexities of Famine Relief." In *Matters of Life and Death,* edited by Tom Regan, New York: Random House, 1980: pp. 260–298.

OTTESON, JAMES R."Limits on Our Obligation to Give." *Public Affairs Quarterly* 14, no. 3 (July 2000): pp. 183–203.

RACHELS, JAMES."Killing and Starving to Death." *Philosophy* 59 (1979): pp. 159–171.

SINGER, PETER."Famine, Affluence and Morality." In *World Hunger and Moral Obligation,* edited by William Aiken and Hugh LaFollette, Englewood Cliffs, N.J., 1977: pp. 22–36.

UNGER, PETER. *Living High and Letting Die.* Oxford: Oxford University Press, 1996.

WHELAN, JOHN M., JR., "Contractualism and the Right to Aid." *Journal of Philosophical Research* 17 (1992): pp. 427–442.

www.hungersite.com

CHAPTER 14

Gambling

PETER COLLINS, Is Gambling Immoral?

JEFFRIE G. MURPHY, Indian Casinos and the Morality of Gambling

Is Gambling Immoral?

Peter Collins

Peter Collins notes that gambling, historically, has been deemed a "vice." But is it really immoral? He prefaces his discussion of this question with an examination of what gambling is. He makes it clear he is concerned primarily with commercial gambling rather than social gambling. He considers three theoretical ethical approaches to gambling.

First, drawing on John Stuart Mill, he examines the matter from a utilitarian perspective. He responds to two Millian utilitarian arguments that might be advanced against gambling: (1) that self-indulgence in activities like gambling may impede utility production; and (2) that gambling constitutes a "lower pleasure" and thus ought to give way to "higher pleasures." The author argues that neither of these arguments is convincing, even though he concedes that both may have some force against some instances of gambling.

Second, he considers a Kantian approach to gambling. From such a view, it might be objected that gambling is an irrational or, at least, mindless activity. But this line of argument, he argues, is also unpromising.

Next, the author examines the puritan argument that gambling is wrong because all worldly pleasures are morally suspect. He takes this view to be untenable but suggests that one component of it—what he calls the "stewardship" view—constitutes part of the most compelling theoretical approach to gambling.

This final approach is that of eudaimonic ethics—the view that the good life is the life that is conducive to one's true inner well-being. On this view, most notably associated with Aristotle, the pleasures of gambling can have a morally acceptable role to play in the lives of some people. Such pleasures only become vicious when they are taken to excess.

Peter Collins, "Is Gambling Immoral?" is printed by permission of the author.

1. INTRODUCTION

The question of whether gambling should be prohibited or legalised and, if legalised, how it should be regulated has received considerable attention from people who think about public policy. It is no part of my purpose here to try to contribute to answering those questions. Clearly, in as far as these questions raise moral issues, they are issues of public rather than private morality. That is, they are about what governments should or should not use their coercive powers to do rather than about how we individually should conduct our lives in conformity with what morality requires.

Historically, gambling along with other activities deemed to constitute vices has been legally proscribed because two beliefs were widely held: first that gambling is immoral and second, that it is the business of government to try to stamp out activities which are immoral. The second of these beliefs, however, has for better or for worse been largely discredited in pluralist societies committed to the principles of liberal democracy, on the grounds that it is neither morally defensible nor politically practicable. As a consequence, advocates of banning or limiting legal gambling tend to avoid invoking the claim that gambling is intrinsically immoral even though this is a belief which many of them hold. Instead they focus on trying to show that prohibition or legal restriction is justified on the basis of the illegitimate harm that legalised gambling does to gamblers themselves, to third parties and to society as a whole.

But is gambling immoral? Suppose it were agreed, on the purest libertarian grounds, that the State should do absolutely nothing to try to prevent or discourage people from gambling as much as they like; would there still be any good reasons why you and I should nevertheless decide on moral grounds that gambling ought to play little or no part in the way we conduct our daily lives?

I want to anchor this discussion by identifying three reasons why this question deserves substantial attention from moral philosophers and certainly more attention than it has recently received.[1] I shall in fact be directly concerned only with the first two and in particular with the light which a consideration of the second question throws on the answer to the first. The third, however, is sufficiently important to need acknowledgment even though it cannot be adequately addressed here.

First, the role which pleasure and pleasures should play in our lives is a fundamental issue in moral philosophy to the extent that it addresses the question of how ordinary people ought to conduct their everyday lives. Gambling

---

[1]Amongst the articles which have addressed recently this issue, the following deserve mention: Barrett, Will: "Gambling and Public Policy" *Public Affairs Quarterly*. Vol. 14. No 1, January 2000; Lorenz, Valerie C: "Gambling" in *Encyclopaedia of Applied Ethics*. San Diego Academic Press. 1998; Newton, Lisa: "Gambling, A Preliminary Inquiry." *Business Ethics Quarterly*. Vol. 3. Issue 4. 1993. Murphy, Jeffrie: "Indian Casinos and the Morality of Gambling." *Public Affairs Quarterly*. Vol. 12. Jan 1998. Versions of all the anti-gambling arguments discussed here can also be found in a form which repays philosophical analysis in MacKenzie, W. Douglas: *The Ethics of Gambling*. (4th Edition). The Sunday School Union. London 1899.

furnishes a particularly good case study for this kind of philosophising since it not only tends to consume considerable time and money which could arguably be better spent but also has a propensity to become addictive. For reasons which may be largely self-serving we tend to avoid reflection on this kind of question when it applies to our own pleasures or those of our friends. But it becomes inescapable when we think about the need to offer rational guidance to children about how they should conduct themselves in relation to different kinds of pleasure. And as soon as we ask: "What should we teach children about gambling?" we confront the question of the morality or otherwise of gambling.

Secondly, it is clear that gambling provides an interesting case against which to test different types of ethical theory. As we shall see, some people argue that gambling violates the principle of utility. Others claim on Kantian grounds that it is inconsistent with conduct of a rational and autonomous person. Gambling has also, of course, been condemned by those who espouse a puritan ethic whether based on religious convictions or on secular considerations.

Finally we need to consider the claim that gambling is incompatible with living the best or most fulfilling kind of life of which human beings are capable.

A third reason for taking the question of whether gambling is immoral seriously is that one of the most important *moral* decisions which ordinary people make concerns their choice of work. There may be reasons, either deriving from or independent of the reasons why people should not gamble, why other people should not choose on moral grounds to earn their living by catering to the desires of others to gamble. That is, it may be wrong to be either a professional gambler or to work in the gambling industry. In the same way it might be thought immoral to be a prostitute or a pimp even if it were not thought immoral—or at any rate *as* immoral—to be someone who seeks sexual pleasure by paying for it.

I shall not deal with this third consideration here because it relates to the morality of making money in various ways rather than to the morality of enjoying oneself in various ways and, as such, falls beyond the scope of what can be attempted here. I believe, however, that the importance as well as the complexity of this kind of question become clear if we ask analogous questions about smoking: "Would it be wrong not only to fail to try to discourage our children from smoking? Would it also be wrong to take a job with a tobacco company?"

2. WHAT IS GAMBLING?

Before we can properly address questions about the morality of gambling we need to make some conceptual points about the nature of the activity we are discussing.

The standard definition of gambling is that it involves three components:

- Something valuable is placed at risk (staked).
- With the prospect of winning something more valuable if one set of events occurs and of losing one's stake if another set of events occurs.
- Where the outcome is wholly or partly unpredictable by the gambler.

This definition, however, seems to leave some important questions unanswered amongst which I wish to single out two because of their relevance to the moral issues.

First there is the question of whether buying stocks and shares is gambling. The thought here is that a pro-gambling argument might be developed along the following lines. If there is no difference between speculating on the stock market and gambling in a casino, the latter activity can only be morally culpable if the former is too. But it would obviously be absurd to condemn investing on the stock exchange as immoral. Therefore it is absurd to condemn gambling in casinos as immoral.

In order to refute this argument it is not necessary to rebut the full (and considerable) force of Marx's arguments to the effect that those who make money out of the mere ownership of capital in the form of shares are robbing workers of the private property which is rightfully theirs because it was created by their labour. All that is necessary is to point out that the stock exchange is not in its essence a provider of gambling services but rather of opportunities for genuine investment. The stock exchange thus differs from a casino or lottery in at least two crucial ways. First, success on the stock exchange depends primarily on the exercise of rational judgment. Second, investing in the stock market is not a zero sum game. That is, making profits on the stock exchange does not necessitate the making of losses by others: in the normal case it depends on the creation of new wealth. It is true that some investing on the stock exchange is, from the point of view of the investor, exactly like gambling—for example, if they pick their investments using a pin. Similarly, some gambling is indeed like investing on the stock exchange: the professional poker player or the bettor on horse races who is an expert on form is trying to make money out of superior knowledge and judgment. But the essence of investing in the stock market does not consist in people literally "trying their luck" in circumstances where one person's gain is always another's loss. The essence of gambling—or at least of the most widespread forms of gambling with whose morality this essay is mainly concerned—consists in just this.

This is why some of the most telling arguments against gambling are that, unlike investing, it is an irrational activity which is unproductive, at best, and destructive of wealth, at worst.

The second distinction which needs to be added to the standard definition of gambling is that between social gambling and commercial gambling. In the heyday of temperance movements, opponents of gambling argued that playing low-stakes social bridge was no less to be condemned on moral grounds than betting on horses, playing roulette or going to a gambling den. For the purposes of the present discussion, however, I shall assume that there could be a great deal of difference from a moral point of view between:

- games of skill engaged in as a social pastime and spiced up with wagers which all participants have a formally equal chance of winning, and
- gambling on games where the outcome is unavoidably and mainly dependent on luck, in commercial contexts where the games are set up so as to make it certain that the players will in the long run lose.

Thus the morality of gambling on slot machines, as opposed to having a bet on a game of golf, may be significantly affected by the fact that anyone who plays gaming machines ought to know that over time they are bound to lose. This may, for example, strengthen the claim that such gambling must be irrational and as such morally wrong. Note also that such an argument would not be affected by whether the amount wagered was large or small.

A very important question for conceptual analysis which underlies the question of what principles we should adopt in shaping both personal conduct and public policy in regard to gambling is: "To what extent is gambling like and unlike other pleasures which have historically been banned on the grounds that they are immoral?" At one extreme some would claim that gambling is like taking hard drugs and should be eschewed on the grounds that it is immoral and banned on the grounds that it is highly dangerous. At the other extreme, people argue that gambling is no more vicious or dangerous than going to the theatre or cinema which was also once much disapproved of by puritans. Rather than discussing these questions fully here, I simply note that to the extent that gambling is both similar to and different from other pleasurable activities to which we devote time and money we will benefit in our thinking about both public and private morality if we accept the demands of consistency in this area, i.e., if we accept that we should take the same position with respect to all pleasures except to the extent that we can demonstrate relevant differences between them. The discussion which follows, therefore, is implicitly though not explicitly concerned that a satisfactory answer can be given to the question: "What are the morally relevant differences, if any, between gambling and, say, dancing, playing golf (on the Sabbath), watching sexually exciting movies or consuming psychotropic drugs for pleasure?"

To summarise these considerations, then, I shall be here predominantly concerned with the morality of individuals' playing games of chance in commercial contexts where the odds are systematically stacked against them. The paradigm will be games like roulette or slot machine gambling. I shall also be concerned with table games played in casinos such as poker or blackjack where the opportunities to exercise skill are rendered systematically nugatory, as well as with lotteries and other number games like keno and bingo. With respect to most sports- and other event-betting I take it that ignorance of the relevant facts for most punters is sufficient to make the outcome the equivalent to one which is predominantly determined by luck. By contrast, I shall not concern myself with the morality of either professional gamblers who rely on superior knowledge and skill in order to make money or of the suppliers of gambling services who earn their money by offering only games in which the odds always favour the House.

I shall proceed by considering what light may be shed on the first question I identify above, namely how does gambling relate to a general moral theory of pleasure, by considering what light may be shed on this question by the four types of ethical theory alluded to above. Not only does applying these theories illuminate the ethics of gambling but we also learn something about the power of the theories by testing them against the case of gambling.

In general, I shall argue that a strong puritan position—it is always good to deny oneself pleasure—is indefensible. I shall also argue against a weaker puritan position which says that it is wrong to engage in any wasteful and addictive activities of which gambling is clearly one. On the other hand, I do not take the view—though I do take it seriously—that gambling is unconditionally good for one's moral health. Perhaps rather tamely, I conclude by adopting what I take to be an Aristotelian view of the morality of gambling and I hope that this position is sustainable with respect to all those pleasures which have been and continue to be deemed by some to be "vices."

3. MILL, UTILITARIANISM AND VICE

A good place to begin considering whether we ought to refrain from or restrict our indulgence in gambling even if the law does not oblige us to do so is with John Stuart Mill's extraordinarily rich, subtle and sensible Chapter 5 of *On Liberty*. Here he treats of each of fornicating, gambling, drunkenness and drugs. Under the title "Applications," Mill addresses the question of what would happen in terms of actual policy and legislation if his two great principles were adopted by government. The principles are that:

- "That the individual is not accountable to society for his actions, in so far as these concern the interests of no person but himself"
- "That for such actions as are prejudicial to the interests of others, the individual is accountable and may be subjected either to social or to legal punishment if society is of the opinion that the one or the other is requisite for its protection"[2]

Clearly on Mill's view, we cannot outlaw consensual fornication, gambling or self-intoxication. Nor, according to Mill can we subject people who engage in such activities to social sanctions such as ostracism. This is because in an ideal libertarian society, the State makes no attempt to stop people enjoying themselves in whatever way they choose provided only that they do not illegitimately harm others. In such a state anyone may do as they please within the limits of the harm proviso; and in particular, there are no restrictions on indulgence in all manner of pleasures deemed to be vices, no matter how widespread and deeply ingrained the conviction may be that these activities are immoral. But this does not mean, according to Mill, that there are no good moral grounds for refraining from indulgence in vicious pleasures. His felicific ethics as expounded in *Utilitarianism* allow him at least two arguments.

The first is that vicious self-indulgence may be contrary to the principle of utility to the extent that it is self-damaging and conducive for the individual to a preponderance of misery over pleasure in the long run. The second is that fornication, gambling and drunkenness are "lower pleasures" which ought to be abstained from in favour of higher pleasures such as enjoying works of great art.

Neither of these reasons is very convincing as they stand. The first turns on matters of empirical fact: for example, will my indulgence in drugs or gambling

---

[2]J.S. Mill: *On Liberty*. (1859) Everyman's Library Edition Edited by H.B. Acton. 1910. New Edition 1972. pp. 162–3.

ultimately lead to the madness and misery of addiction? The answer in at least many cases is "No" and as Mill himself says, "no-one but the person himself can judge of the motive which may prompt him to incur the risk."[3] Consequently, the most others may legitimately do is to ensure that "he be warned of the danger."[4]

With regard to the argument from higher pleasures, apart from the well-known difficulty which this notion creates for the utilitarian calculus generally, it is also far from clear that the vices would always fail Mill's own test. This test consists in asking moral or hedonic experts who have experience of both higher pleasures such as reading poetry and lower pleasures such as playing pushpin, which of the two activities afford them the greater pleasure. Unfortunately for puritans, however, plenty of people who thoroughly appreciate Picasso's paintings, nevertheless rate the pleasures of fornication even more highly. (Perhaps Picasso himself did.)

On the other hand, I think both kinds of argument have some force in relation to at least the commonest forms of gambling, namely wagering on mechanical devices like roulette wheels or slot machines. Even non-pathological gambling consumes significant amounts of time and money on an activity which arguably affords no significant intellectual or physical stimulation, which, in other words is literally mechanical and mindless. On a purely utilitarian calculus of maximising personal pleasure it is probably easy for most people to get a bigger bang for their leisure buck. I also think that gambling fares poorly in relation to the question of higher pleasures and that it ought to be possible for most people to get a better as well as a bigger bang for their buck.

However, as far as Mill is concerned, the truth is, I believe, that the logic of his position really supports the hedonistic, "whatever-turns-you-on" permissivism. However, Mill didn't embrace such an ethic himself partly because he was concerned to defend utilitarianism against criticism from high-minded Victorian moralists but more because he was himself largely in sympathy with their puritanism, at least in relation to traditional vices. He would almost certainly have regarded modern permissivism as decadent.

However, even if Mill's arguments against vices in general are inadequate to shore up a general defence of puritanism against permissivism, there may be some other and better arguments against unrestrained self-indulgence at least in relation to gambling even though these arguments do not support stronger forms of puritanism or a moral requirement for teetotalism in respect of gambling. Kantian moral reasoning might furnish such arguments.

4. KANTIAN ARGUMENTS AND GAMBLING

The general form of Kantian arguments vetoing particular practices is that one could not rationally desire the world to be a place in which everyone acted in accordance with the principle of conduct which informs the particular practice

---

[3]Ibid., p. 165.
[4]Ibid.

under discussion. Thus, one could not rationally want the world to be a place where everyone told lies or broke promises whenever it suited them. This seems plausible to the extent that there does seem to be something very like a piece of self-contradiction in asserting: "It would be a good thing if people always told lies when they felt like it" or "Everyone ought to break their promises if they think they will gain thereby." It also seems plausible to claim that there would be something not just bad but mad about someone who asserted without any further explanation that it is just or right for blue-eyed people to be paid much more than brown-eyed people for doing the same job.

The most plausible way in which Kantian reasoning has been used against gambling is by focussing on the fact the whole point of gambling is to distribute property randomly: to make some people richer who have done nothing to deserve it and others poorer simply as a consequence of chance. Allied to this is the thought that gamblers are people who want something for nothing. A Kantian might then argue that one could not rationally desire a world in which what people possess bears no relation to what they deserve in terms of their natural endowments, the talents they cultivate and deploy, theft industry and/or their general contribution to the welfare of society.

One objection to this line of reasoning would be a sort of socialist argument which pointed out that, as a matter of fact, property in society mostly has been and mostly still is distributed according to accidents of birth. It might then be further urged that it would be much fairer and perhaps less divisive if, instead of allowing people to inherit wealth (and otherwise benefit materially from fortunate accidents of birth), differences in at least unearned wealth should be entirely determined by a literal lottery rather than the so-called "lottery of life."

This is perhaps fanciful. A more down-to earth objection to the Kantian anti-gambling argument is to deny that gambling is all about wanting something for nothing. On the contrary, it may plausibly be urged, gambling is merely a pastime in which some people take pleasure and for which they are willing to pay in the form of the losses which they incur as a result of the fact that the odds are set, to a modest degree, against the player and in favour of the House. Surely, there is nothing irrational about the principle that people should be able to spend their own time and money on entertainments of their own choosing.

A stronger line of argument which seems to be properly located in the philosophical terrain where Kant's "transcendental" reasoning converges with Mill's utilitarianism starts by asking the question: "If we were able to do so, would we disinvent gambling?" A more particularised variant of this kind of thinking is: "If someone can easily live without gambling, would they be well-advised to do so?"

Part of what disposes us to answer these questions affirmatively is the fact that we know that some people gamble addictively or compulsively, that is, they gamble to the point where they do serious damage to their lives and are unable to stop or otherwise control their gambling. If we could disinvent smoking cigarettes we almost certainly would and it would surely be morally wrong not to advise people who could easily live without smoking to do just that. The other consideration which might make us wish to disinvent gambling is that it

apparently serves no useful purpose. Again the parallel with cigarettes is the se-
ductive one. Is it true of gambling, what is alleged about cigarette smoking, that
it does some people a lot of harm and no-one any serious good, apart from
those who make a living out of exploiting people's vulnerabilities?

The answer to this question obviously depends mainly on the force of the
parallel and this force is substantially diminished if one thinks that gambling is
much less like cigarettes and much more like alcohol. For the vast majority of
people who drink it, alcohol is a source of harmless pleasure in itself and one
which enhances many other aspects of their lives as well, in particular by facilitating sociability, conviviality and a loss of inhibitions. That a minority of
drinkers become addicted or otherwise harm themselves and others is something that should be addressed in its own right but certainly doesn't compel the
conclusion that it would be better to disinvent alcohol if we could, or that
morality requires a life of total abstinence. (Still less, of course, does it provide
ethical justification for a policy of prohibition which penalises the innocent
many who drink or gamble harmlessly in order to contain the damage caused
by the minority who inflict and suffer harm.)

Indeed with gambling there are good grounds for thinking that the case for
disinvention, abstinence and prohibition is even weaker than it is for alcohol.
This is not only because there seem to be more addicted drinkers than addicted
gamblers at least in the Western world. It is also and more importantly because
there is no equivalent with gambling to driving, starting fights or otherwise
causing mayhem while intoxicated.

There may, however, be a more persuasive and subtle argument against at
least the forms of gambling whose paradigm is the gambling machine. This argument is usually couched in Kantian terms and suggests that gambling is an
anti-rational activity which runs counter to our character as autonomous agents
and, in some sense, requires us to surrender our freedom of will, something
which it can no more be rationally right to do than to choose to submit to a condition of slavery. It can, however, also be articulated in utilitarian terms, employing Bentham's notion of the importance of the fecundity of pleasures and
pains in doing the felicific calculus as well as noting the role of the principle of
diminishing returns. On this view, we should judge pleasures and pains in respect of their propensity to spawn other pleasures and pains, as well as in the
tendency of pleasures to grow stale on us the more we indulge in them.

Thus, the kinds of reason that one is intuitively most disposed to urge
against regularly gambling on slot machines is that it is a vapid, pointless and
mindless activity. As such, it may actually undermine or degrade the intelligence,
given that there is no skill involved and that perhaps one becomes inveigled into
deceiving oneself into believing that one may actually win in the long run. From
a Kantian point of view, this may be thought to be inconsistent with living as a
fully rational and autonomous human being. From a utilitarian point of view, it
is at least a waste of time and money which could be more usefully employed. It
may also actually blunt one's capacity for more profound pleasures.

The difficulty with this line of reasoning is partly that so are many of the
other activities—playing solitaire, watching soap operas etc.—which human beings divert themselves in their moments of leisure in the interval between birth

and death. It is not obvious that it is more *rational* to spend time listening to Beethoven rather than playing roulette. On the other hand for many people who enjoy gambling, Beethoven's music sadly remains mere noise no matter how sincerely they attempt to appreciate it. What is obviously true as a matter of fact is that lots of people actually do get a lot of pleasure from gambling, that it does them no harm, and that they get as much benefit from it as others (such as Wittgenstein) get from other forms of recreation such as reading thrillers.

Of course, any time or money whatsoever which we spend on enjoying ourselves could in principle be used to improve ourselves or the lot of our fellow human beings, often in a manner that would be required of a fairly narrowly construed felicific calculus. Perhaps this means that we should regard gambling as indeed but one among many available diversions. However, in this case we might say, with Pascal, that any diversion which serves to distract us from the business of contemplating our ultimate destiny and thereby learning the truths which are necessary for the salvation of our immortal souls is *eo ipso* sinful. This brings us directly to a consideration of the religious case against gambling and secular versions of the same case.

5. PURITAN ARGUMENTS AND GAMBLING

The view that all indulgence in worldly pleasures is immoral is associated with the more fundamentalist and ascetic strands of all religions. It has a secular counterpart in the views of people who ascribe to political commitment the same importance as others ascribe to religious faith: the pursuit of private pleasure distracts from the work of establishing the political kingdom of heaven. An interesting, if eccentric, puritan view about gambling is to be found in Freud's claim that gambling is really a substitute for masturbation and, as such, an impediment to achieving the ideal of full genitality.

It is perhaps also worth mentioning that some people are puritanical about some pleasures on grounds that are more akin to aesthetic than moral ones. Very obviously people have objections of this kind to all sorts of sexual practices probably preferring to describe those who engage in them as disgusting rather than wicked. It is certainly true that many people who disapprove of Las Vegas would now be inclined to describe it as a monument to crassness and vulgarity rather than as a den of iniquity.

It must be conceded that by far the most common objections to gambling come from people who are in principle opposed to it on religious grounds which they take to possess the self-evidence of revealed truth. Typically they feel the same about sexual activity outside marriage as well as about getting drunk or high. Since, in the nature of the case, puritans tend to appeal either to contested authority or to faith or to taste, it is not clear what arguments could effectively be urged against them. Clearly, they would be right if in fact it turns out that those who indulge themselves in certain kinds of pleasure are going to suffer greatly after they are dead while those who abstain receive great blessings. But this seems equally clearly to be in the realm of the publicly unshowable even if it is not strictly unknowable.

Against puritanism one can urge but not demonstrate that pleasure is always a good and, as such, always a good prima facie reason for action. Thus, if there is anything morally wrong about indulging in any alleged vice, this cannot be a function of the character of the pleasure it offers, let alone of the fact that it offers pleasure at all. It is difficult to see how gambling could be rationally adjudged immoral merely on the grounds that people enjoy it. Like any other activity in which people take pleasure, if it is immoral this must be because of its propensity for corrupting character or otherwise doing damage to those who engage in it or to others. This must be to a significant extent an empirical issue and on this the evidence seems to be that in most cases gambling does not do any harm including harm to people's character.

A much more persuasive basis for arguments against dissipation of all sorts derives from the idea of stewardship. Here the religious version claims that our minds and bodies, our time and our talents, are all gifts of God. We are the stewards of our lives and our nature is such that we can only find true fulfillment and happiness by living in a manner befitting the creatures of God. We do this by attending to the workings of divine grace within us and engaging in works which are pleasing in the sight of our Creator. At all events we should not squander our lives in trivialities and we should acknowledge that a life given over to self-indulgence is an ultimately unsatisfying one.

The secular version of the stewardship argument sometimes appeals to the general economic well-being of society which allegedly requires a good deal of self-denial. More generally it appeals to our alleged obligations to future generations. In its simplest and, I think, strongest form it asserts that this life is all we have. Consequently, we should do everything in our power to ensure that we live it as well as we can and do not waste the only chance at living which we shall ever get.

Thinking in either of these ways enables us to make sense of what people have been getting at in their hostility to drugs, gambling and promiscuity. In each case a plausible argument can be made for the view that loveless sex is not a right use of the body, that consigning one's property to chance is improper stewardship of one's possessions, and that altering one's state of mind with chemicals is an abuse of one's mind. Arguments of this kind will never be decisive but that does not mean they are without rational force. And the force of these stewardship arguments is to alert us in what may be a very salutary way to the dangers of squandering our lives. It does not, however, support the view, nor is it usually taken as supporting the view, that any particular pleasures are in themselves wrong, including gambling.

6. EUDAIMONIC ETHICS AND THE PLACE OF PLEASURE IN THE GOOD LIFE

At this point I think the stewardship argument becomes part of what I take to be the most convincing of all ethical theories, namely what I call eudaimonic ethical theory which most explicitly characterises Greek ethical thought but which is also at the basis of all moral systems which derive from religious creeds or secular belief systems such as Marxism or Psychoanalysis. The fundamental tenet of this kind of theory is that the answers to ethical questions are to be found by discovering what is the best kind of life that a human being can lead. Here the best kind of life is understood as the one which is most conducive to true inner well-being or happiness. This may be thought to have a different answer for different people or a general answer which is true for everyone. It is also clear that there are many different views about what constitutes the *summum bonum* or supreme good for human beings.

The great strength of such theories is that they make all ethical judgments ultimately a matter of enlightened self-interest and thus render the facts about human nature and human experience crucial for determining how we ought to live. In technical terms, it is analytic that one ought to live the best possible life of which one is capable and it is also analytic that the best possible life is the one which most conduces to eudaimonia or true happiness.

If this line of reasoning is to be helpful in answering the question: "Is gambling immoral?" we need to ask the question which is asked by the Greeks in a self-consciously philosophical way and to which all religions and secular ideologies offer (usually dogmatic) answers, namely: "What is the role of pleasure generally and of individual pleasures specifically in the life of a truly happy man?"

At this point I want to claim that, in general, the view of Aristotle is superior to that, not only of later religious puritans, but also to that of other secular philosophers in both the ancient and the modern worlds. For Aristotle, pleasure is indeed an important part of the best kind of life which a human being can lead, as is wealth. A life in which there is no fun can no more be accounted a happy life than a life of grinding poverty.

But pleasure, like money, is not the only ingredient in a truly happy human life nor is it the most important ingredient. And indeed a life which is exclusively devoted to the pursuit of either pleasure or money will not be a happy one. Hence the famous doctrine of the golden mean which in this case would require finding the right median course between the opposing vices of an excessive asceticism, on the one hand, and of hedonistic over-indulgence on the other.

Obviously for many people gambling will not be an important source of pleasure in their lives. But for those who do derive significant pleasure from gambling, what Aristotle defends in respect of pleasure generally seems to be a sensible view to take in respect of gambling. This is the Delphic injunction: "Nothing in excess."

The virtue of temperance which this maxim recommends is one which it is highly plausible to see as an essential ingredient in living the best kind of life of which we are capable, especially in respect of the commonest sources of pleasurable recreation. Not only does temperance obviously avoid the dangers of addiction but it is not unreasonable to suppose that it issues in a life which is better than one of total abstinence. Thus it may in fact be the case that more people who drink in moderation, have temperate sex lives, and even enjoy the occasional game of chance have lives which are not only more enviable but also more admirable than those who eschew all such pleasures. Their obvious advantages over both the hedonist and the ascetic is that their wants are tempered to their ability to satisfy them. Moreover, they do not find themselves in the condition of permanent tantalization which Schopenhauer believed to be our natural lot.

At least this is a way I can imagine we might talk to our children about "adult pleasures" with honesty and helpfulness.

7. CONCLUSION

I want to conclude by first trying to express as forcefully as I can what I take to be a synthesis of all the anti-gambling views we have considered from all philosophical standpoints and then to say some things which seem to me to be relevant to a defence of gambling against these charges.

The worst that can be said about the sort of gambling which is typified by repetitively inserting money into gambling machines is that as a way of spending time and money it is mindless, anti-social, boring, dehumanizing, vulgar, ugly, degrading, depraving, cretinising, soul-destroying, feckless and stupid.

Against this need to be set a number of considerations which relate to why people actually engage in this activity and what the actual effect on their character may be supposed to be.

In the first place people who spend money on gambling are buying three distinct kinds of product. The first is the pleasure of play. People play slot machines and table games pretty much as they play pinball machines or games of patience. Precisely because it is not intellectually or physically taxing, some people find this an especially relaxing form of amusement. It is hard to make a serious moral case against indulging in the pleasures of playing games for recreation or entertainment. Secondly, people who gamble on machines which offer large jackpots, who buy lottery tickets or do the pools are really buying (through theft losses) fuel for their fantasies of getting suddenly and fabulously rich beyond the dreams of avarice. In itself this puts gambling in the same morally trivial category as other forms of innocuous escapism such as watching soap operas or reading sex-and-shopping novels. From one point of view, indeed, buying a lottery ticket may not only be a harmless form of escapism but also a rational investment. For the poor who have no other prospect of ever becoming really rich no matter how hard they work, it is better to have a very remote chance of attaining great wealth than no chance at all. Thirdly, people pay for the ancillary pleasures they associate with gambling—the conviviality of the bingo hall or the betting shop, the glamour of the casino or the racetrack, and in all cases the defence against loneliness. This seems to be not just harmless but positively benign.

We should perhaps also consider the view that gambling may actually be good for the character. Perhaps gambling accustoms us to sit more loosely than we otherwise would towards money and material possessions and this may be morally desirable. Perhaps, too, gambling inculcates the virtues of courage, equanimity, and graciousness in adversity and good fortune alike. It was after all the supreme poet of traditional Victorian virtue and values, Rudyard Kipling, who tells us that we shall attain to his ideal of moral perfection not only:

> If you can meet with triumph and disaster
> And treat those two impostors just the same[5]

But also:

> "If you can make one heap of all your winnings
> And risk it on a turn of pitch and toss
> And lose, and start again at your beginnings
> And never breathe a word about your loss.[6]

In some ways it would be nice to conclude with the suggestion that not only is gambling generally good for the moral character but that gambling for very high stakes is particularly likely to develop moral heroism. The truth of the matter, however, is almost certainly much duller. This is that for the vast majority of people who engage in it gambling has no significant impact on their moral character at all. Moreover, when it appears to, it is more likely to be an expression of character traits which for better or worse are already established rather than being the cause of the emergence of new vices or virtues which otherwise would not have developed.

If this is so, then it looks as if the truth about gambling is that, despite all the passion which continues to inform the attacks of opponents of gambling, it is in fact for the most part a morally trivial issue. What is of course not morally trivial is that no one ought to devote too much of their time, their talents, their energies and their resources to activities which are morally trivial, and that includes gambling.

Questions

1. What, according to Peter Collins, is the difference between buying stocks and shares, on the one hand, and gambling, on the other? What does he think is the difference between social gambling and commercial gambling?
2. What are the differences and similarities between gambling and other activities that have traditionally been termed "vices"?
3. Why might some Kantians argue that gambling is irrational? Why does the author think that this view is mistaken?
4. Can pleasure in itself be bad?
5. Which of the ethical theories mentioned in the introduction to this book is most closely associated with what the author calls "Eudaimonic Ethics"?

---

[5]Rudyard Kipling, "If" in *Rudyard Kipling's Verse 1885-1918,* Hodder and Stoughton [no date], p. 645.
[6]Ibid.

Indian Casinos and the Morality of Gambling

Jeffrie G. Murphy

Jeffrie Murphy and Peter Collins both discuss the morality of gambling by examining what various moral theories would say about it. Although their papers have this approach in common and both consider utilitarian, Kantian, and eudaimonic or Aristotelian accounts, they do so quite differently. Moreover, Jeffrie Murphy examines a cultural relativist approach to gambling (which Peter Collins does not do).

Jeffrie Murphy argues that at least some Native American cultures are not opposed to gambling, and he suspects that most Americans are not categorically opposed to gambling. In such contexts gambling cannot be judged immoral on cultural relativist grounds.

He then considers three utilitarian arguments against gambling: (a) that it tends to attract organized crime; (b) that it tends to compromise, at least aesthetically, the character and appearance of a community; and (c) that gamblers might squander their money on gambling rather than using it for better purposes. Jeffrie Murphy argues that none of these objections succeed in demonstrating that gambling is always wrong.

Nor does he think that gambling is unjust. More specifically, he denies that it violates considerations of distributive justice or exploits vulnerable people.

He then considers the question of whether gambling is an addictive vice that corrupts one's character. He concedes, given a particular understanding of addiction, that it may have this effect on some people, but suggests that "weakness of will" might be an alternative diagnosis of their character. In any event he suggests that most gamblers are occasional recreational gamblers rather than self-destructive ones.

Finally, the author raises a number of empirical questions that would need to be settled in order to reach a more definitive conclusion about the morality of gambling.

Jeffrie Murphy, "Indian Casinos and the Morality of Gambling," *Public Affairs Quarterly,* vol. 12, no. 1 (January 1988): 119–136. Copyright 1998. Reprinted by permission.

INTRODUCTION

The recent development and success of Indian casinos has generated substantial public policy debate on gambling. Those who oppose casino gambling often base their opposition on the claim that gambling is, in some often not clearly specified sense, *immoral.* The purpose of the present essay is to make a start toward understanding and assessing this claim.[1]

Let me note at the outset that I shall in my remarks always use the term "gambling" and never the euphemistic term "gaming" that is favored by casinos and those who support them. No sane person could object to all games, but it is quite possible for a reasonable person to object to games that involve putting significant amounts of one's money and property at risk. These are the games that involve what we ordinarily call gambling, and they will be the focus of my remarks here.

Let me also note that I will not presume to make any *legal* judgments about such matters as tribal sovereignty or the degree to which citizens and their legislators have a *legal* right to shut down or curtail tribal casinos. Such matters would carry me far outside of my areas of expertise. Sometimes citizens and legislators can attempt to act in a good moral cause but find themselves legitimately prevented from following through on their attempt because, for example, of constitutional restraints. So, while I have great moral sympathy with those who seek to eliminate pornography that degrades women, I also accept that the First Amendment quite properly precludes most coercive uses of state power to attain this end.

Thus even if tribal gambling is judged to be immoral, and citizens and their legislators thereby act properly in doing what they can to curtail it, there may—for all I know—be statutory, constitutional and treaty barriers that will place great limits on their activities here. I am concerned in this essay simply with the issue of what we, as rational and moral citizens of some American state, ought to *think* about gambling. I will leave it to others to determine the degree to which such thinking can be realized in our own legal system.

GAMBLING AS A MORAL ISSUE

What does it mean to claim that a practice is immoral? I think that it can mean any or all of the following:

---

[1]This paper is a slightly revised transcript of a public lecture that was presented at a Symposium on Indian Gaming that was held at the Arizona State University College of Law on October 11–12, 1996. The lecture benefitted enormously from earlier discussions with Ellen Canacakos, Peter de Marneffe, Ira Ellman, and Rebecca Tsosie; but it was never intended as—nor does it now pretend to be—a deep or final scholarly analysis of the moral and social policy implications of gambling. Its purpose is simply to get some ideas on the table for discussion. For various legal perspectives on Indian casinos, see the essays in *Arizona State Law Journal,* Volume 29, Number 2, Spring 1997.

1. *The practice is contrary to the accepted cultural and/or religious mores of the community.* I will call this the *cultural relativist* account of immorality.
2. *The practice, on balance, causes more social harm than social good.* I will call this the *utilitarian* account of immorality.
3. *The practice is unjust in that it violates the basic rights of those whom it affects.* In homage to the philosopher who brought this vision to its highest level of sophistication, I will call this the *Katian* account of immorality.
4. *The practice tends to exploit or—even worse—create traits of character that are vices—traits that undermine the proper and healthy flourishing of human beings.* In homage to the philosopher who brought this vision to its highest level of sophistication, I will call this the *Aristotelian* account of immorality. Like utilitarianism, this notion of immorality may be called teleological or consequentialist in that it bases moral assessment on results or effects. Its scope is much narrower than utilitarianism, however, in that it focuses mainly on only one object: character.

In summary, to call a practice immoral is to say at least one of the following: it contravenes community values, it causes more social harm than social good, it unjustly violates important rights of persons, or it corrupts the characters of persons. If Indian-sponsored gambling is immoral, then, it must be because it falls victim to at least one of these arguments. Does it?

It would be efficient to move immediately to a consideration of this question, but three additional preliminary distinctions will, I think, ultimately, prove useful.

First, it is important to distinguish between what I call an *internal* and an *external* scope of the above arrangements. On the latter, it is argued that the practice is immoral because of its impact on persons outside the tribe—e.g., non-Indian citizens. On the former, it is argued that the practice is immoral because of its impact on tribal members themselves.

Second, it is important to distinguish between the immorality of an activity itself and the immorality of offering opportunities for that activity to others or assisting others in its performance. A person who commits suicide out of clinical depression is perhaps not morally responsible and thus perhaps should not be morally condemned. A person who assists this depressive to commit suicide, however, may be a legitimate target for moral blame. And consider our present topic: Suppose that there are only two sorts of gamblers—those who pursue gambling as occasional recreation and those who are compulsive. One could hold that neither sort is subject to moral condemnation—the first because he acts legitimately, the second because he is sick and not fully responsible. Such a judgment would be consistent, however, with the moral condemnation of someone who offers the opportunity to gamble to persons of the second sort (compulsives)—either by targeting them explicitly or by targeting those of the first sort but failing to take adequate precautions to screen out those of the second sort.

Third, it is important to distinguish between the immorality of a practice and the legitimacy of the state interfering with or prohibiting that practice. That a practice is immoral always, I think, counts as a good reason in favor of the

state interfering with or prohibiting it; but often this reason is not sufficient because it is outweighed by other values. These values might be legitimate liberty
interests, the costs of prohibition, the unfairness of prohibition, or the corruption of character that prohibition might itself create. Some persons oppose the
existence of criminal laws against the sale of crack cocaine, for example, by arguing (whether rightly or wrongly) that criminalizing such an admittedly immoral practice represents an overly costly and inefficient use of limited police
resources, unjustly burdens racial minorities encourages such corrupt police
practices as entrapment, and (though fewer would argue this) perhaps even
compromises what ought to be regarded as a legitimate liberty. (In dealing with
the perceived immoralities of a sovereign nation, of course, we might find even
additional reasons for resisting prohibition.) Thus even a showing of immorality does not by itself justify state interference or prohibition. That would require
a separate argument.

But is the practice of gambling immoral in any of the previously noted
senses? I will now move to a consideration of this question. The final answer to
the question is not, of course, merely a matter of philosophy but will be heavily
dependent upon empirical facts—e.g., the percentage of gamblers who are compulsive and the degree to which casinos could or would screen them out. All I
can do here is lay out some general principles relevant to the moral evaluation
of gambling and thereby indicate what kinds of facts or research are necessary
in order to support a final moral judgment.

Let me begin by noting that, by my lights, the most persuasive argument
that gambling is immoral is that the practice corrupts or exploits the already
corrupted characters of those persons who are involved with the practice. Thus
I will spend the most time on this argument. Before doing this, however, I will
briefly discuss the arguments from relativism, general social utility, and justice.

GAMBLING AND CULTURAL RELATIVISM

Consider the argument that gambling is immoral for relativist reasons—that it
is contrary to the accepted norms of the population. But *which population*—Indian or non-Indian? If the latter, the relevance or the point might be challenged.
Normally, one would not even consider interfering with the affairs of another
culture unless one could argue that one of that culture's practices is *objectively
immoral*—something on a par, say, with the female genital mutilation practiced
by some African cultures. But if all one can say against a practice is that our own
culture simply has a different norm, this hardly seems to provide the basis either for action against the other culture or for an attempt to prohibit citizens
from our own culture from visiting the other culture and taking part in its practices. This is, I think, how most Americans deal with the Mexican sport of bullfighting. Our norms do not countenance this sport—indeed, because it is a
blood sport that causes great animal suffering it might even be regarded by
some as objectively immoral—but we make no efforts to intervene in the affairs
of Mexico to prevent this activity. Nor do we do anything formal to dissuade

our own citizens from going to Mexico in order to attend bullfights. Thus if non-Indians are going to mount a rational case against Indian casinos, they might need a stronger argument than merely noting that there is a difference between Indian and non-Indian norms here.

But perhaps this is too quick. Might not a culture have a right to attempt to preserve its own normative structure and to defend that structure against external challenges? (Those who speak for Indian tribes often make this claim on their behalf; and, if this is a legitimate claim for them to make, it must surely—in consistency—for non-Indian cultures as well.) Thus our general indifference to Mexican bullfighting may be based in large part on the fact that it is a form of amusement aimed mainly at Mexican citizens and one that does not tend to target large numbers of Americans and thus poses no real threat to our own normative structure. If the Mexicans started marketing bullfighting in a radically different way or if they started opening up casinos near the border, however, and if those businesses started to have a significant impact on America's normative structure, then American society might understandably attempt to bring pressure to bear on Mexico or on our own citizens to curtail the activity in an attempt to preserve our own normative structure. Mexico is, of course, a sovereign nation and thus no doubt has a right to do whatever it wants with respect to either bullfighting or casinos. This does not mean, however, that America could not do many things that would make these business options highly unattractive to them.

But *is* strong opposition to gambling a part of non-Indian America's normative structure—strong enough to justify seeing Indian casinos as a threat to that normative structure? I am not sure. Perhaps I run in nonrepresentative circles, but I know very few people who regard recreational gambling as contrary to any very important norms. When my friends and I encounter a person who has returned from Las Vegas for a weekend at the casinos, we do not normally treat this person as a social pariah. One must not make the mistake of thinking that a certain kind of uptight Protestantism (Puritanism)—suspicious of all forms of pleasure—defines the cultural norms for all Americans. The recent catechism of the Catholic Church, for example, teaches that gambling is morally harmless so long as it is practiced with moderation and remains consistent with the satisfaction of one's obligations. My hunch is that most Americans—including most American Protestants—hold a similar view.

Also, if the dominant culture clearly had a strong norm of opposition to gambling in general, it is hard to see how that norm could be squared with dog tracks, horse racing, bingo nights at religious or charitable organizations, or—most obviously—state lotteries. When the state itself is in the business of running a gambling enterprise, it is hard not to suspect that its cries against Indian casinos are more an expression of fear at its own loss of revenue than any genuinely normative objection. Perhaps lotteries are different in some significant way from casinos—e.g., perhaps they attract fewer compulsive gamblers—but unless this can be shown, it is hard not to charge with hypocrisy any state government that simultaneously runs its own lottery while seeking to block Indian casinos on the grounds that they are immoral.

I might mention in passing, by the way, that state lotteries initially strike me as much harder to justify than tribal or private gambling. If the state is running its own gambling operation, it is in effect endorsing and encouraging gambling. (Note the TV ads that many states—including my own state of Arizona—use to lure their citizens into regular play.) State toleration is not the same as state endorsement, however, and may be based on values—e.g., respect for freedom of choice or tribal autonomy—that in no way express approval of the tolerated practice. The government, although it tolerates the sale of tobacco and pornography, may consistently mount campaigns to discourage those practices—something it could not consistently do if it decided to raise revenue by manufacturing and selling its own cigarettes or by producing its own sex films. Thus if the state wants to condemn and discourage gambling, it should probably first get out of the gambling business itself.

So far I have discussed the degree to which, if at all, casino gambling is contrary to the norms of non-Indian America. But what about the Indian tribes themselves? Is casino gambling contrary to any of their important norms? This is, of course, a question that it would be presumptuous for an outsider to attempt to answer with any confidence. My hunch, however, is that the answer probably varies from tribe to tribe. Some tribes, with gambling games as a part of their traditions, may well see casinos as simply an extension of those traditions. Other tribes may have traditions that condemn gambling; and these tribes, presumably, would simply not open casinos—the course so far chosen by the Navahos—unless driven to by grave economic necessity. I assume that all tribes however, would at least worry that the extensive development of casino gambling and its associated life styles might undermine over time some of their venerable traditions—traditions already hard to maintain given the pressures of the outside world.[2] This is their worry and a matter for them to decide, of course, and I doubt seriously that they need any counsel from outsiders in the matter.

THE SOCIAL DISUTILITY OF GAMBLING

Let me now move from cultural relativism to a consideration of the utilitarian objections to gambling. What about the argument that the practice of gambling produces more bad than good social consequences? The good consequences are, I take it, obvious: recreational pleasure for many of those who do gamble and economic benefit for those who profit from lotteries and casinos.

Putting aside the possible effect of gambling on character—a point to be considered separately later—what might the *bad* consequences be? I can think of only three: (1) the tendency of gambling to attract organized crime and all the social problems that this occasions; (2) the tendency of gambling—at least casino gambling—to change the character and appearance of a community (the public environment) in ways that are, at the very least, unaesthetic; and (3) the

---

[2]See, for example the *New York Times* story on June 17, 1996, concerning the way that casino gambling is disrupting tribal governance among the Oneidas.

tendency that gamblers might have to spend their resources on gambling rather than on more socially productive objects—e.g., providing for their families.

There is no doubt that casino gambling has historically been associated with organized crime. Even when organized crime is not running the casinos, it seems to surround casinos with the criminal activities that tends to follow gambling—e.g., prostitution and loan sharking. But surely the fact that an activity attracts immorality does not show that the activity itself is immoral. Those who condemn gambling as immoral because it attracts prostitution should then condemn professional baseball as immoral because it has in the past attracted excessive gambling. But we have on the whole successfully severed the corrupt connection between professional baseball and gambling, and I think that the burden of argument should be on those who claim that we could not—with a set of thoughtful regulations—sever the connection between gambling and such activities as prostitution. If the sole problem connected with gambling is organized crime, a free society would probably be better advised, at least as an initial strategy, to attack organized crime itself rather than to attack gambling. The reason for this is that free societies—by definition—have a preference for the least intrusive remedies and will adopt more intrusive remedies only if the least intrusive ones fail—as might, for all I know, turnout to be the case with respect to casino gambling and organized crime.

Of course, when people fear the collateral activities associated with casino gambling, it is not always organized crime that they have in mind. Sometimes their worries are aesthetic and cultural. At the risk of revealing myself as a cultural snob, I must confess that my own revulsion at casino gambling is partly of this nature. I despise Las Vegas—regarding it as a monument to all that is shallow and superficial in our consumerist culture—and dread the thought of my own city becoming a carbon copy of that city—with all the neon lights, prostitution, and (worst thought of all, perhaps) the visible presence of Wayne Newton and Liza Minnelli. I would see this as, at the very least, a kind of aesthetic pollution; and I suspect that many of my fellow Arizonans agree with me here.

But what does this have to do with Indian casinos, you might well ask. Just this: It is perhaps not unreasonable to fear the spread of casino gambling from the Indian communities to non-Indian communities—a spread that might arise because of the pressure of competitive economics. If Indian casinos begin to draw away significant business from local resort industries, then—in order to compete—these resorts might exert enough pressure on state legislatures that they would be allowed to open casinos also. Thus casinos, of no great interest to many non-Indians while confined to the reservations, may become an object of dread if one comes to think that their presence might eventually impact the quality of the non-Indian environment. In short: What might promote utility within the Indian communities might well be disutilitarian for surrounding communities and thus provide a rational basis for non-Indian opposition to Indian casinos.

What about the final utilitarian argument—the argument that gamblers waste their resources on gambling and neglect such important social responsibilities as care for their families? First of all, I would want to ask of what percentage of gamblers this is true? I suspect that it is true only for those gamblers who are compulsive, and thus I will postpone a full discussion of this group until I explore the general issue of gambling and character. I have no doubt, of course, that much of the money spent on even non-compulsive recreational gambling could be spent instead in more socially productive ways, but it is unthinkable that we adopt—as a *general* principle—the use of state power whenever so doing will coerce people into spending more of their time in ways that optimize social and economic utility. If we did, what would happen to people who spend a great deal of their time watching mindless sitcoms on television?

So much for the relativist and utilitarian objections to gambling. Let me now consider the Kantian worry: the possibility that gambling is unjust because it violates the rights of people.

THE INJUSTICE OF GAMBLING

We normally think of injustice or rights violations when the state interferes with a freedom that we regard as legitimate. Censorship of legitimate speech, for example, is a clear unjust and rights-violative use of state power. Gambling, however, *expands* rather than contracts freedom—allowing one more source of recreational amusement. Thus it seems that gambling is not an injustice in the most obvious sense of injustice.

There are, however, two less obvious ways in which a practice can be unjust. It may (1) upset just patterns of economic distribution or it may (2) take advantage of the helpless vulnerability of certain people. This is why we void some contracts as *unconscionable* even if those contracts were, in some sense, freely signed. It is also why we regard the crack dealer as involved in injustice since he caters, not to genuine free choice, but rather to helpless and hopeless addiction. Might gambling then be unjust either because it upsets just patterns of distribution or because it involves unfairly taking advantage of the vulnerabilities of those people who do gamble?

What is a just pattern of distribution? Let us suppose, for a moment, that John Rawls is correct in his suggestion that all just societies will satisfy his Difference Principle—a principle that requires that the economy of a society be structured to benefit the representative most unfortunate of its members.[3] Someone who subscribes to this principle of social justice might well use it to condemn gambling as a practice that, rather than benefitting the representative most unfortunate members of society, actually gives false illusions of "something for nothing" to the poor while it takes from them the little that they have for the benefit of the rich.

Is this a powerful objection to gambling? I have my doubts. It is certainly true that the chances of very poor people hitting it big through gambling are exceptionally small but I suspect that their chances of doing this—or even making a decent living—in any other way are also exceptionally small. The thrills of

---

[3]John Rawls, *A Theory of Justice* (Harvard University Press, Cambridge, 1971), Chapter 2.

fantasy are sad, but perhaps not as sad as no thrills at all—the only realistic alternative for many such people. It would, of course, be nice to live in a world where destiny is determined solely by hard work and never by luck; but this is not the world we live in. The world we live in is one in which our social and economic location is highly dependent on what Rawls has called our luck on "the natural and social lottery," and thus what are we to say to those who gamble in the hope that they will get lucky: that they should abandon dreams of luck and realize that it is hard work that gets people where they want to go?

Let us not delude ourselves and forget that we live in a society that generally manifests a callous indifference to the poor. I would personally welcome some radical and comprehensive programs for their betterment, but I do not think that a ban on gambling—unaccompanied by anything else—is a very promising beginning. Also I am inclined to think that a state lottery is much more adequately characterized as taking from the poor to give to the rich than is Indian casino gambling. Given the historical poverty of some Indian tribes, the presence of their tribal casinos is—at worst—the poor taking from the poor and is more often, I suspect, the poor taking from the middle class. (This will change, of course, if Indian casinos are so successful that the Indians who control them become rich.) Thus I am not persuaded by the argument that gambling is immoral because it upsets just patterns of distribution captured by Rawls's Difference Principle. We currently do not have such patterns, and I do not see that gambling is a major obstacle in the way of our achieving them. Our selfishness and meanness are quite adequate for that.

What then of the argument that gambling is unjust because it involves taking advantage of human vulnerability? Well, there are vulnerabilities and there are vulnerabilities. Advertising a car in such a way that it leads insecure and lonely men to think that its purchase will make them sexually successful is take advantage of a vulnerability, but our society (whether rightly or wrongly) has decided that this kind of advantage taking is fair game—certainly not to be outlawed. Selling cocaine is perceived to be different but why? The answer, I think, is that a vulnerability to sexy cars is considered ordinary human weakness whereas vulnerability to cocaine is considered a serious vice, or character defect—in part because it is an *addiction*.

This point now places me at the final issue I want to discuss—the issue that generates what is, I think, the most common and also the most compelling objection to gambling: *gambling is an addictive vice.*

GAMBLING AS AN ADDICTIVE VICE THAT DEGRADES CHARACTER

According to the Aristotelian tradition in ethics, the most important moral value is the exemplary flourishing of the human personality—the rich development of the most essentially human of our potentialities. This tradition regards as *vices* any actions or traits of character that are in themselves contrary to exemplary human flourishing or that tend to undermine such flourishing.

In Anglo-America civilization, the idea that gambling is a vice sometimes rests on puritanical notions of contempt for material values or on the idea that the proper stewardship of property precludes putting it at speculative risk. It is hard to see how these notions could condemn gambling without condemning capitalism itself, however—a point raised by Alexis de Tocqueville when he noted in 1835 that the American economy is like "a vast lottery." The forces of virtue that are quick to condemn gambling tend to be silent on the activities of those who speculate in stocks and real estate, and one cannot help wondering about their consistency here. A more consistent honesty was perhaps revealed by Sir Earnest Cassell, the banker to King Edward VII, when he wrote: "When I was young, people called me a gambler. As the scale of my operations increased I became known as a speculator. Now I am called a banker. But I have been doing the same thing all the time."

Of course, the devices of capitalism could be defended in terms of the many trickle down benefits to those on the lower rungs of the economic ladder; but one could make a similar claim on behalf of those tribal members who benefit from their casinos. Thus I do not think that, given the nature of the American economy, we can make a serious case against gambling by arguing that it involves the vices or greed, material focus, and a failure of stewardship. The most we could argue is that some greedy exercises of economic risk taking are required for capitalism's success in a way that casino gambling is not. Since this would at most show the fundamental unimportance of gambling and not its immorality, however, a different sort of argument would be required to make a case that gambling is a vice.

It might be that such an argument is to be found in the concept of addiction. Many people who regard gamblers with some mixture of pity and contempt do so, I think, because they regard gamblers as lacking in virtue in a way far more serious than is present in most players in the great game of capitalism. They see them instead as possessing a deep vice or character defect that is degrading or debasing to their very humanity—one which, in its most extreme form, constitutes an addiction. On this view, gambling is to be condemned morally because it either creates or exploits or allows expression of a debasement or degradation in the human personality. Persons holding this view do not see the state as needing a very powerful justification to interfere with gambling because they see the activity itself, being a vice, as intrinsically unworthy of protection. It represents not a legitimate freedom but rather a debasement of freedom.

At the risk of being asked to surrender my credentials as a political liberal, I must confess that I am not unsympathetic to all claims that would justify state action to control vice and would indeed argue that state *paternalism*—the use of state power to protect people from themselves—is sometimes justified. I would, for example, be strongly inclined to oppose any movement to generate wealth by legalizing brothels or sponsoring dwarf-tossing contests. This is because I currently believe—although I could possibly be argued out of it—that both prostitution and dwarf-tossing involve personal degradation (of all involved parties) and that a decent society will attempt to discourage such degradation even if in some sense those persons being degraded consent to their degradation. I would also oppose attempts to generate wealth by producing and selling hard drugs, since extensive use of such drugs strikes me as both degrading and addictive— as lacking even the most basic element of voluntary choice and control.

But is gambling like prostitution, or dwarf-tossing, or cocaine use? At first glance, I found it hard to see any important analogies here. Although casino gambling strikes me as a pretty silly way to spend time, I generally feel—cultural snob that I am—that this is true of most of the things average Americans do for amusement. But surely the fact that I and people like me find an activity silly is no argument that it is degrading or in any other important sense a vice. (We must all be careful not to let the biases that go with our particular educational and social class be taken as evidence of anything deep or important.) I tend to see casino gambling as somewhere in the general category that includes professional wrestling and tractor pulling contests—not my cup of tea, surely, but hardly matters of moral debasement. Thus my initial inclination was to opt for a society that allows me to sip fine wine during the intermission at the opera at the same time other people are tossing down a few brews at the racetrack or tossing quarters into a slot machine. To those who would interfere with any of this, I was tempted to be flip and simply quote Jimmy Durante: "What a wonderful world this would be if everybody would leave everybody else the hell alone."

Such was my initial response but not, after further reflection, my considered response. In reaching a considered response, I was forced to consider and weigh with some care the possibility that gambling is not simply a silly amusement but is truly an *addiction—compulsive behavior* that represents powerlessness on the part of the gambler. If this is so, then gambling is not just a silly pastime. If it is more like cocaine use—something that I have already admitted is a legitimate target of state interference—then the Jimmy Durante quotation is rendered quite beside the point.

But is gambling compulsive behavior—an addiction? This is a difficult question to discuss in the present age of psychobabble, since we live in times when there is a tendency to medicalize all human problems and to make victims out of everyone. Those who in more sexually repressed times were called "promiscuous" and in more sexually liberated times were called simply "randy" or "horny," are now called "addicted to sex." These changes in labels probably tell us more about underlying currents in society than about the behavior in question.

Related to this is the problem that we often confuse psychological claims of compulsion with normative claims of disapproval—pretending to base our disapproval of the behavior on the fact that it is compulsive or addictive but really calling it compulsive because, on other grounds, we disapprove of it. Who, for example, would have referred to Mother Teresa as *compulsive* in her good works, or as *addicted to charity*— this in spite or the fact that she would probably have found it just as hard to give up her works of love as a heavy drinker would find it hard to give up his booze?

Of course, some behavior probably merits being called addictive or compulsive in a less controversial sense because there is a physiological dependence with associated physical withdrawal symptoms. This seems to be true of addiction to cocaine, alcohol, and nicotine. We may think of this as *true addiction*.

Is gambling an instance of *true addiction?* I am not sure about the answer to this question. Some researchers claim that persons can become addicted to their own adrenaline. If this is true, then the adrenaline rush that some people get from gambling could—for all I, a non-scientist, know—give them a physical dependence on gambling and force them to experience withdrawal symptoms if separated from gambling.

Even in the absence of a full scientific understanding of the underlying causal mechanism, however, I am prepared to concede a point to the opponents of gambling and grant that gambling may be addictive in this sense: that some gamblers (perhaps in part for physiological reasons) systematically act contrary to their own best rational judgments of what their lives ought to be, deeply regret such actions, and yet characteristically return to these actions in spite of the regret. If one prefers moral language over therapeutic language, one might not call such gamblers addicts but rather say that they exemplify the vice that Aristotle called *akrasia*—weakness of will. Of course, if one thinks of gamblers as addicts, one will be inclined to regard their acts of gambling—not as responsible moral failings—but as symptoms of illness. If one simply thinks of them as weak-willed, however, one may be inclined to subject them to moral condemnation when they gamble.

When our concern is to assess the morality of offering inducements and opportunities to gamble, however, the difference between addiction and moral weakness may not be so crucial. For one is surely open to some moral criticism for putting temptation and opportunity in the way of either the mentally sick or the morally weak.

But what is the scope of this addiction or weakness? Is it more like susceptibility to cocaine and nicotine or more like susceptibility to alcohol? According to some apparently reputable studies, cocaine and nicotine are addictive to all normal humans; alcohol, however, is addictive only to that minority of humans who have an unusual genetic susceptibility to such addiction.[4] Thus: If the state intervenes to prohibit cocaine or nicotine consumption, it is limiting the freedom of all for the good of all. If it intervenes to prevent alcohol, however, it is limiting the freedom of all for the good of a few—a much more difficult policy to justify in a free society. As Mill argued long ago in *On Liberty*, a free society will target those who abuse a freedom and not shut down for all an entire domain of freedom simply to deal with the minority who cannot be trusted with it. For example: If a free society is concerned with the problem of drunken driving, it imposes aggravated penalties for drunken driving; it does not ban alcohol.

My own hunch is that gambling is more analogous to alcohol use than to cocaine or nicotine use—namely, that those gamblers who are in any meaningful sense addicted or compulsive or extremely weak with respect to its temptations represent a minority of all gamblers. Thus state policies of prevention here will be more difficult to justify. We attempt to deal with alcohol abuse through regulation—on advertising, on serving to minors and to those who are clearly

---

[4]The empirical support for this claim is summarized by Robert E. Goodin in his book *No Smoking.* University of Chicago Press, Chicago, 1989. My own thinking about addiction has been greatly influenced by this book.

intoxicated—and we could perhaps deal with the problems of gambling abuse in a similar way. We might, for example, place limits on betting, on the use of credit cards for betting, on the number of hours allowed at the casino, and (at least for Indian tribes not burdened by constitutional restraints) on the residency of those who are allowed to gamble at the casino—a practice followed by some European casinos. Of course, if casinos are unwilling to cooperate in weeding out the compulsive gamblers—as many critics claim that they are—this is some evidence that they indeed depend upon them and are in the business of exploitation rather than merely recreation.

If regulation will not work to solve the problems posed by compulsive gamblers, then the moral case against casinos becomes more compelling. An important fact about freedom—a fact sometimes forgotten by Mill—that not all freedoms are of equal value or worth. On any plausible hierarchical scale of freedom, the freedom to gamble is surely not to be regarded as one of our most important freedoms. Thus, while it is clearly improper to restrict a really important freedom (such as political speech or religious worship) for the good of a few, it is not so obviously improper to do this when the freedom itself is fairly trivial. So why not advocate, on paternalistic moral grounds, the elimination of gambling in order to protect those who will otherwise have their lives and the lives of their families destroyed by it?

Of course, the freedom to consume alcohol is also fairly trivial; and so it would seem that the above pattern of thought might justify the prohibition of alcohol in order to protect those alcoholics who will otherwise have their lives destroyed by alcohol. But this is clearly absurd, many would argue, since one thing we all now supposedly know for sure is that Prohibition was wrong. But do we really know this? Prohibition failed, of course, but this does not mean that it was wrong in principle. Its failure may have resulted from the fact that it was an unpopular attempt on the part of the state to interfere with a deeply embedded traditional American practice—an activity that people had become accustomed to enjoying. Casino gambling does not—in most states—have the force of such history behind it, however, and thus the failure of Prohibition with respect to alcohol is probably largely irrelevant to the debate over casino gambling. There are powerful reasons that counsel restraint in attempts to weed out old vices, but such reasons do not apply with respect to new vices.

But what about nicotine? Nicotine is highly addictive to all users and its use often leads to horrible and expensive death. And yet we tolerate the use of nicotine, in part because of the economic pressure brought to bear by those states that grow tobacco. Thus should we not, as a matter of fairness, cut Indian tribes the same break that we currently cut the tobacco farmers of North Carolina—farmers whose product addicts the youth of America and sentences many of them to death by cancer?

This is a difficult claim to assess, but at least two points can be raised to challenge the analogy between tobacco and gambling. One—noted above with respect to alcohol—is that it is much harder to justify overthrowing an established practice than it is to prevent the development of a new practice. The second is concerned with economic reliance. The farmers in tobacco growing states have relied on the income from tobacco for many generations and have built a whole way of life around the practice— a claim that Indian tribes cannot make with respect to casinos. And I would not, by the way, look with too much envy on those tobacco farmers of the American south. The social and governmental vice tightens on them a little more each year, and I think that even they see that their days are numbered. The process of closure is slow—in part to give them time to make economic adjustments—but I would not be at all surprised to see a total ban on tobacco sales in America some years down the road.

In summary: It is hard to make a case that the occasional recreational gambler exhibits a vice or that one who offers the opportunity to gamble to such persons exploits a vice and therefore acts immorally. The real moral problems arise with respect to those gamblers who gamble as an exercise in self-destruction. Perhaps not all such gamblers are to be morally blamed for their behavior—some of them may be sick—but surely those who offer them both temptations and opportunities for such behavior are, at the very least, involved (like those who provide drugs, alcohol or tobacco) in a situation of great moral complexity. They cannot say—like someone who simply runs an amusement park—that their activities involve *nothing but* innocent and harmless recreation.

SOME CONCLUDING REMARKS

What is my tentative answer to the question "Is gambling immoral?" My tentative answer—something of a letdown, I fear—is: "It all depends."

The final answer depends on a variety of factual claims, and some of these are highly contested. Those who favor casinos can amass empirical research to support their claims, and those who oppose casinos can do the same thing. As we learned with respect to tobacco industry funded research on the dangers of nicotine, we need research that is truly disinterested—research that is not driven by economic interest and ideology. I hope we can get such research and do not instead merely get confirmation of W. H. Auden's counsel "Thou shalt not sit with statisticians nor commit a social science."

What would we want to learn from such research that would have a bearing on the morality of gambling? Here are a few questions that need answering:

1. *What percentage of gamblers are compulsive in the sense that they gamble to self-destructive excess?* Casinos probably like to underestimate the number of such gamblers, and moralistic critics of gambling probably like to overestimate the numbers. It would be nice to know the actual facts.
2. *Is the number of compulsive gamblers generally fixed or does their number expand as opportunities to gamble expand?* If casinos create more compulsive gamblers, this is obviously more of a social problem than if casinos simply shift the location of gamblers from dog tracks and the lottery to casinos instead.
3. *If the number of compulsive gamblers is sufficiently large to constitute a genuine social problem, are there reasonable steps that casinos could and would take to reduce those numbers?* Many critics of casinos claim that they are highly

dependent on compulsive gamblers and actually do things to encourage and further tempt them. If this is so, then casinos may be crossing the line that separates recreation from exploitation.

4. *Do those who develop casinos suffer from a level of economic hardship sufficient to justify their development in spite of the moral problems associated with them?* Activities that may be judged immoral viewed in isolation may sometimes be judged morally acceptable when all relevant considerations have been surveyed. Killing another human being, viewed as an isolated act, must be regarded as immoral. But under certain circumstances—legitimate self-defense, for example—what is normally immoral becomes morally justified. Could a comparable argument be made for gambling—that, all things considered, it is justified in spite of its obvious moral downsides?

I am doubtful that such an argument can be made for state sponsored gambling such as lotteries. Lotteries are not a state's only possible source of income; indeed, their attractiveness often lies in their use as politically expedient alternatives to taxation. States are hardly driven to lotteries by necessity. Thus: Unless it can be clearly demonstrated that lottery play is almost totally low stake and tends to attract almost no compulsive gamblers, I do not see how a morally decent state can justify its use of lotteries.

The situation maybe quite different for Indian tribes, however. With respect to them, a case can perhaps be made that their development of casinos is, all things considered, justified. There is a possible legal argument based on tribal sovereignty—one that I am not competent to discuss—and a possible moral argument. The moral argument would be based on the claims that (1) casino gambling is the only way out of the extreme poverty in which many tribes find themselves and (2) that this poverty results from their historical exploitation at the hands of non-Indian America—the very culture that seeks to curtail their casinos while maintaining its own lotteries. Such claims are empirically and historically complex—and may vary remarkably in plausibility from tribe to tribe—and I would not presume to judge their accuracy. In any instance where they are accurate, however, then perhaps a case has been made for the moral legitimacy of casino gambling—a case that maintains that the morally relevant downsides of casinos (such as a failure to screen out compulsives) are outweighed by such morally relevant upsides as (at long last) economic viability for some historically oppressed people. Sometimes morality involves choosing the lesser of two evils, and the evils associated with casino gambling are arguably not nearly as great as the evils involved in extreme poverty.

Of course, economic necessity cannot justify just anything. If a particular tribe could avoid abject poverty for its members only by selling heroin or opening brothels or robbing banks, then it would no doubt be morally required to remain in poverty. For all the badness of casino gambling, however, it does not seem—given the arguments I have developed above—*that* bad, and thus it does seem to represent an issue where the moral argument of lesser evils might well apply.

Let me close with one radical (and no doubt unworkable) thought: If the larger society decides it is unwilling to bear the impact of gambling on non-Indian citizens and communities and thus seeks to stop or curtail tribal casinos, perhaps the larger society should be viewed as under an obligation to pay money to the tribes to compensate them for the costs of their lost opportunity.

Consider an analogy with third world countries and environmental destruction. Having for centuries raped the natural world for their own benefit, it seems terribly unfair if developed nations now go to third world countries and tell them that they must not (for example) destroy their rain forests and thereby increase global warming. The only fair way to treat these nations, it seems to me, is to transfer some of the wealth that developed nations got from raping the environment (a kind of unjust enrichment) to the developing nations as compensation for lost opportunity.

If gambling is seen as some combination of moral and aesthetic pollution, it is perhaps understandable that the larger society would want to prevent tribes from generating this pollution. If it was indeed the larger society that put them in the position of having no realistic choice but to generate this particular pollution, however, some substantial compensation should perhaps be viewed as owed to them. Obligatory compensation would be fair and would also, I suspect, deter the larger society from attempting too hastily to eliminate tribal casinos in the first place. Stinginess is a powerful motive, and the desire to interfere with perceived vice is much more attractive when such interference is cost-free than when it carries a high price tag.

A moral obligation to compensate tribes for lost opportunity is one thing; but a legal requirement of such compensation is, of course, quite a different thing. Such a legal requirement would, I suspect, have to be generated from some model of international law and the relations between sovereign nations. Since I know almost nothing about international law, however, I will leave that line of inquiry to those who—to borrow a contrast from Plato—possess knowledge and not mere opinion.

Questions

1. What is the difference between addiction and *akrasia?* Can one be addicted to gambling?
2. Some arguments against gambling, if correct, would entail the wrongfulness not only of gambling but also of other practices that are widely accepted. What are those arguments, and how would they apply to the currently accepted practices?
3. In what way does Jeffrie Murphy think that gambling differs from prostitution and drug use?

Suggestions for Further Reading on Gambling

BARRETT, WILL."Gambling and Public Policy." *Public Affairs Quarterly* 14, no. 1 (January 2000): pp. 57–71.

LORENZ, VALERIE C."Gambling." in *Encyclopedia of Applied Ethics*, vol. 2, edited by Ruth Chadwick, San Diego: Academic Press, 1998: pp. 341–355.

NEWTON, LISA."Gambling: A Preliminary Inquiry." *Business Ethics Quarterly* 3, no. 4 (1993): pp. 405–418.

CHAPTER 15

Tipping

Mark P. Maller, The Morality of Tipping

The Morality of Tipping

Mark P. Maller

Mark Maller argues for a view that will make him unpopular with taxi drivers everywhere! He argues that the practice of tipping certain service providers, such as taxi drivers and waitresses, is grounded only in custom. The practice, he says, although it may sometimes be acceptable, is not morally justified or required.

He distinguishes between egoistic and sympathetic reasons for tipping. Among the egoistic reasons are (a) avoiding guilt feelings, (b) making oneself feel generous, and (c) ensuring good service in the future. Sympathetic tipping is not motivated by any benefit for oneself, but rather by either sympathy with the person tipped or by a belief that tipping is morally right. He argues that tipping does not have the effect of improving service. Moreover, it is arbitrary, irrational, and unjust that some service providers, such as taxi drivers, waitresses, porters, and hair stylists receive tips, whereas others, such as retail sales clerks, do not. He rejects the argument that tipping is morally required because service workers depend on tips for their living. Finally, he argues that because most customers will have earned their money through their labor, tipping entails the customer's "working for" both the worker whom he tips and the employer of the tipped worker.

The custom of tipping service workers is frequently considered a moral obligation, and though rarely a subject of moral disclosure, it deserves closer scrutiny and understanding. The intention here is to challenge why tipping is justified by discussing its most common reasons, and to show that there is no moral justification for it, that it is grounded in custom, but not in sound moral judgment.

Why, then, do people tip service workers who perform a personal service, such as waiting at their table, driving to a destination, or carrying their luggage in a hotel? Almost all people feel that workers expect to be tipped, regardless of

Mark Maller, "The Morality of Tipping," *Public Affairs Quarterly*, vol. 7, no. 3 (July 1993): 231–239.

the service, and 71% of those surveyed feel obligated to tip, even if service does not meet their standards.[1] If customers do not tip (or significantly under tip), they risk embarrassment to others in their party and the worker—in the event of future business. Most people would rather not offend, or at least shun disapproval, verbal or nonverbal, or other negative reactions, such as less friendly behavior and slower service. Some tip to avoid guilty feelings, and many others derive pleasure from their generosity. Of course, speedy, friendly service is the major motivator. In fact, the work tip is derived from "To Insure Promptitude."[2]

These reasons and others like them are grounded in the customer's own self-benefit, not the worker's, and thus in a hedonistic egoism. The egoist's sole moral obligation is to create as much pleasure and least suffering for himself. Even when the egoist tips generously, far from having the worker's welfare in mind, he is buying the kind of personal service he wants in that business, that which pleases him the most. Minimally, he will gain more respect or esteem from his recipients, and that can be worth the money itself.

The other type of tipping is based primarily on sympathy toward the service worker, and is distinguished from egoistic tipping. Sympathetic tipping occurs when customers expect no personal benefit, such as better service, preferred seats or products—when traveling, for instance—nor do they derive special pleasure from it, or feel guilt from *not* tipping. They tip because they believe it is morally right, and not to do so would be less than virtuous and possibly immoral. An affinity of feeling is struck toward the worker, perhaps because of the notion that they work hard and earn less. (Female workers particularly seem to elicit more sympathy from other females who identify with them.) For these customers, a sense of common feeling for/with the service worker justifies a tip, and this justification engenders their moral judgment confirming this action right.

It is not argued here that this tipping is unjustified (assuming acceptable service), but only that it cannot be claimed to be *morally* justified. This kind of claim must be stricter and defined in its ethical implications for all, but this has not been done, and the case is difficult. Customers may suggest that tipping is morally obligatory even with average or below average service, and though tips may be reduced, they're usually not withheld. These customers hold that this moral obligation, based on their sympathy, is sound regardless of the establishment, the relative wealth of the customer and worker and other factors. This type of tipping presents the strongest defense, as egoistic tipping is less controversial, and besides, is open to the weaknesses of ethical egoism itself.[3] My arguments concentrate more on sympathetic tipping but apply to both types.

There are several reasons for holding that tipping is morally obligatory.

1. It is said tipping encourages better service, specifically and overall, which in turn permits the worker to keep his/her job, keeps the company in business

---

[1]According to a survey conducted by Tippers International of a cross-section of people, in Schein, J., *The Art of Tipping* (Wausau, WI: Sun Press, 1984), p. 31.

[2]*Ibid.* preface.

[3]William Frankena suggests some of the weaknesses of this position in his *Ethics* (Englewood-Cliffs, NJ: Prentice-Hall, 1963), pp.16–18.

with lower prices, and ultimately improves the retail economy of the community and nation. Is this claim true? Consider, that as tipping has become so standard and universal, regardless of the service, superior excellent service then becomes devalued and not as well rewarded. The incentive to excel is sharply reduced, and even when meritorious work is no longer the aim, excellence becomes only occasional, contingent (on numerous factors), not the rule. Just as the purpose of tipping is to reward or encourage good service, not tipping shouldn't necessarily suggest poor service, but simply that competence alone will not be rewarded. Generally, as a business rule one is not specially rewarded simply for doing one's job. Work competence alone is not a sufficient condition for monetary bonuses. Yet certain occupations, usually in the hospitality business, are the exceptions by the force of custom. Truly exceptional service, as defined by each individual, (recognized by top management as a high priority for business), is worth tipping well.

If competence becomes the necessary and sufficient condition, every worker within certain occupations will receive tips as a rule, and those who are satisfied with their 15%–20% have no incentive to strive beyond (in many cases) to a mediocre competent level.[4] Also, reducing or withholding tips doesn't imply the business will lose money, as customers may spend more on products and services. Free enterprise, based on keen competition, naturally weeds out (or should) less than competent service, and in the end, management with better service earns more profit, while the others, ideally, wither away. Some might argue that without tips the cost of services would increase, perhaps significantly. However, it is also possible that many businesses (especially large and financially sound) will not have to raise prices, and prudently find other ways to absorb the cost which won't (or minimally) affect customers. But assuming prices are raised and enough customers choose not to patronize those services, prices may have to be lowered to their original level, or if necessary, businesses might create new services for their additional profit.[5]

2. Although tipping sometimes appears rational and logical, appealing to common sense, it is equally arbitrary, irrational and unjust. Consider, for example, retail sales clerks. They are never tipped, and yet often spend more time on each customer, receive about the same wages (working without commission) as waitresses, bartenders, cabdrivers, etc., and work at least as hard, depending on their employers. They're expected to know their merchandise, operate cash registers, and persuade customers to make purchases. Yet waiters usually do little more than take the order and bring it to you. Bartenders do not even need to walk the floor. Gas station attendants with full service, repairmen, other restaurant staff, and airline attendants all provide personal services yet never receive

---

[4]Schein, president of Tippers International, writes "People lose out on good service in the future when they fail to use tipping as a way for encouraging good service, but keep tipping about the same no matter what kind of service or treatment they receive." (Schein. p. 31.)

[5]Since tipping occurs in non-essential services, those customers who will not or cannot accept the higher prices will make alternative choices. For instance, travelers may choose motels, not full service hotels, buses instead of taxis. In order to keep their customers, businesses may find it necessary to expand or enhance their existing services.

tips, though their work is just as deserving. Generally, this is a cross-cultural world custom, excepting those governments which discourage or limit tipping. So, what do waiters/waitresses, porters, hair stylists, cabdrivers, doormen, etc. have in common, besides providing personal services? Apparently, only the time-honored custom of receiving tips, whether earned or not, whether they're well-paid or not, educated or illiterate, first day on the job, or a seasoned professional.[6]

I do not argue that these workers shouldn't receive tips, but that the entire custom is grounded purely and solely on tradition (including implied expectation), not on moral obligation, duty, or rights. That they *ought* to receive tips cannot be derived from the factual premise that they do receive them and have done so in the past. Yet this shift from a sociological observation to a moral conclusion is exactly what so many tipping customers and workers hold true and valid. Yet this shift is unsound, despite the weight of public opinion and policy which seems to indicate otherwise. Ask a regular tipper why he or she tips, and after repeated questioning, they will imply or suggest that it's the right thing to do, *not* because service was exceptional, or to ensure future good service, or due to a liking for the worker. Yet why is this the right action? After all, tradition alone often lacks the sufficient moral ground for such strong beliefs and actions. Justice, equality, and most of all, merit are all important virtues which would ground and establish moral precepts for a more rational custom concerning wages.

3. The most commonly held reason for tipping is that service workers *depend* on tips for a living. This economic reason entails that without such tips, the worker would suffer from inadequate income, which in turn entails a poorer lifestyle (lower quality of food and housing, perhaps), and possibly unable to earn a living at all in that occupation. Let us assume this unproven assumption is true in the majority of cases anyway, that hourly wages alone would not sustain them. We also assume that they have an agreement with management to keep all the tips they receive. Does this imply that such workers have a *right* to receive them? The right to receive money must be distinguished from the right to keep it. I have a right to keep a gift from a stranger on my block, but I certainly have no right to a gift *from* him, just as he has no obligation to give me one. Society recognizes rights to keep property as owned, but there's no moral contract for someone to simply give me one. And what is a tip, but a small gift or gratuity? Suppose, furthermore, that I help this stranger cross the street and carry his packages. Does this action entitle me to a gift from him? Could I claim a right to a gift? Would the stranger be obligated to give me one?

The answers are negative. Only in extenuating circumstances might a token gratuity be anticipated, and then only to reward the unexpected kindness from someone who might have ignored the stranger without feeling obligated. (For instance, if the stranger collapsed on the street and I called an ambulance and assisted him.) In these cases, one stranger may offer a gratuity to another in exchange for a benevolent service.

In a business transaction, however, workers often virtually make a living from their tips, basically for satisfactorily doing their jobs. Yet the average

---

[6]Approximately $5 billion are spent on tips annually.

customer is more likely to reward a worker for doing his or her job, which *must* be done under fear of termination, rather than offer a similar reward to someone whose kindness was purely voluntary, done without any incentive, out of respect and obligation to another's predicament.

In neither case can it be claimed that the recipient has a right to receive tips. No verbal or nonverbal contract exists, though custom often encourages it. Of course, workers have a right to their *earned* wages, and when tips are truly earned, one can argue that they have a right to the tips, too. But it is precisely the worker's customers who decide if a tip is earned. For some customers, tips are earned *a priori,* automatically, as it were, regardless of the quality or speed of service, while others, using stricter guidelines, evaluate the service prior to making their judgments. All along, tipping is intended to be an evaluative process, not a simple addition to the bill, a kind of service tax. Some choose not to make specific evaluations; that is their choice. In choosing to forego this value judgment, they are being no more or less virtuous than those who do make these evaluations. For clearly guided by custom and conscience, we have a difference of opinion on the methods of tipping and the standards for what constitutes "good" or acceptable service. It is unfortunate that those with stricter standards suffer social embarrassment (especially when labeled cheap or tight, as if that was a low vice.) This social labeling has become an effective way in which service workers and their generous tippers exert social power against the rest. This intent to exert a sense of guilt from financially conservative customers is specifically unjust in light of the pervious discussion.

Furthermore, such workers have a right to their earned tips, but in the same way they earn gratuity gifts from customers, or a bonus from their employer for improved or superior service. These rewards, far from being guarantees, are responses to earned work, representing a higher value or esteem. Such workers deserve these bonuses according to the employer, and customers will confirm that with greater tips, or disprove it with less or none.

Some will still argue that these workers must depend on tips, *regardless* of the quality of their competent service, and this necessitates a reasonable tip by each customer for every service performed. The relative financial status of the worker is not the issue. The point is that he or she is in a dependent relation to customers for 15–20% of the bill.

Does this also include customers living on government assistance? The homeless? The poor? Those with huge debts, lacking the means to pay back? The exceptions are numerous and legion, so apparent that analysis shouldn't be required. For these groups, tipping in most instances is an immoral action, insofar as their tips are needed for their survival and/or rudimentary happiness, and spending the extra money would create a hardship. The tip would be trivial or insignificant to the worker but very important to these customers. This principle of utility is central here, and service workers cannot claim the Utilitarian principle in their defense, or with a rather weak argument. For clearly, 'the greatest good for the greatest number of people' will be achieved when these groups of above-mentioned customers refrain from tipping, and the 'greatest good' is more likely to be achieved when all other customers do the same, when the tipping situations are evaluated from the perspectives of the customer and worker. When this is done, in most instances, the majority of the factors[7] which would induce or decrease happiness cannot be known by the customer, so that the full consequences of giving the tip will remain unknown. The Utilitarian happiness principle, as espoused by Mill, therefore, cannot be applied with reasonable accuracy in most of the cases. Among the most affluent customers, the principle will weigh in favor of the workers, among the lower classes, against the workers, but in the large middle classes, the question usually appears much less certain, as the workers themselves are in the middle class. Who can say who will most benefit by a sizeable tip, or not? The Utilitarian principle is not usually argued probably because of this dubious uncertainty, and because service workers do not perceive this as a key issue.

This relationship of dependence between customer and worker is a collective one, moreover, not individualized. That is, the dependence is based on customers as a general group, giving to designated service workers. These workers consider their income from customers as a collective whole, a constantly changing group. All customers are actual/potential tippers. Each individual may or may not contribute to the tipping whole. An important question here is: what are the necessary and sufficient conditions for this relationship or dependence to continue? This Kantian way of putting the question recognizes that this relation has survived and will be part of wage economics, of a public policy, and it's significantly interesting to analyze its minimum requirements, (a philosophical L.C.D.), especially in light of the fact that so many customers and workers are unhappy with this relationship. That is, it is minimally sufficient that enough customers contribute just enough to keep the worker satisfied to the point where he is not so unhappy as to quit the occupation or become too alienated from himself or his work to perform satisfactorily. In this way, the dependent relationship still survives. This dependence, guided by custom and sympathy, does not entail the necessity of each individual contributing each time he is expected to do so—to these pools of gratuities. The regular customer notices the worker's unhappiness, and may feel guilty for not tipping enough, sympathy, and even vicarious alienation. But if these sentiments become the basis and reason for tipping, service may never excel and the game continues.

Arguably, this dependent relationship is fundamentally unjust to customer and worker, as the worker's wages ought not be the responsibility of the customer, contingent on his generosity. Public opinion strongly resists this objection however unjust it seems.

This dependent relationship is similar, in certain aspects, to charitable giving. It is meaningful to think of tips as small donations, contributions to a worthy service. Tips and donations are given to people who might not survive, or have a poorer existence without them. They are voluntarily given in degrees of frequency and amount partly determined by the level of sympathy and the contributor's finances. Although the charity depends on and requires donations

---

[7]We have in mind factors such as the number of children supported by the worker and customer, family income, other dependents, the suffering possibly caused by lack of tips, or the pleasure gained by the tips, weighed against the relative happiness of both parties. This can be figured for the cumulative effect of all tips.

from the collective action of donors, this is in no way necessitates, morally or economically, that every donor or potential donor donate something each time requested to do so, or at every opportunity.

Let us assume that Jones volunteered to be on a list of donors to the Lupus Foundation. However, this doesn't obligate her to contribute some change each time she sees a can labeled 'lupus' on the counters of stores she patronizes. Nor is she obligated each and every time she is asked to pledge a donation by telephone or mail. By consent, though, she is obligated to donate a designated amount some time during the year. Like all donors, she is aware that the charity depends on individual donations to supplement major corporate gifts. The custom of giving will stand unviolated even when only a sufficient number of customers (or donors) and sufficient money validate the custom and the charity survives. Large tips and large donations reinforce this dependence and may make it much stronger, (though it's recognized that small amounts add up.) No doubt, there are important differences between the system of tipping and charities, (such as giving to a whole, as opposed to an individual in decent health), but the idea of morality presupposes sufficient similarity. Furthermore, if enough customers tip large enough sums regularly to specific workers (or charities), then their income will not suffer from those customers who under tip or do not tip. The ethics of charitable giving deserves a more detailed study.

My last argument against the moral justification of tipping is more radical, and has its roots in the Marxist analysis of the wage-labor system.[8] Consider:

A. Service workers often depend on tips for a significant portion of their wages.
B. Through tipping, customers are then paying the wages of these workers.
C. The vast majority of customers of a service business earned their wages by laboring at work. By paying a portion of these worker's wages, customers are therefore spending their labor for them.

Whether the gratuity is added directly to the bill, or given to the workers, there is no difference between paying for the purchase with their labor, or for the tip with their labor; for both, customers worked for the money spent a determined amount of time. (Perhaps a tiny fraction of the customer's wages, but maybe a significant sum over a year or several, depending on individual habits and lifestyle. For example, a teen who works for $5.00 an hour purchases a meal for $10.00 and leaves a 15% tip—$1.50. He has worked over 15 minutes to pay for this tip.)

D. It follows directly, then, that the customer is "working for" the worker whenever he leaves a tip and in proportion to its size.
E. In so doing, the customer is also working for the worker's employer— management which pays his wages. This is not a symbolic relationship; it is very real. Customers are quite literally working for these workers, and in this way, for management itself.

---

[8]S. Jhally, *The Codes of Advertising* (New York: St. Martin's Press, 1987), pp. 83–90. Jhally develops a similar argument for viewers watching commercials and their sponsors from a Marxist perspective.

This relationship prescribes or permits an implied, free and autonomous power to evaluate each worker's performance in order to determine the tip, i.e., the labor spent to support the worker. Each customer may well ask: "how many minutes do I wish to work to pay the wages of this worker?" "Or all workers?" This power of choice and questioning is within each of us to use as we wish. Thus, as management sets the hourly wages and service standards, and just as we work for management in our own small way through tipping, we also determine this part of their wages and service standards in situations where tips are expected. In fact, when the tip is determined by the price of goods purchased (as in restaurants), the tip can often be in disproportion to the actual work involved. Tipping seems unobjectionable to many customers probably because one spends a relatively small amount each time, and the total spent is usually not calculated. It could total several hundred annually, or more, depending on the individual, and one doesn't consider the goods or services which could've been purchased instead.

The reasons for tipping combine sympathy with the customer's personal gratifications, and it can be difficult to clarify one's true motives. Tipping for egoistic reasons, such as from guilt, fear of disapproval, for friendly speedy service, or the pleasure in giving, is individually relative, and establishes no strong valid universal principle. So, too, sympathy, though an admirable virtue, by itself in this context, is based on an emotional consciousness, and thus too subjective and insufficient to ground or imply a prescriptive moral rule for all.

The practice of tipping has always been a matter of personal judgment, grounded in custom and expectation in most industrialized nations though some have a public policy against it.[9] In certain circumstances, tipping appears mandated, as if it was a moral obligation which ought not be ignored or violated. But this sense or obligation is based only on custom, the collective praxis of ordinary individuals. From this custom, no universal moral obligation should be inferred.

Questions

1. Can the expectations of taxi drivers and porters that they will be tipped, no matter how unreasonable, provide moral grounds for tipping?
2. Are there reasons for thinking it morally *unreasonable* or *wrong* to tip people like taxi drivers (for quite ordinary service)?
3. Can Mark Maller's Marxist-inspired argument be applied equally well to non-tipping payments for services? For instance, in paying the electrician for his services are we not working for the electrician, according to Mark Maller's argument? If so, is that a *reductio ad absurdum* of his argument?

Suggestions for Further Reading on Tipping

SCHEIN, J. *The Art of Tipping*. Wausau, WI.: Sun Press, 1984.
VISSER, MARGARET. "Tipping." In *The Way We Are*. London: Viking, 1995.

[9] New Zealand, the former Soviet Union, China, and many South Pacific nations have or have had policies against tipping. The Chinese considered tipping to be rude according to Schein, p. 138.

PART SIX

Body and Environment

CHAPTER 16

Substance and Sustenance

The Moral Status of Smoking

Keith Butler

Keith Butler argues that it is morally wrong for smokers to smoke in the presence of non-smokers. He says that in a situation in which smokers and non-smokers share a space, the smokers, by smoking, do something to the non-smokers whereas the non-smokers do not do anything to the smokers. The smokers perform an act. The non-smokers are passive. Thus, if it is the case that smoking harms the non-smokers, the smokers cannot be said to have a right to smoke in their presence. He gives the analogy of a right to discharge firearms. Such a right cannot exist where firing the weapon would harm somebody.

The author then addresses the question of whether smoking harms. He argues that smoking in the presence of non-smokers causes the non-smokers (1) annoyance, (2) irritation, and (3) disease. Even the least severe of these—annoyance—is a form of harm, argues the author. He then lists some additional ways in which smoking can have pernicious effects on non-smokers.

It is well known that cigarette smoking[1] is dangerous to one's health; 350,000 Americans die prematurely each year from the effects of smoking, and millions more live on in ruined health with crippled lungs and overstrained hearts.[2] Non-smokers often question the rationality of smoking in light of these enormous health risks: Why engage in an activity that will ruin your health and

---

[1] Though I will explicitly talk only about cigarette smoking, the points I shall make apply to all other forms of tobacco smoking as well: pipes, cigars, and clove cigarettes.

[2] Tobacco industry advocates vocally question these claims; in spite of the findings of over 50,000 studies on the issue, they maintain that there is no consensus on the health risks of smoking within the scientific community. It is beyond the scope of this paper to rebuke the arguments of tobacco industry advocates on this matter, though I think it is worth noting that the hypothesis that smoking causes cancer, heart disease, and other illnesses is as well-confirmed as just about any accepted scientific hypothesis where it is infeasible to trace casual lineages directly.

Keith Butler, "The Moral Status of Smoking," *Social Theory and Practice,* vol. 19, no. 1 (Spring 1993): 1–20. Copyright 1993 by *Social Theory and Practice.*

perhaps eventually kill you? Smokers defiantly, if evasively, respond with the claim that they have the right to smoke, even if it is not the most rational thing to do. But do they? This is a moral issue, one that has immediate implications for public policy regarding smoking.

For the purposes of this paper, I will assume that individuals at least sometimes have rights,[3] and that these rights place corresponding duties on others to respect those rights. I will demonstrate, within this context, that smokers do not have the right to smoke, in a wide variety of cases, because it is inconsistent with their duty to respect the right of others (to be free from harm). There are many to whom this claim is obvious; this paper is not written for them (though there are many subtleties to this issue that are often overlooked by even non-smokers). It is instead directed at those who regard smoking to be a matter of personal choice outside the normal boundaries of ethical inquiry. . . .

SOME GROUNDWORK

Activity vs. Passivity

There are differences between shooting someone and being shot. Among these differences is that the shooter, A, has done something to the one who has been shot, P; with respect to the shooting, ceteris paribus, A is active while P is passive. One can imagine cases where P has jumped in the path of a speeding bullet that would otherwise have missed him, in which case he is not passive; but this is the deviant case. In the normal case, there is an asymmetry between A and P that corresponds to the difference between activity and passivity. I am not yet claiming that A has done something wrong in shooting P; I only mean to say that A, in shooting P, has done something to P. P, on the other hand, in so far as he is shot by A, has done nothing to A. With respect to other activities, P may be quite active; he might have provoked A, thrust guilt upon A, or ruined A's life. But whatever P has done to A, and P may have done many things, being shot is not one of them.

It is important that this distinction between activity and passivity not be confused with the more controversial philosophical distinction between doing something to another and letting something happen to another. The moral relevance of this distinction is often debated in the context of euthanasia. The distinction I want to draw is not at all concerned with such issues as killing vs. letting die. Rather it is concerned with such issues as killing vs. being killed. This may be an obvious distinction, but it will be crucial to the arguments that

---

[3]There are well-known conceptual issues involving the nature of rights (see Becker, 1992, p. 1103 ff.). I do not wish to rest the thesis of this paper on any particular outcome of these disputes. Because this issue is usually couched in terms of rights, I will not be considering issues that arise only when it is looked at from a Utilitarian perspective. Some cost/benefit analysis, however, will clearly be relevant. See L. Becker, *The Encyclopedia of Ethics*, Volumes I and II, (New York: Garland Publishing Inc., 1992), p. 1103 ff.

follow. For when we move to cases involving smoking, it is easy to forget that smokers are doing something to non-smokers in a way that non-smokers are not doing anything to smokers.

The Harm Principle

Let us grant that one has the right to discharge firearms. A may justifiably exercise this right in a shooting gallery and, possibly, in the woods hunting for food; the right may even be exercised justifiably in a state of war and in situations that require self-defense. A, however, may not justifiably exercise this right when the discharged bullet is directed at another person, P, who has not provoked the assault. The right to discharge firearms has limits, and those limits are fairly obviously marked in cases of shooting: When A's shooting is going to harm P, the right to shoot must yield to P's right to be free from harm. P may forfeit his right to be free from harm by provoking A (by shooting first, or trespassing, or fleeing from a crime, etc.). But if the shooting is unprovoked, then it would seem clear that A has violated P's right to be free from harm.

The general rule here seems to be that one's rights to pursue an activity survives only so long as the exercise of that right does not infringe upon the right of another to be free from harm. The right to be free from harm is in some sense more basic than the rights one may have to perform certain activities. This "harm principle" is perhaps the fundamental liberty-limiting principle.

The crucial issue, however, involves the application of this principle to particular cases. It is difficult to interpret this general rule without some understanding of sorts of harms it is intended to protect against. For not all harms are within the purview of the harm principle; harms inflicted in most sporting contexts are surely excluded, as are harms in cases of self-defense, just wars, and the like. These are excluded, of course, because the one harmed has forfeited his right to freedom from harm. But even where this right is not forfeited, there are some harms that the principle cannot reasonably be expected to protect against. A severe homophobe may, in some sense, be harmed by the mere mention of homosexual activity, but that is no license to restrict the mention of homosexual behavior.

Some draw a distinction between harm and offense, and this can be used to do some work in separating cases that fall within the purview of the harm principle from those that do not. Harms set back the interests, or are otherwise injurious to the welfare, of those who are harmed,[4] while offenses merely violate the sensibilities of those offended, but leave them otherwise undamaged. While disturbances of the peace and such intrusions are not harmful, they do affect others in something like the way that offenses do. The strict harm principle would seem to be uncontroversial, and would protect against unprovoked assaults, bodily injury, and the like. Our homophobe, however, is not harmed; and while he may be offended, he cannot seek protection under the harm principle.

---

[4]Joel Feinberg, *Harm to Others* (Oxford: Oxford University Press, 1984).

Might there also be a weakened version of the harm principle, though, one that protects against intrusions like offenses in the way that the harm principle protects against harm?[5] The concern here is to distinguish between intrusions and offenses that are morally significant, and hence have a role in forging a public policy, and those that are more properly a matter of etiquette, best dealt with privately on a voluntary basis. Some offenses are quite clearly sufficiently significant to warrant legal restraint, for example, being taunted by a flasher for several hours a day. The offenses may collapse back into a variety of harm; one's interests are set back, one's welfare is not maintained. Other offenses, like our homophobe's, seem either too trivial or too unreasonable to warrant restraint. We might, as a matter of etiquette, not flaunt our disrespect for the homophobe by continuing to talk about homosexuality, but even that is to be left to our discretion.

But presumably there is a range of cases that fall between these two extremes, where the applicability of some sort of liberty-limiting principle will be difficult to determine. Feinberg[6] considers several factors that should be considered in determining the extent of an offense and the applicability of a liberty-limiting principle. These factors include such things as the magnitude of the offense, the reasonableness of avoiding the offense, the extent to which incurring the offense was voluntary, the extent to which incurring the offense was owing to abnormal susceptibility, and several others. Given the complexity of the calculations involving these and other parameters, it is not likely that we are going to settle on clear and uncontroversial criteria according to which intrusions and offenses may be subsumed under a weakened version of the harm principle. Offensive and intrusive behavior will have to be judged on a case-by-case basis. And in the absence of any straightforward application of a liberty-limiting principle, we will have to be very careful to take account of all factors that play a role in the offense or intrusion.

As a matter of principle, then, we will assume that one does not have the right to inflict unprovoked harm upon others, where "harm" is understood to be injurious to the welfare of those who are harmed. In applying this principle to particular cases where the harms are not blatant, however, we must pay particular attention to specific details of the cases in question. There is significant slack in the move from a general principle regarding intrusions and offenses to a verdict regarding a particular case. Those intrusions that collapse into harms would seem to be uncontroversially limited, while those that do not are for the most part the subject of controversy. In the case of smoking there will be some respects in which exposure to secondhand smoke is a clear harm, in which case the harm principle can be applied uncontroversially. In other cases, though, the effects of secondhand smoke are more difficult to assess, though there still remains a sense in which secondhand smoke remains an affront to the non-smoker. In either case, I will be focusing throughout this paper on specific aspects of the practice of smoking and its relation to non-smokers.

[5]Joel Feinberg, *Offense to Others* (Oxford: Oxford University Press, 1985).
[6]Feinberg, *Offense to Others*, pp. 7–9 and 35.

So much for the groundwork on which the following discussion will be based. I turn now to a direct consideration of the practice of smoking against this backdrop. I will first lay out the form the argument will take, which gets broken down along three not altogether unrelated dimensions; I discuss each in turn. Following this, I will consider additional factors that weigh against smokers' rights, and policy options suggested by the various versions of the argument.

THE BASIC ARGUMENT

Suppose there is a public room, say a bar, populated by smokers and non-smokers, and individuals of both groups have the right to be present in the room. The air in the room is filled with smoke, and it is clear that the cause of this is the activity of the smokers. Since the non-smokers have to breathe the smoky air they had no part in producing, the smokers are doing something to the non-smokers (in the way that a shooter is doing something to the one who is shot). Since both the smokers and the non-smokers have equal right to be present in the room, the non-smokers stand to smokers as victims stand to those who shoot them. The non-smokers have actively placed themselves in the room, presumably, but they have not actively done anything to the smokers in the way that the smokers have actively done something to them. Nor have they actively sought to place themselves in a smoky environment (except, of course, in the deviant case where a non-smoker wishes to breathe smoky air); that responsibility belongs to the smokers.

If the non-smokers are harmed by the presence of the smoke, then the smokers have violated the harm principle. The right to smoke persists only so long as the act of smoking does not conflict with the more basic right of non-smokers to be free from harm. On the condition that they are causing harm, the smokers are obliged to refrain from smoking, and this remains true even if those doing the harm are unaware of the harm they are causing.[7] This places a burden on smokers to change their behavior to comply with the rights of non-smokers. This inconvenience to smokers, which is often viewed as harm to smokers, is asymmetrically related to the harm caused to non-smokers; it is the smokers who are doing something to the non-smokers, while the reverse is not true. This point is crucial in determining an appropriate policy when the interests of smokers and non-smokers conflict. If harm is indeed being caused, public policy should prevent the smoker from smoking in this room.

The issue now turns on whether the smokers are harming the non-smokers. There are at least three levels on which smoking may harm non-smokers. The first involves the distasteful odor of cigarette smoke, in the air and in the clothes and hair of even non-smokers who are in the same room as a smoker; let us call

---

[7]It even remains true if those being harmed are unaware of the harm brought on them so long as they would object if they were aware of that harm (imagine industrial polluters claiming the right to pollute the fishing waters of an uninformed public on the grounds that the public doesn't realize the harm being done to them). More on this later.

this the level of annoyance. The second involves the short-term physiological irritation of the eyes, nose, mouth, throat, and lungs caused by the inhalation of smoke; let us call this the level of irritation. The third involves the longterm risk of disease caused by repeated exposure to secondhand smoke; let us call this the level of disease. At each of these three levels we must determine whether the harm is sufficiently significant to warrant the application of the harm principle, and where it is not true, we must focus on specific features of actual situations to determine if the right to smoke should be curtailed.

LEVELS OF HARM

I will now consider, in order of increasing severity, each level of harm caused to non-smokers by smokers.

Annoyance

Smoke is annoying when one would simply prefer not to breathe it. This is an offense to, or intrusion upon, the non-smoker, rather than an obvious harm, so it is unlikely that we are going to get a straightforward application of the harm principle. We must therefore be very careful to examine specific features of the situations in which this offense arises; only in this way will we be able to determine if annoyance is sufficient to militate against the moral right to smoke. I will argue that what might appear to be a trivial matter best left to etiquette is often quite the contrary. I will take it that the weight of the following considerations from annoyance, taken individually, is limited; but weight accumulates, and the sum total is rather more than trivial. Consider a non-smoker in his own home. Here the rights of property ownership and autonomy give weight to one's preferences beyond what they might otherwise enjoy. Should someone be smoking in a non-smoker's home, the smoker surely must respect the non-smoker's preference to be free from secondhand smoke. In this respect, smoking is no different from other activities one simply does not want performed in one's own home.

But suppose that the smoker is a friend, a business associate, or a superior. Because of these relationships, the non-smoker may, as a matter of course, be made to feel some pressure to acquiesce to the smoker's desire to smoke. For example, if it is his boss, he may be made to feel that his job or working conditions will be jeopardized if he "sticks to his guns" and refuses to allow smoking in his home. If it is a friend, he may feel that the friendship will be strained if he insists on his right to be free from secondhand smoke. Social pressures of this sort are significant features of many actual situations and should be given moral weight. The non-smoking homeowner has the moral (and legal) right to stipulate policy in his or her home, and an offender should not be allowed to exert pressure, knowingly or otherwise, on the homeowner. When forming a policy on the practice of smoking, we should take into account that, even on his own property, there are situations where a non-smoker can be forced by real and significant pressures to sacrifice his right unwillingly. Widespread tolerance of smoking will only increase the probability that non-smokers will face such pressures unjustifiably.

Suppose that a smoker challenges this result on the grounds that the annoyance caused by secondhand smoke is too small to be of moral concern. This sort of worry can be met in two ways: First, the smoker probably doesn't know how the non-smoker reacts to the presence of smoker, and since smoking destroys olfactory sensitivity,[8] the smoker probably cannot know how distasteful smoke can be to a non-smoker. And because smoking induces a thick mucus film in the lungs of smokers that dilutes possible irritants, smokers are less likely to suffer the sort of physiological irritation that compounds the extent to which a non-smoker is annoyed by exposure to secondhand smoke. Former smokers are often surprised to discover that when one is not smoking, the extent of the annoyance is rather more than trivial. It is unlikely that the smoker can have any justification to claim that some particular amount of annoyance is insignificant; how would she know? Second, in actual situations, we do not find an isolated instance of a non-smoker being annoyed by a smoker. Each non-smoking individual is affected by every smoker with whom he comes into contact. This includes smoke in the workplace, restaurants, bars, and other public forums. The level of annoyance can be much greater than any smoker might realize since it is not an individual smoker, but a team of smokers with which the non-smoker must contend; and as a team, smokers constitute a powerful collective source of annoyance. Whether an annoyance can reach the level of moral status depends on just how annoyed one can get. If one is sufficiently annoyed at the presence of secondhand smoke, then it might very well be a moral issue, and it is hard to see how the smoker is in a position to challenge this.

So suppose that in a bar or public room where both the smoker and the non-smoker have the right to be, the non-smoker objects to the smoke because it just plain smells bad; it is annoying and he prefers not to have to smell it in the air, in his hair, or in his clothes.[9] Is this offense analogous to the homophobe's offense mentioned above, or is it analogous to, say, disturbing the peace, which is actionable under law?[10]

There would seem to be several crucial disanalogies between the case of smoking and the case of the homophobe. First, the annoyance in the case of smoking is a physiological reaction, one that seems to fall well within the range of biologically normal reactions to one's environment, while the homophobe's reaction is cognitive and idiosyncratic. Cognitive reactions depend directly on what else one believes, while physiological reactions typically do not. Given this, there is likely to be a range of biologically normal reactions to one's environment in a way that there is not likely to be a range of cognitively normal reactions. Most non-smokers find the smell of smoke to be unpleasant (though some to a greater extent than others), while there is no corresponding

---

[8]G. Kittel, "Results of Clinical Olfactometric Studies," *Rhinology* 14 (1976): 99–108.
[9]We mustn't forget that in the context of annoyance, the effects of smoking extend well beyond the immediate olfactory distress; these effects can linger, and can cause one to make a trip to the laundromat that one would rather not make, and otherwise wouldn't have made.
[10]Goodin, *No Smoking*, p. 64.

agreement in attitude toward homosexuality. Preferring not to breathe second-hand smoke is not idiosyncratic in the way that preferring not to hear talk of homosexuality is. And in any case, cognitive reactions fall within the purview of reason, and can be examined accordingly. Such is not the case with physiological reactions. Second, the behavior that the homophobe wants restricted involves the expression of one's beliefs. Typically this sort of restriction involves censorship. The non-smoker, however, is not looking to censor the smoker's freedom of expression.[11] Smoking restrictions no more involve censorship of smoking than shooting restrictions involve censorship of shooting.

On the other hand, there are some interesting similarities between the case of smoking and the case of disturbing the peace (for example, loud music). In neither case does the impetus for restriction have anything to do with cognitive content; both involve mere physiological reactions to the environment. And in each case, the sort of reaction that calls for restriction is within the range of biologically normal reactions, and is hence not idiosyncratic. On balance, then, it would seem that the case of smoking is rather more analogous to cases of disturbing the peace than it is to the case of the homophobe. If there is a moral mandate to restrict disturbances of the peace and other like offenses, then there should be a moral mandate to restrict smoking.

Suppose that smokers grant the disanalogies between the case of smoking and the case of the homophobe, and even the analogies between smoking and disturbing the peace. This still leaves unaddressed the extent to which smoking is analogous to, say, the smell of perfume, cologne, or even food. There are no restrictions on the use of perfume and the smell of food even though these affect people in the same way as smoking, and may be objectionable to some people; why should there be restrictions on smoking if there are no restrictions on perfume or cologne?

Again, we have to look carefully at actual situations involving both to determine the extent of the analogy. Though there are similarities in the way smoke and perfume affect individuals (that is, olfactorily), there are many more differences in the nature and magnitude of that effect. First, perfume is normally pleasing to smell. Though there may be individuals who prefer not to smell perfume, they are certainly in the minority. And given that the whole point of perfume is to smell good to people, it is hard to see how the perfume industry could flourish if its products were widely distasteful and offensive. Secondhand smoke, on the other hand, is widely distasteful and offensive. These statistical and biological norms are certainly relevant when it comes to implications for public policy. Second, in most cases where restrictive measures are needed, there is a difference in the magnitude of secondhand smoke as against the magnitude of perfume. A single cigarette in a hallway, office, or common room will have an impact greater than perfume or cologne. And in the

---

[11]Except in so far as the smoker views her behavior as having some cognitive content that the smoking restriction prevents her from expressing. In that case, however, any infringement on expression is incidental; the smoking behavior is restricted for reasons that have nothing to do with the putative content of the 'expression.'

absence of restrictions, it will not be a single cigarette, but many, in which case the level of smoke and its impact on others will far exceed that of perfume or cologne; the persistently hazy atmosphere in bars and taverns will attest to this.

The annoyance of secondhand smoke would seem to carry some moral weight in the determination of a public policy regarding smoking. I have tried not to quantify too precisely how much weight should be given to this consideration, except to argue that it deserves some moral weight as against no moral weight. Nor have I attempted to carefully define appropriate sorts of restrictions. After we have examined the more obvious harms of irritation and disease, we will take stock of the strength of the total case, and what sort of restrictions are called for.

Irritation

The most obvious and common forms of physiological irritation due to secondhand smoke affect the eyes, nose, mouth, throat, and lungs of non-smokers. Speer[12] reports that 69% of nonallergic subjects complained of eye irritation during passive exposure to cigarette smoke, while 32% complained of headache, 29% of nasal symptoms, and 25% of cough. With respect to eye irritation, it may take the form of lachrymation, or a stinging of the eyes, depending upon how quickly the precorneal tear film is broken up by the secondhand smoke. This may also result in an impairment of the optical properties of the corneal surface,[13] and also conjunctive infection.[14] With respect to nasal irritation, complaints range from foul odor, nasal discharge, and nasal obstruction[15] to itching, dryness, and frequent rubbing;[16] smoke-induced post nasal drip may provoke coughing as well. These symptoms may also contribute to mouth-irritation by causing mouth-breathing, which can in turn lead to throat irritation. Irritation can also be felt in the lungs, since only a very modest exposure to cigarette smoke will retard the activity of the cilia and promote the development of mucus, thus leading to cough.

The point here should be plain: Quite apart from the annoyance non-smokers experience at the foul smell of cigarette smoke, there are real and certain physiological irritations caused by passive exposure to cigarette smoke. There is no question that these are harms and that smokers are causing these harms. We can now expect a straightforward application of the harm principle. Smokers harm non-smokers, and therefore violate the right of non-smokers to be free from unprovoked harm. Given the uncontroversial application of the harm principle, we

[12]"Tobacco and the Non-Smoker: A Study of the Subjective Symptoms," *Archives of Environmental Health* 16 (1968): 443–46.

[13]M. Grayson and R. Keates, *Manual of Diseases of the Cornea* (Boston: Little, Brown, and Co., 1969).

[14]C. H. Dohlman, J. Friend, B. Kalevar, D. Yagoda, and E. Balazs, "The Glycoprotein (mucus) Content of Tears from Normal and Dry Eye Patients," *Experimental Eye Results* 22 (1976): 359–65.

[15]P. Pimm, R. Shepard, and F. Silverman, "Physiological Affects of Acute Exposure to Cigarette Smoke," *Archives of Environmental Health* 33 (1978): 201–213.

[16]A. Weber, C. Jermini, and E. Grandjean, "Irritating Effects on Man of Air Pollution Due to Cigarette Smoke," *American Journal of Public Health* 66 (1976): 672–76.

have a touchstone with which to probe complex and controversial arguments concerning the nature of the interaction between smokers and non-smokers.

Consider first the surprisingly popular attitude that if non-smokers experience irritation when exposed to secondhand smoke, they are free to leave the room, and thereby put an end to their irritation. No one, of course, will dispute that non-smokers are free to leave, but so too are smokers. The pertinent question is, Who is it who ought to leave? In laying out the groundwork for this paper, we considered carefully the asymmetry in the contributions made by active and passive participants in certain situations (for example, shootings). This asymmetry is present in situations involving smokers and non-smokers and the conflict over secondhand smoke. It is the smokers who actively infringe upon the rights of the non-smokers in the way that a gun-wielder actively infringes upon the rights of an innocent victim. And just as no one would treat the gun-wielder's right to discharge his or her firearm on a level with the victim's right to be free from harm, we should not treat the smoker's right to smoke on a level with the non-smoker's right to be free from harm. The application of the harm principle depends on this asymmetry. And given that the principle does indeed apply to this case, it is the smoker who is duty-bound to respect the right of the non-smoker, either by leaving or refraining from smoking.

The smoker may at this point charge that, by preventing her from smoking, the non-smoker is causing her harm, namely, the discomfort brought on by nicotine deprivation. Certainly, she may claim, a smoker has as much right to avoid discomfort as a non-smoker. Therefore, by application of the harm principle, a compromise must be reached that allows the smoker to cause harm to the non-smoker in proportion to the amount of discomfort the smoker experiences in abstaining for a substantial length of time. After all, what we have here is a conflict of rights, and in such cases the conflict has to be resolved by compromise.

There are two lines of resistance open to the non-smoker in this case. First, the asymmetry in the contributions of the smoker and non-smoker to this conflict again justifies the application of the harm principle in such a way that protects the rights of the non-smoker, and not the reverse. It is a common but peculiar mistake of smoking advocates to the frame issue in such a way as to simply assume that the rights of smokers and non-smokers should be treated as equal. The whole point of applying the harm principle to this case, however, is to show that these rights are not equal, any more than the gun-wielder's right to shoot is equal to the victim's right to be free from harm. A person's right to engage in an activity must, if it causes harm to others, yield to the other's right to be free from harm. There is simply no provision in this principle that says that it only applies if the offender is not put out by ceasing the activity. It just doesn't matter whether ceasing that activity is somehow uncomfortable to the offender, and it is a red herring to argue as if it does.

Second, relatedly, the discomfort caused by the smoker's abstention is entirely self-inflicted. It would not occur if the smoker had not taken steps that have resulted in his addiction to nicotine. It is, in fact, identical to the misery of abstention suffered by any drug addict who cannot indulge his habit (this is not surprising, of course, since the cigarette smoker is a drug addict, that is, a nicotine addict). It is obvious, I take it, that it is not within a drug addict's right to steal from a drug store to indulge his habit and relieve his discomfort. Such self-inflicted discomfort does not justify violating the rights of others (for example, to retain their property). Similarly, a smoker's self-inflicted discomfort does not justify violating the rights of others' (for example, to be free from harm). The smoker has put himself in such a position, and once in that position, he is not entitled to violate the rights of others to get out of that position. Never mind that the smoker may have put himself in that position without realizing what he was doing; the same may be true of drug addicts and we are not likely to allow them to trample on the rights of others to make up for this lack of foresight. We might, in some cases, want to extend some compassion toward people in these pitiable positions; but that is a far cry from claiming that such people have rights on equal footing with the right to be free from harm.

Given this, what is the appropriate response to the smoker who implores others to be tolerant? Everyone has vices, this person will maintain, and we should all be tolerant of others' weaknesses. After all, in many of the cases I have described, the inconvenience to the non-smoker is only minimal and hardly life-threatening. Why worry so much about such a little problem?

I have argued above that the smoker is in no position to argue about the size of the problem, but even if the issue of secondhand smoke is minor when compared to other public health hazards (which is a plausible position given the recent finding regarding fluorocarbons and the ozone layer), that is absolutely no reason to consider it morally irrelevant. That there are more serious problems bodes ill for society in general, but it does not weaken or even address the problems we have already seen regarding secondhand smoke. I don't get any shorter if there are tall people around; the problems with involuntary exposure to secondhand smoke don't get any smaller if there are bigger problems around. Some problems may be more pressing, but that doesn't meant that nothing should be done about this problem; it may just have to wait its turn for policy consideration.

Also, the smoker is himself as much in need of tolerance as anyone. He or she is under moral obligation to "tolerate" our desire to remain free of foul and hurtful secondhand smoke? After all, most instances of public cigarette smoking are hardly trivial, especially when one considers that an overwhelming majority of the time it takes to smoke a cigarette (perhaps 95%) is spent with the cigarette fouling the air of everyone around, and only a small percentage of the time is it serving its destructive but gratifying function for the smoker. In fact, it is not clear why the non-smoker should be at all tolerant, even in the most trivial of cases. If I should bottle car exhaust and give people a little spritz just for grins, should I be tolerated? It is probably no more or less harmful or annoying than cigarette smoke, but because it doesn't enjoy the morally irrelevant but timehonored sanction of social tolerance and apathy, no one would be inclined in the least to tolerate it. The situation with smokers should be treated no differently. The bottom line, after all, is that it is the smokers who are violating the rights of others. If tolerance is called for, I suggest that it is the smokers who are obliged to be so.

So far, the discussion of physiological irritation has assumed that the smoker and the non-smoker have equal right to be present in the room or bar where the conflict arises. How are the moral dynamics altered when the non-smoker is at the home or in the office of the smoker? Hasn't the smoker got the right to smoke at home, even if it is to the detriment of the non-smoker? Here we have a real conflict between the legal rights of property ownership, with their attendant moral rights regarding autonomy, and the moral right of the non-smoker to be free from harm.

In its baldest form, this sort of situation does seem to constitute an instance where legal rights preserve for the smoker the moral right to smoke even when that activity causes harm to others. But there are permutations on even this sort of situation that may have a moral bearing. As we noted above, there are myriad pressures at play in typical social and professional situations: The non-smoker may unwillingly find himself in the home or office of smokers, and is only able to leave on pain of offending a friend or co-worker, or some other such consequence. For the non-smoker simply wishing not to be harmed, the burden to take matters into his own hands seems unfairly steep. In the more drastic case of shooting, the right to discharge a firearm is not preserved simply on strength of the autonomy given by property ownership; one wonders what relevant difference there is in the case of smoking. If the non-smoker were truly free to leave, there would seem to be no problem with the right to smoke on private property. But that is very often not the case, and policy decisions must take this into account.

There are also those instances involving the acutely vulnerable; for example, asthmatics and others allergic to cigarette smoke may deserve special consideration, in which case it is not clear that smokers have the moral right, even on their own property, to inflict harm on people of unusual vulnerability. There is also substantial public ignorance on the short-term (and long-term) risks of cigarette smoking and its effect on others, so there is some question whether smokers are even aware of the sort of discomfort their smoking inflicts on their guests. An element of thoughtlessness is evident in some cases; this may not be a moral consideration of great weight, but it does demonstrate to a certain extent the need for restrictions that are a matter of policy rather than etiquette. Perhaps some sort of educational policy is in order so that the risks of unwanted exposure to second-hand smoke are minimized.[17]

There is a general point that seems not to be affected by the autonomy provided by property ownership: It is not the responsibility of the person harmed to have to take steps to see that his right to freedom from harm is respected (though he surely has the right to do so if need be). For if it were, people not terribly outspoken or aggressive would have their right (even more) routinely trampled upon by the ambitious and powerful. The non-smoker may simply believe (incorrectly) that she has no right to protest, and so remain conscientiously silent so as to avoid overstepping her rights, or she may be forcefully conditioned by years of public tolerance of smoking to repress any urge to do something about the irritation caused by cigarette smoke. The point of legal restrictions is to protect the rights of all people, including those who, for whatever reason, are unable to protect themselves; this includes non-smokers who unfairly would have to face unwanted consequences for defending their right to be free from harm. Without such protection, the powerful would have all the rights, and the vulnerable

[17]Contrast this with Goodin's discussion of the right to smoke on private property. *No Smoking*, p. 71.

would have none.[18] This responsibility to protect non-smokers is not unlike the responsibility to protect those who are particularly vulnerable in society. Goodin[19] argues that the special responsibilities parents have to protect their children, or societies have to protect those who cannot take care of themselves, are really instances of a more general responsibility to protect those who are vulnerable. There is good reason for a public policy that protects non-smokers in all places where they may rightfully roam, including the private property of a smoker.[20]

Physiological irritation justifies application of the harm principle to cases involving passive exposure to secondhand smoke. The moral weight from these considerations, as well as the previous considerations based on annoyance, is beginning to accumulate. We now turn to the level of disease and the now famous statistics about the health risk of secondhand smoke. For in the case of disease, the moral weight is dramatically greater than either of the cases we have discussed so far.

Disease

The issue first reached public consciousness in the USA with the 1986 Surgeon General's Report on passive smoking, but the information can now be found in any brochure or pamphlet from the American Lung Association, the American Heart Association, or the American Cancer Society. The facts are these: According to a report sponsored by the EPA, over 53,000 non-smoking Americans die each year from lung cancer and heart disease caused by secondhand smoke.[21] No doubt these figures are initially shocking, but in light of the fact that cigarette smoke contains some 4,000 pollutants, 200 of which are known poisons, and 50 of which are carcinogenic,[22] it becomes almost expected. Moreover, and this is important, sidestream smoke (the smoke from the burning end of a cigarette) is more dangerous than mainstream smoke (the smoke inhaled by the smoker) because sidestream smoke does not pass through a filter in the manner of mainstream smoke. Sidestream smoke contains more carcinogens, more tar and nicotine, and up to fifteen times more carbon monoxide (which robs the blood of oxygen) than mainstream smoke.[23]

These figures only begin to tell the story; there remains the question of non-fatal diseases and ailments caused by secondhand smoke. Consider first that only a few puffs of a cigarette will increase the heart rate, increase blood pressure, and upset the flow of blood and air in the lungs. In small doses this will only cause mild discomfort; but prolonged exposure will lead to an overstrained

[18]Contrast this with Goodin who, in my view, doesn't fully appreciate this point. *No Smoking*, p. 70.
[19]R. Goodin, *Protecting the Vulnerable: A Reanalysis of Our Social Responsibilities* (Chicago: University of Chicago Press, 1985).
[20]Non-smokers may not be able to rightfully roam into a smokers convention, or a bar that is designated for smoking. It is interesting to note, however, that if a public policy is invoked that fully protects the non-smokers' rights, then bars (at least) that permit smoking might be immoral. More on this later.
[21]*Wisconsin State Journal,* May 30, 1991, p. SA.
[22]American Lung Association, 1990.

heart, hardened or blocked arteries and decreased efficiency of organs that rely on blood flow for oxygen. Perhaps more importantly, however, this little exposure to cigarette smoke will begin to paralyze the cilia in the lungs, the hairlike bodies that normally sweep out germs, mucous, and dirt from the lungs.[24] This leaves the lungs exposed to infections of all kinds. In sinus cavities, too, tissue irritation brought on by exposure to secondhand smoke can cause swelling that obstructs normal draining, thus increasing the risk of sinusitis. Sidestream smoke also contains significantly increased amounts of carbon monoxide, which, when it enters the bloodstream, restricts one's ability to transport oxygen from the air to the working tissues of the body. Very small does of carbon monoxide are known to reduce endurance time for hard physical work,[25] and this is unwelcome news for those who enjoy endurance athletics, where even an extremely modest 1% reduction in oxygen transport could significantly impair performance.[26] Given that sidestream smoke is more destructive than mainstream smoke, it would not take long in the presence of a smoker for one to intake the equivalent of a few puffs of a cigarette, and for the ill-effects of smoke to significantly weaken one's defenses against disease and infection. There is simply no way to estimate just how large the number is of colds and other respiratory problems that could be prevented if secondhand smoke could be eliminated.

In light of this, it is no surprise that young children of smoking parents are twice as likely to develop acute respiratory illnesses (for example, bronchitis and pneumonia) as compared with children of non-smoking parents, and that smoking by parents aggravates symptoms in asthmatic children, and can even trigger asthmatic episodes. Children ages five to nine whose parents smoke show impaired lung function as compared to children whose parents don't smoke.[27] Cigarette smoke in the bloodstream of a pregnant woman alters the heart rate, blood pressure, oxygen supply and acid balance of the unborn infant; pregnant women who smoke have more stillbirths, spontaneous abortions, and low-weight babies than do non-smoking mothers.[28] Figures are not available describing the extent of disease, infection and impaired function of the lungs and heart for adults exposed to secondhand smoke, but the sheer number of deaths and the known effects on children provide a clear picture of what those figures will look like. Secondhand smoke is a serious health risk to non-smokers. Professor Nicholas Ward of St. Bartholomew's hospital in London says flat out that there is "no longer any disagreements among scientists that passive smoking is harmful to adults and children, and can be fatal."

---

[24]T. Dalhamm, "Effects of Cigarette Smoke on Ciliary Activity," *American Review of Respiratory Disorders* 93 (1966): 108–14.

[25]A. Seppanen, "Smoking in Closed Space and Its Effect on Carboxyhaemoglobin Saturation of Smoking and Non-smoking Subjects," *Annual Clinical Results* 9 (1977): 269–74.

[26]R. Shepard, *The Risks of Passive Smoking* (New York: Oxford University Press, 1982), p. 58.

[27]American Lung Association, *The Facts about Secondhand Smoke,* American Lung Association Printing, 1987.

[28]American Lung Association, *Cigarette Smoke: The Facts about Your Lungs,* American Lung Association Printing, 1987.

The application of the harm principle is clear: Even if cigarette smoke isn't irritating to a non-smoker, its detrimental effects on non-smokers can be felt in a very big way for a very long time. The sort of harm at issue is dramatically greater than the irritation and aggravation caused by secondhand smoke. There can be no question that any government has a moral obligation to protect its citizens against such uncalled-for, blatant harm. Prolonged and regular exposure to secondhand smoke must be eliminated.

ADDITIONAL FACTORS

The various ways in which exposure to secondhand smoke is harmful have given us a rather compelling collection of reasons to limit smoking in order to protect the non-smoker from harm. These harms are each rather straightforward consequences of exposure to secondhand smoke. But exposure to secondhand smoke is not the only way in which smoking can have a pernicious impact on non-smokers. Let us inventory several often overlooked consequences of smoking.

First, consider pollution—not air pollution, but litter. I have urged throughout this paper that, when looking at the moral status of smoking, we look at actual features of the practice of cigarette smoking. Though it is by no means a necessary byproduct of smoking, the fact of the matter is that cigarette smokers litter a lot. It is now impossible to walk down a city street without encountering hundreds or thousands of disposed cigarette butts. There are moral grounds for opposing litter, some of which are similar to those we have explored in this paper. It should not go unnoticed that those same moral considerations apply with the same force to smokers. Smokers unfairly destroy urban environments; their litter is invasive, uncalled-for, and unacceptable.

Even a smoker who assiduously avoids smoking in the presence of others (probably contrary to any actual situation) may affect others in a rather less obvious way. While non-smokers exposed to secondhand smoke are at increased risk of respiratory infection, colds and the like, smokers themselves are at even greater risk. With such a weakened defense against this sort of sickness, smokers are several times more likely to contract and then spread these illnesses to those around them. This is a dubious privilege, and apparently unfair to those who are unavoidably infected.

Smokers also tax health care systems to the tune of $22 billion per year in the United States alone, with a loss of work-years and productivity estimated at $43 billion annually.[29] This is not a trivial burden for smokers and non-smokers alike.[30] The question, of course, is whether this is fair to non-smokers who many times have to bear this financial burden through work-related health care programs or government subsidies for health care institutions. The loss of work years is no doubt to the detriment of the nation as a whole. Non-smokers are responsible for none of this, yet still must absorb many of the consequences. No

---

[29]American Cancer Society, *Smoke Signals,* American Cancer Society Printing, 1987.
[30]L. Breslow, "Control of Cigarette Smoking from a Public Policy Perspective," *Annual Review of Public Health* 3 (1982): 129–52.

doubt that there are other drains on public health maintenance (for example, automobile exhaust), but smoking is unique in that it serves no function (for example, transportation) necessary for normal membership in the social community. These consequences of smoking unfairly place nontrivial burdens on non-smokers . . . [31]

Questions

1. Why does Keith Butler think that the annoyance smoke causes to non-smokers is a harm? How does he say that it differs from the annoyance some people feel at the mention of homosexuality? Do you agree?
2. What is the difference, for the author, between annoyance and irritation?
3. How does he respond to the objection that non-smokers whose presence prevents smokers from smoking harm the smokers by causing them nicotine deprivation?

[31] I am indebted to Robert Goodin, Carolyn Morillo, and Norton Nelkin for helpful comments on an earlier draft.

Morality and Smoking

Tibor R. Machan

Although Tibor Machan briefly considers the morality of smoking in the presence of others, his main focus is on whether the health of smokers themselves provides grounds for a categorical moral condemnation of smoking. He argues that it does not.

To this end he argues that although the virtue of prudence supports an imperative to look after one's health, that imperative can often be overridden by other values.

Our duty, he says, is not simply to live but to live well. Part of living well is to enjoy certain pleasures. For some people smoking is a considerable pleasure. If it is done in moderation, then it could contribute to such people's flourishing, even though in other people's lives it would impede flourishing. He argues further that it is not always wrong for parents to allow their children to smoke.

INTRODUCTION

In this discussion I plan to focus on whether smoking can be morally unobjectionable, that is, something some persons morally may do, or is it in fact something from which everyone ought to refrain. The issue of whether what is morally objectionable ought also be banned by law is one of political theory, not of ethics per se.[1]

As to whether smoking is morally unobjectionable, views have varied from one extreme to the opposite. Ayn Rand, in her best selling and influential novel, *Atlas Shrugged*, praised the symbolic significance of smoking cigarettes. It is supposed to signify the power human beings have over nature. One character says, "I like to think of fire held in a man's hand. Fire, a dangerous force, tamed

---

[1] I am on record objecting to any bans on smoking or consuming any other stimulants or narcotics or even the advertising of such practices and products. See, Tibor R. Machan and Mark Thornton, "The Re-legalization of Drugs," *The Freeman* (April 1991), pp. 153–155, and Tibor R. Machan, *Private Rights and Public Illusions* (New Jersey: Transaction Books, 1995), Chapter 9, "Advertising."

Tibor R. Machan, "Morality and Smoking," is printed by permission of the author.

at his fingertips. . . . I wonder what great things have come from such hours. When a man thinks, there is a spot of fire alive in his mind—and it is proper that he should have the burning point of a cigarette as his one expression."[2]

On the other hand there are those who object to smoking cigarettes and consider it morally wrong to light. Some also believe that the government ought to prohibit smoking, although I won't dwell on that issue here.[3] As a posting on one anti-smoking web site states, "We think smoking is too wide spread [a] vice and too [few] things have been told about [the] danger and harm of smoking."[4] Furthermore, "If we look at smoking from a very rational side, we can say there is nothing good in it except the joy and maybe habit."[5]

Teens these days are given tickets in certain states for smoking cigarettes on public sidewalks and adults are prohibited from smoking in private restaurants, bowling alleys and other commercial places! But more importantly, many consider smoking morally wrong and they ostracize smokers not only because they may find the activity nauseating, with the prospect of some bad side effects, but because they deem it a private vice.

The gist of what I will defend is this: Adult human beings are not bound by any categorical imperative to refrain from smoking despite the evident health hazards of the practice because health, though vital, is by no means most important in human living. Flourishing as a human individual is most important.

MORAL OBJECTIVISM AND PLURALISM

Most of us often make ethical, political, and aesthetic claims,[6] yet many doubt that such claims can be true. Instead, such claims are said—by some of the most prominent figures in the social sciences and philosophy—to be "subjective" or "relative" or even beyond the pale of reason. Political economist Milton Friedman, for example, states that "of course, 'bad' and 'good' people may be the same people, depending on who is judging them,"[7] and philosopher Richard

---

[2]Ayn Rand, *Atlas Shrugged* (New York: Random House, 1957), p.61.

[3]As with the consumption of many substances and as with much private conduct to which there is widespread opposition in a robust democracy—for example, marijuana smoking and prostitution—tobacco smoking, once it is widely regarded as morally objectionable, is likely to be prohibited. But there is another argumentative step that needs to be made before that conclusion can be validly reached. An activity may be morally wrong, yet not by a long shot subject to prohibition or bans—e.g.,betraying a friend, laziness or sloth. To prohibit conduct it needs to be shown that apart from its wrongfulness it is also a violation of some just interpersonal principle such as a basic or derivative right or against the public interest. The First Amendment protects even wrongful publishing from prohibition or bans, such as offensive pornography or fascist, Nazi and communist propoganda.

[4]See, http://library.thinkquest.org/17360/text/tx-e-zac.html.

[5]Ibid. There may be a clue here, in the offhand denigration of joy, as to what often drives the more zealous elements in the anti-smoking movement. Joys, it seems, count for hardly anything as far as many who insist on a puritanical life style seem to be concerned.

[6]Even those who object to the claim that norms can be objective make purportedly objective claims when they say that others, too, ought to reject this claim. The "ought" may be only a very mild moral rebuke in this instance, yet judging by the intensity and seriousness with which it is advanced, it is hardly to be taken as an expression of a mere preference.

[7]Milton Friedman, *Capitalism and Freedom* (Chicago: University of Chicago Press, 1962), p.12.

Rorty tells us that concerning political principles, we cannot say that democratic institutions reflect a moral reality and that tyrannical regimes do not reflect one, that tyrannies get something wrong that democratic societies get right."[8]

This view of subjective truth is widespread,[9] even as nearly universal agreement can be found regarding some norms. People in different cultures and at different periods of history clearly treat some of them as "objective"; that is, they think that the truth of such claims could be known.[10] For example, it is nearly universally agreed that parents ought to rear their children so as to ready them for adulthood; that life-preserving actions are superior to life-destroying ones, at least in nonextraordinary circumstances; and even that one ought to stay out of the way of angry beasts and powerful, angry persons.[11] I say "nearly" only to make room for cases where someone refuses to ascent to the truth of such claims because, for example, he or she wishes to disguise a failing or is airing a wholly contrarian philosophical position.[12] In the main, however, such claims, as well as many others, are treated as if they were true, at least for specific circumstances involving particular persons and their choices.[13]

---

[8]Richard Rorty, "The Seer of Prague," *The New Republic,* 1 July 1991, p. 37. By "we" Rorty means "non-metaphysicians," that is, those who understand that words and ideas do not represent some reality "out there."

[9]Just how prominent it is can be gleaned from the proclamation offered by Richard Posner, judge of the Ninth Circuit Court of Appeals and professor at the University of Chicago School of Law, that he subscribes to pragmatism "in approximately the sense in which pragmatism is expounded and defended by the philosopher Richard Rorty" (Richard Posner, "Pragmatism and the Rule of Law," lecture given at the American Enterprise Institute, Washington, D.C., 7 July 1991).

[10]"Objective" is used, in ordinary discourse, as a way to distinguish claims that are unbiased from those that are not. But in the philosophical sense, to call claims "objective" is to focus on the possibility of knowing what they assert, since these claims supposedly rest on what is "out there," that is, features of objective reality—the properties, relationships, attributes, aspects, and so forth of what exists in the world, as distinct from what we feel about them, prefer them to be, desire from them or of them, and so forth.

[11]It might be objected here that what I have listed are at most "good policies" and that a policy cannot be true. Yet arguably, the claim that these are good policies could be either true or false, and the objectivist would try to show that it is true that they are good.

[12]Those who deny the objectivity of moral principles usually contrast this with their view that other claims, pertaining to what science discovers or what we observe in the world around us, are capable of being true or false, that what is being asserted in these areas, in contrast to ethics, politics, or aesthetics, is knowable, or cognitively significant. Yet in these areas there is rarely universal agreement about the truths that can be ascertained, nor do all those who address the issues involved make identical knowledge claims. But those who uphold this thesis would tend to account for the lack of universal agreement not in terms of the impossibility of reaching it but, rather, in terms of certain impediments some people face as they attempt to figure out what is true or come to know what is the case. Of course, there are those, including Rorty, who would extend their skepticism not just to value judgments and moral claims but also to claims advanced in the sciences and other nonnormative areas. They would hold that even in these the possibility of objective truth is an illusion. See, for example, Rorty's essays "Solidarity or Objectivity?" and "Science and Solidarity," in Richard Rorty, *Objectivity, Relativism and Truth* (Cambridge: Cambridge University Press, 1991), pp.21–45.

[13]I mean here that as we discuss what we should or should not do in personal, social, political, international, and other contexts, we do adduce reasons and sometimes even reach agreements because of these reasons, despite what such thinkers as Posner tell us, namely: "I am denying the priority of reason in human [moral] judgment. I am suggesting that we can, because we do, have confident beliefs without reasoning to them from unimpeachable truths, unimpeachable or

While I will not defend the following view in detail here, I wish to suggest that objective ethical claims appear to be subjective because, briefly, ethical claims pertain to how individual human beings ought to act, and that, in turn, depends to a considerable extent on who these individuals and their particular circumstances are. Only at the most fundamental level—vis-à-vis some very rare universal considerations—can we expect what is objective to be also universally applicable. As far as I can assess this, the best candidate for such a universal imperative is "One ought to think, be thoughtful, use one's mind conscientiously." Wittgenstein, for example, makes the point—one many other philosophers, from Socrates, Aristotle, Spinoza to Kant and Rand have made— that it is vigilant thinking through which someone becomes a good human being. He says, in a letter to Paul Engelmann, "I work diligently enough but wish that I were better and wiser. And these two things are the same."[14]

---

non-unimpeachable, because I haven't suggested and don't mean to suggest that our strong moral intuitions are true. They are merely undislodgeable at the time, an undislodgeable part of our grounds for action, and that is good enough for me, because I don't think we can do better" (Posner, op cit.). Of course, these intuitions are dislodged aplenty, for example, by people who do horrible things, for which Posner and those who agree with him give no explanation. One reason many think moral judgments do not lend themselves to being established as true is that they mistakenly assume that truths in non-normative disciplines can be established with timeless, unchanging, infallible certainty. Yet truth everywhere is different from this. When we know something, or when we have shown some claim to be true, we have the best possible cognitive grasp of it. Although this is difficult to explain by analogy since such a feat is unique—not surprisingly, since the human capacity for conceptually knowing the world is, so far as we know, unique—one might get some assistance for grasping the idea by thinking of how some object can be (literally) covered up. To cover up an object does not require having done so totally, fully, perfectly, completely, only adequately for the purposes at hand. Covering something up *absolutely* may be impossible, in the sense that no conceivable improvement on the task is possible, whereas covering it up is possible. Thus knowing something absolutely is impossible, but knowing it is possible. We can also fail to cover something up, just as we can fail to know something.)

[14] Paul Engelmann, *Letters from Ludwig Wittgenstein. With a Memoir.* (March 31, 1917) Ed., B. F. McGuinnes (London: Oxford University Press, 1967), p. 4. By "wiser" I take it that he means something along lines of "think more rationally, carefully and conscientiously."

To illuminate this a bit, I wish to call attention to what Simon Blackburn says about judgment: "[Kant] is talking about 'an art [of judgment] concealed in the depths of the human soul, whose real modes of activity nature is hardly likely ever to allow us to discover, and to have open to our gaze.' That art is the art of judgment, and the reason that it is concealed in the depths of the soul is precisely that it cannot be reduced to the grasp of rules, or recipes, or criteria. Nor can it be reduced to the presence, before the mind, of a thing like a picture or even word, and for Wittgenstein's reasons. Even when pictures, diagrams, and words float before our mind's eye, judgment only comes about when we have taken them the right way. Judgment then requires something spontaneous, outside the domain of reason; but this 'something' is a precondition making any application of reason." (*The New Republic*, February 7, 2000, page 37)

I submit that this allegedly mysterious something is actually oneself, the agent or the will of a person—the personal, chosen or initiated act of focusing one's mind—and the reason Kant, Blackburn and others cannot make sense of it and regard it as something concealed is that these philosophers have a mistaken picture of what it must for something to be natural, non-mysterious. To grasp something, for these philosophers, must amount to some type of empirical contact. When that isn't available, then the judgment of the being of something must be concealed.

Yet, not even the natural sciences are so empiricist about understanding the world as to demand that everything be explainable in empirical terms. I would suggest that there is something *sui generis* about meaning or judgment. Or is everything reducible to something else?

In some respects this idea is close to the way human health-related claims could appear to be but are by no means subjective. Even though we most often encounter claims in the discipline that apply to people in terms of their special or even unique situations, some basic claims concerning human health are universally applicable. More broadly, the relationship between applied engineering fields and the broad principles underlying them is similar.[15] Because of the significance of individuality in human life, the diversity of sound ethical judgments will make it very tempting to conclude that there simply are no universally sound moral ideas at all.

THE MORAL IMPERATIVE TO CARE FOR ONE'S HEALTH

In the context of the ethics of virtue, there is an imperative to care for one's health as well as other matters of benefit to oneself. The moral virtue of prudence supports this unequivocally. The exception would be if some value, say the spiritual life or preparing for the life hereafter, requires that prudence vis-à-vis one's mundane existence be superseded by prudence vis-à-vis such an overriding value. Another sort of exception would be if some higher virtue might override prudence, such as courage or justice.

Is there some value pertaining to one's mundane life—leaving aside now the troublesome matter of whether an afterlife or purely spiritual life could be shown to be of value to human beings—that might require or at least permit neglecting one's health?

We can consider some examples to show that this is not an implausible suggestion. Athletics, sports, the arts, politics and adventure all may be values in support of which health might not be of primary value for a human being. It is, after all, not an unfamiliar idea that some good persons have pursued the goals of such ways of life in the face of very serious risks to their health, even their sheer lives. A dedicated mountain climber, race car driver, soldier and movie stunt person often takes such risks and is sometimes admired for it.

It perhaps strains credibility to compare smoking cigarettes to risking one's health for some higher purpose. Yet, it is not uncommon for people to take reasonably serious health risks in order to celebrate a birthday, attend a sports

---

[15]For a very well worked out application of this model, see Martha Nussbaum, *The Therapy of Desire* (Princeton, N.J.: Princeton University Press, 1994). See, also, Ayn Rand, "The Objectivist Ethics," in *The Virtue of Selfishness, a New Concept of Egoism* (New York: New American Library, 1964). See, also, Tibor R. Machan, *Classical Individualism* (London: Routledge, 1998), especially Chapter 4, "Why Objective Ethical Claims Appear Subjective." For additional metaethical issues involved here, see, Douglas Rasmussen, "Ethical Individualism, Natural Law, and the Primacy of Natural Rights," *Social Philosophy & Policy* (Winter 2000). In this paper and other works, individualists stress their serious disagreement with the characterization of ethics or morality as necessarily of the impartial observer type, where such bizarreness arises that parents aren't morally correct in taking special care of their own rather than others' children, that one is morally remiss in caring for oneself and one's loved ones instead of the poor in Bangladesh, etc. (For these latter results of the impartial observer position, see note 13.)

event or go to the barber shop. Most such activities involve driving a car, and accidents are always possible. Individuals with health problems routinely take risks to take part in family and fraternal celebrations.

If all this risk taking were morally objectionable, then human beings would have to be said to routinely be living morally disreputable lives. Indeed, some of the best things about human living would turn out to be morally vicious, which seems rather paradoxical (unless the ethics of asceticism is true). But we recognize that we are not responsible merely to live, but to live well, to flourish. Flourishing, moreover, requires that different people will adopt different ways of life. This is what Isaiah Berlin meant when he said that the values of human life are both objective and not universalizable. And while I do not go so far as to maintain, mostly because of certain metaphysical considerations Berlin did not seem to fully appreciate, that the plurality of values often lands us with contradictory commitments,[16] I would wish to argue, as I have already suggested, that the diverse contexts of judgment created by our individual circumstances will often result in moral assessments that are by no means universal imperatives.

INTEGRITY AND MODERATION

Although certain moral theories do not regard the virtues as prime candidates for guidelines to moral excellence, it is still arguable that a morally good life is a virtuous life. This is not something I can defend here, although I have developed the position elsewhere. Its essence is that to live morally virtuously is to have cultivated good character traits that guide one, in a principled but not robotic way, toward human flourishing.[17] This often requires finding flexible policies of moderation and prudence rather than following rigid rules. What makes such an approach to morality different from and more realistic than following a system of rules is the attention to and cultivation of rules of thumb, on economization in the face of uncertainties. Although human beings are rational agents in that they guide their actions with theories, we are not the perpetual calculators that rule-driven moral systems depict. It is our unrelenting, open-ended thinking that will apprehend what flourishing requires, often with novel answers, so that the guidelines we learn cannot become rigid lest they turn against the very goal they are meant to further.

Instead it is more plausible to view morality more on the analogy of a skill, such as driving or carpentry or being a business executive. In all these endeavors human beings must initially acquire some measure of proficiency by means of concentration and focus, only to have that proficiency turn into what

---

[16]See, for a refutation of Berlin's type of moral pluralism, Gregory R. Johnson, "The Non-Sequitur of Value Relativism: A Critique of John Gray's 'Post-Liberalism'," *Reason Papers*, No. 19 (Fall 1994), pp. 99–107.

[17]See, Machan, *Classical Individualism*. See, for an earlier argument, Tibor R. Machan, *Human Rights and Human Liberties* (Chicago: Nelson Hall, Inc., 1975).

we might refer to as second nature. And while our conduct should always be monitored and supervised by reason, conduct itself is not the product of constant calculation or cost-benefit analysis. Rather we gain confidence in the principles that become our virtues, even though we have the added responsibility to make sure that they are used in proper measure and we do not become fanatical about any of them as we use them to guide us in our lives.

PLEASURES AND MODERATION

Barring the prospect that a morality of self-denial—such as championed by Peter Singer and Peter Unger,[18] as well some religions[19]—is sound, it is a feature of the moral life for every human being to develop oneself in all benign respects, major and minor. According to an ethics of self-actualization, happiness requires that we cultivate our capacities for excellence. Excellence requires that we have serious purposes in life—that we become artists, merchants, parents, friends, athletes, citizens, educators, and so forth. But there is also a dimension of self-development, as Aristotle noted long ago, that pays heed to pleasures. To put the matter bluntly, for some people there is pleasure that comes from smoking—as from drinking, gourmet eating, exotic or even dangerous travel, entertainment and so forth. All these may be enjoyed well or badly, moderately or immoderately. There is nothing blameworthy about the sensible and moderate enjoyment of life and there is no honest way of using these arguments to rationalize senseless and immoderate conduct.

The issue, then, is whether morality makes room for smoking or other possibly idiosyncratic pleasures in life that may be good for some but bad for others. What I have been proposing calls attention to the fact that there can be a difference between imperatives about, for example, smoking as far as they concern an opera singer or frequent lecturer versus someone who writes novels, directs movies, studies the structure of the atom or does accounting for a career.

Of course when we turn to the social dimensions of smoking, other variables, such as whether one has people in one's home who are sensitive to the irritation smoke can produce for some person or who have emphysema, would enter the discussion. I have dealt elsewhere with some of these issues.[20] For present purposes, however, the issue is whether as a matter of one's private conduct smoking could be morally justified.

---

[18]Peter Singer, *Practical Ethics* (London: Cambridge University Press, 1993), and Peter Unger, *Living High and Letting Die: Our Illusion of Innocence* (London: Oxford University Press, 1996). Both of these works suffer from serious metaethical problems. Singer, especially, rests his ethics on quicksand. See, Peter Berkowitz, "Other People's Mothers," *The New Republic*, January 10, 2000, pp. 27–37.

[19]By virtue of the fact that our mundane life is inferior to the spiritual afterlife that follow it and the demands of the former must not overshadow the prospects of the latter.

[20]Tibor R. Machan, "Coping with Smoking," *More Controversial Issues* (New York: NewsSource Unit, 1996). See, also, the essays in Robert D. Tollinson, ed., *Smoking and Society* (Boston, MA: Lexington Books, 1986), especially, Douglas J. Den Uyl, "Smoking, Human Rights, and Civil Liberties."

BAD SMOKING, WHOSE FAULT?

Let me turn briefly to cases of bad smoking—people who should not smoke at all or who smoke immoderately. The issue here is not simply what is wrong and who is at fault but also whether fault can be ascribed at all and to whom it may be assigned. First of all, the issue arises of who is responsible for the behavior in question?

There has been an attempt on the part of many—including legal authorities and some victims of smoking related ailments who have sued tobacco companies—to blame the tobacco company executives for ill effects smokers experience from smoking. The issue goes back to one frequently discussed in connection with advertising.

The most prominent advocate of the idea that the evil that follows encounters with advertisements for any product or service, including smoking, has been John Kenneth Galbraith. In his book, *The Affluent Society*,[21] he advanced the view that advertisers create a dependence effect by producing desires in potential consumers who then become hooked on what is being sold to them. This is especially true in the case of products and services that are by many experts considered to be addictive. Thus, if smokers, especially, cannot help themselves in the face of the "pressure" exerted on them by advertisements by tobacco companies, aren't the executives at least morally—but perhaps also legally—guilty of causing their ailments?

Let me for now ignore the reply to Galbraith given by F. A. Hayek, who did not so much deny that advertising creates desires but did undermine the claim that we are helpless in the face of this. (He argued that all creative activity by human beings produces desires in us but we are able to determine which desires to satisfy, which to ignore or reject.[22]) What is more important for my purposes here is that the Galbraithian thesis of how potential consumers are caused to depend on products and services being advertised to them has within it an implicit determinism that can then be applied equally to the tobacco executives.

Are we, in other words, going to blame company executives for causing people's smoking habits, only to have these executives defend themselves by pleading that they were, of course, helpless in the face of their upbringing—for example, when they went to college and took classes in marketing, advertising, and sales? If potential consumers are victims of manipulation, were not arguably the executives brainwashed into peddling their tobacco wares? So they had no control about becoming tobacco and other product peddlers, so they cannot be blamed either. And their teachers, too, went to various universities and learned how to teach their own students effectively, so they would do well at their professions. And so on and so forth—everyone is a victim of someone

---

[21]John Kenneth Galbraith, *The Affluent Society* (Boston, Houghton Mifflin 1958). The section in question, "The Dependence Effect," is reprinted in many business ethics texts, including in T. L. Beauchamp and N. B. Bowie, eds., *Ethical Theory and Business* (Englewood Cliffs, NJ: Prentice-Hall, 1983), p. 360.

[22]F. A. Hayek, "The Non-Sequitur of the 'Dependence Effect'," *Ibid.*, p. 508.

else's influence, ad infinitum. Which is to say, in the end none us is responsible for anything and all the moral blaming is pointless: *que sera, sera*.

In this entire discussion the determinist thesis that leaves no room for moral praise or blame or, more importantly, for moral responsibility, has to be precluded. It is surely impossible to consider whether what people do is morally right or wrong if they have no power to decide about their conduct at all. One might speak of behaving badly, just as one can speak of this in connection with animals that cause much hurt or damage, without impugning any moral blame. Neither whether one smokes or not, nor the moral professional issues of whether to market, advertise and sell tobacco products could be considered as moral issues if human beings lacked free will.[23]

HEALTH AND THE HUMAN GOOD

I wish to return here to something hinted at before, namely, that health is really not all there is to human life. A piece in *The New Republic*[24] makes the point beautifully—smoking has been with us way before advertising made its marketing so visible. Millions choose to smoke not without awareness that it is dangerous to their health (meaning it is going to reduce their lives by an average of 2.2 years).

There are purely recreational smokers who will light up, maybe once a day, with a cup of espresso or a brandy, so clearly addiction, assuming that it is a genuine phenomenon,[25] is not a universal reaction to taking up the practice. People quit all the time, so tobacco is not for everyone a special kind of commodity with which people who try it necessarily endanger their health.

Yet even apart from the fact that one could engage in recreational smoking that is morally unobjectionable, for some persons even the sort of smoking that is clearly a health hazard could be morally permissible. The reason is that health, while undeniably one of the clear cut human goods that is to be promoted in a

---

[23]It is generally understood that to advertise and sell hard drugs, ones that are either immediately very dangerous to—or produce a desire for continued use that is eventually very dangerous to—anyone's health is morally wrong. It is on par with encouraging some innocent person with much to live for to commit suicide. This is especially morally objectionable when directed at young persons not generally deemed capable of deciding for themselves. Even to adults it should not be done for it offers support for something they should not do. This is so especially when clothed in the normal garb of advertising, namely, gimmickry, celebrity endorsement, and the bias that all promotional activity contains. We could explore whether the advertising and selling of cigarettes on par with the advertising and selling of hard drugs or similarly immediately dangerous or addictive and eventually very dangerous drugs. But I leave that issue to be considered in the investigation of professional or business ethics, not here. (See, for more along these lines, Tibor R. Machan and Douglas J. Den Uyl, "Should Cigarette Advertising Be Banned?" *Public Affairs Quarterly*, Vol. 2 [1988], pp. 19–30.)

[24]*The New Republic*, October 20, 1995. See, also, Tibor R Machan, "Smokers Stand Alone in Blame," *The Los Angeles Times* (March 5, 1988).

[25]See, for a dissenting view on whether addiction even exists, Stanton Peele and Archie Brodsky, *The Truth About Addiction and Recovery* (New York: Simon and Schuster, 1991), and Thomas S. Szasz, *Ceremonial Chemistry* (New York: Learning Publications, Inc., 1987).

morally good, flourishing life, is far from the highest good for human beings to pursue. That would be happiness, in the eudaimonist sense, meaning success or excellence as the kind of individual, namely, a human being, one is.[26]

PARENTAL RESPONSIBILITY AND SMOKING

Perhaps one of the most explosive public issues, with distinct moral dimensions, is what parents are responsible for in their children's behavior, including health-impeding ones such as smoking, drinking, and other matters. Although in some states it is illegal for those under 18 to smoke in public, never mind what the parents' views are on the matter, we can consider the issue apart from this fact of the law.

Once again the issue is one of context, not of categorical moral principles. Parents often rightfully expose their children to hazards that are as great if not greater than exposing them to various health hazards. They take them on long weekend vacations when the risk of automobile crashes are greatest. They let them swim in the ocean, go rafting in roaring Colorado rivers, and encourage them to take part in sports that sometimes cause serious injuries, even deaths.

Of course, many of these practices can be understood as quite justifiable, consider the importance of the goals they serve to achieve. Visiting grandparents or other family on vacations, building character through sports and so forth can all be seen as not only permissible but valuable aspects of child raising. Can one say the same thing about allowing one's children to smoke, drink, even use some narcotics (apart from their sometimes being illegal)?

We might start addressing this issue by noting that certainly people in various cultures around the globe bring up their children differently, including allowing them to smoke, drink and otherwise indulge, at least in moderation. Hungarian children routinely drink wine at the dinner table when they are only 8 years old. And that is but a rather mild instance of the diversity involving the raising of children around the world. It would be very difficult to argue that in each case child abuse is going on. Even child labor, which in the United States is outlawed or officially regulated, cannot sensibly be uniformly condemned.

It is arguable, of course, that the context of American culture is such that given the information most parents could obtain about the health risks of various practices and given that taking certain health risks, such as those arising from smoking cigarettes, serves no overriding valued purpose, parents in America and similar cultures are morally irresponsible if they allow their children to smoke and indulge in similar risky practices. Yet America and many other developed societies are these days multicultural, despite the fact that information about health risks are nearly universally available. If, thus, some persons consider it valuable to encourage or permit independent decision making

---

[26]For the underlying ethics here, see David L. Norton, *Personal Destinies, A Philosophy of Ethical Individualism* (Princeton, NJ: Princeton University Press, 1976) and, op. cit., Machan, *Classical Individualism*.

on the part of their, say, teen aged children, who then decide to smoke, this could be seen as no less morally justifiable than encouraging or permitting children to ride horses, play ice hockey, surf, ski, or even gamble a little for enjoyment. Similarly, letting children smoke or drink especially in moderation, would be no parental malpractice.

MORALITY AND SMOKING

Adults and even children might well choose to moderately indulge in smoking, drinking and similar practices, even granting the health hazards of such activities. Health is not the highest good and guarding it is not a categorical imperative for anyone. It cannot be said apart from knowing a reasonably detailed context of someone's life situation whether the person ought to or ought not to smoke. For some smoking would be morally wrong, self-destructive, impede personal growth and flourishing, for others this would not be the case. In most instances a moderate degree of such indulgence is morally unobjectionable.

When it comes to imposing the side effects of smoking on others, this too cannot be condemned categorically. If a proprietor of a restaurant or bowling alley or personal home consents, patrons and guests, respectively, may indulge, taking the permission to indicate a judgment on the owner's or host's part that for him or her the side effects of smoking will not be a serious impediment or injury. To know if there is anything morally amiss, we would need to gain detailed enough information about the smokers and companions so as to see if what they ought to strive for in their lives is undermined through their indulgence in the practice.

Questions

1. Why does Tibor Machan think that smoking can be morally permissible for some people but not for others?
2. Why does the author think that it may not always be wrong for parents to allow their children to smoke?
3. Do you think that the author has adequately represented the dangers of smoking to the smoker?

The Use of Drugs for Pleasure: Some Philosophical Issues

Dan W. Brock

In considering the use of drugs for plea-sure, Dan Brock examines some philosoph-ical theories about the nature of pleasure and some arguments about the value of pleasure. He distinguishes between two major theories about the nature of pleasure: (1) the property of conscious experience theory (PCET) and (2) the preference the-ory (PT). According to PCET, "pleasure is a sensation, feeling or quality of conscious experience that is liked or found agreeable for its own sake." According to PT, one takes pleasure in an experience "if, at the time, one likes it for its own sake, in the sense of wanting to sustain and repeat it for its felt qualities and apart from its con-sequences." Dan Brock suggests that it is not clear which theory is preferable or even which provides the best analysis of drug use for pleasure.

Turning to the moral issues, he notes that few people who oppose drug use for pleasure do so because they oppose all pleasure. Drawing on the two theories of pleasure, he then rejects the view that the pleasure from drugs has no value, before considering the view that the pleasure de-rived from drugs is a qualitatively lower rather than higher form of pleasure. He ar-gues that PT, unlike PCET, can make sense of the claim that the pleasures of drug use are qualitatively lower than other pleasures. He argues that there is a prima facie case that the use of drugs for pleasure is part of some people's good on each of three theories he mentions. He sug-gests, though, that this prima facie case would be defeated if it were shown that drugs interfered with important aspects of a person's good. The extent to which drugs do interfere with the list of goods he men-tions is an empirical matter and is best left to scientists.

Dan W. Brock, "The Use of Drugs for Pleasure," in *Feeling Good, Doing Better*, edited by Thomas H. Murray, Willard Gaylin, and Ruth Macklin, pp. 83–106. Copyright © 1984 by Humana Press, Inc. Clifton, N.J.

I intend to outline here some philosophical theories of the *nature* of pleasure, and in turn some philosophical arguments concerning the *value* of pleasure, in the hope that doing so will aid in the assessment of attitudes towards the use of drugs to produce or enhance pleasure. In particular, a significant source of the support for continuing strong legal prohibitions on the use of drugs merely for pleasure is the common public attitude that such use is bad. Is there any sound basis for this disapproval of pleasure that is produced by drug use, and if so what can that basis be? And more specifically, is there any sound basis for the disapproval of the use of drugs for pleasure *in itself,* as opposed to disapproval because of other consequences such use has, or may be thought to have?

Although I shall be examining philosophical issues and arguments here, I believe it would be a mistake to think that popular attitudes toward the use of drugs for pleasure rest largely on any well-founded and thought-out philosophical position . . . [M]any historical and political factors have contributed to present attitudes toward the use of drugs for pleasure in ways that often do not stand up to rational scrutiny. It would, consequently, be a further mistake to suppose that philosophical confusions are the principle source of more general confusions and irrationalities in attitudes towards the use of drugs for pleasure, and in turn that removal of this philosophical confusion would clear up most of the more general confusion and irrationality found in the area. In particular, and as I shall elaborate briefly at the end of the article, most such confusion is probably of an empirical rather than philosophical sort—confusion in the form of myths and other unfounded or false beliefs about the nature of these drugs and the various circumstances and consequences of their use. There may, nevertheless, be room for some illumination of the area if we can clear up some of the philosophical confusions that have a part in attitudes about the use of drugs for pleasure.

I should note that the focus of my concern is limited in another way. I shall not discuss the general issue of when the state may rightly regulate or prohibit behavior, the different justifications for its doing so, nor, more specifically, which if any of these justifications may apply to the use of drugs for pleasure. These are obviously important issues of moral and political philosophy for the larger project addressed in this volume. My concern then will be the modest and limited one of attempting to gain some philosophical clarity about the value or disvalue, goodness or badness, of the use of drugs for pleasure.

When we consider opposition to the use of drugs for pleasure, there are two obvious sorts of objections that we might expect to find. First, it may be that *pleasure* is what is opposed. It is the goodness of pleasure, or its place in a sound account of the good for persons that is being questioned. But that is unlikely since, except perhaps for extreme ascetics, few person oppose pleasure generally, or all pleasure. Second, it might be the use of *drugs* that is opposed, but that too would be problematic since the use of drugs for other purposes, such as to alleviate pain, is rarely opposed. So it must be the particular combination of the use of *drugs* in order to produce *pleasure* that is opposed. To evaluate whether there is any sound philosophical basis for this opposition, we need to consider several issues. First, we need to get clearer about the concept of pleasure, what value is to be assigned to pleasure, and whether and if so, how that value may vary according to the source of the pleasure. Finally, we will then need to consider the place of pleasure, and then specifically the use of drugs for pleasure, in a conception of the good for persons.

THE NATURE OF PLEASURE

First, then, the nature of pleasure. It may be that we all know pleasure, and even more clearly pain, when we experience it, but to give an account of what pleasure is—an analysis or definition of the concept of pleasure—is no easy task. There are a variety of experiences of pleasure or enjoyment that any analysis of pleasure should cover. For example, there is the pleasure from sexual orgasm or a good meal, as well as the rather different enjoyment from reading a good book or spending a day in the country. These two different classes of cases in each turn lend plausibility to two major alternative philosophical theories about the nature of pleasure. The first theory I shall call the property of conscious experience theory (PCET). On this account pleasure is a sensation, feeling, or quality of conscious experience that is liked or found agreeable for its own sake.[1] Thus, a back rub, sexual orgasm, or smoking a marijuana cigaret may produce pleasurable feelings or sensations. It is on this sensation or feeling sense of pleasure that pain is naturally taken to be the opposite of pleasure, a sensation or feeling disliked or found disagreeable for its own sake. It is probably this sense of pleasure that people usually have in mind when they think of drugs used for pleasure, that is, drugs used to produce particular pleasurable feelings or sensations, or to enhance the pleasure from already present feelings or sensations.

It is on this first view of the nature of pleasure that it may seem natural to think that activities are undertaken *for* the pleasurable feelings or sensations they produce, and in turn to think that, were it possible to have these same pleasurable feelings and sensations without having to undertake the activities that produce them, then we would do just as well without the activities. The hedonist, who attributes value to all pleasure, and only to pleasure, is on this account of pleasure correctly viewed as attaching no intrinsic value to the activities that persons normally pursue and that produce pleasure. On this account of plea-

---

[1]Gilbert Ryle in *The Concept of Mind*, London, Hutchinson & Co., 1949, criticized extensively the view that pleasure is some kind of sensation or feeling, and few recent philosophers have defended a form of the property of conscious experience theory. J. J. C. Smart in *An Outline of Utilitarian Ethics*, Carlton, Melbourne University Press, 1961, reprinted in a revised edition in J. J. C. Smart and Bernard Williams, *Utilitarianism: For and Against*, Cambridge, Cambridge University Press, 1973, seems committed to such a view. Other philosophers, such as J. C. B. Gosling, *Pleasure and Desire*, Oxford, Oxford University Press, 1969, and Anthony Kenny, *Action, Emotion and Will*, London, Routledge & Kegan Paul, 1963, argue that there is one sense of pleasure in which it is a sensation, but that not all pleasure is a sensation. Part of this theory's importance is that probably most ordinary persons implicitly hold some version of it, and so it in turn underlies such persons' attitudes towards the use of drugs for pleasure.

sure, pleasure seems to have what might be called a detachability from the activities that produce it. It is the pleasurable sensations or feelings that are liked for their own sake, and the activities that produce the pleasure only happen to be contingently necessary to the pleasure. A hedonist's life filled with pleasure on this view could as well merely contain the feelings or sensations without the activities, if that turned out to be empirically possible.

Enjoying or taking pleasure in reading a book or spending a day in the country, however, seem not to fit the sensation or feeling view. Once we look at enjoyable activities, like these, that tend to last a significant period of time and to contain significant variety, it seems difficult to locate any sensation, feeling, or other quality of conscious experience that is the pleasure. We enjoyed the whole book or day in the country, but there was no sensation or feeling that continued throughout each experience that was the pleasure. In general, if we look at the enormous variety and duration of experiences that we enjoy or take pleasure in, there seems no unitary sensation, feeling, or quality of conscious experience that is present throughout them and that can be identified as the pleasure. This has led philosophers to an alternative account of pleasure that I will call the preference theory (PT). On this account, one is enjoying (taking pleasure in) an experience if, at the time, one likes it for its own sake, in the sense of wanting to sustain and repeat it for its felt qualities and apart from its consequences.[2] Pleasure on this second view refers not to a property of conscious experience, but to a relation holding between an experience and a person's preferences or desires. To say that one enjoys *x*, is to say that one has a non-evaluative, pro-attitude towards *x* at the time one undergoes *x*; to say that the attitude in non-evaluative is to say that the positive attitude or preference is not based on any evaluation (moral or otherwise) of the person that he ought to prefer or have a positive attitude towards experiences of this kind.

There are many refinements in either the conscious experience or preference conceptions of pleasure that would be necessary before we could fairly evaluate whether either is a satisfactory account of the nature of pleasure, but I shall not concern myself with most of them since they are not central to my concerns in this paper. But a few points should be noted. First, on the preference theory, since pleasure refers to a relation that holds between a person's preference and his or her experience, there should be less temptation to believe, as I noted above did seem plausible on the conscious experience view, that one could get the pleasure without the experience or activity in which one takes pleasure. As I shall discuss further below, one basis for the objection that a life filled with pleasure is not a good life is that on the conscious experience view that seems consistent with a life without all the various activities with which we in fact seek to fill our lives, so long as we could get the conscious experiences without the activities. The philosopher J. J. C. Smart has imagined being able to hook

---

[2]Among the more extensive discussions of pleasure sympathetic to some form of the preference theory are J. L. Cowan, *Pleasure and Pain*, New York, St. Martin's Press, 1968, and D. L. Perry, *The Concept of Pleasure*, The Hague, Mouton, 1967. An excellent, shorter review of alternative theories of pleasure is William Alston, "Pleasure," in Paul Edwards, ed., *The Encyclopedia of Philosophy*, New York, Macmillian, 1967.

oneself up to electrodes that would stimulate parts of the brain so as to produce the conscious experience or feeling of pleasure without the usual activities necessary for such feelings.[3] If a life hooked up to such electrodes fails to conform to the conception of the good life than many of us have, as I believe it does, a life filled with pleasure on this conception of pleasure need not be a good life. That sort of objection is not as easily made against a life filled with pleasure on the preference conception, since the activities are logically necessary to the pleasure, given that the pleasure refers to a relation holding between the person's preferences and his activities.

Second, the preference theory allows a hedonist to meet the common objection against hedonism on the conscious experience account that there seem to be many activities that we seek and value that do not produce any identifiable feelings or sensations of pleasure. We have already mentioned two examples, reading a good book and spending a day in the country. Examples could, obviously, be multiplied indefinitely, since on the preference view *any* experience that, at the time one undergoes it, one likes for its own sake—that is, for its own felt qualities and apart from its consequences—is an experience in which one is taking pleasure or enjoying. In particular, all of the so-called "higher" or "distinctly human" activities that persons like for their own sake, such as understanding a philosophical argument, good conversation between friends, and so forth, are experiences in which we take pleasure on the preference view. J. S. Mill considered the objection to hedonism that it was a doctrine fit only for swine, in that it attributed value for humans to only the lowest or basest animal pleasures.[4] And some such view may well underlie the distrust and disapproval with which, many Americans regard pleasure and hedonism. Mill rightly noted that this objection was misplaced, in that it rested on a conception of humans as only taking pleasure in the experiences shared with swine, whereas because humans are the kinds of being that enjoy experiences, of intellectual and other sorts, of which swine are incapable, the hedonist can appropriately ascribe value to our pleasure in these "higher" experiences.

Earlier we noted that disapproval of the use of drugs for pleasure might have its source in general disapproval of pleasure. When it does, it often takes some form of the "swine objection" above, that is, that persons are capable of many higher activities, and to view persons as merely pleasure-seeking beings is to debase their nature. But we can see now that such an objection rests on the same confusion as did the swine objection, and is to be answered in the same manner as Mill answered it. Just in case human beings are capable of, *as they are,* and in turn take pleasure in, *as they do,* "higher" activities, then disapproval of pleasure is not justified by a belief that it is only "lower" activities that lead to, or are associated with, pleasure. It is worth adding that even if it were true that only "lower" activities lead to pleasure, this would seem to be a reason to value other things ("higher" activities) besides pleasure but not a reason to assign disvalue to pleasure.

[3]Smart and Williams, p. 19.
[4]John Stuart Mill, *Utilitarianism,* S. Gorovitz, ed., Indianapolis, Bobbs-Merrill, 1971, pp. 18–19.

With these two broad philosophical accounts of the concept, and nature, of pleasure before us, it is worth briefly asking how these philosophical theories are related to recent neurochemical advances concerning pleasure, and in particular the discovery of endorphins. As discussed elsewhere in this volume, recent research has shown that the body contains specific receptors for the opiates, such as morphine. This suggested that the artificial opiates must have their analogs in natural substances, the endorphins, that are "manufactured by" or at least present in the body naturally and that bind to these receptors. Perhaps then these natural opiates are the more general pleasure producer/pain inhibitors in the body, just as morphine may be an externally induced artificial pleasure producer/pain inhibitor. Suppose future research allowed us to isolate specific neurochemical changes that occur in the brain every time a person undergoes a pleasant or unpleasant experience, every time he/she has a pleasure or a pain. The implications of such a finding would likely be many, but what specifically would they be for the philosopher's concept of pleasure? And that means as well, for the ordinary person's concept of pleasure, since the philosopher's concept is intended to be an analysis of it. Would it, for example, be the case that we would then know what pleasure *really is*, and could dispense with the philosopher's and ordinary man's prescientific account? I would suggest not. What we would be faced with would be a specific instance of what has traditionally and more generally been called in philosophy the mind–body problem.[5] The philosopher's and ordinary person's concept of pleasure concerns their conscious experience, referring either to a property of a person's conscious experience or to a relation between this conscious experience and one's preferences. The "new conception of pleasure" would concern our physical states, and be formulated in physical, specifically neurochemical terms. The two conceptions operate at two different levels of discourse and of reality, one at the mental level of the conscious experience of persons, the other at the level of physical states or organisms. The philosophical problem would then be how the two, the mental and physical, are related. On one view, usually called materialism or physicalism, the relation is one of identity with the mental being in some sense reducible to and nothing more than the physical.[6] But this is only one position, and a highly controversial one, concerning the nature of the relation. The issues and literature concerning the mind–body problem are enormously complex, and need not detain us here. The point to be stressed is that advances in our physical understanding of humans do not uncontroversially give us reason to give up the language of the mental in which the concept of pleasure is found. Rather, it would be more accurate to say that such advances increase our understanding of what physical, and specifically neurochemical, changes take place in the body when a person experiences pleasure. More specifically, we may be able to compare what differences there are between the neurochemical

---

[5]For readers unfamiliar with the philosophical literature and positions on the mind–body problem, two useful starting points are Richard Taylor, *Metaphysics*, Englewood Cliffs, NJ, Prentice-Hall, 1963, Chapters 1–3, and the entry, "The Mind–Body Problem," by Jerome Shaffer in Paul Edwards, ed., *The Encyclopedia of Philosophy*, New York, Macmillian, 1967.
[6]Taylor and Schaffer also contain introductory discussions of materialism and physicalism.

effects accompanying pleasurable experiences at an ordinary, "natural" sort, as opposed to pleasure induced by ingestion of artificial opiates. If the latter have some harmful consequences, for example, in the developmental process of young adolescents because of the large doses of endorphins introduced, that may give us good reason to be cautious about uses of opiates in those cases. None of this, however, would establish that the philosophical accounts of plea-sure are mistaken, or that attitudes toward pleasure itself, as opposed to differ-ent sources of pleasure, are in need of revision.

Given the two philosophical theories of pleasure that we have noted, PCET and PT, which one is correct? As I have noted earlier, attempting to answer that question would require us to introduce many refinements into the two theories, and to assess many issues and arguments, most of which would not serve my purposes in this paper. So we must be content here to leave that question unan-swered, but we can consider the more restricted question of which theory is ap-propriate when we consider the use of drugs for pleasure. The narrower, property-of-conscious-experience theory, which holds that pleasure is a sensa-tion, feeling, or other property of conscious experience, seems to fit many uses. Descriptions of the pleasurable effects of drug use by drug users are often in terms of sensations or feelings that the drugs produce. On the other hand, sometimes the descriptions do not focus on unique sensations or feelings from the drugs, but rather on the way in which the drugs enhance the pleasure ob-tained from experiences that were pleasurable independent of the drug use. For example, the effects of marijuana in focusing one's attention and shutting out distracting thoughts or sensations in order to enhance the pleasure of sexual ac-tivity or listening to music is of this sort. The pleasure is still in the experience of sex or listening to music, but is intensified and focused by the drug effect. The drug is a pleasure enhancer, rather than a pleasure producer. And that may be true even for "long term" experiences that seem best to fit the preference the-ory, for example, "being stoned" during the day in the country. It is thus unclear that only one of these two theories provides the most plausible analysis of plea-sure in all its "drug use" instances, much less in all instances, and both theories must here be left in contention for the position of correct theory.

HIGHER AND LOWER PLEASURES

I shall turn now to some of the normative or moral issues that we need to ad-dress here. These can be formulated in a number of ways, keeping in mind the aim of attempting to clarify whether there is any philosophical basis to the op-position to the use of drugs for pleasure. Few of the opponents of the use of drugs for pleasure oppose all pleasure, so one issue can be put as, is there any basis for evaluating some pleasures as better than others, such that pleasure from drugs might come out lower on the value scale? Mill, for example, made a well-known distinction between higher and lower pleasures, higher and lower in an evaluative sense, which would seem relevant here. And a second question, which I shall take up in the next section, is what place does pleasure have in a sound theory of the good for persons, what is the proper role of pleasure in the good life? I believe these questions turn out to have a different form and meaning depending on which of the two accounts of pleasure we are using, and that the plausibility of different answers to them depends in part on how pleasure is understood.

Before directly addressing whether pleasure from drug use can plausibly be taken to be a lower pleasure, we need to bring out more explicitly a difference in the two theories of pleasure that was implicit in some of our discussion of them, a difference in the components of their respective analyses of pleasure. On the property of conscious experience theory (PCET) there are the following components:

1. The pleasure, which is a sensation, feeling or other property of conscious experience.
2. The conscious experience of the person, of which the pleasure is a part or aspect.
3. The source of the pleasure.

The source of the pleasure will be some activity or behavior, for example playing a game of tennis or smoking a marijuana cigaret, that produces component 2 above, the conscious experience, and component 1 above, the pleasure that is a part or aspect of that experience. On the preference theory (PT) there are these components:

1. The person's experience, which can include two components:
   a. A conscious experience, e.g., thinking thoughts, feeling hot or tired, and so on.
   b. An activity, e.g., playing tennis, having sexual intercourse, reading a book, and so on.
2. The person's liking the experience, in the sense of desiring or preferring at the time of undergoing it to continue and repeat it because of its felt qualities and apart from its consequences.
3. The pleasure, which just is component 2 holding of component 1, that is a positive desire or attitude towards the experience.

On this second theory, pleasure is nothing over and above the relation between a person's experience and likings, where the likings are analyzed in terms of the person's desires.

Now an *extreme opponent* of the use of drugs for pleasure would be one who denied that pleasure having its source in drug use was good *at all* or had any intrinsic value. He or she would be denying the first of the following two claims, which I have noted together define ethical hedonism:

1. All pleasure has intrinsic value (is good, desirable).
2. Only pleasure has intrinsic value (is good, desirable).[7]

---

[7]For a general discussion and evaluation of ethical hedonism, see Richard Brandt, *Ethical Theory*, Englewood Cliffs, Prentice-Hall, 1959, Chapters 12, 13.

The denial of claim 1 would rest, at least in part, on the example of drug use. But it is very difficult to see what *argument* the extreme opponent could offer to establish that pleasure having its source in drug use has *no intrinsic value at all*. This difficulty can perhaps best be brought out by briefly considering one kind of case that *has* been taken to present a strong objection to the first claim of hedonism, and how the hedonist may answer that objection.

Consider malicious or sadistic pleasures, cases where one person's pleasure is in the misfortune or suffering of others. In general, philosophers have argued that pleasure always takes an object, pleasure must be *in* or *with* something, and here the object is another's suffering. The usual response to the objection that there is *no* value in sadistic or malicious pleasures turns on the distinction between intrinsic and extrinsic value. Roughly, that distinction is between the value a state of affairs or experience has in itself, or because of its own nature, as opposed to the value it may have on account of its consequences or relations to other things. We might then say that sadistic or malicious pleasures will always have the *consequence* of the suffering or misfortune of another, and in general the latter might be thought likely to be greater than the former. This line of reasoning is a way of explaining one's opposition, all things considered, to sadistic or malicious pleasures, without abandoning the ethical hedonist's position that all pleasure has some intrinsic value. On PCET, where pleasure is the logically detachable component 1 noted above, this line of response seems plausible. On PT, where pleasure is a relation between components 2 and 1, and where 1 includes an activity, one might think that the causing of suffering of another could not be separated from, and so merely an extrinsic consequence of, the pleasure. But such pleasures need only be at the *thought* of the suffering or misfortune of another, and need not involve one's doing anything to cause that suffering. And, perhaps more important, since such pleasures require only the belief that others are suffering, that belief could be false and so the sadistic pleasure occurs without anyone else suffering. J. J. C. Smart has asked us to

> . . . imagine a universe consisting of one sentient being only, who falsely believes that there are other sentient beings and that they are undergoing exquisite torment. So far from being distressed by the thought, he takes a great delight in these imagined sufferings. Is this better or worse than a universe containing no sentient beings at all? Is it worse, again, than a universe containing only one sentient being with the same beliefs as before but who sorrows at the imagined tortures of his fellow creatures?[8]

Smart's example is designed to focus more precisely the question of whether the sadistic pleasure, in itself and apart from its consequences, is bad, and I believe he is correct in suggesting that it is not. But if the distinction between intrinsic and extrinsic value, coupled with the method of analysis employed in Smart's example, are sufficient to defend the intrinsic value of even sadistic pleasures, or at least to undermine the force of sadistic pleasures as objections to the first claim of hedonism, then they will probably be sufficient against any argument the extreme opponent of the use of drugs for pleasure might offer. It is highly unlikely that the extreme opponent of the use of drugs for pleasure can make

[8]Smart and Williams, p. 25.

out a plausible case that pleasure from the use of drugs either has *no* positive intrinsic value *at all*, or has intrinsic *dis*value.

A more *moderate opponent* of the use of drugs for pleasure is one who does not deny the first of the two theses of ethical hedonism (or at least does not deny it for the case of drug use), but rather claims that some pleasures are better or more valuable than others, and that pleasure from the use of drugs is a lower value or quality pleasure. As already mentioned, J. S. Mill made a well-known distinction between the qualities, as well as quantities, of pleasures, though he did not apply the quality distinction to the case of drug use.[9] All hedonists have agreed that pleasures can differ in quantity, in particular in amount at a point in time, and in duration over time. Mill's claim, and the claim of our moderate opponent of drugs used for pleasure, is that pleasures can differ in quality as well as in quantity, where "quality" denotes evaluative differences, not merely differences in kind that do not mark nonquantitative evaluative differences. On this view, though pleasure A might be of greater quantity than pleasure B, B might be of higher quality, and so of overall higher value than A. Mill's criterion for which pleasures were of higher or lower quality was to appeal to the preferences of those who had experienced both sorts of pleasures; where such qualified judges preferred B to A, though A was of equal or greater quantity than B, then B was a higher quality pleasure than A. There are many difficulties of both a practical and theoretical sort with such a proposal, and I shall mention only those that are important for the position of our moderate opponent of the use of drugs for pleasure, and will illuminate the core of plausibility in the quality of pleasure distinction.

A common objection to Mill's introduction of a distinction between qualities of pleasure is that it was inconsistent with his acceptance of ethical hedonism and its two theses noted above. Now since it is no part of my aim in this paper to defend ethical hedonism, we might simply conclude that if the "quality of pleasure" distinction is sound, then so much the worse for ethical hedonism. But both what makes appeal to some "quality of pleasure" distinction plausible for a hedonist, as well as what generates the supposed inconsistency, *are* important for our moderate opponent's position, and so we must look more carefully at the difficulty here. The supposed inconsistency can be brought out most clearly on the PCET account of pleasure. On that account, pleasure is a sensation, feeling, or other quality of conscious experience. And it is usually understood to be a single, unitary sensation, feeling, or property of conscious experience, single or unitary because it is an unanalyzable quality, much as color qualities of experience, such as redness, are taken to be; pleasure is a property of our conscience experience that cannot be broken down in analysis into other properties. The hedonist claims that it is the presence of this, and only this, unanalyzable property of pleasure in an experience or state of affairs that gives value to the experience or state of affairs. But to claim that pleasures differ in quality (evaluative sense) as well as quantity, seems to be to require some *other*

---

[9]Mill, pp. 19–21. A contemporary defense of hedonism that employs the distinction between different quality pleasures is Rem Edwards, *Pleasures and Pains: A Theory of Qualitative Hedonism*, Ithaca, Cornell University Press, 1979.

property besides pleasure to be the *basis* for the difference in value, and so which itself gives value to states of affairs or experiences. But this seems inconsistent with the hedonist claim that *only* the property of pleasure gives value to states of affairs or experiences.

Moreover, apart from this inconsistency with hedonism, on PCET it is difficult to see how pleasures in themselves could differ qualitatively as Mill's distinction supposes, if pleasure itself is in fact a basic, unanalyzable property of our conscious experience. We can see easily enough how components 2 and 3 of the PCET analysis above could differ qualitatively, but they are not, on this analysis, strictly speaking the pleasure. Thus, on PCET, the position of the moderate opponent of the use of drugs for pleasure is not merely inconsistent with hedonism, in which case one might simply give up hedonism, but is thoroughly obscure concerning how, on that view of the nature of pleasure, there could possibly *be* higher and lower pleasures, pleasures whose differences in intrinsic value were of a qualitative and not merely quantitative sort. This strongly suggests that, on the PCET account of the nature of pleasure, differences in the overall value of experiences or states of affairs that are not based on differences in quantity of pleasure in that state of affairs will be differences in the extrinsic, not intrinsic, value of those states of affairs. And this means that on the PCET account of the nature of pleasure, pleasure from the use of drugs is not in itself a lower quality or value pleasure than pleasure from any other source, but is of lower value overall (if it is) only because of its consequences or, as it might be put, side effects. The defense of this latter position would require appeal to empirical claims about the nature of the consequences or side effects of the use of drugs for pleasure, and I shall say something about such claims later in Section III, but it is not an explication of the position of the moderate opponent as we have understood him here.

If we turn now to the PT account of pleasure, we can perhaps make more sense of the quality of pleasure distinction, and bring out more clearly what makes the distinction plausible. On this view, recall, to say that a person is taking pleasure in an experience just is to say that he is undergoing that experience, with its conscious and activity components noted above, and that he likes that experience, in the sense of desires to continue and repeat it, for its own sake and apart from its consequences. The pleasure consists in the relation holding between his experience and his liking, "liking" analyzed in terms of his desires or preferences. One of the elements of this relation, his experience, with its two components of his conscious experience and his activity, is clearly such that it can vary in quality in a multitude of ways that can affect the pleasure relation by affecting his liking of the experience. For example, compare two sexual experiences: masturbation and sexual intercourse. Although this sensation of sexual orgasm might be the same with each, because the latter can involve emotions, feelings, beliefs, commitments, and so forth, that the former does not, we can speak of the two varying in quality in an evaluative sense, and of sexual intercourse being the richer and higher quality experience. But is it a higher quality pleasure, independent of differences in quantity of pleasure? There are two interpretations open to us here. If the quantity of pleasure is determined by the degree of liking of the experience, which is in turn determined by the strength of desire to continue and repeat it, and if the differences in kinds of experience merely contribute to differences in degree of liking them, then it seems we may still have here only a difference in quantity of pleasure. On the other hand, perhaps further elaboration of this theory of pleasure would show this to be a difference of quality rather than quantity. But on either interpretation, the important point is that the PT account of pleasure can accommodate the underlying intuition that supports the plausibility of distinguishing qualities of pleasure in the first place, namely that in the actual valuing that persons perform, many features or properties of an experience contribute to our overall evaluation of it. And this, I believe, is a crucial advantage of the PT account for a defender of hedonism. In general, objections to the second thesis of ethical hedonism, that only pleasure has intrinsic value, take the form of arguments that many things besides pleasure have intrinsic value. Persons value friendship, commitments, the respect of others, making their own choices, and many other features or properties of experiences or states of affairs, besides pleasure. Ethical hedonism on the PCET account of pleasure seems to fail to attribute intrinsic value to these features of experience, and to be an inadequate theory of value for that reason. Ethical hedonism on the PT account of pleasure does not reflect this diversity or plurality in most persons' actual values. The PT account of pleasure makes sensible the evaluation both of some pleasures as better than others, and of some sources of pleasures as better than others. Some pleasures can be better than others, whether this is, in the end, in a qualitative or quantitative sense, because the experience that the pleasure relation holds with regard to, contains properties or features to which is ascribed independent, nonderivative value. And some sources of pleasure can be better than others in the very same way—the different experiences that are the sources of our pleasures, that is the causes of our liking the experiences in varying degrees, can themselves contain other valued, that is liked, elements. If the above is sound, it explains how it can be sensible to talk of some pleasures, and of some sources of pleasure, being better than others. But the moderate opponent of the use of drugs for pleasure, while of course requiring that such talk be sensible, makes the additional specific claim that pleasure having its source in drug use is among the lower quality pleasures. What particular features of drug-induced pleasure may underlie the moderate opponent's view, I shall suggest later in the next section, but the general structure of his view can be noted now. Our earlier example of sexual activities is instructive. Masturbation is thought to be a lower quality source of pleasure than sexual intercourse because it does not contain elements of love, commitment, and so forth, that sexual intercourse can contain, and that can contribute (whether finally, in a qualitative or quantitative way) to the latter's value. Sexual intercourse is "value rich," as we might put it, in a way that masturbation is not. Likewise, the moderate opponent of the use of drugs for pleasure will hold that drug-induced pleasures are "value poor" in comparison with many other common pleasures, in that they lack valued features or properties of experience that such other pleasures contain. Again, I shall suggest what some of these valued features are in the next section. But it should be added here that the moderate opponent of the use of drugs for pleasure often holds not merely that such pleasure is of a lower quality kind, but that it tends to replace pleasures of a higher quality kind in the lives of persons who resort to it. This too, of course, is an empirical claim for which evidence is needed. Let me emphasize that I am not arguing that pleasure from the use of drugs in fact *is* a lower quality pleasure, but am only explicating how we can make sense of such a view. I shall note in the next section some of the empirical claims that would have to be supported if one wanted as well to defend the moderate opponent's view. But it should be stressed that even if the pleasure from drug use is a lower quality pleasure, it is still a pleasure and so, even on the moderate opponent's view, an intrinsic good, albeit a lesser one.

THE PLACE OF PLEASURE FROM DRUGS IN THE GOOD LIFE

We must now try to clarify the second major normative or moral issue that I noted earlier in this paper—what place does pleasure, and then more specifically the use of drugs for pleasure, have in a sound theory of the good for persons, or what is their proper role in the good life? The problem with these questions posed in this way (and of course I am responsible for posing them in this way) is that, certainly on the PT account of pleasure, they are misleading. Asking what place or role pleasure has in the good life seems to assume that pleasure is one goal or end among others that we seek in our action, and the question is then how much pleasure, as opposed to other things, we should seek. This question about pleasure seems analogous to such questions as what is the proper place or role of playing tennis or playing with one's children in the good life. How much time should I devote to tennis or my children, and likewise how much should I devote to pleasure. But clearly on the preference theory of pleasure this is a confusion. Pleasure is a relation between my experience and my desire to continue and repeat the experience for its felt qualities and apart from its consequences. The goal or end is the experience, for example, playing tennis or playing with my children, and the pleasure is not one experience, and so one goal among others to which we must assign proper weight, as our question above suggested. I shall try shortly to give some sense to this question, but whatever sense it has is not to be found along these lines.

There is a related confusion that should be removed before we directly address the place of the use of drugs for pleasure in the good life. I have spoken often in this paper of the use of drugs for pleasure, and the implicit comparison is with their use for other purposes, specifically therapeutic purposes in the treatment of illness and disease. This comparison too can misleadingly suggest that some activities of life are aimed at pleasure, whereas other activities are aimed at something(s) else, and the problem of the proper role or place of pleasure in the aims of a good life again arises. But this is not a proper understanding of what is usually meant by the distinction between doing something for pleasure as opposed to for some other end. Consider two tennis players. Player A plays tennis for pleasure, which on the PT account of pleasure just means that at the time A plays tennis he or she likes it, in the sense of desiring to continue and repeat the experience of playing tennis for its own sake and apart from its consequences. Player B plays tennis not for pleasure—in fact B rather dislikes playing—but for the entree it provides to otherwise unavailable social circles and activities that B enjoys. It is not as if pleasure has a greater place in A's life than in B's. Rather, playing tennis is a direct source, is itself a source of pleasure for A, where as for B it is not a direct source, or itself a source of pleasure, but it is only instrumental as a means to something else, and only that something else, the social activities, is itself a source of pleasure for B. This is a distinction between an experience desired or enjoyed for its own sake, as opposed to desired as a means to some other experience that is desired or enjoyed for its own sake. In each case there is an experience desired or enjoyed for its own sake, an experience in which the person takes pleasure, and so pleasure does not have a more prominent place in A's life, and in particular in A's scheme of ends, than in B's. If one is to talk of using drugs for pleasure, the less misleading comparison is with the use of other things for pleasure, that is, with other experiences also liked for their own sakes, rather than with the use of drugs for other things or other ends instead of pleasure.

The above is not to say, however, that any experience desired for its own sake must be an instance of pleasure. The preference theory's analysis of pleasure in terms of desire—specifically the desire to continue and repeat an experience at the time one undergoes it, and for its felt qualities and apart from its consequences—commits the preference theory to all pleasure being desired. But it does not commit the preference theory to *only* pleasure being desired, as an analysis of desire in terms of pleasure might do. It is consistent with the preference theory's analysis of pleasure that one desire something that it will not produce pleasure. I can today desire to have an experience tomorrow that I now correctly believe I will not like, that is, not desire to continue and repeat for its felt qualities when I have the experience tomorrow. For example, I may believe that it is my duty to have the experience, though I know I shall find it distasteful, and more generally, I may desire other things besides pleasure because I can have other reasons to desire to have an experience besides the reason that I will like its felt qualities when I have it. When other things besides pleasurable experiences are desired for their own sakes, the idea of pleasure as one end among others is sensible.

What can we now say of the place of pleasure whose source is drug use in the good for persons or the good life? One difficulty, as we shall see, in attempting to provide an answer to this question is that the major alternative philosophical theories of the good for persons are at too general or abstract a level to have much in the way of clear implications on this question. The differences between these theories concern theoretical issues that are at a considerable remove from the question of drugs used for pleasure. And within any of the major theories considerable empirical data, largely concerning the effects of drug use, will be necessary before any of the theories would have any clear implications concerning the use of drugs for pleasure. I believe that most of the disagreement concerning the desirability of the use of drugs for pleasure rests not on philosophical, and more specifically moral, differences concerning the good for persons, but rather on the dispute over the empirical facts concerning the consequences of the use of drugs for pleasure. In the remainder of this paper, I shall elaborate these points and suggest where I believe the controversial issues do lie.

What are the major alternative philosophical theories of the good for persons? I shall distinguish three: the pleasure or happiness theory; the desire theory; the perfectionist theory. It is common, and for historical accuracy within the history of philosophy, necessary to distinguish between pleasure and happiness, in turn between pleasure and happiness theories of the good. I shall not do so, however, because they are similar, if not identical, in the respects in which I am now interested. Both can be construed along the lines of the account of pleasure in the PT theory. To promote a person's good on the pleasure or happiness theory is to promote one's having experiences that, at the time they are undergone, are liked for their own felt qualities.[10] When having such experiences, one experiences pleasure, enjoys oneself, or is happy, and the more one likes the experiences, the more pleasure one has or the happier one is. In a crude nutshell, on this first theory, a person should attempt to have as much experience that pleases or makes one happy, when he or she has it, as possible.

On the desire theory, what is good for a person is for his or her desires to be satisfied to the maximum extent possible.[11] It might seem that since we have construed pleasure, on the preference theory, in terms of desiring to continue and repeat an experience, that there is no substantial difference between a pleasure/happiness theory of the good and a desire theory. However, that is not the case. As noted above the preference theory is committed to all pleasure being desired for its own sake, but not to only pleasure being desired for its own sake. The difference between the pleasure/happiness and desire theories of the good for persons is perhaps most obvious in the case of desires whose objects are not one's own conscious experiencings, e.g., my desire that my children thrive, and thrive not just while I am alive to take pleasure in their thriving, but after I die as well. This desire is satisfied by it being true that my children do thrive, both before and after my death, though in the latter case I will not be around to receive satisfaction from their thriving. More importantly for our purposes, it seems possible that a person desire something even though he or she, correctly, does not expect it to give pleasure or make one happy, either at all, or as much as something else that one does not desire or desires less. Although the desire theory enjoys considerable popularity among the contemporary moral philosophers, and in fact has important attractions, serious difficulties have been raised concerning whether it is even a coherent, much less a morally attractive, conception of a person's good.[12] Moreover, there are significantly different versions

---

[10]A recent statement and defense of a happiness theory of the good for persons can be found in Richard Brandt, *A Theory of the Good and the Right*, Oxford, Oxford University Press, 1979.

[11]A recent statement and defense of the desire theory of the good for persons can be found in John Rawls, *A Theory of Justice*, Cambridge, Harvard University Press, 1971, Ch. 7.

[12]See, for example, the criticisms of desire theories made by Brandt, *Good and the Right*, pp. 247–253.

of the desire theory; there are various constraints one can plausibly put on which desires are such that their satisfaction is for a person's good, e.g., only the desires that have a place within a person's rational plan of life. But I shall leave all these difficulties and details aside here. The main point of contrast is that *if* we want other things besides what will make us happy, or want things that will not make us happy or give us pleasure, the desire theory takes account of this in its account of a person's good.

The third sort of theory of the good for persons is a perfectionist or ideal theory. On this view, some experiences or states of affairs may have a place in a person's good at least in part independent of any pleasure or happiness they will produce for that person, or of whether they are desired by that person.[13] Perfectionists theories will vary according to which particular ideals are defended, and how the ideals are argued for or defended. Examples of such ideals include developing one's special talents, serving God's will, being an autonomous chooser, being nice to people you don't like and so forth. It is to be emphasized that perfectionist theories generally allow that happiness and/or desire satisfaction are *part* of our good, and the ideals then either constrain the production of happiness or desired satisfaction, *and/or* serve as additional elements of our good.

The above is only the merest indication of the general form of these three sorts of theories of the good for persons. But to know the place of drug use in the good for persons on any of these theories of the good for persons, it is clear that we also need considerable empirical information of two sorts: (1) information about persons, in particular about what makes them happy, or what they desire; and (2) information about drugs, in particular about the various effects that use of drugs for pleasure has. Without such data, the different theories of the good for persons are simply at too high a level of generality to have definite implications concerning the use of drugs for pleasure. But even without such information, we can note that there is a *prima facie* case that the use of drugs for pleasure is part of some person's good on all three sorts of theories. This is most obvious on the pleasure/happiness theory, since persons who take drugs because they in fact produce pleasure are producing what that theory takes to be good. On desire theories, when a person freely takes the drug because he or she desires the experience it produces, its use is again *prima facie* for the person's good. On perfectionists theories, its use may be part of a person's good if enjoyed or desired for the same reason as above. Perfectionists theories would differ from pleasures/happiness and desire theories only if they contained a specific ideal according to which the use of drugs for pleasure was *in itself* either intrinsically good or bad. So far as I can tell, no plausible perfectionist theory has contained such an ideal.

---

[13]Systematic statements and defenses of perfectionist theories are difficult to find in recent philosophical literature. Nevertheless, many persons are committed to some form of perfectionist theory, as I have construed such theories in the text, by their substantive views about the good for persons. For example, anyone who holds that it is good for a person not to read pornography and not to engage in exploitative personal relations, even if that person desires to or is made happy by doing so, is committed to what I have called a perfectionist theory.

The issue would then appear to be what, if anything, might defeat the *prima facie* case that the use of drugs for pleasure is a part of the good of those persons who do in fact enjoy and/or desire their use? I would suggest that any rational basis for the position of the critic of such drug use must lie in arguments that the consequences of the use of drugs for pleasure are such that they interfere with or inhibit realization of other important aspects of a person's good. Such arguments must include two different sorts of claims: first, claims that particular things are, on some general theory of the good for persons of the sort noted above, components of a person's good; second, empirical claims that use of drugs for pleasure has the consequence of inhibiting or interfering with the promotion and realization of these other aspects of a person's good. If we move down one step from the high level of generality of theories of the good for persons noted above, I believe we would find fairly widespread agreement among proponents of all three theories that the following are components of a person's good. I shall very briefly state these components, but not argue for their being part of a person's good, though I believe such arguments could (at some length) successfully be made; this sort of argument necessary would vary according to which general theory of the good is adopted. All of the following then, I believe, are part of the good for persons on any of the usual theories of the good for persons:

1. Participation in social relations of friendship, love, and intimacy.
2. Development and exercise of certain distinctive human capacities, especially intellectual capacities.
3. Being responsible in one's relations to other persons.
4. Being an active person, actively participating in a full array of activities and experiences.
5. Being autonomous, at least in the sense of having and exercising the capacity to act in the manner that on reflection one values or most wants to act.

I shall not elaborate the precise meaning of any of these components of a person's good, but shall rely on the reader's loose understanding of them, and agreement that they *are* part of our good. The point is that there is a widespread popular image of the user of drugs for pleasure, on which the realization of each of these components of our good is interfered with by such drug use. This popular image is clearest probably concerning the heroin user, but I believe it exists as well in a somewhat attenuated form for users of drugs like cocaine and marijuana. On this image, the drug user is:

1. Withdrawn from others, existing in his or her own "private world," and so having, at best, impoverished social relations with others.
2. Dominated or consumed by drug use, in a way that precludes the development and exercise of one's other human capacities, including especially intellectual capacities.
3. Irresponsible in one's relations with others. This is because of both the extent to which drugs are thought to dominate or "take over" the user's life (2 above) and to produce strong, irresistible desires for the drugs ("the heroin user would sell his sister to get money to feed his habit").

4. Passive, "doped up," " nodding out," so that one is unable to actively engage in a rich array of life's experiences (recall in *Brave New World* how Soma was used to produce passive persons who avoided many of the experiences most persons value).
5. Addicted, unable to resist the desire for the drug even when one wants to do so, and so under the control of the drug as to be the paradigm of the nonautonomous person.

I have deliberately used some of the vague and evaluatively loaded language of this popular image of the user of drugs for pleasure. But if this popular image is accurate, then the objection to such drug use would, I believe, be sound, for the use of such drugs would interfere with important components of our good. If this popular image is true, we would then have a sound basis for the view that pleasure from the use of drugs is a lower quality pleasure than other pleasurable experiences that either themselves promote, or at least do not interfere with, the five components of person's good noted above. The controversial point is not likely to be whether the five components I have cited are indeed part of the good for persons, but whether drugs (or some drugs, in some uses) do in fact prevent their realization in the way that what I have called the popular image suggests. That can only be determined by empirical studies, not philosophical analysis. . . . But almost certainly, I believe, such an assessment would show that the popular image is vastly oversimplified and substantially, probably largely, false. If that is so, then what is wrong with the popular image is not its implicit philosophical basis, specifically the components of the good for persons that I have noted above and that it implicitly adopts, for those *are* part of a sound account of the good for persons. What *is* wrong is the false empirical claims or assumptions it contains concerning the effects of pleasure producing drugs on their users. It is the task of empirical research, and of social and natural scientists, not of philosophers, to establish where these claims are false and where they have some evidentiary basis. But I believe it is on this issue of the nature of the consequences of the use of pleasure producing drugs that rational controversy concerning the evaluation of their use must largely turn, and not on philosophical and evaluative differences about the intrinsic value or disvalue of the use of drugs for pleasure.

Questions

1. Why does the author think that PCET cannot distinguish between higher and lower pleasures?
2. Why does the author think it cannot be argued that drug-induced pleasure has no intrinsic value at all?
3. If, as Dan Brock suggests, most of the disagreement about the use of drugs for pleasure stems from disagreement about empirical issues, what bearing does his philosophical discussion have on the problem?
4. To what extent can Dan Brock's analysis of the pleasure of drug use be applied to other pleasures that have been termed "vices"—such as gambling and fornication?

The Pleasures of Eating and Drinking

Elizabeth Telfer

Many people have criticized the pleasures of eating and drinking—or, at least, of that eating and drinking which exceeds what is needed for our survival and good health. Elizabeth Telfer offers a defense of such pleasures. Her argument consists of responses to a variety of criticisms that are leveled against the pleasures of eating and drinking.

Among these criticisms are the claims that: (a) the quest for gastronomic pleasure is self-defeating; (b) indulgence in eating and drinking has undesirable effects; (c) the pleasures of eating and drinking are unreliable in that a meal may prove disappointing; (d) the capacity for enjoying food and drink is particularly vulnerable, as one may lose the teeth, digestion, or money necessary for such enjoyment; (e) the pleasures of eating and drinking are short-lived; (f) the pleasures of food and drink are too costly given their short duration; and (g) the pleasures of eating and drinking are unworthy and trivial in comparison with allegedly higher pleasures.

Having responded to these criticisms, the author concludes that eating and drinking can be an aesthetic experience that, although simple in comparison with other aesthetic experiences, has the capacity to enrich our lives.

In this essay I wish to examine one possible answer to the question of whether we are justified in attaching so much importance to eating and drinking. This question might seem odd at first sight. Surely, it might be said, the answer is obvious; we attach great importance to eating and drinking because eating and drinking are necessary for survival, and we do not need a justification (in normal circumstances) for trying to stay alive. But these obvious answers do not meet the case. For most people spend very much more time, money and attention or some combination of these, on eating and drinking than is necessary to stay alive, or indeed to stay healthy and active. We could eat healthily on very

Elizabeth Telfer, "The Pleasures of Eating and Drinking" in *Virtue and Taste: Essays on Politics, Ethics & Aesthetics*, edited by Dudley Knowles and John Skorupski, (Oxford: Blackwell, 1993), pp. 98–110.

simple cheap food which did not need much preparation. But, instead, most people spend considerable sums of money on food and/or a great deal of time preparing it, and care very much about what it is like. This expenditure of time, money and attention cannot be justified by trying to stay alive, and so the question does arise: 'Are we justified in making such a fuss, or would it be better to bother less about our food, and perhaps more about other things?'

This question is probably one which strikes the regular cook in a household with particular force. But I think many people must have been struck with it at one time or other. If, for example, we come across people who eat very much more simply than we do ourselves, we may wonder (unless this is due to poverty) whether this is simply a different way of life, or whether it is better than ours in this respect. The asking of this question does not imply that the asker could do anything about changing his behaviour; it may be that in the sphere of eating and drinking people are governed by compulsions of various kinds. Nor does it imply that the asker would modify his food behaviour if he could do so and became convinced that he should; there are traits of character, such as greed, which might militate against this. But, of course, it may be that a person who compares his food expenditure with that of others might conclude that he is justified in spending more time, money or effort and drink than they do. And one obvious way in which he might not explain but seek to justify his policy is by claiming that eating and drinking can bring a great deal of *pleasure* if sufficient time, money or though is spent on them. It is this answer to my initial question which I wish to examine.

One immediate reaction to the claim that it is pleasure which justifies the attention we pay to eating and drinking takes the justification in question to moral justification, and objects that it is very difficult to justify this expenditure on one's own pleasure in moral terms; the money or time could be put to much more worthy use helping someone else. As a preliminary reply, I would point out that the question of expenditure on food does not arise only about one's own food: people can equally well consider whether it is important to take a lot of trouble with others' food, or whether one should benefit them in other ways instead. But if it is only our own pleasure that is in question, we can say that we have a right to an area for ourselves which is immune to the demands of others, and the question (to see whether it is to be called a moral one or not) is: what are the most worthwhile ways of spending that time and money which are in the sense ours?

If this is the question, there might be an opposite reaction: in a sphere in which, *ex hypothesi*, I have no obligations, how can the question of justification arise at all? Obviously, food and drink can be great sources of pleasure, and if this is how an individual chooses to spend his time and money, there is no more to be said.

But this reaction would be too hasty. The idea that in comparison with many other things eating and drinking are not good sources of pleasure, contrary to appearances, has a long history. This idea has two forms. On the one hand, the doctrine is that the net *quantity* of pleasure produced by eating and drinking is not as great as it seems. On the other hand, there is the idea that somehow the kind of pleasure to be got from eating and drinking is inferior to that from many other pursuits: a deficiency of quality, rather than quantity. What exactly this means is a question to which I shall return. For the moment I shall consider some of the quantity arguments. Is there any plausibility in the claim that eating and drinking do not produce as much pleasure as we are apt to think, so that if quantity of pleasure is our aim we should choose other pursuits instead?

Someone might object here that there is no point in considering specific arguments belittling the quantity of pleasure in eating and drinking, because we are not in a position to choose between these pleasures and others: we have to eat and drink in any case. But this objection would be a mistake. It is true that we have to eat and drink, but we do not have to eat and drink pleasantly. The question at issue, therefore, is whether we should choose to minimize our expenditure on food and drink because we get more pleasure spending our time and money on other things. And this is a real issue.

There are, however, two problems about any enquiry into quantities of pleasure. The first concerns the difficulty of isolating the pleasures of eating and drinking from other pleasures with which they may be associated. In some typical situations where good food is enjoyed, it may be very difficult to work out how much of the enjoyment derives from the food, how much from the pleasures of company, friendship, conversation and so on. Moreover, these pleasures are not simply distinct but contemporaneous experiences; they may enhance and modify each other. This seems to me to be a real difficulty. I think the best we can do is to try to pinpoint the food pleasures by focusing on those occasions when we eat alone with pleasure and by comparing the pleasures of eating with friends with the pleasures of sharing other activities with them. The arguments against the view that eating and drinking provide a large quantity of pleasure presuppose that we can isolate the food pleasures in this way. But I shall consider later whether this assumption loads the dice unfairly against the food pleasures, by omitting the possibility that their chief role may be as enhancers of other kinds of pleasure—the monosodium glutamate among pleasures, if we may use an apposite metaphor.

The second difficulty about enquiring into quantities of pleasure is that the enquiry might seem to be an empirical rather than a philosophical one, and one, moreover, which has as many answers as there are people. Can there be an answer to a question about how much people enjoy food, as distinct from the question about how much particular individuals do? Again, this seems to me to be a problem, and one of a kind which philosophers tend to ignore. But the traditional arguments would claim to appeal to general considerations about the nature of these pleasures which are sufficiently cogent to elevate any differences between individuals.

What, then, are the traditional arguments against eating and drinking as rich sources of pleasure? First, it is said that this is a self-defeating quest; a person who seeks pleasure from eating and drinking is never satisfied and gets less and less pleasure each time. The pleasures of eating and drinking are seen as a kind of addiction. But it is important to distinguish various possibilities here.

The addict, for present purposes, is the person who feels compelled to eat or drink more and more of a particular food or drink or perhaps of food and drink in general but who does not enjoy the food or drink; it is precisely the lack of enjoyment which leads us to see this behavior as compulsive rather than merely greedy. We can distinguish the addict both from the greedy person, who always wants to be eating but who enjoys his food, and from the jaded gourmet who no longer gets as much pleasure as he did from ordinary food and has to have something quite out of the ordinary before he can enjoy what he eats.

All these types are distinct from the normal eater who eats and enjoys his food. We might describe all of them, including the normal eater, as 'never finally satisfied.' But this would mean different things in the different cases and would not always show that eating and drinking were an unsatisfactory source of pleasure. Thus the addict is always unsatisfied in that he always craves for more of the substance to which he is addicted, the jaded gourmet in that nothing is ever quite good enough; and for both of these people it is true that the pleasures of eating or drinking constantly diminish. The greedy eater is like the addict in that he always wants more; the normal eater satisfies his desire to eat only for the time being and later wants to eat again. Both these eaters, therefore, can be seen as never satisfied. But they are unlike the addict and the jaded gourmet in that they can continue to get pleasure from their food. Provided we can avoid becoming addicted or jaded, then, we can always gain pleasure from eating and drinking.

One problem, of course, is that there may be a tendency for people who appreciate the pleasures of eating and drinking to *become* either jaded or addicted. This is a difficulty which we would need to guard against, but it may be a risk worth taking if the pleasures of eating and drinking are great, as they are. In any case, these are dangers which beset so-called mental pleasures too; people can be compulsive readers or jaded culture-vultures. Another problem might be that a pleasure whose source is so impermanent might seem an unworthy or undignified kind of pleasure. But this consideration belongs with my second section.

A second type of argument against eating and drinking as fruitful sources of pleasure refers to after-effects: those who indulge in the pleasures of the table suffer from indigestion and hangovers in the short term, ugliness and ill health in the long term. But these ill effects can probably be avoided with care, and in any case someone might think the risks worth taking—the bet a good one in terms of quantity of pleasure—if he enjoyed his food and drink sufficiently. As before, there might be objections that a person ought not to risk his health or his looks for his food, but this argument does not belong with these considerations about the quantity of pleasure.

A third type of argument concerns the alleged unreliability of eating and drinking as a source of pleasure; one can never be sure that some meal eagerly awaited will come up to expectation. This is no doubt true, but it does not differentiate eating and drinking from many other sources of pleasure: a favourite author's new book does not come up to standard, a play is poorly performed or perversely produced, and so on. Nor are pleasures safe if they are familiar, because *we* change: the grandeur of the mountains seems merely bleak and lonely, the coziness of a friend irritatingly vapid. I hesitate to say whether our tastes for food are more or less unvarying than for other things; it is certainly not obvious that food pleasures are more unreliable than their competitors.

A fourth and related argument against the food pleasures is that they are particularly vulnerable, or rather a way of life based only on them is so: a person may lose his teeth or digestion, or the money which enables him to eat and drink pleasantly rather than merely adequately. Now this argument rests on several assumptions. The first is that pleasurable styles of life may need training, or at least habituation. This assumption is required because if it were not so a person who lost his capacity for the food pleasures could simply turn to another kind of pleasant life, and their vulnerability would not matter. This first assumption is probably sound: it takes a while to 'get into' aesthetic or intellectual pleasures or to make friends. Granted these facts, the prudent policy seems to be to lead a mixed life, in which one develops several different sources of pleasure. If this is possible, the alleged vulnerability of the food pleasures would not matter after all. So a second assumption behind the vulnerability argument must be that one needs to specialize in one's sources of pleasure and the mixed life is not possible. Now it may be that a certain amount of concentration maximizes pleasure, by enabling the habituation and training to take place more quickly. But excessive specialization is counterproductive because our moods vary. A person does not necessarily enjoy the same things all the time, and needs to have different possibilities to turn to. If this is so, why should the pleasures of food not be one of these? The reply might be that there is bound to be pain at losing a source of pleasure, even if there are others to compensate; some of the vulnerability of the food pleasures makes it wiser to leave them out of the combination. But this conclusion rests on a third assumption, that the pleasures of food and drink are not only vulnerable, but more vulnerable than other kinds of pleasure. And this is by no means obvious. Certainly, extravagant food pleasures are vulnerable to changes of material fortune, but then so are extravagant intellectual or aesthetic pleasures. But there are simple food pleasures which are almost as difficult to rob someone of as the contemplated mental pleasures which can seem absolutely safe. True, people can lose their teeth and digestion. But they can also lose their sight, hearing and mental capacities. Which is more likely, that we become blind, deaf and senile, but still able to enjoy our food or that we become unable to enjoy food (that is, needing to be fed artificially) but able to think, see and hear and talk to our friends? This is an empirical question, and the answer is not obvious.

A fifth argument is that the pleasures of eating and drinking are short-lived: you cannot go on enjoying them all day, as you can a good book, a country walk or the company of friends. This contrast is probably sound, if the pleasures are considered in isolation, though, it is possible to extend the pleasure of eating and drinking by mixing it with other pleasures such as those of conversation. But it is not clear why short-livedness should be seen as a defect, unless two hidden assumptions are both true; that the food pleasures are to be the only pleasures in someone's life and that he has long periods of time in which to seek pleasure. If a person has almost no leisure time, a short-lived pleasure may be perfectly appropriate, rather as the brevity of a squash game in comparison with a golf game is no drawback to someone who has time only for squash games. And if he has a lot of leisure time and many leisure pursuits, then the short-lived pleasures can be interspersed with longer-lived ones without causing the hazards of time without pleasure.

A sixth argument is that food pleasures are too costly, given their relatively brief span. The cost is in money, time or attention, or all three; and the theory is that this expenditure spent some other way could have procured far greater pleasure. For example, I can either spend three-quarters of an hour slaving over a hot stove preparing a meal which I then enjoy eating for ten minutes, or I can spend the three-quarters of an hour enjoying reading, listening to music or talking to friends and then open a tin. I can spend ten pounds on a meal in a restaurant which gives me great pleasure for an hour, on a theatre ticket which gives me pleasure for two and a half hours, or on a paperback of a classic novel which gives me pleasure for many hours. Isn't food the poorest bargain in these cases?

The supporter of the pleasures of food may say that as far as the expenditure of time and effort is concerned, this contrast is misleading: he enjoys preparing food as well as eating it. This reply is unconvincing because the champion of the food pleasures is ignoring what Bentham called the fecundity of the competing pleasures. If I learn a piece of music, see a fine play or read a good novel, these experiences live in my mind and produce other pleasures. I can remember the works and contemplate them again. I see the world in a different way because of them. It seems that none of this is possible with the pleasures of eating and drinking. I can recall flavours and textures, but it does not seem possible to contemplate them or to gain a new idea of the world in terms of them. In the light of these considerations, the claims of aesthetic and intellectual pleasures to be cost-effective relative to eating and drinking must be high.

Despite these considerations, which are after all fairly obvious, a great many people spend a lot of time and trouble and money on nice food. This may be because they have never stopped to think about the best ways to maximize their pleasure. But some people who seem to think very carefully about enjoying themselves give a prominent role to eating and drinking. Perhaps others are greedy or compulsive eaters, who regret their eating habits and would rather spend their time or money on other things if they could manage to do so. But although it is commonplace to find people who eat too much for their health and seem unable to stop themselves, I have never met a person who thought he would increase his pleasure by paying less attention to his food and more to other things. It may be that the pleasures of eating and drinking are so intense that this compensates for their lack of duration and fecundity. But they are not normally spoken of as having great intensity, in comparison with sexual pleasure, say, or some aesthetic pleasures.

There are, I think, three reasons why the pleasures of eating and drinking retain their place despite their apparent lack of cost-effectiveness. First, they mix very well with some other great pleasures, notably those of conversation and of sightseeing. This means that, whereas they may not rank high in isolation, they enable time spent talking or soaking up the sights of a lake, garden or piazza to double its pleasure score, as it were. Secondly, many occasions of eating and drinking are symbolic occasions. This means that the pleasure of eating and drinking as such may be combined with the pleasure of performing the action which they symbolize: the pleasure of celebrating a friend's birthday or the success of an enterprise, for example. Thirdly, the pleasure of eating and drinking may simply be a popular *kind* of pleasure. I have written hitherto as though pleasure were a commodity which could be desired independently of its source, so that anyone who is seeking pleasure must prefer what gives more pleasure to what gives less. We certainly do sometimes talk in this way: 'I decided I got more pleasure out of golf than out of the clarinet—I haven't time for both, so I've given up the clarinet.' But pleasure is so closely bound up with its source that it may be coherent to say of two activities that, although both are pursued for pleasure, and although A might give more pleasure then B, B gives a kind of pleasure which the pleasure of A cannot replace. Notice that I am not here saying that the pleasure of B might be better. I am claiming rather that we may not be willing to give up food pleasure by concentrating on other things instead, and this may be a deliberate preference which is not agonized over or seen as shameful.

But there is a school of thought which would depict this kind of preference as mistaken, and maintain that the pleasures of eating and drinking are not merely *different* in kind from others but also unworthy or trivial in comparison. Eating and drinking, to this school, may or may not be a good source of pleasure, but it is not a source of good pleasure.

The best known example of this kind of idea is, of course, Mill's doctrine of higher and lower pleasures in *Utilitarianism*.[1] Mill says that we know which of the higher pleasures are by seeing which the competent judges prefer, competent judges being those who are 'equally capable of appreciating both kinds of pleasure'.[2] Notoriously, this notion of competent judges is beset with difficulties, and I propose to leave it on one side for the time being and consider some of the arguments that might be put forward for regarding the pleasures of eating and drinking as lower pleasures: arguments which may be partly what influences the competent judges in any case, since Mill depicts them as being moved by pride and dignity;[3] in other words, they do not simply consider what they like, they consider what they ought to like.

The idea of higher and lower pleasures (which is, of course, an idea which goes back to the Greeks) is in a nutshell the idea that some types of pleasure are better than others and that the person whose pleasure is in question is not necessarily the best judge of its quality. The assumption is also that intellectual, aesthetic and moral pleasures are of higher quality than physical pleasures, and that when there is a choice one should prefer the higher pleasures. But what sort of 'should' is this? For Plato and Aristotle, writing within a framework of what might be called Higher Egoism, the higher pleasures are more worth having

[1] J. S. Mill, *Utilitarianism*, ed. Mary Warnock (Collins Fontana, Glasgow, 1962), ch. 2.
[2] Ibid., p. 259.
[3] Ibid., p. 260.

than the lower, and the person whose life is rich in them is more fortunate than the person who enjoys only lower pleasures. We tend to think that the claim is either that the higher pleasures give us more pleasure or that they are part of the moral life, that we have some duty to cultivate them. I suggest that there may be something in between, concerned with what is worth while or worth having. It would, of course, be possible to link this conception with the others, by arguing that we will not be pleased with our lives unless we think they contain what is worth having or that we have a duty (to ourselves?) to pursue what is worth having, or both.

The next question which arises about higher pleasures is this: in calling a type of pleasure higher or lower, are we talking about the pleasure we take in something, our reaction, or about the experience or activity to which we react? The word 'pleasure' can be used in either way ('reading gives me great pleasure' or 'reading is one of my pleasures in life') and so the phrases 'higher pleasures', 'lower pleasures' are ambiguous. It might be argued, however, that it makes no difference in practice whether 'pleasure' stands for a reaction or for its source, on the grounds that the only way of evaluating a reaction is in terms of an evaluation of its source: it is good to take pleasure in something good, bad to take pleasure in something bad, just as the desire for a good thing is a good desire, for a bad thing a bad desire. The trouble is that pleasure seems to have some independent value: a baby's enjoyment of a trivial piece of play seems to be a precious thing. I shall, however, assume that the value of pleasure does relate to the value of the activities or experiences which give rise to it, though this is a big assumption.

The first group of arguments which aim to demote the pleasures of eating and drinking all relate in some way to the notion of eating and drinking being necessary to fulfill a physical need. The most striking is that found in Plato's *Republic:* that many so-called pleasures, among them the pleasures of eating and drinking, are illusory and are really only a relief from pain; the only genuine pleasures are those which do not depend on a previous craving.[4] This argument can be viewed at two levels. At one level, the 'pain' in question may be the physical discomfort of pangs of hunger and Plato may be saying that we mistake the relief of the pangs for a positive pleasure. There are several things wrong with this. First, it fails to distinguish a physical state from a mental reaction to it. I can be pleased that my hunger pangs have subsided, or indifferent (something else claims my attention) or even distressed (if it is the symptom of some disorder). Secondly, it assumes that the relief of hunger pangs necessarily coincides with eating. But this is not the case: my hunger pangs could also be relieved some other way, for example by drugs. Thirdly, it assumes that the pleasures of eating and drinking are dependent on having felt hungry previously. But this is not so either. There are unexpected but very keen pleasures of eating, such as eating wild blackberries or raspberries on a country walk, which do not depend on previous hunger and are, in fact, closely parallel to the example of

[4]Plato, *Republic*, trans. H. D. P. Lee (Penguin Classics, London, 1955), ss. 583–4.
[5]Ibid.

the pleasure of smell which Plato gives us as a genuine pleasure.[5] Of course, there is a relationship between being hungry and enjoying one's food. But the relationship is a complex one: one can be too hungry to enjoy one's food and one is probably more discerning and appreciative when not too hungry.

As I said earlier, Plato's argument about illusory pleasures can also be taken at another level. The 'pain' which is relieved may be, not hunger pangs, but desire for food. The thesis then would be a general one: many so-called pleasures in a thing are really only the absence of the painful desire for the thing which disappears once the thing is obtained; genuine pleasure exists only when its source is not something previously desired. But this is not satisfactory either. First, desire is not necessarily painful. Secondly, it can disappear without being satisfied. Thirdly, getting what one previously wanted does not always bring pleasure, or even what Plato would call illusory pleasure; it would be truer to say that to feel pleasure is to want now to hold on to one's present experience rather than to have wanted it previously.

I conclude then that we cannot argue that the pleasures of eating and drinking are illusory. But a second line of attack, still based on the importance of eating as fulfilling a need, is that the pleasures of eating and drinking, though they exist, are false in another sense: they depend on the body's being in a disordered state or needing replenishment. As before, this argument presupposes that the pleasures of eating and drinking all depend on need. But this is not the case, and indeed the more the pleasure concerns the quality of the food, the less is this so. Think of a person sipping a fine port during an evening. What disorder is presupposed by this pleasure?

The same sort of reply can be made to anyone who says that eating and drinking are merely a means to an end, not valuable in themselves, and their pleasure must therefore have a lower status than those of activities which are ends in themselves. This account of eating and drinking begs the question. Certainly eating and drinking are a necessary means to survival. But the eating and drinking which goes on in an affluent society consists of a great deal more, both in quantity and quality, then is necessary for survival. In other words, eating and drinking are also a pastime, entered into for its own sake. If the argument is that eating and drinking are only a means to an end, it fails. But, of course, it might be argued that eating and drinking should be treated only as a means to an end. I turn now to some arguments for this view.

One pervasive idea is that the pleasures of eating and drinking are lower pleasures because they are physical rather than mental. But what does this mean? All pleasures are mental in the sense that they depend on consciousness; this is partly what distinguishes the restoration of blood sugar level, which does not depend on consciousness, from the pleasure of eating which does. It is true that the pleasures of eating and drinking have a physical source, in the sense that they depend on input from the senses. But then so do a great many so-called higher pleasures, such as looking at beautiful things in art or nature or listening to music. It might be argued that food pleasures are more crudely physical than these, in that they involve actual physical contact between the body and what it enjoys, but this point loses a lot of its force in the light of the thought that something physical (light or sound waves) mediates between the thing enjoyed and the sense organ even in the cases of the sights and sounds.

It is difficult, then, to characterize the 'lower' pleasures purely non-mental pleasures. But it has often been maintained that the pleasures of eating and drinking, as of sex, are at any rate subrational pleasures, which can be enjoyed equally by animals and do not employ man's distinctive endowment of reason, imagination, taste etc. But this pervasive argument is very unsatisfactory. First, it is obvious that a human being's food pleasures are usually quite different from those of a pig at a trough. The human being uses his mind to appreciate combinations of flavours and textures, the suitability of the food for the season, the craftsmanship of the well-prepared dish and so on. (I am deliberately mentioning only features which could be relevant to a solitary, non-celebratory meal). Secondly, the assumption that it is better to act in ways distinctive of one's species needs supporting. If we believe in a good God or purposeful Nature who designed us for a task which other creatures cannot fulfil, we have a justification. But without these assumptions it is not obvious that we should not try to cast off the burden of rationality and aspire to a more pig-like condition. Thirdly, even if we accept that we should try to behave in ways characteristic of our species, we might argue that our species has a dual nature: we are rational animals, not angels, and it is as appropriate to human beings to enjoy animal pleasures as it is to enjoy intellectual pleasures. Of course, we would be living a non-human life if we had no intellectual activities: but, as I have said, even the life of the 'physical pleasures' will not be completely pig-like.

What about John Stuart Mill's claim that 'few human beings would consent to be changed into any of the lower animals, for a promise of the fullest allowances of a beast's pleasures'?[6] Mill attributes this refusal to a sense of dignity, which in most people is such that nothing which conflicts with it is compatible with happiness. Now it is probably true that most people would prefer a less contented life of human quality than a perfectly contented pig's life. But the human life can have the so-called lower or physical pleasures as part of it. The real question raised by Mill's account is this: suppose one had the choice between a normal human life, with both 'higher' and 'lower' pleasures in it, and a life which as far as possible consisted purely of 'higher' pleasures, would the latter be the choice demanded by the sense of dignity? Suppose, for example, an eccentric millionaire arranged his life so that he never needed to eat anything (he is fed intravenously by tubes) or to move (because moving can involve physical pleasures). He can see whatever he likes through television cameras, but he never climbs mountains himself or walks round galleries. He can listen to music, but does not play an instrument or sing because there are physical elements in the pleasure of these. Nor does he go to concerts, because they involve the physical proximity of other listeners which introduces an extraneous non-intellectual element. He converses with friends and lovers, but does not touch them. He reads, but does not turn the pages himself because handling crisp paper is a tactile, and therefore presumably 'lower', pleasure. Suppose a person could spend all his life like this, and suppose we waive questions about

---

[6]Mill, *Utilitarianism*, p. 259.

whether he ought to be getting out in the world—is this the perfect life, or is it not a human life at all?

Now, of course, someone might reply that it is both, in an answer reminiscent of Aristotle's claim: that the ideal life, one spent in contemplation, is a life too high for human beings but nevertheless one towards which we should aspire as far as we can.[7] That is a possible reaction: that the less like human beings we are the better. Another reaction is that such a life contains all that is necessary for a valuable human life: to put it another way, there is nothing essentially animal about human life. But my guess is that 'few human beings', to use Mill's phrase, would regard such a life either as human or as better than human. They would say that the animal pleasures, or rather the complex interplay of physical and intellectual which in fact constitutes 'lower' pleasures in a human being, were a valuable part of their experience of life which they would not be without; and the 'sense of dignity' might well lead them to reject the non-physical life as that of only half a person. Of course, we can imagine exceptional cases, where a person's share of physical pain or discomfort is such that he would gladly be without physical sensation altogether. But the ordinary person, I submit, would be as reluctant to exchange his mixed life, with its discontents both mental and physical, for a purely intellectual life as for a purely physical one, and might appeal to his sense of dignity to explain his reluctance.

There lingers a kind of work-ethic prejudice against food pleasures because they are too easily won: pleasure worth having must somehow be the fruits of toil. Now there is a special satisfaction about effortful achievement, but it does not follow that there is something inferior about easy pleasures. Indeed, it might be thought to be a sign of a lack of humility to think that all one's pleasures must also be achievements, that nothing could simply be accepted as 'given'. In any case, the line between what we may call acquired pleasures and what we may call natural pleasures does not coincide with that between what are normally thought of as higher and lower pleasures: the ability to appreciate beauty in a landscape is largely natural, to appreciate a fine wine largely acquired.

One problem about this attempt to rehabilitate the lower pleasures is that it omits the degree to which the pursuit of 'higher pleasures' develops the personality, in a way in which the food pleasures seem not to do. This feature is a counterpart to the greater fecundity of the intellectual pleasures which I noted when considering quantity of pleasures. Where the higher pleasures require effort and long-term projects, the way in which this happens is clear. But we also feel that *natural* aesthetic pleasures, such as the contemplation of a beautiful natural object, are enriching in some way. We are tempted to say that they mean something to us and move us, and that the experiences of eating and drinking do not, unless through symbolism or association, in which case the pleasure concerned is not a pure food pleasure. We also feel that 'higher pleasure' involves contact with something universal, whereas food and drink are merely particulars. (Interestingly we are much readier to think of universality,

[7]Aristotle, *Nicomachean Ethics,* trans. W. D. Ross, rev. edn, J. L. Ackill and J. O. Urmson (World's Classics, Oxford University Press, Oxford, 1980), bk. X, ch. 7.

meaning and being moved in connection with *sexual* pleasure, which is also supposed to be a lower pleasure.)

But is this perhaps only a difference (albeit perhaps a great difference) of degree? Even if food and drink do not have *meaning*, they can have a kind of beauty. And here I do not mean visual beauty, but their own beauty of taste and texture and smell which can be appreciated only by consuming them. For example, it seems possible to regard a lovely natural taste like that of a ripe strawberry as a beautiful element of a similar aesthetic status to that of a lovely natural colour such as that of the Mediterranean on a sunny day. If we cannot exactly be moved by food or drink, we can be stirred or excited by fine tastes. We can also appraise a particular interpretation of a classic dish rather as we can a particular performance of a classic play or piece of music.

In short, I am suggesting that eating and drinking can be an aesthetic experience; simple, undoubtedly, in comparison with some others, but genuine none the less. And this experience need not be dependent in any obvious way on symbolism or association, or on the accompaniment of other pleasures such as conversation and fellowship. But the very simplicity of the aesthetic experience associated with food and drink makes it one which can be combined with others: we sip wine as we read or listen to music, we picnic as we gaze at a landscape, we eat as we converse. If we despise the pleasures of eating and drinking, we ignore a way of enriching our lives. We have to eat in any case; so we may as well cultivate this bit of our garden.

Questions

1. What two difficulties with inquiring into the quantities of pleasure does Elizabeth Telfer mention?
2. How does the author distinguish between the addict, the greedy person, and the jaded gourmet?
3. Which of the criticisms of gastronomic pleasures considered in this essay can be leveled at the pleasures derived from smoking and drugs? Could the pleasures of smoking and drug use be defended with the same arguments that the author employs?

Suggestions for Further Reading on Substance and Sustenance

FEINBERG, JOEL. Review Essay on Robert Goodin's *No Smoking: The Ethical Issues.* *Bioethics* 5, no. 2, (1991): pp. 150–157.

FIELDING, JONATHAN. "Smoking: Health Effects and Control" (first of two parts). *New England Journal of Medicine* 313, no. 8 (22 August 1985): pp. 491–498.

———. "Smoking: Health Effects and Control" (second of two parts). *New England Journal of Medicine* 313, no. 9 (29 August 1985): pp. 555–561.

GOODIN, ROBERT E. *No Smoking: The Ethical Issues.* Chicago: University of Chicago Press, 1989.

HUSAK, DOUGLAS N. *Drugs and Rights.* Cambridge: Cambridge University Press, 1992.

REPACE, JAMES."Tobacco Smoke: The Double Standard." *Report from the Center for Philosophy and Public Policy* 4, no. 1 (winter 1984).

SCHALER, JEFFREY A., AND MAGDA E. SCHALER, eds. *Smoking: Who Has the Right?* Amherst: Prometheus Books, 1998.

SHAPIRO, DANIEL."Smoking Tobacco: Irrationality, Addiction, and Paternalism." *Public Affairs Quarterly* 8, no. 2 (April 1994): pp. 187–203.

SHAW, DAVID. *Choose Your Pleasure*. London: Tandem, 1972.

TOLLISON, ROBERT D., ed. *Smoking and Society: Toward a More Balanced Assessment*. Lexington, Mass.: Lexington Books, 1986.

www.cdc.gov/tobacco/

CHAPTER 17

The Environment, Cars, and Consumption

JAMES C. ANDERSON AND RONALD SANDLER, The Least We Can Do

JULIA MEATON AND DAVID MORRICE, Individual Freedom and the Ethics of Private Car Use

JUDITH LICHTENBERG, Consuming Because Others Consume

The Least We Can Do

James C. Anderson and Ronald Sandler

James Anderson and Ronald Sandler discuss the question of what duties we have to the environment. They first outline arguments that moral consideration ought to be extended not only to humans and other conscious beings but also to all living things. In response to the difficult question of how much weight the interests of non-human living things should have, they propose a 'Principle of Alternatives'. According to this modest principle, if an agent can satisfy his interests without killing or injuring a being with moral standing, then such killing or injury ought to be avoided. The authors then spell out the implications of adopting such a principle. Next they consider how judgments generated by such a principle might be overridden by an "all things considered" judgment. They note that human interests can conflict with the interests of other living things. They argue that the least we can do is to act in accordance with their 'All Things Considered Principle'—to sacrifice our non-serious or peripheral interests when these conflict with the basic interests of other living things.

PART I: INTRODUCTION

People are becoming increasingly aware of their responsibilities to the environment. Recycling, avoidance of pesticides and herbicides, buying local organic produce, taking care not to waste or pollute the water and air, are all becoming more prevalent practices in our culture. The common sense thinking behind these practices is that the world is a shrinking place and we need to conserve its resources for ourselves and for future generations of people. The arguments of this paper, while not incompatible with these common sense concerns, will make no appeal to human interest. We will argue for environmentally conscious practices on the basis of the interests of non-humans.

James C. Anderson and Ronald Sandler, "The Least We Can Do," is printed by permission of the authors.

Our arguments will be neutral on a number of controversial issues in environmental ethics. They are compatible both with the views of those who argue from the basis of animal interests—that animals experience conscious states and we have certain duties to them in virtue of that fact—and those who propound what is called a life-ethic—the view that all living things have interests worthy of moral consideration. Further, our argument can be formulated either in terms of the direct killing and suffering caused to morally considerable beings or in terms of the unfair distribution of common resources of the earth's inhabitants caused by human uses of the environment. While these two aspects of our treatment of the environment are not entirely separable, they do represent somewhat different moral concerns. It is one thing for a person to directly kill or cause suffering to another living thing; it is something else to deprive, by way of our everyday activities, such a living thing of habitat, water or other necessities. As we shall see, this second concern becomes particularly problematic when we are taking more than our fair share of those resources. We will be employing both of these formulations when defending the practical conclusions of Part II, that from the perspective of environmental ethics we ought, particularly in the industrialized world, either to limit severely the number of children we have or radically alter our patterns of consumption (or both).

The arguments in Part II advocate extending moral considerability from the human domain to the domain of nature—of conscious creatures and even all living things. However, that some practice or way of living is required from the perspective of environmental ethics is not to say that *all things considered* a particular agent ought to act accordingly. There might be countervailing reasons that lie outside the purview of environmental ethics that mitigate or override the requirements established from the perspective of environmental ethics. These sorts of concerns, which we investigate in Part III, are found in the common sense views of ordinary people who think of some environmentalists as "too radical" or "overly moralistic." We will argue that in spite of the arguments in Part II, there is something important to be said in favor of "toning down" the conclusions of Part II. We will argue for this *without* undermining the reasonableness, from the point of view of environmental ethics, of the conclusions reached in Part II.

The arguments of Parts II and III generate a sort of tension. Morality, understood as applying beyond the human domain, requires that we accept certain restrictions on our ways of life. On the other hand, our individual and cultural goods, as expressed in those aspects of our lives which are central to who we are and as required by certain relationships central to our lives, might require that we not abide by the point of view of environmental ethics. This tension will not and quite possibly cannot, be resolved in any general way. Certainly we will not attempt such a general resolution in this paper. Instead, in Part IV, we will articulate examples of what, for most people in our culture, can be thought of as the least we can do with respect to the non-human environment. We will provide a practical principle of action that we believe expresses the *minimal* constraint on human action all things considered—the least we can do—given all that has been argued for in Parts II and III of this paper.

PART II: ENVIRONMENTAL ETHICS

The fabric of our common sense moral beliefs includes not only concern for other human beings but concern for animals as well. It is wrong to kick the family dog. Animals ought not to be raised in slovenly conditions or without adequate nourishment. It is wrong to torture the rabbit that lives in the raspberry bushes. Even those philosophers who deny that we have true and direct duties to animals recognize that *in some sense* we have obligations with regard to how we treat both domesticated and wild animals[1]. It is an easy step for us to see that these duties cannot plausibly be accounted for in terms of the effects such actions have on *humans*. The explanation of what is wrong with kicking the family dog, torturing the rabbit that lives in the raspberry bushes, must include the pain of the dog, the suffering of the rabbit. Jeremy Bentham expressed this common sense moral belief in his now famous series of questions from *The Principles of Morals and Legislation*, "The question is not, Can they *reason?* Nor, Can they *talk?* but, Can they *suffer?*"[2] With his final question, Bentham takes us from ethical theories that are human-centered into the domain of ethical theories that directly consider the moral relevance of a wide variety of animals. Animals share with us the morally relevant characteristic of being able to suffer; we are, in the moral sense, kin to any such animal.

A similar argumentative strategy has increasingly been employed by moral philosophers who have argued that moral consideration ought to extend beyond the realm of conscious creatures to all living things.[3] Each of these philosophers begins by describing a characteristic or set of characteristics which is possessed by all living things (including, of course, us). The proposed common characteristics vary somewhat from philosopher to philosopher. Attfield focuses on common capacities and their corresponding interests in terms of which we can specify the goods proper to various organisms.[4] Taylor[5] and Rodman[6], while they go on to develop significantly different moral theories, agree that the metaphysical ground for the attribution of moral standing to all living things is

---

[1] Both Aquinas and Kant deny that we have direct duties to animals. But both philosophers believe that the common sense duties we ordinarily suppose we have to animals can be explained without explaining them away. That is, they both think that while the common sense duties are binding, such duties are actually indirect duties to oneself and other human beings. Saint Thomas Aquinas, *Summa Theologica*, translated by the English Dominican Fathers (Chicago: Benziger Brothers. 1918). Immanuel Kant, "Duties to Animals and Spirits," in *Lectures on Ethics*, trans. Louis Infield (New York: Harper and Row, 1963).

[2] Jeremy Bentham, *The Principles of Morals and Legislation* (1789), Chapter XVII, Section 1.

[3] Robin Attfield, "The Good of Trees." *The Journal of Value Inquiry* 15 (1981). John Rodman, "Ecological Sensibility." *Ethics and the Environment*, edited by Donald Scherer and Thomas Attig (Englewood Cliffs, N.J.: Prentice-Hall, 1983). Paul Taylor, *Respect for Nature* (Princeton: Princeton University Press, 1986). Kenneth E. Goodpaster, "On Being Morally Considerable," *The Journal of Philosophy*, Vol. LXXV, No. 6 (June 1978), pp. 308–25. Holmes Rolston III, "Environmental Ethics: Values in and Duties to the Natural World," *Reflecting on Nature*, ed. Lori Gruen and Dale Jamieson (New York: Oxford University Press, 1994), pp. 65–84.

[4] *Ibid.*

[5] Taylor, *op. cit.*

[6] Rodman, *op. cit.*

that such beings are characterized teleologically in the life sciences and have goods of their own. It is, therefore, rational for us to view them as beings that can be benefited or harmed. The various functional parts of these organisms are organized in such a way as to promote the good of the organism. The root functions to provide nutrients to the tree; the bark functions to protect the tree; the cell membrane functions so as to allow harmful chemicals to pass out of the organism. All these biologically specifiable functions presuppose that organisms—all living things—can be benefited or harmed.

Granted that there are non-human beings with interests, organisms that can be benefited or harmed, why should we take these characteristics into account from a moral point of view? It is one thing to say that an animal suffers; it seems quite another thing to say that this suffering ought to be of moral concern for me. It is one thing to say that a tree has an interest in staying alive, it is another thing to say that this interest ought to be of moral concern for me. Some philosophers who embrace the life-ethic answer this objection by arguing that the relevant characteristic (or set of characteristics) possessed by all living things is of recognized moral significance in the human domain. Since it is, it would be irrational to deny its moral significance in the domain of other living things. Attfield, for example, in a passage reminiscent of Bentham's famous questions, asks,

> Are the similarities [between humans and other living things] really negligible? . . . If then their interests are partially similar to interests of acknowledged moral relevance (i.e., our own), can we disregard them totally?[7]

Other philosophers, such as Taylor, argue more directly that when we adopt a scientific view of ourselves and our place in nature—seeing ourselves as one kind of organism among many others in the Earth's community of life—it becomes irrational for us to regard our human goods as morally privileged. If our goods are of legitimate moral concern to us as moral agents, so too must be the goods of others. Finally, there are those such as Routley who, by the use of various thought experiments, attempt to show that all living things have some intrinsic value and so are deserving of our moral regard.[8]

Here we offer an argument common to each of the above strategies. It is also an argument shared by those, such as Singer and Regan, who argue that moral concern ought only to extend to sentient beings. We will call our argument the Argument from Moral Consistency. If one were to say that one's own pain (or one's own life) was morally relevant but not the pain or life of another, one would have to provide some reason for saying so. To answer that demand by saying "because it is mine!" surely begs the question. In the absence of morally compelling differences, if a characteristic counts morally in one's own case, it counts in any case in which it occurs. If it counts in some other case, it counts in one's own case. If a characteristic warrants moral concern *anywhere*, it merits it *everywhere* it is found. It is important to see that this line of reasoning

---

[7] Attfield, *op. cit.*, p. 50.
[8] Richard Roufley, "Is There a Need for a New, an Environmental Ethic?" in *Proceedings of the Fifteenth World Congress of Philosophy* (Varna, 1973), pp. 205–10.

(a) is not unique to the view that only sentient beings deserve moral concern nor to the life-ethic view, and (b) does not depend on the nature of the characteristic in question. It is a general argument from consistency in moral consideration. If any of the above strategies for isolating morally relevant characteristics of all living things is successful, and if the Argument from Moral Consistency is sound, we can conclude that all living things deserve our moral concern—that the interests of these others ought not be ignored by moral agents such as ourselves.

It is a much more difficult question to determine how much moral weight one should give to non-human living beings. Some argue that each organism should be given equal moral weight. Among these philosophers there are disagreements regarding the relevant meaning of "equality." Others argue that some organisms deserve more moral weight than other organisms depending, for example, on the complexity of the organism.[9] To arrive at our conclusions, however, we will not have to adjudicate among the various equality and superiority claims. We simply propose the following plausible moral principle which we will call the Principle of Alternatives:

> P1: When there is an alternative, A, to killing or injuring a being with moral standing and A satisfies the same agent interest without killing or injuring a being with moral standing then one ought to do A.

This principle does not adjudicate cases where a human life is pitted against an animal life (lifeboat cases). It is not meant to adjudicate all of the possible sorts of conflicts that can arise between humans and other members of their environment. The Principle of Alternatives is meant to reflect common sense and be a moral requirement acceptable to both the utilitarian and rights-based views of animal moral consideration, as well as to those who propound some version of the life-ethic.

While the above formulation of the principle of alternatives appeals to the immorality of direct killing and causing injury to beings with moral standing, the principle can also be formulated to reflect a particular sense of moral fairness or justice as it applies to such organisms. Here we are concerned with cases in which our activities harm other organisms indirectly by our consuming resources required for their survival and flourishing. The sense of justice involved is that of distributive justice and we will call this argument The Argument from Distributive Justice. The concept of distributive justice requires that when a resource is basic to the lives of various living things, humans and non-humans, each organism ought to have a fair share of the resource. All organisms have certain requirements for their survival; some organisms require the same things to fulfill those needs. For example, many organisms in a given geographical region might require the very same water in order to survive. Sometimes resources are so short that there simply is not enough of a given resource for all basic needs to be met. We are not, initially, concerned with such cases. We are

---

[9]For a discussion of these issues see James C. Anderson, "Species Equality and the Foundations of Moral Theory," *Environmental Values* (Cambridge, UK, 1993), pp. 347–365.

concerned with cases in which all interests *can* be met but where humans, by taking more than their fair share, are precluding the fulfillment of the basic interests of other living things.

In order to make clear the force and content of this argument, we introduce the following plausible moral principle—yet another version of what we have called the Principle of Alternatives:

> P2: If there is an alternative, A, to a person taking an unfair share of some basic interest-satisifying resource and A still satisfies the person's interest, one ought to do A.

These two principles (Pl and P2), combined with the limited resources of the planet and the current consumptive patterns of human beings, have far reaching implications for virtually all persons. Some of these implications have already been popularized and have attracted widespread support. For example, P1 and P2 imply that it is wrong for humans to raise and kill animals for food[10]. But other implications, implications for activities that are every bit as fundamental to how we live our lives, remain, for the most part, unrecognized. These implications include how we construct our homes, how we conduct business, how we travel and how we recreate[11]. And, if our behavior cannot be suitably modified, P1 and P2 might even require that we reduce, though in morally acceptable ways, the population of humans. This means that people may be obligated to have few if any children.

In order to emphasize the scope of the implications that P1 and P2 have for how we live our lives, let us consider the implications they have for how we take our recreation. According to the Principle of Alternatives, persons should satisfy their interest in recreation by engaging in recreational activities which minimize environmental impact and usage of what ought to be seen as shared resources. On this standard a number of popular recreational activities, as they are now commonly practised, are immoral. Golf courses use an average of one half ton of chemical pesticides per year. In the United States alone that amounts to 8000 tons of pesticide (there are approximately 16,000 golf courses) annually which damage wildlife and contaminate water through runoff and seepage[12]. Snowmobiles dump millions of gallons of raw fuel into the national parks of the

---

[10]It takes roughly ten times as much of the surface of the earth to produce a pound of meat as it does to produce a pound of protein from vegetables such as beans and peas. Five times the acreage is used in the production of meat protein as compared with the production of proteins from cereal grains. The land we use to produce these meat proteins could be used to satisfy the basic interests of wild plants and animals, for in all of the places in which we raise cattle, hogs, and chickens for food, and on which we raise food for those animals, other natural systems of life once lived and flourished. The distributive justice versions of the principle of alternatives morally requires that we radically change our methods of food production and consumption. It is unfair to do otherwise.

[11]For a thorough discussion of how we can build our homes, our cars and our industry in ways which are far more fair, according to the standards of P1 and P2, than at present see *Natural Capitalism* by Paul Hawken, Amory Lovins and L. Hunter Lovins (New York: Little, Brown and Company, 1999).

[12]Golf courses can also use upwards of 250,000 gallons of water per day. And consumption is often highest when waterfall and water levels are lowest. These numbers are from Texas Parks and Wildlife at *www.tpwd.state.tx*.

United States and have carbon monoxide emission levels 500–1000 times higher than modern cars. In fact, carbon monoxide emissions from snowmobiles led to the west entrance to Yellowstone National Park having the highest carbon monoxide levels in the nation. This resulted in, among other things, illness among park rangers. Furthermore, both the millions of miles of groomed snowmobile trails and the engine noise alter migratory patterns and cause habitat desertion by wildlife.[13] Similar problems with migratory patterns and habitat abandonment arise in connection with large alpine skiing resorts such as the Vail Ski Resort in Colorado which recently opened 885 new acres of national forest terrain on top of its previous 4000 skiable acres. In these cases we need to recognize, first, that there are alternative forms of recreation available to people in our culture; second, that some of these alternatives are less taxing on the environment and less destructive to flora and fauna. Once these two facts are recognized, we see that our present recreational activities violate both P1 and P2. Such recreational practices, then, are immoral from the point of view of environmental ethics.

The form of recreation that perhaps most flagrantly violates the Principle of Alternatives is sport hunting. Again, we need only point out that there are alternative forms of recreation available. One could take a walk through the woods and fields; one could even track animals and "shoot" pictures of them in their natural habitats. This being the case, it seems clearly immoral to kill these animals for recreational purposes.

It might be argued, however, that the human interest involved in recreational hunting is such that nothing short of killing the animal can satisfy that interest. Thus, there is no alternative to killing these animals. Similarly, in the cases of snowmobiling, golfing and skiing one might argue that the human interest involved is simply that of snowmobiling, golfing, or skiing (rather than the more generic interest of recreating). The problem with this line of argument is that it ignores our earlier considerations concerning the moral status of non-human beings. It is true that the above activities fulfill a serious interest (the human interest in recreation); but, given the options available in our culture, they do not constitute serious interests in their own right. They express mere *preferences* for ways of satisfying a serious interest. When morally considerable beings are at stake, mere preferences on our part are not sufficient to justify the frustration of their interests.[14]

---

[13]According to the Wisconsin Department of Natural Resources, the Canadian Parks and Wilderness Society, and the Environmental News Network websites.

[14]Could it be that our mere preferences are weightier than the basic interests of some other living things are? Isn't that a possibility? If different interests can be ranked, why can't the interests of different beings be ranked? Perhaps even the most basic interests of some beings are such that they weigh less than the weakest interests of others. if this line of argument is accepted, if our mere preferences can outweigh the basic interests of other organisms, what sense can be made of attributing moral standing to these organisms at all? Sacrificing the basic interests of other morally considerable beings to satisfy our whims is equivalent to denying the moral relevance of their interests altogether. More will be said about this in Part IV.

Simply stated, if the above moral requirements (P1 and P2) are to be met, our consumptive practices must be drastically altered. When we consider the mere numbers of people consuming resources which satisfy their every interest, basic and non-basic, and when we realize the amount of destruction of habitat of other living things entailed by that consumption, we find it difficult to avoid the conclusion that we are we are harming and killing morally considerable beings and using a disproportionate amount of the earth's common resources. (In many cases the two go hand in hand. It is often because of the over consumption of humans and the concomitant destruction of habitat that morally considerable beings are harmed and killed).

So many of our environmental problems come down to this, it seems. Why are we driven to cut down the last remaining redwood forests of the Pacific Northwest? Why are we driven to mine for copper at the risk of destroying the ecosystem of a lake or river? Because there is a demand for these resources. Meeting that demand is the means for the satisfaction of various human interests. If not Redwoods then lumber produced on a timber plantation will be used to satisfy those interests; but, in either case, habitats are destroyed—whole ecosystems are destroyed. The destruction of habitats throughout the world to meet the interests of humans has resulted in species extinctions of unprecedented numbers.[15] We, especially in the industrialized world, are taking a disproportionate share of the planet and this taking is not benign.

We emphasize the destruction caused by those of us in the industrialized world for two reasons. First, there is a tendency on the part of those of us in the industrialized world to look elsewhere when it comes to population problems—to assume that the locus of the problem is in places where the raw numbers of people are greatest and where population growth is on the increase. But each of us uses many times more of the planet's resources than do those in the so-called, Third World. Second, while there is plenty of environmental damage going on in the non-industrialized world, there is plenty going on here as well. It is likely, to say the least, that a reduction in human population as well as radical changes in our patterns of consumption, are necessary to rectify this injustice.

PART III: ALL THINGS CONSIDERED

In the previous section we argued for a number of environmentally friendly practices from the environmental ethics point of view. We argued, for example, that persons should refrain from hunting (except for subsistence cases), snowmobiling, chemically maintaining golf courses and acting so as to increase the human population of the Earth. But that is just the environmental ethics point of view. Is it not possible that there are considerations which can override or

---

[15]Of course, there have been other periods in the history of the earth when there have been mass extinctions. But those have not been at the hands of moral agents; they did not result from the unfair practices of humans or any other moral agents.

mitigate those responsibilities? It is certainly the case that those practices come into conflict with legitimate human ground projects. By ground projects we just mean those projects which make life meaningful. Here in Wisconsin, hunting and snowmobiling are often defended on the grounds that the activities are meaningful traditions to many of those who participate in them and are occasions for promoting intimate familial relationships, particularly between fathers and sons. For example, there is apparently—as non-hunters we cannot speak first hand—a special kind of closeness that is fostered by the long quiet hours spent together tracking in the wilderness. To many who engage in it, hunting is much more than a mere recreational activity.

Such claims are by no means limited to Wisconsinites nor to deer hunters. Native Americans have long asserted the importance of hunting to their cultural and spiritual well-being. The Makah tribe in the Pacific Northwest, for example, recently revived the tradition—suspended in the 1920s—of hunting gray whales, in hopes that it would restore cultural pride and purposiveness particularly among the tribe's men; the absence of the hunting practice having stripped the Makan men of their traditional role and identity. The Whale hunt, limited in scale as it must be by law, is intended to revitalize not by means of an economic boom, but by restoring communal pride and suspended heritage[16]. The ground projects of the Makah are in conflict with the moral prohibition against hunting for non-subsistence purposes.

A person's ground projects can likewise give rise to reasons that conflict with the prohibition against increasing the human population of the planet. The most common of such projects are the deep religious commitments that orient many peoples' lives and define their worldviews. These commitments are in some cases taken to involve an obligation to have a large number of offspring. So to the extent that one takes having many children to be a tenet of the religion to which one is committed, one has a reason for non-compliance with the environmental ethics prescription to avoid human population growth.

The above cases not only provide examples of reasons for action which conflict with the environmental ethics point of view; they indicate the source of such reasons. They originate in the complexities of human character and well-being. Persons are not one-dimensional; they are not merely environmental agents. What makes human life meaningful involves a variety of commitments and projects. And reasons which arise out of persons' ground projects and commitments often give rise to reasons for action which are not included in the environmental ethics point of view. And these reasons, just as they can conflict with each other (as in the case when one has reason to spend time with one's family and reason to spend time on one's career though there is not time for both), can conflict with environmental ethics reasons.

It by no means follows from the fact that there are, for some people, reasons for having large families, golfing, snowmobiling, or hunting for non-subsistence purposes that the policies justified from the environmental ethics point of view

---

[16]"Reviving Tradition, Tribe Kills a Whale", *New York Times*, May 18, 1999.

are to be ignored. It merely demonstrates that the question "what is the least we should do for the environment?" is not fully answered by attending to the environmental ethics point of view *alone*. There are other considerations. These considerations can and do conflict with the policies and practices advocated from the environmental ethics point of view. What remains is to develop a method for adjudicating such conflicts. In the next section we will offer what we find to be the most plausible principle of adjudication for conflicts between persons' duties to the environment and considerations generated from persons' particular ground projects.[17]

PART IV: THE LEAST WE CAN DO

In Part II of this paper we argued that a number of common practices in our culture are, from the perspective of environmental ethics, immoral. In Part III, we argued that not every such practice must, all things considered, be abandoned by everyone under every sort of condition. We even suggested that the practices shown to be immoral in Part II might well be among the practices which, all things considered, should persist in the lives of some people some times. The question we must address here is whether there is *a principled way* of deciding when we ought to abandon those practices and when we may, perhaps with an attitude of regret, persist in those practices. If we are, for example, individually in a position to define what is one of our "ground projects" can we not simply assert that snowmobiling or golfing is one of our "ground projects"? And if a practice which is immoral from the perspective of environmental ethics is part of our cultural tradition, can we not simply assert that, for example, recreational hunting is, all things considered, permissible?

Our dilemma is this: while environmental reasons can sometimes be overridden by other concerns, they, being moral reasons, still carry, in our common sense thinking, a certain *general* unassailability. If we abandon moral reasoning to *mere* personal assessment of what does or does not count as a "ground project" we abandon this *general* unassailability. If we abandon moral reasoning to what is *merely* culturally acceptable, we abandon the very possibility of any practical importance for the moral assessment of cultural practices. On the other hand, we have already argued in Part III that in some instances environmental reasons part company with what we have called "all things considered" reasons. We are in need of a principled way of resolving this dilemma. The project of articulating any such principle is complicated by the fact that ground projects do differ from individual to individual; moreover, cultural practices vary widely and perhaps not in systematic ways. These facts seem to offer further resistance to the project of finding a solution to our dilemma.

---

[17]We have left out of the discussion the possibility of observer independent aesthetic value. In theory it is possible that such values will lower the standard which is the least we should do. However, it is more likely, given that favorable aesthetic responses to nature among person are ubiquitous, that such values would raise the standard.

Because of the formidable task before us, we will make only a modest start toward finding a solution to the dilemma we face. This is why we have entitled this part of our paper, and the paper as a whole, "the least we can do." We will argue here for the *minimal* circumstances under which environmental reasons outweigh other reasons; we will remain silent on the issue of whether, in other sets of circumstances, environmental reasons might outweigh non-environmental reasons. As will become evident, even our modest suggestion is not without *practical* difficulties (even if it proves to be theoretically sound.)

The examples in Part III are all cases in which the human goal or interest involved is what we might call a *serious* human interest. Developing a close relationship with one's child in a natural setting, passing on knowledge that has permeated the history of one's family, not alienating one's self from one's parents and family and living in accord with one's religious beliefs are all instances of serious human interests. What do we mean by a "serious interest"? Following VanDeVeer,[18] we define a serious human interest as one such that though the person could survive without its being satisfied, it would be difficult or costly to the persons' well-being to do so.

Let us anticipate two objections at this point. First, the above definition is (admittedly) vague and consequently any subsequent use of it to solve our dilemma will inherit that vagueness. Second, the above definition allows the possibility that what is a serious interest for one person might be less than serious for another. This variability seems to run contrary to the very idea of finding even a modest *principled* resolution to our dilemma. With respect to the vagueness objection, we point out that the principle we will be offering will be stated in contrast to the notion of a serious interest and will be so minimal in its "all things considered" requirements, that the vagueness of this initial concept will not be threatening. With respect to the variability of serious interests from person to person, we will argue that this is actually a theoretical, if not a practical, advantage of our position. The practical difficulties will be dealt with in our concluding remarks.

Our modest solution is as follows. The least we can do, all things considered, with respect to our treatment of non-humans who have moral standing, is to sacrifice our non-serious or peripheral interests when they conflict with the basic interests of those beings. A nonserious, or peripheral, interest is one the sacrifice of which poses little or no cost to the well-being of the person in question.[19] It is sometimes permissible, all things considered, to override environmental concerns in favor of our serious interests. However, it seems clear that environmental reasons ought, all things considered, to override reasons which reflect nothing more than our peripheral interests—our *mere* preferences. We can state this all things considered judgment in the following principle:

> P3: Never sacrifice the basic interests of beings with moral standing to satisfy one's non-serious (peripheral) interests.

---

[18]VanDeVeer, "Interspecific Justice", Inquiry, Vol. 22, Nos. 1–2 (Summer 1979), p. 60.
[19]*Ibid*, p. 59.

We call this the All Things Considered Principle. P3 reflects *the least we can do* with respect to our actions regarding non-human morally considerable beings. Let us consider the implications of this modest principle for the moral conclusions we reached in Part II.

First of all, we must recognize that for most of us, most of the time, snowmobiling and golfing, for example, satisfy only a peripheral interest. They are, then, for most of us, most of the time, all things considered impermissible activities. The least we can do, then, is to refrain from these activities (at least as they are presently constituted). For many recreational hunters, hunting satisfies a mere peripheral interest; so it is for many hunters an all things considered impermissible activity. The least they can do, then, is to refrain from that activity. The same is true of the other recreational activities discussed in Part II.

On the other hand, for some people, at least some times, these activities might represent the satisfaction of a serious interest. P3 does not preclude, all things considered, these activities in those cases. The arguments in Part III, for example, suggests that for some people, at least some times, recreational hunting represents a serious interest. P3 does not preclude, all things considered, hunting in those cases. Again, the same can be said of snowmobiling, maintaining golf courses, and alpine ski resorts. If there are cases where these activities represent more than a mere peripheral interest then, according to P3, they are not impermissible.

The case of having children is surely more difficult to deal with. Having children is serious business and decent parents take a serious interest in the well being of their children. But at the same time, many adults judge that their interest in having children (or more children) is peripheral. Some even judge that they have a serious interest in *not* having children (or more children.) It is not inconceivable that someone might reasonably assert that, yes, it would be fun to have (more) children but that other considerations might conflict with their preference for having (more) children. In such cases, P3, together with the arguments from Part II, would imply that it is, all things considered, impermissible to have (more) children. We believe that such cases are quite real. A person might have an inclination to have a third or fourth child and reason that having such a child would undermine their desire to travel to far away places. That desire might reasonably override the person's interest in having another child. But if the desire to travel to far away places can reasonably override such an interest, surely environmental reasons of the sort we have adduced in Part II should, all things considered, override this peripheral interest. Again, it is the least the person can do.

Determining the level of one's interest in doing a certain thing under certain circumstances is indeed a difficult task. One must be perceptive and, just as important, honest with oneself. Is my interest serious or is it peripheral? In part, this depends on accurate projections of how satisfaction or nonsatisfaction of the interest in question will affect my well-being. In these matters, we can make honest mistakes in either direction. We can be dishonest with ourselves, as well. For an individual to act on even this modest principle, P3, requires a commodity which philosophers have always sought and always found to be elusive—

self-knowledge. Given the difficulties in one's own case, how much more difficult is it to assess whether the actions of another express her serious or peripheral interests? How much more difficult to judge her level of honesty? If the required *self-knowledge* is as difficult to come by as we suspect it is, it would perhaps be prudent, when assessing the all things considered judgments of others, to bear in mind the important differences between people which can issue in different all things considered judgments.

Questions

1. What is the authors' Argument from Moral Consistency? What characteristic or set of characteristics is it that is deemed morally considerable in the case of humans and that humans share with all living things?
2. What is the difference between the first and second version of the Principle of Alternatives?
3. Do you think it is true, as the authors say in footnote 14, that sacrificing "the basic interests of other morally considerable beings to satisfy our whims is equivalent to denying the moral relevance of their interests altogether"?

Individual Freedom and the Ethics of Private Car Use

Julia Meaton and David Morrice

Julia Meaton and David Morrice argue that while a government ban on the private use of cars would be justified in principle even from a liberal perspective such a ban, would be both impracticable and unfair at present. However, they argue that although private car use may continue to be legal, individuals face the moral dilemma of whether to abandon or limit their own use of cars.

The authors note that according to John Stuart Mill's principle of liberty, an individual's freedom, although it ought to be respected in what John Stuart Mill calls "self-regarding" actions, ought to be restricted when the individual engages in harmful "other-regarding" actions. The authors then highlight numerous ways in which the use of cars causes harm to others, both directly and indirectly. They note that using cars also poses many dangers to the drivers themselves—dangers of which drivers are often not fully informed and to which they do not freely consent. For the authors, this suggests that there are moral problems with car use even within the "self-regarding" sphere. They conclude that individuals ought to restrict their private use of cars by limiting how much they drive, the kind of cars they drive, and the manner in which they drive.

INTRODUCTION

We all make moral choices in our everyday life: whether or not to return mislaid valuables; whether to lie; whether to drop litter. For most people the decision to use the private car for work, leisure or shopping is not a moral choice, but one made out of convenience and habit. Car use, for most, is not seen as a matter of good or bad, but as a simple aspect of everyday life. It is seen as a very convenient mode of private transport, which can take one where one wishes,

Julia Meaton and David Morrice, "Individual Freedom and the Ethics of Private Car Use," is printed by permission of the authors.

when one wishes. For many people the car is seen as an essential part of everyday life, as indispensable as other manufactured goods, such as the telephone, the television, and the washing machine. As is often remarked, the car is the second most expensive purchase which most people will make, and as such is an object of pride and joy. It is even accorded the status of an aesthetically pleasing object. Above all, the private car is perceived as a symbol of individual freedom.[1] As Ellwood says: 'cars are the mechanical embodiment of personal freedom, of the ability to be in control, to go where you want when you please'.[2] On the other hand, as we propose to argue, the private car is not an innocent pleasure but, rather, the cause of a number of problems which have become increasingly important over the past forty years. As the cause of serious problems, private car use is, we argue, a moral problem.

Many people may be aware of the range of problems and harms associated with car use: road congestion, death and injuries, and environmental pollution. However, few people seem to relate this awareness to their own decision making, and so few seem to appreciate that car use is a moral matter. As the evidence of congestion and environmental damage accumulates, transport experts suggest that we are moving into an era when restrictions on private car use will have to be made.[3] There has been a gradual but noticeable shift in the attitudes of some governments across the world, away from road building and provision for the motorist towards policies which restrict car access in certain areas at certain times, and other policies designed to encourage the use of public transport. Attitude research has shown that while people might agree with such policies in a general and abstract way, when their lifestyles and everyday behaviour are directly affected people tend to become less tolerant and in some cases aggressively opposed to what they perceive as restrictive and punitive transport policies.[4] Thus, any proposed restriction on the use of private cars is likely to be very unpopular and to be seen as a restriction of inviolable individual freedom. Even if governments fail to introduce 'greener' transport policies, and individuals retain their lawful freedom to choose to drive their cars, we argue that individuals must now face up to a moral dilemma: should they continue to use their private cars for their personal convenience, without moral scruple, or should they voluntarily restrict their use for the sake of the good of all.

Faced with this moral dilemma, a few individuals may abandon private car use. Many more, whilst acknowledging the harm of car use in general, may argue that their personal contribution is insignificant; that they have no alternative; and that they use their cars responsibly. Some individuals may doubt that

---

[1] J. Whitelegg, *Critical Mass; Transport Environment and Society in the Twenty-first Century* (Pluto Press/WWF, London, 1997).

[2] W. Ellwood, 'Car Chaos', *New Internationalist*, no. 195, 1989, pp. 4–6.

[3] J. Roberts, J. Cleary, K. Hamilton, and J. Hanna, *Travel Sickness: the need for a sustainable transport policy for Britain* (Lawrence and Wishart, London, 1992). See also, Royal Commission on Environmental Pollution, *Transport and the Environment, 18th Report* (HMSO, CM2674, London, 1994).

[4] M. Anderson, J. Meaton, C. Potter, and A. Rogers, "Greener Transport Towns: Publicly Acceptable, Privately Resisted", in D. Banister ed., *Transport Policy and the Environment* (E. and F.N. Spon/Routledge, London, 1998), pp. 267–297.

there is sufficient evidence to demonstrate that their car use is harmful. Those individuals who continue to use their private cars may be tempted, in the face of opposition, to fall back on the argument that their choice is a matter of individual freedom, of concern only to themselves. The freedom of the road is, as already noted, one of the reasons why the car is so popular, even in the face of growing congestion, and why other means of transport fail to provide acceptable alternatives. The attitude that private car use is a matter of freedom of choice, of concern only to the individual, can be associated with John Stuart Mill's highly influential liberal theory of freedom. We consider the ethics of private car use within the framework set by Mill and argue: a) that even on Mill's terms there is good reason to question the morality and right of unlimited freedom of private care use; and b) that Mill's theory of freedom is vulnerable to criticism such that private car use may be seen to lack adequate moral justification. We conclude that although private car use may lack adequate moral justification, nevertheless an immediate total ban would be impracticable and unfair in operation. Private car users are left with a set of moral dilemmas which they should consider seriously and respond to responsibly.

MILL'S THEORY OF LIBERTY

Mill defines civil or social liberty as 'the nature and limits of the power which can be legitimately exercised by society over the individual'.[5] The problem of liberty is, therefore, where to draw the line between the freedom of the individual and the authority of society or the state. Mill proposes a solution based on 'one very simple principle'.

> That principle is, that the sole end for which mankind are warranted, individually or collectively, in interfering with the liberty of action of any of their number, is self protection. That the only purpose for which power can be rightfully exercised over any member of a civilised community, against his will, is to prevent harm to others. His own good, either physical or moral, is not a sufficient warrant.[6]

Mill's simple principle rests on a distinction between a) what he terms self-regarding action, over which society has no authority and the agent has absolute freedom; and b) what is usually termed other-regarding action, over which society has authority to prevent the agent doing harm to others. In accord with this distinction Mill identifies two maxims which sum up his theory of liberty.

> The maxims are, first, that the individual is not accountable to society for his actions, in so far as these concern the interests of no person but himself. . . . Secondly, that for such actions as are prejudicial to the interests of others, the

[5]J. S. Mill, *On Liberty and other writings,* S. Collini ed. (Cambridge University Press, Cambridge, 1989), p. 5.
[6]*Mill, On Liberty,* p. 13.

individual is accountable, and may be subjected either to social or legal punishment, if society is of the opinion that the one or the other is requisite for its protection.[7]

Mill links liberty and ethics by means of the concept of harm and the distinction between self-regarding and other-regarding actions. There is room for debate about what exactly Mill means by the concept and the distinction. Clearly, harm may result from an action done by an agent. But in addition to the harm of acts of commission, Mill also recognises the harm of acts of omission. 'A person may cause evil to others not only by his actions but by his inaction, and in either case he is justly accountable to them for the injury.'[8] Harm, or evil, undoubtedly includes physical harm, such as assault on the body. It may be noted that in one of the quotes from Mill above he refers to physical or moral good, and so implies both physical and moral harm. Does Mill mean, then, that society has the authority to prevent an individual doing not only physical but also moral harm to another? He is ambiguous on this matter. On the one hand, he says clearly that acts which are 'directly injurious only to the agents themselves, ought not to be legally interdicted,' but that if done in public these acts are 'a violation of good manners, and coming thus within the category of offences against others, may rightly be prohibited'.[9] On the other hand, Mill is also clear that even though others may consider an agent's conduct to be 'foolish, perverse, or wrong, 'the action may not actually harm them and so may not be restricted.[10] Thus, it would seem that for Mill, the giving of moral offence may not constitute harm. The harm which Mill is clearly concerned with is that which damages 'the permanent interests of a man considered as a progressive being'.[11] For the purposes of this chapter, the harm done by private car use—accidents, congestion, and environmental pollution—surely constitutes harm of the permanent interests of human beings, in so far as it directly threatens human life, or the quality of life, or the conditions for sustaining flourishing life.

When Mill refers to self-regarding action he surely cannot mean action which has no effect whatsoever on others. As members of society individuals cannot remain completely isolated from others, and their behaviour cannot be completely insulated against some sort of effect on others. In a wide-ranging survey of interpretations of Mill, C.L. Ten[12] argues that Mill's concept of self-regarding action is designed to show that there is a range of actions which, although they might attract the disapproval or disgust of others, do not directly harm the interests of others, and so should remain a matter of personal liberty. Other-regarding action which directly effects the interests of others and causes harm is properly subject to authoritative intervention and control.

We return to the distinction between self-regarding and other-regarding action later in the chapter and argue that Mill fails to sustain it and so undermines

---

[7]Mill, *On Liberty*, p. 94.
[8]Mill, *On Liberty*, p. 14.
[9]Mill, *On Liberty*, p. 98.
[10]Mill, *On Liberty*, p. 15.
[11]Mill, *On Liberty*, p. 14.
[12]C. L. Ten, *Mill on Liberty* (Oxford University Press, Oxford, 1980), chapter 2.

his own theory of liberty. We now consider the application of Mill's categories of self-regarding and other-regarding activity to the ethics of private car use.

PRIVATE CAR USE AS OTHER-REGARDING HARMFUL ACTIVITY

Mill's concept of other-regarding activity facilitates the formation of a very strong argument that private car use lacks moral justification: if by using a car we cause harm to others, our action is wrong, and we cannot properly claim unlimited freedom to engage in it.

One of the major disadvantages of private car use is the damage it causes to both global and local environments This environmental damage takes several forms including air and noise pollution.

On a global scale the pollution caused by transport has an acute environmental impact. Global warming, arguably one of the greatest environmental challenges of all time, is caused by a buildup of greenhouse gases that prevent heat from leaving the Earth's atmosphere. The most important of these greenhouse gases is carbon dioxide, which is a waste product derived from the burning of fossil fuels. Road traffic accounts for one fifth of all fossil energy consumed world wide.[13] In the United Kingdom energy used by all transport accounted for one third of all energy demand in 1994. Cars accounted for 67% of road transport related carbon emissions; large goods vehicles were responsible for 21%; light vans, 9%; and buses and coaches, 3%.[14] Teufel et al. estimated that carbon dioxide equivalent emissions arising from all stages of car manufacturing and use were 4.4 billion tonnes in 1995, with a projected increase to over 10 billion tonnes in 2030.[15] If the carbon emissions related to the exploration, transportation, refining and distribution of fuel are also included, the transport sector can be seen to be making an even greater contribution to global warming.

Other gases that cause global and transboundary environmental problems include chlorfluorocarbons (CFCs), nitrogen oxide emissions, methane and ozone. Private car use makes a contribution to all of these. For example, CFCs are produced in motorised vehicles' air conditioning, which accounts for 25% of the CFCs produced in the United States of America.[16] CFCs are a cause of the destruction of stratospheric ozone, the layer of gas that blocks harmful ultraviolet radiation from the sun reaching the Earth. Such high-level ozone depletion has serious implications for human health, particularly with regard to the risk of skin cancer.

---

[13]R. Pfleiderer and M. Dieterich, "New Roads Generate New Traffic", *World Transport Policy and Practice*, vol. 1, no. 1, 1995, pp. 29–31.

[14]M. Acutt and J. Dodgson, "Transport and Global Warming: Modelling the Impacts of Alternative Policies", in D. Banister ed., *Transport Policy and the Environment* (E. and F. N. Spon/Routledge, London, 1998).

[15]D.Teufel et al., *Folgen einer globalenMotorisierung* (Umwelt and Prognose Institut, Heidelberg, 1995).

[16]K. Burton and W. Rothengatter, "Global Environmental Degradation: The Role of Transport", in D. Banister and K. Button eds., *Transport, the Environmental and Sustainable Development* (E. and F.N. Spon/Routledge, London, 1993).

Transport accounts for about half of nitrogen oxide emissions, which are the primary ingredients of low level ozone formation that causes smog. Nitrogen oxides also contribute to acid rain which in turn has a serious impact on the natural environment.[17] Global warming, holes in the ozone layer, and acid rain are threats to present and future generations. Private car use, by making such a major contribution to them, is clearly a harmful other-regarding activity.

Apart from the global impacts, private car use contributes to the degradation of our more immediate environments. A car produces over 1,000 pollutants whose complete impact on the environment is still not fully understood.[18] Among the pollutants produced by motorised transport are lead, benzene, carbon monoxide, nitrogen oxides (see above), hydrocarbons, ozone and diesel particulates. The air pollution that these cause seriously affects human health.

Until relatively recently lead was routinely added to petrol as an anti-knocking agent. However, concerns about health-related impacts of exposure to lead have resulted in the widespread introduction of lead free petrol. Lead has been linked to poor development in children[19] and there are concerns about its general effect on humans, including the circulatory, kidney, reproductive and nervous systems.[20] Although most new cars use unleaded petrol, the leaded variety is still widely available and widely used across the world.

Benzene, produced from road vehicle emissions and fuel evaporation, is a carcinogen thought to cause leukaemia. There is no known safe threshold level and the World Health Organisation is not able to recommend any "safe" levels for airborne benzene. Cars produce 65% of world emissions of carbon monoxide.[21] Carbon monoxide reduces the oxygen carrying capabilities of the blood and exposure to it can cause reduced awareness, slower reflexes, headaches and, in extreme cases, death.

It has already been noted that nitrogen oxides contribute to global environmental problems in terms of acid rain and smog. On a more localised level, smog can result in respiratory problems for humans, including oedema, bronchitis, pneumonia and death. It can also cause severe damage to crops and trees. The United States Environmental Protection Agency estimate that 2.5–3 billion dollars are lost each year because of smog related crop damage and Los Angeles estimates that damage done to health and agriculture in that region alone totals 3.65–7.3 billion dollars.[22]

Hydrocarbons are unburned or partly burned fuels emitted from traffic exhausts and can cause drowsiness, eye irritation, and coughing. Hydrocarbons

---

[17]D. Banister, "Introduction", in D. Banister ed. *Transport Policy and the Environment*.

[18]K. Sandquist, "Are Automobiles Really Benign Members of the Modern Family?", *World Transport Policy and Practice*, vol. 4, no. 3, 1998, pp. 4–7.

[19]World Health Organisation, *Air Quality Guidelines for Europe* (WHO Regional Publications, European Series 23, 1987).

[20]J. Whitelegg, *Transport for a Sustainable Future: the Case for Europe* (Belhaven Press, London and New York, 1993).

[21]Organisation for Economic Co-operation and Development, *The State of the Environment* (OECD, Paris, 1991).

[22]E. Deakin "Policy Responses in the USA", in D. Banister and K. Button eds. *Transport, the Environmental and Sustainable Development*.

react with nitrogen oxides to form tropospheric ozone, which is thought to be one of the most significant pollutants affecting vegetation and consequent economic loss. Road traffic is a main source of these hydrocarbons and accounts for 39% of the hydrocarbon pollution in the world.[23] Photochemical smog, produced by low-lying ozone, causes eye, nose and throat irritation, headaches, coughing and impaired lung function.

Diesel particulates are fine particles resulting from the incomplete combustion of fuel. The main health concerns focus on those particulates measuring under 10 microns in diameter (PM10). Because of their small size they are able to penetrate deep into the lungs causing bronchitis and asthma. They are also carriers of cancer causing agents. Bown estimated that every year up to 10,000 people died prematurely from PM10 emissions in the United Kingdom,[24] and Ginsberg et al. calculated that PM10 emissions are the cause of around 293 premature deaths each year in Tel-Aviv-Jafo.[25]

Noise can be defined as unwanted sound, which is a source of irritation and stress for many people.[26] Noise pollution from cars is a severe irritant that normally commands less attention than the problem of car related air pollution, yet road traffic noise is one of the most widespread sources of noise pollution and is also one of the more difficult to control.[27] Apart from the permanent physical damage to hearing, the main problem with noise pollution is the stress it causes and the consequences of that stress. Stress affects an individual's ability to function in both mind and body, and the combined impact of direct noise disturbance and the frustrations of lack of concentration and sleep severely affect the quality of life.[28]

Pollution from road traffic, therefore, affects our environment in many ways and has, as a consequence, a significant impact on our health. Whitelegg and Gatrell investigated the association between health and the level of traffic near people's homes. They looked at seven symptoms of illness and concluded that living in proximity of high levels of traffic damages health.[29]

There are also other less direct environmental and social consequences of road traffic. The manufacture of cars, for example, contributes widely to environmental damage, but is largely ignored.[30] Iron and steel making require large amounts of coal and limestone, and produce sulphur dioxide, acids and slag waste.[31] Aluminium production causes soil degradation and produces sulphur

---

[23]Friends of the Earth, *Roads to Ruin* (FOE, London, 1987).

[24]W. Bown, "Dying From Too Much Dust", *New Scientist*, 141, 1994, pp. 12–13.

[25]G. Ginsberg, A. Serri, G. Fletcher, J. Shemer, D. Koutik, and E. Karsentry, "Mortality from Vehicular Particulate Emissions in Tel-Aviv-Jafo", *World Transport Policy and Practice*, vol. 4, no. 2, 1998, pp. 27–31.

[26]National Society for Clean Air, *Noise Pollution* (NSCA, Brighton, 1998).

[27]Friends of the Earth, *Road Transport and Air Pollution* (FOE Trust, London, 1999).

[28]J. Whitelegg, *Transport for a Sustainable Future: the case for Europe*.

[29]J. Whitelegg and A. Gatrell, "The Association Between Health and Residential Traffic Densities", *World Transport Policy and Practice*, vol. 1, no. 3, 1995, pp. 28–30.

[30]J. Whitelegg, *Critical Mass: Transport, Environment and Society in the Twenty-first Century*.

[31]United Nations Environment Programme, *Environmental Impacts of Iron and Steel Production* (UNEP, Paris, 1987).

dioxide when smelted.[32] Zinc and lead, copper smelting, and platinum production are all required in order to produce cars, and all, in turn, contribute to environmental production.[33]

Motor vehicles are using up an increasing amount of the world's oil and its energy. In 1992 the United Kingdom transport sector used more than 43 million tonnes of petroleum products, 54% of the UK total.[34] In the United States two-thirds of annual petroleum usage is by transport vehicles.[35] Global fuel consumption is expected to rise from 650 million tonnes in 1995 to 1.3 billion tonnes in 2030, and cumulative oil consumption by the car fleet alone will amount to 41.6 billion tonnes.[36] Finding and transporting this oil impacts severely on the natural environment in a number of ways. Exploration and exploitation of oil reserves causes habitat loss. Oil spills, which are estimated to average a million gallons every month,[37] cause damage to marine and bird life and pollute the air and water. On a grander scale, wars involving loss of human life as well as environmental damage are waged over oil (for example, the Gulf War of 1990).

Old unwanted vehicles have to be dumped and stored. In the United States of America there has been a move to recycle old cars and Holt estimates that about three quarters of the weight of each car is recycled but that at least 3.5 million tonnes of scrapped cars end up in landfill sites each year.[38] Morgan estimated that cars sent for scrap in the European Union would create a 3 kilometre queue of juggernauts filled with shredder waste every day.[39] In the United States 230 million tyres are worn out each year,[40] and in the United Kingdom the Environment Agency estimates that about 26% of old tyres are disposed of in landfill sites. The Environment Agency removes a further 30,000 tyres each year from rivers and watercourses.[41] Disposal of tyres is a major problem as they are not biodegradable and most storage options cause visual pollution. Tyre dumps are also prone to fire, which, when it occurs, is almost impossible to extinguish. Car dumps are also sources of other types of pollution. For example, surveys in Belgium have estimated that each dumped car contains on average six litres of oil, three litres of fuel, five litres of cooling liquid, and three litres of sulphuric acid.[42]

In the United Kingdom, transport infrastructure accounts for 20% of the surface of urban areas and in the United States public roads occupy 25,000

[32]United Nations Environment Programme, *Environmental Aspects of Aluminium Production* (UNEP, Paris, 1981).

[33]*Research and Technology Strategy to Help Overcome the Environmental Problems in Relation to Transport: Resource Users Study* (SAST-MONITOR, Brussels, 1992).

[34]D. Banister ed., *Transport Policy and the Environment*.

[35]E. Deakin, "Policy Responses in the USA", in D. Banister and K. Button eds., *Transport, the Environment and Sustainable Development*.

[36]J. Whitelegg, *Critical Mass: Transport, Environment and Society in the Twenty-first Century*.

[37]D. Kelso and M. Kendiziorek, "Alaska's Response to the Exxon Valdez Oil Spill", *Environment, Science and Technology*, vol. 25, no. 1, 1991.

[38]D. Holt, "Recycling and the Automobile", *Automobile Engineering*, 101(10), 1993.

[39]R. Morgan, *Planet Gauge: The Real Facts of Life* (Earthscan, London, 1994).

[40]Greenpeace, *The Environmental Impact of the Car* (Greenpeace International, Amsterdam, 1991).

[41]Environment Agency, *Road Transport and the Environment* (Environment Agency, London, 1998).

[42]Greenpeace, *The Environmental Impact of the Car.*

square miles of land, rising to 29,000 square miles if off-street parking, garages and driveways are included.[43] Road building itself is very destructive; it removes land from other uses (one mile of motorway requiring about 25 acres of land), damages ecosystems, changes watercourses, kills wildlife, and requires vast amounts of quarrying and gravel extraction (one mile of motorway uses 250,000 tonnes of sand and gravel). Social disruption caused by community severance is an additional impact of road construction.[44]

Congestion and traffic jams on roads, apart from exacerbating the amount of pollution caused by car engines, also produce further social costs ranging from damage to historic buildings to the social and economic costs of increased travel time. For example, it has been estimated that 100,000 hours a day are spent in traffic jams by Los Angeles drivers.[45] The Confederation of British Industry claims that delays to deliveries and hold-ups to the travelling public cost businesses in London as much as £15,000,000,000 a year,[46] while congestion costs to London Buses have been estimated at £220 million per year.[47]

So far, we have demonstrated that private car use, by contributing to the amount of motorised traffic, causes many environmental and social and economic problems. Perhaps, however, the strongest argument concerning private car use as an other-regarding harmful activity is that the car injures 10 million people and kills over a quarter of a million people in the world each year.[48] In the United States alone, 40,000 people are killed each year in car accidents.[49] In Germany, half a million people have been killed on the roads since the end of the Second World War,[50] and in the United Kingdom, seventy people are killed on the roads each week.[51] Apart from the pain, grief, and other emotional costs of these accidents, which are impossible to quantify, additional social and economic costs include working days lost and the cost of health care.

In conclusion, private car use contributes significantly to serious problems that affect many people: it threatens the long-term viability of the planet; it pollutes our more immediate environment; and it regularly maims and kills people. Thus, private car use cannot be categorised as a purely self-regarding activity. It is, in fact, a harmful other-regarding activity which, in Mill's terms, lacks adequate moral justification and is liable to social and political control. Even if political control is not exercised, individuals have a moral obligation to limit their harmful use of private cars.

---

[43]D. Banister, "Introduction", in D. Banister ed., *Transport Policy and the Environment*.

[44]Transport and Health Study Group, Public Health Alliance *Health on the Move: Policies for Health Promoting Transport* (Transport and Health Study Group, Birmingham, 1991).

[45]M. Renner, "Rethinking the Role of the Automobile", *Worldwatch Paper*, no. 84, 1988.

[46]Confederation of British Industry, Taskforce Report, *Transport in London* (CBI, London, 1989)

[47]MVA Associates, *Report to London Regional Transport* (MVA Associates, London, 1989).

[48]Greenpeace, *The Environmental Impact of the Car*.

[49]E. Deakin, "Policy Response in the USA", in D. Banister and K. Button eds., *Transport, the Environmental and Sustainable Development*.

[50]H. Holzapfel, "Violence and the Car", *World Transport Policy and Practice*, vol. 1, no. 1, 1995, pp. 41–44.

[51]BRAKE, Road Safety Campaign, 2000.

PRIVATE CAR USE AS SELF-REGARDING HARMFUL ACTIVITY

Although private car use can never be an entirely self-regarding activity, there are a number of ways in which it can cause harm to those who drive. The obvious harm that can be incurred is death or injury while driving a car. Less obvious, and less well known, is the danger of in-car vehicle emissions. Jefferies et al. found that drivers and passengers travelling in cars were being exposed to dangerous levels of air pollution.[52] Levels of vehicle-derived pollutants including benzene, carbon monoxide, and nitrogen dioxide were found to be substantially higher inside vehicles than in air 50–100 metres from the road. More recently Taylor and Fergusson reviewed the growing research evidence and concluded that car drivers travel through a 'tunnel of pollutants' and are exposed to significantly higher levels of pollution than background readings would suggest.[53] Although the direct health impact of in-car pollution on drivers and passengers has yet to be fully explored, this paper has already noted the general health effects of these pollutants.

Another harmful result of car travel is the health risk from lack of exercise. The more we travel by car, the less we walk, run or cycle, all of which contribute to health and general well-being and reduce the risks of heart disease.[54] It is increasingly recognised that the way we travel is directly 'linked to our levels of physical activity and that our transport choices directly affect our health.[55]

Private car use is, then, a harmful, self-regarding activity, but as such might seem to be a matter of individual freedom, beyond moral censure or social control. We have already noted that for Mill there can be no justification for social intervention to prevent an individual harming himself, either physically or morally. Mill writes:

> The only part of the conduct of anyone, for which he is amenable to society, is that which concerns others. In the part which merely concerns himself, his independence is, of right, absolute. Over himself, over his body and mind, the individual is sovereign.[56]

Mill confirms: 'Each is the proper guardian of his own health, whether bodily, or mental and spiritual.[57]

---

[52]P. Jefferies, A. Rowell, M. Fergusson, *The Exposure of Car Drivers and Passengers to Vehicles' Emissions* (Greenpeace UK, London, 1992).

[53]D. Taylor and M. Fergusson, "The Comparative Pollution Exposure to Road-Users—A Summary", *World Transport Policy and Practice*, vol. 4, no, 2, 1998, pp. 22–26. Research which supports these conclusions includes: W. Rudolf, "Concentrations of Air Pollutants Inside Cars Driving on Highways in Downtown Areas", *Science of the Total Environment*, vol. 146/147, 1994, pp. 433–444 and S. Kingham and J. Meaton, "Exposure to Traffic-Related Pollutants During the Journey to Work", *Transportation Research D*, vol. 3, no.4, 1998, pp. 271–274.

[54]Coronary Prevention Group, *Exercise, Heart and Health* (Coronary Prevention Group, London, 1987).

[55]A. Davis, "Developing a New Consensus for Physical Activity in England: Evidence of the Growing Convergence of Transport and Public Health Policies", *World Transport Policy and Practice*, vol. 3, no. 2, 1997, pp. 4–10.

[56]Mill, *On Liberty*, p. 13.

[57]Mill, *On Liberty*, p. 16.

We now propose to show that even on Mill's terms there are serious moral problems with so-called self-regarding harm, that is, harm done to individuals by themselves. Moreover, and more critically, we propose to question the very concept of self-regarding harm and so challenge Mill's notion of the freedom of the individual to harm oneself.

(a) Informed Choice

If, as Mill would have it, the individual is to be the guardian of his or her own health and well being, both physical and moral, it would seem to be important that the individual be well informed. Any choice requires some information, and good choices would seem to be more likely if based on good information. The supposed liberty to harm oneself is very doubtful if the individual is in fact ignorant of the harm being done. Mill would seem to agree that information and wisdom are valuable for human beings and their good. In his famous essay, *Utilitarianism*, Mill introduces a standard of excellence when be writes:

> It is better to be a human being dissatisfied than a pig satisfied; better to be Socrates dissatisfied than a fool dissatisfied. And if the fool, or the pig, are of a different opinion, it is because they only know their own side of the question. The other party to the comparison knows both sides. [58]

According to Mill, then, the better informed being makes the better judgements and choices.

It would seem that on Mill's terms it is possible to question the liberty of private car users if they choose to drive on the basis of ignorance of the dangers involved. Few would argue that motorists are unaware of the carnage caused on the roads by motorised transport. However, few motorists are aware of the real dangers that they personally face each time they drive their cars. Even fewer are aware of the full environmental impact of their activities and hardly any are aware of the potential dangers they are exposing themselves to in the form of in-car pollutants. Car companies advertise their products as safe and environmentally friendly and so compound the misinformation of the public. True facts about the real risks, both bodily and environmental, should be given a higher profile in order that drivers are put in a better position to make informed choices. Drivers cannot claim moral immunity for their choices if these are based on ignorance.

(b) Freedom of Choice

If motorists are to be free to make their own informed choices, it is necessary, of course, that these choices be truly free. We have already touched on the role of advertising in encouraging private car use, but perhaps the more pernicious encouragement comes from socialisation. From the moment we are born we are taught to live in a world that embraces the car. We are given soft, cuddly car toys in our cradles; as we grow up we learn to play with miniature metal models; we read about and watch films and videos about cars with loveable natures; and

---

[58]J. S. Mill, *Utilitarianism, Liberty and Representative Government* (Everyman's Library, J. M. Dent and Sons Ltd, London, 1971), p. 9.

some of our national heroes are famous because they drive fast cars the fastest. It is not surprising that before we even reach our teens, car culture is so ingrained that we make judgements about people according to the cars they drive, and that for many of us the main goal in life is to pass the driving test and purchase a car as soon as possible.

Such strong societal and peer pressure is hard to resist and each year more new drivers appear on the roads. Even if individuals were to resist and reappraise the role of the car in their lives, few alternatives are available. As car ownership and use has increased, there has been a resulting decrease in the demand for, and consequently provision of, public transport. For groups such as the old, the young, the poor, and the disabled, who are unable for various reasons to own and drive cars, the alternatives, and consequently their choices, are limited.[59] As public transport services are reduced, more people strive to afford a car, producing a vicious spiral of demand for cars and a lack of alternative services. For those groups of people whose car ownership and use is restricted, this lack of alternatives severely affects their freedom. The choices of individuals who simply do not want to own or drive a car also become limited. Thus, this increase in private transport ultimately becomes another case of harmful, other-regarding action. However, even if we are lucky enough to not to be run over and killed, most of us will grow old, infirm, and incapable of driving our own cars, and we will then need the public transport services which we have helped make scarce. Thus, a harmful, other-regarding activity ultimately becomes a harmful, self-regarding activity of which we are often ignorant.

There are other examples of freedom of choice producing unintended harmful consequences. Traffic jams are generated by individuals choosing to travel by car to reach their destinations in the quickest, most convenient way. Similarly, parents concerned about the safety of their children drive them to school, thereby aggravating the traffic problems and increasing the dangers.[60] These are examples of what are known in the literature of political philosophy as collective action problems. The uncoordinated, self-interested actions of each individual may not produce the best outcome they could achieve. Attempts at voluntary cooperation may lead only to what is known as the free-rider problem. Here, an individual calculates that whilst others pay the costs of securing a common good, he or she may also enjoy it without payment. For example, whilst other parents encourage their children to walk to school or use public transport, the free-riding parent has a clearer road on which to drive his or her children to school. The only solution to the free-rider problem may be that imposed by a public authority. [61]

---

[59]I. Ker and P. Tranter, "A Wish Called Wander: Reclaiming Automobility from the Motor Car", *World Transport Policy and Practice*, vol. 3, no, 2, 1997, pp. 10–16.

[60]Mayer Hillman, John Adams, and John Whitelegg, *One False Move: a study of children's independent mobility* (London, Policy Studies Institute, 1990). See also, M. S. Joshi et al.,"Children's Journeys to School: New Data and Further Comments", *World Transport Policy and Practice*, vol. 3, no. 4, 1997, pp. 17–22; and J. Whitelegg, *Critical Mass*.

[61]For further discussion of such matters see E. Ostrom, *Governing the Commons* (Cambridge University Press, Cambridge, 1990), and D. Green and I. Shapiro, *Pathologies of Rational Choice Theory* (New Haven, Yale University Press, 1994).

In conclusion, our freedom of choice has been manipulated by the pro-car society in which we live. This car-orientated society has loaded the dice in favour of car use by restricting the choice of alternatives. Our ignorance of the full consequences of our actions serves to perpetuate the problem. Thus, our status as moral decision makers has been compromised. Private car users cannot claim full moral justification for their choices if these have been heavily influenced by societal pressures, and if the full range of choice has been denied them by various forces, including some of their own making.

(c) Self-Harm of Private Use Is Not Entirely Self-Regarding

By working with Mill's categories, we might seem to accept that the self-harm of private car use is entirely self-regarding. We doubt that this is the case. Even if an individual could make, fuel, and drive his or her own car in isolation from others, without causing them any harm, it is not clear that the self-harms of driving private cars could be entirely self-regarding. Car accidents resulting in deaths and injuries only to the driver are always accompanied by grief and distress of friends, relatives, neighbours, and passers-by. Surely it is the case that few, if any, serious self-harms are entirely self-regarding. Mill acknowledges this. 'I fully admit that the mischief which a person does to himself may seriously affect, both through their sympathies and their interests, those nearly connected with him and, in a minor degree, society at large.'[62] We take this crucial admission to undermine the crucial distinction between self-regarding and other-regarding actions, and so to undermine Mill's theory of liberty. If harmful self-regarding activity is also harmful other-regarding activity, it is liable to moral criticism and social control, and the realm of absolute freedom is much, if not fully, diminished.

(d) Prevention of Self-Harm Is Permissible and Compatible with Liberal Culture and Society

Mill's position on self-harm is clear: one should be free to do harm to oneself if one knows what one does and one does not harm others. We now propose to challenge this position. If there is evidence that an activity is harmful, why should individuals be allowed to do it, or, as in the case of private car use, be encouraged to do it? If it is agreed that individuals should not harm others, why should they be allowed to harm themselves? It cannot be that individuals consent to harm themselves, whereas others refuse their consent, for the morally significant concept is not consent, but harm.[63] There seems to be no moral problem about doing good to others without their consent. It is not clear that

---

[62]Mill, *On Liberty*, p. 81.

[63]Aspects of the British criminal law seem to embody the belief that consent cannot condone a supposed wrong. The offence of gross indecency, which was introduced in 1885, applies to sexual activity between one man and another, even if they are both consenting adults, above the age of consent. The law applies only to male homosexual, and not heterosexual or lesbian, activity. In 1967 the sexual offences act decriminalised male homosexual activity done in private between consenting

individuals have any right to do harm or wrong, to whosoever, including themselves.

Perhaps individuals should be encouraged to accept responsibility for their own actions, if only to encourage them to act responsibly. But perhaps, also, there are some actions, for example potentially fatal ones, which are so serious as to justify restriction of individual freedom. It seems that within our generally liberal culture, we are already prepared to accept that public authorities may legitimately attempt to prevent individuals doing harm to themselves: witness existing legislation on the use of car seat belts by drivers and passengers; the use of helmets by motor cycle riders; possession of certain dangerous drugs; and issues of health and safety at work. Prevention of self-harm seems to be compatible with liberal culture. If we accept legislation that car drivers must wear seat belts to prevent harm to themselves, should we not also accept control of private car use for similar reasons? The problem, of course, is that many people mistakenly regard private car use as a matter of absolute individual freedom.

In conclusion, we argue that the harm one can do to oneself by private car use is not purely self-regarding. Self-harm is usually also an other-regarding harmful act, and so lacking moral justification. Even if it could be considered as self-regarding, there is need for serious moral consideration of issues such as the control of information and the influences on behaviour. Regardless of Mill's distinction, private car use, as an avoidable and potentially fatal act, is an act which requires serious moral consideration by those who engage in it.

CONCLUSION

Private car users often use something like Mill's theory of freedom to justify their activity. We have argued that private car use is an activity which harms drivers and all others to some extent. Thus, even on the basis of Mill's principles, private car use lacks adequate moral justification. Massive restriction, and indeed a total ban, on private car use is morally justifiable. We appreciate that many other harms may go unnoticed and uncontrolled, for various reasons. But this is not a good reason to do nothing about harms that are now being recognised and that can be controlled. However, an immediate ban on private cars would be impracticable and unfair. It would be unwise to enact legislation

---

adults. Private was defined in the act as meaning that no more than two men were present during the sexual activity. This left open the possibility of prosecution for gross indecency in cases where three or more consenting male adults engaged in homosexual activity. In November 1996 a British man was convicted of gross indecency, and given a two year conditional discharge, following a trial in which it was established that he had engaged in consensual sexual activity in the presence of up to four other men, in his own bedroom. An appeal against the conviction, on the grounds of invasion of privacy, has recently been heard by the European court of human rights, where a representative of the British government defended the conviction, noting that there was no breach of privacy because the sexual activity had taken place in the presence of other men and had also been videotaped, which posed the risk that others might be able to view it. See the report in *The Guardian* newspaper, December 1, 1999.

likely to be so unpopular as to cause serious political unrest. It would be unfair on those without adequate alternative transport to deprive them of the use of private cars. Much requires to be done in preparation for a total ban, and most important is the provision of adequate public transport for all. Public transport is not, of course, without its own contribution to environmental pollution. But by its nature it permits a large number of people to travel in one motorised vehicle, and so, with the possible exception of air transport, it pollutes the environment much less than private cars.

Given our argument that private car use lacks adequate moral justification, and our acknowledgement that a total ban is not yet feasible, we conclude that individual private car owners and users face a number of moral considerations. In short, individuals should adopt a more ethically responsible attitude to private car use. They should make less rather than more use of private cars. If they must travel, they should make as much use as possible of public transport rather than private cars. If public transport is not available or is very inconvenient, individuals should consider car sharing. If they must own and use a private car, they should, as far as possible, buy one that is environmentally friendly, in terms of engine capacity, fuel type, exhaust emissions, etc. If they must drive a private car, individuals should adopt environmentally responsible driving behaviour, in terms of acceleration, speed, and braking. By encouraging individuals to adopt an ethically responsible attitude to the use of private cars, it may be possible to build a popular, democratic solution to the problem of their harm, and so avoid the need for the painful consequences of authoritative political intervention, which would otherwise become necessary.

Questions

1. List some of the ways in which driving a car can cause harm to others. Do you think that the benefits of private car use outweigh the costs? Does it matter if the costs we consider are only short-term ones or also long-term ones?
2. Given that all one's actions have some effect on others, what do you think that John Stuart Mill means by "self-regarding" actions?
3. What are collective action problems? In what way is the issue of private car use a collection action problem?
4. Considering only the costs to the environment (and not, in addition, the negative effects on humans), what would James Anderson and Ronald Sandler's All Things Considered Principle imply about private car use?

Consuming Because Others Consume

Judith Lichtenberg

The central thesis of Judith Lichtenberg's paper is that at least part of the explanation why we consume is that others consume. The defense of this claim is intended neither to support current levels of consumption nor to condemn them unequivocally. Instead, the author argues for some intermediate position: that though we could live more simply without living less happily, consumption is not as morally troubling as is often suggested.

There are a few explanations why one can come to consume because others consume. One of these is that the practices of others can determine whether a particular commodity is a luxury or a necessity (or something in between). Thus, having a car, for example, may be a luxury in some contexts but could be a near necessity in other contexts—where the social infrastructure has adapted to most people's having cars. A second explanation is that the consumption by others can serve as an important form of publicity for a product, thereby stimulating a desire for that product. Finally and probably best recognized, people sometimes (but not always) consume in a bid to elicit respect from others.

The author examines each of these explanations and argues that none of them necessarily require a morally condemnatory response (even though there may be some instances in which such a response would be fitting).

Critics have long decried the levels of material consumption and indulgence prevalent in advanced industrial societies, but over the last several decades their voices have become more insistent. In the press and in the political arena, the matter came to a head during the 1992 Rio Earth Summit, when (to put it succinctly) the North accused the South of overpopulation, and the South accused the North of overconsumption.

Judith Lichtenberg, "Consuming Because Others Consume," *Social Theory and Practice,* vol. 22, no. 3, (fall 1996): 273–297. Copyright 1996 by *Social Theory and Practice.*

Contemporary concerns about consumption and materialism have three different, although not mutually exclusive, roots. One is increasing international interdependence and the resulting sense that we inhabit a global community, which makes it hard to ignore the juxtaposition of so much wealth in some places with dire poverty elsewhere. Another is growing environmental awareness, which raises the possibility that our levels of consumption are irreparably harming the planet and its inhabitants. Finally, technological progress combined with the bombardments of the media have given us the sense that we are increasingly in the grip of having and owning—that we have more than anyone really needs, and that this access is incompatible with virtue or true human flourishing.

Not everyone agrees, of course, that we middle-class North Americans and others similarly situated consume too much, and indeed it is not easy to say by what standards one decides how much is too much.[1] But the feeling that we might be living at a higher level of material dependence and indulgence than we ought to is prevalent enough in our culture, even if the dictum that "Action speaks louder than words" forces us to say it is not *that* prevalent. The concern has dominated moral philosophy over the last twenty years.[2] What has driven the philosophical debate, in addition to the reigning (but practically unbearable) interpretation of utilitarianism as requiring one to maximize the good, is the palpable presence of millions or perhaps billions of people worldwide who live in serious poverty, combined with the knowledge that we (individually, and even more, collectively) could do something to alleviate that poverty if we chose. The question is whether or in what sense we ought to do something about it—whether, in particular, we are morally obligated to do something, and that therefore we are morally blameworthy or deficient when we continue to live in relative or absolute luxury while others struggle to survive or subsist.[3]

I do not want to enter into this debate here, but rather to change its focus. This is partly because I think the debate is becoming stale, with one side arguing that we do have strong moral obligations to do more for others, even if it means lowering our own standards of living significantly, and the other side arguing that the threat to personal integrity, to the concept of a life with which one may, within certain crucial constraints, pretty much do as one chooses, would be too great if we acknowledged such demanding moral obligations. Each of these

---

[1]That is because, as I shall argue below, the concept of "too much" is partly relative to what others have. And so to know what too much is, we first must decide on a frame of reference—on the community to whom comparison is being made.

[2]One might take Peter Singer's essay "Famine, Affluence, and Morality," *Philosophy and Public Affairs* 1 (1972): 229–43, to mark the beginning of the contemporary philosophical debate.

[3]I am leaving aside questions about whether we have had a role in bringing about the situation in which the poor find themselves. If one thinks A is causally responsible for B's plight, that gives a strong (perhaps undeniable) reason for thinking A must do something to remedy it. But the question is raised and vigorously discussed in the philosophical literature, even where it is not assumed that A is causally responsible for B's plight. I shall describe both these situations as raising questions of justice, although some would reserve the term for the first situations, describing the second instead in terms of benevolence or decency.

points of view pulls hard on us. The latter has "common sense" on its side, but it arouses our suspicions just because it is altogether too convenient to believe. The former, even if theoretically persuasive, moves too few people to action. This leads some, who assumed ethics must be practical and take into account "human nature," to think that the morally strenuous view cannot be right; it leads others, committed to social change, to conclude that even if right, it is ineffective and thus irrelevant. But where do we go from here?

This debate turns out to be partly otiose if the general view set forth here is correct. I think we have been missing features of the social and psychological landscape with important implications for our moral and practical views. My aim in what follows is to go some way toward establishing the thesis that, to a large extent, people consume because others around them do. There are a variety of reasons for this relational feature of consumption. Among them are the aim of gaining status and superiority that the notion of "consuming because others consume" tends to evoke, an aim that has been cited almost to tedium ever since Thorstein Veblen published *The Theory of the Leisure Class* in 1899. Even this idea, I shall argue, is more complex, and less clearly damning, than is usually thought. But there are other reasons for consuming because others do—some having to do with the pursuit of status, but with the desire for equality rather than superiority, and some having nothing at all to do with status. In what follows I describe and evaluate the various other-regarding reasons for consuming.

This thesis about the relativity of the desire to consume has implications of two kinds, which are explored below. One is practical: to the extent that a person consumes because others do, she could consume less if others did too, without diminishing her well-being. It follows that the handwringing about how much we can reasonably demand that people sacrifice for the well-being of others is exaggerated, for reductions in consumption, when effected in a concerted way, need not involve deprivation in the way generally envisioned. It is not a matter of "sacrificing because others sacrifice," but rather of not having to sacrifice when material compensation falls collectively.

The other implication is moral. Critiques of consumption often amount to indictments of human character: the view that people consume because others do seems to suggest they are conformist, greedy, preoccupied with material things, status, and one-upmanship. Although we should not discount these traits altogether, an appreciation of the complexities of consumption shows why it is often reasonable and respectable for a person to consume when others do; more generally, it illuminates certain puzzles about human desires and well-being.

THE RELATIVITY OF ABSOLUTE WELL-BEING

How are people's desires for and consumption of things dependent on what others have? We can best answer this question by considering how their desires for and consumption of things are *not* dependent on what others have. It is natural to think here in terms of basic needs or minimum requirements—conditions that must be met if a person is to lead a minimally decent life. A person's need to consume some number of calories and nutrition, or to have clothing and shelter against the elements, exists independently of what other people have or do. Without food one dies; what other people do is irrelevant.

Even biological needs, however, are not wholly independent of context or circumstance; they may depend, in particular, in part on what other people do. In a society in which strenuous physical exertion is important—either because physical activity is socially valued or because scarcity requires strength or speed to acquire necessities—a greater caloric intake might be needed to function effectively or well.

Whether all needs are partly relative to what others do, and thus in some cases to "ways of life," is a question we need not answer here. Two points are worth noting, however. First, a great deal depends on how we specify or describe needs. Suppose, for example, we agree that people have a basic need for enough food to survive or thrive. Stated in this way, the need is absolute in the sense of being invariant to circumstances, including the behavior of others. But how much food is enough to survive or thrive will vary depending on the circumstances. Thus, although we can describe the need absolutely, its satisfaction may depend on relational facts. As Amartya Sen argues, "the absolute satisfaction of some . . . needs might depend on a person's relative position *vis-à-vis* others."[4]

Second, some needs are much more relative than others. The need for air is quite nonrelative. Think, by contrast, of the ability to work, or, even more simply, to get around and do things (acquire food and the like) for oneself. In many contemporary communities, it is difficult to perform these tasks without private transportation. The need for a car is not "absolute" in the sense of existing irrespective of context. The economic system and the infrastructure could have evolved differently so that a car would not be an indispensable item of modern life. A well-functioning system of public transportation creates and perpetuates demand: the larger and finer the net it casts (that is, the more places you can get to using it), the more people use it; the more people use it, the greater its economies of scale; the greater its economies of scale, the better and cheaper it gets. In such cases, people have purely economic and practical reasons for doing as others do.

In many communities today, however, a car is a virtual necessity; indeed, for a suburban or rural family two cars are often required. A person's desire for a car, then, although dependent on what other people have and do, need not be rooted in greed, envy, or the desire for status.[5] Many items once thought of as high-tech luxuries—television, cable television, computers, on-line databases—become nearly indispensable in a technologically sophisticated society. Invention is the mother of necessity.

Just how far the point illustrated by this example extends is a difficult question. The danger on one side is being led to say that every deprivation relative

[4]Amartya Sen, "Poor, Relatively Speaking," *Oxford Economic Papers* (New Series) 35 (1983): 153–69, esp. pp. 155–63.

[5]Of course, cars have acquired a great deal of significance apart from their utility. One may want a particular kind of car to express something about oneself or to demonstrate one's status. The point is simply that these motives could be entirely absent and one would still have reason to want a car.

to others in one's society is the frustration of a basic or important need. On the other side, critics of contemporary Western culture—those who decry "conspicuous consumption" and materialistic values—often pay insufficient attention to the significance of relative deprivation for absolute well-being.

Even when it would be an exaggeration to say that a particular item has moved from the status of luxury to necessity, new goods often become entrenched in a society—become more like needs—in a subtle and interesting process. We can observe this transformation with many recent innovations: microwaves, answering machines, VCRs, electronic mail. When first introduced, such items may appear frivolous, at least to those not mesmerized by gadgets. Gradually—but really very quickly—even the skeptics start to notice the thing's uses. For example, while the benefits to owners of answering machines were immediately apparent, some callers at first found the devices awkward or even insulting. Soon, however, even skeptical callers began to notice the advantages to themselves: not having to call back repeatedly when no one answered; avoiding unwanted and unnecessarily prolonged conversations. Complaints about "talking to a machine" are rarely heard anymore. Similarly, car phones, which when first introduced were widely viewed as mere status symbols, are now recognized for their convenience and safety-enhancing features (in a dangerous world of carjackings and other crimes).

How does this phenomenon of the entrenchment of new products bear on the relational aspects of consumption? Acquisition of a good by many people can render it more necessary in an absolute sense, even if not always a "necessity." In some cases—public versus private transportation—this is a question of infrastructure: where others take buses, there will be buses, available to all, and I will have less need for a car. In other cases, such as electronic mail and on-line databases, we have what economists call networking effects: one lacking the service is made worse off by being cut off from the flow of information. Even the humdrum answering machine can affect how people conduct business, so that those lacking them may both suffer disadvantages themselves and also inconvenience others. So, for example, where it is assumed that most people have answering machines, it might be reasonable to ask someone to make a dozen phone calls, on the assumption that messages can be left if no one answers. The person without an answering machine forces the messenger to work harder by calling repeatedly, and is more likely not to be reached at all. This may be more than an inconvenience: it may cost a businessperson her livelihood if the caller is a customer with alternative providers.

SALIENT THINGS

The process by which new goods get entrenched in a culture bears in a second way on the relational aspects of consumption: the acquisition of goods by others serves as a crucial form of publicity. Leaving aside for the moment questions about status and the need to "keep up with the Joneses," the fact that one's friends and neighbors have something new acts as a stimulus if the good has intrinsic appeal of any kind. Advertisers have always been fully aware of the phenomenon, which can be understood in terms of what cognitive psychologists call "salience": the physical presence of an item makes it more available to consciousness. The economist James Duesenberry describes this process in terms of what he calls "the demonstration effect":

> In given circumstances, . . . individuals . . . come into contact with goods superior to the ones they use with a certain frequency. Each such contact is a demonstration of the superiority of those goods and is a threat to the existence of the current consumption pattern. It is a threat because it makes active the latent preference for these goods. . . . For any particular family the frequency of contact with superior goods will increase primarily as the consumption expenditures of others increase.[6]

In our zeal to find sophisticated or deep explanations for people's desires to raise their level of material well-being, we have neglected the simple yet powerful effect of firsthand experience on wanting. It stands to reason that a person is more likely to want something if he sees it than if it exists for him merely as an abstract possibility. (Indeed, an abstract possibility is usually an unconceived possibility, which moves us not at all.) Familiarity breeds desire more often than contempt.

This desire-stimulating process seems perfectly respectable, as plausibly attributable to human curiosity, to being alive to one's surroundings, as to greed or envy or status-seeking—the explanations more commonly offered by critics of consumption. Some might argue that, on the contrary, this fact about human beings is precisely what terms like "greed" and "envy" are meant to denote—wanting things when you see them, being moved by the consumption habits of others. How should we resolve this dispute, where both sides agree on the evidence but disagree about what it shows? It seems wrong to say the disagreement is merely terminological (how you define greed or envy), since the two sides make very different moral judgments about the human qualities in question. One solution is to have it both ways: to acknowledge an element that is morally neutral or even praiseworthy (curiosity, aliveness to one's surroundings), but also an element worthy of criticism (lack of self-sufficiency, overdependence on material things). Yet whether moral criticism is appropriate depends partly on other issues that await resolution. Under what circumstances, and for what reasons, does attraction to material things constitute a vice? Some issues relevant to answering this question are discussed briefly below.

However we resolve these questions, it is clear that as a matter of fact, salience—here constituted by the possessions of my neighbors[7]—acts as a

---

[6]James Duesenberry, *Income, Saving and the Theory of Consumer Behavior* (Cambridge, Mass.: Harvard University Press, 1949), pp. 26–27. Duesenberry describes some of the same phenomena discussed here in terms of the "interdependence of preferences." As I hope my discussion makes clear, no significant questions are begged by allowing Duesenberry's description of the new goods as superior.
[7]Here and elsewhere the word "neighbors" must be understood partly metaphorically. Who the reference group is to which I compare myself varies from person to person and context to context. Sometimes it is literally my neighbors; sometimes my coworkers; sometimes those who share my occupation; sometimes the parents of my children's friends. Literal neighbors sometimes have a special significance because, particularly in the suburbs, one is confronted by their houses, their yards, and their cars. As the sentence immediately following shows, there are, at least in the contemporary world, few constraints that can be imposed in advance on the class of neighbors.

powerful stimulus to the desire to consume. Now that the world's poorest people have instant and constant access, through television and other mass media, to the style of life of their affluent "neighbors," the significance of the demonstration effect can hardly be exaggerated.

This is not to beg the question whether, all things considered, having more things necessarily makes a person happier or better off. We may acknowledge that getting what one's neighbors have enhances one's welfare, without denying that everyone might be happier living more simply. The explanation for these seemingly conflicting facts rests on the interaction of three phenomena: salience, opportunity costs, and collective action problems. Thus, if we assume (what the true aesthetic presumably would not) that the life of things enhances one's well-being in certain respects, then, beginning from the status quo of a consumption-oriented culture and acquaintance with some new thing, having it may improve one's welfare, even though a different bundle of experiences inconsistent with having it (that is, beginning from a different baseline) might improve one's well-being even more. Given that my neighbors have it, and that the thing possesses at least some small utility or aesthetic virtue, I may be better off having it. It is hard to explain the pull that material things exert on most people's desires without acknowledging their intrinsic attractions, however shallow or transitory these might be.[8]

Other things being equal, then, more is often more. But the qualification is crucial. I could admit that I would be better off having an item my neighbors have, and still maintain that a world in which we both had fewer things would be better still—that in such a world we would all be better off. This claim involves a view about the overall worth of alternative ways of life—about how high-consumption "life-packages" compare with others emphasizing nonmaterial goods instead. The present discussion of the benefits of consumption, however, is about micro, not macro, partial, not complete, compliance, the world of second-best: about the reasons for consuming when others around you do.[9]

CONSUMPTION AND SELF-RESPECT

I turn now to the reasons for consuming that probably loom largest when people think about consumption in modern society—and certainly if they hear of

The concept of a reference group to whom one compares oneself, extensively analyzed in the sociological literature, is central to our understanding of the processes described here. See, for example, Robert K. Merton and Alice Rossi, "Contributions to the Theory of Reference Group Behavior," in Robert K. Merton, *Social Theory and Social Structure*, 1968 enlarged ed. (New York: Free Press, 1968).
[8]For discussion and defense of the attractions of consuming, see Michael Schudson, *Advertising, the Uneasy Persuasion: Its Dubious Impact on American Society*, afterword to the new English edition (originally published in the United States by Basic Books, 1984); and Colin Campbell, "Consuming Goods and the Good in Modern Consuming," in David Crocker (ed.), *The Ethics of Consumption and Global Stewardship* (Lanham, Md.: Rowman and Littlefield, forthcoming 1997).
[9]This is one reason for thinking that, as Robert Goodin puts it, "voting green but living brown" is not necessarily hypocritical. See his *Green Political Theory* (Cambridge, Mass.: Polity Press, 1992), pp. 78–83, 120–23.

"consuming because others consume." We think of conspicuous consumption, keeping up with the Joneses, the ostentatious display of wealth and the excessive reliance on material goods as a way of attaining status. But the contemptuous attitude revealed in these descriptions depends partly, I believe, on a misunderstanding of other-regarding consumption. I have already given two reasons for thinking so. First, because of a society's way of life or infrastructure, or because of networking effects, the satisfaction of needs and interests that most people would agree are basic depends in part on other people's consumption practices. Second, acquaintance breeds desire: it is not necessarily a sign of greed or envy to want things when you see them.

None of this is to deny that the desire to improve one's position *vis-à-vis* others plays an important part in the urge to consume. We want to have things, and to have others know we have them, in part in order to *say something* about ourselves to others. It is this expressive function that we now need to analyze more carefully.

First, we should note that not all expressive consumption need involve the desire to say something about one's worth. A person who wears one earring or long hair, or drives a Jeep Cherokee or a battered bicycle, is *expressing* himself— we might even say he is *making a statement* about himself and his values—but he need not be attempting to secure a place in a hierarchy.[10] It may even be questioned whether his behavior is communicative. Terms like "self-expression" and "making a statement" can be understood to imply communication to others, but they can also be understood in a more private way—perhaps as an outpouring of inner feeling. Let us assume, however, that for most people such forms of self-expression as fashion do include a crucial communicative component. In part, this communicative component is rooted in practical aims: it is useful to tell others what one is like, in order to find those with similar interests. (This function is discussed further below in terms of ability-signaling.)

But acts of consumption are sometimes designed[11] to communicate to others something about one's own worth, and it is this expressive function in which we are interested. Such status seeking has a bad reputation. A long tradition of moralists advises that what other people think of us is not important, that one should not base one's actions on the opinions of others, and so forth. If this were true, then all consumption aimed at sending a message, especially a message about one's worth, would be less than reputable as a motive. But although it is easy to describe situations where one shouldn't care what others think (for instance, where there is a right thing to do, and one must brave public opinion and do it), it seems too sweeping a judgment to say that it is always disreputable to care. The person wholly unconcerned with how others see her seems at best too saintly to serve as a model for the ordinary person; at worst, she may be pathological, or contemptuous of other people.

---

[10]See A. Strudler and E. Curlo, "Consumption as Culture," in Crocker (ed.) for a discussion of non-status-related expressive aspects of consumption.

[11]I do not mean to imply that these choices are consciously designed to impress other people; almost certainly the processes are less than conscious much of the time.

At least in part, consumption designed to send a message about one's worth has a bad reputation because it masks a morally significant ambiguity. We imagine a world in which everyone is trying to outdo everyone else—trying not merely to keep up with the Joneses but to surpass them. Veblen certainly did much to promote this interpretation:

> . . . the end sought by accumulation is to rank high in comparison with the rest of the community in point of pecuniary strength. . . . However widely, or equally, or "fairly," it may be distributed, no general increase of the community's wealth can make any approach to satiating this need, the ground of which is the desire of every one to excel every one else in the accumulation of goods.[12]

But although a person may consume to show that he is better than others, he may also consume simply to show that he is as good as others. Veblen fails to draw this distinction, which I believe is both morally significant and psychologically real. Let us first ask why it is acceptable and important for people to attain some measure of perceived equality with their fellows, then ask to what extent people want not merely equality but superiority.

For all but the most extraordinarily self-sufficient individuals, self-respect requires respect from one's fellows; it requires that one not be shamed before them. I take this kind of self-respect and the respect from others it implies to be fundamental human needs; a person cannot have a decent life without them.[13] As Veblen himself puts it: "Only individuals with an aberrant temperament can in the long run retain their self-esteem in the face of the disesteem of their fellows."[14] The satisfaction of these needs calls for a certain kind of equality, not superiority; it means having certain things that others have, not more than others have.

Adam Smith articulated this point—and its connection with consumption practices—two centuries ago, and his formulation has not been surpassed:

> By necessaries I understand, not only the commodities which are indispensably necessary for the support of life, but whatever the custom of the country renders it indecent for creditable people, even the lower order, to be without. A linen shirt, for example, is, strictly speaking, not a necessary of life. The Greeks and

---

[12]Thorstein Veblen, *The Theory of the Leisure Class* (Mineola, N.Y.: Dover, 1994), chap. 2, pp. 20–21. Veblen describes the point of this kind of accumulation as "invidious comparison," although he hastens to add that "there is no intention to extol or depreciate, or to commend or deplore any of the phenomena which the word is used to characterise. The term is used in a technical sense as describing a comparison of persons with a view to rating and grading them in respect of relative worth or value" (p. 22). Whether Veblen meant to "depreciate" or not, that is certainly the way his words have been taken. It is not hard to see why.

[13]Self-respect is among the Rawlsian primary goods—things that anyone would want no matter what their values or their plan of life. See John Rawls, *A Theory of Justice* (Cambridge, Mass.: Harvard University Press, 1971).

[14]Veblen, *The Theory of the Leisure Class*, p. 20. Veblen speaks of self-esteem, not self-respect. Although the terms are often used interchangeably, there are reasons for distinguishing them. See David Sachs, "How to Distinguish Self-Respect from Self-Esteem," *Philosophy and Public Affairs* 10 (1981): 346–60. Following what I take to be Sach's main idea, I understand self-esteem to mean having a high opinion of oneself or one's accomplishments, while self-respect involves having a proper regard for one's rights, deserts, or entitlements—having a sense that one person of value whose interests and wishes ought to be taken seriously. These concepts are clearly related, and are not always easily distinguishable. Nevertheless, my point is about self-respect, and I employ Veblen's assertion in support of it.

Romans lived, I suppose very comfortably, though they had no linen. But in the present times, through the greater part of Europe, a creditable day-labourer would be ashamed to appear in public without a linen shirt, the want of which would be supposed to denote that disgraceful degree of poverty, which, it is presumed, no body can well fall into without extreme bad conduct. Custom, in the same manner, has rendered leather shoes a necessary of life in England. The poorest creditable person of either sex would be ashamed to appear in public without them.[15]

Extrapolating from Smith's analysis, we might say that the need for self-respect—or, put negatively, the need to avoid shame—is basic and universal. But what it takes to satisfy that need varies widely from time to time and from place to place. This point could have far-reaching implications. In Smith's society, self-respect meant leather shoes; in some circles in the 1990s it means Nikes.

Why some goods—such as shoes, of all things!—should have the kind of significance that Smith describes is an interesting question, but one I shall not pursue here. We can see at least that goods functioning as markers of self-respect or other status must be "conspicuous"—visible and public—which explains the prominence of clothing and cars. What the inside of a person's house looks like matters less, since most others will not see it.

At the same time, it is plausible to think that in mass societies the opinions and respect of subgroups, rather than the general public, assume greater importance. Two reasons might be offered in support of this claim. First, beyond the crudest indicators individuals are not noticed by the "general public." Second, it is psychologically difficult for individuals themselves to care about what "everybody" thinks; instead they focus on achieving respect from particular reference groups to whom they compare themselves.

The path by which certain goods become "necessaries" must involve the processes of entrenchment discussed in the last section. It would seem that wherever there is material or technological progress, new goods will gradually assume the role of "signifying decency"—and others will assume the role of signifying superiority—that Smith describes. (This is not to say that in less dynamic societies no goods play this role, only that they are less often superseded.) This is important, for it suggests that technological progress combined with the need for self-respect tend to up the consumption ante.

EQUALITY AND SUPERIORITY

Two questions cast shadows over the foregoing account. First, how much equality does self-respect require? One might argue that all significant material inequalities are damaging to the self-respect of those who have less. The improbability of radical egalitarianism could render this point a *reductio ad absurdum* of the self-respect argument. But it would have to be shown that material inequalities generally do undermine self-respect. No doubt this is a matter of degree, and reasonable people will disagree about how damaging

---

[15]Adam Smith, *An Inquiry into the Nature and Causes of the Wealth of Nations,* originally published 1776 (New York: Modern Library), book V, chap. 2, pp. 821–22.

inequalities are. My point has been only that the absence of certain—circum-scribed—goods undermines self-respect, and that it is therefore reasonable for people to want those things when others have them. How far-reaching the implications of this argument are remains to be seen.

The second question concerns the distinction between the desire for equality and the desire for superiority. There are at least two reasons for thinking these differ in ways that matter. One is moral: to want to be (and to seem) as good as others seems clearly respectable; to want to be better than or to outdo others arouses our suspicions. In Kantian terms, it is possible to will everyone to succeed in their striving for equality, but not in their striving for superiority (or more simply, it is possible to will that everyone be equal but not that everyone be superior).[16] Some critics of egalitarianism would insist that to eradicate the desire for superiority would be to discourage excellence and individuality. Egalitarians can respond by distinguishing the desire to excel from the desire to outdo others: one can aim to do as well as one can or achieve a goal defined by the activity at hand rather than by the achievements of others.

Whether this argument can succeed in throwing out the bathwater (the desire to surpass others) without the baby (excellence and individuality), and, more generally, whether the desire to surpass others is morally objectionable, are questions we cannot settle here. But there is another difference between the desire for superiority and the desire for equality. The first can lead to prisoner's dilemma situations, which are among the primary reasons for thinking consumption in the contemporary world problematic. (It need not always lead to them, however, whether it does or not will depend partly on the rate of technological change and changes in fashion.) We envision the ever-escalating spiral of acquisition among consumers all intent on proving their superior status. The desire for equal status does not appear to generate such vicious spirals.

Do people want merely to be equal to others, or do they want to be better? No doubt there is wide variation in this matter, both among people within a society, and between cultures more generally.[17] Variation exists also within individuals: we are content to be merely as good as others in many respects, even if we want to excel in some. It would be foolish to deny the existence of the desire for superiority, but it is also a mistake to exaggerate its extent.

A classical social-psychological study conducted during and after World War II, *The American Soldier*, sheds light on these issues.[18] It was found that in the Military Police, opportunities for promotion were poor, yet satisfaction was higher than in the Air Corps, where opportunities for promotion were much better. The explanation is nicely summarized by W. G. Runciman:

[16]I owe this point to Thomas Pogge.

[17]In addition, societies differ in the goods that serve as markers of status. The Veblenesque critique of consumption practices can mask two different (although not mutually exclusive) complaints: that people care about status and superiority; and that these concerns manifest themselves crudely, in the display of material things, rather than, say, in intellectual, aesthetic, or spiritual values. I discuss this point further in the final section.

[18]Samuel A. Stouffer et al., *The American Soldier. I: Adjustment During Army Life* (Princeton: Princeton University Press, 1949). The authors of this study coined the central and now common term "relative deprivation."

> Those who were not promoted in the Military Police tended to compare them-
> selves with the large number of their fellows who were also not promoted,
> while those few who had been promoted were likely to appear to themselves to
> have done relatively better. In the Air Corps, by contrast, the man who was not
> promoted would be likely to compare himself with the large number of his fel-
> lows who had been promoted, while these, though successful, would appear to
> themselves to have done relatively less well.[19]

This conclusion is intuitively plausible and borne out by casual observation. In
a professional school with one endowed chair, the unendowed will be relatively
content; if half the members of the department have endowed chairs, the situation of the unendowed will rankle. A person's position can seem tolerable and
even satisfactory to her as long as most other members of her reference group—
those to whom she compares herself—are in the same boat.[20] The sense of deprivation is largely relative to one's expectations, and these in turn depend on
what others around one have.

This claim supports the view that equality is a satisfactory outcome for
many people in many situations. Interestingly, the same line of reasoning suggests that even the desire for superiority can often be satisfied by superiority
relative to one's reference group. This emphasis on relative endowment contrast
with a view of human beings as craving more and more, period. Even where
people desire superiority and not just equality, the relativized view implies that
consumption can be constrained. For to the extent that a person's aim is relative
rather than absolute endowment, having more than others—rather than more
and more and more—will suffice.

Both the moral concern about the desire for superiority (that it is reprehensible) and the practical concern (that it may escalate without surcease) will be
more serious if there are reasons for doubting the stability of the distinction between the desire for equality and the desire for superiority. We turn now to this
question. The discussion leads to more general questions about the extent to
which the quest for status informs decisions about consumption.

STATUS AND OTHER GOODS

To think that by having or owning or showing certain things a person can
demonstrate his status is to acknowledge that such things constitute the outward signs of some nonvisible condition.[21] This idea is so fundamental to the
way material goods are viewed in our society that it is difficult to imagine not

---

[19]W. G. Runciman, *Relative Deprivation and Social Justice: A Study of Attitudes to Social Inequality in Twentieth-Century England* (Berkeley: University of California Press, 1966), p. 18. For a discussion of the significance of relative deprivation in envy, with references to the social-psychological literature, see Aaron Ben-Ze'ev, "Envy and Inequality," *Journal of Philosophy* 89 (1992): 551–81.

[20]A full account of these matters would have to explain how the reference group gets chosen: how people decide which—that is, whose—boat they are in. Sometimes this will be fairly obvious, but not always.

[21]Perhaps this is not strictly true: one might think that the possession of things was itself tantamount to status or superiority. But I believe that the relationship is commonly taken to be an evidentiary

viewing them in this way. The economist Robert Frank calls this crucial function of consumption "ability signaling." It is worth quoting him at some length:

> In societies in which economic and social interactions between people are pervasive and important—that is, in every known human society—information about people with whom we might interact has obvious value. . . . Many of the most important decisions ever made about us depend on how strangers see our talents, abilities, and other characteristics.
>
>   . . . People's various talents and abilities are not like numbers tattooed on their foreheads, there for all the world to observe at a glance. Their assessment is a subtle and complicated task, which to accomplish with reasonable accuracy requires a heavy investment of time and effort. Time and effort, however, are valuable for other purposes as well, and so we are led to seek ways of economizing on the evaluation process.
>
>   . . . The importance of consumption goods as signals of ability will be different for different occupations. Earnings and the abilities that count most among research professors are not very strongly correlated, and professors think nothing of continuing to drive a 10-year-old automobile if it still serves them reliably. But only in a very small town, where people know one another well, might it not be a mistake for an aspiring young attorney to drive such a car in the presence of his potential clients. Good lawyers generally earn a lot of money, and people with a lot of money generally drive fashionable new cars. The potential client who doesn't know better will assume that a lawyer with a battered car is not much sought after.[22]

If it is true that we need information about each other that would ordinarily be impossible or inefficient to acquire directly, we must read it off from more visible signs. We can, of course, argue about the reliability of different signs, but that is another matter. Individuals do not decide what the signs are or should be; they must pretty much take them as given. If you want to convey information, you have to speak the language. One decides to drive an Acura Legend or to wear Guess jeans, but not what information is conveyed by these choices. Sometimes, of course, the information will be misinformation. So if one cares what other people think, one must be sure to learn what different consumption choices are taken to signify.

The purely informational aspect of ability-signaling obviously performs a useful function. Reading surfaces is a shortcut, and especially in mass societies where typically we are strangers to one another, we need shortcuts.[23] This func-

---

one: possessions (which of course may be thought also valuable and desirable in themselves) are taken as a sign of worth. Compare the Protestant idea that emerged during the rise of capitalism that economic enterprise and wealth (although not material display) were the signs of spiritual salvation. See Max Weber, *The Protestant Ethic and the Spirit of Capitalism* (New York: Scribner's, 1958), and R. H. Tawney, *Religion and the Rise of Capitalism* (New York: Penguin, 1980).

[22]Robert Frank, *Choosing the Right Pond: Human Behavior and the Quest for Status* (New York: Oxford University Press, 1985), pp. 148–49. I am indebted to Frank's book and to Fred Hirsh, *Social Limits to Growth* (Cambridge, Mass.: Harvard University Press, 1976) for stimulating my thinking generally about these matters.

[23]Things are not quite so simple. The informational aspect of ability-signaling is conjoined with a disinformational aspect. I may want to communicate my abilities, or I may want to fool people into thinking that I have abilities that I don't.

tion of consumption extends to its purely expressive aspects, unconnected with status considerations. How you dress, what kind of car you drive, what you eat—these choices tell people about your tastes, interests, and values. It is not necessarily a matter of status-seeking to want other people to know such things.

Yet when consumption services to signal abilities, the distinction between consuming to demonstrate one is as good as others and consuming to show one is better, and between either of these and consuming simply to convey information, begins to blur. Insofar as a person is attempting to convey information about his abilities, he is saying "I have these traits, these talents, I am this good (. . . so hire me, or let me into your university)."He is serving the useful function of providing information about himself, but he is also trying, in a competitive world, to obtain a scarce commodity.

The consumption of education provides illuminating examples of these complexities. (It also shows that the consumption of nonmaterial goods like education is in important ways just like the consumption of material goods.) What is the good that we desire, and that we hope to obtain for ourselves or our children by enriched educational programs, private schools, prestigious colleges, advanced degrees? There are three kinds of possibilities. First, I may want my child to acquire the intellectual resources to appreciate Shakespeare or Einstein. What I seek here is a nonrelative good. To attain it, my child will need a certain quality of education. Theoretically, at least, everyone could have such an education; there is plenty of Shakespeare to go round, and her gain need be no one else's loss.

Perhaps, though—instead or in addition—the good I seek through education is a chance at one of society's better jobs. Better jobs are scarce, and we can assume that those with more and better education have an advantage in obtaining them. But better jobs can be scarce in two quite different ways. A job can be better because it is more interesting or rewarding (defined however one chooses), so that a person with a better job will have a better or richer life. Here again, what is wanted is a nonrelative good; it is a good that happens to be scarce, however, because of certain unfortunate accidents of the world we inhabit, and so one person's having the good excludes others from having it. There is no necessity that a person who wants a better job in this sense wants status—certainly no superiority, not necessarily even equality; status may not enter as a consideration at all. Nevertheless, such a person will want to be better than others so that she rather than one of them will get the job.

A job can be better in a different sense: it can occupy a higher position in the social hierarchy. A person who wants a better job in this sense clearly seeks superiority over others; the good sought is what Fred Hirsch calls a positional good, one that is inherently scarce.[24] Only in this case do we find the concern with status that has so dominated thinking about consumption.

Of course, I have been arguing that the concern with status, insofar as it represents a desire for equality rather than superiority, is not reprehensible. Yet

[24]My discussion of education owes much to Hirsch's account. See *Social Limits to Growth*, chap. 3. The distinction between the intrinsic and the positional advantages of a job can sometimes be hard to draw. A person who feels his work is unappreciated or unrecognized, because it lacks a certain status, may be unable to enjoy what would otherwise be an intrinsically rewarding job.

educational goods illustrate the instability of the distinction. We can further clarify this point with the example of so-called "gifted and talented" programs in the public schools. As a parent, I may believe that the educational needs of my children and of children generally are better served by an environment that deemphasizes tracking, and that does not label academically talented students and segregate them from other students in special programs. I may hold this view even if my children are among those chosen by the elite system. Nevertheless, given the existence of a "gifted and talented" program, I will want my children to be selected for it. For once the system is in place, if they are not labeled as better, they are thereby labeled as worse. It is simply rational to hope they are chosen, even if I disapprove of the system. A similar analysis can be given of the flight from public to private schools, "white flight" from integrating neighborhoods, and many other phenomena. In such situations, one who fails to practice what she preaches has at least a partial defense against the charge of hypocrisy.

We come back to the prisoner's dilemma situations mentioned in passing earlier. Just how large a range of consumption practices should be understood in these terms is a question that needs further investigation. But it is clear at least that some such practices do fall into this category: if you don't move ahead, you fall behind. So the decision not to acquire more of the good in question is not simply a decision not to improve one's well-being; it is in effect a decision to lower it. When high school diplomas are a dime a dozen, employers will start to require college degrees; even if the additional education is not necessary to do the job, it serves as a sorting device. When college degrees are a dime a dozen, employers will require MBAs or law degrees; even though the additional education is not necessary . . . , and so on. As Hirsch puts it, when everyone stands on tiptoe, no one sees any better. But if you don't stand on tiptoe, you won't see at all. If you want to see better, you'll have to get stilts. But when everyone gets stilts . . .

Another way in which the line between the desire for equality and the desire for superiority blurs emerges from a more careful examination of the idea of the reference group. It may be true that people often want only equality with respect to those groups to which they aspire or to which they think they belong. But sometimes it is part of the group's identity to derive satisfaction from what Veblen calls "invidious comparison" with other groups. A member of Mensa may be content so long as his IQ equals that of other members. But he may also derive satisfaction from knowing he is smarter than others who do not qualify for membership. Some would argue that class membership works similarly: a person's satisfaction with being middle class rests partly on knowing there is a lower class. The instability of the line between the desire for equality and the desire for superiority depends on how central invidious comparison is to a group's identity. It is probably safe to say that feeling superior is central to the identity of some groups but not others.

WHAT'S WRONG WITH CONSUMING, ANYWAY?

How much space do the relational aspects of consumption occupy in the totality of reasons for consuming? It is not easy either to interpret this question concretely, or to know how to go about answering it. My own view is that the relational aspects of consumption are extremely important: that the reasons people want things have a great deal to do with what others around them have. This proposition has not been fully established by the foregoing arguments; but I believe that observation of and reflection on social phenomena support the conclusion that consuming because others consume explains a great deal.

An important corollary is that to the extent that people's desires to consume depend on what others around them consume, collective reductions in consumption will be less painful to individuals than reductions individuals effect in isolation. And the reason is not simply that it is easier for people to make personal sacrifices if they know that others are doing likewise. It is also that, to the extent that consumption is relational, having less does not constitute a sacrifice if others also have less. We can put the point more strongly: to the extent that the desire to consume is relative, two societies could differ markedly in their overall level of consumption without differing in overall well-being, however well-being is understood.

This view helps explain the common observation that people in societies less affluent than our own are not necessarily worse off, and often do not seem less happy or satisfied, than we are. Relative deprivation—deprivation relative to those around you—is crucial. This is *not* to say that deprivation is wholly relative, or that there are not certain privations that are absolutely bad and to be avoided. Such a conclusion would be comforting yet pernicious. Nevertheless, for a society acting in concert, the pain of reducing consumption should exceed the pain of reduced consumption, since what we are used to and what we are exposed to centrally affects our desires and degree of satisfaction. Collective, concerted efforts are less painful not simply because welfare is relational in the ways I have described, but also because typically, they do not require the same kind of full awareness that individual efforts do. Legally-mandated taxes, deducted like clockwork from one's paycheck (and from everyone else's), do not hurt—because we do not notice them—in the way that individual choices to donate money often do. The latter may be purely voluntary, but because these acts are done deliberately and in full consciousness, we are constantly reminded of our sacrifice.

It is worth noting that I have not addressed the question whether we ought to consume less or not. Partly as a result, this discussion might seem to have a certain ambiguous, "half-empty or half-full?" quality. Looked at in one way, it might appear to be an apology for consumption; looked at in another, it seems a call for the simpler life. It looks like the first because in explaining the relativity of consumption practices I have also been defending these practices to some extent. It looks like the second because the questions raised get their force from the assumption that consumption is somehow problematic.

Both impressions have some warrant. Let us see why.

First, let us consider the (partial) defense of consuming because others consume against the charges of conformity, greed, envy, or one-upmanship. I have argued that the desire to consume rests partly on factors that have nothing at all to do with status, and that even the desire for status is not always reprehensible—that we consume partly to satisfy the desire for a certain kind of equality that is essential to self-respect. Do these arguments commit the naturalistic fallacy? Just because people behave in a certain way or possess certain traits (assuming they do) does not amount to a justification. Perhaps we should conclude instead that human beings are contemptible or at least morally weak.

To some extent this dispute will remain immune to rational solution. When all is said, there will still be serious disagreements about how much we can or should expect of mortal human beings—disagreements that cannot be analyzed further into soluble bits. But we can make some headway by distinguishing the different ways in which consumption is relational, for these differ morally. Consider the four categories that emerge from the foregoing discussion: (a) consumption dependent on infrastructure and networking effects; (b) consumption dependent on salience and the demonstration effect; (c) the status-related desire for equality; (d) the status-related desire for superiority. The first is least problematic morally, because it affects needs that almost everyone will agree are basic and whose fulfillment therefore typically does not reflect vice. The last is most problematic, which is not to say that no defense of the desire for superiority can be made. I myself would not make it, however, and insofar as Veblen is right empirically I think he is wrong evaluatively: we should "depreciate" and "deplore" the tendency.[25]

It is the two intermediate cases that are most difficult to resolve. As I argued above in the discussion of salience, one person's greed is another's openness to new experiences, and it is not easy to see what further information could get them to see eye to eye. What this may show is just that their disagreement does not depend on divergent factual beliefs, but rather on differing judgments about the moral value of certain character traits or behavior. Similar things can be said about equality and self-respect: facts about human psychology aside, we may disagree about how much a virtuous person should care about what others think.

Facts about human psychology aside? Here, it seems clear, we cannot dispense with naturalism. What we count as virtue must take heed of psychology; if the great mass of people cannot thrive or be happy without a certain degree of respect from their fellows, then it is at best only the remotest kind of virtue, fit for the very few, to go without it. There is still room for disagreement, of course, about how much we should care about what others think. This disagreement is rooted partly in disputes about or ignorance of the psychological facts, and partly in evaluative issues.

The moral heart of the question about what consuming because others consume indicates about our character may rest, finally, on the importance of self-sufficiency as a moral ideal.[26] Self-sufficiency can be viewed in terms both of things and of people. Salience and the demonstration effect involve dependence on things; the desires for equality and superiority involve dependence on other people and public opinion.

---

[25]See n. 12 above and the text accompanying it.

[26]For a discussion of the virtue of self-sufficiency, see Michael Slote, "Virtue Ethics and Democratic Values," *Journal of Social Philosophy* 24 (1993): 5–37.

In these matters I would urge moderation. With respect both to things and to people, too much self-sufficiency is eerily inhuman and remote; too little is slavish. It is for this reason, among others, that I take the foregoing arguments to constitute a defense of human character, but only a partial defense. We are made to respond to the stimuli around us, and to care about the opinions of others; but that doesn't mean that we don't often care more than we should. We do.

The preoccupation with status and the opinions of others can manifest itself, and often has manifested itself, in value systems that place less emphasis on material goods. Are these other outlets superior? Some would argue that material inequalities constitute a more benign and democratic manifestation of inegalitarianism than other forms, at least in part because material things are more easily separable from a person's identity. Others would insist on the intrinsic superiority of spiritual, moral, intellectual values, even if they do not solve the hierarchy problem and even if, because they are less separable from the self, they give rise to greater problems of self-respect and deep inequality.

These are large questions that I cannot address here. They matter insofar as we are interested in the intrinsic moral value of material consumption and in the implications of consumption for character. But—to come back to the beginning—we worry about consumption for other reasons too: because it seems wrong for some to have so much while others have so little, or because we think that those who have so much are partly to blame for others having too little, or that by consuming so much themselves they impoverish others. Insofar as we worry about consumption for these reasons—reasons of justice—or for environmental reasons, consuming less materially could make a big difference.

To know whether it will for certain would require us to analyze and evaluate these reasons carefully. I hope at least to have shown why such changes, once effected, might be less significant and traumatic than those of us who have become accustomed to a certain level of material comfort might suppose.[27]

Questions

1. What phenomena does Judith Lichtenberg describe when she says that (*a*) "invention is the mother of necessity" and (*b*) "familiarity breeds desire more often than contempt"?
2. What does the author mean by "salience"?
3. Given that it is harder for an individual to consume less while others do not reduce their consumption, what responsibility, if any, does a person have to consume less unilaterally?
4. How, if at all, do the consumption issues discussed by Judith Lichtenberg relate to the environmental issues raised by James Anderson and Ronald Sandler?

[27]This essay was written with support from the Pew Charitable Trusts. I am grateful to audiences at the University of Illinois, the University of Connecticut, Yale University, and Wesleyan University for helpful discussion. I especially want to thank my colleagues at the Institute for Philosophy and Public Policy, and, in particular, Karla Hoff, David Luban, Thomas Pogge, Jerome Segal, Alan Strudler, Leonard Waks, and David Wasserman for their conversations and comments.

Suggestions for Further Reading on the Environment, Cars, and Consumption

CAFARO, PHILIP. "Less Is More: Economic Consumption and the Good Life." *Philosophy Today*, spring 1998: pp. 26–39.

CAMPBELL, COLIN. "Consuming Goods and the Good of Consuming." *Critical Review* 8, no. 4 (fall 1994): pp. 503–520.

CROCKER, DAVID, AND TOBY LINDEN, eds. *Ethics of Consumption: The Good Life, Justice, and Global Stewardship*, Lanham, Md: Rowman and Littlefield, 1998.

ELLIOT, ROBERT. *Faking Nature: The Ethics of Environmental Restoration*. London: Routledge, 1997.

ROLSTON, HOLMES III. *Environmental Ethics*. Philadelphia: Temple University Press, 1988.

TAYLOR, PAUL. *Respect for Nature*. Princeton: Princeton University Press, 1986.

PART SEVEN

Virtues and Vices

CHAPTER 18

Forgiveness

JEFFRIE G. MURPHY, Forgiveness, Reconciliation, and Responding to Evil

NORVIN RICHARDS, Forgiveness

PAUL M. HUGHES, Moral Anger, Forgiving, and Condoning

Forgiveness, Reconciliation, and Responding to Evil

Jeffrie G. Murphy[1]

Jeffrie Murphy follows Bishop Joseph Butler in understanding forgiveness as essentially a change of inner feelings rather than of external behavior. The relevant feelings are vindictive passions such as resentment, anger, hatred, and the desire for revenge, which arise when another responsible agent has wronged one. The author distinguishes forgiveness from justification, excuse, mercy, and reconciliation. He then argues that forgiving too hastily and uncritically will often threaten the values of respect for self and respect for the moral order. Nevertheless, says the author, forgiveness can also be virtuous. It can prevent one from becoming consumed by vindictiveness, it can inhibit cruelty, and it can foster the restoration of valuable personal relationships. He then discusses the important role that the wrongdoer's repentance can play in facilitating virtuous forgiveness. Finally, he suggests three ways in which a Christian perspective might somewhat facilitate forgiveness.

. . . I shall begin by attempting to explain what forgiveness is and, in the process, distinguish it from various other things it is not but with which is has often been confused. After that, I will explore what can be said against forgiveness and then close with a discussion of what can be said in its favor.

THE NATURE OF FORGIVENESS

I think that one of the most insightful discussions of forgiveness ever penned is to be found in Bishop Joseph Butler's 1726 sermon "Upon Forgiveness of Injuries."[2] In that sermon, Bishop Butler offers a definition of forgiveness that

[1] Regents' Professor of Law and Philosophy, Arizona State University.

[2] Sermon IX, *Sermons of Joseph Bulter*, ed. W. E. Gladstone, Oxford: The Clarendon Press, 1897, pp. 127–141.

Jeffrie Murphy, "Forgiveness, Reconciliation, and Responding to Evil," *Fordham Urban Law Journal*. Reprinted by permission. Fordham Urban Law Journal, Volume XXVII, June 2000, Number 5, pp. 1353–1366.

I have adapted in my own work on the topic.[3] According to Butler, forgiveness is a moral virtue (a virtue of character) that is essentially a matter of the heart, the inner self, and involves a change in inner feeling more than a change in external action. The change in feeling is this: the overcoming, on moral grounds, of the intense negative reactive attitudes—the vindictive passions of resentment, anger, hatred, and the desire for revenge—that are quite naturally occasioned when one has been wronged by another responsible agent. A person who has forgiven has overcome those vindictive attitudes and has overcome them for a morally creditable motive—e.g., being moved by repentance on the part of the person by whom one has been wronged. Of course, such a change in feeling often leads to a change of behavior—reconciliation, for example; but, as our ability to forgive the dead illustrates, it does not always do so.

On this analysis of forgiveness, it is useful initially to distinguish forgiveness from other responses to wrongdoing with which forgiveness is often confused: justification, excuse, mercy, and reconciliation. Although these concepts are to some degree open textured and can bleed into each other, clarity is—I think—served if one at least starts by attempting to separate them. I will discuss each of them briefly.

1. Justification

To regard conduct as justified (as in lawful self defense, for example) is to claim that the conduct, though normally wrongful, was—in the given circumstances and all things considered—the right thing to do. If I have suffered because of conduct that was right—e.g., had my nose bloodied by someone defending himself against my wrongful attack—I have not been wronged, have nothing legitimately to resent, and thus nothing to forgive.

2. Excuse

To regard conduct as excused (as in the insanity defense, for example) is to admit that the conduct lacked substantial capacity to conform his conduct to the relevant norms and thus was not a fully responsible agent. Responsible agency is, of course, a matter of degree; but to the degree that the person who injures me is not a responsible agent, resentment of that person would make no more sense than resenting a sudden storm that soaks me. Again, there is nothing here to forgive.

3. Mercy

To accord a wrongdoer mercy is to inflict a less harsh consequence on that person than allowed by institutional (usually legal) rules. Mercy is less personal

---

[3]My adaptation of Butler is free, and I make no pretense that what follows is a solid piece of Butler scholarship. I have been inspired by Butler's discussion; and thus, even when I have modified or added to that discussion, I hope that I have always been loyal to its essential spirit.

than forgiveness, since the one granting mercy (a sentencing judge, say) typically will not be a victim of wrongdoing and thus will not have any feelings of resentment to overcome. (There is a sense in which only victims of wrongdoing have what might be called *standing* to forgive.) Mercy also has a public behavioral dimension not necessarily present in forgiveness. I can forgive a person simply in my heart of hearts, but I cannot show mercy simply in my heart of hearts. I can forgive the dead, but I cannot show mercy to the dead. I can forgive myself, but I cannot show mercy to myself.

This distinction between mercy and forgiveness allows us to see why there is no inconsistency in fully forgiving a person for wrongdoing (that is, stop resenting or hating the person for it) but still advocate that the person suffer the legal consequence of criminal punishment. To the degree that criminal punishment is justified in order to secure victim satisfaction, then—of course—the fact that the victim has forgiven will be a relevant argument for reducing the criminal's sentence and the fact that a victim still resents and hates will be a relevant argument for increasing that sentence. It is highly controversial, of course, that criminal punishment should to *any* degree be harnessed to victim desires. Even if it is, however, it must surely be admitted that the practice serves other values as well—particularly crime control and justice; and, with respect to these goals, victim forgiveness could hardly be dispositive. In short: It would indeed be inconsistent for a person to claim that he has forgiven the wrongdoer and still advocate punishment for the wrongdoer in order to satisfy his personal vindictive feelings. (If he still has those feelings, he has not forgiven.) It would not be inconsistent, however, to advocate punishment for other legitimate reasons. Of course, the possibilities for self deception are enormous here.

4. Reconciliation

The vindictive passions (those overcome in forgiveness) are often a major barrier to reconciliation; and thus, since forgiveness often leads to reconciliation, it is easy to confuse the two concepts. I think, however, that it is important also to see how they may differ—how there can be forgiveness without reconciliation and reconciliation without forgiveness.

First let me give an example of forgiveness without reconciliation. Imagine a battered woman who has been repeatedly beaten and raped by her husband or boyfriend. This woman—after a religious conversion, perhaps—might well come to forgive her batterer (i.e., stop hating him) without a willingness to resume her relationship with him."I forgive you and wish you well" can, in my view, sit quite consistently with "I never want you in this house again." In short, the fact that one has forgiven does not mean that one must also trust or live again with a person.

As an example of reconciliation without forgiveness, consider the example of the South African Truth and Reconciliation Commission.[4] In order to negotiate a viable transition from apartheid to democratic government with full

---

[4]For a survey of the operation of the Commission, see Minnow, *supra* note 2, Chapter 4, pp. 52–90.

black participation, all parties had to agree that there would in most cases be no punishment for evil acts that occurred under the previous government. Wrongdoers, by making a full confession and accepting responsibility, would typically be granted amnesty. In this process the wrongdoers would not be required to repent, show remorse, or even apologize.

I can clearly see this process as one of reconciliation—a process that will allow all to work toward a democratic and just future. I do not so easily see this process as one of forgiveness, however. No change of heart was required or even sought from the victims—no overcoming of such vindictive feelings as resentment and hatred. All that was required of them was a willingness to accept this process as a necessary means to the future good of their society.

In my view, this counts as forgiveness only if one embraces what is (to me) a less morally rich definition of forgiveness: forgiveness merely as the waiving of a right. Examples of this are found in a private law idea of forgiving a debt or in Bishop Desmond Tutu's definition of forgiveness as "waiving one's right to revenge."[5] But surely one can waive one's rights for purely instrumental reasons—reasons having nothing to do with the change of heart that constitutes forgiveness as a moral virtue. One can even waive one's rights for selfish reasons—e.g., the belief that one's future employment prospects will be better if one simply lets bygones be bygones. I am not saying that it is wrong to act for instrumental reasons—indeed, for South Africa, it may have been the only justified course. Neither am I saying that instrumental justifications can never be moral justifications. To attempt reconciliation for the future good of one's society, for example, is surely both instrumental and moral. I am simply saying that, however justified acting instrumentally may sometimes be, it is—absent the extinction of resentment and other vindictive passions—something other than what I understand as the moral virtue of forgiveness. In short: If all we know is that two parties have decided to reconcile, we do not know enough to make a reliable judgment about whether the moral virtue of forgiveness has been realized in the reconciliation.

Another point worth making about the relation between reconciliation and forgiveness is this: If one always delayed reconciliation until forgiveness had taken place, then some vitally important kinds of reconciliation might not be possible. Thus the realization that forgiveness is often a helpful step toward reconciliation should not lead us into the mistaken belief that forgiveness is a necessary condition for reconciliation. Indeed, it is surely sometimes the case that reconciliation, coming first and adopted for instrumental reasons, opens the door to future forgiveness. After learning that one can work with one's victimizer toward a common goal, a sense of common humanity might emerge and one's vindictive passions toward that person might over time begin to soften.

Let me now discuss the evaluation of forgiveness as I—following Bishop Butler—have defined it.

---

[5]Bill Moyers interview, PBS, April 27, 1999.

THE DANGERS OF HASTY FORGIVENESS

In addition to his powerful sermon on forgiveness, Bishop Butler authored an equally powerful sermon with the title "Upon Resentment."[6] In that sermon, Butler started to make a case for the legitimacy of resentment and other vindictive passions—arguing that a just and loving God would not have universally implanted these passions within his creatures unless the passions served some valuable purpose. The danger of resentment, he argued, lies not in having it, but rather in being dominated and consumed by it to such a degree that one can never overcome it and acts irresponsibly on the basis of it. As the initial response to being wronged, however, the passion stands in defense of important values—values that might be compromised by immediate and uncritical forgiveness of wrongs.

What are the values defended by resentment and threatened by hasty and uncritical forgiveness? I would suggest two: respect for self and respect for the moral order. A person who never resented any injuries done to himself might be a saint. It is equally likely, however, that his lack of resentment reveals a servile personality—a personality lacking in respect for himself and respect for his rights and status as a free and equal moral agent. (This is the point behind S. J. Perelman's famous quip: "To err is human; to forgive, supine.") Just as indignation or guilt over the mistreatment of others stands as emotional testimony that we care about them and their rights, so does resentment stand as emotional testimony that we care about ourselves and our rights.

Related to this is an instrumental point: Those who have vindictive dispositions toward those who wrong them give potential wrongdoers an incentive *not* to wrong them. If I were going to set out to oppress other people, I would surely prefer to select for my victims persons whose first response is forgiveness rather than persons whose first response is revenge. As Kant noted in his *Doctrine of Virtue*, "One who makes himself into a worm cannot complain if people step on him."[7]

Resentment does not simply stand as emotional testimony of self-respect, however. This passion—and the reluctance to hastily transcend it in forgiveness—also stands as testimony to our allegiance to the moral order itself. This is a point made forcefully by Aurel Kolnai in his important essay on forgiveness.[8] According to Kolnai, we all have a duty to support—both intellectually and emotionally—the moral order, an order represented by clear understanding of what constitutes unacceptable treatment of one human being by another. If we do not show some resentment to those who, in victimizing us, flout those understandings, then we run the risk (in Kolnai's words) of being "complicitous in evil."

---

[6]Sermon VIII, *supra* note 6, pp. 115–126.
[7]Immanuel Kant, *The Doctrine of Virtue* (Part II of the *Metaphysics of Morals*), trans. Mary J. Gregor, New York: Harper Torchbooks, p. 103 (p. 437 Academy Edition).
[8]Aurel Kolnai, "Forgiveness," *Proceedings of the Aristotelian Society*, 1973–74, pp. 91–106.

If I had more time, I could say many more things in defense of the vindictive passions. (Indeed, I am soon to publish an essay with the title "Two Cheers for Vindictiveness."[9]) I hope I have said enough, however, to support Butler's claim that these passions have some positive value. Having such value, these passions are unlike, say, *malice*—pure delight in the misfortunes and sufferings of others. Malice is by no means universal but is, where present, intrinsically evil or diseased or both. Butler essentially wants to apply Aristotle's idea of the mean to the passion of resentment—developing an account of the circumstances that justify it and the degree to which it is legitimate to feel and be guided by it. But the doctrine of the mean does not apply to malice; for the proper amount of this passion is always zero.

Uncritical boosters for quick forgiveness have a tendency to treat resentment and the other vindictive passions as though, like malice, they are intrinsically evil—passions that no decent person would acknowledge.[10] In this, I think that they are quite mistaken. In the *Oresteia*, Athena rightly made an honorable home for the Furies (representatives of the vindictive passions)—so constraining their excess by due process and the rule of law that they become the Eumenides (the Kindly Ones), protectors of law and social stability. There is no honorable home for malice, however.

Let me summarize what I have argued to this point: The problem with resentment and other vindictive passions is not (as with malice) their very existence. In their proper place, they have an important role to play in the defense of self and of the moral and legal order. The problem with these passions is rather their tendency to get out of control—to so dominate the life of a victimized person that the person's own life is soured and, in his revenge seeking, he starts to pose a danger to the very moral and legal order that rightly identifies him as a victim of immorality. It is here—as a limiting and overcoming virtue—that forgiveness has its important role to play.

FORGIVENESS AS A VIRTUE

It is, of course, possible to take one's revenge against others in measured and proportional and peaceful ways—ways as simple as a cutting remark before colleagues or a failure to continue issuing lunch invitations.

Very often, however, a victimized person will allow vindictiveness to take over his very self—turning him into a self-righteous fanatic so involved—even joyous—in his outrage that he will be satisfied only with the utter annihilation of the person who has wronged him. Such a person is sometimes even willing to destroy, as symbolic stand-ins, persons who have done him no wrong or who

---

[9]Forthcoming in *Punishment and Society*.

[10]I sometimes think I find such uncritical boosterism among certain voices within what might be called the "forgiveness movement" in clinical psychology. See my "Forgiveness in Counseling: A Philosophical Perspective" in my *Character, Liberty and Law: Kantian Essays in Theory and Practice*, Dordrecht: Kluwer, 1998, pp. 223–238.

may even be totally innocent. (The von Kleist story *Michael Kohlhaas*—retold by E. L. Doctorow in his novel *Ragtime*—is a famous illustration of this.[11]) Such a person is a danger to himself—very like, as I think Nietzsche once said, a scorpion stinging itself with its own tail—and poses a threat to the morality and decency of the social order. A person under the power of such vindictiveness can, often unconsciously, even use the language of justice and crime control as a rationalization for what is really sadism and cruelty. I cannot help thinking, for example, that many of the unspeakably brutish conditions that we tolerate in our prisons flow, not from the stated legitimate desires for justice and crime control, but rather from a vindictiveness so out of control that it actually becomes a kind of malice.

Against such a background, forgiveness can be seen as a healing virtue that brings with it great blessings—chief among them being its capacity to free us from being consumed by our angers, its capacity to check our tendencies toward cruelty, and its capacity to open the door to the restoration of those relationships in our lives that are worthy of restoration. This last blessing can be seen in the fact that, since each one of us will sometimes wrong the people that mean the most to us, there will be times when we will want to be forgiven by those whom we have wronged. Seeing this, no rational person would desire to live in a world where forgiveness was not seen as a healing virtue. (This is, I take it, the secular meaning of the parable of the unforgiving servant at Matt. 18:21–35.)

We are faced, then, with a complex dilemma: How are we to reap the blessings of forgiveness without sacrificing our self respect or our respect for the moral order in the process?

One great help here—and I make no claim that it is the only help or even a necessary condition for forgiveness—is sincere *repentance* on the part of the wrongdoer. When I am wronged by another, a great part of the injury—over and above any physical harm I may suffer—is the insulting or degrading message that has been given to me by the wrongdoer: the message that I am less worthy than he is, so unworthy that he may use me merely as a means or object in service to his desires and projects. Thus failing to resent (or hastily forgiving) the wrongdoer runs the risk that I am endorsing that very immoral message for which the wrongdoer stands. If the wrongdoer sincerely repents, however, he now joins me in repudiating the degrading and insulting message—allowing me to relate to him (his new self) as an equal without fear that a failure to resent him will be read as a failure to resent what he has done. In short: It is much easier to follow St. Augustine's counsel that we should "hate the sin but not the sinner" when the sinner (the wrongdoer) repudiates his own wrongdoing through an act of repentance.[12]

---

[11] A good English translation of Heinrich von Kleist's 1808 novella *Michael Kohlhass* may be found in Heinrich von Kleist, *The Marquise of O and Other Stories*, trans. by David Luke and Nigel Reeves, London: Penguin Books, 1978, pp. 114–213. E. L. Doctorow, *Ragtime*, New York: Random House, 1974.

[12] St. Augustine's remark, so often rendered as it is here, more literally reads "with love of mankind and hatred of sins." According to *The Oxford Dictionary of Quotations*, Revised Fourth Edition (Oxford: Oxford University Press, 1996, p. 37), the remark appears in Letter 211 in J. –P. Minge, editor, *Patrologiae Latinae* (1845), Volume 33.

My point here is that sincere repentance on the part of the wrongdoer opens the door to forgiveness and often to reconciliation. This is not to suggest, however, that we should always *demand* repentance as a condition for forgiveness and reconciliation. When a person comes to repentance as a result of his own spiritual growth, we are witness to an inspiring transformation of character. Any repentance that is simply a response to a demand or external incentive, however, is very likely to be fake. In what could be read as a commentary both on certain aspects of the Federal Sentencing Guidelines and on remarks made by some of our current crop of elected officials, Montaigne wrote: "These men make us believe that they feel great regret and remorse within, but of atonement and correction or interruption they show us no sign. . . . I know of no quality so easy to counterfeit as piety."[13] Montaigne's observation also suggests that the South Africans were perhaps wise in not making repentance a condition for amnesty under their Truth and Reconciliation Commission.

So let us welcome repentance when we find it, and let us do what we can to create a climate where it can flourish and open the door to the moral rebirth of the wrongdoer and to forgiveness by the wronged. But, out of respect for the genuine article, let us not demand or otherwise coerce it. Demanding tends to produce only lying and may even be degrading to the wrongdoer—inviting his further corruption rather than his moral rebirth. David Lurie, the central character in J. M. Coetzee's recent novel *Disgrace*, could save his job if he simply expressed the kind of repentance demanded of him by the university disciplinary board that has authority over him. I find myself sympathizing with the reasons he gives for not giving them what they want when he says:

> We went through the repentance business yesterday. I told you what I thought. I won't do it. I appeared before an officially constituted tribunal, before a branch of the law. Before that secular tribunal I pleaded guilty, a secular plea. That plea should suffice. Repentance is neither here nor there. Repentance belongs to another world, to another universe of discourse. . . . [What are you asking] reminds me too much of Mao's China. Recantation, self-criticism, public apology. I'm old fashioned, I would prefer simply to be put against a wall and shot.[14]

There has in recent times been much cheap and shallow chatter about forgiveness and repentance—some of it coming from high political officials and some coming from the kind of psychobabble often found in self-help and recovery books. As a result of this, many people are, I fear, starting to become cynical about both. For reasons I have developed here, repentance may pave the way for forgiveness. It is less likely to do so, however, in a world where

---

[13]Michel de Montaigne, "On Repentance" (1585–1588) in *The Complete Essays of Montaigne*, trans. Donald Frame, Stanford: Stanford University Press, 1958, p. 617.
[14]J. M. Coetzee, *Disgrace*, New York: Viking, 1999, p. 58 and p. 66.

we come to believe that too many claims of repentance are insincere and ex-pedient—talking the talk without (so far as we can tell) walking the walk. . . .

FORGIVENESS AND CHRISTIANITY

[I shall] . . . close with a few general remarks about the relationship between re-ligion—particularly Christianity—and forgiveness. As someone who is neither devout nor trained in theology, I am hardly the best person to do this—either spiritually or intellectually. However, I will take a brief stab at it none the less.

There are, I think, at least three ways in which a Christian perspective on the world might make the struggle toward forgiveness—not easy, surely—but at least slightly less difficult than it otherwise might be. (Similar perspectives might also be present, of course, in other religions and world views.[15])

First, I think that Christianity tends to introduce a *humbling* perspective on one's self and one's personal concerns—attempting to counter our natural ten-dencies of pride and narcissistic self importance. According to this perspective, we are all fallible and flawed and all stand in deep need of forgiveness. This perspective does not seek to trivialize the wrongs that we suffer, but it does seek to blunt our very human tendency to magnify those wrongs out of all reason-able sense of proportion—the tendency to see ourselves as morally pure while seeing those who wrong us as evil incarnate. By breaking down a sharp us-them dichotomy, such a view should make it easier to follow Auden's counsel to "love your crooked neighbor with your crooked heart."[16] This should make us more open to the possibility of forgiving those who have wronged us and should also help us to keep our justified resentments from turning into mali-cious hatreds and our demands for just punishment from serving rationaliza-tions for sadistic cruelty.

Related to this is a second Christian teaching that might help open the door to forgiveness—a teaching that concerns, not the status of the victim, but the status of the wrongdoer. According to Christianity, we are supposed to see the wrongdoer, as we are supposed to see each person, as a child of God, created in His image, and thus as ultimately precious. This vision is beautifully expressed by the writer William Trevor in his novel *Felicia's Journey*. He speaks with com-passion and forgiveness even of the serial killer who is a central character of that novel and writes of him: "Lost within a man who murdered, there was a soul like any other soul, purity itself it surely once had been."[17] Viewing the wrongdoer in this way—seeing in him the innocent child he once was—should

---

[15]See, for example, the discussion of the background world view that underlies the Judaic concep-tion of forgiveness in Louis E. Newman's "The Quality of Mercy: On the Duty to Forgive in the Ju-daic Tradition," *Journal of Religious Ethics*, Volume 15, Fall 1987, pp. 155–172. For the context provided by Stoicism, see Seneca's essays "On Anger" and "On Mercy" in *Moral Essays*, Volume I, trans. John W. Basore, Cambridge: Harvard University Press, 1994, pp. 106–449.

[16]W. H. Auden, "As I Walked Out One Evening," in *Collected Poems*, New York: Vintage, 1991, p. 135.

[17]William Trevor, *Felicia's Journey*, London: Viking, 1994, p. 212.

make it difficult to hate him with the kind of abandon that would make forgiveness of him utterly impossible.

Third and finally, Christianity teaches that the universe is—for all its evil and hardship—ultimately benign, created and sustained by a loving God, and to be met with hope rather than despair. On this view, the world may be falling, but—as Rilke wrote—"there is One who holds this falling/with infinite softness in his hands."[18]

If I could embrace such a view of the universe and our place in it—a view for which there is surely no proof and thus requires a faith that is properly called religious—then perhaps I would not so easily think that the struggle against evil—even evil due to me—is my task alone, all up to me.[19] If I think that I alone can and must make things right—including making sure that the people I have branded as evil get exactly what is coming to them—then I take on a kind of self-importance that makes me not only unforgiving but dangerous—becoming the kind of person Nietzsche probably had in mind when he warned that we should "mistrust those in whom the urge to punish is very strong"[20] If I were capable of a certain kind of faith, then perhaps I could relax a bit the clinched fist with which I try to protect myself, sustain my self respect, avenge myself, and hold my world together all alone. . . .

Questions

1. Why does Jeffrie Murphy think that forgiving too quickly and uncritically can threaten the values of respect for self and respect for the moral order?
2. In what three ways does the author think that Christianity might make forgiveness at least slightly less difficult than it otherwise might be?
3. Do you think that, according to Jeffrie Murphy, forgiveness can ever be justified in the absence of repentance by the wrongdoer?

---

[18]From "Autumn" by Rainer Maria Rilke in his *The Book of Images*, translated by Edward Snow. New York: Farrar, Straus, and Giroux, 1991.

[19]I came to see the value of this perspective when it was used by philosopher-theologian Marilyn Adams in her critique of some of my earlier writing on forgiveness. See Marilyn Adams, "Forgiveness: A Christian Model," *Faith and Philosophy*, Volume 8, Number 3, 1991, pp. 277–304. I have also recently come to see the wisdom in Herbert Morris's use of the thought of Simone Weil on these matters. See Herbert Morris and Jeffrie G. Murphy, "Exchange on Forgiveness," *Criminal Justice Ethics*, Volume 7, Number 2, 1988, pp. 3–22.

[20]Thus *Spoke Zarathrustra*, Second Part, "On the Tarantulas," in *The Portable Nietzsche*, trans. Walter Kaufmann, New York: Viking, 1970, p. 212. I pursue Nietzsche's thoughts on punishment in somewhat greater detail in my "Moral Epistemology, the Retributive Emotions, and the 'Clumsy Moral Philosophy' of Jesus Christ." supra note 1.

Forgiveness*

Norvin Richards

Norvin Richards rejects a common definition of forgiveness as the forswearing of resentment. On this view it is impossible to forgive somebody whom one does not resent but whose mistreatment of one has caused contempt, anger, or sadness instead. Thus, he says, the definition needs to be broadened to include the forswearing of other negative attitudes that one has toward those who mistreat one. But not every elimination of such negative attitudes can be forgiveness. It matters how and why the change in attitude occurs. To forget, for instance, is not to forgive.

Next the author considers the question of when we should forgive. He says that to have hard feelings of a particular degree of intensity for having been sub-jected to a particular mistreatment is an expression of one's character. To forgive, by overruling such feelings, expresses another part of one's character. Forgiveness is required when it overrules a flaw in one's character. By contrast, to overrule a feature of one's character that is acceptable is not required, but neither is it wrong, says the author. When forgiveness would overrule a trait that is essential to decent character, it would be wrong. He then responds to a popular contrasting view that is always wrong not to forgive. Finally, the author considers various reasons often given in particular circumstances for forgiving. These include excuses and good intentions, repentance, and "old times' sake."

What is it to forgive someone? What would be a good reason to do so? Could the reason be so good that one would be wrong not to forgive, or is forgiveness a gift one is always free to withhold?

The first section of this paper criticizes the standard definition of forgiveness and offers a replacement. The second sets out an approach to the moral

*I am greatly indebted to Scott Hestevold for many helpful discussions of this topic. This work was supported by University of Alabama research grant 1328.

Norvin Richards, "Forgiveness," *Ethics* 99 (October 1988): 77–93. Copyright 1988. Reprinted by permission of the University of Chicago Press.

questions. The third considers the place this approach finds for the usual reasons to forgive—repentance, old times' sake, and so on—and for some less usual reasons as well. . . .

I

In the following passage, Jeffrie Murphy opts for the account of forgiveness favored by most writers on the topic: "I shall . . . argue (following Bishop Butler) that forgiveness is the foreswearing of *resentment*—where resentment is a negative feeling (anger, hatred) directed toward another who has done one moral injury."[1] This conception ably distinguishes forgiving someone from merely forgetting what he did. And, since it makes forgiving a matter of controlling powerful emotions, it also explains why this can be a lengthy, effortful process, imperfectly successful or entirely beyond one's powers. Even so, I want to argue against it.

Notice, first, that it precludes forgiving anyone you do not first resent. Suppose that someone's especially treacherous behavior made you not resentful but contemptuous of her. Contempt is an abiding attitude, no less than resentment, but quite a different one: contempt is dismissive, in a way anger and hatred are not.[2] Since contempt is not resentment, if forgiving is *foreswearing* resentment it is impossible for you to forgive such a person. Of course, she might entreat you to view her differently, speaking perhaps of how sorry she was to have acted as she did, and her plea might move you. But it could not be forgiveness to which it moved you, according to the definition.

Similarly, it is possible for mistreatment to make one not angry or contemptuous but just very sad, if it is mistreatment at the hands of a loved one. Imagine, for example, that your grown son had badly let you down. This might make you angry, of course, but it might also make you feel deeply disappointed in him, instead. You are hurt that he should act in this way, not angry, not moved to hatred. Accordingly, if you were to abandon these feelings you would not be forgiving your son, on the definition in question, no matter how natural you and he might find it to say that you were, since you would not be abandoning an attitude of the specified kind. Again, the limitation seems arbitrary. It should also count as forgiveness to abandon negative feelings of these other kinds.

---

[1] Jeffrie Murphy, "Forgiveness and Resentment," *Midwest Studies in Philosophy*, vol. 7, ed. Peter French, Theodore Uehling, and Howard Wettstein (Minneapolis: University of Minnesota Press, 1982) p. 504. See also R. J. O'Shaughnessy, "Forgiveness," *Philosophy* 42 (1967): 344; H. J. N. Horsbrugh, "Forgiveness," *Canadian Journal of Philosophy* 4 (1974): 271; Aurel Kolnai, "Forgiveness," *Proceedings of the Aristotelian Society* 74 (1973–74): 93 ff. (but see also p. 104, where forgiveness is defined as "re-acceptance"); Elizabeth Beardsley, "Understanding and Forgiveness," in *The Philosophy of Brand Blanshard*, ed. P. A. Schilpp (LaSalle, Ill.: Open Court, 1981), pp. 249–50, 252; Martin P. Golding, "Forgiveness and Regret," *Philosophical Forum* 16 (1984–85): 134.

[2] Certainly Murphy himself would accept the distinction. See, in particular, his agreement with Nietzsche that having contempt for someone is incompatible with resenting him (Murphy, "Forgiveness and Resentment," p. 505).

Finally, imagine a woman whose husband frequently belittles her in public. Most recently, he has done this in the company of some new acquaintances whose opinion was especially important to her. The episode has made her furious, and the anger has stayed with her. She seethes at the sight of her husband, entertains thoughts of violent revenge, and so on. However, such feelings and thoughts themselves distress her, for she believes we should always forgive those who wrong us, lest the Lord not forgive us our own misdeeds. So, she does her best to forgive her husband, and she does manage a certain shift in her emotions: she no longer wants to hit the man or to wring his neck. However, she can't seem to get any further than this. Now, the thought of him makes her laugh scornfully—and, sometimes, a little ruefully at herself as well, for putting up with such treatment all these years."What a contemptible pair!" she says to herself, and resolves to leave the man as a first act of self-respect.

Is this woman *forgiving* her husband? She does qualify under the definition, since she has foresworn hatred and anger, abandoning resentment through an act of will. But I doubt he would think he was being forgiven, as she ridiculed his urgings that things should return to "normal" and went on packing her bags. And I doubt that *she* should consider that she had forgiven him, either. After all, her efforts to do so were founded in the hope that God would later do for her as she did for her husband. Surely she does not hope the Lord will merely move from hating her to holding her in icy contempt? She wants an embrace, not a different kind of rejection.

Evidently, then, abandoning resentment does not constitute forgiving, because a person can stop resenting and still have a hostile attitude of another kind: here, the dismissive one of contempt. The earlier examples suggested that neither must it be resentment that one is forswearing: it should also count as forgiveness to abandon contempt for someone or disappointment in him. Taken together, these suggest that to forgive someone for having wronged one is to abandon all negative feelings toward this person, of whatever kind, insofar as such feelings are based on the episode in question.

One might have other reasons to take a dim view of him, of course. To forgive him for having done X is not to forgive him for everything he has done. So, we are not here equating forgiving with "re-accepting," as Kolnai is sometimes inclined to do.[3]

A broader difficulty with seeing forgiveness as reacceptance is that some wrongdoers were not "accepted" to begin with: there is no relationship to reestablish. Consider the stranger whose car drenches you with mud. Having seen this in her mirror, she stops to apologize, insists on paying your cleaning bill, and so on. Surely it is possible to forgive this woman, just as it would be if she were an equally repentant friend. But to call this "reaccepting" her or "reestablishing our relationship" is rather strained: there was no relationship, and there is none after she drives away.

This is not to deny that when, say, a husband wants his wife to forgive him he wants their relationship restored, wants things to be as if he had never

[3]Kolnai, p. 104.

misbehaved, and doesn't feel forgiven if they are not. Since there was a warm relationship prior to the misdeed, there will be many reasons for his wife to treat him with affection. If she is cool and distant instead, this will show that she has not forgiven him. For, if there really were no vestiges of the hard feelings founded on his one misstep, her behavior would be more affectionate. This is not because forgiveness is reacceptance, though, but because it amounts to abandoning all hard feelings founded on the incident, and her coolness shows she has not done that.

Thus far, we have widened the range of negative attitudes one can banish in an act of forgiveness but have put no restrictions on one's reasons for changing one's attitude. Regardless of why I change my attitude toward you, it will count as forgiving you. This is not quite right. Suppose that I do so as an act of mental hygiene. I am sick and tired of being so angry that my sleep is restless and my stomach upset. I resolve not to endure another day of it, and I manage, with professional help, to end this disruptive state of mind. Am I extending forgiveness to you in this instance?

It seems not, precisely because the process is so entirely self-absorbed. When we forgive we are concerned with other people, or with a more appropriate response to what they did. So we forgive them because they are genuinely sorry, or because we realize they were not malicious but only careless, or for the sake of the children, and so on. To change one's attitude entirely out of self-interest might be (sensibly) to forget what someone did, but it is not to forgive him for having done it.[4]

II

What about the moral questions concerning this banishing of hard feelings? When should one do this? When should one not? And, how strong are these "shoulds"?

My answers turn on viewing acts of forgiveness and refusals to forgive as displays of character. I follow the lead of ordinary practice here, as when we think a person hard for refusing to forgive a particular supplicant, or weak for continuing to forgive someone who continues quite relentlessly to mistreat him. My idea is to take this apparently natural approach much further.

It will turn out that some acts of forgiveness (and, some failures to forgive) do enact flaws of character, just as we think. That is important, since it is always at least prima facie wrong to enact a flaw of character, whether the flaw is cowardice, or arrogance, or something with no simple name. This is not the only thing that can be wrong with an action, of course, not is it always the worst thing.[5]

---

[4] This may be Jeffrie Murphy's point in following a similar example with this stipulation: "Forgiveness is not the overcoming of resentment *simpliciter*; it is rather this: to foreswear resentment on moral grounds" ("Forgiveness and Resentment," p. 506). I am grateful to Gary Watson for convincing me of the need for some such restriction.

[5] A model for combining an action's several moral credentials is offered in Norvin Richards, "Moral Symptoms," *Mind* 89 (1980): 49–66

Still, that behavior is, for instance, *arrogant* is a serious mark against it, and in lieu of unusual circumstances it is simply wrong to act arrogantly. In the same way, it is wrong to refuse to forgive when that enacts arrogance or some other flaw of character. And it is wrong to extend forgiveness when *that* does so.

On other occasions forgiving someone expresses a highly admirable trait of character, not a defect. Obviously, forgiving is not then wrong in the way described. But, neither would it be wrong *not* to forgive on such an occasion, just as it would not be wrong to fail to perform a rescue which demanded a true hero, for example. There are good reasons to do such deeds, and a person of a certain disposition will find them compelling, but no one is obliged to do them, no one acts wrongly in failing to do them. In the same way as the heroism is beyond duty, when forgiving requires a positive virtue it is admirable to do but not wrong to omit.

What determines whether forgiving (or failing to forgive) would enact a virtue or a defect of character? As we have seen, to forgive someone for something is to abandon all the hard feelings one bases on this particular episode. Were this positive effort not made, the feelings would continue. Their presence, and their precise tendency to continue, is itself an expression of one's character. It is because of the sort of person you are that you are *this* angry with me for having done *that* to you.

Now, to forgive is to overrule this part of your character. The overruling expresses a different part of one's character: you are not only a person who will be this angry with me for having done that, you are also a person who will abandon such feelings in light of certain considerations (or, a person who will not). This second-level, self-regulatory part of one's character is what is in play in acts of forgiveness and refusals to forgive. When forgiving enacts a (self-regulatory) flaw of character, it is wrong to forgive; when it does not, it is not wrong to forgive. Similarly, a refusal to forgive is wrong if it enacts a flaw at this second, self-regulatory level, *not* wrong if it enacts a virtue or a neutral trait.

These matters will turn on what sort of character one would be overruling (or failing to overrule). There appear to be three possibilities.

1. It might be that in forgiving, you would overrule a flaw in your character. For example, perhaps your still hating me for the careless remark I made years ago expresses an intolerance for weakness in others, or a deep suspicion that people secretly dislike you, or some other trait without which your life would be a far happier one. The countertendency to overrule that unfortunate trait would at least diminish its impact, if not lead to your eventual reform. Thus the countertendency, expressed in forgiving, is itself a good trait. So, it would not be wrong to forgive on such an occasion—that is, to forgive would not enact a flaw of character.

What about refusing to forgive in such a case? This would amount to a disinclination to check what is (by hypothesis) a flaw in your character, either failing to see it as a flaw or being quite content to remain flawed in this particular way. That is itself a defect of character at a second level, it seems to me, at least where the first-level flaw is a relatively serious one. For one thing, it perpetuates the first-level flaw, increasing thereby its negative contributions to one's life. For another, to be blind to your serious flaws (or, content with them) adds an extra offensiveness of its own: an arrogance, a self-centeredness which is hard to swallow. In short, to refuse to overrule a (relatively serious) flaw is to enact a second flaw. That makes the refusal wrong: it is wrong not to forgive, when forgiving would abandon feelings which themselves express a (relatively serious) defect of character.

2. Alternatively, forgiving could overrule not a defect in one's character but something perfectly in order. Perhaps, for example, there is nothing at all wrong with taking remarks of the kind I once made as seriously as you do: we are not dealing with intolerance or paranoia on your part, but with a perfectly acceptable level of self-respect. If you were to have no tendency to overrule such feelings, that would hardly be a flaw in your character. It would serve to perpetuate, not a defect, but something perfectly acceptable. In short, to refuse to forgive would not be wrong in a case of this kind.

On the other hand, although it is not a flaw to be content with an acceptable feature of one's character, neither must it be a flaw to be dissatisfied with such a feature. Perhaps you aspire to be more than merely acceptably kind, or more generous than a person need be to rise above the miserly. Such aspirations need not collapse into narcissism or involve ignoring traits in a greater need of attention. Thus, the inclination to overrule an acceptable feature of character need not be a flaw. It needn't be wrong to forgive, then, when this overrules feelings it is perfectly acceptable to have. Nor, as noted earlier, is it wrong to decline to forgive, under those circumstances.

3. Finally, suppose that forgiveness would overrule a trait which is not merely acceptable but is essential to decent character: something it would be a defect to be without. Perhaps, for example, to feel no anger toward someone who had just swindled your aged mother out of her life's savings is like this. It is not merely "perfectly acceptable" to be angry at the swindler, that is: there is something wrong with you if you are not.

The inclination to banish feelings without which one would not be a decent human being can hardly be a virtue. It fosters bad character, no less than being satisfied with bad traits one already has. Enacting such an inclination is enacting a flaw in one's character. In short, it is wrong to forgive, when doing so overrules a trait which it would be bad character to lack.

I believe that each of these categories has instances, and thus that it is sometimes wrong to forgive, sometimes wrong not to forgive, and sometimes admirable to forgive but acceptable not to do so. There is a powerful tradition which denies this, however, teaching that one is never wrong to forgive, and, indeed, always wrong not to do so. I will close this section by explaining why I do not find that view compelling.

The point in dispute is not whether people of good character should be repelled by immoral behavior: both sides will agree that they should. Moral wrongs themselves are rather evanescent, however; they cease to exist once they are done. Hard feelings toward the wrongdoer serve to express one's feelings about the (now completed) wrong. In my view, there is nothing inappropriate about this. On the opposing view, there is: one should always hate the sin, but never the sinner.

Why not? Well, such feelings do have costs. They can be distressing, they can preclude certain close relationships, and they can dominate a person's life. However, it would be a mistake to conclude that they *must* be costly on balance. For one thing, there simply are people against whom it is better to be on one's guard, and there are pairs of people who seem to bring out the worst in each other if they attempt a close relationship. For another, it is a considerable exaggeration to think that unless we forgive we must burn with resentment, our lives consumed by bitter feelings and angry schemes. Resentment is a disposition which varies considerably in its intensity and in the length of its natural tenure. And, as Bishop Butler pointed out, some levels of resentment are perfectly compatible with a general good will toward the wrongdoer.[6] (Think here of the parent who is angry at a child for disobeying, but is certainly not transformed into a spiteful, single-minded avenger unless moved to forgiveness.)

Notice too that when we do hate the sinner, as well as the sin, we are not indulging some isolated quirk but are implementing a broad feature of human psychology. If you had been assaulted, you would feel differently not only about the person who assaulted you but also about the place in which the assault occurred and, perhaps, about a particular instrument your assailant used. The park where you loved to ramble would become a place you dreaded. Similarly, suppose you had been attacked in you own home, with your own kitchen knife. You would scarcely return it to the drawer with the others as just the thing for carving this year's turkey. Instead, the very sight of it would distress you, and the idea of using it would be repugnant. Are we only wrong to change our feelings toward wrongdoers, on the view that we must always forgive, or are we also wrong to feel differently about places and instruments? Neither answer seems particularly attractive.

Instead, how strongly you are repelled by the places, instruments, and agents of a harm is one measure of how bad a thing it was for you. How long such feelings last is another. There is a basis here for speaking of such feelings as in keeping with what happened, or as out of proportion to it. That would provide a way of speaking about your character, of judging that you take deeds of the kind in question as a person of good character would, or, that you do not. Such judgments make important points about us, it seems to me: points that are lost in thinking that good character simply requires immediate forgiveness on every occasion.

III

What place have the various standard reasons for forgiving, if we take the approach I have suggested? The pleas commonly offered are strikingly different. Some invoke special features of the misbehavior: it wasn't meant to turn out as it did; or, it was intentional but really only a rather minor misdeed; and so on. Other reasons ask that the deed be taken in a certain context: it was bad

[6]Joseph Buttler, "Upon Forgiveness of Injuries," in *The Works of the Right Reverend Father in God, Joseph Butler, D.C.L, Late Bishop of Durham*, ed. Samuel Halifax (New York: Carter, 1846), pp. 106–7. See also William R. Neblett, "Forgiveness and Ideals," *Mind* 73 (1974): 270.

behavior, but she's your oldest friend; or, you've treated her this way yourself, quite often; and so on. Still others emphasize new developments: the wrong-doer is now very distressed over the way she acted, despises herself for it, and hopes you'll forgive her.

Often, the person seeking forgiveness is able to offer several of these reasons at once. Certain of them go together in a way, strengthening each other: *since* she's an old friend she probably is *genuinely* sorry for what she's done . . . But the more basic question is why each is itself a reason to forgive. So, it will be better to consider each in turn, as if it were the only consideration put forward.

A. Excuses and Good Intentions

In his sermon, "Upon Forgiveness of Injuries," Bishop Butler maintains that we very seldom injure each other out of malice. Nearly, always, says he, the harm is not done purposely but through ignorance or inadvertence.[7] Perhaps he is right about this. What is of current interest, though, is that he regards these excuses as reasons to forgive: he thinks the fact that you were wronged inadvertently or through a misunderstanding ought to change your feelings about the wrongdoer.

It might be replied that although such discoveries could call for a change in one's feelings, they could not call for forgiveness. The argument would run as follows. Excuses fall into two categories. Some are so good as to mean the 'wrongdoer' was not at all responsible for what befell the victim. In that case, there is nothing for the 'victim' to forgive this particular person. Such excuses are not reasons to forgive, exactly, but reasons to stop acting as if one had been wronged.

Jeffrie Murphy writes as if all excuses were of this kind: "To excuse is to say this: What was done was morally wrong; but, because of certain factors about the agent (e.g., insanity), it would be unfair to hold the wrongdoer responsible or blame him for the wrong action . . . we may forgive only that which it is initially proper to resent; and, if a person . . . was not responsible for what he did, there is *nothing to resent* (though perhaps much to be sad about."[8] But, although the insanity excuse perhaps does erase all responsibility, not every excuse is so powerful. Commonly, excuses do not exonerate but only mitigate by showing that one acted less badly than it appears. Since they do leave one having acted somewhat badly, could they perhaps be the reasons to forgive which Butler thought they were?

Again, it might be argued that they could not. To forgive someone for having wronged one is not merely to reduce the intensity of one's hard feelings but to abandon such feelings altogether (insofar as they are based on the incident in question). As we just noted, the excuse leaves it the case that the agent did wrong the person. But if so, the argument continues, hard feelings of *some* intensity are called for: to abandon them would be both a poor defense against

---

[7]Butler, p. 111.
[8]Murphy, "Forgiveness and Resentment," p. 506.

repetitions and a display of inadequate aversion to what was done. In short, only someone of bad character fails to resent a wrongdoer, and a wrongdoer with the common sort of excuse is still a wrongdoer. So, the argument concludes, the common sort of excuse cannot be a reason to forgive, any more than the exonerating excuse could be.

The flaw in this argument, I believe, is the premise that only someone of bad character fails to resent a wrongdoer. That is certainly a contention Murphy would advance, and it seems to appeal to R. S. Downie as well.[9] However, although perhaps it is tautological that one should be averse to any wrong, no matter how minor, it does not follow that this aversion should always find expression in sustained hard feelings toward the source of the wrong. Compare here the man who dislikes the beach because that is where he dropped his ice cream cone in the sand. There is certainly nothing wrong with his regretting having lost his cone, but these feelings about the beach should show that he takes its loss too seriously. Certainly, there is no appeal whatever in the idea that unless he continues to hate the beach, he does not take the loss of the cone as seriously as he should.

Similarly, suppose our man dropped his cone not because a bully viciously twisted his arm but because he was jostled by a careless teenager. The jostling is mistreatment, and one should be averse to being mistreated. But it does not follow that our man will exhibit bad character unless he continues to harbor bad feelings toward the teenager—unless he refuses to forgive him, that is.

The idea is that even if, as Murphy and Downie would urge, good character does require being averse to all forms of mistreatment, it might not require sustained hard feelings toward the sources of the minor kinds. Conceivably, an excuse could show that a misdeed was a very minor one. It would thereby provide a reason to abandon those unwarranted hard feelings without contradicting the intuition that one should always be averse to mistreatment.

We can add to this Bishop Butler's own ideas concerning why excuses are reasons to forgive. Mistake, inadvertence, and so forth "we ought all to be disposed to excuse in others, *from experiencing so much of them in ourselves.*"[10] Tu quoque: but, why should this be a reason to forgive when the deed is done to me? Well, either I am also hard on myself for this same behavior, or I am not. To be hard on myself (as well as on others) over even minor mistakes and inadvertencies amounts to a broad intolerance of human limitations. No one can meet my expectations, since I expect perfection, and this must make me a very impatient, frustrated, and generally objectionable fellow.

Alternatively, suppose I am not hard on myself for minor bungles, but only on others. This suggests that I am not actually averse to the wrong as such but to my being wronged (however slightly) myself. Here I am flawed in a different way. I take myself too seriously, and I draw in my own favor a distinction without a relevant difference.

---

[9]Ibid., p. 505; R. S. Downie, "Forgiveness," *Philosophical Quarterly*, vol. 15 (1965).
[10] Butler, p. 111 (emphasis added).

In short, not to forgive minor misbehavior to which one is oneself prone exhibits either a general intolerance of human frailty or an unwarranted exaltation of oneself. It is wrong to enact either trait, for both are flaws of character. Thus, it is wrong not to forgive a person whose excuse makes the misdeed a minor one of a kind to which one is prone oneself.

Let me note that although this argument makes use of Bishop Butler's thinking concerning excuses, it does not reach as sweeping a conclusion as he did. He believed we should always forgive those who had excuses for wronging us (which, in his view, covered virtually everyone who did so). However, not all excuses do reduce the wrong done to a minor misstep of a kind to which one is prone oneself. Some only reduce murder to manslaughter, for example. Unlike Bishop Butler, then, my argument takes only some excuses to be reasons to forgive.

The fact that the wrongdoer had your best interest at heart appears to function in the same way. His good intentions can reduce the behavior to something trivial and familiar, and then they are a reason to forgive. But they can also fail to effect such a reduction, and then they provide no reason to forgive. Murphy, in contrast, sharply distinguishes excuses (which he believes cannot be reasons to forgive) from paternalistic motives (which he believes can be). His discussion of paternalistic motives, however, supports the idea that they are reasons to forgive only insofar as they effect the reduction I have described:

> A person who interferes with my liberty for what he thinks is my own good is, in my judgement, acting wrongly. . . . His grounds for interfering, however, are well-meaning (i.e., he seeks to do me good) even if his actions are misguided and morally insensitive. . . . It is hard to view the friend who locks up my liquor cabinet because he knows I drink too much as on the same moral level as the person who embezzles my funds for his own benefit; and thus the case for forgiving the former may have some merit.[11]

Again, just as not all excuses make misbehavior sufficiently minor that it ought to be forgiven, neither do all realizations that the behavior was only "misguided and morally insensitive" paternalism. Some acts of paternalism remain sufficiently serious mistreatments that it is certainly not bad character to take them sufficiently seriously to hold them against their perpetrators. So, it will not always be wrong not to be moved to forgiveness by the news that a certain person meant to be acting in your own best interest.

On the other hand, neither must it be bad character to accept another's effort to look after one. A fierce independence is hardly the only alternative to spinelessness. So, it can also reflect perfectly acceptable character to forgive someone who (after all) only meant to help.

B. Repentance

So far, we have been focusing on pleas that one's behavior was not really bad enough to merit the victim's attitude. It is a different move altogether to agree that the behavior was very bad and ask to be forgiven because one now *repents*.

---

[11]Murphy, "Forgiveness and Resentment," p. 509.

Repentance is perhaps the most familiar of the grounds for forgiveness. The question is, why should it work? What is it about the wrongdoer's repenting that justifies (or even mandates) forgiving him?

Actually, I think, repentance can present appeals of two distinct kinds. At least some forms of repentance involve a change in the wrongdoer from someone who saw nothing wrong with mistreating you in a certain way to someone who joins you in condemning that behavior. This alone might seem to make hard feelings against him rather pointless and forgiveness the only reasonable course.

Murphy and Kolnai both testify to the attractiveness of this line of thinking, though neither accepts it in the end. [12] There are two good reasons not to. First, repentance does not guarantee that there will be no future misbehavior. It is always possible that the wrongdoer will revert to his earlier views, or be vulnerable to temptations to violate his new ones. There might also be forms of behavior which his new view does not condemn but against which a general vigilance would provide a defense. (Think here of someone who now agrees that it was wrong to lie to you as he did but still has nothing against a very broad range of deceptive practices.) Since repentance thus does not obviate the need for defensive postures, it does not mandate forgiveness.

Second, the question whether to forgive does not turn entirely on whether defenses against repetition are needed. If it did, one would always be wrong not to forgive a villain who had passed out of one's life: the rapist who was killed while escaping, for example, or the embezzler using your funds to dwell happily in Brazil. Such people are not future threat to you. But, the fact remains that they have done you wrong, and that issues its own call for hard feelings against them.

Wouldn't the same be true of the wrongdoer who was very much at hand, but now repentant? Just like the rapist and the embezzler, even if such a person poses not future threat, he remains someone who did you wrong. That is a second reason to resent him, which is not erased by his repentance. Thus the change undergone in repenting does not render hard feelings pointless after all and does not mandate forgiveness.

It does accomplish something less dramatic, however. It provides a reason to forgive repenters who have changed in the way described. It makes forgiving them an option appealing to persons with one sort of good character: it makes forgiveness morally permissible. How it does this requires a bit of explanation.

First, to repent in the way I have been discussing it is not merely to have newly negative feelings about what one had done, but to have these feelings as part of a change in one's moral views. To know all along that one is misbehaving and only have misgivings about it the next day does not qualify. Rather, we are speaking here of the person who has "seen the light," who has come to disapprove of a kind of behavior which she had thought of as perfectly permissible. A new moral principle is acquired, or there is a new realization that her old principles are inconsistent and that her behavior violated the more important of them.

Now, in such a case, the wrongdoer's permissive former principles are one reason why she acted as she did: she did it, in part, because she did not think it

---

[12]Ibid., p. 511; Kolnai, pp. 101–2.

wrong to do. So, a change in her views would be a change in something which was partly responsible for the wrong. Her repentance is thus like repairing that part of a house which contributed to an accident. The child took a nasty fall right here, in part because the steps were uneven, but now I have fixed them; I shouted at the secretary in part because I did not think there was anything wrong with shouting at secretaries, but now I realize that there is.

Despite the change, this is still the house where the child fell and I am still the person who shouted at the secretary. So, there is still a question whether the victims ought not to have hard feelings in both cases. However, there has been a change in them qua source of suffering; there has been a replacement of (part of) what was responsible for the suffering with something which promises to be harmless. Accordingly, there would be nothing amiss in the association being broken—in the child feeling good about the house again, or in the secretary dropping her resentment of me now that I am (clearly) more respectful of her. Forgiveness has become a permissible option with appeal to persons of perfectly good character, rather than something which shows a failure to take the episode as seriously as one should, because the wrongdoer has changed something about himself which contributed to the wrong.

On the other hand, neither would there be anything amiss in the hard feelings continuing, despite the repairs to the stairs and to the wrongdoer's moral views. For one thing, it might not be so clear that the flaw has been repaired, particularly where this consists in reforming one's moral views. (Hence the significance of the allegedly repentant person's apologies, efforts to "make up for it," to be on especially good behavior, and so on.) For another, it might be that the harm was too serious for the change to relieve one's other associations between this person (that face, those hands, that smirk) and what she did to you, despite those features having not even partly caused the harm. So, there needn't be a flaw of character in being unmoved by the change in the repentant person, any more than there must be one in being so moved. On the view I am offering, it is permissible either to forgive or not to do so.

That brings us to the second way in which someone's repentance might provide a good reason to extend forgiveness: a way which applies not only to those who have undergone moral reformation but also to those who knew all along they were misbehaving, and whose repentance consists in their later feeling very sorry. Part of both scenes is emotional: remorse over what was done before the change occurred. In the classic description the repentant wrongdoer is contrite, or "bruised in the heart."

Exactly why the victim's forgiveness should relieve the pain of remorse is somewhat curious, especially if one takes the view that wrongdoing is an offense not just against its most obvious victim but against an abstract moral order and/or against all who refrain from the misbehavior.[13] Perhaps what

---

[13]See, e.g., J. Finnis, "The Restoration of Retribution," *Analysis* 32 (1972): 131–35 (Finnis attributes the view to Thomas Aquinas, as well as advancing it himself); Herbert Morris, "Persons and Punishment," reprinted in *Punishment and Rehabilitation*, ed. Jeffrie Murphy (Belmont, Calif.: Wadsworth,

bothers us about having done wrong is not the abstract fact that we have done it, but the fact that a particular person has suffered a wrong at our hands.

At any rate, the fact is that repentant wrongdoers are pained by their victims' hard feelings toward them. They are unhappy, sometimes deeply so, in a way which the victim could relieve by extending forgiveness. That is a reason to grant the forgiveness: an appeal to the victim's compassion for someone he can rescue from unhappiness. Of course, sometimes the rescue is enormously difficult, because the offense was deeply aversive to the victim and occurred quite recently. Moreover, sometimes the forgiveness seems unlikely to do the wrongdoer all that much good. Perhaps his unhappiness over the misdeed is genuine but not terribly deep, and seems likely to pass of its own accord before too long; and, perhaps it would do him good to suffer over this a bit longer. So there are surely times when there would be nothing wrong with being unmoved by the appeal the repentant person makes to one's compassion.

By the same token, however, generally speaking there are also times when there *is* something wrong with being unmoved by an appeal to one's compassion. Imagine that it would be quite easy to relieve considerable suffering, as when a single word from you would save the postman from a vicious dog. Wouldn't you be very wrong not to say the word? Shall we say that you would also be wrong not to forgive whenever a single word from you would rescue the wrongdoer from agonies of remorse?

I think not. The postman is simply an object of compassion. The wrongdoer is something more: a wrongdoer. The postman's troubles befell him through no fault of his. The wrongdoer is suffering because he did you wrong. You have thereby a reason not to be compassionate toward him, which you do not have regarding the poor postman.

That is enough, I think, to justify rejecting the idea that it is simply heartless to withhold forgiveness from anyone who is genuinely repentant. The reply is that it is not heartless to resist their appeal to one's compassion because they are not simply objects of compassion. However, it is worth considering more closely why their past behavior does make them so different and why compassion should not simply overrule this further consideration.

There is one (ultimately mistaken) account of this with considerable initial appeal. According to it, the key difference between the postman and the wrongdoer is that the latter deserves his current unhappiness. To leave him to stew in his own juice will not be simply uncompassionate but will be an exercise of your sense of justice. As Butler urged, it is absolutely vital that we have a firm sense of justice to supplement our tender feelings of compassion.[14]

However, there is a certain awkwardness in thinking of hard feelings as penalties one imposes in the interest of justice, on the same order as fines and

---

1973), esp. pp. 43 ff.; Herbert Morris, *Guilt and Innocence* (Berkley: University of California Press, 1976), esp. pp. 33–34; M. P. Golding, *Philosophy of Law* (Englewood Cliffs, N. J.: Prentice-Hall, 1975), p. 92; Jeffrie Murphy, "Three Mistakes about Retributivism," reprinted in his *Retribution, Justice, and Therapy* (Dordrecht: Reidel, 1979).

[14]Butler, "Upon Resentment," in *The Works of the Right Reverend Father in God*, pp. 99–100.

imprisonments. They seem instead to be natural consequences of the misbehavior. The victim's resentment is rather like the sore muscles and occasional scratches which a mugger might find to be occupational hazards. Certainly we feel no sympathy for the thug who gets sore or scratched in the process of mugging, and we might express that by saying he "had it coming," or that it was "no worse than he deserved," just as we say such things about the victim's hating him. There's even something satisfying about his having come by these aches and pains in the process of his wrongdoing. But, this is not to say such things are part of what a person deserves for mugging. We are not in the least inclined to have scratches and soreness imposed on muggers who do not suffer these in plying their trade, or to reduce the sentences of other muggers on the ground that (after all) they are scratched and sore. Rather, we treat these as extra misfortunes which we are not sorry the mugger suffers. It is just so, I am suggesting, with any regrets he suffers over his victim's hard feelings for him.

If we do stop thinking of the hard feelings as deserved penalties, however, how will we explain why the wrongdoer's having wronged us matters? How will we explain, that is, why his misbehavior distinguishes him from the simple object of compassion, such as the mailman whom it would be wrong not to save from the vicious dog?

The explanation I want to develop begins from the premise that we are right to be averse to what happens to us when we are wronged and, when the wrong is not trivial, to express this aversion in hard feelings toward its source. The fact is that there is a degree of incompatibility between having hard feelings toward someone and being moved by that person's suffering to go to his or her aid. If I hate a certain man, the news that he is having some minor misfortune does not make me unhappy and might even provide a certain satisfaction. I need not be proud of this—I might wish to be kinder or more generous. Still, part of hating him is wanting him not to flourish, just as part of liking someone is wanting that person to fare well. One measure of the strength of my hatred is the point at which I begin to sympathize instead. Another is the point at which my sympathies are sufficiently strong that I will exert myself to relieve this person's plight, despite disliking him.

Now, suppose that my hard feelings are not merely present, but are called for by his having wronged me, and that my imperviousness to his plight expresses those hard feelings. Then, that imperviousness is also not just present, but called for. His having wronged me is a reason not to go to his aid—it makes him not simply an object of compassion, like the postman under attack from the dog.

Of course, this does not collapse into saying that his having wronged me means I should never be moved by his troubles, no matter how grave they are or what form his mistreatment of me took. The claim is only that to be victimized by someone creates a perfectly proper obstacle to compassion toward that person. How substantial an obstacle it *should* create would largely depend on how grave the mistreatment was. (I think it would also depend, to some extent, on how recently the wrong was committed: at least some feelings should lessen in intensity as time passes.) How substantial an obstacle it *would* create would depend instead on how aversive the event was for the victim, which is quite another thing. It is obviously possible to take something more seriously than one should, and thus to be impervious to suffering that should move one.

I have argued that even though a repentant wrongdoer does make an appeal to compassion, it is not necessarily a flaw of character to be unmoved to forgiveness, even if it would be easy for you to forgive and a great relief to him. Depending on how badly he acted and how recently, it might be a flaw of character if you *were* moved. Thus, there are times when it would be wrong to forgive such people, but this is not because even repentant wrongdoers deserve to suffer one's wrath. It is because even repentant wrongdoers are wrongdoers, hard feelings are called for toward wrongdoers as sources of wrong, and hard feelings are incompatible with a certain degree of compassion.

Although it is thus sometimes wrong to respond sympathetically to the repentant wrongdoer, by the same reasoning it is also sometimes wrong not to. Suppose the wrong was done long ago and was not extremely serious, and it is quite plain by now that the wrongdoer has undergone a change of character and that your forgiveness would be a considerable relief to him. As Murphy urges, it is possible to take too lightly oneself and the wrong done to one; but, it seems to me, it must also be possible to take these too seriously. I have just sketched what would be involved in doing so.

Between these extremes lies the broad range of cases in which the wrong was neither dreadful nor trivial and happened neither a few minutes nor a few years ago, and over which the (apparently) repentant wrongdoer is remorseful but not devastated. Within this range it is neither wrong to forgive nor wrong not to do so. As Kolnai so nicely puts it, here forgiveness is "a venture of trust"—a venture not always equal in its risks.

C. Old Times' Sake

> I will forgive the person who has willfully wronged me because . . . of old times' sake (e.g., "He has been a good and loyal friend to me in the past").[15]
>
> *Old Times' Sake.* As with repentance we have here a clear case of divorce of act from agent. When you are repentant, I forgive you for what you *now are.* When I forgive you for old times' sake, I forgive you for what you *once were.* Much of our forgiveness of old friends and parents, for example, is of this sort.[16]

Although Murphy says here that we can properly forgive people for old times' sake, for what they once were to us, he does virtually nothing to explain why. Why should your having "been a good and loyal friend to me in the past" be a reason to forgive you for wronging me, rather than something which deepens the hurt? Does it matter whether you had been my friend at least until this episode, or are only someone to whom I was once close, long ago? What, if anything, is it about past or present friendly relationships that provides a reason to forgive?

Suppose we begin with the current friend. Such a person is entitled to have her actions interpreted with a certain generosity, it seems to me. It isn't only that

---

[15]Murphy, "Forgiveness and Resentment," p. 508.
[16]Ibid., p. 510.

one should not be positively suspicious of one's friends, expecting the worst of them. More than that, they should have the benefit of the doubt. Even when it does appear they have mistreated you, your inclination should be to disbelieve the appearances. To regard someone as a friend is to trust that this person wishes you well and thus would not have acted as it seems. To be incapable of such trust, of regarding people as friends, is a serious failing.

In my view, this means it is sometimes morally wrong not to disbelieve the evidence that a certain person has mistreated you. That is not a point about forgiving friends, however, but one about assuming that there is nothing to forgive. Your friend is entitled to the assumption that she has not wronged you—but that differs from her being entitled to your forgiveness when, in fact, you know that she has wronged you.

Perhaps we can bring the two together in the following fashion. Part of someone's being your friend is her wishing you well. Part of that is being especially averse to doing you ill. If such a person has wronged you, it is safe to assume there must have been some powerful reason for it, or that she did not fully understand what she was doing. And, it is also safe to assume that she is now quite unhappy over what she has done, in a way your could relieve by extending your forgiveness.

In short, her being a friend is a reason to suppose that you have one of the *other* reasons to forgive her. That is not the same as "old times' sake" being a reason in itself, of course. And, it is less compelling for the merely former friend than for the current one. Still, evidently someone's being your friend can be indirectly a reason to extend forgiveness, and that is at least a role for old times to play.

Consider next this stronger argument. Throughout, I have contended that a person ought to be averse not only to wrongs but to the sources of (nontrivial) wrongs. It seems equally plausible to hold that one should have positive feelings toward morally good actions and toward the sources of such actions, at least insofar as the actions are beyond minimally good behavior. Friendships involve many such actions—the doing of favors, small and sometimes large sacrifices of self-interest, and so on. Hence, one ought to have good will toward a friend, by virtue of the events constituting the friendship, just as one ought to have hard feelings toward a villain, as an expression of one's aversion to what the villain has done to one.

Earlier, it was suggested that hard feelings are incompatible with being easily moved to sympathy. By the same token, wouldn't warm feelings be incompatible with being easily moved to hostility? If so, a part of the good will which a past friendly relationship should have engendered would call for not taking offense at a certain range of wrongs. You simply would not be resentful over such matters if your friends meant what they should to you.

On finding that you *were* resentful, your proper course would be to strive to banish such feelings straightaway—to extend forgiveness, that is. Anyone who did not do this would show an inability to appreciate friends for their kindness and affection—an inability which would surely impoverish life in many ways. In other words, it would be bad character not to forgive a friend a certain range of small wrongs, just because he or she was your friend.

This is certainly not an argument that one should forgive a friend everything. The idea is that friendship is incompatible with being easily provoked to hostility, which suggests that the deeper the friendship, the more tolerant one should be. That does not deny that there is behavior so egregious that one's warm feelings should be overcome. . . .

Questions

1. How does Norvin Richards respond to the view that it is always wrong not to forgive? Do you think his response is adequate? Do you think that forgiving can sometimes be wrong?
2. When does the author think it is wrong not to forgive somebody for whose wrongdoing there is an excuse?
3. Two reasons are mentioned for not forgiving the repentent. What are they?
4. When, if ever, is "old times' sake" a good reason to forgive somebody?

Moral Anger, Forgiving, and Condoning

Paul M. Hughes

Moral anger, says Paul Hughes, is what Peter Strawson calls a "reactive attitude" and is characterized in part by the belief that a moral subject has been wrongfully harmed. Moral anger is personal *when it is aroused by a wrong done to the self, and it is* vicarious *when it arises in response to a wrong done to another. Resentment, unlike other reactive attitudes such as indignation, wrath, hatred, and ill will, cannot be vicarious, the author says. Renouncing personal moral anger, in his view, is an essential part of what forgiving is, but other conditions also have to be met. These include: (a) the reason for renunciation of moral anger must be compatible with morality; (b) the renunciation must involve self-activity or effort (overcoming moral anger by taking drugs, for example, is not forgiveness); (c) the belief that one has been wrongfully harmed must be* true;

(d) the moral anger one overcomes must be directed against a moral agent; (e) although typically it is resentment that will be overcome, other forms of moral anger might be renounced (sometimes instead of resentment).

The author recognizes that there may be forms of moral reactive attitudes to wrongdoing that are not anger. Forgiveness, he says, may involve renouncing (some of) these, but it does not require it. Although moral anger is also overcome when one condones *an action, condoning, argues the author, is usually distinct from forgiving. He argues that when condoning is indistinguishable from forgiveness it is unvirtuous because in such circumstances it is done for reasons that are incompatible with the demands of morality.*

INTRODUCTION

Forgiving wrongdoing is at least sometimes a virtue, while condoning it is usually thought to be a vice. Both may be strategies for dealing with anger, a

Paul Hughes, "Moral Anger, Forgiving, and Condoning," *Journal of Social Philosophy*, vol. 25, no. 1 (spring 1995) 103–118. Copyright 1995. Reprinted by permission of *Journal of Social Philosophy*.

morally important emotion that has been given little attention by contemporary moral philosophers.

In this essay I seek to clarify forgiving and condoning and their relationship to anger. Specifically, I argue that an important type of forgiving involves overcoming *moral anger* directed toward a wrongdoer. But condoning may also involve overcoming moral anger aimed at an offender, and to this extent condoning resembles forgiving. Moreover, condoning is routinely defined as a kind of forgiving,[1] and people frequently caution one another against excessive forgiving; as if forgiveness admits of some limit beyond which it becomes condonation or some comparable vice. The underlying truth upon which such warnings are based is surely the recognition that renouncing moral anger directed at a wrongdoer sometimes amounts to collusion with evil. These considerations suggest that because forgiving and condoning are ambiguous, overlapping notions, they may at times be conceptually and morally indistinguishable. I suggest that a sufficiently fine grained account of more anger is the key to clarifying whether and in what sense this is ever the case.

I. MORAL ANGER AND MORAL SUBJECTS

Anger is a reactive attitude. P. F. Strawson argues that reactive attitudes are "human reactions to the good or ill will or indifference of others towards us, as displayed in *their* attitudes and action." Further, reactive attitudes involve personal feelings which "depend upon, or involve" our beliefs about the attitudes, intentions, and actions of others towards us.[2] For example, gratitude is a reactive attitude typically felt toward another you believe intended to help you out. By contrast, gratitude is not typically felt toward those who benefit you inadvertently, for accidental benefits bespeak nothing in particular about the benefactor's feelings or attitudes toward you. Similarly, resentment is a reactive attitude typically felt toward another you believe has wrongfully harmed you, while it is not usually felt toward those who harm you accidentally.[3] There are

---

[1]The *Oxford English Dictionary* (Second Edition, Volume III, p. 688) defines *condone* as "to forgive or overlook (an offense) so as to treat it as non-existent; especially to forgive tacitly by not allowing the offense to make any difference in one's relations with the offender," while Webster's *Third New International Dictionary* (1986, p. 473) defines *condonable* as "excusable" or "forgivable"; and *condonation* as "pardon of an offense; voluntary overlooking or implied forgiveness of an offense by treating the offender as if it had not been committed."

[2]P. F. Strawson, *Freedom and Resentment*, Methuen, 1974, p. 10. Note that Strawson's conception of reactive attitudes does not account for cases of anger that do not involve beliefs about others. Bishop Butler, however, distinguishes between "hasty and sudden" and "settled and deliberate" anger, and claims that the former is connected to the impulse for self-preservation and has nothing to do with beliefs about how others perceive or treat us. For reasons that will become clear presently, I consider this to be a type of non-moral anger that even infants and, perhaps, some higher animals are capable of experiencing. See Bishop Joseph Butler, *Fifteen Sermons Preached at Rolls Chapel* (London, 1726); Sermon VIII, "Upon Resentment."

[3]I am speaking here of one common form of resentment. See Butler, *op. cit.* The Nietzschean notion of *ressentiment*, a type of resentment grounded by envy, is an altogether different concept.

many reactive attitudes, both positive and negative, but as the following considerations make clear, only a relatively small set of such attitudes count as *moral anger*.

Sophisticated reactive attitudes such as resentment, humiliation, or guilt are recognizable by virtue of the beliefs that partially constitute them. Such indentificatory beliefs are essential for the intelligibility of any complex reactive attitude, and they enable us not only to recognize, say, humiliation for what it is, but to distinguish it from similar, though different, emotions, such as embarrassment or shame. My contention is that moral anger is a reactive attitude characterized in part by the belief that a moral subject has been wrongfully harmed. A *moral subject* is anything that has moral standing, that is, anything that is vested with moral rights, interests, or claims to respect. Thus, individuals, groups of persons, animals, and perhaps (other parts of) the natural environment are moral subjects, and moral anger may be aroused for the sake of any of them. When moral anger is generated primarily on behalf of one's self, it is *personal* moral anger; when it is aroused primarily for the sake of moral subjects other than the self, it is *vicarious* moral anger.[4]

Resentment, indignation, wrath, hatred, and ill will are reactive attitudes that are potential forms of personal moral anger. But while you may be indignant over an injustice done to another, furious with your spouse, hate ware and poverty, and display a generalized animosity toward all persons, only resentment necessarily involves the belief that you have been wrongfully harmed. That is, the belief that *you* have been wrongfully harmed is a necessary condition of resentment, while in other reactive attitudes it is not. This difference between resentment and other angry or disapproving attitudes emerges clearly when we examine more closely what is at issue in each case.

Ill will need not be directed toward others you believe have caused you harm. Literature is replete with misanthropes whose general animosity toward all human beings is legendary, yet these characters need not regard the whole of mankind as either potentially or actually harmful to themselves in any way.

What of hatred? The objects of hate are, indeed, numerous. One may hate many things or people, but again it is surely not the case that in order to hate you must regard the hated object as actually or even potentially harmful to yourself. You may, for example hate apartheid or any system of racial segregation, and yet believe that such systems have benefited rather than harmed you. Or you may hate the stubbornness of a friend or a political idea or rainy days in

---

[4]This account of moral anger is oversimplified. Moral anger is anger partially constituted by the belief that a moral subject has been (a) wrongfully harmed, or (b) wrongfully put at the risk of harm, or (c) has been or is the object of an intended wrongful harm or has been or is the object of an intended wrongful risk of harm. These complex qualifications are needed to fully articulate the possible constitutive beliefs of moral anger. Moreover, these beliefs are only "partially" constitutive of moral anger, for any one of them is but a necessary condition of moral anger. The "feelings" which partly constitute the emotion must be present as well. For more on the background theory of emotions I rely upon in my analysis of moral anger see Gabriele Taylor, *Pride, Shame, and Guilt: Emotions of Self Assessment*, (Oxford, 1988).

San Francisco. None of these cases of hate need involve the belief that you have been harmed.[5]

Moreover, rage, fury, or wrath need not involve the belief that you have been harmed, even though these reactive attitudes are varieties of anger. One may "fly into a rage," become furious with another, or have one's wrath inspired by many things, yet such strong emotional episodes may occur even though you believe you have not been harmed, or are in any danger of being harmed. People are notorious for flying into a rage for reasons even they regard as of no moral significance. Thus, this sort of sudden anger is frequently *non-moral* anger.

Finally, isn't indignation, necessarily, directed toward those persons, things, or events you believe have harmed you? This is clearly not the case, for one may become indignant over the maltreatment of another, as for example when one witnesses an injustice done to a stranger. It may be tempting to think of such cases as involving harm to the self, since there is a sense in which an injustice done to one is an injustice done to all. But this construal of indignation renders it fundamentally self regarding, and robs that emotion of its "other-directed" nature in many cases. When I learn that an innocent vagrant has been framed by the authorities for the murder of the prominent politician, I boil with indignation not because this despicable event has harmed me, but because that other person has suffered unjust treatment. I am not, in other words, always indignant because of *my* suffering, real, potential or imagined, but sometimes because of another's suffering.

The point of these examples is to show that an essential difference between resentment and other reactive attitudes, including other forms of anger, is that the belief that you have been wrongfully harmed is not a necessary condition of these other attitudes. You cannot, however, experience resentment without believing that you have been wrongfully harmed. Resentment is, therefore, a central case of *personal* moral anger precisely because it necessarily involves this belief.[6]

But while resentment is a central case of personal moral anger, it is not the only case. Personal moral anger ranges over other kinds of anger so long as the belief that you have been wrongfully harmed is partly constitutive of them. If, for example, I become indignant over a wrong done to me, then my indignation is personal moral anger. In general, any form of anger that is partially constituted by the belief that you have been wrongfully harmed counts as personal moral anger. Thus, the essential difference between personal moral anger and

[5]Strictly speaking, hatred is not a form of anger, though it may involve the belief that you have been wrongfully harmed and therefore take a "moral" form. Cf. Jean Hampton's notion of "moral hatred" in Jeffrie Murphy and Jean Hampton *Forgiveness and Mercy*, (Cambridge University Press, 1988), chapter 2.

[6]Howard McGary makes a similar point in claiming that resentment is necessarily "self pertaining" because its focus is, directly or indirectly, the self. Note also Strawsons' conception of resentment as a reactive attitude that serves to protect certain "values of the self." Howard McGary, "Forgiveness," *American Philosophical Quarterly* 26.4, October, 1989, pp. 343–350, and Strawson, *op.cit.*

other reactive attitudes, including other forms of (moral and nonmoral) anger is that the belief that you have been wrongfully harmed is not a necessary condition of these other attitudes.

It might be objected that since forms of anger other than personal moral anger *could* involve the belief that you have been wrongfully harmed, it is very difficult for this "belief condition" to be the essential difference between personal and other forms of (moral and nonmoral) anger.[7] In other words, the belief that you have been wrongfully harmed is a *necessary* condition of personal moral anger, but some forms of anger that only *contingently* involve this belief are said to be instances of personal moral anger. So how can a belief that is only contingently involved in anger mark an essential difference between personal and other forms of (moral and nonmoral) anger?

The fact that certain forms of anger are contingently, not necessarily, personal moral anger, may be odd in light of the claim that all personal moral anger necessarily involves the belief that you have been wrongfully harmed, but it is neither incoherent nor implausible. If an "essential" difference between X and Y is that which makes something an X but not a Y (and vice versa), then with respect to anger this is precisely the function served by the belief that you have been wrongfully harmed. It may be helpful to reiterate that one reason for articulating the difference between personal and other forms of (moral and nonmoral) anger in terms of the identificatory belief that you have been wrongfully harmed is to clarify the moral parameters of anger. For anger to be personal moral anger, its subject must be the self (a moral subject) while its object must be a perceived moral agent. The fact that resentment necessarily evidences this logical structure does not imply that other forms of anger cannot assume this structure; and the fact that forms of anger other than resentment only contingently involve this belief does not, so far as I can tell, pose any special problem for the theory I am propounding.[8]

II. PERSONAL MORAL ANGER AND FORGIVENESS

One common type of forgiveness involves overcoming personal moral anger; that is, anger directed toward another you believe has wrongfully harmed you. For example, suppose you find yourself on the receiving end of an insult, and you respond angrily. Upon learning that the author of the insult mistook you for someone else, you might renounce the personal moral anger you bear toward him, especially if he is apologetic. Renouncing personal moral anger is surely part of what is involved in forgiving.

---

[7] I am indebted to an anonymous reviewer of this journal for raising this issue.

[8] It must be acknowledged, of course, that not all cases of moral anger are unambiguously personal or vicarious, for the belief that you have been wrongfully harmed may coexist with the belief that other moral agents have been wrongfully harmed, or that you have been wrongfully harmed *because* other moral agents (e.g., your family, friends, colleagues) have been wrongfully harmed, and so forth, and these beliefs may be jointly involved in constituting one's moral anger.

But overcoming personal moral anger is not all that is involved in forgiving, for not just any manner of overcoming such anger counts as forgiveness. Two issues are germane here. First, forgiveness seems to require overcoming personal moral anger for a reason that is compatible with morality. Overcoming one's anger toward a repentant wrongdoer because he has apologized counts as forgiving for a reason that is *prima facie* compatible with the demands of morality, while renouncing one's anger simply to curry favor with a wrongdoer is not. Secondly, forgetting one's anger, or overcoming it via therapy, are not ways of renouncing anger that make for forgiveness, however beneficial they might be for those who bear the anger and those at whom it is aimed. This is because forgiving involves overcoming personal moral anger in the sense of conquering, overpowering, or prevailing over it, and these notions imply self-activity or effort. Examples of overcoming in this sense abound, as for instance when a person successfully overcomes a physical or mental handicap, or the untoward consequences of social and economic injustice, or the deleterious effects of an internalized stereotype. Forgiveness, therefore, presupposes an effort or struggle to get beyond one's personal moral anger.[9]

But overcoming personal moral anger, even when it involves a direct effort of will and is done for a moral reason, is still not sufficient for forgiveness, since personal moral anger may be grounded in the *false* belief that you have been wrongfully harmed. While the belief that you have been wrongfully harmed is a necessary condition of any sort of personal moral anger, forgiveness requires the *true* belief that you have been wrongfully harmed. This is important, for though it is possible to bear personal moral anger toward another one falsely believes has done one wrong, it is impossible to forgive someone for a wrong that was never committed. Consequently, one way of overcoming personal moral anger is to discover that the belief that you have been wrongfully harmed is false. But this way of overcoming personal moral anger is not forgiveness.[10]

The true belief that you have been wrongfully harmed presupposes that the cause of harm is a responsible agent, and this means that another condition of forgiveness is that personal moral anger must be directed a *moral agent*. Animals, small children, mental incompetents, and natural events like hurricanes do not count as moral agents, while mature adults and perhaps even nations, corporations, and other human collectives do. This notion of moral agency permits us to distinguish forgiveness from a variety of phenomena with which it is

[9]It should be noted that not all uses of psychotherapy, behavior modification, or other clinical psychological techniques for overcoming anger fall outside the pale of forgiveness. The use of such techniques *could* be involved in forgiving so long as they are part of one's attempt to forgive a perceived wrongdoer. This will depend in part on one's intentions *vis a vis* the wrongdoer and one's reasons for seeking professional help in an effort to manage one's anger. My point is that such techniques are often, perhaps typically, used to get rid of anger rather than to forgive wrongdoers (though such efforts may be an important first step in forgiving wrongdoers). See note 23 below.

[10]Bearing personal moral anger toward another one falsely believes has harmed one may itself amount to wrongfully harming that person, depending on whether the false belief was reasonably or unreasonably held. Furthermore, to claim to *forgive* another who has done nothing wrong is an insult, if in taking the moral high road one unjustly misrepresents the moral positions of the parties involved.

frequently confused. Specifically, forgiveness is often confused with justification, excuse, or mercy. It is none of these, since if a person has done nothing wrong (i.e., is justified in what she did), or is not responsible for what she did (i.e. has an excuse), then there is nothing at which to be morally angry, and therefore nothing to forgive.[11] Moreover, forgiveness is not the same as mercy, for one who has not been wronged can show mercy (e.g., a judge in dispensing punishment for a crime) in virtue of his position of authority (and mercy can even be shown in the absence of wrongdoing), but I cannot forgive another *for you*, no matter my position.[12] Furthermore, mercy is primarily a matter of how one person treats another, whereas forgiveness is essentially a matter of how one *feels* about another. Forgiveness, therefore, requires overcoming personal moral anger, and personal moral anger presupposes that its object is a moral agent.

Finally, since resentment necessarily involves the belief that you have been wrongfully harmed and is thus a central case of personal moral anger, forgiveness will paradigmatically involve overcoming resentment. Other forms of anger count as personal moral anger just in case the belief that you have been wrongfully harmed is partially constitutive of them, and so overcoming these forms of anger may also be involved in forgiving.[13] The following examples should further clarify this point and help illustrate what, on my view, counts as forgiveness.

Suppose your lover betrays you. In response you hold him in contempt, or regard him with disgust, or treat him scornfully. None of these reactive attitudes is resentment, which I have argued is the central case of personal moral anger. But were you to overcome (in the appropriate way and for moral reasons) these sorts of emotional states directed at your lover you *would* have forgiven him just in case those angry attitudes were partially constituted by the belief that you had been wrongfully harmed.

Now imagine a case in which you respond to your lover's misdeeds with resentment. In struggling to overcome this negative emotional state you succeed; your resentment, however, is replaced by scorn. You no longer wish to

---

[11]It is important to stress that even where there is justification or excuse there may well be much to be *nonmorally* angry about. Thus, while justification or excuse render (personal or vicarious) moral anger impossible, they do not entail the impossibility of some other form of anger or other sorts of negative feelings (e.g., rage, frustration, disappointment). Note also that not all excuses erase moral responsibility. Some excuses function to mitigate wrongdoing, and in such cases there remains a wrongful harm that is resentable (i.e., the object of moral anger).

[12]One might suppose that it is at least sometimes the case that a third party might forgive a wrongdoer on behalf of the person wronged. Aside from cases in which the third party acts as a proxy, so to speak, for the person harmed and merely conveys the message of forgiveness on behalf of the wronged party, there are at least two reasons, one conceptual and the other psychological, why this cannot be the case. First, if forgiveness is overcoming personal moral anger, then whatever message is conveyed by a proxy cannot itself be "overcoming" such anger. No mere utterance can by itself do this. Second, personal moral anger is an ineliminably personal psychological state, and no other person can overcome a psychological state of mine *for me* any more than another person can feel my pain or ecstasy, fall in and out of love for me, and so on. Hence, with the possible exception of God, it is impossible for a third party to forgive wrongdoing on behalf of the wronged.

[13]For more on the conditions of forgiving see my "What is involved in forgiving?," *The Journal of Value Inquiry* Vol. 27, December, 1993, 331–341.

"wring his neck" or upbraid him for what he had done; instead, you now feel that you are a foolish couple and that such a relationship should be abandoned because it involves a fundamental lack of mutual respect. Forgiveness does *not* occur in this case if the scornful attitude is, as the example implies, personal moral anger caused by the wrongdoing of one's lover. After all, I hardly forgive you if I overcome my resentment in favor of holding you in contempt, or viewing you with disdain; and this is because a change from one reactive attitude of anger to another is not always overcoming "personal moral anger" toward a perceived wrongdoer.

This is not to deny the possibility that a change from one type of anger to another may constitute forgiveness. Suppose, for example, one holds one's neighbor in mild contempt, and that this is as it were the emotional status quo *vis à vis* your neighbor. Now suppose your neighbor deliberately insults you for no apparent reason. You are indignant, but he implores you to forgive him, explaining perhaps that he has had a very bad day and was simply taking it out on the nearest person. In the end he convinces you that he is repentant, and so you forswear your indignation and return to the usual state of holding him in mild contempt. Since the pre-existing contemptuous attitude has no connection to the infuriating insult, overcoming the indignation caused by that insult could be a genuine case of forgiveness.

But now imagine two neighbors, Jim and Ed, who dislike one another intensely, though neither believes the other has ever harmed him. They may simply rub one another the wrong way. Jim, disturbed that he dislikes Ed for no apparent reason, attempts to overcome this negative feeling. After much reflection and effort Jim succeeds in eradicating his dislike of Ed. Jim and Ed are not now friends, and Jim has not replaced his negative feelings with kind ones. He is, instead, indifferent toward Ed. The change from dislike to indifference involves overcoming negative feelings, but it is hardly forgiveness, since Ed has done nothing to Jim for which Jim might forgive him. Moreover, in the absence of further information about Jim the moral status of his emotional transformation is unclear. And if it turns out to be virtuous, it is decidedly not the virtue of forgiveness. My point is that while angry reactive attitudes and, in general, negative emotional states, *may* involve the belief that one has been wrongfully harmed, they need not. Where this belief is absent, overcoming those states can hardly constitute forgiveness, for there is nothing to forgive. Put differently, the belief that one has been wrongfully harmed is *essential* to the moral nature of forgiveness. Without it, one's emotional transformations *vis-à-vis* other people are morally obscure.

These cases make it clear that personal moral anger ranges over a variety of emotional responses to perceived wrongdoers, and that the idea that forgiveness involves overcoming personal moral anger allows us to draw an intuitively plausible line between what is to count as forgiving and what is not, at least when the reactive attitudes at issue are angry ones.

Still, not all emotional responses to perceived wrongdoers are cases of personal moral anger. Just as it is possible to be angry at someone or something and not believe that anyone has been wrongfully harmed, so it is possible to believe that a moral subject has been wrongfully harmed and not be angry. One may, instead, be disappointed, depressed, heartbroken, and the like. Hence, that forgiveness frequently involves overcoming personal moral anger does not entail that it may not also be overcoming or forswearing other negative feelings caused by a wrongdoer.

I suggest that non-angry reactive attitudes such as sadness or disappointment count as *moral* reactive attitudes (what we might call "moral unhappiness") just in case the belief that a moral subject has been wrongfully harmed is partially constitutive of those attitudes. Extrapolating from the earlier analysis of moral anger, we can add that such attitudes will be either personal or vicarious, depending on who is believed to have been wrongfully harmed. Thus, disappointment or sadness count as "personal moral unhappiness" when they are partially constituted by the belief that you have been wrongfully harmed; and they count as "vicarious moral unhappiness" when partially constituted by the belief that someone else has suffered a wrongful harm. That is to say, it is possible to respond to wrongful harms suffered by others with sadness, disappointment, or some other (non-angry) vicarious moral reactive attitude such as sympathy, compassion, and the like.

Does this imply that overcoming "personal moral unhappiness" over perceived wrongdoing counts as forgiveness? I am inclined to think that *some* such overcoming for moral reasons counts as forgiveness, but that the proper analysis of such emotions and their transcendence is quite different from that which is appropriate for moral anger. Let us return to an earlier example to illustrate this point.

Suppose your lover has betrayed you and you respond with great anger. You are furious with her. Now suppose she explains the circumstances and asks your forgiveness. Convinced that she is truly sorry for what she has done you "let go" of your anger. But your anger is replaced with a sense of disappointment that such an unfortunate event should ever have happened and/or that your lover could have found it in herself to mistreat you so. Is this a case of forgiveness? I think it is, for to hold otherwise is to assume that to forgive another is to utterly wipe the emotional slate clean; to "feel," that is, as if the misdeed were never committed.[14] This strikes me as too restrictive a requirement of forgiveness, and thus that the view I have been urging all along is closer to the truth of the matter: forgiveness typically involves overcoming personal moral *anger* caused by the wrongdoing of another. While the eradication of *all* negative non-angry feelings is not required of forgiveness, overcoming all personal moral anger is. In other words, the existence of a residual unhappiness or disappointment is consistent with forgiveness, but lingering personal moral anger is not.

---

[14]Norvin Richards argues that forgiveness involves renouncing all "hard feelings" toward those who mistreat us. But if sadness and the like are to count as "hard feelings," then it must be the case that forgiveness only occurs when all such feelings have been overcome. This seems implausible. I think part of the problem with this view is that it is not clear that sadness, and other unhappy feelings, count as "hard feelings" or that they are *directed toward* perceived wrongdoers. See Richards, *op.cit.*, and section II of my "What is involved in forgiving?," *op.cit.*

III. FORGIVING AND CONDONING

To condone is to overlook or forgive an offense by treating the offender as if he had done nothing wrong.[15] This standard definition of the term, while explicitly equating condoning with forgiving, is ambiguous between at least two *types* of condoning. Condoning may mean (a) overlooking and thereby approving of wrongdoing, and (b) overlooking while nevertheless disapproving of wrong-doing. We might label these distinct senses "condoning as accepting" wrong-doing versus "condoning as tolerating" it, where the former implies no opposition to wrongdoing but the latter does in the sense of putting up with, bearing, or enduring wrongdoing. More specifically, while "condoning as ac-cepting" involves the belief that wrongdoing has occurred and a willingness to refrain from holding the wrong against the wrongdoer, "condoning as tolerat-ing" involves the belief that wrongdoing has occurred along with continued op-position to it in the form of a reactive attitude against it."Condoning as tolerating" wrongdoing thus implies an attitude of disapproving permissive-ness with regard to whatever is being tolerated.[16] By contrast, "condoning as ac-cepting" involves an attitude of approving permissiveness, which is not a manner of tolerating wrongdoing but a way of acquiescing in, affirming, or em-bracing it. Condoning in this sense therefore involves *complicity* in wrongdoing.

"Condoning as accepting" wrongdoing appears to be the core meaning of the concept. Familiar examples include accepting such relatively minor wrong-doing as the theft by one's friends or associates of hotel towels, restaurant glass-ware, or even pencils, letterhead, and other supplies from one's employer. Acquiescence in more significant wrongs, frequently of a political nature, come to light on a nearly daily basis in the mass media. A recent *New York Times* report describing a new law which would make euthanasia easier in The Netherlands further illustrated this sense of condoning in its claim that "although ending a patient's life or helping in suicide is illegal, and would remain so under the new law, Dutch courts have condoned the practices in a series of rulings for more than a decade."[17]

But "condoning as tolerating" wrongdoing has its instances as well. For ex-ample, if an employee is morally repulsed by the wrongdoing of a superior, has a moral (and perhaps legal) obligation to report it to authorities, yet fails to do so because he is lazy or because he does not want the inconvenience of getting involved, then he is condoning the wrongdoing even while he remains silently

---

[15]See note 1 above. Also note that both the *Oxford English Dictionary* and *Webster's Third New Inter-national Dictionary* distinguish between condoning in general and the legal doctrine of condonation relevant to the duties of matrimony. The O.E.D. defines the latter as "The action of a husband or wife in the forgiving, or acting so as to imply forgiveness, of matrimonial infidelity" (p. 688); and Webster's defines it as "the expressed or implied forgiveness by a husband or wife of a breach of marital duty (as adultery) by the other with an implied condition that the offense shall not be re-peated" (p. 473).

[16]This definition of toleration is articulated and explored in detail in *Toleration*, Nick Fotion and Ger-ard Elfstrom, University of Alabama Press, 1992.

[17]*The New York Times*, February 9, 1993, p. A7.

opposed to it. This sense of condoning involves *duplicity* as well as complicity, for while the condoner's overt behavior conveys the impression of agreement with the wrongdoing, his silent opposition to it means he holds the offense *against* the wrongdoer.

While the standard dictionary definition admits of these senses of condoning, it also equates condoning with *forgiving*. This is puzzling, for though forgiving and condoning are frequently assumed to be synonymous, one would not expect this fact about common usage to reflect anything more than a superficial resemblance, especially since forgiving and condoning are two very different *moral* phenomena. Moreover, in light of the earlier analysis of forgiveness as overcoming personal moral anger, it should be clear that "condoning as tolerating" wrongdoing is very different from forgiving, since is does *not* involve abandoning one's negative attitude toward a wrongdoer. The question, then, is whether "condoning as accepting" wrongdoing is conceptually indistinguishable from forgiving.

According to Aurel Kolnai, condoning and forgiving may be indistingishable if condoning involves deliberately refraining from a "retributive response" to wrongdoing.[18] On Kalnai's definition, condoning involves (a) awareness of wrongdoing, (b) *per se* disapproval of it, and (c) consciously refraining from any retributive response to it. A "retributive response" is a reactive attitude of opposition; it is akin to what I have called moral anger. Kolnai's point, in other words, is that the absence of an oppositional attitude toward the wrongdoer is a necessary condition of condoning. This definition accords with "condoning as accepting" which implies that while one believes a wrong has been committed, one accepts or endorses it by not holding it against the wrongdoer. Refraining from holding a wrong against a wrongdoer may be accomplished by squelching one's attitude of opposition to it, and so this sense of condoning *seems* a lot like forgiveness, especially since the silencing of moral anger is "a . . . consciously decisional act" in both.

But Kolnai's claim that condoning involves deliberately refraining from a retributive response to wrongdoing may mean either (a) not reacting with moral anger in the first place, or (b) consciously ridding oneself of such anger. These are not the same, for one may not experience moral anger when faced with wrongdoing, and this may be the result of a prior decision to deal with wrongdoing in a dispassionate manner. A parent might respond to her child's wrongdoing with patience rather than any form of anger, and this might be a policy she has adopted for raising her child. Moreover, some parents do not become upset when confronted with the wrongdoing of their children, either because they do not care enough about it, or because they have rationalized the behavior as something all children do. Such attitudes will sometimes amount to condoning wrongdoing, but these will be cases of condoning quite unlike those that involve overcoming moral revulsion, anger, disgust, or some other retributive response to wrongdoing. Because such cases involve no retributive attitude, and thus no moral anger, accepting wrongdoing in this way is another type of

[18]Aurel Kolnai, "Forgiveness," *Proceedings of the Aristotelian Society*, Vol. LXXIV, 1973/74, pp. 95–96.

condoning that is easily distinguished from forgiving. This leaves the sort of condoning that involves (b), overcoming moral anger, as potentially indistinguishable from forgiveness, but there are good reasons for thinking that even this sort of condoning is not easily confused with forgiving. Consider the following case.

George is a lawyer who has just learned that an alleged drug dealer has accepted a plea bargain on the advice of his attorney. George knows that the defendant's attorney, who happens to be George's brother, has suppressed evidence that might lead to the defendant's acquittal (the defendant actually has an alibi that might lead to the charges being dismissed), and he is furious about it. We might further suppose that the reason George's brother recommends the plea bargain to his client is that he has an extremely heavy case load and is impatient to get on with it. Because the defense attorney is his brother, George decides to ignore the wrongdoing rather than risk tense family relations for the indefinite future. With some effort and a good bit of rationalizing George manages to neutralize his anger toward his brother. This is a case of "condoning as accepting" wrongdoing that involves overcoming a retributive attitude. But is this sort of condoning indistinguishable from forgiving?

George does not forgive his brother if the sort of moral anger that he overcomes is anger felt on behalf of a third party who has been wronged. As the earlier analysis of moral anger makes clear, anger felt on behalf of a wronged third party is *vicarious*, not personal, moral anger. Since forgiveness involves overcoming *personal* moral anger, it is impossible for this to be an instance of George forgiving his brother, even though it involves silencing a "retributive response" to wrongdoing.[19] Hence, George condones, but does not forgive, his brother's wrongdoing.

This case helps illuminate two important differences between condoning and forgiving, even when condoning involves repudiating a retributive attitude. First, since forgiving involves overcoming personal moral anger, it follows that one cannot forgive *for* another.[20] But it is possible to condone wrongs done to third parties, as the case involving George and his brother aptly demonstrates. The possibility that condoning can be impersonal in this way suggest, secondly, that even though it may involve overcoming negative feelings, the principal *moral* element of condoning seems to be the condoner's overt behavior, not his feelings. Condoners "treat" wrongdoers as if they have done nothing wrong, and this is surely the main reason condoning is thought to be morally objectionable. This focus on overt behavior makes condoning a closer conceptual cousin of *mercy* than it is of forgiveness, since forgiveness is primarily a matter of feelings while mercy has to do with how people (or other moral subjects) are treated.[21]

---

[19]Let me remind the reader that this will be a case of forgiveness only if George believe *himself* to be the victim of wrongdoing, in which case his moral anger will be "personal." If George construes the injustice done to the defendant as a wrong done to humanity or to the state or to his profession, then he may see it as a wrong done to himself in virtue of his membership in these groups.
[20]See note 12 above.
[21]See the earlier discussion in section II.

It appears, then, that condoning and forgiving are potentially indistinguishable only in those cases where the sort of retributive attitude to be overcome is *personal* moral anger. Let us consider such a case.

> A woman marries a man with a stern, rather rigid father who is getting on in years. The father comes to stay with the couple for a visit, and finds his daughter-in-law's conduct irritating, the food less than perfect, the house less than clean, the conversation rather dull; in small ways he makes it clear that he considers the daughter-in-law to blame for the imperfections in his son's house. Whatever the motivations for the old man's attacks, let us suppose that they are unfair and give pain to the daughter-in-law. However, her husband says to her: "Look, he is my father and we should be on good terms with him. I know you think he is behaving badly, but be good and forgive him so that family peace can be preserved." [22]

Jean Hampton claims that were the woman to "drop" her judgment that the father-in-law is a wrongdoer and overcome the accompanying resentment for moral reasons (for the sake of preserving family harmony) she would be condoning, not forgiving, the wrongful behavior of her father-in-law. But recall that "condoning as accepting" wrongdoing involves complicity in wrongdoing, and complicity is not *necessarily* a feature of this case. Renouncing anger at a wrongdoer and abandoning the judgement that the wrongdoer is a wrongdoer does not necessarily entail collusion with evil, at least if "colluding" with wrongdoing means *enabling* a wrongdoer to continue his evil ways. Though the unfortunate daughter-in-law may view peaceful family relations as the greater good in the name of which she is willing to accept her father-in-law's abuse, this need not mean that she views the abuse as morally right or justifiable. Perhaps she is simply making the best of a bad situation that she cannot realistically do anything about. If overcoming personal moral anger in such a case is not forgiveness, it does not follow that it must be condonation. Surely there is middle ground between forgiving and condoning. If one's choice is between overcoming personal moral anger and silently bearing it, the rational (and moral) thing to do may well be to neutralize or overcome it rather than have the anger fester indefinitely, and this need be neither condoning nor forgiving wrongdoing. [23]

Alternatively, if we suppose that the young woman must either be forgiving or condoning the behavior of her father-in-law, but construe the disjunction as inclusive, it follows that she is either forgiving her father-in-law, condoning his behavior, or forgiving *and* condoning his behavior. Given the options, I don't know why we wouldn't call this a case of forgiveness, especially if she overcomes her personal moral anger for a moral reason (to preserve family peace). As I argued earlier, for forgiveness to count as a virtue, it must be done for

---

[22]Jean Hampton, *Forgiveness and Mercy*, p. 39.

[23]There is a burgeoning psychological self-help literature devoted to "healing" oneself that focuses on just the sort of middle ground I am alluding to between condoning and forgiving. Some of this material suggests that overcoming personal moral anger and dropping the judgment of another as a wrongdoer may be done not for the sake of restoring a relationship, but for the purpose of getting on with one's life and healing emotionally. Thus, letting go of one's moral anger is not always done to free a wrongdoer from that anger, but to free oneself from the grasp of an ultimately destructive emotion.

a moral reason. Neutralizing one's personal moral anger in the name of peaceful family relations will sometimes, but not always, count as overcoming moral anger for a good enough moral reason. What will count as a good moral reason depends, to some extent, on one's moral and professional duties. In the case in which George the attorney condones the wrongdoing of his brother, it is plausible to suppose that George has a professional and/or moral duty to challenge this brother's wrongdoing, even at the cost of long-term family peace. No such duty may apply in the case of the young woman with the irascible father-in-law. If this is right, then condoning may be indistinguishable from forgiving only in those cases where it is morally wrong to forgive. If we imagine that George interprets his brother's misdeed as wrongfully harming him (George) in virtue of their common membership in the legal profession, then George's ridding himself of personal moral anger toward his brother may be a case of forgiving that is equivalent to condoning. But this just means that *unvirtuous* forgiving is tantamount to a specific form of condoning, and so the standard dictionary definition which equates condoning with forgiving perhaps turns out to be true when and only when repudiating personal moral anger is done for the wrong reason.

IV. CONCLUSION

I have urged in this essay that moral anger is anger partially constituted by the belief that a moral subject has been wrongfully harmed, that if the wronged moral subject is one's self, then moral anger is "personal," otherwise it is "vicarious," and that this analysis of moral anger helps illuminate what is involved in forgiving and condoning wrongdoing. In at least one important type of forgiving, personal moral anger must be renounced. This required an effort of will and, frequently, an inner struggle to come to terms with the sense of violation or wrong suffered. It turns out, though, that one type of condoning involves neutralizing personal moral anger, and so it seems that in some cases forgiving and condoning are indistinguishable. I have urged, however, that we can distinguish four ways of condoning wrongdoing, and that only one of these is potentially indistinguishable from forgiving. Because forgiveness requires nullifying personal moral anger toward a wrongdoer, and "condoning as tolerating" wrongdoing presupposes an unrenounced retributive attitude toward a wrongdoer, condoning in this sense is not forgiving. Furthermore, "condoning as accepting" wrongdoing may not involve any retributive attitude (moral anger) at all, or it may involve overcoming vicarious rather than personal moral anger. In either case, these forms of condoning are not equivalent to forgiving. A fourth sense of condoning which involves overcoming personal moral anger toward a wrongdoer *is* potentially indistinguishable from forgiveness. I have claimed, though, that there may be middle ground between forgiving and condoning, and thus that not all renouncing of personal moral anger need to be either forgiving or condoning. Finally, I have suggested that where forgiveness *is* synonymous with condoning, it is unvirtuous forgiving insofar as it is done for a reason incompatible with the demands of morality.

Questions

1. What is a "reactive attitude"?
2. If the reason for renouncing moral anger must be compatible with morality in order to count as forgiveness, which Paul Hughes seems to suggest, can there be *unvirtuous* forgiveness to which he later refers?
3. Why does the author think that one cannot forgive *for* another person?

Suggestions for Further Reading on Forgiveness

GOLDING, MARTIN, "Forgiveness and Regret." *Philosophical Forum* 16, nos. 1–2 (fall–winter 1984–85): pp. 121–137.

LANG, BEREL, "Forgiveness," *American Philosophical Quarterly* 31, no. 2 (April 1994): pp. 105–117.

McFALL, LYNNE, "What's Wrong with Bitterness?" In *Feminist Ethics*, edited by Card, Lawrence: University Press of Kansas, 1991: pp. 146–160.

MURPHY, JEFFRIE G., AND JEAN HAMPTON. *Forgiveness and Mercy.* New York: Cambridge University Press, 1988.

MURPHY, JEFFRIE G. "Forgiveness in Counseling: A Philosophical Perspective." In *Character, Liberty and Law: Kantian Essays in Theory and Practice.* Dordrecht: Kluwer, 1998: pp. 223–238.

————. "Jean Hampton on Immorality, Self-Hatred and Self-Forgiveness." *Philosophical Studies* 89 (1998): pp. 215–236.

NORTH, JOANNA, "Wrongdoing and Forgiveness." *Philosophy* 62, (1987): 499–508.

SMITH, TARA, "Tolerance & Forgiveness: Virtues or Vices?" *Journal of Applied Philosophy* 14, no. 1, (1997): pp. 31–41.

WIESENTHAL, SIMON, *The Sunflower.* New York: Schocken Books, 1976.

CHAPTER 19

Modesty

Julia Driver, Modesty and Ignorance

G. F. Schueler, Why *Is* Modesty a Virtue?

Modesty and Ignorance*

Julia Driver

Julia Driver defends what she calls an un-derestimation *account of modesty. On this view, modest people are those who, in some respect, underestimate their self-worth to a limited degree. Where the ex-tent of the underestimation is not limited, then there is not the virtue of modesty but the vice of self-deception. The author re-sponds to the objection that if modesty is characterized by ignorance, then it cannot be a virtue. She argues that ignorance is not always bad and that modesty is one example of valuable ignorance.*

The author then suggests three possi-ble ways that her account of modesty could be developed: (1) epistemic modesty (EM), according to which the agent is modest if she underestimates self-worth to some limited extent but relative to the available evidence; (2) objective modesty (OM), according to which the agent is modest if she underestimates self-worth to some limited extent; and (3) combination modesty (CM), according to which the agent is modest if she is disposed to under-estimate self-worth to some limited extent, even in spite of available evidence.

The author applies these accounts to an interesting case of somebody who un-derestimates himself relative to the evidence available to him, but whose estimation of himself is, as a matter of fact, an overesti-mation. She concludes that CM is the best account. Finally, the author raises some problems for G. F. Schueler's account of the modest person as one who does not care about impressing others.

Modesty has turned out to be a surprisingly interesting virtue—or vice, de-pending on one's theoretical proclivities. Some years ago I offered an account of modesty which characterized the trait as a disposition to underestimate

*I thank Jonathan Adler, John Deigh, Walter Sinnott-Armstrong, and Roy Sorensen for their very helpful comments on an earlier draft.

Julia Driver, "Modesty and Ignorance," *Ethics* 109 (July 1999): 827–834. Copyright 1999. Reprinted by permission of the University of Chicago Press.

self-worth in some respect.[1] This account is an epistemic one since it character-izes modesty as involving some incorrect belief—actual ignorance—on the part of the modest agent. In a recent article, G. F. Schueler presents an intriguing new account of modesty and its value, offering an alternative to my belief-based ac-count of the trait.[2] In this article I would like to respond to Schueler' criticisms of my view by offering an advance on my previous analysis. In addition, I will argue that Schueler's account has some fairly serious flaws of its own.

I have argued that the best account of modesty is an *underestimation* ac-count. On this view, modesty involves—or at least can involve—an agent un-derestimating self-worth in some respect, to some limited degree. The degree of underestimation must be limited in order to differentiate modesty from a vice such as self-deprecation. For example, the woman who sinks into depression and views herself as a completely inadequate mother is not modest—she is ex-hibiting the vice of self-deprecation because her estimate dramatically misses the mark. However, if Albert Einstein viewed himself as a great physicist, just not the greatest physicist of the twentieth century—that's modesty. He is mis-taken but not dramatically off the mark.

The underestimation account has the advantage of distinguishing false from sincere modesty. A falsely modest agent knows full well how good she is at, let's say, math, but presents herself as less good. To the observer who detects the de-ception this behavior, or understatement of self-worth, is often patronizing and condescending. The person who is genuinely underestimating, however, does not provoke such a response. Yet another advantage of the account is that it cap-tures a wide range of cases which seem paradigmatic of modesty. For example, James Clark Maxwell was undoubtedly one of the greatest scientists of his time, yet this was not his own opinion. He is mistaken, and this is taken as modesty on his part. Note that the account I present is not a "low estimation" account—un-derestimation and low estimation are not the same. A modest person can still have a rather high opinion of herself on my view, just not as high as she is enti-tled to. Schueler seems to conflate the two in his criticism of my account.[3]

Criticism of this view can take two forms: one could argue that this is the correct account of modesty but that modesty is not a virtue, or, as Schueler has decided to argue, modesty is a virtue by my account is not the correct one. Though he agrees that modesty is a virtue, Schueler argues that my account cannot capture what is truly valuable in modesty.

One difficulty raised by Schueler is the following: if modesty does involve ignorance in some crucial way, why do we value it? After all, in general we seem to place great disvalue on ignorance. Indeed, Owen Flanagan, as Schueler notes, considers this enough to dismiss my account out of hand.[4] This is too quick. We sometimes do value ignorance. For example, ignorance of one's own

---

[1]Julia L. Driver, "The Virtues of Ignorance," *Journal of Philosophy* 86 (July 1989): 373–84.
[2]G. F. Schueler, "Why Modesty Is a Virtue," *Ethics* 107 (1997): 467–85.
[3]Schueler writes on p. 470, for example, "It may be worth nothing that the (or a) Christian view of the virtue called "humanity' accepts a 'low opinion" account somewhat similar to Dirver's."
[4]Owen Flanagan, "Virtue and Ignorance," *Journal of Philosophy* 87 (1990): 420–28.

beauty is often said to enhance it. The term "unaffected" is used as a compliment and refers to a person's lack of awareness, or ignorance, of their own personal charm. In addition, we certainly value innocence in children, which is a form of ignorance. So, the general principle that ignorance is always bad seems to be violated by a number of counterexamples. My account of modesty as a virtue would constitute simply another counterexample.

But there is the additional question of *what* makes modesty as ignorance valuable. My claim is that a person who is modest stops problems from arising in social situations. If we adopt a corrective view of the virtues, then we can see how it accomplishes this.[5] People in general have a tendency to rank and estimate worth relative to others, and this tendency is destructive. The modest person is one who does not spend a lot of time ranking, who does not feel the need to do so, and thus remains ignorant to the full extent of self-worth (to a limited extent). The analogy with beauty is helpful. The modest person has a charm similar to the unaffected person. Someone who doesn't compare his appearance to those around him, and, even better, seems unaware of it, seems less likely to provoke an envy response in others.

Given a refinement of this account, the modest person is someone who has accomplished something, and the accomplishment is such that it would normally generate envy or jealousy in those around her. This should be understood relative to specific reference classes. That is, the modesty works in cases where the person of accomplishment is similar enough to generate the negative emotions. I am not envious of Michael Jordan, for example, since his athletic talents—though far, far superior to mine—don't reflect badly on me. If my sister, on the other hand, were to begin winning all the time at neighborhood tennis matches, then I would start feeling a bit envious, I suspect.

Modesty helps us to avoid the vice of overranking. A person who tends to avoid ranking will not have this problem. Those who are ignorant of the full value of their accomplishments have obviously not put a great deal of time into thinking about it, given the tendency of people to overrank. Thus, modesty involves ignorance, and the ignorance is valuable because of what it indicates about a person's ranking behavior.

Imagine the following case: suppose Albert is a scientist who has put a great deal of thought into ranking, ranking himself the fifth best physicist in the world. He stands up at the next department meeting and so declares it. However it turns out that, unbeknowst to him, he is actually third best. Further, he has plenty of evidence that he is, in fact, third best. Is he modest? Yes, he is modest, but the modesty in his case is anomalously not preventing the bad because it isn't functioning normally in the case of this person. He is modest *in spite of* his overzealous ranking behavior.

A critic at this point may try the following: you haven't shown that it is the ignorance itself we value, only something else—the restraint, or failure to rank—that is correlated with the ignorance. There are two strategies for me to pursue here. In writing my original paper I had intended simply to argue

---

[5]Philippa Foot in *Virtues and Vices* (Oxford: Blackwell, 1978) discusses such a strategy in understanding the virtues.

against the thesis that no virtue can involve ignorance in any way. If even some cases of modesty involve ignorance, then I will have established counterexamples to that general claim. However, I would like to go further than this and claim that it is the ignorance that we value. Imagine someone who believes that he's the best, though he hasn't gone through a ranking exercise. He may know because God told him, or his mom told him, or he read it in the *New York Times*. It is correct, too. Thus, he knows he is the best. Any professions of inferiority on his account would constitute false modesty. If one were to find out that he knew and professed an even slight inferiority, one would be offended. I think this has to do with feeling as though one has been patronized, or condescended to.

Schueler also challenges me to distinguish underestimation from other forms of ignorance, such as stupidity and self-deception. The view that underestimation would be valuable but that these other types of ignorance would not be valuable seems in need of justification. Genuine stupidity, or a sort of general dull wittedness, has numerous bad effects, and it is difficult to see what good effect it would produce sufficiently to outweigh the bad. The form of underestimation that I argue for as a virtue in the form of modesty is *limited*, both in depth and in scope. Persons are typically modest only in some respect or other—that is, they are modest regarding their work accomplishments, or hobbies, or specific skills, and so forth. Further, modesty involves underestimation only to a certain limited degree to distinguish it from self-deprecation. These features distinguish it from stupidity. Self-deception, however, is somewhat different. Like deception itself, self-deception may be considered good and valued, depending upon the ends. Consider the case of a parent who engages in self-deception so that she has a view of her children which is slightly more elevated than the evidence would warrant. She displays a selective attentiveness to evidence, paying attention primarily to evidence of her children's precociousness, while downplaying the countervailng evidence. Suppose also that this behavior had very good effects—suppose children need a parent's praise in order to properly develop their potential and that a parent who genuinely believed in his or her child's precociousness did a better job of praising. Under these circumstances I don't think that such forms of self-deception would be considered bad. Likewise, the ignorance associated with modesty is not bad. Note that this does not mean that ignorance, in some global sense, is good, any more than the above case would illustrate that self-deception understood globally is good. The point simply is that limited ignorance may be good.

Still, the account of modesty I am offering to this point does seem underdetermined. There are three possible ways to develop an underestimation account: there is an epistemic version and an objective version and one which combines objective and epistemic features:

> Epistemic modesty (EM) is when an agent is modest if he underestimates self-worth to some limited extent but relative to the available evidence.
>
> Objective modesty (OM) is when an agent is modest if he underestimates self-worth to some limited extent.
>
> Combination modesty (CM) is when an agent is modest if he is disposed to underestimate self-worth to some limited extent, even in spite of the available evidence.

Consider the following case which points out the importance of the distinction between EM and OM. Suppose that Roger is a gifted physicist in midcareer at MIT. He has published influential articles, but none that have had tremendous impact. His colleagues in the physics department decide to play a joke on him. They would like to make him believe that he has won the Nobel Prize. One member of the department sends a phony telegram from Stockholm; another pretends to be the president of the university, calling to congratulate; yet another pretends to be a reporter from the *New York Times* calling for an interview, and so on. The evidence accumulates, and Roger comes to the conclusion that he has indeed won the Nobel Prize. He begins thinking to himself, "Maybe that essay on quantum flarks was much better than I had thought," "Maybe the new research I've been conducting in the area of *phlidiston* is very, very promising," "I hadn't recognized my own brilliance until now," and so on. Roger is overestimating self-worth in terms of the value of his accomplishments, but let's suppose that he is doing so to a lesser extent than the evidence available to him would warrant, so that even though he is objectively overestimating self-worth, relative to available evidence he is still underestimating. Is Roger modest? On the epistemic view he is, but on the objective view he is not. Note that this case is not a problem for an underestimation account—indeed, it supports an underestimation account since in either case he is underestimating.

I believe that this case best supports OM, which would hold that the agent is not modest. The reason for this would be that when he discovers the truth he will feel very embarrassed and even ashamed. The difficult case for OM, however, is that of a person who underestimates self-worth, but only because he does not have access to evidence that would improve his opinion of himself. This does not seem like genuine modesty, since the "modest" belief seems accidental. This counterexample can be handled by appealing to CM, which would hold that not only must the agent underestimate, he must be disposed to do so in order to have the virtue of modesty, even against available evidence. I find this alternative to be the most plausible because it is committed to the view that the agent is objectively underestimating but also requires that he be disposed to do so against the evidence which would rule out accidental underestimations.

The underestimation account so construed can avoid the difficulties raised by Schueler, while preserving intuitions regarding sincere versus false modesty. In avoiding the vice of overranking, this person displays a character trait that exhibits ignorance of self-worth without falling into the vice of self-deprecation. This may also help to explain why the blustery braggart who vocally overestimates himself, while secretly underestimating, seems like he is immodest. He is displaying behavior characteristic of immodesty. If his true views are revealed he will seem pathetic, and one might say of him "he doesn't act modest, but really he is." Once again, in this case, the modesty is not functioning properly to prevent the overranking behavior. Thus, the ignorance account of modesty can account for the value of the trait as a corrective for undesirable behavior.

Schueler does present his own positive account of modesty and why it is valuable. His account is intended to solve or avoid problems he has raided for my account. However, the account he presents is subject to fairly significant problems. Schueler argues that the modest person is someone who does not care whether her accomplishments impress others or not. Just any "not caring" will not do, of course, since the slovenly person does not care about her appearance impressing others, and slovenliness and modesty are distinct traits. Thus, Schueler claims that the modest person must have some genuine accomplishment and not care "whether people evaluate one highly because of these genuine accomplishments."[6] More fully, he writes: "Someone who is genuinely modest is someone who doesn't care whether people are impressed with her for her accomplishments. That is, she lacks a certain desire or set of desires, namely, that people be impressed by her for what she has accomplished."[7] It is compatible with modesty that the person care how things appear to others to some extent, it's just that the modest agent won't care about impressing others. For example, a modest writer may be distressed by a critic's cutting remarks and would care about her work, but the modest writer would not care what people thought about her for writing it. On this account, the modest person is not ignorant; the lack is affective, and there is simply an absence of caring in a certain way which accounts for the modesty.

I believe that Schueler's account is misguided. He fails to make an important distinction between not caring *intrinsically* and not caring *derivatively*. For example, Martha may not care (intrinsically) about what her colleagues think of her regarding her accomplishments and yet care (derivatively) insofar as it affects her merit raise.

Consider how the distinction is relevant to Schueler's analysis: imagine a Ghandi-like figure, someone who is deeply concerned with promoting freedom and peace and who is mild and unassuming regarding his own accomplishments. However, this person cares intensely about how others perceive him and his work because he realizes that the success of his mission depends upon their perception of it as worthwhile, and to some extent, their perception of *him* as a morally worthy individual. He needs to set a good example. He needs others to think well of him.[8] Surely such a person could still qualify as modest.

Schueler could respond by appealing to the distinction above. He could say that modesty involves not caring intrinsically about how people evaluate one in light of one's genuine accomplishments. However, this will not solve another problem. The account, even so modified, is too broad. It would include cases of manifest immodesty.

Consider the following case: Robert is a very talented artist, regarded to be the best new painter in America. Robert is also convinced of his own supreme worth and the worth of his works, which are genuine accomplishments. It is also the case that he doesn't care at all about what people think of him in terms of these accomplishments, he isn't concerned with impressing others with his work or with the fact that he is the one who created it. This is because he has

---

[6]Schueler, p. 479.

[7]Ibid., pp. 478–79.

[8]See Julia L. Driver, "Caesar's Wife: On the Moral Significance of Appearing Good," *Journal of Philosophy* 89 (July 1992): 331–43.

contempt for their puny capacities for aesthetic appreciation. I doubt such a person could accurately be called modest, yet such a person fulfills Schueler's criteria.

Schueler challenges me to explain how it is that modesty, as ignorance, is valuable. A similar challenge could be leveled against his account. He writes that his view accounts for the value of modesty because the modest person is, rightly, not taking credit where she doesn't in fact deserve it, even though her accomplishments are true accomplishments. He writes:

> The more one looks into the various cultural, social, educational, and other factors that explain any of one's accomplishments (including genetic ones, of course), the less of one's self one finds and the more important these external explanatory factors seem to be. . . . If that is so, then the desire to be given credit for one's accomplishments . . . will be a desire for something one does not deserve. . . . The modest person on my account is one who perfectly well understands that her accomplishments are genuine . . . and yet who does not care whether she is evaluated highly for these accomplishments. She lacks the illegitimate . . . desire to be evaluated highly for her accomplishments and she does so in spite of the temptation to think that she does deserve credit.[9]

Thus, the value seems to consist in not desiring underserved credit. However, Schueler's account of the value of modesty seems a bit rough to me. He seems to be assuming a sort of determinism that is controversial, and this raises the issue of whether or not the modest person must have the view that credit for her accomplishments is undeserved (because her accomplishments are really due to factors beyond her control) in order to be modest. That is, must she in some sense realize that the credit is undeserved? If so, then there will be few genuine cases of modesty.

Schueler characterizes the modest person as one who doesn't care about being evaluated highly for genuine accomplishments or who doesn't care about things like "credit" or how she looks, though she may be concerned about the accomplishments themselves. But concern regarding how one, or one's accomplishments, appears to others does not seem bad at all. Indeed, it seems considerate of others. Concern for appearances need not be vicious, or nonvirtuous. I have argued elsewhere that there will be cases where failure to be concerned about moral appearances is morally questionable.[10] For example, if one's behavior sets an example for others, then even the appearance of defect can have serious negative consequences.

A further, and perhaps deeper, point can be made about sensitivity to what others think. After all, this is a form of evidence that should be considered. Such evidence might help one keep one's perspective and serve as a check on tendencies to be dismissive of others. Thus, in the absence of a more detailed description, I don't see that Schueler has accounted for the value of modesty.

Contrary to Schueler, I believe that one of the characteristics of the modest person is that she is giving up, in effect, something like credit that she *is* entitled

---

[9]Schueler, pp. 484–85.
[10]Driver, "Caesar's Wife."

to or belief as to her self-worth in some (limited) respect. In this way the modesty can function as a corrective of ranking behavior discussed earlier. It is this feature which serves to distinguish modesty from traits such as a ponderous sense of humor which may produce some social good, but which don't seem particularly virtuous. Modesty, as I have described it, is not debilitating.

Thus, in spite of qualms raised by Schueler, among others, regarding the underestimation account, I still believe that it offers the best overall account of modesty and what makes modesty a valuable trait. The additional clarification of the account offered here, I hope, will stimulate further discussion of the role controlled ignorance can play in virtue. To deny it any role, as Schueler and others such as Owen Flanagan would seem to do, begs the question in favor of a strongly intellectualist account of virtue. Like lying, ignorance may be something which is almost always very bad and generally to be avoided. But that doesn't make it bad all the time, when the ends morally justify it.

Questions

1. How does Julia Driver think that her account can distinguish false from sincere modesty? If a person did not underestimate herself, would it be better to present herself as though she did or as though she did not?
2. Do you think the author has satisfactorily defended her account of modesty against the charge that modesty (as she understands it) cannot be a virtue because it involves a degree of ignorance?
3. What objections does the author raise against G. F. Schueler's account of modesty?

Why Is Modesty a Virtue?

G. F. Schueler

G. F. Schueler responds to Julia Driver's paper. He raises a counter-example to her Combination Modesty account. In criticizing her claim that the modest person is one who does not spend a lot of time ranking people and thus remains ignorant of his worth, he notes that a person who does not rank people at all cannot rank himself lower than he deserves. By contrast, he notes, failure to rank oneself is a natural outcome of his own view of what modesty is: not caring whether people are impressed with one's accomplishments.

The author suggests that it will not do to understand the value of modesty, as Julia Driver does, as being derived from its positive social consequences. There are many other personal attributes that can have these consequences but that we do not consider to be virtues. Moreover, because false modesty can have exactly the same positive consequences as the genuine kind, it would have to be equally virtuous on this account. The author then suggests that the reason why immodesty is a vice is that it entails a "hollowness of self": the immodest person's goals and purposes are dependent on what will elicit the approval of others. The modest person is one who effects his own goals and purposes. Finally, the author responds to an apparent counter-example Julia Driver gives to his account of modesty.

> Talking of successful rackets
>
> modesty deserves a mention.
>
> Exclamation points in brackets
>
> never fail to draw attention.
> [PIET HEIN][1]

[1]Piet Hein, *Grooks* (Cambridge, Mass.: MIT Press, 1966), p. 47.

G. F. Scheuler, "Why IS Modesty a Virtue?" *Ethics* 109 (July 1999): 835–841. Copyright 1999. Reprinted by permission of the University of Chicago Press.

An account of modesty should explain both what modesty really is, that is what character trait the term 'modesty' actually refers to, and why this trait is (or is thought to be) a good thing, a virtue. Julia Driver's account stumbles over the first issue, mine over the second.

Driver's revised "underestimation" account of modesty, which she calls CM, is this: "An agent is modest if he is disposed to underestimate self-worth to some limited extent, even in spite of the available evidence"[2] (p. 830). This trait is valuable, she writes, because "a person who is modest stops problems from arising in social situations" (p. 828). A modest person "seems less likely to provoke an envy response in others" (p. 828) for instance.

But CM can't be correct, since someone could be disposed to underestimate her own worth, due to some systematic, minor miscalculation, say, and yet still be a full-blown, loud-mouthed, braggart, that is, a paradigm of someone who is definitely not modest. Driver herself suggests a perfectly good example of this. Albert, the world's third best physicist, believes he is the world's fifth best physicist and brags about this ranking. Driver's account entails that Albert is modest, though it seems quite clear that he is not.[3]

Part of what leads Driver into this problem becomes clear if we ask why she holds that someone who underestimates her own worth should, just by that fact, be thought to stop social problems such as envy form arising. Intuitively there is no connection between these two things, as the case of Albert shows. Someone could underestimate her own worth and still think very highly indeed of herself, brag about her accomplishments, and so on. When discussing why she thinks there is a connection here Driver says, "The modest person is one who does not spend a lot of time ranking, who does not feel the need to do so, and thus remains ignorant to the full extent of self-worth" (p. 828). And a bit later she refers to the modest person as a "person who tends to avoid ranking" (p. 829).

But this is quite a different thought, arguably not even compatible with the idea that modesty is essentially underestimating one's own worth. It is one thing to rank oneself a bit lower than one deserves; it is another thing entirely not to do any ranking at all. Someone who does not do any ranking will not be someone who ranks herself lower than she deserves. She will not rank herself at all. And, for the same reason, someone who ranks herself a bit lower than she deserves is not someone who avoids ranking herself.

So if it is failure to do any ranking (especially of oneself, presumably), or failure even to feel any need to do any ranking, that leads to the lessening of envy, jealousy, and the like, then it is not at all clear that Driver has given us any reason to think that someone who ranks herself lower than she deserves will produce these sorts of socially beneficial results. Ranking oneself lower than

---

[2]Julia Driver, "Modesty and Ignorance," in this issue, pp. 827–34. References to this article appear in the text in parentheses.

[3]Michael Ridge, in an unpublished paper which he was kind enough to show me, suggests that it is a necessary condition for modesty that one be disposed to de-emphasize one's accomplishments, at least in the minimal sense of doing nothing to emphasize them. Driver's underestimation account doesn't seem to meet this condition. Michael Ridge, "Modesty as a Virtue" (University of North Carolina at Chapel Hill, unpublished manuscript, 1998), p. 7.

one deserves is not the same as not ranking oneself at all and is perfectly compatible with ranking oneself pretty high, and hence compatible with the sort of boasting and the like that exacerbates, rather than lessens, feelings of envy and jealousy.

In contrast (I modestly point out), failure to rank oneself or one's accomplishments, or even to want to do so, is quite a natural outcome of the trait I claimed was referred to by the term 'modesty', namely, not caring whether people are impressed with one for one's accomplishments. So if Driver is right in thinking that what is good about modesty is that it leads to the lessening of various unhappy social emotions such as envy and jealousy, and that is does this because the modest person tends not to rank herself or even not to want to rank herself, then the account of modesty I gave earlier is actually much better positioned to make use of this fact than is Driver's underestimation account.

And a lucky thing, too, because I think Driver is right in the central criticism she makes of my explanation of why modesty (as I describe it) is a good thing. I claimed that what is good about not caring whether one is given credit for one's accomplishments is that a desire to be given this sort of credit would be illegitimate. And it would be illegitimate, I claimed, because whatever accomplishment we pick there will always be numerous genetic, social, cultural, and other factors for which one is in no way responsible that explain this accomplishment, that is, explain it in such a way that one really deserves no credit for it. Driver rightly points out that this is a controversial thesis and, even worse, that it would be very surprising if the value of modesty, what makes it a virtue, depended on the truth of a thesis that held that no one ever really deserves credit for any of her accomplishments.[4] So, some rethinking seems in order.

One possible tack would be simply to accept, in the way described above, Driver's suggestion that the value of modesty is in the positive social consequences it has, that is, in lessening envy and the like among people who know about the modest person's accomplishments. I suppose that modesty does indeed have such consequences, typically at least, and perhaps it should even be regarded as a condition of a successful account of modesty that it should make clear sense of why this should be so. But that would still leave a bit of a puzzle. There seem to be lots of other positive character traits, charm, for instance, or a sprightly wit, that have very much the sorts of positive social consequences Driver claims for modesty but which we do not regard as virtues. And by the same token there seem to be virtues, genuine, undoubted virtues such as honesty, whose value doesn't seem to reside in their positive social consequences. So it seems at best unclear that adopting the "positive social consequences" story of what is good about modesty really does show it to be a virtue. (Of course one might in the end decide that it was just a mistake to think that modesty is a virtue as opposed to merely a positive character trait, analogous to charm or wit.)

---

[4]Ridge makes a similar point. Ridge, p. 9. This is not really "a sort of determinism" though, as Driver calls it, since one could hold that causal explanations of the sort mentioned always undermine claims of credit for any accomplishment without holding that such explanations were deterministic. But this is a quibble.

Much the same point can be made in a slightly different way. False modesty, or at least undetected false modesty, should have exactly the same positive social consequences as genuine modesty. The lessening of envy and so on that Driver mentions depend not on the actual modesty of the agent in question but on the perception or belief that the agent is modest by those around her. But then why is false modesty, at least in a very clever person in whom it is never detected, not thought to be just as much a virtue as genuine modesty? It would seem that it should be if what is good about modesty is just the positive social consequences it has. One would think that false modesty should be at least a reasonable "second best" for those not blessed with the real thing if it were only the positive social consequences of modesty that made it a good thing. Yet we do not find authors of biographies, for instance, praising the subjects of their works for managing all their lives to maintain an undetected facade of false modesty.[5]

Intuitively, at least, the reason for this seems to be that there is something about the modest person that is intrinsically virtuous, that is, something that does not depend on the social consequences of this character trait, indeed does not depend on anyone even being aware of its existence. If that is right, then whatever that trait is, it will have to be something that falsely modest people, and, in general, immodest people lack. This suggests a way of approaching the issue of why exactly modesty is a virtue. The question to ask, I suggest, is this: what is it that one finds out about an immodest person, in noticing that she is bragging or the like, that makes one think less well of this person? What weakness or flaw in this person's character is revealed by the action or actions that convinced one that she lacked modesty?

I have argued that someone who is genuinely modest is someone who does not care whether people are impressed with her for her accomplishments (where 'accomplishment' should be read very broadly so as to include possessions, abilities, etc., anything about which one might be or fail to be modest). If that is on the right track, then someone who is not modest will be someone who does indeed care about whether people are impressed with her for her accomplishments. And I suppose someone who is actually immodest (and not merely not modest) will be someone who cares a lot about whether people are impressed with her for her accomplishments. So, the question is, what is wrong with that?

Notice that immodest behavior, such as bragging and the like, does not automatically involve lying or dissimulation. This might be common for someone who is immodest, and would be explained by the account I want to give, since a strong desire to impress people will presumably tempt one to exaggerate one's accomplishments. But still, someone who frequently reminds others of her accomplishments and the like might never speak anything but the literal truth and still be quite immodest. So it would be a mistake to think that immodest people are necessarily liars, for instance. So then what *is* wrong with immodesty?

The answer, I (now) think, is this. On my account, not being modest means caring about whether people are impressed with one for one's accomplishments.

---

[5]Supposing, for instance, that the biographer herself detects the facade by reading her subject's private diary after his death.

Of course there is a continuum (or actually more than one) here. There may be a few, or some, or many sorts of accomplishments where one cares whether people are impressed. And the amount one cares in any particular case can range from only a little to quite a lot. But, and this is the point, to have desires of this sort is to have a certain kind of character flaw. This is quite clear in the paradigm case of immodesty where the desire to impress others with one's accomplishments is strong and, so to speak, pervasive (i.e., it applies to virtually everything one does). The fact that such a person cares about whether others are impressed with her for her accomplishments reveals, as one might say, a certain hollowness of self.

Someone who cares a lot about what others think of her in this way is the sort of person whose direction in life, whose goals and purposes and so on, are generated not from herself but from those around her. In the most extreme case, at least, the whole structure of purposes that make up such a person's life will be built on whatever it is that impresses those around her. She will, one might say, care about her own accomplishments, whatever they are, only to the extent that others are impressed with her for having achieved them.

So, on this view the immodest person, or at least the paradigmatically immodest person at the very far end of the continua mentioned above, will be someone who has no goals or purposes of her own at all, someone for whom all of her direction in life comes from others. Of course it is unlikely that there could even be anyone who fits this extreme description. But looking at this extreme case tells us what is wrong to a less extreme degree with immodesty generally, that is, what sort of character flaw is revealed by more garden-variety cases of bragging and the like. To the extent that someone cares about whether people are impressed with her accomplishments, the direction of her life comes not from within herself but from others.

If that is what is wrong with immodesty we can now see what is good about modesty itself. On this account, modesty is not good for anything it causes (as on Driver's account). But modesty is a virtue, according to this view, because of what it reveals about the person who has it, namely, that her goals and purposes come from herself, not from others. Someone who is genuinely modest is thus seen to have a kind of substance to her character, just the sort of substance that the immodest person lacks.

Let me conclude by looking at quite a different objection Driver raises against my account of modesty, one aimed not at my explanation of why modesty is a virtue but at my description of the trait of character referred to by the term 'modesty'. Discussion of this objection will, I hope, make clearer what my account is supposed to be. Driver's example of the person who doesn't care whether people are impressed with his accomplishments (which are artistic creations in the case Driver describes) but only "because he has contempt for their puny capacities for aesthetic appreciation" (p. 833) seems to be intended as a straight counterexample to my account. Such a person, Driver says, seems far from modest, and yet my account of modesty seems to entail that he is modest. But this is based on a misunderstanding. We need to distinguish the question of whether this person cares at all, so to speak, from the question of whether he cares, all things considered.[6]

Here is an analogy. I have been drooling for weeks over the expensive new car in the showroom. Finally a salesman, having seen my nose pressed to the showroom window day after day, comes out and asks whether I want to buy this car. "No," I say, thinking of the fact that I already have a perfectly service-able car, that I would need to go far into debt to buy this new one, and so forth. Was I lying? Of course not, but there is another question to which the true an-swer was "yes." I certainly had a strong desire to buy that car, but this was a de-sire I had to balance against the many (alas) better reasons I have not to buy it. It was only "all things considered" that I did not want to buy it. This is quite dif-ferent from the case in which I am utterly indifferent to the car in the first place.

In thinking about Driver's example of the person who does not care whether people are impressed with his artistic creations "because he has con-tempt for their puny capacities for aesthetic appreciation," we need to make a similar distinction. There will be two sorts of case.

1. Someone might think that people certainly should, if they had any sense, be very impressed with his accomplishments, but also think that they do not, in fact, have any sense. That sounds like the case that Driver is describing, and though I agree it is not a case of modesty, I do not agree that it fails to fit the ac-count of modesty I suggested but just the reverse. Such a person certainly does care whether people are impressed by his accomplishments, but he also has the extra, contemptuous belief about their aesthetic abilities to explain why they in fact are not impressed, a belief that thus lets him totally discount their actual aesthetic judgments. So it is only "all things considered" that he does not care whether they are impressed, in the way it was only" all things considered" that I did not want to buy the car.

2. Someone might not be concerned at any level what people think of his artistic accomplishments, that is, be completely indifferent to whether they are impressed with these accomplishments and, as an extra fact so to speak, be of the opinion that their aesthetic judgments were all quite worthless. Such a per-son would on my account be modest, but this sort of case does not even appear to be a counterexample to this account. There is nothing about being modest that rules out thinking that the judgments of others about one's accomplish-ments are quite bad.

The difference between these two cases is in whether or not the person fails to care, all things considered, whether people are impressed with his accom-plishments only "because" he has contempt for their judgments. If the answer is "yes," as in the case Driver describes, then he will, of course, have to care in some way what people think of his accomplishments, otherwise his contempt will not figure into the explanation of his all-things-considered view (i.e., he will not fail to care only "because" of his contempt for their judgments). On my

---

[6]I try to sort out this distinction and some others of relevance to 'want' and its cognates in my book, *Desire* (Cambridge, Mass.: MIT Press, 1985), esp. chap. 1.

view, such a person does indeed care whether others are impressed with his accomplishments. He is not indifferent to this (as I was not indifferent to buying the car) and so will not be modest.

However, if he fails to care, all things considered, whether people are impressed with his artistic accomplishments because he is utterly indifferent in the first place about whether they are impressed (analogous to my being left totally cold by the new car in the showroom) then on my account he will indeed be modest about these accomplishments. But so far as I can see, that is perfectly consistent with his having the opinion that the aesthetic judgments of others are totally without merit. Their aesthetic judgments might after all really be totally without merit, and there is nothing to prevent him from noticing this fact.

The account of modesty I am suggesting essentially includes the claim that the modest person does not care whether people are impressed with her for her accomplishments. That does not mean that she does not care "all things considered," since that is compatible with it being the case that she cares deeply but that this care gets outweighed or "trumped" by some other view, such as contempt for the ability of others to make reasonable judgments on the topic in question. It means that she does not care at all, she is just indifferent to whether people are impressed with her for her accomplishments.

Questions

1. Do you think the value of modesty lies in its consequences? Does modesty always have positive consequences? Is modesty valuable if it has good consequences for society and has either no good consequences or only bad consequences for the modest person?
2. Is it true that immodest people tend to generate their goals and purposes from those around them? Could an immodest person generate his own goals and purposes but relish the adulation others accord him for attaining them?
3. What is G. F. Schueler's distinction between whether a person cares *at all* and whether he cares, *all things considered*?

Suggestions for Further Reading on Modesty

BEN-ZE'EV, AARON. "The Virtue of Modesty." *American Philosophical Quarterly* 30, no. 3 (July 1993): pp. 235–246.

DRIVER, JULIA. "The Virtues of Ignorance." *Journal of Philosophy* 86 (July 1989): pp. 373–384.

NUYEN, A. T. "Just Modesty." *American Philosophical Quarterly* 35, no. 1 (January 1998): pp. 101–109.

RIDGE, MICHAEL. "Modesty as a Virtue." *American Philosophical Quarterly* vol, no. 3 (July 2000): pp. 269–283.

SCHUELER, G. F. "Why Modesty Is a Virtue." *Ethics* 107 (April 1997): pp. 467–485.

SNOW, NANCY. "Humility." *Journal of Value Inquiry* 29, no. 2 (June 1995): pp. 203–216.

STATMAN, DANIEL. "Modesty, Pride and Realistic Self-Assessment." *Philosophical Quarterly* 42, no. 169 (October 1992): pp. 420–438.

TIBERIUS, VALERIE, AND JOHN D. WALKER, "Arrogance." *American Philosophical Quarterly* 35, no. 4 (October 1998): pp. 379–390.

CHAPTER 20

Politeness

FELICIA ACKERMAN, Politeness as a Virtue

SARAH BUSS, Appearing Respectful: The Moral Significance of Manners

Politeness as a Virtue[1]

Felicia Ackerman

Felicia Ackerman first examines some existing definitions of politeness and points to their shortcomings. Then she provides a list of four conditions she thinks are relevant to (but not decisive in determining) whether a rule is a rule for politeness. Not all these conditions apply all the time. For instance, sometimes (contrary to her condition 2) a rule of politeness is legally enforced. The author notes that because of vagueness in the concept of politeness, it is unclear how many of the conditions are sufficient to subsume something under the concept.

Having given an account of what politeness is, the author asks whether it is a virtue. She distinguishes between politeness that is ulteriorly motivated from that which is not, and focuses on the latter, which she calls "intrinstic politeness." She argues that insofar as there are moral grounds for the various conditions of politeness, being polite can be morally good. She cautions against giving politeness undue weight. We should be less impressed, she ways, by somebody's manners than by morally weighter aspects of character and behavior.

Politeness and rudeness are important dimensions in social life and in day-to-day evaluations of people's behavior and character. But these concepts have received little philosophical attention. This paper aims at remedying that lack by explicating the concept of politeness and discussing the status of politeness as a virtue and its relation to other virtues.

---

[1]"The gentle mind by gentle deeds is known / For a man by nothing is so well bewrayed / As by his manners." (Edmund Spenser, *The Faerie Queene*, Book VI, Canto 3, Stanza 1.)

Felicia Ackerman, "A Man by Nothing Is So Well Betrayed as by His Manners? Politeness as a Virtue," *Midwest Studies in Philosophy* 12 (1988): 250–258.

I

Politeness is one of a family of concepts whose members include such notion as civility, good manners, courtesy, and etiquette, along with their opposites of rudeness, incivility, bad manners, and discourtesy. Within each group are concepts that have subtle differences of nuance. This paper concentrates on politeness/good manners as the central notion and uses the terms 'politeness' and 'good manners' interchangeably.

For attempts at general characterizations of good manners, it seems natural to consult etiquette books. As a sample, consider *Drebett's Etiquette and Modern Manners*, which describes good manners as follows:

> The object [of manners] is to put everybody at ease, whatever their [*sic*] age or rank.[2]
>
> Good manners mean showing consideration for others—a sensibility that is innate in some people and has to be carefully cultivated in others.
>
> Whatever its sources, however, its purpose is to enable people to come together with ease, stay together for a time without friction or discord, and leave one another in the same fashion. This is the role of custom and of courtesy: the first stimulates personal confidence and reduces misunderstandings, the latter reassures us that our associates mean to be friendly.[3]

This account has a number of strengths. It recognizes that manners inherently involve some notion of consideration for others and of helping social encounters flow smoothly. It also recognizes that manners have both a conventional side (as illustrated by the fact that handshaking is a customary greeting in American but not in Indian society), which seems to be what *Drebett's* means by 'custom', and a non-conventional side, which seems to be what *Drebett's* means by 'courtesy' and which sets down limits on the aims and functions a rule can have in order to count as a rule of good manners at all. Thus, regardless of which society one is considering, a system of rules for eating will not count as a system of table manners unless it has certain ends (preventing sudden death from choking or food poisoning would not qualify, for example), but how these appropriate ends are to be implemented will, of course, vary from society to society.

The term 'custom' is actually a bit misleading here. What counts as polite behavior in a given society is less a matter of how people in that society customarily behave than of how whatever authorities the society recognizes on the subject of manners say good manners require people to behave. (Note the parallel here with rules of correct usage of a language. Whether 'ain't' counts as correct English is not a matter of whether English speakers customarily use it, but of whether it would be sanctioned by the sources English speakers recognize as authorities on correct usage.)

---

[2]*Drebett's Etiquette and Modern Manners*, edited by Elsie Burch Donald (London, 1982), 7.
[3]Ibid., 10.

An important weakness of *Drebett's* account is that the purpose specified for good manners is too broad. Rules of good manners do not aim to prevent just any kind of discord; for example, they do not aim to prevent political discord in Congress. Similarly, they do not always aim to enable people to "come together with ease"; for example, they may aim to make it difficult to approach the Queen. *Drebett's* itself notes elsewhere that rules of good manners may be designed partly to exclude and confuse "*arrivistes*." [4] Moreover, good manners can often be used on specific occasions to make one's enemies feel guilty, inferior, or otherwise uncomfortable, a practice often advocated by etiquette writer Judith Martin (a.k.a. Miss Manners), who delights in recommending "faultlessly polite and cheerful ways to drive others into the madhouse." [5]

Social scientists have suggested somewhat more sophisticated accounts. Thus, Goffman characterizes ceremonial rules (as opposed to substantial rules) as follows:

> A ceremonial rule is one which guides conduct in matters felt to have secondary or even no significance in their own right, having primary importance—officially, anyway—as a conventionalized means of communication by which the individual expresses his character or conveys his appreciation of other participants in the situation . . . in our society, the code which governs ceremonial rules and ceremonial expressions is incorporated into what we call etiquette.[6]

This overlooks the rules for conventional expressions of aspects of one's character whose violation would not constitute a breach of manners or etiquette. For example, it is conventional (at least on college campuses) to wear buttons with slogans expressing one's political (or other) views, but is not automatically a breach of manners or etiquette to wear a button proclaiming views one opposes instead. Similarly, during an election campaign, it is conventional to wear a button bearing the name of one's favored candidate, but it is not automatically a breach of manners or etiquette to attempt to mislead by wearing a button for a candidate one opposes. Also, there are rules of good manners or etiquette that originally had (and sometimes still have) important "substantial" purposes beyond the ceremonial ones Goffman allows. The rule about not talking with one's mouth full has an aesthetic purpose. Rules of manners or etiquette regarding asking permission to smoke in social gatherings seem as much concerned with people's physical comfort as with their sensibilities. But there are limits. It may be impolite to smoke and make a mildly allergic person cough or to smell up a room with a cigar, but where the expected physical consequences are drastic enough (for example, in a case where one knows someone

---

[4]Ibid., 9. See also Judith Martin, *Miss Manners' Guide to Excruciatingly Correct Behavior* (New York, 1982), 7, and Judith Martin, *Miss Manners' Guide to Rearing Perfect Children* (New York, 1984), 327–28.
[5]Ibid., 288. See also ibid., xviii and 178, and Martin, *Guide to Excruciatingly Correct Behavior*, 7, 195, and 215, as well as Peg Bracken, *I Try to Behave Myself: Peg Bracken's Etiquette Book* (New York, 1963), 72.
[6]Erving Goffman, "Deference and Demeanor," in Erving Goffman, *Interaction Ritual* (Garden City, N.Y., 1967), 54–55.

would drop dead instantly upon being exposed to one's cigar smoke), speaking of rudeness and politeness seems ludicrous.[7]

How might an improved account go? The following conditions seem relevant to whether a rule is a rule for polite behavior.

1. The rule concerns social behavior, i.e., behavior between people or between people and other sentient beings normally capable of grasping rules of the system.[8]
2. The rule is extra-legal and is not enforced by legal sanctions.
3. The rule is part of a system of rules (or may be the whole system as a limiting case) having the original purpose and/or current function for the intended beneficiaries of making social life orderly, predictable, comfortable, and pleasant, over and above considerations of survival, health, safety, economy, religious edicts, or playing a game,[9] and doing this by such means as:
   a. making social life aesthetically appealing and avoiding situations perceived as aesthetically repellent;
   b. minimizing embarrassment, hurt feelings, and unpleasant surprises;
   c. showing consideration for others, respecting and defining their social privacy and autonomy;
   d. providing the security of conventional forms and rituals;
   e. reflecting distinctions of rank and privilege considered important.
4. It is socially sanctioned to take a violation of the rule by other people in situations involving oneself as an affront to oneself.

Note that rules of polite behavior help define as well as reflect what counts as aesthetically repellent, embarrassing, instrusive, etc. I suggest that being a rule of polite behavior is a concept that has what Alston calls combination-vagueness;[10] i.e., in order for something to fall under the concept, "enough" of a series of conditions must be satisfied where it is unclear in principle how many are enough, and they may be unequally weighted. Thus, the rules relating to American eating habits that concern which utensils to use, when and who is served in what order, as well as such matters as chewing with closed mouth, not pressing others to violate their diets, or grabbing food from other's plates, etc.,

---

[7]Thus, see Bracken's facetious remark about "Good Manners for the Smoker": "He mustn't smoke where there are NO SMOKING signs, for these usually mean business. It is bad form to explode a planeload of people or to blow a hospital sky-high." Bracken, *I Try to Behave Myself*, 41.

[8]Thus, Martin seems right in saying that "the whole concept of proper and improper behavior does not apply between people and machines" (Martin, *Guide to Excruciatingly Correct Behavior*, 202) and that it is ludicrous to speak of politeness toward one's dog (Ibid., 191). But simply someone's status as a human being seems adequate to make him a suitable object of polite behavior even if his particular cognitive capacities are not up to understanding or reciprocation. (For example, see Martin, *Guide to Rearing Perfect Children*, 336–37, on polite behavior toward, "senile" people.)

[9]The qualifier here reflects the insight behind Goffman's view about the limitations on the "substantial" function of ceremonial rules of etiquette, although my above counterexamples show that his view is too strong.

[10]See William P. Alston, *Philosophy of Language* (Englewood Cliffs, N.J., 1964) 87 ff.

are clearly rules of good manners. Laws against murder and rules for playing solitaire clearly are not.

Matters can be less clear when only some of the conditions are satisfied. Conditions 1, 3b, 3c, 3e, and 4 seem particularly important, the others less so. For example, rules of polite behavior in medieval Japan violated condition 2. They were enforced by law,[11] as are contemporary rules against loud night parties in some cities (which does not seem to keep annoying one's neighbors by having such parties from being rude). But the reason rules of grammar or rules for playing a musical instrument, unlike rules restricting the use of obscene language, do not count as rules of polite behavior seems to lie in conditions 3b, 3c, and 4. Rules of grammar or musical performance do not seem rooted in consideration for the feelings of others, and it is not socially sanctioned to take violation by others of these rules in social interaction with oneself as an affront. There is some social sanction, however, for feeling affronted by one's dinner companion's poor table manners, although the sanction for this decreases as the manners in question become more esoteric (using the wrong fish fork, for example). Note that condition 1 does not commit us to Martin's extreme view of the social nature of manners, that "In manners, as distinct from morals, . . . the only [act that counts] is one that has been witnessed [by someone else]."[12] Such a view seems excessive, as it precludes attributing rudeness to someone who says to his comatose grandfather in no one else's hearing, "Hurry up and croak, you old idiot, so I can inherit your money."

Some of the most interesting problems in characterizing rules as rules of polite behavior have to do with the qualification in condition 3 that mentions the intended beneficiaries of the rules. This, along with condition 3e, allows for the possibility that a system of manners may not only be hierarchical but may not benefit or even be intended to benefit all the categories of people to which it applies. Several cases can be distinguished here. First are such cases as the rules of manners for showing "respect" for women or old people. While it can, of course, be argued that this sort of respect is actually a form of condescension whose function is to reinforce the subordinate role of its recipients, as long as there is an official rationale that these rules benefit and show respect for the recipients, the rules clearly count as rules for good manners, although not necessarily desirable rules. But what about such cases as the practice that a lord is to walk through the door ahead of a commoner, or the elaborate "Jim Crow" set of rules of social segregation in the pre-1960s American South? "Jim Crow" rules had components that were legally enforced (such as blacks having to sit in the back of the busses) and components that were not (such as blacks not entering the homes of whites through the front door or being entertained as guests in the living room). Limiting consideration to the cases that did not involve legal sanctions, we can distinguish three sorts of cases. The first would involve a rationale (however preposterous) that the rules in some sense benefited subordinates as

[11]See Myra Waldo, *Myra Waldo's Travel Guide: Orient and Asia* (New York, 1965), 53–54.
[12]Martin, *Guide to Excruciatingly Correct Behavior*, 249.

well as superiors, for example, by making for a more orderly society[13] or one where people would not be embarrassed by being strained beyond their "true capacities." This still seems to count as a system of politeness, and one where there are politeness-obligations from the members of the superior class to those of the subordinate class, as well as vice-versa. An even more debased case would involve no claim that the rules benefit the commoners or blacks, but would claim that members of the subordinate class are natural inferiors who accordingly owe deference to their natural superiors. At most, this seems to be a one-way system of politeness, where members of the subordinate class have politeness-obligations to members of the superior class, but not vice versa. A final case involves inegalitarian rules with no rationale at all beyond the power of the superior class to enforce them. It seems doubtful that this would count as a system of politeness at all, in which case condition 3 should be amended to require that an appropriate rationale (of one of the sorts mentioned above) for the social distinctions in question be part of the system.

My account, like *Drebett's*, allows for both conventional and non-conventional sides of politeness. There are actually three levels here. At the most general level are my conditions 1–4 that can be used cross-culturally to decide whether a given rule is to count as a rule of politeness at all. Second is the room for cross-cultural variations in the specifics of aims and functions in condition 3. For example, societies may differ as to what distinctions of rank and privilege are to be respected. Finally, there are the conventional expressions of polite social gestures, such as my earlier example that a handshake is a common greeting in the United States but not in India (even if the two societies have similar cultural values about the importance of greeting a stranger with friendliness and respect.)

These distinctions allow for the possibility of some polite behavior even from a person who does not know the conventions of a society he is visiting: he can at least stay off any topic that he has reason to believe his listener will find embarrassing or unpleasant and that there is no overriding need to discuss. Someone who is largely ignorant of the conventions of another society may still happen to know of a topic some particular person in that society would find embarrassing or unpleasant.

These distinctions also point to a way there can be a split between what one might call the letter and the spirit of good manners, as in the popular anecdote about a host who drinks the water in his fingerbowl to set at ease his guest who has made a similar move out of ignorance. Another, more interesting split of this sort involves flaunting one's pleasantness, professed interest, and considerateness as a means of making another person uncomfortable. As I have mentioned, Martin gives cases where one can (and on her view should) use

---

[13]"When Dr. Johnson declared that it makes things much simpler to know that a lord goes through a door ahead of a commoner, he was no more striking a blow against individualism than against equality: he was only interested in saving everybody's time." Louis Kronenberger, quoted in Bracken, *I Try to Behave Myself*, 17. The obvious objections to this rationale (why not have the commoner or the taller man go first?), like the obvious objections to racist claims that segregation benefited blacks, need not concern us here.

politeness in this way, for example, by frustrating unsolicited advice-givers by repeatedly requesting ever-more-detailed suggestions, listening quietly, and then ignoring the advice ("one of Miss Manners' favorite faultlessly polite and cheerful ways to drive others into the madhouse")[14] or by making someone who did not invite one to her birthday party "feel terrible and remorseful—and all by behaving like a perfect lady!"[15] (in this case by telling her one hopes she had a wonderful birthday and inviting her to one's own birthday party). Is this genuinely polite behavior? Consider another case. Normally, greeting one's colleagues is polite, but suppose someone knows one of his colleagues would resent being subjected to his greeting, perhaps because she knows he was instrumental in denying her tenure. It seems clear that it would be kinder for him not to greet her, but would it also be more polite? In both cases, the answer seems to hinge on what, if anything, the society's rules of politeness have to say about what to do when the usual forms of politeness appear to defeat some of their own ends. Martin seems right that our society's concept of politeness allows unkindness in the sorts of cases she presents. For my question about the case involving the colleagues, the answer seems less clear.

II

Is politeness a virtue? If so, how is it related to other virtues? It may seem that if politeness is a virtue, it differs from the usual cases of moral virtues in a way illustrated by Philippa Foot's remark that "moral judgment concerns itself with a man's reasons for acting as well as with what he does. Law and etiquette require only that certain things are done or left undone, but no one is counted as charitable if he gives alms 'for the praise of men', and one who is honest only because it pays him to be honest does not have the virtue of honesty."[16] This is certainly oversimplified for the case of law, which takes into account someone's intentions as well as what he does. It may be oversimplified for politeness as well. A person's actions my count as polite provided they accord with society's rules of polite behavior, but it seems at least questionable whether habitually acting politely is enough to make him count as a polite person. Suppose he aims at being rude but inevitably ends up doing what counts as polite through misinformation about this society's conventions. Is he a polite person? "In a sense, yes, in a sense, no?" Someone who follows the conventions of politeness "for the praise of men," on the other hand, clearly does count as a polite person. As long as he habitually acts with deliberate politeness, ulterior motives seem irrelevant to the question of whether he is a polite person. Thus, it is politeness that is not ulteriorly motivated whose status as a virtue should be examined. I will call this "intrinsic politeness."

---

[14]Martin, *Guide to Rearing Perfect Children*, 288.
[15]Ibid., 178.
[16]Philippa Foot, "Morality as a System of Hypothetical Imperatives," *Philosophical Review* 83 (1972): 312–13.

Precisely what is the connection between intrinsic politeness and morality? Eugene Valberg has pointed out that "it is obvious that statements of etiquette are not in and of themselves moral statements."[17] But, of course, there can still be moral grounds for obeying the rules of polite behavior, insofar as there are moral grounds for such ends as those in conditions 3a–e and for avoiding actions that will give other people social sanction for feeling affronted (condition 4). The diversity of these ends shows some of the complexity of this issue. For example, it is obvious that both moral defenses and moral objections can be made concerning the distinctions of rank and privilege embodied in a given system of manners. What is less obvious is that these distinctions may involve priorities that are a matter of gradations less standard that distinctions of age, gender, social class, or social caste. Martin, for example, is a staunch believer that good manners require unhappy people, even those who "have had a genuine tragedy in their lives,"[18] to put on a happy social face in order to avoid blighting the day of anyone who might be better off—a position that might be criticized as the equivalent of taxing the poor to support the rich. A related objection can be raised to the stricture that requires the newly bereaved to pen handwritten replies to (possibly hundred of) sympathy notes. But it might also be claimed that the pressure to maintain conventional forms and rituals is diverting and beneficial for the sufferer.

To the extent that intrinsic politeness is a virtue, it is presumably so because either the distinctions embodied in condition 3e, the forms of consideration embodied in 3a–c, the security embodied in 3d, or the avoidance of making people feel affronted (condition 4) are things that are intrinsically good. Thus, it seems doubtful that there is much virtue in forms of intrinsic politeness that involve obeying the letter of conventionally polite forms that defeat the spirit of politeness in other conditions, except insofar as there is some virtue in upholding the system of rules itself (for example, to discourage defections by others or to provide the security of convention, as indicated in condition 3d, which cannot be defeated when the letter of conventionally polite forms is followed).

Common sense suggests that insofar as is serves the aims of conditions 3a–d, intrinsic politeness is a virtue, but not one of the most important ones.[19] It seems ludicrous, for example, to attach weight to whether someone who successively and painlessly murdered six wives in their sleep was an intrinsically polite person (let alone whether he was polite to his wives!). But apparently not everyone finds this sort of consideration ludicrous. Newspaper stories from the

---

[17]Eugene Valberg, "Phillipa Foot on Etiquette and Morality," *Southern Journal of Philosophy* 15 (1977): 388.

[18]Martin, *Guide to Excrutiatingly Correct Behavior*, 243. See also ibid., 678–79 and Martin, *Guide to Rearing Perfect Children*, 319–20. A similar rule is supported by Emily Post. See *Emily Post's Etiquette: The Blue Book of Social Usage*, revised by Elizabeth L. Post (New York, 1965), 41.

[19]"Think of situations like 'I *know* Emily Post wouldn't approve, but etiquette hasn't got anything to do with this. This is *serious*,'" Lawrence Becker, "The Finality of Moral Judgments: A Reply to Mrs. Foot," *Philosophical Review* 82 (1973): 369. (Italics in original.) Even using the less trivial-sounding terms 'good manners' or 'courtesy' does not militate against the view that "For all practical purposes, we may ignore considerations of [good manners] in life-or-death situations." (Ibid.)

1950s and 1960s frequently quoted neighbors of a newly discovered ex-Nazi torturer as objecting to his extradition or prosecution on the grounds that he had rehabilitated himself as a decent person living a decent life, as witnessed by his good manners, neat appearance, and well-tended lawn.

The limited importance of intrinsic politeness as a virtue leads to moral dangers in giving it undue weight. One way this can happen is by giving someone's manners undue weight in judging him as a person. Even Martin grants that "there is a ridiculous emphasis on the superficial [in the fact that] people will be judged more on their manners . . . than on their character,"[20] and quotes Somerset Maugham's remark that "few can suffer manners different from their own without distaste. It is seldom that a man is shocked by the thought that someone has seduced another's wife, and it may be that he preserves his equanimity when he knows that another has cheated at cards or forged a check . . . but it is hard for him to make a bosom friend of one who drops his aitches and almost impossible if he scoops up gravy with his knife."[21]

Even adherence to the spirit of politeness can be overrated in judging a person. For example, someone may be overvalued for his good manners, when his intrinsic desire to maintain pleasant surfaces and avoid embarrassing others keeps him from speaking out against injustice. Similarly, politeness can be overvalued in making one's own decisions about how to behave. Another virtue that can conflict with intrinsic politeness is honesty, although it is often unclear how this conflict should be resolved. Martin holds that "Hypocrisy is not generally a social sin, but a virtue"[22] in explaining why one should answer someone's question about the merit of her granddaughter's unmeritorious performance with insincere praise. But a natural objection to this sort of tact is that once it becomes a social practice, it undermines trust about the relevant situation. If politeness requires an affirmative answer to 'Did you like my flute solo?' an affirmative answer will not be a reliable guide to the speaker's opinion. This problem is inherent in the nature of tact as a social practice, rather than being an avoidable result of taking polite conventions too literally, as in the sort of person who gives a literal answer to 'Hello. How are you?' 'How are you?' (as opposed to 'Tell me how you've been; I really want to know') is not intended to be taken literally, but tactful praise is intended not only to be polite, but to be believed. That is what makes it reassuring. And tact also requires a polite lie in response to, 'Tell me, what did you *really* think of my flute solo? I really want to know.' It might also be argued that it is condescending to assume someone "really" wants or needs reassurance when he appears to be asking for an opinion.

Any virtue (other than loyalty itself) seems able to conflict with loyalty, since its requirements may conflict with the interests or desires of someone

[20]Martin, *Guide to Rearing Perfect Children*, 186.
[21]Ibid., 185–86, quoted from Somerset Maugham, *The Narrow Corner*.
[22]Ibid., 85. Compare Ze'ev Chafets' affectionate description of manners in Israel: "Excessive displays of . . . good manners are considered suspect, manifestations of superficiality or worse. If you are in a good mood, you show it; if your feet hurt, you show it, too." Ze'ev Chafets, *Heroes, Hustlers, Hard Hats, and Holy Men: Inside the New Israel* (New York, 1980), 201.

to whom one is or should be loyal. But politeness, with its usual stress on widespread impersonal agreeability, provides an especially fertile field for such conflicts. Suppose a man's wife wants him to "cut" (i.e., snub) someone who has done her a serious wrong. The spirit of politeness requires that the husband greet this person pleasantly (and even the letter of politeness may afford no means for a snub in this situation), but the wife may reasonably see such politeness as a breach of loyalty—and, of course, it may be a breach of loyalty even if she is not there to witness it. Politeness can also conflict with loyalty when there is no prior act of wrongdoing to be given its due (?) by a snub. Consider the following case.[23] A woman is emotionally devastated by the unexpected discovery that she is going blind and a few hours later is impetuously rude to a waitress in a restaurant. Her lover is far more upset by her rudeness than by her fear of impending blindness and in her presence apologizes to the waitress for this rudeness—a move which the first woman considers a betrayal. 'A man by nothing is so well betrayed as by his manners' here can have, not its original import that one can betray his boorishmess and crudeness by his bad manners, but the import that one can also betray his superficiality and small-mindedness by his overemphasis on good manners where their display is incompatible with deeper values.[24]

Questions

1. What does Felicia Ackerman mean by "conventional" and "non-conventional" sides of politeness?
2. How does the author suggest that manners can be used to make people feel guilty, inferior, or otherwise uncomfortable?
3. How important do you think that each of the author's conditions for politeness are?
4. On Felicia Ackerman's account, is politeness an attribute of character, or behavior, or of both?

[23]See Felicia Ackerman, "A Man by Nothing is So Well Betrayed as by His Manners," *Mid-American Review* 6 (1986): 1–12.
[24]I am deeply grateful to Marilyn McCord Adams, Katrina Avery, Sara Ann Ketchum, and James Van Cleve for graciously discussing various issues in this paper with me.

Appearing Respectful:
The Moral Significance
of Manners*

Sarah Buss

Sarah Buss disagrees with a common view that manners are to be distinguished from morality. She argues that (1) manners play an essential role in our moral life; and (2) playing this role is the essential function of manners. Many moral philosophers have thought that to respect or acknowledge a person's intrinsic worth or "dignity" is to allow her to pursue her own goals. The author says that such treatment is an indirect acknowledgement of a person's worth. She argues that acknowledging a person's value also requires that one treat her politely. Good manners, she says, encourage people to behave morally by making us agreeable to one another and by building a conception of human beings as deserving of moral concern. Good manners have an expressive function. By treating somebody politely we are implicitly saying she is deserving of respect. This direct way of acknowledging somebody's dignity, the author says, is necessary. The indirect ways do not suffice.

The author considers the question of when the obligation to be polite is overridden. Because it is often appropriate to override rules of polite behavior, such rules are less binding in this sense. There is another sense, however, in which they are more binding. They leave less room, says the author, for "neutral" behavior than other moral rules and are thus far more pervasive in our lives.

*Many people have given me helpful comments on this article: Jonathan Adler, Julia Driver, Maggie Little, Mark Migotti, Elijah Millgram, Amy Mullin, Alexander Nehamas, Martha Nussbaum, Gabrielle Richardson, Mathias Risse, Connie Rosati, Johathan Vogel, the members of Philamore, and an audience at the University of California, Riverside. I am also grateful for the many insightful suggestions offered by two referees and three editors for this journal. They forced me to clarify my position at a point when I would otherwise have been content to settle for less.

Moral philosophers constantly remind us how very important it is to treat one another with respect. After all, we are persons; and persons have a special dignity. Persons are ends in themselves—and must be acknowledged as such.

Experts on manners have a strikingly similar drum beat. They tell us how very important it is to treat one another respectfully. We must not offend the dignity of others if we can possibly avoid doing so. We must treat other people with as much consideration as possible.

When the same words are used in very different contexts, they often mean very different things. Nonetheless, it seems to me that the "respect" and "dignity" of such importance in moral philosophy are the very same "respect" and "dignity" of such importance in manners. Systems of manners play an essential role in our moral life. What's more, playing this role is the essential function of good manners.[1]

This, at any rate, is the two-part thesis I hope to defend in the pages that follow. I will not argue that it applies to each particular rule in a code of etiquette. Rather, I will focus on the virtue that is essential to good manners: the virtue we call "courtesy." Codes of etiquette tell us how to set the fork, the knife, and the spoon. But the most important lessons in manners are the lessons in how to avoid being discourteous, impolite, rude, inconsiderate, offensive, insulting. I will argue that someone who flouts these lessons behaves in a manner that is immoral as well as impolite. And if a system of manners encourages such immorality, then it can be criticized from the point of view of manners itself: it is a code of bad manners as well as a code of bad morals.

To most people uncorrupted by philosophy this will probably not be a surprising thesis: in appraising one another's behavior we are not committed to a clear division of labor between rules of manners and rules of morality. Many philosophers, however seem to take it for granted that manners lie outside the scope of morality. They assume that doing one's moral duty is one thing, being polite quite another. In defending the moral function of manners I will at the same time be challenging the assumption that in order to treat other persons as ends in themselves, it suffices to pursue one's own ends in a way that permits them to pursue theirs. I will, that is, be making the case for a more inclusive conception of the moral duty to treat other persons with respect.[2]

---

[1] Notice that this thesis is perfectly compatible with the view that the most important function of manners is to maintain social stability and order. After all, it may well be that maintaining social stability and order is the most important function of morality! In claiming that treating people with respect is the point of manners, I mean to be focusing attention on the fundamental *internal* aim of manners. This aim is compatible with, and may even contribute to, other desirable or undesirable goals—just as the internal aim of religious rituals (very roughly: to promote the worship of God) is compatible with and contributes to many other desirable and undesirable goals.

[2] David Brink expresses a widely shared view when he claims that requirements of etiquette differ from moral requirements because "their inescapability is not grounded in facts about rational agents as such." "Perhaps," Brink speculates, "rational agents . . . need not live under the rule of etiquette at all" (David O. Brink, "Kantian Rationalism: Inescapability, Authority, and Supremacy," in *Ethics and Practical Reason*, ed. Garrett Cullity and Berys Gaut [Oxford: Clarendon, 1997], pp. 255–91, p. 281), If, as seems to be the case, Brink means to include rules of manners among the rules of

To treat someone "with respect" is to treat her in a way that acknowledges her intrinsic value, or "dignity."[3] This is a value she has no matter what her deeds and accomplishments may be; it is tied to what she *is*, not to what she *has done*. Many of us believe that what makes someone valuable in this respect is not that she is a duchess, or some member of a privileged class, but that she is a person, capable of evaluating her situation for herself and setting her own goals accordingly. On this view, the obligation to acknowledge the intrinsic value of everyone who is intrinsically valuable is the obligation to acknowledge the intrinsic value of everyone.

But how is this acknowledgment accomplished? There is widespread agreement that we acknowledge the intrinsic value of persons by permitting them to constrain our decisions in a special way: in deciding what to do, we accommodate ourselves to the fact that other persons have their own interests and

etiquette, then the burden of my article is to show that he is wrong about etiquette, at least where the rational agents at issue are anything remotely like us. In defending a broader conception of our duty to treat people with respect, I will, in effect, be defending a broader conception of the right to be treated with respect. According to Joseph Raz, "one can, and people often do, show disrespect to others, including disrespect which amounts to denying their status as persons, by acts which do not violate rights" (Joseph Raz, *The Morality of Freedom* [Oxford: Clarendon, 1986], p. 191). Similarly, Judith Jarvis Thomson speculates that respect for persons may be "something other than respect for their rights. Then the work would remain to be done of saying what it is, and how this or that in morality issues from it" (Judith Jarvis Thomson, *The Realm of Rights* [Cambridge, Mass.: Harvard University Press, 1990], p. 211). To my mind, however, to divide disrespectful acts into those that violate a person's rights and those that merely "deny his status as a person" is to obscure the intimate connection between respecting a person's rights and acknowledging his moral status. At the very least, this sort of taxonomy encourages the false belief that we have fulfilled our duty to treat others as ends in themselves as long as we have enabled them to pursue their own morally permissible ends. (Though I agree with Raz that respect for persons should not be confused with respect for their rights, I am persuaded by Cora Diamond's suggestion that a person has rights only *because* she has moral standing. See Cora Diamond, "Eating Meat and Eating People," in Diamond's *The Realistic Spirit: Wittgenstein, Philosophy, and the Mind* [Cambridge, Mass.: MIT Press, 1991]. Raz is wrong, I think, to insist that moral rights are "based on" our interests and not, ultimately, on the independent fact that we are persons, ends in ourselves (Raz, p. 189). The moral significance of a person's *interests* depends on the fact that *she* has moral significance; our respect for a person's rights is based on the fact that we respect the person herself. (For more on this point, see Sarah Buss, "Respect for Persons," unpublished manuscript.)

[3] According to Kant, "The respect which I bear others or which another can claim from me . . . is the acknowledgment of the dignity (*dignitas*) of another man, i.e., a worth which has no price, no equivalent for which the object of valuation (*aestimii*) could be exchanged" (Immanuel Kant, *The Metaphysics of Moral, Part II: The Metaphysical Principles of Virtue*, in *Ethical Philosophy*, trans. James W. Ellington [Indianapolis: Hackett, 1983], p. 127).There are passages in which Kant suggests that in order to acknowledge a person's dignity, it is not enough to accommodate our ends to hers. Thus, he writes, "Holding up to ridicule real faults or faults attributed as real with the intention of depriving a person of his deserved respect, and the propensity to do this, may be called bitter derision (*spiritus causticus*). . . .[It is] a severe violation of the duty to respect other men" (p. 132). (I thank an editor of this journal for calling my attention to this passage.) At the same time, however, Kant seems to reject my interpretation of the relation between morals and manners insofar as he claims that "I am not bound to venerate others (regarded merely as men), i.e., to show them positive reverence. The only respect which I am bound to by nature is that for the law generally (*reverere legem*)" (p. 133).

concerns, their own ends. Of course, philosophers disagree about just what the necessary accommodation requires. My point about manners, however, is that whatever we must do in order to accommodate our ends to the ends of others, we must do something more in order to acknowledge the intrinsic value of others. Acknowledging a person's intrinsic value—treating her with respect—also requires that one treat her politely (considerately, respectfully). If we treat someone rudely, then we fail to treat her with respect—even if we do not prevent her from pursuing her most fundamental goals. Having defended this claim, I will consider what it implies about one of our own most basic rules of polite behavior.

If I am to have any hope of convincing anyone that good manners are an essential aspect of a morally decent life, I must confront those features of manners that seem to distinguish them from morals. Though there are surely many such features, I will focus on the three which, to my mind, are the most significant.

First, then, one of the primary objectives of systems of manners is to encourage us to make ourselves *agreeable*. This feature is closely related to the second: insofar as one's aim is good manners, acting from a good will is less important than *appearing* to be good willed. As Miss Manners succinctly puts it: "Manners involve the appearance of things, rather than the total reality."[4] Finally, everyone seems to agree that what counts as good manners in one culture does not necessarily count as good manners in another culture; when the subject is manners, relativism is an uncontroversial thesis.

Despite these obvious respects in which rules of manners differ form moral commands, I want to argue that a moral life would be severely impoverished without good manners. What's more, I want to argue that it would be impoverished because good manners have an important moral function—a function only they can perform. It is, I believe, a striking fact that people who are boorish or sulky or obnoxious or otherwise *disagreeable* are *morally* deficient precisely because they make so little effort to please. Why should this be? The simplest answer is that we believe that, all else being equal, people have a basic moral obligation to make themselves agreeable to others. This seems to have been Hume's view in the *Enquiry*. A quick glance at his discussion, however, suggests that this answer is, at best, incomplete. Making oneself agreeable to others is not only an end in itself; it is also, and more importantly, a means to treating them with respect.

---

[4] Judith Martin, *Miss Manners' Guide to Excruciatingly Correct Behavior* (New York: Warner Books, 1983), p. 13. There are actually two points here, each of which Miss Manners stresses on many occasions. First, as Philippa Foot points out, "moral judgment concerns itself with a man's reasons for acting as well as with what he does. Law and etiquette require only that certain things are done or left undone" (Philippa Foot, "Morality as a System of Hypothetical Imperatives," *Philosophical Review* 81 [1972]: 305–16, p. 312). Second, "in manners, as distinct from morals . . . the only recognized act is one that has been witnessed" (Martin, p. 249). In an interesting article, Julia Driver challenges the view that the stress on appearance distinguishes etiquette from morality. Appearing to be virtuous, she argues, can be essential to really being virtuous (see her "Caesar's Wife: On the Moral Significance of Appearing Good," *Journal of Philosophy* 89 [1992]: 331–43).

According to Hume, the primary difference between rules of polite behavior and laws of justice is the sphere to which they apply: "As the mutual shocks, in *society*, and the oppositions of interest and self-love have constrained mankind to establish the laws of *justice*, in order to preserve the advantages of mutual assistance and protection: in like manner, the eternal contrarieties, in *company*, of men's pride and self-conceit, have introduced the rules of Good Manners or Politeness, in order to facilitate the intercourse of minds, and an undisturbed commerse and conversation."[5]

Hume lists some of the ways in which expressions of pride and self-conceit are constrained by good manners: "Among well-bred people, a mutal deference is affected; contempt of others disguised; authority concealed; attention given to each in his turn; and an easy stream of conversation maintained, without vehemence, without interruption, without eagerness for victory, and without any airs of superiority."[6]

Notice the priority Hume gives here to *appearances*: he speaks of "affecting" mutual deference, of "disguising" contempt, of avoiding "airs." This suggests another, more important, difference between the rules of manners and the laws of justice: whereas the latter impose limits on an individual's pursuit of her own self-interest, the former impose limits on an individual's doing things that *suggest* she *would* pursue her self-interest at the expense of others if given half a chance. The point of good manners is to create a certain appearance, to show others that one does not care overly much for one's own dear self.[7]

Hume is right to stress that the best way to accomplish this goal is to be considerate of others. He is also right that the things people do to show consideration are often "immediately agreeable," and that this is what makes them suitable modes of showing consideration. Nonetheless, it seems to me that Hume's account of good manners is seriously inadequate; for it fails to do justice to the fact that good manners have a value independent of the pleasure they directly inspire. More particularly, Hume underestimates the contribution that good manners make to good morals; and (more importantly) he fails to appreciate the extent to which both this contribution and the more immediate pleasure we experience when we are treated politely reflect the fundamental moral purpose of polite behavior. I will take up each of these points in turn.

Try to consider, for a moment, what it would be like to live in a society in which there were no conventions of politeness. As Hume suggests, there would be much less social harmony: people would find one another's company far less tolerable; they would not be so favorably disposed toward one another; they would be far more likely to get on one another's nerves. It seems to me, moreover, that such social disharmony could not fail to adversely affect people's willingness to regulate their behavior according to certain principles of justice,

---

[5]David Hume, *An Enquiry concerning the Principles of Morals*, in *Enquiries concerning Human Understanding and concerning the Principles of Morals*, 3d ed. (Oxford: Oxford University Press, 1979), sec. 8, pp. 169–346, p. 261.

[6]Ibid.

[7]It may well be, of course, that a person will have a better chance of creating this appearance if she really does care about the others. I owe this point to Jonathan Adler.

and this for at least three reasons. First, people who feel anger and resentment toward one another are far less inclined to go out of their way to avoid harming one another. Second, people so ill equipped to be agreeable to one another are likely to keep at a distance from one another; and people thus alienated are less likely to care about one another's well-being. (I will come back to this point when, in the article's last section, I discuss the requirement to "mind one's own business.") Finally, and most importantly, people who have never developed the habit of treating one another with courtesy are not constantly encouraged to take it for granted that people *deserve* to be so treated; that is, they are not conditioned to regard people as having a special dignity that imposes limitations on what it is reasonable for other people to do.

The importance of such conditioning has recently been called to our attention in a thought-provoking article by Cora Diamond. In "Eating Meat and Eating People," Diamond suggests that our conventions of courtesy influence our assumptions about the moral status of human beings. The countless little rituals we enact to show one another consideration are, she argues, the means whereby we "build our notion of human beings."[8] They are "the ways in which we mark what human life is,"[9] and, as such, they "belong to the source of moral life."[10] From our earliest childhood, we learn that *Homo sapiens* is the sort of animal whose death it is appropriate to mark with a funeral, the sort of animal it is inappropriate to eat, the sort of animal it is inappropriate to kill for convenience or sport. These lessons contrast sharply with our lessons about nonhuman animals: as children we "see insect pests killed, or spiders or snakes merely because they are distasteful; [we] hear about the killing of dangerous animals or of superfluous puppies and kittens, and are encouraged early to fish or collect butterflies—and so on."[11]

Again, the point is that human and nonhuman animals "are not given for our thought independently of such a mass of ways of thinking about and responding to them."[12] Though Diamond does not herself stress the extent to which conventions of polite behavior figure among these ways of responding, she certainly means to include them. Indeed, she notes the moral significance of the fact that human beings are the only animals whose company we accept at the dinner table.[13]

Good manners, then, not only inspire good morals. They do so by constructing a conception of human beings as objects of moral concern. To learn that human beings are the sort of animal to whom one must say "please,"

---

[8]Diamond, p. 324.

[9]Ibid., p. 325.

[10]Ibid., p. 326. A difficulty for this account of the moral status of human beings is that it does not seem to allow for the possibility of a moral critique of the practices which contribute to the conception of what it is to be human. My own view is that our practices are not the only thing to which we can appeal to defend our views about what we owe one another. I take this for granted at the end of the article, when I call into question the requirement that people "mind their own business."

[11]Ibid., p. 330.

[12]Ibid., p. 331.

[13]Ibid., p. 324. ("we are around the table and they are on it.")

"thank you," "excuse me," and "good morning," that one ought not to interrupt them when they are speaking, that one ought not to avoid eye contact and yet ought not to stare, that one ought not to crowd them and yet ought not to be standoffish, to learn all this and much more is to learn that human beings deserve to be treated with respect, that they are respectworthy, that is, that they have a dignity not shared by those whom one does not bother to treat with such deference and care.

It is a small step from noting *that* manners play a key role in our moral education to understanding *why* they are so well suited to play this role. With this step, we arrive at the second, more fundamental, moral function of polite behavior: polite behavior not only has important moral *consequences*; it has an essentially moral *point*. Though Hume did not fully appreciate this point, he did remark upon it. Thus, consider the following observation in his discussion of "qualities immediately agreeable to others": "Many of the forms of breeding are arbitrary and casual; but the thing expressed by them is still the same. A Spaniard goes out of his own house before his guest, to signify that he leaves him master of all. In other countries, the landlord walks out last, as a common mark of deference and regard." [14]

I would like to make three comments about this brief passage. First, Hume calls attention to the *expressive* function of manners: by behaving politely, we are, in effect, "saying" something to one another. Second, by Hume's own account, the message expressed is that we defer to another person because we hold him in regard. Third, Hume's insistence to the contrary notwithstanding, such expressive behavior is *not immediately* agreeable. The pleasure it inspires is *mediated* by the guest's appreciation of what is expressed. If this guest were ignorant of the symbolic significance of his host's behavior, his host would be powerless to please him with this behavior. Indeed, if the guest were a Spaniard in one of those "other countries," he might even experience considerable *dis*pleasure.

Hume's remarks thus suggest that the reason why manners play such an important role in moral education is simply because they enable people to acknowledge one another's special dignity. This is their most basic purpose. An act of politeness may be intrinsically agreeable to others; and if it is intrinsically agreeable to others, this may be why it came to be regarded as a "mark of deference." What *makes* it a mark of deference, however, is *not* that it is agreeable. Rather, it is a mark of deference because this is the expressive function that has been assigned to it. Though there is an obvious sense in which the point of behaving politely is to be agreeable, the point of being agreeable in this way is to acknowledge the dignity of others. Indeed, it is often only if this more basic point is appreciated that the behavior is capable of giving pleasure.

But why should we care so much about whether someone acknowledges our dignity? Why should we find it so disagreeable when someone fails to exhibit some mark of deference? The answer, I wish to suggest, is simply that we believe we are worthy of respect, we believe that because we are respectworthy

---

[14]Hume, p. 262.

[15]Note that this answer is compatible with the fact that the pain we experience in being treated rudely is often, in part, the pain of being shunned, rejected, treated as an outsider. I will refer later

we deserve to be *treated with respect*, and we believe that being treated with *courtesy*—being *treated respectfully*—is a very important way—indeed, a necessary condition for the possibility—of being treated with respect. [15]

To treat people with respect is to act in a way that acknowledges their dignity, and to act this way *because* they have dignity. Moral philosophers have investigated the various ways we can make this acknowledgment *indirectly*. Very roughly: we indirectly acknowledge a person as respectworthy whenever we treat his interests and goals as constraints on our own most basic aims. There is, however, more to treating someone with respect than accommodating our ends to his. It is also essential that we more *directly* acknowledge that he is worthy of this accommodation; and in order to satisfy this requirement, we must treat him *politely*. When we treat one another politely, we are directly expressing respect for one another in the only way possible. We are, in effect, saying: "I respect you," "I acknowledge your dignity." [16]

The only way possible? Is there really no other means of acknowledging people directly? Instead of speaking the more subtle language of good manners, one could, of course, pepper one's conversation with the explicit assurance: "You are worthy of respect." As far as I can tell, however, this would not be an alternative method of direct acknowledgment. For if the phrase really did function to directly acknowledge people's respectworthiness, it would, in effect, be a stand-in for "please," "thank you," and so on. When you wanted someone to pass you the salt, you would say, "Pass the salt, you are worthy of respect"; and when someone passed you the salt, you and she would tell each other, "You are worthy of respect," "You are worthy of respect." This would be rather odd, to be sure, but not deeply different from the more specialized tokens of politeness with which we are familiar. Perhaps subtle alterations in tone of voice could pick up much of the slack. In any case, the practice would not be an alternative to being polite but just an alternative way of being polite. Nor would things be different for any other apparent alternative mode of direct acknowledgement: either it, too, would just be a different means of being polite, or it would not be a means of direct acknowledgment, after all.

Still, one might wonder whether treating people with respect really requires directly acknowledging their respectworthiness. I doubt whether this is the sort of thing that can be proved. Nonetheless, I hope to build on my discussion of Hume to show that a conception of treating people with respect which includes treating them politely is more compelling than the alternative conception, according to which treating people with respect is one thing, and behaving respectfully is another.

First, then, once we see polite behavior as essential to acknowledging the dignity of others, we can better understand the moral consequences of treating

---

to the capacity of manners to define in-groups. For now, it suffices to stress that the reason why it is so painful to be treated as an outsider is that this is one way of being treated as though one has less intrinsic worth than the insiders.

[16]Note that an acknowledgment of dignity can be both direct and indirect. Thus, e.g., asking permission to smoke is both a way of saying, "You are worthy of respect," and a way of adjusting one's ends to the ends of others.

people rudely. I have already noted that when people treat one another rudely, they are less likely to accommodate their actions to others, or even to believe that they ought to. It is difficult to see why this would be so, if treating people rudely were not at odds with acknowledging their intrinsic value, their dignity, their worthiness of being treated with respect.

So, too, unless good manners are essential to acknowledging another's dignity, it is difficult to see why treating someone politely so often plays an essential role in enabling her to pursue her own ends. As John Rawls reminds us, when a person doubts that others regard her as respectworthy, she tends to doubt that her "plan of life" is "worth carrying out," and that she has what it takes to carry out any life plan of value.[17] But why does rude behavior have the power to create doubts of this sort? Because, I submit, good manners are essential to acknowledging the intrinsic value of anyone who deserves to be treated with respect. It is precisely because treating people with courtesy is a direct way of acknowledging their dignity that treating them rudely can undermine their belief in their own intrinsic worth.

Additional support for the moral importance of direct acknowledgment comes from cases of nonmoral acknowledgment. Consider, for example, what is required to acknowledge that someone (A) is an expert on some topic (X). When doing a research project on X, one ought to look up A's papers. But surely this indirect acknowledgment is not sufficient. If, for example, when one is discussing X with A (and others), one repeatedly interrupts A's attempts to explain something about X or responds to her comments with a sniff of the nose, a roll of the eyes, or a "That's what *you* say," then one has failed to acknowledge her expertise (or has not acknowledged it enough, which comes to the same thing where giving people their due is concerned). Similarly, one does not adequately acknowledge A's skill at doing X if one hires her to do X, and yet in her presence enthusiastically praises the ability of others (and only others) to do X, gives them (and only them) awards for doing X, and so on.

To my mind, the most compelling reason for thinking that good manners have an essentially moral function and that this function is essential to treating persons with respect is that this is what is revealed by a simple exercise of the imagination. Consider what things would be like if there were a human community in which no human being violated the Kantian Categorical Imperative or had the least worry that others would do so. Would courtesy be pointless under these ideal conditions? Would polite behavior have no moral value? Would this imaginary kingdom be a "kingdom of ends," in which the intrinsic value of each is acknowledged by all? The answer, it seems to me, is clearly "no." Even if every citizen of the realm enabled every other citizen to exercise his capacity for rational choice, it would still be possible for these people to fail to treat one another with respect. For they would still be capable of hurting one another's feelings, offending one another's dignity, treating one another discourteously, inconsiderately, impolitely.

---

[17]John Rawls, *A Theory of Justice* (Cambridge, Mass.: Harvard University Press, 1971), p. 440.

In short, even if I were confident that everyone in my community respected my right to choose and act "autonomously," someone could still fail to treat me with respect if she stared off into the middle distance, or carefully examined her fingernails, whenever I tried to engage her in conversation. Someone can value me as a person without valuing my opinions. She can acknowledge my dignity as a person even if she condemns my opinions and actions on moral grounds. But she fails to treat me with respect if she makes no effort to hide her disinterest in, or contempt for, my feelings. When she treats me this way, she implies that my concerns, my feelings, my point of view do not matter, that is, that I have no intrinsic value, after all.[18]

Whereas acknowledging people *indirectly* involves considering how they feel about certain things, people, and projects, acknowledging people *directly* involves considering how they feel about having their feelings ignored. Prominent among this second group of feelings are shame and humiliation. When our words and deeds tell someone that it does not matter whether we hurt her feelings, we offend against her dignity by directly offending *her*.

But couldn't there be a "kingdom of ends" in which no behavior counted as rude? If this were a kingdom in which all behavior counted as polite, then it would not be a counterexample to the moral importance of direct acknowledgment. But what if it were a world in which no behavior counted as polite? In trying to imagine such a world, the best I can come up with is the "world" of many small children: though small children can easily provoke one another to tears, they generally do not take offense as readily as most adults; they say harsh things to each other, or ignore each other, without seeming to notice that there is anything amiss. The "world" of small children is not, however, a counterexample to the moral importance of direct acknowledgment. For it is, essentially, a child's world, and so it is not populated by full-fledged moral agents. Good manners matter less to the inhabitants of this world because these little people have not figured out what they and their comrades are really worth, and because, as a consequence, they do not yet treat one another with respect.

Not only are good manners essential to treating people with respect, but this is the essential point of good manners. In making this claim, I do not mean to be saying anything about the origin of rules of courtesy. Like our moral code, our code of manners may have originated as a way to encourage peaceful coexistence among people, or as a way for the powerful to maintain control over the resentful weak, or as a way for the resentful weak to claim power for themselves. Even if one or more of these stories is true, and even if the code continues to serve its original purpose, we can still ask: what does the code mean now? what do its rules signify to those who accept its authority? If, as seems obvious, the essential point of these rules is to instruct people on how to treat each other respectfully, and if, as I have argued, treating people respectfully is essential to treating them with respect, then the essential point of good manners is a moral point: to enable us to treat one another with respect.

---

[18]As Henry Richardson has reminded me, international negotiations provide a vivid example of how important good manners are in this regard.

Of course, one can directly acknowledge someone's dignity, and then go right off to plot her murder. But notice that the "polite" behavior of such a person would almost surely be deemed hypocritical; and this judgment only makes sense if the behavior does, indeed, have the moral significance I am attributing to it. More importantly, this moral significance is perfectly compatible with my earlier concession that manners involve *appearances* and so may not be in harmony with reality. For this concession is perfectly compatible with the fact that *appearing* to respect people is essential to *really* respecting them.

The fact that being polite has a moral point is compatible with the fact that in order to acknowledge a person's dignity *indirectly*—that is, in order to accommodate our own ends to hers—we may sometimes have to treat her rudely. For example, we may have to violate certain rules of politeness in order to save someone's life. Situations in which one must be rude in order to do what is right are situations in which one has a more pressing moral obligation than the moral obligation to directly acknowledge another person's dignity, and so it is not possible to treat her with respect. Lawrence Becker has argued that in this sort of situation it is permissible for us to "ignore" considerations of good manners.[19] It seems to me, however, that, as in the most straightforward cases of conflicting moral claims, we are simply forced to recognize that other considerations have greater weight.[20]

When the behavior required in order to acknowledge another person *directly* conflicts with the behavior required in order to acknowledge her *indirectly*, the requirements of indirect acknowledgement are usually overriding. My account of manners helps explain why this is so. Take, first, the case in which the conflict concerns the treatment of a single person. As I already noted, it is hypocritical to express one's belief in someone's respectworthiness while doing what one can to set back her most serious interests. If one' harmful behavior is evident to her, then it devalues one's expressions of courtesy, for it in-

---

[19]Lawrence Becker, "The Finality of Moral Judgments: A Reply to Mrs. Foot," *Philosophical Review* 82 (1973): 364–70, p. 369.

[20]Julia Driver has called my attention to a second situation of this sort. Suppose that Bob is a master criminal whom many young men admire and wish to emulate. And suppose that near the end of his life, he has a change of heart and wishes to discourage this administration. Bob might ask others to treat him disrespectfully in order to make his position seem less desirable. Driver suggests that those who honored Bob's request would, in fact, be treating him with respect. It seems to me, however, that this is not the right way to describe the situation. Even if one's reason for treating someone rudely is because this is necessary to save his life or to accommodate his wishes, in treating him rudely one fails to treat him with respect. Examples such as Driver's simply show that direct and indirect acknowledgment are sometimes incompatible, and that it is thus not always possible to treat someone with respect. Polite behavior's essential role in treating people with respect is compatible with the fact that a person can "betray his superficiality and small-mindedness by his overemphasis on good manners where their display is incompatible with deeper values" (Felicia Ackerman, "A Man by Nothing Is So Well Betrayed as by His Manners: Politeness as a Virtue," *Midwest Studies in Philosophy* 13 [1998]: 250–58, p. 257).

[21]It is unclear to me just when failures of indirect acknowledgment render attempts at direct acknowledgment fruitless. It seems, e.g., that a master can succeed in treating his slave politely, despite failing to accommodate her most basic interests. But perhaps this is true only insofar as the rights violation consists of the basic fact that he owns her. If he were to rape her, his courteous behavior the next day would surely add insult to injury.

dicates that these expressions do not really mean what they normally say. Since in such circumstances, one's polite gestures are nothing but empty gestures, they are not a form of direct acknowledgment.[21] So the choice in such cases is between acknowledging someone indirectly and not acknowledging her at all.

There are, of course, cases in which directly acknowledging someone's dignity plays a key role in preventing her from discovering that she is not being acknowledged indirectly: one's oh-so-polite behavior can convince the beneficiary of this behavior that one is truly committed to accommodating oneself to her interests and goals, even though nothing could be further from the truth. In such cases, nothing subverts the symbolic meaning of the polite behavior, however insincere it may be. Nonetheless, as far as I can tell, there is no reason for someone to favor direct acknowledgment over indirect acknowledgment in such cases; for in such cases one is not forced to choose between the two sorts of acknowledgment.

But what about those rare occasions on which no reconciliation is possible, occasions on which one must treat someone rudely in order to accommodate her capacity for rational choice—or in order to accommodate this capacity in others? It seems to me that to determine which requirements have priority in such cases we must simply employ whatever balancing test we use to adjudicate among competing rights. Perhaps it will turn out that it is always more important to acknowledge people *indirectly* than to acknowledge them *directly*. But I doubt it. There are probably many occasions on which we ought to break a promise, or trespass on someone's property, or even cause someone minor physical pain in order to avoid hurting someone's feelings, or offending her in some other way.

The fact that rules of manners tend to be trumped by other moral rules have been attributed to the fact that demands of manners have weaker "binding force" than most demands of morality.[22] But is this explanation is meant to add something to the one I have just offered myself, then it is (at best) misleading. To avoid confusion, we need to distinguish the ways in which rules of manners are "less binding" than other moral rules from the ways in which they are at least as binding. First, then, if rules of manners are less binding, this is *not* because they are any less authoritative: whether they apply to us is no more a matter of choice than whether any other moral demands apply to us. It is no more up to us whether we ought to behave rudely than it is up to us whether we ought to break a promise: if we know that a given action would be rude in a given context, or obligation to refrain from performing it is no more nor less negotiable than our obligation to keep our promises.[23] Like the obligation to keep our promises, the obligation to behave politely is not always overriding; but clearly this does not disqualify it as a genuine obligation.

Rules of polite behavior are less binding in the sense that it is often appropriate to override them. They are also less binding in two other respects. First, as I noted earlier, particular rules of polite behavior vary from social group to

[22]The phrase comes from Foot.

[23]Foot herself makes this point when she calls attention to the sense in which imperatives of etiquette are categorical.

social group far more than do other moral rules; they bind the members of one group without necessarily binding anyone else. Again, my account of manners helps to explain why this is so: good manners are morally significant because they have *symbolic* significance, and there are few limits to the symbolic meaning that a group of people can assign to any given act.

This also explains why the requirements of manners are less binding in the further respect that our code of manners counsels us to violate its own rules on occasion, even when these rules are not in conflict with one another. Since the point of good manners is to let someone know that one recognizes her dignity, one must be sensitive to how she will interpret one's behavior. If she is likely to mistake one's courtesy for discourtesy, it may be advisable to break the rules— *not*, again, because it may be advisable to "ignore" considerations of manners altogether but precisely because in order to treat her politely, one must ignore one's own particular code of polite behavior. (I will return to this point later when I discuss the "code of the street.")

There is, finally, one respect in which codes of manners are *more* binding than other moral codes: they leave less room for "neutral" behavior, which is neither morally praiseworthy nor morally criticizable. As long as we refrain from harming others, and as long as we come to the aid of some of them some of the time, we satisfy the demand to acknowledge other persons indirectly. In contrast, there is hardly a human interaction in which a code of manners does not require certain quite specific behavior. Are we meeting someone for the first time? Then we had better look him in the eye, offer our hand, and say, "Hello. How do you do? Nice to meet you," or something pretty similar to this. Are we visiting a friend (at home, at work, in the hospital)? eating at a restaurant? driving through town? asking for directions? On each of these occasions, and on most others too, there is something in particular (and usually *several* things) we must do to avoid being rude. My point is not that the rules of manners apply on more occasions than do other moral rules; after all, there are very few occasions on which it is appropriate to kill someone. Rather, my point is that whereas a wide range of behavior counts as "refraining from killing someone," there are far fewer ways to assure someone that she has the sort of value that makes it unthinkable to kill her, except in self-defense.[24] This feature of manners is linked to its importance as a *constant* reminder that persons are worthy of respect: it cannot serve this function unless there are many occasions on which there is something rather particular people must be sure to do in order to be polite to one another.[25]

According to Miss Manners, when we violate some code of polite behavior, we typically feel "embarrassment" rather than a "troubled conscience."[26] Para-

---

[24]At the end of the article, I remind the reader that though our options for avoiding rudeness are relatively restricted, codes of polite behavior provide us with more than one script for most occasions.

[25]The importance of this point was called to my attention by Alexander Nehamas.

[26]Martin, p. 10. According to Gabriele Taylor, embarrassment is occasioned by "failures to present oneself in an appropriate manner to a given audience" (Gabriele Taylor, *Pride, Shame, and Guilt: Emotions of Self-assessment* [Oxford: Oxford University Press, 1985], p. 74). "The overall demand of the situation [that inspires embarrassment] is always that [the person] make a certain impression or correct a certain impression which he thinks the audience is left with either because of his own behavior or because of the behavior of the member of his group with whom he thinks he will be identified" (p. 75).

digmatic *moral* failures are not of this sort. But this obvious contrast between violations of paradigmatic moral laws and violations of rules of manners does not show that manners have less "binding force" than morals; nor, more generally, does it challenge the moral status of manners. Manners are morally significant, I have argued, because appearing respectful is morally significant. This does not mean that a mistake in manners has the same significance as other moral mistakes. But is does mean that someone ought to have a troubled conscience if the reason why she made a mistake in manners is because she was indifferent to the moral value of appearances. Being indifferent—being immune to feeling embarrassed or ashamed or remorseful about lapses in courtesy—is not a moral option. . . .

Questions

1. What three features of manners does Sarah Buss mention that seem to distinguish them from morality?
2. What do you think the author would say about Felicia Ackerman's conditions for politeness?
3. Can polite behavior that does not stem from real respect really be thought to express an acknowledgment of somebody's dignity?

Suggestions for Further Reading on Politeness

BELL, LINDA. "Gallantry: What It Is and Why It Should Not Survive." *Southern Journal of Philosophy* 22 (1984): pp. 165–174.

HEYD, DAVID. "Tact: Sense, Sensitivity, and Virtue." *Inquiry* 38, no. 3 (1995): pp. 217–231.

WHITE, PATRICIA. "Decency and Education for Citizenship." *Journal of Moral Education* 21, no. 3 (1992): pp. 207–216.

CHAPTER 21

Gratitude

FRED R. BERGER, Gratitude

PATRICK BOLEYN-FITZGERALD, Gratitude and Justice

Gratitude[*]

Fred R. Berger

Fred Berger first reflects on the conditions under which gratitude is due. He notes that gratitude is not owed in every instance in which a person is benefited. A person might be benefited accidentally, for instance, in which case there would be no grounds for gratitude. Gratitude is owed in response to benevolence. It is accordingly to be distinguished from reciprocity, which may be owed in the absence of benevolence.

The author then suggests that in expressing gratitude we demonstrate certain attitudes. More specifically, (a) the grateful person shows that he recognizes the value of the benefactor's act; (b) the grateful person shows that he does not regard the donor as having value only as an instrument of his own welfare; and (c) a relationship of moral community is established, maintained, or recognized, consisting of mutual respect and regard.

The author notes that one reason why gratitude has been neglected by philosophers is that it involves not just acting in certain ways but having certain attitudes and that much contemporary philosophy has (unlike Aristotle) given very little attention to character.

Gratitude is not a subject much discussed in the philosophical literature, though hardly a book or article is published without some expression of gratitude by the author for the help of others. From the literature, one would have to conclude that gratitude plays a role in our moral life which, with only a few exceptions, philosophers have not seen fit to explore. Later I shall have a few suggestions as to why this is so. I cannot help but speculate now, however, that one

[*]I should like to record some of my own acknowledgments of aid: I first discussed some of these matters a number of years ago with H. L. A. Hart, from whom I gained important insights; I also benefited greatly from discussion of these matters with Torstein Eckhoff, of the University of Oslo Law School.

Fred R. Berger, "Gratitude," *Ethics* 85 (1975): 298–309. Copyright 1975. Reprinted by permission of the University of Chicago Press.

source for this neglect has been the view that gratitude does not play an important role in morality and thus does not deserve extended treatment. I want to show in this essay that the study of gratitude is indeed fruitful, in that it reveals important aspects of our moral life. Gratitude may or may not itself be important to our morality; it is, however, intertwined with an aspect of our moral relations which I believe has been unjustly neglected and on which the analysis of gratitude sheds light.

The paper is divided into three sections. In the first, I shall explore important aspects of the duty to *show* gratitude: under what conditions that duty does or does not hold, precisely to what gratitude is a response, and ways in which this duty differs from other principles invalving reciprocation. Using these results, I shall then, in the second section, turn to an analysis of the "internal" aspects of gratitude—that is, to an analysis of what it is that is shown or expressed in a demonstration of gratitude. In the concluding section, I shall attempt to show what the analysis reveals concerning the nature of morality. In particular, I shall hold that the analysis of gratitude shows that our feelings and attitudes (as well as our actions) play a role in our moral life which has been insufficiently acknowledged and stressed. Thus, I believe, we have not understood very well the morality of interpersonal relations.

I

In this section I shall concentrate on the duty to show gratitude. I shall assume there is (at least in our culture) a general duty to show gratitude under certain conditions, though it is, to be sure, a somewhat unusual "duty." I shall not seek to elucidate the *sense* in which we recognize a duty to show gratitude; in a final section, though, I shall try to deal with some of the anomalies the notion of a duty to show gratitude presents.

The first point I want to make about the duty to show gratitude is that a show of gratitude is not simply a response to other persons having done things which benefit us. That this is so can be seen by exploring the questions of the conditions under which gratitude is due and what factors affect the issue of what is required in the way of specific performance.

Two such factors suggest themselves immediately: the value of the benefit to the recipient and the degree of sacrifice or concession made by the grantor. There are other important factors, however. Suppose someone does something involving a sacrifice on his part which benefits us, but he was forced by threats to do it. In such a case, gratitude is not due; the appropriate response may be to return the gift, if possible, or to make sufficient restitution or replacement of it. The voluntariness with which the benefits are produced for us is thus a factor in determining if gratitude is appropriate when others benefit us.

Suppose further that someone did something which benefited us, but he was utterly unaware of this fact. That we are benefited is a fortuitous and unforeseen consequence of something he has done without any intention on his part to help us. Where it is clear that such intention was lacking, gratitude is not due. Insofar as he did not choose to do something to give us benefits (which he could not do if he had no foresight of the consequences), he did not *grant* them to us. Similarly, if the person knew he was creating benefits for us, but engaged in the behavior only because it also brought him benefits, gratitude is not due; the benefits were a mere by-product of acts done for self-gain. We may be glad for the benefits, but no gratitude is owed. Of course, in actual cases, motivation may not be entirely clear, or singlefactored, and perhaps we owe one another the benefit of the doubt; but in the clear sense, gratitude is not involved.

These facets of our practice with respect to gratitude reveal something important. The kinds of considerations cited are indices that the act was or was not done in order to help us. If the act was done only because the actor chose the lesser of two evils or sacrifices to himself, or without any knowledge or thought that it would benefit us, or solely because it would bring him benefits, there is no debt of gratitude, because nothing was done in order to help us. Gratitude, then, does not consist in the requital of benefits but in a response to *benevolence*; it is a response to a grant of benefits (or the attempt to benefit us) which was motivated by a desire to help us.

This fact about gratitude can be used to decide difficult cases in ways which seem plausible. For example, we might want to know if we owe gratitude for benefits which are *owed* us, that is, in which those providing them are fulfilling their duties to us. The answer is complicated by cases which incline us toward divergent answers. We owe gratitude to our parents for the sacrifices involved in their caring for us and giving us a decent upbringing, though it is their duty to provide this to the best of their ability. On the other hand, with regard to most contractual transactions, we do not usually feel we owe gratitude to the other contracting party when he fulfills his part of the deal. Of course, we owe him the performance of our part of the bargain, but that is not, in itself, a show of gratitude. All this becomes easily dealt with once we see gratitude as the requital of benevolence. Though our parents are under a duty to give us a decent upbringing and to care for us, it is almost never solely for this reason that parents make the sacrifices requisite for proper care and rearing. These sacrifices are normally made because our parents care for us and love us and want us to have the benefits of a good upbringing. On the other hand, many a contemporary novel has made capital out of the justified lack of gratitude in situations in which parents have given children the outward manifestations of a good rearing in our society (e.g., clothes, good schools, etc.) but solely for selfish reasons such as keeping up the family name or social standing. Indeed, to the extent that a *really* good rearing cannot be given without love at its base, it is something which by its nature deserves gratitude. In contrast to this, contractual arrangements are usually thought to be means for advancing the interests of both parties and hence tend not to be cases of benefits granted in order to help another, and gratitude would be out of place. This is not to say, however, that one cannot enter into a contract to help another. People quite often accept unfavorable terms of a contract in order to help the other party. When this happens, we *do* think there is an obligation to show gratitude. These features of our moral practices are readily understood once we perceive gratitude as a response to benevolence.

Even more subtle features of the duty to show gratitude are explicable in these terms. While we have no hesitation in saying there is an obligation to show gratitude for help or for a gift, we do not feel at ease in saying it is something owed the grantor in the sense that he has a right to demand it.[1] Such a demand shows the help or gift to be something less than a show of benevolence; it appears to be something done in order to gain favor, and to the extent we feel this to be case, the duty to show gratitude is diminished.

The analysis of gratitude as a response to benevolence is also important because it forms part of the basis on which the duty to show gratitude is to be distinguished from other duties involving reciprocity. Consider a principle dubbed by H. L. A. Hart "mutuality of restrictions": "When a number of persons conduct any joint enterprises according to rules . . . those who have submitted to these restrictions when required have a right to a similar submission from those who have benefited by their submission."[2]

This principle, underlying cooperation, differs from gratitude in a crucial respect. Cooperation does not imply benevolence; it is compatible with complete, but enlightened, self-interest. Selfish motivation on the part of the participants in no way diminishes the obligation to reciprocate with the requisite behavior when one has enjoyed the benefits of the practice. The point of such an activity is to produce *mutual* benefits. One who has enjoyed the benefits of a cooperative scheme would not present an adequate justification for his refusal to cooperate if he merely pointed out that the others restricted their behavior in order to obtain the benefits of the practice. Unlike gratitude, such a fact is not a rebuttal to the claim that a duty of reciprocation is owed. In fact, it is part of the ground on which the duty to do one's share in the production of the benefits is based. The benefits were *not* a gift to him.

Thus we are led to our first major conclusion: showing gratitude is a response to the benevolence of others. I want now to turn to the question of what it is that is shown or expressed in gratitude.

II

Thus far we have dealt only with the external aspects of gratitude—the duty to show or express gratitude. What *is* it that we show or express? And why can we distinguish "sincere" from "insincere' expressions? Moreover, we speak of "feeling" grateful and of having "feelings" of gratitude. All this suggests that when we express gratitude we simply show or give vent to certain internal

---

[1]*Other* parties may rightly criticize the failure to discharge it, and even the person to whom it is owed may be entitled to complain of the *insult* such a failure represents.

[2]H. L. A. Hart, "Are There Any Natural Rights?" *Philosophical Review* 64 (1955): 185. This principle should be compared with one called John Rawls "the duty of fair play." He has discussed it in numerous places. See, for example, "Legal Obligations and the Duty of Fair Play," in *Law and Philosophy*, ed. Sidney Hook (New York: New York University Press, 1964), pp. 3–18. No doubt Hart's statement of his principle requires important qualifications to be acceptable.

states. Even if this were correct, it would not go very far toward explaining why we regard gratitude as part of our moral relations—why ingratitude has been regarded by philosophers as a vice.[3] Nor would it explain why gratitude should be proportionate in the ways it is expressed, rather than in relation to the intensity of one's feelings. And it would not explain why sometimes mere verbal expression of one's feelings is not enough to constitute a sincere demonstration of gratitude. In what follows in this section, I want to attempt an account which goes some way toward dealing with these issues.

We should begin by noting that an act of benevolence evinces certain things about the actor. If I am the recipient of another's benevolence, his action indicates he cares about me, he values me, he respects me.[4] This is especially the case where any measure of sacrifice or concession or consideration is shown; he has been willing to incur a sacrifice of his own convenience or welfare to assist me. This shows that my welfare is valued by him in addition to his own.[5] I am an object of his concern.

When we show gratitude, then, it is this display of the other's attitude toward us to which we are responding. Note that in each of the cases in the last section in which we said gratitude is *not* due, no such indication of concern or valuing of the recipient was involved. A sincere expression of gratitude thus involves at least the recognition of the other's having done something which indicates he values us. Clearly, more than just this is involved, however. It seems to me that all of the following are accomplished by sincere, adequate expressions of gratitude: (*a*) the recipient shows he recognizes the value of the donor's act—that is, that it was an act benefiting him and done *in order to* benefit him; (*b*) the recipient shows that he does not regard the *actor* as having value only as an instrument of his own welfare; and (*c*) a relationship of moral community is established, maintained, or recognized, consisting of mutual respect and regard. Reciprocation makes the relationship two-way.

If this account is right, then expressions of gratitude are demonstrations of a complex of beliefs, feelings, and attitudes. By showing gratitude for the benevolence of others, we express our beliefs that they acted with our interests

[3]See Immanuel Kant, *Lectures on Ethics,* ed. Lewis White Beck (New York: Harper & Row, 1963), p. 218, in which ingratitude is described as one of the three vices which "are the essence of vileness and wickedness."

[4]There is an important ambiguity in this which I shall ignore in this paper. Benevolence can take a *general* and a *specific* form. Someone who cares about humanity (supposing this to be possible) may be motivated to act because he wishes to help people. *I* just happen to be the object of his largess by virtue of my humanity. On the other hand, it may be me he cares about, independently of any concern for humanity. In some contexts, this might be an important distinction. There is also some discussion of the issue by C. D. Broad in his treatment of Butler's ethics, as sometimes Butler seems to have supposed benevolence to be a concern for humanity and at other times a concern for the well-being of particular persons. See C. D. Broad, *Five Types of Ethical Theory* (Paterson, N.J.: Littlefield, Adams & Co., 1959), pp. 70 ff. But also see the discussion of Butler in T. A. Robert's *The Concept of Benevolence* (London: Macmillan Co., 1973).

[5]We sometimes distinguish ordinary men, great-hearted men, and saints according to how much they value the welfare of others in relation to their own. (Of course, we assume that they do not hate themselves.)

in mind and that we benefited; we show that we are glad for the benefit and the others' concern—we appreciate what was done; we indicate that we also have an attitude of regard for them, at least in the respect that we do not look on them as objects in the world whose movements have happened to bring us benefits (for then no response would be necessary). And we show that we do not regard their sacrifices and concessions as mere instruments of our welfare. The donor has shown his valuing of the recipient; the donee shows the relationship is mutual by some form of reciprocation, an each has demonstrated attitudes appropriate to members of a moral community.

It is important to note two features of our actual practice which this account is meant to tie in with. First, while some form of reciprocation is requisite, this need not be, and often *ought not to be,* the giving of the same or an equivalent benefit to the grantor. Not only is this not always possible, but sometimes it would destroy the force of the original gift. When someone grants us a benefit because of his concern for us, or because he wishes to make us happy, it can be an insult to return it or to show that we feel obligated to make a like return. The grant was made with no strings attached, with no desire to obligate us. To show that we feel we are obligated demonstrates that the gift misfired to a certain extent or, at worst, gives reason to think the donee misread the intentions of the grantor. It is one thing to show that we think we owe a sign of appreciation; it is quite another thing to show we think we owe a gift in return. Sometimes the most adequate display of gratitude is a loving hug or a warm handshake, and anything more would be inappropriate in some degree.

On the other hand, there are times when a mere "thank you" or warm handshake will not do, when an adequate showing of gratitude requires putting ourselves out in some way, at least a little. The sort of continual sacrifice and caring involved in a decent upbringing is not reciprocated to parents by a warm handshake at the legal age of independence. While the notion of gratitude to one's parents can easily be overdone, it is clear enough that an adequate showing of gratitude to them cannot be made with mere verbal expressions.

The explanation of gratitude I have provided can give a partial explanation to these features of our practices. First of all, on the account given, a crucial aspect of the practices associated with gratitude is the showing of one's recognition of the value of the donor's act. But, if one scrupulously attends to reciprocating in kind, that may undercut this showing, since part of the value of the act is constituted by its being given with no objective of a return. Furthermore, it is not only a set of beliefs and feelings which are involved in gratitude but attitudes as well: appreciation for the gift and the actor's caring, along with mutual respect for himself. But having an attitude or expressing through behavior also, and *certain* behaviors are the appropriate, concomitant expressions of attitudes. One does not take or have that attitude without some appropriate behavior. One cannot claim truly to care for someone and never act in certain appropriate ways. Indeed, gratitude is not so much the *expression* of our appreciation and respect as it is the *demonstration* of these attitudes. Sometimes we can demonstrate those attitudes by expressing them verbally; sometimes more is required for the demonstration to be adequate to the situation. Thus an adequate demonstration of our appreciation and concern for our parents could never be a mere handshake. A kiss on the cheek might suffice for a particular birthday present, but it is not an adequate demonstration of appreciation for years of care, inconvenience, and, perhaps, sacrifice. It is very hard to say just what is appropriate, and it may be that there can be no answer in the abstract, that it will depend on the nature of the particular family and the nature of the particular relationships within it. It is clear, however, that a handshake or kiss on the cheek normally will not do. The account of gratitude I have provided can explain, in part, why not.[6]

I have acknowledged that gratitude to one's parents can be overstressed, and that one's response to others' benevolence can be overdone in various ways. These points indicate that the practices associated with gratitude my take what I shall call "pathological" forms. By considering some of these, I believe we can bring into sharper focus the features of gratitude and will be better able to see its role in our moral life.

The first kind of pathology I wish to pick out takes the form of the man who does favors for others in order to place them in his debt. Where it is clear that something is expected in return, of course, there need be nothing wrong. But the debt, then, will not be one of gratitude. On the other hand, the act may be one in which the actor plays on, and takes advantage of, the conventional practices associated with gratitude and the recipient's inclination to be grateful for favors and to demonstrate his gratitude. Such an act involves deception (at least with respect to motivation) and is pathological in that respect. But it is also pathological in the deeper sense that the practices involved in gratitude presuppose that the agents are manifesting their mutual valuing of one another as ends in themselves, whereas *this* act treats the recipient as an instrument of the donor's welfare and thus as having instrumental value only.

A second form of the pathological practice of gratitude involves the tendency to overemphasize it and to ritualize it, so that every act under the sun which benefits someone else is viewed as requiring gratitude, and the constant display of gratitude is insisted on. In its mildest form, this consists in reducing giftgiving and returning to the level of matters of etiquette of no greater moral importance than simple social amenities. There are, however, more trenchant forms. In Western cultures with a strong family life, it is a familiar story for young people to be in rebellion at the constant insistence that they behave in traditional ways, or assume certain roles, or take up certain religious practices, in order to show gratitude to their parents for the sacrifices made in bringing them up. Any act of disobedience is viewed by the parent so as ingratitude, and everything done for the children is viewed as deserving gratitude. The combination of these two beliefs, of course, makes it impossible for the children ever to be properly grateful, unless they are willing to cater to every wish of the

---

[6]The question of the "appropriateness" of a response if complicated by cases in which only *part* of the complex of beliefs, feelings, and attitudes involved in being grateful are present, e.g., when we resent the other's benevolence because we personally dislike him and do not wish to be indebted to him, or where we do not desire the benefit sufficiently to warrant the sacrifice made, or a commensurate response. Here, the duties to be sincere and to show gratitude are in conflict. My account can help to explain this, though, of course, it does not show how to resolve it.

parents.[7] Such situations, when carried to extremes, are pathological in a number of respects. Even loving parents cannot claim that everything done for their children springs from their concern. Moreover, if truly done from love, these deeds would not be viewed as giving the right to make incessant demands on the children's life styles. The constant expectation of concessions as a sign of gratitude can be an oppression; and departure is a source of guilt, and the relations with the parent become clouded with feelings of resentment. All of this destroys love. In addition, this is a pathological misuse of the practices involved in gratitude, because it undercuts the moral relations presupposed by those practices (at least this is the case when the children have reached a certain age). To treat someone as a person in his own right entails granting him the right to work out the plan of his life as he sees fit. To use the fact of one's past aid in order to control another's life is to deny him the independence befitting a moral agent. A set of practices which function to demonstrate mutual regard is employed by one party to impose behavior on another as the price of his past regard and to demand the signs if regard, irrespective of the party's own judgment as to the appropriateness of those particular expressions. If we really have a concern with the well-being of someone, there are some aspects of his life which we ought not to seek to control and which we cannot obligate him to let us control.

To summarize my main points briefly: (*a*) being grateful to someone involves having a set of beliefs, feelings, and attitudes which are manifested when we show gratitude; (*b*) but showing gratitude involves a *demonstration* of those beliefs and attitudes and, thus, may require forms of behavior in addition to verbal expression; (*c*) such a demonstration of gratitude is a response to another's (perceived) benevolence; (*d*) as such, it involves the mutual demonstration of respect and regard—the indication that neither treats the other, or the sacrifices of the other, as a mere means to his own welfare; (*e*) thus the practices associated with gratitude are a manifestation of, and serve to strengthen, the bonds of moral community—the sharing of a common moral life based on respect for each person as having value in himself.

Much more needs to be said about gratitude before we can be content that we have very full understanding of it, even if the account I have given is correct. It would be important to know, for example, to what extent gratitude is conventional, whether there could be a community having a shared morality which did not incorporate gratitude is conventional, whether there could be a community having a shared morality which did not incorporate gratitude in some recognizable form, the role of spontaneity in gratitude, the necessary and sufficient conditions of sincerity, etc. Without seeking to explore these issues further, I shall turn in the concluding section to speculate on the significance for moral philosophy of the points already made.

III

What I find most significant about gratitude, as I have analyzed it, is that it involves in a crucial way our feelings and attitudes toward people. Requisite be-

[7]For a case history, see Philip Roth, *Portnoy's Complaint* (New York: Random House, 1969).

havior is involved primarily as a demonstration of those feelings and attitudes or as natural concomitants of them. This suggests the ancient view, held by Aristotle, that the moral life of a creature of a composite nature—having both rational and affective aspects—involves the right ordering of both elements. The moral virtues, then, involve not merely acting in certain ways but also having appropriate attitudes and feelings toward others.[8] Certain actions have value, than, *as* expressions of attitudes.

The recent history of moral philosophy shows great emphasis on such concepts as "right," "wrong," and "duty." These are notions applicable primarily to action. Goodness tends to be treated either as something it is our duty to act to produce or as a property of actions themselves. Moreover, the notion of one's having a *duty* to have certain feelings and attitudes is problematical, at the least. There seems no room left for the affective life in our moral world; it is entirely ancillary or incidental, helping or hindering us from performing our duties, possibly the basis for excuses, but forming no essential part of the basic concepts of morality. Even in views which emphasize a good will or proper motivation as basic to morality, the subjective factor emphasized is that of intention, and it is the intention to *act* in particular ways which is involved. Missing almost completely in the literature is the idea of certain attitudes as underlying a common moral life and actions as being natural or conventional expressions and demonstrations of those attitudes.

It is for such reasons as these, as well as others, that gratitude is not much dealt with in the literature. Consider that we do not, generally, *punish* people for failing to show gratitude; there is rarely a *particular* act which *must* be done if we are to show gratitude; there are no acts which the benevolent person may *demand* as a grateful return for his largess; and, though we sometimes speak of an act as entailing a *debt* of gratitude, it is a debt which differs in important ways from others, and there seem to be no acts which differs in important ways from others, and there seem to be no acts which it is our duty to perform in order to discharge the debt, even though a range of acts may be sufficient.

Far from showing that gratitude has nothing to do with morality, I think such facts show that the traditional ways of talking about morality, in which the concepts of "right," "wrong," "duty," "punishment," etc., are central, has led to an insufficient picture of what it is to have a morality. The sorts of feelings and attitudes involved in gratitude *do* play an important role in our moral life. Though we do not punish ingratitude, and though it *may* be logically impossible to make the having of certain feelings and attitudes (and thus their sincere display) a matter of duty, we nonetheless do not ignore gratitude in moral training. We teach that certain feelings and attitudes are appropriate and in *some* sense *ought* to be had in certain situations. Moreover, a statement like "You

---

[8]Aristotle stated his view in this way: "I mean moral virtue; for it is this that is concerned with passions and actions, and in these there is excess, defect, and the intermediate. For instance, both fear and confidence and appetite and anger and pity and in general pleasure and pain may be felt both too much and too little, and in both cases not well; but to feel them at the right times, with reference to the right objects, toward the right people, with the right motive, and in the right way, is what is both intermediate and best, and this is characteristic of virtue" (*Nicomachean Ethics* 1106b25)

should be glad for his gift," while not a demand that one should be glad, is a criticism of moral character and does play a role in moral education. We do not blame people for character defects, but blame is not the only form of criticism and not the only impetus to reform; and we certainly do *praise* those who display exemplary character. We can, to be sure, encourage and develop in people certain feelings and attitudes and the sort of characters in which these are appropriately displayed. We do this through example, exhortation, being pleased when those feelings and attitudes spontaneously show through, etc. In any particular culture, many kinds of affective and attitudinal responses become appropriate in certain situations, and a well-developed moral personality is expected, as a matter of course, to display these. In Western cultures, worried concern is appropriate to the difficulties faced by friends and associates (would one *be* a friend if he did not have a concern for our tribulations?); distress is appropriate to the ill fare of loved ones, joy or gladness is appropriate to great gains made by those close to us, anger is appropriate to situations in which an individual does great harm to another.[9] Not only do we strive to develop the affective life in certain ways rather than others, expressing appropriate approval or disapproval at proper or improper displays of attitudes, but we regard the failure to have the requisite responses as a defect of character. Consider the judgment one would make of one who finds the pain of others humorous, or who is incapable of pitying the unfortunate, or who does not feel pride in the accomplishments of his offspring, or feels no genuine gratitude for the sacrifices made for him by others. There is something lacking in these cases in the relations held with others, and the attitudes of the individual are deficient. These lackings are not punishable *offenses* (nor, by themselves, do they seem grounds for saying the persons are *immoral*), but they are not mere personality defects, either, in the way that, say, being boring is merely a defect of personality. Ingratitude, in particular, may rightly prompt castigation and reproval—the marks of a moral defect.

In addition, gratitude shows the role of the affective life in morality in an especially cogent way. If my account is correct, among the feelings and attitudes expressed in gratitude are those of appreciation of the other person and one's attitude of respect for the other person as someone of value in himself, and not merely as the source of one's own welfare. Having this kind of regard, taking these attitudes toward others is essentially involved in having a morality. Those with whom we share moral relations are not merely creatures whose behavior exhibits certain patterns but whose behavior manifests attitudes of valuing, respect, and concern.

It may be that these points, though important in themselves, can readily enough be accounted for on traditional conceptions of morality, even that of the utilitarian tradition. For example, John Stuart Mill often emphasized the importance of the development of moral character, and that this involves the cultiva-

---

[9]One writer who has stressed the idea that attitudes are appropriate to take and express to certain situations is J. N. Findlay. See his important article, "The Justification of Attitudes," *Mind* 63 (1954): 145–61.

tion of appropriate feelings and desires. Indeed, he criticized Bentham and the utilitarian tradition for ignoring this aspect of morality.[10] Mill's reason for stressing the development of the affective aspects of man was that these have consequences for our actions.[11] We must get men to feel and desire properly in order to get them to act properly. Indeed, he advocated inculcating in people desire for things other than the general welfare, for the reason that by acting from such desires they will, in fact, produce the general welfare more perfectly than if they always and solely acted from the desire to maximize the general welfare.[12]

There is no question that the practices associated with gratitude and the feelings and attitudes which comprise it are useful in these ways. An amateur sociologist would have little trouble pointing out the ways in which such displays reinforce dispositions to giftgiving and enlarge the degree of concession and concern people show one another. This, however, seems to me an unsatisfactory account of why reflective people seek to maintain the conventions of gratitude. Quite without regard to any further consequences, we care how people feel toward us and how they regard us. It is not enough that our friend does the right things in our interrelationship; it is equally important that he does them (at least in part) because he *likes* and *cares* for us. We are not satisfied if a friend does a favor for us if we think he begrudges it to us for some reason. Gratitude plays a role in our interrelationships precisely because it involves the demonstration of our feelings toward another. Thus it has value quite without regard to any further contribution to the good of society, quite without regard to any further actions it tends to produce. Our conception of our status with respect to others involves our view of how they *feel* toward us, what their *attitudes* are toward us, how they *regard* us.[13] Our idea of how we are valued, how we are thought of by others, and, thus, our view of the basis of our moral relations with them, is bound up with these perceptions. We can put this point another way: having regard for someone as of value, as deserving respect and concern, involves having certain feelings and attitudes; thus when we display these, we exhibit what their moral status is in our eyes.

Still, it may seem, even these points can be accommodated within the utilitarian framework. It may be thought that what this shows is that our *happiness* requires that we perceive that others have certain feelings and attitudes toward us. Thus the practices involved in gratitude have value, since they produce an essential element of happiness directly. Mill, it seems to me, regarded our sense

---

[10] John Stuart Mill, "Remarks on Bentham's Philosophy," in *Collected Works*, vol. 10, ed. J. M. Robson (Toronto: University of Toronto Press, 1969): pp. 7–8.

[11] Ibid.

[12] See "Utilitarianism," in *Collected Works*, 10:238–39. Also, the later editions of Mill's *A System of Logic* contain a passage at the very end which makes this point.

[13] I would be remiss were I not to mention an important article by Peter Strawson, in which he stresses the great importance to us of others' attitudes and feelings toward us. And he interprets gratitude, as I have, in terms of what he calls "reactive attitudes" toward another's benevolence. Of "reactive attitudes," he writes: "What I have called the participant reactive attitudes are essentially natural human reactions to the good or ill will of others towards us, as displayed in their attitudes and actions" (P. F. Strawson, "Freedom and Resentment," in *Studies in the Philosophy of Thought and Action*, ed. P. F. Strawson [London: Oxford University Press, 1968], p. 80).

of our own dignity as human beings to be an essential element of human happiness, and so may well have found a view such as this acceptable.[14] I do not wish to speculate further as to whether happiness can be properly viewed this way, or whether some further aspect of gratitude resists utilitarian treatment or can be brought within the rubrics of traditional philosophical concepts. For my purposes, it will suffice to have shown that demonstrations of our feelings and attitudes and the proper ordering of our affective lives are importantly involved in morality, whether or not there is a way of dealing with these points in traditional terms.

I shall close by pointing out that, if the present analysis is correct, a number of similar topics bear serious philosophical treatment, as there are large patterns of our moral relations which involve elements of the kinds I have isolated in gratitude. Among such related topics are: friendship, trust, loyalty, fidelity, pity, charity, disgust, resentment, hatred, etc. These and other such notions are importantly involved in the morality of our interpersonal relationships, and some of them can be more important for us to understand in our daily lives than, say, the logic of promising or even the principles of justice.

Questions

1. Why is that reciprocity can be owed in the absence of benevolence?
2. What "pathological" forms of practices associated with gratitude does Fred Berger mention?
3. Do you think that utilitarians can adequately account for the value of gratitude, as the author understands it?
4. Is gratitude required where somebody intended to benefit one but failed?

---

[14]See especially "Utilitarianism," p. 212. I should note, however, that on this view it would appear that there is no moral difference between an insincere show of gratitude, in which the insincerity is completely concealed, and a sincere display.

Gratitude and Justice*

Patrick Boleyn-Fitzgerald

Patrick Boleyn-Fitzgerald takes issue with Fred Berger's view of gratitude, which he argues is the dominant contemporary philosophical view about gratitude. It is, he says, because this view focuses only on the conditions under which we owe gratitude that gratitude has been thought to be peripheral to morality.

Instead of asking when we owe gratitude, we should ask, the author suggests, when we have good moral reasons for gratitude. He argues that there are (or can be) good moral reasons for being grateful to: (1) those who harm you and (2) those whom you benefit. These "anomalous" cases of gratitude, he notes, do not fit three features of the dominant view about gratitude: (a) that gratitude ought to be a response to a benefit; (b) that this benefit be motivated by benevolence; and (c) that this benefit was either wanted or accepted by the beneficiary.

The author discusses six possible justifications for the anomalous cases of gratitude: (i) juridical—when gratitude is owed; (ii) non-maleficent—when gratitude will prevent a harm; (iii) beneficent—when gratitude benefits; (iv) caring—when gratitude promotes or preserves special relationships; (v) civic—when gratitude promotes or preserves communal relationships; and (vi) perfectionist—when gratitude facilitates the development of virtues or helps thwart the formation of vices. The contemporary view of gratitude, he says, considers only juridical justifications. If, however, we consider the other sorts of moral reasons for gratitude, we can conclude, he argues, that we should sometimes be grateful to those who harm one and to those whom one benefits.

Patrick Boleyn-Fitzgerald, "Gratitude and Justice," *Ethics* 109 (October 1998): 119–153. Copyright 1998. Reprinted by permission of the University of Chicago Press.

*I would like to thank Lawrence Becker, Philip Bennett, Miriam Bowling, Claudia Card, David Schmidtz, Kit Wellman, members of the Louisiana State University Philosophy Club, and several anonymous editors and referees from *Ethics*. Their comments and concerns considerably improved the quality of this article. I am grateful to all of these individuals because of their goodwill. Given the thesis of this article, however, I would be remiss if I only mentioned those who have been beneficent.

More than two decades ago Fred Berger noted the scant attention philosophers had shown the concept of gratitude. It has received more attention since then, but even those who analyze gratitude do not consider it an important concept in ethics. Terrance McConnell, who devoted a whole book to the subject, described gratitude as "on the edge" and only having a "peripheral nature" to moral theory. If we agreed with McConnell, we might wonder why we should look at gratitude at all, but he contends that we can learn much from an investigation into one of morality's side issues.[1]

One reason McConnell and others consider gratitude peripheral to morality is that they believe individuals owe gratitude only in a very restricted set of conditions. If these theorists are right and we are only infrequently called to gratitude, then gratitude does indeed deserve the appellation "on the edge." I will contend, however, that contemporary philosophers give gratitude far too narrow a scope. The problem lies in the questions they try to answer. Philosophers often try to uncover our "debts of gratitude" or figure out when we "owe" gratitude rather than merely asking when we have good moral reasons to be grateful. When we try to discern when we "owe" gratitude we constrain our moral thinking to issues of justice and ignore other relevant moral concerns. To support my view I will analyze two cases where some Buddhists argue for gratitude: gratitude to those who harm you and gratitude to those whom you benefit. In both cases strong moral reasons support gratitude, but neither of these cases fits the contemporary philosophical analysis. The conclusion I draw is that sometimes we should be grateful even when justice does not demand it. Looking at gratitude in this way helps us to see it as one of the most common ways that morality asks us to relate to others.

I. GRATITUDE IN CONTEMPORARY MORAL THEORY

Gratitude is an emotion or a set of feelings. One *feels* grateful. This emotion has three components. Gratitude is (1) a warm sense of appreciation for somebody or something, (2) a sense of goodwill toward that individual or thing, and (3) a disposition to act which flows from appreciation and goodwill. Gratitude is not merely an emotion; however, we describe it as a virtue when it contributes to living one's life well. The question of when gratitude is a virtue is controversial, and this is where we will focus most of our attention.

The emotional component of gratitude poses a difficulty that philosophers commonly recognize. Many duties require us to perform particular actions but do not require us to feel any particular way. Gratitude is not like that. One cannot be grateful without feeling grateful. To be grateful for all that my mother had done for me may require actions, such as calling her on her birthday, but it also

---

to me. I would also like to thank everyone I have ever hated (they are far too numerous to list) and everyone who has ever granted me the opportunity to give. I could never have written this article without them.

[1]Terrance McConnell, *Gratitude* (Philadelphia, Pa.: Temple University Press, 1993), p. 12.

requires feeling a certain way about her. If, for example, I call my mother on her birthday purely out of a sense of duty, then I am not grateful though I have done all of the *actions* that gratitude may require. I am not grateful to my mother until I appreciate her. Claudia Card noted that this feature of gratitude strikes many oddly."A duty to be grateful sounds like a joke," she states, pointing out that the obligation involves not only what we do but the spirit in which we do it.[2] This may strike us oddly because, she notes, "according to deontological ethics, I can conscientiously fulfill my obligations even if my heart isn't in it."[3]

The emotional component of gratitude is what differentiates it from the virtue of reciprocity. Many cases of reciprocity are also cases of gratitude. You help me move into my new apartment and I am grateful—I feel appreciation, I have goodwill toward you, and I am disposed to act on my appreciation and goodwill. Consequently, I invite you over to dinner because I think you will enjoy it. Here my gratitude is also reciprocity—my gratitude is also a return for the favor you have done me. Nevertheless, this overlap need not always exist. We can, for example, have reciprocity without gratitude. Suppose again that you help me move into my apartment, but I feel no appreciation toward you. I have just started a new job, and it has captured all of my attention. I realized you did me a great favor, but my worries about my new job fill my mind. Or perhaps the day before my move I attended the funeral of a dear friend and grief overwhelms me. If I invite you to dinner anyway (perhaps because I habitually return favors), then I have reciprocated without being grateful. The emotional state appropriate for gratitude is not present. Anytime we try to reciprocate a benefit, but lack appreciation or goodwill, we have reciprocity without gratitude.[4]

When should we have these feelings of gratitude and express them? When should we be grateful? Contemporary philosophical analyses of gratitude agree on three general points. Philosophers agree that gratitude ought to be a response to a benefit (or perhaps an attempt to provide a significant benefit), a benefit given from an appropriate motivation (usually benevolence), and a benefit that was either wanted or accepted by the beneficiary. These three important areas of agreement are the very areas that I wish to challenge. Before I voice my challenge, however, I will spend the rest of this section fully describing them.

First, gratitude is a response to a favor, a benefit, or an attempt to provide a significant benefit. A. D. M. Walker, for example, argues, "What, first, is the 'proper object' of gratefulness: for what can one be grateful? In a word, gratefulness is a response to favour. That is to say: (I) Gratefulness is a response to what one sees as good; being grateful for what one takes to be unmitigated evil is a logical impossibility."[5] Terrance McConnell offers a similar analysis choosing the term 'benefit' rather than 'favor'. Usually McConnell believes that there must be a benefit provided, but he does make an exception. If someone tries to

---

[2]Claudia Card, "Gratitude and Obligation," *American Philosophical Quarterly* 25 (1988): 115–27, p. 117.
[3]Ibid., p. 117.
[4]See Lawrence C. Becker, *Reciprocity* (New York, N.Y.: Routledge & Kegan Paul, 1986), p. 105.
[5]A. D. M. Walker, "Gratefulness and Gratitude," *Proceedings of the Aristotelian Society* (1981): 39–55, p. 48.

give another a significant benefit but fails, gratitude may be owed. Gratitude might be owed, for example, when a colleague nominates you for an award even if it turns out that you do not get it. He states, "It must be the case that the person to whom gratitude is owed provided a benefit or through great effort or sacrifice tried to provide a significant benefit."[6] Others presume this condition but do not discuss it directly. Those who endorse the claim that a benefit must be given out of benevolent motivation, for example, presume that some benefit must be given.

Second, obligations of gratitude are only created when benefactors cause a benefit with an appropriate attitude. Fred Berger, for example, argues that the benefactor must not have been *forced* to grant the benefit. If someone benefits us because he was forced to, we need not be grateful. He imagines, "Suppose someone does something involving a sacrifice on his part which benefits us, but he was forced by threats to do it. In such a case, gratitude is not due; the appropriate response may be to return the gift, if possible, or to make sufficient restitution or replacement of it. The voluntariness with which the benefits are produced for us is thus a factor in determining if gratitude is appropriate when others benefit us."[7] Berger also argues that the benefactor must be *aware* that he benefited the beneficiary. Berger states, "Where it is clear that such intention was lacking, gratitude is not due." In general, Berger claims that gratitude is a response to *benevolence* and so when a benefactor does not have a benevolent attitude a beneficiary need not be grateful. He states, "Gratitude, then, does not consist in the requital of benefits but in a response to *benevolence*; it is a response to a grant of benefits (or the attempt to benefit us) which was motivated by a desire to help us."[8] Berger's analysis was very influential. More recent papers on gratitude often take his paper as a starting point. Some writers simply endorse his position outright. Nancy Jecker endorsed the position in a paper she wrote on the subject.[9] Card also endorsed it when she stated, "In an illuminating paper on this topic Fred Berger says one's gratitude is a response to another's benevolence, more specifically, to the valuing of oneself presupposed in another's benevolence: gratitude acknowledges and reciprocates that valuing, thereby demonstrating that one does not value others merely as useful for one's own ends."[10] A. John Simmons argues for a similar condition when he discusses gratitude as a possible source of political obligation, but he breaks the point down into three components:

> These features concern the benefactor's reasons for granting the benefit. First, his provision of the benefit must be intentional if we are to owe him a debt of gratitude for his performance; a benefit which he gives us unintentionally will not bind us to any repayment. Second, he must have given the benefit voluntarily. A man who benefits me because of the gun at his back does not

[6]McConnell, p. 44.
[7]Fred R. Berger, "Gratitude," *Ethics* 85 (1975): 298–309, p. 299.
[8]Ibid., p. 299.
[9]Nancy S. Jecker, "Are Filial Duties Unfounded?" *American Philosophical Quarterly* 26 (1989): 73–80, p. 74.
[10]Card, p. 117.

earn my gratitude, although he may, for instance, be entitled to ask for a return of the benefit (if possible) when the gunman no longer is in control. Third, the benefactor must not have provided the benefit for reasons of self-interest.[11]

McConnell agrees with this general condition and provides a more complete analysis of what kind of intention is necessary. He maintains that the intentional provision of benefit is required only in a weak sense. Jones rescues a drowning man without realizing his identity. Afterward Jones discovers that he has rescued his enemy and reports that he would not have rescued him if he had known who he was at the time. Jones only intended to give his enemy a benefit in a weak sense, but McConnell still thinks that gratitude is owed. Hence, McConnell claims that "the benefit must be granted voluntarily, intentionally (at least in the weak sense), freely, and not for disqualifying reasons."[12]

Third, contemporary theorists argue that beneficiaries must want the benefit, or at least accept it, before they would owe gratitude. Simmons describes the reaction in terms of want. First, "we must *want* the benefit which is granted" and, second, "we must not want the benefit *not* to be provided *by the benefactor*."[13] McConnell agrees that gratitude is due only when the beneficiary responds to a benefit in a particular way, but he believes that Simmon's conditions are too narrow. What if, for example, a wealthy benefactor pays for Bonnie's college tuition, and she accepts the gift not because she wants to go to college but merely because she wants to please her parents. McConnell thinks Bonnie owes her benefactor gratitude even though she didn't want the benefit provided to her. Consequently, McConnell proposes a standard focusing on acceptance rather than want. He states, "3'. The benefit must not be forced (unjustifiably) on the beneficiary against his will. 4'. The beneficiary must accept the benefit (or would accept the benefit if certain impairing conditions were corrected.)."[14]

When we stand back and look at contemporary philosophical discussions of gratitude we see that, while there are disputes, the disputes are minor. Philosophers seem to have reached a consensus on the general approach to when we should be grateful. Moreover, this approach to gratitude makes the virtue insignificant. Philosophers generally agree that we ought to be grateful only when very restricted conditions are met. Consequently, gratitude is thought to have a minimal role in our moral life.

II. TWO ANOMALOUS CASES

There are many cases where I believe we ought to be grateful that do not fit within the contemporary philosophical analysis of gratitude. Instead of listing every such case and instead of moving directly to the alternative theory that I

---

[11]A. John Simmons, *Moral Principles and Political Obligations* (Princeton, N. J.: Princeton University Press, 1979), pp. 171–72. See also P. F. Strawson, "Freedom and Resentment," in *Studies in the Philosophy of Thought and Action*, ed. P. F. Strawson (Oxford: Oxford University Press, 1968), pp. 75–76.
[12]McConnell, p. 44.
[13] Simmons, pp. 177, 178.
[14] McConnell, p. 44.

favor I will take two cases that dramatically conflict with the contemporary analysis. Both cases are found in Buddhist writings, revealing the inspiration for my alternative theory. The cases illustrate a very different way of looking at gratitude. In this section I will describe the cases and some motivation for them. In the next section I will describe the cases and some motivation for them. In the next section I will flesh out more systematically the theory that could provide justification for the examples.

A. Gratitude to Those Who Harm You

Given the Christian heritage of the West, it does not strike us as strange that we might forgive our enemies. Being grateful to our enemies, on the other hand, sounds absurd. When Jesus was crucified, he asked God to forgive those who crucified him, but he never thanked them. He asked his followers to turn the other cheek, but he never requested that they do so with appreciation for those who slapped them. The idea of practicing gratitude toward one's enemies is not, however, without precedent.[15] Indeed, it is a common ideal within Buddhism. The Dalai Lama often repeats this Buddhist teaching by telling his audiences that he is grateful to the Chinese for giving him the opportunity to practice love for his enemies.[16] In one instance he expressed gratitude for a different but related reason: because the Chinese gave him training in patience and helped his development as a person.

> Even our enemies give us the best training in patience. When we reflect on these holy instructions, in a way we should feel grateful to the Chinese. If we were still living in the same old system, I very much doubt that the Dalai Lama could have become so closely acquainted with worldly reality. I used to live in a very sheltered environment, but now that we are in exile there is no stigma attached to facing reality. In our own country, we could pretend that everything was in order because it was shrouded under a cloak of pomp and show. I had to sit on a high throne assuming the attitude of being the Dalai Lama. . . . It is quite possible that I could have become narrow minded, but because of the Chinese threats and humiliations, I have become a real person. So what happened in Tibet can be seen as a blessing in disguise.[17]

The Dalai Lama's expression of gratitude strikes many as strange, but before we look at possible justifications for his position, we should look at another example so that the details of the Tibetan case do not color our analysis.

Nichiren, a controversial thirteenth-century Japanese Buddhist monk, offers another example. Nichiren gave unyielding criticisms of Japanese religious leaders, governmental support of established religions, and the Japanese religions

[15]Nietzsche seems to suggest an analogous position. He states, "But if you have an enemy, do not requite him evil with good, for that would put him to shame. Rather prove that he did you some good" (*The Portable Nietzsche*, trans. Walter Kaufman, [New York: Viking, 1968], p. 180).

[16]Malcolm David Eckel, "Gratitude to an Empty Savior: A Study of the Concept of Gratitude in Mahayana Buddhist Philosophy," *History of Religions* 25 (1985): 57–75, p. 59.

[17]His Holiness the Dalai Lama, *Awakening the Mind, Lightening the Heart: Core Teachings of Tibetan Buddhism*, ed. Donald S. Lopez, Jr. (San Francisco, Calif.: Harper Collins, 1995), p. 38.

themselves. Nichiren believed that they had abandoned what he considered the highest Buddhist teaching—the Lotus Sutra. Because of his outspoken manner, the Japanese government twice exiled him and nearly executed him. Nonetheless, Nichiren claimed that he was grateful to the Japanese government and its ruler (during this period in Japanese history the real authority rested neither in the hands of the emperor nor the shogun, but in members of the Hojo family who held the office of regent for the shogun). During his exile to Ito on the Izu Peninsula, Nichiren wrote to a follower, "Those people who slandered me and the ruler [who had me banished] are the very persons to whom I owe the most profound debt of gratitude."[18]

While the ruler had clearly harmed Nichiren through exiling him and attempting to execute him, Nichiren considered these difficulties as essential to his own spiritual progress. He considered the persecution an essential part of a larger picture, a step on his own road to enlightenment. Consequently, he considered the harm the ruler caused as insignificant. He states, "Moreover, in this lifetime, I have been able to take faith in the Lotus Sutra and to encounter a ruler who will enable me to free myself in my present existence from the sufferings of birth and death. Thus how can I dwell on the insignificant harm that he has done me and overlook my debt to him?"[19]

The gratitude expressed by Nichiren and the Dalai Lama clearly does not fit the contemporary philosophical model.[20] First, both Nichiren and the Dalai Lama express gratitude to people who harmed them. While both claim that the very people who harmed them have also benefited them, that benefit is indirect. Both claim spiritual progress: Nichiren could "take faith in the Lotus Sutra," and the Dalai Lama could become "a real person." We should note that neither the Japanese nor the Chinese was the sufficient cause for either of these Buddhists to develop spiritually. The Japanese and the Chinese created conditions, created the opportunity, where a particular kind of spiritual progress was possible. In other words, the benefits accrued by Nichiren and the Dalai Lama were significantly due to their own efforts. Neither was given a direct benefit. If we

---

[18]Nichiren Daishonin, *The Major Writings of Nichiren Daishonin*, vol. 5 (Tokyo: Nichiren Shoshu International Center, 1988), p. 8; brackets in quoted translation.

[19]Ibid., p. 9.

[20]Similar examples can be found in other spiritual traditions. The Sufi poet Rumi writes about a priest who prays for thieves and muggers, "because they have done me such generous favors. Every time I turn back toward the things they want I run into them. They beat me and leave me in the road, and I understand again, that what they want is not what I want. Those that make you return, for whatever reason, to the spirit, be grateful to them. Worry about the others who give you delicious comfort that keeps you from prayer" (quoted in Jack Kornfield, *A Path with Heart: A Guide Through the Perils and Promises of Spiritual Life* [New York: Bantam Books, 1993]. p. 74). In the Christian tradition the Christian Desert Fathers use a parable that relates a similar sentiment. A student is told by his master to give money to anyone who insults him. After three years of this practice he is told to go to Alexandria and truly learn wisdom. When he gets to the gates of Alexandria he meets a wise man who insults everyone who enters. After the wise man insults the student, the student bursts out laughing. The wise man asks him why he laughs and the student says, "For years I have been paying for this kind of thing, and now you give it to me for free!" The wise man tells the student to enter the city, "It's all yours" (ibid., p. 64).

really wanted to define benefit broadly, we could say that both the Dalai Lama and Nichiren were benefited. This broad sense of benefit, however, is not what the contemporary philosophical analysis typically intends. I will say, therefore, that the Dalai Lama and Nichiren were harmed and given opportunities. Both capitalized on those opportunities by creating benefits out of them.

Second, neither party was benefited intentionally. The Chinese did not try to make the Dalai Lama "a real person," and the Japanese did not try to make Nichiren "the votary of the Lotus Sutra." The Dalai Lama's and Nichiren's expressions of gratitude are clearly not responses to benevolence.

The third criterion, acceptance, is a bit more complicated. While both Nichiren and the Dalai Lama accepted what happened to them in one sense, this sense of acceptance is not the kind envisioned by contemporary moral philosophers. First, the object of acceptance is a benefit in contemporary philosophical analysis, but no benefit is given in these cases. At best we can say opportunities are given. Second, in an important sense both Nichiren and the Dalai Lama did not accept even these opportunities. Neither Nichiren nor the Dalai Lama wanted what happened to them before it happened. Both men do accept the events in retrospect, but neither would choose the persecution if they could. Indeed, if they chose to be persecuted, it would no longer be persecution and would become masochism. An essential part of each of these stories is that hardship was *forced* on these men against their will. In this sense neither accepted even the opportunities that their hardships presented. Instead, they chose to see their hardships as opportunities after they occurred so that they could make the best out of a bad situation or, in the terms of the traditional Buddhist metaphor, "turn poison into medicine."

Thus, in this first case we have two examples of gratitude that do not meet any of the necessary conditions proposed by contemporary philosophers. These two examples are clearly anomalous to the contemporary analysis.

B. Gratitude to Someone Whom You Benefit

A second anomalous case for contemporary accounts of gratitude is the case of benefactors who feel grateful to those they benefit. This again is a Buddhist theme, but it is also common in non-Buddhist writings. Individuals who perform volunteer work or community service sometimes speak of the benefits they gain from the service and express gratitude to those who present them with the opportunity to serve. This often occurs with volunteers, but sometimes it also occurs with individuals who are members of service professions. One example of the latter case can be found in a recent article in the *Journal of the American Medical Association* by Dr. David Hilfiker: "I am beginning to realize that we in medicine need the poor to bring us back to our roots as a servant profession. Medicine drifts understandably yet ominously toward the technical and the economically lucrative, and we find it difficult to resist. Perhaps we *need* the poor at this very moment to bring us back to ourselves. The nature of the healer's work is to be with the wounded in their suffering. Can the poor in their very vulnerability show us how?"[21] Hilfiker expresses feelings of gratitude for the poor, but it is not because of any beneficent actions that the poor take on behalf of doctors. Instead the poor create an opportunity for members of the medical profession to define their working lives around helping the vulnerable rather than getting lost in technical details or money making. Without the poor to serve, the profession would lose itself and move away from its professional ideal.

Buddhists often advocate a similar attitude toward those that one serves. Here the reason for a debt of gratitude toward those in need comes from the importance of compassion. Having compassion is thought to be essential for one's happiness. Jack Kornfield explains, "There's a tremendous sorrow for a human being who doesn't find a way to give. One of the worst of human sufferings is not to find a way to love, or a place to work and give of your heart and your being."[22] Ram Dass and Paul Gorman explain the Buddhist view of compassion in terms of self-discovery: "Caring for one another, we sometimes glimpse an essential quality of our being. We may be sitting alone, lost in self-doubt or self-pity, when the phone rings with a call from a friend who's *really* depressed. Instinctively, we come out of ourselves, just to be there with her and say a few reassuring words. When we're done, and a little comfort's been shared, we put down the phone and feel a little more at home with ourselves. We're reminded of who we really are and what we have to offer one another."[23] Because compassion is thought to be immensely beneficial to those who feel it, it is considered appropriate to feel grateful to those who cause one's compassion. There can be no rescuer without someone to rescue; there can be no benefactor without a beneficiary. If giving to those in need enriches one's life, then one owes a debt of gratitude to those who needed the gift. Consequently, Buddhism enshrines a debt of gratitude to all living beings. Nichiren comments, "One who studies the teachings of Buddhism must not fail to repay the four debts of gratitude. According to the *Shinjikan* Sutra, the first of the four debts is that owed to all living beings. Were it not for them, one would find it impossible to make the vow and same innumerable living beings."[24]

Here again the expression of gratitude need not fit *any* of the conditions found in the contemporary philosophical model. First, beneficiaries need not give benefactors any benefits. A benefactor may benefit from a beneficiary trying to return the favor he received or a benefactor may get emotional benefits from a beneficiary expressing gratitude, but neither of these benefits always occurs. Beneficiaries often do nothing to try to help their benefactors. If one is grateful for the opportunity to give in these cases, then one is grateful to someone who does not *give* benefits. Hilfiker's suggestion to the medical com-

---

[21]David Hilfiker, "Unconscious on a Corner," *Journal of the American Medical Association* 258 (1987): 3155–56, p. 3156.

[22]Jack Kornfield, *Roots of Buddhist Psychology*, quoted in Frederic Brussat and Mary Ann Brussat, *Spiritual Literacy: Reading the Sacred in Everyday Life* (New York: Scribner's, 1996), p. 327.

[23]Ram Dass and Paul Gorman, *How Can I Help? Stories and Reflections on Service* (New York: Knopf, 1985), p. 7.

[24]Nichiren, p. 8.

munity is an example of this. He does not argue that poor patients perform actions that benefit doctors. Indeed the lack of an ability to give doctors the typical benefit they receive for their services—money—is the very reason Hilfiker sees serving the poor is important. The plight of poor patients gives the medical profession an opportunity—an opportunity to return the medical profession to a servant profession. Like our previous case of gratitude to those who harm you, gratitude to those whom you benefit is gratitude for opportunities (which if not taken are merely harms or burdens) rather than gratitude for benefits.

Second, the benefits derived from giving need not be intended by those who receive. It is unlikely that a poor person will receive aid merely because it might help the giver develop compassion. Even less likely is the case of a person becoming poor, or in need of other assistance, merely because it might help self-absorbed individual rise to a higher moral or spiritual plane. Those who receive aid rarely do so out of beneficent intentions. This kind of gratitude is not a response to beneficence.

Third, it is again hard to talk of a benefactor accepting the benefits of giving. No one is intending to give her anything, and all that she receives is an opportunity for a benefit (that if not developed is merely a burden) rather than an actual benefit. Any kind of acceptance that we could attribute to this kind of gratitude would not be the kind suggested by the contemporary philosophical analysis. Being grateful to those whom one aids is, like being grateful to those who harm you, an anomaly for the contemporary philosophical analysis of gratitude. It is anomalous because none of the three conditions thought necessary for gratitude need be present.

III. POSSIBLE JUSTIFICATIONS FOR GRATITUDE

We could respond to these two anomalous cases in three general ways: (1) we might criticize those who feel grateful because we think they ought not be grateful; (2) we might praise the grateful for their gratitude; or (3) we might neither criticize nor praise the grateful, maintaining that their gratitude is neither favored nor disfavored by moral reasons. If we take option (1) and we criticize the grateful, then the two cases that I presented pose no problems for the contemporary philosophical analysis. The same is true if we take option (3), and we conclude that morality neither favors nor disfavors these cases of gratitude. Since the contemporary philosophical analysis tries to identify only those cases where gratitude is owed, these cases—where people feel gratitude even though they do now owe it—are no problem. These cases are only a problem if we think that morality favors gratitude in the two cases. If morality favors gratitude and the contemporary philosophical analysis can give no account of this, then the contemporary philosophical analysis is incomplete. I support (2). I think morality favors the expressions of gratitude in the cases I have described.

A. Six Possible Justifications

Before arguing that gratitude is justified in the two anomalous cases, it will be helpful to categorize the kinds of moral reasons we might have for gratitude at any time. There are at least six distinct types of moral reasons one might have for gratitude. Usually we will have more than one moral reason for gratitude, so we could use a single example to illustrate many or all of them. Still, even when there is overlap, one reason may dominate or be more important than another. I am not sure that this list is exhaustive, but the most important point may be that there is a list at all, that there are many possible moral reasons for gratitude. As I will argue in the next section, moral philosophers (probably reflecting common-sense morality) often seem to assume that only one kind of moral reason is relevant for gratitude—reasons of justice. This assumption, however, is not justified.

We can begin with the most common type of moral reason cited in favor of gratitude—justice. In these cases we have *juridical* reasons for gratitude. The recipients of gratitude "deserve" it, "merit" it, are "entitled" to it, or ingratitude may be somehow "unfair." Those who ought to be grateful "owe" gratitude or have a "debt of gratitude." Suppose George stops to jump my car one cold winter morning, and I give him a perfunctory "thank you." The next morning I see George in the same perdicament—now he is in need of a jump—but instead of stopping I drive on, aspiring to get first pick of the free donuts that await me at my office. Some would say that I owe George a jump or that he deserves my help, or that he is entitled to my help or that I treat him unfairly if I do not help. If any of these reasons is correct then I have a juridical reason to be grateful. My ingratitude would be a case of injustice.

Gratitude might also be called for because it will prevent a harm or burden. In these cases we have *nonmaleficent* reasons for gratitude. When, my father tells me "don't forget your mother's birthday or you will break her heart," he is giving me a nonmaleficent reason for a particular expression of gratitude. Unless I express gratitude to my mother by recognizing her birthday, I do her harm or cause her distress. If, however, my father tells me, "You could bring your mother a lot of joy if you could show your appreciation," then my father points to a different moral reason for gratitude. Here my gratitude will benefit my mother. In these cases we have *beneficent* reasons for gratitude.

Gratitude might be useful to promote or preserve a special relationship such as a relationship with a friend or a lover. Since the ethic of care emphasizes these kinds of relationships, we can say that in these cases we have *caring* reasons for gratitude. Suppose I come home, and my friend has made me dinner. Of course, I have many moral reasons to be grateful, including the ones discussed above. My gratitude may prevent my friend's distress (nonmaleficent) or cause my friend joy (beneficent), but my gratitude may also be essential for preserving the friendship. Most people do not enjoy being friendly with the ungrateful. If I am not grateful to my friend and show no appreciation or show appreciation only out of a sense of duty, then my friend may not want to remain my friend. So ingratitude may be cause for severing or weakening the friendship. If I treasure the relationship then I have a good reason to be grateful, and if I consider the relationship morally important (because of its intrinsic value, its instrumental value in shaping my character, or for another reason), then I have a good moral reason to be grateful.

Gratitude might be useful for promoting or preserving communal relationships. In these cases we have *civic* reasons for gratitude. Cases like this often arise when we look at norms of gratitude. What might be a moral justification for the norm of being grateful to someone who holds the door open for you? We might try to explain it in terms of beneficence (it reinforces a practice that brings joy) or nonmaleficence (it protects against hurt feelings), but a better explanation is probably communal. The practice of being grateful to strangers who hold doors open produces a small communal feeling, a slight feeling of solidarity or connectedness. When we take care to prevent a door from coming between us the act brings us together both literally and figuratively. This is a better explanation than a juridical one. It sounds very strange to say that I owe something to Joe for holding the door open, or that Joe is entitled to something because he held the door open, or that I treat Joe unfairly if I am not grateful for his holding the door open. But this does not mean that the practice of holding doors open is irrelevant to morality, it only means that the practice of holding doors open is irrelevant to justice. Gratitude, then, has the potential of reinforcing communal ties, and some norms of gratitude may find their primary justification in this very feature.

Finally, gratitude also may aid in the development of virtues or help prevent the formation of vices. In these cases we have *perfectionist* reasons for gratitude. Gratitude may be especially important as an antidote to feelings of anger and resentment and thus to the formation of an angry or resentful character. Suppose that I have a friend who has given me many benefits, but just last week harmed me significantly. Although we have discussed last week's incident, and he has apologized and done what we we could to make things better, I am unable to forget it. Whenever I see him, I feel my fists and jaw clench, my blood pressure rise, and my mind returns again and again to the wrong that he did me. In the presence of my friend I become an angry and resentful person. If I reflect on my mental life, I may wish I were not so resentful, and I may realize that my character would improve if I could overcome my resentment. Gratitude is a potential antidote to these unwanted emotions. If I focus on the benefits that my friend has given me, and if I can focus on those benefits with appreciation, then I will find it difficult to feel angry, at least for a moment. Gently returning my attention to the broader perspective where the presence of my friend is a benefit competes with my mind's tendency to focus on the incident of harm. Cultivating gratitude (by focusing my attention on the wider perspective where I receive benefit), therefore, reduces anger and resentment. The more that I do this the more grateful and the less angry my character becomes.

B. The Case for Gratitude to Those Who Harm You

I have described six different kinds of moral reasons that one may have to be grateful. Now what should we say of our two anomalous cases? What moral reasons might favor feeling grateful to those who harm you? The primary reason cited by both Nichiren and the Dalai lama is perfectionist. According to the Dalai Lama, for example, the purpose of Buddhist practice is to combat disturbing emotions: "It is important to remember that all the Buddha taught was meant to help sentient beings and guide them on their spiritual path. His philosophical teachings were not just abstract speculation but part of the processes and techniques for combating disturbing emotions."[25]

From the perspective of someone who is working to eliminate their own disturbing emotions, incidents where people harm you can be an important opportunity. Those who irritate us the most give us the opportunity to develop our patience and extend the boundaries of our compassion. Hence, it is the very antagonistic attitude, the absence of beneficence in the "enemy"—a general term in Buddhism used to refer to any individual with whom one has a conflict—that enables the individual to develop virtue. The Dalai Lama states, "It is sometimes the case that beings with actively hostile intentions can help us to the highest realizations. Enemies are very important, because it is only in relation to them that we can develop patience. Only they give us the opportunity to test our patience. Not your spiritual master, your friends, or your relative give you such a great opportunity. The enemy's antagonism would normally arouse your anger, but by changing your attitude you can transform it into an opportunity to test and practice patience."[26] When we deal with an "enemy" we can focus on the harm that they have done us and become angry. Alternatively, we can focus on the opportunity that the "enemy" gives us and develop gratitude and compassion. The Dalai Lama argues that it would be better to focus on the opportunity that our "enemy" gives us."We need to appreciate that the kindness of sentient beings is not confined to when they have been our parents or friends; it extends to when they have been our enemies as well. This is something to be pondered deeply. It will serve as a great inspiration for cultivating compassion. When you recollect the special kindness of sentient being in this way, your wish to repay them will be much stronger." [27]

I have quoted extensively from the Dalai Lama because I began with the example of his gratitude toward the Chinese, and because I think his writings give the readers a good sense of how gratitude to those who harm us may be useful. However, the Dalai Lama's teaching is not unique in this respect. It is a central tenet of Buddhism. In Buddhist thought, anger is one of our most destructive emotions (classified as one of the "three poisons" of the mind) and consequently calls out for our attention. Because anger is so powerful we will probably have to use many methods to deal with it if we are to bring it under our control, but the cultivation of gratitude is one important way. Gratitude can be an antidote to a mental state that causes suffering in ourselves and those around us. Putting this argument more formally might be helpful:

[25]Dalai Lama, p. 17.
[26]Ibid., p. 108.
[27]Ibid.

1. We have good moral reasons to overcome our anger or hatred.
2. Sometimes cultivating gratitude will be the most effective way to overcome anger or hatred.
3. Therefore, in some cases of anger or hatred we have good moral reasons to cultivate gratitude.

The support for premise 1 has thus far been cast in perfectionist terms—cultivating gratitude is an antidote to the vice of anger. Additional support can be crafted from nonperfectionist moral reasons. Again the Dalai Lama's gratitude toward the Chineses illustrates this. The Dalai Lama is not merely concerned about his own character and the characters of those who listen to him. He is moved by a desire to create peace in Tibet and China, and he believes that responding to the Chinese occupation with gratitude would be more effective than anger. By cultivating gratitude he and others can refrain from action motivated by resentment and thus refrain from committing or supporting violent acts. Anger threatens peace and gratitude is an antidote for anger. Consequently, this one case of gratitude might be justified in many different ways. It might be justified in civic terms because the Dalai Lama wants to create communal ties between Tibetans and Chinese, in nonmaleficent terms because he wants to prevent the harm that my come from Chinese/Tibetan hostilities, in beneficent terms because he wants to create the benefits of peace, in caring terms because he thinks he may have a better relationship with his students if he dispels his own anger, or in perfectionist terms because he thinks that his own gratitude will make him a better person.

Support for premise 2 must be contextual. Sometimes the suggestion of cultivating gratitude to those who harm you may be unhelpful. The very idea may seem psychologically impossible or undesirable, and suggestions to the contrary may only create psychological resistance. Even if cultivating gratitude would help a resentful person, it may not help to tell her to cultivate gratitude. Furthermore, gratitude's value in each case lies in its effectiveness as a psychological strategy, and we have no reason to believe that the gratitude strategy is equally effective in all cases. Sometimes approaching one's anger in a different way may be better. So premise 2 does not and should not read, "Gratitude is always the best way to counteract anger" and the conclusion does not and should not read, "All individuals should try to cultivate gratitude for those who harm them." It would, I believe, be a better world if we were all grateful to those who harmed us, but sometimes trying to cultivate gratitude may do more harm than good. So premise 2 does not speak to everyone in every situation. It does, however, speak to some people in some situations, and perhaps it speaks to everyone in at least some situations. When one notices anger arising or resentment festering, and if cultivating gratitude is the most effective way to counteract these feelings, then one has good moral reasons for gratitude.

C. The Case for Gratitude to Those You Benefit

We can now turn to the justification for being grateful to those whom you benefit. Those who claim this kind of gratitude rarely give intricate justifications, but we should consider three. First, gratitude to beneficiaries is sometimes justified by referring to the importance of compassion. This is the justification that Nichiren gives when he cites the bodhisattva's debt of gratitude to all living beings. Without those individuals in need there would be no way to become a bodhisattva—an individual who vows to liberate innumberable living beings from suffering. Since the bodhisattva is a *perfectionist* ideal in Buddhism, we may describe this reason in perfectionist terms.

We might describe a similar sentiment in *juridical* terms. If not caring for others inevitably leads to suffering, as Jack Kornfield maintains, then the individual who becomes the object of one's caring has done one a great service. "If it weren't for you," the benefactor might say to the beneficiary, "I would be miserably self-absorbed." The reasoning her is juridical. The beneficiary does the benefactor a great service, though it was probably not intentional, and gratitude is due.

A third possible justification focuses on preventing harm. Consider a common criticism of charitable giving. Some say charitable giving disempowers or otherwise psychologically harms beneficiaries. Rousseau, for instance, worries that if one individual always receives help and is never allowed to give it then he is likely to feel powerless. Kant claims that helping out a poor man "involves a dependence of his welfare upon my generosity, which humiliates him."[28] If giving has this consequence, or creates a similarly unhealthy relationship between benefactor and beneficiary, then it poses a difficult problem for a genuinely beneficent benefactor. If one truly wishes another well, how can one provide material support without also degrading the very individual one desires to help? Card notes that this may convince benefactors that they do not want their beneficiaries to feel indebted: "Sensitive benefactors may want their beneficiaries *not* to feel indebted to them, for it alters their relationship."[29] But how are benefactors to do this as they provide material support? Must one refrain from giving to prevent such an unhealthy interpersonal dynamic? One might conclude that nonmaleficence, the desire not to harm, argues against giving (except in such dire cases where the material benefits of the aid outweigh the psychological harm).

Such a strong conclusion is unwarranted, however, because the problems associated with giving do no always occur. Rather, the problems associated with giving depend on both the attitudes of the beneficiary and the benefactor. Consider the effects of the attitudes of a benefactor with a simple thought experiment. Suppose that you collect stamps, and you strongly want to acquire rare stamps when you seem them. Also suppose that someone else has a stamp that you want, and they will give it to you but have no interest in letting you buy it. Now imagine the different reactions you might have for each of the following individuals giving you the stamp you want: a longtime friend whom you have often helped; an associate whom you have always felt is trying to prove that he is better than you; a Jehovah's Witness who has just knocked at your door to tell

---

[28]Immanuel Kant, *Metaphysical Principles of Virtue, in Ethical Philosophy*, trans. James W. Ellington (Indianapolis, Ind.: Hackett, 1983), pp. 112–13.
[29]Card, p.117.

you about the true path to salvation; an associate who always resents giving but typically does give out of a sense of duty; a lover; a family member. The obvious implication of this thought experiment is that the value you place on getting your desired stamp may vary widely with who your benefactor might be. What may the benefactor want or expect in return? Is that something you want to give? The effect of receiving a gift, even when it is the same material object in each case, varies when the benefactor is someone who wants to see you happy, someone who wants you to join their religion, or someone who wants to see you in a position subservient to them. The general point, then, is that the attitude of the benefactor can significantly affect the well-being of the beneficiary. Consequently, the ethics of giving cannot stop at the material object given but must extend to the attitude with which it is given.

One attitude that may harm is a feeling of superiority. If the benefactor looks at his beneficiary as something pitiful or thinks of himself as better than the beneficiary, then acceptance of a material gift may come at the price of self-respect. So, if you are about to offer help to another and you realize that you are likely to feel superior to your beneficiary, or if you are in the midst of helping another, and you come to notice feelings of superiority, or if you realize that the person you are about to help could easily believe that you want to help in order to feel superior, and you don't want to harm or challenge another's self-respect—what should you do? On one occasion Kant suggested that a benefactor should "carry out his beneficence completely in secret." But it is unclear that this is really a solution. The beneficiary is still likely to feel pitiful, perhaps even more so since the benefactor had to hide his activities. The very secrecy seems to reinforce the idea that the recipient should feel pitiful or deeply indebted to receiving this aid. Perhaps for these very reasons Kant prefers a different approach. He states, "The benefactor must express himself as being obligated or honored by the other's acceptance, treating the duty merely as a debt he owes."[30] It is only if a benefactor cannot do this that he should resort to giving in secrecy. The idea here seems to be that the benefactor should try to transform the giving relationship into something that does not degrade recipients.[31] Gratitude in giving offers an analogous approach. What if we truly valued the opportunity to help another individual because we considered it essential for our own happiness? When we see an instance where we know we really can be of help, what if we felt thankful to the chance to rise out of our self-absorption or simply thankful for the chance to do something worthwhile? Kornfield's description of Buddhist psychology seems to suggest such a sentiment. If one of the worst human sufferings is not finding a way to love then the benefactor may get as much, if not more, out of giving than the beneficiary receives. Consequently a feeling of gratitude transforms an act of giving into a trade—"I will support you materially and in the process you will help me rise above my self-centeredness" (or, ". . . and you will help me do something worthwhile," or

[30]Kant, p. 118.
[31]For a discussion of gratitude in Kant's writing, see Jean P. Rumsey, "Re-Visions of Agency in Kant's Moral Theory," in *Feminist Interpretations of Immanuel Kant*, ed. Robin May, Schott (University Park, Pa.: Pennsylvania State University Press, 1997), pp.125–44.

simply, " . . . you will help me love"). This trade means that no debts linger after material aid is given. No inferior position is required of the beneficiary. Charity does not wound.

This is not the only way to counter the asymmetries of the gift relationship. Often it may be more important to create opportunities where a beneficiary can pay back aid in kind or feel that the aid is part of a larger system of mutual aid to which she could later make contributions. But this may be difficult or impossible to achieve. Sometimes the opportunity to pay a benefactor back may be impossible or unlikely, and the beneficiary may be unable to contribute to any system of mutual aid. Imagine a hospice volunteer who continually gives services to strangers who are terminally ill. If this volunteer want to help those whom she serves then she clearly would not want to leave them with feelings that they owed her something for her help. It would be cruel to create feelings of unpaid debts in people who are about to die. In these and other cases gratitude in giving may be invaluable in preventing psychological harms that may come about from receiving.

IV. OUGHT VERSUS OWE

Contemporary philosophical analyses of gratitude are too narrow. They give gratitude too limited a place in our moral life and argue for the cultivation of gratitude on too few occasions. The two anomalous cases that I chose were designed to be the most dramatic demonstration of my claim. In these cases we have good moral reasons for gratitude, but the contemporary philosophical analysis has no means to account for them. If I am right about these extreme cases, then there should be many more that are less dramatic. The reasons why the contemporary philosophical analysis fails also seem to suggest this conclusion. The contemporary philosophical analysis fails because it only entertains juridical reasons for gratitude and ignores others. This assumption is rarely articulated but is typically apparent in the limited range of moral terms that philosophers use to discuss the morality of gratitude. This seems especially clear in one passage in Card's article. She states, "It should be noted, however, that gratitude need not be deserved to be in order. Gratitude is not always *to* someone, although is if *for* something. I may be grateful *that* the weather 'cooperated' with plans for the picnic, or *that* the highway patrol officer was distracted as I sped by, without being grateful to anyone for either event. . . . My interest, however, like Berger's, is in deserved gratitude."[32] Notice the move that Card makes here. She doesn't want to discuss cases of gratitude that seem irrelevant to morality,[33] but instead of merely excluding gratitude that is morally irrelevant she narrows the discussion to a particular kind of moral reason—

[32]Card, p. 117.
[33]It is questionable, however, that these cases are morally irrelevant. The case of being grateful for good weather may be entirely appropriate for a deep ecologist who excludes nothing from the moral sphere. Others may think that developing gratitude to things or processes is a virtuous character trait that holds in check a tendency to exploit the environment.

desert. Card is not alone in making this move. She attributes the same position to Berger, and others use similar moral language. Jecker asks which persons merit gratitude, and McConnell tries to answer the question of "When gratitude is owed?"[34] This common move sets the terms of the debate by limiting the kinds of moral reasons we might have to be grateful. The question asked is not, "When do we have good moral reasons to be grateful?" but, instead, "When do we have the specific moral reasons of desert, merit, or debt?"

In one sense it is understandable why Card and others might frame the issues in this way. The limitations reflect common moral intuitions or at least common moral language. Terms like 'desert', 'merit', and 'debt' are commonly used to discuss cases of gratitude and ingratitude. If we were interested in merely uncovering the modern moral intuitions regarding gratitude, then it might seem plausible to limit our discussion in the way philosophers have.

In another sense, however, this limitation seems quite mysterious. What moral justification is there to believe that gratitude is only supported by juridical reasons? Why should we only be worried about ingratitude that is unjust? When reflecting on whether to cultivate gratitude, this limitation is clearly arbitrary and artificial. A moral agent ought to be concerned with all relevant moral reasons, not just whether gratitude is deserved, merited, or owed. If gratitude is not owed but can nonetheless cause great benefit or prevent great harm or repair communalties, then the agent has a good moral reason to be grateful. The question of whether gratitude is owed is simply not the whole story. So if the contemporary philosophical discussion of gratitude accurately reflects common moral beliefs about when we should be grateful, then those beliefs are wrong. . . .

Questions

1. What is the difference between Fred Berger's and Patrick Boleyn-Fitzgerald's accounts of how gratitude and reciprocity differ?
2. What do you think of the objection that although reasons (ii) to (vi) may provide moral reasons for gratitude, these reasons are outweighed (at least usually) by other moral considerations, such as the inappropriateness of responding to evil with gratitude? Do you think it makes a difference whether the wrong done is to oneself or to another person?

Suggestions for Further Reading on Gratitude

CARD, CLAUDIA. "Gratitude and Obligation." *American Philosophical Quarterly* 25 (1988): pp. 115–127.

McCONNELL, TERRANCE. *Gratitude*. Philadelphia: Temple University Press, 1993.

WALKER, A. D. M. "Gratefulness and Gratitude." *Proceedings of the Aristotelian Society*, 1981: pp. 39–55.

WEISS, ROSLYN. "The Moral and Social Dimensions of Gratitude." *The Southern Journal of Philosophy* 23 (1985): pp. 491–501.

WELLMAN, CHRISTOPHER HEATH. "Gratitude as a Virtue." *Pacific Philosophical Quarterly* 80 (1999): pp. 284–300.

[34]Jecker, p. 73; McConnell, p. 13.

CHAPTER 22

Jealousy and Envy

IMMANUEL KANT, Jealousy and Its Offspring—Envy and Grudge

DANIEL FARRELL, Of Jealousy and Envy

Jealousy and Its Offspring— Envy and Grudge

Immanuel Kant

According to Immanuel Kant, there are two ways people arrive at an opinion of their worth: (1) by comparing themselves with perfection and (2) by comparing themselves with others. The first of these he considers good, but not the second, because when somebody compares himself with somebody who has more good features than himself, he usually becomes jealous of the other and tries to minimize the value of the other person's good features. Immanuel Kant calls this kind of jealousy "grudge" and distinguishes if from a rare form of jealousy, "emulating jealousy," which occurs when a person attempts to emulate the person with better qualities than himself.

Grudge, the author further contends, is to be distinguished from envy. Whereas grudge occurs when one resents some advantage another has over one, envy occurs when one begrudges a person his fair share of happiness. The envious person is the one who desires the unhappiness of others, not because it will advance his own position but because he wants to be the only happy one. Envy, in Immanuel Kant's view, is one of three vices that, in their extreme forms, are "devilish." The other two are ingratitude and malice.

There are two methods by which men arrive at an opinion of their worth: by comparing themselves with the Idea of perfection and by comparing themselves with others. The first of these methods is sound; the second is not, and it frequently even leads to a result diametrically opposed to the first. The Idea of perfection is a proper standard, and if we measure our worth by it, we find that we fall short of it and feel that we must exert ourselves to come nearer to it; but if we compare ourselves with others, much depends upon who those others are

Immanuel Kant, "Jealousy and Its Offspring—Envy and Grudge," in *Lectures on Ethics*, translated by Louis Infield (London: Methuen, 1930), 215–223.

and how they are constituted, and we can easily believe ourselves to be of great worth if those with whom we set up comparison are rogues. Men love to compare themselves with others, for by that method they can always arrive at a result favourable to themselves. They choose as a rule the worst and not the best of the class with which they set up comparison; in this way their own excellence shines out. If they choose those of greater worth the result of the comparison is, of course, unfavourable to them.

When I compare myself with another who is better than I, there are but two ways by which I can bridge the gap between us. I can either do my best to attain to his perfections, or else I can seek to depreciate his good qualities. I either increase my own worth, or else I diminish his so that I can always regard myself as superior to him. It is easier to depreciate another than to emulate him, and men prefer the easier course. They adopt it, and this is the origin of jealousy. When a man compares himself with another and finds that the other has many more good points, he becomes jealous of each and every good point he discovers in the other, and tries to depreciate it so that his own good points may stand out. This kind of jealousy may be called grudging. The other species of the genus jealousy, which makes us try to add to our good points so as to compare well with another, may be called emulating jealousy. The jealousy of emulation is, as we have stated, more difficult than the jealousy of grudge and so is much the less frequent of the two.

Parents ought not, therefore, when teaching their children to be good, to urge them to model themselves on other children and try to emulate them, for by so doing they simply make them jealous. If I tell my son, 'Look, how good and industrious John is', the result will be that my son will bear John a grudge. He will think to himself that, but for John, he himself would be the best, because there would be no comparison. By setting up John as a pattern for imitation I anger my son, make him feel a grudge against this so-called paragon, and I instil jealousy in him. My son might, of course, try to emulate John, but not finding it easy, he will bear John ill-will. Besides, just as I can say to my son, 'Look, how good John is', so can he reply: 'Yes, he is better than I, but are there not many who are far worse? Why do you compare me with those who are better? Why not with those who are worse than I?' Goodness must, therefore, be commended to children in and for itself. Whether other children are better or worse has no bearing on the point. If the comparison were in the child's favour, he would lose all ground of impulse to improve his own conduct. To ask our children to model themselves on others is to adopt a faulty method of upbringing, and as time goes on the fault will strike its roots deep. It is jealousy that parents are training and presupposing in their children when they set other children before them as patterns. Otherwise, the children would be quite indifferent to the qualities of others. They will find it easier to belittle the good qualities of their patterns than to emulate them, so they will choose the easier path and learn to show a grudging disposition. It is true that jealousy is natural, but that is no excuse for cultivating it. It is only a motive, a reserve in case of need. While the maxims of reason are still undeveloped in us, the proper course is to use reason to keep it within bounds. For jealousy is only one of the many motives, such as ambition, which are implanted in us because we are designed for a life of activity. But so soon as reason is enthroned, we must cease to seek perfection in emulation of others and must covet it in and for itself. Motives must abdicate and let reason bear rule in their place.

Persons of the same station and occupation in life are particularly prone to be jealous of each other. Many business-men are jealous of each other; so are many scholars, particularly in the same line of scholarship; and women are liable to be jealous of each other regarding men.

Grudge is the displeasure we feel when another has an advantage; his advantage makes us feel unduly small and we grudge it him. But to grudge a man his share of happiness is envy. To be envious is to desire the failure and unhappiness of another not for the purpose of advancing our own success and happiness but because we might then ourselves be perfect and happy as we are. An envious man is not happy unless all around him are unhappy; his aim is to stand alone in the enjoyment of his happiness. Such is envy, and we shall learn below that it is satanic. Grudge, although it too should not be countenanced, is natural. Even a good-natured person may at times be grudging. Such a one may, for instance, begrudge those around him their jollity when he himself happens to be sorrowful; for it is hard to bear one's sorrow when all around are joyful. When I see everybody enjoying a good meal and I alone must content myself with inferior fare, it upsets me and I feel a grudge; but if we are all in the same boat I am content. We find the thought of death bearable, because we know that all must die; but if everybody were immortal and I alone had to die, I should feel aggrieved. It is not things themselves that affect us, but things in their relation to ourselves. We are grudging because others are happier than we. But when a good-natured man feels happy and cheerful, he wishes that every one else in the world were as happy as he and shared is joy; he begrudges no one his happiness.

When a man would not grant to another even that for which he himself has no need, he is spiteful. Spite is a maliciousness of spirit which is not the same thing as envy. I may not feel inclined to give to another something which belongs to me, even though I myself have no use for it, but it does not follow that I grudge him his own possessions, that I want to be the only one who has anything and wish him to have nothing at all. There is a deal of grudge in human nature which could develop into envy but which is not itself envy. We feel pleasure in gossiping about the minor misadventures of other people; we are not averse, although we may express no pleasure thereat, to hearing of the fall of some rich man; we may enjoy in stormy weather, when comfortably seated in our warm, cozy parlor, speaking of those at sea, for it heightens our own feeling comfort and happiness; there is grudge in all this, but it is not envy.

The three vices which are the essence of vileness and wickedness are ingratitude, envy, and malice. When these reach their full degree they are devilish.

Men are shamed by favours. If I receive a favour, I am placed under an obligation to the giver; he has a call upon me because I am indebted to him. We all blush to be obliged. Noble-minded men accordingly refuse to accept favours in order not to put themselves under an obligation. But this attitude predisposes the mind to ingratitude. If the man who adopts it is noble-minded, well and good; but if he be proud and selfish and has perchance received a favour, the feeling that his beholden to his benefactor hurts his pride and, being selfish, he cannot accommodate himself to the idea that he owes his benefactor anything. He becomes defiant and ungrateful. His ingratitude might even conceivably assume such dimensions that he cannot bear his benefactor and becomes his enemy. Such ingratitude is of the devil; it is out of all keeping with human nature. It is inhuman to hate and persecute one from whom we have reaped a benefit, and if such conduct were the rule it would cause untold harm. Men would then be afraid to do good to anyone lest they should receive evil in return for their good. They would become misanthropic.

The second devilish vice is envy. Envy is the highest degree detestable. The envious man does not merely want to be happy; he wants to be the only happy person in the world; he is really contented only when he sees nothing but misery around him. Such an intolerable creature would gladly destroy every source of joy and happiness in the world

Malice is the third kind of viciousness which is of the devil. It consists in taking a direct pleasure in the misfortunes of others. Men prone to this vice will seek, for instance, to make mischief between husband and wife, or between friends, and then enjoy the misery they have produced. In these matters we should make it a rule never to repeat to a person anything that we may have heard to his disadvantage from another, unless our silence would injure him. Otherwise we start an enmity and disturb his peace of mind, which our silence would have avoided, and in addition we break faith with our informant. The defence against such mischief-makers is upright conduct. Not by words but by our lives we should confute them. As Socrates said: We ought so to conduct ourselves that people will not credit anything spoken in disparagement of us.

These three vices—ingratitude (*ingratitudo qualificata*), envy, and malice—are devilish because they imply a direct inclination to evil. There are in man certain indirect tendencies to wickedness which are human and not unnatural. This miser wants everything for himself, but it is no satisfaction to him to see that his neighbor is destitute. The evilness of a vice may thus be either direct or indirect. In these three vices it is direct.

We may ask whether there is in the human mind an immediate inclination to wickedness, an inclination to the devilish vices. Heaven stands for the acme of happiness, hell for all that is bad, and the earth stands midway between these two extremes; and just as goodness which transcends anything which might be expected of a human being is spoken of as being angelic, so also do we speak of devilish wickedness when the wickedness oversteps the limits of human nature and becomes inhuman. We may take it for granted that the human mind has no immediate inclination to wickedness, but is only indirectly wicked. Man cannot be so ungrateful that he simply must hate his neighbor; he may be too proud to show his gratitude and so avoid him, but he wishes him well. Again, our pleasure in the misfortune of another is not direct. We may rejoice, for example, in a man's misfortunes, because he was haughty, rich and selfish; for man loves to preserve equality. We have thus no direct inclination towards evil as evil, but only an indirect one. But how are we to explain the fact that even young children have the spirit of mischief strongly developed? For a joke, a boy will stick a pin in an unsuspecting playmate, but it is only for fun. He has no thought of the pain the other must feel on all such occasions. In the same spirit he will torture animals; twisting the cat's tail or the dog's. Such tendencies must be nipped in the bud, for it is easy to see where they will lead. They are, in fact, something animal, something of the beast of prey which is in us all, which we cannot overcome, and the source of which we cannot explain. There certainly are in human nature characteristics for which we can assign no reason. There are animals too who steal anything that comes their way, though it is quite useless to them; and it seems as if man had retained this animal tendency in his nature.

Ingratitude calls for some further observations here. To help a man in distress is charity; to help him in less urgent needs is benevolence; to help him in the amenities of life is courtesy. We may be the recipients of a charity which has not cost the giver much and our gratitude is commensurate with the degree of good-will which moved him to the action. We are grateful not only for what we have received but also for the good intention which prompted it, and the greater the effort it has cost our benefactor, the greater our gratitude.

Gratitude may be either from duty or from inclination. If an act of kindness does not greatly move us, but if we nevertheless feel that it is right and proper that we should show gratitude, our gratitude is merely prompted by a sense of duty. Our heart is not grateful, but we have principles of gratitude. If, however, our heart goes out to our benefactor, we are grateful from inclination. There is a weakness of the understanding which we often have cause to recognize. It consists in taking the conditions of our understanding as conditions of the thing understood. We can estimate force only in terms of the obstacles it overcomes. Similarly, we can only estimate the degree of good-will in terms of the obstacles it has to surmount. In consequence we cannot comprehend the love and good-will of a being for whom there are no obstacles. If God has been good to me, I am liable to think that after all it has cost God no trouble, and that gratitude to God would be mere fawning on my part. Such thoughts are not at all unnatural. If is easy to fear God, but not nearly so easy to love God from inclination because of our consciousness that God is a being whose goodness is unbounded but to whom it is no trouble to shower kindness upon us. This is not to say that such should be our mental attitude; merely that when we examine our hearts, we find that this is how we actually think. If also explains why to many races God appeared to be a jealous God, seeing that it cost Him nothing to be more bountiful with His goodness; it explains why many nations thought that their gods were sparing of their benefits and that they required propitiating with prayers and sacrifices. This is the attitude of man's heart; but when we call reason to our aid we see that God's goodness must be of a high order if He is to be good to a being so unworthy of His goodness. This solves our difficulty. The gratitude we owe to God is not gratitude from inclination, but from duty, for God is not a creature like ourselves, and can be no object for our inclinations.

We ought not to accept favours unless we are either forced to do so by dire necessity or have implicit confidence in our benefactor (for he ceases to be our friend and becomes our benefactor) that he will not regard it as placing us under an obligation to him. To accept favours indiscriminately and to be constantly seeking them is ignoble and the sign of a mean soul which does not mind placing itself under obligations. Unless we are driven by such dire necessity that it compels us to sacrifice our own worth, or unless we are convinced that our benefactor will not account it to us as a debt, we ought rather to suffer deprivation than accept favours, for a favour is a debt which can never be extinguished. For even if I repay my benefactor tenfold, I am still not even with him, because he has done me a kindness which he did not owe. He was the first in the field, and even if I return his gift tenfold I do so only as repayment. He will always be the one who was the first to show kindness and I can never be beforehand with him.

The man who bestows favours can do so either in order to make the recipient indebted to him or as an expression of his duty. If he makes the recipient feel a sense of indebtedness, he wounds his pride and diminishes his sense of gratitude. If he wishes to avoid this he must regard the favours he bestows as the discharge of a duty he owes to mankind, and he must not give the recipient the impression that it is a debt to be repaid. On the other hand, the recipient of the favour must still consider himself under an obligation to his benefactor and must be grateful to him. Under these conditions there can be benefactors and beneficiaries. A right-thinking man will not accept kindnesses, let alone favours. A grateful disposition is a touching thing and brings tears to our eyes on the stage, but a generous disposition *is* lovelier still. Ingratitude we destest to a surprising degree; even though we are not ourselves the victims of it, it angers us to such an extent that we feel inclined to intervene. But this is due to the fact that ingratitude decreases generosity.

Envy does not consist in wishing to be more happy than others—that is grudge—but in wishing to be the only one to be happy. It is this feeling which makes envy so evil. Why should not others be happy along with me? Envy shows itself also in relation to things which are scarce. Thus the Dutch, who as a nation are rather envious, once valued tulips at several hundred of florins apiece. A rich merchant, who had one of the finest and rarest specimens, heard that another had a similar specimen. He thereupon bought it from him for 2, 000 florins and trampled it underfoot, saying that he had no use for it, as he already possessed a specimen, and that he only wished that no one else should share that distinction with him. So it is also in the matter of happiness.

Malice is different. A malicious man is pleased when others suffer, he can laugh when others weep. An act which willfully brings unhappiness is cruel; when it produces physical pain it is bloodthirsty. Inhumanity is all these together, just as humanity consists in sympathy and pity, since these differentiate man from the beasts. It is difficult to explain what gives rise to a cruel disposition. It may arise when a man considers another so evilly-disposed that he hates him. A man who believes himself hated by another, hates him in return, although the former may have a good reason to hate him. For if a man is hated because he is selfish and has other vices, and he knows that he is hated for these reasons, he hates those who hate him although these latter do him no injustice. Thus kings who know that they are hated by their subjects become even more cruel. Equally, when a man has done a good deed to another, he knows that the other loves him, and so he loves him in return, knowing that he himself is loved. Just as love is reciprocated, so also is hate. We must for our own sakes guard against being hated by others lest we be affected by that hatred and reciprocate it. The hater is more disturbed by his hatred than is the hated.

Questions

1. Is "emulating jealousy" the only kind of jealousy in which a person does not attempt to depreciate another's attributes or possessions?
2. What, according to Immanuel Kant, is spite? How does this differ from jealousy?
3. How, if at all, do you think ingratitude is related to jealousy?

Of Jealousy and Envy

Daniel Farrell

Daniel Farrell gives an account of what jealousy and envy are. He then argues that although envy is bad, jealousy is not always as bad as it is usually thought to be. Jealousy, he says, occurs when (1) A has a desire to be favored by B, in some respect, over C; (2) A believes that he is not so favored; and (3) A is bothered by this. Envy, he says, occurs when (1) B has something that A does not have but would like to have, and (2) A is bothered by the fact that B has the good while A does not have it. One difference between jealousy and envy, then, is that jealousy occurs in three-party con-texts, whereas envy occurs in two-party contexts.

The author then considers the nature of the "botherment" in each of these emotions before discussing what each of these emotions do and do not say about the person who has them. He denies that jealousy must be thought to exhibit childishness, insecurity, or possessiveness. There can be quite good reasons why somebody would want to be favored by somebody over somebody else in a given respect. The author thinks that envy, by contrast, exhibits a kind of meanness that makes it undesirable.

Few emotions are looked upon with more opprobrium in our society than jealousy and envy. And few emotions cause more trouble in interpersonal relationships: jealousy (typically, but not exclusively, as we shall see) in sexual and romantic relationships, envy in these as well as in relationships of other sorts. Particularly significant in this connection is the fact that we are so often told that it is wrong to be jealous or envious of others, or that the fact that we sometimes experience these emotions reveals something bad or objectionable about our character.

In what follows I try to determine why it is that we think of these emotions in the way we do and how plausible it is to so regard them. I proceed by saying,

Daniel Farrell, "Of Jealousy and Envy," in George Graham & Hugh LaFollette (eds.) *Person to Person* (Philadelphia: Temple University Press, 1989), pp. 245–268.

first, roughly what I think each of these emotions involves—that is, roughly what it is to be jealous and roughly what it is to feel envy. I then show how an understanding of what each of these emotions is can help us to get clear on what attitudes it might be reasonable to have toward someone who is feeling one or the other of them if a given situation. In connection with this latter task, I am particularly concerned with evaluating certain common claims about what each of these emotions shows about the person who is experiencing it. And, very roughly, what I suggest is that envy is decidedly deserving, at least in full-bodied form, of its ill-repute, but that jealousy is in fact not as objectionable as it is generally made out to be.

I

Let us begin with jealousy. Suppose I'm at a party with my friend Linda and I happen to see her chatting with a particularly good-looking man on the other side of the room. He tells a long and evidently very funny story, she laughs appreciatively and tells a story of her own, and eventually they walk off to the kitchen for more drinks. A bit later I notice that Linda and her new friend are dancing and that he cuts a considerably better figure on the dance floor than I. Finally, when the time comes to leave, Linda suggests we stay a while longer. The night is young, she says, and she's having a particularly good time. I continue talking to friends, while Linda wanders off to spend more time with Prince Charming.

If certainly would not be surprising if I felt a twinge of jealousy under these circumstances. I might not be jealous, of course, and if I am jealous, this may show something awful about me. Nonetheless, I have felt just a bit jealous in situations like this in the past, and I suspect that I am likely to suffer mild recurrences in similar situations in the future. More important, whether or not I would be jealous in a situation like this, it is certainly the sort of case in which it is plausible to talk about the possibility of jealousy. An ordinary person will have no difficulty, in other words, in seeing it as a case in which one might be jealous.

Consider next a case of what I call *professional* jealousy. Suppose I am a *professional* tennis player and one important source of gratification for me is the fact that I am considered one of the best players on the pro circuit. Surely if some younger player suddenly begins to attract a lot of attention, and people gradually seem to be coming to the conclusion that he is a better player than I, it is possible that I will start to feel something akin to what we imagined I was feeling in the case just described. No doubt it will not be exactly like what I felt in that case, and the differences may turn out to be more important than the similarities. Nonetheless, it is interesting, I think, that we can imagine an old pro acting in ways which in some very straightforward sense suggest that he is jealous because of the attention a younger pro is starting to receive. He talks about the latter's bad days a little too much, let us suppose, and about his own good days a little too often. My point, as before, is not that the one player *must* experience feelings of jealousy when beginning to see what people think of the other player, but that the one player *might* be jealous of the other in a case like this and that we certainly have no trouble imagining such a case.

What sorts of general truths do cases like these suggest? Notice first that in each of these cases jealousy occurs in a very similar and rather special context: In each case our protagonist is jealous because some third party seems to be getting from some second party something that the first party (our protagonist) wants. This fact about jealousy—that is seems always to occur in a context involving three or more independent parties—is important in distinguishing jealousy from envy, as we shall see.[1]

Notice second, though, that cases like these suggest another, quite important general point; namely, that jealousy presupposes a certain kind of desire, on the part of the jealous individual, and a certain kind of *belief*. In a typical case of sexual jealousy, for example, one person, A, is desirous of retaining the (perhaps exclusive) affection of another person, B, but is fearful that B is beginning to feel more affection (or whatever) for some third person, C. Similarly, in a typical case of professional jealousy we find one person, A, who wants something—esteem or admiration, for example—from some other person (or group of persons), B, and who is fearful that B is beginning to feel more esteem (or whatever) for some other person, C. As we shall see, even in cases that don't involve three people—as when we speak of an animal feeling jealous—something like a belief that is not favored in some way in which it wants or desires to be favored seems to be necessary if the concept of jealousy is to apply.[2]

Suppose we try to generalize these remarks, putting them in the form of a two-part thesis about what I call the conceptual presuppositions of jealousy. We would then want to say, first, that jealousy is, necessarily, an emotion that arises only in what we may call a three-party context: A is jealous of C because B seems to be favoring C (in respect R) rather than A. We would also want to say, second, that jealousy is, again necessarily, something that one feels only when one has a desire to be favored by some other person (or by some group), in some respect R, to some third person (or whatever), and only when one believes—or at any rate suspects—that one is not so favored As we shall see, thinking of jealousy in this way enables us both to understand and to assess some of the many things that are said about this emotion and what it tells us

---

[1]The party of whom I am jealous need not actually exist, of course, nor need she be (imagined to be) some *one* person or group (see note 4 in this connection). What is important is that I think I have a rival (or a set of rivals). Notice, too, that the party of whom I am jealous doesn't have to be a *person;* nor, for that matter, does the jealous party or the party whose affections the jealous party wants. I might be jealous because of your interest in some animal or in a hobby; and my dog might be jealous because of my interest in you, just as I might be jealous because of *his* interest in you.

[2]Notice, by the way, that the clearest cases of jealousy are cases where A not only *wants* to be favored in some way over C, but also believes that until now he or she *has* been so favored. It is more problematic, I think, to speak of jealousy in cases where A wants to be favored by someone in some way but has never been favored in that way by the person by whom he or she wants to be favored. Nonetheless, for simplicity's sake I refer in what follows to A's desire to be favored rather than—as would no doubt be more accurate, at least for most cases—to A's desire to *continue* to be favored.

about the jealous person.[3] Before pursuing these matters, though, we need to pause in order to consider an important objection to what has just been said, an objection that centers on the fact that there seem to be cases where we find jealousy in two-party contexts and, what's more, in contexts that do not involve the sorts of desires and beliefs that our present analysis requires. Consideration of this objection enables us to introduce the other object of our attention in this essay—envy—and helps us to indicate exactly how it is that jealousy and envy differ.

II

We can begin with the undeniable fact that we sometimes talk about jealousy in two- rather than three-party contexts. For instance, when you learn that I have just gotten a year's sabbatical you might say, "That's terrific! I'm really jealous!" Or, painfully aware of how difficult it is for me to do, when I see how easy it is for you to write up your ideas I might say, "I'm really jealous. I wish I could write as easily as you." These are perfectly ordinary uses of the word "jealous," it seems to me, and yet they do not conform at all to the three-party paradigm just suggested.

Now, what I want to say here, despite the apparent propriety of speaking in the ways just described, is that in cases like these we are really talking about *envy* rather than jealousy. In saying this, of course, I am implicitly suggesting that common usage is to some extent misleading in this connection, since we do indeed use the word "jealous" in just these ways. This is certainly not a fatal objection to my contention, however—or so it seems to me—since it often happens that common usage fails to honor distinctions that themselves emerge only from an analysis of common usage.

Let us begin, then, by asking when the concept of envy is most appropriately and least controversially used in ordinary discourse. The clearest sort of case, it seems to me, is a two-party case where one person has something— some thing, literally, or some trait or capacity, say—that another person doesn't have but would very much like to have, and where the one person is somehow *bothered* by the fact that the second person has the relevant good while the first does not. Thus I can be envious of your wealth, your good looks, or your physical prowess, and I will be envious of you in these respects if, in contemplating the fact that you have them while I do not, I experience a certain negative affect because this is so. To be sure, we sometimes say the one party is jealous of the other in cases like this, and that is the point with which we are now concerned. But leaving aside for a moment exactly, what we would say in such cases, notice that there are important differences between cases like these and the paradigms

---

[3]Unless otherwise indicated, when I say "the jealous person" or "the jealous individual," I am referring to someone who is *occurrently* jealous, as we might say: someone who is actually experiencing this emotion in some specific situation. I do not mean to refer, as these locutions might be thought to suggest, to the person who is *prone* to jealousy.

of jealousy mentioned earlier. To begin with, notice that in these new cases it is not literally your money or good looks or physical prowess that I want, nor is it necessarily the case that I want you to have any less money or to be any less handsome or physically adept. I just want more money——and it may very well be a matter of complete indifference to me whether or not you retain yours. In the earlier cases, by contrast, you have something that I want and that we cannot both have. For example, in the sexual case I want Linda's primary affections and I don't want you to have them. Similarly, in the tennis-pro case I want the attention that you are getting; *ex hypothesi* we can't both have that attention, and I want for me rather than you to have it.

What is perhaps even more significant than the difference just mentioned, however, is what I call the difference in focus between the two sorts of cases. In the latter cases I'm upset because you have something I want—money, good looks, or whatever—and don't have (or at any rate don't think I have). In the cases of sexual and professional jealousy, by contrast, I am upset not just because of what the person of whom I'm jealous *has*—namely, the affection or esteem of someone else who matters to me—but also because the subject of my jealousy has been given that affection or esteem, freely, by that other party. Of course, in both sorts of cases I am upset because, among other things, in some sense you have something I want. What bothers me in the case of jealousy, however, is not just that you have something I want—namely, a certain person's or group's esteem—but that you have been given that affection or esteem by someone who is important to me and from whom I want that esteem or affection. And herein lies the difference in focus to which I wish to call attention. In cases of envy, there are just you and I, so to speak, and what you have and I don't. In genuine cases of jealousy, on the other hand, there are you and I *and* the person who is giving *you* what I want *that person* to give *me*.[4]

III

We can summarize our conclusions thus far as follows. Jealousy is an essentially three-party emotion, in which one party, *A*, is bothered by the fact that some other party, *B*, seems to favor some third party, *C*, in some respect in which A desires to be favored by B instead.[5] Envy, by contrast, while sometimes occurring in three-party contexts, is in essence a two-party emotion, in which one

---

[4]For the sake of simplicity, I am writing as though *you* always exist, in cases of jealousy, and are some one specific person. However, this is not really accurate, since you may *not* exist (being a mere figment of my imagination, for example), or you may exist but without my really knowing you (I just know or suspect that there's someone competing with me). Or I may be jealous not of any particular person but of any and all of a whole series of real or imaginary rivals. I ignore these complications here for ease of expression, though they should of course be borne in mind.

[5]Note that while one's desire to be favored over another party, in the relevant sorts of cases, is usually a desire to be *preferred* over that party in some respect, it is possible for this desire to be thought just as highly of, or to be treated in the same way as, the other party or parties.

party is bothered by the fact that another party has something that the first party wants but does not seem to have.[6]

Obviously, there are plenty of questions one might want to raise at this point, just as there are plenty of problems one might want to urge against the claims that have just been made. Here, however, I want to focus on just one of the many questions that might be thought to need attention; namely, the question of exactly what is meant when we say that, in the case of each of these emotions, we are dealing with a situation where someone is bothered by the perception that something or other is or is not the case. What, we want to ask, is the nature of the botherment in each case? And why, for that matter, should we suppose that we must *be* bothered or pained in such cases in order to be either envious or jealous? It is not enough, for jealousy, to believe we are not favored in some way in which we want to be favored? And, similarly, are we not already envious on noticing that another has something that we want for ourselves but do not have? Unless we can answer these and a number of related questions, we can hardly claim to have said what it is to be envious or jealous, much less to have put ourselves into a position to be able to address the many claims we hear made about what these emotions show about the person who is feeling them.

Let us begin with jealousy. And let us note at once that we actually have two questions before us rather than just one. The first is the question of why we must suppose we need to be bothered or pained by something—that is, by one of our beliefs or perceptions—if we are plausibly going to be said to be jealous. The second is the question of what, supposing we must be bothered or pained in order to be jealous, is the nature of the botherment or pain in question.

Now, the first of these is a question I am afraid I simply cannot answer at the present time. If you say you believe I can plausibly be said to be jealous, once I begin to suspect I am not being favored in some way in which I want to be favored, and can plausibly be said to be jealous in such a case even though I am not the least bit bothered by the fact that I am not favored as I want to be favored, I have no argument to show you are mistaken. Indeed, it may be that common usage occasionally supports such a way of speaking. However, I think that many of us would say, upon reflection, that if I really am not bothered by the fact that I am not favored as I want to be favored, then I really am not jealous. After all, if this were not so, how would we distinguish between the people who are jealous when they believe they are not favored in some way in which they want to be favored and the people who, discovering this, just don't care?

Far more interesting, it seems to me, is the question of just what it means to say that jealousy consists in being bothered by the fact that we are not (as we believe) favored in some way in which we want to be favored. What exactly do we mean by "bothered" here, we want to ask, and what exactly is the difference

---

[6]Note that I am speaking somewhat loosely here, for the sake of simplicity, when I say that in the case of envy A wants something that B has. It may be that A wants that very thing and they cannot both have it. Typically, though, what A wants is the *kind* of thing B has; for example, money or good looks. For more on this, see section V.

between someone who *is* bothered (or pained) by the fact of not being favored in some way and someone who is not (someone, say, who just doesn't care)?

One answer, of course, would be to say that we are bothered or pained by the fact that we are not favored by another in some way just in case we *feel bad*—that is, just in case we are consciously experiencing a certain negative affect—as a result of our belief. Aside from being intolerably vague, however, this answer is unacceptable because it fails to account for cases in which, consciously at any rate, we are utterly unaware of being jealous, but where we certainly are jealous and where everyone else around can see that this is so. No doubt, we typically do feel something when we are jealous, something very painful. But we can evidently be jealous without realizing it, and indeed without feeling it, and our account must somehow make sense of the fact this is so.

Our account must be able to explain, therefore, not only what it is to be bothered by the fact that we are not favored in some way, in cases where our being bothered is something we are quite well aware of, but also what it is to be bothered by this sort of thing in cases where we are *not* aware of being bothered by it. And for this, it seems to me, we need a very general notion. Indeed, it seems to me we need a notion that is not necessarily *experiential* at all. We need to be able to say, in other words, that a person can be bothered by something, in the sense of the term that interests us, even though we are not strictly speaking *feeling* anything at all in connection with the object of our concern.

What sense of bothered, then, is available to us? One possibility is the quasi-mechanical notion of disruption: We might say that we are bothered by the thought that something is or is not the case, just in case our normal pattern of thoughts or actions or feelings is somehow disrupted by the thought that such and such is or is not the case. This is, or course, a rather vague way of speaking, and, unfortunately, we cannot at present afford the time and space to make it any less vague. Still, I think it is clear enough for present purposes: We are bothered or pained by the thought that we are not favored in some way in which we admittedly want to be favored, on this view, just in case the thought that this is so disrupts in some way the regular flow of our thoughts, feelings, or actions.

Now, with just two qualifications, I think this account is right. The first qualification is this. In order to capture the fact jealousy is a painful emotion, at least when consciously felt, I think we need to say that the disruption caused by the relevant belief must be a kind that would be experienced as painful, if it were consciously experienced, or at least as otherwise negative rather than as pleasurable or somehow positive. Thus the woman who is delighted at the fact that (as she believes) her lover has been unfaithful cannot be said to be jealous because of what she is experiencing, even if her delight is so intense as to disrupt her normal pattern of thoughts, feelings, or actions.[7]

The second qualification we need to add to the foregoing (disruption) account of jealousy is this: We need to say something about what the *object* of our state of mind has to be if that state of mind, supposing all the other conditions

---

[7]This, of course' is arguably already entailed by the fact that, for jealousy, the jealous party must *want* the favoring that she believes (or suspects) she is not now getting.

have been met, is plausibly to be said to warrant saying we are jealous. To see this, it will suffice to note that we can become *angry*, say, or *fearful*, as a result of coming to believe we are not favored, and thus can become bothered as a result of coming to have this belief, without its following that we are jealous. For suppose we are angry and our anger is focused entirely on the fact that we believe our partner's choice of the third party is stupid. Or suppose we are afraid, as a result of what we have come to believe, but our fear is focused entirely on the fact that we will be at grave risk of contracting some venereal disease as a result of our partner's depredations. In such cases, it seems implausible to me to say we are jealous, supposing conditions are just as we have imagined, even though it is true that we are bothered by the fact that we are not favored in some way in which we want to be favored. What we need, I think, is to suppose that, whatever else we feel, we are bothered not simply by some special aspect or consequence of the fact that we are not favored as we want to be favored but, rather, that we are bothered by the very fact that we are not favored as we want to be favored. Given this—for example, given that we are angry not because of our partner's *stupidity* in choosing another, but because of the very fact that another has been chosen—I think we have enough to say that we are jealous and to say this regardless of whether our jealousy is experienced, phenomenologically, as anger, fear, or whatever.[8]

We can now take up the case of envy. We argued that to be envious of another is to be bothered by the fact that (as we believe) you have something (or some kind of thing) that I want for myself but believe I do not have. Our current question, then, is this: What can we say about how I must be bothered in the relevant sorts of circumstances in order for my botherment to qualify as envy rather than, say, anger, indignation, irritation, or whatever?

One answer to this question, of course, is analogous to the first answer we considered when we raised the same sort of question about jealousy. This answer, which is supported to some extent by ordinary usage, holds that I do not in fact have to be bothered by my perception of your advantages in order to be envious of you for having those advantages. Recall, in this connection, the sorts of cases mentioned in our discussion of the difference between jealousy and envy. We said that people sometimes say they are jealous of someone else when, in our terms, what they really mean to say is that they are envious of them. What's relevant about these sorts of cases here, of course—supposing for a moment that what the parties in question are reporting is in fact envy rather than jealousy—is this: When you say to me, "I envy you your ability to [do such and such]," it's not at all clear that what you are saying would be falsified if we were to discover that in fact you were not the least bit bothered or pained by the fact that (as you believe) I can do such and such while you cannot. It is not at all

---

[8]One important consequence of my view is that there is no special phenomenological feeling that is the feeling of jealousy. Provided all our other conditions are met, what the jealous person feels may be phenomenologically indistinguishable from what the person who is merely angry or afraid is feeling. The *objects* of their respective emotions, however, will differ and will be what accounts for the fact that their emotions are different.

clear, that is to say, when we are thinking about cases of this sort, that you really do have to be bothered by your perception of another's advantages in order for you plausibly to say that you are envious of those advantages.

Let us call cases of the sort we are imagining here cases of apparently friendly envy. Does the existence of such cases show what the argument just sketched suggests—namely, that it is possible to envy others because of some good they have without at the same time being bothered, in any way, by our realization that they have that good while we do not? I think not. Rather, I think that what such cases show is that we sometimes attribute envy to ourselves in what I shall call a "purely formal" way. On such occasions, it seems to me, we are not really attributing envy to ourselves at all. Instead, we are simply indicating to our interlocutor that she has something that we admire and would very much like to have ourselves. We do say on such occasions, of course, that we envy the individual in question. It does not follow from this, however, that we are actually envious of her, much less that we are in fact feeling—or have in fact felt—the emotion that currently interests us. And to the degree that we are not feeling something in such cases—or, at any rate, are not in some sense bothered by our perception that the other person has what she has—it seems to me to be reasonable to say we are not really feeling envy.[9]

Suppose this is right. Suppose, that is to say, we cannot be said to be feeling, or to have felt, envy unless we are feeling, or at some point have felt, some generally negative affect because of what we believe about what others have and we lack. This, of course, leaves entirely untouched the question with which we began; namely, the question of exactly what that generally negative affect has to be if, given the other circumstances we have associated with envy, the party who is affected is rightly to be said to be feelings envy as opposed to mere anger, say, or indignation, or whatever.

Now here, I think, it will be useful to turn away from polite or friendly contexts for a moment and look, instead, at a somewhat more dramatic example of someone who we would all agree is clearly feeling envy: an actor, say, who, witnessing the consummate skill of one of his fellows, is green with envy, as we might say. I think it's obvious that we would say that such an individual's envy is *constituted*, in part, by the fact that he is indeed bothered or pained by what he perceives as the other actor's superior skills. But what more can we say about the nature of this botherment and about how being thus bothered in cases of envy differs from being similarly bothered, in other cases, but not envious?

One answer is suggested by most dictionaries and by the etymology of "envy": To be envious of another is to look askance at that person because of what the person has and one does not. The *Oxford English Dictionary*, for example, tells us that to envy is, among other things, to "look maliciously upon. The

---

[9]I am not suggesting here that any case of apparently friendly envy is a case in which one is attributing envy to oneself in a "purely formal" way. My point is merely that one can attribute envy to oneself in this way without actually feeling envy and that this will be so precisely when one attributes envy to oneself in these kinds of circumstances without at the same time feeling at all bothered by the fact that the other party has what one wants but doesn't have.

feeling of mortification or ill will occasioned by the contemplation of superior advantages possessed by another."[10] The suggestion here that envy involves malice or ill will is one that has to bear considerable scrutiny. Notice, though, that the idea that envy involves something like malice or ill will is supported, to some degree at least, by certain strains in popular thinking about this emotion. For if we did not think that envy involves some such feeling, why would we think of it as something objectionable and, in its extreme forms, even sinful?

One problem with this line of thought has to do with cases of apparently friendly envy like those described earlier. To be sure, if our previous remarks are right, many cases of this sort are not really cases of *envy* and hence do not pose a problem for the view that envy presupposes something like ill will or malice toward the ones of whom we are envious. I think it is clear, however, that in come cases of apparently friendly envy, we are in fact envious—not because we say we are but because we are in fact *bothered*, however mildly, by the fact that they have what we want but do not have. And cases like these, it seems to me, which are quite possible even if our earlier remarks are right, do indeed pose a problem for definitions of envy like the one that we have culled from the O.E.D. For it would be quite implausible, I think, to suppose that in these sorts of cases one's botherment takes the form of anything even remotely resembling malice or ill will.

What, then, shall we say affective side of envy involves, if we are not to say that it involves anything quite so strong as malice or ill will? As in the case of jealousy, I want to suggest what some may consider a surprising answer to this question: I want to suggest that there is no *one* feeling or inner experience that we all undergo when we are feeling envy. Rather, I think that any of a number of different affects will qualify as envy provided that they occur in circumstances of the sort that we have sketched and are directed at the very fact that another has what we want but do not ourselves have.

The proof of this claim, it seems to be, is exactly analogous to our earlier line of argument, where we showed that unless we are bothered by the very fact that we are not favored as we want to be favored, we will not be feeling jealousy. Thus suppose that I am situated in a two-party case where I see that you have something I want—a huge amount of money, let's say—and suppose that, upon perceiving that this is so, I begin to feel anger or ill will toward you. Does it follow that I am feeling envious of you? It seems to me that it does not. For suppose I believe you have gotten this money unfairly—indeed, suppose I believe that the money is rightfully mine, having been cunningly embezzled from me by you. In such a case, I might well feel ill will, anger, or whatever, toward you without at the same time feeling envy. My anger is perfectly understandable, that is to say, as an expression of indignation over the fact that, as I believe, I have been wronged by you. And we can imagine ourselves feeling anger (or whatever) in exactly the same circumstances without feeling envy at all.

---

[10]This definition fails to make it clear that for envy we have to suppose that the person in question *wants* the superior advantages in question. Without this assumption, it is possible that we will have, not envy, but what we might call *Freudenschadde,* or sorrow at another's good fortune, which is the obverse of the familiar *Scitaddenfreude.*

Of course, as in the case of our discussion of jealousy, it is tempting to suppose that what the preceding argument shows is that botherment in the sorts of cases that interest us is envy only when it has a certain unique feel—for example, that mere anger in such circumstances differs from envy, or from envy and anger, by virtue of being some special and quite possibly unique feeling that the relevant person has. As I said, however, think that this conclusion is unwarranted. For I think that what makes our pain or botherment envy, as distinct from any of the other things we might be feeling in such a situation, is not some special qualitative tone but, rather, the fact that the pain is occasioned by the mere fact that (as we believe) they have the money and we do not. Thus if we suppose, in the case imagined, not only that I am bothered by the fact that you have money that belongs to me, but also that I am bothered simply because you have money while I do not, we can say that I am both indignant over the fact that you have money that does not belong to you and envious of the money that you have and I want.

We may now return to the phenomenon of so-called "friendly" envy and the problem it appeared to pose for the conception of envy that presupposes that this emotion involves something like malice or ill will. If our remarks are right, we can now resolve this problem quite straightforwardly, and we can do so without invoking the possibility that what we have here are importantly distinct kinds of envy. For if our remarks are right, neither malice nor ill will nor anything like these feelings is *required* for a person's emotional state to qualify—in the sorts of circumstances that interest us—as envy. I *may* feel ill will toward you as a result of my belief that you have what I want but do not have, just as I may feel anger, without ill will, or a mild form of annoyance, or whatever. But no one of these affective states is essential, on our analysis, for my feeling to qualify as envy. Rather, what's essential, as we have seen, is that my negative feelings, whatever precisely they involve, be focused on the very fact that you have what I want but apparently do not have. Thus whenever we have any negative affect in a two-party context of the sort we have described, we will have envy, on our view, provided that the object of that affect is the *very fact* that the one party apparently has something or some kind of thing that the other party wants.

IV

Let us assume that our remarks thus far are right: To be jealous is to be bothered or pained by the fact that, as we believe, we are not favored by others in some way in which we want to be favored (some other party apparently being so favored by those other people instead); to be envious is to be bothered or pained by the fact that (as we believe) someone else has something that we want but do have.[11] The question I want to raise now is this: In light of our analysis of what

---

[11]For the sake of simplicity I am speaking loosely here. One needn't, on our view, want the very thing the other person has in order to be envious. One merely needs to want it *or* something that is like it in relevant respects. See note 6 in this connection.

they are, what can we say about these emotions and what they do and do not show about the person who is experiencing them?

We can begin with the case of jealousy. And we can note at once that in at least one respect it is easy to see how our analysis can help us to advance the discussion over what this emotion does and does not show about the jealous person. For inasmuch as our analysis enables us to distinguish the various components of jealousy, it enables us to examine the various claims that are made about this emotion in a rather more systematic way than would otherwise have been possible. Consider in this connection the rather common claim that jealousy is a particularly *childish* emotion or, alternatively, that it is an emotion that only emotionally immature people would be likely to feel. On our analysis this has to come down either to the claim that only immature people could want to be favored in any of the various ways the jealous people necessarily want to be favored on our account, or to the claim that only immature people would be bothered by the fact that they are apparently not favored in some way in which they want to be favored. For on our account, to be jealous is just to be bothered by the fact that (as we believe) we are not favored in some way in which we want to be favored, and hence what's objectionable about jealousy must either be the desire to be so favored or the botherment that constitutes the affective part of the jealous response.[12]

Now, I do not wish to pursue this particular allegation here—I mean the allegation that jealousy is necessarily a sign of childishness or immaturity—since it's not clear to me exactly how one is to settle arguments about whether something is or is not a mark of immaturity. I do, however, want to note two points in passing. First, it seems to me that it would be quite implausible to suppose that it is the jealous people's *affective response*, given the apparent frustration of their presumed desire, that shows them to be somehow childish or immature. For given a desire to be favored in a certain way, it seems quite natural to imagine people being pained or bothered by the fact that (as they believe) this desire is not being met. To be sure, we can imagine someone's affective response being out of all proportion to what we would expect of an adult individual. This, however, is an independent point. For here we are concerned only with the question of whether the mere fact that someone is bothered in the relevant circumstances is itself enough to convict that person of childishness or immaturity. And, offhand at any rate, it seems to me to be clear that it is not.

The second point I want to make in this connection concerns the evaluation of the sort of desire that our analysis shows is involved whenever we feel jealousy in a given set of circumstances. Is the fact that we want to be favored in some respect—favored with sexual exclusivity, for example, or favored by our professional colleagues in some way—necessarily a mark of childishness or immaturity? As I have already indicated, it seems to me that answers to questions of this sort are virtually impossible to defend. However, I do think it is hard to

---

[12]Of course, another thing that might be wrong or objectionable about a person's jealousy on our account is this: The belief that one is not favored in the relevant way may be unfounded—perhaps ludicrously so. I ignore this problem here only for the sake of brevity.

see, offhand, why we should suppose that there is anything necessarily immature about wanting to be favored in some way by some particular person or
group. There certainly seems to be nothing intrinsically objectionable, or childish, about wanting to be favored in some way *professionally*, nor is it clear—
again, offhand—why it should be thought to be odd or otherwise objectionable
to want to be favored sexually in certain ways: to want you, for example, to
share your sexual favors only with me.[13]

The charges made against the jealous person, though, do not always
amount to charges of childishness or immaturity. Sometimes it is said, instead,
that jealousy is a sign of possessiveness, or of insecurity, or of a belief in what
we might call the limited-commodity view of love and affection, according to
which each of us has only limited amount of love and affection to give to others
and hence according to which it would perhaps make sense to want you to limit
your affections to me (the fault in this last instance, of course, lying not in having this desire, given one's belief in the limited commodity view, but in actually
accepting that view in the first place). These are much more serious and much
more interesting charges, it seem to me, quite independently of the fact that, if
proven, they might or might not tend to suggest that there is something childish or immature about wanting to be favored in the ways that, on our account,
a jealous person necessarily wants to be favored. Before leaving the subject of
jealousy, therefore, and what it does and does not show about the jealous person, I want to consider some of these other charges, at least in a brief and programmatic way.

Consider first the claim that jealousy is a sign of insecurity. If the account
developed earlier is right, there is of course at least one respect in which this
claim is trivially true: The jealous people[14] are—*ex hypothesi*, on our account—
people who believe or suspect that they are not favored in some respect in
which they desire to be favored; hence jealousy is indeed a sign of insecurity, in
this sense, inasmuch as it occurs, necessarily, only when we doubt that we are
desired or favored in some relevant respect. Surely this, however, is not what
people mean to say when they say that jealousy is a sign of insecurity. Presumably, at least some people who make this kind of claim mean to make a far more
radical claim about the interconnections between jealousy and insecurity. I assume, in particular, that they mean to say that jealousy somehow betokens a
kind of insecurity that is independent, logically, of our doubts about whether
we are favored as we want to be favored, and that is merely signaled, as we
might say, by our concern with whether or not we are favored.

---

[13]Notice, though, that if it were made clear that a person wanted to be favored by another in every
respect imaginable, we would be inclined to think there was something wrong with the person. One
virtue of our analysis, it seems to me, is precisely that it enables us to distinguish this sort of case
from the less immoderate sorts of cases imagined earlier.

[14]I mean, of course, someone who is experiencing jealousy at a given time, not someone who is
prone to jealousy and in *that* sense a jealous person. (See note 3.) People who are prone to jealousy
may well tend to be insecure in the sense—described later—which I argue is not necessarily connected with jealousy (as an occurrent emotion, that is). This is one of the many very interesting
questions that space prohibits us from taking up in the present paper.

What is this insecurity, then, that jealousy supposedly betokens, and how plausible is it to suppose that in fact jealousy does betoken it? As for the first of these questions, I think what people have in mind is something like the following. Jealous individuals are pictured as being unable to stand on their own; they have a bad self-image, as we might say, and need—to an unhealthy degree—reassurances of some sort in order to feel good about themselves. Since one kind of reassurance would be the thought that other people—at least certain other people—think more highly of these individuals than they do of others, such people want to be thought more highly of—their insecurity thus explaining their desire—and will understandably be disturbed when they are not.

Now, I think it is reasonable to suppose that we have here a good explanation of why some people care about whether they are favored in the ways in which we have shown a jealous person will necessarily want to be favored. However, the question we need to ask here is whether this is the only possible explanation—that is, whether, as we often hear, the jealous person is *necessarily* an insecure person. And in order to see that this is not the only possible explanation, it seems to me we simply have to ask why—feelings of insecurity aside—people do in fact care about whether they are favored in any of the various possible respects. Why does it matter to them, if it is not because they are insecure in the sense explained?

Consider first the case of an animal or a young child. Obviously, animals and children sometimes care in the relevant way. Is it plausible to suppose that this concern is always based on insecurity in the sense explained? It seems obvious to me that it is not. For one thing, it *feels good* to be favored, or to be treated as though one is somehow special, and hence it should not surprise us that humans and nonhumans alike sometimes seem to want to be so treated, independently of whether or not they suffer from the sort of personal insecurity discussed. For another thing, it is not at all clear that nonhuman animals and very young children are capable of the rather sophisticated process of forming—consciously or unconsciously—a bad self-image in the sense our account requires. Again, it is far simpler, and much closer to the facts, it seems to me, to say that these creatures just like being favored—they find it intrinsically pleasurable, as we might say—and hence want to be favored for the pleasure that's in it.[15]

Of course, someone might claim that mature adults would want to be treated as special in these ways only if they were insecure or only if they were afraid of a loss and wanted reassurance. But without further argument, and some convincing evidence, this would seem to be either ad hoc or unwarrantably dogmatic. After all, if it is plausible to suppose that it is similarly pleasurable, in and of itself, for children and animals, it seems plausible to suppose that it is similarly pleasurable for adults. And if this is so, I think we can

---

[15]Perhaps it would be more accurate to say that they find it pleasurable—in and of itself—for reasons that we haven't explained. This removes the perhaps objectionable notion of intrinsic desirability and leaves it open to behavioral scientists to determine why a given person desires to be favored in a given way. The answer to the advocate of the insecurity analysis would then be that it seems terribly implausible to suppose that we will find the same explanation in every case; namely, personal insecurity.

conclude that the likely truth of the matter is that some people have the relevant sorts of desires because they are pathologically insecure, others because they are—perhaps understandably—fearful of loss and hence want or need reassurance, and still others simply because it feels good to be treated as special. On this account there turns out to be all sorts of reasons—and very different reasons in different cases—for why people desire to be favored in the relevant ways. The point is simply that no one of these explanations—for example, the insecurity explanation—is necessary implicated in any one case.

Consider next the claim that jealousy is a sign of an objectionable kind of possessiveness: When we feel jealous because people we care about show that they care about someone else, we are revealing that we think of them as ours, it is sometimes said, or as somehow bound to us in ways that make it inappropriate for them to share their love with others. But, then, to admit to jealousy, this argument continues, is surely to admit to an ugly and very objectionable view of our standing vis-à-vis the relevant person to persons. For no one belongs to another in the way jealousy shows we think another belongs to us, and to think otherwise is to show that we don't appreciate this elementary truth.

Now, before we can assess this line of thought, it will be useful to begin by asking what we generally mean by possessiveness, independently of cases where jealousy is involved, and why it is that we generally think of possessiveness as wrong. One very obvious answer, it seems to me, it this: We picture a possessive man as a man who is excessively concerned about his possessions and who makes too much of the fact that they are his—that is, of the fact that it is he who has the say, so to speak, about who uses them or about what shall or shall not be done with them. It's not so much that the possessive man literally won't let go of his possessions as that he insists on the importance of the fact that they are his—has as objects he owns and thereby his to regulate and control.

Now imagine the case of the man for whom it is very important that his wife have sexual relations with only him. One would think that if the idea of possessiveness has anything at all to do with jealousy, it is in just this sort of case that it does. And if fact I think there is something like possessiveness, in the sense just described, in at least some cases of this sort. For the man for whom it is important to be the only person with whom his wife has sexual relations may—and probably often does—think of his wife in something like the way he thinks about his car or his favorite fishing rod: "That's mine," he might say; "leave it alone." Moreover, and perhaps even more important, such a man's possessiveness—his feeling that a thing is his—itself suggests some of the other sins that are commonly laid at the jealous person's door. For in trying to say a moment ago wherein his possessiveness resides, we were driven to talk about the possessive man as a man who is much concerned about the things he owns—thus introducing the possibility that our exclusionist really thinks about his wife as a mere thing or object rather than as a person—and in reflecting on the notion of ownership we were in turn driven to talk about the notion of control: His possessions are his, among other things, only insofar as it is he who gets to say who uses them and when; in other words, only if he controls them in some sense.

Despite the fact that there are these similarities, however, between the notions of possessiveness, control, and treating another person as an object rather than a person, on the one hand, and some cases of sexual jealousy, on the other (cases, that is, in which the jealousy presupposes a desire for sexual exclusivity), it is far from clear that these notions are necessarily connected with the possibility of jealousy. For one thing, of course, it is not clear how any of the points we have just been making is relevant to professional jealousy. How is my wanting to be considered a better teacher than Professor *K*, for example, a sign of possessiveness or a sign that I think of my students as mere objects or that somehow I am concerned with controlling them or their likes and dislikes? For another thing, it is not clear how these sorts of considerations are relevant to all the other sorts of cases of sexual jealousy, the cases where we are concerned not about sexual exclusivity, in and of itself, but about our lovers' opinions of us—as lovers, say, or as thinkers, charmers, or whatever. In these cases, one is certainly not thinking of one's lover as a mere object; indeed, it is hard to see how even possessiveness and a need to control others are relevant here, except in trivial ways.

Perhaps, though, the point intended here is that, these sorts of cases aside—professional cases, that is, and nonexclusivist sexual cases—in cases where jealousy *is* connected with a desire for sexual exclusivity, the jealous people are necessarily possessive and controlling or controlseeking people and also people who, inasmuch as they want what they want, think of their mates more as objects than as people. To see that even this is not so, let us begin with the charge that inasmuch as the sexual exclusivist seems to think of his partner in some sense as one of his possessions, he treats her more as an object than as a person. Is this really an accurate characterization of what's going on in such cases?

It seems to me that it is not. A man who thought of his wife strictly as an object wouldn't in fact feel jealousy, it seems to me, when he suspected her of infidelity (or, rather, of having been bedded by another, as we would have to say). On the contrary. I should think he would feel something more like indignation, say, or some similar emotion, in the way that we feel indignant or somehow wronged when someone uses something of ours without our permission or against our will. To the degree that a man does feel jealous when he suspects his wife of infidelity, on the other hand, it seems to me it's precisely because he is thinking of her as a person, in at least this respect: What bothers him is that she *chose* to sleep with the other man (assuming that she did sleep with another man). If we think of choosers as necessarily people, then we must say that to be jealous presupposes that one thinks of the other as—to that extent at least—a person.[16]

---

[16]Notice in this connection how odd it would be for a man to react to the fact that his wife has been raped by another man by being jealous of the rapist. Of course, some husbands *may* experience feelings of jealousy in such cases. It seems to me that their jealousy is intelligible, however, only if we assume that they suspect the woman *wanted* sex with the rapist or possibly enjoyed it. (Unfortunately, there is some reason to believe that many husbands are in fact inclined in such cases to just such suspicions.) Notice, too, that if I am jealous because my dog Poldy seems to prefer Linda's company to mine, this is no counterexample to the claim, advanced earlier that if *A* is jealous of *C*,

It will be clear by now how I think we should approach the problem of interpreting and evaluating the various things that people are inclined to say about jealousy and what it shows about the jealous person. For if I am right, jealousy can be thought of as a rather special kind of threat-response—a response, that is, to the possibility that one's status as a favored individual is in jeopardy. And if this is right, one way to approach the claims that interest us is to ask, of any given claim that jealousy shows this or that, why the fact that you care about your status in the relevant ways should be thought to suggest this or that. Unfortunately, because of limitations of time and space, further illustration of this way of analyzing the various claims made about jealousy must be left as an exercise to reader to perform on their own.

V

If the argument of the preceding section is right, jealousy does not deserve the unqualified opprobrium with which it is often regarded. I have not, of course, defended jealousy, in any positive sense. I have merely tried to show that many of the charges that are commonly made against it will not withstand scrutiny, at least when they are understood as general claims about what jealousy necessarily shows us about the jealous person.

What about envy, though? What is the received wisdom about this emotion, and what can we say about it in light of the foregoing remarks?

Notice first of all that envy does not, in our own culture, come in for anything like the abuse that jealousy tends to receive. To be sure, to give in to envy is generally thought to be a fault, and a proneness or general disposition to experience this emotion would presumably be thought to be a serious defect of character. Still, in contrast to the case of jealousy, envy is not generally thought to be suggestive, in and of itself, of any other (further) vices of deficiencies of character.[17]

Now, this, I think, is actually rather odd. For if our remarks are right, there is at least this to be said against envy: It shows a kind of meanness, at least in one somewhat old-fashioned sense of the term. For while envy is not displeasure felt *simply* because of another's good fortune—this would be meanness of an even worse sort—it is nonetheless displeasure at another's good fortune *given that the person enjoys the good fortune and one does not (also) enjoy it oneself.* The displeasure or negative affect we have identified with envy, that is to say, is

---

then *A* is necessarily thinking of *B* as having freely *chosen C* and hence, to that extent at least, is necessarily thinking of *B* as a person. For my jealousy would be crazy if it weren't for the fact that at such times I am thinking of Poldy as a chooser and in that sense as a person.

[17]This has not always been the case. In the Middle Ages, for example, Roman Catholic theology counted envy a capital sin. And in Dante's *Purgatorio,* those who had been guilty of this sin remained on the Second Terrace until they were purged of it. (See especially Cantos XIII and XIV and the very interesting remarks that Dante makes about this emotion.) The remarks that follow can be thought of, in significant part, as an attempt to determine where envy was thought to be, if not the most serious of sins, a fairly serious sin nonetheless.

not simply the displeasure consequent upon my realization that I do not have something I want to have. Rather, it is a displeasure generated by my perception or belief that you have what I want but do not have myself. And this, it seems to me, is a rather suspect state of mind, since it suggests that your good fortune does indeed offend me, not in and of itself, but in the context of my realization that my own desire is unfulfilled while yours is not.

It might be objected to this, of course, that in cases of what we called friendly envy, we do not find displeasure—at another's good fortune—of the sort we are discussing here. And this much, at least, it true: For those cases where, as we said, the verbal expression of envy is playing a purely formal role, there is indeed no displeasure at another's good fortune. But, of course, in such cases, as we also said, we are not really dealing with envy: The speaker is not describing emotional feelings in such cases, but simply pointing out the desirability of what the interlocutor has. Thus cases like these, at any rate, do not undermine our claim, according to which the actual occurrence of envy suggests a certain meanness or smallness of spirit.

What about cases of apparently friendly envy, though, where I really am feeling at least slightly envious but where, as we granted earlier, it would be unreasonable to say the feeling is ill will? In what sense is the fact that I am experiencing negative affect in these circumstances a sign of meanness or of anything else that might plausibly be thought to render me something less than wholly admirable?

Here, I think, we need to recognize two related points. First, we must note that the negative feelings that constitute the affective side of envy will tend to vary enormously from case to case. Thus in a case of the sort alluded to earlier, it may be that I am pained—and hence actually feeling envy—only slightly and only for a moment or so. And while it might be said to be undesirable, morally, to be the sort of person who is even slightly and very briefly pained in such circumstances—we would admire people who were not even momentarily pained at the thought that others have what they don't have but want—one would hardly want to inveigh at length against the character of someone who was susceptible to such brief and superficial feelings of displeasure at another's good fortune. In other cases, by contrast, we can imagine a man who is consumed with anguish because of the fact that, as he believes, another has something—some thing, literally, or some trait or capacity—that he lacks but very much wants to have. And here, I think, we would see fit to make a strong displeasure at not having the thing he wants to have, but because of the presence of the super-added displeasure that constitutes his feeling of envy—the displeasure generated, that is, not by his perception that he lacks something he wants but by his perception that he lacks it while someone else has it.

So the first point we need to note in connection with the problem posed by genuine cases of apparently friendly envy is that there is nothing surprising in the fact that the negative feelings that constitute the affective side of envy will tend to vary in intensity in different sorts of cases. The second point we need to note is this. The relevant feelings will indeed vary in intensity in the way just described. It nonetheless remains true that they are negative feelings—feelings of displeasure or discontent, if not of resentment and ill will—and that they are negative feelings occasioned by our perception (or, at any rate, belief) that someone else has something that we (also) want for ourselves but don't have (or, at any rate, don't believe we have). Thus if I am right in supposing that to be thus discomfited by the fact that another has what one wants but doesn't have is to be less virtuous than, ideally, one ought to be, we can say that even if one's degree of meanness of viciousness is small in certain cases, one is nonetheless always somewhat mean when one experiences the feeling that is the feeling of envy.

My argument here presupposes, of course, among other things, that it is mean or vicious—inconsistent with ideal moral virtue, that is to say—to be susceptible to displeasure at the thought that another has something that one wants but does not have. And someone might deny this. It might be argued that it is only human or perfectly natural to be susceptible to, and then to feel, this sort of displeasure in the relevant circumstances, and hence that it is unreasonable to think less of someone for being so disposed, much less to hold that person liable to change these dispositions to the degree that they can be changed.[18]

Now, answering the objection adequately would take more space than is in fact available to us here. For one thing, we would have to work out in a great deal more detail the implications of the fact that feelings of the sort that interest us vary enormously in their intensity and hence, presumably, in the degree to which, even on our account, they detract from a person's virtue. And, for another thing, we would have to say much more about the sense in which feeling displeasure at another's good fortune, even in the sorts of circumstances we have in mind, is arguably vicious or mean. In the absence of this fuller account, however, it is reasonable to assume, it seems to me, that the burden is on anyone who would defend envy against the charges made earlier. For we do ordinarily think less of me for begrudging you such good as I happen to enjoy. And, as we have seen, if our analysis of envy is correct, something very much like this is going on when one person actually *feels* envy because of the advantages that another person enjoys.

VI

I have certainly not *proved* here that envy is somehow more objectionable than jealousy, even supposing what we are comparing are cases of each emotion that are in most respects roughly on a par (in intensity, for example, or extent, or duration). Indeed, it is not clear to me exactly what a proof of such a proposition would involve. Still, I have tried to establish, to the best of my ability, at least this much: Many of the things that are frequently said against jealousy do not in fact appear to be things we can actually say against this emotion, once we reflect

---

[18]Another objection would hold that the relevant dispositions are not something over which we have any control and hence are not something one can in any sense hold against us, even as regards our virtue in the sense suggested. (See Adams, 1985, for useful reflections.)

on what jealousy is and on what the charges against it are; in the case of envy, by contrast, while little is typically said against it, there do in fact appear to be a number of things that *can* be said against it and that, so far as I can see, do not disappear once we are clear on what it is to feel envy and what the charges against it, thus conceived, really are. Barring a deeper account of these matters, therefore—which account I hope the present remarks can be said to serve—I think we can conclude that, first appearances notwithstanding, envy really is, morally at least, rather more objectionable than jealousy.

Questions

1. In what ways, if any, do Daniel Farrell's accounts of jealousy and envy differ from Immanuel Kant's?
2. What does Daniel Farrell mean by "apparently friendly envy"? Why does he think that this is not a threat to his account of envy?
3. Can you think of some instances in which jealousy, as the author understands it, can be morally acceptable? In other words, in what sorts of circumstances is it acceptable to desire that one be favored over another in a particular respect?

Source Cited

ADAMS, ROBERT M. 1985, "Involuntary Sins." *Philosophical Review*, 94, 1, 3–31. *Oxford English Dictionary*. 1933. Oxford: Clarendon Press.

Suggestions for Further Reading on Jealousy and Envy

BEN-ZEEV, AARON."Envy and Jealousy." *Canadian Journal of Philosophy*, vol. 20, no.4 (December 1990): pp. 487–516.

ROBERTS, ROBERT C. "What Is Wrong with Wicked Feelings?" *American Philosophical Quarterly* 28, no. 1 (January 1991): pp. 13–24.

TAYLOR, GABRIELE. "Envy and Jealousy: Emotions and Vices." In *Midwest Studies in Philosophy*, vol. 13, edited by Peter French, Theodore E. Uehling Jr., and Howard K. Wettstein, 1988. Notre Dame, IN, University of Notre Dame Press.